CUSTOMER SERVICE EXCELLENCE

Kent
County
Council

Libraries & Archives

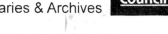

I N T E R P E T   P U B L I S H I N G

C152710492

CONTENTS – *Practical Section*

ISBN-13 978 184286 100 4
ISBN-10 1 84286 100X

Credits

Created and compiled: Ideas
into Print, Claydon, Suffolk
IP6 0AB, England.
Design and Prepress: Stuart
Watkinson, Ayelands, New Ash
Green, Kent DA3 8JW, England.
Practical photography: Geoff
Rogers © Interpet Publishing
(Also see Credits page 208.)
Production management:
Consortium, Poslingford, Suffolk
CO10 8RA, England.
Print production: Sino Publishing
House Ltd., Hong Kong.

Printed and bound in China.

This reprint 2005

Author

Dick Mills, author of many aquarium books, is a former editor of The Aquarist and Pondkeeper magazine and also a Vice-President of the Federation of British Aquatic Societies. He has kept aquarium and pond fish continuously for the last 40 years, but also finds time to travel, when — as if by accident — he always manages to come across a public aquarium or two.

Other contributors:
Colin Grist
Andrew Caine
Steve Halls

CONTENTS – *Fish Profiles*

PART ONE

The marine aquarium is different

If your fishkeeping experience has been confined to tropical freshwater fish, the biggest difference you will find when you start keeping marine species (apart from the salt) is the fact that the number of fishes you can keep in a tank of any given size is far fewer than you have been used to.

A second difference, especially in a basic marine setup, is the absence of aquarium plants. Although synthetic corals may be a reasonable substitute as a means of providing sanctuary for the fishes, they are nothing more than static objects. However, once you have gained experience, you can progress from a simple marine setup to a reef aquarium. This will enable you to enjoy the vibrant background provided by macro-algae, living corals and other invertebrate life.

The major impact of setting up a marine aquarium is that it places exacting responsibilities on its owner. Successful marine fishkeeping is in direct proportion to the amount of effort you are prepared to put into maintaining optimum conditions.

Although marine fishkeeping may be considered a relatively recent introduction within the fishkeeping hobby, there is more pioneering work to be done, particularly in the area of captive breeding. Experience built upon the efforts of others in the past, together with the technological advances in aquarium equipment, have provided us with a much firmer foundation from which to advance. Every marine fishkeeper has something worthwhile to contribute.

Marine fishkeeping is no longer in the 'hit and miss' or 'try and hope' categories of years gone by. Modern air transportation systems ensure that livestock arrives in far better condition, aquarium equipment is completely reliable and there is a wider range of suitable aquarium foods available. And, with the vast amount of information available in publications and on the Internet, both the experienced fishkeeper and the novice have a wealth of back-up advice and guidance at their disposal to help them in the quest for success.

Bringing the natural world into your home

Switch on the television or go on holiday to a sun-drenched island and the chances are that you will see (or be offered) an underwater journey on which you will encounter the brilliant colours and dazzling shoals of fish as they cruise around the coral reefs.

Modern day technology, while allowing you to view and visit such sights, also enables you to create a living souvenir in your own home. The fast jet transport that so effortlessly carried you away is also likely to be bringing thousands of fish to your aquatic dealer. No longer quite so dramatically stressed by the protracted journey, these living jewels are soon thriving in almost identical conditions to those of their native homes as they await your interest. But is it as easy as it sounds?

All it takes is to provide the fish with the same conditions as they would enjoy in nature – excellent water conditions, enough living space and a steady supply of nutritious foods. Fortunately, all the old problems encountered in the early days of marine fishkeeping have been resolved. Crucially, the ability to create synthetic seawater has removed the risk of introducing pathogens into the aquarium by using natural seawater. Modern equipment and practical knowledge make maintaining the water in optimum condition an easy task, while a greater appreciation of the lifestyle and needs of the animals themselves means that they will not be doomed to a short aquarium life as was the case in earlier times. A further encouragement (should you need one) is that since most marine aquarium fishes are caught in shallow waters from coastal fringing reefs, the fishes that you enjoyed seeing in the wild will be readily available for your home aquarium, too.

Left: *Looking down on the coral reefs may be a beautiful experience in itself, but to the marine fishkeeper nothing beats getting down among the fishes or, by following the steps described in this guide, bringing them into your own home.*

The bountiful oceans

The Indo-Pacific Ocean is the natural home of a very large proportion of marine fishes suitable for the aquarium. Despite the huge areas of very open water, most are collected in shallow waters from local reefs.

Fish collected from almost anywhere on this map will all be satisfied by one set of water conditions – so stable is their world-ranging environment.

The Philippines are a rich source of fishes for the marine aquarium.

Singapore and Hong Kong are important hubs of the fish collecting and exporting trade.

The Great Barrier Reef is visited by thousands of tourists each year – all potential marine fishkeepers.

If you add to these reassuring facts the existence of suitable aquarium materials well able to withstand the effect of proximity to corrosive seawater, then the possibility of a successful marine aquarium becomes a reality rather than a dream.

Although it is tempting to assume that recreating a coral reef in the home is within everyone's reach, remember that there is still a lot to learn before you can provide just the right environment in which the underwater panorama of your imagination will thrive. By keeping, caring for and observing the fishes in your aquarium, you could be making a contribution to their conservation. The more we know about the fascinating animals in our charge, the more we can perhaps replicate their needs for captive culture. In this way, we could reduce the need to catch them from the wild, denuding their natural homes and, at the very least, sparing them the long flights that, no doubt, they find as exhausting and tedious as we do.

Seawater – simulating the real thing

As 71% of the Earth's surface is covered by seawater, you might expect it to be one of the most convenient commodities to obtain. Unfortunately, it is not often suitable for the domestic marine aquarium, for several reasons.

For most aquarists it is totally impractical to make regular trips to the coast to collect and transport large quantities of natural seawater. Secondly, relatively few marine aquarists have the luxury of living in the tropics and being able to collect local water. For most, collecting cooler local water and converting it to 'tropical water' can present a number of problems. Warming up natural seawater could cause plankton either to die off, creating potentially toxic conditions, or rapidly multiply and use up vital oxygen. In addition, coral reef fishes are unlikely to have the natural means to fight off disease pathogens that occur in water from other parts of the world. Should you wish to establish an aquarium to house fishes from your local shores,

then it is acceptable, but not always convenient, to use seawater from the same locality.

Another important point to consider is the difficulty of finding a source of unpolluted natural water. The increasing volume of seagoing commercial traffic and effluent from industrial activity around the world means that coastal waters are not likely to be entirely pure, to say the least!

It is clear from this that using natural seawater in a home aquarium can generally create more problems than it is worth.

Synthetic seawater

The best way of providing suitable water for the marine aquarium is to use an artificial mix that is carefully balanced and combined with good quality tapwater so that the final composition approximates as closely as possible to natural seawater. These commercially available mixes of dry salts, minerals and essential trace elements are sterile and should

Right: The constant movement of the sea caused by tides and wind-driven waves means that it is always saturated with oxygen.

The 'salt mix' of seawater

Chloride 55%

Sodium 30.5%

Sulphate 7.5%

Magnesium 3.5%

Calcium 1%

Potassium 1%

Bicarbonate 0.5%

Other chemicals and trace elements 1%

Seawater is not simply a solution of sodium chloride; it also contains sulphates, magnesium, calcium and potassium, plus many trace elements in very small amounts. The very best synthetic seawater mixes are indistinguishable from natural seawater.

be manufactured from scientific-grade materials, so that there is no risk of inadvertently introducing diseases and other problems into the aquarium. Also, because you only purchase the dry mix and add it to freshwater when needed, it is very convenient in terms of carrying and storing.

Modern mixes are so exact in their formula and manufacturing process that you no longer need to use up an entire package at once in order to produce a given volume of water with the desired

specific gravity (or density) and correct chemical composition. These days you can use up part of a package and still be sure of obtaining the correct chemical composition regardless of what specific gravity you wish to attain. (Reseal partly used bags and store in a cool, dry place.) This offers a great deal of flexibility and is an ideal solution for preparing small amounts of seawater for partial water changes. This is the medium your fishes and invertebrates have to live in, so quality is essential.

Living in a salt solution

The key difference between marine fish and freshwater fish, both coldwater and tropical, is the level of salt found in the water they inhabit, and their ability to survive in their environment. While some freshwater fish may adapt to life in saltwater, and some marine fish will survive at low salinity levels, their inability to cope with the level of salts both in their body and in the surrounding water is one major reason why marine fish and freshwater fish will not generally survive in each other's environment. The process by which the salts are absorbed and excreted from the fish's body and the way in which they control their salt levels is known as osmoregulation.

How osmoregulation works

In all fish there is a natural difference between the level of salts found in the fish's body fluids and the level of salts in the surrounding environment, whether it is freshwater or saltwater. Only very thin membranes, such as the gills, separate the differing levels, so there is a tendency for water and salts to flow constantly into and out of the fish. This two-way movement is caused by diffusion and osmosis, natural processes that occur wherever two solutions of different concentrations are separated by a partially permeable membrane. The salt ions move from the more concentrated solution through the membrane and into the weaker solution; this is diffusion. The water molecules will move in the opposite direction and dilute the stronger solution; this is osmosis.

Marine fish differ from their freshwater relatives in the way they balance the levels of salts and fluids in their bodies. The bodies of freshwater fish contain a

Above: *Marine fishes are well adapted to thrive in their highly salty environment. They can absorb water and excrete the salt to maintain their internal bodily fluids at the right concentration for life.*

higher level of salts than the surrounding water. There is a tendency for salts to be lost through the tissues as water flows in. To combat this, freshwater fish have extremely efficient kidneys that are able to excrete water very quickly, while retaining the salts in the water by reabsorbing them from the urine. Additionally, freshwater fish have specially structured gills that allow them to retain salts circulating in the blood that have been ingested with food.

In marine fish the situation is reversed. Their environment has a higher salt level than is found in their body fluids. As a result, they face a constant battle against dehydration, as water is lost to the surrounding seawater and salts are retained in the body. Marine fish deal with this situation by consuming large amounts of water and excreting very little urine. Only a few salts are absorbed from the seawater they drink and special chloride cells in the gills actively excrete salt.

Freshwater osmoregulation

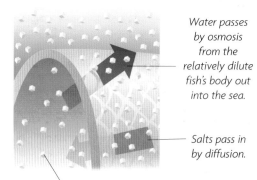

Water passes by osmosis from the relatively dilute freshwater into the fish's body.

Salts pass out by diffusion.

The body fluids have a higher salt concentration than the surrounding water.

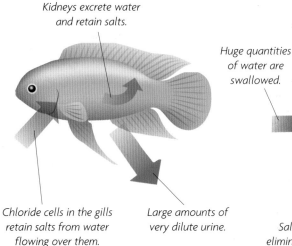

Kidneys excrete water and retain salts.

Huge quantities of water are swallowed.

Chloride cells in the gills retain salts from water flowing over them.

Large amounts of very dilute urine.

Saltwater osmoregulation

Water passes by osmosis from the relatively dilute fish's body out into the sea.

Salts pass in by diffusion.

The body fluids have a lower salt concentration than the surrounding water.

Water, but not salts, absorbed in the gut.

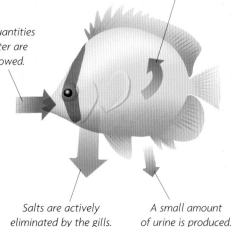

Salts are actively eliminated by the gills.

A small amount of urine is produced.

Salinity, specific gravity and pH

The salinity of water is a measure of the total amount of dissolved salts it contains; it is usually quoted as gm/litre (parts per thousand). Within the fishkeeping hobby, however, it is more usual to talk in terms of the specific gravity (S.G.) of water, since this is more easily tested and clearer to understand.

Specific gravity is simply a ratio of the weight of a water sample compared to the weight of an equal volume of distilled water at 4°C (39°F), which is assigned a specific gravity of 1. Since adding salts to water increases its weight as well as its salinity, the two scales are directly comparable. Thus, a salinity of 35gm/litre is equivalent to a specific gravity of 1.026 at 15°C (59°F), measured by means of the traditional floating hydrometer or the easy-to-use swing-needle types.

Seawater generally has an S.G. of between 1.023 and 1.027, depending on

Left: *The correct specific gravity (S.G.) is indicated when the chosen value coincides with the meniscus (water level) as shown on the coloured part of*

the location. Once properly acclimatised, many fish and invertebrates seem happy to accept a constant S.G. in a fairly wide range. For most purposes, a reading between 1.021 and 1.024 is acceptable. The key factor is to keep the S.G. as constant as possible. Using a hydrometer, take regular readings and ensure that they do not vary by more than one point (between 1.022 and 1.023, for example). Although this seems a minor shift, it is still many times that which occurs in even the most extreme circumstances in any one natural location.

In an established tank, the main cause of changes in specific gravity are evaporation and the addition of new stock. Over a period of time, the water level in the tank tends to drop as fresh water evaporates and thus, the salt water become progressively more saline. Compensate for this by regularly adding a small quantity of *fresh* water. It is not a good policy to wait until a large amount (more than 0.5 litre /approximately a pint, say) is needed as the change in salinity will harm delicate invertebrates and algae. Two common and dangerous sequences of events can lead to a continual increase in the S.G. of the water in your tank. In the first scenario, you allow the water level in the tank to drop through evaporation and then decide to carry out a partial water change. Having drained out 10-20 percent of the water, you replace exactly the same amount with newly made up seawater, plus extra seawater to make up the evaporation loss. Since the reduced volume in the tank was more concentrated, this will cause an increase in S.G. Alternatively, the water level drops and you then add more stock (and its attendant seawater), thus filling the tank and also raising the S.G. Be sure to guard against these pitfalls

How pH is measured

The pH scale registers the acidity or alkalinity of water. The scale is logarithmic, so that each unit change in pH, say from 7 to 8, is a ten times change, while 7 to 9 is a hundred times change, etc. This is why a sudden change in pH is very stressful and harmful to fish.

Water molecule

Water (H_2O) is made up of positively charged hydrogen ions (H^+) and negatively charged hydroxyl ions (OH^-). The pH level is a measure of the ratio of these two ions in a body of water. Acidic water has more hydrogen ions; alkaline water more hydroxyl ions. Neutral water has an equal number of both.

pH 9: 100 times more alkaline than pH 7.

pH 8: 10 times more alkaline that pH 7.

pH 7: neutral.

Left: Test the water regularly to monitor the pH level, which in a marine tank should remain fairly stable. Most tests involve adding chemicals to a measured sample and comparing the colour change to a printed chart.

Above: The final stage of testing the pH, showing a correct reading of between 8.0 and 8.4. When you compare the sample colour against the card, follow the directions; not all tests are the same.

The nitrogen cycle

The nitrogen cycle is an extremely important biological process on the reef – and in all ecosystems, for that matter. It is an important purification system, but it is more than that, because it is also the source of primary food production, without which nothing on earth would survive.

How the cycle works

The nitrogen cycle is the 'driving force' that removes harmful nitrogenous compounds that gradually build up in the aquarium water, starting with free ammonia (NH_3) and ionised ammonia (NH_4^+). Fishes and invertebrates produce ammonia as a waste product from their metabolic processes. This is added to the ammonia produced by bacteria 'working on' other waste materials in the aquarium, such as uneaten food and faeces. Ammonia is highly toxic to fishes and invertebrates; if it is not removed, or converted into other less harmful substances, your aquarium subjects will soon perish. Fortunately, in Nature's Grand Plan, a substance that is poison to one living organism is food for another and so there

is a natural way of dealing with ammonia removal.

Aerobic (oxygen-loving) bacteria, such as *Nitrosomonas* species, convert ammonia to nitrite (NO_2), a slightly less toxic substance, but one that is still dangerous to fishes and invertebrates. A second group of bacteria, such as *Nitrobacter* species, transform the nitrite to nitrate (NO_3), which is a much safer substance but one that can still cause some problems if allowed to build up too much. It is not fully understood to what level nitrate can cause problems for aquarium subjects, although it seems to be detrimental to delicate fish species and some invertebrates. The important thing is that nitrate does not occur on the natural coral reef other than in the smallest quantities, so we should not make compromises but strive to keep it to an absolute minimum in the aquarium. Nitrate is a primary nutrient for algae and the mainstay of primary food production right at the beginning of the food chain from which all other living organisms benefit. (It is worth noting that undesirable algae flourishes in the presence of excess nitrates, as well as phosphates.)

Left: *Marine ('macro') algae, such as the* Caulerpa *sp. shown here, will thrive in a marine aquarium. The nitrates produced as part of the nitrogen cycle are absorbed as food by these and other less welcome forms of algae.*

How the nitrogen cycle works

Nitrogen is recycled in the natural world through the digestion of nitrogen-containing proteins by animals and the action of bacteria in the environment. Here is how the cycle works in the marine world.

Fish and other marine creatures digest and metabolise protein as part of their varied diets.

Nitrates are absorbed by plants, such as algae, as a fertiliser.

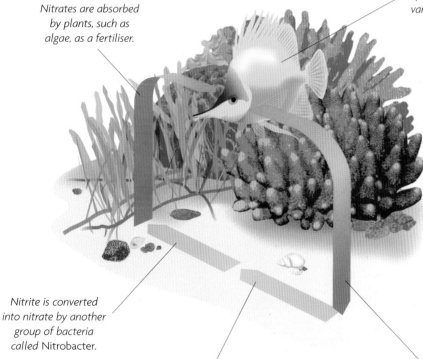

Nitrite is converted into nitrate by another group of bacteria called Nitrobacter.

Ammonia is converted by Nitrosomonas bacteria into nitrite. These bacteria thrive in oxygenated conditions in the substrate and on the surface of rocks.

The main waste product of protein digestion is ammonia. Fish excrete this in urine and directly from the gills. Ammonia also builds up as faeces, plant matter and uneaten food decay.

Protein skimmers

Most fishkeepers consider protein skimmers to be essential for the long-term success of a marine aquarium, but what do they do and how do they work? Originally designed for the sewage treatment industry, protein skimmers, or foam fractionisers as they are sometimes called, remove harmful organic substances from the aquarium before they can cause the water quality to deteriorate.

A protein skimmer works on the principle that dissolved matter, including bacteria and plankton, as well as organic material resulting from fish waste and food, will adhere by surface tension to the outer layer of air bubbles. The rising column of air bubbles reaches the top of the skimmer's 'reaction chamber', where it falls away, leaving the protein waste to collect at the top of the skimmer. This protein manifests itself as a thick, yellowish, smelly liquid.

A triple-pass protein skimmer

Protein-laden foam overflows into this cup and settles out into a discardable liquid.

Cleaned water returns to the aquarium from the outer cylinder of the skimmer.

Air bubbles rising up the central tube attract protein from the water. The foam progresses upwards, while the cleaned water continues its longer path towards the outlet.

Air drawn into the venturi creates a mass of bubbles in the water flow.

Contact time

Certain factors play an important role in the efficiency of a protein skimmer. One of them is contact time, the period during which air and water are mixed together in the skimmer chamber. The longer this period is, the more effective the skimmer becomes. The triple-pass, Berlin-type system represents best available.

Types of protein skimmer

Protein skimmers are available in three main forms. **Air-operated protein skimmers** are mounted inside the aquarium or sump and are generally better suited to smaller aquariums. **Venturi skimmers** are high-powered workhorses, operated by a water pump that takes water either from the aquarium or the sump and pushes it into the bottom of the skimmer through a venturi tube that draws in air to create a mass of bubbles. **Turbo skimmers** have air injected directly into a turbo pump with a modified 12-blade impeller that chops up the air and water into a super-fine concentrated mix. Turbo skimmers, especially those using Berlin technology, have set new standards for removing protein from aquariums. **Convergent-divergent flow skimmers** employ a unique method of mixing air and water, while still using the turbo method of air injection.

An advanced turbo skimmer

This advanced skimmer maximises the contact time between the tank water and a constant stream of fine air bubbles. Protein wastes stick to the bubble surfaces and can be collected and removed as the bubbles collapse.

Collection cup in which the protein-laden foam collapses.

A pipe can be connected to this port to drain off the protein waste.

Cleaned water returns to the tank over this cascade.

Optional basket for chemical or biological filtration media.

Reaction chamber in which the water and air bubbles remain in close contact.

Optional surface skimmer attachment on the inlet pipe.

Pump with an 18-blade impeller that generates fine air bubbles in the incoming air/water flow.

External filters

Although protein skimming is a type of filtration, it is important enough to be discussed in its own right. But, generally speaking, 'filtration' refers to mechanical, biological or chemical filtration, which are all used in various ways to provide marine fishes with stable, healthy water.

The filter is the life-support system of any aquarium. It not only prevents debris from remaining within the aquarium by physically removing it into a filter chamber or some other container (mechanical filtration), but also breaks down the toxic ammonia compounds released into the aquarium by fish excreta and the decay of excess food (biological filtration). If carbon or phosphate removers are used, the filter also performs chemical filtration. Over the next few pages, we look at filtration systems and consider their advantages and disadvantages.

External power filters

Also known as canister filters, external power filters are fairly large filters situated outside, usually below, the aquarium. Canister filters enable you to use different filter media (usually two or three) in one filter. By varying the filter media, you can incorporate all three forms of filtration – mechanical, biological and chemical.

Ideally, the filter has an initial prefilter foam to remove particulate waste. The foam is usually followed by a filter media with a high surface area, such as sintered glass, which is quickly populated by millions of beneficial bacteria that break down ammonia and nitrite into less harmful nitrate (see page 16). Finally, carbon may be used to remove any slight discoloration from the water and give the aquarium an extra 'sparkle'.

An external canister filter

These plastic tubes carry water to and from the aquarium.

Shut-off taps disconnect the filter without water spillage.

An electric water pump is housed in the top part of the filter.

Incoming water passes upwards through the filter media, packed in a plastic basket inside the canister. Maintain water flow at all times to prevent the media turning anaerobic, as would quickly happen following any failure of the power supply.

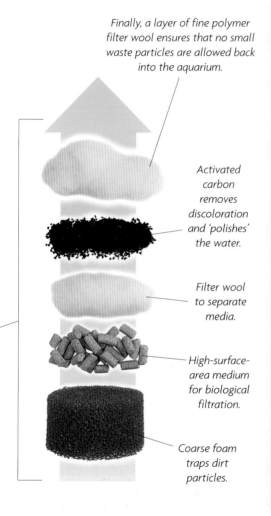

Finally, a layer of fine polymer filter wool ensures that no small waste particles are allowed back into the aquarium.

Activated carbon removes discoloration and 'polishes' the water.

Filter wool to separate media.

High-surface-area medium for biological filtration.

Coarse foam traps dirt particles.

Algae filters

As excess nitrate/phosphate levels encourage algal growth, it seems a sensible plan to turn this fact around and deliberately use algae to remove these unwanted 'pollutants.' A separate shallow container can be placed within the water flow pumped from the aquarium. In it, and under fairly bright lighting, a healthy crop of algae can be grown without it interfering with the designed beauty of the main tank. By regularly harvesting the algae, nitrates and phosphates can be effectively removed from the aquarium water; as this main algal growth develops it out-competes any would be algal growth within the main aquarium in the race for nutrients in the water. One drawback of this system is that any herbivorous fish in the main aquarium served by an algae filter will be denied their necessary green diet; arrange for these fishes to get their 'green' food by other methods. To be effective, such filters need to be of considerable size, which may be problematical when it comes to disguising them, lest they detract from the inherent beauty of the otherwise well-presented main aquarium.

Right: This shows the basic principle of an algae filter, but the shape and scale must be matched to the display aquarium.

Fluidised bed filter system

Fluidised bed units take biological filtration out of the tank and supersede outdated substrate systems. Silica sand is held in suspension in aquarium water pumped through an external cylindrical container. Because the sand granules are free to move, and not packed together, they offer a much larger surface area for bacterial colonisation and this results in a much more efficient conversion of ammonia through nitrite and into nitrate.

In some models, an incorporated carbon filter cartridge removes any coloration from the water before it returns to the aquarium. The fluidised bed system is oxygen-consuming and water emerging from such units should be given every chance to re-oxygenate before returning to the main aquarium. This may be achieved by using a spraybar as a return tube, a venturi system fitted to the outlet or even an airstone placed at the point of the returning water.

Coping with power failures

Some thought should also be given as to what happens should the electricity supply be cut off or debris block the inlet of the fluidised bed unit. The water flow through the unit will stop but, more importantly, the 'filter bed' will physically collapse from its previous 'in suspension' form to a solid mass of sand. On the resumption of power, the pump may not have enough energy to 're-suspend' the sand without a little help, with consequent damage to the pump. (If possible, adjust the flow to maximum on restarting, and then reset it to normal flow rate.) Equally problematical for the aquarium would be the rapid demise of the bacterial colony should the power failure last an appreciable length of time. When restarting after a lengthy period, run the unit in a monitored 'closed system' situation until tests show the bacterial bed has become re-established.

Refugium

A refugium is a body of water, separate from the main tank but sharing its water source. On one hand, it can live up to its name and be nothing more than an area of shelter. Alternatively, and more likely, the refugium can be used in several ways in conjunction with the main aquarium. It provides ideal growth conditions for food items, such as copepods and amphipods. Depending on design and installation, these animals can be continuously swept back into the main tank to feed both invertebrates and fish. It can also be a controlled growing area for macro-algae. Caulerpa and other macro-algae will not only consume ammonia/nitrates and phosphates that accumulate due to overstocking or overfeeding but, because they are grow in isolation, they avoid being predated upon by vegetarian-minded fish. Other uses include acting as a convenient parking area for heaters, UV sterilisers, etc., a temporary isolation area for a bullying species or as a breeding tank. It has been suggested that daily pH fluctuations can be avoided by running the refugium in a reverse photoperiod operation. A further adaptation uses a special substrate that provides a continuing supply of vital trace elements to the main tank and also harbours beneficial anaerobic denitrifying bacteria.

A *fluidised bed filter*

Above: A typical fluidised bed filter in operation. The sand's moving biological bed is held in suspension (the two lines show the upper and lower levels of the medium). A valve in the unit prevents sand siphoning back into the pump if the power fails.

Control the rate of water flowing into the filter by rotating this cap.

Water from the aquarium

This cartridge is filled with activated carbon to adsorb impurities from the water.

Water returning to the aquarium

An optional cartridge can be fitted to remove phosphates from the water.

The media used in the filter is a special silica sand. Once in suspension, it forms a 'biological bed' with an enormous surface area.

Ultraviolet light sterilisation

Ultraviolet (UV) light is capable of eliminating algae spores and bacteria that are freely suspended in the water and sometimes cause cloudiness. A germicidal-grade lamp can also destroy disease pathogens, but is only effective on pathogens with a free-swimming stage that may find their way through the UV unit, so do not rely on it for total disease control. Bear in mind that UV light is dangerous to the eyes: NEVER look directly at the lamp without eye protection.

The UV steriliser consists of a UV lamp fitted inside a sealed clear quartz sleeve, mounted within a water jacket. Aquarium water fed into the outer jacket is sterilised as it flows from one end to another. The efficiency of sterilisation depends, among other factors, on the length of time the water is exposed to the UV light. The effectiveness of the lamp can be optimised by prefiltering the water mechanically before passing it through the steriliser. This prevents organic material and suspended matter from obscuring the quartz sleeve and thus lessening the effect of the UV rays. Even so, the lamp has a definite useful lifespan; used continually, most lamps will require replacement every six months. After this period, the lamp may still appear to be functioning, but in fact the UV light is no longer able to penetrate the quartz sleeve and sterilise the water.

Above: *This is a typical UV unit used to treat aquarium water. The water hose connectors are translucent so that you can see the 'glow' of the UV tube when in operation. This is a safety measure to make sure you do not open the unit and damage your eyesight by looking directly at the lamp.*

How a UV steriliser works

High-energy ultraviolet light disrupts living cells in a number of ways. The genetic material (DNA) in the nucleus and tiny 'power packs' called mitochondria dotted around the cell are all damaged by the rays. In algae cells, the light ruptures the chlorophyll-containing plastids that carry out essential photosynthesis.

The fluorescent tube in the middle produces ultraviolet light with a wavelength of 253.7 nm. This UVC is harmful to living tissue.

This quartz sleeve encases the tube but allows UV light to pass through.

Water flows though this outer glass tube.

Above: *Aquatic dealers run several filter systems to sustain their livestock, including heavy duty UV sterilisers such as these.*

Using ozone

Ozone (O_3) is an unstable form of oxygen (O_2). The extra atom of oxygen readily separates from the molecule and oxidises toxins and other compounds in the aquarium water. This oxidising action makes ozone an effective disinfectant; it will kill bacteria, disease pathogens, algae spores and other free-swimming microorganisms that come into close contact with the gas. Ozone is used by many large public aquariums as part of their overall water quality management systems.

Ozone is formed by passing air (ideally dried) over an electrical discharge in a device known as an ozoniser, converting some of the oxygen in the air to ozone. The ozonised air is then passed through a special water/ozone contact chamber or a protein skimmer. Providing this is made from ozone-resistant materials, it makes an ideal ozone reactor. Since ozone is harmful to the aquarium inhabitants, it must only be applied in a separate vessel, never directly into the aquarium. Ozone-treated water should be passed through a carbon filter before being returned to the aquarium in order to remove any residual ozone or any harmful byproducts of excessive ozonisation. It is advisable to use an ozoniser together with a redox (or ORP – oxidation, reduction potential) controller. A probe in the aquarium monitors ozone concentration in terms of the redox potential of the water and switches on the ozoniser only when the water conditions require it.

As you might imagine, ozone is a dangerous gas and must be used with the utmost care. Always follow the manufacturer's instructions to the letter. Ozone is also capable of damaging materials, such as rubber piping and pump diaphragms, and excessive levels can also make plastics turn brittle.

Left: With their crowns of feathery tentacles, tubeworms make attractive subjects for the marine aquarium. They will thrive in strong currents of clean water, but need fine forms of food to sustain them.

Ozone and protein skimming

Froth carrying organic waste overflows into this collecting cup.

The waste can be drained from the base of the collecting cup through this tube.

The ozone generator uses a high-energy electrical discharge to bond an extra atom to oxygen molecules to create ozone (O_3).

A check valve prevents water siphoning back into the ozoniser. Renew this regularly.

Above: Activated carbon placed in a compartment on top of the collecting cup prevents any excess ozone entering the atmosphere.

Ozone passes into the water flow through the venturi device located here.

This probe hangs in the aquarium. It measures the redox potential of the water and regulates the amount of ozone produced by the ozoniser.

The Jaubert system

Until relatively recently, marine aquariums relied on mechanical, chemical and biological methods of filtration using long-established conventional units. One innovative progression in the 1980s was the Jaubert system, best described as a subgravel system without any uplift tube or any deliberately engineered water flow through it. Primarily designed for use in Dr Jaubert's own Monaco Oceanographic Aquarium, this system's basics soon attracted interest and several American marine fishkeepers, such as Bob Goemans, adapted it with some success for use in the more modest-sized home aquarium.

A plastic grid (fluorescent light diffusing grids are ideal) is held off the bottom of the tank by plastic supports to create a static void (plenum). A thin layer of synthetic floss material covers the grid to prevent material trickling downwards and the rest of the substrate placed over it. The natural diffusion of oxygen downwards from the main, additionally-aerated body of water towards the oxygen-depleted plenum sustains the biological filtration action within the substrate, whilst bacteria in the anaerobic plenum act as denitrifiers, reducing nitrate levels and completing the full nitrogen cycle.

The top layer of substrate – about 4cm (1.5in) deep – is aerobic because of the oxygenated water above it.

A layer of plastic mesh prevents disturbance of the substrate by digging or burrowing fish.

The lower level of substrate, and the water-filled void beneath, are anaerobic due to the lack of water movement through the substrate.

A layer of filter floss prevents substrate trickling through the 'egg-crate' grid.

Grid formed of criss-crossed plastic slats.

Short pillars support the grid to create a void about 2.5cm (1in) deep beneath the substrate.

Using living rock in the aquarium

While a basic aquarium has a protein skimmer and an external filter, the 'biological' purification of the water can also be achieved by using another natural method making use of 'living rock'. This is simply rock collected from the wild with living organisms already in situ. The base material is usually of a labyrinthine, highly-porous nature and provides both aerobic and anaerobic areas inhabited by the various minute animals and bacteria. These actively purify the water in much the same way as the bacteria in an external filter. This system has become known as the 'Berlin method'.

In the Berlin method, more reliance is placed upon living rock and protein skimming in the aquarium to rid it effectively of unwanted toxic materials. The theory is that the protein skimmer removes organic matter before it degenerates into ammonia and therefore obviates the need for its subsequent conversion to nitrite and nitrate by bacteria. The inclusion of large areas of live rock also reduces the load on biological filtration systems. One drawback of using live rock is that it is expensive and furnishing the aquarium with a suitable amount may prove to be a financial deterrent to many fishkeepers.

Live rock is maintained at the aquatic store and may even be inoculated with new living cultures during this time. Obviously, taking the usual pre-cleaning precautions as described for ordinary 'decorative' rocks would not apply in this instance. It is vital that living rocks are introduced into oxygenated water as soon as possible. Depending on their quality (a known history is highly preferable) you may put them into your main collection immediately, although treating them to a quarantine period (as you would with any new additional livestock) could be a prudent measure. During quarantine, it may be likely that some organisms will die off and new ones re-emerge. Fluctuations in nitrite and nitrate levels will occur and the conditions should be left to stabilise before transferring the rocks to their new permanent home.

Unless the aquarium is to be set up with living rock from the outset (as shown in the setting up sequence starting on page 46), only small amounts should be introduced into an established system at a time to avoid fluctuations in redox potential.

Reverse osmosis

Thus far we have only discussed equipment required for treating water once it is in the aquarium. However, one of the easiest ways to get ahead in the quest for good water quality is to ensure that only the very best water is used in the first place. To make it safe for human consumption, tapwater contains not only chlorine and chloramine, but also pesticides, nitrates, phosphates and silica, all of which are detrimental to the health of marine animals. To prevent these substances from ever entering the aquarium, you are strongly advised to use a reverse osmosis unit.

Reverse osmosis is a process that removes salts and minerals from the water, plus the toxins mentioned above, as well as some bacteria, viruses and fungal spores. The key to a reverse osmosis unit is a partially permeable membrane that allows water to pass through, but repels all the other substances. Typically, a reverse osmosis unit will have a carbon prefilter to remove chlorine from the incoming water.

An R.O. unit is usually simple to plumb into a domestic coldwater supply. The only real drawback is that typically three to four times as much 'reject' water has to be discarded for every measure of 'good' water. However, the discarded water is suitable for watering plants, as it is high in useful nutrients.

Using a good-quality salt mix will ensure that the correct trace elements and minerals are restored to the R.O. water before it is added to the tank. If you are using R.O. water for a freshwater top-up, you must use a marine buffer and trace element additive in conjunction with the water change.

Above: *Tapwater is processed for human consumption. Chemicals added to it by the local water company make it safe for us to drink but dangerous for aquarium use without prior treatment.*

Right: *Tapwater can contain contaminants that can be removed using a reverse osmosis unit such as this. The efficiency of such units depends on the concentration of pollutants present in the water supply. Be sure to buy the correct unit for your usage.*

How reverse osmosis works

When separated by a partially permeable membrane, the natural tendency is for solutions to equalise in concentration by osmosis. Applying pressure to reverse this process creates very pure water.

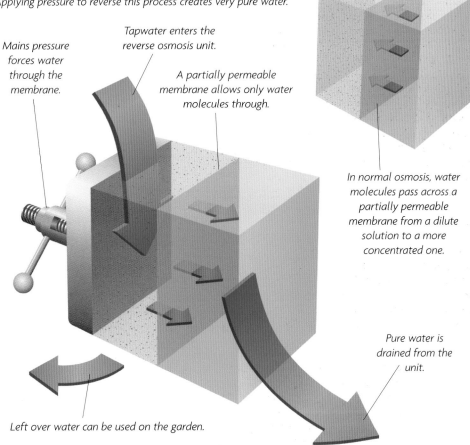

Tapwater enters the reverse osmosis unit.

Mains pressure forces water through the membrane.

A partially permeable membrane allows only water molecules through.

In normal osmosis, water molecules pass across a partially permeable membrane from a dilute solution to a more concentrated one.

Pure water is drained from the unit.

Left over water can be used on the garden.

Complete water management systems

The sump beneath a reef aquarium is a 'high-tech' environment full of tubes and boxes that maintain the water conditions in the display tank above it. Water reaches the sump by overflowing from the main aquarium and, once cleaned, is returned by a pump situated in the sump. In the 'wet-and-dry' filter, the incoming aquarium water is fed over a mass of plastic balls on its way to the other water treatment components. Being in the atmosphere rather than totally submerged, the nitrifying bacteria that flourish here are well provided with oxygen and so operate more efficiently.

Nitrates can be removed by means of a denitrator unit in which bacteria live in anaerobic conditions. As they 'feed' they take their necessary oxygen from the nitrates, thus reducing them back to nitrogen gas.

Biofilter   Mechanical filtration   Protein skimmer

Left: *Complete systems house filtration and other water management devices, including protein skimmers, phosphate removers, freshwater 'topping up' reservoirs and even the heating system.*

Above: *Where the aquarium is housed in a cabinet, it makes good sense to have the water treatment equipment assembled in one convenient place - out of sight but easily accessible for maintenance tasks.*

Calcium reactors

A calcium reactor is not a filter, but it is included here because it is normally used in tandem with a filtration system. Invertebrates need calcium carbonate in order to grow their skeletons or shells, and regularly take these elements out of the water. As aquarium water ages and its calcium buffering capabilities diminish, the pH has a tendency to drop. This can cause metabolic problems for fishes and invertebrates, such as respiration difficulties. It is vital to maintain the pH at 8.3 for reef animals. A calcium reactor can help to achieve this. The apparatus is usually a sealed acrylic container filled with calcareous material such as aragonite. (Shown here empty.) Aquarium water is delivered to the unit fairly slowly via a bypass system from the main filter. The system is injected with carbon dioxide gas and its acidic nature slowly dissolves the more alkaline aragonite, thus charging the aquarium water with calcium. The carbon dioxide gas is used up in the process.

Temperature control

The marine aquarium must be kept at a reasonably constant temperature if fishes and invertebrates from tropical coral reefs are to survive. In some places, measures to cool down the tropical aquarium may be required, particularly during summer months.

Types of heating equipment

The most popular method of heating aquarium water is by means of small, individual electric immersion heaters combined with a thermostat control, commonly known as heaterstats. These units are generally protected inside a glass sleeve, although you can also buy more rugged types made from materials such as titanium. Some external, canister filters also incorporate a heating system, but be sure to check these out carefully as most are only safe for use in freshwater systems because the elements and thermostat connections could corrode in saltwater. Undergravel heating cables controlled by an external thermostat are also available.

Heating equipment may also be incorporated within the water treatment compartment (or sump) of a built-in 'total system'. This can make more efficient use of your heater, as it is heating a smaller body of water at any one time.

Controlling heat

In a standard aquarium heaterstat, the built-in thermostat controls the supply of electricity to the heating element by sensing the temperature of the water. This sensing is achieved by means of a bimetallic strip that bends and straightens, making and breaking contact as the temperature changes, or by microchip circuitry. Microchip thermostats are normally a separate unit from the heating element and temperature control is achieved by a probe in the water that sends a message to the thermostat, which regulates the power to the heating element.

For most tropical marine aquariums, the ideal temperature is around 75°F (24°C). The familiar heaterstats are usually factory preset to this temperature, but can be adjusted if necessary.

Heaterstats are available calibrated in °C or °F, or both scales side by side.

Right: *Heaterstats are easy to adjust by turning the knob at the top until you reach the desired temperature. Some units have a light to indicate whether it is on or off. Make sure you can see it. Always keep a spare heaterstat handy in case of failures.*

External thermostat units can be either analogue or digital. Analogue units are set manually, but digital models allow you to programme a variety of temperature parameters and often have automatic features, such as emitting an alarm if the temperature gets too high or too low. Some include a display that records the maximum and minimum temperature reached in a time period, as well as showing the current temperature. Such digital units can offer the degree of control and accuracy that will provide extra protection for aquarium subjects and peace of mind for you, the aquarist.

Computerised aquarium systems that can control temperature along with a variety of water quality testing features from a single unit are also available. Such equipment often includes software and connecting cables to link with a personal computer, allowing you to plot trends and store other information that you will find useful.

What size heaterstat?

Allow about 10 watts per 4.5 litres (1 gallon) of water content. An aquarium measuring 90x30x38cm (36x15x12in) has an approximate volume of 110 litres (24 gallons) and would therefore require 240 watts of heat. A smaller-sized heater would be sufficient if the room is permanently heated. Following the guidelines described above, a single 250-watt heater should suffice, but two separate 150-watt heaters would be better and afford some margin for error or in the event of heater failure.

Keeping it cool

Chillers contain a compact refrigeration unit that cools the incoming water to a preset temperature. Always choose one designed specifically for use with marine aquariums. Ask your dealer for advice on the correct size and type of chiller to use.

Above: *The in and outflow pipe connectors are visible at the front of this chiller.*

Right: *Various thermometers are available for aquarium use, including easy-to-read liquid crystal types that stick to the outside surface of the tank. A digital model is shown being used on page 57.*

Lighting the aquarium

Lighting in a fish-only aquarium is really down to personal taste. Two fluorescent tubes will usually suffice, with perhaps a third, blue lamp for night viewing. However, if there are invertebrates in the tank, lighting becomes far more important. Many corals, anemones and molluscs rely on algae known as zooxanthellae for food. As well as good water quality, the main requirement of zooxanthellae and macro algae, such as caulerpa, is high intensity light at the correct wavelength. In fish-only systems with relatively low light intensities, zooxanthellae will not grow. In a reef aquarium, the correct lighting is therefore of paramount importance and this usually means using metal-halide lamps.

There are two key elements that contribute to the suitability of a particular lamp for a given marine aquarium setup: light intensity and colour temperature Understanding these factors will help you to choose the best lighting system for a fish-only tank or a reef aquarium with invertebrates.

Light intensity

The electrical power of a lamp is measured in watts, whereas the intensity, or brightness, of a light source is quoted in lumens. (You may also see light intensity quoted in terms of lux – lumens per square metre.)

The intensity of a lamp is usually indicated on the packaging. Most fluorescent tubes rarely exceed 5,000-6,000 lumens, and some are far lower. On the other hand, metal-halide lamps commonly emit in excess of 10,000 lumens.

Light intensity also depends on the efficiency of the lamp and it is difficult to achieve high levels of illumination with fluorescent tubes. This is especially true in deeper tanks, where tube light fades quickly.

Colour temperature

Any type of lamp appears to give off light in a particular colour. In fact, the colour we perceive is made up of many different colours, each with their own spectral wavelengths. This is called the 'colour temperature' of the lamp and is measured in degrees Kelvin (°K). The higher the Kelvin rating, the more white and 'cool' the light appears. A low Kelvin rating produces a 'warm' appearance, usually mainly red or yellow. For example, a candle flame has a colour temperature of 1,800°K, a cool white fluorescent tube is 4,000°K and a very bright metal-halide lamp can be 14,000°K. By contrast, looking up into a clear blue sky over a tropical reef can register up to 30,000°K.

The real colours of white light

A rainbow reminds us that white light is made up of a spectrum of colours. They are produced by different wavelengths; violet is short, red is long.

Right: *Various wavelengths of light penetrate to different depths in the sea. Blue light can reach depths of over 250m (820ft), while red light fades at about 10m (33ft). Ultraviolet light (invisible to us) can reach 100m (330ft).*

Below: These new forms of the standard white and blue tubes produce 80% more light. Reflectors boost the light even more.

Above: These standard marine white and actinic blue tubes are 60cm (24in) long and consume 18 watts of power.

Spectral power distribution

The output of the various wavelengths of light produced by a lamp is referred to as its spectral power distribution. In effect, this represents the strength of light in the different colour 'bands' and forms a convenient way of graphically illustrating and comparing the colour performance of a lamp. The graphs shown below compare the output of two light sources set against the sun's complete spectrum. You will see similar graphs on packaging of aquarium lamps. Wavelengths are in nanometres (nm) – billionths of a metre.

White triphosphor fluorescent tube

These spectral output curves show that this type of fluorescent tube produces useful levels of light at a wide range of wavelengths, providing bright illumination for all creatures in the aquarium. (The vertical scale on these graphs reflects comparative output levels.)

nm   400   500   600   700

Blue actinic 03 fluorescent tube

This tube is 'strong' in the blue area of the spectrum, especially in the so-called 'actinic' range peaking at 420nm, which is vital for zooxanthellae to thrive. It also supplies some UV for a fluorescent effect.

nm   400   500   600   700

37

Lighting the aquarium

Left: The familiar fluorescent tubes used across the world in homes and offices are fine for aquarium use. The development of a triphosphor coating has boosted the output across a wide range of light wavelengths.

Above: The biax tube is like a conventional fluorescent tube folded back on itself with the two sets of double pins in a row of four. These tubes save space and provide high light outputs for aquarium use.

Left: A narrow-bore form of fluorescent tube provides intense light and saves space in the aquarium canopy. These are triggered with an electronic starter (ballast) system and are available in a range phosphor types.

Right: Powered up, a biax tube glows just like a conventional fluorescent tube. The twin tubes close together produce an intense light for the space they occupy. Another benefit of these lamps is that the tubes can be coated with different phosphor formulations, making it possible to recreate the effect of two separate (and different) tubes in one fitting.

Right: Metal-halide lamps for aquarium use are fitted into housings such as this and suspended above the open tank. They provide very bright illumination, but must have some ventilation space around them because of the heat they generate.

Metal-halide lamp

Metal-halide lamps generate a wide output with high levels at 400-480nm (good for zooxanthellae) and 550nm (to simulate sunlight). The volume of the curves in the spectral output shown below indicates a bright lamp.

Above: The provision of white and blue fluorescent tubes in combination with a metal halide lamp offers the fishkeeper the facility of creating separate day and night lighting effects, together with a 'hot' highlighted area to feature specially chosen decor or invertebrate life in the tank.

| nm | 400 | 500 | 600 | 700 |

Lighting the aquarium

The final piece in the lighting jigsaw is the length of time the lighting is left on – the 'photoperiod'. There are no hard and fast rules about this, as every aquarium differs slightly in its requirements. The best way is to learn from nature and try to replicate life on the reef in your aquarium.

Around the equator, the period of sunlight is about 12 hours each day, whereas in tropical latitudes (up to about 20° north and south of the Equator), full sunlight is only experienced between about 9am to 3pm (i.e. six hours). As a starting point, if you are using fluorescent tubes, try setting your lighting

period to about 12 hours. A blue lamp or one of the less bright lamps should come on one to two hours before the main lighting and go off one to two hours after it has been turned off. This creates a feeling of dusk and dawn and avoids stressing nervous fish.

If you are using metal-halide lamps, try starting with a photoperiod of about eight hours, again with blue lamps that come on before the main lights and remain on after the halides have been turned off for the day. Sophisticated lighting setups include a programmable timer and a special 'moonlight' lamp that matches the cycle of the moon!

Light in nature

In tropical regions, the sea receives about 10-12 hours of strong light every day for most of the year.

The most intense light occurs during the middle part of the day.

In the subtropics there is a dusk and dawn.

Light in the aquarium

Aquarium lighting should be similar to natural light, but can be altered slightly for practical purposes.

An actinic blue lamp coming on before the others provides a dawn effect each day.

At the end of the day, the white lamps go out before the blue actinic one, creating a dusk effect.

How light is lost in the aquarium

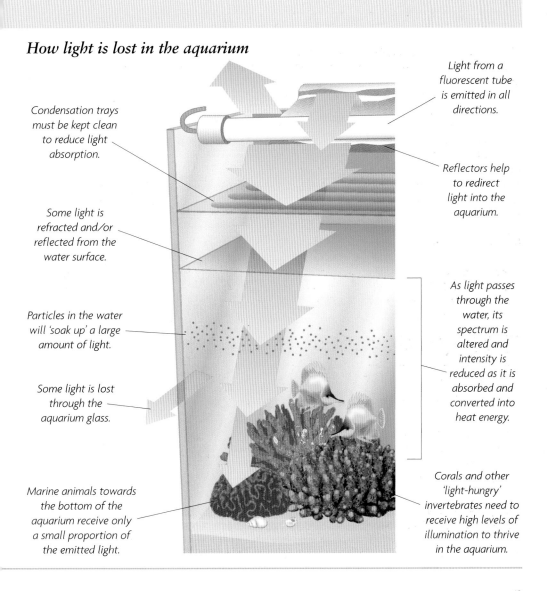

Light from a fluorescent tube is emitted in all directions.

Condensation trays must be kept clean to reduce light absorption.

Reflectors help to redirect light into the aquarium.

Some light is refracted and/or reflected from the water surface.

Particles in the water will 'soak up' a large amount of light.

As light passes through the water, its spectrum is altered and intensity is reduced as it is absorbed and converted into heat energy.

Some light is lost through the aquarium glass.

Marine animals towards the bottom of the aquarium receive only a small proportion of the emitted light.

Corals and other 'light-hungry' invertebrates need to receive high levels of illumination to thrive in the aquarium.

Choosing rocks

Newcomers to marine fishkeeping may be forgiven for thinking that decorating the tank with substrate and rocks, etc. is done solely for aesthetic purposes. However, in modern marine aquariums, these items play an integral role in maintaining water quality and providing the fishes and invertebrates with habitat to live in or on. Generally speaking, these materials require thorough cleaning, or curing, before use and must be prepared in advance of setting up the tank.

When you come to decorate the aquarium, always work from the bottom up. First put in the rockwork or living rock directly on the tank base and then build up the substrate on top. (This is the approach used in the practical sequence of setting up a basic marine aquarium, starting on page 46.) An obvious statement perhaps, but if you intend to use biological filters, such as a plenum, that are often situated below the substrate, then you must fit these before any other work is carried out.

The substrate

In the case of a tropical marine aquarium, coral sand and gravel are the only real choices if you wish to

Left: Coral gravel and sand (shown here) are the most suitable and easily available substrates for a marine aquarium. They not only look right but also help to maintain a stable pH and high buffering capacity.

establish a 'natural' look. In temperate marine systems, you could use soft beach sand, gravel or small pebbles, or a combination of these materials.

Sand on the reef is mostly produced by animals such as boring worms and parrotfishes, which crunch up coral to extract tiny organisms and algae. Their crunching activities are so thorough that they eventually excrete fine sand that falls to the seabed. Coral gravel is created by wave action, whereby the coral is broken and the fragments are slowly worn down. In nature, myriad organisms, such as worms and crustaceans, some microscopic, live in the sand and keep it clean and aerated to a certain depth. In the aquarium, too, these organisms can become very useful when the sand is allowed to become 'live'.

Choosing rocks

Apart from deciding how to set out the tank, you must choose the correct materials to put into it. Once again, remember the importance of water quality control and choose from the wide range of calcareous and inert substances available. Fortunately, there is no difficulty in obtaining materials such as lava rock, ocean rock and so-called 'living rock' (see the panel on page 29) for use in the tropical marine aquarium. Where temperate or coldwater marine tanks are concerned, you could use a wider variety, such as sandstone, granite, some slates (grey is safe) and limestone. Whichever you decide on, you must examine the pieces before use to make sure there is no evidence of metallic-ore veins in the rock. Ores have occasionally been found in tufa and volcanic lava rock, in particular.

How you design the habitat in your aquarium is largely a matter of taste, but it is worth taking a bit

Rocks for a marine aquarium

Calcareous oceanic rock will help to maintain pH levels in the aquarium.

This ocean rock has been smoothed off and will provide an excellent footing for algal growth.

This porous rock has been sculpted by hand to provide 'swim-throughs'.

of time to consider the needs of the animals you want to keep. Fishes certainly need somewhere to go at night, unless they are nocturnal and the reverse applies. Shrimps and other crustaceans require overhang ledges to get under, and some fishes, such as lionfishes, often hang upside-down under ledges. Territorial animals, as the name implies, must be able to establish their own territories, whilst cruising species, such as triggerfishes, batfishes and angelfishes, need a reasonable amount of open space. By including caves, crevices, ledges and arches along with plenty of swimming space, you will be able to cater for a wide range of needs.

Building a lava rock cave

Press the 'roof' onto the siliconed areas of two side pieces. Allow to set a few days before use.

Synthetic forms of aquarium decor

Thanks to wildlife TV programmes, our ideas about corals for the marine aquarium have not only changed but become more informed over recent years. No longer are the dead skeletal remains of coral considered either decorative or even representative of nature. Nowadays, we appreciate corals for the living creatures they are and go to great lengths to ensure the necessary aquarium conditions are set up almost as much for their benefit as for the fishes.

For those that wish to simulate the undersea world their imaginations provide, without resorting to worrying about keeping real corals alive, there are very realistic replica models of coral heads with which to decorate the aquarium. Closely modelled to represent the real thing, these replicas soon lose their artificiality when covered with a little aquarium detritus or algae growth. They still provide natural-looking refuges and sanctuaries for the fish as they do in nature and have one advantage over live corals in that they can be taken out and given a good scrub should they get too unattractive!

Very natural structures can be built up using artificial rocks by using cable-ties; actually hanging some pieces from cross-struts over the aquarium can avoid the risk of rocks collapsing – especially if there is only a shallow substrate in which to imbed them or if you are trying to create overhangs.

Try to avoid creating dead-spots where there is little or no water flow; it is important that all parts of the aquarium receive well-oxygenated water, particularly in a reef-type aquarium where water currents will bring food to the sedentary invertebrate life. Judicial placings of small extra powerheads will ensure ideal water movement for this purpose.

Grouping these artificial barnacle shells in a cluster creates a more natural effect.

Left: *Whether the rockwork is natural or synthetic makes no difference to any fish seeking a sanctuary within its many crevices. As darkness falls, most fish will find a hiding place for the night.*

Right: By choosing contrasting shapes, sizes and colours, even these clearly synthetic models of coral heads can add extra dimension to the aquarium's decorations. Bear in mind that these structures will not grow but make sure you have enough room for the live soft and hard corals to do so.

Although it looks garish out of water, this simulated tree coral will soon lose its harsh appearance and add colour and interest to any display.

This synthetic seafan looks surprisingly realistic, and its elegant sweeping form will contrast well with more upright shapes.

Right: Models of corals moulded in resin are incredibly lifelike and will soon take on the patina of realism as they become covered in algae and detritus in a marine aquarium. They are the only choice if we are to conserve the real thing in the wild.

Siting and preparing the tank

On the following pages we consider the stages involved in setting up a basic marine aquarium using separate pieces of equipment to achieve the three main types of filtration – biological, mechanical and chemical – along with heating and lighting. Our customised aquarium includes substrate, some living rock and a compatible selection of fishes and invertebrates.

Our setup will feature an externally fitted fluidised bed sand filter, an external protein skimmer for removing organic and chemical waste, an external power filter with foam and filter wool to remove particles from suspension and improve water movement in the aquarium. As some of the equipment will be situated outside the tank, make sure there is enough room on the stand (or along the back panel of the tank) to accommodate it.

It is a good idea to compile a list of all the items you will need before beginning the setting up process. Make sure that both the floor and the tank stand or cabinet are strong enough to take the weight of an aquarium full of water. Follow the guidelines for positioning the tank and place a sheet of expanded polystyrene or plastic foam mat on top of the stand to help support the tank evenly. Then sit the tank on top of that.

Cleaning the tank

It pays to clean the aquarium thoroughly before setting it up and you can do this fairly conveniently once it is in its final position. You will find that aquarium accessories attached by 'sucker caps' stick much better to clean glass. First remove any packaging tapes, fingermarks and so on. Wash the inside of the tank with warm, slightly salty water and dry it off with a lint-free cloth or paper towel. A final polish with a cloth soaked in methylated

spirits will remove any stubborn grease or packaging adhesive. Polish the outside of the glass with proprietary glass cleaner if you wish – but never the inside!

Check the level of the tank in both directions. It must be perfectly level to avoid stresses in the glass panels when it is filled with water. Remember that it is impossible to make levelling adjustments once the tank is full.

Siting the aquarium

Good position

Even if an aquarium is next to a chimney, the amount of heat that penetrates the wall is insignificant.

Bad position

A hallway is not the best place for an aquarium because of draughts caused when the door is opened and closed and because of disturbance caused by people passing by.

Good position

A quiet alcove is good, provided you have access to an electricity supply and room to service the aquarium.

Bad position

Close to a door is not a good place to put an aquarium because the fish will be disturbed by the sound and vibration of the door closing.

Good position

A quiet corner of a room that is, perhaps, too dark to grow a houseplant can be enhanced by an attractive display aquarium.

Bad position

In a kitchen, cooking fumes may affect the fish.

Bad position

In a bright sunroom there is too much light on the tank and it will get too hot during the day and cold at night.

Good position

In this position, the tank is far enough away from the doors not to be affected by people passing by.

Adding heaters and filtration

Of all the essential technical requirements in a marine aquarium, heating is the easiest to fit and the least demanding to maintain. As explained on page 34, a simple, thermostatically controlled electric immersion heater (heaterstat) hangs in the tank and switches itself on and off as needed. In tanks over 60cm (24in) long, it is usual to divide the total wattage of heat required into two, and install two heaterstats, one at each end of the tank. As well as ensuring an even spread of heat, you can be reassured that if one of the heaterstat should fail, the other will act as a back-up.

Heaterstats are wired into the electricity supply, usually through a 'cable tidy' connecting box. Unlike pumps and lights, they are NOT serviced by switched circuits. When carrying out maintenance within the aquarium, switch off the power supply at the power outlet before putting your hands into the tank. Allow some minutes to elapse following 'switch off' for any residual heat in the heaters to expend itself before you work on the tank, especially if it is to be drained.

Fitting heaters is an easy task; simply attach their supporting suction caps to the glass of the aquarium. To ensure long-lasting suction, fix the suckers to the dry glass before adding the water. As water is added, it will increase the pressure on the suckers. Fitting suction caps under water is not so successful, as there is always a small amount of water trapped between the suction cap and glass that minimises the cling-on effect.

Always make sure that heaters are mounted clear of the substrate material to allow maximum circulation of water around the heater.

Heating options

The options when heating the aquarium fall between two choices. You may choose to have the heating equipment either in the aquarium itself or as part of a separate water management sump sited below the aquarium. In this case, it may be prudent to put one heater in the sump and one in the tank, just to be safe.

The temperature scale is clearly marked along the top section of this heaterstat. Remember that this shows the heat setting you choose, not the actual temperature of the water.

Left: *Sometimes fishes, especially those of a nervous disposition, may attempt to shelter too near a heater, with the result that they may suffer burns. Heater guards can be fitted around the heater units to prevent this occurring.*

1 In all but the smallest of aquariums, it is best to use two heaters placed at opposite ends of the tank to ensure even heat distribution and as a safeguard against heater failure. These units combine a heating element with a small electric water pump to distribute heat.

2 Place the return pipe from the external power filter at one end of the tank and try to arrange it so that it can be easily hidden by your habitat.

3 Place the inlet filter pipe at the opposite end of the tank from the return pipe to provide the most efficient water circulation.

Installing a power filter

If the heater is allowed to lie on the surface of the substrate, local boiling action could occur, with the result that the glass tube containing the heater element may crack. Similarly, do not crowd tank decorations around the heater unit or otherwise restrict water movement around it.

There are other methods of heating the water. Some external canister power filter units have heating elements incorporated into their design. Where the filtration system is made up of a separate sump unit, often housed immediately below the aquarium, heaters may be placed in the sump rather than in the aquarium itself.

To adjust the water temperature, simply turn the control at the top of the heaterstat. A quarter turn is the most you will need in any direction to effect a change. Allow at least 30-60 minutes to elapse before re-reading the water temperature. The action of the heaterstat is generally indicated by a small neon lamp within the heater body; when it is lit, the heater is working.

Do not confuse the heater's 'temperature-set' indicator with the actual temperature of the water – always check the thermometer in or on the tank.

4 *Connect hoses to the external power filter. Take care to fit these securely so that they do not come apart when the filter is running under full pressure – otherwise water in the tank ends up on the floor!*

External filter taps

Always fit isolating taps on any external filter. They make filter cleaning simple and mess-free! If you fill the filter body almost full with water after cleaning, there will be very little air to purge from the system once you reconnect and open the taps. Keep a close watch on the water emerging from the return pipe – any slowing down indicates the need for a filter clean.

5 *Connect the hoses to the external filter securely, making sure they are not tangled and, if necessary, mark them IN and OUT.*

6 *If you choose to place your aquarium on a cabinet, then it is easy to hide away external equipment such as this power filter.*

Installing other filtration systems

7 There are several designs of protein skimmer available. This one needs to be hung on the back panel of the aquarium. Make sure you provide easy access to such equipment for regular cleaning.

8 This aquarium makes use of a fluidised bed sand filter for biological filtration. This particular unit is driven by a small submersible water pump. Attach this by suckers inside the tank on the back glass.

9 Hang the fluidised bed sand filter on the outside of the back glass and connect it to the internal pump with a hose. Always make sure that the chamber containing the sand is fitted in a truly vertical position.

10 Here is how the aquarium looks with the heating and filtration equipment fitted.

Water return from external power filter. Direct this to suit the tank decoration layout. Can be fitted with a spraybar.

Protein skimmer. Slim models easily fit between tank and wall. Empty the collection chamber regularly.

Fluidised bed sand filter. The massive surface area of the continuously agitated suspended sand provides super efficient bacterial action

Intake for external power filter. Ensure water flow to it is unobstructed.

Heating unit. Mount well clean of any substrate and ensure water can circulate around them unhindered.

Heating unit. One at each end for better heat spread and insurance against failure.

53

Adding living rock and substrate

Providing you have a supply of previously matured saltwater to hand that has the correct temperature, specific gravity and pH of 8.3, you can now introduce pieces of living rock. Add the water immediately after placing your rocks and laying the substrate. If you only have newly mixed saltwater available at the setting up stage, wait until the aquarium is fully operational before adding the living rock to avoid damaging the organisms in it.

In this aquarium we are using a coral sand substrate to a depth of about 2.5cm (1in). This is equivalent to about 4.5kg (10lb) per 900cm^2 (1ft^2); any deeper and you will run the risk of anaerobic conditions developing in the lower layers.

You will probably need to wash the substrate before use and this is best done in advance of starting the setting-up process. Wash a small amount at a time in a fine mesh hand net. Hold the net over a bucket and run water through from a tap or hose until all the detritus has been flushed out of the sand. Dispose of the waste, but try to avoid clogging the trap in your sink. When you are happy that all the sand is clean, spread it over the base of your tank and around the habitat so that the rocks appear to be rising out of the substrate.

11 *Fit a background to the outside of the back glass to hide the equipment. Blue is the best choice, as the colours of fishes and invertebrates stand out well against it. Black can also be used to good effect in a display aquarium.*

12 *Add the first pieces of living rock directly onto the tank floor. Place them carefully so that you can build up a stable display. In this setup we are using high-quality living rock only and have opted not to include any form of base rock or other aquarium decor.*

13 Create the habitat in a way to provide plenty of retreats for the inhabitants and to hide pieces of equipment placed internally. However, leave open swimming space for those fishes that require it. It is vital that the rock is not allowed to dry out.

14 The best substrate for this aquarium setup is coral sand. Spread it around the base of the tank and against the rocks to give the appearance of the habitat rising up from within the sand.

Adding the water

If you have already mixed the water in another container or spare aquarium, then it is simply a case of pouring it carefully into the tank. It is a good idea to pour the water onto a rock or into a container placed on the substrate to avoid the sand being moved out of place. Now connect the pumps for the fluidised bed sand filter and protein skimmer to the electricity supply and switch on in order to fill their chambers and start circulation. Carry this out in full accordance with the manufacturer's instructions. The water level in the aquarium will drop a little and will need to be topped up. Switch on the power filter and heater.

If you do not have pre-matured water ready you will have to mix a new batch before setting up. When mixing, the temperature should be at the normal aquarium operating level of 24°C (75°F), as the salts will dissolve more readily. A thermometer stuck to the outside of the mixing container is good as a quick reference, but to be accurate use a glass thermometer that reads directly from the water. Once you are certain the salts have completely dissolved take a specific gravity reading using a hydrometer. If it is low, add more salts and continue doing this while taking further specific gravity tests, until the S.G. is 1.022-1.023.

Remember, once the aquarium is fully operational and has animals living in it, you must never mix saltwater directly in the tank again. Always perform this task in a separate container.

When you are happy that everything is correct, add the water to the aquarium and connect up the heating and filtration systems.

Left: Always use non-metallic containers in which to mix the marine salts with water. Ideally, food-quality plastic buckets are the best. Look out for nitrate and phosphate-free salt mixes.

Keep a suitable bucket solely for aquarium use.

Mixing techniques

Modern salt mixes are carefully researched and accurately contain everything to replicate 'seawater' for the aquarium. You should use a spare aquarium heaterstat in the mixing container to ensure that the mix is at the correct temperature before you check the specific gravity. Aerate the mix strongly for 24 hours before using.

15 Because this setup includes living rock, it is important to add matured saltwater, i.e. from another established aquarium. New saltwater can harm the many tiny invertebrates already living on the rock. Pour the water gently onto the rocks to prevent displacing the substrate. Keep living rock wet until ready for use in the tank.

16 Attach the readout unit of a digital thermometer to the outer glass and place the probe in the water, ideally some distance away from the heating units.

Adding lights and maturing the tank

The lighting canopy must be able to accommodate two white 10,000°K fluorescent tubes and one blue actinic 03. It is also important that it can have sections cut out of it to allow filter fittings, hoses and cables to be routed through. A wooden hood laminated with plastic, or painted with several coats of polyurethane varnish, is ideal. Site any control gear for the lamps away from water and splashes.

It is worth connecting the power cables for the lights into a remote control box or power strip with the pumps and heaters so that there is only one cable running to the electricity supply socket.

17 *Position the tubes in the hood (blue at the back) so they provide the best coverage within the aquarium. Place each tube as far apart as possible from its neighbour to allow for good air circulation between them, which prevents overheating.*

18 *When using fluorescent tubes it is important they are secured properly into the hood by clips designed for this purpose. Do not use metal clips.*

Maturing the filters

Even though there are no animals in the aquarium at this stage, leave the lights on for the normal photo-period, i.e. 12 hours per day, as this will help the maturation process. It is essential once the living rock has been introduced.

It is absolutely critical that you do not introduce any more livestock into the aquarium until the filters have matured. This means you must wait until there is a large enough population of nitrifying bacteria to deal with ammonia and nitrite. As the 'living rock' in this setup may have bacteria already living on it, the process could be faster than in other arrangements. Make daily tests for ammonia and nitrite levels until the readings show zero for both. It is likely you will not see any evidence of ammonia or nitrite right away, but this does not mean the coast is clear, as the levels will build up gradually, with ammonia peaking first. Be patient and wait until you have had several consecutive days of zero readings before considering adding livestock. When you are certain that all is clear make a 20-25% saltwater change to dilute the resulting levels of nitrate that may form.

Two triphosphor white tubes

One actinic 03 'blue' tube

How your aquarium matures

It is vital to understand how the levels of nitrogenous waste products rise and fall during the first few weeks.

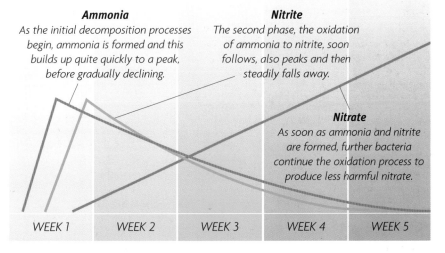

Ammonia
As the initial decomposition processes begin, ammonia is formed and this builds up quite quickly to a peak, before gradually declining.

Nitrite
The second phase, the oxidation of ammonia to nitrite, soon follows, also peaks and then steadily falls away.

Nitrate
As soon as ammonia and nitrite are formed, further bacteria continue the oxidation process to produce less harmful nitrate.

WEEK 1   WEEK 2   WEEK 3   WEEK 4   WEEK 5

Monitor the water quality and do not introduce any fish until ammonia and nitrite levels have been zero for several days.

19 Connect the heating and filtration units to the electricity and turn them on. Introducing a 'cleaning gang' of hermit crabs and/or snails controls any developing algae growth while the tank is fish-free and lit 12 hours a day.

Patience at this stage will ensure that your aquarium gets off to a healthy start.

59

Choosing fish and invertebrates

Several factors must influence your choice of animals for the aquarium; their compatibility, both with their own kind and unrelated species; their diet; their tolerance of captivity; their appearance and even their cost. It is, therefore, very important to research thoroughly all the species you would like to keep.

Obtaining healthy stock

Observe fishes and invertebrates carefully before buying them. They should be alert and free from any sort of damage. Avoid fishes that look thin, or have pinched stomachs, as they often have trouble recovering. Freshwater fishkeepers are used to seeing their healthy fishes swim with erect fins, but many marine fishes naturally keep their fins down, so this is not necessarily a sign of ill-health. With invertebrates, it is more difficult to tell whether they are in good condition or not. In the case of corals (ideally attached to rock), anemones and other polyp animals, look out for tissue damage or even decay. The same applies to sponges, but with crustaceans and starfishes it is usually a case of making sure all their limbs are intact. Sea urchins should not be showing any signs of shedding their spines. Generally speaking, it is worth avoiding any invertebrates that appear to be shedding unusual mucus-like substances, unless you know for sure that this is a normal trait in that species.

Stressed fishes will often produce excessive skin mucus that usually has the appearance of white slimy patches. Avoid these fish, even though the temptation may be to transfer them to your own tank, where conditions are much better.

Left: When faced with the wide range of fishes to choose from at the aquatic store, you should know what to look for, so that you only buy healthy stock. Avoid buying fish simply because you like the look of them; they might not be compatible.

Many tropical marine fishes and invertebrates are brilliantly coloured. Make sure their colours are as they should be and avoid specimens with an unnaturally dull appearance or any with poorly defined markings. Cloudy or swollen eyes, ulcerations and abnormal swimming or instability are bad signs. In particular, look out for signs of scratching or unusually high respiration, as these indicate parasite infections or other possible ailments, as well as toxic water conditions.

Some species, particularly those caught directly from the wild, may take a while to start feeding in captivity, so it is worth asking if you can observe them eating before you buy. Most aquarium dealers will not have any problem with this. However, one problem arising from this is the risk of the food being regurgitated or the fish defecating in the transit container on the way home and causing an ammonia problem. Once you have seen the animal feed, it is worth leaving a deposit and arranging to collect it the following day. For these reasons it is always worth developing a good relationship and level of trust between yourself and your chosen dealer.

Using the same source for your fishes and invertebrates will help to ensure a consistent quality of livestock and service. If you obtain specimens from a variety of sources it can be difficult to trace where a problem may have originated and you will not be able to alert the relevant people, or expect any one source to take responsibility.

The journey home

Once you have obtained your chosen specimens you will be taking them, presumably, on the final stage of their journey from natural habitat to the aquarium. The best, and standard, way of transporting most fishes and invertebrates is in plastic bags filled with one-third aquarium water and two-thirds air. If your journey home is a long one, explain the situation to the dealer so that you can arrange for oxygen to be injected into the bag instead of air. If the weather is cold, or very hot, you may be able to buy or borrow an insulating polystyrene shipping box to transport your animals.

Whilst in transit, never subject your fish to bright light, but keep them calm in the dark. The plastic bags should be wrapped in paper or kept in a dark paper bag or box. Likewise, do not subject them to sudden movements and vibrations. If travelling in a vehicle, cushion the transit container to prevent excessive vibrations from the engine or uneven road surfaces disturbing the animals.

Right: Once caught from the dealer's tank and bagged up, fish are usually placed into a brown paper bag. Being in dark surroundings usually calms them down and prevents undue stress occurring during the journey home.

Introducing the fish

Continue to keep the new animals in dimly lit conditions throughout the introduction process. Unpack the bags and float them in your aquarium for approximately 15 minutes to allow any differences in temperature to equalise. If you have had a long journey, there is a risk that the pH of the water in the transit bags will have dropped. Sudden changes in pH are dangerous to marine animals, so gradually mix the transit water with the aquarium water until equalisation has been achieved. Open the floating bags and introduce a small amount of aquarium water at a time until the bag is full, making sure it does not sink, then pour two-thirds back into the tank and repeat the process. By the time you have filled the bag a second time, you should find that
the pH, S.G. and temperature have all equalised. Nevertheless, you must take some tests to be absolutely certain before releasing the animals.

To avoid further stress on the fishes and invertebrates you should carefully balance the need to acclimatise them with the length of time it takes to do so. Carefully monitoring respiration will indicate to some degree the level of stress a fish is experiencing, but it is much more difficult to assess with invertebrates.

As living rock actually includes living organisms, it is necessary to acclimatise it to your aquarium in exactly the same way you would fishes and invertebrates. The same also applies to algae.

Quarantining new stock

If you are not certain about the health of new animals, it may be advisable to quarantine them in a tank designed for this purpose before introducing them to the aquarium. Always maintain such a tank to the same standard as your main aquarium. Despite the best intentions, it may be argued (with some degree of logic) that any extra transference of animals from one situation to another can cause stress. The extra quarantining stage may be an example of this and will require that you acclimatise the animals in the usual ways when transferring them. Careful handling of healthy stock from a reputable dealer will reduce the number of occasions where quarantining is necessary.

Above: *Equalise the transport water with that in the aquarium by floating the unopened bags in the tank, preferably with the lights off, as this will help the fishes or invertebrates stay calm during this process.*

Left: *After the bags have floated for 15 minutes you can open them and start gradually mixing in some aquarium water as described in the main text. Doing this will equalise differences in pH, salinity and 'fine tune' the temperature before release.*

The first days

After the animals have been successfully introduced into the aquarium, leave them with the lights off, but not in total darkness, for about an hour. After this the lights can be turned on in stages, and it is often a good idea to offer a very tiny amount of food. For many animals, eating when in a new situation is what is known as a displacement activity and the fact that food is available helps them to settle. Obviously, the presence of healthy living rock will provide a number of suitable food items in the form of microorganisms and algae. However, some fishes may not feed for a couple of days while they are settling in and, in most cases, this will not cause undue harm. The most notable exceptions are surgeonfishes and seahorses, which must keep eating virtually constantly.

Whether you are introducing animals to a newly set up aquarium or an established system, add only one fish at a time to avoid overloading the capabilities of the biological filtration. Gradually the bacteria population will catch up with the extra loading and you will be able to make another addition. For corals and other invertebrates, you can count a cluster of polyp animals on a rock as the equivalent of one animal, providing it is not a massive piece. In fact, invertebrates can be added in pairs at weekly intervals.

It is worth bearing in mind that any animals known to exhibit particularly aggressive territorial behaviour are best introduced last of all. If established in the tank any earlier, these animals could mercilessly attack newcomers that are introduced after them.

Introducing invertebrates

The same general guidelines that apply to fishes should be observed when introducing invertebrates to the aquarium. These include sea anemones, crabs, shrimps and prawns, tubeworms, featherdusters, starfishes, sea cucumbers, sea slugs and sea urchins. To keep invertebrates you will need to learn different skills; many are normally sedentary, hardly moving from their coral or rockbound sites. Feeding can be a collective affair for filter-feeding species, but you will need to feed sea anemones by hand, placing morsels of food into their tentacles with tweezers.

Invertebrates will reproduce in the aquarium; sea anemones, for example, will simply divide, or expel young forms to increase their numbers. Hermit crabs are fascinating to observe when they hunt for larger 'premises' as they outgrow their former dwellings. Even at night there is activity in the aquarium; many of the soft corals and similar animals emit small points of light in the darkness.

Above: *Avoid placing individual corals and anemones too close to each other and never touch their living tissue with your fingers as you position them, as this may cause serious damage to the animals.*

Left: *The same approach applies to living rock, algae and corals. Take care not to damage other invertebrates when placing new items into your habitat formation. Place them onto the rockscape in stable positions to prevent other tank inhabitants from easily dislodging them.*

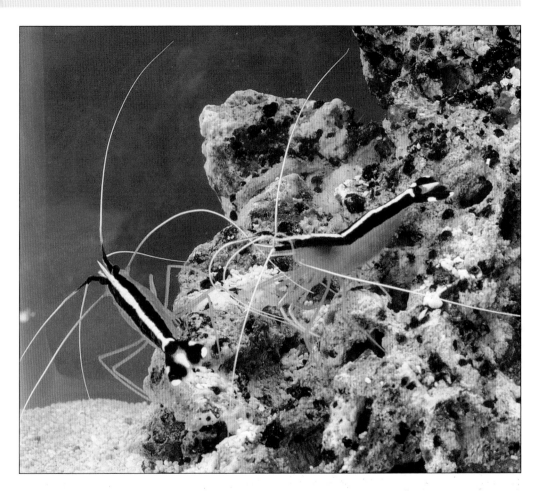

Above: *A pair of cleaner shrimps. All kinds of invertebrates require the same type of careful treatment as marine fishes when being introduced to the aquarium.*

The finished display

The finished aquarium, including the initial livestock. Only introduce one fish or invertebrate at a time, unless they are small enough to allow more – please use good judgement! Always monitor the water quality before making any further introductions to avoid overburdening the filter system and in turn stressing the animals.

In addition to playing an important role in water quality control, the living rock habitat supports its own community of living organisms, but also provides retreats for other aquarium subjects and a base for adding live corals, anemones and other sessile creatures.

Yellow sailfin tang, a hardy fish ideally suited to this type of aquarium setup.

Compatibility

It is important to consider the compatibility of both the fishes and invertebrates you intend to keep together in the same aquarium. Nature seems cruel when you think about a large predatory fish eating a smaller species, which in turn may eat a yet smaller fish or invertebrate; and certain invertebrates are quite capable of devouring fishes. Sadly, tank inmates do not necessarily become docile in the home aquarium where food is more easily available, so food chain trends continue.

If you are not certain about the normal lifestyle of a species, work on the principle that if one fish is bigger than the others in the aquarium and has a large mouth, then the chances are that smaller fishes will be eaten. Groupers, lionfishes, anglerfishes and moray eels are typical of those in this category. Likewise, invertebrates with large claws are potentially going to do some serious damage, and anemones with powerful stinging cells can easily catch slow, weak- swimming fishes, such as seahorses.

Less obvious threats are butterflyfishes that eat the stinging cells of corals, filefishes that often bite out the eyes of less robust species and triggerfishes that have jaws adapted to eating spiny sea urchins. Another consideration is that when a fish that naturally lives in a shoal is kept as an individual, it may change its defence tactic by becoming aggressive and territorial because it can no longer rely on the safety of numbers. The best strategy against predation in the aquarium is to read about the lifestyles of the animals you are interested in before obtaining them.

To avoid other types of aggression, it is a good idea to learn how to tell sexes apart. In the case of damselfishes, for example, males that have established a nest site will fiercely fight with one another, and other fishes that get too close for that matter, whilst females are happier living together out in the water column. Male damsels often have colour in their fins, but the females' fins are transparent.

Corals, anemones and marine algae

Living hard corals (or stony corals), the reef-building corals, are controlled by C.I.T.E.S. (Convention for the International Trade in Endangered Species) but licenses to import them can be obtained. Clams (*Tridacna* spp.) are also controlled, but soft corals, anemones and other polyp animals are not. Commercial coral propagation farms now exist and you should try to buy pieces that have originated from such sources whenever possible. Many aquarists have successfully propagated their own corals and swapping pieces with fellow enthusiasts is quite common. You can also obtain artificial coral 'skeletons' moulded in resin (see page 45).

Adding corals and related animals to the marine aquarium is not as difficult to achieve as it was some years ago. However, hard corals are still not for the inexperienced and you should begin with other, tougher, related polyp animals. Always bear in mind that certain species of fishes will eat corals and other invertebrates, even those found on living rock, so some forethought will be required when considering what mix of animals you wish to keep.

Marine algae

The sheer mass of algae on a reef is quite enormous. Apart from the more recognisable types of macro-algae that grow on one substrate or another, there are the zooxanthellae that live within the tissues of corals, particularly hard corals, and clams. It is because of these algae that corals can only survive in areas of very strong sunlight. Like other plants, zooxanthellae need light to photosynthesise.

By including macro-algae in the reef aquarium, you can provide the plant element that many aquarists miss if they have moved from keeping a freshwater aquarium to a marine tank. Macro-algae can also be very useful for marine fishes that like to graze, such as herbivorous surgeonfishes. The algae derive much of their nourishment from waste products in the aquarium water, but you may have to add trace elements, fertilisers and even extra carbon dioxide, which is perhaps the most important nutrient for plants. One drawback of achieving a lush growth is that it may suddenly 'crash', releasing toxins into the aquarium water as it dies back. To avoid this, harvest your algae periodically. Macro-algae, especially some of those in the genus *Caulerpa*, are capable of rapidly taking over the tank, as their daily growth rate is quite phenomenal when conditions are right.

Above: *Caulerpa comes with many 'leaf' shapes, but these grapelike clusters instantly identify the species shown here as* Caulerpa racemosa. *This is an attractive and relatively slow-growing form.*

Left: When the normally extended polyps of this leather coral are retracted, all that is visible are these leathery-textured fingers. There are many forms available for the hobby and they thrive in brightly lit tanks.

Above: Similar in appearance to mushroom coral, the polyps of finger coral Sinularia are displayed on separated lobes rather than on an undulating plate.

Left: Large anemones, such as this giant carpet anemone, Stichodactyla gigantea, require intense lighting if they are to reach these proportions in a marine aquarium.

A reef aquarium

The ultimate type of aquarium for most marine hobbyists is a reef aquarium populated by an abundance of corals and macro-algae. Such aquariums often contain very few fish, as the main focus is on invertebrates. A reef aquarium is often best decorated using a base of tufa with live rock placed on top. Alternatively, glass shelves can be siliconed into the aquarium, with live rock placed on top. This method has the added advantage that valuable water space is not displaced by tufa or ocean rock.

When buying live rock, always ensure that it has been properly treated before adding it to an established aquarium. Uncured rock will give off high levels of toxic ammonia. Once it has become established, the rock will develop attractive algae, coral and sponge growths. Reef aquariums are best illuminated by metal-halide lamps, in order to provide the correct intensity and light wavelengths for the zooxanthellae required by many corals and other invertebrates to grow (see page 39).

Water quality in a reef aquarium must be of a high quality and it is fortunate that once it has become established, living rock is capable of nitrate reduction in the aquarium. Not only do hard corals require the correct lighting and good water quality, they also benefit considerably from a high water flow, provided by suitable powerheads. Furthermore,

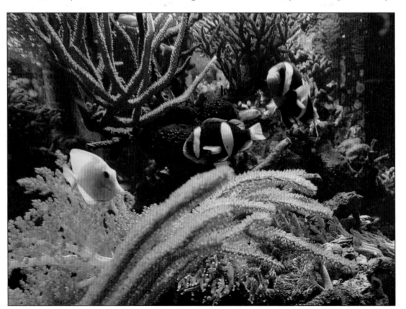

Right: A successful marine aquarium will allow each of the inhabitants to establish its own territory within it. This means providing plenty of safe retreats.

Left: In the modern reef aquarium, the emphasis is more often centred around coral growth than on the fish population.

powerheads provide a flow of water that washes away any detritus from the surface of corals, and prevents them from rotting away.

Given the amount of equipment generally required to maintain a reef aquarium, it is a good idea to use a sump system and to house the protein skimmer, heating units, filtration and recirculation pumps outside the aquarium. The only pieces of equipment required inside the aquarium are the powerheads to provide strong water currents, which can easily be hidden amongst rocks.

Reef tanks with a capacity of less than 450 litres (100 gallons) are not recommended, especially for less experienced hobbyists, as the exacting water requirements of hard corals are extremely difficult to maintain in a small aquarium.

Feeding marine fish

Ideally, the best diet for any animals in captivity should be based on the food they would have enjoyed in nature, so we should not be surprised that the best diet for the majority of marine fishes is fish! The exceptions to this general rule are fish that are herbivorous by nature or those whose tiny mouths mean that they feed on microscopic animals such as plankton.

The shape of a fish's head or snout is a good clue as to how it obtains its food. For example, butterflyfishes often have elongated snouts, ideally suited to picking food from crevices within the coral reef. Parrotfishes have strong fused teeth with which

they crunch up the coral in search of food. The fearsome jaws of groupers and lionfish are obviously designed for copious food-gathering. The mouths of blennies and gobies are located at the very front of the head and the flat ventral surface of the body brings the mouth into efficient proximity with the food-laden substrate.

A feeding regime

Other considerations are when – and how often – to feed fish, and here again, observing nature will help the fishkeeper. Large-mouthed, predatory fish may gorge themselves initially and then fast for a

Frozen foods

Whole cockle
This natural food is accepted by all marine fishes.

Marine mix
This is a mixture of various natural marine invertebrate and fish meats.

Krill
A nutritious food for larger fish; break up for small fishes.

Fish
These small fish make excellent 'one-gulp' food for larger fishes.

Shrimp
Many wild-caught foods are irradiated to destroy disease pathogens.

Above: Frozen foods are sold in single slabs (simply break off pieces as required) or in individual push-out 'servings'. Thaw frozen foods before use to prevent fish eating ice.

Ease of feeding in the aquarium

Group	Easy	Reasonable once feeding	Difficult	Difficult, need livefoods
Angels		●	●	
Basses	●			
Blennies	●	●		
Butterflyfishes	●	●	●	●
Cardinals		●		
Catfishes	●			
Clownfishes	●	●		
Damsels	●			
Eels	●			
Filefishes			●	
Gobies	●			
Jawfishes		●		
Lionfishes		●		●
Seahorses		●	●	●
Squirrelfishes		●		●
Surgeons	●			
Tangs	●			
Triggers		●		
Wrasses	●			

Feeding for groups with multiple entries depends on species.

few hours; herbivorous grazers appear to be active as long as there is daylight. However, the majority of fishes in the aquarium will be satisfied with one or two regular feeds each day. Do not neglect the needs of the more nocturnal species. They should be fed after the aquarium lights have been switched off for a little while.

On balance, the fishkeeper would be well-advised to underfeed, rather than to give food every time the fish appear to indicate that they require it by their behaviour at the front glass. You will know if you are feeding the correct amount of food because the fish will consume it all within a few minutes and there will be none left to pollute the water.

Feeding marine animals other than fish in the aquarium may require special techniques. For example, in the case of filter-feeding invertebrates in a reef tank, it may be best to turn off the filtration system briefly, so that the action of the filter does not remove the food from the aquarium before the invertebrates can make use of it.

Feeding marine fishes

All suitable foods for marine aquarium fishes should be processed in one form or another. Unless the source is meticulously screened, providing live food runs the risk of introducing undesirable pathogens to the aquarium. There is a school of thought that believes that offering live fish, such as goldfish, to the larger, more predatory marine fish in the aquarium may lead to the marines 'learning' to be predatory towards their smaller tankmates.

Given that the ideal diet should be marine-based, you will find all manner of frozen fish- and shellfish-based foods available from your aquatic retailer. These have probably been processed using gamma irradiation to safeguard against the introduction of disease. The freeze-drying process may also be employed to preserve aquatic animals as prospective food, and such products are also readily available.

Much research has been done by the fish food manufacturers and a whole range of recipes suitable for marine fish will be available in many forms: flake food, tablets, granules or even sticks. While such foods may appear expensive, it is false economy to buy a large amount, especially if you only have one aquarium. Once the food container has been opened, the quality of the food (and the important vitamin content) will gradually deteriorate, thus denying your fish all the benefits the manufacturers have engineered into the food.

Feeding herbivorous marine fish

Dealing with the needs of herbivorous species is not as difficult as you might imagine. If the lighting level is sufficiently strong, a healthy growth of algae should soon manifest itself over the surface of the aquarium walls and decorations, and herbivorous species will be only too glad to graze on this green matter. Alternatively, culture algae-covered rocks in a separate tank standing in a sunny position and filled with discarded aquarium water following a water change. Transfer each 'green' rock to the main aquarium in rotation, and replace the 'grazed upon' rocks in the culture tank. This should ensure a steady vegetable diet for those fish that need it.

Provide further vegetable matter in the form of peas, spinach and blanched or lightly bruised lettuce leaves. Clamp the leaves between the two halves of a magnetic algae scraper to prevent them circulating around the aquarium in the water currents.

Right: This decorated dartfish (Nemateleotris decora) is a midwater feeder and clearly has no problems in taking food as it falls through the water. Here, it is about to 'capture' a fragment of thawed-out shrimp.

Flakes and granules

Flake foods fall slowly through the water and are ideal for most midwater and upper water level species.

Brineshrimp flakes

Mixed flakes

Granular food
This sinks quickly for the benefit of bottom-dwellers.

Tablet food
Excellent for sticking on the tank glass.

Above: *To prevent green foods becoming stuck in filter inlets, secure them to the aquarium glass using a sucker and clip.*

Freeze-dried foods

Based on fresh natural foods, most freeze-dried portions can be stuck onto the interior glass panels at any level.

Freeze-dried krill

Freeze-dried river shrimp

Freeze-dried brineshrimp

Routine maintenance

Once your aquarium is completely up and running, the time taken by routine maintenance is relatively small, yet it is something you can still enjoy.

Routine checks

There are several checks that you should make on a regular basis. First and foremost are daily temperature checks, along with a 'head count' of your aquarium subjects. Counting fishes is best done at feeding time, when they tend to be the most visible, although some invertebrates may be more difficult. Over time, you will develop an 'eye' for what is right and wrong, so that you can tell almost instinctively if any animals are more than just missing. Do your best to locate them and immediately remove any that have died. If an animal dies and the cause is unlikely to have been old age, you must try

to discover the cause and take action accordingly. Marine fishes and invertebrates are generally sensitive to disturbances and the potential stress they cause, so do your best to use your eyes rather than searching around the tank with your hands. Some species are capable of jumping, so if an animal is not evident in the aquarium, it is worth looking on the floor, especially if the tank is not covered.

As the aquarium gradually becomes more established, its subjects will settle down into their natural behavioural patterns. If you take time to observe the animals' normal activities, you will soon be able to recognise any irregularities that may be early indications of trouble.

In a fully established aquarium, you should check pH weekly, making sure it remains stable at around 8.3 – but no higher – and no lower than 8.1. If it

Testing for ammonia, nitrates and nitrite

Testing the water involves adding chemicals to a measured sample and comparing the colour change to a printed chart. Some tests involve adding two or three chemicals in stages. Allow the correct time period to elapse between adding reagents. Wear protective gloves when using chemicals, as they may cause skin irritation.

Above: Any indication of the presence of nitrite does at least mean that the bacteria are doing their job in the conversion process but, like ammonia, nitrite is still very toxic and a zero reading is what you need.

starts to drop, adjust it by adding buffering materials (see pages 33). The situation may require some water renewal, especially if the pH continues to drop after you have attempted to adjust it. Siphoning off debris from the substrate on a weekly basis will go a long way in preventing a decline in water conditions, especially pH. Most of this debris is likely to be organic, so as it breaks down it will be releasing carbon dioxide into the water and affecting its buffering capabilities.

Take a specific gravity reading once a week and test for ammonia and nitrite levels once every two weeks. It is also a good idea to keep a check on the nitrate and phosphate levels weekly. Fishes generally appear to have a higher tolerance of nitrate than many invertebrates, and experienced marine aquarists have suggested 40 mg/litre is an

acceptable upper limit. However, it is always best not to make any compromises and try to keep nitrate levels below 5 mg/litre.

It is important to carry out regular partial water changes. Do not change too much at any one time as it may cause a sudden drift in environmental conditions and cause some stress to the animals. Around 10% change each week is good, although smaller amounts on a daily basis would be more efficient, but far less convenient, for most aquarists. As already discussed elsewhere, never mix new supplies of saltwater directly in the tank once there are living organisms in it. Occasionally, it may be necessary to top up due to evaporation loss. As only water evaporates, leaving the salts behind, you must only top up using freshwater. Always use the best quality freshwater available to you for this purpose.

Above: *When testing for ammonia, the aim is to achieve a reading of zero. Not until this reading is consistently at the lowest possible value, is it safe to introduce any fish into the aquarium. Test the water regularly.*

Left: *With some original nitrate already present in the mixing water, readings are likely to be high. Although nitrate can be tolerated by some species, it should not be allowed to exceed 10mg/litre. Here, the reading is very low.*

Routine maintenance

Occasionally things can go wrong. If a heater fails, causing a serious drop in temperature, it is a good idea to float plastic bottles filled with hot water in the aquarium, taking care that the displacement of aquarium water does not overflow. If you own an enamel pan, you could also heat up some aquarium water and return it to the tank very carefully and gradually. In the meantime, either repair the heater or replace it with a new unit – the latter being the most likely course of action.

On the other hand, should your heater's thermostat stick in the 'on' position, causing the temperature to rise, switch off power to the unit and apply extra aeration. In a reverse of the method described above, you could fill plastic bottles with ice in order to reduce the temperature gradually.

Phosphate test

Add phosphate reagent to a sample of tank water and mix. After five minutes look down the tube to compare the colour of the solution with the chart.

Should your electricity supply fail, such as in a power cut, the relatively large body of water in the aquarium can act as a heat reserve and will take a while to cool down. Lagging the tank with insulating material will help if there is concern that the power outage will last a long time. If you have other means of heating water, you could use bottles as described above. It is more critical to keep the filters running and to provide extra aeration. If the nitrifying bacteria die off due to a lack of oxygenated water, you run the serious risk of deadly ammonia build-up. In such an event, one or two battery-powered airpumps would be very valuable investments and could maintain both water movement and the filter system until power is restored.

Back-up systems are worth considering. To avoid disaster from a sticking thermostat, you could connect a second one in line to the power supply. Set the second thermostat at a couple of degrees higher than the first, so that if the main one sticks, the other one will turn off the heater. Otherwise, you could install two units as a precaution against one failing and causing a temperature drop. A further refinement would be to install a battery-operated buzzer alarm to indicate power failures.

Look on the bright side

Finally, remember not to look on routine tasks as chores to be avoided; most of them should be part of the pleasurable task of providing your aquarium subjects with the care and attention that they undoubtedly deserve. They will repay you in the best manner possible – with a living picture of beauty and colour that is both entertaining and educational. As a hobbyist, this is your reward.

Practical tips for a healthy aquarium

Choose healthy stock and quarantine all new additions. Avoid stressing the fish in any way during transportation and subsequent handling.

Bear in mind the feeding habits of different species, their compatibility with fish of the same or different species and their eventual mature size.

Remove uneaten food at the earliest opportunity. Acclimatise fish to any new food over time.

Learn to recognise symptoms of impending water problems: frothy, cloudy, yellowing and smelly water are all signs of deteriorating conditions.

Keep cover glasses clean. Salt spray soon renders them opaque, which prevents the full light intensity reaching right down into the water.
Make all changes to the water conditions gradually. Power-heads or other motorised

equipment may be left 'high and dry' as water levels fall; turn them off during water changes but turn them on again!

Do not neglect regular partial water changes. Changing 20-25% each month is a rough guide; an invertebrate tank may require more frequent changes.

Check that the waterflow rate from filters remains high. Clean external mechanical filters and replace (or rinse out and re-use) the filter medium together with the activated carbon frequently – at least once a week if necessary. Wash filter media in some aquarium water to avoid killing any bacterial colonies. Fit isolating taps in filter hoses to lessen the risk of spillage when cleaning filters.

After cleaning external power filters, make sure that the hoses are securely attached ñ a filter pump will just as easily empty a tank as filter it!

Remove algae from the front glass with a non-metallic scraper; nylon or plastic scourers are very effective for this purpose. Algae scrapings can be fed to herbivorous fish in less algae-covered tanks. Thin out excessive macro-algae growths, as a sudden 'algae death' could cause pollution.

When treating fishes with disease remedies, follow the maker's recommendations. Most treatments are designed to be added to the whole aquarium but remember that copper-based cures will kill most invertebrates in the tank. (This is why it is difficult to keep fishes and invertebrates together. A practical ratio would be 80% invertebrates to 20% or even fewer, fishes.) Do not mix medications. Sterilise all equipment after use and do not share a net between two tanks.

Top up evaporation losses in the aquarium with fresh water.

Health care

Even assuming that your fish were in the best condition when they became your responsibility, it is nevertheless a fact of life that, at some time or another, you will have to face up to an outbreak of disease in the aquarium.

Look and learn

Get into the habit of learning from what you see. Once you can recognise each fish's normal behaviour, you will soon be able to detect any abnormalities, such as erratic swimming, sulking and hiding away. Concave profiles (especially on a new fish) should be regarded with suspicion.

Remember that many marine fish, such as the birdmouth wrasse, swim with their fins folded down as a matter of course, and in any case, some species lack some fins found on other fishes!

First things first

When dealing with disease, you should not only identify the ailment, but also look for the causes. Always check the aquarium conditions (especially water parameters) first. Attention to aquarium hygiene, modest stocking levels and quarantining all new stock will do much to ensure that your aquarium remains stress- and disease-free.

Copper remedies

It is not possible to treat fishes in the aquarium if invertebrates are also present. Although fish respond well to copper-based remedies, invertebrates have no tolerance to them at all and will be killed.

The treatment tank

One reason for using a separate treatment tank is that some medications can affect the nitrifying bacteria, with the result that the main tank needs time to 'remature' once treatment is complete. A further problem occurs if you are using filters that employ carbon, which removes the treatment from the aquarium water. Always remove carbon from the filtration system before dosing with treatments.

Setting up a quarantine tank

Use a heaterstat to maintain the water temperature. Fit a guard to protect fishes that might rest against the heating element.

Use a clean tank with no substrate.

A clay flowerpot will provide shelter and security.

Intake and return pipes connected to an external filter to maintain water quality.

Right: *Accurate dosing is essential, so it helps to know the exact volume of water in your aquarium. Pre-mix medication in a little tank water before adding it to the treatment tank. Never add another remedy immediately should the first one not work, as combining several remedies may be toxic.*

Many common problems have easily detectable, external, visible symptoms, such as tiny white spots, etc. These can be treated successfully using commercially available treatments. Internal disorders, with external symptoms that may not become apparent until the disease has progressed too far for successful treatment, are more difficult to deal with and usually result in the loss of the fish concerned. Some remedies are not always available worldwide due to differing regulations on drug sales.

Tread carefully

Treat your fish in a methodical way and make notes if necessary. Be confident of your diagnosis before embarking on a course of treatment. In an emergency, some parasitic attacks can be dealt with by a simple freshwater bath. Although it sounds contradictory, a bath in freshwater for some minutes (less if the fish shows signs of discomfort) can bring relief to marine fish.

It might not be possible to arrive at an accurate diagnosis straightaway, since there may be more than one explanation for any given symptom. For example, fishes with breathing difficulty may not be the subject of a parasitic attack at all; it may be that there is simply not sufficient oxygen in the water available to them. (That is why it is so important to check the water conditions first.) However, if the fish's gills really are covered with parasites, then this will cut down the efficiency with which they can extract oxygen from the water and results in their rapid, gasping breathing actions.

Health care

Detecting and treating health problems

Symptoms	Cause	Treatment
Opaque patches on skin.	Chilodonella	Anti-parasite treatment effective as a host is needed; an uninhabited aquarium should be clear after 5 days.
Triangular spots.	Benedina	Proprietary treatments effective. Use brief freshwater baths with caution.
White spots, fish scratch against rocks.	Cryptocaryon irritans	Use copper-based remedy in separate tank if invertebrates present.
Dusty, velvet-like spots; fish scratch, gills inflamed, breathing affected.	Amyloodinium ocellatum	Proprietary remedies effective but avoid copper-based treatments if invertebrates present.
Emaciation – but eating regularly.	Ichthyosporidium or Tuberculosis	No effective cure. Antibiotics may help; isolate sick fish.
Eyes – Bulging, pop-eye.	Exophthalmia	No definite remedy but fish often not distressed by condition.
Fins – Ragged with wasted tissue.	'Finrot', bacterial infection Usually secondary infection	Use copper-based remedy. in separate tank if invertebrates present. Improve water conditions.
Gills – Open, inflamed.	Gill flukes, Dactylogyrus	Brief formalin bath.

Symptoms	Cause	Treatment
Cotton wool-like tufts.	Saprolegnia fungus.	Immediate partial water change; brief freshwater baths and antibiotic treatment. Improve water conditions.
'Cauliflower' growths.	Lymphocystis.	Fish either waste away or recover completely.
Slimy faeces.	Diarrhoea; poor diet.	Raise tank temperature a few degrees; starve fish for two days then feed high roughage foods.
Swellings.	Bacterial infection or, in severe cases, dropsy.	Use copper-based remedy in separate tank if invertebrates present.
Wounds.	Physical damage. Poor handling. Bullying. Ulcers caused by Vibrio bacteria.	General antibacterial treatment, local swab medication. Consult veterinarian.
Rapid breathing coupled with dashing about, dull eyes.	Poisoning.	Immediate partial water change with total change later if needed.
Gaping gills.	Gill flukes (see 'Gills').	Brief formalin bath.
Listlessness.	Associated with several other disorders.	Diagnose and treat accordingly.
Loss of balance, cannot maintain position in the water.	Swimbladder disorder.	Isolate fish in warmer water. Try medicated foods.

Breeding marine fish

The art of breeding marine fishes in captivity is still in its infancy. However, well over 100 species have been bred in aquarium conditions and some of these are available commercially. Successfully breeding and rearing a species must be the ultimate achievement for any marine aquarist, and the results are crucial for the future of the hobby and for conservation. The knowledge gained from such experience will in time help to reduce the demand for wild-caught specimens and the conservation of natural habitats. Just as importantly, this information could be used to teach those who are currently collecting for the aquarium hobby to set up breeding stations in the fishes' countries of origin as an alternative means of income should the demand for wild stock diminish. There are tried and tested methods for breeding and rearing some marine species, but there is still a great deal of experimentation to be done for most.

Anemonefishes – egglayers

Anemonefishes are amongst the most popular of marine aquarium fishes and, although not the hardiest, they are probably the most likely to breed in a home aquarium. The common clown anemonefish, Amphiprion ocellaris, *has been bred in captivity over and over again since the early 1950s and has fascinated even novice marine fishkeepers with its characteristic breeding behaviour.*

Right: *A pair of common clownfish (*Amphiprion ocellaris*) guard the eggs they have laid on a tile in their otherwise bare tank. In the wild, they clean a flat rock surface on which to lay their eggs.*

A clownfish breeding tank

Provide a flat surface such as a piece of slate for the eggs to be laid on.

Use a tank measuring 75x30x38cm (30x12x15in).

Make regular partial water changes of 10% every few days.

Install a simple bubble-up sponge filter.

Remove the adults and slate once the fry are free swimming.

A synthetic 'anemone' placed near the slate will make the clownfishes 'feel at home'.

Cardinalfishes – mouthbrooders

One cardinalfish has captured a great deal of interest in recent times – the Emperor, or Banggai, cardinalfish, Pterapogon kauderni. This species appears to be very restricted in its distribution, being found at only a couple of locations around the Banggai Islands off the coast of Sulawesi in Indonesia. Because of its limited distribution, there has been some concern that collecting for the aquarium hobby will impact on the wild population, so breeding the fish in captivity is a worthy initiative. Fortunately, they reproduce readily in the aquarium and it is hoped that in the near future all specimens offered for sale will be captive bred.

Above: The male mouthbroods the fertilised eggs. Once hatched, the free-swimming fry take newly hatched brineshrimp as a first food.

PART TWO

Introduction to fish profiles

Although nearly three-quarters of the earth's surface is covered by salt water, relatively few marine fishes are kept in the aquarium. And of these, by far the most are tropical species. Nevertheless, such is the appeal of this small group of fishes that the marine fishkeeping hobby has flourished and continues to attract more hobbyists around the world.

The most striking tropical marine fishes are native to the coral reefs and coastal waters, where collection is quite easy. Fishes from the deepest waters usually grow too large for the aquarium, and also present too many collection and transportation problems. The majority of suitable fishes come from the Indo-Pacific Oceans, the Caribbean area of the Northern Atlantic Ocean, and the Red Sea.

The water conditions on a tropical reef are extremely stable – the water is well oxygenated and almost completely free from waste products due to the constant cleansing action of the sea. The water is relatively shallow and this means that the fishes are quite used to fairly high light levels. One distinct advantage of simulating these brightly lit conditions in the aquarium is that grows of green algae (usually shunned by freshwater fishkeepers) can be encouraged, much to the appreciation of the fishes, many of which are herbivorous by nature.

Coral reef fishes are extremely territorial, each fish's chosen 'living space' in nature being much larger than that possible in the average indoor aquarium. This makes keeping shoals difficult in many cases because the fishes are intolerant of other members of the same species, although they rarely regard different 'neighbours' as a threat.

These are the challenges facing the tropical marine fishkeeper: maintaining clean, stable conditions; providing enough space; and choosing compatible species. Achieve these successfully and you can then sit back and admire these wonderful 'living jewels of the sea'.

Anemonefishes & damselfishes

The family Pomacentridae contains two groups of fishes kept by most marine fishkeepers as initial stock fish when first setting up the marine aquarium. The reasons for this are easy to understand; the fish are hardy, inexpensive and readily available. Because of their hardiness, they can tolerate early introduction into a newly set up aquarium that may not be sufficiently established to support more delicate species. However, this is no excuse for the impatient fishkeeper to skimp on preparing the aquarium properly before introducing any fish.

The family consists of two distinct groups of fishes, both of which need to feel secure within the aquarium. Anemonefishes, as their name implies, seek refuge within the tentacles of a sea anemone, while damselfishes tend to congregate around the branches of any stands of coral. Each group has an individual swimming style: anemonefishes waddle about, while damselfishes tend to have a more vertical bobbing action.

Caring for these fish is straightforward. They will accept most foods and are not too antagonistic towards other fishes in the aquarium. Damselfishes may squabble amongst themselves, so provide an aquarium large enough to give each fish a reasonable amount of territory. Several species are likely to breed within the confines of the aquarium, depositing and guarding their eggs in much the same way as freshwater cichlids.

Above: This spinecheek
anemonefish (Premnas
biaculeatus) *is the largest of
the anemonefishes, but still
seeks the reassurance of
safety amongst the
tentacles of a sea anemone.*

COMMON CLOWNFISH • *Amphiprion percula*

For most people, the definitive anemonefish is the common clown. It is able to live within the tentacles of the sea anemone with impunity, because the mucus on its skin prevents the sea anemone's stinging cells from operating. The ability to dash into the tentacles when pursued by predators stands the clownfish in good stead, as its pursuers will not be similarly immune. Some authors are of the opinion that as a reward for acting as a safe haven, the sea anemone benefits from particles of food accidentally (or perhaps purposely?) dropped by the returning clownfish. Although this mutual friendship may be classed by some as symbiosis, neither of the animals is strictly dependent on the other and perhaps the more correct term for this association would be commensalism.

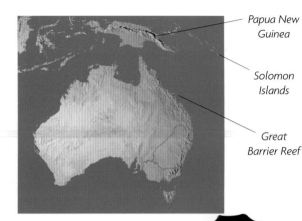

Papua New Guinea

Solomon Islands

Great Barrier Reef

▶ Origins

One of the most widespread species in the genus, ranging from Papua New Guinea to the Solomon Islands and Australia's Great Barrier Reef.

▶ Breeding

Eggs are deposited and fertilised on a firm surface such as a nearby rock. The parents guard them until the fry hatch. Clownfishes are often increasingly available from captive-bred stocks, thus lessening the need for wild-caught specimens.

The distinctive body pattern is shared by the almost identical species, A. ocellaris, the false clown anemonefish. However, it is easy to distinguish between them, because the common clownfish has the wider black markings.

Size: 11cm (4.3in); females are generally larger

▶ *Fishkeeping data*

Number per aquarium: Two to three, plus a suitable sea anemone.
Community/species tank: Community.
Swimming area: Middle and lower levels.
Food: All prepared foods, including freeze-dried and frozen, plus some vegetable matter.
Compatibility: Peaceful.
Availability: Regularly available (tank-bred and wild-caught).
Captive breeding: Possible.

Clownfishes and anemones

Buying clownfish complete with an associated anemone is much the best strategy. It is not possible to guarantee mutual acceptance between the anemone and clownfish of your choice if you buy them separately. Anemones of the Entacmaea *and* Macrodactyla *species seem to be widely accepted by many clownfish.*

RED SADDLEBACK ANEMONEFISH • *Amphiprion ephippium*

This clownfish, also known as the tomato clown or fire clown, is slightly larger than the common clown (page 10) and lacks the vertical white banding found on some species. Its red-orange body is merely marked by an oval, dark brown patch two thirds along the flank. All the fins are plain red-orange in colour. It has been reported that juveniles have a vertical thin white line passing down over their head, just behind the eye, but this fades with maturity.

Compatibility

While happy to be associated with the sea anemone, this species is a bold feeder and at times may become aggressive towards any other fish entering its territory.

Ungainly swimmers

The name 'clownfish' has been applied to these fishes because of their waddling swimming action. In some literature they may even be called clown anemonefish.

The composition of the mucus covering the skin prevents the stinging cells (nematocysts) of the sea anemone's tentacles from 'firing', thus providing the fish with immunity.

Size: 14cm (5.5in)

▶ Origins

The Andaman
and Nicobar
Islands, Malaysia
and Java.

Andaman
and   Malaysia
Nicobar
Islands   Java

▶ Fishkeeping data

Number per aquarium: Two to three,
plus a suitable sea anemone.
Community/species tank: Community.
Swimming area: Middle and
lower levels.
Food: All prepared foods, including
freeze-dried and frozen, plus some
vegetable matter.
Compatibility: Peaceful.
Availability: Regularly available
(wild-caught).
Captive breeding: No information.

BLACK-FOOTED CLOWNFISH
AMPHIPRION NIGRIPES

Although similar in appearance to
Amphiprion ephippium *and* A. frenatus,
A. nigripes *is much more subtly coloured.
It is a soft golden-brown, with a white
stripe just behind the head. The pelvic fins
are black, but the anal fin is not always so,
hence the common name.* A. nigripes,
*found off the Maldives Islands in the
Indian Ocean, grows to 8cm (3.2in). In the
wild it eats plankton and crustaceans, but
finely chopped foods are ideal in the
aquarium. Although a bold feeder,* A.
nigripes *is a shy fish and best kept with
other anemonefishes. It is an ideal subject
to keep with invertebrates.*

Above: *The colours of* A. nigripes *are
not as rich as some other clownfishes,
and in this respect it is very similar to*
A. perideraion.

PINK SKUNK CLOWNFISH • *Amphiprion perideraion*

As its popular name suggests, the body colour of this clownfish is more subtle than the garish hues of the preceding species. A thin, vertical white stripe crosses the body at the rear of the gill cover and another white line runs from the top of the head right along the top of the dorsal ridge to the caudal peduncle. The pectoral, pelvic and anal fins are the same colour as the body, but the dorsal and caudal fins are almost colourless, with just a tinge of yellow. The skunk anemonefish, *Amphiprion akallopisos*, is similarly coloured, but lacks the white vertical stripe on the head.

Over its natural distribution range, it is usually found within the tentacles of the sea anemone *Heteractis magnifica*.

Sex reversal

The genus is also noted for its sex reversal characteristics. However, in this instance, all fish mature as males, only changing into a dominant female in order to head small colonies.

▶ Origins

From Thailand to Samoa, including waters south of Japan down as far as the Great Barrier Reef and New Caledonia.

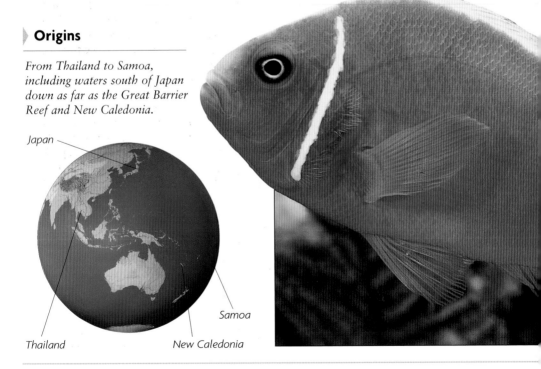

Japan

Samoa

Thailand

New Caledonia

▶ *Fishkeeping data*

Number per aquarium: Two to three, plus a suitable sea anemone.
Community/species tank: Community.
Swimming area: Middle and lower levels.
Food: All prepared foods, including freeze-dried and frozen, plus some vegetable matter.
Compatibility: Peaceful.
Availability: Less frequently available (wild-caught).
Captive breeding: No information.

TOMATO CLOWNFISH
AMPHIPRION FRENATUS

The tomato clown, also known as the fire clown and the bridled clownfish, is very similar to A. ephippium, but it has the white stripe behind the head (sometimes two in juveniles) and the body blotch is often larger. The confusion is not helped by the fact that some authorities call this fish A. ephippium or A. melanopus. Another name is A. polylepis. The tomato clown is found in the Pacific Ocean and grows to 7.5cm (3in). It is a bold feeder that accepts small crustaceans, small live foods, algae and vegetable-based foods. It may be quarrelsome in confined spaces, but perfectly compatible with invertebrates.

Below: *Adult specimens of the tomato clown retain the vertical white stripe into adulthood. As with all fishes with similar features that are gathered over very wide areas by collectors not aware of other's efforts or descriptions, there is bound to be confusion with classification.*

MAROON CLOWNFISH • *Premnas biaculeatus*

This is one of the largest clownfish. In addition to this identifying factor, it also has two rearward-facing sharp spines on each cheek just below the eye. This feature accounts for its alternative common name of spinecheek anemonefish. The orange and red body colour is more intense in the male fish and is crossed vertically by three narrow white bands. The female fish is much more likely to attain the maximum size and her body colour can be much darker, almost black, with less distinct bands. These may almost disappear in some specimens.

Like all wild-caught anemonefishes, the maroon clownfish is susceptible to stress arising from poor handling and poor aquarium conditions. However, specimens obtained commercially from captive breeding programmes are said to be much hardier.

It is usually found exclusively with the bubbletop sea anemone, *Entacmaea quadricolor*, although in the aquarium it may not be quite so dependent on a sea anemone as its relatives.

Its larger size, deep orange-red coloration and three white stripes makes the maroon clownfish easy to identify.

▶ Origins

Western Indonesia as far north as Taiwan and south to the northern end of the Great Barrier Reef.

▶ Fishkeeping data

Number per aquarium: One.
Community/species tank: Community.
Swimming area: Middle and lower levels.
Food: All prepared foods, including freeze-dried and frozen, plus some vegetable matter.
Compatibility: May bully.
Availability: Frequently available (wild-caught).
Captive breeding: Possible.

Size: *17cm (6.6in), males are usually smaller*

Taiwan

Western
Indonesia

Great Barrier
Reef

TWO-BANDED ANEMONEFISH
AMPHIPRION CLARKII

*Also known as the banded clown and
Clark's anemonefish, this species is highly
variable in coloration depending on its
location in the Indo-Pacific. Generally, the
body is predominantly dark brown but for
the ventral regions, which are yellow. All the
fins, with the exception of the paler caudal
fins, are bright yellow. Two tapering white
bars divide the body into thirds; in juvenile
forms, there is a third white bar across the
rear of the body. A. clarkii grows
to 12cm (4.7in) and enjoys a diet
of small crustaceans, small
live foods, algae and
vegetable-based
foods. It is peaceful
and makes an
ideal choice
for a mixed
aquarium.*

Above: *Clark's anemonefish can be
found in many colour variations and
identification is therefore sometimes
difficult. This bold fish is excellent for the
community aquarium with little need for
a host anemone in most cases.*

SERGEANT MAJOR • *Abudefduf saxatilis*

Look out from a glass-bottomed boat anywhere in the tropics and you are bound to see an oval, silvery fish with a number of vertical dark bands across its sides. In military terms, the sergeant major has an enormous parade ground, being found on rocky shores and coral reefs in both the Atlantic and Indo-Pacific areas, although to be accurate, there is more than one species with this common name. For example, *A. saxatilis* is from the Atlantic, while *A. vaigiensis* is found from the Red Sea eastwards to Lord Howe Island in the Pacific, but *A. abdominalis* is restricted to the Hawaiian islands.

   The body coloration is similar (give or take a blotch or two) from species to species. The body shape is very reminiscent of the freshwater sunfish, although the caudal peduncle is much shorter. Sergeant majors can be territorially aggressive.

▶ *Fishkeeping data*

Number per aquarium: One.
Community/species tank: Community.
Swimming area: Middle and upper levels.
Food: All foods.
Compatibility: May bully.
Availability: Usually available (wild-caught).
Captive breeding: No information.

Spacious aquariums can contain more fish from one species, providing they each have ample 'territorial space'.

Size: 15cm (6in)

Pacific
Ocean

Atlantic
Ocean

Indian Ocean

▶ **Origins**

*The Atlantic and
Indo-Pacific areas.*

BLUE VELVET DAMSELFISH
NEOGLYPHIDODON OXYODON

*A vertical yellow stripe crosses the deep
blue-black body just behind the head.
The electric-blue wavy lines on the
head and upper part of the body fade
with age. This handsome but aggressive
fish from the Pacific Ocean can be
safely kept with invertebrates. It requires
a diet of finely chopped meats, algae and
greenstuff and grows to 13cm (5in). It may
not adapt well if it is in less than first-class
condition when you buy it.*

99

GOLDTAIL DEMOISELLE • *Chrysiptera parasema*

With the demoiselles we enter a veritable minefield of identification problems, because there are so many similar-looking, brilliantly blue-coloured species from several different genera – without counting the blue-only juvenile forms. *C. parasema* has a touch more yellow to its posterior end than most, which should make identification slightly less problematical.

All damselfish are territorial and on the aggressive side. They will quarrel if there is not enough room (or too few hideaways) in the aquarium. Introducing lone specimens (often of any species of fish, not just the same species) into an aquarium already inhabited by damsels is asking for trouble. The best way to encourage them to settle in is to introduce a small number at once. Another trick is to relocate the aquarium decorations just before making any new introduction, so that everyone is too busy choosing new territories to pick a fight.

Electric blue, although a strikingly dazzling colour, is common amongst several similar species of damselfishes.

Philippines

Ryuku Islands

Sulawesi

Papua New Guinea

▶ Origins

Philippines, Sulawesi, New Guinea, Solomon Islands and Ryuku Islands.

Solomon Islands

Size: 7cm (2.75in)

GREEN CHROMIS
CHROMIS VIRIDIS

This hardy, colourful shoaling species has a brilliant green-blue sheen to the scales. The caudal fin is more deeply forked than in some damselfishes. Keep these gregarious fishes in a shoal of at least six; individuals may go into decline in the aquarium. This lively and attractive species from the Indo-Pacific and Red Sea grows to 10cm (4in), is generally peaceful in the aquarium and can safely be kept in a mixed fish and invertebrate set-up. It is a shy feeder; offer it chopped meats.

Below: Chromis viridis *is a 'cheap and cheerful' species and an ideal beginner fish that usually weathers early aquarium teething troubles better than most.*

Fishkeeping data

Number per aquarium: Two or three (or maybe two or three single specimens from different genera).
Community/species tank: Community.
Swimming area: Middle and upper levels.
Food: All foods.
Compatibility: Territorial, pugnacious.
Availability: Often available (wild-caught).
Captive breeding: No information.

HUMBUG • *Dascyllus aruanus*

This fish's common name may intrigue anyone who is unfamiliar with the black-and-white striped peppermint confection of the same name.

The high-backed white body is crossed vertically by three black bands, which are united by a thick black edge along the top of the dorsal fin. The pelvic and anal fins are also black, but the pectoral and caudal fins remain clear. *Dascyllus melanurus* is often confused with this species. Although it lacks the black edge to the dorsal fin, it does have a black area across the caudal fin.

Damselfish congregate around coral heads and are only too quick to dash into the safety of the coral's branches. There is bound to be a wealth of such sanctuaries in this fish's natural range, from the Red Sea eastwards to Lord Howe Island in the Pacific.

▶ Fishkeeping data

Number per aquarium: Two to three (or maybe two to three single specimens from different genera).
Community/species tank: Community.
Swimming area: Middle and upper levels.
Food: All foods.
Compatibility: Peaceful.
Availability: Regularly available (wild-caught).
Captive breeding: No information.

Domino, or three-spot damselfish
The three white spots on the jet black body of D. trimaculatus *are very reminiscent of a domino piece. A white spot appears on each side of the body just below the dorsal fin, with a third spot located on the dorsal surface just above the forehead. This coloration is limited to the juvenile form, as the adult fish is a sooty-grey, with less distinct (if at all visible) white markings.* D. trimaculatus *has a similar distribution to* D. aruanus *and the same requirements in captivity.*

A feature of the juvenile fish's behaviour is its association with large sea anemones, a trait it loses when adult.

Size: 8cm (3.2in)

Red Sea

▶ Origins

*From the Red
Sea eastwards
to Lord Howe
Island in the
Pacific.*

Lord Howe Island

Above: *As with all aggressive and territorial
species, it is best to introduce* Dascyllus
melanurus *to the aquarium last of all.*

BLACK-TAILED HUMBUG
DASCYLLUS MELANURUS
*This fish is very similar to D. aruanus,
except that the black bars are more
vertical and, as indicated by the common
name, a black bar crosses the caudal fin.
It is a shoaling species from the Western
Pacific around the Philippines and
Melanesia, and grows to 7.5cm (3in). In the
aquarium the fish are aggressive and
territorial and are best housed with other
fish that can take care of themselves.
They are bold feeders that will accept
both chopped and dried foods, frozen
mysis and brineshrimp.*

Angelfishes

The Family Pomacanthidae contains many brilliantly coloured fishes that range in size from very small to species that would feel more at home in a public aquarium. For example, members of the genus *Centropyge* can be accommodated quite easily in the home aquarium, whereas members of the genus *Pomacanthus* require much larger living quarters. A distinguishing physical feature of these fishes is the backward-projecting spine on the rear of the gill cover. Another characteristic of some members of this family is the complete difference in colour patterning between juvenile and adult specimens.

Many angelfish are specific feeders and, unfortunately, it may not always be possible to acclimatise them to aquarium life. In the wild, some restrict their diets to sponges and similar non-replicable foods, and it is difficult to provide a continuous supply of their required food.

Spawning usually occurs in the early evening, when pairs of fishes come together to release free-floating eggs at the climax of their courtship manoeuvring. However, this is not likely to happen within the aquarium.

Above: *The majestic angelfish,* Euxiphipops navarchus, *certainly lives up to its name. Suitable for the aquarium only as a young fish, when it is dark blue with vertical white stripes.*

BICOLOR ANGELFISH • *Centropyge bicolor*

As can be deduced from its distribution range, this species is a common occurrence. Its very distinctive patterning – forward half and caudal fin bright yellow, the remainder royal blue – makes identification simple. The blue area on the forehead helps to distinguish it from the very similar Coco's pygmy angelfish, *C. joculator*, which has a more swept-back forward edge to the blue area of coloration and orange-edged dorsal and anal fins. As it often feels insecure, the bicolor angelfish prefers areas of rocky rubble that offer welcome boltholes.

The coloration of this fish is not dissimilar to that of the much larger rock beauty, Holacanthus tricolor, *which lacks the dark patch above the eye.*

Cherubfish

The elongated oval body of C. argi (8cm/3.2in) is a deep royal blue that extends into all the fins except the pectorals, which share the bright daffodil-yellow colour of the head. The cherubfish frequents rocky rubble around the coral reefs of Bermuda, Florida and the Caribbean. It feeds mostly on algal growths, so provide some vegetable matter within its diet.

Size: 15cm (6in)

▶ Origins

From Malaysia to Samoa, Japan to northwestern Australia.

Japan

Malaysia

Northwestern Australia

Samoa

▶ *Fishkeeping data*

Number per aquarium: One or an established pair.
Community/species tank: Community.
Swimming area: Middle and lower levels.
Food: Appreciates some vegetable matter.
Compatibility: Peaceful.
Availability: Frequently available (wild-caught).
Captive breeding: No information.

CORAL BEAUTY
CENTROPYGE BISPINOSUS

In young specimens, the head and body are outlined in deep purple; red flanks are vertically crossed by many thin purple lines. Adult fish, measuring 12cm (4.7in), have much larger areas of gold/yellow on the flanks, again crossed by dark vertical stripes. The pattern is very variable, however; for example, specimens from the Philippines have more purple and red coloration than those from Australasian waters. The fish will settle down in the aquarium if retreats are close at hand and are generally well behaved with invertebrates. They are grazers that appreciate meat foods and plenty of greenstuff in their diet.

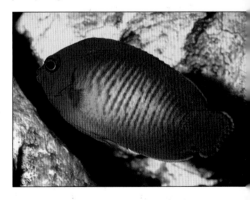

Above: *This coral beauty shows the typical colour pattern of young fish. Adult colour varies depending on the location from which the fish have been collected.*

LEMONPEEL ANGELFISH • *Centropyge flavissimus*

The distinctive coloration of this species can lead to a little confusion between it and its relative, Herald's angelfish *(C. heraldi)*, but the latter lacks the outlining blue of the dorsal, anal and caudal fins and the blue lips. However, just to make things difficult, a local population around the Cocos-Keeling and Christmas Islands in the Indian Ocean does lack the blue outline. Add to this the fact that the juvenile form of the mimic surgeonfish, *Acanthurus pyroferus*, which shares it distribution area (which also reaches as far as Easter Island), is also a plain yellow colour, and you have even more opportunity for confusion.

Closer examination reveals that the lemonpeel hybridises with the pearlscale angelfish *(C. vroliki)*, and Eibl's angelfish *(C. eibli)*.

▶ Origins

Cocos-Keeling and Christmas Islands; Ryukyu, Marianas to Rapa Island. Usually absent from Indo-Australian waters.

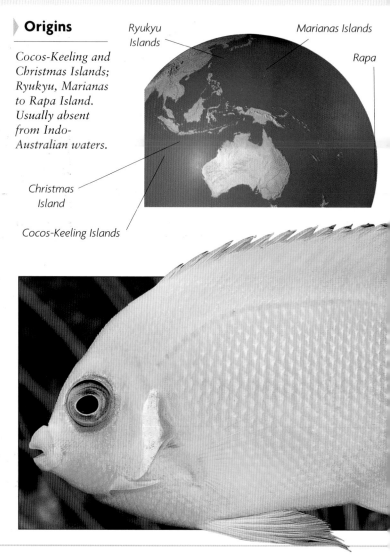

Ryukyu Islands

Marianas Islands

Rapa

Christmas Island

Cocos-Keeling Islands

Size: 14cm (5.5in)

> ## Fishkeeping data

Number per aquarium:
One or an established pair.
Community/species tank:
Community.
Swimming area: Middle
and lower levels.
Food: Appreciates some
vegetable matter.
Compatibility: Peaceful.
Availability: Frequently
available (wild-caught).
Captive breeding: No
information.

Below: Look for the
blue-edged fins if you
are seeking this
species, otherwise you
might end up with
something completely
different, such as a
juvenile surgeonfish.

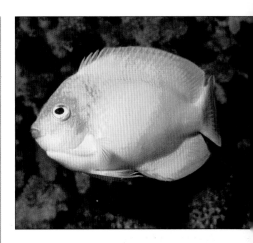

Above: Angelfish are spectacular fishes,
but many are just too large for the average
aquarium. Centropyge species, however,
are ideally suited to the home aquarium.

HERALD'S ANGELFISH
CENTROPYGE HERALDI

C. heraldi *is plain yellow, lacking even the
blue details of* C. flavissimus. *Specimens
collected from around Fiji have a black
edge to the dorsal fin. In the world of
marine fishes, monocoloration is quite
exceptional. This makes the totally yellow
Herald's angelfish from the Indo-Pacific
easy to identify, and a popular choice. It
grows to 10cm (4in) and is a peaceful fish,
generally well behaved in the invertebrate
aquarium. This grazing fish feeds mainly
on greenstuff, but also takes meaty foods.*

FLAME ANGELFISH • *Centropyge loriculus*

The coloration of the bright-orange body with its bright-yellow central area is further enhanced by vertical bands of deep blue-black. The edges of the soft-rayed portions of the dorsal and anal fins also have this blue-black coloration, but the caudal fin is red, shading to yellow. This species is somewhat shy and prefers to stay close to any convenient sanctuary-offering coral outcrop.

Male fish tend to be larger than females. All the fish start out as females, then males develop amongst a harem later.

Fishkeeping data

Number per aquarium: One or an established pair.
Community/species tank: Community.
Swimming area: Middle and lower levels.
Food: Appreciates some vegetable matter.
Compatibility: Peaceful.
Availability: Frequently available (wild-caught).
Captive breeding: No information.

Size: 10cm (4in)

Palau

Hawaii

Samoa

Great Barrier
Reef

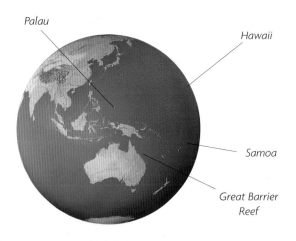

▶ Origins

*From Palau, just east
of the Philippines, to
Samoa and the Great
Barrier Reef, although
less frequent
around Hawaii.*

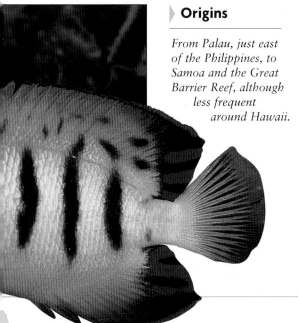

POTTER'S ANGELFISH
CENTROPYGE POTTERI
C. potteri *should not be regarded as an
easy fish to keep; it demands excellent
water quality and a varied diet. At first it
may be a difficult feeder that needs
tempting with live foods. However, once
settled, it will usually accept the usual
frozen marine food. Be sure to provide
plenty of algae for the fish to graze on,
as this makes up an important part of this
species' diet.* C. potteri *is a peaceful fish
that can often be kept with its own kind in
pairs or in small groups in a sufficiently
large aquarium. It is only found in the
Hawaiian Islands. Measuring 10cm (4in), it
falls somewhere in the middle size range
between dwarf angels and the larger angels.*

Above: Centropyge *species are found
at varying water depths. Potter's
angelfish lives in 15m (50ft) of water.*

111

EMPEROR ANGELFISH • *Pomacanthus imperator*

This fish is a favourite (and very recognisable) species with fishkeepers. The body is traversed with diagonal, alternating stripes of blue and yellow, the snout is grey, the eye is hidden within a blue-edged dark stripe and a yellow face mask is interrupted by a further dark area down across the gill cover. The anal fin is purple with red streaking, while the dorsal and caudal fins are yellow. It is reported that specimens from the Indian Ocean have rounded dorsal fins, not pointed as in other cases. However, all this gorgeous patterning is in the future because, like many of its relatives, the juvenile form is dark blue with white markings, in a vaguely concentric form in this particular species.

Juveniles tend to keep in or around boltholes and ledges in coral outcrops, but the adults are much bolder on the seaward coral faces of reefs that occur throughout its large distribution area.

Above: *Like many juvenile angelfish, the young emperor angelfish does not resemble the adult coloration form in any way.*

▶ Origins

From the Red Sea to Hawaii, Japan to south of Tahiti.

Japan

Hawaii

Red Sea

Tahiti

Size: 40cm (16in)

BLUE RING ANGELFISH
POMACANTHUS ANNULARIS

In adult blue ring angelfish, blue lines run from either side of the eye diagonally across the brown body. The lines rejoin at the top of the rear portion of the body. A dominant blue ring lies behind the gill cover. Juveniles are blue, with a distinctive pattern of almost straight transverse white lines. It is not hard to understand why juveniles and adults were once considered to belong to different species. Blue-ring angelfish, from the Indo-Pacific, grow to 40cm (16in) and are territorial. Although they are safe to keep with invertebrates when young, they become destructive with age. The fish are grazers that feed on meat foods and greenstuff.

Below: *If you have sufficient tank space, try keeping this reliable species.*

Fishkeeping data

Number per aquarium: One.
Community/species tank: Community.
Swimming area: All levels.
Food: Appreciates some vegetable matter.
Compatibility: Peaceful.
Availability: Frequently available (wild-caught).
Captive breeding: No information.

FRENCH ANGELFISH • *Pomacanthus paru*

Most marine fishkeepers will be more familiar with the juvenile form of this species and its black body (and fins) crossed by vertical yellow stripes, as shown here. This is a far more interesting pattern than the adult fish's rather drab grey-black ground colour with a faint dusting of yellowish flecks. Again, the adult fish is a rather large proposition to take on for the average domestic aquarium.

Fishkeeping data

Number per aquarium: One.
Community/species tank: Community.
Swimming area: All levels.
Food: Appreciates some vegetable matter.
Compatibility: Peaceful.
Availability: Frequently available (wild-caught).
Captive breeding: Fry have been produced using the 'hand-stripping' method similar to that used for goldfish.

Breeding

French angelfish tend to pair-bond in nature. The actual spawning process is a leisurely affair conducted in deeper water, with eggs being expelled and fertilised as the two fish swim upwards through the water. Reports indicate that breeding through 'hand-stripping' adult fish of eggs and sperm (in a similar fashion to goldfish) is possible.

Size: 38cm (15in)

Left: This is a splendid example of an adult queen angelfish. Juveniles often act as 'cleaners' to other fish visiting their locality.

QUEEN ANGELFISH
HOLACANTHUS CILIARIS

This angelfish from the Western Atlantic looks very beautiful in the aquarium. Variations in colour pattern occur and the body hues also appear to change under varying lighting conditions. Young fish have curving, royal blue vertical markings on a dark blue, gold-finned body. Adult coloration may also be adopted at half the fish's maximum size, given the proper diet and a spacious tank. H. ciliaris grows large – up to 45cm (18in), grazing on meat foods and greenstuff. It is aggressive when young, intolerant of its own species and can be very territorial. Although juveniles are safe with invertebrates, they become destructive with age. Queen Angelfish are reported to be prone to outbreaks of whitespot disease, but can be successfully treated with copper-based remedies. They are quite resistant to such treatment and may even withstand some degree of overdosing without ill effects.

▶ Origins

A far-ranging species covering waters of the northern Gulf of Mexico to Brazil. There are even some reports of central Atlantic sightings around Ascension Island.

Gulf of Mexico

Ascension Island

Brazil

Butterflyfishes

Members of the Family Chaetodontidae are not dissimilar in shape or coloration to the angelfishes, but lack the spine on the gill cover. Furthermore, feeding can present similar problems (see page 73). Most of the butterflyfishes have sharply pointed heads, often with elongated snouts that are ideal for picking among the coral for their food. They are typically active during daylight hours and retreat amongst the coral heads at night.

Although this group contains some of the most beautiful fishes to be seen around the coral reef, it is in their own best interests that they are left in their natural habitat. However, their expensive price tag will always mean that they are desired by the ambitious fishkeeper, who in all probability will be disappointed at their relatively short life in captivity, usually due to feeding problems. Because they are grazers of polyps and sponges, there is the added problem of keeping them in a reef tank containing live corals.

On the credit side, established pairs of butterflyfish generally do well, although their degree of 'hardiness' is often due to their method of capture – net-caught specimens being far hardier than those captured using drugs.

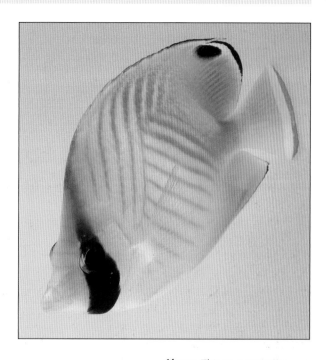

Above: *This young specimen of the elegant, boldly marked threadfin butterflyfish,* Chaetodon auriga, *has just a small extension to the rear of the dorsal fin from which the common name is derived.*

THREADFIN BUTTERFLYFISH • *Chaetodon auriga*

Many species of *Chaetodon* within the same distribution range are similarly coloured and the threadfin butterflyfish shares its 'herring-bone' striped patterning of grey-black stripes on a silvery yellow background with two or three relatives. Additionally, the hiding of the eye in a vertical dark band is a common feature amongst butterflyfishes in general, serving to protect this vital organ from attack. It is especially effective when supplemented by a replica, or decoy, eye marking elsewhere on the body.

The common name refers to a threadlike extension to the rear of the yellow rear portion of the dorsal fin. While threadfins usually have an 'eyespot' in the dorsal fin's yellow area, some populations on the seaward side of reefs do not. Normal foods include polyps, anemones and algae.

Fishkeeping data

Number per aquarium: One.
Community/species tank: Community.
Swimming area: All levels.
Food: Polyps, anemones and algae, but will take prepared foods.
Compatibility: Peaceful.
Availability: Frequently available (wild-caught).
Captive breeding: No information.

Vagabond butterflyfish

Chaetodon vagabundus *may be distinguished from the threadfin by the black border running around the rear edge of the body and around the rear edges of the dorsal and anal fins. Two vertical black bars appear on the yellow caudal fin. The forehead is less steeply inclined. The diet follows that for the threadfin and the distribution area is similar.*

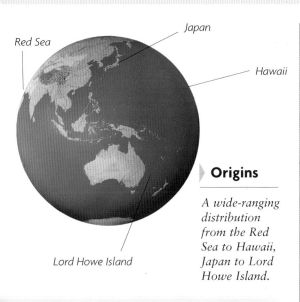

Red Sea

Japan

Hawaii

Lord Howe Island

▶ **Origins**

*A wide-ranging
distribution
from the Red
Sea to Hawaii,
Japan to Lord
Howe Island.*

DOUBLE-SADDLED BUTTERFLYFISH
CHAETODON FALCULA

*Two dark saddle markings cross the top of
the body (developing on this young fish).
The dorsal, anal and caudal fins are yellow,
and there is a black spot or bar on the
caudal peduncle. The body and head are
white. A vertical black bar runs down the
side of the head and there are many thin
vertical lines on the body. C. falcula, found
in the Indian Ocean, grows to 15cm (6in) and
is often confused with C. ulietensis, which
occurs in the wider-ranging Indo-Pacific
waters, and has slightly lower reaching
'saddles' and less yellow on top of the body
and dorsal fin. Like most species in this
family, C. falcula, which also goes by the
common name of pig-faced butterflyfish, is
not suitable for the beginner. It requires a
diet of crustaceans, coral polyps and algae.
It is aggressive towards similar species and
cannot be trusted with invertebrates.*

COPPERBAND BUTTERFLYFISH • *Chelmon rostratus*

While many butterflyfishes have almost identical coloration, namely bright yellow bars on a silvery background, the copperband is in a class of its own, except maybe for the very similar ocellate coralfish, *Parachaetodon ocellatus*, found further westwards. However, its body shape is more rhomboid, while the copperband's is oblong.

The silvery body is crossed vertically by five black-edged orange bands that reach into the yellow-and-blue-edged pelvic, anal and dorsal fins. There is a false eyespot in the rear portion of the dorsal fin. The main physical characteristic (apart from the coloration) is the long beaklike snout – ideal for reaching into coralline crevices for food.

The copperband may be slow to acclimatise to tank conditions and appears to do best in a well-established reef aquarium, where it can find enough to satisfy its coral-pecking instincts.

Andaman Sea

Japan

Papua New Guinea

▷ Origins

Great Barrier Reef

Found either as a solitary specimen or in pairs from the Andaman Sea, Papua New Guinea, Australia and Great Barrier Reef north towards Japan.

Size: 20cm (8in)

Fishkeeping data

Number per aquarium: One.
Community/species tank:
Community.
Swimming area: Middle and
lower levels.
Food: All 'meaty' foods.
Compatibility: Peaceful.
Availability: Frequently
available (wild-caught).
Captive breeding: No
information.

*If you had to design a tool
for collecting food from
coral reef crevices, you
would be hard pushed to
come up with something
better than this.*

ADDIS BUTTERFLYFISH
CHAETODON SEMILARVATUS

The yellow body of Chaetodon
semilarvatus *is crossed by thin orange
vertical lines. A blue-black inverted
teardrop patch covers the eye. Specimens
from the Red Sea are difficult to obtain
and therefore very expensive. This species,
also known as lemonpeel butterflyfish and
golden butterflyfish, grows to 20cm (8in)
and grazes on crustaceans, coral polyps
and algae. The bright coloration and
distinctive markings make it an attractive
fish to look at, but in the aquarium it may
be intolerant of other members of its own,
or other, species and cannot be trusted
with invertebrates. Nevertheless, it settles
down readily in captivity.*

LONGNOSED BUTTERFLYFISH • *Forcipiger longirostris*

This species not only looks extremely similar to its relative, *F. flavissimus*, but also shares much of its distribution area. For those wishing to differentiate between the two species, *F. longirostris* has the longer snout and the steeper forehead, while *F. flavissimus* has a larger gape to its mouth.

The head coloration serves two purposes: the black upper half protects the eye (there is a small eyespot on the rear of the anal fin to divert attack away from the real eye), while the silver lower half effectively breaks up the fish profile, again perhaps to prevent detection from would-be predators. The whole body rearwards of the gills, together with the pelvic, dorsal and anal fins, is bright yellow, with bright blue on the edges of the single fins. The caudal fin is colourless.

Note that the real eye is hidden in a dark area with a 'decoy' eye prominently displayed just below the caudal peduncle.

This is another instance of disruptive coloration, with bold areas of different colour that break up the fish's outline.

Size: 22cm (8.5in)

East Africa

Japan

Hawaii

Austral Islands

Great Barrier Reef

▶ Origins

From East Africa to Hawaii, Japan to the Austral Islands, including the Great Barrier Reef.

▶ *Fishkeeping data*

Number per aquarium: One.
Community/species tank: Community.
Swimming area: Middle and lower levels.
Food: All 'meaty' foods.
Compatibility: Peaceful.
Availability: Frequently available (wild-caught).
Captive breeding: No information.

WIMPLEFISH
HENIOCHUS ACUMINATUS

Two wide, forward-sloping black bands cross the white body. The rear parts of the dorsal, pectoral and anal fins are yellow, while the pelvic fins are black. The front few dorsal fin rays are much extended. H. acuminatus, from the Indo-Pacific and Red Sea, varies little in juvenile and adult coloration. Young specimens act as cleanerfishes. They grow to 18cm (7in), grazing on most frozen marine foods and greenstuff. Heniochus is easier to keep than the lookalike Moorish idol (Zanclus canescens). It is a companionable shoaling fish, but the natural leader in a group in captivity may develop into a bully. Do not keep these fish with invertebrates.

Wrasses

The Family Labridae contains very many species of all shapes and sizes, although usually it is only juvenile members of the species that are suitable for the home aquarium. Again, there may be a vast difference both in colour and patterning between juvenile and adult forms.

All wrasses appear to rest at night, often burying themselves in the substrate or spinning a cocoon of mucus to form a 'sleeping bag'. An aquarium furnished with many nooks and crannies is ideal for wrasses.

Perhaps the best-known species is the cleaner wrasse, *Labroides dimidiatus*, which feeds off parasites on other fishes. Unfortunately, this habit pushes the species into a 'specific feeder' category, which means that in the average aquarium (containing few parasites) there may well not be enough food for this fish to thrive. For this reason ask your aquarium dealer for advice on buying this fish.

Many wrasses are brilliantly coloured and would make attractive aquarium subjects. The larger species are not recommended for a reef-type tank, although smaller species are much more satisfactory in this respect.

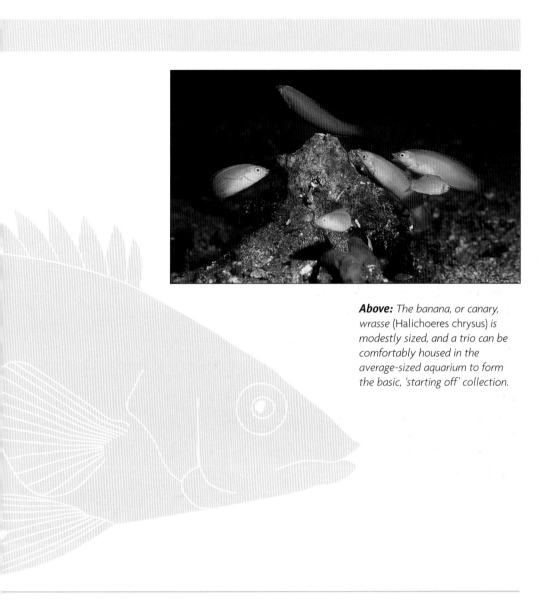

Above: *The banana, or canary, wrasse (*Halichoeres chrysus*) is modestly sized, and a trio can be comfortably housed in the average-sized aquarium to form the basic, 'starting off' collection.*

CUBAN HOGFISH • *Bodianus pulchellus*

The stocky but streamlined body is bright crimson-red for most of its length; only the top half of the caudal peduncle is bright yellow. The pelvic, dorsal and anal fins are also scarlet, while the caudal fin is mostly yellow; only the bottom edge carries the remainder of the red colour from the body. The clear pectoral fins feature a black blotch at their tips. In some specimens, a lateral white stripe may be present.

This bold species acts as a cleanerfish when young and is often found in close association with the bluehead wrasse, *Thalassoma bifasciatum*.

▶ Origins

Wide-ranging across the Caribbean, from Florida to Brazil.

Florida

Caribbean Sea

Brazil

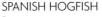

Fishkeeping data

Number per aquarium: One.
Community/species tank: Community, but not with invertebrates.
Swimming area: Middle and lower levels.
Food: All 'meaty' foods.
Compatibility: Usually peaceful but intolerant of its own kind.
Availability: Frequently available (wild-caught).
Captive breeding: No information.

Below: The spotfin hogfish takes its name from the black blotch on the end of each pectoral fin.

SPANISH HOGFISH
BODIANUS RUFUS

Juvenile specimens are yellow with an area of blue along the upper body. Adult fishes show the standard red and yellow coloration, although the proportions may vary according to the habitat and depth of water. These brightly coloured wrasses from the Western Atlantic grow to 20cm (8in), feeding boldly on crustaceans and shellfish meat at the bottom of the tank. They are peaceful community fish and safe to keep with invertebrates when young, but become destructive with age and size. Like other members of the genus, juveniles perform cleaning actions on other fishes.

Above: The change between juvenile (as shown here) and adult coloration is probably in order to adapt to the differing light levels in deeper water, where the adults eventually live.

127

HARLEQUIN TUSKFISH • *Choerodon fasciatus*

The coloration of this fish is quite stunning, with blue-edged bright orange bands crossing the blue-silver body vertically. The pelvic, dorsal and anal fins are also orange-red with blue edges. The body area around the caudal peduncle is dark blue and the caudal fin is white with a red final edge. The teeth are protrusible, ideal for moving rocks around in order to get at the invertebrate food beneath them, or for wrenching molluscs from rocks.

Fishkeeping data

Number per aquarium: One.
Community/species tank: Community, but not with invertebrates.
Swimming area: Middle and lower levels.
Food: All 'meaty' foods.
Compatibility: Usually peaceful but intolerant of its own kind.
Availability: Frequently available (wild-caught).
Captive breeding: No information.

This adult tuskfish has lost the 'eyespots' seen on the dorsal, anal and pelvic fins of the juvenile form.

Size: 25cm (10in)

Origins

Taiwan

Ryukyu Islands

Often found as solitary specimens in their native waters, ranging from Taiwan, Ryukyu Islands to Australia and the Great Barrier Reef.

Barrier Reef

TWIN-SPOT WRASSE
CORIS AYGULA

A spectacularly coloured species, both as a juvenile and as an adult. When young, this fish is white with two prominent orange spots on the dorsal surface. The front of the body together with the fins, is covered with dark spots and there are two white-edged black blotches on the dorsal fin. The adult is green with yellow-edged purple fins and is referred to as the Napoleon wrasse. This peaceful, bottom-feeding fish accepts small frozen marine animals and live foods. It can be safely kept with invertebrates when young, but becomes destructive with age and size. It quickly grows to 20-30cm (8-12in).

Below: *Do not confuse the Napoleon wrasse with the Napoleonfish at three times its size!*

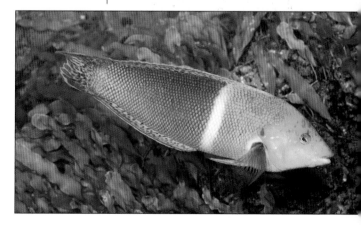

129

BIRDMOUTH WRASSE • *Gomphosus coeruleus*

The birdmouth wrasse is aptly named, for not only does it have an extended snout reminiscent of a bird's beak, but also a curious swimming action that gives the impression that the fish is 'flying' through the water with a swooping action that is more avian than piscine.

The body of the male fish is green-blue, with a semicircle of yellow in the caudal fin. The dorsal and anal fins have yellow borders and the pectoral fins are black. The female is a dull brown colour.

This constantly active species does not burrow into the substrate at night, but hides up amongst the coral.

▶ Origins

A wide natural distribution, ranging from the Red Sea to Hawaii, Ryukyu Islands to Lord Howe Island.

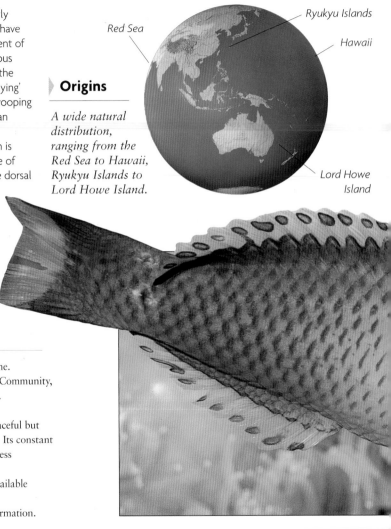

Red Sea

Ryukyu Islands

Hawaii

Lord Howe Island

▶ *Fishkeeping data*

Number per aquarium: One.
Community/species tank: Community, but not with invertebrates.
Food: All 'meaty' foods.
Compatibility: Usually peaceful but intolerant of its own kind. Its constant activity may worry other less boisterous species.
Availability: Frequently available (wild-caught).
Captive breeding: No information.

Above: The legendary cleanerfish regularly services most fishes visiting its coral reef.

CLEANER WRASSE
LABROIDES DIMIDIATUS

This is the most familiar of the wrasses because of its cleaning activities. This cleaning process, also practised by some gobies and cleaner shrimps, is almost ritualistic. When approached by a cleaner wrasse, the subject fish – or host – often remains stationary with fins spread, in a head-up or head-down attitude. Sometimes the colours of the host fish fade, maybe so that the cleaner wrasse can see any parasites. The cleaner wrasse is found in the Indo-Pacific and grows to 10cm (4in). In the wild it feeds on the skin parasites of other fishes, but in the aquarium, finely chopped meat foods make an excellent substitute for this bold feeder. This constantly active but peaceful fish is safe with invertebrates.

Wolf in sheep's clothing

The elongate blue body of the cleaner wrasse has a horizontal dark stripe from snout to caudal fin. The mouth is terminal, and it is this feature that distinguishes Labroides dimidiatus *from the predatory lookalike* Aspidontus taeniatus, *the so-called false cleanerfish, which has an 'underslung' mouth.*

BANANA WRASSE • *Halichoeres chrysus*

The brilliant yellow coloration, coupled with the shape of the body, should leave nobody in doubt as to the inspiration for this species' popular name. It has three black spots on the dorsal fin and one on the caudal peduncle. This helps to distinguish it from a similar-looking species, *H. leucoxanthus*, known as the canary-top wrasse, in which only the top half of the body is yellow; the lower half is silvery-white.

▶ Origins

From Christmas Island to Marshall Islands, south Japan to southeastern Australia.

Japan

Marshall Islands

Christmas Island

▶ Fishkeeping data

Number per aquarium: Two to three.
Community/species tank: Community, but not with invertebrates.
Swimming area: Middle and lower levels.
Food: All 'meaty foods'.
Compatibility: Usually peaceful, but may quarrel amongst themselves.
Availability: Frequently available (wild-caught).
Captive breeding: No information.

Above: However you look at it, the sixline wrasse is a smart character, from its horizontally striped eye to the tip of its green tail fin.

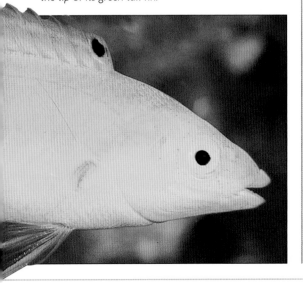

SIXLINE WRASSE

PSEUDOCHEILINUS HEXATAENIA

The body shape of this species from the Indo-Pacific is one of classic symmetry, with the dorsal and ventral profiles mirroring each other perfectly. The coloration consists of horizontal stripes of alternating yellow and purple. The dorsal and caudal fins are yellow, while the pelvic and anal fins are purple. There is a white-edged black spot on the caudal peduncle. Despite the fish's attractive features, it tends to shy away from exhibiting them, preferring to frequent the coral branches rather than more open water. It grows to 7.5cm (3in) and readily accepts most marine frozen, live and flake foods. Keep them in a community tank, where they constantly inspect the rockwork for titbits and, maybe, worry the snails. They are generally peaceful, except with the same or similar species. The sixline wrasse is an interesting, inexpensive and disease-resistant species that can be heartily recommended to any newcomer to the hobby.

Think ahead

Many of the wrasse family are attractive fishes in their juvenile forms, but become quite large, outgrowing their living quarters and losing their colours as they mature. This is something to bear in mind when selecting wrasses for your collection.

Surgeonfishes & tangs

Members of the Family Acanthuridae have oval or disc-shaped bodies, edged with long-based dorsal and anal fins. The head has a steeply rising forehead with the eyes mounted high up. The aptly named surgeonfishes carry an erectile scalpel on each side of the caudal peduncle, which can be used either offensively or defensively.

Members of this group are usually active during daylight hours and mostly herbivorous, requiring a good proportion of vegetable matter in their diet. Most are intolerant of their own kind, especially those of similar colours or shapes, but in a large aquarium, it is possible that oval-shaped fish will co-exist with the disc-shaped species without constant quarrelling.

The popular name of 'tang' is likely to be an abbreviation of the German 'seetang', meaning seaweed. This reflects the fishes' fondness for consuming large quantities of algae and kelp as its natural diet. In addition to offering such a diet, it is also important to provide a flow of well-oxygenated water by means of a powerful filtration system with, perhaps, extra aeration.

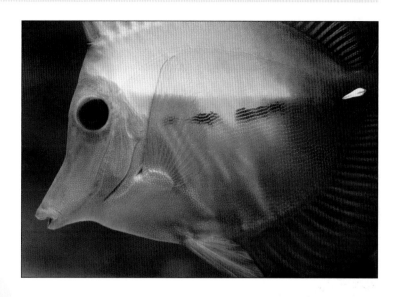

Above: *What better common name could there be for these fishes than 'surgeonfish'. The 'scalpel' near the junction of the tail and body shines white here as a warning to would-be predators to keep away.*

POWDER BLUE SURGEON • *Acanthurus leucosternon*

The steeply rising forehead and oval body are typical of the genus. Furthermore, the black head, white throat and blue body surrounded by yellow dorsal and anal fins, plus a black-decorated caudal fin make recognition of this species easy. The 'scalpel' is disguised in the yellow background of the caudal peduncle. The small, pointed mouth, well-equipped with teeth, is set well forward for efficient grazing on algae or capturing planktonic food. Although the fish often occur in large colonies in nature, most aquatic dealers separate young specimens from one another as they have a penchant for squabbling. Powder blues (and the related powder brown, A. japonicus) have a wide distribution area.

When buying surgeons and tangs, look out for 'pinched-in' bodies, especially in the head region. These fishes are constantly eating in the wild and need adequate, vegetable-based diets.

Despite the fish's overall 'blueness', the scalpel is visible against its bright yellow border.

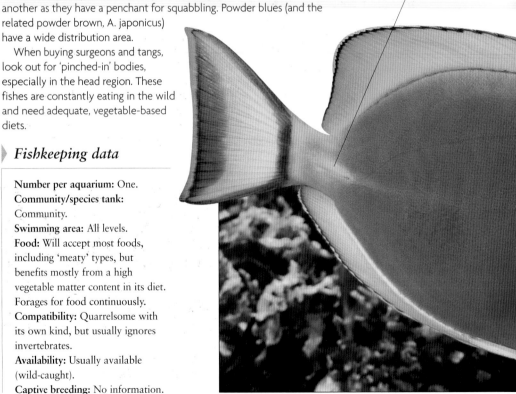

▶ Fishkeeping data

Number per aquarium: One.
Community/species tank: Community.
Swimming area: All levels.
Food: Will accept most foods, including 'meaty' types, but benefits mostly from a high vegetable matter content in its diet. Forages for food continuously.
Compatibility: Quarrelsome with its own kind, but usually ignores invertebrates.
Availability: Usually available (wild-caught).
Captive breeding: No information.

Size: 23cm (9in)

▶ Origins

From East
Africa to
southwest
Indonesia.

East Africa

Indonesia

BLUE TANG
ACANTHURUS COERULEUS

*Young fishes are yellow with blue
markings around the eye – do not confuse
them with Zebrasoma flavescens (see page
142). Small specimens can be quite
aggressive and may become bullies if
established in the aquarium before other
fishes, but this tendency generally
decreases with time. Do not keep blue
tangs with invertebrates. As they age, the
fish develop narrow blue lines, the adult
fish being darker blue than the 'almost
adult' fish. The scalpels on the caudal
peduncle are ringed with yellow or white
in mature fishes. Its dark blue coloration
defies the bright yellow of the juvenile.
Blue tangs are found in the Western
Atlantic and grow to 15cm (6in). They
feed mainly on algae.*

Above: *The scalpels of surgeonfishes are
usually well hidden, but the colour scheme
of this species gives the game away.*

137

ORANGE-SPINE UNICORNFISH • *Naso lituratus*

Although this species is technically classified as a surgeonfish in most literature, it is also known as a member of the unicornfish group (Nasinae), some of which have a single hornlike projection from the forehead. Additionally, the 'scalpels' are permanently erected and are arranged as a pair of bony projections on each side of the caudal peduncle.

The body coloration is olive-brown, while the whitish face has black markings and bright red lips that account for the fish's popular name of lipstick tang. The long-based dorsal fin is bright yellow and the almost equally long anal fin is brown. There is a black border around the caudal fin. As may be surmised by its size, it is an ocean-going species and naturally requires adequate aquarium space to contain its constant movements.

Origins

From the Red Sea to Hawaii, Japan to the Great Barrier Reef.

Japan

Hawaii

Red Sea

Great Barrier Reef

Fishkeeping data

Number per aquarium: One.
Community/species tank: Community.
Swimming area: All levels.
Food: Will accept most foods, including 'meaty' types, but benefits mostly from a high-vegetable matter content in its diet. Forages for food continuously.
Compatibility: Quarrelsome with its own kind but usually ignores invertebrates.
Availability: Usually available (wild-caught).
Captive breeding: No information.

Size: 30cm (12in)

Left: *The scalpels on this species are not as large as their disguising colour panel.*

ACHILLES TANG
ACANTHURUS ACHILLES

The brown, oval body is offset by yellow-red baselines to the dorsal and anal fins. The white marking on the gill cover behind the eye and the dull white patch on the chest are shared by other members of the family, but the feature that positively identifies this fish is the teardrop-shaped orange-red area on the caudal peduncle, in which the scalpels are set. Young fish do not have nearly as many red markings as adults. They grow to 25cm (10in). The Achilles tang is normally peaceful but very delicate. It is compatible with most fish, but may fight at first with other members of its own family. Do not add it to the tank until the first fish are established and do not keep it with invertebrates. The fish are found in the Pacific and graze on growths of algae (the high forehead makes this easy). In the aquarium they are shy grazers that will accept the usual protein foods, such as gamma-irradiated frozen foods and live brineshrimp, plus algae and other greenstuff.

139

REGAL TANG • *Paracanthurus hepatus*

This aquarium favourite is easily identified by its royal blue body, decorated with the familiar painter's palette outline, and the bright yellow caudal and pectoral fins.

All surgeons and tangs are very dependent on well-oxygenated water and are also warmth-loving; a temperature of 26-28°C (79-82°F) suits them fine. Keep the specific gravity as near to the level they would experience in nature and also ensure that the pH is consistently stable at about 8.3.

Like all members of this family, they can be territorially minded, so adequate tank space with plenty of retreats is called for.

▶ Origins

A wide-ranging species, from East Africa to the mid-Pacific Line Islands, southern Japan to the Great Barrier Reef, New Caledonia and Samoa.

The 'palette' pattern on the body is instantly recognisable, but the dorsal fin pattern and bright yellow caudal fin also deserve appreciation.

East Africa

Japan

Samoa

New Caledonia

Great Barrier Reef

▶ Fishkeeping data

Number per aquarium: One.
Community/species tank: Community.
Swimming area: All levels.
Food: Will accept most foods, including 'meaty' types, but benefits mostly from a high-vegetable matter content in its diet. Forages for food continuously.
Compatibility: Quarrelsome with its own kind, but usually ignores invertebrates.
Availability: Usually available (wild-caught).
Captive breeding: No information.

Size: 31cm (12.25in)

CLOWN SURGEONFISH
ACANTHURUS LINEATUS

This is one of the species of the Acanthuridae family with a split level of coloration: there is a lighter area to the lower body, with dark-edged, parallel longitudinal lines above. The pelvic fins are yellow. This striped pattern accounts for the fish's other common names – blue-lined surgeonfish and pyjama tang. Ideally, keep only one of these fish in an aquarium (unless you have a very large tank with space for several), as small specimens, in particular, can be quarrelsome. Like other surgeonfishes, A. lineatus appreciates some coral or rockwork to provide welcome shelter. The fish are found in the Indo-Pacific and require a diet of algae. They will grow to 15cm (6in).

Left: *The colourful patterning of the clown surgeonfish looks quite stunning under aquarium lighting, but may appear very different when viewed 'down in the depths'.*

YELLOW TANG • *Zebrasoma flavescens*

This brightly coloured yellow fish has a high profile and stands out well in the aquarium. It relishes vegetable matter and will happily munch on scalded lettuce leaves. These can be conveniently secured between the jaws of a magnetic algae-scraper to anchor them into an 'easy-eating' position.

This species cannot be confused with other all-yellow fishes, such as the lemonpeel angelfish *(Centropyge flavissimus)*, Herald's angelfish *(C. heraldi)* or even the related juvenile mimic surgeonfish *(Acanthurus pyroferus)*, because of its distinguishing tall finnage and more laterally compressed body.

Fishkeeping data

Number per aquarium: One.
Community/species tank: Community.
Swimming area: Middle and lower levels.
Food: Will accept most foods, including 'meaty' types, but benefits mostly from a high-vegetable matter content in its diet. Forages for food continuously.
Compatibility: Quarrelsome with its own kind, but usually ignores invertebrates.
Availability: Usually available (wild-caught).
Captive breeding: No information.

Size: 20cm (8in)

▶ Origins

Ryukyu Islands

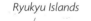

Hawaii

From Ryukyu Islands eastwards, although most frequently found around Hawaii.

This is a fine specimen of yellow tang. Avoid tangs with concave bodies, especially in the head and dorsal areas.

Algae-eaters

Keeping a tang in your aquarium is an ideal way of keeping unwanted growths of algae under control. However, some macro-algae is beneficial, as it removes nitrates and adds trace elements.

SAILFIN TANG
ZEBRASOMA VELIFERUM

At first glance this species, from the Indo-Pacific, is reminiscent of the freshwater discus, Symphysodon *sp., but a closer look will reveal that the actual body shape is not round but a tapering, forward-sloping oval. It is the large, wide dorsal and anal fins that add the illusory 'roundness.' It grows to 40cm (16in).*

The pale cream background colour is crossed vertically by five or six brown bars, the darkest two of which are found at the front, crossing the eye and the gill cover. Some bars also carry gold-red streaking along their lengths. The fins repeat the alternate brown-and-cream patterning in what appears as almost concentric circles around the body. The caudal peduncle is light blue with a dark blue scalpel; the caudal fin is yellow. Juveniles (shown here), which are yellow with alternating dark bars, frequent shallower waters than adults.

The fish appreciate a diet with a high vegetable content, as well as 'meaty' foods. The may be quarrelsome with their own kind, but usually ignore invertebrates.

Triggerfishes

Members of the Family Balistidae have deep, triangular, tapering bodies, with only rudimentary stumps where the pelvic fins would normally emerge. However, their main characteristic is the locking action found on the first of the two dorsal fins. The second spine of the first dorsal fin locks it up into a vertical position, which can effectively lodge the fish into a crevice or, alternatively, prevent it being swallowed by another larger fish. (Remember that it may also catch in the fishkeeper's net!) The first dorsal fin can only be unlocked by releasing the 'trigger', thus allowing the fin to settle back into a groove on the back of the fish, where it is normally carried flat and out of sight until needed.

Do not keep these fish with invertebrates on which they prey in nature. In captivity, they are often quite quarrelsome amongst themselves, so are best kept as single specimens. They have a rather unusual swimming action, propelling themselves through the water using a side-to-side action of their dorsal and anal fins, rather than their tails. In nature, breeding occurs on the seabed, where eggs are deposited in shallow pits dug out by the male fish.

Above: In this clown triggerfish, Balistoides conspicillum, *the first dorsal fin has been locked in an upright position by the second spine, aptly called the 'trigger'. Normally, this fin is carried flat against the body.*

CLOWN TRIGGERFISH • *Balistoides conspicillum*

Like many marine species, the clown triggerfish has very disruptive colour patterning. The lower half of the dark body is covered with large white ovals, while the upper body immediately beneath the dorsal fin has a bright-yellow 'saddle'. The eye is hidden, but a bright-yellow stripe crosses the snout below it. The mouth is accentuated by a bright-yellow surround and an additional white line beyond it. The teeth are very sharp, so handle this fish with care. Although triggerfishes have two separate dorsal fins, the first fin is normally folded flat and carried in a groove immediately above the yellow saddle marking.

▶ *Fishkeeping data*

Number per aquarium: One.
Community/species tank: Community, with larger fishes but not invertebrates. Often best kept as individuals in a species aquarium.
Swimming area: Middle and lower levels.
Food: All 'meaty' foods.
Compatibility: Territorial.
Availability: Frequently available (wild-caught).
Captive breeding: No information.

Japan

East Africa

Samoa

Lord Howe Island

▶ **Origins**

The clown triggerfish has a wide natural distribution, frequenting waters as far apart as East Africa to Samoa, Japan to Lord Howe Island.

146

Size: 50cm (20in)

REDTOOTH TRIGGERFISH
ODONUS NIGER

The body is a uniform dark blue-green, with the dark-centred scales creating a reticulated effect. The head region may be a shade or two lighter. Some facial markings may be visible, running from the snout up towards the eye. As the common name implies, the teeth are bright red. The outer margins of the fins are a bright blue, and the caudal fin is often very well produced, giving the fish a lyretail appearance. In the wild, when frightened, this is the only part of the fish to be seen, as it dashes into a coral crevice for shelter, leaving its tail sticking out. It is generally considered to be a peaceful species in the aquarium, but do not keep it with invertebrates. It accepts all 'meaty' foods and grows to 40cm (16in).

Above: Note the 'waviness' of the rear dorsal and anal fins; these are providing propulsion rather than the caudal fin.

Right: The swimming action of triggerfishes is different to that of most fish. They wave their dorsal and anal fins from side to side, rather than use their caudal fin.

147

PICASSOFISH • *Rhinecanthus aculeatus*

With a native common name – Humuhumu – as striking as its colour patterning, this species always invites attention. Although the mouth is relatively small, the yellow lips and elongated yellow line that runs horizontally rearwards across the gill cover give the impression of an immense gape – maybe a defensive coloration? The top of the head is yellowish, the throat and ventral area white. The lower half of the body from the pectoral fins to the caudal peduncle is decorated with diagonal alternate stripes of white and black. The caudal peduncle itself has horizontal black-and-white lines. A blue-edged dark stripe straddles the eye and covers the rear edge of the gill cover, while the upper half of the body is creamy white. The dorsal surface is separated from the diagonal stripes by brown-grey smudges through which brown stripes rise to meet the rearward of the two dorsal fins.

Despite appearances, the Picassofish's mouth is quite small. Note this fish's erect dorsal fin, which is not often seen.

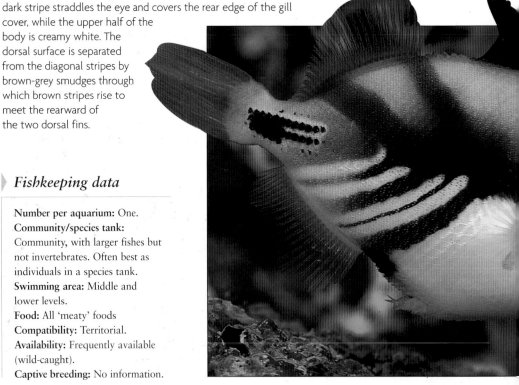

Fishkeeping data

Number per aquarium: One.
Community/species tank: Community, with larger fishes but not invertebrates. Often best as individuals in a species tank.
Swimming area: Middle and lower levels.
Food: All 'meaty' foods
Compatibility: Territorial.
Availability: Frequently available (wild-caught).
Captive breeding: No information.

Size: 25cm (10in)

▶ Origins

Indo-Pacific
waters from
East Africa to
Hawaii,
Japan to
Lord Howe
Island.

Japan

Hawaii

East Africa

Lord Howe Island

Below: Triggerfish spawnings may be feasible if their aquarium is sufficiently large.

QUEEN TRIGGERFISH
BALISTES VETULA

Dark lines radiate from around the eyes and there are striking blue facial markings. The tips of the dorsal fin and caudal fins become filamentous with age, especially in the male, which is larger and more colourful than the female. This beautifully marked species may become hand-tame in captivity. However, take care when hand-feeding, as the fishes' slightly obtrusive teeth are very sharp. Try impaling pieces of food on a cocktail stick before offering them to the fish. They are bold feeders, accepting good-sized pieces of smaller frozen fishes, crustaceans and molluscs, plus the usual frozen foods. B. vetula is found in the tropical western Atlantic and grows to 25cm (10in). Do not keep it with small fishes or invertebrates. Although peaceful with other species, it will quarrel with its own kind.

Groupers & basslets

The Family Serranidae is very large, containing both brilliantly coloured, modest-sized specimens and drab-coloured monsters of the deep. Body shape tends to be stockily cylindrical, with spiny dorsal fins.

Many members are bottom-loving fish that constantly patrol the rubble at the base of coral reefs, while others may lie in wait, ready to pounce on any passing 'meal'. Sex reversal is common, with a female likely to change into a male as the need occurs, say, should the dominant male of a group of fishes cease to fulfil his function for whatever reason.

With the larger specimens, the production of large amounts of waste material demands an efficient filtration system and more frequent partial water changes to keep water conditions at their optimum.

The smaller specimens are especially suitable for the home aquarium. Such species include the royal gramma and its lookalike royal dottyback, both of which make excellent and highly colourful reef tank inhabitants. Whilst they are included within this section for convenience, they are not strictly serranids but are actually members of the Grammidae and Pseudochromidae families respectively.

Above: *Huge shoals of these wreckfish (Pseudanthias squamipinnis)* are a common sight in their native habitat. Most will be females in a 'harem' with their attendant solitary, dominant male.

PANTHERFISH • *Chromileptis altivelis*

Despite its large size, there is something very graceful about this species as it cruises slowly around its necessarily large aquarium. The creamy-white body and fins are covered with black spots, which give rise to the alternative popular name of polkadot grouper. Yet another name, the humpbacked grouper, is inspired by the smallness of the head, which accentuates the height of the dorsal profile. Juvenile forms have larger black blotches that become smaller but more numerous with increasing adulthood.

In its natural home, this species is a valued food fish. Despite its apparently small mouth, it would be prudent not to keep it with small fishes, just to be on the safe side.

The large fins are used to control this fish's slow and graceful movement around the aquarium.

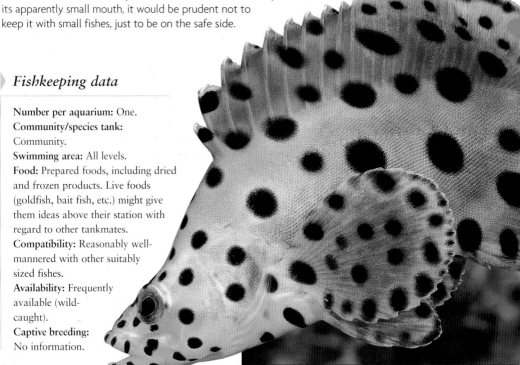

Fishkeeping data

Number per aquarium: One.
Community/species tank: Community.
Swimming area: All levels.
Food: Prepared foods, including dried and frozen products. Live foods (goldfish, bait fish, etc.) might give them ideas above their station with regard to other tankmates.
Compatibility: Reasonably well-mannered with other suitably sized fishes.
Availability: Frequently available (wild-caught).
Captive breeding: No information.

Japan

East
Africa

Vanuatu

New Caledonia

▶ **Origins**

*From East Africa to
Vanuatu, southern Japan
to New Caledonia.*

MARINE BETTA
CALLOPLESIOPS ALTIVELIS

*When looking at this very beautiful and
deceptive fish, the trick is to decide which
way it is facing, since the dorsal fin has a
'false-eye' marking near its rear edge. The
dark brown body is covered with light blue
spots and the very elongated fins are
similar to those of the freshwater Siamese
fighting fish,* Betta splendens, *hence the
common name. The tail allegedly
resembles the head of the moray eel – a
useful defence against predators. This
species from the Indo-Pacific spends much
of its time in a 'head-down' hunting
position. Offer it a diet of frozen smaller
fishes and meaty foods. It grows to 15cm
(6in). Although this predatory fish is an
ideal choice for the invertebrate aquarium,
err on the side of caution and do not keep
it with small fishes.*

Right: *By the time
potential predators
have made up their
minds which end to
attack, the marine
betta will have taken
evasive action.*

ROYAL GRAMMA • *Gramma loreto*

This is one of the most brilliantly coloured fishes to come from the Western Atlantic and Caribbean waters. The body boasts two highly contrasting colours: bright cerise on the front half and an equally bright yellow to the rear. A thin black line runs from the snout upwards through the eye, and there is a black dot at the front of the long-based dorsal fin. The pectoral and pelvic fins are cerise, the caudal fin is bright yellow, and the dorsal and anal fins share both colours.

Gramma loreto shares its waters with a lookalike species, the bicolor basslet *(Liopropoma klayi)*, in which the cerise colour is confined to the head region. It also lacks the eyestripe and dorsal fin dot. The royal gramma is far more frequently confused with the royal dottyback *(Pseudochromis paccagnellae)* from Indonesian and Pacific waters. Its two similar colours are separated by a hardly discernible thin white line.

> ### Fishkeeping data
>
> **Number per aquarium:** One, but established pairs could be kept in very large tanks.
> **Community/species tank:** Community.
> **Swimming area:** Middle and lower levels.
> **Food:** Most foods, including live brineshrimp.
> **Compatibility:** Peaceful, but can be territorial.
> **Availability:** Usually available (wild-caught, but tank-bred numbers increasing).
> **Captive breeding:** Possible.

Below: G. loreto *dislikes any intrusion by other fishes into its chosen home. An aquarium stocked with many hideaways suits it perfectly.*

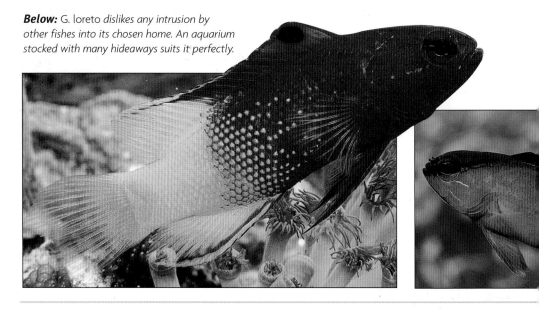

Size: 8cm (3.2in)

Bahamas

▶ Origins

The Bahamas, Venezuela, Lesser Antilles but not Florida.

Lesser Antilles

Venezuela

FALSE GRAMMA
PSEUDOCHROMIS PACCAGNELLAE

This brilliantly coloured species, a member of the Pseudochromidae family, is almost a replica of the royal gramma (Gramma loreto). However, it is not quite so striking, as its dorsal and anal fins are colourless, and there is no black eyestripe. The giveaway clue to positive identification is the thin white line that runs vertically downwards across the body to separate the cerise and yellow areas. It is similar in habit to the basslets, keeping close to the sea wall on reefs and swimming slowly over coral rubble in its native waters.

Below: G. melacara grows to 10cm (4in). It is a shy fish that seeks out crevices on the reef and rests upside-down against the ceiling of a cave.

Above: *The false gramma, or dottyback as it is also known, requires similar conditions to its lookalike relative, the royal gramma. It appreciates convenient retreats for security.*

SWISS GUARD BASSLET • *Liopropoma rubre*

How quick we are to assign descriptive names to fishes without giving too much thought to their suitability! This species, for example, with its alternating stripes of reddish brown and yellow arranged horizontally along the body obviously reminded its describer of the colours of the uniform of the Papal Swiss Guard in the Vatican City (even though their stripes go vertically!). There are two dorsal fins, the second of which, like the anal fin, carries a black dot. The caudal fin has black areas in its two shallow lobes, smartly terminating the striped patterning of the body. Although it is common in its native habitat, being a secretive species, it is not actually seen very often.

Fishkeeping data

Number per aquarium: Two to three.
Community/species tank: Community.
Swimming area: Middle and lower levels.
Food: All foods.
Compatibility: Generally peaceful.
Availability: Often available (wild-caught).
Captive breeding: No information.

The slim body form makes 'crevice-creeping' an easy task.

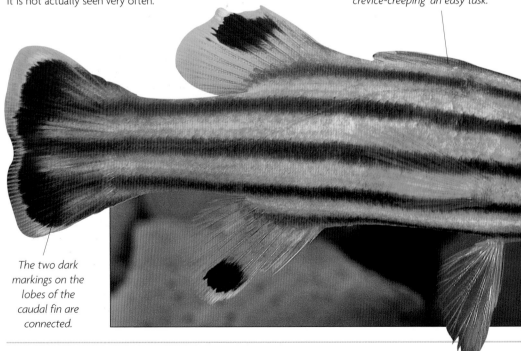

The two dark markings on the lobes of the caudal fin are connected.

Size: 8cm (3.2in)

Left: *Unsuspecting fish find it difficult to see the coral trout as it lurks under a coral overhang waiting for the next meal to come into range.*

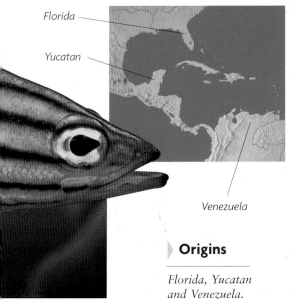

Florida

Yucatan

Venezuela

Origins

Florida, Yucatan and Venezuela.

CORAL TROUT

CEPHALOPHOLIS MINIATUS

The body and the dorsal, anal and caudal fins of C. miniatus are bright red and covered with bright blue spots. However, the pectoral and pelvic fins are plain red. Other fishes bear a resemblance to this species, but they do not have the distinguishing rounded caudal fin. It often hides away in caves or under edges, denying the fishkeeper a view of its spectacular colouring. A large, well-filtered aquarium is essential for this fast-growing fish that can grow to 45cm (18in). Ranging from the Red Sea to the mid-Pacific, the predatory coral trout inhabits the coral reefs in search of a meal. Offer it smaller frozen fishes and meaty foods in the aquarium. It is safe with invertebrates, but do not keep it with small fishes.

LYRETAIL ANTHIAS • *Pseudanthias squamipinnis*

This very large genus, containing many species, occurs in massive numbers in the wild, usually with a multitude of females acting as a harem to a very few males. If the dominant male is removed from such a group, another female will change sex to fill the gap. The Midas blenny *(Ecsenius midas)* uses its similar colouring to associate within the shoal for safety.

The body of the female fish is a golden-orange, with a pink-cerise stripe running from the eye rearwards and downwards across the gill cover. The fins are a golden-yellow. The male fish is more of a violet-pink with a reddish head. The gill cover decoration is yellow, and the edges of each fin are purple. The dorsal fin has an elongated third ray and the caudal fin is produced at each tip to form a lyretail. Although obviously gregarious in the wild, within the confines of the aquarium there may not be enough room for several fish to live together peacefully, so try keeping a solitary male or just a couple of females.

Natural surfers

As these fish inhabit coral reef cliff faces near the 'surf zone', the aquarium should incorporate not only suitable rocky formations, but also fairly vigorous water movement in order to make the fish feel at home. Some authorities regard anthias as 'desirable but delicate' and recommend coaxing them with live adult brineshrimp to acclimatise them to captive feeding.

Fishkeeping data

Number per aquarium: One (more in a spacious species tank).
Community/species tank: Community.
Swimming area: All levels.
Food: Most foods, especially 'meaty' foods and live adult brineshrimp.
Compatibility: Unless the aquarium is large enough to maintain an established 'pecking order' shoal, frequent altercations will occur between rival males.
Availability: Frequently available (wild-caught).
Captive breeding: No information.

Size: 15cm (6in)

Right: Even in a display aquarium, lyretail anthias form up into groups to roam around the territory. Marine divers will see shoals of these colourful fish near wrecks and reefs.

The male has an elongated third ray on the dorsal fin and a lyre-shaped caudal fin.

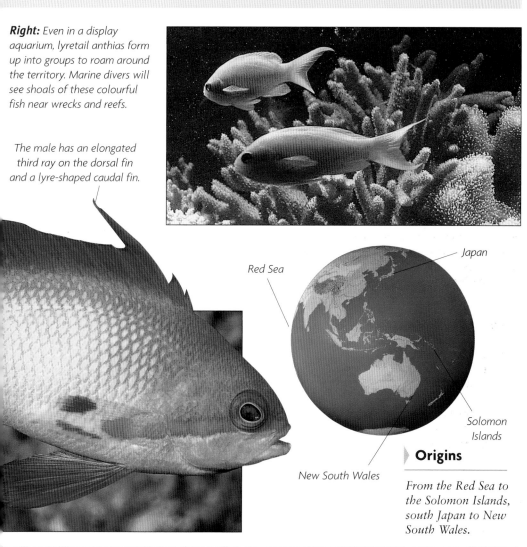

Red Sea

Japan

New South Wales

Solomon Islands

▶ Origins

From the Red Sea to the Solomon Islands, south Japan to New South Wales.

Blennies & gobies

Members of the Blenniidae and Gobiidae Families share many characteristics. All are small, cylindrical fish that inhabit the seabed. Generally carnivorous, they constantly dash about in search of a meal, but are always ready to rush back to the sanctuary of a nearby cave or pile of rocks should they feel threatened.

Outwardly, they could be mistaken for members of the same family, but closer examination reveals quite distinct differences. Blennies generally have a continuous, long-based dorsal fin, whereas gobies have two separate dorsal fins. Another characteristic is that blennies have separate pelvic fins, while in gobies these are fused together to form a suction disc with which the fish anchor themselves into position. A further aid to positive identification is that some blennies have 'cirri' – peculiar eyebrowlike growths on the head that gobies lack.

Several gobies have been bred in captivity. Many species live in substrate burrows and some even share these homes with invertebrates, such as pistol shrimps. A number of blennies are mimics; some, such as the Midas blenny *(Ecsenius midas)*, in order to associate with other fishes for safety reasons, others for more ulterior motives (especially the sabre-tooth blenny, *Aspidontus taeniatus*, which mimics the cleanerfish in order to procure a quick meal!) Always choose carefully before you buy.

The similarly shaped dartfishes have been included in this section for convenience, although they strictly belong to the Family Microdesmidae and, unlike either blennies or gobies, spend more time away from the substrate area of the aquarium. They are easily distinguished by the very long extended rays in the dorsal fin.

Above: *The decorated dartfish (*Nemateleotris *sp.) is a stunning sight in a marine display. The colours are intense and almost glow in the aquarium lighting.*

BICOLOR BLENNY • *Ecsenius bicolor*

The popular name of this species could, conceivably, be taken in two ways: either as a straightforward description of the two-part coloration of the body, or as a reference to the various colour phases seen in the fish. In general, the front half of the body is dark blue and brown and the rear portion is bright yellow. The two sections of the continuous dorsal fin correspond in colour to the part of the body they adjoin, while the anal and caudal fins are yellow. Two curly 'eyebrows' appear in front of the eyes.

Variations in colour include an all-brown form, and a dark-topped body with silvery blue lower flanks separated by a horizontal white band. The caudal fin and most rearward section of the body are yellow. Further colour variations occur during spawning, when the male turns red with white transverse bars, and the female becomes yellow.

Ryukyu Islands

Maldives

▶ Origins

From the Maldives, eastwards and northwards to the Ryukyu Islands and south to the Great Barrier Reef.

Great Barrier Reef

Sharp teeth

When they leave the relative safety of the substrate, this group of fishes is less likely to be predated upon because they have canine teeth, from which they derive not only protection, but also their popular name of fang, or sabre-tooth, blennies.

Size: 10cm (4in)

Fishkeeping data

Number per aquarium: One – maybe more in a separate, spacious species tank.
Community/species tank: Quiet community tank or species tank with plenty of hideaways.
Swimming area: Substrate level.
Food: All foods.
Compatibility: Shy and peaceful; do not keep with larger fishes.
Availability: Generally available (wild-caught).
Captive breeding: No information.

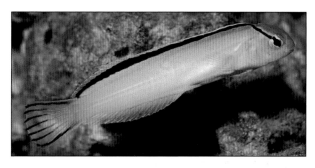

The body colours of male and female may be variable, as both change colour at breeding time.

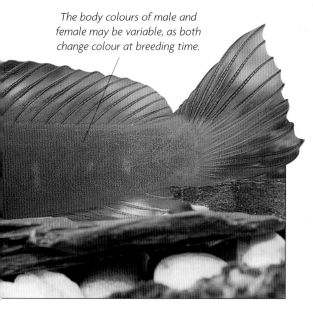

SMITH'S FANG BLENNY
MEIACANTHUS SMITHI

This very smart fish measuring 8cm (3.2in) has a smoky-grey-blue body topped with a white-edged, dark blue dorsal fin. The anal fin is blue. Unlike some members of the genus, the black-streaked caudal fin is rounded and not lyre-shaped. There is a diagonal blue-edged black band running upwards through the eye.

This genus is far more adventurous than most blennies; because it has a fully-functional swimbladder, it can venture up into midwater with greater ease than its more substrate-bound relatives.

Another fang blenny (Plagiotremus phenax) is a mimic of this species, but can be differentiated from M. smithi by the slightly broader dorsal fin with a more rounded front, a black-edged anal fin and a squared-off caudal fin. It lacks the eye-bar. This differentiation is vital, because whereas M. smithi is a peaceful species, P. phenax is definitely not.

163

RANDALL'S PRAWN GOBY • *Amblyeleotris randalli*

The blue-grey body is crossed vertically by seven orange-red bands. The two dorsal fins are yellow, the foremost one having a dark ocellus, or 'eyespot', at its base. The pectoral, pelvic, anal and caudal fins are the same colour as the body.

This body colour and patterning is shared by several other species, including Steinitz' prawn goby (*A. steinitzi*), which has a dark area above the mouth and no dorsal fin eyespot, and Magnus' prawn goby (*A. sungami*), which has plain fins and no dark area.

Spotted prawn goby

Members of this genus live in burrows with a shrimp or prawn of the Alphaeid group. Since these invertebrates are usually blind or only partially sighted, the association works well; the prawn digs the burrow, the fish acts as lookout. The creamy-yellow body of A. guttata (below) is covered with reddish brown spots that extend into the dorsal, anal and caudal fins.

▶ Fishkeeping data

Number per aquarium: One.
Community/species tank: Community or species tank with a sufficiently deep substrate to accommodate burrowing.
Swimming area: Substrate level.
Food: Meaty foods.
Compatibility: Peaceful.
Availability: Often available (wild-caught).
Captive breeding: No information.

▶ Origins

From the Moluccas eastwards to the Solomon Islands, Ryukyu Islands south to the Great Barrier Reef.

Ryukyu Islands

Moluccas

Great Barrier Reef

Solomon Islands

BLUE STREAK

VALENCIENNEA STRIGATA

At first glance, the delicate blue body and yellow head of this species resemble the coloration of the yellow-headed jawfish (Opisthognathus aurifrons). However, the presence of two dorsal fins (the first often carries extended rays in adults) marks the fish as a goby, while the bright blue streak running obliquely upwards across the gill cover is another distinguishing feature.

In nature, a characteristic action of this burrowing, prawn-independent genus is its substrate-chewing, as it sifts through particles searching for tiny worms and crustaceans. It prefers a quiet community or species tank and grows to 18cm (7in).

V. strigata is normally classed as a sleeper goby, a group of gobies previously referred to as Eleotridae, and usually regarded as having a sedentary lifestyle. Specimens of this genus also appear to communicate through movements of the mouth. Whether these 'signals' are audible or simply visible signs is not clear.

OLD GLORY • *Amblygobius rainfordi*

This species is very reminiscent of the Swiss Guard basslet (*Liopropoma rubre*, page 156) in its coloration, but the body ground colour is a greenish yellow and the red horizontal stripes are much thinner. Two dark ocelli appear, one at the base of the second dorsal fin and another at the top tip of the caudal peduncle. The first dorsal fin and the anal, pectoral and pelvic fins are clear. The body shape is less blunt-headed than that of *L. rubre* and its symmetrical dorsal and ventral profiles indicate that it may spend as much time in midwater as on the substrate.

▶ *Fishkeeping data*

Number per aquarium: One.
Community/species tank: Community, or species tank with a sufficiently deep substrate to accommodate burrowing.
Swimming area: Middle and lower levels.
Food: Meaty foods.
Compatibility: Peaceful.
Availability: Often available (wild-caught).
Captive breeding: No information.

Brown-barred goby

The heavily built, streamlined body of A. phalaena has a greenish grey background crossed by alternating vertical bands of brown and white. It grows to 15cm (6in) and lives in western Pacific waters, from Sumatra to the Great Barrier Reef and New South Wales.

166

Size: 6.5cm (2.5in)

▶ Origins

From the Philippines southwards to northwestern Australia and the Great Barrier Reef.

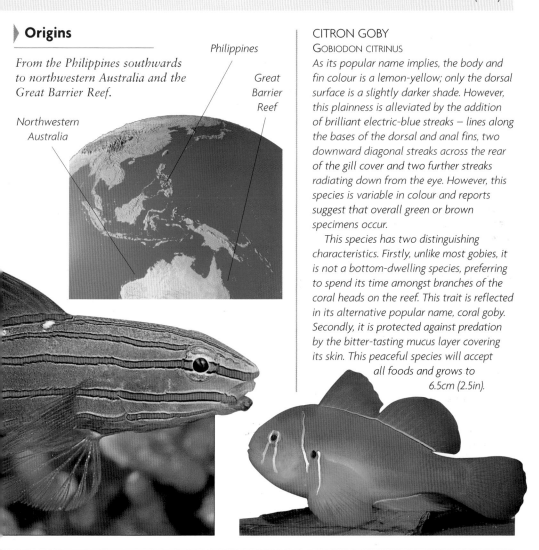

Philippines

Great Barrier Reef

Northwestern Australia

CITRON GOBY
GOBIODON CITRINUS

As its popular name implies, the body and fin colour is a lemon-yellow; only the dorsal surface is a slightly darker shade. However, this plainness is alleviated by the addition of brilliant electric-blue streaks – lines along the bases of the dorsal and anal fins, two downward diagonal streaks across the rear of the gill cover and two further streaks radiating down from the eye. However, this species is variable in colour and reports suggest that overall green or brown specimens occur.

This species has two distinguishing characteristics. Firstly, unlike most gobies, it is not a bottom-dwelling species, preferring to spend its time amongst branches of the coral heads on the reef. This trait is reflected in its alternative popular name, coral goby. Secondly, it is protected against predation by the bitter-tasting mucus layer covering its skin. This peaceful species will accept all foods and grows to 6.5cm (2.5in).

NEON GOBY • *Gobiosoma oceanops*

Despite the growing numbers of gobies becoming available in the hobby, the neon goby remains one of the most popular, although it could be classed as a veteran.

The dark blue body, with a white underside, is highlighted by a glowing electric-blue line running from the snout the whole length of the body. Such a simple design, yet so attractive. The species – one among a number of so-called cleaner gobies in the genus – can be distinguished from similar species by the gap on the snout between the two blue lines. In other species, the lines may be joined across the snout or have a 'pip' marking in the gap.

In nature, this goby sits in crevices or caves waiting for food or, perhaps, a customer for its cleaning services. Its coloration is reminiscent of the cleaner wrasse (Labroides dimidiatus) and it has been known to 'clean' divers' hands.

Unfortunately, although the neon goby makes an excellent aquarium subject, being hardy and easy to keep and breed, it is rather shortlived. If you want to have them for a reasonable time, it is best to buy several juveniles rather than just one or two obviously adult fish.

Florida   Atlantic Ocean
Belize
Honduras

Origins

Western Atlantic waters around Florida, Belize and Honduras.

Fishkeeping data

Number per aquarium: Two to three.
Community/species tank: Quiet community or species tank with rocky caves.
Swimming area: Substrate level.
Food: All foods.
Compatibility: Peaceful and maybe even bold with larger fish.
Availability: Generally available (tank-bred).
Captive breeding: Long-standing aquarium-bred species.

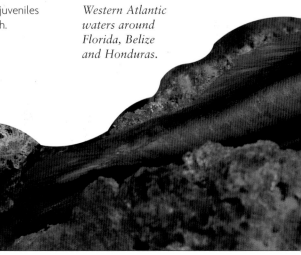

Size: *5cm (2in)*

▶ *Breeding*

One of the earliest gobies to be bred in captivity. It lays its eggs in holes in rocks, in vacant 'tubes' of feather-duster worms, plastic pipes or on any convenient firm surface. The male guards the eggs. Once the fry are free-swimming, they develop quite rapidly and appear to mature within a few months.

BLUE-BANDED GOBY
LYTHRYPNUS DALLI

Understandably, this gorgeously coloured goby is a long-standing aquarium favourite. The body is a glowing red, overlaid with a number of vertical bright blue stripes. The first few rays of the first dorsal fin are elongated. There is a similar-looking species (L. pulchellus), but its body is not such a deep red and it has more vertical stripes. The blue-banded goby accepts meaty foods, but prefers small live foods, and grows to 5.7cm (2.25in). It is peaceful, although it can be territorial amongst its own kind.

It might be said that this fish is the equivalent (in terms of its lifespan) of many of the freshwater killifishes, living, as it does, not much longer than a year or so. As its natural home is quite a distance northwards from that of most 'tropical' marine species, it does not require quite such a high water temperature in the aquarium, which would probably shorten its naturally brief life even more. It has been bred in the aquarium.

DECORATED DARTFISH • *Nemateleotris decora*

It is no wonder that this genus has become so popular. The fishes' colours (and their willingness to display them) are simply stunning. The creamy-yellow cylindrical body is framed by purple and red finnage, with the first rays of the front dorsal fin carried permanently erect like a banner. A purple mask covers the forehead and is led by a thin line upwards over the back to join the dorsal fin.

Although happy to hover in groups in midwater, where water currents bring their food, these fish also require immediate access to safe boltholes should they feel threatened. An aquarium suitably decorated with rocks is a prerequisite to making these beautiful fishes become settled in captivity.

Fishkeeping data

Number per aquarium: Two or three.
Community/species tank: Quiet community or species tank.
Swimming area: Middle and lower levels.
Food: Most meaty foods.
Compatibility: Shy and peaceful.
Availability: Generally available (wild-caught).
Captive breeding: No information.

▶ Origins

From Mauritius eastwards through the Maldives, Ryuku Islands south to New Caledonia.

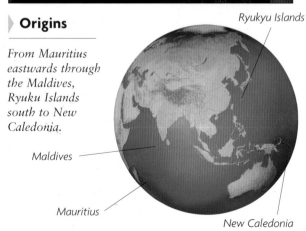

Ryukyu Islands

Maldives

Mauritius

New Caledonia

A feature of the genus is the long first dorsal fin.

A slender body makes speedy entries into caves easy to accomplish.

Left: N. magnifica (7cm/2.75in) has an even higher dorsal fin than N. decora. The fish may be found as single specimens, as pairs or in groups across their wide distribution.

Boxfishes, cowfishes & pufferfishes

This group of fishes encompasses several families, but we have collected them together for convenience, as they share almost a common body shape and similar physical characteristics.

It is the exterior coverings of these fish that provide the interest. In the boxfishes and cowfishes there is a covering of bony plates that form an exoskeleton. The pufferfishes have two characteristic features: erectile spines and the ability to inflate their bodies to a size that will deter any foes. Some members of this group can further defend themselves when threatened or under stress by releasing self-generated toxins into the water. Handle them with care and always transport specimens alone in their own bag. Should a specimen die unnoticed in the aquarium, it is possible that the whole population of the aquarium will be wiped out as a result of the toxins from the corpse.

Despite all these warnings, do not be left with the impression that these fishes are not suitable inmates for your aquarium. On the contrary, they soon become 'tame' and get to know when it is feeding time. Due to their adult size, only juvenile specimens are likely to be available commercially, which is no bad thing for fishkeepers with modest-sized — and invertebrate-free — tanks.

Below: *Cowfishes are pretty strange-looking creatures, even more so when seen from the front! Approach the front glass of their aquarium and they will slowly come to have a look at you.*

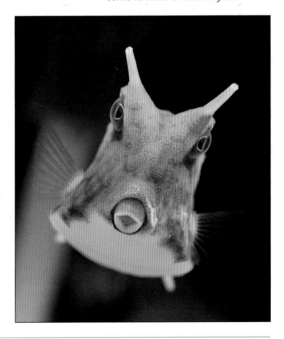

COWFISH • *Lactoria cornuta*

Many aquarium fish are kept for their curiosity value and none is more curious than the cowfish. Here is a fish that wears its skeleton on the outside as a suit of rigid bony plates. The only apparent area for growth is the part of the fish that sticks out from the caudal peduncle. Naturally, the fish gets its popular name from the two 'horns' that project from the top of a square head that rises steeply from a terminal mouth. The mouth is conveniently situated right at the bottom corner of the head, which makes for easy feeding on invertebrates on the substrate. The fish flips them up with a jet of water from its mouth and seizes them as they fall.

Two 'horns' adorn the head of the aptly named cowfish.

The caudal fin (along with the dorsal fin) is the only 'active' part of the fish, protruding from the bony, boxlike body.

▶ *Fishkeeping data*

Number per aquarium: One.
Community/species tank: Species collection or community with very peaceful and slow-moving tankmates.
Swimming area: Middle and lower levels.
Food: Almost everything; appreciates green matter, plus shellfish. The shells help to keep the teeth worn down.
Compatibility: Do not keep with small fishes or invertebrates.
Availability: Frequently available (wild-caught).
Captive breeding: No information.

Size: 45cm (18in)

▶ Origins

From the Red Sea to the
Marquesas and
Tuamotu Islands, South
Korea, South Japan and
to Lord Howe Island.

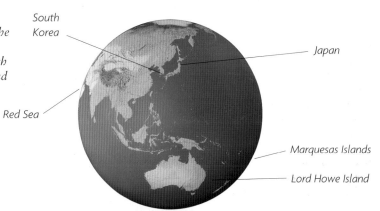

South
Korea

Japan

Red Sea

Marquesas Islands

Lord Howe Island

Right: *This view
highlights the
mouth at the
front 'corner' of
this fascinating
fish. It uses this to
take invertebrates
from the substrate.*

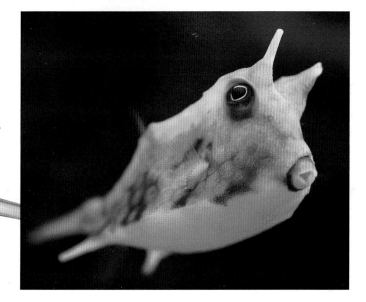

SPOTTED BOXFISH • *Ostracion meleagris*

This species was responsible for much confusion until it was realised that two differently patterned fish were not, in fact, different species, but merely male and female of the same species!

The male has the best coloration, with the two distinct areas of the body being separated by a yellow line. The dorsal surface is black, the area below the yellow line is blue and the body (excluding the blue head) is speckled with black-edged yellow spots. The pelvic fins are missing and propulsion is achieved by the rear-located dorsal and anal fins only. The female has a black body covered with white spots.

In the wild, this species feeds on sponges and bottom-dwelling invertebrates.

The male fish has a two-patterned body, while the female (below) is uniformly spotted.

Size: 16cm (6.2in)

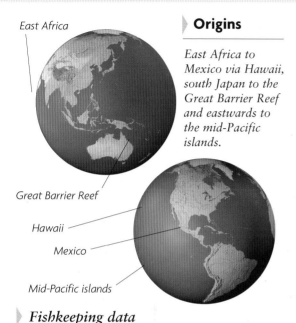

East Africa

Great Barrier Reef

Hawaii

Mexico

Mid-Pacific islands

▶ Origins

East Africa to Mexico via Hawaii, south Japan to the Great Barrier Reef and eastwards to the mid-Pacific islands.

▶ *Fishkeeping data*

Number per aquarium: One.
Community/species tank: Species collection, or community with very peaceful and slow-moving tankmates.
Swimming area: Middle and lower levels.
Food: Almost everything; appreciates green matter, plus shellfish. The shells help to keep the teeth worn down.
Compatibility: Do not keep with small fishes or invertebrates.
Availability: Frequently available (wild-caught).
Captive breeding: No information.

SPOTTED CUBE
OSTRACION CUBICUS

Young specimens of these fish from the Red Sea and tropical Indo-Pacific, resemble little yellow dice. Their bold black spots on a bright yellow background may serve as a warning to predators. When attacked or frightened, the fish will release poisonous ostracitoxin into the water. Adult fish, measuring 18in (45cm) lose much of their bright livery, becoming a drab brown. This fish is relatively easy to keep and will enjoy most foods that are offered. However, take care when introducing it into the aquarium so that it does not become unduly stressed. If this happens it will secrete its poison into the water, thereby killing all the tank inhabitants, including itself. For the same reason, it should not be housed with aggressive or boisterous fishes.

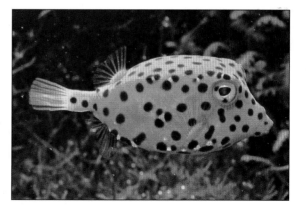

SPINY BOXFISH • *Chilomycterus schoepfi*

The body shape is much like a horizontally elongated teardrop, with a slightly flattened, broad top and the large eyes set high up. The yellow body is covered with a series of dark brown stripes, and several large, dark ocelli are distributed over the body. The spines are held erect as a permanent deterrent to would-be predators and this stands the fish in good stead, as it does not inflate itself as do most members of this group. It is not regularly seen at aquatic outlets.

▶ Origins

Common in Florida (and occasionally northwards), plus coastal waters south to Brazil (excluding the Caribbean islands).

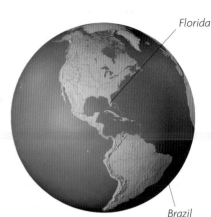

Florida

Brazil

The relatively shallow body allows the fish to lurk in caves and narrow crevices.

Above: *These smoothed-down spines can soon be erected to form a spiky defence.*

Fishkeeping data

Number per aquarium: One.
Community/species tank: Species collection, or community with very peaceful and slow-moving tankmates.
Swimming area: Middle and lower levels.
Food: Almost everything; appreciates green matter, plus shellfish. The shells help to keep the teeth worn down.
Compatibility: Not with small fishes or invertebrates.
Availability: Frequently available (wild-caught).
Captive breeding: No information.

BALLOONFISH
DIODON HOLOCANTHUS

The body has a yellowish tinge with a white ventral surface. A number of short dark bars straddle the dorsal surface, while a much longer one covers the eye and gill cover. The dorsal, anal and caudal fins are yellow. A feature of the Diodontidae family is the fusing together of the two front teeth on each jaw ('diodon' meaning two teeth) to form a bony beak for crushing shelled invertebrates. The fish is a poor swimmer and its large eyes may denote that it does its feeding more by night than by day.

One problem with all 'inflatable' fish is that they can inflate with air, rather than water, especially if lifted from the water. In such cases, the fish may find it very difficult to deflate itself afterwards.

Balloonfish grow to 50cm (20in) and are found worldwide in all warm seas. Keep them in a species collection or a community with very slow-moving tankmates, but not with smaller fishes or invertebrates. Provide the same diet as for the spiny boxfish.

Handle with care

Stress will cause all the porcupinefishes and burrfishes to exude toxins and thus 'self-destruct'. Do not 'net' them (watch out for those spines!) or expose them to the air – they might 'inflate'. Capture them in a water-filled plastic bag.

BLACK-SADDLED TOBY • *Canthigaster valentini*

The white body of this fish has unusual coloration imposed upon it. Four dark, triangular blotches appear on the dorsal surface, from the top of the head to the caudal peduncle, the middle two extending down the flanks almost to the ventral surface. Additionally, the lower half of the body is peppered with yellowish brown spots, and the yellow caudal fin has a black top and bottom edge.

Distinctive as it may sound, this patterning is not exclusive to this species. The black saddle filefish *(Paraluteres prionurus)* has exactly the same markings, with the exception of the caudal fin, which lacks the black top and bottom edges.

Males surround themselves with a harem of females with whom they mate on a rotational and regular basis; eggs are laid in a nest of algae.

The dark markings reach further down the body than on the similar-looking species, Canthigaster coronata.

Fishkeeping data

Number per aquarium: One.
Community/species tank: Species collection, or community with very peaceful and slow-moving tankmates.
Swimming area: Middle and lower levels.
Food: Almost everything; appreciates green matter, plus shellfish. The shells help to keep the teeth worn down.
Compatibility: Not with small fishes or invertebrates.
Availability: Frequently available (wild-caught).
Captive breeding: No information.

▶ Origins

Wide distribution including the Red Sea to Tuamotu Islands, South Japan to Lord Howe Island.

Red Sea

Tuamotu Islands

Lord Howe Island

SHARPNOSED PUFFER
CANTHIGASTER SOLANDRI

This spectacularly patterned fish from the Indo-Pacific and Red Sea has a gold-brown body and a caudal fin covered with pale spots. A blue wavy line replaces the spots on the upper part of the body and a large white-edged black spot appears at the base of the dorsal fin. The fish swims with its caudal fin folded. The pelvic fins are absent. In the aquarium, C. solandri is peaceful, except towards members of its own kind, but do not keep it with invertebrates, as it will eat them. Feed it on finely chopped meat foods. It grows to 5cm (2in).

Above: *Do not give pufferfish the opportunity to live up to their name. Avoid exposing them to the air, and when handling them, transfer them in water-filled plastic bags and not via 'open-air' nets.*

Miscellaneous species

This final section of the book features fish from a number of families. Cardinalfishes (Apogonidae) are ideal for the marine aquarium. They are undemanding, and amenable to aquarium conditions and foods. A common characteristic is the presence of two separate dorsal fins. Hawkfishes (Cirrhitidae) like to perch on a rocky outcrop as they await any passing prey, typical behaviour of species lacking a swimbladder. Hawkfishes should settle down quickly in captivity, but mixing hawkfish species in the tank may lead to quarrels.

The slow-moving lionfishes (Scorpaenidae) present a false picture of serenity. A sudden gulp from the huge mouth can engulf any passing prey and a sting from their venomous spines can seriously incapacitate the careless handler. As these fish are naturally active at dusk and dawn, the aquarium need not be too brightly lit. Filefishes (Monocanthidae) have two dorsal fins, the posterior one being used with the anal fin for propulsion. The skin is rough to the touch and often causes problems when netting; using a plastic bag to capture them is recommended.

Jawfishes (Opisthognathidae) need a reasonably 'quiet' aquarium with peaceful tankmates, and a soft substrate in which they can build a burrow. They normally hover vertically, tail-down, around the burrow entrance into which they can retreat – backwards – like lightning. Dragonets (Callionymidae) are hard to see against the substrate, where they make their permanent living space. They need copious amounts of live foods; do not keep them with sizeable tankmates who would out-compete them in the hunt for food.

Above: With its venom-filled spines, the lionfish (Pterois volitans) is a favourite public aquarium exhibit, where its graceful drifting form of locomotion belies a more sinister motive – looking for food.

BANGGAI CARDINALFISH • *Pterapogon kauderni*

Every so often, a species comes along that finds instant appeal amongst fishkeepers, and so it is with the Banggai cardinalfish. It has striking silver-and-black coloration, very reminiscent of the freshwater angelfish, *Pterophyllum scalare*, with one or two extra adornments. The top and bottom parts of the caudal peduncle have a white-edged black stripe that continues to the tips of the caudal fin. The large pelvic fins, together with the anal fin, seem to mirror the two separate dorsal fins, while the whole body is overlaid with white dots.

Discovered in 1990 in the Banggai Islands of Sulawesi in Indonesia, this fish has proved to be extremely amenable to life in captivity and many public aquariums are able to breed them freely (they are mouthbrooders). This means that future supplies to the aquatic trade should be secure, thus allowing the original wild stock to continue their natural existence without the threat of fish collectors hunting them down. In the light of this, do not be surprised if home aquarium breeding suddenly takes off.

Fishkeeping data

Number per aquarium: Two or three.
Community/species tank: Species or community, but not with large fishes.
Swimming area: Middle and lower levels.
Food: All 'meaty' foods, fresh or frozen, plus live brineshrimp.
Compatibility: Peaceful, sometimes a little quarrelsome between themselves.
Availability: Recent introduction but plentiful (wild-caught, but soon tank-bred).
Captive breeding: Regularly in public aquariums and increasingly in hobbyists' tanks, too.

Banggai Islands

Origins

The Banggai Islands off Sulawesi in Indonesia.

Size: 8cm (3.2in)

White spots are part of the natural coloration of this fish – not symptoms of disease!

Above: A square, deeper jaw usually indicates a male incubating a new batch of eggs in his throat.

Breeding Banggai cardinalfishes

It is sometimes possible to acquire proven pairs, but it is best to obtain a small group and hope that there is a male and female among them and that pairing occurs.

Eggs are produced and fertilised in the normal way for egglayers, but are then taken into the mouth of the male for incubation. Even after hatching, the juvenile fishes remain in the mouth for protection from predators. When they emerge – as tiny, fully formed replicas of the adults – juveniles immediately seek the protection of the long-spined sea urchins (Diadema sp.) with which they associate in the wild. It is not essential to keep sea urchins in order to rear this species successfully, but if they are not available, separate the juveniles from the adults, at least until they have grown larger. Some aquarists use artificial urchins with good results. Juvenile Banggai cardinals will sometimes protect themselves in anemones if urchins are not present in the aquarium.

Newly hatched brineshrimp and very finely chopped mysis shrimps, etc., are good foods for these relatively large juveniles. As they grow, offer them larger food particles.

Breeding this, and similar, species can be carried out in an aquarium as small as 90 litres (20 gallons). This is due to the very small brood sizes and the fact that you can easily separate adults from juveniles by using a partition that allows a flow-through of aquarium water.

PYJAMA CARDINALFISH • *Sphaeramia nematoptera*

In common with the previously described species, the body shape of this fish is quite stocky and deep, with the dorsal and ventral contours being quite convex. The patterning is quite unusual in that the dark-spotted rear half of the body is separated from the unadorned front section by a broad, dark brown vertical band. The front dorsal fin has some patterning and the large pelvic fins are yellowish edged with white. The large eye, indicative of a nocturnally active species, is red-rimmed with two vertical white stripes.

Origins

From Java to Papua New Guinea, and Ryukyu Islands south to Great Barrier Reef.

Ryukyu Islands

Java

Papua New Guinea

Great Barrier Reef

Fishkeeping data

Number per aquarium:
Two or three.
Community/species tank:
Community, but not with large fishes.
Swimming area: All levels.
Food: All 'meaty' foods, fresh or frozen, plus live brineshrimp.
Compatibility:
Peaceful, shy and sometimes a little quarrelsome between themselves.
Availability: Often available (wild-caught).
Captive breeding: No information, but may occur unnoticed.

Size: 8cm (3.2in)

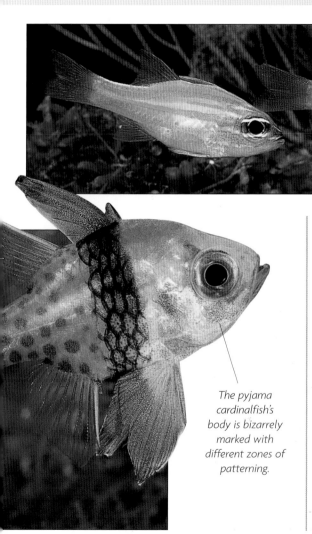

YELLOW-STRIPED CARDINALFISH
APOGON CYANOSOMA

True to its common name, the streamlined body carries five or six horizontal yellow lines along the flanks. The eye is large. When the fish is viewed from the side, the pectoral, pelvic and the first (of two) dorsal fins all line up vertically. All the fins are colourless. A similar-looking species, the blue-spot cardinalfish (A. nitidus), is found over much of the same distribution area (Red Sea to the Marshall Islands and south Japan to the Great Barrier Reef), but it has a somewhat brown tinge to the yellow areas and a dark line running centrally through the caudal fin.

The yellow-striped cardinalfish is peaceful, sometimes shy and will not bother other fishes. Keep it in a community tank, but not with large fishes. It accepts all 'meaty 'foods, fresh or frozen, plus live brineshrimp, and grows to 8cm (3.2in).

The pyjama cardinalfish's body is bizarrely marked with different zones of patterning.

LONGNOSED HAWKFISH • *Oxycirrhites typus*

At one time, this was the only hawkfish likely to be found in dealers' tanks. The long snout and jawline, together with the squares of bright red covering the whitish body, make the longnosed hawkfish instantly recognisable. The long-based dorsal fin has a spiny front section, and tiny growths at the tips of the dorsal spines are often visible. These growths, known as cirri, account for the derivation of the Family name, Cirrhitidae.

This species, along with others in the genus, is not an active fish, spending its time on an outcrop of coral or any suitable aquarium decoration, waiting for a feeding opportunity to present itself. This apparently peaceful occupation may seem innocent enough, but small fishes and non-sedentary invertebrates may be at risk.

Fishkeeping data

Number per aquarium: One.
Community/species tank: Community, but not with very small fishes or invertebrates.
Swimming area: Middle and lower levels.
Food: All foods.
Compatibility: Fairly peaceful, may be territorial; certainly an opportunistic, rather than predatory, feeder.
Availability: Regularly available (wild-caught).
Captive breeding: No information.

Origins

The natural distribution of the longnosed hawkfish ranges from the Red Sea to Panama, including Japan, Hawaii and New Caledonia.

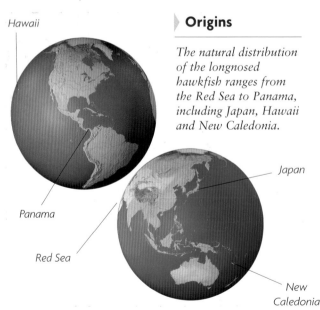

Hawaii

Panama

Red Sea

Japan

New Caledonia

Size: 13cm (5in)

Left: *The flat lower contour of the body makes perching on rocky outcrops easy, as the longnosed hawkfish waits for a passing meal.*

Below: *A red line on the lower edge of the jaw may indicate a female.*

ARC-EYE HAWKFISH • *Paracirrhites arcatus*

With its high, arched back and flatter ventral surface, the body contour of this fish is not entirely symmetrical, but obviously an efficient design for a fish that does not do a lot of swimming around. The head and dorsal surface are red, the flanks below the median line are yellow and separated by a bright white band (not present in all cases) running from mid-dorsal fin to the end of the caudal peduncle. Some radiating, red-edged, blue bands emerge from the rear edge of the gill cover. All the fins are yellow. The species takes its common name from a blue, red and yellow-edged dark area on the head just above, and to the rear of, the eye. Other species share this decoration.

The 'eye patch' is not exclusive to this species, but the white body stripe (when present) helps with positive identification.

On the lookout
The high-set eyes of the hawkfishes enable them to spot potential prey easily. Their body shape is ideally suited to their sedentary life; they prefer their meals to come to them, rather than chase their food.

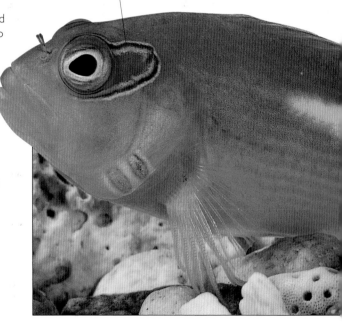

Fishkeeping data

Number per aquarium: One.
Community/species tank: Community, but not with very small fishes or invertebrates.
Swimming area: Middle and lower levels.
Food: All foods.
Compatibility: Peaceful.
Availability: Often available (wild-caught).
Captive breeding: No information.

Size: 14cm (5.5in)

Origins

From East Africa
to Hawaii, south
Japan to Norfolk
Island.

Japan

Hawaii

East Africa

Norfolk Island

SCARLET HAWKFISH
NEOCIRRHITES ARMATUS

*This extremely attractive 7.5cm (3in)-fish
from the Central and Western Pacific is
much sought after by aquarists and
usually commands quite a high price as
a consequence. It is not a good swimmer,
and in the wild it spends much of its time
resting on rocks and gorgonians waiting
to ambush small crustaceans and
plankton. Fortunately, it is not a threat in
the home aquarium and seems to fare
best in a mixed fish and invertebrate
system, where it also tends to look more
natural. It accepts most marine frozen and
live foods of a suitable size. Once settled
in the aquarium it will also accept marine
flake. An ideal community addition.*

Above: 'Hawkfish' is an apt name for
these species, which are always perched
on rocks on the lookout for food.

191

DWARF LIONFISH • *Dendrochirus zebra*

Such are the proportions of the intricately patterned fins, that it is often hard to determine the exact body shape of these fishes. In fact, the body is sturdily built, with a high dorsal arch and, unsurprisingly for a genus that spends some time around the substrate level of the aquarium, a flattened ventral surface.

Deep reddish brown bands, alternating with lighter brown, cross the body vertically, and this patterning appears to extend concentrically into all fins. The large, fan-shaped pectoral fins have connecting tissue membrane right to the tips of the fin rays. The first few rays of the dorsal fin are separate and there is a pair of 'hornlike' growths above the eyes. A distinguishing characteristic of this species is the dark ocellus spot on the lower part of the gill cover.

Below: *The pectoral fins have much more connecting tissue between the spines than is seen in other species in this family group.*

The coloration of the winglike fins is just as impressive as that of a butterfly.

Origins

From South Africa to Samoa, south Japan to Lord Howe island.

Japan

Samoa

Lord Howe Island

Size: *18cm (7in)*

Fishkeeping data

Number per aquarium: One.
Community/species tank: Species.
Swimming area: Middle and lower levels.
Food: A wide appetite for all foods,
especially 'meaty' derivatives.
Compatibility: Predatory with small fishes
and some invertebrates.
Availability: Often available (wild-caught).
Captive breeding: No information.

OCELLATED LIONFISH
DENDROCHIRUS BIOCELLATUS

Compared to related Pterois *species, the
smaller (around 12cm/4.7in) Dendrochirus is
poorly equipped when it comes to extended
finnage. However, the ocellated lionfish has
the distinction of being the only lionfish
with 'eye-spots' on the rear soft portion of
the dorsal fin, and the large butterfly-wing
pectoral fins have dark concentric rings.
Another exclusive feature is the presence of
two barbels on the upper jaw.*

*The fish is not often seen in the general
day-to-day activity on the reef due to its
habit of lurking (often upside-down)
beneath overhangs n the coral, only
venturing out to feed at night. It may lose
out in the feeding race if kept with more
lively fish, and shrimps, etc. in a reef tank
may be at risk.*

LIONFISH • *Pterois volitans*

Unlike the previous species, which is classed as a dwarf lionfish by fishkeepers, this is the real thing and quite fantastic in all its enlarged beauty.

Once again, the reddish brown-striped body is surrounded by a huge 'plumage' of fins. Although separated, each one of the first dozen rays of the dorsal fin has a backing of membranous tissue, giving them the appearance of feathers. Similarly, the rays of the huge pectoral fins are separate, with decorated tissue along their length. The function of these large fins is to herd prey into a convenient area for feeding on, and it is not hard to imagine a number of lionfish acting collectively, using their impressive fins as capes to round up their next meal.

This species, usually seen 'drifting with intent' around rock faces and under coral ledges in public aquariums, seems to spend more time off the seabed than its smaller relatives.

Below: *The large mouth is just waiting to engulf any passing prey – in one gulp!*

Origins

From Malaysia to Pitcairn Island, south Japan to Lord Howe Island.

Malaysia

Japan

Lord Howe Island

Pitcairn Island

Fishkeeping data

Number per aquarium: One.
Community/species tank: Community (with large fish) or species tank.
Swimming area: All levels.
Food: All 'meaty' foods.
Compatibility: Predatory.
Availability: Regularly available (wild-caught).
Captive breeding: No information.

Size: *38cm (15in)*

Keep your hands well away
from the venom-filled fin rays.

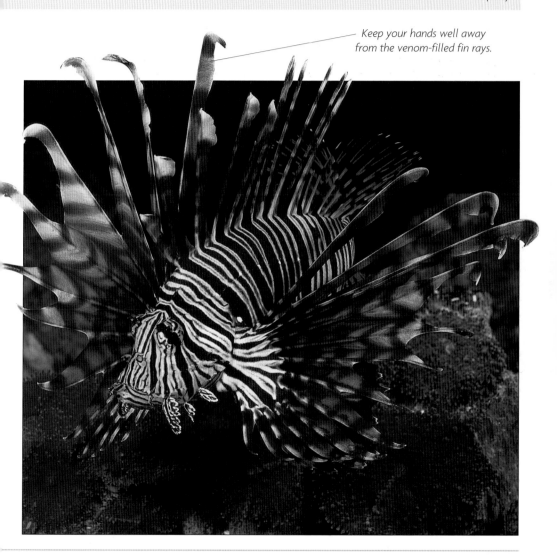

195

TASSELLED FILEFISH • *Chaetoderma pencilligera*

It is hard to describe the characteristics of a species that frequents floating seaweeds and models itself accordingly. The body shape, once determined, is greyish white with a few brown blotches on the lower flanks and a couple of dark spots higher up. Its outline and actual surface is further disguised by a covering of tassel-like appendages, and a number of thin brown lines also cross the body in a branchlike network. The fins are mostly clear with a little speckling, and the caudal fin is attached to the body by a very short and narrow caudal peduncle. The pelvic fins are but a single spine. The tiny snout is beaklike, ideal for browsing and grazing on algae and polyp growths.

Once acclimatised to aquarium foods, this fish is a popular favourite. Fortunately, it is unlikely to attain its full natural size in the home aquarium.

The tassel-like appendages disguise the fish's presence amongst seaweeds.

Fishkeeping data

Number per aquarium: One.
Community/species tank: Community.
Swimming area: Middle and lower levels.
Food: Most foods (including vegetable matter and meaty foods) once acclimatised. If necessary, offer live foods at first.
Compatibility: Fairly peaceful, but may nibble enquiringly at other fish without causing physical damage – only annoyance.
Availability: Often available (wild-caught).
Captive breeding: No information.

Size: *25cm (10in)*

Japan

Malaysia

Great Barrier Reef

▶ Origins

*Waters around
Malaysia, south
Japan and the
Great Barrier Reef.*

PINK-TAILED FILEFISH
PERVAGOR MELANOCEPHALUS
*The tail of this fish is pink to orange-red,
and the body shades from orange-green
to a deep purple. The dorsal fin may be
limited to just one or two strong rays. A
dark bar extends upward from the
pectoral axil to a point behind the eye.
This slow-moving fish from the tropical
Indo-Pacific is quite secretive by nature.
Its main habitat is among weed beds and
algal growths, where its body colour gives
it an ideal camouflage.*

*There may be some initial difficulties
when the fish is first introduced into the
aquarium, but then it usually settles in
well and will accept all the usual
aquarium foods. Like most filefishes, it
grows quite fast, but not too large for the
average aquarium, reaching 15cm (6in).
Provide plenty of rocks and hiding places
into which the fish can retreat at night.*

YELLOW-FACED JAWFISH • *Opisthognathus aurifrons*

For a good look at this species you will need to be patient until it is confident enough to emerge fully from its burrow. Then you can see that the long, cylindrical body is a most delicate blue, with a bright yellow, blunt head. The dorsal fin runs almost the complete length of the body and is mirrored by the anal fin, which occupies two-thirds of the ventral length. The pectoral fins are yellow, the pelvic and caudal fins blue. The dark eye is very large and the mouth, terminally situated at the tip of the blunt snout, is ideally placed for shifting grains of substrate material during excavation of the burrow.

Sex differentiation is difficult, but should breeding occur, then it is reported that the male takes on the incubating duties of this mouthbrooding species.

▶ Origins

Opisthognathus *contains several species other than this one and all are found in waters ranging from Florida and the Bahamas to Barbados and Venezuela.*

Florida Bahamas

Venezuela Barbados

When it ventures outside its burrow, the yellow-faced jawfish 'hovers' just above its safe retreat.

▶ Fishkeeping data

Number per aquarium: One (possibly more in a species tank).
Community/species tank: Community or species tank.
Swimming area: Lower levels.
Food: Meaty foods. It is a good idea to mince these up and distribute them near to the fish's burrow.
Compatibility: Peaceful and shy.
Availability: Regularly available (wild-caught).
Captive breeding: No information.

Size: 10cm (4in)

The rear blue portion of the fish's body is usually hidden from view as it sits vertically in its burrow.

Above: Keeping the burrow entrance free from falling particles is a constant chore, but having a muscular mouth helps the yellow-faced jawfish to cope with the problem.

MANDARINFISH • *Synchiropus splendidus*

The scaleless body of this fish is covered with an amazing tangle of contrasting colours that obviously reminded the original describer of the brilliantly coloured robes worn by ancient Chinese dignitaries. Golds, reds and greens are all intertwined across the body; nor are the fins excluded from this rainbow effect, having purple edges in addition to those colours spreading from the body. The caudal fin has gold lines radiating from the caudal peduncle and the large pelvic fins are decorated with purple/green spots. The first ray of the first dorsal fin is projected and carried like a flag.

▶ Origins

Waters around the Philippines and Java, from the Ryukyu Islands south of Japan to the Great Barrier Reef.

Philippines

Ryukyu Islands

Japan

Java

Great Barrier Reef

Size: *6cm (2.4in)*

Fishkeeping data

Number per aquarium: One or two.
Community/species tank: Suitably stocked community aquarium, but a species tank is probably better.
Swimming area: Lower level.
Food: Requires copious amounts of live foods.
Compatibility: Shy, but constantly on the lookout for food.
Availability: Often available (wild-caught).
Captive breeding: Has spawned in captivity, but not a regular occurrence and no reports of surviving fry are known.

Breeding

From very limited reports of aquarium breeding, it seems that internal fertilisation of eggs occurs before their release as floating eggs into open water. While this may be true, there are no reports of any viable fry being raised to maturity.

PICTURESQUE DRAGONET
SYNCHIROPUS PICTURATUS

Being blunt-headed, flat-bottomed and almost cylindrical, the body shape of this fish is very similar to that of the better-known bottom-dwelling species, such as blennies and gobies. There are two dorsal fins, the first of which is usually carried like a banner.

The basic body colour is light green, but this is overlaid with patches of dark green ringed with gold, black and blue. These blotches also appear in the dorsal, anal and pelvic fins, while the caudal and pectoral fins are a plain yellowish green. The high-set eye has a gold and black rim.

Males are generally equipped with brighter colours and extensions to the dorsal and anal fins. There is some belief that any highly coloured species (fish or invertebrates) are necessarily poisonous and advertise this fact accordingly; whether this toxicity risk actually applies to the mucus of this species is subject to conjecture. S. picturatus requires the same general care in the aquarium as the mandarinfish and also grows to 6cm (2.4in).

GENERAL INDEX

Page numbers in **bold** indicate major entries; *italics* refer to captions, annotations and panels; plain type indicates other text entries.

FISH INDEX

CREDITS

The publishers would like to thank the following photographers for providing images, credited here by page number and position: (B) Bottom, (T) Top, (C) Centre, (BL) Bottom left, etc.

Aqua Press (M-P & C Piednoir): 8, 32-33(C), 39(BL), 93(R), 99(R), 101(BR), 107, 109(TR), 111, 113(BR), 115, 123, 127, 129, 131(T), 137, 139(T), 141(B), 149(BR), 153(BR), 157(T), 181, 193(B), 197(B), 199

Bioquatic Photo — Alf J. Nilsen (bioquatic@biophoto.net): 71

Bruce Coleman Collection: 200-201 (Jane Burton)

Les Holliday: 85(T), 177(BR)

Photomax (Max Gibbs): 90-91, 92, 94-95, 96-97, 98-99, 100-101, 102(L), 102-103(C), 106(T,B), 108-109, 110-111, 112, 112-113, 114, 118, 119(BL), 120-121, 122, 125, 126-127, 128-129, 130-131(B), 132-133(B), 133(T), 136-137, 138-139, 140-141(T), 142, 143, 146-147(T), 147(B), 148-149, 152-153, 154, 154-155(C), 155, 156-157(B), 158-159, 162-163, 163(TR), 164(T), 164-165, 165(BR), 166(T), 166-167, 167(BR), 168-169, 169(TR), 170, 171(BR), 174, 176, 178, 179, 180-181, 184-185, 186-187(B), 187(T), 189(T), 190-191, 192-193, 195, 198-199, 201

Geoffrey Rogers © Interpet Publishing: *Title page, Contents pages,* 7, 10, 12, 16, 26, 29, 68, 69, 70, 74, 85(B), 87, 89, 91(R), 95(R), 97(R), 103(TR), 105(R), 117, 119(TR), 121(T), 135, 145, 151, 159(TR), 161, 171(TL), 173, 175, 183, 188-189(B), 191, 194, 196-197

Tropical Marine Centre: 32(BL), 33(BR), 35(L)

Computer graphics by Phil Holmes and Stuart Watkinson © Interpet Publishing.

Index compiled by Amanda O'Neill.

The publishers would like to thank the following for their help: Swallow Aquatics at Colchester, East Harling, Rayleigh and Southfleet; Arcadia, Croydon, Surrey; Aquaworld, Warringtom, Cheshire.

Publisher's note
The information and recommendations in this book are given without guarantee on the part of the author and publishers, who disclaim any liability with the use of this material.

HIMACHAL PRADESH
Pages 108–133

UTTAR PRADESH & UTTARANCHAL
Pages 166–211

KT-415-922

ASSAM & THE NORTHEAST
Pages 322–339

EASTERN INDIA

• Lucknow

• Patna

Guwahati

WEST BENGAL & SIKKIM
Pages 284–303

CENTRAL INDIA

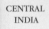

KOLKATA
Pages 224–239

Bhubaneswar •

0 km   250

0 miles   250

MADHYA PRADESH & CHHATTISGARH
Pages 226–255

ORISSA
Pages 304–321

ANDHRA PRADESH
Pages 658–683

KERALA
Pages 624–657

TAMIL NADU
Pages 576–615

ANDAMAN & NICOBAR ISLANDS (INDIA)

Port Blair

ANDAMAN ISLANDS
Pages 616–623

EYEWITNESS TRAVEL

INDIA

HIMACHAL PRADESH
Pages 108–133

UTTAR PRADESH & UTTARANCHAL
Pages 166–211

ASSAM & THE NORTHEAST
Pages 322–339

Lucknow

• Patna

CENTRAL INDIA

EASTERN INDIA
Guwahati •

KOLKATA
Pages 224–39

WEST BENGAL & SIKKIM
Pages 284–303

Bhubaneswar •

0 km   250

0 miles   250

MADHYA PRADESH & CHHATTISGARH
Pages 226–255

ORISSA
Pages 304–321

ANDHRA PRADESH
Pages 658–683

KERALA
Pages 624–657

TAMIL NADU
Pages 576–615

ANDAMAN & NICOBAR ISLANDS (INDIA)

• Port Blair

ANDAMAN ISLANDS
Pages 616–623

EYEWITNESS TRAVEL

INDIA

EYEWITNESS TRAVEL

INDIA

DK

LONDON, NEW YORK,
MELBOURNE, MUNICH AND DELHI
www.dk.com

MANAGING EDITOR Aruna Ghose
MANAGING ART EDITOR Bindia Thapar
PROJECT EDITOR Nandini Mehta
EDITORS Madhulita Mohapatra, Vandana Mohindra,
Ranjana Saklani, Alissa Sheth
DESIGNERS Benu Joshi, Mugdha Sethi, Priyanka Thakur
CARTOGRAPHERS Uma Bhattacharya, Kishorchand Naorem
PHOTO EDITOR Radhika Singh
PICTURE RESEARCHER Kiran K Mohan
DTP COORDINATOR Shailesh Sharma
DTP DESIGNER Jessica Subramanian

MAIN CONTRIBUTORS
Roshen Dalal, Partho Datta, Divya Gandhi, Premola Ghose,
Ashok Koshy, Abha Narain Lambah, Annabel Lopez, Sumita Mehta,
George Michell, Rudrangshu Mukherji, Meenu Nageshwaran,
Rushad R Nanavatty, Ira Pande, Usha Raman, Janet Rizvi,
Ranee Sahaney, Deepak Sanan, Darsana Selvakumar,
Sankarshan Thakur, Shikha Trivedi, Lakshmi Vishwanathan

CONSULTANT George Michell

PHOTOGRAPHERS
Clare Arni, Fredrik & Laurence Arvidsson, M Balan, Dinesh Khanna,
Amit Pasricha, Bharath Ramamrutham, Toby Sinclair, BPS Walia

ILLUSTRATORS
Avinash Ramsurrun, Dipankar Bhattacharya, Danny Cherian, R
Kamalahasan, Surat Kumar Mantoo, Arun P, Suman Saha, Ajay Sethi,
Ashok Sukumaran, Gautam Trivedi, Mark Warner

Reproduced by Colourscan, Singapore
Printed by KHL Printing Co. Pte. Ltd., Singapore

First published in Great Britain in 2002
by Dorling Kindersley Limited
80 Strand, London WC2R 0RL

Reprinted with revisions 2005, 2008

ISBN 978 1 40532 944 6
Throughout this book, floors are numbered
according to local usage, ie "first floor" is one flight up.
Front cover main image: Humayun's Tomb, New Delhi

**The information in this
DK Eyewitness Travel Guide is checked regularly.**

Every effort has been made to ensure that this book is as up-to-date as
possible at the time of going to press. Some details, however, such as
telephone numbers, opening hours, prices, gallery hanging
arrangements and travel information are liable to change. The
publishers cannot accept responsibility for any consequences arising
from the use of this book, nor for any material on third party websites,
and cannot guarantee that any website address in this book will be a
suitable source of travel information. We value the views and
suggestions of our readers very highly. Please write to:
The Publisher, DK Eyewitness Travel Guides,
Dorling Kindersley, 80 Strand, London WC2R 0RL.

**The external boundaries of India as shown in this book are
neither correct nor authentic.**

Ashokan Capital, Sarnath

CONTENTS

◁ **Pilgrims taking an early morning ritual bath in the waters of the Ganges, Varanasi *(See pp202–203)***

Mehrangarh Fort, towering over the city of Jodhpur

Fruit vendors on the pavements of
George Town, Chennai

Kandariya
Mahadev Temple
at Khajuraho,
Madhya Pradesh

INTRODUCING
INDIA

DISCOVERING INDIA

India is one of the most diverse nations in the world. In area, it is the seventh largest country and in population second only to China. Within its geographical confines, stretching from the Great Himalayas in the north to the tropical southern peninsular, there is a dizzying variety of cultures,

Intricately painted wall mural

languages, ethnic groups, beliefs and lifestyles that few countries or continents possess. The past is ever-present and centuries-old forts and temples happily coex-ist with the modern. The following six pages give highlights of each region, to help visitors make the most of this incredible country.

The graceful Qutb Minar in Delhi, a UNESCO World Heritage Site

DELHI

- **Magnificent monuments**
- **Bustling Chandni Chowk**
- **Imperial grandeur of Lutyens's New Delhi**

Delhi, India's capital, lies at the heart of northern India and has been an important site for about 1,000 years. Remains of its past lie scattered within both Old and New Delhi. Among its famous monuments are the **Qutb Minar** tower *(see p94)*, **Humayun's Tomb** *(see p83)* – inspiration for the Taj Mahal – and the **Red Fort** *(see pp86–7)*, all UNESCO World Heritage Sites.

Chandni Chowk's lanes in Old Dehli *(see pp84–5)* are filled with shops and eating places. Stop by for some country-renowned Mughlai cuisine at **Karims's** *(see p720)* near **Jami Masjid** *(see p86)*.

Imperial architect Lutyens designed much of New Delhi; begin a tour at **Rashtrapati Bhavan** *(see p74)*.

HARYANA & PUNJAB

- **The glittering Golden Temple in Amritsar**
- **Patiala's palaces and forts**
- **Vibrant crafts bazaars**

An area of flat plains and friendly towns, this region is also home to the glorious **Golden Temple**, the sacred shrine of the Sikhs *(see pp106–7)* and a must-see in the holy city of **Amritsar** *(see pp104–5)*. Another splendid city is the former princely state of **Patiala** *(see p102)*, with fine 18th- and 19th-century forts, palaces and gardens. The bazaars here offer a choice of the city's famed leather shoes *(juttis)* and embroidery *(phulkari)*. **Surajkund's** *(see p100)* famous crafts fair *(mela)* is held each February.

Architecture fans should not miss the region's capital, **Chandigarh** *(see p100)*, designed by Le Corbusier.

HIMACHAL PRADESH

- **Shimla: summer capital of the British Raj**
- **Little Tibet**
- **Scenic treks**

Shimla *(see pp110–12)* is now the state capital and a walk through The Mall offers glimpses of charming 19th-century Colonial archi-tecture. From the Ridge there are splendid views of the Himalayas.

In **Dharamsala** *(see pp122–3)*, the seat of the Dalai Lama, is the Tibetan

enclave of McLeodganj. Here, the Government-in-Exile maintains the monas-teries, performing arts centre and archives to keep the spiritual culture of Tibet alive. The state also offers great trekking options around the beautiful region of the **Sangla Valley** *(see pp118–19)* and the hill station of **Manali** *(see 128)*.

LADAKH, JAMMU & KASHMIR

- **Srinagar's houseboats**
- **Monasteries along the Indus**
- **Ancient caravan routes**

This Himalayan state is home to Hindus, Muslims and Buddhists. In the pre-dominantly Muslim Valley of Kashmir, a paradise of rice fields and waterways, is **Srinagar** *(see pp154–5)*, where ornate houseboats can be seen moored on the lakes, and graceful

Buddhist monasteries against the dramatic landscapes of Ladakh

◁ Miniature painting of a Rajput prince, surrounded by female attendants in a garden pavilion

The Taj Mahal at sunrise, a sublime experience

shikaras sell flowers and vegetables on the backwaters. Ladakh, where the Indus flows, is a cold desert whose inhabitants practise Tibetan Buddhism. This incredibly beautiful region is home to ancient monasteries such as **Alchi** *(see pp144–6)* and **Hemis** *(see p140)*. Ladakh's ancient caravan routes that linked India to the Silk Route now function as popular **trekking trails** *(see pp152–3)* or as tour routes, such as the one passing through the remote and intriguing **Nubra Valley** *(see p143)*.

UTTAR PRADESH & UTTRANCHAL

• **The superlative Taj Mahal**
• **Nawabi Lucknow**
• **Varanasi: City of Light**
• **The Great Himalayas in the Garhwal region**

Uttar Pradesh, one of India's largest and most populous states, is watered by the country's great rivers – the Yamuna and Ganges. Three great cities lie along these riverine paths: **Agra** *(see pp168–77)*, the city of the **Taj Mahal** *(see pp172–5)* and other magnificent monuments built by the Mughals; **Lucknow** *(see pp196–8)*, the city of the nawabs, is famous for its refinement, stately architecture and superb cuisine; and **Varanasi** *(see pp202–8)*, the world's oldest city and Hinduism's holiest place of worship.

The Great Himalayas in Kumaon and the **Garhwal** *(see p187)* are full of sacred peaks and provide excellent trekking terrain. Adventurers will love expeditions such as the **Gaumukh Trail** and the challenging **Curzon Trail** to the **Nanda Devi Sanctuary** *(see pp188–9)*.

BIHAR & JHARKHAND

• **The Buddhist Route**
• **Forests of Jharkhand**
• **Sonepur's elephant fair**

It was in Bihar that the earliest empires emerged, and this antique land derives its name from *vihara* or monastery. The Buddhist Route includes **Bodh Gaya** *(see pp222–3)* where the Buddha attained enlightenment; **Rajgir** *(see p220)*, where the Buddha lived and taught and the earliest imperial capital; and the great university of **Nalanda** *(see pp218–19)*. Jharkhand is made up largely by the Chhota Nagpur Plateau, a

thickly forested area home to the Munda and Oraon tribes. **Palamau National Park** *(see p224)* offers glimpses of wildlife and some tribal villages. More local colour can be had at **Sonepur** *(see p216)*, where Asia's largest live-stock fair is held.

MADHYA PRADESH & CHHATTISGARH

• **The Great Stupa at Sanchi**
• **Khajuraho's temples**
• **Wildlife sanctuaries**

The hill of **Sanchi** *(see pp242–3)* is one of the best preserved sites of Buddhist India. Its crowning glory is the UNESCO World Heritage Site, the **Great Stupa** *(see pp244–5)* with its four impressive gateways and intricate carvings. The town's environs are also rich in ancient ruins.

Khajuraho's group of temples *(see pp236–8)*, also a UNESCO World Heritage Site, boasts not only splendid architecture, but a marvelous wealth of sculpture, including the much-talked-of erotic friezes. Its greatest temple is Kandariya Mahadev, dedicated to Shiva.

It is said that Rudyard Kipling set his classic, *The Jungle Book*, in the deciduous forests of **Kanha National Park** *(see pp254–5)*, still considered one of the best places to see the elusive tiger. The state's other important national park is **Bandhavgarh** *(see p239)*.

Tiger resting at the Bandhavgarh Park, Madhya Pradesh

Victoria Memorial, Kolkata's most celebrated landmark

KOLKATA

- **The Raj revisited**
- **Victoria Memorial**
- **India's oldest museum**

Kolkata, capital of the British Empire until 1911, saw a brilliant cultural and intellectual renaissance in the 19th century. At the heart of this fascinating city is **BBD Bagh** *(see pp270–71)*, which contains some of the finest buildings of the 18th and 19th centuries.

To its south is the **Maidan** park *(see p273)* and **Victoria Memorial** *(see pp274–5)*, the Raj's finest architectural legacy, named after Queen Victoria. On view here is an excellent selection of Raj memorablia. India's oldest museum, the 19th-century **Indian Museum** *(see pp276–7)*, has a superb collection of miniatures and stone and bronze sculptures.

WEST BENGAL & SIKKIM

- **The Ganges delta**
- **Terracotta temples**
- **The eastern Himalayas**

West Bengal and Sikkim's varied landscape ranges from the steamy delta area to the icy Himalayas bordering Tibet. In the vast Ganges-Brahmaputra Delta is the **Sunderbans** *(see pp288–9)*, the world's largest mangrove swamp and habitat of the Bengal tiger.

The terracotta temples of **Bishnupur** *(see pp290–91)*, built in the 17th century, are unique and have no equal in India. The most famous is the richly decorated Shyama Raya Temple.

Traversing the Teesta River, the **North Sikkim Tour** *(see p300)*, which begins at **Gangtok** *(see p298)*, the capital of Sikkim, provides breathtaking views of the eastern Himalayas, including **Kanchendzonga** *(see p302)*, the world's third highest peak.

Orchid from Sikkim

ORISSA

- **Konark's Sun God temple**
- **Great bird-watching**
- **Temples of Bhubaneshwar**

This beautiful state of forests and coastline boasts an incredible artistic and cultural heritage and is the birthplace of one of India's most exquisite classical dances, Odissi.

Konark *(see pp310–12)*, the temple to the Sun God, stands on the coast and is a marvel in stone. Built in the 13th century, it was conceived as a gigantic chariot. Further down the coast is the great lagoon, **Chilika Lake** *(see p316)*, a paradise for birds and aquatic life, especially dolphins. It is also noted for its seafood.

Bhubaneshwar *(see pp306–9)*, the state capital, is a city full of temples, including the impressive Lingaraj and the lyrical Rajarani temples. The city's environs are well known for their archaeological sites and craft villages.

ASSAM & THE NORTHEAST

- **Rhino-watching**
- **Tawang Monastery**
- **Colourful Kohima**

Seven states form this large and diverse part of India. The mighty Brahmaputra river flows through this area, dominating life in Assam. **Kaziranga National Park** *(see pp330–31)* lies on its banks and is home to the one-horned rhinoceros. **Tawang Monastery** *(see p327)* in Arunachal Pradesh is the largest Buddhist monastery in India and belongs to the Yellow Hat sect. Nearby is the Bramdungchung Nunnery, set in a landscape of snowy peaks and Monpa villages. **Kohima** *(see p339)*, the capital of Nagaland, is an introduction to tribal India as is evident in the boldly patterned textiles, dramatic woodcarvings and spirited dances. The War Cemetery here commemorates one of the most decisive battles of World War II.

Rhino-watching at Assam's Kaziranga National Park

Jaisalmer, one of the world's largest and most dramatic forts

RAJASTHAN

- **Jaipur & Amber**
- **Desert fortresses**
- **The Lake City of Udaipur**

India's most popular region for tourism, Rajasthan continues to haunt the imagination with its stark landscapes, fortresses and the colour and drama of its people. The 17th-century city of **Jaipur** *(see pp352–63)* is both picturesque and a shopper's paradise. Around **Badi Chaupar** *(see pp354–5)* are colourful bazaars, the **City Palace** *(see pp356–7)*, still the residence of the Jaipur kings, and **Hawa Mahal** *(see p352–3)*, the fanciful Palace of Winds. Crowning the crest of a hill just outside Jaipur is the magnificent old fort-palace of **Amber** *(see pp364–6)*. Dating from the late 16th century, this was the capital of the Jaipur rulers for almost 200 years.

In the arid Thar Desert is **Jaisalmer** *(see pp386–91)*, a town and fort built of gold sandstone. Among its many attractions are palaces and houses *(havelis)* that have been intricately carved like jewels. Jaisalmer also has a vibrant folk music tradition.

Around the shores of Lake Pichola is the fairytale city of **Udaipur** *(see pp398–401)*. Traditional *havelis*, palaces, *ghats*, temples and bazaars make this city and its equally interesting environs a rare experience. One of the world's great hotels, the **Lake Palace** *(see p705)*, is located on an island on the lake. Nearby is another small palace, Jag Mandir.

GUJARAT

- **Bustling Ahmedabad**
- **The stepwells of Gujarat**
- **Modhera's Sun Temple**

Gujarat's leading city and commercial and industrial centre, **Ahmedabad** *(see pp410–13)*, has a rich heritage. The Old City, a maze of towering gateways,

Sculptures at the Rani ni Vav stepwell

bazaars, mosques and temples can be seen on a walking tour organized by the Ahmedabad Municipal Corporation. The city's unique **Calico Museum** *(see pp412–13)* is also worth a visit for an overview of India's rich textile traditions. Beyond the city centre is **Sabarmati Ashram** where Mahatma Gandhi lived during the days of India's Freedom Movement.

Water scarcities have plagued Gujarat for centuries. An ingenious answer to this perennial problem were stepwells. These elaborately decorated underground wells conserved water as well as provided a cool place for social interaction. The finest, **Adalaj Vav** *(see pp414–15)*, was built in 1499 by Queen Rudabai and boasts 800 individual sculptures. Others are **Dada Harir Vav** in Ahmedabad and **Rani ni Vav** in Patan *(see p417)*. The **Sun Temple at Modhera** *(see pp418–19)*, built in 1026, is laid out with astronomical precision. The temple's richly carved exterior and interior depict Hindu deities in great detail and are fine examples of medieval sculpture. Some of the most outstanding carvings can be seen on the walls and pillars of the inner sanctum.

The ancient rock-cut caves of Ajanta, near Aurangabad

MUMBAI

- **Magnificent Victoria Terminus**
- **Elephanta Island**
- **Bollywood magic**

Cosmopolitan Mumbai is a city of contrasts, where skyscrapers stand next to stately Victorian edifices. A walk through the eclectic **Kala Ghoda** district *(see pp448–9)* emphasizes this fact. Further north, **Victoria Terminus** *(see pp454–5)* is a riot of domes, spires and arches, and a star of Victorian Gothic architecture.
Off the coast is **Elephanta Island** *(see p461)*, with its 6th-century AD rock-cut temples dedicated to Shiva. Mumbai is also the home of India's vibrant film industry, **Bollywood** *(see pp32–3)*, and in sprawling **Film City** *(see p460)* extravagant, big-budget films are made.

MAHARASHTRA

- **Ancient frescoes at Ajanta**
- **Island-forts of the sparkling Malvan Coast**

The Western Ghats separate the slim **Konkan Coast** *(see pp438–9)* from the volcanic lava of the cotton-growing Deccan Plateau. The tradition of rock-cut caves was widespread in this region and at **Ajanta** *(see pp479–81)* visitors can see the world-famous 5th-century frescoes on Buddhist themes. **Ellora** *(see pp476–8)* has Jain, Buddhist and Hindu caves, the highlight of which is the **Kailasanatha Temple**. A UNESCO World Heritage Site, it is intricately carved out of a massive cliff. The picturesque Malvan Coast in South Konkan is dotted with sandy beaches, fishing villages and island forts, such as **Murud-Janjira** and Kolaba near **Alibag** *(see p466)*.

Narasimha sculpture at Hampi

GOA

- **Portuguese flavour in Old Goa**
- **Panaji Old Town**
- **Idyllic beaches**

Goa is a tourist haven with stunning beaches, grand mansions, such as **Braganza House** *(see pp508–9)*, Indo-Portuguese culture and delicious cuisine. **Old Goa** *(see pp496–501)*, the first capital of the Portuguese, is a showcase of imperial Portuguese architecture, clearly visible in the state's cathedrals, churches and monasteries.
Panaji Old Town *(see pp488–9)*, especially São Tomé and Fontainhas, is typically Latin, with tile-roofed houses, gardens and restaurants. **Goa's beaches** *(see p491)* are splendid and stretch over 106 km (66 miles) from north to south.

KARNATAKA

- **Palaces of Mysore**
- **Hampi: a heritage site**
- **Bijapur's Gol Gumbad**

Strikingly varied in landscape, Karnataka is rich in history and the arts. The former princely state was ruled from **Mysore**, a city which has lovely palaces, such as the 19th-century **Amba Vilas** *(see pp518–519)*. Nearby is **Srirangapattana** *(see p516)*, once the head-quarters of Tipu Sultan.
Amid huge boulders near the Tungabhadra river are the evocative ruins of **Hampi** *(see pp530–33)*, once the capital of the richest kingdom in South India, the Vijayanagara Empire. To the north is **Bijapur** *(see pp542–3)*, where the Deccani sultans' superb artistic legacy can be seen in the monumental tomb, the **Gol Gumbad**.

One of Goa's many idyllic beaches

CHENNAI

- **Fort St George**
- **The Pantheon Complex**
- **Traditional Mylapore**

Chennai entered history as Madras, India's first British settlement, centred around **Fort St George** *(see pp560–61)* and nearby **George Town** *(see p561)*. Both contain fine examples of British Colonial architecture. The **Pantheon Complex** *(see pp564–5)* includes the Indo-Saracenic Government Museum, which has a rare collection of Buddhist sculptures from Amaravati, the Bronze Gallery and the Contemporary Art Gallery.

St Thomas, the apostle of Christ who came to India in AD 52, died in Chennai. The **Little Mount** *(see p573)*, where the saint was mortally wounded, has an imprint of his hand near the entrance. He is buried at the Gothic-style **Basilica of San Thomé** at **Mylapore** *(see p570)*, a busy, traditional quarter.

TAMIL NADU

- **The great Chola temples**
- **Spectacular Mamallapuram**
- **Charming Pondicherry**

In this state of great stone temples and lush rice fields in the Kaveri Delta, is the city of **Thanjavur** *(see pp596–9)*, where the Chola kings built the magnificent **Brihadishvara Temple** *(see pp598–9)*. In the same district are the temples at **Chidambaram** *(see p590)* and **Darasuram** *(see p593)*.

Along the Bay of Bengal, **Mamallapuram** *(see pp578–9)* was once a major port of the 7th-century Pallava kings. The dramatic Shore Temple sits precariously on the coast, while inland are the rock-cut **Panch Rathas** *(see pp580–81)*. **Pondicherry** *(see pp586–9)*, a former French colony, is also home to the Aurobindo Ashram.

Snorkelling in the waters off the Andaman Islands

ANDAMAN ISLANDS

- **Coral reefs and crystal clear water**
- **Sinister history of Port Blair**

An idyllic archipelago, the Andamans encompass several ecosystems including mangrove swamps, tropical forest and coral reefs. Glimpses of aquatic life can be had while snorkelling or scuba diving, especially around Jolly Buoy Island in the **Wandoor Marine National Park** *(see pp620–21)*.

In the 19th century the islands served as a penal colony; the Cellular Jail in **Port Blair** *(see p618)* is a dark symbol of those times.

KERALA

- **Sparkling coastline and picturesque backwaters**
- **Virgin rainforests**
- **Wooden architecture**

Kerala offers an appealing mosaic of landscapes and cultures, as well as some fantastic coastline. No visit here is complete without a **Backwaters Tour** *(see pp634–5)* through the labyrinthine network of lush waterways. In the virgin rainforests of the **Wynad District** *(see p654)*, glimpses of wild elephants and giant Malabar squirrels can be seen.

For an insight into the area's tumultuous past visit **Fort Kochi** *(see pp644–5)* in this bustling port-city. Also don't miss the **Padmana-**

bhapuram Palace *(see pp630–31)* one of the finest examples of Kerala's unique wooden architecture.

ANDHRA PRADESH

- **Hyderabad's Old City**
- **The ruins of Golconda**
- **Buddhist sites**

Hyderabad *(see pp660–65)* is a city of grand palaces, mosques and bazaars. The **Charminar** area *(see pp662–3)* is the best place to view the legacy of the city's incredibly rich Nizams. Outside the city are the vast ruins of **Golconda** *(see pp666–7)*, a legendary 16th-century citadel. Along the Krishna river are the remains of the state's Buddhist settlements at **Amravati** *(see p675)* and **Nagarjunakonda** *(see p676)*, named after a 2nd-century Buddhist philosopher.

The sprawling ramparts of Golconda Fort outside Hyderabad

Putting Northern India on the Map

Encompassing an area stretching from the Greater Himalayan Range in the north to the upper part of the Deccan Plateau, northern India covers 2,331,318 sq km (900,127 sq miles). It is watered by three rivers – the Indus, the Ganges and the Brahmaputra – all of which originate in the Himalayas. The vast, densely-populated Indo-Gangetic Plains form its heartland. Some 705 million people, who speak 10 major languages, live here. The two largest cities are Delhi, the capital, and Kolkata (formerly Calcutta), both well-connected internationally by air.

JAMMU & KASHMIR
Indus
Wular Lake
Srinagar
Jhelum
NH1A
Shayok
Leh
Chenab
Pangong Tso
Tso Morin
Jammu
NH20
Kullu
Ravi
Amritsar
HIMACHAL
Lahore
PRADESH
NH15
PUNJAB
NH22
Shimla
Manasarovar Lake
Chandigarh
Mussoorie
Dehra Dun
UTTARANCHAL
NH1
Nainital
HARYANA
Yamuna
Ganges
DELHI
NH24
PAKISTAN
Bikaner
NH11
NH65
NH2
UTTAR
NH15
PRADESH
Jaisalmer
RAJASTHAN
Lucknow
Agra
NH15
Ajmer
Jaipur
Kanpur
Jodhpur
Chambal
NH14
Gwalior
NH25
NH12
Allahabad
Luni
Gandhi Sagar
Khajuraho
NH27
Udaipur
NH8
Bhuj
MADHYA PRADESH
Kandla
Gandhinagar
Bhopal
NH26
Jamnagar
Ahmedabad
NH12
Jabalpur
GUJARAT
Rajkot
NH8A
Vadodara
NH7
NH88
Indore
Narmada
I N D I A
Bhavnagar
Tapti
Surat
Raipur
NH6
Nagpur
Durg
NH43
KEY
Ajanta
Nasik
MAHARASHTRA
NH8
NH3
Ellora
Aurangabad
NH50
NH4
Ahmadnagar
Jagdalpur
Mumbai
Pune
Nizamabad
Karimnagar
Satara
Bidar
Warangal
NH17
Solapur
NH9
Godavari
Panaji
Hyderabad
NH7
Krishna

KEY

▨	Central city area
✈	International airport
☒	Domestic airport
⛴	Ferry port
═	National highway
▬	Major road
– –	International border
– –	State border
x x x	Disputed border

DELHI & ENVIRONS

NH10
Civil Lines
Chandigarh
The Ridge
New Delhi
NH24
Yamuna
Indira Gandhi International Airport
NH8
Hauz Khas
Siri Fort
NH2
Agra
Mehrauli
0 km   3
0 miles   3
Tughluqabad

PUTTING INDIA ON THE MAP

KAZAKHSTAN
MONGOLIA
UZBEKISTAN
TURKMENISTAN
CHINA
IRAN
AFGHANISTAN
NEPAL
BANGLADESH
PAKISTAN
MYANMAR
SAUDI ARABIA
UAE
OMAN
YEMEN
INDIA
PACIFIC OCEAN
ARABIAN SEA
BAY OF BENGAL
THAILAND
LAOS
VIETNAM
CAMBODIA
See next page
SRI LANKA
MALAYSIA
MALDIVES
SINGAPORE
INDONESIA
INDIAN OCEAN

C H I N A
T I B E T
Tsangpo
Lhasa

NORTHEAST STATES

N E P A L
Ziro
Dibrugarh
KATHMANDU
SIKKIM
THIMPHU
Itanagar
NH37
Raxaul
Gangtok
BHUTAN
Tezpur
NH52
Bagdogra
NH37C
Kohima
Patna
NH31
NH84
NH37
Guwahati
NH56
Varanasi
NH28
NH29
NH30
Shillong
Silchar
Imphal
NH2
BIHAR
NH57
Brahmaputra
NH53
NH39
Son
BANGLADESH
DHAKA
Aizawl
JHARKHAND
NH44
JHARKHAND
Shantiniketan
NH54
Agartala
Ranchi
NH23
WEST BENGAL
MYANMAR
NH32
CHHATTIS-GARH
NH6
Kolkata
Haldia
Yangon
ORISSA
NH42
Bhubaneswar
NH5A
Port Blair
NH5
Puri
0 km   200
0 miles   200
Visakhapatnam

KOLKATA & ENVIRONS

Netaji Subhash Chandra Bose International Airport
0 km   2
NH2
Jorasanko
0 miles   2
Hooghly
Shibpur
Central Kolkata
Tangra
Park Circus
Alipore
Kalighat

The external boundaries of India as shown on this map are neither correct nor authentic.

Putting Southern India on the Map

The six states of Southern India lie within the triangular peninsula that forms the lower part of the Indian subcontinent. With a population of 322 million, speaking six major languages, they cover an area of 955,945 sq km (369,092 sq miles) – larger than France and Germany combined. The western coast is flanked by the Arabian Sea, and the eastern coast by the Bay of Bengal, while the southern tip juts into the Indian Ocean. The rocky Deccan Plateau forms southern India's heartland, bordered on either side by the wooded hills of the Western and Eastern Ghats. The two largest cities are Mumbai (formerly Bombay) and Chennai (formerly Madras).

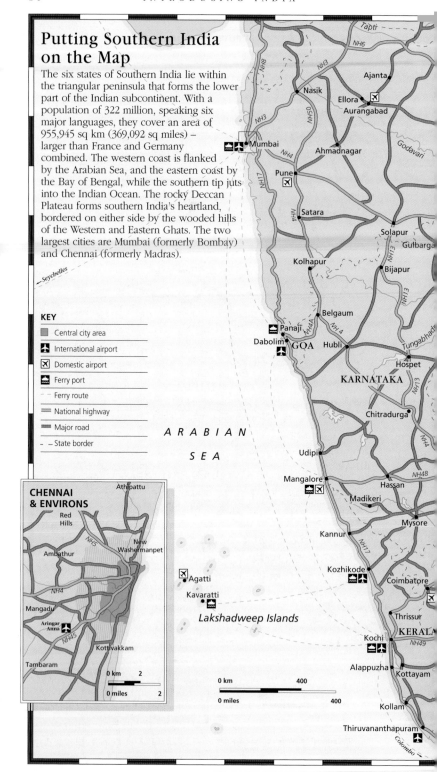

KEY

- ▨ Central city area
- ✈ International airport
- ☒ Domestic airport
- ⛴ Ferry port
- - - Ferry route
- ═ National highway
- ▬ Major road
- – – State border

ARABIAN SEA

CHENNAI & ENVIRONS

Red Hills
Athipattu
New Washermanpet
Ambathur
NH5
Mangadu
NH4
Aringar Anna
NH45
Kottivakkam
Tambaram

0 km   2
0 miles   2

Tapti
NH6
NH3
NH8
Ajanta
Nasik
Ellora
Aurangabad
NH50
NH3
Godavari
Mumbai
NH4
Ahmadnagar
Pune
NH17
Satara
NH4
Solapur
Gulbarga
NH13
Kolhapur
Bijapur
NH13
Belgaum
Panaji
NH4A
NH4
Dabolim
GOA
Hubli
Tungabhadra
Hospet
KARNATAKA
NH13
Chitradurga
NH4
Udipi
Mangalore
NH48
Hassan
Madikeri
Mysore
Kannur
NH7
Kozhikode
Coimbatore
Agatti
Kavaratti
Thrissur
Lakshadweep Islands
KERALA
Kochi
NH49
Alappuzha
Kottayam
Kollam
Thiruvananthapuram
Colombo

Seychelles

0 km   400
0 miles   400

Landscape and Wildlife

Plum-headed parakeet

India has an extraordinary diversity of landscapes and vegetation, supporting a rich variety of wildlife. The country is bounded on the north by the majestic Himalayas. Along their foothills, sweeping the breadth of Central India, are the fertile, densely populated Indo-Gangetic Plains, while the arid Thar Desert covers much of Western India. South of the Gangetic Plains is the Deccan Plateau, flanked by the hills of the Eastern and Western Ghats. India's 7,516-km (4,670-mile) long coastline borders on the Arabian Sea, the Indian Ocean and the Bay of Bengal.

The Himalayan landscape *features snowcapped peaks, glacial streams and pine-covered slopes* (see pp64–5).

THE ARID WEST
The Thar Desert and the semi-arid scrublands adjoining it support a surprising variety of flora and fauna. The sand dunes of Rajasthan give way further west to the barren salt-flats and marshes of the Rann of Kutch.

THE GANGETIC PLAINS
The rich alluvial soil of these vast plains, which stretch across India from the northwest to the east, has been cultivated for thousands of years. Today rice, as well as wheat, sugarcane and pulses are grown here.

Blackbucks *are among the swiftest animals, covering up to 80 km (50 miles) per hour.*

Asian elephants *number only 45,000 in comparison to a quarter of a million African elephants, making this smaller species the more endangered one.*

Asiatic lions, *once found all over northern India, are now seen only in the Gir Sanctuary in Gujarat* (see p423).

Painted storks *migrate to lakes and swamps during their breeding season, between July and October.*

Crested serpent eagles *are large raptors with a distinctive pattern of black and white bands on their underwings.*

Wild boars *are common in most deciduous forests in India. The males have tusks and can be very aggressive.*

Avocets *migrate to the coasts and marshes of Gujarat and Maharashtra in November.*

THE COASTS

The diverse landscapes of the coasts include sandy beaches in Goa and Kerala, fringed by coconut palms, coral reefs in the Andamans, and mangrove forests in West Bengal and Orissa. The east coast is often hit by cyclones.

Starfish, *which cling tenaciously to rocks, can be seen in tidal pools all along the Indian coastline.*

THE DECCAN PLATEAU

Separated from the Gangetic Plains by the scattered ranges of the Vindhyas, the Deccan Plateau is covered with black volcanic soil and ancient crystalline rocks. The plateau's mineral wealth includes gold and diamonds.

THE GHATS

The hills of the Western and Eastern Ghats are covered with forests of teak, rosewood, sal (*Shorea robusta*) and sandalwood (*Santalam album*), prized for its fragrant wood. Many orchid species also grow here.

Tigers, *an endangered species and numbering only 3,500 in the country, are found across peninsular India.*

Nilgiri tahrs *live in the higher elevations of the Western Ghats (see p649).*

Daniel butterflies *are common in the region.*

Bullfrogs *display their large vocal sacs during their mating season in the monsoon.*

Langurs *or Hanuman monkeys* (Semnopithecus entellus), *live in large groups, led by an adult male.*

Peacocks, *India's national bird, perform a spectacular dance when rain clouds appear.*

Spectacled cobras *have characteristic spectacle-shaped markings on their hoods. Another reptile is the king cobra, the world's largest venomous snake.*

Sacred Architecture

Ceiling panel from a Jain temple

India's 2,000-year-old architectural heritage is intrinsically linked to the country's major religions. Indigenous forms include Buddhist stupas and monasteries and Hindu and Jain temples *(See pp396–7)* in diverse styles. Many Indian temples, however, share common structural characteristics, being mostly built of stone columns and horizontal blocks, often richly carved with sacred imagery and decorative motifs. The true arch and the dome, as well as the use of mortar, were introduced in the 12th century by the Muslim conquerors.

Sculpted column, Narayana Temple, Melkote

BUDDHIST ARCHITECTURE

India's earliest religious monuments are stupas, hemispherical funerary mounds, and rock-cut shrines *(chaityas)* and monasteries *(viharas)*. While *chaityas* were places of worship, *viharas* were dwelling places for Buddhist monks and consisted of small residential cells arranged around four sides of an open court.

Entrance / Vaulted ceiling / Model stupa

Chaityas *served as halls* (grihas) *for congregational worship and enshrined a model stupa at one end.*

Circumambulatory path / Hemispherical mound / Torana *(gateway)* / Railing

Stupas *were monumental reliquaries in which the ashes of Buddhist teachers, including the Buddha, were interred. The Sanchi Stupa (see pp244–5) is faced in stone, and surrounded by a high railing with gateways* (toranas).

Rock-cut *chaityas have distinctive barrel-vaulted ceilings, expressed on the exterior as a horseshoe-shaped arch.*

HINDU TEMPLES

Vimana **(pyramidal spire)**

In North India, the soaring tower above the inner sanctum takes the form of a curving *shikhara* (spire) topped with a circular ribbed motif, the *amalaka*. South Indian temples, however, have multi-staged, pyramidal spires *(vimana)* crowned with a hemispherical or barrel-vaulted roof. Worship in both types takes place in a small dark sanctuary known as the *garbhagriha* (womb chamber).

Mandapa **(hall or pillared pavilion)** / Entrance

South Indian temples, *such as Thanjavur's Brihadishvara Temple (see pp598–9), have corridors and spacious halls* (mandapas), *with a profusion of decorated columns. These lead to the garbhagriha, above which rises the multi-staged spire.*

Kalasha **(pot finial)** / *Amalaka* **(circular ribbed motif)** / *Shikhara* **(curved temple spire)** / Carvings of deities

Khajuraho's *Kandariya Mahadev Temple's* shikhara *(see pp236–7) is considered the finest in North India.*

ISLAMIC ARCHITECTURE

Mosques and tombs represent an imported tradition that was absorbed into Indian architecture. Mosques have domed prayer halls at one end of an open courtyard. The *mihrab* (arched niche) faces west, towards Mecca. The Mughals introduced the garden tomb, raised on a high plinth in the centre of a *charbagh*, an enclosed garden divided into four quarters. Decorative elements include Persian and Arabic calligraphy, geometric patterns and floral motifs, typical of Islamic art.

Mihrab, Bidar mosque *(see p545)*

Chhatri **(domed rooftop pavilion)**

An onion-shaped dome surmounts the central space.

Plinth

Intricate *jalis*

Minarets

Taj Mahal *(see pp172–3),* the zenith of Islamic architecture

GURDWARAS

The Sikh gurdwara, a prayer chamber where the *Granth Sahib*, or Holy Book, is housed, is often roofed with a dome flanked by arcades. Based on the late-Mughal style prevailing in North India in the 18th century, gurdwaras blend Islamic and Hindu architectural styles.

Gold plated dome

The prayer chamber houses the Holy Book.

The Golden Temple in Amritsar *(see pp106–107)*

CHURCHES

Though church architecture in Kerala predates the arrival of Europeans, most Christian places of worship, such as those in Goa *(see pp496–7),* are built in European styles. A common design has a Neo-Classical portico topped with a tapering steeple. Many Indian churches are also built in a Neo-Gothic style, such as the Afghan Memorial Church of St John the Evangelist *(see p447).*

Tower with thin tapering steeple

Pointed arched windows

Entrance

Afghan Memorial Church, Mumbai

Amalaka

Kalasha (pot finial)

Jagamohana **(assembly hall)**

Deul **(temple spire)**

Pot finial

Conical roof

Wooden screen

Metal tiles

Brass bells

The Mukteshwar Temple (see p307) *typifies Orissa's temple architecture. The sanctuary has a curving spire (deul) and an adjoining assembly hall (jagamohana).*

Kerala's temples, *such as the one at Ettumanur (see p638), have a distinctive form. The sanctums are often circular with roofs of sloping tiers of metal sheets or terracotta tiles. Carved woodwork and murals embellish the structure.*

Secular Architecture

Detail from a mirrored room

Magnificent secular buildings, such as forts, palaces and mansions (*havelis*) were built by powerful ruling and aristocratic families. Many of these, especially in Rajasthan and Gujarat (*see pp346–7*), harmoniously combine monumental scale with superb decorative elements. The British imposed their own architectural stamp, a fusion of East and West. A variety of indigenous domestic forms that have remained unchanged through the ages can be seen throughout rural India.

Windows are inspired by Rajput palaces.   **Mughal dome**

Laxmi Vilas in Vadodara (*see p419*), built in the late 19th century

CIVIC ARCHITECTURE

Sculpture, Churchgate Station, Mumbai

In the mid-19th century, the British began to incorporate elements from Indian Islamic architecture into European Neo-Classical or Gothic Revivalist styles. Known as Indo-Saracenic, this style reflected imperial and civic pride. Indo-Saracenic public buildings include Victoria Terminus (*see pp454–5*) and Mumbai University, and the High Court and Egmore station in Chennai. This culminated in the building of the new capital at New Delhi (*see pp72–3*), where Sir Edwin Lutyens and his associates evolved a grand architectural style which was a more elegant synthesis of Indian and European traditions.

Gothic window, Mumbai University

End towers are surmounted by small bulbous cupolas.

Colonnaded verandahs run the length of the building.

A dome crowns the central chamber.

The entrance porch has a balcony above.

Prince of Wales Museum, Mumbai (*see pp450–51*), inspired by Bijapur's Gol Gumbad (*see p543*)

THE COURTYARD

Domestic architecture in India is governed by public and private spaces. The front portion of the house was open to visitors and guests, but just beyond that was the courtyard, the heart of the house, restricted to the family. Larger mansions, such as those at Shekhawati (*see p372*), Jaisalmer (*see p387*) and Chettinad (*see p612*), had several courtyards surrounded by elaborate colonnades. The separation of private and public spaces within the home grew out of social conventions that secluded women from the public gaze.

Courtyard with wooden pillars and carved doors

VERNACULAR ARCHITECTURE

A painted niche

Rural houses in India reflect the country's varied climate and the range of available materials. In spite of the diversity, certain overall principles prevail. A typical dwelling is approached from the street through a formal doorway, often sheltered by a verandah, flanked by raised seating. The first room is usually used for both living and sleeping, and is thus larger. Cooking and eating take place to the rear, on the other side of an inner courtyard, near the well, or water supply. Hindu homes have a small masonry stand (*vrindavan*), in the courtyard, where the sacred *tulsi* (basil) plant is grown for daily worship.

Walls are made with strips of bamboo.

Extended timber acts as supports.

Tribal houses *in the forested northeast are quickly constructed from wood and bamboo. Rooms are added on as the family grows.*

Slate slabs are used to build strong, protective roofs.

Wooden pillars in the upper verandah.

Mountain homes *are built on high ground, and are double-storeyed, with the ground floor serving as a stable for livestock in winter.*

Central Indian villages *are tightly packed with houses that are either one-roomed tiled structures or larger ones. Some have flat-roofs where the family sleep at night in summer.*

Coastal houses *have sloping tiled roofs as protection from sun and rain. The* tulsi *(basil) plant indicates that this is a Hindu home.*

Mud walls are reinforced with straw and cowdung.

Thatch roofs, made of local elephant grass, are replaced every year.

Desert dwellings *are built with mud and consist of a single thatched room, enclosed by a wall. The circular* kothi *is used to store grain. Designs in white lime embellish the outer walls.*

MATERIALS FOR CONSTRUCTION

Circular thatch ceiling

Traditionally, most houses were built of locally available material. Bamboo and thatch were employed in house construction in Bengal, Orissa and the northeast, while stone and terracotta tiles were preferred in Madhya Pradesh, Maharashtra and South India. Sadly, such materials are now rapidly being replaced by steel and concrete. However, mud is still the most common material and is either applied directly or mixed with cowdung and straw.

Woven bamboo panel for walls

Coconut palm leaf roof

Thatched roof made of grass

Half-cylinder tiles

Terracotta sun-dried bricks

Stone slabs, ideal for walls

Hindu Mythology

Garuda, the great sun-eagle

The vast pantheon of Hindu gods, goddesses and their divine exploits is best explored through sculpture. The principles of temple architecture were defined and established under the imperial Guptas (4th–6th centuries AD). Indian temples are adorned by a profusion of sculptures that are not merely decorative but also provide a visual interpretation of Hindu mythology. The numerous manifestations of deities, such as Shiva, Vishnu and Devi (the goddess also known as Parvati, Durga, Kali) are depicted in great detail. Semi-divine beings, such as devotees, nymphs and musicians complete the picture.

Dvarapala *is the armed guardian who stands outside the entrance of the temple or by the door of the inner sanctum. These forbidding figures carry weapons to protect the deity from intruders.*

Karttikeya is mounted on his peacock vehicle *(vahana).*

Vedic gods, *such as Surya the Sun God, were manifestations of nature and the elements. They were absorbed into the Hindu pantheon of deities almost 2,000 years ago.*

Indra, the Vedic God of the Heavens, sits on Airavata, the four-trunked white elephant representing the rain-cloud.

Female attendant

Lakshmi, the consort of Vishnu

Garuda, the vehicle *(vahana)* of Vishnu, is half man and half eagle.

Lakshmi, *the Goddess of Wealth, appears as Gajalakshmi in this panel from Mamallapuram* (see p579). *She is seen with two elephants* (gaja) *who bathe her with their upturned trunks.*

Vishnu's *dwarf incarnation, Vamana* (see p679) *transforms himself into a giant to measure out the universe in three steps. This panel from Badami* (see pp536–7) *shows him with one leg raised skywards.*

Mohini, *the female form of Vishnu, is described as an enchantress, the most alluring maiden imaginable. Courtesans and nymphs are also carved as bracket figures.*

VISHNU ANANTASAYANA

This 5th-century panel from Deogarh *(see p233)* depicts Vishnu asleep on the serpent Ananta, whose hood shelters him. Brahma on a lotus rises from behind, while Shiva sits with Parvati on his *vahana*, the bull Nandi. Attendants and celestial beings surround the figure. The mace, discus, shield and sword, Vishnu's attributes, are personified below to ward off demons.

Brahma, *the Creator, is part of the holy Trinity (Trimurti) of gods that also include Vishnu and Shiva. He is depicted with four heads, of which only three are usually visible, and holds a sceptre, a spoon, a string of beads and the Vedas. He is seen here with his consort, Saraswati, the Goddess of Learning.*

Shiva, *the God of Destruction, is seated with his wife, Parvati, who represents his peaceful and domestic aspect. Shiva holds an elephant goad and drum (dumroo), while Parvati has a lotus (kamal) in her hand.*

Shiva and Parvati

Flying celestial figure

Ananta, the Many Headed Serpent, is also known as Adishesha.

Vishnu, the Preserver

Durga, *the fierce form of gentle Parvati, slaying the buffalo-demon, Mahishasura. This panel from Mamallapuram, known as Mahishasuramardini, shows Durga riding a lion with a deadly weapon in each of her eight arms, given to her by the gods to annihilate the demon.*

Karttikeya, *Shiva's warrior son, has a peacock as his vahana. He is also known as Skanda, Subramanya and Murugan in South India. The other son of Shiva is Ganesha (see p467).*

Attendants, the personifications of Vishnu's four attributes, protect the god from demons.

Dancers, musicians and other performers, usually carved on the lower plinths of temples

Devotees *are often elevated to the status of saints and are honoured for their devotion to either Shiva or Vishnu. This 11th-century bronze is of a Shaivite boy-saint holding cymbals in his hands.*

The Great Epics

The two great epic poems, the *Ramayana* and the *Mahabharata*, have had an abiding impact on Indian culture and philosophy. Over the centuries, their stories have inspired a great deal of art, music, dance, theatre and, more recently, popular TV serials. Containing a fund of wisdom about human behaviour, emotions and moral dilemmas, the epics continue to guide the daily lives

Pandava hero on *ganjifa* card

of millions of Indians. Though known in their oral form since at least 500 BC, they were only put into writing around the 4th century AD.

Arjuna *shot the eye of a fish reflected in water, and won the hand of Draupadi, who then married all five brothers.*

In a game of dice *with the Kauravas, the Pandavas lost their kingdom and Draupadi. She was saved from the shame of being disrobed by the Kauravas when her sari kept growing magically to cover her.*

THE MAHABHARATA

This epic recounts the rivalry between the five heroic Pandava brothers – Yudishthira, Bhima, Arjuna, Nakul and Sahdeva – and 100 members of the Kaurava clan, headed by Duryodhana, and culminates in a great battle. Several other fables, legends and discourses are woven into the main story, making the *Mahabharata* eight times longer than the *Iliad* and the *Odyssey* put together.

Forced into exile *after the game of dice, the Pandavas wandered all over India for 13 years. In the final year, Arjuna lived in disguise as a eunuch, giving dance lessons.*

The Bhagavad Gita *is a sermon given to Arjuna by Lord Krishna, who acted as Arjuna's charioteer, on the battlefield of Kurukshetra. It is a famous discourse on ethics and morality, that contains the essence of Hindu religion and philosophy.*

In the final battle *the Kauravas created a cobweb-shaped defensive formation called the* chakravyuha, *inside which Arjuna's son was trapped and killed. However, on the 18th day of this fierce battle, the Pandavas, with Krishna's divine guidance, finally emerged victorious, and regained their kingdom, which they ruled with Draupadi as their queen.*

THE RAMAYANA

Rama, the ideal hero, was prevented from becoming king of Ayodhya by the intrigues of his stepmother, and sent into exile with his wife Sita and brother Lakshman. The demon-king, Ravana, abducted Sita, who was then rescued by the two brothers with the help of the monkey god, Hanuman. Rama is worshipped as an incarnation of Vishnu *(see p679)*.

The wedding of Rama and Sita *took place after Rama succeeded in breaking the great bow of Shiva, which other suitors for her hand could not even manage to lift off the ground.*

Exiled to the forest *for 14 years, Rama, Sita and Lakshman lived simply and visited the hermitages of many holy sages.*

Sita was abducted *from her forest hut by Ravana, the demon-king of Lanka, who came disguised as a mendicant. The brave vulture Jatayu tried to save her, but his wings were slashed by Ravana. However, Jatayu was able to tell Rama what had happened before he died.*

Ravana's ten heads *and 20 arms signify his great intellectual and physical strength.*

Hanuman, the Monkey God, *is a much-loved figure in the pantheon of Hindu gods, worshipped for his miraculous powers, his courage and physical prowess.*

Ravana's palace at Lanka *was attacked by Rama and Lakshman who, with the help of Hanuman and his army of monkeys, rescued Sita and killed Ravana. Lakshman was gravely wounded in the battle, but saved by the magical mountain herb, Sanjivini, brought by Hanuman.*

Rama's triumphant return *to Ayodhya is celebrated in the festival of lights, Diwali (see p37), which symbolizes the victory of good over evil.*

Classical Music and Dance

Indian music and dance are simultaneously modes of worship and a joyous celebration of life. Based on ancient codified texts, they originated as a form of worship in the temples, and gradually acquired a more secular character with royal patronage. Different regions of India have their own classical dance forms, while classical music is distinguished by two main styles – Hindustani and Carnatic (*see p595*), the latter specific to South India.

Sarangi and bow

Kuchipudi *is a highly dramatic dance form from Andhra Pradesh, which often enacts scenes from the great epics.*

The tiara is shaped like a temple spire.

Sensuous and spiritual at the same time, Odissi has sinuous movements and highly sculptural poses.

Frieze of a dancer from an 11th-century South Indian temple

Complex footwork and rhythms, and multiple pirouettes characterize this dance form.

Fan pleats decorate the front of the sari.

CLASSICAL DANCE

A wide range of hand gestures, facial expressions and body postures, codified in the *Natya Shastra*, a 4th-century treatise, constitute the "language" of Indian classical dance forms. Their themes are mostly based on religious mythology, and percussion and music play an important role.

A swirling skirt is worn over tight pyjamas.

Ghungroos (bells) help mark the rhythmic beat.

Kathak *was a favourite dance at the royal courts of northern India.*

Odissi *developed in the temples of Orissa as an offering to the deities.*

HINDUSTANI MUSIC

The origins of Hindustani classical music date to about 3000 BC. The raga (melodic line) and the *tala* (rhythmic cycle) are its foundation, and there is no formal written score. This gives artistes great latitude to improvise within the melodic framework of a raga. There are more than a 100 ragas, each assigned to a particular time of day or season, according to the mood or images its melody evokes. Royal patrons founded different *gharanas* or schools of music, which have preserved their individuality by passing knowledge down orally from guru (teacher) to *shishya* (disciple).

Ravi Shankar, *one of India's foremost sitar players, introduced Indian classical music to the West.*

Amjad Ali Khan *plays the sarod, an instrument developed by his grandfather from the rabab, a medieval Central Asian lute.*

Nine rasas *(moods) are mentioned in the 4th-century treatise* Natya Shastra. *From the erotic, comic and pathetic to the odious, marvellous and quiescent, the* rasas *cover every mood and expression, whether in music, dance or painting. This 17th-century miniature painting depicts the serene mood of the morning* Raga Todi.

Kerala's Kathakali dance featuring spectacular masks *(see p657)*

Fresh flowers adorn the hair.

Elaborate jewellery

Red colour on the hands and feet draw attention to intricate movements.

Diaphanous veil

Crinoline-like skirts and gentle swaying movements are typical of Manipuri dance.

Chiselled movements and symmetrical stances are typical of this dance form.

Beautiful silk sari

Bharat Natyam, *from Tamil Nadu, has eloquent eye and hand movements* (mudras).

Manipuri, *from the northeast, enacts the legend of Radha and Krishna* (see p179).

Bismillah Khan *played the* shehnai, *a ceremonial reed pipe, which the late maestro popularized into a concert instrument.*

Zakir Hussain *plays the* tabla, *a pair of drums that provide percussion at most music and dance performances.*

Kishori Amonkar *is a leading singer. A concert usually begins with a slow evocation of the raga, followed by an elaboration of the melodic line, and culminating in a fast-paced climax.*

Costumes of India

One of the most remarkable features of Indian apparel is the ingenious way in which a simple length of unstitched cloth is used. Gracefully draped as a sari, or wrapped around the head as a turban, the length of fabric is versatile, and is worn by both men and women. Stitched garments include the *kurta*, pyjama, sherwani, the voluminous skirt *(ghaghara or lehenga)*, and of course, the trouser, shirt and ubiquitous blue jeans. Today, despite the growing influence of contemporary Western fashion trends, most Indians continue to dress traditionally. The sari, particularly, is still worn all over India, even though the style of draping it differs from region to region.

The Veil (odhni *or* dupatta) *is an essential part of dress in conservative societies.*

The sari, *usually 5.5 m (6 yd) long, is tied around the waist, with the pleats tucked into an under-skirt. The* pallav *(end-piece) is either drawn over the left shoulder or draped over the head.*

Safa (turban)

Angavastram is the unstitched mantle draped over the shoulder.

Sari blouse

Sari

Salwar-kameez, *consisting of a baggy pyjama (salwar), a loose tunic (kameez) and* dupatta, *are worn by women in Punjab. This outfit is now worn all over India.*

THE INDIAN WEDDING

Festivals and weddings are glittering events that showcase the range and variety of clothes worn by both men and women in India. Such occasions are what keep traditional customs and attire alive today.

Bracelet-like folds of the *churidar.*

Maharashtrian *women wear 8-m (9-yd) saris in a style very similar to a dhoti. The extra fabric is pleated in front, drawn between the legs and tucked in at the back, to allow freedom of movement.*

In Kerala, *women wear a two-piece sari (mundu-veshti), of which the* mundu *forms the lower garment, while the* veshti *is tucked into the waist to form the* pallav. *Men just wear the lower garment, with an* angavastram.

HEADDRESSES

For Indian men, the most important accessory is the turban, *(pagri* or *safa)*, an unstitched length of cloth that is deftly tied around the head. More than just a fashion statement, the turban's style and colour also indicates the wearer's social, religious, caste and regional status. Rajasthani turbans are intrinsic to the cultural ethos of the land, whereas in Punjab, the Sikh turban is characteristic of their identity as a martial community *(see p103)*. From the mid-19th century onwards, *topis* (caps) became popular, especially among courtiers in the Muslim courts. Even today, men wear plain or ornamental caps in mosques or during festivals.

Topi, **worn by a young Muslim boy**

A turbaned patriarch from Jodhpur, Rajasthan

Choli (tight-fitting blouse)   **Odhni (veil)**   **Kurta**

The bridegroom wears a formal sherwani-*churidar* in ivory silk.

The bride's *lehenga* is red silk, heavily encrusted with gold embroidery.

Sherwani, *a long coat with a high collar, is worn above the* churidar *pyjama, so-called because of the bracelet-* (churi-) *like folds near the ankles.*

The dhoti-kurta *is the traditional male attire and comprises a dhoti* (loincloth) *or* lungi, *either tied around the waist or tucked between the legs. The upper garment is the stitched, long-sleeved* kurta.

Ghaghara, *the ankle-length, gathered skirt worn in Rajasthan and Gujarat, is tied with a drawstring. A* choli *(tight-fitting blouse) is worn on top, while the* odhni *has one end tucked into the waistband and the other taken over the right shoulder to cover the head.*

In Manipur, *women wear the sarong-like* phanek, *while men wear a garment known as the* khudei. *Each tribe, however, is identified by its distinctive colours and stripes. This couple is from the Paite tribe.*

Bollywood's Magic Formula

Hindi films from Bollywood (Bombay or Mumbai) are a fascinating mix of romance, violence, comedy, and tragedy, interspersed with song and dance sequences, and with a clear social or moral message. Ever since its inception in 1899, fashions in Bollywood have swung from mythological epics to action thrillers to family dramas. But the basic *masala* (spicy mix) formula, which appeals to a large and diverse audience, remains unchanged.

Romance *trickles down into almost every plot that a film explores. The hero wooing the heroine always forms a very popular sequence.*

Heroines *add an essential touch of glamour. Slim, fashionable and gorgeously dressed film stars, such as Miss World 1994, Aishwarya Rai, set the standard for feminine beauty and grace.*

Star-studded, high-budget films usually ensure a box-office hit.

Abhishek Bachchan is among India's top young actors.

The hero cult *and Shah Rukh Khan are synonymous. Affectionately called King Khan, he is popular both in India and abroad, even boasting a wax statue at Madame Tussaud's in London. Aishwarya Rai and superstar Amitabh Bachchan share the honour with him.*

THE HINDI FILM INDUSTRY

It costs anywhere between US$1.75 million and $30 million to produce a Bollywood film. The budget is spent on massive fees for the stars, exotic locations, special effects, and on huge promotional campaigns. Of the more than 100 films produced every year, some are dubbed into regional Indian languages, or subtitled in English for international audiences.

Song and dance *sequences range from duets between the hero and heroine to spectacular set pieces with lots of male and female dancers. These are released before the film as music videos for TV, and often become hits, even if the film flops at the box office.*

Family values *form the core of most films. The home can be the scene of great happiness or discord, and in the end everyone comes together.*

Villains *are portrayed as evil incarnate. In* Omkara *(2006), which was based on Shakespeare's* Othello, *the villain is a loyalist turned traitor who seeks to avenge himself at the cost of many innocent lives.*

Violence *can often be of the comic-book variety. Dramatic fights are staged between the hero and villain at the climax, and invariably end with the triumph of good over evil.*

Fashion statements made by Bollywood stars inspire youngsters to follow suit.

The hero usually anchors the film, with the plot and other characters revolving around him. Hrithik Roshan is one of Bollywood's most sought-after stars, with electric good looks and a powerful physique that have earned him a huge fan following.

Aishwarya Rai as the heroine represents the fun-loving, urban, Westernized youth.

NEW WAVE CINEMA

In the 1950s and 60s parallel or "art" cinema was dominated by Satyajit Ray *(see p260)*, whose thought-provoking films portrayed everyday life in Indian villages and small towns. By focusing on realism and social issues rather than fantasy and entertainment, he paved the way for internationally acclaimed directors such as Deepa Mehta and Mira Nair to make films that made an impact on society.

Deepa Mehta with the star cast of her Oscar-nominated film *Water*

Youth, *the prime focus of Bollywood films, saw a paradigm shift with* Rang De Basanti *(2006), a commercial film that didn't just set fashion trends but made a case for a better society with the participation of the younger generation.*

INDIA THROUGH THE YEAR

Indians love celebrations and the year is filled with innumerable fairs and festivals. Almost every day marks a religious or social event celebrated by the diverse religious or local communities, where ritual fasting and feasting go hand in hand. Some festivals are linked to the pantheon of gods and goddesses, others follow the changing seasons and mark pastoral occasions. Some

Orchids in full bloom

commemorate anniversaries and events of national importance such as the Republic Day (*see p75*). Hindu festivals usually follow the lunar calendar and both the full moon (*purnima*) and the new moon (*pradosh*) are considered auspicious. Muslim festivals, too, are determined by the new moon. This means that the dates of most religious festivals vary from year to year. See also special festival columns in each chapter.

Holi celebrations in the area around Mathura

SPRING (FEB–MAR)

From Mid-February to the end of March, spring (Basant) is India's most glorious season with flowers in full bloom and pleasant, not-too-hot temperatures. It is also the main season for weddings, parades, cricket matches, horse racing, flower shows and other events.

Basant Panchami *(Feb)*. Considered to be the first day of spring, Basant is celebrated all over North India. People dress in shades of yellow, echoing the yellow mustard blossoms that are in bloom. In Eastern India, the same day is celebrated as Saraswati *puja*, honouring the Goddess of Learning and Wisdom.

Vasantahabba *(Feb)*, Nrityagram. One of Bangalore's most awaited dance festivals. Acclaimed artistes from all over India

perform from dusk till dawn.

Elephanta Festival *(Feb)*, Elephanta Island. An open air festival of classical dance and music, with performances by renowned artistes.

Kala Ghoda Festival *(Feb)*, Mumbai. A two-week extravaganza of the visual and performing arts is held in Mumbai's main cultural district of Kala Ghoda. The National Gallery of Modern Art and the Jehangir Art Gallery, as well as the area's sidewalks, become venues for sitar and tabla performances, dance recitals and exhibitions of paintings, prints, photographs and installation art.

Nishagandhi Dance Festival *(Feb)*, Thiruvanan-thapuram. Artistes of almost all classical dance

forms perform at the open air Nishagandhi Auditorium.

Shivratri *(Feb/Mar)*. Devotees of Shiva observe the night of his celestial wedding to Parvati.

Delhi Dhrupad Samaroh *(Mar)*, Delhi. Leading exponents of Dhrupad, a classical musical tradition, present a series of recitals.

Holi *(Mar)*. One of the most important Hindu festivals, Holi takes place on a full moon night and marks the end of winter. On the eve of Holi, bonfires are lit, and an effigy of the demon Holika is burnt to signify the triumph of good over evil. The next day, people swarm the streets, sprinkling coloured water and powder (gulal) on each other. This exuberant festival is especially dear to Lord Krishna, and around Mathura, his birthplace (see p178), it is celebrated with great abandon.

Nauchandi Mela *(Mar)*, Meerut. Held around the shrine of a Muslim saint and a temple, this fair has come

Show jumping at the Delhi Horse Show

Namaaz (prayers) being offered during Id-ul-Zuha

to symbolize Hindu-Muslim unity. Its origins date to the late 17th century when local leaders decided to merge festivities held concurrently at both shrines. Today, this is more a fun-filled carnival than a religious event.

Jamshed-e-Navroz *(Mar)*. Celebrated by the Parsi community as their New Year's Day, the festival is named after the Persian king Jamshed, who is believed to have first introduced the solar calendar. Devotees visit fire-temples and make offerings of sandalwood.

Ramnavami *(Mar)*. Nine days of fasting *(navaratris)*, precede the birth of the hero-god Rama *(see p27)* on Ramnavami (the ninth day). During this period, many Hindu households maintain a strict vegetarian diet, and prepare special food cooked in ghee (clarified butter) without garlic or onions.

International Film Festival of Kerala *(Mar/Apr)*, Kerala. This event invites films from around the world, in categories such as world cinema, short films, documentary and Malayalam cinema.

Shankarlal Sangeet Sammelan *(Mar/Apr)*, Delhi. This is the capital's oldest classical vocal and instrumental music festival.

Delhi Horse Show *(Mar/Apr)*, Delhi. A two-day sporting event, where thoroughbred horses from all over the country take part in show-jumping, tent-pegging and dressage events.

Four Square White-Water Rafting Challenge *(Mar/Apr)*, Rishikesh. The premier white-water rafting event in India, this is also one of the richest competitions in the world with a cash prize of US$25,000.

Mahavira Jayanti *(Mar/Apr)*. Jains celebrate the birth of the founder of Jainism, Mahavira *(see p396)*. This is celebrated on a large scale in Rajasthan and Gujarat. Devotees offer prayers to the 24 *tirthankaras*.

Milad-ul-Nabi *(Mar/Apr)*. Prophet Mohammed's birthday is observed with prayers and readings from the holy Koran.

SUMMER (APR–JUN)

From early April until June, the northern plains, and much of the south, undergo a hot and dry summer. By May and June, the heat in the north builds up to a scorching 40° C (104° F) and above – a signal for those who can afford it to move up to the hill stations in the Himalayas. Meanwhile, temperatures in the Deccan Plateau and the south rise to about 38° C (100° F). Most festivities come to a halt.

Baisakhi *(13 Apr)*. This festival heralds the harvest season in the north.

Himachal Hang Gliding Rally *(May)*, Kangra. An

Symbol of National School of Drama

international competition that draws professionals from around the world.

Buddha Jayanti *(May)*. The Buddha was born, attained enlightenment and died on the full moon of the fourth lunar month. Buddhists gather in *viharas* for prayers.

International Flower Festival *(May)*, Gangtok. A rare show of exotic flowering plants found in Sikkim, including almost 500 varieties of orchids.

NSD Repertory Festival *(May/Jun)*, Delhi. This all-India festival is organized by the National School of Drama.

Procession of Buddhist lamas on Buddha Jayanti

Women teams participating in the Nehru Trophy Boat Race, Kerala

MONSOON (JUL–SEP)

July, August and September make up the monsoon season, celebrated in India for the magical transformation of the earth. The south, especially the coastal areas, and the northeast, experience very heavy rains. Rainfall is fairly scanty in the northern plains, which remain hot and humid.

International Mango Festival *(Jul)*, Delhi. Held at the peak of the mango season, over 1,000 varieties of mangoes grown in North India are exhibited and sold at the Talkatora Stadium.

Kanwar Mela *(Jul/Aug)*, Haridwar. The largest religious congregation after the Kumbh *Mela (see p211)*, Thousands of Kanwarias (Shiva devotees), converge for a dip in the Ganges. During this period, devotees are seen travelling by cycle and on foot, carrying gaily decorated *kanwars* (vessels hung on bamboo poles).

Independence Day *(15 Aug)*. This is a national holiday, commemorating India's freedom from British rule in 1947. The Prime Minister addresses the nation from the ramparts of the historic Red Fort in Delhi.

Raksha Bandhan *(Aug)*. Young girls tie sacred threads *(rakhis)* on their brothers' wrists as a token of love, and receive in exchange gifts and a promise of everlasting protection.

Bangalore Flower Show *(Aug)*, Bangalore. A spectacular flower show is held in the Glass House of the Lalbagh Gardens.

Nehru Trophy Boat Race *(Aug)*, Kerala. About 40 lavishly decorated snake boats *(see p633)* take part in a thrilling race at Alappuzha.

Janmashtami *(Aug/Sep)*. The birth of Lord Krishna is celebrated with abandon. Festivities reach their peak at midnight, while the day is given to fasting. The merrymaking in Mathura *(see p178)* and Brindavan *(see p179)* is especially grand.

A gaudy modern day rakhi

WINTER (OCT–FEB)

This is the most perfect season. The monsoon is over, and the days now begin to grow cooler. It is also the most auspicious period in the Indian calendar and ushers in a number of festivals. Winter also marks the sowing of crops such as mustard and wheat. The chill is at its worst in the northern plains and hills between mid-December and mid-January, and though temperatures often fall below 3° C (37° F), the days are sunny. The southern region does not experience very low winter temperatures, the minimum being around 19° C (66° F).

Dussehra *(Sep/Oct)*. For nine days, episodes from the *Ramayana (see p27)* depicting Rama's adventures against Ravana are enacted. The tenth day, Vijaya Dashami, celebrates Rama's defeat of Ravana, and huge effigies of the demon-king, his brother and son are burnt. In Delhi, the Shriram Bharatiya Kala Kendra's month-long dance-drama encapsulates the epic. Bengalis celebrate Durga Puja *(see p281)* at this time.

Gandhi Jayanti *(2 Oct)*. Mahatma Gandhi's birthday is widely celebrated as a national holiday.

Id-ul-Fitr *(Oct)*. This festival marks the end of Ramzan or Ramadan, the 40-day long period of fasting for Muslims, that marks the period when the Prophet received the message of the Koran from Allah. The actual day varies

Huge effigies of Ravana and his son during Dussehra, Delhi

according to the sightings of the new moon. A special *namaaz* is held at Delhi's Jami Masjid. It is also called Mithi (sweet) Id, as *sewian,* a delicacy made with sweetened vermicelli, is prepared on the occasion.

Diwali *(Oct/Nov).* Oil lamps illuminate each home to commemorate Rama's return to Ayodhya after 14 years of exile. Firecrackers are lit and sweets exchanged. Every locality holds Diwali *melas.*

Pushkar Fair *(Oct/Nov),* Pushkar. Asia's largest camel, horse and cattle fair takes place in this pilgrim town.

Guru Parab *(Nov).* On the first full moon night after Diwali, Sikhs celebrate the birthday of Guru Nanak, the founder of Sikhism.

Prithvi International Theatre Festival *(Nov),* Mumbai. Prithvi Theatre is one of Mumbai's best known theatres. This week-long festival brings international theatre groups to the city, who perform a variety of contemporary plays, along with a handful of Indian theatre groups.

International Trade Fair *(14–21 Nov),* Delhi. In this major event for Indian industry, goods manufactured in India and abroad are exhibited at Pragati Maidan. Cultural events are also held in the fair grounds.

International Film Festival of India *(Nov/Dec),* Goa. India's premier film event, showcasing state-of-the-art films by Indian as well as international directors.

Madras Music Festival *(Dec),* Chennai. The city celebrates its rich heritage of Carnatic music and dance with recitals by numerous well-known artistes.

Id-ul-Zuha *(Dec).* The Muslim feast of sacrifice popularly known as Bakr Id, commemorates Abraham's willingness to sacrifice his own son, Ismail. Since then, a goat is sacrificed to Allah

Immaculate vintage cars at the Kolkata rally

on this day, prayers are offered in mosques and special delicacies are served.

Mamallapuram Dance Festival *(Jan/Feb),* Mamallapuram. Leading Indian classical dancers, perform Bharat Natyam, Kuchipudi, Kathakali and Odissi against a backdrop of the famous Pallava rock-cut sculptures.

Lohri *(13 Jan),* Punjab. Bonfires and merriment mark what is believed to be the coldest day in winter.

Makar Sankranti *(14 Jan),* Jaipur. Kites are flown to celebrate the return of the sun from the Equator to the Tropic of Capricorn. This day coincides with the Tamil festival of Pongal *(see p589).*

Decorative paper kite

Republic Day *(26 Jan).* A national holiday. Pomp and pageantry mark India's birth as an independent republic. In Delhi, a colourful military parade is held at Rajpath.

Beating of the Retreat *(29 Jan),* Delhi. This beautiful

ceremony recalls the end of the day's battle when armies retreated to their camps. A grand display of regimental bands perform against the spectacular backdrop of North and South Blocks. As the sun sets, a bugle sounds the retreat, fireworks are lit and the buildings are framed with fairylights.

Vintage and Classic Car Rally *(Jan),* Kolkata. *The Statesman* group of newspapers organizes this event when vintage cars, or the "grand old ladies", are flagged off on a short race. Their owners often dress up in period costumes. A similar rally is held in Delhi, in March each year.

Thyagaraja Aradhana Festival *(Jan),* Thiruvaiyaru. An eight-day music festival is held in honour of the saint composer Thyagaraja, attracting eminent musicians from all over the country.

Island Tourism Festival *(Jan/Feb),* Port Blair. A ten-day festival of dance, theatre and music reflects the multi-cultural population of the Andaman Islands. There are also exhibitions of local crafts, flora and marine life.

Desert Festival *(Jan/Feb),* Jaisalmer. A cultural festival, held on the sand dunes over three days, with camel races, camel polo, folk dances and music performances.

Bagpipers of an army regiment at the Beating of the Retreat ceremony

The Climate of India

Summer, monsoon and winter, with a brief but glorious spring and autumn, span the seasons in India. The climate changes with latitude and geographical location. In the north, temperatures soar in the vast Gangetic Plains, though the Himalayan belt remains pleasantly cool in summer. In winter, the high mountain passes remain snowbound. The central Deccan and deep south, however, have a tropical monsoon climate, with high temperatures and virtually no winter. India's coastal belts, on the other hand, remain humid and warm, with torrential rain. The semi-arid regions of Rajasthan and Kutch, as well as the rain shadow areas east of the Western Ghats, are among the country's worst drought hit areas, while the coasts and the northeast states, face the full onslaught of the monsoon, and are devastated by cyclones and floods each year.

Giant cacti growing in the arid Thar Desert, Jaisalmer

This arid region receives little rainfall.

India's highest temperatures, recorded in the Thar Desert in Rajasthan, rise above 48° C (118° F).

Srina

Jaisalmer   Jaipu

KEY

- ☐ Tropical rainy region: consistently high temperatures and heavy summer rainfall.
- ☐ Humid subtropical region: hot summer followed by heavy rainfall. Dry winter.
- ☐ Tropical savannah region: long, dry season with high summer temperatures. Mild winter.
- ☐ Tropical and subtropical steppe region: semi-arid. Low and erratic rainfall leading to drought.
- ☐ Tropical desert region: high summer and very low winter temperatures. Scanty rainfall.
- ☐ Mountain region: cold and dry climate. Short summer.
- ☐ Mountain region: cold, humid winter. Short summer.

JAIPUR

	°C/°F			
	37/99	34/93	33/91	
		26/79		22/72
	21/70		18/64	
				8/46

☼	9.3 hrs	4.4 hrs	9.6 hrs	8.6 hrs
☂	4.2 mm	193 mm	19.3 mm	14 mm
month	Apr	Jul	Oct	Jan

MUMBAI

	°C/°F			
	32/90	30/86	32/90	29/84
	25/77	25/77	25/77	
				19/66

☼	9.6 hrs	2.5 hrs	8.3 hrs	9.1 hrs
☂	2.8 hrs	710 hrs	88 hrs	2 hrs
month	Apr	Jul	Oct	Jan

Mumbai

ARABIAN SEA

Torrential showers typify Kerala's monsoon

THE MONSOON

The word monsoon, from the Arabic *mawsim* (season), refers to South Asia's seasonal moisture-laden winds. In India, the Southwest Monsoon hits Kerala in end May. Simultaneously, one branch sweeps across the Bay of Bengal towards the Eastern Himalayas and the northeast, while the other, deflected westwards by the vast Himalayan barrier, moves towards the Gangetic Plains and gradually spreads across the mainland. At the end of September, the Southwest Monsoon begins to retreat southwards, and during October and November, southern Andhra Pradesh and the eastern coast of Tamil Nadu receive heavy rain. Nothing in India is awaited more eagerly than these annual rains; and songs and poems celebrate the months of Sawan and Bhadon (July and August), as a time of renewal and hope.

Lakshadweep Islands

Thiruvananthapu

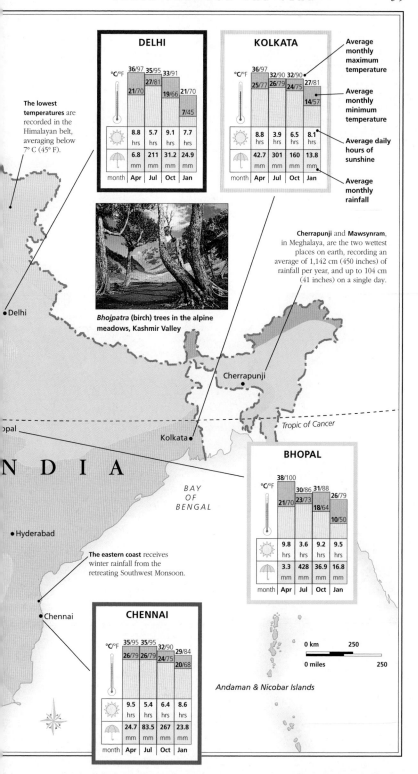

DELHI

°C/°F	36/97	35/95	33/91	
	21/70	27/81	19/66	21/70
				7/45
☀	8.8 hrs	5.7 hrs	9.1 hrs	7.7 hrs
☂	6.8 mm	211 mm	31.2 mm	24.9 mm
month	Apr	Jul	Oct	Jan

KOLKATA

°C/°F	36/97	32/90	32/90	
	25/77	26/79	24/75	27/81
				14/57
☀	8.8 hrs	3.9 hrs	6.5 hrs	8.1 hrs
☂	42.7 mm	301 mm	160 mm	13.8 mm
month	Apr	Jul	Oct	Jan

Average monthly maximum temperature

Average monthly minimum temperature

Average daily hours of sunshine

Average monthly rainfall

The lowest temperatures are recorded in the Himalayan belt, averaging below 7° C (45° F).

Bhojpatra (birch) trees in the alpine meadows, Kashmir Valley

Cherrapunji and **Mawsynram**, in Meghalaya, are the two wettest places on earth, recording an average of 1,142 cm (450 inches) of rainfall per year, and up to 104 cm (41 inches) on a single day.

• Delhi

Cherrapunji •

Tropic of Cancer

opal

Kolkata •

I N D I A

BAY OF BENGAL

• Hyderabad

The eastern coast receives winter rainfall from the retreating Southwest Monsoon.

BHOPAL

°C/°F	38/100	30/86	31/88	
	21/70	23/73	18/64	26/79
				10/50
☀	9.8 hrs	3.6 hrs	9.2 hrs	9.5 hrs
☂	3.3 mm	428 mm	36.9 mm	16.8 mm
month	Apr	Jul	Oct	Jan

CHENNAI

°C/°F	35/95	35/95	32/90	
	26/79	26/79	24/75	29/84
				20/68
☀	9.5 hrs	5.4 hrs	6.4 hrs	8.6 hrs
☂	24.7 mm	83.5 mm	267 mm	23.8 mm
month	Apr	Jul	Oct	Jan

• Chennai

Andaman & Nicobar Islands

0 km 250
0 miles 250

THE HISTORY OF INDIA

*he name India comes from "Indoi", a Greek word for the
people who lived beyond the Indus river. The roots of Indian
civilization lie in the country's precise and awesome natural
boundaries, formed by the Himalayas in the north, and seas to the
east, south and west. These have fostered a remarkable physical and
cultural unity, despite the size and diversity of the area they enclose.*

INDUS VALLEY CIVILIZATION

Prehistoric sites in India date
back to at least 250,000
BC, with agricultural settlements appearing around
7000 BC. By 2500 BC, a
sophisticated urban civilization
emerged, stretching across the
Indus Valley and northwest India,
all the way down to Gujarat. Its
main cities were marked by
solid brick structures, roads in
a grid pattern, and elaborate
drainage systems. Stone seals
with an as yet undeciphered
script, and standardized weights and
measures were among the artifacts
found in this culture (also known as
Harappan Civilization), which had a
thriving trade with Mesopotamia.
Remains of two of these cities can
be seen at Lothal and Dholavira in
Gujarat. By 1800 BC, these cities
declined, perhaps because of
tectonic or ecological changes.

**Dancing girl,
2500 BC**

THE VEDIC AGE

Around 1500 BC, a people commonly
known as Aryans, who were
probably migrants from Central Asia,
settled in the Indus region. Described
in the *Rig Veda*, a Sanskrit text of that
period, they had a mixed pastoral

and agrarian economy. Three later
Vedas, written between 1000–600
BC, and associated Sanskrit
texts, record the extension of
their settlements across the
Gangetic Valley. This was also
the time of the *Mahabharata*
epic *(see p26)*, which
describes a great war between
two clans.

While the Rig Vedic religion
worshipped nature gods, the
deities of the later Vedic
period were more complex.
Later Vedic literature
included a remarkable set of
Sanskrit treatises called the
Upanishads, which advocated a
philosophical quest for truth,
through enquiry. By this period, a
social structure based on the caste
system had developed. It was earlier
occupational, but was now
becoming hereditary and
increasingly rigid. At the apex were
the Brahmins or priests, followed by
the *kshatriyas* (rulers and warriors).
Below them were *vaishyas* (farmers
and traders), and *shudras* (servants
and labourers). Sacrifices and rituals
to appease the gods were prescribed by the Vedas, and became a
part of daily life.

TIMELINE

Early Stone Age relics		**1500 BC** Aryans migrate to northwest India	**1000–600 BC** Later Vedic Age. Painted Grey Ware and iron used		*Megalithic stone dolmens, South India*
	6000–1000 BC Neolithic or New Stone Age				
7000 BC	**6000**		**1000**	**900**	**600**
		2500–1800 BC Harappan culture flourishes in the Indus Valley	**1200 BC** Iron discovered	**950 BC** Mahabharata war supposed to have been fought	
8000–4000 BC Mesolithic or Intermediate Stone Age	*Indus Valley seal*	**1800–800 BC** Farming communities emerge	**1500–1000 BC** Period of the *Rig Veda*		**1000 BC–AD100** Megalithic grave sites in southern India

◁ **Miniature painting of the Battle of Panipat, 1526, which established the Mughal dynasty in India**

THE AGE OF MAHAVIRA AND BUDDHA

The 6th century BC saw the rise of several urban centres in the north, accompanied by widespread trade. Urbanization led to changes in social stratification, and encouraged the emergence of new religious sects which challenged Brahmin dominance. Chief among these were Buddhism and Jainism, founded respectively by Gautama Siddhartha (566–486 BC) who became the Buddha, and Vardhamana Mahavira (540–467 BC). These religions gained popularity as they had neither caste nor sacrifice, and were open to everyone, including women. The Buddha's simple yet profound teachings *(see p221)* had particularly wide appeal. Mahavira believed in an ascetic life accompanied by truth and non-acquisitiveness *(see p396)*. Both religions disregarded god, discussed the laws of the universe, and advocated ahimsa – not harming any living being. Merchants, traders and others who adopted these religions gained new social status.

Ajanta painting of the Buddha with a monk

THE MAURYAN EMPIRE

The first empire in India was founded in 321 BC when Chandragupta Maurya, an unknown adventurer, defeated the ruling Nanda dynasty of Magadha (in Bihar) and established an empire extending down to the Narmada river in the Deccan.

Lion capital of Ashokan pillar

Chandragupta's grandson, Ashoka (269–232 BC) became one of India's greatest rulers, extending the Mauryan Empire to reach from Afghanistan to Karnataka. But after his bloody conquest of Kalinga *(see p309)*, Ashoka gave up violence and became a great patron of Buddhism. He recorded his ethical code on rocks and pillars all over his vast empire, enjoining his subjects to respect others' religions, give liberally to charity and avoid the killing of animals. These edicts were written in the Brahmi script, from which most Indian scripts have evolved. Ashoka also built many stupas enshrining Buddhist relics, including the one at Sanchi *(see pp244–5)*.

CENTRAL ASIAN INVADERS

After Ashoka, the Mauryan Empire soon declined. Local kingdoms arose across North India, while from the northwest a series of invaders, all from Central Asia, established successive dynasties. These included

TIMELINE

566–486 BC Age of Buddha	**327–325** Alexander the Great invades northwest India but soon retreats	**321 BC** Accession of Chandragupta Maurya, founder of Mauryan dynasty	**269–232 BC** Ashoka's reign

189–75 BC Rule of Shunga dynasty

500 BC	400 BC	300 BC	200 BC	100 BC

540–467 BC Age of Mahavira

Jain votive plaque from Mathura

315 BC Megasthenes, the Greek writer, visits India

260 BC Ashoka's conquest of Kalinga (now Orissa)

165 BC Menander, Indo-Greek king, rules in northwest India

100 BC–AD 220 Rule of Satavahanas in Deccan

the Indo-Greeks from Bactria (200–80 BC), the Scythians or Shakas with many branches (from 80 BC), the Parthians (1st century AD), and the Kushanas (AD 50–300). The territory of Kanishka, the greatest Kushana king, covered the northwest, Kashmir, and most of the Gangetic Valley. He too was a patron of Buddhism. Mahayana Buddhism developed at this time, reflected in two great schools of art, with Buddha sculptures in the Graeco-Roman Gandhara style in the northwest, and in a more indigenous style at Mathura.

As the Kushanas declined, the Gupta dynasty emerged in northern India, to establish another great empire (AD 320–500). The Gupta period saw a great cultural flowering, with fine sculptures, classical Sanskrit poetry and drama,

Buddha head, Gupta period

and learned treatises on mathematics and astronomy produced at this time. In religion, the two Hindu sects of Vaishnavism and Shaivism (followers of Vishnu and Shiva) became prominent, and the Buddhist university of Nalanda was established (see pp218–19). But inroads by the Huns, marauding tribes from Central Asia, contributed to the decline of the Guptas after AD 450.

The next major empire was established by Harsha (AD 606–647) at Kanauj. His long and enlightened rule is described by the Chinese traveller Hiuen Tsang (see p219).

RULERS IN THE SOUTH

Meanwhile, in the Deccan region, numerous dynasties arose after the decline of the Mauryas. They included the Satavahanas (100

BC–AD 220), and the Ikshvakus (AD 225–310) in the eastern Deccan, under whom Buddhist stupas were constructed at Amravati (see p675) and Nagarjunakonda (see p676). Another Deccan dynasty were the Vakatakas (AD 250–550), during whose reign many of the superb sculptures and paintings at Ajanta (see pp479–81) were made. In the western Deccan, the Chalukyas came to power and built great temples at Badami (see pp536–7), Pattadakal (see pp538–9) and Aihole (see pp540–41). Their most powerful ruler, Pulakeshin II (AD 608–642), defeated Harsha, and stopped his southward advance.

In the far south, the three kingdoms of the Cheras (now Kerala), Cholas and Pandyas ruled between 400 BC and AD 400. The people of this region were of non-Aryan origin and were known as Dravids. Another major dynasty in the south were the early Pallavas, who ruled from AD 275–550, with their capital at Kanchipuram. During these centuries, cities, craft guilds, and inland and foreign trade flourished across India. The South Indian kingdoms grew rich on trade with Rome till AD 300, exporting luxury goods such as spices, fine silks, precious gems, and exotic creatures such as monkeys and peacocks.

The Drunken Courtesan, 2nd-century Kushana panel

4th-century Iron pillar, Delhi

AD 52 St Thomas in India	250–300 Buddhist stupas of Nagarjunakonda and Amravati are built	300–399 *Ramayana* and *Mahabharata* are compiled 320–500 Gupta dynasty	476 Birth of Aryabhata, great astronomer and mathematician	606–647 Harsha's reign 630–644 Hiuen Tsang in India
AD 100	**200**	**300**	**400**	**500**	**600**

| AD 78–110 Reign of Kushana king Kanishka | *Statue of Kanishka* | 335–375 Reign of Samudra Gupta
Gold coin of Samudra Gupta | 450 Hun invasions begin | 608–642 Reign of Pulakeshin II, Chalukyan king |

Ceremonial procession of a Rajput prince

NORTHERN KINGDOMS (AD 750–1200)

Kanauj, once the capital of Harsha's empire, centrally located in the Gangetic Plains, had by 750 become the focus of conflict between three major dynasties – the Pratiharas, the Rashtrakutas and the Palas. The Pratiharas were a Rajput clan who ruled in Rajasthan and Malwa, while the Rashtrakutas (740–973) ruled in the northern Deccan. The Palas (750–1150), who were a Buddhist dynasty, ruled Bengal. Each captured Kanauj for a short while, but finally around 836, the Pratiharas gained control and held it for nearly two centuries. Soon other Rajput clans began to establish independent kingdoms.

The origins of the Rajputs are shrouded in mystery, but they are known from the 7th century AD in Western India. Some of them may have been descended from Central Asian tribes who settled in India in the wake of the Hun invasions *(see p43)*. They called themselves *rajaputra* or "sons of kings", and their 36 clans claimed descent from the sun and moon, from fire, or from mythical ancestors, in order to enhance their political

Woman writing a letter, Khajuraho

and social status. Early Rajput dynasties included the Paramaras in Malwa, the Solankis in Gujarat, the Tomars in Delhi, the Chandelas in Central India, and the Chauhans in Rajasthan, whose best known king, Prithviraj, is still extolled in Rajasthani ballads for his legendary valour and chivalry. During this period, independent kingdoms also existed in Kashmir, the northwest, the northeast, and in Orissa, where the Eastern Ganga dynasty, builders of the great temples at Konark and Puri *(see pp310–12)* ruled.

All these Rajput and non-Rajput dynasties fought frequent wars with each other to gain control of strategic areas, setting the stage for their downfall – they would be unable to form a united front to defend themselves against outside attack. In between wars, however, the rulers and princes lived in great luxury, in grand forts and richly ornamented palaces. Agriculture was well-developed, with over 100 types of cereals cultivated. Trade with the Arab lands flourished, bringing new prosperity to cities, merchants and craftsmen, and leading to the emergence of many new towns. This period also saw a flowering of literature, as well as sculpture and temple architecture. Outstanding examples, apart from those in Orissa, are the Khajuraho temples of the Chandelas *(see pp236–7)*, the Modhera Sun Temple *(see pp418–19)* and the Dilwara marble temples *(see p394)*, which were built under the Solankis of Gujarat.

TIMELINE

Rajput shield with sun emblem

700
Arab merchants arrive in Western India

783–1036
Pratiharas rule Rajasthan and Kanauj

871–1216
Rule of Imperial Cholas of Thanjavur

700	750	800	850	900

736
Dhillika (Delhi) founded by Tomars

740–973
Rule of Rashtrakutas of the Deccan

750–1150
Palas rule Bengal and Bihar

800 Adi Shankaracharya preaches his philosophy

900–1192
Rule of Western Gangas, builders of Shravana Belagola

916–1203
Rule of Chandelas, builders of Khajuraho

SOUTHERN DYNASTIES (AD 600–1200)

In the Deccan and South India too several dynasties existed between 600 and 1200. A new Pallava dynasty had risen to power in the 6th century, at Kanchipuram. In 642, the Pallava ruler Narasimha Varman I defeated and killed the Chalukya king Pulakeshin II, after which the great Chalukya kingdom declined.

In the late 9th century, the Cholas *(see pp46–7)*, who had gone into decline in the 4th century, reasserted their power. They defeated the Pallavas, the Western Ganga dynasty which ruled near Mysore, and the Pandyas of Madurai, and established their supremacy in the south. They would later be challenged by the Hoysalas of Karnataka *(see p523)* who came to power in the 12th century.

As in northern India in this period, trade flourished in the south, despite constant wars. The Pallavas' maritime trade extended as far as Cambodia, Annam, Java, Sumatra, Malaysia and China.

In religion, this was a period of questioning and ferment. From the 7th century, itinerant Tamil poet-saints known as Alvaras and Nayannars, devotees of Vishnu and Shiva respectively, preached against caste divisions and orthodox Brahmanical practices, and emphasized a personal union with god through love and devotion *(bhakti)*. Their teachings had great popular appeal. Other influential sages were Adi Shankaracharya *(see p648)* who travelled across the country, elaborating on the ideas contained in the *Upanishads (see p41)* and challenging Buddhism, Jainism and the *bhakti* cult; and the 11th-century philosopher Ramanuja, who expanded on Shankaracharya's teachings. By the 12th century, with the reforms and revival that had taken place in Hinduism, Buddhism went into decline, except in Eastern India.

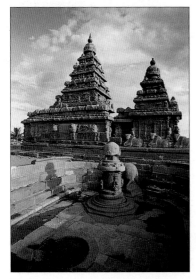

Great monuments were built in the Deccan and South India in this period, among them the magnificent temples of the Pallavas at Mamallapuram *(see pp578–81)* and Kanchipuram *(see p582)*, and the monolithic image of the Jain saint Bahubali at Shravana Belagola *(see p522)* erected by the Western Ganga kings. In the south-west, the superb rock-cut Kailasanatha Temple *(see pp476–7)* was built at Ellora by the Rashtrakutas.

Bronze image of a Nayannar saint, 13th century

The Shore Temple of the Pallavas, Mamallapuram

Image of Surya from Konark

	974–1233 Rule of Paramaras of Malwa	998–1030 Invasions of Mahmud of Ghazni	1032 Adinatha Temple, Mount Abu, built under Solankis		1110–1342 Hoysala rule	1192 Prithviraj Chauhan defeated by Muhammad of Ghur
950		**AD 1000**	**1050**	**1100**	**1150**	**1200**
973–1192 Rule of Chauhans of Ajmer	974–1238 Rule of Solankis of Gujarat	1050 Ramanuja preaches his Vaishnava philosophy	1076–1438 Eastern Gangas of Orissa build Konark and Puri		*Prithviraj Chauhan*	

The Chola Dynasty

Between the 9th and 13th centuries, South India was dominated by the Chola dynasty, whose extensive empire covered much of peninsular India. Their two greatest kings were Rajaraja I (985–1014) and Rajendra I (1014–1044), under whom literature, architecture and sculpture reached new heights. They built magnificent temples, endowed with land and enormous wealth, and these became the focal point of their economy, as well as their social and cultural life. In 1216, the Cholas were defeated by the Pandyas, who then became the dominant power in South India.

Chola queen

King Rajaraja I
The first great Chola king, Rajaraja I (left) *subdued other southern kingdoms and conquered Sri Lanka.*

Infrastructure
The Cholas' irrigation dams on the Kaveri river (see p601) ensured the fertility of their lands. Civil and military officials, provincial chieftains, and elected village committees formed part of their efficient administration.

Wrestlers formed part of the Chola army.

Two faces of a copper coin of Rajaraja I

CHOLA WARRIORS
This panel from the temple at Darasuram *(see p593)* celebrates the martial skills of the Cholas. Rajaraja I had a huge army of 31 regiments, which included elephant and horse cavalry, as well as foot soldiers.

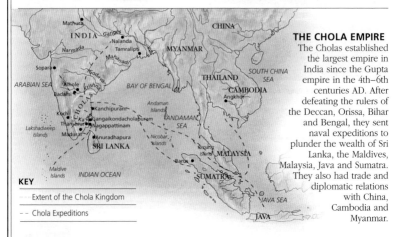

THE CHOLA EMPIRE
The Cholas established the largest empire in India since the Gupta empire in the 4th–6th centuries AD. After defeating the rulers of the Deccan, Orissa, Bihar and Bengal, they sent naval expeditions to plunder the wealth of Sri Lanka, the Maldives, Malaysia, Java and Sumatra. They also had trade and diplomatic relations with China, Cambodia and Myanmar.

KEY

--- Extent of the Chola Kingdom

-- Chola Expeditions

THE HISTORY OF INDIA

Architecture
The Brihadishvara Temple (see pp598–9) at Thanjavur, King Rajaraja I's capital, represents the zenith of Chola temple architecture, which is distinguished by its monumental scale and towering sculpted spires and gateways.

Sculpture
This Ardhanarishvara *(half man, half woman) image of Shiva, symbolizing the union of male and female aspects, exemplifies the superb grace of Chola bronze sculpture (see p566). Other famous sculptures portray princely queens, princely warriors, scenes from Shaivite texts, and Shiva as Nataraja, the God of Dance.*

Soldiers
used swords and shields with great skill.

Religion
The Chola kings, who spent lavishly on religion, worshipped Shiva, but Vishnu worship was also popular in South India. This stone sculpture of Harihara, a composite of Shiva and Vishnu, symbolizes a bridge between the two sects.

Seat of Power
Gangaikondacholapuram (see p592) was built in 1035 by King Rajendra I as his new capital, after his successful military expedition to the Gangetic Valley in northern India. The temple here, watched over by Shiva's bull Nandi, also served as a treasury, and a cultural and educational centre.

Dance and Music
Hundreds of musicians and dancers performed at the Chola temples every evening, under royal patronage.

THE COMING OF ISLAM (1206–1555)

Constant internal warfare between the different kingdoms, in the north as well as the south, had left them vulnerable to outside attack. From the 11th century, a volatile political situation in Central Asia, coupled with tales of India's fabulous wealth, fuelled a new wave of invasions by Muslim Turkic rulers from the northwest. Many of them stayed on in India to found dynasties, and with them came soldiers, scholars and merchants, artists and Sufi preachers, who brought new ideas in art, architecture, theology and warfare from the Islamic world. These were to have a lasting impact on religion, art, culture and history in the Indian sub-continent.

Ceramic tile detail, Lodi period

The first major invader was Mahmud of Ghazni who raided India repeatedly between 998–1030, and took back vast wealth from its temples. He was followed by Muhammad of Ghur, who conquered Punjab and Delhi, and established his control over areas earlier dominated by Rajputs, after defeating Prithviraj Chauhan in 1192. He was succeeded by his slave, Qutbuddin Aibak (1206–1210), who founded the first of many Muslim dynasties, collectively known as the Delhi Sul-tanate. Qutbuddin built the towering Qutb Minar in Delhi. His successors included Iltutmish and Balban (see p93). Next came the Khiljis (1290–1320), whose ruler Alauddin conquered Gujarat, Rajasthan and Bengal, and made the kings of the Deccan and South India his tributaries. After the Khiljis came the Tughluqs (1320–1414), whose second ruler, Muhammad bin Tughluq, completed the conquest of the Deccan (see p475) and South India, and annexed them. But he was unable to maintain control over these distant areas, which soon began to reassert their independence. This process was accelerated by the devastating invasion of northern India by Timur of Samarkand in 1398, which further weakened the power of the Delhi Sultans. The last two Sultanate dynasties, the Sayyids (1413–1451) and the Lodis (1451–1526), were riven with infighting among their nobles, and had only a tenuous hold over their territories.

INDEPENDENT KINGDOMS

During the early years of the Delhi Sultans, a number of independent kingdoms, such as the Solankis in Gujarat, the Eastern Gangas in Orissa, and the Kakatiyas, Pandyas and Hoysalas of the Deccan and South India had been absorbed into the Sultanate. However, as the Tughluqs began to decline, many new independent states emerged. In 1336, the Hindu Vijaya-nagar Empire (see pp530–31) in southern India established its independence,

The 13th-century Qutb Minar in Delhi

TIMELINE

Tughluq coin

Sultanate weaponry

| 1206–1290 Rule of first dynasty of Delhi Sultans | 1288–93 Venetian traveller Marco Polo visits South India | | 1336–1565 Vijayanagar Empire | |
| | 1228 Ahoms rule in Assam | 1320–1414 Rule of Tughluqs | 1347–1518 Bahmani kingdom | |

| 1250 | 1300 | 1350 | 1400 | 1450 |

	1296–1316 Reign of Alauddin Khilji	1327 Transfer of capital from Delhi to Daulatabad	1398 Timur's invasion	1440–1518 Kabir, saint-poet of the *bhakti* movement
1206–1210 Qutbuddin Aibak builds the Qutb Minar			1394–1505 Rule of Sharqis of Jaunpur	
			1345–1538 Rule of Ilyas Shahis of Bengal	

The 14th-century Sufi saint Nizamuddin

while in 1347 the Muslim kingdom of the Bahmani sultans was founded in the Deccan, by a Tughluq noble. By the early 16th century, the Bahmani kingdom had broken up into the five smaller Muslim kingdoms of Bijapur, Ahmadnagar, Golconda, Berar and Bidar. In 1565, the combined forces of three of these kingdoms defeated the Vijayanagar forces, after which this powerful Hindu empire declined.

Meanwhile, as the Delhi Sultanate declined, its nobles and governors rebelled and founded their own kingdoms in Bengal (1388), Gujarat (1407), Mandu (1401) and Jaunpur (1408). In northeast India, the Ahoms who had migrated from Myanmar in 1228, established a kingdom in Assam *(see p332)*. In Rajasthan too, several Rajput kingdoms, such as Mewar *(see p398)* and Marwar *(see p380)*, reasserted their independence.

NEW CULTURAL INFLUENCES

Despite the turbulence throughout India between the 13th and 15th centuries, several new methods and technologies in agriculture, irrigation, administration, arts and crafts were introduced, many of them by the Muslim rulers. Trade flourished with Iran, the Arab countries, Southeast Asia, China and Europe, and a 14th-century historian records that Delhi was the largest city in the eastern Islamic world. The mosques, tombs and forts built by the Delhi Sultans ushered in new trends in architecture; and distinct regional styles, fusing Islamic and Hindu elements, developed at places such as Ahmedabad, Mandu, and the Muslim kingdoms of the Deccan.

In religion, mystical Sufi sects of Islam and saint-poets of the *bhakti* movement, such as Meerabai and Kabir, popularized the practice of religion as devotion to god, rejecting caste hierarchies. Guru Nanak (1494–1530) founded the Sikh religion *(see p103)*, taking elements from the *bhakti* movement and Islam.

THE COMING OF THE MUGHALS

In 1526 Babur, a Central Asian prince descended from Timur, and a brilliant military campaigner, marched into India, overthrew the Lodis at the historic battle of Panipat, and laid the foundations of the Mughal Empire. Mughal rule was briefly interrupted when Babur's son Humayun was overthrown in 1540 by an Afghan chieftain, Sher Shah Sur. But Humayun regained his throne in 1555, and it was left to his son Akbar to consolidate and expand the Mughal Empire. The next two emperors, Jahangir and Shah Jahan, left a legacy of magnificent art and architecture. Aurangzeb, the last great Mughal, expanded the empire by adding new territories in the south.

Frieze of an elephant hunt from Hampi, Vijayanagar

Bara Gumbad, a 15th-century Lodi tomb

1500	1550	1600	1650	1700
1451–1526 Reign of Lodi sultans of Delhi	**1555** Reconquest of Delhi by Humayun	**1643** Shah Jahan begins Taj Mahal	**1674** Shivaji crowned Chhatrapati	
1469–1539 Guru Nanak, founder of Sikhism	**1571–85** Akbar builds Fatehpur Sikri		**1690** Calcutta founded by Job Charnock	
1498 Portuguese Vasco da Gama reaches Calicut	**1540** Sher Shah Sur defeats Humayun and takes Delhi	**1600** Queen Elizabeth I grants charter to East India Company	**1661** Bombay transferred from the Portuguese to the English	
1526 Babur defeats Ibrahim Lodi at Panipat	**1530** Humayun succeeds Babur	**1556** Akbar becomes Mughal emperor		

The Great Mughals

Mughal helmet

The Mughals, like their contemporaries the Ottomans of Turkey, the Safavids of Iran and the Tudors of England, were a powerful and influential dynasty. They ruled India for over 300 years, their empire extending at its height from Kandahar in the northwest to Bengal in the east, and from Kashmir in the north to the Deccan in the south. Great patrons of literature, architecture, and arts and crafts, which reached new heights under their patronage, the Mughals established a rich pluralistic culture, blending the best of Islamic and Hindu traditions.

Decorative Arts
Sumptuous objects, such as this blue glass and gold enamelled hookah base, were made in the royal Mughal workshops.

A nobleman presents a gift to the emperor.

Court robes and turbans indicated status and religion.

Rajput princes were loyal allies.

Diwan-i-Khas was the special audience hall.

Emperor Akbar
The greatest Mughal, Akbar (r.1556–1605) was a brilliant administrator and enlightened ruler. He built the city of Fatehpur Sikri (see pp180–83).

Weaponry
War elephants formed an important part of the Mughal army. They were controlled and commanded with sharp but beautifully crafted goads.

Mughal Coins
Gold mohurs struck during the reigns of Akbar and his son Jahangir are renowned for their fine calligraphy.

The Nine Jewels
Akbar gathered at his court brilliant men from different professions, whom he called his "nine jewels". They included the musician Tansen (centre) who, it is said, could light a lamp with the power of his voice.

Political Alliances
Raja Man Singh I of Amber gave his daughter in marriage to Akbar, beginning a tradition of Mughal-Rajput alliances that would bring peace and prosperity to the Mughal Empire.

Nur Jahan
A formidable combination of brains and beauty, Jahangir's Persian-born queen (b.1577) was the real power behind the throne.

Architecture
A monument of ethereal beauty, built by Shah Jahan for his wife, the Taj Mahal (see pp172–5) represents the zenith of Mughal architecture.

Jewellery
The legendary wealth of the Mughals included fabulous jewellery, such as this pendant encrusted with large, flawless diamonds.

Illuminated Manuscripts
Works of literature, history and biography were produced on gilded paper with beautiful calligraphy and illustrations.

Shah Jahan on his splendid throne.

SHAH JAHAN'S COURT
The splendour of the Mughal court is illustrated in this 17th-century painting of Emperor Shah Jahan, with his nobles grouped in strict hierarchical order around the throne. Mughal emperors, whose capitals were at Agra and later Delhi, used glittering court rituals and pageantry to display their supreme authority, as they took stock of the state of affairs in their empire.

Wars of Succession
Aurangzeb, the last great Mughal, came to power after imprisoning his father Shah Jahan, and killing his brothers. Ruthless and bigoted, he alienated many of his Hindu subjects, but expanded the Mughal Empire.

THE MUGHAL DYNASTY
The Mughal Empire flourished from 1526 until Aurangzeb's death in 1707. After that, the dynasty gradually declined under weak rulers, and finally ended in 1857. Its first six rulers were:
Babur (r.1526–30)
Humayun (r.1530–56)
Akbar (r.1556–1605)
Jahangir (r.1605–27)
Shah Jahan (r.1627–58)
Aurangzeb (r.1658–1707)

THE DECLINE OF THE MUGHALS

The death of Emperor Aurangzeb, the last great Mughal, in 1707, heralded the decline of the Mughal Empire. He left a ruined economy and weak successors, and independent states now began to be established by the Rajputs in Rajasthan, the nawabs of Avadh and Bengal, the nizams of Hyderabad, and the Wodeyars of Mysore. Two new powers were the Marathas in the Deccan and the Sikhs in the north. The Marathas under their leader Shivaji *(see p471)* expanded their territories after 1647. The Sikhs, originally a religious group, began to acquire territory in the hill states of the north, Jammu and Punjab. Under Ranjit Singh *(see p104)*, they became a powerful state in the early 19th century.

Sahib and mahout on elephant

THE EUROPEANS

But India would no longer remain a battleground for indigenous groups and dynasties – European traders, who had begun to arrive in the 16th century, were to change the course of its history. To set up trading factories in areas where their agents had settled, the Europeans began to acquire land, and fought numerous wars, both against one another and against Indian rulers. The trading groups were organized into companies, and included the Portuguese, French, Dutch and English. The Portuguese, who were the first to arrive, lost most of their territories to the Dutch and English by the end of the 17th century, retaining only Goa and a few adjacent enclaves. The Dutch, in turn, lost out to the English. The 18th century saw major conflicts between the French and English, with three Carnatic Wars fought between 1740 and 1763, in South India and involving Indian powers on both sides. Ultimately, the English were the victors, the French retaining only Pondicherry and a few small settlements.

THE RISE OF THE BRITISH

Meanwhile, the English East India Company was acquiring territory in the north by gaining trade concessions from the Mughal emperors from the early 17th century onwards. They defeated the nawabs of Bengal in the Battles of Plassey (Palasi) in 1757 and Buxar in 1764. By this time, the invasions of Nadir Shah of Persia in 1739, and Ahmad Shah Abdali of Afghanistan in 1761, had further weakened the Mughals. In the battle with Abdali the Marathas, who had gained control of Delhi, suffered a crushing defeat. From these beginnings, the British began to expand their power. Robert Clive *(see p561)*, responsible for many of their successes, became Governor of Bengal in 1757. From 1773, the Parliament in England started to

Rachol Church in Portuguese Goa

TIMELINE

1707 Death of Mughal emperor Aurangzeb	**1739** Nadir Shah of Persia invades Delhi	**1761** Ahmed Shah Abdali of Afghanistan defeats Marathas in the Third Battle of Panipat	**1774–85** Warren Hastings, first Governor General *A Maratha soldier*

Nadir Shah's battle axe

1750   **1775**

1727 The city of Jaipur founded by Sawai Jai Singh II

1764 Battle of Buxar, British granted Diwani of Bengal

1757 Battle of Plassey, British defeat Siraj-ud-daulah, Nawab of Bengal

1789 Marathas occupy Delhi

1799 Tipu Sultan defeated

Sepoys (Indian foot soldiers of the East India Company) rebelling at Fatehpur during the Mutiny of 1857

exercise some control over the Company. Warren Hastings, appointed Governor in 1772, was soon given the title of Governor General of Bengal (1774–1785), with supervisory powers over all the Company's territories. Under him and his successors (who from 1833 onwards were known as governors general of India), expansion continued, with major wars being fought against the Marathas, the Punjab, and Haider Ali and Tipu Sultan in Mysore. Other states too were conquered or brought under British control by various policies, such as the Subsidiary Alliance, under which Indian states had to maintain British troops and allow a British official to reside in the state and advise them. Another policy was the Doctrine of Lapse, under which states "lapsed" to the Company if a ruler died without a direct male heir. Thus by 1857, the Company's control extended over much of India, and obtained them vast profits. After the

Industrial Revolution, raw materials from India were exported to Britain, and machine-made British goods, particularly textiles, flooded the country. Artisans were impoverished, and crafts, towns and cities declined. Discontent with the alien rulers was growing. Unlike earlier conquerors of India, the British maintained their separateness, and their base in another country. In 1857, a combination of factors led to a major revolt, which began as a soldiers' mutiny, but soon had widespread civilian participation. Thousands of rebels marched towards Delhi in May and proclaimed the titular Mughal ruler, Bahadur Shah Zafar, emperor of India. By September the British had regained control over Delhi. Bahadur Shah was exiled to Rangoon (Yangon), and his young sons executed. Other rebel areas were also brutally taken over, ending the first major challenge to British rule.

Toy showing Tipu's tiger mauling a British soldier

| 1803 British capture Delhi from the Marathas | | *Queen Victoria's head on a Company coin* | 1853 First railway from Bombay to Thana | 1857 The Indian Mutiny |
| | | | | 1863 Simla becomes summer capital of the Raj |

1800   **1825**   **1850**

| 1799–1839 Reign of Ranjit Singh | 1818 Rajasthani kingdoms accept British control | 1829 Governor General Bentinck bans *sati*, the Hindu practice of widow burning | 1856 Annexation of Avadh

Nawab Wajid Ali Shah of Avadh | 1858 Crown takes over the East India Company, Lord Canning becomes the first Viceroy |

Pax Britannica

The Victoria Cross

The foundations of British rule, or the Raj, were laid after the Indian Mutiny of 1857, which revealed the unpopularity of the East India Company's rule. By an Act of Parliament in 1858, the Company's rule ended, and its Indian territories became part of the British Empire, to be ruled through a viceroy. Though the *raison d'être* of the Raj was economic profit and political control, its abiding legacy was the political unification of the subcontinent, together with the introduction of Western education, a centralized administrative system, and a network of railways.

BRITISH INDIA

☐ *British territory, 1858*

Indian attendants in viceregal livery re-enact a Mughal procession.

Caparisoned elephants carry Raj officials.

Administration

Some 2,000 British officers, members of the prestigious Indian Civil Service, ruled over 300 million Indians. Dubbed the "Steel Frame of India", they brought British-style law and order to the remotest corners of the country.

A Sahib Travelling

A vast rail network was set up to facilitate commerce and travel. This 19th-century print shows first-class travel, a privilege of "whites only". The sahibs travelled in style, with several servants in attendance.

Lord Curzon

Viceroy from 1899 to 1905, Curzon believed British rule was necessary to civilize "backward" India. Paradoxically, the Western-style educational institutions set up by the Raj helped make Indians more aware of the injustices of colonial rule.

Raj Cuisine
The British soon developed a taste for Indian curries, toned down to make them a bit less spicy. Restaurants such as London's Chutney Mary *have been popular in Britain ever since.*

Memsahib and Tailor
Despite the climate, the British clung to their own dress and lifestyle. Children were sent "home" to study, and a large Indian staff enabled a leisurely lifestyle.

The Viceroy, Lord Curzon, and his wife lead the procession.

Crowds line the streets to see the grand spectacle.

Cemeteries of the Raj
The harsh Indian climate took a heavy toll on British women and children. Their tombs fill the Raj's graveyards.

THE IMPERIAL DURBAR, 1903
This painting of Curzon's Delhi Durbar (1903), held to celebrate the coronation of Edward VII in London, shows a procession winding through the historic streets of Delhi. Held periodically, such assemblies announced the grandeur and the political might of British Rule in India.

Colonial Architecture
The most imposing edifice in New Delhi, built as the imperial capital between 1911 and 1931, was the viceroy's sprawling residence.

The Company School
Paintings by Indian artists, such as this fanciful portrait of King Edward VII and Queen Alexandra in Indian royal attire, were specially commissioned for the British market.

Crowds of supporters around Mahatma Gandhi

THE NATIONAL MOVEMENT

After 1857, nationalist aspirations began to grow, and the founding of the Indian National Congress in 1885 gave Indians a platform from which to demand self-goverment. A turning point came in 1919, when General Reginald Dyer's troops fired on an unarmed crowd in Jallianwala Bagh in Amritsar, which was protesting against the suppression of civil liberties. More than 300 people died, and Indians of every caste, class and religion united in their outrage at British brutality. By 1920, the leadership of the National Movement was taken over by Mohandas Karamchand Gandhi, a Gujarati lawyer who had recently returned from South Africa. Popularly known as Mahatma or "great soul", Gandhi's charismatic appeal and identification with the poor of India converted the freedom struggle into a mass movement. His strategy was to launch a moral crusade of non-violent resistance *(satyagraha)* to British laws and institutions, followed by

A popular poster of political heroes, past and present

periods of constructive village work. Working alongside Gandhi were several outstanding Indians, among whom was Pandit Jawaharlal Nehru.

At first, the movement for freedom was ruthlessly suppressed, but after World War II, Britain no longer had the strength or the will to enforce its rule. Meanwhile, from 1940 onwards, the Muslim League, led by Mohammad Ali Jinnah, had been demanding an independent state of Pakistan for Muslims.

Finally, at midnight on 14/15 August, 1947, the era of British rule ended, and the new nations of India and Pakistan were born. Casting a dark shadow over the celebrations was the Partition of the Indian subcontinent into two countries, accompanied by mass migrations of millions of Hindus and Muslims across the borders, and communal riots in which thousands were killed.

INDEPENDENT INDIA

After Independence, the new government integrated more than 550 princely states, which had been semi-independent in British days, into the Indian Union. In late 1947, a war between India and Pakistan took place over the accession to India of the princely state of Kashmir, and this continues to be a major point of dispute between the two countries. In 1948, Mahatma Gandhi was assassinated by a Hindu fanatic who felt he favoured Muslims. This so shocked and grieved both communities that peace was finally restored.

As India's first prime

TIMELINE

1942 Quit India Movement

1885 Indian National Congress founded

1911 Transfer of capital to Delhi announced at the Delhi Durbar

1920 Non-cooperation Movement launched by Gandhi

1940 Muslim League adopts the Pakistan Resolution

1948 Mahatma Gandhi assassinated

1910 **1920** **1930** **1940** **1950**

1905 Partition of Bengal

Gandhi's spinning wheel

1919 Jallianwala Bagh massacre

1913 Rabindranath Tagore wins Nobel Prize

1930–32 Civil Disobedience movement

1947 India attains Independence, Partition

The Indian flag

1952 First General Election, with universal suffrage

Nehru, with his daughter Indira and grandson Rajiv

minister, Jawaharlal Nehru laid the foundations of a modern nation state, with a democratic, secular polity, a strong industrial base and a planned economy, with Non-alignment as the keystone of its foreign policy. In 1962, China invaded northeast India and then withdrew after inflicting a humiliating defeat on the Indian army. This brought about much-needed modernization of India's military machine. Nehru died in May 1964, and in 1966 his daughter Indira Gandhi became prime minister. She continued his pro-poor and socialist policies, and in 1971, she stripped the Indian princes of their titles and abolished their privy purses. Later in the same year, she aided East Pakistan in its struggle against West Pakistan, leading to the formation of Bangladesh. But in 1975, perceiving a threat to her power and popularity, she declared a State of Emergency, under which the press was censored and dissidents imprisoned. When the general elections took place, in 1977, she was defeated, and the Congress party lost power for

Rural women learning to read during a literacy campaign

the first time since Independence. By 1980, Indira and the Congress were back in power, but a military action against Sikh terrorists holed up in their sacred Golden Temple led to her assassination by her Sikh guards in 1984. Her son, Rajiv Gandhi, took over in a sympathy wave, and began liberalizing the economy. He was assassinated by a Sri Lankan Tamil separatist during the 1991 election campaign, but economic reforms encouraging private enterprise and foreign investment continued. Since 1996, a series of coalition governments have been in power, with the Hindu nationalist Bharatiya Janata Party (BJP) emerging as a major force to challenge the Congress.

Significant progress has been made in the 60 years since Independence, though unemployment and poverty

A newly-built Info-tech park in Hyderabad

continue to exist. The literacy rate has risen from 18 per cent in 1951 to 66 per cent in 2001. In urban areas, women can be seen working in all professions. From frequent food shortages in the 1950s, India now has a food surplus, and its industrial base has expanded to produce a wide range of goods, from toys to aircraft. Economic reforms have flooded the market with consumer goods, and helped the rise of a prosperous middle class. In the field of information technology, there has been a veritable revolution, with India now established as a world leader in software development.

1960	1970	1980	1990	2000
1961 Goa liberated from Portuguese rule	**1971** Birth of Bangladesh	**1992** Destruction of Babri Masjid leads to communal riots	**1998** BJP comes to power. AB Vajpayee becomes Prime Minister	**2004** Tsunami hits coastal Tamil Nadu and the Andamans
1962 India-China war		**1991** Rajiv Gandhi assassinated	**2001** Gujarat Earthquake	
1965 War with Pakistan	**1975** Indira Gandhi declares Emergency	**1998** Amartya Sen wins the Nobel Prize for Economics	**2000** Population reaches 1 billion	**2007** Pratibha Patil becomes the first woman President of India
1971 Princes lose titles and privy purses	**1982** India sends scientific team to Antarctica	**1999** India-Pakistan conflict in Kargil		

DELHI &
THE NORTH

Introducing Delhi & the North

As rich in natural beauty as in historic
sites, North India is a much visited region. A
wide variety of landscapes can be enjoyed
here, from the snowcapped peaks, alpine
valleys and pine forests of Ladakh and Himachal
Pradesh, to the flat plains of Haryana and Punjab,
dappled with fields of golden mustard and wheat.
In sharp contrast is the urban sprawl of Delhi, a
bustling metropolis and the nation's capital. Ladakh's
dramatically sited cliff top monasteries and pristine
trekking trails are major attractions for visitors, as
are Shimla's Raj-era ambience and Dharamsala's
distinctive Tibetan flavour. Amritsar's great Sikh
shrine, the Golden Temple, and Delhi's magnificent
Mughal monuments are other popular destinations.

The lush green landscape of Srinagar, in the Kashmir Valley

Punjabi farmers enjoying a ride in a tractor-trailer

GETTING AROUND

Delhi has good air, rail and road links to the rest of the region. There are
daily flights to Leh, Srinagar, Amritsar and Chandigarh. Amritsar and
Chandigarh are also connected to Delhi by fast trains and a National Highway. From Chandigarh, there are air services to Shimla and Manali as well
as road links with frequent bus services. A particularly charming journey
is on the Toy Train, "Shivalik Queen" *(see p777)*, which goes from Kalka,
near Chandigarh, to Shimla. Other great journeys, with spectacular
mountain scenery en route, include the trip by road from Manali to Leh,
and the journey along the old Hindustan-Tibet Road (National Highway
22), which runs from Shimla to the India-China border near Shipkila.

◁ **A local woman crossing a barley field, nestled between the barren hills of Spiti *(see p130),* Himachal Pradesh**

LADAKH
JAMMU
& KASHMIR

HIMACHAL
PRADESH

HARYANA
&
PUNJAB

DELHI

KARGIL

NUBRA
VALLEY

LAMAYURU   LEH   THIKSE
ALCHI

ZANSKAR
VALLEY   HEMIS

Pang-gong
Tso

Chenab

Tso
Moriri

CHAMBA   LAHAUL AND SPITI

DHARAMSALA
MANALI
NH20

KANGRA
VALLEY   KULLU
VALLEY   TABO

Beas

SHIMLA   KINNAUR

Satluj

NH1   CHANDIGARH

PATIALA   NH1   Yamuna

PANIPAT

NH10

DELHI

NH8

Jaipur

Agra

SEE ALSO

KEY

━━ National highway

▬▬ Major road

▬▬ River

– – State border

Autumn colours along the banks of the Indus river in Ladakh

| 0 km | 100 |
| 0 miles | 100 |

A PORTRAIT OF DELHI & THE NORTH

The peaks of the Himalayas, the most spectacular natural barrier in the world, mark the boundaries of the area that extends northwards from Delhi. A variety of cultures and landscapes lies within this region. Delhi's bustling urban sprawl gradually gives way to the lush, flat farmlands of Punjab and Haryana, north of which are the serene mountainous lands of Himachal Pradesh and Ladakh.

In geological terms, the Himalayas are very young *(see pp64–5)*, but for humans, they evoke a feeling of timeless eternity, and have been a source of spiritual inspiration for Indians for thousands of years. The monasteries and temples situated on their slopes perfectly complement the profound beauty of these mountains.

Saffron flowers

Most visitors to the region start out from Delhi, the country's capital, a city that is a blend of several historical eras. Its grand Mughal past is evident in its many superb monuments and tombs. The elegant tree-lined avenues and bungalows of New Delhi evoke the period of the British rule. Yet both coexist alongside the modern world of internet cafés, shopping arcades and posh multiplex cinemas.

Delhi's population swelled massively to accommodate the millions of people displaced by the Partition of India in 1947, when the western portion of Punjab became part of Pakistan. Homeless refugees from west Punjab have since prospered in Delhi, and now dominate the city's commercial life. As the nation's capital, Delhi continues to attract people from all over India, giving this vibrant city a resolutely cosmopolitan air.

The hardworking, resilient Punjabis have also transformed their home state with modern farming techniques, introduced in the 1960s. As a result of this "Green Revolution", Punjab and

A deep blue glacial lake near Thamsar Pass in Himachal Pradesh

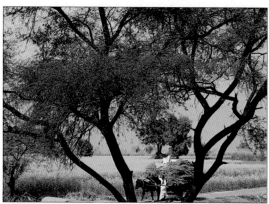

Mustard fields in the fertile plains of Punjab

Haryana today produce much of India's wheat and rice, and one-third of its dairy products. Punjabis are also among the most successful immigrant communities in the world, and today, almost every family has at least one member living abroad, whether in London, New York, Vancouver or Hong Kong, as portrayed in Mira Nair's film, *Monsoon Wedding* (2001).

The name "Punjab" refers to the five *(panch)* rivers *(ab)* which traverse this green land. The sixth "river", if one can call it that, is the legendary Grand Trunk Road *(see p179)*. Travelling almost anywhere north of Delhi, one is bound to use this route. The kind of traffic may have changed since Rudyard Kipling's *(see p255)* day, and it is now rather prosaically rechristened National Highway 1, but it still lives up to the author's description: "Such a river of life exists nowhere in the world".

During the Raj-era, the British would escape from the summer heat of the plains and head for the hills. Today's visitors follow

A Delhi wedding procession

in their footsteps all year round. Himachal Pradesh has a number of delightful hill stations, such as Shimla, Kasauli and Dalhousie. The hillsides are covered with orchards, and apple farming is an important part of the state's economy. Himachal Pradesh also offers spectacular treks, some of which start from Dharamsala, a town with a distinct Tibetan flavour as the home of the Dalai Lama *(see p122)*

Jammu and Kashmir, which includes Ladakh, is India's northernmost state. Tragically, the militant separatist movement in the beautiful Kashmir Valley has effectively put an end to tourism there. But Ladakh remains an oasis of peace. Often perceived as having a purely Buddhist culture, its population is, in fact, almost equally divided between Buddhists and Muslims, who coexist here in harmony. Ladakh's uniquely syncretic culture, together with its astonishing natural beauty and the dramatic architecture of its monasteries, make it one of India's most fascinating areas.

A Kashmiri family gathered around their samovar

The Great Himalayas

Himalayan magpie

The highest and youngest mountains in the world, the Himalayan Range stretches for 2,500 km (1,553 miles) along the Indian subcontinent's northern borders, separating it from Central Asia and the Tibetan Plateau. The Himalayas were formed about 30 million years ago, when the Indian plate broke away from Gondwanaland, drifted northwards and collided with the Eurasian landmass, driving the earth's crust up to form three parallel ranges, which include 30 of the world's highest peaks.

LOCATOR MAP

▨ The Himalayas

▨ Area illustrated below

High altitude desert, *where little grows except lichen, is found above the tree line. One such area is between Diskit and Hundar in Ladakh's Nubra Valley (see p143), which has sand dunes and camels.*

Glaciers *are especially abundant in the Western Himalayas. They are the source of three great Indian rivers – the Indus, the Ganges and the Brahmaputra.*

THE HIMALAYAS

Fourteen peaks in the Himalayas tower above 8,000 m (26,247 ft), including Mount Everest, the world's highest peak at 8,848 m (29,029 ft). The two highest peaks in India are Kanchendzonga (*see p302*) at 8,598 m (28,209 ft), and Nanda Devi (seen above) at 7,817 m (25,646 ft).

Bandar Punch ("Monkey Tail"), 6,316 m (20,722 ft), attracts many mountaineers. This peak is visible from Dodital (*see p188*).

Jaonali Peak, 6,633 m (21,762 ft)

Pithwar Peak, 6,904 m (22,651 ft)

Kedarnath, 6,940 m (22,769 ft), is regarded as Shiva's sacred mountain. Below it is the famous Kedarnath Temple.

A traditional Himalayan dwelling *is generally built of stone and wood, or sun-dried mud bricks. Typically it has two or three storeys, the lowest level filled with stone to provide stability during earthquakes, the next level housing livestock, and the top floor where the family rooms are laid out.*

FLORA AND FAUNA

Subtropical jungles, temperate coniferous forests and alpine meadows are among the varied vegetation zones in the Himalayas. They support a rich and abundant variety of plant and animal life.

Brahma Kamal (Saussurea obvallata) *is a popular offering at most hill temples.*

Deodar (Cedrus deodara) *is a towering conifer found in temperate forests in the Western Himalayas.*

Bar-headed geese (Anser indicus) *are attractive water birds that breed in high altitude lakes in Ladakh.*

Bharal (Pseudois nayaur) *are called blue sheep because of the blue sheen on their grey coats. They inhabit the harsh, stony slopes above the snow line.*

Marine fossils *and rocks that have been found in high altitudes in the Himalayas, and even on peaks such as Mount Everest, testify that these mountains were once a part of the Tethys seabed.*

Trishul ("Trident"), 7,120 m (23,360 ft)

Nanda Devi, 7,817 m (25,646 ft)

The snow leopard (Uncia uncia), *now endangered, lives above 4,000 m (13,123 ft). It preys on wild sheep and hares.*

The Flavours of Delhi & the North

Several culinary strands cross the region of Delhi and the Punjab, which, despite national boundaries, begins at the Khyber Pass, now in Pakistan. Wheat is the staple food and a variety of breads *(rotis)* are baked in a *tandoor*, the domed clay oven, also used to barbecue marinated meats and vegetables. Rich curries, legacies of the imperial kitchen, are still prepared as is the post-Partition cuisine of butter chicken, *tikkas* and *dal makhani*. Kashmiri flavours are a delicate blend of yoghurt, spices, aniseed, dried ginger powder, red chillies and a pinch of asafetida (Hindus) or garlic (Muslims). Rice and mutton are the standard fare of both communities.

Strands of saffron

Today, Delhi is a city of immigrants and each community has brought its own food. By far the most dominant is Punjabi and "Frontier" cuisine. The ubiquitous *tandoori* chicken, served with pickled onions and mint chutney was "invented" in Daryaganj's Moti Mahal restaurant in 1947. Other popular foods are the *dosa* and *idli* from South India *(see pp554–5)*.

Delhi has an abundance of street foods. *Bhutta* (corn-on-the-cob) roasting on makeshift stoves, fruit juices and cooling sherbets sold from handcarts and the range of *chaat* (savoury snacks) are legendary. Equally famous are *jelabis* (crisply fried batter in syrup) *phirni* (rice pudding) and crushed almond or pistachio *kulfi* (ice cream), garnished with noodle ribbons.

Mangoes and other fruit on sale in a Delhi fresh produce market

DELHI

Centuries of Muslim rule have given Delhi its succulent *shami* and *burra kebabs*, as well as creamy *kormas* and *salans*, rich *biryanis* and *pulaos*, all delicately spiced main dishes. Once served at the courts of kings, emperors and sultans, this imperial cuisine is still eaten by most people.

Murg zafrani (spiced chicken)　*Reshmi kebab* (chicken kebab)　*Seekh kebab* (lamb kebab)

Tandoori murg　　　　　　　　　　　　　　*Burra kebab* (char-grilled lamb)

A tandoori platter with a selection of barbecued meats

LOCAL DISHES AND SPECIALITIES

From the old city of Delhi comes the *nahari*, the delectable mutton (which can mean goat meat too in India) dish that is cooked through the night and served at breakfast with *naans*. Snacks include the popular *chhole-bhatura* and vegetable *pakora* (Indian tempura). Specialities of the Punjab include *dal makhani*, *baigan ka bharta* (smoked and puréed aubergines (eggplant)), and various stuffed breads. Vegetarian dishes in Kashmir are few, the most famous being *haaq* (a special spinach), *aloo dum* (potatoes in yoghurt), and *chaman* (cottage cheese in gravy). Lamb or mutton dishes include *rishta* (meatballs) cooked in a sauce and *tabak maz* (fried ribs cooked in milk).

Mint and chillies

Aloo puri *is a spicy potato dish eaten with puffy deep-fried bread and a mint and coriander chutney.*

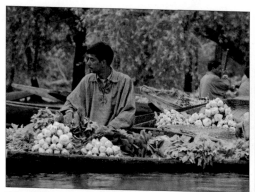

Shikras (skiffs) carrying fresh vegetables, Dal Lake, Srinagar, Kashmir

PUNJAB

Punjabi food is robust and linked to the lifestyle of the largely farming communities. It is dominated by milk and its products, such as yoghurt and *paneer* (cottage cheese), prepared in innumerable ways. Popular drinks are *lassi* (buttermilk) and a variant, *chhach*, made with ginger, coriander and powdered cumin. Wheat is the staple cereal and dishes include *aloo parathas* (fried bread stuffed with potatoes and other vegetables and eaten with yoghurt) and the seasonal *sarson ka saag* (mustard greens) and *makke* (corn) *ki roti*.

Although vegetarian food is the main fare, the non-vegetarian dishes from this state are a mixture of Northwest Frontier and Mughlai cuisines. The hub of Punjabi cuisine is Amritsar, famous for its batter-fried fish. The *dhabas* (eateries) that dot the main highways offer the best local food as lorry drivers demand a fresh, hot and tasty meal.

Winnowing wheat, a common sight in the Punjab

KASHMIR

Food here ranges from a simple family meal to a 36-course wedding banquet, the *wazawan*, where guests are seated on cushioned rugs in groups of four, in front of large silver platters. Rice, grown in the Kashmir Valley, mutton, chicken or fish are of prime importance. The generous use of yoghurt in the sauces gives the dishes a creamy consistency, while the locally-grown saffron adds flavour and colour. Walnuts and almonds are also added for texture and flavour. A meal ends with *kahva*, a green tea flavoured with cardamom and cinnamon.

ON THE MENU

Aloo tikki Potato cutlets.

Chhole-bhatura Spiced chickpeas and puffy bread.

Dal makhani Lentils flavoured with ginger, garlic, spices and a dollop of cream.

Gushtaba Large meatballs flavoured with fresh mint.

Phirni A sweet rice pudding, garnished with nuts.

Shami kebab Mincemeat patties flavoured with spices.

Tandoori murg Barbecued spring chicken.

Yakhni A yoghurt and mutton or lotus root curry with a delicate hint of fennel.

Rogan josh *has pieces of mutton simmered in yoghurt which is then thickened with* khoya *(solidified milk).*

Dal *combines lentils with a heady mix of onions, garlic and spices. It is considered India's "soul food".*

Gulab jamuns *are deep-fried milk and flour balls in a sweet syrup flavoured with rosewater and cardamom.*

DELHI

Delhi, the capital of India, is also its third largest city, with a population of about 16 million. Its strategic location along the north-south, east-west route has given it a focal position in Indian history, and many great empires have been ruled from here. The monuments and ruins of these are scattered throughout the city, often cheek by jowl with modern structures and highrise towers.

The vast urban sprawl of contemporary Delhi is, in fact, a conglomeration of several distinct enclaves, chief among which are Old Delhi, with its 16th- and 17th-century Mughal-built monuments and congested souk-like bazaars; and New Delhi with its wide avenues, grand vistas and colonial mansions, built by the British in the 1930s as their imperial capital. New Delhi has government buildings and also houses the Diplomatic Enclave where all the embassies are located. The picturesque 12th-century ruins of citadels built by the first Islamic rulers can be seen in the Qutb-Mehrauli area, and the affluent new middle class suburbs of South Delhi lie close by. Slums and shanty towns dot the outer fringes of the city.

All the contrasts and contradictions of India are particularly visible in the capital: denim-clad youngsters rubbing shoulders with robed sadhus (holy men), and bullock carts travelling alongside the latest luxury cars. Adding to Delhi's fascinating diversity is the fact that it is largely a city of migrants. After the violent Partition of India and Pakistan in 1947, millions of refugees, mainly from West Punjab, flocked here in search of a new life. Since then there has been a steady influx of people from all over India. Yet each regional community has retained its distinct cultural identity, making Delhi less a melting pot than a *thali* (platter) whose offerings may be savoured singly or in interesting combinations.

A view of the old city around Jami Masjid, with its bustling streets and crowded buildings

◁ India Gate and the elegant Statue Canopy designed by Sir Edwin Landseer Lutyens, completed in 1931

Exploring Delhi

Some of Delhi's most impressive buildings can be seen in the area shown in this map. Vijay Chowk is the vantage point for the grand sweep of Raj buildings grouped on Raisina Hill. To the north, the magnificent Jami Masjid with its busy hive of lanes, is the focus of Old Delhi. To the southeast, the medieval quarter around the tomb of the Sufi saint Nizamuddin Auliya leads along Mathura Road to the ruined fort, Purana Qila. And to the south, the Mehrauli area (shown on the Greater Delhi map), has a fascinating cluster of monuments built in the 12th and 13th centuries.

Vijay Chowk (see pp72–3), at the base of Raisina Hill, surrounded by government offices

SIGHTS AT A GLANCE

Historic Buildings, Streets & Neighbourhoods
Around Kashmiri Gate ㉒
Around Vijay Chowk pp72–3 ❶
Chandni Chowk pp84–5 ⓱
Coronation Memorial ㉓
Feroze Shah Kotla ㉑
Hauz Khas ㉘
Humayun's Tomb p83 ⓰
Jahanpanah ㉚
Jantar Mantar ❾
Khirkee ㉙
Mehrauli Archaeological Park pp92–4 ㉛
Nizamuddin Complex ⓯
Purana Qila ⓭
Raisina Hill ❸
Rajghat ⓴
Rajpath ❹
Rashtrapati Bhavan ❷
Red Fort ⓳
Safdarjung's Tomb ㉖
Tughluqabad ㉝

Churches, Temples & Mosques
Baha'i House of Worship ㉞
Jami Masjid ⓲
Lakshmi Narayan Mandir ❿

Museums
Crafts Museum pp80–81 ⓮
National Gallery of Modern Art ❻
National Museum pp76–7 ❺

Nehru Memorial Museum and Library ⓫
Sanskriti Museum ㉜
The National Rail Museum ㉕

Shops & Markets
Connaught Place ❽
INA Market ㉗

Parks & Gardens
Lodi Gardens ⓬
The Ridge ㉔

Theatres & Art Galleries
Mandi House Complex ❼

LOCATOR MAP

KEY

	Around Vijay Chowk: *see pp72–3*
	Chandni Chowk: *see pp84–5*
R	Railway station
M	Metro station
Bus	Bus station
i	Tourist information
P	Parking
+	Hospital
	Police station
	Temple
C	Mosque
	Gurdwara
	Church
	Tomb
⊠	Post office
—	National highway
—	Major road

GETTING AROUND

The areas shown here are best covered by the metro, taxi, auto-rickshaw or a hired car and driver. Guided coach tours run by Delhi Tourism *(see p761)* also cover many sights. Avoid buses!

GREATER DELHI

SEE ALSO

- **Where to Stay** pp690–91

- **Where to Eat** pp720–21

Street-by-Street: Around Vijay Chowk ❶

Vijay Chowk or "Victory Square", a large piazza at the base of Raisina Hill, was planned as a commanding approach to the Viceroy's House, now the Indian President's residence. This is where the "Beating of the Retreat" ceremony takes place each year on 29 January *(see p37)*. Vijay Chowk is flanked by two long, classical Secretariat buildings (the North and South Blocks), which house several ministries as well as the Prime Minister's Office. Ministers and government officials live in spacious bungalows on the tree-shaded avenues nearby. From Vijay Chowk, Lutyens's grand Central Vista lies ahead – large trees and fountains line the lawns of Rajpath up to India Gate, the Statue Canopy and the National Stadium at the far end.

★ **Vijay Chowk**
This piazza, flanked by red sandstone obelisk-shaped fountains, faces a grand vista.

North Block, designed by Herbert Baker, has an imposing Central Hall.

Sansad Bhavan is also known as Parliament House.

The Iron Gates
Copied from a pair Lutyens saw in Chiswick, England, these are set into ornamental sandstone gateposts. They lead to Rashtrapati Bhavan (see p74).

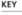

KEY

- - - Suggested route

SIR EDWIN LANDSEER LUTYENS

Architect Sir Edwin Landseer Lutyens (1869–1944), President of the Royal Academy from 1938 to 1944, was commissioned to design India's new capital in 1911. With Herbert Baker, his colleague, it took him 20 years to build the city in a unique style that combined Western Classicism with Indian decorative motifs. The result is an impressive and harmonious synthesis, with Neo-Mughal gardens and grand vistas meeting at verdant roundabouts. Delayed by World War I and quarrels between Baker and Lutyens, spiralling costs met by Indian revenues led Mahatma Gandhi to term it a "white elephant". Ironically, the British lived here for only 16 years.

The red sandstone National Archives, designed by Lutyens

★ **South Block**
The Prime Minister's Office and the Defence Ministry are located within this section of the Secretariat.

Sunehri Bagh Mosque
This simple 18th-century mosque, built by a saint called Sayyid Sahib, makes for a picturesque roundabout. The adjoining Sunehri Bagh Road is lined with shady trees – a feature of all Lutyens's avenues.

LOCATOR MAP
See Delhi Map pp70–71

Roundabout
Beautifully landscaped road intersections are a haven for workers during lunch.

India Gate

Vayu Bhavan (Air Headquarters)

Udyog Bhavan (Ministry of Commerce)

MOTILAL NEHRU MARG

KAMARAJ ROAD

SUNEHRI BAGH ROAD

DUPLEIX ROAD

KRISHNA MENON MARG

| 0 metres | 25 |
| 0 yards | 25 |

Statue of Kamaraj
K Kamaraj was Congress Party President (1963–6).

★ Bungalow-lined Avenues
Strict building bylaws preserve the original architecture of the colonial bungalows in the tree-lined avenues of this area.

STAR SIGHTS

★ Vijay Chowk

★ South Block

★ Bungalow-lined Avenues

Ornate iron gates leading to Rashtrapati Bhavan, designed by Lutyens

Rashtrapati Bhavan ❷

Tel (011) 2301 5321. 📷 9:30am –1pm, 2–4:30pm Mon, Wed, Fri & Sat. **Change of Guard Ceremony** Tel (011) 2301 3592. Apr–Oct: 8am; Nov–Mar: 10am Sat only. **Mughal Gardens** ◯ Feb–Mar.

Designed by Sir Edwin Lutyens *(see p72)* as the British Viceroy's Palace, Rashtrapati Bhavan, situated at the crest of Raisina Hill, is now the official residence of the President of India. A vast, copper-clad cupola soars over this elegant beige and red sandstone building which covers an area of 2 ha (5 acres). The *pièce de résistance* is the circular Durbar Hall, situated directly beneath the dome, where all important state ceremonies and functions are held.

To the west, the beautifully landscaped grounds include Rashtrapati Bhavan's famed **Mughal Gardens**. These terraced gardens with water-courses and fountains built on three levels, are open to visitors in the spring months.

Raisina Hill ❸

Cathedral Church of the Redemption *Tel* (011) 2309 2396. ◯ 8am–noon; 4–6pm daily.

The barren, treeless grounds around Raisina Hill were selected by the British as the site of the new capital. Now a heavily-guarded, verdant area, it is dominated by stately

buildings such as the twin North and South Blocks *(see p72)* of the **Secretariat**. The two virtually identical buildings that rise from the top of Raisina Hill, were designed by Sir Herbert Baker, who also designed the grand circular **Sansad Bhavan** (Parliament House) to the north of Vijay Chowk. Both the Rajya Sabha (Upper House) and the Lok Sabha (House of the People) convene here when Parliament is in session. After the December 2001 terrorist attack, Sansad Bhavan is now closed to visitors.

Behind Sansad Bhavan is the Anglican **Cathedral Church of the Redemption**, inspired by Palladio's Church of Il Redentore in Venice. Originally built for senior British officials in 1931, it is now the diocese of the Bishop of the Church of North India.

Rajpath ❹

National Archives Janpath. *Tel* (011) 2338 7509. ◯ 9:30am–6pm Mon–Fri. 🔴 Public hols. **Indira Gandhi National Centre for the Arts** Janpath. *Tel* (011) 2338 4938. ◯ 9am–5:30pm Mon–Fri.

Running east of Vijay Chowk is Rajpath, a two-mile-long avenue used for parades, with ornamental fountains, canals and lawns on either side. The **National Archives**, situated at the intersection with Janpath, houses a major collection of state records and private papers. Opposite is the **Indira Gandhi National Centre for the Arts** with an archive of rare manuscripts. It holds many national and international exhibitions and symposia.

At Rajpath's eastern end is **India Gate**, a massive red

India Gate

sandstone arch, built to commemorate the Indian and British soldiers who died in World War I, and those who fell in battle in the North-West Frontier Province and the Third Afghan War. An eternal flame burns in memory of the soldiers who died in the 1971 India-Pakistan War. Facing India Gate is the sandstone canopy where a statue of King George V was installed in 1936. The statue is now at Coronation Park *(see p88)* and the canopy stands empty.

National Museum ❺

See pp76–7.

Sansad Bhavan, where the Constitution of India was drafted

National Gallery of Modern Art ❻

Jaipur House, near India Gate.
Tel *(011) 2338 5378.* ☐ *10am–5pm
Tue–Sun.* 🌑 *Mon & public hols.*
🖼 🏛

Jaipur House, the former
residence of the maharajas of
Jaipur, is one of India's largest
museums of modern art,
covering the period from the
mid-19th century to the
present day. Its excellent
collections include works
by modern Indian painters
such as Jamini Roy,
Rabindranath Tagore, Raja
Ravi Varma and Amrita
Shergill, as well as contemporary artists such as Ram
Kumar and Anjolie Ela
Menon. Also on display are
works by British artists such
as Thomas Daniell and his
nephew William Daniell, and
an interesting group of
"Company Paintings" – 18th-
and 19th-century works by
Indian artists commissioned
specially for the British market.

Mandi House Complex ❼

Triveni Kala Sangam Tansen Marg.
Tel *(011) 2335 6139.* ☐ *9:30am–
5pm Mon–Sat.* 🌑 *public hols.* 🖼
🖼 **Rabindra Bhavan** Ferozeshah
Rd. **Tel** *(011) 2338 1833.* 🖼
Kamani Auditorium Copernicus
Marg. **Tel** *(011) 2338 8084.*
Shri Ram Centre Safdar Hashmi
Marg. **Tel** *(011) 2335 2410.* 🖼 🖼
National School of Drama Bhagwan
Das Rd. **Tel** *(011) 2338 8249.*
For **Tickets** see **Entertainment** p96.

Mandi House, today the
offices of the state-owned
television centre, lends its
name to this cultural complex
encircling the roundabout.
Triveni Kala Sangam has
contemporary art galleries, an
open air amphitheatre for
concerts and plays, a popular
café and a bookshop
specializing in Indian arts
publications. The state-
sponsored **Rabindra Bhavan**
arts complex houses the
national academies of
literature (Sahitya Akademi),
fine arts and sculpture (Lalit

Connaught Place, the British-built shopping complex in New Delhi

Kala Akademi), and the
performing arts (Sangeet
Natak Akademi) in separate
wings. All three have libraries
and display
galleries that sell
reproductions.
Regular exhibitions
of photography
and ceramics are
also held here.
**Kamani
Auditorium**, the
Shri Ram Centre
and the **National
School of Drama** are vibrant
centres for theatre, music and
dance performances.

Mirrorwork skirts on sale
at Janpath

Connaught Place ❽

Shops ☐ *10:30am–8pm Mon–Sat.*
🌑 *public hols.*

Opened in 1931 and named
after the Duke of Connaught,
this shopping complex, with
its Palladian archways and
stuccoed colonnades, was
designed by Robert Tor

Russell as a deliberate contrast
to the noises and chaos of an
Indian bazaar. The central
circle of Connaught Place has
now been renamed
Rajiv Chowk, and
the outer circle
Indira Chowk. Its
arcades and pave-
ments spill over
with *paan* kiosks,
book stalls and
shoe shine boys,
while the eclectic
mix of shops is
interspersed with eateries and
cinema halls. Though no
longer Delhi's premier shopping area, its shaded arcades
are pleasant to stroll through.
The recently built Central
Park features an amphitheatre, 21 fountains and plush
lawns. Nearby popular shopping centres include the state
emporia at **Baba Kharak
Singh Marg** and the stalls
along **Janpath**. **Cottage
Industries** *(see p97)* is also
located on Janpath.

REPUBLIC DAY PARADE

Ever since 1950, when
India became a
republic, this parade
on 26 January has
attracted large crowds
despite the often chilly
weather. Soldiers and
sailors, war veterans
and school children,
and even elephants
and camels, march

Republic Day Parade

smartly down Rajpath. Especially popular are the folk
dancers and the inventive floats representing each state of
the country. A ceremonial flypast by the Indian Air Force
signals the end of the always colourful parade.

The National Museum ❺

Five millennia of Indian history can be explored at the National Museum, with a collection of more than 200,000 pieces of Indian art. The nucleus collection of about 1,000 artifacts was sent to London in the winter of 1948–9 for an exhibition at the Royal Academy's Burlington House. After its return, it was housed in the Durbar Hall of Rashtrapati Bhavan until the present building, built of the same beige and pink stone as the imposing new capital, was complete in 1960. The Museum's collection of Indus Valley relics and Central Asian treasures from the Silk Route is considered among the finest in the world.

Dancing girl from 2500 BC

★ Dara Shikoh's Marriage Procession
An 18th-century Mughal miniature painting in gold and natural pigments.

★ Nataraja
This 12th-century Chola statue of the cosmic dance of Lord Shiva is the centre-piece of the museum's South Indian bronzes.

The Coins and Indian Scripts Gallery displays an impressive collection of coins and the evolution of the Indian script.

Ground floor

★ Kubera
A rare example of a Hindu god shown as a 2nd-century Kushana (see pp46–7) grandee with marked Central Asian features is among a large collection of Mathura Art.

Entrance

THE SERINDIAN COLLECTION

Almost 700 years after the Silk Route fell into disuse, Sir Aurel Stein, a British archae-ologist, led a series of expeditions (1900–16) to un-cover its treasures. On view at the National Museum, Stein's Central Asian collec-tion of the artifacts he found in the Taklamakan Desert has silk paintings, Buddhist manuscripts and valuable records of life along this ancient trade route.

Silk painting, 7th–8th century

Terracotta Mask
This unusual human mask made of terracotta dates back to 2700 BC, and was unearthed in Mohenjodaro in the early 20th century.

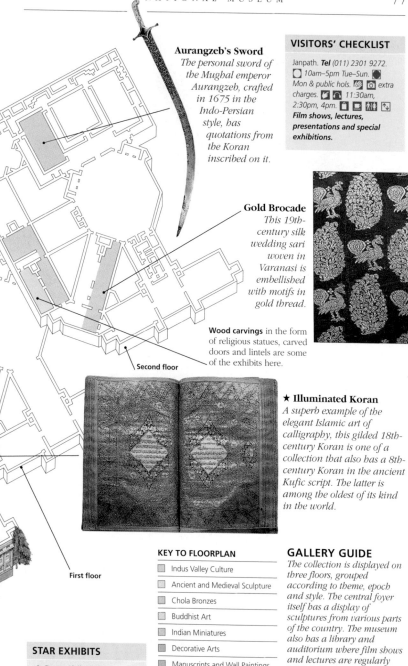

Aurangzeb's Sword
The personal sword of the Mughal emperor Aurangzeb, crafted in 1675 in the Indo-Persian style, has quotations from the Koran inscribed on it.

VISITORS' CHECKLIST

Janpath. **Tel** (011) 2301 9272.
🕐 10am–5pm Tue–Sun. ⬤
Mon & public hols. 🎫 📷 extra
charges. 🎥 📞 11:30am,
2:30pm, 4pm. 🚻 🚻 ♿ 🔼
**Film shows, lectures,
presentations and special
exhibitions.**

Gold Brocade
This 19th-century silk wedding sari woven in Varanasi is embellished with motifs in gold thread.

Wood carvings in the form of religious statues, carved doors and lintels are some of the exhibits here.

Second floor

★ Illuminated Koran
A superb example of the elegant Islamic art of calligraphy, this gilded 18th-century Koran is one of a collection that also has a 8th-century Koran in the ancient Kufic script. The latter is among the oldest of its kind in the world.

First floor

KEY TO FLOORPLAN

☐ Indus Valley Culture
☐ Ancient and Medieval Sculpture
☐ Chola Bronzes
☐ Buddhist Art
☐ Indian Miniatures
☐ Decorative Arts
☐ Manuscripts and Wall Paintings
☐ Central Asian Antiquities
☐ Textiles, Arms and Armour, Musical Instruments
☐ Coins and Indian Scripts
☐ Jewellery
☐ Wood carvings

STAR EXHIBITS

★ Dara Shikoh's
Marriage Procession

★ Nataraja

★ Kubera

★ Illuminated Koran

GALLERY GUIDE
The collection is displayed on three floors, grouped according to theme, epoch and style. The central foyer itself has a display of sculptures from various parts of the country. The museum also has a library and auditorium where film shows and lectures are regularly held. Information on these is published in the newspapers. Information regarding catalogues and souvenirs can be had at the ticket office in the foyer. The display is changed from time to time for variety, and special exhibitions are also mounted.

The brick and plaster astronomical instruments in Jantar Mantar

Jantar Mantar ❾

Sansad Marg. ◯ *daily.* 🖼️

Sawai Jai Singh II of Jaipur, a keen astronomer, built this observatory in 1724 because he wanted to calculate planetary positions and alignments accurately, in order to perform sacred rituals and *pujas* at propitious moments. One of the five observatories he built *(see pp358–9)*, Jantar Mantar's instruments are large and fixed, making them resistant to vibration and therefore exact. The Samrat Yantra, a right-angled triangle whose hypotenuse is parallel to the earth's axis, is a gigantic sun-dial, with two brick quadrants on either side of it to measure the sun's shadow. The Ram Yantra, reads the altitude of the sun, and the Jai Prakash Yantra (invented by Jai Singh II himself) verifies the time of the spring equinox. Now obsolete, the observatory lies in the centre of a pleasant park surrounded by high-rises.

Lakshmi Narayan Mandir ❿

Mandir Marg. ◯ *daily.*

Built in 1938 by the industrialist BD Birla, this was one of the earliest Indian temples without caste restrictions, and Mahatma Gandhi attended its first *puja*. A fairly typical example of modern Indian temple architecture, with its marble entrance and ochre and maroon *shikharas* (spires), the Birla Mandir, as it is popularly known, has images of Vishnu and his consort Lakshmi in its main shrine. Subsidiary shrines set around the courtyard, are inscribed with verses from sacred Hindu texts and are decorated with paintings depicting scenes from the *Mahabharata* and *Ramayana*.

Nehru Memorial Museum and Library ⓫

Teen Murti Marg. *Tel (011) 2301 4475.* ◯ *Tue–Sun.* ⬤ *public hols.*
Nehru Planetarium *Tel (011) 2301 2944.* 🖼️ *Shows 11:30am, 3pm.*

The residence of Jawaharlal Nehru, India's first prime minister, Teen Murti Bhavan was converted into a museum and library for research scholars after Nehru's death in 1964. This house has a special place in modern Indian history because it was also the home of two future prime ministers – Nehru's daughter Indira Gandhi and his grandson Rajiv Gandhi, both of whom were assassinated *(see p57).* Nehru's bedroom and study, still exactly as he left them, reflect his austere yet elegant personality and his eclectic taste in books.

Teen Murti Memorial

The extensive grounds are home to the **Nehru Planetarium** and the square, three-arched **Kushak Mahal**, a 14th-century hunting lodge built by Sultan Feroze Shah Tughluq *(see p87).* On the roundabout in front of the house stands the **Teen Murti** ("Three Statues") **Memorial**. This is dedicated to the Indian soldiers who died in World War I. The house derives its name from this landmark.

Teen Murti Bhavan, Nehru's official residence, now the Nehru Memorial Museum and Library

For hotels and restaurants in this region see pp690–91 and pp720–21

Athpula, the 17th-century bridge near the entrance to Lodi Gardens on South End Road

Lodi Gardens ⑫

Entrance on Lodi Rd & South End Rd. ○ *daily.* **11**

Lodi Gardens is one of Delhi's most picturesque parks, and a favourite haunt of joggers, yoga enthusiasts, political bigwigs accompanied by their bodyguards, and families who come to picnic on weekends. Landscaped at the behest of Lady Willingdon, the vicereine, in 1936, the park acts as a "green lung" for the people of Delhi. Its tree lined pathways and well-kept lawns and flowerbeds are laid out around the imposing 15th-century tombs of the Sayyid and Lodi dynasties, Delhi's last sultans. Many of them still have traces of the original turquoise tilework and calligraphy. The elegantly proportioned octagonal **Tomb of Muhammad Shah** (r.1434–44), the third ruler of the Sayyid dynasty, is said to be the oldest in the garden. The largest of the structures is the **Bara Gumbad** ("Big Dome") with an attached mosque built in 1494, and a guesthouse. At the South End Road entrance to the gardens is a lovely stone bridge called **Athpula** (literally "eight piers"), said to date from the 17th century. To its west are ramparts that enclose the **Tomb of Sikander Lodi** (r.1489–1517).

Purana Qila ⑬

Mathura Rd. **Tel** *(011) 2435 4260.* ○ *sunrise–sunset daily.* **Museum Tel** *(011) 2435 5387.* ○ *10am–5pm.* ● *Friday.* 🎫 **Tickets:** *from site and the Delhi Tourism office.* **Tel** *(011) 3320 005.*

Purana Qila, literally "Old Fort", stands on an ancient site that has been continuously occupied since 1000 BC, as archaeological excavations have revealed. The brooding ramparts of the fort now enclose the remains of the sixth city of Delhi, Dinpanah *(see p91)*, which was begun by the second Mughal emperor, Humayun. His reign, however, was short and in 1540 he was overthrown by the Afghan chieftain Sher Shah Sur *(see p49)*. Sher Shah added several new structures and renamed the citadel Shergarh ("Lion's Fort"). After Sher Shah's death Humayun regained his throne. Of the many palaces, barracks and other edifices built by these two rulers, only Sher Shah's mosque and a building that was probably Humayun's library remain standing today.

The **Qila-i-Kuhna Mosque**, built in 1541, is a superbly proportioned structure with fine decorative inlay work in

Chhatri with decorative tilework

red and white marble and slate. To the south of the mosque is Humayun's library, known as **Sher Mandal**. A double-storeyed octagonal tower of red sandstone, it is crowned by an elaborate *chhatri* (open pavilion) supported by eight pillars. This was the tragic spot where the devout emperor, hurrying to kneel on the steps for the evening prayer, missed his footing and tumbled to his death in January 1556. The ramparts of the Purana Qila have three principal gateways, of which the imposing red sandstone **Bara Darwaza** on the western wall is the main entrance. Humayun's Tomb *(see p83)* can be seen from the southern gate.

Bara Darwaza, Purana Qila

Crafts Museum ⑭

For centuries, Indian craftsmen such as potters, weavers, masons and carvers, have created a range of objects for everyday use that are both beautiful and practical. A unique project was started in 1956 to promote indigenous artisans by giving them a place to display their work, and by the early 1980s, over 20,000 objects had been collected. This was the core around which India's first Crafts Museum developed.

Wooden doll on toy swing

Sarota, a 19th-century betel nut cracker from South India

★ Bandhini Odhni
This exquisite veil is the work of the Bhansali tribe in Kutch, Gujarat. Tie-and-dye (bandhini) is done by tying threads around grains to form a pattern, and dyeing the cloth in different colours.

Mukhalinga
This rare, late 19th-century phallic image (linga) with a human face (mukha) is made of brass and silver. The third eye and tiny snake-earrings are symbols of Shiva.

Amphitheatre

STAR EXHIBITS

- ★ Bandhini Odhni
- ★ Charraku
- ★ Bhuta Figure

Crafts Demonstration Area
Artisans from all over India set up workshops each month (barring the monsoon) to display their skills to visitors.

KEY

☐	Gallery of Aristocratic Arts
☐	Gallery of Ritual Arts
☐	Gallery of Folk and Tribal Cultures
☐	Gallery of Textiles
☐	Non-exhibition space
☐	Temporary exhibitions gallery
☐	Visual store

For hotels and restaurants in this region see pp690–91 and pp720–21

Yashoda and Krishna
This mid-20th-century plaster cast statuette from South India is an interesting example of popular kitsch, inspired by gods and mythology. It is cheap and easy to reproduce for use in a domestic shrine.

VISITORS' CHECKLIST

Bhairon Marg. **Tel** (011) 2337 8876. ◯ Tue–Sun. ● public hols. 🏠 🖥 👬 ♿
Crafts demonstration ◯ Oct–Jun: daily.

★ Charraku
These enormous, circular vessels are cast of an alloy known as bell metal. They are still used in Kerala for wedding feasts or at temples for making payasam *(a type of rice pudding) for devotees during festivals.*

Madhubani Painting
This traditional wall painting in natural pigments, depicting a wedding scene, is by Ganga Devi, a famous 20th-century woman painter from Bihar (see p217).

★ Bhuta Figure
These life-sized wooden figures, artifacts from the Bhuta cult of spirit worship in the southern state of Karnataka (see p526), date back to the early 19th-century.

Library

Entrance

GALLERY GUIDE
The museum's exhibits are spread over two floors of the complex, divided into separate areas by courtyards that also double up as exhibition spaces. A large open area is used for live art displays by visiting artisans each month, except during the rainy season.

The Crafts Museum Shop
This shop sells a fine selection of items made by indigenous artisans, including household objects, decorative pieces and textiles.

Nizamuddin Complex ⑮

W of Mathura Rd. **Dargah** ☐ daily.
Qawwali performance 7pm Thu.
📷 Urs (Jul & Dec).

This medieval settlement, or *basti,* is named after Sheikh Hazrat Nizamuddin Auliya, whose grave and hospice are located here. Nizamuddin belonged to a fraternity of Sufi mystics, the Chishtis, respected for their austerity, piety and disdain for material desires, and was a spiritual descendant of Moinuddin Chishti *(see p376).* His daily assemblies drew both the rich and the poor, who believed that he was a "friend of God" who would intercede on their behalf on Judgement Day. He died in 1325 but his disciples call him a *zinda pir* (living spirit) who continues to heed their pleas. A three-day Urs is

Congregational area, Nizamuddin

observed, with qawwalis sung, on the anniversary of his death, and another on the death of his disciple Amir Khusrau.

A winding alley leads to the saint's grave. It is crowded with mendicants and lined with stalls selling flowers and *chadors* (ceremonial cloths), poly-chrome clocks and prints of Mecca. The main congregational area is a marble pavilion (rebuilt in 1562) where, every Thursday evening, followers sing devotional songs composed by the celebrated Persian poet, Amir Khusrau (1253–1325). Women are denied entry beyond the outer verandah but may peer through *jalis* into the small, dark chamber where the saint's grave lies draped with a rose petal strewn cloth, surrounded by imams who continuously recite verses from the Koran. Amir Khusrau is buried in the complex, as

Tomb of the famous poet Mirza Ghalib

Colourful stalls in the alley leading to Nizamuddin's tomb

are other eminent disciples, such as Jahanara Begum.

Across the western side of the open courtyard is the red sandstone Jama't Khana Mosque, built in 1325. To its north is a *baoli* (stepwell), excavated in secret while Tughluqabad *(see p95)* was being built, because Ghiyas-uddin Tughluq had banned all building activities elsewhere. Legend has it that labourers worked here at night with the help of lamps lit not with oil but with water blessed by Nasiruddin, Nizamuddin's successor. The early 16th-century **Tomb of Atgah Khan** is to the north. A powerful minister in Emperor Akbar's court, he was murdered by Adham Khan, a political rival *(see p93).* The open marble pavilion, **Chaunsath Khamba** ("64 pillars"), is close by and just outside is an enclosure containing the simple grave of Mirza Ghalib (1786–1869). One of the greatest poets of his time, Ghalib wrote in both Urdu and Persian, and his verses are still recited. Nearby is the **Ghalib Academy**, a repository of paintings and manuscripts.

Despite its crowds, the *basti* preserves with miraculous serenity the legend of Nizamuddin, described by Khusrau as "a king without throne or crown, with kings in need of the dust of his feet".

NIZAMUDDIN COMPLEX

One of Delhi's historic necropolises, many of the saint's disciples, such as Amir Khusrau and Jahanara Begum, Shah Jahan's favourite daughter, are buried close to their master. Jahanara's epitaph echoes her master's teachings: "Let naught cover my grave save the green grass, for grass well suffices as a covering for the grave of the lowly".

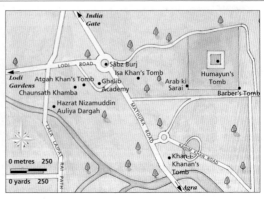

India Gate

LODI ROAD · Sabz Burj
Isa Khan's Tomb
Lodi Gardens · Atgah Khan's Tomb · Ghalib Academy
Chaunsath Khamba
Hazrat Nizamuddin Auliya Dargah
Arab ki Sarai
Humayun's Tomb
Barber's Tomb
MATHURA ROAD
LALA LAJPAT RAI PATH
Khan-i-Khanan's Tomb
KARIM KHAN ROAD
0 metres 250
0 yards 250
Agra

Humayun's Tomb ⑯

Marble star inlaid on panel

Humayun, the second Mughal emperor *(see p79)*, is buried in this tomb, the first great example of a Mughal garden tomb, and inspiration for several later monuments, such as the incomparable Taj Mahal *(see pp172–3)*. Built in 1565 by Persian architect Mirak Mirza Ghiyas, it was commissioned by Humayun's senior widow, Haji Begum. Often called "a dormitory of the House of Timur", the graves in its chambers include Humayun's wives and Dara Shikoh, Shah Jahan's scholarly son. Also in the complex are the octagonal tomb and mosque of Isa Khan, a 16th-century nobleman, and the tomb of Humayun's favourite barber. The Arab ki Sarai was a rest house for the Persian masons who built the tomb.

VISITORS' CHECKLIST

Off Mathura Rd, Bharat Scout Guide Marg. **Tel** *(011) 2461 9861.* ☐ *daily.*

The perfectly symmetrical Humayun's Tomb as seen from the entrance

The Dome
This imposing white marble double dome is a complete half-sphere, and is surmounted by a finial with a crescent in the Persian style. Later Mughal finials, such as the one at the Taj Mahal, added a lotus base.

Geometric designs inlaid on panels

Jalis
Fine trellis work in stone later became a signature Mughal feature.

The imposing plinth is decorated with red sandstone arches and consists of multiple chambers, a departure from the single chamber of previous tombs.

The Tomb Chamber
The plain white marble sarcophagus stands on a simple black and white marble platform. The grave itself, no longer accessible, lies in the dark, bat-filled basement below.

Street-by-Street: Chandni Chowk ⓱

Once Shahjahanabad's *(see p91)* most elegant boulevard,
Chandni Chowk ("Silvery, Moonlit Square"), laid out in
1648, had a canal running through it, and was lined with
grand shops and mansions. Today, it is still the heart of Old
Delhi, where religious and commercial activity mix easily.
At the entrance to Chandni Chowk is the Digambar Jain
Temple, the first of many shrines along its length. Built in
1656, it also houses a unique hospital for birds.

Charity box for donations
at the Bird Hospital

Sisganj Gurdwara
*Guru Tegh Bahadur, the
ninth Sikh guru, was be-
headed at this site in 1675.*

CHANDNI CHOWK

Fatehpuri Masjid
(built in 1650)

KINARI BAZAAR

DARIBA KALAN

Nai Sarak

Sunehri Masjid
*The "Golden Mosque",
with three gilt domes,
was built in 1722. On
22 March 1739, Persian
invader Nadir Shah
stood on its roof to
watch the massacre
of Delhi's citizens.*

BAZAAR GULIYAN

CHEL PURI

Shiv
Temple

STAR SIGHTS

★ Kinari Bazaar

★ Lahore Gate

★ Dariba Kalan

★ Jami Masjid

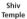

★ Kinari Bazaar
*Tightly packed stalls sell
all manner of glittering
gold and silver trimmings
such as braids, tinsel
garlands and turbans for
weddings and festivals.*

★ **Lahore Gate**
This imposing red sandstone gateway is the main entrance to the Red Fort (see p86). The Prime Minister addresses the Independence Day rally here.

LOCATOR MAP
See Delhi Map pp70–71

★ **Dariba Kalan**
Gold and silver ornaments are sold along this lane. Gulab Singh's famous perfume shop (see p96) is located here.

★ **Jami Masjid**
India's largest mosque, Jami Masjid, with its soaring minarets and vast marble domes, is grandly positioned on top of a mound (see p86).

Government Girls
Senior Secondary
School

Karim's

| 0 metres | 25 |
| 0 yards | 25 |

KEY

- - - Suggested route

Karim's
Tucked away in a narrow lane to the south of Jami Masjid is Delhi's most authentic Mughlai eatery (see p720). Named after a legendary 19th-century chef, the restaurant is now run by his descendants.

The sandstone and marble Jami Masjid, India's largest mosque

Jami Masjid ⑱

Off Netaji Subhash Marg. ⬤ *for non-Muslims during prayer time and after 5pm.* 📷 *extra charges.*

This grand mosque, with three imposing black and white marble domes, and twin minarets framing its great central arch, was built in 1656 by the Emperor Shah Jahan, on a natural mound. It took six years and 5,000 workers to construct, at a cost of nearly a million rupees. A magnificent flight of sandstone steps leads to the great arched entrances. In Aurangzeb's time, the area attracted horse sellers and jugglers; today, shoe minders and beggars mill around. The huge 28-m (92-ft) square courtyard can accommodate up to 20,000 people at Friday prayer sessions and at Id, when it looks like a sea of worshippers. Next to the *dukka* (water tank) for the ritual ablutions, is the platform where, before loud-speakers took over, a second

prayer leader echoed the imam's words and actions for worshippers too far from the pulpit for a clear view.

Red Fort ⑲

Chandni Chowk. ***Tel*** *(011) 2327 7705.* ⬛ *Tue–Sun.* ⬤ *public hols.* 🎦 **Son et Lumière** *Sep–Oct & Feb–Apr: 8:30–9:30pm daily; Nov–Jan: 7:30–8:30pm daily; May–Aug: 9–10pm daily.* 🎦 **Museum** ⬛ *Tue–Sun.* 📷

Red sandstone battlements give this imperial citadel its name, Lal ("Red") Qila ("Fort"). Commissioned by Shah Jahan in 1639, it took nine years to build and was the seat of Mughal power until 1857 when the last Mughal emperor, Bahadur Shah Zafar, was dethroned and exiled. Today, the Red Fort remains a powerful symbol of Indian nationhood.

The throne canopy at the Diwan-i-Aam

It was here that the national flag was hoisted for the first time when India became an independent nation on 15 August 1947.

Entry is through **Lahore Gate**. One of the fort's six gateways, this leads on to the covered bazaar of **Chatta Chowk**, where jewels and brocades were once sold. Beyond this lies the **Naqqar Khana**, a pavilion where ceremonial music was played three times a day.

A path from here leads to the **Diwan-i-Aam**, a 60-pillared, red sandstone hall where the emperor gave daily audience to the public. The emperor sat beneath the lavishly carved stone canopy, while the low bench in front of it was for his chief minister. Beyond this hall is the **Rang Mahal**. Inside its gilded chambers, once exclusively for women, is an inlaid marble fountain shaped like an open lotus.

Nearby, is the **Khas Mahal**, the emperor's royal apartments with special rooms for private worship and for sleeping. The Robe Room ("Tosh Khana") has a superb marble *jali* screen carved with the scales of justice, a motif seen in many miniature paintings. North of the Khas Mahal is the **Diwan-i-Khas**, built completely of white marble. The legendary Peacock Throne, embedded

RED FORT

1　Delhi Gate
2　Lahore Gate
3　Naqqar Khana
4　Diwan-i-Aam
5　Rang Mahal
6　Moti Mahal
7　Khas Mahal
8　Diwan-i-Khas
9　Hamams
10　Shah Burj
11　Sawan
12　Bhadon
13　Zafar Mahal
14　Moti Masjid

0 metres　　　200

0 yards　　　200

with priceless jewels was kept here until it was taken away as war booty by the Persian chieftain Nadir Shah in 1739. The walls and pillars of this exclusive pavilion, where the emperor met his most trusted nobles, were once inlaid with gems. The ceiling was of silver inlaid with precious stones.

A little further away are the **Hamams** (Royal Baths) with inlaid marble floors and three enclosures. The first chamber provided hot vapour, the second scented rosewater through sculpted fountains, and the third cold water.

To the west of the baths is the elegant little **Moti Masjid** ("Pearl Mosque"), named after the pearly sheen of its marble. It was built by Emperor Aurangzeb in 1659.

The Ashokan Pillar, rising above the ruins of Feroze Shah Kotla

Gandhi's *samadhi* at Rajghat

Rajghat ⓴

Mahatma Gandhi Rd. ◯ *daily.*
Prayer meetings *5pm Fri.*
Gandhi National Museum
Tel *(011) 2332 8310.* ◯ *Tue–Sun.*
◉ *public hols.* **Film shows** *4–5pm Sat & Sun.*

India's most potent symbol of nationhood, Rajghat is the site of Mahatma Gandhi's cremation. A sombre, black granite platform inscribed with his last words, *He Ram!* ("Oh God") now stands here. The only splash of colour comes from the garlands of orange marigolds that are draped over the platform. All visiting heads of state are taken to this *samadhi* (memorial) to lay wreaths in memory of the "Father of the Nation". On Gandhi's birthday (2 Oct) and death anniversary (30 Jan), the nation's leaders gather here for prayer meetings.

Just across the road is the **Gandhi National Museum**, crammed with memorabilia, including Gandhi's letters and diaries. A framed plaque on the wall sets out his simple philosophy: "Non-violence is the pitting of one's whole soul against the will of the tyrant... it is then possible for a single individual to defy the might of an unjust empire".

Feroze Shah Kotla ㉑

Bahadur Shah Zafar Marg. ◯ *daily.*

Only some ramparts and ruined structures remain of Feroze Shah Kotla, the palace complex of Ferozabad, Delhi's fifth city *(see p91)*, erected by that indefatigable builder Feroze Shah Tughluq. Entry is from the gate next to the Indian Express Building. At one end of the walled enclosure stand the roofless ruins of the Jami Masjid, of which only the rear wall is still extant. This was once Delhi's largest mosque and according to popular legend, Timur, the Mongol conqueror from Samarkand who sacked Delhi in 1398, came here to say his Friday prayers.

Next to the mosque are the remains of a pyramidal structure, topped by one of the Mauryan emperor Ashoka's polished stone pillars *(see p42)*. Brought from the Punjab, it was installed here in 1356 by Feroze Shah. It was from the inscriptions on this pillar that James Prinsep, the Oriental linguist, deciphered the Brahmi script, a forerunner of the modern Devanagari, in 1837.

Khuni Darwaza (the "Bloodstained Gate"), oppo-site the Express Building, was built by Sher Shah Sur as one of the gates to his city *(see p79)*. This was where the Emperor Bahadur Shah Zafar's sons were shot by Lieutenant Hodson after the Mutiny of 1857 was quashed *(see p53)*.

THE BAZAARS OF OLD DELHI

Old Delhi's bazaars are legendary. An English visitor over a 100 years ago, wrote in praise of the "Cashmere shawls, gold and silver embroidery, jewellery, enamels and carpets" found here. Today the great wholesale bazaars of Chandni Chowk still retain a souk-like quality. Their narrow streets are lined with shops, whose goods spill out onto the pave-ments. Each lane specializes in a commodity: Dariba Kalan, for instance, is the lane of jewellers and silversmiths, while Kinari Bazaar *(see p84)* sells a bewildering array of tinsel and sequins.

Indian spices on sale in Khari Baoli, Asia's largest spice market

Around Kashmiri Gate ㉒

Between Nicholson Rd, Ramlal Chandok Marg & Church Rd.
St James's Church Lothian Rd.
***Tel** (011) 2386 0873.* ☐ *daily.*
✟ *English: 9am Sun.*

This landmark, from where the Mughals would set off to spend their summers in Kashmir, resonates with memories of the Mutiny of 1857 *(see p53)*. The short stretch between Kashmiri Gate and the Old Delhi General Post Office (GPO) witnessed bitter fighting, as the city of Delhi lay under siege by the British. A final assault led to the blasting of the Gate, and a plaque on its western side honours "the engineers and miners who died while clearing the gate for British forces on September 14, 1857". In the 1920s, this area was also a favourite haunt of the British residents living in nearby Civil Lines.

The historic **St James's Church**, Delhi's oldest, is the most striking sight in the vicinity. It was consecrated in 1836 by Colonel James Skinner. A flamboyant adventurer of mixed parentage who was rejected by the British Army, Skinner raised his own cavalry regiment which proceeded to fight with great distinction. The church was erected in fulfilment of a vow Skinner made on the battlefield. An unusual structure, the church is in the shape of a Greek cross, surmounted by an imposing eight-leafed dome. Its two stained-glass windows were installed in the 1860s. A marble tablet in front of the altar marks Skinner's simple grave.

Statues of former viceroys around the Coronation Memorial

Coronation Memorial ㉓

S of NH1 Bypass. ☐ *daily.*

The Royal Durbar, held in 1911 to proclaim the accession of George V as King Emperor of India, was held at this site. A red sandstone obelisk commemorates the coronation. More than 100,000 people thronged to see the King Emperor and Queen Empress sit beneath a golden dome mounted on a crimson canopy. Today, it is a dusty and forlorn spot, surrounded by statues of former viceroys, including Lords Hardinge and Willingdon (distinguished for their role in the construction of New Delhi). Towering over them all is the 22-m (72-ft) high statue of the King Emperor himself, which was removed from the Statue Canopy at India Gate *(see p74)* and installed here in the 1960s. About 3 km (2 miles) southeast is a forested park area known as the **Northern Ridge**, cut through by Ridge

Coronation Memorial

Road and Rani Jhansi Road. At its southern end lies the **Mutiny Memorial** (known locally as Ajitgarh), a Victorian Gothic tower which commemorates the soldiers "both British and native ... who were killed" in 1857. Panoramic views of Old Delhi can be enjoyed from here.

Running parallel to the Northern Ridge is the sprawling **Delhi University** area. St Stephen's College, the most distinguished of the colleges dotting the campus, was designed by Walter George in 1938. The office of the Vice Chancellor, once the guesthouse for British officials, is also the spot where the young Lord Louis Mountbatten proposed to Edwina Ashley in 1922. A plaque celebrates the event. They eventually became India's last viceroy and vicereine.

The Ridge ㉔

Upper Ridge Rd. ☐ *daily.* **Buddha Jayanti Park** ☐ *daily.*

Delhi's ridge, the last outcrop of the Aravalli Hills extending northwards from Rajasthan, runs diagonally across the city from southwest to northeast. The area was originally developed by Feroze Shah Tughluq in the late 14th century as his hunting resort. The ruins of his many lodges can still be seen here. This green belt of

The impressive yellow and white edifice of St James's Church undulating, rocky terrain is covered by dense scrub forest consisting mainly of laburnum *(Cassia fistula)*, kikar *(Acacia arabica)* and flame of the forest *(Butea monosperma)*, interspersed with bright splashes of bougainvillea.

A large area in the centre is now the **Buddha Jayanti Park**, a peaceful, well-manicured enclave, with paved paths. Pipal *(Ficus religiosa)* trees abound, and on a small ornamental island is a simple sandstone pavilion shading the large gilt-covered statue of the Buddha, installed by the 14th Dalai Lama in 1993. An inscription nearby quotes the Dalai Lama: "Human beings have the capacity to bequeathe to future generations a wealth that is truly human". Every year in May, Buddhist devotees celebrate Buddha Jayanti here *(see p35)*.

The National Rail Museum ㉕

Chanakyapuri. *Tel (011) 2688 0804.* ◻ *Tue–Sun.* ● *public hols.* ▨ *extra for train rides.* ▯

India's railway network can boast some astonishing statistics. It has a route length of 63,360 km (39,370 miles) and tracks that cover 108,513 km (67,427 miles). There are about 7,150 stations, 12,600 passenger trains, and 1,350 goods trains that run every day. The railways employ 1.6 million people, while 13 million passengers travel by train each day, consuming 6 million meals through the course of their journey.

This museum encapsulates the history of Indian railways. Steam locomotive enthusiasts

will appreciate the collection that traces the development of the Indian railways from 1853, when the first 34 km (21 miles) of railway between Bombay (now Mumbai) and Thane was laid. The wealth of memorabilia on display inside includes the skull of an elephant that collided with a mail train at Golkara in 1894, and a realistic model of an 1868 first-class passenger coach with separate compartments for accompanying servants. Outside, are several retired steam locomotives built in Manchester and Glasgow in the late 19th century, and the salon that carried the Prince of Wales (later King Edward VII) on his travels during the 1876 Royal Durbar. A "toy train" offers rides around the compound, and the shop sells a range of model locomotives.

Safdarjung's Tomb ㉖

Aurobindo Marg. *Tel (011) 2301 7293.* ◻ *daily.* ▨ ▢ *extra charges for video photography.* ♿

This is the last of Delhi's garden tombs and was built in 1754 for Safdarjung, the powerful prime minister of Muhammad Shah, the Mughal emperor between 1719 and 1748. Marble was allegedly stripped from the tomb of Abdur Rahim Khan-i-Khanan in Nizamuddin to construct this rather florid example of late Mughal architecture. Approached by an ornate gateway, the top storey of which houses the library of the

Archaeological Survey of India (ASI), the tomb has an exaggerated dome and stands in a *charbagh*, a garden cut by water channels into four parts. Its façade is extensively ornamented with well-preserved plaster carving and the central chamber has some fine stone inlay work on the floor.

A well-stocked shop selling imported foodstuffs at INA Market

INA Market ㉗

Aurobindo Marg. **Shops** ◻ *Tue–Sun.*

This lively bazaar retains all the trappings of a traditional Indian market but also sells imported foodstuffs such as cheese, pasta and exotic varieties of seafood. The stalls are crammed together under a ramshackle roof, mostly corrugated iron and oilcloth, and sell every manner of stainless steel utensils, spices, Punjabi pickles, readymade garments and even live chickens. Tiny restaurants in between offer Indian fast food. Diplomats, out-of-town shoppers and locals all patronize this market for its reasonable prices and wide variety of products.

The name is derived from Indian National Airports, as the adjacent colony used to house employees of the nearby Safdarjung Aerodrome. Built in the 1930s, the aerodrome was the headquarters of the South Eastern Command Air Wing during World War II. It now contains the offices of the Ministry of Civil Aviation and the Delhi Gliding Club. Indian Airlines also has a 24-hour booking office here *(see p773)*.

A late 19th-century steam engine at the National Rail Museum

The double-storeyed *madrasa* (college) at Hauz Khas

Hauz Khas 28

W of Aurobindo Marg. **Monuments** 🔾 *daily.*

Beyond the boutiques, art galleries and restaurants that have taken over the village of Hauz Khas, are the medieval monuments from Feroze Shah Tughluq's reign. In 1352, the sultan erected a number of buildings on the banks of Hauz Khas, the large tank which was excavated by Alauddin Khilji for his city of Siri. The tank, which shares its name with the surrounding village, is now dry.

Contemporary accounts claim that Feroze Shah was a prolific builder, and during his 37-year reign he constructed an astounding 40 mosques, 200 towns, 100 public baths and about 30 reservoirs.

Among the buildings around Hauz Khas are a *madrasa*, Feroze Shah's tomb and the ruins of a small mosque. The *madrasa* is built close to the edge of the tank. Plaster carvings and niches for books can be seen inside. The *chhatris* (open pavilions) in the entrance forecourt are said to cover the teachers' burial mounds. At one end of the *madrasa* lies the austere tomb of Feroze Shah. Wine-red painted plaster calligraphy decorates its interior.

The complex is best viewed in the afternoon, when sunlight filters through the *jalis* to cover the graves of the sultan, his sons and grandson with delicate star-shaped shadows.

East of Hauz Khas, off Aurobindo Marg, is a small tapering structure called **Chor Minar** ("Tower of Thieves") dating back to the 14th-century Khilji period. Its walls, pockmarked with holes, are said to have held the severed heads of thieves, intended to deter others from crime.

Close by, to the northwest, is the **Nili Masjid** ("Blue Mosque"). Named after the blue tiles above its eaves, it was built in 1505 by a certain Kasumbhil, nurse to the governor of Delhi's son.

Khirkee 29

N of Press Enclave Marg. **Monuments** 🔾 *daily.*

The unusual two-storeyed Khirkee ("Windows") Mosque, built by Feroze Shah Tughluq's prime minister, Khan-i-Jahan Junan Shah, in

The fortress-like Khirkee Mosque

the mid-14th century lends its name to this little village in South Delhi. The mosque has a fortress-like appearance, broken by rows of arched windows, which give the mosque its name. Its innovative design was not repeated again as its many pillared divisions were found impractical for large congregations.

Further down is **Satpula**, the seven-arched stone weir built by Muhammad bin Tughluq in 1326. It formed part of a reservoir used for irrigation, and also made up a portion of the fortified wall enclosing Jahanpanah.

An arched window with a carved stone *jali*, Khirkee Mosque

Jahanpanah 30

S of Panchsheel Park. **Monuments** 🔾 *daily.*

In the heart of Jahanpanah, Muhammad bin Tughluq's capital, stands **Begumpuri Mosque**, also built by Khan-i-Jahan Junan Shah. (Ask specifically for the old mosque, as a new one is located nearby.) The mosque is remarkable for its 44 domes which surmount the cloisters surrounding the central courtyard. It is said that in times of need, this mosque also functioned as a treasury, a granary and a general meeting place.

To the north is the palace of **Bijay Mandal**, from where, according to the 14th-century Arab traveller Ibn Batuta, Muhammad bin Tughluq reviewed his troops. The upper platform offers a grand view of Delhi, extending from the Qutb Minar to Humayun's Tomb and beyond.

Early Capitals of Delhi

Delhi's famous "seven cities" range from the 12th-century Qila Rai Pithora, built by Prithviraj Chauhan, to the imperial Shahjahanabad, constructed by the Mughals in the 17th century. Each of these cities comprised the settlements that grew around the forts erected by powerful sultans with territorial ambitions.

Purana Qila

As the Delhi Sultans consolidated their territories, they moved their defensively situated capitals in the rocky outcrops of the Aravallis, to the northeast, towards the open plains by the banks of the Yamuna. Today, Delhi is an amalgam of ruins of medieval citadels, palaces, tombs and mosques, and an ever-expanding, modern concrete jungle.

Ferozabad (see p87), *stretching north from Hauz Khas to the banks of the Yamuna, is Delhi's fifth city built by Feroze Shah Tughluq (r.1351–88).*

Shahjahanabad

Shahjahanabad *was Delhi's seventh city, built between 1638 and 1649 by Shah Jahan who shifted the Mughal capital here from Agra (see pp168–77).*

Ferozabad

Purana Qila

Siri, *Delhi's second city can still be seen near the Siri Fort Auditorium and the adjacent village of Shahpur Jat. The once prosperous city of Siri was built by Alauddin Khilji in 1303.*

Purana Qila (see p79), *the citadel of Delhi's sixth city, Dinpanah, was built by Humayun. It was captured and occupied by the Afghan chieftain, Sher Shah Sur (r.1540–45) who called it Shergarh.*

Siri

Jahanpanah

Qila Rai Pithora

Tughluqabad

Jahanpanah *was built by Muhammad bin Tughluq (r.1325–51) as a walled enclosure to link Qila Rai Pithora and Siri. The ruined battlements of Delhi's fourth city stand near Chiragh.*

Qila Rai Pithora *was the first of Delhi's seven cities, built by the Chauhans in about 1180. In 1192, it was captured by Qutbuddin Aibak who established his capital here (see pp92–3).*

Tughluqabad (see p95), *a dramatic fort on the foothills of the Aravallis, was Delhi's third city built during Ghiyasuddin Tughluq's four-year reign (1321–5).*

Mehrauli Archaeological Park ㉛

Chhatri outside Jamali-Kamali

Best known for the Qutb Minar, a UNESCO World Heritage Monument, Mehrauli was built over Rajput territories called Lal Kot and Qila Rai Pithora. In 1193, Qutbuddin Aibak, then a slave-general of Muhammad of Ghur *(see p48)*, made it the centre of the Delhi Sultanate. By the 13th century the small village, Mehrauli, had grown around the shrine of the Sufi saint, Qutb Sahib. Later, Mughal princes came here to hunt and some 19th-century British officials built weekend houses, attracted by the area's orchards, ponds and game. Many of Delhi's rich and famous now own sprawling retreats in the area.

Dargah Qutb Sahib
The 13th-century dargah of Sufi saint Qutbuddin Bakhtiyar and the nearby Moti Masjid ("Pearl Mosque") attract many pilgrims.

Hauz-i-Shamsi reservoir was built in 1230 by Sultan Iltutmish *(see p48)*, who is supposed to have been guided to this site by the Prophet in a dream.

Zafar Mahal is a palace named after the last Mughal emperor, Bahadur Shah Zafar.

Mehrauli village

★ **Jahaz Mahal**
Venue of the Phoolwalon ki Sair (a colourful flower procession), this square pleasure pavilion, built during the Lodi era (1451–1526), seems to float on the Hauz-i-Shamsi tank.

Jharna (waterfall) was so-called because after the monsoon, water from the Hauz-i-Shamsi would flow over an embankment into a garden.

Bagichi Mosque

Madhi Masjid
Surrounded by bastions and a high wall, this fortress-like mosque, dating back to 1200, has a large open courtyard and a three-arched, heavily ornamented prayer hall.

STAR FEATURES

★ Jahaz Mahal

★ Qutb Minar

★ Jamali-Kamali Mosque and Tomb

Adham Khan's Tomb
The son of Emperor Akbar's wet nurse, Adham Khan murder-ed a political rival and was executed by the emperor for his crime. Akbar later built this large tomb for mother and son.

VISITORS' CHECKLIST

Delhi-Gurgaon Rd. ◯ *daily.*
Conservation Assistant's Office,
(011) 2664 3856.
Phoolwalon ki Sair (early Oct).

★ Qutb Minar
India's highest single tower, Qutb Minar (Arabic for pole or axis), marked the site of the first Muslim kingdom in North India, established in 1193 (see p94).

| 0 metres | 250 |
| 0 yards | 250 |

Dilkusha Gardens

New Delhi

Rajon ki Baoli
This dramatic three-storeyed stepwell was also called Sukhi Baoli (dry well). Nearby is the five-storeyed Gandhak ki Baoli, named after its strong sulphur (gandhak) smell. These baolis once supplied fresh water to the area.

Balban's Tomb
The 13th-century tomb of Balban, Qutbuddin's successor, lies in a square rubble-built chamber.

★ Jamali-Kamali Mosque and Tomb
The tomb of Jamali (the court poet during the late Lodi and early Mughal age) is inscribed with some of his verses. Its well-preserved interior has coloured tiles and richly decorated painted plasterwork. The second grave is unidentified but is widely believed to be that of his brother, Kamali.

Mehrauli: The Qutb Complex

Floral motif

The Qutb Minar towers over this historic area where Qutbuddin Aibak laid the foundation of the Delhi Sultanate *(see p48)*. In 1193, he built the Quwwat-ul-Islam ("Might of Islam") Mosque and the Qutb Minar to announce the advent of the Muslim sultans. The mosque is a patchwork fusion of decorative Hindu panels, salvaged from razed temples around the site, and Islamic domes and arches. Later, Iltutmish, Alauddin Khilji and Feroze Shah Tughluq added more structures, heralding a new architectural style.

VISITORS' CHECKLIST

Mehrauli, Delhi-Gurgaon Rd.
7am–6pm, 7–9:30pm daily.
Qutb Festival (Oct/Nov).

Iron Pillar
This 4th-century pillar, originally made as a flagstaff in Vishnu's honour, is a tribute to ancient Indian metallurgy.

Qutb Minar
The five-storeyed Victory Tower started by Qutbuddin Aibak was completed by his successor, Iltutmish.

Carved Panels
Panels carved with inscriptions from the Koran embellish the gateway.

Entrance

Alai Darwaza
This gateway to the complex, erected in 1311 by Alauddin Khilji, is one of the earliest buildings in India to employ the Islamic principles of arched construction.

Quwwat-ul-Islam Mosque
Hindu motifs, such as bells and garlands, are clearly visible on the pillars of this mosque.

Pots displayed at Sanskriti Museum

Sanskriti Museum ③

Anandgram, Mehrauli-Gurgaon Rd. *Tel* (011) 2650 1796. ☐ *daily*. ● *public hols*.

This unusual museum is set amid beautifully landscaped, spacious grounds. Exhibits are displayed both in the garden and in specially constructed rural huts. The collection itself is equally unusual in its devotion to objects of everyday use, that have been exquisitely crafted by unknown, rural artisans. OP Jain, whose personal collections gave birth to this museum, has donated combs, nutcrackers, lamps, toys, foot-scrubbers and kitchenware, to demonstrate how even the most utilitarian objects can possess an innate beauty. Terracotta objects from all over India, in every shape and size, are also on display. They include striking pots made in traditional techniques unchanged for centuries, and towering figures of South Indian village deities.

Tughluqabad ③

Off Mehrauli-Badarpur Rd. **Monuments** ☐ *daily*.

The third of Delhi's early capitals *(see p91)*, Tughluqabad is dominated by its spectacular fort, built by Ghiyasuddin Tughluq early in the 14th century. The fort was so sturdily constructed that its rubble-built walls, following the contours of the hill, survive intact all along the 7-km (4-mile) perimeter. Rising from the citadel to the right of the main entrance are the ruins of the Vijay Mandal ("Tower of Victory"). To the left is a rectangular area where arches are all that remain of a complex of palaces, houses and halls. Legend has it that when Ghiyasuddin tried to prevent the building of the *baoli* at Hazrat Nizamuddin Auliya's *dargah (see p82)*, the saint cursed him, saying that one day only jackals and the Gujjar tribe would inhabit his capital.

A good view of the fort and of the smaller, adjoining Adilabad Fort, is possible from the walls. Adilabad was built by Muhammad bin Tughluq, who is believed to have killed his father Ghiyasuddin by

Ghiyasuddin Tughluq's Tomb

contriving to have a gateway collapse on him. Both are buried in **Ghiyasuddin's Tomb**, attached to the Tughluqabad Fort by a causeway that crossed the dammed waters of a lake. Constructed in red sandstone and inlaid with white marble, the tomb's sloping walls pioneered a style that was used in all subsequent Tughluq architecture.

Baha'i House of Worship ③

Bahapur, Kalkaji. *Tel* (011) 2644 4029. ☐ *Tue–Sun*. ● *public hols*. **Prayer services** *10am, noon, 3pm & 5pm*.

Delhi's most innovative modern structure, the Baha'i House of Worship is a world where silence and order prevail. Designed by Iranian architect Fariburz Sahba and completed in 1986, the arresting shape of its unfurling, 27-petalled, white marble lotus has given it its more popular name, the Lotus Temple. The edifice is circled by nine pools and 92 ha (227 acres) of green lawns.

The Baha'i sect originated in Persia and is based on a view of humanity as one single race. Followers of all faiths are invited to meditate and attend the daily 15-minute services in the lofty auditorium, which can seat up to 1,300 people.

The lotus-domed Baha'i House of Worship, one of Delhi's most spectacular sights

Shopping & Entertainment in Delhi

The hallmark of shopping in Delhi is the bewildering variety of merchandise, markets and styles. Besides Connaught Place, almost every residential colony boasts a market. Old, established shops, bazaars and markets co-exist happily with glitzy, high-end boutiques and department stores and one can buy anything from seasonal fruits and traditional handicrafts to designer clothes and the latest imported electronic items. Delhi also has a rich and varied cultural life. The city's cultural calendar livens up between October and March when the season is in full swing. The number of events multiply as all major festivals of music, dance, theatre and cinema are held at this time of the year.

SHOPS AND MARKETS

New Delhi's main shopping centres are in and around Connaught Place and Janpath where the state emporiums and Cottage Industries offer an exciting and varied range of textiles, jewellery and souvenirs at fixed and reasonable prices. In the north is Chandni Chowk (see pp84–5), the traditional market, while to the south are Khan Market, Sundar Nagar and Santushti, the old urban villages of Hauz Khas, Shahpur Jat and Mehrauli, and Dilli Haat, a crafts bazaar on Aurobindo Marg. The five-star hotels also have convenient shopping arcades selling carefully selected goods.

ANTIQUES, JEWELLERY AND SILVER

Genuine antiques are rare to come by and, in any case, cannot be taken out of the country unless certified by the ASI *(see p759)*. However, the **Crafts Museum Shop**, hotel boutiques and Sundar Nagar market stock excellent reproductions of miniature paintings, woodcarvings and bronzes made by artisans today. Superb pieces of traditional jewellery, including *kundan* and *meenakari,* are available at Sundar Nagar market, especially at **Bharany's**. Silver jewellery, both traditional and modern, can be found in the gullies of Dariba Kalan, in Chandni Chowk and Sundar Nagar. **Ravissant** and **Cooke & Kelvy** are the best places for contemporary silverware.

TEXTILES, SHAWLS AND CARPETS

Traditional textiles are available in most of the better shops and emporiums, particularly **Cottage Industries** on Janpath. A wide and exclusive selection of personal care products are on offer at **Forest Essentials** in Defence Colony. **The Shop, Anokhi** and **FabIndia** are the best places for good quality ready–made garments, linen and light cotton quilts. Lodi Colony market has several boutiques offering eclectic Indian designer-wear, including the stylish **Abraham & Thakore. Shyam Ahuja** sells linen, textiles and *dhurries,* while **The Carpet Cellar** is an excellent outlet for Afghan and Kashmiri carpets and pashmina shawls.

HANDICRAFTS AND GIFTS

The Crafts Museum Shop, **Tulsi, Kamala** and Dilli Haat have a wide selection of Indian handicrafts and other gift items, while **Tibet House** has woollen shawls, jackets, *thangkas* and carpets. For quality leather goods such as, handmade shoes and jackets, the many Chinese-owned outlets in Connaught Place, set the standards for comfort and durability. For trendier goods there is **Da Milano**.

In Chandni Chowk's Dariba Kalan is **Gulab Singh Johari Mal**, a marvellous old-fashioned shop where one can test Indian perfume *(attar)* from cut-glass bottles. Their soaps are also worth buying. Herbal cosmetics, incense sticks, perfumed candles and aromatherapy oils and lotions are available in many of the larger stores, including **Good Earth**, which also stocks towels, bathrobes and massage mats. Cosmetics by Vama Ayurveda, Biotique and Shahnaz Herbal are found at most chemists.

Spices and fresh seasonal fruit are found at INA Market *(see p89)* and Indian tea is sold in Kaka Nagar Market (near the Oberoi Hotel on Zakir Hussain Marg), Khan Market and at **Mittal Tea House** in Lodi Colony market.

ENTERTAINMENT GUIDES, TICKETS AND VENUES

All newspapers list the day's entertainment on their engagements page. Other useful sources of information on events, restaurants, sports and related activities are the weekly *Delhi Diary*, and the monthly magazine, *First City*.

At several venues in the city, such as the **India International Centre**, entry is free. At others, such as the **Indian Council for Cultural Relations** (ICCR), it is by invitation only. Tickets for selected music and dance festivals and theatre, however, are advertised and sold at certain bookshops or at the box office.

Most of Delhi's cultural activities are clustered around Mandi House *(see p75)*. The largest auditorium, **Kamani** on Copernicus Marg, hosts concerts, plays and classical music and dance performances throughout the year. During the season, music and dance events are also held at FICCI Auditorium, on the roundabout, **Triveni Kala Sangam**, on Tansen Marg, and at Azad Bhavan, the main venue for performances organized by the state-run ICCR. Excellent plays, in both Hindi and English, are held at the open air auditorium of the **National School of Drama**, the main repertory company at Bhawalpur House, and at the **Shri Ram Centre** nearby. Colourful folk dances from all over India, organized by the

Trade Fair Authority of India, are held during the annual Trade India Fair in November, at Pragati Maidan, the huge exhibition grounds on Mathura Road.

Both the **India Habitat Centre** and the India International Centre, on Lodi Road, organize a variety of events that include films, plays, concerts, exhibitions, lectures and discussions. The mega **Siri Fort Complex**, in South Delhi, is the venue for most prestigious events.

Popular Indian and foreign films are screened at the many cinema halls dotted all over the city. Among the better equipped halls are **PVR Anupam** in Saket and **PVR Priya** in Vasant Vihar.

PERFORMING ARTS

Delhi is the best place to experience the range and richness of classical dance and music. Performances by the best exponents of the major styles of Odissi, Kathak, Bharat Natyam and Kathakali take place during the high season, between October and March. The same is true of concerts of Hindustani and Carnatic classical music. India's vibrant folk dance and music traditions, such as the devotional music of the Sufis, dance-dramas from Kerala, puppet shows from Rajasthan and Karnataka, can also be seen at various venues. Check newspapers for details on location and tickets.

EXHIBITIONS

Major exhibitions are held at the **National Museum**, **National Gallery of Modern Art**, **Art Heritage** and the Crafts Museum. These include special collections of rare sculpture and paintings from museums all over India, as well as from abroad. Recent years have seen exhibitions of Picasso's paintings, the Nizam of Hyderabad's fabulous jewels and Mughal paintings from Queen Elizabeth II's private collection.

Regular exhibitions of contemporary art and craft, photography and graphics are also held in the many art galleries around Mandi House.

DIRECTORY

ANTIQUES, JEWELLERY AND SILVER

Bharany's
Sundar Nagar Market.
Tel (011) 2435 8528.

Cooke & Kelvy
Janpath.
Tel (011) 2372 1081.

Crafts Museum Shop
Pragati Maidan.
Tel (011) 2337 1269.

Ravissant
Oberoi Hotel.
Tel (011) 2436 3030.

TEXTILES, SHAWLS AND CARPETS

Abraham & Thakore
31, Lodi Colony Main Mkt.
Tel (011) 2460 3455.

Anokhi
Khan Market.
Tel (011) 2460 3423.

The Carpet Cellar
1 Anand Lok.
Tel (011) 2626 1777.

Cottage Industries
Janpath.
Tel (011) 2332 0439.

FabIndia
Greater Kailash I,
N-Block Market.
Tel (011) 2621 2183.

Forest Essentials
46-B, Khan Market.
Tel (011) 4175 7057.

The Shop
Connaught Place.
Tel (011) 2374 6050.

Shyam Ahuja
Santushti.
Tel (011) 2467 0112.

HANDICRAFTS AND GIFTS

Da Milano
Connaught Place.
Tel (011) 2341 5490.

Good Earth
Santushti.
Mehrauli.
Tel (011) 2685 1757.

Gulab Singh Johri Mal
Dariba Kalan,
Chandni Chowk.
Tel (011) 2327 1345.

Kamala
Rajiv Gandhi Handicrafts
Bhavan, Baba Kharak
Singh Marg.
Tel (011) 2374 3322.

Mittal Tea House
8-A, Lodi Colony Mkt.
Tel (011) 2461 5709.

Tibet House
Lodi Rd.
Tel (011) 2461 1515.

Tulsi
Santushti.
Tel (011) 2687 0339.

ENTERTAINMENT VENUES

India Habitat Centre
Lodi Rd.
Tel (011) 2468 2222.

India International Centre
40, Lodi Estate,
Max Mueller Marg.
Tel (011) 2461 9431.

Indian Council for Cultural Relations
Azad Bhavan,
IP Estate.
Tel (011) 2337 9309.

Kamani Auditorium
Copernicus Marg.
Tel (011) 2338 8084.

National School of Drama
Bhawalpur House.
Tel (011) 2338 9402.

PVR Anupam
Community Centre,
Saket.
Tel (011) 2686 5999.

PVR Priya
Basant Lok,
Vasant Vihar.
Tel (011) 2614 0048.

Shri Ram Centre
Safdar Hashmi Marg.
Tel (011) 2371 4307.

Siri Fort Complex
Asian Village Complex.
Tel (011) 2649 3370.

Trade Fair Authority of India
Pragati Maidan.
Tel (011) 2337 1540.

Triveni Kala Sangam
205, Tansen Marg.
Tel (011) 2371 8833.

EXHIBITIONS

Art Heritage
Triveni Kala Sangam.
Tel (011) 2371 9470.

National Gallery of Modern Art
Jaipur House,
India Gate.
Tel (011) 2338 2835.

National Museum
Janpath.
Tel (011) 2301 9272.

HARYANA & PUNJAB

Haryana and Punjab cover the vast plains that stretch between the River Indus and the Gangetic belt. Fertile soil and the improved agricultural techniques of the 1960s Green Revolution (*see p62*), have made this region the granary of India, producing more than half the wheat, rice and millet grown in the country. Industrial development followed the success of the Green Revolution, and the two states now also have flourishing dairy and wool-based industries. Most visitors pass only briefly through Haryana and Punjab, usually on their way to Himachal Pradesh, taking in en route the states' two best known attractions: Chandigarh, the planned city built by the famous architect Le Corbusier, which is the shared capital of Haryana and Punjab, and the Golden Temple at Amritsar, the holiest shrine of the Sikhs. For those who care to explore further, there are the former princely states of Patiala and Kapurthala, with their distinctive architecture, and the holy *dargahs* at Panipat and Sirhind. Above all, the warmth and hospitality of the people is this area's special attraction.

SIGHTS AT A GLANCE

Towns & Cities
Chandigarh ❸
Kapurthala ❼
Panipat ❷
Patiala ❹
Sirhind ❺
Surajkund ❶

Temples & Holy Places
Amritsar ❽
Anandpur Sahib ❻

KEY

✈	Domestic airport
═	National highway
▬	Major road
—	Major railway
--	International border
-·-	State border

◁ **A view of the Hari Mandir or Golden Temple from across the sacred pool, Amrit Sarovar, at Amritsar**

Sufi saint Qalandar Shah's *dargah* at Panipat, built in the 14th century

Surajkund ❶

Faridabad district. 21 km (13 miles) S
of Delhi. 🚌 **ℹ** *Haryana Tourism,
Chanderlok Building, 36, Janpath,
New Delhi, (011) 2332 4910.* 🎭
Surajkund Crafts Mela (Feb).

This historic reservoir, built
between the 10th and 11th
centuries by King Surajpal of
the Rajput Tomar dynasty, is
today a popular picnic spot.
The original embankment of
stone terraces
surrounding the
tank, specially
built to trap rain-
water, still exists.
Nearby, an
artificial lake is
well-equipped
with boating
facilities. The
area comes alive
in the first two
weeks of February, when an
excellent crafts *mela* is held
here, with artisans from all
over India selling their wares
in a specially created village.
Puppets from Rajasthan, bell
metal beasts from Orissa, and
mirrorwork from Gujarat are
displayed alongside a variety
of food stalls, while musicians
and folk dancers weave
through the crowds, giving
the fair a joyous, carnival air.

Folk singers performing at the
Surajkund Crafts Mela

Panipat ❷

Panipat district. 85 km (53 miles) N
of Delhi. 🚌 🚏 🎭 *Urs of Qalandar
Shah (Jan/Feb).*

The site of three decisive
battles that changed the
course of Indian history,
including one which led to
the founding of the Mughal
Empire *(see pp50–51)* in
1526, Panipat is situated on a
flat, dusty plain and traces its

history to the epic age. The
older part of the town has
some interesting *havelis*, and
a 14th-century tomb-shrine
dedicated to the Sufi saint
Qalandar Shah. The new
town is a busy, bustling
settlement, strung along
National Highway 1, which
follows the route of the
historic Grand Trunk Road
(see p179). Today, Panipat is
well-known for its furnishing
fabrics and carpets.

Environs
Karnal, 34 km
(21 miles) north
of Panipat, lies
at the heart of a
rich pastoral
region and is an
important
agricultural and
cattle breeding
centre. The
National Dairy Research
Institute is situated here.
Some 90 km (56 miles) north
of Panipat, the pilgrim town
of **Kurukshetra** is dotted with
temples and marks the
mythical site of the epic battle
between the Pandavas and
Kauravas, the heroes of the
Mahabharata (see p26).

**Ritual prayers at the sacred
temple tank at Kurukshetra**

Chandigarh ❸

Chandigarh district. 238 km (148 miles)
N of Delhi. 🚶 *750,000.* ✈ *11 km (7 miles)
S of city centre.* 🚉 🚌 **ℹ** *Interstate
Bus Terminal, Sector 17, (0172) 272
1173.* 🎭 *Rose Festival (Feb).*

The state capital of both
Haryana and Punjab,
Chandigarh was built in the
early 1950s by the inter-
nationally renowned architect
Le Corbusier. It is considered
the first modern city of post-
Independent India and is laid
out on a grid, divided evenly
into 57 blocks or sectors.

Le Corbusier conceived the
city along the lines of a mod-
ular man, with the **Capitol
Complex**, which includes the
Secretariat, Assembly and
High Court buildings, as its
"head". The main shopping
area, **Sector 17**, is the
"heart" of Le Corbusier's plan,
and is set around a central
plaza and fountain, lined
with shops indicating that
Chandigarh's affluent citizens
are extremely fond of good
food and clothes. Adjoining
this sector is a gently
undulating stretch of green,
the city's "lungs", with an
enormous **Rose Garden**
that is at its best in February.
Over a 1,000 varieties of
colourful roses bloom amidst
winding paths, fountains
and sprawling, beautifully
tended lawns.

The city's extensive
residential sectors make up its
"torso", with neat houses and
gardens showing impressive
evidence of the residents'
green fingers. Each road is
lined with a different species
of flowering tree – laburnum,
jacaranda, *gulmohar* – adding
colour to the cityscape.

Chandigarh's **Museum and
Art Gallery** in Sector 10
houses one of the country's
finest collections of
Gandharan sculpture *(see
p43)* and miniature paintings.
Among the best exhibits are a
serene 6th-century Standing
Bodhisattva in the Gandharan
style, and a rare 11th-century
statue of Vishnu holding a
conch shell from Kashmir.
The miniatures section has a
comprehensive selection of
Pahari paintings *(see p121)*

Chandigarh's Capitol Complex, typical of Le Corbusier's functional style

from the Kangra, Basohli and Guler schools, while modern art includes mountainscapes by the Russian painter Nicholas Roerich (see p128).

Lying opposite the Capitol Complex, the **Rock Garden** is one of the city's most popular tourist spots. Spread over 1.6 ha (4 acres) in Sector 1, it was created in the 1970s by an ex-road inspector, Nek Chand, and is a refreshing contrast to Le Corbusier's severely symmetrical cityscape. The area encloses a unique "kingdom", a labyrinth with hills, waterfalls and caves, and serried ranks of sculptures crafted from such

Ceramic figures at Nek Chand's Rock Garden

unlikely material as discarded neon lights, fuse switches, broken crockery and glass.

A short distance away is the man-made **Sukhna Lake**, where a pleasant promenade attracts joggers and walkers.

This is one of Chandigarh's prettiest areas, especially in the evenings, when visitors can enjoy dramatic sunsets and views of the twinkling lights of the nearby hill station, Kasauli (see p113).

🏛 **Museum and Art Gallery**
Tel (0172) 274 2501. ☐ Tue–Sun. 🎫

Environs
The **Pinjore Gardens**, lying 22 km (14 miles) north of Chandigarh, were designed in the 17th century by Fidai Khan, foster brother of the Mughal emperor Aurangzeb. They are terraced in the Mughal style and dotted with domed pavilions, fountains and water chutes. **Sanghol**, 40 km (25 miles) west of Chandigarh, has an excavated site of a 2nd-century Buddhist stupa with an interesting museum of Kushana sculpture.

LE CORBUSIER'S CITY

The "open hand", Chandigarh's emblem

In 1950, India's first prime minister, Jawaharlal Nehru, commissioned the French-Swiss architect Charles Edouard Jeanneret ("Le Corbusier"), to create a new capital for Punjab, as the old capital, Lahore, had become a part of Pakistan after Independence in 1947. The result was a city of concrete blocks and straight arterial roads, projecting Le Corbusier's philosophy of functional efficiency, free of unnecessary ornamentation such as domes and arches. Without any crowded bazaars, Chandigarh lacks the typical bustle and vitality of older Indian towns, and some of Le Corbusier's buildings now look weather-beaten. Yet it remains the country's cleanest and most orderly city and this, perhaps, is Le Corbusier's lasting legacy.

FESTIVALS OF HARYANA & PUNJAB

Qalandar Shah's Urs (Jan/Feb), Panipat. This festival honours the Sufi saint Qalandar Shah with qawwali singing and a colourful fair at his shrine.
Surajkund Crafts Mela (1–15 Feb), Surajkund. Craftsmen from all over the country congregate with a fine selection of their wares, from hand-woven fabrics to folk toys.
Rose Festival (Feb), Chandigarh. The city's gigantic Rose Garden is at its best with flower shows and a weekend carnival of dance and music.

Skilled swordsmanship at the Hola Mohalla festivities

Hola Mohalla (Mar/Apr), Anandpur Sahib. The highlight of this fair, held the day after Holi, is a spectacular display of fencing and tent-pegging, as the Nihang Sikhs show off their legendary martial and equestrian skills.
Baisakhi (14 Apr). Gala processions, dancing and feasting take place all over Punjab to mark the spring equinox and the beginning of the harvest. Lively melas are held at all the major gurdwaras.
Guru Parab (Nov). Celebrated across Punjab on the first full moon night after Diwali (see p37), the birthday of Guru Nanak, the founder of Sikhism, is particularly spectacular at the Golden Temple at Amritsar. Thousands of lamps illuminate the temple every night from Diwali onwards.

The splendid Durbar Hall at the Qila Mubarak, Patiala

Patiala ❹

Patiala district. 63 km (39 miles) SW of Chandigarh. ⚑ 269,000. ⚑ ⚑ ⚑ Basant (Feb). ⚑ Mon–Sat.

Patiala, situated between the Satluj and Ghaggar rivers, was formerly a princely state, ruled by a string of flamboyant rulers in the 19th century, who made its name a byword for everything larger than life. Thus, the "Patiala Peg" is a whopping measure of whisky, the Patiala *salwar* three times the width of an ordinary one, and the gargantuan palace, to quote an overawed English visitor, "makes Versailles look like a cottage". Its rulers were also enthusiastic patrons of the arts, architecture and sports, and the city's gracious ambience and its rich folk crafts owe a great deal to their generous encouragement.

The present city has grown around the **Qila Mubarak**, a fort built in 1763. Its oldest part, Qila Androon, though derelict, has traces of fine wall paintings. The **Durbar Hall**, added later, stands to the right of the entrance gates and is now a museum with a beautifully ornamented ceiling and well-preserved murals. Inside it, is a spectacular display of cannons and arms, including the sword of the Persian ruler Nadir Shah (see p52) who invaded India in 1739. The lively bazaar around the fort offers the city's

famous hand-crafted leather shoes *(jutties)*, tasselled silken braids *(pirandis)* and brightly embroidered *phulkari* fabric.

The enormous **Old Moti Bagh Palace**, completed in the early years of the 20th century in the Indo-Saracenic style, has as many as 15 dining halls. Counted as one of the largest residences in Asia, it is set amidst terraced gardens and water channels, inspired by Mughal gardens. The terraces lead to the Sheesh Mahal, where the **Art Gallery** displays miniature paintings, rare manuscripts, objets d'art, and hunting trophies from the former royal collection. Pride of place is given to a collection of medals, some awarded to, and some collected by, the former rulers. The Art Gallery overlooks a large tank flanked by two towers, with a rope suspension bridge to connect them. The main palace has

Hand-embroidered *jutties* on sale in Patiala's bazaar

A typical *phulkari* motif

now been given over to the National Institute of Sports and the large pleasure pool where the maharaja once watched dancing girls cavorting has been converted into a wrestling pit.

In the north of the city are the **Baradari Gardens**, laid out in the late 19th century by Prince Rajinder Singh, an avid horticulturist, who also created a rock garden and fern house here. The splendid **Kali Temple**, which is located within the walled city, has a large marble image of Kali, brought here all the way from Makrana in Rajasthan.

🏛 **Durbar Hall Museum**
⚑ Tue–Sun. 📷 with permission. ⚑
🏛 **Old Moti Bagh Palace**
⚑ Tue–Sun ⚑

Sirhind ❺

Fatehgarh Sahib district. 55 km (34 miles) W of Chandigarh. ⚑ 31,000. ⚑ ⚑ ⚑ Punjab Tourism, (01763) 22 9170. ⚑ Urs at Rauza Sharif (Aug), Shaheedi Jor Mela (Dec).

The town of Sirhind was one of the most important settlements in North India between the 16th and 18th centuries. Once the capital of the Pathan Sur sultans, the ruins of whose massive fort can still be seen, Sirhind was also a favourite halting place for the Mughal emperors on their annual journeys to Kashmir. In the 11th century, Mahmud of Ghazni (see p48) expanded his empire up to this area, thus giving the town its name, which in Persian means "Frontier of India".

The Mughals constructed several beautiful buildings here, in the area now called **Aam Khas Bagh**, which today is a tourist complex run by the government. Especially interesting is the **Royal Hamam**, a complex structure for hot and cold baths, that uses water drawn from wells nearby through an intricate system of hand pulleys. Close to the baths are the ruins of Shah Jahan's double-storeyed palace, the **Daulat Mahal**, and the better preserved **Sheesh Mahal**,

Rauza Sharif, Shaikh Ahmad Faruqi Sirhindi's *dargah* in Sirhind

whose walls still have traces of the original tilework and decorative plaster.

To the north of Aam Khas Bagh is the white **Fatehgarh Sahib Gurdwara**, standing in the midst of bright yellow mustard fields, which bloom in January. It was built to honour the memory of the martyred sons of the tenth Sikh guru, Gobind Singh, who were walled in alive at this spot by the Mughal emperor Aurangzeb in 1705, for refusing to convert to Islam.

Adjacent to the gurdwara is an important pilgrimage site for Muslims, the tomb-shrine of the Sufi saint and theologian, Shaikh Ahmad Faruqi Sirhindi, who is also known as Mujaddad-al-Saini ("The Reformer of the Millennium"). This magnificent octagonal structure, with its dome covered in glazed blue tiles, was built in the 16th century. Known as the **Rauza Sharif**, it is considered as holy as the

Dargah Sharif in Ajmer (*see p376*). Standing close to it is a striking tomb from the same period, the **Mausoleum of Mir Miran**, son-in-law of one of the Lodi kings. Also of interest is the **Salavat Beg Haveli**, a fascinating and exceptionally well preserved example of a large Mughalera house.

🏛 **Aam Khas Bagh**
⭕ *Tue–Sun.*

Anandpur Sahib ➅

Roopnagar district. 73 km (45 miles) N of Chandigarh. 🚊 31,000. 🚉 🚌
📅 *Hola Mohalla (Mar/Apr).*

Guarded by the Shivalik Hills and a ring of impos-ing forts, Anandpur Sahib is a complex of historic Sikh gurdwaras. It was here that

the severed head of the ninth guru, Tegh Bahadur, was brought to be cremated, at a site now marked by the **Sisganj Sahib Gurdwara**. The gurdwara also marks the place where the tenth and last guru, Gobind Singh, founded the Khalsa or "Army of the Pure" in 1699, along with five volunteers to help him defend the faith. The **Kesgarh Sahib Gurdwara**, which was built to commemorate this event, is regarded as one of the four *takhts* or principal seats of the Sikh religion – the others are at Amritsar (*see p104*), Nanded in Maharashtra, and Patna (*see p214*) in Bihar. A week-long celebration was held here in April 1999, to mark the 300th anniversary of the Khalsa.

A series of forts surround Anandpur Sahib on all sides – **Lohagarh Fort** was used as the armoury of the Khalsa army, **Fatehgarh Fort** guarded the route between Delhi and Lahore, and **Taragarh Fort** protected it from attacks by the hill states lying to the north.

A Nihang Sikh in full regalia

Anandpur Sahib comes to life every year during the Hola Mohalla festival (*see p101*) when thousands of devotees congregate here to watch the blue-robed Nihang Sikhs, descendants of the gurus' personal guards, display their formidable martial and equestrian skills.

A mid-19th-century painting of Guru Nanak with his disciples

SIKHISM

With their characteristic turbans and full beards, the Sikhs are easy to identify. The Sikh religion is a reformist faith, founded by Guru Nanak in the 15th century. Strongly opposed to idol worship, rituals and the caste system, it believes in a formless God. Sikhism is also called the Gurmat, meaning "the Guru's Doctrine" and Sikh temples are known as gurdwaras, literally "doors to the guru". Nanak, the first of a series of ten gurus, chose his successor from among his most devout disciples. Gobind Singh (1666–1708), the tenth and last guru, reorganized the community in 1699 as a military order, the Khalsa, to com-bat religious persecution by the Mughals. He gave the Sikh community a distinctive religious identity, and from then onwards they were meant to wear the Khalsa's five symbols: *kesh* (long hair), *kachha* (underwear), *kirpan* (small sword), *kangha* (comb) and *kara* (bracelet). Their holy book, the *Guru Granth Sahib*, is kept in the Golden Temple (*see pp106–107*).

Detail of a marble sculpture, Elysée Palace, Kapurthala

Kapurthala ❼

Kapurthala district. 165 km (103 miles) NW of Chandigarh. 🚆 🚌

This former princely state owes its extraordinary architectural heritage to the eccentric Maharaja Jagatjit Singh, who created amidst the rich agricultural fields of Punjab, a corner that will be forever France. In 1906, this passionate Francophile, commissioned a French architect to build him a palace modelled on Versailles, with elements of Fontainebleu and the Louvre added on. This amazing structure, which he grandly named the Elysée Palace (now the **Jagatjit Palace**), sits amidst gardens embellished with stone statuary and fountains, and is surrounded by villas built for his officials, modelled on those that were in vogue in the suburbs of Paris in the late 19th century. The palace is now a school, but the building with its ornate interiors and Renaissance-style painted ceilings, is open to public.

After this palace was built, the maharaja went through a Spanish phase. This found expression in the **Buena Vista Hunting Lodge**. Located on the outskirts of the town, it is occupied by his descendants. Another impressive sight is the town's **Moorish Mosque**. Inspired by the grand Qutubiya Mosque in Marrakesh, this was designed by yet another French architect employed by Jagatjit Singh. Its inner dome has been beautifully painted by Punjabi artists.

🏛 Jagatjit Palace
⏰ Tue–Sun. 📷

The Jagatjit Palace at Kapurthala, modelled on Versailles in France

MAHARAJA RANJIT SINGH

Maharaja Ranjit Singh (r.1790–1839)

Maharaja Ranjit Singh was one of North India's most remarkable rulers. By persuading rival Sikh chieftains to unite, he established the first Sikh kingdom of the Punjab. A military genius, his strong army kept both the British and ambitious Afghan invaders at bay, making Punjab a prosperous centre of trade and industry. A devout Sikh who did much to embellish the Golden Temple, the one-eyed Ranjit Singh was an enlightened ruler who liked to say "God intended me to look at all religions with one eye". A decade after his death, the British annexed the Punjab and seized his fabulous treasures, including the famous Kohinoor diamond.

Amritsar ❽

Amritsar district. 217 km (135 miles) NW of Chandigarh. 🚶 1,000,000. 🏨 Palace Hotel opp railway station, (0183) 240 2452. ✈ 12 km (8 miles) NW of city centre. 🚆 🚌 🎦 Guru Parab (Nov).

Founded in 1577 by the fourth Sikh guru, Ram Das, Amritsar was built on a site donated by the Mughal emperor Akbar. Located in the heart of the city is the **Golden Temple** (see pp106–107), the Sikh community's holiest shrine, surrounded by a maze of lanes and 18 fortified gateways. In 1984, parts of the Golden Temple were badly damaged during an army operation to flush out extremists holed up inside, who were demanding a separate Sikh homeland. It has now been repaired and carefully restored to its original glory.

The temple complex is actually a city within a city, and the main entrance is through its northern gateway, known as the **Darshani Darwaza**, which also houses the **Central Sikh Museum**. On display are paintings, coins, manuscripts and arms, that combine to create a vivid picture of Sikh history. Steps lead down to the **Parikrama** (marble path-way) which encircles the **Amrit Sarovar** ("Pool of Nectar", after which the town is named), and the main shrine, the golden-domed **Hari Mandir** ("Temple of God"). Several holy and historic sites line the Parikrama, among them a tree shrine called the **Dukh Bhanjani Ber**, said to have miraculous powers for healing diseases, and the **Athsath Tirath** which represents 68 of the holiest Hindu pilgrim shrines.

The Parikrama continues on to the Akal Takht, the seat of the Sikh religious order. Its construction began in 1589 and was completed in 1601 by the sixth guru, Guru Hargobind, when he began organizing the Sikh community into a political entity. The upper floors were built by Maharaja Ranjit Singh.

View of the Golden Temple complex, with the central shrine and main entrance

As part of the daily ritual, the Holy Book of the Sikhs, the *Guru Granth Sahib*, is carried out of the Akal Takht to the Hari Mandir at daybreak. The head priest then opens it for the *vaq*, the message for the day. From dawn till late at night the temple echoes with the music of *ragis*, musicians employed by the temple trust to sing verses from the Holy Book. Every visitor entering the Hari Mandir (including non-Sikhs) is given a dollop of sweet *prasad* (holy offering), and no visit is considered truly complete without a meal at the **Guru ka Langar**, a free kitchen where all visitors are fed a simple meal of *dal-roti* (lentil curry and bread). Run by volunteers, this kitchen can feed 10,000 people a day. Its vast hall, which can seat 3,000 people at a time, serves as a symbol of the caste-free, egalitarian society that the Sikh gurus strove to create. The notion of *kar-seva* (voluntary manual labour for a cause) is an important part of the Sikh order. Tasks such as sweeping the temple pre-cincts, cooking at the *langar* or looking after the pilgrims' shoes, are enthusiastically performed by volunteers. The final evening prayers are over by 9:45pm, when the Holy Book is reverently closed and carried in a silver palanquin

Memorial, Jallianwala Bagh

back to the Akal Takht. The floors of the temple are then washed with milk and water before the doors of the Darshani Deorhi are closed. A few other shrines are found just outside the Temple complex. These include a shrine dedicated to Guru Hargobind Singh, as well as the nine-storeyed **Baba Atal Tower** which marks the spot where Atal Rai, the son of Hargobind attained martyrdom. The 16th-century **Durgiana Temple**, visited by Hindus, is dedicated to Durga. It lies 2 km (1.3 miles) northeast of the Golden Temple.

Jallianwala Bagh, also a short distance from the Golden Temple, is the site of an infamous massacre that took place in 1919. Hundreds of unarmed demonstrators were gunned down in this enclosed garden on the orders of General Reginald Dyer, who arrived heading a platoon of infantry from Jalandhar. It was an event which helped hasten the end of British rule in India. A memorial to those killed stands at the east end.

Environs
The last checkpost on the Indian border is at **Wagah**, just 9 km (6 miles) from Amritsar, separated from Attari in Pakistan by a thin road. Each evening, as buglers sound the last post, two splendidly uniformed guards on either side of the border goose step across to the flagpoles to lower their respective national flags. Their steps are matched so perfectly that it is like watching a mirror image of the same exercise. The ceremony, which attracts crowds of spectators on both sides, is a poignant reminder of the Partition of 1947 *(see p56)*, when Punjab was divided between two nations.

Ceremonial guards accompanying the Holy Book outside the Akal Takht

Amritsar: The Golden Temple

Pietra dura detail

The spiritual centre of the Sikh religion, the Golden Temple was built between 1589 and 1601, and is a superb synthesis of Islamic and Hindu styles of architecture. In keeping with the syncretic tradition of those times, its foundation stone was laid by a Muslim saint, Mian Mir. It was virtually destroyed in 1761 by an Afghan invader, Ahmed Shah Abdali, but was rebuilt some years later by Maharaja Ranjit Singh, ruler of Punjab, who covered the dome in gold and embellished its interiors with lavish decoration.

First Floor
The marble walls have pietra dura inlay and decorative plasterwork, bearing animal and flower motifs covered in gold leaf.

★ Sheesh Mahal
The Hall of Mirrors on the top floor has a curved bangaldar roof, and its floors are swept with a special broom made of peacock feathers.

Hari Mandir
The holiest site for Sikhs, the three-storeyed temple, decorated with superb pietra dura, is where the Holy Book is kept during the day.

The dome, shaped like an inverted lotus, is covered in 100 kg (220 lbs) of gold donated by Ranjit Singh in 1830.

The lower wall of the temple is made of white marble.

STAR FEATURES

★ Sheesh Mahal

★ Guru Granth Sahib

★ Guru Granth Sahib
Covered by a jewelled canopy, the Holy Book lies in the Durbar Sahib ("Court of the Lord").

Darshani Deorhi
This gateway provides the first glimpse of the temple's inner sanctum. It has two splendid silver doors and sacred verses carved on its walls.

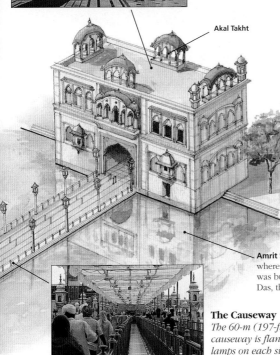

Akal Takht

Akal Takht
The seat of the supreme governing body of the Sikhs, it houses the gurus' swords and flagstaffs, as well as the Holy Book at night.

Amrit Sarovar, the pool where Sikhs are baptized, was built in 1577 by Ram Das, the fourth guru.

The Causeway
The 60-m (197-ft) long marble causeway is flanked by nine gilded lamps on each side, and leads to the temple across the Amrit Sarovar.

GOLDEN TEMPLE COMPLEX

1. Temple Office
2. Cloakrooms
3. Darshani Darwaza and Clocktower
4. Hari Mandir
5. Athsath Tirath (68 Shrines)
6. Guru ka Langar (Dining Hall)
7. Baba Karak Singh's Residence
8. Assembly Hall
9. Baba Deep Singh's Shrine
10. Darshani Deorhi
11. Arjun Dev's Tree
12. Akal Takht
13. Nishan Sahibs (Flagstaffs)
14. Gobind Singh's Shrine
15. Dukh Bhanjani Ber (Tree Shrine)

| 0 metres | 50 |
| 0 yards | 50 |

KEY

▢ Area illustrated above

HIMACHAL PRADESH

Himachal, the "Abode of Snow", covers over 56,000 sq km (21,622 sq miles) of the Western Himalayas. The state's terrain rises from the foothills of the Shivaliks bordering the plains of Punjab, and extends to the trans-Himalayan heights of the Zanskar Range, bordering Ladakh and Tibet. Himachal's capital Shimla, famous as the summer capital of the British Raj, remains a popular destination for visitors. Manali, the state's other big hill station, is in the heart of the idyllic Kullu Valley. Watered by the Beas river, it is an excellent base for treks and excursions. West of Kullu, with the magnificent Dhauladhar Range as its backdrop, is the Kangra Valley, dotted with apple orchards. Its main town is Dharamsala, home to the Dalai Lama and a vibrant Tibetan community, and the seat of the Tibetan Government-in-Exile. In the eastern part of the state is Kinnaur with its green pastures and enchanting villages, while Lahaul and Spiti to the north are lands of rugged grandeur, with Buddhist monasteries clinging to steep, rocky cliffs.

SIGHTS AT A GLANCE

Towns & Cities
Mandi ⑩
Nahan ⑤
Rampur ⑥
Sarahan ⑦

Hill Stations & Areas of Natural Beauty
Bharmour ⑮
Chail ②
Chamba ⑭
Dalhousie ⑬
Dharamsala ⑫
Kasauli ④

Manali ⑲
Narkanda ③
Shimla ①

Monasteries
Tabo Monastery ㉑

Valleys & Districts
Kangra Valley ⑪
Kinnaur ⑨

Kullu Valley ⑯
Lahaul and Spiti ⑳
Parvati Valley ⑰

National Parks
Great Himalayan
     National Park ⑱

Tours
Sangla Valley Tour ⑧

KEY

✕	Domestic airport
═══	National highway
▬▬	Major road
══	Minor road
—	Major railway
‑ ‑	International border

Chenab
Keylong
Hansa
Pathankot
Kaza
Kotla
Gaggal
Manikaran
NH 20
NH 21
Jwalamukhi
Beas
NH1A
Rekong Peo
Jalandhar
Govind Sagar
NH 22
Bilaspur
Yamunotri
Gangotri
Solan
Chandigarh
Uttarkashi
Mussoorie
Ambala
Dehra Dun

0 km   50
0 miles   50

◁ Buddhist prayer flags fluttering in the wind, in the rugged mountains of Spiti

Shimla

Stained glass, Christ Church

A popular hill station in North India, Shimla's spectacular location, thickly forested slopes and invigorating climate have attracted countless visitors since the small village was discovered by Captain Charles Kennedy in the early 19th century. In 1864, it became the summer headquarters of the British government in India. Today it is the fast-growing capital of Himachal Pradesh. Though many of the surrounding spurs and forests are now covered with concrete buildings, Shimla still retains much of its colonial charm.

Christ Church and the Municipal Library on the Ridge

🚇 The Ridge

N of The Mall.

A popular promenade and the centre of Shimla's busy social and cultural scene, the Ridge, situated at a height of 2,230 m (7,316 ft), is an open stretch of land on the western shoulder of Jakhu Hill. From here, the snowcapped peaks of the Himalayan Range stretch in an arc across the northern horizon. Ceremonial parades and official state functions are also held here.

🔒 Christ Church

🕐 daily. ✝ 8am, 11am Sun.
Contact caretaker if church is closed.
Dominating the eastern end of the Ridge is the Gothic Christ Church, a prominent landmark. Constructed in 1846, it was one of the first churches built in North India. Its fine stained-glass windows and impressive organ were acquired in the 19th century. The fresco around the chancel window was designed by Lockwood Kipling, Rudyard Kipling's father. Shimla's mock-Tudor **Municipal Library** is nearby.

🔒 The Mall

Shops 🕐 Mon–Sat. Restricted vehicular movement.
This 7-km (4-mile) long thoroughfare, running from Boileauganj in the west to Chhota Shimla in the southeast, demarcates the original limits of the town. The central section of The Mall, flanked by rows of half-timbered buildings, has always been, and still remains, its most fashionable area with a profusion of restaurants, bars and upmarket shops. The Mall's highest spot, Scandal Point, is marked by a statue of Lala Lajpat Rai, the famous freedom fighter. The so-called "scandal" refers to the reputed abduction of an English lady in the late 19th century from this spot by Maharaja Bhupinder Singh of Patiala *(see p102)*. Nearby are the timber-framed Post Office, the Town Hall and the jewel-like Gaiety Theatre, opened in 1887, and still a popular venue for amateur dramatics. A favoured pastime for both local residents and visitors, is to stroll along The Mall, from Scandal Point to Combermere Bridge. Further ahead on this stretch lies the charming mock-Tudor Clarkes Hotel.

🔒 Lower Bazaar

Shops 🕐 Mon–Sat.
Below the central section of The Mall is the Lower Bazaar, which Kipling once referred to as "that crowded rabbit warren catering to the native population of Shimla". Offering the option of cheaper wares and less fashionable hostelries and eating places, it remains the poor man's Mall. Lower still is the **Ganj**, a congested bazaar where the town's wholesale trade in groceries takes place. This, more than any other part of town, retains a flavour of times gone by. Customers and coolies mingle in crowded lanes redolent with the aroma of the many spices on display.

🏛 State Museum

Chaura Maidan. *Tel* (0177) 280 5044.
🕐 Tue–Sun. 🔵 public hols. 🚫 📷
The State Museum, housed in a reconstructed Raj building called Inverarm, was opened to the public in 1974. It has, since then, built up a fairly good collection of almost 10,000 artifacts from various parts of Himachal Pradesh. The exhibits, displayed in 15

The interior of the Gaiety Theatre, a focal point of Shimla's cultural life

galleries, include stone sculptures dating from the 6th to 11th centuries, belonging to the Gupta and Pratihara periods, and a collection of Kangra miniatures *(see p121)* representing various themes, based on the seasons *(Baramasa)*, musical modes *(Ragamala)* and episodes from the *Gita Govinda*, a devotional poem. Most impressive, however, is a spectacular series of mid-19th-century wall paintings from Chamba, housed in the ground floor galleries.

Jakhu Hill Temple
Jakhu Hill. ◯ *daily.*
The forested dome of Jakhu Hill, at 2,450 m (8,038 ft) is the highest point in Shimla. At its peak stands a temple dedicated to the monkey god, Hanuman. According to the epic *Ramayana (see p27)*, Hanuman rested here during his journey to fetch the Sanjivini herb from the Himalayas to save the wounded Lakshman's life. A steep 2 km (1.3 miles) climb from the Ridge to the summit through deodar and oak forests offers panoramic views of Shimla and its suburbs. Monkeys are a common sight all over Shimla but Jakhu is their kingdom. Visitors should watch out for simian hands rifling through their pockets and belongings.

🏛 Viceregal Lodge
The Mall. *Tel* (0177) 283 1375.
◯ *daily.* 📷 ⊘
The most imposing British-built building in Shimla is the former Viceregal Lodge. Situated atop Observatory Hill, this grey stone structure in the English Renaissance style was built under the guidance of Lord Dufferin in 1888, as a suitable summer residence for the viceroys of India. Well-maintained gardens surround the stately mansion on three sides. The interior is as impressive, with two rows of

balconies overlooking the magnificent teak-panelled entrance hall. A bronze plaque behind the building lists the peaks visible at a distance. It is now called Rashtrapati Niwas and houses the Indian Institute of Advanced Studies. Only the entrance hall and the gardens are open to the public.

The stately Viceregal Lodge, set amid manicured lawns

SHIMLA CITY CENTRE

Christ Church ②
Lower Bazaar ④
The Mall ③
The Ridge ①

0 metres 200
0 yards 200

Annandale

Rivoli Bus Stand
CIRCULAR

VICTORY TUNNEL

THE MALL

SCANDAL POINT

Town Hall

Gaiety Theatre

The Ridge ①

② Christ Church

LAKKAR BAZAAR ROAD

Mashobra, Naldehra

ROAD

Boileauganj, State Museum, Viceregal Lodge

Airport 21 km (13 miles)

CART

③ THE MALL

④ Lower Bazaar

Branch Railway Station

Inter State Bus Terminal

ROAD

Jakhu Hill Temple

RAJ BHAVAN

Chhota Shimla

Key to Symbols *see back flap*

Campsite at Kufri, under a heavy blanket of snow in winter

Exploring Shimla

The best way to explore Shimla is to walk along the many meandering roads and byways. Beyond the centre *(see pp110–11)*, the meadow of **Annandale** is 5 km (3 miles) north of the Ridge. During the Raj, all major social events, including races, cricket matches and fêtes, were held here. The **Glen**, another popular picnic spot, is further west and is reached by a path near the Oberoi Cecil *(see p693)*. This grand colonial structure, built on a precipice, is reminiscent of Raj-era luxury. Across the spur from here are the scenic **Chadwick Falls**. A 4-km (2.5-mile) long forest road, starting from Christ Church on the Ridge, continues along the wooded slopes of Jakhu Hill. This road winds southeast to end near one of Shimla's oldest educational institutions, St Bede's College for Women, en route overlooking the quaint bazaar of Chhota Shimla.

Musk deer in the Himalayan Nature Park

Deeper into the hills and along the same ridge system as Shimla, are a number of places to visit. At Charabra, 13 km (8 miles) north of Shimla, **Wildflower Hall**, the former retreat of the Commander-in-Chief, Lord Kitchner, is now a plush hotel *(see p693)*. About 10 km (6 miles) north along the old Hindustan-Tibet (HT) Road, just above the diversion to the left leading to the village of **Mashobra**, a gravel road barred by a gate to the right, indicates the entrance to the **Seog Wildlife Sanctuary** and the old Seog rest house. The sanctuary is home to local species of wildlife, including deer, hill fox and monal pheasants. At Mashobra, a steep forest pathway leads to a lovely little temple dedicated to a local goddess, set in a grove of deodars. The annual Sipi Fair is held here.

Continuing north from Mashobra, 3-km (2-mile) along a motor road, is the **Craignano Rest House**. Once the home of an Italian count, it commands superb views from its hilltop garden. Further north (10 km/6 miles) is **Naldehra** with a nine-hole golf course set amidst sloping meadows and fringed by deodar and blue pine. A British legacy dating from the 19th century, the golf course was

designed by the viceroy, Lord Curzon. About 16 km (10 miles) east of Shimla, is the picturesque little village of **Kufri**. At an altitude of 2,650 m (8,694 ft), it is now becoming a popular venue for winter sports. Kufri's small zoo, the **Himalayan Nature Park**, counts the Himalayan black bear and the musk deer among its residents.

🦌 Seog Wildlife Sanctuary
For permission contact: Divisional Forest Officer, Shimla Municipal Corporation. **Tel** *(0177) 265 2911.*

🦌 Himalayan Nature Park
Kufri. ◻ *daily.* 🖼

Chail ❷

Solan district. 45 km (28 miles) SE of Shimla. 🚌 ℹ *Hotel Chail Palace, (01792) 248 141.*

This tiny hill station is situated on a wooded ridge at a similar altitude to Shimla. Chail was developed as the summer capital of the Patiala maharajas *(see p102)* in the 1920s. **Chail Palace**, a stone mansion occupying a flattened hilltop, amid beautiful orchards and garden, is now a deluxe hotel *(see p692)*. The cricket pitch, near the top of a hill, is said to be the highest in the world. The Patiala rulers, enthusiastic cricketers themselves, invited the Marylebone Cricket Club (the MCC) to play here in 1933. Walks through the deodar forests of the Chail Wildlife Sanctuary, where Scottish red deer were introduced, are the best way to discover Chail's natural beauty.

Naldehra's scenic golf course

A temple on Hatu Peak, a day's hike from Narkanda

Narkanda ❸

Shimla district. 64 km (40 miles) N of Shimla. 🚌

Narkanda, at a height of 2,750 m (9,022 ft), stands on the HT Road as it winds along the edges of the ridge-line dividing the Satluj and Yamuna catchments. From here, the Himalayan peaks are even closer, and the walks through dense temperate forests where spruce, fir and high-altitude oak take over from the deodar and blue pine, are quite spectacular. The best walk is the 6-km (4-mile) hike to Hatu Peak (3,300 m/10,827 ft), where the Gurkhas made one of their last stands against the British in 1815. The area around Narkanda is lush with apple orchards. In winter, the slopes are ideal for skiing.

Kasauli ❹

Solan district. 77 km (48 miles) S of Shimla. 🚶 5,000. 🚌

The closest hill station to the plains, Kasauli offers the charm of quiet walks shaded by *chir* pine, oak and horse chestnut trees. It is at its best just after the monsoon, when colourful dahlias cover the hillsides. As an army cantonment, restrictions imposed by the authorities have prevented the old town from being taken over by concrete modern structures. As a result, old-fashioned buildings with gable roofs and wooden balconies remain intact on the **Upper** and **Lower Malls**, the two main streets that run right through the town. **Monkey Point**, the highest spot in the town, is 4 km (2.5 miles) from the bus station. From here there are clear views of Shimla, the meandering Satluj and Chandigarh. A particularly lovely trail across the hills is the 5-km (3-mile) walk to the **Lawrence School** at Sanawar, a public school founded by Sir Henry Lawrence (see p197) in 1847.

Postbox, Kasauli

Environs
About 60 km (37 miles) northeast of Kasauli is **Nalagarh**, the seat of the former princely state of Hindur. The palace is now a heritage hotel called the Nalagarh Resort (see p693).

HILL STATIONS
By the late 19th century, when the British had consolidated their rule in India, families began to come over from Britain to join their menfolk. In the years that followed, more than 80 settlements were established in the lower hill ranges, as summer retreats for the burgeoning expatriate population, keen to escape the intense heat of the plains. Hill stations endeavoured to recreate a way of life reminiscent of the home country, complete with half-timbered houses, clubs, churches, hospitals, parks with bandstands and a main street invariably known as The Mall. Boarding schools, were also set up for children who were unable to go back to study in England.

Kennedy's Cottage, by Captain J Luard, Shimla, 1822

FESTIVALS OF HIMACHAL PRADESH
Shivratri *(Feb/Mar)*, Mandi. Local deities are carried down from the surrounding hills on elaborately decorated palanquins, to pay homage to Lord Shiva at the Bhootnath Temple.
Summer Festival *(May/Jun)*, Shimla and Dharamsala. This recently inaugurated festival coincides with the tourist season and attracts singers and dancers.
Minjar *(Jul/Aug)*, Chamba. Maize shoots or *minjars*, strung on silken threads, are cast into the Ravi river at the start of this week-long festival to seek blessings for a bountiful harvest.
Manimahesh Yatra *(Aug/Sep)*, Bharmour. The pilgrimage to the sacred Manimahesh Lake draws thousands of Hindu devotees. Its waters are believed to cleanse the sins of a lifetime.
Dussehra *(Sep/Oct)*, Kullu *(see p127)*.
Lavi Fair *(Nov)*, Rampur. Products from remote Tibet and Ladakh were once bartered with those from the plains and lower hills at this fair. Today, woollen goods and pashmina from Tibet, *chilgoza* nuts and shawls from Kinnaur and Changmurti horses from Spiti are briskly traded.
Renuka Fair *(Nov)*, Nahan. People from the surrounding villages gather at the shores of the Renuka Lake to celebrate the completion of the harvest, at this fair.

Colourful Kinnauri shawls on sale at the Lavi Fair, Rampur

Trekking in Himachal Pradesh

This mountainous state, with its vast variety of terrains, offers a wide range of treks from easy, one-day hikes to week-long routes. At lower altitudes, trails wind through forests of oak, deodar (*Cedrus deodara*) and pine, while steeper climbs lead to flower-strewn

A cone from a deodar tree

alpine meadows above the tree line. The towns of Manali and Dharamsala are starting points for several popular treks. The best season for trekking is during the month of June, and then later between mid-September and October, after the monsoon. During the rains (June–September), the trans-Himalayan cold deserts of Spiti (*see p130*) and Upper Kinnaur are ideal destinations, completely shielded from monsoon showers.

LOCATOR MAP

▨ Area shown below

0 km   20

0 miles   20

Dharamsala to Macchetar

A challenging 75-km (47-mile) route crosses rocky terrain to the meadows at Triund. A steep ascent leads to the Indrahar Pass, with views of the Pir Panjal peaks, and ends at the small town of Macchetar, connected by road to Chamba.

Duration: *5 days*
Altitude: *4,350 m (14,272 ft)*
Level of difficulty: *moderate to tough*

KEY

▪▪ The Pin Valley Trek

▪▪ Naggar to Jari

▪▪ Manali to Beas Kund

▪▪ Dharamsala to Macchetar

══ National highway

▬▬ Major road

— Minor road

△ Peak

⌣ Pass

Starting at Palchan near Manali, a 30-km (19-mile) round trip to the glacial lake of Beas Kund, leads past the ski station at Solang and over glacial moraine to the lake, surrounded by snow-clad peaks.

Duration: *3 days*
Altitude: *3,980 m (13,058 ft)*
Level of difficulty: *easy*

*Map labels:* Gepang Goh (6,050 m/19,849); Chamba; Bharmour; Kailash (5,656 m/18,556 ft); Beas Kund; Rohtang Pass (3,985 m/13,0...); Macchetar; Indrahar Pass (4,350 m/14,272 ft); Kuarsi; Solang; Palchan; Hanuman Tibba (5,930 m/19,455 ft); Manali; Dharamkot; Triund; Dharamsala; Palampur; Naggar; Chanderkhani Pa... (3,500 m/11,483); Malana; Manikar; Jari; Pulga; Kullu; Beas; NH21; Satluj; Mandi; Bilaspur

Naggar to Jari

This 40-km (25-mile) trek crosses the Chandrakhani Pass, offering fine views of the peaks surrounding Solang Nala, and leads past the isolated Malana village (see p128) to end at Jari in Parvati Valley.

Duration: *4 days*
Altitude: *3,500 m (11,483 ft)*
Level of difficulty: *moderate*

The Pin Valley Trek
Starting at Manikaran, famous for its hot springs, the 130-km (81-mile) path goes over the Pin-Parvati Pass to the cold desert region of the beautiful Pin Valley. It ends at Mikkim, 40 km (25 miles) from the main roadhead at Kaza.

Duration: 7 days
Altitude: 5,319 m (17,451 ft)
Level of difficulty: tough

Kaza

Spiti

Dankar

Mikkim

Sangam

Mud

Dankar

Pin Valley

Mantalai

andav Bridge

hirganga

Parvati

Pin Parvati Pass
(5,319 m/17,451 ft)

PRACTICAL TIPS

Be prepared: *Acclimatization is essential for areas over 3,000 m (9,843 ft). See p767 for tips on altitude sickness. Guides are needed as maps are insufficient for safe passage across glaciers. For details on trekking see p751.*

On the trek: *Drink plenty of water. Carry a first aid kit and cooking fuel. Never burn wood, which is a scarce resource. Put out all fires properly, leaving no burning embers. Do not litter, and carry your rubbish back with you.*

Permits: *Foreign visitors require travel permits for parts of Spiti and Kinnaur, obtainable from the district or subdivisional magistrate's offices in Shimla (see p111), Rekong Peo (see p119), Kaza and Kullu (see p126). The offices at Kaza, (01906) 222 302 and Rekong Peo, (01789) 222 253 are the most efficient. For general details see p758.*

Equipment hire & operators: *The Institute of Mountaineering and Allied Sports in Manali (01902) 252 342, and Yeti Trekking in McLeodganj (01892) 221 887, organize treks. The Regional Mountaineering Centre in McLeodganj, (01892) 221 787, offers mountaineering courses. In Manali, Himalayan Adventurers, (01902) 252 365, is a reputable rafting agency, the Himalayan Institute of Adventure Sports, (01902) 253 050, offers paragliding, and Himalayan Journeys, (01902) 252 365, offers mountain biking. See also p755.*

Caution: *Trekkers have gone missing in Parvati Valley. It is advisable to trek in groups and to take an experienced guide along.*

OTHER ADVENTURE ACTIVITIES

Climbing a rock face, Tirthan Valley

Himachal Pradesh has several peaks over 3,000 m (9,843 ft), suitable for climbing. The Institute of Mountaineering and Allied Sports at Manali offers three-week courses. Skiing is possible at Narkanda, Kufri and at Solang Nala near Manali. Summer is the best season for rafting and kayaking on the Beas river at Manali, and for paragliding at Solang and Billing in Kangra. Himalayan Journeys *(see p752)* in Manali offers mountain biking near the Rohtang Pass.

Renuka Lake, venue of the Renuka Fair held in November

Nahan ⑤

Sirmaur district. 100 km (62 miles) S of Shimla. 🚌 🖼 *Renuka Fair (Nov).*

Lying in the lower Shivalik Hills close to the plains, Nahan nestles sleepily on a low wooded ridge at 930 m (3,051 ft). The old town retains its network of narrow cobbled streets and has an interesting bazaar dating to the 17th century. The old palace (Raja Mahal) is closed to visitors. Other attractions include the Ranzore Palace facing the Chaugan (the royal polo ground), the lively Jagannath Temple in the bazaar, and the quiet walks through the *chir* pine forests on the Villa Round. Nahan serves as a convenient stop-over for visiting the popular Renuka Lake nearby.

Environs
Lying 42 km (26 miles) east of Nahan, is the sacred **Renuka Lake**, whose shoreline traces the shape of a sleeping woman. According to Hindu mythology, Renuka was the wife of the sage Jamdagni and mother of Parasurama, an incarnation of Lord Vishnu *(see p679).* She was killed by her son at his father's command, and miraculously came back to life, only to disappear again, leaving behind an imprint in the shape of her body. At the far end of the lake is a small wildlife park housing a pride of lions, Himalayan black bear and antelope. Nearby lies a smaller lake called Parasurama Tal, and below this, an open area where the Renuka Fair *(see p113)* is celebrated every year in November.

The pavilion in the spacious gardens of Rampur's palace

Rampur ❻

Shimla district. 130 km (81 miles) NE of Shimla. 🚌 🚗 *daily.* 🎪 *Lavi Fair (Nov).*

Once on the main trade route between India and Tibet, Rampur is today a big commercial town. It comes alive in November each year when the vibrant Lavi Fair (*see p113*) takes place.

The early 20th-century palace of the old kings is still their private residence, though visitors are allowed to walk around the sprawling gardens. A Hindu temple and a small pavilion are set in their midst.

Sarahan ❼

Shimla district. 198 km (123 miles) NE of Shimla. 🚌 🚗 *daily.* 🎪 *Dussehra (Sep/Oct).*

Perched high above the left bank of the Satluj, Sarahan was once the summer residence of the Rampur Bushahr kings. At 2,165 m (7,103 ft), it has a pleasant climate enhanced by the vista of the Srikhand Range across the valley, with the twin peaks of Gushu-Pishu and the holy mountain Srikhand Mahadev standing out prominently. Sarahan's most interesting sight is the spectacular tower temple, **Bhimakali**. It also has a short nature trail leading to a pheasantry. The many pheasants housed here include the monal and the near-extinct Western Himalayan tragopan.

Sarahan: Bhimakali Temple

Carved tiger

The palace-cum-temple complex of the Rampur Bushahr kings, Bhimakali owes its origin to the tradition of housing the family deity on the top floor of the feudal chief's home. Its elaborate layout consists of a series of courtyards connected by beautiful gateways. The presiding deity, Bhimakali, one of the myriad forms of the goddess Kali, is housed in the first floor of the pagoda-style temple. Although the exact age of the temple is not known, it is associated with historical events dating to the 7th century, while parts of it are around 800 years old.

View of the Bhimakali Temple Complex
The twin towers of the Bhimakali Temple, covered in snow and framed against the backdrop of the Srikhand Range, present an awesome sight.

The Ram Mandir is located in the second courtyard.

Slate roofs

Narasimha Temple

Main Entrance
An elaborately decorated metal door, at the entrance, opens into the first courtyard.

STAR FEATURES

★ Carved Balconies

★ Tower Shrines

★ Silver Doors

★ Carved Balconies
The uppermost storey of the renovated temple is fringed by overhanging balconies with exquisitely carved panels.

VISITORS' CHECKLIST

☐ daily. 📷 🎭 Janmashtami (Jul/Aug), Dussehra (Sep/Oct). Obligatory to wear the saffron cap, available outside. Shoes and leather objects not allowed.

★ Tower Shrines
The Leaning Tower (on the right) was the main temple until it was damaged during an earthquake in 1905. The adjoining tower has since become the main shrine.

Golden Finials
The finials, a combination of symbols of the sun and the moon, represent the deity and the royal patrons.

Alternating bands of stone and timber

Wooden Skittles
Carved wooden skittles hang from the eaves of the temple roofs.

Carved tiger statue

★ Silver Doors
The silver doors that lead to the second courtyard are embellished with panels depicting various Hindu gods. They were added during the reign of Padam Singh (1914–47), a Rampur Bushahr king.

Dussehra Festival
Dussehra is the only time of the year when the original 200-year-old image of Bhimakali is actively worshipped.

Sangla Valley Tour ❽

The largest village in Kinnaur, Sangla, often lends its name to the whole Baspa Valley. A drive through this area takes two to three days and encapsulates a dramatic transition in landscape, from the spectacular river gorge at the entrance to Kinnaur to alpine valley pastures. It takes in awesome mountain scenery and mixed forests of oak and rhododendron, before reaching charming slate-roofed villages that nestle amidst orchards and fields.

Temple at Sungra Maheshwar ③
The temple's pagoda-like roof and the fine wooden carvings on its doorways and walls make this an interesting stopover.

Kafour ①
Strung out along a little spur below the road, scenic Kafour is the first inhabited village in Kinnaur. The Hirma Temple, dedicated to a local mother goddess, stands out amid the slate rooftops.

| 0 km | 5 |
| 0 miles | 5 |

The Satluj Gorge at Tranda ②
From the road there are striking views of sheer rock walls falling 500 m (1,640 ft) to the river. On the other side, cliffs of equal magnitude enclose the Satluj in a narrow impenetrable gorge.

Kinnaur ❾

Kinnaur district. 244 km (152 miles) NE from Shimla to Rekong Peo. 🚌 19,250. 🚐 🚡 daily. 🎎 Sazi (Jan). **Travel permits** are required for parts of Kinnaur. Contact the Subdivisional Magistrate's office in Rekong Peo, (01786) 222 253. For details see p115.

Kinnaur, the remote north-eastern corner of Himachal Pradesh fringing the Tibetan Plateau, is a region of awesome grandeur. In the past, difficult terrain made Kinnaur inaccessible to all but the most intrepid of travellers, while in the 1950s, its proximity to the international border with Tibet resulted in restrictions on entry. However, these restrictions have been eased since 1992.

The variations in terrain, vegetation, climate and wildlife have broadly divided this region into Lower, Middle and Upper Kinnaur. Lower

View of the Kinner Kailash on a clear winter day

Kinnaur hugs both banks of a gorge-like Satluj river. The left bank's forested mountain slopes, contour-hugging terraced fields and tightly packed rows of houses clinging to the hillsides are picturesque in contrast to the right bank which is steeper, with higher peaks and a smaller population. Middle Kinnaur is much more rugged.

Dominating its heart are the majestic heights of the Kinner Kailash Range, while to its south is the gentler valley of the Baspa, one of the Satluj's largest tributaries. The arid sweep of the Zanskar peaks makes Upper Kinnaur a cold desert country of stark, barren mountains interspersed with occasional villages and irrigated fields.

Sapni ④
Sapni village has a tower temple that contains some of the finest examples of wooden sculpture in Kinnaur.

KEY

▨▨▨ Tour route

══ Road

── River

Urni

REKONG PEO

NH2

④
⑤
⑥

Rukti Khad

Baspa

Shaune Garang

⑦

Sangla ⑥
The largest among the villages that dot the Baspa Valley, Sangla has some beautiful walks to offer.

Chitkul ⑦
The tour ends at the village of Chitkul, just before the pastures of the Upper Baspa Valley. The valley's blue poppy was admired by the explorer Marco Pallis in 1933.

Kamroo ⑤
The tower of the Kamroo Narayan Temple commands a picturesque view of the valley. Fields and orchards slope down to the Baspa on one side of the river, while on the other side, thick forests rise up to pasturelands.

Rekong Peo, the new district headquarters, is a bustling little township on the right bank of the Satluj river, with some shops and adequate transport connections. About 13 km (8 miles) higher up on the same mountain is **Kalpa**, the old headquarters. With its panoramic view of the Kinner Kailash Range, Kalpa is a must in any Kinnaur itinerary. The choice of walks include one to the upland pastures through deodar and *chilgoza* pine (*Pinus gerardiana*) forests. Some old temples can be seen in the nearby Chini village.

About 20 km (12 miles) from Rekong Peo, the Baspa river joins the Satluj at its left bank. The beauty of the **Sangla Valley** (or Baspa Valley) has been extolled both in local legend and by visitors over the years, and the region lends itself to a lovely trip by road. Apart from a furious rush in its

last stretch of its course, the Baspa river ambles along a wooded valley past serene villages. Stupendous gneiss faces and forests of deodar, pine and birch reaching up to long swards of pasture and snow-covered peaks surround the valley. Every village in this valley, from Sangla to Chitkul, offers glorious walks and a choice of festivals to celebrate with the local people.

Buddhism holds complete sway throughout Upper Kinnaur. Fluttering prayer flags and mud-walled Buddhist temples with clay images and wall paintings dot the region, reflecting its proximity to Tibet. Many temples are credited to the 11th-century

scholar Rinchen Zangpo, revered in Tibetan Buddhism as the Lotsawa (Translator), who initiated the mammoth task of translating Indian texts into Tibetan. He was also the main force behind a great temple-building movement and supposedly built 108 monasteries in one night. **Nako**, 100 km (62 miles) from Rekong Peo, has a small lake and is close to Reo Purgyal, the highest peak in Himachal Pradesh at 6,816 m (22,362 ft).

Young Buddhist monks in a monastery, Kinnaur

A cluster of village houses with sloping roofs in Mandi

Mandi ⑩

Mandi district. 156 km (97 miles) N of Shimla. 🏠 26,900. 🚉 Joginder Nagar, 53 km (33 miles) NW of Mandi, then taxi or bus. 🚌 🎭 Shivratri (Feb/Mar).

Often referred to as the gateway to the Kullu Valley (see p126), Mandi is situated at the confluence of the Beas river with a small rain-fed tributary. The capital of the erstwhile princely state of Mandi, this small market town once functioned as a vital link between the hill communities on either side of it. The busy market located in a sunken garden in the centre of town, where all manner of merchandise is sold, is one of the more interesting sights here. Also situated in the town centre is the former residence of the Mandi kings, built in the colonial style, and now the heritage Rajmahal Palace Hotel. Several 16th- to 17th-century temples with beautiful stone carvings can be found all over the town. The most famous among these are the Madho Rai Temple, the Tarna Devi Temple and the Bhootnath Temple where the Shivratri festival is celebrated.

Environs

Rewalsar, a peaceful village at a height of 360 m (1,181 ft) is 24 km (15 miles) southeast of Mandi. On the shores of the Rewalsar Lake, resting in the hollow of a mountain spur, are a Buddhist monastery, three temples and a gurdwara commemorating the month-long stay of the tenth Sikh guru, Gobind Singh, in 1738. It is said that Padma-sambhava, the 8th century Indian apostle credited with bringing Buddhism to Tibet, used his legendary powers to fly from here to Tibet. His spirit is believed to reside in the tiny floating reed islands on the lake.

Mandi district apple orchard

Mandi's hinterland contains many other places of scenic beauty. To the east, **Jhanjheli** and **Karsog**, both about 100 km (62 miles) away in apple orchard country, offer the possibility of lovely treks to the hilltop temples of Shikari Devi and Mahunag.

Kangra Valley ⑪

Kangra district. 222 km (728 miles) NW of Shimla. 🏠 9,200. ✈ Gaggal, 10 km (6 miles) N of Kangra town. 🚉 Joginder Nagar and Una. 🚌

Located in the western part of Himachal Pradesh and spread between the Shivalik foothills and the Dhauladhar Range, the Kangra Valley is a land of gentle beauty. Undulating expanses of tea gardens and terraced paddy fields are crisscrossed by sparkling snow-fed rivulets. Kangra is the most populated district of Himachal Pradesh, and is well connected with the plains as it is situated along the border with Punjab.

The valley derives its name from the ancient town of Kangra, even though Dharamsala (see p122) is the present district headquarters. The history of the town goes back 3,500 years when it was called Nagarkot and was the capital of the kingdom of Trigartha. In 1620, Kangra and its fort were captured by Emperor Jahangir, after which it became a Mughal province. Dominating the town today are the ruins of the once formidable Kangra Fort, perched on top of a steep cliff overlooking the Banganga and Majhi rivulets. Within the fort's compound are two Hindu temples

The square-shaped Rewalsar Lake resting in the hollow of a mountain spur

The towering spire of Brajeshwari Devi Temple in Kangra town

dedicated to Ambika Devi (a local goddess) and Lakshmi Narayan, and a Jain temple with a stone image of Adinath. Behind the crowded bazaar is the Brajeshwari Devi Temple, whose fabled riches were plundered by Mahmud of Ghazni *(see p48)* in 1009. The present structure was built in 1920, after the terrible earthquake of 1905 destroyed the city and original temple.

Some 40 km (25 miles) southwest of Kangra town, are the 15 monolithic rock-cut temples of **Masroor**, dating to the 10th century and carved in a style similar to those at Ellora *(see pp476–8)*. The picturesque **Jwalamukhi**

Temple, 35 km (22 miles) southwest of Kangra, is one of North India's most important pilgrimage sites.

Further east of Kangra, the beauty of the tea garden country unfolds around **Palampur**, 45 km (28 miles) away. East of Palampur, are the 9th-century stone Baijnath Temple dedicated to Shiva, Bir with its Tibetan Buddhist monastery, and Billing, well-known as a take-off point for paragliding over the valley.

About 40 km (25 miles) southeast of Palampur, is the fortress of **Sujanpur-Tira**, located on the right bank of the Beas. Built by the Kangra kings in the early 18th century, it was the favoured

residence of Raja Sansar Chand, the renowned patron of Kangra miniature painting. The fortress also preserves some excellent wall paintings.

At the far end of the Kangra Valley is **Jogindernagar**, 55 km (34 miles) south of Palampur, the terminus of a narrow gauge railway line that winds up the valley from Pathankot in the west.

The **Maharana Pratap Sagar Lake**, created in 1979 by the construction of the Pong Dam across the Beas, lies to the southwest of Kangra district. This large wetland, spread over 45,000 ha (111,200 acres) when full, is a favoured stopover for migratory birds from Central Asia.

Terraced paddy fields in the Kangra Valley

PAHARI MINIATURE PAINTINGS

Pahari or "hill" painting refers to the various schools of miniature painting such as Kangra, Basohli, Mankot and Guler, that flourished between the mid-17th and the late 19th centuries in the Rajput kingdoms situated in the long, narrow region of the Himalayan foothills. Although there is evidence of painting in this region as early as 1552, the earliest group of distinctive Pahari style paintings appeared in about 1650 in the small state of Basohli. These miniatures, horizontal in format, use flat planes of bold colours, mainly reds and yellows.

Stylized architecture and figures with large eyes and straight profiles wearing elaborate costumes and jewellery, are typical of these miniatures, which illustrate the *Rasamanjari*, a Sanskrit poem on the behaviour of lovers. In the 18th century, the neighbouring state, Mankot, developed an equally vibrant style, remarkable for a series of portraits of grandees of the court. By the late 18th century, the vitality of local tradition had mellowed under Mughal influence and a lyrical, more tranquil palette with a naturalistic rendering of forms characterized the miniatures from Guler and Kangra. Guler's painting tradition was dominated by one family of artists of whom the most talented was Nainsukh. Painting in Kangra flourished under the reign of Raja Sansar Chand (r.1775–1823). The highly refined style that emerged during this period concentrated on the lush, idyllic landscape as the backdrop for romantic scenes. Other centres of Pahari painting included Mandi, Jammu, Nurpur, Chamba and Kullu.

Kangra miniature, 1788, depicting Krishna killing the serpent-demon, Kaliya

Dharamsala ⑫

Kangra district. 238 km (148 miles) NW of Shimla. 🚌 19,100. ✈ Gaggal, 11 km (7 miles) S of town centre. 🚉 Pathankot, 80 km (50 miles) NW of Dharamsala, then bus or taxi. 🚌 ℹ HP Tourism, McLeodganj (01892) 221 205. 🅰 daily. 🎫 Summer Festival (May), Bodh Festival (Oct/Nov).

Tibetan nuns in their red robes, a common sight in Dharamsala

This hill station, established by the British in the mid-19th century, is today the home of the Dalai Lama and the Tibetan Government-in-Exile. Located on the lower spurs of the Dhauladhar Range, the town consists of two sections – the lower town with the main bus stand and bazaar, and the upper town, known as **McLeodganj**, 9 km (5 miles) to its north, which is the destination of most foreign visitors. There is little of interest in the lower town, apart from the lively **Kotwali Bazaar** and the **Museum of Kangra Art**. The museum has an excellent collection of Kangra miniatures *(see p121)*, and also houses a school which teaches the art of miniature painting.

McLeodganj, the upper town, named after David McLeod, the lieutenant governor of Punjab in 1848, is primarily a Tibetan settlement. Its focal point is the **Tsuglagkhang Complex**, located at the southern edge of the town, which contains the residence of the Dalai Lama (not open to visitors), the **Namgyal Monastery** where monks can be seen debating in the afternoons, and the important

Tsuglagkhang Temple. A simple hall, painted in yellow, the temple has a raised dais from where the Dalai Lama holds discourses, and three beautiful images from the Buddhist pantheon – Sakyamuni (the Historical Buddha), Avalokitesvara *(see p141)*, and Padmasambhava *(see p120 & p139)*. The Dalai Lama is believed to be an incarnation of Avalokitesvara. Another temple in the complex has an intricate mural of the Kalachakra ("Wheel of Time") and beautiful sand mandalas, painstakingly created by the monks over a period of time and then ritually destroyed.

Situated at the northern edge of town are the **Tibetan Institute of Performing Arts**, and the beautiful **Norbulingka Institute**, where traditional arts and crafts are promoted. **Gangchen Kyishong**, the administrative centre of the

Stained glass, St-John-in-the-Wilderness

Tibetan Government-in-Exile, is midway between the upper and lower towns. This complex includes the excellent **Library of Tibetan Works and Archives**, a museum on the first floor with bronze images and *thangkas*, as well as the **Institute of Tibetan Medicine**. Nearby is the **Nechung Monastery**, the seat of the Tibetan State Oracle, whose predictions about major events in the coming year carry great weight in the Tibetan community. Also on the road to Kotwali Bazaar, just below McLeodganj, is the picturesque **Church of St-John-in-the-Wilderness**, a grey stone structure built in 1852. Brass plaques and superb Belgian stained-glass windows can be seen inside the church. The tomb of Lord Elgin, the British viceroy who died here in 1863 while on holiday, lies in the churchyard.

🏛 **Museum of Kangra Art**
Main Rd, Dharamsala. **Tel** (01892) 224 214. ◯ Tue–Sun.

🏛 **Library of Tibetan Works and Archives**
Gangchen Kyishong, McLeodganj Rd. ◯ Mon–Fri.

⛪ **St-John-in-the-Wilderness**
◯ daily. 🕆 11am Sun.

Environs
The pretty village of **Dharamkot**, north of McLeodganj, is reached by a 3-km (2-mile) long road, lined with deodar and oak trees. There are superb views of the Kangra Valley from the village.

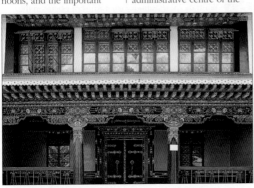

The brightly-painted façade of Namgyal Monastery, McLeodganj

Little Tibet

Butter lamp

When the 14th Dalai Lama, Tenzin Gyatso, fled Tibet in 1959 after the Chinese occupation, Dharamsala became his new home, and the base of the Tibetan Government-in-Exile. The town is today often called Little Tibet, preserving Tibet's religious and cultural heritage, keeping the Tibetan cause alive internationally, and serving as the focal point for the 100,000 Tibetans scattered in refugee settlements all over India. Dharamsala also attracts Buddhists from across the world, such as the Hollywood actor Richard Gere.

The Tibetan flag *is dominated by a snow-covered mountain representing Tibet. The six red bands symbolize the six Tibetan tribes.*

RELIGION AND CULTURE

Dharamsala's many monasteries and crafts centres, and its performing arts school, ensure that Tibet's distinctive religion and culture continue to flourish.

Tibetan opera, *known as lhamo, has traditional folk tales, legends and myths as its themes.*

The Dalai Lama, *who won the Nobel Peace Prize in 1990, is head of the Gelugpa or Yellow Hat sect (see p139) and is revered as Tibet's god-king.*

Thunderbolt sceptre

The altar *in a Tibetan monastery includes, apart from images of the deities, seven ritual bowls of water, butter lamps, intricate butter sculptures, as well as a bell and a thunderbolt sceptre used during prayers and special rites.*

Butter sculpture   **Prayer bell**

Thangkas, *or scroll paintings framed in silk depicting Buddhist divinities, are among the traditional arts kept alive by the refugees.*

Sand mandalas *symbolizing the universe are meticulously created and then ceremonially destroyed. They help monks to meditate.*

See also features on Buddhist Iconography (p141) and In the Buddha's Footsteps (p221).

Sylverton, one of the many colonial houses in Dalhousie

Dalhousie **⓭**

Chamba district. 336 km (209 miles) NW of Shimla. 🏠 7,400. 🚌 🚹 *Geetanjali Hotel, near bus stand, (01899) 242 136.* 🟢 *daily.* 🎎 *Summer Festival (Jun).*

Sprawling over five hills that range in height from 1,525 m to 2,378 m (5,003 ft to 7,802 ft), Dalhousie still retains its Raj-era ambience, with spacious, gable-roofed bungalows and churches flanking its leafy lanes. Originally conceived as a sanatorium for the expatriate population rather than as a fashionable summer retreat, it was founded in 1853 and named after Lord Dalhousie, the governor-general of British India between 1854 and 1856. The most popular walks are the twin rounds of **Garam Sarak** ("Warm Road") and **Thandi Sarak** ("Cold Road"), so called because one path is sunnier than the other. A shorter walk from the Circuit House to Gandhi Chowk – the central part of town where a school, church and the post office are situated – offers spectacular views of the Pir Panjal Range. From Gandhi Chowk, another pleasant ramble, about 3 km (2 miles) long, leads south to the pretty picnic spot of Panjpula or "Five Bridges".

For Raj aficionados, a track leading off to the right from the main bus stand moves past the old British cemetery in the woods, before reaching the cantonment. One of the two churches here boasts pretty stained-glass windows and sandstone arches.

Environs

A scenic road through dense forests of pine, deodar, oak, horse chestnut and rhododendron leads to the **Kalatope Wildlife Sanctuary**, about 8 km (5 miles) east of Dalhousie. With prior permission from the wildlife authorities at Chamba it is possible to take a diversion at Bakrota and drive to a rest house deep inside the sanctuary. About 26 km (16 miles) east of Dalhousie is **Khajjiar**, situated at a height of 2,000 m (6,562 ft). This saucer-shaped expanse of green meadow, bordered by towering deodars, has a picture postcard beauty, comparable with the finest views in Kashmir or Switzerland. In the centre is a small lake with a golden-domed Devi temple built on a floating island.

🦌 Kalatope Wildlife Sanctuary
For permission contact: Forest Department, Chamba. **Tel** *(01899) 222 639.*

Chamba **⓮**

Chamba district. 378 km (235 miles) NW of Shimla. 🏠 20,300. 🚌 🟢 *daily.* 🎎 *Sui (Apr), Minjar (Jul/Aug).* **Travel permits** *Contact the Deputy Commissioner, (01899) 225 371. For details see p758.*

This town was chosen as the capital of the former princely state of Chamba in the 10th century, when Raja Sahil Varman moved here from Bharmour. He named it Chamba after his favourite daughter, Champavati, who legend says, sacrificed herself to provide water for the parched city. During the Sui festival, women and children sing her praises in the town's many temples.

A bridge over the Ravi river leads up to the town, situated on the ledge of a mountain, overlooking the right bank of the river. In the town's centre is the **Chaugan**, a huge expanse of meadow, that is the focal point of all cultural and social life. Clustered around it are a number of imposing buildings, including the old **Akhand Chandi Palace**, part of which is now a college. The Chaugan is also the main marketplace with shops that sell a variety of merchandise, ranging from traditional silver jewellery with enamelled clasps to embroidered Chamba *chappals* (sandals) that may look flimsy but are excellent for walking up hillsides.

Chamba's towering stone temples are some of the finest in the region. The most

Silver mask of Parvati, Chamba

Images of deities on the walls of Lakshmi Narayan Temple, Chamba

Hillsides around Chamba ablaze with the colours of autumn

important are the six North Indian *shikhara*-style temples *(see p20)* that comprise the **Lakshmi Narayan Temple** complex, to the west of the Chaugan. Of these, three are dedicated to Vishnu and three to Shiva. The white marble image of Lakshmi Narayan, in the main temple, was brought from Central India in the 10th century. The carved panels on the temple walls illustrate mythological scenes as well as animal and floral motifs.

Other temples include the **Madho Rai Temple**, near the palace, with a bronze image of Krishna, and further up, the **Chamunda Temple**.

A glimpse of Chamba's rich heritage can be seen at the **Bhuri Singh Museum**, set up in 1908 by the king of Chamba at the time. His rare collection of miniature paintings formed the nucleus of the museum. Today, it has a fine collection of Pahari paintings *(see p121)*, murals, inscribed fountain slabs, carved stone panels and other artifacts, such as Chamba *rumals*, metal masks, copper plates and silver jewellery.

🏛 **Bhuri Singh Museum**
S of Chaughan. *Tel (01899) 222 590.* ☐ *Tue–Sun.*

Bharmour ⑮

Chamba district. 64 km (40 miles) SE of Chamba. 🚌 🖼 *Manimahesh Yatra (Aug/Sep).*

The Bharmour region, homeland of the semi-nomadic, sheep-herding Gaddis and the first capital of the Chamba rulers, spreads across a steep mountainside, high above Budhil, a large tributary of the Ravi river. Bharmour's main attraction is the fascinating **Chaurasi** (literally, "Eighty-Four") **Temple** complex, built in the 10th century under Raja Sahil Varman, to honour the 84 saints who visited Bharmour. The major shrines are dedicated to Narasimha, Ganesha, and the local deities Larkana Devi and Manimahesh. The intricate wooden carvings on the temple lintels and the images of the main deities are outstanding, and it is said that the sculptor's hands were cut off to prevent him from replicating such remarkable work.

Environs
Situated at a height of 3,950 m (12,959 ft), **Manimahesh Lake**, 35 km (22 miles) from Bharmour, is the area's most sacred lake, as its holy waters are believed to cleanse all sins. In August/September, thousands of pilgrims converge here to participate in the annual Manimahesh Yatra *(see p113)*. The main motor road continues up to Hadsar, 16 km (10 miles) beyond Bharmour, and from there the *yatra* (procession) ascends in two stages via Dhanchho to the lake, nestling at the base of the Manimahesh Kailasa.

For the adventurous, Bharmour also offers a tough five-day trek over the Kugti Pass (5,040 m/16,535 ft) to Lahaul *(see p129)*. Holi, 26 km (16 miles) away in the main Ravi Valley, is the base for a number of trails over the Dhauladhar Range to the Kangra Valley. It offers the option of a longer walk to the Kullu Valley as well. Down the course of the Ravi, on the road to Chamba, the **Chatrari Temple** with its exquisite bronze image of Shakti Devi, is also worth a stop.

Well-preserved 10th-century temples at Bharmour

CHAMBA RUMALS

Chamba *rumals*, exquisitely embroidered handkerchiefs or coverlets, generally square in shape, were used primarily to wrap gifts, either for temple offerings or for ceremonial exchanges during wedding rituals. At times, they also formed the canopies draped above deities in temples. Pale colours, silk thread, and a double-sided satin stitch and an unbleached muslin base were the framework within which intricate compositions, inspired by delicate Pahari miniatures, were created. Originally the work of the ladies of the court, the themes were religious, interspersed with animal and plant motifs, and enclosed within floral borders.

Hand-embroidered Chamba *rumal*

Brightly coloured tiger guarding the Jagannathi Devi Temple, Kullu

Kullu Valley 16

Kullu district. 240 km (149 miles) N
of Shimla. 👥 18,300. ✈ Bhuntar,
10 km (6 miles) S of Kullu town. 🚌
ℹ HP Tourism, near Maidan,
(01902) 222 349. 🎭 Dussehra
(Sep/Oct). **Travel permits** Contact
Deputy Commisioner, (01902) 222 727.
For more details see p115.

The Kullu Valley in central
Himachal Pradesh, watered
by the Beas river, has long
been a site of
human habita-
tion. In ancient
Sanskrit texts it is
referred to as
Kulantapith, or
"end of the
habitable world"
– an apt
description when
one compares

**Typical geometric pattern on
the border of a Kullu shawl**

the lush fields and apple
orchards of this 80-km (50-
mile) long valley with the
desolate expanse of Lahaul
(see p129), which is separated
from it by the Pir Panjal Range.
The local name for Kullu is the
"Valley of the Gods" – its
alpine setting is the gathering
place for 360 gods from different temples in the region,
who congregate here for the
famous Dussehra festival.

Unlike British-built hill
stations in the Himalayas,
Kullu remained unknown to
the outside world until it was
"discovered" in the 1960s by
the flower children, who were
enchanted as much by its
hillsides covered with
marijuana plants (Cannabis
sativa), as by its gentle beauty,
superb mountain vistas and
amiable people. The men of

Kullu Valley usually wear the
distinctive Kullu topi, a snug
woollen cap with a colourful
upturned flap. The women
weave thick shawls with
striking geometric designs on
their borders, and few visitors
can resist acquiring these
attractive products, now a
flourishing local industry.
Equally attractive are the
village houses, their slate
roofs rising above green
meadows. **Kullu**, the district
headquarters
and the largest
settlement in the
valley, is located
on the right
bank of the
Beas. The town's
chief attraction is
the 17th-century
**Raghunath
Temple**,
dedicated to Rama and Sita,
whose richly adorned images
lead the processions at the
Dussehra festival. Also worth
exploring is the Akhara
Bazaar, at the northern
end of the town, famous
for its handicrafts
shops, selling shawls
and traditional silver
jewellery. At the
southern end of town
is the large green open
space called **Dhalpur
Maidan**, where the
colourful Dussehra
festivities take place.

A number of temples,
all with superb stone
carvings and impressive
images, lie in the
vicinity of Kullu town –
the **Vaishno Devi Cave
Shrine** is 4 km (2.5
miles) to the northeast;

the **Jagannathi Devi Temple** at
Bekhli, 5 km (3 miles) to the
north; and the **Vishnu Temple**
at Dayar, 12 km (8 miles) to
the west. The huge, pyramidal
Basheshwar Mahadev Temple
at Bajaura, 15 km (9 miles) to
the south, has superb images
of Vishnu, Ganesha and
Durga. However, the most
famous is the **Bijli Mahadev
Temple**, dedicated to the "Lord
of Lightning", 14 km (9 miles)
to the southeast. Located on a
high spur on the left bank of
the river, opposite the town,
this temple has an 18-m (59-ft)
high staff, which periodically
attracts lightning during
thunderstorms especially in
the monsoon. This is regarded
as a divine blessing, even
though it shatters the
Shivalinga in the sanctum
of the temple. The stone
fragments are then painstakingly put together again with a
mortar of clarified butter and
grain, by the head priest.

Environs
Jalori Pass, about 70 km (44
miles) south of Kullu, on the
ridgeline forming the divide
between the Beas and Satluj
rivers, offers two beautiful
walks through dense, high-
altitude oak forests and
meadows. The first walk goes
through a path with gentle
gradients to the tarn of
Saryolsar, 5 km (3 miles)
away. The other walk, up a
neighbouring hill, leads to the
picturesque ruins of a fort
occupied by the Gurkhas in
the 19th century.

A waterfall in Kullu Valley

Hot springs in Manikaran, a popular pilgrim spot

Parvati Valley ⓱

Kullu district. 180 km (112 miles) NE of Shimla (via Jalori Pass). 🚌
ℹ HP Tourism, near Maidan, Kullu, (01902) 222 349.

The scenic Parvati Valley, with its green, terraced rice fields and apple orchards, draws an increasing number of visitors. However, because of illegal marijuana cultivation in the surrounding countryside, the Parvati Valley has, in recent years, gained notoriety as a centre for the narcotics

trade, and several foreign visitors have gone missing from the area. It is advisable to take guides and porters available from Naggar (see p128) and **Manikaran**, for treks in this region.

The main settlement in the Parvati Valley is Manikaran, famous for its hot springs. It is also the starting point for a number of treks (see pp114 –15). An interesting legend explains the origins of the hot springs. A serpent stole the earrings of Parvati, the consort of Lord Shiva, and disappeared with them into a deep burrow. On witnessing Shiva's terrible anger, the snake was too terrified to come out of its hole, but managed to snort the earrings out through the earth, thus creating vents from which the hot springs bubble out. A bath here is said to be good for the body and the soul, and local people sometimes boil rice in the geo-thermal steam. The Rama Temple and the Shiva Temple next to a Sikh gurdwara is always thronged with sadhus.

Great Himalayan National Park ⓲

Kullu district. 205 km (127 miles) N of Shimla, (via Jalori Pass). **Entry points:** Saing, Gushani. 🚌 Shamchi, 15 km (9 miles) S of Kullu, then jeep. ℹ For bookings & permits contact Director, GHNP, Shamchi, (01902) 265 320. 📷

The great Himalayan National Park, covering an area of 754 sq km (291 sq miles), ranges in altitude from 1,300 m (4,265 ft) to 6,100 m (20,013 ft), and abuts the cold desert region of Pin Valley National Park (see p130). The variety of flora and fauna found here represents the entire Western Himalayas. A vast range of subtropical species along with alpine grasslands are covered with edelweiss and oak forests. Mammals include the Himalayan tahr, musk deer and the elusive snow leopard. Among the 300-odd species of birds, there are at least six kinds of pheasant.

Monal pheasant

A number of trekking trails and forest huts in the buffer zone offers an opportunity to explore the park.

GATHERING OF THE GODS

Kullu celebrates the festival of Dussehra with unique gusto. All over India, this festival commemorates the defeat of the demon-king, Ravana, by the god Rama, a story recounted in the Hindu epic, *Ramayana (see p27)*. In Kullu, local traditions add their own piquancy to this pan-Indian myth. These traditions originated in the 17th century, when the ruler, Jagat Singh, inadvertently caused the death of a Brahmin priest. To expiate his sin, he installed the deity Raghunath (an incarnation of Rama), on his throne and vowed that thereafter he and his descendants would rule Kullu only as regents. The image of this god was brought all the way from the holy town of Ayodhya (see p199), the birthplace of Lord Rama. From then on, every September/October, Raghunath "invites" all the local gods of the valley, to celebrate Dussehra in Kullu. These gods, 360 of them,

Image of Vashishtha Devta, a local god

include Hadimba, the patron deity of the Kullu rajas from Manali (see p128), and Jamlu, the reigning deity of Malana who administers justice via the village priest. The gods are carried on palanquins from their own temples and arrive at the Dhalpur Maidan in a cheerful procession accompanied by the frenzied beat of drums. Nine days of festivities follow, when a temporary market is set up, which sells everything from locally-made shawls and shoes, to brightly-hued plastic toys. The graceful *natti* dance, performed amidst a lot of friendly rivalry by several local groups, can also be watched.

Preparing for the Dussehra festival celebrations

Manali ⑲

Kullu district. 281 km (175 miles) N of Shimla. 🏠 6,300. 🚌 ℹ The Mall, (01902) 253 531. 🛍 daily. 🎭 Winter Carnival (Jan), Dhungri Mela (May).

Picturesque Manali, situated along the west bank of the Beas river, is a prime destination for visitors, offering a variety of scenic walks and treks through dense forests. Though a profusion of hotels and shops in recent years has overrun downtown Manali, its environs still retain much of the natural beauty that gives this hill station a unique flavour. Particularly charming is the original village, about 3 km (2 miles) north of the main bazaar, with its temple dedicated to Manu, the Hindu sage after whom Manali is named.

Located 1.5 km (1 mile) north of the main bazaar is the sacred **Hadimba Temple**, shaded by a grove of stately deodars. This four-tiered wooden temple with its pagoda-style roof was built in 1553 around a small natural cave enshrining the footprints of the demoness Hadimba, wife of Bhima, the mighty Pandava brother *(see p26)*.

On the left bank of the Beas, about 3 km (2 miles) north of the bazaar, the hot sulphur springs in the village of **Vashisht** are piped into Turkish-style baths. Further up, the lovely **Solang Valley**, 14 km (9 miles) from downtown Manali, is the scene of most of the area's outdoor activities. Treks lead up to the pastures of Dhumti and the small

The 16th-century wooden Hadimba Temple in Manali

snow-fed lake of Beas Kund *(see p114)*. Paragliding, a popular activity, takes place on the nearby slopes, which also attract skiers in the winter.

Environs

Rohtang Pass, the perilous pass crossing into Lahaul, at an altitude of 3,980 m (13,058 ft), is 52 km (32 miles) north of Manali. It is a day's excursion, possible only in summer, with a brief halt at the spectacular Rahalla Falls along the way.

The first capital of the Kullu kings, **Jagatsukh** is 6 km (4 miles) south of Manali, on the left bank of the Beas. The two *shikhara*-style *(see p21)* stone temples here possibly date back to the 6th century. **Naggar**, further south, on the same side of the river, succeeded Jagatsukh as the capital till it was moved to Kullu *(see p126)* in the 17th century. The Naggar Castle, built in the 15th century, is now a hotel. It is an excellent

Woodcarving on a door in Malana

example of traditional local architecture with walls composed of alternate layers of wooden beams and evenly hewn stone. It commands a fine view of the Beas Valley. Nearby is the **Roerich Art Gallery** displaying the work of the Russian painter Nicholas Roerich. Lying across the river from Naggar, is scenic **Katrain**, surrounded by orchards. Trout fishing is a popular pastime here. The remote village of **Malana**, beyond Chanderkhani Pass, is 25 km (16 miles) southeast of Naggar. Malana's isolated people live by their own code of conduct and shun contact with outsiders. Their unique culture, language and system of government set them apart from the rest of the valley. Visitors should enter the village only if invited.

🏛 **Roerich Art Gallery**
Naggar. ⬜ daily. 📷

A tiny stream crisscrossing the lush landscape around Manali

NICHOLAS ROERICH (1874–1947)

This multi-faceted Russian who painted, wrote poetry and expounded a universalist philosophy distilled from many religions, travelled extensively through Tibet and the Himalayas. He is best remembered for the colourful celebration of nature in his trans-Himalayan landscapes. Roerich lived in Naggar where he died in 1947. His old home is now the Roerich Museum. His son Svyatoslav, also a painter, made India his home as well.

A mountainscape by Roerich

Lahaul and Spiti ⑳

Lahaul and Spiti district. 610 km (379 miles) N from Shimla to Keylong via Kunjam Pass. 🏔 *33,200.* 🚌
🎪 *Ladarcha Festival, Spiti (Aug).*

At an altitude of 2,750 m (9,022 ft), Lahaul and Spiti, bordering Tibet and Ladakh's Zanskar Valley, comprise the trans-Himalayan regions of western Himachal Pradesh. Unlike the lush meadows of the Kullu Valley, this is a barren land of rocky massifs and hanging glaciers, enclosed by the Himalayas to the north and the Pir Panjal to the south. Rainfall is scarce and the region is dependent upon glacial melt for the cultivation of its main crops, barley, millet and seed potato.

While the difficult terrain inhibits many travellers from going to Spiti *(see pp130–31)*, Lahaul is more accessible. Upper Lahaul is a stark land of high mountains enveloping the deep valleys of the Chandra and Bhaga rivers, while Lower Lahaul lies below Tandi, where the two rivers meet and become the Chandrabhaga, or Chenab.

Today, Lahaul's social structure is an interesting mix of Buddhism and Hinduism, reflecting the close ties the region had with Tibet, Ladakh and neighbouring Kullu.

Keylong, the district head-quarters on the Bhaga river,

The meandering Chenab river, near Gondhla village

is the region's principal town. With many basic facilities, it is widely used as a stopover by travellers en route to Leh *(see pp136–7)* or as a base for treks. Across the river, opposite Keylong, a steep tree-shaded pathway leads to **Drugpa Kardang Gompa**, the largest monastery *(gompa)* in Lahaul. It has a fine collection of *thangkas (see p123)*, musical instruments and old weapons. Nearby is the 16th-century **Shashur Gompa**. This monastery is renowned for its long 4.5 m (15 ft) *thangka*.

On the road to Manali, about 16 km (10 miles) south of Keylong, the eight-storeyed tower of the Gondhla chiefs

Detail of a prayer wheel at Keylong

dominates the landscape. The oldest monastery in Lahaul, the 800-year-old **Guru Ghantal Gompa** at Tandi, 11 km (7 miles) southwest of Keylong, is believed to have been etablished by Guru Padmasambhava, the founder of Tibetan Buddhism. Other places worth visiting are the carved wooden Mrikula Devi Temple at **Udaipur**, in the Pattan Valley, 44 km (27 miles) west of Tandi, and **Trilokinath**, with its marble image of Avalokitesvara *(see p141)*.

Beyond Keylong, the road to Leh passes the last Lahaul village of **Darcha** with a trekking route to Zanskar *(see p152)* via the Shingo-la.

Suraj Tal, the glacial lake that is the source of Bhaga river, one of the main rivers in Lahaul

Spiti: The Sacred Valley

The heart of Himachal's cold desert, Spiti is a land of fascinating contrasts. Monasteries and prayer flags are dotted along the banks of glacial streams, while blue sheep and ibex graze amidst sparse pastures sprinkled with marine fossils. Once part of a West Tibetan kingdom, Spiti submitted to Ladakhi rule in the 17th century and became a part of British India in the 19th century. Through these changes in its political history, Spiti remained a locked land, enclosed between tall mountain ranges and international borders. Though now part of Himachal Pradesh, it has retained its Tibetan character and is an important preserve of ancient Buddhist heritage.

Bare multi-hued rock faces, a typical feature of the Spiti area

Chandra Tal, *or the "Moon Lake", at a height of 4,270 m (14,009 ft), lies at the entrance to Spiti when approached from Lahaul. Oval in shape with deep blue waters, it is overlooked by craggy peaks and hanging glaciers.*

Key Monastery, *possibly founded in the 13th century, is the largest monastery in Spiti. Perched on an escarpment, it has a fine collection of thangkas and is the seat of Lochen Tulku, a reincarnation of Rinchen Zangpo (see p119).*

Kaza is the administrative headquarters of Spiti.

Losar, the first Spiti village encountered en route from Lahaul, is beautifully situated below the wide confluence of the three rivulets that combine to form the Spiti river.

Pin Valley National Park

KEY

▨	Area illustrated
🛕	Monastery
▬	Major road
═	Minor road

0 km   25

0 miles   25

Kungri Monastery in Pin Valley belongs to the Nyingmapa sect *(see p139).* The uppermost hall, in the main temple, contains some ancient wall paintings and wooden sculptures.

The land of the ibex and the snow leopard, *the Pin Valley National Park is an untrammelled pastureland in the shadow of virgin snowcapped peaks. It surrounds the upper reaches of the Pin river and its tributary, the Paraibo. Among the carnivores, the fox and the snow wolf are common, while the beautiful snow leopard is more elusive.*

Chorten at a village in Pin Valley

Dhankar, *the old capital of Spiti, is wedged between the pinnacles of a razor sharp spur of crumbling rock and alkaline deposits. The old monastery here is richly endowed with beautiful frescoes, and a bronze statue of Avalokitesvara.*

Children in Spiti

An impressive image of Guru Padmasambhava, *covered in gold leaf, is the highlight of Lalung Monas-tery. This monastery is one of the 108 structures credited to Rinchen Zangpo.*

Vibrant mural showing a scene from Buddhist mythology, Tabo Monastery

Tabo Monastery ㉑

Lahaul and Spiti district. 460 km (286 miles) NE of Shimla. 🚌 ⬜ Apr–Sep. 🏛 *Monastery Festival (Oct/Nov).* **Travel permits** *required to travel between Tabo and Jangi (in Kinnaur). Contact Deputy Commisioner, Shimla (see p111), or SDM's office in Rekong Peo (see p118). For details see p115.*

Tabo Monastery, Spiti's pride, is linked to an important era in the growth of Buddhism in Tibet. Tibetan Buddhism suffered a major setback during the reign of King Langdarma in the 9th century, and it took a whole century for the religion to recover. The resurgence, also known as the "second diffusion of Buddhism", was spearheaded by Ye-she-od, the Lama king of Guge in Western Tibet. Under his patronage, the legendary scholar Rinchen Zangpo spread the faith by translating Buddhist texts and promoting a tremendous temple-building movement.

The *gompa* at Tabo is one of the products of this movement, established in the 11th century by Rinchen Zangpo himself. Dating from a period when monastic temples were constructed close to villages, it is one of the largest of such centres. The squat, mud structures of Tabo are enclosed within a mud wall about 84 m by 75 m (276 ft by 246 ft) and appear quite unimpressive from the outside. The exquisite wall paintings inside, however, make Tabo one of the most significant art treasures of the Tibetan Buddhist world. The earliest paintings in the *dukhang* (assembly hall) are from the 10th and 11th centuries and depict scenes from various incidents and tales associated with the life of the Buddha. The hall also contains imposing clay sculptures of the chief deities from the Buddhist pantheon. Seven other chapels in the complex contain paintings from the 15th and 16th centuries. One of the shrines houses a huge clay idol of a sitting Maitreya (the Future Buddha). Tabo is also a favourite retreat of the Dalai Lama.

Accessing parts of the Spiti Valley that lie below Tabo remains difficult. Travel is restricted due to the proximity of the border with Tibet.

Monks praying at Tabo Monastery

Fields of buckwheat in the Sangla Valley *(see pp118–19)* ▷

LADAKH, JAMMU & KASHMIR

Lying across six major mountain ranges, and covering an area of 222,000 sq km (85,715 sq miles), Jammu and Kashmir is India's northernmost state, bordering Pakistan and China's Tibetan Plateau. Its three distinct regions – Ladakh, Jammu and the Kashmir Valley – offer a rich diversity of landscapes, religions, and people. The predominantly Muslim Kashmir Valley is a mosaic of forests, ricefields, lakes and waterways, its gentle beauty now shattered by armed insurgency (see p154). Jammu, encompassing plains, mountains and foothills, boasts the famous hilltop shrine of Vaishno Devi, an important pilgrimage site for Hindus. Sparsely populated Ladakh, which accounts for two-thirds of the state's area, is a high altitude desert. Its harsh lines are softened by the emerald green of oasis villages, the crystal light of cloudless blue skies, and the dramatic silhouettes of ancient Buddhist monasteries which, for many visitors, are Ladakh's main attraction.

SIGHTS AT A GLANCE

Towns & Cities
Jammu ⑭
Kargil ⑩
Leh ①
Mulbekh ⑨
Srinagar ⑮

Monasteries & Palaces
Alchi Monastery ⑧
Hemis Monastery ⑤

Matho Monastery ④
Shey ③
Stok ②

Areas of Natural Beauty
Gulmarg ⑯
Pahalgam ⑰
Rangdum ⑫
Southeast Ladakh ⑥

Rivers & Valleys
Suru Valley ⑪
Zanskar ⑬

Tours
Nubra Valley Tour ⑦

KEY

☒ Domestic airport

═ National highway

▬ Major road

═ Minor road

─ Major railway

▬ International border

××× Disputed border

◁ Buddhist monks in Ladakh blowing conch shells to announce the beginning of prayers

The abandoned Leh Palace, once the seat of the royal family

Leh ❶

Leh district. 1,077 km (669 miles) N of Delhi. 🏠 15,000. ✈ 11 km (7 miles) S of town centre. 🚌 ℹ (01982) 252 297. 🎉 Muharram (Mar/Apr), Buddha Jayanti (May), Losar (Dec). **Travel permits** required for certain restricted areas in Ladakh (see p142).

From the 17th century right until 1949, Ladakh's principal town, Leh, was the hub of the bustling caravan trade (see p142) between Punjab and Central Asia, and between Kashmir and Tibet. The large **Main Bazaar**, with its broad kerbs, was clearly designed to facilitate the passage

The Buddha, Leh Palace

of horses, donkeys and camels, and to provide room for the display and storage of merchandise.

The town is dominated by the nine-storeyed **Leh Palace**, built in the 1630s by Sengge Namgyal. A prolific builder of monasteries and forts, with many conquests to his name, he was Ladakh's most famous king. The palace's massive inward-leaning walls are in the same architectural tradition as the Potala Palace in Lhasa which, in fact, the Leh Palace antedates by about 50 years. Sadly, the solidity of its exterior belies the dilapidation inside, although some repair work is now being done. Visitors can go up to the open terrace on the level above the main entrance.

Much of Leh's charm lies in

the opportunities it offers for pleasant strolls and walks. In the heart of town are the Main Bazaar and **Chang Gali**, with their eateries and curio shops selling precious stones and ritual religious objects such as prayer wheels. Along the Bazaar's wide kerb, women from nearby villages sit with large baskets of fresh vegetables, spinning wool on drop spindles and exchanging lively chatter in between intervals of brisk commerce.

The **Jokhang**, a modern ecumenical Buddhist establishment, and the town mosque, built in the late 17th century, are close to each other in the Main Bazaar. Between the Main Bazaar and the Polo Ground, at the eastern end of town, is the fascinating **Old Town**, with its maze of narrow alleys dotted with *chortens* and *mani* walls (see p141), and its cluster of flat-roofed houses constructed of sunbaked bricks.

On the peak above the town are the small fort and monastery complex of **Namgyal Tsemo** (mid-16th century), believed to be the earliest royal residence in Leh. Next to its now ruined fort are a *gonkhang* (Temple of the Guardian Deities) and a temple to Maitreya (the Future

Buddha), both of which have vibrant murals. Those inside the *gonkhang* include a court scene with a portrait believed to be that of King Tashi Namgyal (mid-16th century), the founder of the complex.

At the western edge of Leh is the **Ecological Centre**, which runs development projects in agriculture, solar energy, health and environmental awareness in several of the surrounding villages. The centre also houses a library and a shop selling local handicrafts.

The gleaming white **Shanti Stupa** ("Peace Pagoda"), founded in the 1980s under the sponsorship of Japanese Buddhists, is situated on a hilltop west of the city.

Less than ten minutes' walk, in any direction away from the heart of town, will bring one

Barley fields around Leh

ACCLIMATIZING TO LEH

Visitors flying into Leh, situated at an altitude of 3,500 m (11,483 ft), should allow themselves enough time to acclimatize. Any strenuous physical activity should be avoided for at least the first 24 hours. During the first few days, Leh's high altitude can often cause insomnia, headaches, breathlessness and loss of appetite.

An archery contest near Leh

to barley fields, green or gold according to the season. Down the hill in the village of **Skara**, the massive mud walls of the 19th-century **Zorawar Fort** catch the eye. Another lovely walk is up past the **Moravian Church** to the serene village of **Changspa** with its ancient *chorten*. From here a road turns towards the beautifully-maintained 19th-century **Sankar Monastery**, with its impressive images of Avalokitesvara and of Vajra-Bhairav, Guardian of the Gelugpa order *(see p139)*.

Environs
Choglamsar, 7 km (4 miles) south of Leh, is the main Tibetan refugee settlement in Ladakh. It includes the Dalai Lama's prayer ground, known as Shanti Sthal, an SOS Children's Village, the Central Institute of Buddhist Studies, a solar-heated hospital and workshops that promote colourful Tibetan handicrafts.

Dramatically situated on a hilltop, so close to the airport that the wings of landing aircraft come perilously close to its walls, is the 15th-century **Spituk Monastery**, the oldest establishment of the Gelugpa sect in Ladakh. It houses the library of Tsongkapa, the sect's founder, and a shrine devoted to the goddess Tara *(see p141)* in her myriad manifestations. Situated in one of Ladakh's most charming villages, **Phiyang Monastery**, is one of only two that represent the Drigungpa sect. It was founded by Ladakh's 16th-century ruler, Tashi Namgyal, supposedly as an act of atonement for the violence and treachery by which he came to the throne. Among its many treasures is a large and interesting collection of Kashmiri bronzes of Buddhist deities, dating back to the 13th century, or possibly even earlier.

🏯 **Leh Palace**
◯ daily. ▦ *Book in advance.* ▦

🚩 **Namgyal Tsemo**
◯ daily. ▦ *Book in advance.*

🏛 **Ecological Centre**
◯ *Mon–Fri.* **Tel** *(01982) 253 221.*

🚩 **Jokhang**
◯ *daily.*

🚩 **Sankar Monastery**
◯ *daily.* ▦

🚩 **Spituk Monastery**
◯ *daily.* ▦ 📷 *with permission of the lama-in-charge.*

🚩 **Phiyang Monastery**
◯ *daily.* ▦ 📷 *with permission of the lama-in-charge.*

FESTIVALS OF LADAKH, JAMMU & KASHMIR

Hemis Festival *(Jun/Jul)*, Hemis. Of all Ladakh's monastery festivals *(see p140)* the one at Hemis is the most famous. This spectacular dance-drama, with colourful masks and costumes, offers a wonderfully authentic experience of Ladakhi culture.

Masked dancers performing at the Hemis Festival

Sindhu Darshan *(variable)*, Leh. A recent introduction, this festival is held annually as a homage to the Indus. Held on the river banks, it includes exhibitions, polo matches and archery contests. **Ladakh Festival** *(1–15 Sep)*, Leh and Kargil. Subsidized by the Tourism Department, this is held over two weeks in Leh's Polo Grounds, as well as in Kargil and some selected villages. Apart from the traditional masked dances, the events include polo matches and archery contests – both being popular traditional sports in the region. A handicrafts exhibition is also held. **Thikse Festival** *(Oct/Nov)*, Thikse. The annual festival of the Gelugpa sect takes place in a beautiful setting. The precise dates of monastery festivals are fixed according to the Tibetan lunar calendar and vary every year. **Milad-ul-Nabi** *(Apr/May)*, Srinagar. The Prophet's birthday is celebrated with special fervour at the Hazratbal Mosque, when its sacred relic, a lock of the Prophet's hair, is displayed to devotees.

Spituk Monastery's labyrinth of shrines linked by narrow passages

Monasteries Along the Indus

Maitreya in Thikse

Several of Ladakh's world-famous monasteries are situated along the Indus Valley, the region's historical and cultural heartland. Typically, a Ladakhi monastery *(gompa)* stands on a hill or ridge above the village that adjoins it. Its upper part consists of temples *(lhakhang)* and assembly halls *(dukhang)*, together with the gonkhang, the Temple of the Fearsome Guardian Deities. The monks' dwellings spill picturesquely down the hillside. The monasteries are still active centres of worship, so approach them respectfully.

Monks dancing in the courtyard of Lamayuru Monastery

Likir, *founded in the 12th century, houses a fine collection of* thangkas *and images, the latter enclosed in beautifully carved wooden frames.*

Basgo *has beautiful 16th-century murals in its fort and temple dedicated to Maitreya, the Future Buddha. It was the capital of Lower Ladakh in the 14th and 15th centuries.*

KARGIL

Indus

• Lamayuru

Ri-dzong • Likir

Basgo

Alchi *(see pp144–6)*

NUBRA VALLE

Leh • *(see p136–7)*

Indus

• Shey

ZANSKAR VALLEY

Stok •

Thiks

Hemis *(see p140)* is Ladakh's largest and richest monastery. It has superb murals and *thangkas.*

Stakna •

0 km 15

0 miles 15

• Hemis

Ri-dzong *is built on top of a ridge of glacial debris which blocks a winding gorge. Founded in the 1840s by the Gelugpa sect, its monks follow a particularly austere regime.*

Lamayuru *is dramatically situated on a high spur overlooking an eerily eroded landscape. Believed to date to the 11th century, its oldest temple has a famous image of Vairocana, the Central Buddha of Meditation (see p146). Lamayuru also has a fine collection of thangkas.*

Stakna, *built in the early 17th century, has an exquisite silver chorten in its* dukhang, *surrounded by vividly-coloured murals.*

See also features on Little Tibet *(p123)*, Buddhist Iconography *(p141)*, and In the Buddha's Footsteps *(p221)*.

Thikse, *a 15th-century architectural gem crowning the crest of a hill, is a Gelugpa monastery which also has a modern Maitreya temple, consecrated by the Dalai Lama.*

Chemrey, *perched on a hilltop and dating from the 1640s, houses Buddhist scriptures with silver covers and gold lettering.*

Thak-thok Monastery belongs to the Nyingmapa sect. It is built around a cave which Guru Padmasambhava, the 8th-century saint, is believed to have used for meditation.

KEY

🛕 Monastery

═ Road

Stok Palace, residence of Ladakh's erstwhile royal family

Stok ❷

Ladakh district. 14 km (9 miles)
S of Leh. 🚌 ℹ️ *Leh Tourist Office,*
(01982) 242 010. 📷 *Stok Monastic Festival (Feb/Mar).* **Stok Palace** ⬜
May–Oct. 🚫

The palace at Stok has been the residence of the Namgyals, the former rulers of Ladakh, since its independence in 1843. Part of the palace has been converted into a fine museum of the dynasty and its history. Its collections include a set of 35 *thangkas* *(see p123)* representing the life of the Buddha, said to have been commissioned by the 16th-century king, Tashi Namgyal. Images and ritual religious objects, such as the bell and *dorje* (thunderbolt), are of unsurpassed workmanship. Secular objects include fine jade cups, the queens' jewellery, including a spectacular headdress, the kings' turban-shaped crown, and ceremonial robes. There is also a sword with its blade twisted into a knot, said to have been contorted by the enormous strength of Tashi Namgyal.

Shey ❸

Ladakh district. 15 km (9 miles)
SE of Leh. 🚌 ℹ️ *Leh Tourist Office,*
(01982) 252 297. 📷 *Shey Shrubla (1st week of Sep).*
Shey Palace ⬜ *daily.* 🚫

Shey was the ancient capital of Ladakh. Its abandoned palace contains a temple with a gigantic, late 17th-century Buddha image, surrounded by murals of deities, painted in rich colours and gold. Another beautiful Buddha image is housed in a nearby temple. Just below the palace, are huge 11th-century rock carvings of the Five Buddhas of Meditation *(see p146).*

A Ladakhi couple bringing their baby to be blessed at Shey

BUDDHIST SECTS IN LADAKH

Five sects of Tibetan Buddhism are represented in Ladakh. Thak-thok monastery belongs to the Nyingmapa, which is based on the teachings of the 8th-century saint, Padma-sambhava *(see p120)*, while Matho *(see p140)* with its oracle monks belongs to the Sakyapa. The Drugpa and Drigungpa sects are based on the teachings of a line of Indian masters from the 11th century. The lamas of all these sects wear red hats on ceremonial occasions. The lamas who wear yellow hats belong to the reformist Gelugpa sect, headed by the Dalai Lama *(see p123)*, which exercised political control in Tibet until 1959. Apart from Thak-thok and Matho, and the two Drigungpa monasteries of Phiyang *(see p137)* and Lama-yuru, all Ladakh's monasteries belong to either the Drugpa or Gelugpa sects.

Monks of the Gelugpa sect chanting prayers

Dance of the Oracle at the 16th-century Matho Monastery

Matho Monastery ❹

Leh district. 30 km (19 miles) SE of Leh. 🚌 🚶 *daily.* 📷 📹 *Annual Matho Festival (Feb/Mar).*

The only monastery in Ladakh of the Sakyapa sect *(see p139)*, Matho, built in the early 16th century, is also one of the few that continues to attract many new entrants. Its main importance, however, lies in its Oracles – two monks who, after months of purification by fasting and meditation, are possessed by a deity. This event takes place during Matho's annual festival, held between February and March. The drama of the occasion is tremendous as the Oracles traverse the topmost parapet of the monastery blindfolded, despite the 30-m

(98-ft) drop onto the rocks below. The Oracles answer questions put to them about public and private affairs, and great faith is reposed in their predictions. Matho also has a small museum with a rare collection of 16th-century *thangkas* and costumes.

Hemis Monastery ❺

Leh district. 43 km (27 miles) SE of Leh. 🚌 🚶 *daily.* 📷 📹 *Annual Hemis Festival (Jun).*

Tucked away up a winding glen in the mountains south of the Indus, Hemis is the largest as well as the richest of the central Ladakh monasteries. It was founded in the 1630s as a Drugpa establishment by King Sengge Namgyal, and continued to be the most favoured monastery of the Namgyal dynasty. Of its several temples, the most rewarding is the *tshog-khang*, a secondary assembly hall which contains a fine image of the Buddha in front of a huge silver *chorten* set with flawless turquoises.

Hemis is also renowned for its spectacular annual festival, dedicated to Guru Padmasambhava, the 8th-century Indian apostle who took Buddhism to Tibet. A unique feature of this festival, which is held in the summer and attracts huge crowds, is the 12-yearly unveiling of the monastery's greatest treasure – an enormous, three-storey high *thangka* of Padmasambhava, embroidered and studded with pearls and semi-precious stones. The next unveiling of the *thangka* is due in 2016.

The giant *thangka* unfurled during the festival at Hemis Monastery

THE MONASTIC DANCE-DRAMAS OF LADAKH

The dance-dramas performed at Ladakh's annual monastery festivals are immensely popular events, constituting a link between popular and esoteric Buddhism. Attended by high lamas and novice monks in their ceremonial robes and hats, as well as by local families dressed in their splendid traditional costumes, these events are a vibrant expression of age-old cultural and religious values. The dancers, representing divine or mythological figures, wear colourful brocade robes and heavy masks as they perform ceremonial dances around the monastery courtyard. The solemnity of the occasion is lightened by comic interludes per-

Masked dancers at a monastery festival

formed by dancers in skeleton costumes, who bound into the arena performing agile gymnastics, and caricaturing the solemn rites just enacted, to the delight of the assembled spectators. In the climactic scene the masked figures ritually dismember a doll moulded from barley flour dough (perhaps symbolizing the human soul) and scatter its fragments in all directions. Besides attracting large numbers of outside visitors, these monastery festivals also provide people from far-flung Ladakhi villages an eagerly awaited opportunity to meet each other, and exchange news and views.

For hotels and restaurants in this region see pp694–5 and pp723–4

Buddhist Iconography

The external manifestations of Buddhism are ubiquitous in Leh district and Zanskar – prayer flags fluttering in the breeze, prayer wheels turning in the hands of the elderly, chortens and mani walls inset with stone slabs carved with the sacred invocation Om mani padme hum ("Hail to the Jewel in the Lotus"). Inside the monaster-

Prayer wheel

ies, the iconography is more complex. Each divinity of the Mahayana Buddhist pantheon is depicted in several different manifestations, together with a host of saints, teachers and mythical figures, mandalas and allegorical compositions. Shown below are some images that are encountered most frequently.

THE BODHISATTVAS
Bodhisattvas are supremely compassionate almost-Buddhas who have attained enlightenment, but are willing to forgo nirvana so that they can help others obtain liberation from the endless cycle of rebirths.

Tara *is the female form of Avalokitesvara and is depicted in 21 different forms.*

Avalokitesvara, *the Bodhisattva of Compassion, is often shown with 11 heads and multiple arms, symbolizing his benign omnipresence.*

Manjushri, *the Bodhisattva of Wisdom, bears a flaming sword in his hand, to cut through the fog of ignorance.*

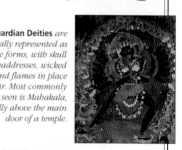

Guardian Deities *are usually represented as fierce forms, with skull headdresses, wicked fangs and flames in place of hair. Most commonly seen is Mahakala, usually above the main door of a temple.*

The Wheel of Life, *with animated human and animal figures on it, is mostly painted on temple verandahs. It shows the temptations and sins that make life on earth an endless misery.*

The Lords of the Four Quarters *guard the four cardinal directions. The Lord of the North is recognized by the banner in his right hand, and a mongoose in his left hand.*

See also features on Little Tibet *(p123)* and In the Buddha's Footsteps *(p221)*.

Glaciers and peaks encircling the blue-green waters of Pang-gong Tso

Southeast Ladakh ❻

Pang-gong Tso Leh district. 150 km (93 miles) E of Leh. **Tso Moriri** Leh district. 220 km (1,137 miles) SE of Leh. ⓘ *Leh Tourist Office, (01982) 252 297.* **Travel permits** *required. Contact Deputy Commissioner, Leh, (01982) 252 010. Permits are granted on condition that visitors travel in groups of not less than four, with the tour organized by a registered travel agent along specific tour routes. For more details see p153.*

Southeast Ladakh, on the sensitive international border with Tibet, is a region with a series of spectacularly beautiful lakes. The two major lakes, **Pang-gong Tso** and **Tso Moriri**, are accessible by road, although there are no scheduled bus services.

The biggest of the lakes is the long and narrow Pang-gong Tso. It is 130-km (81-mile) in length and lies at an altitude of 4,420 m (14,500 ft), extending far into Western Tibet. Visitors may go as far as **Spangmik**, 7 km (4 miles) along the lake's southern shore, from where there are spectacular views to the north of the Chang-chenmo Range, its reflection shimmering in the ever-changing blues and greens of the brackish water. Above Spangmik rise the glaciers and snowcapped peaks of the Pang-gong Range.

Tso Moriri, 30 km (19 miles) to the south of Pang-gong Tso is a 140-sq km (54-sq mile) expanse of intensely blue water. At an altitude of 4,600 m (15,092 ft), it is set among rolling hills behind which lie snow-covered mountains. The region's only permanent settlement is on the lake's western shore, **Karzok** – a handful of houses and a monastery, whose barley fields must be among the highest cultivated areas anywhere in the world.

The lake and its freshwater inlets are breeding areas for many species of migratory birds, such as the rare black-necked crane and the great crested grebe. Wild asses, marmots and foxes can also be seen in the region.

Among the human inhabitants of Southeast Ladakh are the nomadic herders, known as Chang-pa, who brave extreme cold (-40° C/-40° F in winter, and freezing nights even in summer) throughout the year, living in their black yak-hair tents. They raise yak and sheep, but their main wealth is the pashmina goat. The severe cold of winter stimulates the goats to grow an undercoat of soft warm fibre, which they shed at the beginning of summer. This fibre, known as *pashm*, is the raw material for Kashmir's renowned shawl industry and is, in fact, the unprocessed form of the world-famous cashmere wool. The lucrative trade in *pashm* from Ladakh's high-altitude pastures as well as from Western Tibet was the motive behind Ladakh's annexation by the Maharaja of Kashmir in 1834.

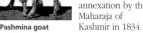

Pashmina goat

Environs

The twin lakes of **Tso Kar** and **Startsapuk Tso** are 80 km (50 miles) north of Tso Moriri, on the road to Leh. Startsapuk Tso has fresh water, but Tso Kar is so briny that the Chang-pa herders regularly collect salt from deposits near its margins.

THE CARAVAN TRADE

For centuries until 1949, Ladakh was the route for a busy trade between Punjab and Central Asia. The caravans invariably halted at Leh *(see pp136–7)*, where a lot of business was transacted, before proceeding to cross the 5,578-m (18,301-ft) high Karakoram Pass, one of the highest points on any trade route in the world. In summer the caravans traversed Nubra, while in winter they crossed the upper valley of the Shayok river. Every year, over 10,000 pack animals – horses, yaks, Bactrian camels, and an especially sturdy breed of local sheep – traversed the Nubra region, carrying Varanasi brocades, Chinese silk, pearls, spices, Indian tea, *pashm* wool, salt, indigo, opium, carpets, and gold.

A Ladakhi horseman taking a break for prayers

Tso Moriri, a breeding ground for the great crested grebe

Nubra Valley Tour ❼

The tour of the Nubra region starts from Leh and follows the old caravan trade route to Central Asia, a "feeder" of the famous Silk Route. It takes in the world's highest motorable mountain pass – the Khardung-la, pretty villages with banks of wild flowers and stands of willow and poplar, valleys covered with seabuckthorn shrubs, stretches of sand dunes and double-humped Bactrian camels, remote monasteries, and medicinal hot springs.

The Karakoram Range, visible from the top of the Khardung-la

Panamik ⑥
A major halt on the caravan trade route, Panamik also has medicinal hot springs. This Panamik lady is seen in her local traditional dress.

Hundar ③
The fascinating vista of sand dunes between Diskit and Hundar can be explored on the back of a Bactrian camel.

LHAYUL GOMPA

Nubra

Shayok

Shayok-Nubra confluence ④
Flat sandy plains surround the confluence of these two rivers.

Samstangling ⑤
Overlooking the green fields of Sumur village, this 19th-century monastery has impressive images.

KARGIL

Shayok

Leh

SHEY

Diskit ②
Diskit, which has the region's only bazaar, also has a 17th-century monastery with exquisite murals.

Khardung-la ①
From the top of this pass (5,578 m/18,301 ft) there are superb views, south over the Zanskar Range, and north to the towering Saser Spur of the Karakoram Range.

TIPS FOR DRIVERS

Length: 195 km (121 miles).
Getting around: This tour takes three days. Diskit, Hundar and Panamik have guesthouses and camps, for overnight stay.
Travel permits: Visitors must obtain an Inner Line Permit from the Deputy Commissioner, Leh, (01982) 252 010, to travel in the Nubra region. Permits are granted only to groups of four or more, and should be carried all the time.

KEY

▬ Tour route

═ Other road

░ River

0 km   8

0 miles   8

Alchi Monastery ❽

Dancing deity in the Sumtsek

Founded in the early 12th century AD, the religious enclave of Alchi is the jewel among Ladakh's monasteries. Because Alchi was abandoned as a site of active worship, for reasons unknown, as early as the 16th century, the 12th- and 13th-century paintings in its temples have remained remarkably well preserved, undimmed by the soot from butter lamps and incense sticks. Of the five temples in the enclave, the finest murals are in the two oldest, the Dukhang and the Sumtsek. These have been executed with great delicacy and skill by master painters who were probably from Kashmir.

Lhakhang Soma
This painting of a Guardian Deity and his female counterpart symbolizes the union of opposites.

Avalokitesvara
The legs of this gigantic statue in the Sumtsek are covered with exquisite miniature paintings of palaces and Buddhist pilgrimage sites.

★ Sumtsek
The carved wooden façade of this temple is in the style of Kashmiri temple architecture.

GREEN TARA

There are several exquisite images of this goddess, variously identified as Green Tara, the Saviour, and Prajnaparamita (the Perfection of Wisdom) in the Sumtsek. Five of them are to the left of the gigantic Avalokitesvara statue, opposite his leg. The Green Tara seems to have held a special place in Alchi, since the goddess is not given such importance in other monasteries.

Green Tara or Prajnaparamita

STAR FEATURES

★ Sumstek

★ Dukhang

View of Alchi
Idyllically located on a bend in the Indus river, Alchi's simple white-washed buildings with their band of deep red trim, stand out against an impressive backdrop of barren mountains.

Chortens containing holy relics are dotted around the complex. They are often built in memory of a great lama.

★ Dukhang
The serene image of the Vairocana Buddha (see p146) is surrounded by elaborate wood-work, decorative friezes and superb mandalas.

Lotsawa Lhakhang

King and Queen
This mural in the Dukhang shows details of royal dress and hairstyles.

Rinchen Zangpo
This rare portrait of Rinchen Zangpo (see p119), an influential Tibetan saint known as the Great Translator, is in the 12th-century Lotsawa ("Translator") Lhakhang.

Manjushri Lhakhang, one of the five temples, contains a large image of Manjushri *(see p141).*

Entrance

Exploring Alchi Monastery

Unknown to the outside world until 1974, when Ladakh was opened up to tourists, Alchi is now one of Ladakh's major attractions, renowned as a great centre of Buddhist art. It was built as a monument to the Second Spreading – the revival of Buddhism that took place in Tibet in the 11th century, on the basis of religious texts brought from Kashmir. The entire Mahayana Buddhist pantheon of deities is represented within its five temples, together with superb paintings of court life, battles and pilgrimages, depicting the costumes, architecture and customs of the time.

The assembly hall, known as **Dukhang**, is the oldest of the five temples and holds some of Alchi's greatest treasures. The beautiful central image of Vairocana, the main Buddha of Meditation, is surrounded by a wooden frame exuberantly carved with dancers, musicians, elephants and mythical animals. It is flanked by four other Buddhas of Meditation. Even more impressive are the six elaborate mandalas painted on the walls, together with small scenes of contemporary life. The space between the mandalas is filled with fine decorative details that have an unexpectedly Rococo look about them.

In the three-storeyed **Sumtsek**, the second-oldest temple, are spectacular images and paintings. The temple's most unique features are the gigantic images of

One of the many prayer rooms in Alchi Monastery

Avalokitesvara, Manjushri (see p141) and Maitreya, that stand in alcoves in three of its walls. Only their legs and torsos are visible from the ground floor, while their heads protrude into the upper storey. From waist to knee they are draped in dhoti-like garments, covered with remarkably animated and sophisticated miniature paintings. It is advisable to take a torch to examine their incredible detail. The Avalokitesvara image is covered with shrines, palaces, and vignettes of contemporary life. The Maitreya image has scenes from the Buddha's life painted within roundels, and the Manjushri image depicts the 84 Masters of the Tantra.

The three other temples probably date from the late 12th to early 13th centuries, and though they would win acclaim in any other setting, they fade in comparison with the Dukhang and the Sumtsek. The **Manjushri Lhakhang** has murals of the Thousand Buddhas and an enormous, recently-repainted image of Manjushri. The **Lotsawa Lhakhang** has rather more austere paintings and images. It is dedicated to the saint Rinchen Zangpo, who was also closely associated with the Thikse (see p139) and Tabo (see p131) monasteries. The **Lhakhang Soma**, the last temple to be built at Alchi, has a profusion of fierce-looking deities on its walls, and scenes showing the Buddha preaching.

Riders, Central Asian in appearance, on the Avalokitesvara image

THE FIVE BUDDHAS OF MEDITATION

Buddhism in the 12th century laid emphasis on the Five Dhyani Buddhas, or Buddhas of Meditation, who feature in several mandalas in Alchi. Each of these Buddhas is associated with a direction and a colour. Vairocana (the Resplendent) is associated with the centre and the colour white; Amitabha (the Boundless Light) with the west and the colour red; Akshobhya (the Imperturbable) with the east and the colour blue; Amoghasiddhi (Infallible Success) with the north and the colour green; and Ratnasambhava (the Jewel-Born) with the south and the colour yellow. The Five Buddhas of Meditation symbolize the different aspects of the Buddha, and the mandalas help devotees to meditate on them.

Mandala with the Five Dhyani Buddhas

Mulbekh ❾

Kargil district. 190 km (118 miles) NW of Leh. 🚌 ℹ️ *Kargil Tourist Office, (01985) 232 721.*

A pretty village in the Kargil district, Mulbekh, spread over the broad green valley of the Wakha river, is the point at which the proselytizing tide of Islam, spreading towards central Ladakh, lost its impetus. As a consequence, Mulbekh has a mixed population of Buddhists and Muslims, and supports a mosque as well as a monastery, perched on a crag above the village. Its main attraction, however, is a giant engraving of Maitreya, the Future Buddha, on a huge free-standing rock by the roadside. It is believed to date back to the 8th century.

The 8-m (26-ft) high Maitreya Buddha at Mulbekh

Kargil ❿

Kargil district. 230 km (143 miles) NW of Leh and NE of Srinagar. 🚌 ℹ️ *Kargil Tourist Office, (01985) 232 721.* 🎭 *Muharram (Mar/Apr), Ladakh Festival (Sep).* **Travel permits** *are required for the Dha-Hanu region, available at Leh (see p142).*

For travellers between Leh and Srinagar, Kargil town is a good place to stop for the night. The second largest urban centre in Ladakh, Kargil was an important trading centre before the Partition of India, when the road to Skardu in Baltistan (Pakistan) was still open. The majority of Kargil's population are Shia

View of the Nun-kun massif from Suru Valley

Muslims, an Islamic sect that regards Muhammad's cousin Ali and his successors as the true imams.

Kargil apricots are famous, and its hillside orchards are an enchanting sight in May when the trees are in bloom, and in July when the fruit is ripe. The town is also the base for expeditions to the Suru Valley, Zanskar and Nun-kun. Kargil suffered shelling during the conflict between India and Pakistan in 1999, so check the situation before a visit there.

Suru Valley ⓫

Kargil district. 19 km (12 miles) S of Kargil. 🚌 *to Sankhu.*

The Suru Valley starts from Kargil and runs 100 km (62 miles) to the southeast. One of Ladakh's loveliest and most fertile regions, it boasts rolling alpine pastures, mud-walled villages and views of majestic snowcapped peaks. Abundant water from melting snows gives the Suru Valley rich harvests of barley and plantations of willow and poplar, especially around **Sankhu** village. Close to Sankhu are the ruins of ancient forts, together with rock engravings of Maitreya and Avalokitesvara from the valley's pre-Islamic past. The upper valley is dominated by the peaks, ridges and glaciers of the Nun-kun massif which is 7,135 m (23,409 ft) high. Expeditions to the mountain take off from the picturesque village of **Panikhar**, whose pastures are covered with alpine flowers in June and July.

Prehistoric rock paintings in the Suru Valley

THE DARDS

A conspicuous sight in the bazaars of Kargil and Leh are the Dards, in their colourful caps adorned with flowers. Their aquiline features and fair complexions set them apart

A Dard in his distinctive cap

from other Ladakhis, as do their customs and traditions. There are several theories about the origins of this small community – among others, that they are the descendants of Alexander the Great's soldiers. Anthropological research, however, indicates that their ancestors migrated from Gilgit in Pakistan before it came under the influence of Islam. There are Dard villages at Dha-Hanu, east of Kargil on the Indus, close to where the river leaves Ladakh for Baltistan (Pakistan).

A view of the dramatically-situated Phugtal Monastery *(see p151)* in Zanskar ▷

Rangdum ⑫

Kargil district. 110 km (68 miles) SE of Kargil. 🚌 ℹ️ *Kargil Tourist Office, (01985) 232 721.*

The village of Rangdum serves as a night halt between Kargil *(see p147)* and Zanskar. Though geographically part of the Suru Valley, its largely Buddhist population and its monastery orient it culturally towards Zanskar. Situated on a wide flat plateau at 3,800 m (12,467 ft), crisscrossed by water courses, and framed by snow peaks and hills of curiously striated rock, Rangdum has a wild, desolate beauty. The fortress-like 18th-century **Gelugpa Monastery** is built on a hillock, and a small temple in the complex has a fine wall painting of a battle-scene, with warriors sporting Mongolian-looking armour and battledress.

Zanskar ⑬

Kargil district. 230 km (143 miles) SE from Kargil to Padum. 🚌 to Padum. ℹ️ *Padum Tourist Office, (01983) 254 017.* 🎭 *Karsha Monastery Festival (Jul/Aug).*

There is a certain mystique about Zanskar. This is no doubt due to its remoteness and altitude, between 3,350 m (10,991 ft) and 4,400 m (14,436 ft), and the fact that the region is difficult to access – the only motorable road into the valley is usually open from around early June to mid-October. But Zanskar's reputation as a Shangri-la also

derives from the grandeur of its landscapes, the simplicity of life in its villages, and the serene ambience in its *gompas*, often built around ancient cliff-top meditation caves.

Zanskar contains the valleys of two rivers, the Stod and the Lungnak which, flowing towards each other along the northern flank of the Greater Himalayas, join to become the Zanskar river. This continues north through a gorge in the Zanskar Range, to join the Indus.

The western arm of Zanskar, the Stod Valley, and its central plain are fertile and well-watered – villages form green pockets and the virtual absence of trees contributes to an extraordinary sense of light and space. The inhabitants of this region are mostly agricultural farmers, growing barley, wheat and peas in the lower villages, and raising livestock – yaks, sheep and *dzos* (a hybrid between cows and yaks) – in the higher villages. In winter, many of these farmers take the only route out of the area, trekking for six gruelling days across the frozen Zanskar river, to sell their highly prized yak butter in Leh. In contrast

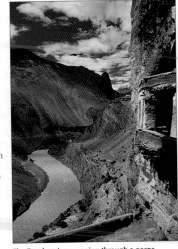

The Zanskar river, running through a gorge

Perak, the traditional female headdress

to the fertile western arm and central plain, the eastern arm of Zanskar – the Lungnak Valley – is a forbidding and stony gorge, with few villages to be found in the vicinity.

The main gateway to Zanskar is the **Pensi-la** (4,400 m/14,436 ft), about 130 km (81 miles) southeast of Kargil. There are spectacular views from the top of this pass, especially of the impressive **Drang-drung Glacier**, which is the origin of the Stod river. The road then continues down to **Padum**, 230 km (143 miles) southeast of Kargil, at an altitude of 3,500 m (11,483 ft). Padum is Zanskar's main village and administrative headquarters. This is the only place in the region with basic facilities including accommodation, transport and a few rudimentary shops. It is also the starting point for a number of treks in the region *(see pp152–3)*. Padum itself has few sites of interest, except for a rock engraving of the Five Dhyani Buddhas *(see p146)* in the centre of the village. A new mosque serves Padum's small community of Muslims. There are a number of interesting sites to explore in the vicinity. Within easy reach

Stucco decoration and images in bas-relief at Sani Gompa, Zanskar on foot, is the village of **Pipiting**, which has a temple and *chorten* on top of a mound of glacial debris, and a pavilion which was specially constructed for the Dalai Lama's prayer assemblies.

A short distance away is **Sani**, 8 km (5 miles) northwest of Padum, one of the oldest religious sites in the Western Himalayas. Within the monastery walls stands the Kanika Chorten, its name possibly linking it to the Kushana ruler Kanishka *(see p43)*, whose empire stretched from Afghanistan to Varanasi in the 1st and 2nd centuries AD. The monastery itself is said to have been founded by Padmasambhava *(see p120)* in the 8th century, and its main temple has some fine murals. Even more interesting is another small temple in the complex, which has unique, beautifully painted stucco bas-relief decorations, and niches in the walls for images. Sani is surrounded by a stand of poplars, conspicuous in this otherwise treeless landscape.

Visible from Padum, the buildings of the Gelugpa monastery of **Karsha**, 10 km (6 miles) northeast of Padum, seem to spill down the mountainside west of the main valley, until they merge with the houses and fields of the village. This site includes ancient rock engravings, and the murals in its Avalokitesvara temple, just outside the main complex, seem to put it in the same period as Alchi *(see pp144–6)*. Tradition, however,

Fertile fields of barley and wheat in the Stod Valley in Zanskar

attributes the monastery's foundation to the ubiquitous Padmasambhava. Karsha has a large community of resident monks, and holds its colourful annual festival between July and August.

Stongde, on the opposite side of the valley, 12 km (7 miles) from Padum, is perched on a ridge, high above the mosaic of the village's fields. Believed to have been founded in the 11th century, it houses no fewer than seven well-maintained temples, some of them containing exquisite murals.

The villages of Sani, Karsha and Stongde are connected by motor transport, though the monasteries in the **Lungnak Valley** are less accessible. The narrow footpath leading up the valley winds along unstable scree slopes high above the river, and the walk is strenuous. It takes a sharp

climb on foot or on horseback to reach **Bardhan** and **Phugtal** monasteries.

Bardhan, 9 km (6 miles) southeast of Padum, is spectacularly located atop a crag jutting out from the mountain and rising some 100 m (328 ft) sheer out of the river. It has fine wall paintings dating back to the time of the monastery's foundation in the early 17th century. Of all Ladakh's many monasteries however, none, not even Bardhan or Lamayuru, can rival

Mandala, Bardhan Monastery

Phugtal, 60 km (37 miles) southeast of Padum, for the grandeur and drama of its location. Its main temples are constructed inside a huge cave on the mountainside above the Tsarap river, at a point where the drop to the water is almost sheer. Yet below the temples the monks' dwellings have somehow been built on or into the cliff-face, and the whole improbable complex is linked by a crazy system of ladders and walkways. There is no record of Phugtal monastery's foundation, but the style of its paintings, some of them quite striking, link it with the Tabo monastery in Spiti *(see p131)* and the traditions established by the Tibetan saint Rinchen Zangpo *(see p119)* in the 11th century. Its monks belong to the Gelugpa order.

Sani, Karsha, Stongde, Bardhan and Phugtal Monasteries

☐ daily.

Phugtal Monastery, built into a sheer cliff-face

Trekking in Ladakh and Zanskar

Trekking in the arid, extremely cold trans-Himalayan desert of Ladakh and Zanskar, very often at altitudes that exceed 5,000 m (16,404 ft), can be a uniquely exhilarating experience. The terrain, as starkly beautiful as any highland setting in the world, has a number of trails, many of which trace ancient trading routes to Central Asia. They lead past spectacularly located monasteries, remote passes, sometimes staggeringly high, deep river gorges and lush meadows scattered with *mani* walls and *chortens*. The best time to trek is between June and September, when the land is not snowbound and the terraced fields are being harvested.

Black-necked crane

LOCATOR MAP

Area shown below

Likir to Tingmosgang is an easy, two-day, 22-km (14-mile) path, past a number of villages at 4,000 m (13,123 ft).

From Lamayuru, a tough five-day, 65-km (40-mile) trek, via Konki-la at 4,905 m (16,093 ft), ends at Alchi *(see pp144–5).*

Padum to Lamayuru

This 160-km (99-mile) path follows the Zanskar river via Karsha, past the impressive Lingshet Monastery and Singe-la ("Lion Pass"), ending at Lamayuru. A slightly easier route past Zangla, joins the main trail at Yelchang village.

Duration: *10 days*
Altitude: *5,000 m (16,404 ft)*
Level of difficulty: *tough*

Padum to Darcha

The 115-km (71-mile) path goes from Zanskar into Himachal Pradesh, along the beautiful Tsarap river, past Phugtal Monastery and Kurgiakh, Zanskar's highest village at 4,100 m (13,451 ft).

Duration: *10 days*
Altitude: *5,100 m (16,732 ft)*
Level of difficulty: *moderate*

Tingmosgang
Lamayuru
Wanlah
Indus
Alchi
Konki-la (4,905 m/16,093 ft)
Skiu
Singe-la (5,000 m/16,404 ft) Zanskar
Lingshet   Yulchung
Zangla
Karsha
Padum
Bardhan   Phu
Reru
Kurgiakh
Shingo-la (5,100 m/16,73...)

Rafting down the Indus river on rubber dinghies, a popular sport

OTHER OUTDOOR ACTIVITIES

White-water rafting on the Indus and Zanskar rivers, is a popular activity from July to mid-September. There are various options to consider on the Indus river, from calm "float trips" between Hemis and Choglamsar, to longer stints between Spituk and Alchi. **Jeep safaris** to the lakes of Tso Kar and Tso Moriri and back, take three days, with tents pitched near Karzok village. The region's rich wildlife include bar-headed geese, black-necked cranes and the *kiang* (Tibetan wild ass).

Dar

Spituk to Hemis

Ladakh's most popular trek, this 105-km (65-mile) path runs along the Indus river through Markha Valley, past Skiu village and the high pass of Kongmaru, and ends at Hemis Monastery (see p140).

Duration: *8 days*
Altitude: *5,274 m (17,303 ft)*
Level of difficulty: *easy*

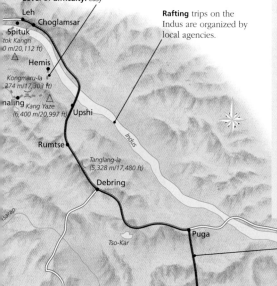

Rafting trips on the Indus are organized by local agencies.

Leh

Choglamsar

Spituk

tok Kangri
0 m/20,112 ft)

Hemis

*Kongmaru-la
274 m/17,303 ft)*

naling *Kang Yaze
(6,400 m/20,997 ft)*

Upshi

Indus

Rumtse

*Tanglang-la
(5,328 m/17,480 ft)*

Debring

Puga

Tso-Kar

Isarap

Karzok

*Tso
Moriri*

*Baralacha-la
(4,892 m/16,050 ft)*

Leh to Tso Moriri is a 230-km (143-mile), ten-hour journey by jeep.

0 km   20

0 miles   20

KEY

- – – Spituk to Hemis
- – – Likir to Tingmosgang
- – – Lamayuru to Alchi
- ▬ ▬ Padum to Lamayuru
- – – Padum to Darcha
- ▬▬ Leh to Tso Moriri
- ═══ Minor road
- △ Peak
- ⌣ Pass

Tso Kar or "White Lake", lying northwest of Tso Moriri

Srinagar's 14th-century Shah Hamadan Mosque, made entirely of wood

Jammu ⑭

Jammu district. 500 km (311 miles) NW of Delhi. 🏠 378,400. ✈ 8 km (5 miles) SW of city centre. 🚉 🚌 ℹ J&K Tourism, Vir Marg, (0191) 254 8172. 🎎 Lohri (13 Jan), Jammu Festival (Apr), Navratra (Sep/Oct).

The winter capital of Jammu and Kashmir state, Jammu is located on a bluff of the Shivalik Range, overlooking the northern plains. The main site of interest is the **Amar Mahal**, once the residence of the maharajas, and today a museum with artifacts relating to the region's culture and history. Jammu is also the base for the pilgrimage to the cave shrine of the goddess **Vaishno Devi** in the Trikuta mountains, 50 km (31 miles) away. The shrine attracts four million Hindus every year.

🏛 **Amar Mahal Museum**
Off Srinagar Rd. ◯ Tue–Sun. 📷

Srinagar ⑮

Srinagar district. 700 km (435 miles) NW of Delhi. 🏠 895,000. ✈ 8 km (5 miles) S of city centre. 🚌 ℹ J&K Tourism, (0194) 245 2690. 🎎 Milad-ul-Nabi (May).

Srinagar, the summer capital of Jammu and Kashmir, is a city of lakes and waterways, gardens and picturesque wooden architecture. The old quarters of the city sprawl over both sides of the Jhelum river, crossed by seven bridges. Although the bridges have their own names (such as Amira Kadal and Zaina Kadal), they are also known by their numbers; an Eighth Bridge, built more recently (in the 20th century) above First Bridge, is known with typical Kashmiri wit as Zero Bridge. This serves the modern part of the city, built in the late 19th century. At the city's edge are the idyllic **Dal** and **Nagin Lakes**, linked by a network of backwaters. Srinagar's mosques and shrines are among the city's most attractive features. Typically, these are built of wood intricately carved in geometric patterns, and instead of a dome they are surmounted by a pagoda-like steeple. The most striking examples are the **Mosque of Shah Hamadan** in the old city, and the **Shah Makhdum Sahib Shrine** on the slopes of Hari Parbat hill. Two conventional stone mosques, the **Patthar Mosque** and the **Mosque of**

Chinar leaves in autumn colours

CAUTION

At present, it is not advisable to visit Jammu and Kashmir, due to continued unrest. In recent years, terrorist activity by militant groups in the area has included bomb blasts, kidnappings and sniper fire. Foreign tourists are sometimes specially targeted.

Akhund Mulla Shah, both beautifully proportioned structures, date from the 17th century. In an altogether different style is the **Hazratbal Mosque**, with its dazzling white dome and single slender minaret. Rebuilt in the Saracenic style after a fire in the 1960s, it contains Kashmir's most sacred relic, a hair from the beard of the Prophet Muhammad.

The Mughal emperors delighted in Kashmir's beauty and further enhanced it by introducing the stately *chinar* tree (*Platanous orientalis*) to the Kashmir Valley. They also created terraced hillside gardens designed around fountains and watercourses, which were formed by channeling water from natural springs or streams. Of the 777 Mughal gardens that reportedly once graced the Kashmir Valley, not many survive. There are three, however, within easy reach of Srinagar, on the eastern shore of the Dal Lake – **Chashmashahi**, **Nishat** and **Shalimar Gardens**. Above

The impressive ruins of the 8th-century Sun Temple at Martand

A house in Gulmarg, one of India's few ski resorts

the pretty Chashmashahi Garden, and rising tier upon tier on the mountainside, are the ruins of a 17th-century religious college. Built by a Mughal prince for his teacher, it is somewhat incongruously known as **Pari Mahal** or "Palace of the Fairies". From this vantage point, there are heart-stopping views of Dal Lake and the snowy ridge of the Pir Panjal Range.

Environs
Vestiges of Kashmir's pre-Islamic past can be seen in the ruins of magnificent Hindu temples at **Avantipora**, 28 km (17 miles) southeast of Srinagar, and **Martand**, 60 km (37 miles) southeast of Srinagar. The Sun Temple at Martand is believed to date from the 8th century AD, while the two Avantipora temples are probably from the 9th century AD. Built with great limestone blocks fitted together without mortar, these temples bear witness to the astonishing degree of technical expertise that prevailed in the early medieval period.

🌺 **Chashmashahi Garden**
☐ *daily.* 🚫

🌺 **Nishat and Shalimar Gardens**
☐ *daily.*

Gulmarg ⑯

Srinagar district. 58 km (36 miles) W of Srinagar. 🚌 🛈 *J&K Tourism, Gulmarg Tourist Office, (01954) 254 439.*

Gulmarg, or the "Meadow of Flowers", at an altitude of 2,730 m (8,950 ft), was developed by the British around a meadow on the northern flank of the Pir Panjal Range. The central bowl has been laid out as a golf course, one of the highest in the world. Around it are fairy-tale cottages with pine forests behind them. Gulmarg, together with **Khilanmarg**, some 300 m (984 ft) higher up in the mountains, is among India's few ski resorts. Its facilities, catering to all levels of proficiency, also include beginner courses.

Pahalgam ⑰

Srinagar district. 96 km (60 miles) E of Srinagar. 🚌 🛈 *J&K Tourism, Pahalgam Tourist Office, (01936) 243 224.*

In the valley of the Lidder river, Pahalgam is on the southern slope of the Great Himalayas. It is the base for several treks to Kishtwar and the Suru Valley *(see p147)*, and for the pilgrimage to the holy cave of **Amarnath**, the destination of several thousand Hindu pilgrims, every August.

Pahalgam, dotted with mustard fields, also offers trout fishing, golf and short expeditions into the nearby mountains. The road from Srinagar to Pahalgam passes by **Pampore**, famous for its fields of saffron *(Crocus sativa)*, which has been cultivated in Kashmir since the 10th century. The saffron flower blooms in late autumn.

Mustard fields surrounding a farmhouse in Pahalgam

HOUSEBOATS AND SHIKARAS

In the 19th century, some of Srinagar's boat-dwelling community started building luxury versions of their own homes to cater to visitors. These houseboats, which remain moored in one place, have become the favoured accommodation for most visitors. Those in the deluxe class are astonishingly elaborate, their plush living rooms and bedrooms a showcase for the celebrated Kashmiri handicrafts – exquisite woodcarving, embroidery, carpets and papier mâché. Mobility between houseboat and shore is ensured by a *shikara*, a skiff propelled by a boatman with a heart-shaped paddle. Whether luxuriating in the comfort of a houseboat, or accommodated more prosaically in a hotel on dry land, there can be no more idyllic way to spend a day in Srinagar than reclining on the cushions of a *shikara* in the shade of its awning, cruising the city's lakes and backwaters.

Houseboats and *shikaras* on Dal Lake

CENTRAL
INDIA

Introducing Central India

Some of India's most visited destinations are in this vast and varied region, which covers the flat Gangetic Plains, several Himalayan ranges and the verdant forests of the Central Indian heartland. These include the Taj Mahal at Agra, the holy city of Varanasi, the exquisitely sculpted temples of Khajuraho, and the great Buddhist sites of Sanchi and Bodh Gaya. Other attractions in Central India include the game sanctuaries of Kanha and Corbett, the medieval forts and palaces of Gwalior and Orchha, and the hill stations of Mussoorie, Nainital and Ranikhet, which are the base for many treks.

SEE ALSO

- *Where to Stay* pp695–9
- *Where to Eat* pp724–7

Luxuriant forested hills of *chir* pine
and alpine meadows in Uttaranchal

0 km   80

0 miles   80

DEHRA DUN RISHIKESH
CORBETT
MEERUT NAINITAL
RAMPUR
ALIGARH
Delhi MATHURA
AGRA
NH2
Yamuna
GWALIOR
SHIVPURI NH25 ORCHHA
NH KHAJURAHO
NH26
UJJAIN NH3 SANCHI
BHOPAL NH12
INDORE *Narmada* JABALPUR
MANDU
PACHMARHI
Mumbai

A view of the cenotaphs of the Orchha rulers, lying along the Betwa river

KEY

▬ National highway

▬ Major road

▭ River

‑ ‑ State border

◁ **The glowing pastoral landscape of rural Kumaon near Mukteshwar *(see p190)*, in the Western Himalayas**

GETTING AROUND

Major destinations and state capitals in this region, such as Agra, Varanasi, Dehra Dun, Khajuraho, Bhopal, Raipur and Patna are served by domestic airlines, as well as fast intercity trains. An air-conditioned special train, the Taj Express, makes a comfortable day trip from Delhi to Agra possible. An extensive road network connects most of the towns in this region. National Highway 2 connects Agra, Allahabad, Varanasi and Bodh Gaya. State highways branch off from National Highway 24 to the hills of Nainital and Mussoorie.

A rustic scene in a provincial town in Bihar

A PORTRAIT OF CENTRAL INDIA

T*hree of India's largest states – Uttar Pradesh, Bihar and Madhya Pradesh – lie in Central India. This vast and densely populated region is the country's Hindi-speaking belt (often called the "cow belt"), an area remarkable as much for its rich historical past and religious and cultural diversity as for its mineral wealth.*

The River Ganges, which flows through Uttar Pradesh (UP) and Bihar, has shaped much of the history and culture of both states. On its fertile banks, civilizations, cities and empires have grown and flourished, from 1500 BC onwards *(see p41)*.

Detail from the great stupa at Sanchi

Today, the river continues to play a crucial role in the economy, culture, religion as well as imagination of the millions of people who live in the surrounding Gangetic Plains.

UP is both the spiritual heartland of Hinduism and the cultural heartland of Indian Islam – the former symbolized by Varanasi, the holiest of Indian cities *(see pp202–208)*, and the latter by the Taj Mahal, the country's greatest Islamic monument *(see pp172–5)*. With a population of 148 million, UP elects more members to the Indian parliament than any other state, and therefore plays a dominant role in national politics. Six Indian prime ministers have been from here,

including Pandit Jawaharlal Nehru, his daughter Indira Gandhi and grandson Rajiv Gandhi and, more recently, Atal Behari Vajpayee. The tides of contemporary politics often hinge on the strength of caste and religious sentiments. One tragic result of this was the demolition of a 15th-century mosque in the town of Ayodhya in 1992, by Hindu religious extremists, because they claimed it stood at the spot where Lord Rama *(see p27)* was born. The incident led to widespread Hindu-Muslim riots and the issue continues to simmer.

In November 2000, several new states were created. In UP, the northernmost section, covering the Kumaon and Garhwal hills, became the new state of Uttaranchal. This is an area of great natural beauty, with picturesque hill stations, trekking trails, and ancient Hindu pilgrimage centres, in the shadow of towering Himalayan peaks.

The Chhota Imambara complex at Lucknow, capital of Uttar Pradesh

Pilgrims on the banks of the Ganges in Bihar

Madhya Pradesh (MP) provides a sharp contrast to the flat, crowded plains of UP and Bihar, with its varied terrain and relatively sparse population. The countryside here is an enchanting mosaic of cotton fields, craggy ravines, rolling hills, and vast tracts of forest and grassland, which are home to at least half of India's tiger population. A tragic industrial disaster in the state capital, Bhopal, in 1984 *(see p240)* has made the people of this state especially active in environmental issues, and many of them have been campaigning against a large dam on the Narmada river *(see p251)*. MP still gets relatively few visitors, yet few other states can rival its range of attractions, which include the World Heritage monuments at Sanchi *(see pp244–5)* and Khajuraho *(see pp236–8)*, and some of India's finest wildlife sanctuaries.

Bihar, like UP, is a densely populated state, and its political agenda too has in recent years been dominated by caste-based issues, at the expense of social and economic development. As a result, rural poverty is still widespread and the literacy rate remains abysmally low, at around 40 per cent. Ironically, this was a state that once had one of the ancient world's greatest universities, at Nalanda *(see pp218–9)*, and was the seat of two of India's greatest empires, the Maurya and Gupta empires *(see pp42–3)*. Bihar also occupies an important place in the history of Indian civilization, as the birthplace of Buddhism – for it was here, at Bodh Gaya *(see p222)*, that the Buddha gained enlightenment. This historic legacy can be seen in the state's famous Buddhist sites. Present-day Bihar has an earthy vitality, which can be experienced at the huge annual cattle fair at Sonepur *(see p216)*, where a prime attraction is the unique elephant bazaar.

The new state of Jharkhand, in what was southern Bihar, came into being in November 2000. An area of great natural beauty, Jharkhand comprises a forested plateau, home to a large population of tribal people with distinctive cultures, who now dominate the political and economic life of their nascent state. Jharkhand is blessed with great mineral wealth, and its rich deposits of coal and iron, in particular, ensure its future prosperity.

At the same time as Jharkhand and Uttaranchal, Chhatisgarh came into being. This southeastern part of Madhya Pradesh is a thickly forested area, populated by different tribal communities, engaged in agriculture and a variety of beautiful crafts *(see p253)*. Facilities are still being developed to welcome visitors to this fascinating part of the country.

A poster depicting Varanasi as the home of Shiva

The River Ganges

Rising in an ice cave, 4,140 m (13,583 ft) high in the Himalayas, the Ganges flows for 2,525 km (1,569 miles) through the mountains of Uttaranchal, and the vast plains of Uttar Pradesh, Bihar and Bengal, before entering the sea in the Bay of Bengal.

Goddess Ganga

Through the ages, great civilizations have flourished on its banks, which are today lined with teeming cities, fertile paddy fields and innumerable temples and ghats. For, above all, the Ganges is India's main spiritual and religious artery, sacred to millions of Hindus who believe that to bathe in its waters is to be absolved of all sins, and to be cremated on its banks and have one's ashes immersed in its waters ensures salvation of the soul.

Gaumukh *("Cow's Mouth") at the mouth of the Gangotri Glacier, is the source of the Ganges. Emerging as an icy torrent, the river is called the Bhagirathi here.*

Rishikesh (*see p184*) has famous ashrams offering yoga and meditation courses where studies in Hinduism are pursued.

Votive offering floated in the river

Devprayag (see p187), *set amidst dramatic mountain gorges, is an important pilgrimage town where the rivers Bhagirathi and Alaknanda meet to become the Ganges.*

UTTAR PRADESH

0 km   100
0 miles   100

Kanpur

Allahabad

KEY

– · – International border

– · State border

Haridwar, *the "Gateway to the Gods" (see p184), is where the Ganges finally descends from the Himalayas and begins its long journey through the plains that constitute India's heartland. Haridwar teems with temples, holy men and pilgrims, especially around its main ghat, Har-ki-Pauri, sanctified by the footprint of Lord Vishnu. It is one of the four sites where the mammoth Kumbh Mela is held every 12 years (see p211).*

Allahabad (see p210) *marks the confluence of three holy rivers, the Ganges, the Yamuna, and the mythical Saraswati. The Kumbh Mela held here in 2001 attracted some 30 million pilgrims.*

The Myth of the Ganges *holds that the celestial River Ganga was brought to earth by sage Bhagiratha so that he could sprinkle her holy water on the ashes of his ancestors, who were struck down by Lord Vishnu for their wickedness. The river water would ensure salvation for their souls. When the Ganga descended, Lord Shiva broke her enormous force by winding her through his hair, to save the earth from being destroyed in a deluge. This myth is often depicted in paintings and sculptures.*

Varanasi (see pp202–208) *is regarded by Hindus as the holiest spot on this holiest of rivers. Around 90 ghats line the river front, where the living come to be purified by the waters of the Ganges, and the dead are brought to attain* moksha *(release from the endless cycle of death and rebirth).*

Fertile fields, *enriched by alluvial soil, can be seen all along the Indo-Gangetic Plains. These fields of wheat and mustard are in Bihar.*

Kanwarias *are devotees of Shiva who make an arduous annual journey every August, to the Ganges on foot, carrying back the river's sacred water in brightly decorated pots, to their temples at home.*

Barges *laden with jute fibre are a common sight around the Gangetic Delta in Bengal.*

Ghaghara

Gandak

Patna

Munger

Varanasi

Son

BIHAR

Patna *(see pp214–5) is always busy with river traffic as the Ganges is wide and easily navigable here.*

Gaur

BANGLADESH

The otter, *about 70-cm (28-in) long, has a brown waterproof coat, webbed paws and stiff whiskers. This playful creature can often be seen gambolling on the banks of the river.*

Nabadwip

WEST BENGAL

Hooghly

Kolkata

Ganga Sagar Mela is a colourful festival *(see p295),* held in January at Sagar Island, close to where the river enters the sea.

Sagar Island

Ganges Delta

Bay of Bengal

The Flavours of Central India

Since a large part of the region falls within the fertile Gangetic Plain, this area is rich in agricultural produce. Stretching across the land are endless fields of rice and wheat as well as vast dark-green mango and litchi orchards. Rice and wheat are both eaten in the so-called Hindi-speaking states, although the food differs from community to community. The two main culinary influences are the sophisticated vegetarian cuisine from the holy city of Varanasi and Lucknow's refined mutton dishes and *biryanis* that evolved in the royal kitchens.

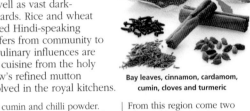

Bay leaves, cinnamon, cardamom, cumin, cloves and turmeric

Street vendor frying *samosas*, a popular snack, in a *tawa* (wok)

UTTAR PRADESH & UTTARANCHAL

Roughly, this region has three types of cuisine: vegetarian, Muslim or nawabi and Uttaranchali. The vegetarian food of the plains is very refined, cooked in pure *ghee* (clarified butter) and tempered with asafetida, *garam masala* (curry powder), cumin and chilli powder. Uttar Pradesh's street food, such as savoury *chaat*, is famous and the best can be found in the lanes of Varanasi.

The states of Awadh (now Lucknow) and Rampur produce an unsurpassable cuisine. Traditional *Dum pukht*, where food is sealed with dough in large pots and cooked on a slow fire, is the essence of Awadhi cuisine, as is the subtle use of spices.

From this region come two exquisite lamb *kebabs*: *galauti* and *kakori*, while the delicately flavoured *pulaos* (rice dishes) are legendary.

In the Himalayan state of Uttaranchal the food leans heavily on lentils, soya beans and *mundua* (buckwheat). Rice is the staple and the food is cooked in either *ghee* or mustard oil. A popular spice in this area is *bhanga* or hemp seeds.

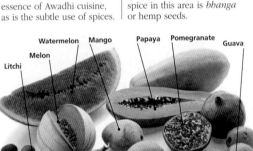

Watermelon   **Mango**   **Papaya**   **Pomegranate**   **Guava**

Melon

Litchi

A selection of fruits grown in Central India

LOCAL DISHES AND SPECIALITIES

Subtlety and refinement are the main features of both vegetarian and non-vegetarian cooking. A regular meal comprises lentils, a vegetable dish, rice or *roti* (bread) with pickles to add piquancy. Typical of Varanasi is *sattvik* or "pure" food, which is strictly vegetarian and lightly spiced, but without onions and garlic. The Muslim courts of Bhopal, Patna and Lucknow further enriched the culinary repertoire with fragrant mutton *biryanis*, rich *kormas* and succulent *kebabs*. Some of the finest sweets from this region include *jalebis* (crisp golden spirals of fried batter), rich *badam halwa* (almond sweet) and the syrup-soaked *malpua* (type of pancake). *Paan* (betel leaf) is served at the end of a hearty meal.

Mung dal

Savouries *include* samosas *(potato-filled turnovers) and* kachoris *(stuffed fried bread, with chutney).*

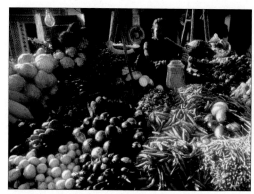

A roadside stall in Agra selling a selection of fresh vegetables

MADHYA PRADESH & CHHATTISHGARH

The food of Madhya Pradesh is as varied as the region. The princely states of Bhopal and Gwalior developed a distinctive cuisine that can be sampled in Gwalior's *barbat* (coriander (cilantro)-flavoured mutton curry), or Bhopal's *rizala* (chicken with yoghurt, green chillies and coriander). A gourmet maharaja from the small state of Sailana even produced his own cookbook, *The Cooking Delights of the Maharajas*, with recipes culled from royal kitchens.

The Malwa Plateau and the city of Indore have a wide array of savouries, sweets and thirst-quenchers that keep the city buzzing until midnight. Here, visitors can savour *bhutta ri kees* (grated corn cooked in *ghee*, milk and spices) or drink the cooling Malwa *kairi pana*, (fresh mango juice). Breads include *baati* and *bafla*, both made from wheat and shaped into balls. *Baati* is roasted and eaten with lentils while *bafla* is fried in *ghee*.

Paan or betel leaf, often eaten as a digestive after a meal

BIHAR & JHARKHAND

An abundance of fruits and vegetables and a simple style makes Bihar's cuisine special. A popular ingredient is *sattu* (roasted chickpea flour), which is energy-giving and nutritious. It can be made into drinks, breads or mixed with wheat, potatoes and mashed aubergine (eggplant).

The tribes of Jharkhand eat cereals and a curry of boiled vegetables, tubers or edible roots, lamb and chillies. A favourite ingredient is the flower of the *mahua (Madhuca indica)* tree which has hallucinogenic properties. It is used to flavour rice in *asur kichdi*.

ON THE MENU

Aloo dum Banarsi Spicy potatoes cooked with cottage cheese, nuts and raisins.

Kele ke kofta Green bananas mashed, made into balls and cooked in a lightly-spiced yoghurt sauce.

Kurwai biryani Steaks are used instead of pieces of mutton in this rice dish, a speciality of Madhya Pradesh.

Mawa-bati A *gulab jamun* (deep-fried milk and flour dumpling) filled with nuts.

Musallam raan Leg of lamb roasted with various spices.

Shabdeg A classic mutton dish slow-cooked with turnips and flavoured with spices.

Mutton korma *has pieces of mutton in a yoghurt and saffron sauce, flavoured with cloves and cardamom.*

Okra *is a favourite summer vegetable, served stuffed and fried or cooked in a yoghurt sauce.*

Shahi tukra *is a royal bread pudding in a rich sauce of thickened milk, garnished with sliced almonds.*

UTTAR PRADESH & UTTARANCHAL

Stretching from the Himalayas to the Indo-Gangetic Plains, Uttar Pradesh (UP) and Uttaranchal cover a vast area of 294,000 sq km (113,514 sq miles), with a population of almost 175 million. Hindi is the main language. Both states offer a wide variety of landscapes and historic monuments. In UP's plains are the famous Taj Mahal and other great Islamic monuments, as well as the holy Hindu city of Varanasi and the Buddhist stupas of Sarnath. The mammoth Kumbh Mela takes place every 12 years at Allahabad as well as Haridwar. In November 2000, the hill areas of Uttar Pradesh became the separate state of Uttaranchal. Its numerous attractions include beautiful trekking trails, the picturesque hill stations of Mussoorie and Nainital, river rafting tours and yoga ashrams around Rishikesh, and Corbett National Park, famous for its tigers.

SIGHTS AT A GLANCE

Towns & Cities
Agra ❶
Aligarh ⑳
Allahabad ㉘
Dehra Dun ❾
Jaunpur ㉕
Jhansi ㉑
Kanpur ㉒
Lucknow ㉓
Rampur ⑲

Hill Stations & Areas of Natural Beauty
Almora ⑬
Kausani ⑯
Lansdowne ⑮
Mussoorie ❿
Nainital ⑫

Ranikhet ⑭
The Garhwal Hills ⑪

Historic Sites
Ayodhya ㉔
Fatehpur Sikri ❺
Kalinjar Fort ㉚
Sarnath ㉗
Sikandra ❷

Temple Towns & Holy Places
Brindavan ❹
Chitrakoot ㉙

Haridwar ❻
Mathura ❸
Rishikesh ❼
Varanasi ㉖

National Parks
Corbett National Park ⑰
Dudhwa National Park ⑱

Tours
River Tour along the Ganges ❽

KEY

✕	Domestic airport
	National highway
	Major road
	Major railway
	International border
- - -	State border

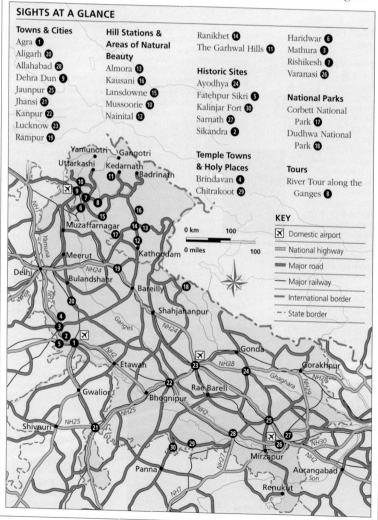

0 km 100
0 miles 100

◁ Fatehpur Sikri's Jami Masjid, built in the 16th century by the Mughal emperor Akbar

Agra ❶

Agra was the seat of the imperial Mughal court during the 16th and 17th centuries, before the capital was shifted to Delhi. The city, strategically located on the banks of the Yamuna and along the Grand Trunk Road, flourished under the patronage of the emperors Akbar, Jahangir and Shah

A pietra dura motif

Jahan, attracting artisans from Persia and Central Asia, and also from other parts of India, who built luxurious forts, palaces, gardens and mausoleums. Of these, the Taj Mahal, the Agra Fort and Akbar's abandoned capital of Fatehpur Sikri have been declared World Heritage Sites by UNESCO. With the decline of the Mughals, Agra was captured by the Jats, the Marathas, and finally by the British, early in the 19th century.

St John's College, designed by Sir Samuel Swinton Jacob

🏯 Agra Fort

See pp170–71.

Ⓒ Jami Masjid

⬜ *daily.* ⬛ *to non-Muslims during prayer times.*

A magnificently proportioned building in the heart of the historic town, the "Friday Mosque" was sponsored by Shah Jahan's favourite daughter, Jahanara Begum, who also commissioned a number of other buildings and gardens, including the canal that once ran down Chandni Chowk *(see pp84–5)* in Delhi. Built in 1648, the mosque's sandstone and marble domes with their distinctive zigzag chevron pattern dominate this section of the town. The eastern courtyard wing was demolished by the British in 1857 *(see p53)*. Of interest are the tank with its

Detail of minaret, Jami Masjid

shahi chirag (royal stove) for heating water within the courtyard, and the separate prayer chamber for ladies.

The area around Jami Masjid was once a vibrant meeting place, famous for its kebab houses and lively bazaars. A stroll or rickshaw ride through the narrow alleys can be a rewarding experience, offering glimpses of an older and very different way of life, reminiscent of Mughal Agra. This is also the city's crafts and trade centre where a vast array of products such as jewellery, *zari* embroidery, inlaid marble objects, *dhurries*, dried fruit, sweets, shoes and kites are available. Some of the main bazaars are Johri Bazaar, Kinari Bazaar, Kaserat Bazaar and Kashmiri Bazaar. Quieter lanes such as Panni Gali have many fine buildings, with

imposing gateways leading into secluded courtyards where the thriving workshops of master craftsmen still exist.

🏯 St John's College

Mahatma Gandhi Rd. **Tel** *(0562) 252 0123.* ⬜ *Mon–Sat.* ⬛ *public hols.*

The unusual architecture of St John's College has been described as "an astounding mixture of the antiquarian, the scholarly and the symbolic". It consists of a group of red sandstone buildings, including a hall and library, arranged around a quadrangle, all designed in a quasi-Fatehpur Sikri style by Sir Samuel Swinton Jacob *(see p353)*, who perfected the Indo-Saracenic style of architecture. Started by the Church Missionary Society, the college was inaugurated in 1914 by the viceroy, Lord Hardinge, and it continues to be one of Agra's most prestigious institutions.

⛪ Roman Catholic Cemetery

Opp Civil Courts. ⬜ *daily.*

Towards the north of the town is the Roman Catholic Cemetery, the oldest European graveyard in North India, established in the 17th century by an Armenian merchant, Khoja Mortenepus.

A number of Islamic-style gravestones, with inscriptions in Armenian, survive today, and include those of the cannon expert, Shah Nazar Khan, and Khoja Mortenepus himself. The cemetery also contains tombs of European

Jami Masjid, built by Shah Jahan's favourite daughter, Jahanara

John Hessing's tomb in the Roman Catholic Cemetery

missionaries, traders and adventurers such as the 18th-century French freebooter, Walter Reinhardt. The largest tomb is that of John Hessing, a British commander in the army of the Scindias, the rulers of Gwalior *(see p228)*. Hessing's red sandstone tomb, built after his death in 1803, is modelled on the lines of the Taj Mahal. One of the oldest tombs belongs to the English merchant, John Mildenhall (1614), envoy of Elizabeth I, who arrived at the Mughal court in 1603 seeking permission to trade. Other interesting graves include those of the Venetian doctor, Bernardino Maffi, and

Geronimo Veroneo (once wrongly regarded by some as the architect of the Taj). Near the chapel, an obelisk marks the grave of the four children of General Perron, French commander of the Scindia forces. Another Frenchman, Jean Philippe Bourbon, a kinsman of Henry IV of France, is also buried here.

🚉 Fort Railway Station
Tel (0562) 236 4131.
This memorable Raj building was constructed in 1891 as a stopping-off point for colonial tourists visiting Agra's monuments. The octagonal bazaar *chowk* that originally connected the Delhi Gate and Agra

Fort to the old city and the Jami Masjid was demolished and this station, with its French château-style slate-roofed platforms, was built in its place. It is still in use today. Agra's two other railway stations are located in the cantonment and at Raja ki Mandi.

Auto-rickshaws parked outside the Fort Railway Station

AGRA CITY CENTRE

Agra Fort ①
Fort Railway Station ⑤
Jami Masjid ②
Roman Catholic Cemetery ④
St John's College ③

The colonnaded arches of the Diwan-i-Aam, the hall used for the emperor's public audiences

🏛 Agra Fort

🕐 daily. 🎫 free on Fri.
Son et Lumière 7:30pm daily. 📷

Situated on the west bank of the Yamuna, Agra Fort was built by Emperor Akbar between 1565 and 1573. Its imposing red sandstone ramparts form a crescent along the river front, and encompass an enormous complex of courtly buildings, ranging in style from the early eclecticism of Akbar to the sublime elegance of Shah Jahan. The barracks to the north are 19th-century British additions. A deep moat, once filled with water from the Yamuna, surrounds the fort.

The impressive **Amar Singh Gate**, to the south, leads into the fort. To its right is the so-called **Jahangiri Mahal**, the only major palace in the fort that dates back to Akbar's reign. This complex arrangement of halls, courtyards and galleries, with dungeons underneath, was the zenana or main harem. In front of the Jahangiri Mahal is a large marble pool which, according to legend, used to be filled in Nur Jahan's time with thousands of rose petals so that the empress could bathe in its scented waters.

Along the river front are the **Khas Mahal**, an elegant marble hall with a vividly painted ceiling, characteristic of Shah Jahan's style of architecture, and two golden pavilions with *bangaldar* roofs (curved roofs derived from Bengali

PLAN OF AGRA FORT

1 Amar Singh Gate
2 Jahangiri Mahal
3 Khas Mahal and Anguri Bagh
4 Sheesh Mahal
5 Musamman Burj
6 Mina Masjid
7 Diwan-i-Khas
8 Machchhi Bhavan
9 Courtyard of the Diwan-i-Aam
10 Nagina Masjid
11 Moti Masjid

A riverside view of the Jahangiri Mahal, the emperor's main harem

St George's Church in Agra Cantonment, built in 1826

huts). These pavilions were once associated with the princesses Jahanara and Roshanara, and have narrow niches which could have been used to conceal jewels. Facing them is **Anguri Bagh** ("Grape Garden") with its lily-pools and candle-niches. The **Sheesh Mahal** and royal baths are to the northeast, near the gloriously inlaid **Musamman Burj**, a double-storeyed octagonal tower with clear views of the Taj. This was where Shah Jahan, imprisoned by his son Aurangzeb, spent the last years of his life. **Mina Masjid** ("Gem Mosque"), probably the smallest in the world and the emperor's private mosque, is nearby. Next to Musamman Burj is the **Diwan-i-Khas**, a lavishly decorated open hall with fine *pietra dura* work on its columns, where the emperor would meet his court. Two thrones, in white marble and black slate, were placed on the terrace so that the emperor could watch the elephant fights below. Opposite is the **Machchhi Bhavan** ("Fish House"), once a magnificent water palace. To its west is the **Diwan-i-Aam**, an arcaded hall within a courtyard. Its throne-alcove of inlaid marble provided a sumptuous setting for the fabled Peacock Throne. To the northwest is the **Nagina Masjid** ("Jewel Mosque") built by Shah Jahan for his harem, and the **Moti Masjid** ("Pearl Mosque").

Musamman Burj

🏵 **Cantonment**

Enclosed by Mahatma Gandhi Rd, Grand Parade Rd & Mall Rd.
The pleasant, tree-shaded army cantonment area, with its own railway station and orderly avenues has many interesting public buildings, churches, cemeteries and bungalows in a medley of styles dating from colonial times. **St George's Church** (1826), a plastered, ochre-coloured building was designed by Colonel JT Boileau, architect of Shimla's Christ Church (*see p110*). **Havelock Memorial Church**, constructed in 1873 in a "trim Classical style", commemorates one of the British generals of the Indian Mutiny of 1857. Other buildings in this area include **Queen Mary's Library**, the **Central Post Office** and the **Circuit House**, which used to accommodate Raj officials.

🞏 **Firoz Khan Khwajasara's Tomb**

S of Agra, on Gwalior Rd. ◯ *daily.*
A signpost on the Gwalior Road indicates the turning to this unusual 17th-century octagonal structure, standing on the edge of a lake. This marks the spot where Firoz Khan Khwajasara, a natural-born eunuch and the custodian of Shah Jahan's palace harem, is buried.
The red sandstone edifice stands on a high plinth and has a gateway attached to the main building. Steps lead to the upper storey where a central pavilion containing the grave is located. Highly stylized stone carvings embellish the surface. Interestingly, unlike other buildings of the period, there is an absence of calligraphic inscriptions. If the tomb is closed, the watchman from the village will open the gate.

A view of the 17th-century tomb of Firoz Khan Khwajasara

GOLD THREAD AND BEAD ZARDOZI

Agra's flourishing traditional craft of elaborate gold thread (*zari*) and bead embroidery is known as *zardozi*. This technique was Central Asian in origin and came to the region with the Mughal emperors. Local craftsmen in the old city developed further refinements and complex new patterns to create garments and accessories for the imperial court. However, with the decline of court patronage, the skill

Detail of an embroidered textile

languished and almost vanished. It owes its recent revival to encouragement from contemporary fashion designers.

Agra: Taj Mahal

Carved dado on outer niches

One of the world's most famous buildings, the Taj Mahal was built by the Mughal emperor Shah Jahan in memory of his favourite wife, Mumtaz Mahal, who died in 1631. Its perfect proportions and exquisite craftsmanship have been described as "a vision, a dream, a poem, a wonder". This sublime garden-tomb, an image of the Islamic garden of paradise, cost nearly 41 million rupees and 500 kilos (1,102 lbs) of gold. About 20,000 workers laboured for 12 years to complete it in 1643.

The Dome
The 44-m (144-ft) double dome is capped with a finial.

★ Marble Screen
The filigree screen, daintily carved from a single block of marble, was meant to veil the area around the royal tombs.

Four minarets, each 40 m (131 ft) high and crowned by an open octagonal pavilion or *chhatri*, frame the tomb, highlighting the perfect symmetry of the complex.

Plinth

★ Tomb Chamber
Mumtaz Mahal's cenotaph, raised on a platform, is placed next to Shah Jahan's. The actual graves, in a dark crypt below, are closed to the public.

Yamuna river

STAR FEATURES

★ Marble Screen

★ Tomb Chamber

★ Pietra Dura

The *charbagh*
was irrigated with
water from the
Yamuna river.

**Main
entrance**

The Lotus Pool
*Named after its lotus-shaped fountain spouts, the
pool reflects the tomb. Almost every visitor is
photographed sitting on the marble bench here.*

Pishtaq
*Recessed arches
provide depth while
their inlaid panels
reflect the changing
light to give the tomb
a mystical aura.*

★ Pietra Dura
*Inspired by the paradise garden,
intricately carved floral designs
inlaid with precious stones embellish
the austere white marble surface to
give it the look of a bejewelled casket.*

Calligraphic Panels
*The size of the Koranic verses
increases as the arch gets higher,
creating the subtle optical illusion
of a uniformly flowing script.*

TAJ MAHAL

1 Main Tomb
2 *Masjid* (mosque)
3 *Mehmankhana*
  (guesthouse)
4 *Charbagh* (quadrifid
  garden)
5 Gateway

KEY

☐ Area illustrated
☐ Charbagh

Decorative Elements of the Taj

Stylized floral motif

It is widely believed that the Taj Mahal was designed to represent an earthly replica of one of the houses of paradise. Its impeccable marble facing, embellished by a remarkable use of exquisite surface design, is a showcase for the refined aesthetic that reached its height during Shah Jahan's reign. Described as "one of the most elegant and harmonious buildings in the world", the Taj indeed manifests the wealth and luxury of Mughal art as seen in architecture and garden design, painting, jewellery, calligraphy, textiles, carpet-weaving and furniture.

Detail of the marble screen with an inlaid chrysanthemum

PIETRA DURA

The Mughals were great naturalists and believed that flowers were the "symbols of the divine realm". In the Taj, *pietra dura* has been extensively used to translate naturalistic forms into decorative patterns that complement the majesty of its architecture.

Flowers *such as the tulip, lily, iris, poppy and narcissus were depicted as sprays or in arabesque patterns. Stones of varying degrees of colour were used to create the shaded effects.*

Marble inlay above the mosque's central arch

White marble, black slate and yellow, red and grey sandstone used for decoration

THE ART OF PIETRA DURA

The Florentine technique of *pietra dura* is said to have been imported by Emperor Jahangir and developed in Agra as *pachikari*. Minute slivers of precious and semi-precious stones, such as carnelian, lapis lazuli, turquoise and malachite, were arranged in complex stylized floral designs set into a marble base. Even today, artisans in the old city maintain pattern books with the fine motifs used on the Taj to recreate 17th-century designs in contemporary pieces.

A contemporary marble inlaid platter

A single flower, often with more than 35 variations of carnelian

CARVED RELIEF WORK

Decorative panels of flowering plants, foliage and vases are realistically carved on the lower portions of the walls. While the *pietra dura* adds colour to the pristine white marble, these highlight the texture of the polished marble and sandstone surface.

Floral sprays, *carved in relief on the marble and sandstone dado levels, are framed with* pietra dura *and stone inlay borders. The profusion of floral motifs in the Taj symbolizes the central paradise theme.*

Jali patterns *on the octagonal perforated screen surrounding the tombs are a complex combination of the geometric and floral. The filtered light captures the intricate designs and casts mosaic-like shadows on the tombs.*

CALLIGRAPHY

Inlaid calligraphy in black marble was used as a form of ornamentation on undecorated surfaces. The exquisitely detailed panels of inscribed Koranic passages, that line the recessed arches like banners, were designed by the Persian calligrapher, Amanat Khan.

Exploring Agra: the East Bank

The picturesque east bank of the Yamuna is dotted with historic gardens, palaces, pavilions and the exquisite tomb of **Itimad-ud-Daulah**. North of Itimad-ud-Daulah is **Chini ka Rauza**, (literally "China Tomb", after its tiled exterior) built by Afzal Khan, a poet-scholar from Shiraz (Persia) who was Shah Jahan's finance minister. This large square structure is Persian in style, and at one time its surface was covered with glazed tiles from Lahore and Multan, interspersed with graceful calligraphic panels. The burial chamber within has painted stucco plaster designs that must have complemented the tiled exterior.

Lying further upriver is the quiet, tree-shaded **Rambagh** or Aram Bagh ("Garden of Rest"). This is believed to be the earliest Mughal garden, laid out by Babur, the first Mughal emperor, in 1526. The garden also served as his temporary burial place before his body was taken to Kabul to be interred. The spacious walled garden, divided by walkways that lead to a raised terrace with open pavilions overlooking the river, was further developed by the empress Nur Jahan.

♠ Chini ka Rauza
1 km (0.6 miles) N of Itimad-ud-Daulah's Tomb. ⬜ *daily.* 📷

♣ Rambagh
3 km (2 miles) N of Itimad-ud-Daulah's Tomb. ⬜ *daily.* 📷 *free on Fri.*

Riverside pavilion at Rambagh

Agra: Itimad-ud-Daulah's Tomb

A stylized floral motif

Lyrically described as a "jewel box in marble", the small yet elegant garden-tomb of Itimad-ud-Daulah, the "Lord Treasurer" of the Mughal empire, was built by his daughter Nur Jahan, Jahangir's favourite wife. Begun in 1622, it took six years to complete. The tomb is a combination of white marble, coloured mosaic, stone inlay and lattice work. Stylistically, this is the most innovative 17th-century Mughal building and marks the transition from the robust, red sandstone architecture of Akbar to the sensuous refinement of Shah Jahan's Taj Mahal.

Tapering pinnacles with lotus mouldings crown the minarets.

Upper Pavilion
The replica tombs of Itimad-ud-Daulah and his wife are placed in the marble-screened upper pavilion.

Mosaic Patterns
Panels of geometric designs, created by inlaid coloured stones, decorate the dado level of the tomb.

★ Marble Screens
Perforated marble screens with complex ornamental patterns are carved out of a single slab of marble.

STAR FEATURES

★ Marble Screens

★ Tomb Chamber

★ Pietra Dura

The dome, with its canopy-like shape, is different from the conventional domes of this period.

The Tomb
The square two-storeyed tomb stands in the centre of a charbagh. At the four corners of the low platform are four squat attached minarets.

Marble latticed balustrade

★ **Tomb Chamber**
The ceiling has incised, painted and gilded stucco and stalactite patterns. The yellow marble caskets appear as if carved out of wood.

Chhatri
Open-pillared domed pavilions top the minarets.

★ **Pietra Dura**
The polished marble surface is covered with stone inlay, the first time this technique was extensively used in Mughal architecture.

Entrance

Painted Floral Patterns
Niches with painted floral bouquets, trees, fruit and wine decanters embellish the interior of the central chamber of the main tomb.

VISITORS' CHECKLIST

E bank of Yamuna. 4 km (2 miles) upstream from the Taj Mahal. ☐ *sunrise–sunset daily.* 🖼

The entrance to Akbar's mausoleum at Sikandra

Sikandra ❷

Agra district. 8 km (5 miles) NW of Agra. 🚌 **Akbar's Mausoleum**
Tel *(0562) 264 1230 (contact for permission to go to the tomb terrace).*
⬜ *daily.* 📷 *free on Fri.* 🎫 📷 📷
Urs at Akbar's Tomb (mid-Oct).

The Mughal Emperor Akbar is buried in this small village on the outskirts of Agra. It is believed that Akbar designed and started the construction of his own mausoleum, which was modified and completed by his son Jahangir. The result is this impressive, perfectly symmetrical complex, with the tomb located in the centre of a vast walled garden. The main gateway, to the south, is a magnificent red sandstone structure with a colossal central arch, finished with an exuberant polychrome mosaic of inlaid white marble, black slate and coloured stone. On each corner are four graceful marble minarets, considered to be the forerunners of those

that can be seen at the Taj Mahal in Agra *(see pp172–3).*

The large garden, where monkeys frolic, is a typical *charbagh,* an enclosed garden divided into four quarters (representing the four quarters of life) by a system of raised walkways, sunken groves and water channels.

The main tomb is a distinct departure from the conventional domed structure of the tomb of Akbar's father, Humayun, at Delhi *(see p83).* The first three storeys of this majestic, four-tiered composition, consist of red sandstone pavilions. Above them is an exquisite marble-screened terrace enclosing the replica tomb, which is profusely carved with floral and arabesque designs, Chinese cloud patterns and the 99 names of Allah.

The upper levels, previously accessible through special permission, are now closed due to security reasons.

Mathura ❸

Mathura district. 62 km (39 miles) NW of Agra. 🚶 *299,000.* 🚉 🚌
ℹ️ *Old Bus Stand, (0565) 240 6468.*
🎭 *Holi (Mar), Hariyali Teej (Jul), Janmashtami (Jul/Aug), Kansa Vadha (Sep), Annakut (Sep/Oct).*

Mathura, on the west bank of Yamuna river, is revered as the birthplace of one of India's most popular gods, Lord Krishna. A dark, cell-like room in the rather modern **Sri Krishna Janmabhoomi Temple**, on the periphery of the city, is reputed to be the actual site of his birth. Further away,

A religious image, Mathura

along the river front, Mathura's 25 ghats form a splendid network of temples, pavilions, trees and stone steps leading down to the water. The **Jami Masjid**, with its striking tilework, lies behind the river front. A charming oddity is the Roman Catholic **Church of the Sacred Heart**, built in 1860, in the army cantonment. It combines Western elements with details taken from local temple architecture.

The **Government Museum** has a superb collection of sculpture in the distinctive local white-flecked red sandstone. These date from about the 5th century BC until the 4th century AD, when Mathura was part of the Kushana empire *(see p43)* and

Vishram Ghat at Mathura, where every evening at sunset oil lamps are floated on the river

flourished as a major centre of Buddhism. Outstanding pieces include a Standing Buddha, and the famous headless statue of the great Kushana king, Kanishka.

🏛 **Government Museum**
Dampier Nagar. **Tel** (0565) 250 0847.
⭕ Tue–Sun. ⬤ public hols. 📷
📷 extra charges.

Brindavan ❹

Mathura district. 68 km (42 miles) N of Agra. 🚌 🚗 daily. 📷 Holi (Mar), Rath ka Mela (Mar), Hariyali Teej (Jul), Janmashtami (Jul/Aug).

Situated along the Yamuna, Brindavan ("Forest of Fragrant Basil") is an important pilgrim centre for devout Hindus who believe that the young Krishna once lived here as a humble cowherd and romanced the beautiful milkmaid Radha. Their love is widely celebrated in dance, art and literature. Brindavan's numerous temples, ashrams and ghats were mainly built by Hindu kings and rich merchants. Many Hindu widows, clad in white with their heads shaven, live in ashrams here, devoting their lives to the worship of Krishna. At the edge of the town is the historic **Govindeoji Temple** (*see p352*), built in 1590 by Raja Man Singh I of Amber. Across is the 19th-century **Sri**

Gopura of the South Indian-style Ranganathji Temple

Ranganathji Temple with a gold-plated ritual pillar and an interesting museum of temple treasures.

Amidst the narrow streets of the old town are the sacred walled groves of **Seva Kunj**, associated with the traditional Raslila dance which narrates the life of Krishna. Other notable temples in Brindavan include the red sandstone **Madan Mohan Temple**, built in 1580, which stands on a hill next to the river, the popular **Banke Bihari Temple**, near the main bazaar, and the 16th-century **Jugal Kishore Temple**. The **ISKCON Temple**, on the outskirts of the town, is a more recent addition to Brindavan.

FESTIVALS OF UTTAR PRADESH & UTTARANCHAL

International Yoga Week (*Feb*), Rishikesh. Yoga is taught on the banks of the Ganges during this rejuvenating week-long festival.

Taj Mahotsava (*Feb*), Agra. This ten-day cultural fiesta of music and dance is held in the vicinity of the Taj Mahal.

Jhansi Festival (*Feb*), Jhansi. A five-day arts and crafts extravaganza unfolds against the backdrop of Jhansi's historic fort.

Rang Gulal (*Feb/Mar*). The festival of colours, also known as Holi, is played with great abandon all over Uttar Pradesh.

Rang Gulal celebrations

Janmashtami (*Aug/Sep*), Brindavan and Mathura. To mark the birth of Krishna, pilgrims perform a circum-ambulation (*parikrama*) of sacred sites. Festivities reach a peak at midnight.

Ganga Festival (*Oct/Nov*), Varanasi. The ancient glory of the Ganges is celebrated by devotees, who pay homage to the sacred river.

Lucknow Mahotsava (*Nov/Dec*), Lucknow. Lucknow's historic past and continuing traditions are celebrated with food, crafts, music and dance.

Buddha Mahotsava (*Dec*), Sarnath and Kushinagar. Religious festivities mark the Buddha's birth, attainment of enlightenment and death. These are held at Sarnath, where he preached his first sermon, and at Kushinagar, where he attained nirvana.

THE GRAND TRUNK ROAD

A roadside *dhaba*

The Grand Trunk Road, Rudyard Kipling's "stately corridor" that linked Calcutta (now Kolkata) in the east with Kabul in the northwest, was laid out by Sher Shah Sur (*see p79*) in the 16th century. In those days, it resounded with the movement of armies on campaign, and in times of peace, with the pomp and pageantry that accompanied the Mughal emperors as their court moved from Agra to Delhi. This remains one of Asia's great roads and North India's premier highway. Some ancient shade-giving trees still stand, but the old caravanserais are now in ruins. Instead, at frequent intervals along the highway, there are *dhabas* where long-distance travellers, especially lorry-drivers, can stop for a cheap and filling meal of *dal* and *roti*, washed down with hot tea or cooling *lassi*. They can also snatch a quick nap on string cots (*charpoys*) thoughtfully provided by *dhaba* owners.

Fatehpur Sikri **❺**

Fretwork *jali*

Built by Emperor Akbar between 1571 and 1585 in honour of Salim Chishti, a famous Sufi saint of the Chishti order *(see p376)*, Fatehpur Sikri was the Mughal capital for 14 years. A fine example of a Mughal walled city with defined private and public areas and imposing gateways, its architecture, a blend of Hindu and Islamic styles, reflects Akbar's secular vision as well as his style of governance. After the city was abandoned, some say for lack of water, many of its treasures were plundered. It owes its present state of preservation to the initial efforts of the viceroy, Lord Curzon, a legendary conservationist.

Pillar in the Diwan-i-Khas
The central axis of Akbar's court, supported by carved brackets, was inspired by Gujarati buildings.

Haram Sa
complex

Jami Masjid

Khwabgah
The emperor's private sleeping quarters, with an ingenious ventilating shaft near his bed, lie within this lavishly decorated "Chamber of Dreams".

Anoop Talao is a pool associated with Akbar's renowned court musician Tansen *(see p228)* who, as legend says, could light oil lamps with his magical singing.

Abdar
Khana

Entrance

★ Turkish Sultana's House
The fine dado panels and delicately sculpted walls of this ornate sandstone pavilion make the stone seem like wood. It is topped with an unusual stone roof of imitation clay tiles.

Diwan-i-Aam
This large courtyard with an elaborate pavilion was originally draped with rich tapestries and was used for public hearings and celebrations.

★ Panch Mahal

This five-storeyed open sandstone pavilion, overlooking the Pachisi Court, is where Akbar's queens and their attendants savoured the cool evening breezes. Its decorative screens were probably stolen after the city was abandoned.

VISITORS' CHECKLIST

Agra district. 37 km (23 miles) W of Agra. 🛈 UPTDC, 64 Taj Rd, Agra, (0562) 236 0517. ☐ daily. 📹 🎫 📷 extra charges for video photography.

★ Diwan-i-Khas

This hall for private audience and debate is a unique fusion of different architectural styles and religious motifs.

Jodha Bai's Palace   Sunehra Makan   Birbal's House

Ankh Michauli

Sometimes identified as the treasury, this building has mythical guardian beasts carved on its stone struts. Its name means "blind man's buff".

Pachisi Court is named after a ludo-like game played here by the ladies of the court.

STAR SIGHTS

★ Turkish Sultana's House

★ Panch Mahal

★ Diwan-i-Khas

PLAN OF FATEHPUR SIKRI

Fatehpur Sikri's royal complex contains the private and public spaces of Akbar's court, which included the harem and the treasury. The adjoining sacred complex with the Jami Masjid, Salim Chishti's Tomb and the Buland Darwaza *(see p183)*, are separated from the royal quarters by the Badshahi Darwaza, an exclusive royal gateway.

KEY

☐	Area illustrated
☐	Other buildings
☐	Sacred complex (Jami Masjid)

Exploring Fatehpur Sikri

Detail of a carved panel

The principal buildings of the imperial palace complex, clustered on a series of terraces along the sandstone ridge, formed the core of Akbar's city. Stylistically, they marked the absorption of Gujarat into the Mughal Empire and reveal a successful synthesis of pre-Islamic, Hindu and Jain architecture (as in the carved brackets) with the elegant domes and arches of Islamic buildings. The concentric terraces clearly separate the public spaces from the private royal quarters. The buildings are mostly in Akbar's favourite red sandstone, which was quarried from the ridge on which they stand.

Stone "tusks" on the Hiran Minar

Aerial view of Fatehpur Sikri, Emperor Akbar's grand capital

Even today, access to the city that was Akbar's capital is provided by a straight road built by the emperor, once lined with exotic bazaars. It leads visitors through the Agra Gate to the triple-arched **Naubat Khana**, where the emperor's entry used to be announced by a roll of drums. Leading off from the Naubat Khana, is the western entrance to the imperial palace complex which opens into the spacious cloistered courtyard of the **Diwan-i-Aam**, where Akbar gave public audiences. A passage behind it leads into the "inner citadel". This contains the **Diwan-i-Khas**, **Khwabgah** and **Anoop Talao**, along with the treasuries and the **Abdar Khana** where water and fruit for the royal household were stored. It also contains the curiously named **Turkish Sultana's House**. Though probably built for one of Akbar's wives, the identity of the "Turkish

Sultana" remains unclear. The great courtyard in front of the Diwan-i-Khas has the **Pachisi Court**, named after the central space that resembles the board of *pachisi*, a traditional game.

The **Haram Sara**, or harem complex, was a maze of interconnected buildings beyond Maryam's House or **Sunehra Makan** ("Golden House"), named after its rich frescoes and gilding. The massive and austere exterior of the harem leads to **Jodha Bai's Palace**, a large inner courtyard, surrounded by pavilions decorated with azure glazed tiles on the roof. A screened viaduct, presumably for privacy, connected the palace to the **Hawa Mahal** facing a small formal garden. The **Nagina Masjid**, adjoining the garden, was the royal ladies' private mosque. The two-storeyed pavilion popularly said to be

Birbal's House, to the east of Jodha Bai's palace, has an unusual layout and fine carvings on its exterior and interior. Beyond this lie a large colonnaded enclosure surrounded by cells, probably meant for the servants of the harem, and the royal stables.

The **Hathi Pol** and **Sangin Burj**, the original gateways to the harem, lead to the outermost periphery of the palace complex. This was laid out in concentric circles around the inner citadel and is made up of ancillary structures, such as the caravanserais, the domed *hamams* (baths) and waterworks. The **Hiran Minar**, believed to be a memorial to Akbar's favourite elephant, was probably an *akash deep* ("heavenly light") with lamps suspended from stone "tusks" to guide visitors.

Entrance to Birbal's House

Jami Masjid

An inlaid panel

This grand open mosque towers over the city of Fatehpur Sikri and was the model for several Mughal mosques. Flanked by arched cloisters, its vast congregational area has monumental gateways to the east and south. The spiritual focus of the complex is the tomb and hermitage of the Sufi mystic, Salim Chishti, as popular today as it was during the time of Akbar.

Tomb of Sheikh Salim Chishti
Exquisite marble serpentine brackets and almost transparent screens surround the inner tomb which has a sandalwood canopy inlaid with mother-of-pearl.

Hujra
Symmetrically flanking the main mosque, this pair of identical cloistered prayer rooms have flat-roofed pillared galleries that run round the complex.

Badshahi Darwaza
Akbar used the steep steps of this royal gateway to enter the complex. The view of the sacred mosque directly across, greeted his entry.

Corridors

Buland Darwaza
Erected by Akbar to mark his conquest over Gujarat in 1573, this huge 54-m (177-ft) gateway later inspired other lofty gateways.

MAKING A WISH IN SALIM CHISHTI'S TOMB

Ever since Akbar's childlessness was ended by the remarkable prediction of Salim Chishti in 1568, the saint's tomb has attracted crowds of supplicants, particularly childless women in search of a miracle. Visitors to the *dargah*, lavishly endowed by both Akbar and his son Jahangir, make a wish, tie a small cotton thread on the screen around the tomb, and go back confident that the saint will make it come true.

A thread tied to a screen in Chishti's tomb

Pilgrims taking a dip in the holy Ganges at Haridwar

A good way to experience Haridwar's ambience, which has changed little since ancient times, is to stroll along the riverside bazaar, lined with small eateries and stalls full of ritual paraphernalia – small mounds of vermilion powder, coconuts wrapped in red and gold cloth, and brass idols. The most popular items with the pilgrims are the jars and canisters sold here. These are used to carry back a vital ingredient of Hindu rituals: water from the Ganges (Gangajal) which, the faithful believe, remains ever fresh.

Haridwar ⑥

Haridwar district. 214 km (133 miles) N of Delhi. 🚉 🚌 🛈 *GMVN Tourist Office, Rahi Motel (01334) 228 686.* 🎎 *Kumbh Mela (every 12 years; Feb–Mar), Ardh Kumbha Mela (every 6 years; Feb–Mar), Haridwar Festival (Oct), Dussehra (Sep/Oct).*

The Ganges, India's holiest river *(see pp162–3)*, descends from the Himalayas and begins its journey through the plains at Haridwar. This gives the town a unique status, making a pilgrimage to Haridwar every devout Hindu's dream.

Surprisingly bare of ancient monuments, Haridwar's most famous "sight", as well as a constant point of reference, is the Ganges itself with its numerous bathing ghats, tanks and temples. These bustling sites of ritual Hindu

Sign of Chotiwala, a popular restaurant

practices, performed by pilgrims for the salvation of their ancestors and for their own expiation, demonstrate their deep faith in the power of the river. The main ghat, **Har-ki-Pauri**, is named after a supposed imprint of Vishnu's feet at the site. Hundreds attend the daily evening *aarti* at this ghat, when leaf boats are filled with flowers, lit with lamps and set adrift on the Ganges. Further south, a ropeway connects the town to the **Mansa Devi Temple** on a hill across the river, which offers panoramic views of Haridwar. Also situated south of the town is the **Gurukul Kangri University**, a renowned centre of Vedic knowledge, where students are taught by their gurus in the traditional oral style. A section here displays archaeological finds.

Rishikesh ⑦

Haridwar district. 238 km (148 miles) N of Delhi. 🚌 🛈 *GMVN Tourist Office Muni-ki-Reti, (0135) 243 1793.* 🎎 *International Yoga Week (Feb).*

This twin city of Haridwar, situated at the confluence of the Chandrabhaga and the Ganges, marks the starting point of the holy Char Dham pilgrim route *(see p187)*. Muni-ki-Reti (literally "Sand of the Sages"), lies upstream from the Triveni Ghat, and is said to be a blessed site since ancient sages meditated at this spot. It has several famous ashrams, including the Sivanand, Purnanand and Shanti Kunj ashrams, which offer courses in India's ancient knowledge systems *(see p754)*. North of Muni-ki Reti are two suspension bridges across the Ganges, Rama or Sivananda Jhula and Lakshman Jhula.

YOGA: THE ANCIENT PATH TO HOLISTIC HEALTH

Over 2,000 years ago, the sage Patanjali formulated a series of physical postures called *asanas* which, along with controlled breathing and meditation *(pranayama)*, were meant to set the individual on the path to self-realization. Ever since, yoga has been practised by ascetics and non-ascetics alike. Essentially, yoga calms and focuses the mind by stimulating blood circulation while relaxing nerves and muscles. This helps to combat the stress of daily life and is particularly suited to modern lifestyles as it does not require equipment or visits to the gym. Yoga entered the wider popular consciousness in the late 1960s when the Beatles paid a visit to the Maharishi Mahesh Yogi's ashram in Rishikesh, and today many schools of yoga have centres in India as well as in Europe and North America. Rishikesh, with its plethora of yoga ashrams, is touted as the yoga capital of the world. An International Yoga Week *(see p179)* is also held here in February.

A woman performing an *asana*

River Tour along the Ganges 8

From September to April, the Ganges, swollen by the monsoon rains of the upper catchment areas, becomes a torrent, gushing over rocky boulders as it hurtles out of the mountains to the plains. During this period a few stretches of rapids, where the flow is rough but safe, become a popular circuit for enthusiasts of white-water rafting. Only organized tours, run by certified experts, are allowed. For the less adventurous, a scenic driving tour meanders through this valley of the sages, whose ashrams nestle in the surrounding forests along the holy river.

The Ganges flowing serenely through a forested valley

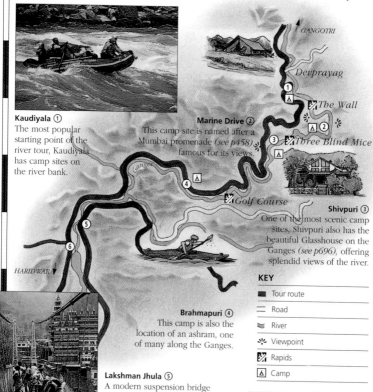

Kaudiyala ①
The most popular starting point of the river tour, Kaudiyala has camp sites on the river bank.

Marine Drive ②
This camp site is named after a Mumbai promenade (see p458), famous for its views.

The Wall

Three Blind Mice

Golf Course

Shivpuri ③
One of the most scenic camp sites, Shivpuri also has the beautiful Glasshouse on the Ganges (see p696), offering splendid views of the river.

GANGOTRI

Devprayag

HARIDWAR

KEY

▰	Tour route
═	Road
⬎	River
☼	Viewpoint
💥	Rapids
Ⓐ	Camp

Brahmapuri ④
This camp is also the location of an ashram, one of many along the Ganges.

Lakshman Jhula ⑤
A modern suspension bridge (jhula) across the Ganges, replaced the old rope bridge in 1929. This lies at the northern end of Rishikesh, and offers fine views of the river.

TIPS FOR RAFTERS

Length: 36 km (22 miles).
Getting around: Rafting can be done over two or three days, with night halts at camps situated at Kaudiyala, Marine Drive, Shivpuri and Brahmapuri. A shorter tour of the same stretch can also be done in one day. For organized tours, tour operators and equipment hire (see p755).

Rishikesh ⑥
An ancient spiritual centre, Rishikesh is serenely located on the banks of the Ganges amid lush, wooded hills.

0 km		10
0 miles		5

The façade of the Forest Research Institute, Dehra Dun, established in 1914

Dehra Dun ❾

Dehra Dun district. 256 km (159 miles) NE of Delhi. 🏠 447,800. ✈ Jolly Grant, 24 km (15 miles) SE of town centre. 🚉 🚌 ℹ GMVN, 74/1, Rajpur Road, (0135) 274 7898.

Fringed by the Shivalik Hills, Dehra Dun lies in the pretty Doon Valley, flanked by the Ganges to the west and the Yamuna to the east. The provisional capital of the newly-formed state of Uttaranchal, the town is also the gateway to the Garhwal Hills. A number of prestigious institutions have their headquarters here, such as the Survey of India and the Forest Research Institute. India's very own Eton, the Doon School, as well as the country's foremost training academy for army officers, the Indian Military Academy, are also situated here. Rajpur Road, the main link to the hills, is lined with bakeries and restaurants and has the old Clock Tower, the town's principal landmark, at one end. Dehra Dun's bracing climate and its proximity to Mussoorie, make it a popular retirement retreat. The Doon Valley is also famous for its fragrant basmati rice, and its mango and litchi orchards.

Environs
The **Rajaji National Park**, 5 km (3 miles) southeast of Dehra Dun, is a picturesque wildlife sanctuary covering over 800 sq km (309 sq miles). It is best known for its birdlife and herds of elephants.

Little blue kingfisher

Mussoorie ❿

Uttarkashi district. 35 km (22 miles) N of Dehra Dun. 🏠 26,000. 🚌 ℹ Uttaranchal Tourist Bureau, The Mall, (0135) 263 2663.

One of the Raj's most popular summer retreats, Mussoorie is perched on a horseshoe-shaped ridge above the Doon Valley at a height of 1,920 m (6,299 ft), and is inundated with Indian visitors in summer. Life in Mussoorie centres around The Mall, the main thoroughfare, which is lined with shops and eating places. The old library lies at the town's western end. About 7 km (4 miles) further west, is a house known as **Everest House**. This was the home of Sir George Everest, the legendary Surveyor-General who mapped Mount Everest,

and one of Mussoorie's earliest residents. The town's small Tibetan community is settled in **Happy Valley**, close to Convent Hill. The **Tibetan Market**, below The Mall, sells a range of woollens. A rope-way from The Mall leads up to **Gun Hill**, which, on a clear day, has fine views of many Greater Himalayan peaks, including Nanda Devi, Kedarnath and Badrinath (*see pp64–5*). **Camel's Back Road** named after a distinctively shaped rock, offers a pleasant walk along the upper ridge, and **Kempty Falls**, lying 12 km (8 miles) northwest of town, is a popular picnic spot.

Landour, a short distance east of Kulri bazaar, was originally a barracks and convalescence area for British soldiers. With its colonial bungalows and relative quiet, it has managed to preserve some of Mussoorie's old character and is the town's prettiest quarter.

THE PUNDITS

Up to the mid 19th-century, Tibet and Central Asia were vast blanks on the map of the world, yet strategically important to the British in their rivalry with Imperial Russia. As foreigners were forbidden from entering these lands, between 1865 and 1885, the Survey of India trained and sent an intrepid group of Indians to survey the region. Known as the Pundits, these men went disguised as Buddhist pilgrims and traders, with compasses and survey notes concealed in their prayer wheels, and mercury thermometers hidden in their hollowed-out pilgrims staffs. The beads of a rosary helped them measure the distance they covered every day. The most remarkable of the Pundits was Nain Singh, who brought back invaluable and accurate topographical information on large tracts of Tibet.

A portrait of Nain Singh (1830–95)

The Garhwal Hills ⑪

Uttarkashi and Chamoli districts. 148 km (92 miles) N from Rishikesh to Uttarkashi. 🚌 ℹ️ *Uttaranchal Tourist Bureau, Uttarkashi, (01374) 274 761.*

The northern stretches of Garhwal (Uttaranchal's western hills) are strewn with pilgrim towns, ancient shrines and forbidding snowbound peaks. **Uttarkashi**, the main town, lies 148 km (92 miles) north of Rishikesh *(see p184),* and is an important starting point for treks to the upper reaches of Garhwal. A leading school for aspiring climbers, the **Nehru Institute of Mountaineering**, is situated in this town, and boasts of having trained Bachendri Pal, the first Indian woman to scale Mount Everest in 1984.

This region also encompasses an area traditionally known as Dev Bhoomi ("Abode of the Gods"). The Char Dham or four major places of pilgrimage, **Gangotri, Yamunotri, Kedarnath** and **Badrinath**, are all situated here at altitudes over 3,100 m (10,171 ft), in the shadow of some awe-inspiring Himalayan peaks. The pilgrimage season lasts from April to early November, after which the snows drive away all but the most devout. All four sites can be reached

Badrinath, Garhwal's foremost *dham* and source of the Alaknanda river

from Uttarkashi, Haridwar and Rishikesh.

Yamunotri, 209 km (130 miles) north of Rishikesh, is the source of the Yamuna, and a 13-km (8-mile) walk from Hanuman Chatti. Its temple was rebuilt in the 20th century after the earlier one was destroyed by floods. The small village of Gangotri, named after the Ganges which flows through it, lies 100 km (62 miles) northeast of Uttarkashi. Its 18th-century temple has images of Hindu deities.

Gaumukh, the source of River Ganges, lies 18 km (11 miles) upstream, below the soaring Bhagirathi peaks, and can be reached via a path that follows the lovely river valley. At this point, the river is known as the Bhagirathi, and only becomes the Ganges proper after it joins the Alaknanda river at **Devprayag** *(see p162).*

The impressive Kedarnath peaks form the backdrop for the pilgrim town of Kedarnath, sacred to Shiva, and 223 km (139 miles) northeast of Rishikesh. A beautifully carved stone temple, said to be 800 years old, lies 4 km (9 miles) north of the road head at Gaurikund.

A mendicant in saffron robes

The most visited of all the Char Dham shrines, Badrinath is situated 298 km (185 miles) northeast of Rishikesh. Its colourfully painted temple, dedicated to Vishnu, is usually packed with pilgrims. The town has a spectacular setting, wedged between the Nar and Narayan ranges. The Neelkanth or "Blue Throat Peak", named after Lord Shiva, towers over Badrinath at a height of 6,957 m (22,825 ft).

Joshimath, lying 250 km (155 miles) northeast of Rishikesh at the confluence of the Dhauli Ganga and Alaknanda rivers at Vishnuprayag, is one of the four *mathas* (seats of learning) established by the great 9th-century sage, Adi Shankaracharya *(see p648).* It is also the junction of two ancient trans-Himalayan trading routes. The town was a gateway to the Nanda Devi Sanctuary *(see p189),* until the sanctuary was closed to the public in 1983. Today, visitors head mostly for the ski slopes of **Auli**, reached via road or cable car from Joshimath. The popular trek to the Sikh shrine of **Hemkund Sahib** and the **Valley of Flowers National Park** *(see p189)* begins 20 km (12 miles) north of Joshimath, from Ghangaria. The Valley of Flowers, best visited between the months of June and September, is a carpet of anemones, roses, primulas and other alpine flora.

Gaumukh, the glacial source of the Ganges, backed by the Bhagirathi peaks

Trekking in Garhwal and Kumaon

No Himalayan ranges are as rich in myth and legend as those of Garhwal and Kumaon (Uttaranchal's eastern hills). Known as Dev Bhoomi ("Abode of the Gods"), every peak, river and trail is either named after a Hindu god or goddess, or finds mention in holy scriptures. Relatively easy to access, Garhwal and Kumaon are a wonderful introduction to the Himalayas. A single walk can lead through forests, valleys bursting with wild flowers, and glacial moonscapes of rock and ice. The best seasons are between February and May and September and November.

Wild irises, Garhwal

LOCATOR MAP

☐ Areas shown below

The Gaumukh Trail

This 26-km (16-mile) path traces the infant River Ganges along an ancient pilgrim trail, from Gangotri to its glacial source at Gaumukh (see p162). The route crosses the Gangotri Glacier and forks, leading to the meadows of Tapovan and Nandanvan, dominated by the imposing Bhagirathi and Shivling peaks.

Duration: 6 days
Altitude: 4,500 m (14,764 ft)
Level of Difficulty: *moderate to tough*

KEY

- – – The Gaumukh Trail
- ░ ░ Dodital
- ─── The Curzon Trail
- – – Pindari Glacier
- – – The Valley of Flowers
- ▬ Major road
- ═══ Minor road
- △ Peak
- ⌣ Pass

Chirbas
Gaumukh
Nandanvan
Gangotri
Tapovan
Kedar Tal
Shivling △
(6,540 m/21,457 ft)
Bhagirathi Parvat
(6,860 m/22,507 ft)
Harsil
Kedarnath
(6,940 m/22,769 ft) △
Gangotri △
(6,670 m/21,883 ft)
Kedarnath
Sanctuary
Chorabar
Tal
Bandar Punch △
(6,316 m/20,722 ft)
Gangnani
Gaurikund
Dodital
GARHWAL
Darwa Top △
(4,130 m/13,550 ft)
Bhatwari
Agoda
Kalyani
Gegari Uttarkashi

Jahnavi
Bhagirathi
Mandakini
Asi Ganga

0 km   10
0 miles   10

Dodital

One of Garhwal's popular treks, the 23-km (14-mile) path from Kalyani follows the Asi Ganga river valley, past Agoda to Dodital. This jewel-like lake, whose waters swarm with trout, is set in a densely wooded bowl. The pine and deodar forests are home to a variety of Himalayan birds.

Duration: 3 days
Altitude: 3,024 m (9,921 ft)
Level of Difficulty: *easy*

The Curzon Trail

The 70-km (44-mile) trail is named after the British viceroy who followed this route. From Ghat, it skirts the western edge of the Nanda Devi Sanctuary, crossing over the Kuari Pass, with clear views of Nanda Devi. It ends at Tapovan, 12 km (8 mile) northwest of Joshimath.

Duration: *6 days*
Altitude: *4,268 m (14,003 ft)*
Level of Difficulty: *tough*

The Valley of Flowers National Park, a 20-km (12-mile) climb from Govindghat, has a profusion of wild flowers (see p187).

Duration: *3 days*
Altitude: *3,352 m (10,997 ft)*
Level of Difficulty: *moderate*

ey of wers
angaria
Hemkund
Bhiundhar
Govindghat
Joshimath
Auli   **Tapovan**

Rishi Ganga

Nanda Devi East
(7,430 m/24,377 ft)

Nanda Devi
(7,817 m/25,646 ft)

Nanda Devi Sanctuary

Pindari Glacier

Kuari Pass
(4,268 m/ 14,003 ft)
Pana
Pipalkoti   **Jhinji**

Gohna Tal   *Chechni Binayak Pass*

Trishul
(7,120 m/23,360 ft)

Phurkiya
Dwali

Sundardhunga

KUMAON

Khati
Loharkhet
Dhakuri
Karmi

Ramni

Chamoli

Nandprayag   **Ghat**

Bekhal Tal

Pindar

Song

TIPS FOR WALKERS

Be prepared: *Acclimatization is essential for altitudes over 3,000 m (9,843 ft). See p767 for information on altitude sickness. For longer routes, guides are necessary. For more details on trekking see p751.*
On the trek: *Drink plenty of water. Carry a first aid kit and cooking fuel. Never burn wood, which is a scarce resource. Put out all fires properly, leaving no burning embers. Do not litter, and carry your rubbish back with you.*
Permits: *In Garhwal, travel permits are required for border areas which can be obtained from the District Magistrate's Office in Uttarkashi, (01374) 222 280 or the GMVN, Rishikesh, (0135) 243 1793. No permits are required for Kumaon. For more information see p758.*
Equipment hire & operators: *In Garhwal, contact Mount Support in Uttarkashi, GMVN (0135) 243 1793, in Rishikesh, GMVN (0135) 274 7898, for trekking assistance; in Dehra Dun (see p186), contact Garhwal Tours and Trekking, (0135) 248 0799. In Kumaon, Parbat Tours in Nainital, (05942) 235 656, and the Nainital Mountaineering Club, (05942) 235 057, organize treks. For more details see p755.*

Pindari Glacier is a 50-km (31-mile) trek from Song, through dense forests with fine views of Trishul Peak.

Duration: *6 days*
Altitude: *3,650 m (11,975 ft)*
Level of Difficulty: *tough*

NANDA DEVI SANCTUARY

The 630-sq km (243-sq mile) Nanda Devi Sanctuary has three splendid peaks – Nanda Devi, Nanda Devi East and Nanda Kot, which form a snowy wall in the north. Nanda Devi (see pp64–5) is India's second highest peak at 7,817 m (25,646 ft). Believed to be the birthplace of Shiva's consort, Parvati, the mountain is revered as a goddess. The area was thought

Nanda Devi and Nanda Devi East

to be impenetrable till British mountaineers Eric Shipton and Bill Tilman discovered a route in 1936. A spate of expeditions followed, to the distress of the local people who believed this would incur the wrath of the goddess. In 1976, American mountaineer Willi Unsoeld, along with his 22-year-old daughter Nanda Devi (whom he had named after the peak), set off for the mountain, but Nanda Devi died tragically during the expedition. The core area of the sanctuary was closed in 1983 to protect its fragile ecosystem, which is the habitat of rare fauna such as the snow leopard and the monal pheasant.

Nainital ⑫

Nainital district. 322 km (200 miles) NE of Delhi. 🚉 *Kathgodam, 35 km (22 miles) S of Nainital, then taxi or bus.* 🚌 ℹ *KMVN, Om Park, (05942) 231 436.*

This pretty hill station, nestled in the Kumaon Hills, is named after the emerald green eyes *(naina)* of Parvati, Shiva's consort. A temple dedicated to the goddess stands on the northern shore of the large freshwater lake *(tal)*. The old summer capital of the British Raj's United Provinces, Nainital is today part of the newly-formed state of Uttaranchal. The lake is encircled by the Mall Road, and the "flats", a large field which is a popular promenade and recreation centre. The **Boat House Club**, set up in 1890 on the water's edge, is the hub of many activities and has a number of sail boats and rubber dinghies for hire. The many attractive colonial buildings include the governor's summer residence (built in 1899), St Joseph's School, the old Secretariat (now the Uttaranchal High Court) and the Municipal Library. **St-John-in-the-Wilderness** is an evocatively named Gothic church, with fine stained-glass windows and dark wooden pews. Nainital also has some beautiful walking trails, one of which leads up from the flats,

The 11th-century complex of stone temples at Jageshwar, near Almora

through the densely wooded Ayarpata Hill, to **Tiffin Top** and **Dorothy's Seat**, lookout points offering panoramic views of the lakeside. Close by, and almost hidden by the forest, is an old public school, the appropriately named **Sherwood College**. The Upper Cheena Mall leads to Naina Peak, with breathtaking views of the mountain ranges. Less energetic visitors can take the cable car up to **Snow View** for scenic views.

Environs
Described as India's Lake District, Nainital's environs have a number of serene lakes, surrounded by thick forests. Excursions are offered to **Bhim Tal**, 22 km (14 miles) east of Nainital; **Naukuchiya Tal**, just 4 km (2.5 miles) from Bhim Tal, is a lake with nine corners, rich in birdlife; and **Sat Tal**, a conglomeration of seven lakes, located 21 km (13 miles) northeast of Nainital. **Mukteshwar**, 30 km (19 miles) northeast of Nainital, is one of the most beautiful spots in the area, along with the orchards at **Ramgarh**, close by.

Sculpture, Jageshwar

Almora ⑬

Almora district. 285 km (177 miles) NE of Delhi. 🚉 *Kathgodam, 90 km (56 miles) S of Almora, then taxi or bus.* 🚌 ℹ *KMVN, Holiday Home, (05962) 230 250.*

The large market town of Almora is the headquarters of the surrounding district. Its curving ridge offers expansive views of the spectacular Greater Himalayan Range, including peaks such as Trishul and the spectacular Nanda Devi *(see p189)*. The cobbled street of Almora's distinctive bazaar lies above The Mall, where locally crafted *tamta* products (hand-beaten copper and brass utensils plated with silver) are on sale. The town's trademark confectionery, the *bal mithai*, is available here as well.

Also of interest are the tall, narrow houses with their delicately carved wooden façades, a hallmark of local architecture. The historic **Almora Jail**, probably one of the few in the country with such picturesque surroundings, once held important political prisoners such as Mahatma Gandhi and Jawaharlal Nehru. A number of temples dot the landscape; the most popular of these are the **Chitai Temple** and the **Udyotchandeshwar Temple**. On the western edge of town, **Brighton End Corner** has fine mountain views.

Environs
Binsar, 34 km (21 miles) northeast of Almora, at an altitude of 2,412 m (7,913 ft), is a wonderful spot from which to view the mountains. The steep drive up through tangy forests of pine is very pretty, and there is a 13th-century Shiva Temple set in the forest, just short of the summit. **Jageshwar**, located 34 km (21 miles) east of Almora, is of great religious significance. This is an

The lake at Nainital, with facilities for boating and water sports

Ranikhet's nine-hole golf course, offering fine mountain views

impressive complex of over 100 splendidly carved stone temples, dating back to the 11th century.

Ranikhet **14**

Almora district. 367 km (228 miles) NE of Delhi. *Tourist Reception Centre, Mall Rd, (05966) 220 893.*

Primarily a cantonment town, Ranikhet is home to the Indian Army's renowned Kumaon Regiment. Not surprisingly, the army is the town's most visible presence, its many red-roofed bungalows spreading across the wide "Queen's Field", a literal translation of the town's name. **Sadar Bazaar** is the main market, while the **Upper Mall** leads away from the bazaar to the quieter part of town. **Chaubatia**, once a British sanatorium, lies further along The Mall and now houses the Government Fruit Garden, which grows 200 varieties of fruit. Ranikhet's true allure, however, lies in its untrammelled Himalayan views that offer a spectacular vista of nearly 350 km (217 miles) of the Greater Himalayan Range. The **Army Golf Course**, 6 km (4 miles) down the Almora Road at Uphat, is one of the country's highest golf courses, and was originally a racetrack. It welcomes visitors who are willing to pay green fees, so take no notice of the signboard that threatens trespassers.

A green bee-eater with its catch

Lansdowne **15**

Almora district. 216 km (134 miles) NE of Delhi. *Kotdwar, 37 km (23 miles) SW of town centre, then taxi or bus.*

The cantonment town of Lansdowne, is one of the few hill stations that has managed to remain wonderfully unchanged over the last century. Away from the main tourist circuit, the town has been spared the frenzied building and modernization that has crept into other popular destinations. A loosely spread out jumble of bungalows and shops, it is set on gentle forested slopes of pine, deodar and silver oak. The Army's Garhwal Rifles have their regimental centre here, and a visit to the beautifully maintained regimental mess is a must. A pleasant walk leads to **Tip-n-Top**, a lookout point 3 km (2 miles) from town, which offers excellent mountain views.

Kausani **16**

Almora district. 385 km (239 miles) NE of Delhi. *Tourist Reception Centre, (05962) 258 006.*

Kausani was Mahatma Gandhi's favourite abode in the hills. After a long stay here at the **Anashakti Yoga Ashram** in 1929, he remarked on how unnecessary it was for Indians to visit the European Alps for their health, when they had the beauty of Kausani at their doorsteps. A 400-km (249-mile) uninterrupted panorama of the Nanda Devi Range can be seen from the old **Circuit House**.

Environs

Baijnath, 20 km (12 miles) north of Kausani, is known for a cluster of temples, now in ruins, built in the 11th century. The main attraction is the **Parvati Temple**, with a 2-m (7-ft) high image of the goddess, dating from the 12th century. **Bageshwar**, 41 km (26 miles) east of Kausani, lies at the confluence of the Gomti and Saryu rivers, and was once a major trading post between Tibet and Kumaon. Although the link with Tibet no longer exists, local merchants still bring wool and animal hide to the town's annual Uttarayani Fair. With its stone temples dedicated to Shiva, Bageshwar is also an important pilgrimage centre in Kumaon. Nila Parvat (the "Blue Mountain"), stands proudly between the two rivers, and locals believe that it is home to all the 330 million deities of the Hindu pantheon. Many visitors to Bageshwar are en route to the Pindari Glacier *(see p189)*.

Pumpkins drying on a slate roof below the peaks at Kausani

Corbett National Park ⑰

Situated along the valley of the Ramganga river and
fringed by the Himalayan foothills in the north,
Corbett is considered one of India's finest wildlife
sanctuaries. The 1,318-sq km (509-sq mile) reserve was
originally a hunter's paradise during the British Raj. In
1936, it became India's first national park, largely due
to the efforts of the great British hunter-turned-
conservationist Jim Corbett, after whom the park is
named. The park encompasses varied terrain, from
savannah grasslands to hilly ridges of deciduous forests
with *chir* pine and *sal (Shorea robusta)*. Corbett is
renowned for its remarkable variety of wildlife,
notably tigers, elephants, *chausingha* (four-horned
antelopes) and an astonishing 600 species of birds.

Paradise Flycatcher
*The male has beautiful
plumage, and measures
50 cm (20 in) in length.*

**Coucal or
Crow Pheasant**
*This striking,
black and brown
bird is found
all over north-
ern India. Its
loud and
resonant call
echoes over the
valleys and forests in
and around Corbett.*

*Sona Nadi
Wildlife Sanctuary*

Kanda

Dhikala   Khinnanauli

Ramganga Reservoir

Paterpani

Chir Choti   Gaujpani

Dam   Kalagarh   Dhara   Jhirna
TAKESWAR

Grasslands
*Vast savannah grasslands (chaurs),
ideal for viewing deer and other wildlife, surround Dhikala, the park's hub,
located by the Ramganga Reservoir.*

Machaans or high
watchtowers, situated
around the park, are
ideal for viewing wildlife.

Gharial
*The gharial (Gavialis
gangeticus) is a species
that can be seen on the
banks of the Ramganga
Reservoir (formed by a
dam on the Ramganga
river). The reservoir also
attracts a variety of water
birds such as geese, ducks,
grebes and storks.*

VISITORS' CHECKLIST

Pauri Garhwal & Nainital districts.
436 km (271 miles) NW of Lucknow. **Entry points:** *Dhangarhi &
Kalagarh.* 🚉 *Ramnagar, 20 km
(12 miles) S of Dhangarhi.* 🚌
ℹ️ *For bookings and permits
contact Ramnagar, (05947)
251 225.* ⬜ *Nov–Jun.* 🎥
📷 *extra charges for video.* 🐘

Ramganga River
*The lifeline of the park's wildlife, the Ramganga river is
surrounded by tall elephant grass* (nall) *and scrub.*

Elephant Safari
*The highlights of a trip
to Corbett are the sunrise
and sunset elephant safaris,
available from Dhikala and
Bijrani. Apart from the
herds of wild elephants
and deer, it is sometimes
possible to encounter a
lone tiger or leopard.*

Gairal — Ramganga

RANIKHET

Sarpduli — Sultan — Dhangathi

Malani

Garjia — Kol

Bijrani

dhang — Dhela

Amdanda

Ramnagar

HALDWANI

Indian Tiger
*Corbett has about 140 tigers. It
became India's first Tiger Reserve
in 1973, under the aegis of
Project Tiger (see p289).*

0 km   5

0 miles   5

KEY

- - Park boundary
- - Trail
= Major road
= Minor road
ℹ️ Tourist information
🔆 Viewpoint
📷 Café
🅰 Accommodation

JIM CORBETT (1875–1955)

Jim Corbett was born in Nainital and developed a keen
interest in the jungles of Kumaon. An avid hunter in his
early years (he shot his first leopard when he
was eight), the turning point came when, on a
duck shoot, he was appalled by the mindless
slaughter of 300 birds. Corbett then decided to
use his rifle solely to kill the man-eating
leopards and tigers that plagued the nearby
villages. Riveting accounts in his first book,
Man-eaters of Kumaon, describe how he
tracked and shot the dreaded
Champawat tigress who had killed 434
people. In 1956, after Corbett's death, the
park was named after him as a tribute to
his pioneering efforts at conservation.

**Bust of Corbett,
Dhikala**

Dudhwa National Park ⑱

Lakhimpur-Kheri district. 220 km (137 miles) N of Lucknow. **Entry point:** *Palia.* 🚉 🚌 ℹ️ *For bookings contact Field Director, Dudhwa, (05872) 252 106.* ⬤ *15 Nov–15 June.* 📷 📷 *extra charges. Jeeps available.* 🏨

Located close to the border with Nepal, Dudhwa National Park covers 490 sq km (189 sq miles) of densely wooded plains. Its forests have some of the finest specimens of *sal* trees in India. In 1988, Dudhwa was recognized as a Tiger Reserve, mainly due to the efforts of Billy Arjan Singh, a legendary environmentalist. Arjan Singh is best-known for the tigress, Tara, he hand-reared and returned to the wild in 1978.

Today, the park has more than 30 tigers. The park is also well known for its herds of swamp deer (*Cervus duvauceli*). Better known as *barasingha* (literally, 12-antlered), these deer find their ideal habitat in the grassy wetlands in the southern reaches of the park.

Other species include leopards, sloth bears and a small herd of rhinos, brought here from Assam and Nepal, in an attempt to re-introduce the species into Dudhwa. The park is also home to nearly 400 species of birds, among them swamp partridges, lesser floricans and hornbills. The park's lakes attract waterfowl such as fishing eagles and ibis.

Rampur ⑲

Rampur district. 310 km (193 miles) NW of Lucknow. 🚶 *281,500.* 🚉 🚌

Earlier a stronghold of the Afghan Rohilla chieftains (highlanders from Peshawar), Rampur became a princely state under the British. It was ruled by a dynasty of Muslim nawabs who were great connoisseurs of the arts. They drew hundreds of scholars and artists to their court, whose books and paintings became part of the state collection. They also established a famous *gharana* (school) of classical music. The Hamid Manzil, built by Nawab Hamid Ali Khan Bahadur who came to the throne in 1896, now houses the renowned **Raza Library**, which has a collection of almost 1,000 Mughal miniatures, over 10,000 books, numerous rare manuscripts, and portraits dating from the 16th to 18th centuries. It is not officially open to the public, but permission to visit can be obtained from the curator. Hamid Ali Khan was also responsible for renovating many of Rampur's palaces, including the sprawling palace and fort complex to the northwest of the town. Rampur is a maze of bazaars and was once known for its fine cotton *khes* (damask). Traces of its Rohilla warrior ancestry are visible in

Rampur knives and daggers, a local speciality

the famous daggers, always on sale, and in the touches of Pashto (the native tongue of Peshawar) which pepper the Urdu that is spoken here.

> 🏛️ **Raza Library**
> For permission to visit contact the curator. *Tel (0592) 232 5045, 232 5346.*

Nawab Hamid Ali of Rampur

Environs
The town of **Moradabad**, lying 26 km (16 miles) west of Rampur, is a small 17th-century settlement, best known for its brass and metal-ware industries. The town's fort and mosque are almost hidden by the many tenements and bazaars.

Aligarh ⑳

Aligarh district. 371 km (231 miles) NW of Lucknow. 🚶 *667,700.* 🚉 🚌 🎎 *Numaish (Feb).*

Historically important because of its location in an agriculturally rich region, Aligarh was a Rajput stronghold from the end of the 12th century onwards, until it was wrested by the Mughals. Its fort, which dates to 1524, fell to the British under Lord Lake in 1803. British presence influenced many of its foremost citizens, such as Sir Sayyid Ahmed Khan who founded the **Aligarh Muslim University** in 1875, for which the town is most famous today. The sprawling campus has many

Swamp deer, also known as *barasingha*, in Dudhwa's grasslands

imposing buildings, such as a mosque that is an exact replica of the Jami Masjid (see p86) in Delhi, only one-third its size.

Jhansi ㉑

Jhansi district. 301 km (187 miles) SW of Lucknow. 🚶 383,200. 🚉 🚌 ℹ️ UP Tourism, Shivpuri Rd, (0517) 244 1267. 🎭 Jhansi Festival (Feb).

The ramparts of Shankar Fort at Jhansi, stormed by British forces in 1858

Most famous for the role that its queen, Rani Lakshmibai, played during the Indian Mutiny of 1857, Jhansi is a key transit point for visitors travelling from Delhi to the temples of Khajuraho (see pp236–8). The main site of interest is **Shankar Fort**, built in 1613 by Raja Bir Singh Deo. It has 9-m (30-ft) high walls built in concentric rings around its centre, and offers fine views from its ramparts.

The **Archaeological Museum**, located outside the fort on the road back to town, has medieval Hindu sculpture, royal artifacts, and some prehistoric tools.

🏛 **Archaeological Museum** 🔲 Tue–Sun. 🔲 2nd Sat. 🎥 📷 extra charges for video photography.

Kanpur ㉒

Kanpur district. 79 km (49 miles) SW of Lucknow. 🚶 2,532,100. 🚉 🚌

One of British India's largest garrisons Kanpur, or Cawnpore as it was then known, witnessed some of

the bloodiest battles in 1857. More than 1,000 British soldiers and civilians were killed when Nana Sahib, the Maratha ruler, broke the British siege held by General Sir Hugh Wheeler in June 1857. When British reinforcements arrived, equally ferocious reprisals occurred.

Today, Kanpur is an industrial city with leather, cotton and oil as its main products. The old garrison, now an enclave of the armed forces, has some interesting relics of the Raj. Among them is the **All Souls' Memorial Church**, a grand Gothic style structure with an intricate stained-glass window over the west door. Built after 1857, it is a memorial to those killed during the siege. East of the church, the pretty **Memorial Garden** has a statue of an angel surrounded by a Gothic screen. This statue originally stood at the site of a terrible massacre, where British women and children were hacked and thrown down a well near Bibighar, in the

town's centre. Northeast of the church, **Sati Chaura Ghat** along the Ganges, is the spot where Indian forces killed 500 British soldiers and civilians. The **Military Cemetery** on the edge of the cantonment has many interesting graves, while in the town, the **King Edward VII Memorial Hall** and **Christ Church** (built in 1840) are also worth visiting.

Environs

Bithur, 25 km (16 miles) west of Kanpur, boasts a fort built by the Peshwas (see p471). It is also the legendary birthplace of Lav and Kush, the twin sons of Rama and Sita (see p27). About 60 km (37 miles) south of Kanpur, lies the beautiful 5th-century brick temple at **Bhitargaon**, built by the Gupta kings. The only one of its kind still surviving, most of the relief panels on the temple have vanished, but some terracotta sculptures inside remain.

Stained-glass window in the All Souls' Memorial Church, Kanpur

---

RANI LAKSHMIBAI OF JHANSI

India's Joan of Arc, Rani Lakshmibai single-handedly defied the British when her husband, Raja Gangadhar Rao, died in 1853 leaving no adult heir. She wished to rule as Regent but the British invoked the infamous Doctrine of Lapse (see p53) and she was driven from her kingdom. While the Indian Mutiny of 1857 brewed in the north, the queen and her general, Tantia Tope, captured Gwalior Fort. She died defending it at Kotah-Sarai near Gwalior in 1858. According to the historian Christopher Hibbert, "she died dressed as a man, holding her sword two-handed and the reins of her horse in her teeth". She remains one of India's best-loved heroines.

Rani Lakshmibai astride her horse

Lucknow ㉓

The fish emblem of the nawabs

As the Mughal Empire disintegrated, many independent kingdoms, such as Avadh, were established. Its capital, Lucknow, rose to prominence when Asaf-ud-Daula, the fourth nawab, shifted his court here from Faizabad (see p199) in 1775. The city was also a great cultural centre, and its nawabs, best remembered for their refined and extravagant lifestyles, were patrons of the arts. Under them music and dance flourished, and many buildings were erected. In 1856 the British annexed Lucknow and deposed its last nawab, Wajid Ali Shah. This incident helped instigate the Indian Mutiny of 1857, when the city witnessed one of the bloodiest episodes in colonial history.

Sikander Bagh's stately gateway, adorned with the fish emblem

View of the Tomb of Khurshid Zadi, Qaiser Bagh

� Qaiser Bagh Palace

Qaiser Bagh. ☐ daily.
Once the most magnificent palace in Lucknow, Qaiser Bagh, was built by Wajid Ali Shah (r.1847–56), the last nawab. When the British recaptured Lucknow in 1858, they demolished many of the complex's more fanciful structures, with their florid sculptures of mermaids and cherubs. However, the remaining buildings, although in ruins, hint at their former splendour. The **Lal Baradari** now houses a fine arts academy as well as the archaeological section of the State Museum; the **Pathar Wali Baradari** is a school for Hindustani music; and the **Safaid Baradari**, now an office building, was where the nawab, dressed as a fakir, used to hold court. Only two wings of the residential quarters that once housed the

nawab's vast harem remain. Carvings of fish, the nawabs' royal emblem, adorn many of the structures. Nearby, lie two grand tombs, the **Tomb of Saadat Ali Khan** (the fifth nawab) and the **Tomb of Khurshid Zadi**, his wife.

Under Nawab Wajid Ali Shah, Lucknow witnessed an artistic flowering. An aesthete who was not interested in governance, he devoted himself to poetry and music and is believed to have introduced the *thumri* (a form of light classical music). Dance forms benefited as well, and the Lucknow *gharana* (school) of Kathak (see p28) reached new heights during his short reign, before he was deposed by the British in 1856 and exiled to Calcutta.

♣ Sikander Bagh

Sikander Bagh. ☐ daily.
Named after Wajid Ali Shah's favourite queen, Sikander Bagh was the royal pleasure garden of the nawabs. In 1857, British troops led by Sir Colin Campbell relieved the

siege of the Residency at this site. The **National Botanical Gardens and Research Centre** are now located in its grounds. To the west, the **Shah Najaf Imambara** has the tomb of Ghazi-ud-din Haidar (the sixth nawab).

♙ Chattar Manzil

NW of Qaiser Bagh. ☐ daily.
Built during Saadat Ali Khan's reign (1798–1814), the Chattar Manzil ("Umbrella Palace"), derives its name from the umbrella-shaped gilt dome (*chattar*) crowning the structure. A basement (*tehkhana*) was built below the level of the Gomti river, so that its waters could keep the area cool in the summer. The building now houses the Central Drug Research Institute.

♙ The Residency

NW of Qaiser Bagh. ☐ daily. 🎟
Lucknow's most haunting monuments are the desolate ruins of the Residency. This complex of buildings which grew around the large brick home of the Resident, was an exclusive British enclave, protected by fortifications. In 1857, all the city's British

The British Residency before it was destroyed during the siege of 1857

citizens took refuge here during the five-month siege. Sir Henry Lawrence, the commander of the troops, expected relief to arrive within 15 days. But, it was 87 days before a force led by Sir Henry Havelock broke through the ranks of sepoys, only to find themselves trapped inside. For the next seven weeks they faced constant bombardment, until Sir Colin Campbell finally retook the Residency on 17 November. By then, almost 2,000 people had died either from bullet wounds or from cholera and typhoid.

Today, the Residency looks just as it did in 1857. In its small museum, the gaping holes made by cannon fire, are still visible. The **Model Room** on the ground floor, has a model depicting British defences during the siege. Lying below, are the cellars where the women and children took shelter. The cemetery near the ruined church, has the forlorn graves of those who died, including that of Sir Henry Lawrence. An **Indian Martyrs' Memorial** stands opposite, on the banks of the Gomti river.

🎐 Bara Imambara

Hussainabad. ◻ daily. ● during Muharram (Mar/Apr). 📷

Lucknow's most distinctive architectural structures are the *imambaras*, or ceremonial halls used during Muharram (*see p669*). The Bara ("Great") Imambara, built by Asaf-ud-Daula in 1784, was essentially a famine relief project providing much-needed employment. It is said that while one group of workers were involved with its construction during the day, another group dismantled it at night. Elaborate gates lead to this sprawling, low edifice. Its most remarkable feature is a large hall, 50-m (164-ft) long and 15-m (49-ft) high, totally unsupported by pillars.

Above it is the *bhulbhulaiya*, a labyrinth of balconies and passages. The **Asafi Mosque** and a stepwell also lie in the compound.

Asaf-ud-Daula also erected the 18-m (59-ft) high **Rumi Darwaza**, just outside. This portal, embellished with lavish decorations, was the Imambara's west facing entrance.

The Bara Imambara complex, built in the late 18th century

LUCKNOW CITY CENTRE

Bara Imambara ⑤
Chattar Manzil ③
Qaiser Bagh Palace ①
The Residency ④
Sikander Bagh ②

Key to Symbols *see back flap*

Lucknow: The Outer Sites

Some of Lucknow's best architectural sites lie beyond the city centre. The religious monuments, such as the *imambaras* and mosques, reveal a distinct Persian influence, while the secular buildings, which include the palaces of the nawabs as well as colonial structures, are more European in style. A particularly extravagant example among the latter is La Martinière. The home and mausoleum of a French adventurer, it later became a school, serving as the model for St Xavier's School which was immortalized in Rudyard Kipling's novel, *Kim*.

Portrait of Nawab Wajid Ali Shah in the Picture Gallery

Close to the Rumi Darwaza *(see p197)*, **Aurangzeb's Mosque** stands on high ground known as Lakshman Tila, the location of Lucknow's original township. To the east is the **Hussainabad Clocktower**, erected in 1887. The 67-m (220-ft) high Gothic tower was built to mark the arrival of Sir George Cooper, Avadh's first lieutenant governor. To its west lies the 19th-century Baradari, built by Muhammed Ali Shah (the eighth nawab), where the **Picture Gallery** is located. Splendid life-sized portraits of the ten nawabs, painted between 1882 and 1885 and recently renovated, are on display here.

To the west of the Picture Gallery is the Hussainabad Imambara, better known as the **Chhota Imambara**. This gem-like structure is surmounted by a delicate gold dome, and its outside walls are engraved with superb calligraphy. The interiors are adorned with gilt-edged mirrors, ornate chandeliers, silver pulpits and colourful stucco decorations. The *tazias* (replica tombs) and *alams* (standards) used during the Muharram festival between March and April, are kept here. The **Jami Masjid**, to the southwest is another striking structure, built by Muhammed Ali Shah in the early 19th century. Its walls are heavily ornamented and its arches are covered with fine stucco work.

Northwest of the Jami Masjid, the **Daulat Khana** was the palace of Asaf-ud-Daula. Constructed in the late 1780s,

Alam, Chhota Imambara

it includes numerous Indo-European buildings. The most prominent of these is the **Asafi Kothi**, its elegant façade marked by semi-circular bays.

Lucknow's main market is situated in the **Chowk**, the city's atmospheric old quarter. Stretching from Gol Darwaza to Akbari Darwaza, this maze of narrow *galis* (lanes) is lined with shops selling a range of goods from colourful kites to *paan* to Lucknow's famed *chikankari* – fine muslin delicately embroidered with threadwork. Wholesale flower markets overflow with roses and jasmine, and *attar* shops sell tiny bottles of fragrant perfume. The Chowk is also the best place to sample some authentic local cuisine (especially the many varieties of succulent kebabs), refined to an art form by chefs attached to nawabi households *(see p165)*.

At the southeastern corner of the city, situated in the Zoological Gardens, is Lucknow's **State Museum**. Its collection includes rare silver and gold coins, 16th-century paintings, and stone sculpture from the 2nd century BC.

The extraordinary **La Martinière** stands further south. It was

built by Major General Claude Martin, a French soldier of fortune and, in 1793, the richest European in Lucknow. A fanciful Gothic château, it has four enormous octagonal towers. The exterior is decorated with animals and mythological figures, including lions, gargoyles and a female sphinx. One of the two cannons on the terrace was cast by Martin, as was the bronze bell. He died in 1800 and is buried in the basement. In 1840, the building, in accordance with Martin's will, became a school for boys. The school was evacuated during the siege of Lucknow, but re-opened a year later.

🏛 **Picture Gallery**
◯ Mon–Sat.

🏛 **State Museum**
Tel (0522) 220 6158. ◯ Tue–Sun. 📷

🏫 **La Martinière College**
Prior permission required from the principal.
Tel (0522) 222 3863.

The elaborate façade of La Martinière College for boys

The colourful Hanuman Garhi Temple in Ayodhya

Ayodhya 24

Faizabad district. 134 km (83 miles)
E of Lucknow. *Kartik Purnima
(Oct/Nov).*

Located on the banks of the
Sarayu river, Ayodhya is said
to be the birthplace of Rama,
the divine hero of the
Ramayana (see p27). Dozens
of temples in this small
pilgrim town commemorate
his birth. Whether this is a
historical fact or simply part
of oral tradition, for devout
Hindu Ayodhya remains
inextricably linked with the
legend of Rama. As a result,
when the Mughal emperor
Babur built a mosque near
the supposed spot of Rama's
birthplace in 1526, he left
behind a bitterly contested
site. Known as the **Babri
Masjid** ("Mosque of Babur"), it
was a long-simmering source
of tension between Hindus
and Muslims. In 1992, a mob
of Hindus tore down the

mosque, leading to rioting all
over the country. Security
personnel now guard the site.
A makeshift temple outside
the security ring still attracts
pilgrims, particularly during
the full moon night of Kartik
Purnima. One of the more
renowned temples, among the
hundreds of shrines on the
river bank, is the **Hanuman
Garhi**. Built within the walls
of an old fort, it is dedicated
to the monkey god, Hanuman.

Environs
Ayodhya's twin city, lying 6 km
(4 miles) to its west, **Faizabad**
has a sizeable Muslim
population and was Avadh's
first capital before it was shifted
to Lucknow in 1775. In the
town's centre is the Jami Masjid,
built by the later Mughals,
while the 18th-century tomb of
Bahu Begum, the wife of
Shuja-ud-Daula (Avadh's third
nawab), is an austere structure
built in marble. Faizabad also
has a pretty rose garden.

Jaunpur 25

Jaunpur district. 60 km (37 miles)
SE of Lucknow. *160,000.*

Though largely bypassed
by visitors, Jaunpur has a
wealth of medieval Islamic
architecture. Located along
the Gomti river, Jaunpur was
established by Feroze Shah
Tughluq *(see p91)* in the late
14th century and soon grew
into an important trading
post. It was subsequently
ruled by the independent
Muslim rulers of the Sharqi
dynasty who held sway for
much of the 15th century,
until Ibrahim Lodi conquered
the city in 1479. It eventually
fell to the Mughals in the
early part of the 16th century.

Jaunpur's many rulers each
left a distinct architectural
stamp on the city. The Mughal
emperor Akbar built the great
Akbari Bridge across the river,
which still stands. To its north
is the **Old Shahi Fort** from the
Tughluq era. It contains a
mosque, built with yellow
and blue enamelled bricks,
and an exact replica of a
traditional Turkish bath or
hamam. The most striking
mosque, the **Atala Masjid**, just
outside the fort, dates to the
Sharqi period. It is embellished with recessed arches
and ornamental fringes, and
square courts surround the
central structure. Though built
on a grander scale, the 15th-
century **Jami Masjid** borrows
its basic architectural inspiration from the Atala Masjid.

THE MANGO: KING OF FRUITS

*Langra mangoes,
available in summer*

The mango *(aam)* is considered the
king of tropical fruits and is the best-
loved fruit of the country. The Mughal
emperor Babur called it the "finest
fruit of Hindostan". The popular
paisley motif is derived from the
shape of the mango fruit, and mango
leaves, considered auspicious, are
used as buntings at festive occasions.
Of the hundreds of varieties grown all
over the subcontinent, few are as
aromatic and juicy as the mangoes of
Jaunpur. The *langra* is arguably the
best among the varieties grown here. It is fleshy, juicy and
sweet, and possessed of a distinct tangy flavour. It sells at a
premium countrywide and is widely exported to the
Middle East and Europe. The *dussehri* from Lucknow, and
the *chausa* from the Rampur region, are also popular
varieties. The raw *chausa* is considered ideal for spicy
chutneys and pickles, without which no meal is complete.

**The grand façade of the Jami
Masjid in Jaunpur**

A view of the Taj Mahal (*see pp172–5*) from across the Yamuna river, Agra ▷

Varanasi ㉖

Also known as Kashi ("the City of Light"), or as Benares, Varanasi is situated on the west bank of the Ganges and is India's holiest Hindu city, with a spiritual and religious legacy that goes back nearly 3,000 years. This is the city of Shiva, the foremost among the 12 places where the god burrowed and then burst into the sky in a fiery pillar of light *(jyotirlinga)*. Sanctified by Shiva's all-pervading presence and the sacred Ganges, the 90 or so ghats along the river define the life and identity of Varanasi. Stretching from the southern Asi Ghat to the northern Adi Keshava Ghat, close to the Malviya Bridge, the ghats cover more than 6 km (4 miles). Lined with temples and shrines they reverberate with the endless cycle of Hindu religious practice – from daily rituals to profound rites of passage.

LOCATOR MAP
Asi Ghat to Shivala Ghat

Tulsi Ghat
One of Varanasi's oldest sites, this ghat (earlier known as Lolarka Ghat), was renamed after the poet-saint Tulsidas, who lived here in the 16th century. His house and temple still stand nearby.

Mural of goddess on the walls at Ganga Mahal Ghat

Asi Ghat
A linga stands beneath a pipal tree on Varanasi's southernmost ghat, which marks the confluence of the Asi and Ganges rivers.

Rewa Ghat

Bhadaini Ghat

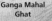

| 0 metres | 50 |
| 0 yards | 50 |

Ganga Mahal Ghat

Janki Ghat
Brick-red steps distinguish Janki Ghat, in keeping with the Varanasi tradition of each ghat having its own distinctive colour.

Chet Singh Ghat
The fort on this ghat marks the spot where Maharaja Chet Singh was defeated by the British in the mid-18th century.

Anandamayi Ghat
The ashram founded by, the Bengali female saint, Anandamayi Ma, draws thousands of devotees.

Niranjani Ghat

Panchkot Ghat

Jain Ghat

Mahanirvani Ghat

Prabhu Ghat

Vatsaraj Ghat

Shivala Ghat
This ghat, dating to 1770, was built by Chet Singh, the maharaja of Varanasi.

VISITORS' CHECKLIST

Varanasi district. 286 km (178 miles) SE of Lucknow. 2,000,000. 22 km (14 miles) NW of the city. Parade Kothi, (0542) 220 8162, Varanasi Junction Station, (0542) 234 6370. daily. Shivratri (Feb/Mar), Ramlila (Sep/ Oct), Ganga Festival (Oct/Nov).

Boat Building
Planks lie waiting to be jointed into boats, which are an essential mode of transportation along the busy river front.

RAMLILA

The Ramlila is a cycle of plays which tells the story of the *Ramayana (see p27)*, in which Lord Rama is exiled from his kingdom for 14 years. The Ramlila tradition was started in Varanasi by Tulsidas, author of the *Ramcharitmanas* (a popular version of the epic). Street performances take place in the evenings at different venues, in September/October, attracting thousands of spectators. The performance at the residence of the former maharaja at Ramnagar Fort is by far the most spectacular of the Ramlilas in Varanasi.

Young boys dressed as the main characters

Varanasi: Digpatiya Ghat to Mir Ghat

These centrally located ghats are the city's most
sacred, and many of them were built under the
patronage of India's erstwhile princely states, such as
Darbhanga, Jaipur and Indore. One of Varanasi's two
cremation ghats, Harishchandra Ghat, lies just to the
south. Behind the holy Dasashvamedha Ghat meanders
a winding lane known as Vishwanath Gali, lined with a
multitude of shops that sell all manner of religious
objects. It leads to the city's principal shrine, the
Vishwanath Temple, said to be over 1,000 years old.

LOCATOR MAP
Digpatiya Ghat to Mir Ghat

Chausatthi Ghat
*Lessons in the scriptures take place at
this ghat, named after the temple of
the Chausath Yoginis or 64
female divinities.*

Digpatiya
Ghat

Harishchandra
Ghat

Rana Mahal
Ghat

Munsi
Ghat

Ahilyabai
Ghat

Prayag
Ghat

Darbhanga Ghat
*The towers and turrets of old
havelis, built in the early
1900s by two princes of Bihar,
dominate this ghat. Some of
the massive pillars in these
havelis are reminiscent of
the Greek style.*

Dasashvamedha Ghat
*This centrally located ghat, Varanasi's holiest spot, is
named after the ten simultaneous horse sacrifices
(dasashvamedh) performed by Brahma the Creator.
Rows of priests sit under bamboo parasols, ready to
perform ritual prayers for the pilgrims that swarm here.*

Vishwanath Gali
*Lacquer jars, vermilion powder,
bottled Ganges water, bangles and
brocade, are all sold in the lane that
leads to the Vishwanath Temple, the
focal point of all worship in Varanasi.*

Vishwanath Temple
*Dedicated to Shiva, this
shrine is topped
by 750 kg (1,654
lbs) of gold. The
present structure
was built in 1777
by Ahilyabai
of Indore.*

Vishwanath
Temple

Man Mandir Ghat
*Jai Singh II of Jaipur built one
of his four Jantar Mantars (see
pp358–9) above Raja Man
Singh's palace in 1710. Its
sundial is visible from the ghat.*

The Palace of the Dom Raja, the king of the
Doms. The Doms are a caste who have
exclusive rights over the cremation ghats. They
sell wood and collect the ashes. The Dom
Raja's wealth derives from the cremation fees
his family have collected for centuries.

**Tripura
Bhairavi Ghat**

**Mir
Ghat**

0 metres 50

0 yards 50

BOAT RIDES

A sunrise boat ride is the highlight of a trip
to Varanasi, when the temples along the
river front are bathed in soft light. The
people of Varanasi trickle out of the labyrinthine lanes and head for the ghats at
dawn. Here, they wash clothes, perform
yoga *asanas*, offer flowers and incense to
the river, and take a ritual dip. The most

Dasashvamedha Ghat at sunrise

fascinating ride is from Dasashvamedha to Manikarnika Ghat *(see p206)*.
Dozens of rowing boats ply up and down the river, and can be hired by
the hour. Rates are negotiable, so do fix the price before hiring one.

Varanasi: Nepali Ghat to Panchaganga Ghat

Along this stretch is the famed Manikarnika Ghat, one of the city's two cremation ghats. According to legend, Shiva's *mani* (crest jewel) and his consort Parvati's *karnika* (earring), fell into the nearby well while they were bathing, hence the name. Dying in Varanasi is a cause of celebration for Hindus, as it is believed to bestow instant salvation or *moksha* (liberation from the cycle of birth and death). It is said that Shiva whispers into the ears of the dying, and the old and infirm, sages and ordinary people, come here to breathe their last.

LOCATOR MAP
Nepali Ghat to Panchaganga Ghat

0 metres   50

0 yards   50

Jalasen
Ghat

Nepali Ghat
A lion stands outside a pagoda-style, woodwork temple, built by the royal family of Nepal.

Scindia Ghat
The elaborate structures on this ghat were so top heavy that they collapsed, and were rebuilt by Daulat Rao Scindia of Gwalior in 1937. A temple stands half submerged in the river, with its sanctum knee deep in the water.

Manikarnika Ghat
Funeral pyres burn day and night at this cremation ghat, while bodies wrapped in shrouds lie on biers besides piles of wooden logs. In the middle of the ghat is the well (kund) that Vishnu carved out with his discus before the Ganges flowed here.

For hotels and restaurants in this region see pp695–7 and pp724–6

RITUALS PERFORMED IN THE GANGES

A vessel for holy water

Although there are over 700 temples in Varanasi, none are more sacred than the river itself. The Ganges is worshipped as a living goddess, with the power to cleanse all earthly sins. Daily baths in her waters are advised by Hindu scriptures to prepare for the soul's final journey to liberation. Offerings of flowers and diyas floating down the river are a common and very pretty sight.

A Ritual Dip
Thousands come to Varanasi everyday, to bathe and pay obeisance to the Ganges.

Evening Aarti
The daily prayers (aarti) at dawn and dusk, serve as salutations to the river. Oil lamps are offered and bells rung while sacred mantras are chanted.

Wayside Shrine
A widow clad in white assembles flowers, incense and Ganges water in a small brass container, for paying homage at a wayside shrine.

Ganga Mahal Ghat
was also built by the king of Gwalior in the early 19th century.

Bhonsle Ghat

Akharas
The city's akharas or wrestling arenas are famous. Men live and train at these centres full time, as part of their tutelage under a guru.

Sankatha Ghat

Mehta Ghat

Aurangzeb's mosque,
built on the site of a Hindu temple that was destroyed, is a grand structure that dominates the skyline.

Jatar Ghat

Panchaganga Ghat
This ghat marks the mythical meeting place of five sacred rivers, and has numerous images of the five river goddesses – Ganga, Yamuna, Saraswati, Dhupapapa and Kirana.

Adi Keshava Ghat

Hanuman, the Monkey God, at Ganga Mahal Ghat

Exploring Varanasi

Varanasi, one of the oldest cities in the world and a contemporary of Babylon and Nineveh, dates to the 7th century BC. This eternal city, where religion is an integral part of daily life, has drawn saints, poets and pilgrims through the ages. Behind the riverside ghats are narrow crowded lanes and bazaars, where people jostle with sacred cows, saffron-robed sadhus and devotees making offerings at roadside shrines. Varanasi is also renowned as a centre of Sanskrit learning and Hindu philosophy, attracting scholars and students from all over India. The Benares Hindu University, established in the early 1900s, perpetuates this tradition.

Dramatic ramparts of the Ramnagar Fort rising from the river bank

The narrow, winding Vishwanath Gali leads to the **Vishwanath Temple**, dedicated to Shiva, who is known here as Vishwanath, "Lord of the Universe". Painted floral carvings adorn its exterior and interior walls, and it is nearly always crowded. Adjacent to it lies the ancient **Jnana Vapi Well** ("Well of Wisdom"), whose waters are said to bring enlightenment. According to legend, this well is believed to contain the linga from the original Vishwanath Temple which was destroyed by the Mughal emperor Aurangzeb in the 17th century. The **Jnana Vapi Mosque** is built on the ruins of the temple.

Further south lies the sprawling **Benares Hindu University**, founded by the eminent Sanskrit scholar, Madan Mohan Malviya. Within the campus is the renowned **Bharat Kala Bhavan Museum**, known for having one of the country's best collections of Indian paintings. About 12,000 in number, they cover the period from the 11th century to the 20th century. Most impressive are the

Mughal miniatures, notably a depiction of the Emperor Shah Jahan. The Indian sculpture section is equally impressive, housing around 2,000 pieces, from 300 BC to AD 1400. Among them are a fine 10th-century sculpture of the marriage of Shiva and Parvati and an 11th-century statue of Vishnu as Varaha (see p679). The display of Gandhara sculpture is also noteworthy.

The 17th-century **Ramnagar Fort**, lying across the river beyond Asi Ghat, has been home to the maharajas of Varanasi for 400 years. Although now in a state of disrepair, the palace still retains its charm. Ornamented swords, photographs of tiger shoots and visits by the King and Queen of Belgium line the walls. The Durbar Hall now houses the museum, where numerous objects are on display including palanquins and elephant howdahs.

🏛 **Bharat Kala Bhavan**
Tel (0542) 230 7621. ☐ Mon–Sat. 📷

🏯 **Ramnagar Fort and Museum**
☐ daily. 📷

Sarnath ㉗

Varanasi district. 10 km (6 miles) NE of Varanasi. 🚌 🚋 *Buddha Mahotsava (May).*

To Buddhists, Sarnath is as sacred as Varanasi is to Hindus. The Buddha came to the Deer Park here in 528 BC, to preach the Dharmachakra, or the Wheel of Law, his first major sermon after gaining enlightenment (see p221). Sarnath was then one of ancient India's greatest centres of learning, visited by Chinese travellers Fa-Hsien and Hiuen Tsang who wrote of its flourishing monasteries.

The central monument of the existing complex is the 5th-century AD **Dhamekh Stupa**, which is built at the site where the Buddha is believed to have delivered his sermon to five disciples. To its west, are the remains of the Dharmarajika Stupa, built by the Mauryan emperor Ashoka (see p42) to preserve the Buddha's relics. The complex also has several smaller monasteries and temples, as well as a Bodhi Tree, planted in 1931, and the statue of Anagarika Dharmapala, the founder of the society that maintained Sarnath and Bodh Gaya (see pp222–3).

The **Archaeological Museum** exhibits a superb collection of Buddhist artifacts. The highlight is the Ashokan lion capital in polished sandstone (see p4), India's national emblem.

🏛 **Archaeological Museum**
Tel (0542) 258 5002. ☐ Sat–Thu. 📷

Dhamekh Stupa, Sarnath's principal monument

Brocades from Varanasi

Varanasi, India's most ancient pilgrimage centre, is also famous for its textiles. Renowned for its gossamer-fine cotton weaves for over 2000 years, its weaving traditions acquired new splendour from the 16th century onwards, with the patronage of the Mughal emperors. Varanasi's weavers soon became adept at weaving silk with gold and silver thread, to create sumptuous

Paisley pattern on silk

brocades for royal costumes and court furnishings, embellished with the exquisite floral, animal and geometric motifs favoured by the Mughals. They also produced brocades for Tibetan monasteries, decorated with Buddhist motifs such as clouds, lotus flowers and flames. Today, a wide range of brocade saris, scarves, and Tibetan-style fabrics are made and sold in the city.

The pallav, *the culminating end piece of a sari (see p30), is the most elaborately designed part of the sari. Its rich and complex weave requires very fine and deft craftsmanship.*

Gyaser textiles *were traditionally woven for trade with Tibet. This contemporary textile has taken a single element (the flame) from a ritual cloth to create a stunning pattern.*

A panel *of more than 600 geometric motifs has been specially created as a design directory for Varanasi's brocade weavers.*

The flower motif, *the classic latifa buta, combines gold and silver threads in a style known as Ganga-Yamuna, after the two rivers whose waters are pale and dark.*

The Panch Ranga sari, *or the five-colour sari, creates a* leheriya *(wave) design in alternating colours of blue, orange, purple, pink and green, with a patterned edging in gold. The sheer richness of the design and colours are its distinguishing features.*

Contemporary brocades *recreate fish scale patterns in gold and silver threads, inspired by* Gyaser *textiles, as well as* jali *or trellis designs used in Mughal architecture.*

The creeper-covered ramparts of Allahabad Fort, built by the Mughal emperor Akbar

Allahabad ❷⑧

Allahabad district. 227 km (141 miles) SE of Lucknow. 🚉 *990,300.* 🚏 🚌 ℹ️ *Tourist Bungalow, 35 MG Marg, Civil Lines, (0532) 260 1837.* 🪷 *Kumbh Mela (every 12 years).*

Allahabad's sacred location at the confluence *(sangam)* of three rivers – the Ganges, the Yamuna and the mythical Saraswati – has given it a cultural, political and religious importance for nearly 3,000 years. Hiuen Tsang, the Buddhist monk and scholar *(see p219),* visited the town, then known as Prayag, in AD 643, and wrote in great detail of its prosperity and fame.

In the 16th century it was captured by the Mughals who renamed it Allahabad. Later, the British maintained a large military presence in the city and established the law courts and the university. Jawaharlal Nehru *(see p57),* India's first prime minister, was born here in 1889, and the city later became a major centre of the Independence Movement. Today Allahabad is a quietly prosperous provincial centre, the broad, tree-lined avenues of the Civil Lines area contrasting with the congested bustle of the old city.

Allahabad Fort was built in 1583 by Akbar, who had a 3rd-century BC Ashokan pillar brought here from Kausambi. The pillar, unfortunately, is in a part of the fort that is not open to the public. On the fort's eastern side, is a temple complex with an undying banyan tree, the **Akshaivata.** Legend has it that anyone who leapt from its branches would achieve salvation from the endless cycle of rebirths. After too many such attempts, the tree was fenced off, and a special permit is required from the local tourist office to view it.

Khusrau Bagh, a tranquil Mughal garden on the western edge of town, is named after Emperor Jahangir's eldest son who led an unsuccessful rebellion against his father and was later murdered during the battle over succession with his brother, Shah Jahan in 1615. His tomb lies next to those of his sister and his mother. The latter, a Rajput princess from Jaipur, distraught by the war between her husband and her son, took an overdose of opium. The *chhatris* on her tomb show Rajput influence.

Anand Bhavan, ancestral home of India's premier political dynasty, the Nehru-Gandhi family, now houses a museum of Nehru memorabilia and chronicles the high points of the Independence Movement. Close by, in the Civil Lines area, is the fantastically arched and turreted **Muir College** built in 1870, and regarded a fine example of Indo-Saracenic architecture. Some glazed blue and white tiles still cling to the dome and a single tower soars to a height of 60 m (197 ft). Across the road is the **Allahabad Museum** which has an interesting collection of terracottas from Kausambi and some 10th- to 13th-century sculpture from the Chandela era. Across Civil Lines to the west stands the **All Saints Cathedral.** Constructed in 1877 and designed by William Emmerson, architect of the Victoria Memorial in Kolkata *(see pp274–5),* it is lined with Jaipur marble inside.

Gothic façade of the All Saints Cathedral

🏰 **Allahabad Fort**
◐ *closed to the public.*

🏛 **Anand Bhavan**
◷ *Tue–Sun.* 🎟️

🏛 **Allahabad Museum**
◷ *Tue–Sun.* 🎟️

The tombs of Prince Khusrau and his sister, Khusrau Bagh

Environs

Kausambi, is 63 km (39 miles) and about an hour's drive from Allahabad on the eastern bank of the Yamuna. Excavated ruins of a stupa, a palace and extensive ramparts lie within a 2-km (1.3-mile) radius. While local legend holds that the city was built by the Pandavas, heroes of the *Mahabharata (see p26)*, excavations reveal that a Buddhist community flourished here between 600 BC and AD 600. The Buddha himself came here to preach. The site contains the remains of a paved brick road, small houses, each with a ceramic drain, and the stump of an Ashokan pillar dating to the 3rd century BC (a second pillar was moved to the Allahabad Fort). Some terracotta artifacts and seals from 200 BC which were found here are now in the Allahabad Museum. Surrounded by fields and villages, with the river in the background, Kausambi has an aura of great serenity.

Chitrakoot's Ramghat, with temples on the banks of the Mandakini river

The remains of mud and brick ramparts at Kausambi

Chitrakoot ⊛

Banda district. 128 km (80 miles) SW of Allahabad. ▣ *Karwi, 8 km (5 miles) NE of town centre, then taxi or bus.* ▦ ⓘ *UPSTDC Tourism Bungalow, (05198) 224 219.* ⌂ *daily.*

This pilgrim town on the banks of the Mandakini river, though in neighbouring Madhya Pradesh, is easier to access from Allahabad. Chitrakoot, literally "the Hill of Many Wonders" refers to the forested **Kamadgiri Hill**, where according to the *Ramayana*, Rama, Sita and Lakshman spent a portion of their 14-year exile. Below the hill lies **Hanuman Dhara**, a natural spring that flows over a delightful image of the monkey god, Hanuman, placed in a recess. Dotted with numerous temples, and full of sadhus, the town has a unique charm. Boat rides from the attractive **Ramghat**, the town's main ghat, provide an impressive view of the temples along the river bank.

Kalinjar Fort ⊛

Banda district. 190 km (118 miles) W of Allahabad. ▣ *Banda, 53 km (33 miles) N of Kalinjar Fort, then taxi or bus.* ▦ ⌂ *daily.*

One of India's oldest forts, Kalinjar was called Kanagora by Ptolemy, the 2nd-century AD Greek geographer. Its strategic location on the route between North and South India made it a coveted target for many rulers. It has thus had a very turbulent history, and was successively occupied by many medieval rulers, until it fell to the Afghan ruler Sher Shah Sur *(see p79)* in 1545.

Seven gateways, named after seven planets, and lined with sculptures and carvings lead to the fort. These include a giant Shiva with 18 arms and a dancing Ganesha. The **Neelkanth Temple** inside the fort, is dedicated to Shiva. Still in worship, the temple's inner sanctum contains an ancient linga.

THE KUMBH MELA

Hindu legend has it that during a war over the urn *(kumbh)* of immortal nectar *(amrit)* between the gods and demons, Vishnu gave the urn to Garuda, his winged mount. During his flight, four drops of the nectar fell on four places, Nasik *(see p474)*, Ujjain *(see p246)*, Haridwar *(see p184)* and Allahabad. A Kumbh Mela is thus held at each spot in turn,

Pilgrims at Allahabad's Kumbh Mela in 2001

every three years, when certain planetary configurations, transform the waters of the Ganges into nectar. Pilgrims from all over India, converge at the Kumbh Mela to wash away their sins, making it the world's largest religious gathering. Specially built tent-cities and stalls spring up to cater to the influx. At Allahabad's Kumbh Mela (Jan–Feb 2001) almost 30 million devotees took a bath on Mauni Amavasya (24 Jan), the most sacred of the six main bathing days. The next Kumbh Melas will be held in Haridwar in 2010 and in Allahabad in 2013.

BIHAR & JHARKHAND

The name Bihar derives from the Sanskrit word *vihara*, or monastery – an apt appellation for a state which was the birthplace of Buddhism. Major sites associated with the life and teachings of the Buddha, such as Bodh Gaya, Nalanda and Rajgir, lie in the dry plains of central Bihar and are the main attractions for visitors to the state. Northern Bihar is a fertile agricultural plain, watered by the River Ganges and its tributaries, where the famous Patna rice is grown. In November 2000, the southern part of Bihar became the new state of Jharkhand, which is dominated by a scenic and thickly forested highland called the Chhota Nagpur Plateau. The game sanctuaries of Palamau and Hazaribagh are located here. Jharkhand is rich in mineral resources, and is also the home of several indigenous tribes, believed to be among the earliest settlers of the Indian subcontinent.

SIGHTS AT A GLANCE

Towns & Cities
Jamshedpur **16**
Munger **5**
Patna **1**
Ranchi **15**

Hill Stations
Netarhat **14**

Historic Sites
Nalanda **7**
Rajgir **8**
Sasaram **2**
Vaishali **4**

Temple Towns & Holy Places
Bodh Gaya **10**
Deoghar **6**

Gaya **9**
Parasnath **11**
Sonepur **3**

National Parks
Hazaribagh Wildlife Sanctuary **12**
Palamau National Park **13**

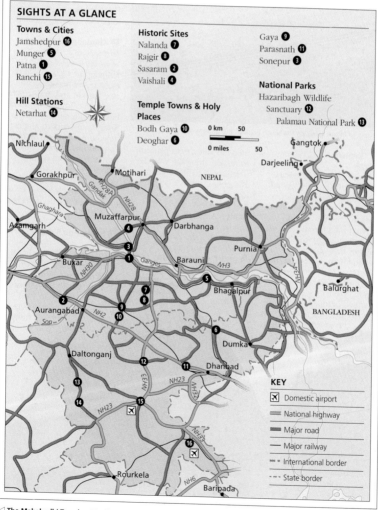

KEY

☒ Domestic airport

National highway

Major road

Major railway

– – International border

- - - State border

◁ The Mahabodhi Temple at Bodh Gaya, the most important Buddhist pilgrimage site

Patna ❶

The capital of Bihar is a modern city with ancient roots going back to 600 BC. During the reign of the Maurya and Gupta empires *(see p42)* Patna, then known as Pataliputra, was renowned as one of the great cities of Asia, but today it is a congested urban sprawl, stretching along the banks of the Ganges. West Patna, laid out by the British, has gracious mansions and administrative buildings, while the eastern end comprises the old city, a warren of crowded lanes surrounding medieval monuments and bustling bazaars.

Didarganj Yakshi

A view of Patna, lying on the south bank of the Ganges

🏛 Golghar

◯ daily.

Patna's signature landmark, the Golghar (literally "round house"), is an extraordinary dome that resembles a giant beehive. Built in 1786 by Captain John Garstin as a silo to store grain during the famines that occurred frequently in those days, the Golghar was never actually put to use. The structure is 125 m (410 ft) wide at the base and gradually tapers up to a height of 29 m (95 ft). Two external staircases spiral upwards

along its sides, with platforms to rest on along the way. The idea was to haul the grain up, and pour it down a hole at the top into the dome's pit, which had a capacity of 124,285 tonnes. A remarkable echo can be heard inside the structure. During the monsoon, the dome's summit offers impressive views of the Ganges which, in this season, can swell to a width of 8 km (5 miles).

🏛 State Museum

Tel (0612) 223 5731. ◯ Tue–Sun. 📷
Some remarkable treasures are displayed in the State Museum. Among them is the Mauryan-era (probably 3rd century BC) polished stone image of the Didarganj Yakshi (female attendant), considered a masterpiece of Indian sculpture. Other highlights include Gandharan style statues of Bodhisattvas; outstanding Buddha images in bronze and black stone, dating from the Pala period (8th–12th centuries); terracotta figurines, ancient Buddhist scriptures and a collection of Tibetan *thangkas*. The museum also boasts a 15-m (49-ft) long fossilized tree trunk, believed to be 200 million years old.

🏛 Khudabaksh Library

Tel (0612) 267 0209.
www.kblibrary.bih.nic.in ◯ Sat–Thu.
Founded in 1900, this library has a renowned collection of rare Persian and Arabic manuscripts, including a group of beautiful illuminated medieval Korans, and superb Mughal miniature paintings. Its rarest exhibits are volumes salvaged from the sacking of the Moorish University in Cordoba, Spain, in the 11th century, though how they found their way to India still remains a mystery.

🚩 Harmandir Sahib

◯ daily.
This historic Sikh gurdwara marks the birthplace of the firebrand tenth guru, Gobind Singh *(see p103)*, who was born here in 1666. Regarded as one of the four holiest Sikh shrines,

The beehive-shaped Golghar, built as a granary in the 18th century

The eclectic private collection at the Jalan Museum

the marble temple was built in the 19th century by Maharaja Ranjit Singh *(see p104)*. On the floor above the main sanctum is a museum with the guru's relics.

🏛 Jalan Museum

By appointment. **Tel** *(0612) 264 1121.*
Also known as Qila ("Fort") House, this museum's eclectic collection, gathered by a 19th-century ancestor of the Jalan family, includes Chinese paintings, Mughal jade and silverware, Napoleon's bed and Marie Antoinette's Sèvres porcelain. Qila House itself is an interesting structure, built

on the ruins of a 16th-century fort constructed by the Afghan ruler, Sher Shah Sur *(see p79).*

🏛 Kumrahar

◯ *Tue–Sun.* 🎟
This site contains the ruins of the ancient city of Pataliputra. Excavations have unearthed elaborately carved wooden ramparts, polished sandstone pillars and the remains of a vast Mauryan assembly hall that is said to have stood here in the 2nd century BC. A museum here displays some of these finds, which date from an era when Patna was described by Megasthenes, the

VISITORS' CHECKLIST

Patna district. 1,015 km (631 miles) E of Delhi. 🚉 *1,377,000.*
✈ *7 km (4 miles) W of the city centre.* 🚌 🚆 🛈 *Bihar Tourism, JP Loknayak Bhavan, Fraser Rd, (0612) 222 5411.* 🛒 *Mon–Sat.* 🎭 *Patliputra Mahotsava (Mar).*

Greek envoy to the Mauryan court, as "a city of light, where even wooden walls shine bright as glass".

🏚 Old Opium Warehouse

Gulzarbagh. ◯ *Mon–Fri.*
Located in a walled compound on the river bank, the opium warehouse of the East India Company is now the Government Printing Press. Opium was packaged in its three long, porticoed buildings and sent by boat to Kolkata.

Environs

Maner, 30 km (19 miles) west of Patna, is a major centre of Islamic learning. It has the fine 16th-century mausoleum of the Sufi saint Hazrat Makhdum Yahya Maneri. It is also famous for *laddoos*, a confection made of gramflour and molasses.

PATNA CITY CENTRE

Golghar ①
Khudabaksh Library ③
State Museum ②

0 metres   500
0 yards   500

MANER

River Ganges

Mahendra Ghat Ferry Terminal

Gandhi Bus Stand

ASHOK RAJ PATH

Khudabaksh Library ③

① Golghar

MAHATMA GANDHI MARG

Gandhi Maidan

MAHATMA GANDHI MAIDAN RD

Birla Mandir

KHANJANCHI ROAD

Old Opium Warehouse, Harmandir Sahib, Jalan Museum

BUDDHA MARG

State Museum ②

BAILEY ROAD

DAK BUNGALOW ROAD

S P VERMA ROAD

EXHIBITION ROAD

FRASER ROAD

RAJENDRA PATH

KRANTI MARG

RAMKRISHNA AVENUE

ARYA KUMAR ROAD

SAIDPUR ROAD

Iskcon Temple

BICHAND PATEL MARG

Patna Junction Railway Station

OLD BYPASS RD

Rajendra Nagar Railway Station

Airport
7 km (4 miles)

Kumrahar

Key to Symbols *see back flap*

The magnificent 16th-century tomb of the Afghan ruler Sher Shah Sur at Sasaram

Sasaram ❷

Rohtas district. 158 km (98 miles) SW of Patna. 🚇 🚌

The dusty town of Sasaram, a three-hour drive west of Patna on the historic Grand Trunk Road *(see p179)*, is famous for the **Mausoleum of Sher Shah Sur**, the great Afghan ruler *(see p79)*. This mid-16th-century architectural masterpiece is, to quote architectural historian Percy Brown, a testament to, "the aesthetic capacity of the Indian architect at its greatest, and his genius at its highest".

With a spectacular setting in the middle of an artificial lake, the pyramidal sandstone structure rises in five tiers to a height of 45 m (148 ft). The first two tiers comprise of a stepped basement and a high terrace that seems to emerge from the water, with a pavilion at each corner. The octagonal tomb is set on this plinth, and tapers towards the dome in three elegant layers of arches, crenellated parapets and small pillared kiosks. The broad dome is crowned by a large gilded lotus finial. All these elements combine to create a superbly proportioned structure that appears to float above the lake.

Curiously, the tomb is orientated eight degrees off its main axis – a mistake that the architect, Aliwal Khan, has skilfully disguised. The brilliant yellow and blue tiles are still seen in places. Nearby is the tomb of Sher Shah's father, Hasan Sur, built by the same architect.

Sonepur ❸

Saran district. 25 km (16 miles) N of Patna. 🚌 ℹ️ *Bihar Tourism, Patna, (0612) 222 5411.* 📅 *Sonepur Mela (Oct/Nov).*

North of Patna, across the 7.5-km (5-mile) long Mahatma Gandhi Bridge over the Ganges, is the little town of Sonepur, known for its annual *mela*, reputedly the largest livestock fair in Asia. The month-long fair begins on the full moon of Kartik Purnima, which usually falls in October or November. The *mela* site is a sandy bank at the confluence of the Ganges and Gandak rivers, and attracts millions of sadhus, pilgrims and local rural families, as well as livestock traders from all over India. On sale are elephants, camels, horses and cows, and an array

A mobile zoo at Sonepur's huge cattle fair

of exotic birds. As a sideshow to the buying and selling of animals, grain and fodder, are several troupes of folk singers and magicians, *nautanki* (vaudeville) groups, dance bands, wrestlers and gymnasts, all exhibiting their skills on the sands. In between trading and entertainment, everyone takes a holy dip in the river during this most auspicious period in the Hindu calendar. The state tourism department sets up a tourist village a week in advance of the fair, and cottages and tents can be booked at their office in Patna.

Even if buying an elephant (prices begin at about US$200) is not on a visitor's agenda, the Sonepur Mela, with its colourful combination of religion, entertainment and commerce, is an unforgettable experience.

Elephants being bathed during the Sonepur Mela

Vaishali ❹

Vaishali district. 55 km (34 miles) N of Patna. 🚌 🏠 *Tourist Information Centre, Vaishali (06225) 284 425.*

Set in the lush green landscape of north Bihar, dotted with groves of banana and litchi trees, Vaishali is an important religious site. Mahavira, founder of the Jain faith *(see p396)*, is said to have been born here in 599 BC. It is also the place where the Buddha preached his last sermon *(see p221)*. In the 6th century BC, Vaishali was a flourishing city under the Lichhavi rulers who established one of the world's first city republics here. A well-preserved **Mauryan Stone Pillar**, dating from the 3rd century BC, with a life-size lion sitting atop it, is located 4 km (2.5 miles) west of the Tourist Lodge.

Close to the pillar is the **Ramkund Tank**, also known as the Monkey Tank, which is now a stagnant pond. According to legend, it was dug by monkeys, who offered the

The renowned Bihar School of Yoga, inside Munger Fort

The lion atop the 3rd-century BC pillar, Vaishali

hungry Buddha a bowl of honey here – a scene often depicted in Buddhist sculpture and painting. Also near the pillar, are the ruins of a 5th-century BC brick stupa. It is believed to have been built by the Lichhavi rulers soon after the Buddha's death to enshrine his ashes. Ongoing excavations have revealed the brick foundations of various other stupas. In 1996, Japanese Buddhists built a temple and a huge white **Vishwa Shanti Stupa** ("World Peace Stupa"), re-establishing Vaishali on the Buddhist pilgrimage circuit.

MADHUBANI PAINTING

The vibrant Madhubani folk paintings *(see p81)* of north Bihar have now gained international acclaim and popularity. Painted on the walls of village homes by women, Madhubani art features motifs and themes inspired by Hindu mythology, nature and festivals, as well as by everyday life. Especially intricate compositions are created for the *kohbar*, or bridal room, for the wedding night, usually featuring a god and goddess surrounded by a host of small birds and animals, and watched over by the sun, moon and stars. In recent years, with Madhubani women having participated in international exhibitions in foreign countries, new motifs have crept into their work, such as skyscrapers, aeroplanes and women in stiletto heels. The vibrant colours used are made of vegetable and mineral dyes, and the paintings are drawn with thin bamboo sticks. Madhubani paintings are now also being done on paper and fabric, and are widely available for sale in many Indian cities.

A Madhubani painting, with its strong lines and colours

Munger ❺

Munger district. 180 km (112 miles) E of Patna. 🚉 🏠 *Tourist Information Centre, Fort Area, Munger (06344) 222 392.*

Picturesquely located on the banks of the Ganges, Munger is home to the famous **Bihar School of Yoga**, established by Swami Satyanand, and now run by his disciple Swami Niranjanananand. The school lies within the 15th-century Munger Fort, and welcomes visitors. The fort was successively occupied by the Mughals, various regional rulers and the British. Near the north gate of the fort is an 18th-century British cemetery with ornate pyramid-shaped tombs.

🏫 **Bihar School of Yoga**
Tel (06344) 222 430. ◯ *daily.*

Deoghar ❻

Deoghar district. 180 km (112 miles) E of Patna. 🚉 🚌 🏠 *Tourist Information Centre, (06432) 222 422.* 🎪 *Mela (Jul/Aug).*

Deoghar's **Baidyanath Dham** is an important Shiva temple in India. It is said to mark the spot where the heart of Shiva's consort Parvati fell, as the grief-stricken Shiva carried her corpse across the earth *(see p279)*. An object of special worship is the linga inside the temple, one of Shiva's 12 *jyotirlingas (see p202)*, believed to have miraculously materialized out of light. The month-long annual *mela* here attracts over 100,000 pilgrims every day.

Nalanda ⑦

Bodhisattva in Temple 3

Once the most prestigious centre of learning in Asia, the Buddhist University of Nalanda, founded in the 5th century AD, had over 5,000 international students and teachers, and a library of nine million manuscripts. Built on a hallowed site where the Buddha had often stayed, Nalanda flourished until AD 1199, when it was looted and destroyed by the Turkish raider, Bakhtiar Khalji. The evocative ruins of its monasteries and temples still convey a vivid impression of the serene and ordered life of contemplation and learning that prevailed here.

Temple 12
The remains of a torana *stand in front of this 7th-century temple, which faces the row of monasteries.*

★ Temple 3
Nalanda's main temple, and its largest structure (31 m/102 ft high), dates to the 6th century. It has a shrine chamber at the top and small stupas at its corners.

Monastery 1A was probably built by a king of Sumatra in the 9th century.

| 0 metres | 50 |
| 0 yards | 50 |

★ Votive Stupas
Located in the courtyard surrounding Temple 3, these have plaster images of standing Bodhisattvas and seated Buddhas.

STAR FEATURES

★ Temple 3

★ Votive Stupas

★ Dado Panels from Temple 2

A View of the Monasteries

Monks' cells surround a courtyard in each of the 11 monasteries. The ruins display skilful brickwork.

Temple 13 has a brick-making furnace to its north.

Temple 14
Traces of painting can be seen here in a niche with a pedestal, where a large image of the Buddha once stood.

Monastery 8 has an imposing shrine in its courtyard. All the monasteries stand on terraces.

Museum

★ Dado Panels from Temple 2
This 7th-century temple's basement, which is all that remains, has an elaborately sculpted dado with over 200 panels carved with deities, animals and floral motifs.

Brickwork
Layers of much earlier construction, some of it dating back to the 3rd century BC, are visible in the brickwork at Nalanda.

HIUEN TSANG IN NALANDA

The great Chinese scholar-monk, Hiuen Tsang, travelled across forbidding deserts and mountains to come to Nalanda in the early 7th century AD. He spent 12 years both studying and teaching here, and was dazzled by Nalanda's "soaring domes and pinna-cles, pearl-red pillars carved and ornamented, and richly adorned balustrades". On his return to China he settled down at the Big Goose Pagoda in Xian, where he translated into Chinese the Buddhist scriptures he had brought back with him from Nalanda.

Chinese print of Hiuen Tsang

Hot sulphur springs at Rajgir, surrounded by temples and rest houses

Rajgir ❽

Nalanda district. 115 kms (72 miles)
SE of Patna. 🚶 33,700. 🚍 🚌
🛈 Bihar Tourism, Kund Market,
(06119) 252 73.

Surrounded by five holy
hills, the picturesque little
town of Rajgir is important for
Buddhists as well as Jains.
Both Buddha and Mahavira,
founder of Jainism, spent
many months meditating and
preaching here. The hills
around are dotted with Jain
temples, the ruins of
monasteries and meditation
caves. Dominating Rajgir is
the large new Japanese-built
marble and sandstone
Vishwa Shanti Stupa on
Ratnagiri Hill, with its four
gilded statues of the Buddha.
Visitors can go up to the
stupa by chairlift. From
here, a path leads to the
adjoining **Griddhakuta Hill**
("Vulture's Peak"), a site
much venerated by Buddhists.
Two rock-cut caves here
were a favourite retreat of
the Buddha, and it was on
this hill that he preached
two of his most famous
sermons. The incident of
the Buddha subduing a
wild elephant, a scene often
depicted in Buddhist art, also
took place in Rajgir.
To the west of Griddhakuta
Hill is **Vaibhava Hill**, at the
foot of which are hot sulphur
springs, crowded with people
seeking a medicinal dip. On
top of the hill are the seven
Saptaparni Caves where the
First Buddhist Council met
soon after the Buddha's
death to record his teachings.
Below them on the hill is the
Pippala Watchtower, a

curious rock and stone
structure, with cells for
guards. It dates to the 5th
century BC, when Rajgir was
the capital of the Magadha
Empire *(see p42)*, ruled by
King Bimbisara who became
a devotee of the Buddha. The
remains of the great drystone
cyclopean wall he built can
still be seen on Rajgir's hills.

Environs
Pawapuri, 38 km (24 miles)
east of Rajgir, is sacred to Jains
as the place where the founder
of their faith, Mahavira, died
in 500 BC. A lotus-filled tank,
with the marble Jalmandir
Temple in the middle of it,
marks the site of his cremation.

Gaya ❾

Gaya district. 100 km (62 miles)
S of Patna. 🚶 383,200. 🚍 🚌
🛈 Bihar State Tourist Office,
Railway Station, (0631) 232 155.

Stretching along the banks
of the Phalgu river, Gaya
along with Varanasi and
Allahabad, is regarded as one
of the three most sacred sites

for performing Hindu funeral
rites. It is believed that Vishnu
himself sanctified Gaya,
decreeing that prayers for
departed souls, performed
here, would absolve all their
earthly sins. Dominating the
religious life of the city is the
Vishnupad Temple, which is
not open to non-Hindus, but
no such restrictions apply to
the picturesque ghats and
shrines along the river front.

Environs
The **Barabar Caves**, cut deep
into a granite hill, are 45 km
(28 miles) north of Gaya, along
a bumpy jeep road. They
were the inspiration for the
Marabar Caves in EM Forster's
famous novel, *A Passage to
India*. Dating to the 3rd
century BC, these are the
earliest examples of rock-cut
caves in India. Of the four
caves, built for ascetics on the
orders of the Mauryan
emperor Ashoka, the two
most impressive are the
Lomas Rishi and **Sudama
Caves**. They are remarkable
for the highly lustrous polish
on the stone, and for the way
in which the caves have been
shaped to imitate the rounded
wood and bamboo dwellings
which were common at that
time. Even the interior walls
have perpendicular grooves
cut into the stone, in imitation
of bamboo strips. The façade
of the Lomas Rishi Cave has
fine lattice-work carving, and
a charming row of elephants
paying homage to stupas.
   It is unsafe to explore this
wild and rugged area without
reliable guides, recommended
by the Bihar Tourism office at
Gaya's railway station.

Rituals being performed at the Phalgu Ghat in Gaya

In the Buddha's Footsteps

The Buddha was born in 566 BC as Siddhartha Gautama, prince of the kingdom of Kapilavastu. Though born in Lumbini, in Nepal, all the places associated with his life and his teachings are in Bihar and Uttar Pradesh. These are now part of a well-travelled circuit for

The Buddha's footprints

Buddhist pilgrims, who follow in the Buddha's footsteps from Bodh Gaya, where he attained enlightenment; to Sarnath where he preached his first sermon; through other places he visited regularly, and finally to Kushinagar, where he died in 486 BC.

Renouncing *his princely life, Prince Siddhartha (represented here by a riderless horse) left his palace and his family at the age of 30, to search for answers to the meaning of human existence and suffering.*

Emaciated *by fasts and penances while he spent six years living with ascetics and wandering as a beggar, Prince Siddhartha found that such self-mortification gave him no answers.*

Enlightenment *came at Bodh Gaya where, after meditating for 49 days under the Bodhi Tree, he discovered that the cause of suffering is desire; and that desire can be conquered by following the "Eightfold Path" of Righteousness.*

The First Sermon, *delivered at Sarnath (see p208), contained the essence of his teachings. Eschewing asceticism, rituals, caste and class distinctions, his Eightfold Path prescribed Right Thought, Understanding, Speech, Action, Livelihood, Effort, Concentration and Contemplation.*

The Buddha's Death *took place in 486 BC. He fell ill after eating wild mushrooms prepared by one of his followers, and died in a grove of sal trees at Kushinagar, where a stupa marks the site of his cremation.*

BUDDHIST PILGRIM SITES

The Buddhist Trail *attracts Buddhists from all over the world, including countries such as Japan and Thailand. Many stupas and temples along the pilgrimage circuit owe their existence to these devotees. This Buddha image was built by the Japanese.*

See also the features on Little Tibet (p123) and Buddhist Iconography (p141).

The Thai Monastery in Bodh Gaya, built like a traditional *wat* (temple)

Bodh Gaya ⑩

Gaya district. 115 km (71 miles) SE of
Patna. 🚶 30,900. 🚆 Gaya, 13 km
(8 miles) N of town centre, then taxi
or bus. 🚌 ℹ️ *Bihar Tourism, 34
Mahabodhi Market Complex, (0631)
240 0672.* 📅 *Monlam Chenmo
Prayers (Jan/Feb), Buddha Jayanti (May).*

The holiest site for Buddhists
from all over the world, Bodh
Gaya is the place where the
Buddha attained enlight-
enment. The focal point of the
town is the **Mahabodhi
Temple**, whose soaring
pyramidal spire dominates
the landscape. The temple is
enclosed on three sides by a
1st-century BC stone railing,
carved with lotus medallions
and scenes from the Buddha's
life, and includes the sacred
Bodhi Tree, under which the
Buddha meditated before he
attained enlightenment.

The original temple at this
spot was a circular stupa, built
by the Mauryan king Ashoka
in the 3rd century BC, but a
major reconstruction in the 7th
century AD gave the temple
its present form. In the 12th
century, it was severely
damaged by Muslim invaders,
but faithfully restored in the
14th century by Burmese
kings, who also added the
replicas of the main spire
at each corner of the
temple. Then, as
Buddhism went into
near eclipse in
northern India, the
temple site was
flooded and silted
over, and
effectively "lost"
for centuries.
Some Burmese
Buddhists
rediscovered it
in the late 19th
century. The temple ruins were
then excavated and restored.

Today, Bodh Gaya once
again flourishes as an international centre for Buddhism.
Temples and monasteries built
by various countries, including

The 25-m (82-ft) Buddha statue,
erected by the Japanese

China, Japan, Sri Lanka, Vietnam, Thailand, Taiwan, Korea,
Bhutan and Nepal, dot the
town. The **Thai Temple** is
the most picturesque, while
the modern **Japanese Temple**
is remarkable for the 25-m
(82-ft) high Buddha statue
that towers in front of it. The
Bhutanese and **Tibetan
Monasteries** are filled with
colourful murals and prayer
wheels, and both are always
thronged by red-robed monks.

In the courtyard around the
Mahabodhi Temple, monks
meditate at the stupas, novi-
tiates have their heads
shaved, and pilgrims pray
before the Bodhi Tree. For
three weeks during the
winter, a tented city springs
up around the temple, as
thousands of monks and
pilgrims congregate here
for the Monlam Chenmo
Prayers, often presided
over by the Dalai Lama
and other venerated
figures from the
Buddhist world.

Across the street,
the **Archaeological
Museum** has
fragments of the
beautiful
original 3rd-
century BC
temple railing,
and bronze and
stone images from the 8th to
12th centuries, which were
excavated during the
restoration of the temple.

🏛 **Archaeological Museum**
🕐 *Sat–Thu.* 📷

Pilgrims gathered around
the Bodhi Tree

Beautifully carved stupas in the
temple courtyard

THE SACRED BODHI TREE

According to local lore, the original Bodhi Tree (*Ficus
religiosa*) was cut down by Emperor Ashoka's wife because
she was jealous of the time he
spent at his Buddhist devotions.
The emperor then revived the tree
by nurturing its roots with gallons
of milk, and built a protective stone
railing around it. The tree that
stands today is said to come from
the same stock as the original tree.
Ashoka's son Mahinda took a
sapling from the original tree to Sri
Lanka on one of his proselytizing
missions. The tree flourished there,
and its sapling was later brought
back to be planted at Bodh Gaya
after the original tree had died.

Bodh Gaya: Mahabodhi Temple

Lotus carving on the Chakramana

The Mahabodhi Temple complex, a UNESCO World Heritage monument, marks the site where, more than 2,500 years ago, Prince Siddhartha meditated on the causes of human suffering, found the answers he was seeking under the Bodhi Tree, and became the Buddha – the Enlightened One. The best time to visit the complex is at dusk, when thousands of oil lamps bathe the temple in a golden light, and the sound of Buddhist prayers fills the air.

VISITORS' CHECKLIST

Mahabodhi Temple Complex.
ℹ️ Temple Office, (0631) 240 0445. ⭕ daily. 📷 extra charges.
🎎 Buddha Jayanti (May).

The Buddha
This gilded stone image (late 10th century) in the main sanctum has an aura of great serenity. The pedestal is carved with alternating lions and elephants.

The Spire, 54 m (177 ft) high, is carved in tiers and capped by an umbrella-like finial.

The Torana
The gateway to the temple is made of granite and covered with inscriptions from the Buddha's teachings. It dates from the 8th century.

The Bodhi Tree under which the Buddha spent 49 days.

The entrance leads to the main sanctum with the Buddha image.

The Chakramana
Carved with lotuses, this sacred promenade was where the Buddha walked, meditating on whether to spread his message to the world.

The Vajrashila
The red sandstone seat beneath the Bodhi Tree marks the spot where the Buddha sat. It probably dates to the 3rd century BC.

Parasnath ⑪

Giridih district. 179 km (111 miles) NE of Ranchi. 🚉 🚌 Madhuban.

An important destination for Jain pilgrims, Parasnath is named after Parsvanatha, the 23rd Jain *tirthankara (see p396)*, who is believed to have attained nirvana here. Clustered on top of Sikayi Hill, the highest peak in Jharkhand at 1,400 m (4,593 ft), are 24 Jain temples, each one dedicated to one of the Jain *tirthankaras*. The temple on the highest point is dedicated to Parsvanatha. Pilgrims begin their climb from Madhuban, a stopover at the foot of the hill, and it takes over three hours, through forested slopes. Palanquins are available to carry those who do not want to walk. The views from the top are magnificent.

Hazaribagh Wildlife Sanctuary ⑫

Hazaribagh district. 107 km (66 miles) N of Ranchi. 🚉 Hazaribagh Rd Station, 67 km (42 miles) S of Pokharia, the main entry point, then bus. 🚌 ℹ️ Tourist Office, near bus stand, Hazaribagh town, located 16 km (10 miles) S of Pokharia. For permission contact Divisional Forest Officer, Hazaribagh, (06546) 22 3340.

Set in the undulating Chhota Nagpur Plateau covered with tropical deciduous forests, this wildlife sanctuary is 16 km (10 miles) from Hazaribagh. Hazaribagh means "Thousand Tigers" and this quiet town's environs were once famous for their tiger population. However, as a result of deforestation, most

En route to Netarhat, through the picturesque Chhota Nagpur Plateau

of the tigers are gone, and spotting a tiger from one of the ten viewing platforms is now rare. The 190 sq-km (73 sq-mile) sanctuary, established in 1954, is bisected by the Ranchi-Kolkata Highway which, with its heavy traffic, has driven away many animals to other habitats. But there are plenty of wild boar, nilgai and leopard, and its thick forests are a haven for birdlife.

Leopard at Palamau Park

Palamau National Park ⑬

Palamau district. 170 km (106 miles) W of Ranchi. 🚉 Daltonganj, 24 km (15 miles) NW of Betla, the main entry point. 🚌 ℹ️ Tourist Office, Betla, (06562) 25 6513. For permits contact the Deputy Director, Palamau National Park, Daltonganj. Jeeps are available at Betla. 🏞️

Also known as Betla National Park, Palamau National Park, on the northwestern edge of the Chhota Nagpur Plateau, is set in hilly tribal country, with the Koel and Burha rivers flowing through it. The park

is dotted with bamboo, *sal (Shorea robusta)* groves, towering *mahua (Madhuca indica)* trees from whose pale yellow flower the area's tribal people (Oraons and Mundas) make a potent liquor, and grassland. The sanctuary is inhabited by wild elephants, deer, leopards, tigers (44 at last count in 1997) and several bird species. There are numerous watch-towers and hides that have been strategically placed around the water holes. The picturesque ruins of two 16th-century forts, hot springs and a few tribal villages also lie within the park.

Netarhat ⑭

Palamau district. 156 km (97 miles) W of Ranchi. 🚌

The only hill station in Bihar and Jharkhand, Netarhat is situated at an altitude of 1,140 m (3,740 ft) and lies deep within the forested Chhota Nagpur hills, just off the Ranchi-Hazaribagh Highway. There are several pleasant rambles in the hills around this little town, and fine views of the surrounding countryside from **Magnolia Point**. The scenic **Burhaga Falls** make an enchanting picnic spot. A curious building here is a huge wooden Swiss-style chalet, formerly the country retreat of the British governors of Bihar, and now a boarding school for boys. The school authorities usually welcome visitors.

Watchtower in the Hazaribagh Wildlife Sanctuary

Fields on the outskirts of Ranchi

Ranchi 15

Ranchi district. 289 kms (180 miles) E of Patna. 846,500. 5 km (3 miles) S of town centre. Birsa Vihar Tourist Complex, Main Rd, (0651) 230 1230. daily. Rath Yatra (Jun/Jul).

The capital of the newly formed state of Jharkhand, Ranchi is a good base from which to explore the natural beauty of the Chhota Nagpur Plateau. The summer capital of Bihar in the days of the British Raj, Ranchi still attracts visitors keen to escape the heat and dust of Bihar's plains. The town's main attraction is the 17th-century **Jagannath Temple**, perched on a hill in the south-western outskirts. Like the Jagannath Temple at Puri (see p313), this temple also holds an annual chariot festival.

The Chhota Nagpur Plateau is the home of the forest-dwelling Munda and Oraon tribes. The wide-ranging exhibits and collections of artifacts in the **Ranchi Museum** provide a comprehensive picture of their lifestyles and social structures.

Oraon tribal girls dancing

Ranchi Museum
Mon–Sat. public hols.

Environs
Hundru Falls, 45 km (28 miles) east of Ranchi, is a picturesque picnic spot. This is the point where the Subarnarekha river drops down dramatically from the Chhota Nagpur Plateau to form a 100-m (328-ft) water-fall, which splashes into the pools below. The sleepy town of **McCluskiegunj**, 40 km (25 miles) northwest of Ranchi, is a quaint relic of the Raj. It was established as a settlement for Eurasians who felt they belonged neither to British nor to Indian society, and wanted a haven of their own. Today, only a handful of the original settlers remain (many have emigrated to Australia), living out their old age in cottages crammed with their treasured collections of English china ornaments, and adorned with pictures of the British royal family.

Jamshedpur 16

East Singbhum district. 130 kms (81 miles) SE of Ranchi. 570,300. Tourist Information Centre, Bistupur, (0657) 243 2892. daily. Founder's Day (Mar).

One of India's major industrial centres, Jamshedpur is a rare oasis of cleanliness and efficiency in this region. The planned township, surrounded by lakes, rivers and the pretty Dolma Hills, was established in 1908 by the Parsi tycoon, Sir Jamshedji Tata (see p446). He is regarded as the father of industrial development in India. The Tata Iron and Steel Company (TISCO) was set up by him in this area because of the rich deposits of iron ore and coal found here. The Tata empire continues to flourish, and several of its research, educational and cultural institutes here are open to visitors.

MADHYA PRADESH & CHHATTISGARH

Covering a vast area of 443,406 sq km (171,200 sq miles), Madhya Pradesh and Chhattisgarh constitute the geographic heart of India. Between them, they border on to seven states, have one-third of India's forest cover, and are home to 40 per cent of the country's tribal population. Madhya Pradesh is crossed by the Vindhya and the Satpura mountains, and its main river is the Narmada. In the state's rugged north are the famous Khajuraho temples, while eastern Madhya Pradesh has two of India's finest game sanctuaries, Bandhavgarh and Kanha. The scenic Malwa Plateau in the southwest has the great Buddhist stupa of Sanchi and the romantic 15th–16th century citadel of Mandu.

In November 2000, the thickly forested and remote southeast, with its predominantly tribal population, became the new state of Chhattisgarh.

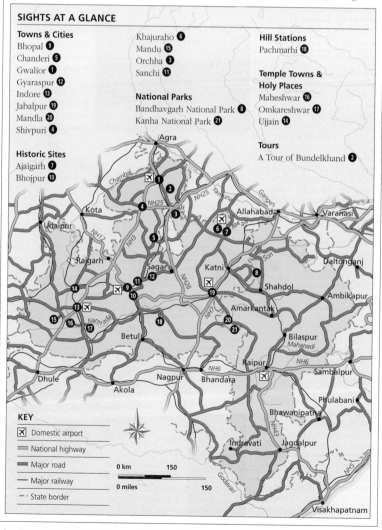

SIGHTS AT A GLANCE

Towns & Cities
Bhopal ⑨
Chanderi ⑤
Gwalior ①
Gyaraspur ⑫
Indore ⑬
Jabalpur ⑲
Mandla ⑳
Shivpuri ④

Historic Sites
Ajaigarh ⑦
Bhojpur ⑩

Khajuraho ⑥
Mandu ⑮
Orchha ③
Sanchi ⑪

National Parks
Bandhavgarh National Park ⑧
Kanha National Park ㉑

Hill Stations
Pachmarhi ⑱

Temple Towns & Holy Places
Maheshwar ⑯
Omkareshwar ⑰
Ujjain ⑭

Tours
A Tour of Bundelkhand ②

KEY
☒ Domestic airport
═ National highway
▬ Major road
— Major railway
-·- State border

0 km   150
0 miles   150

◁ Sculptures of *apsaras* (celestial nymphs) inside the 10th-century Lakshman Temple at Khajuraho

The Durbar Hall of Jai Vilas Palace
with its two gigantic chandeliers

Gwalior ❶

Gwalior district. 321 km (200 miles)
S of Delhi. 🏠 827,000. ✈ 14 km
(8 miles) N of city centre. 🚉 🚌
🏨 TO Hotel Tansen, MG Rd (0751)
223 4557. 🎭 Tansen Music Festival
(Oct/Nov).

Apart from **Gwalior Fort**,
the main attraction for
visitors to Gwalior is the
opulent, Italianate **Jai Vilas
Palace**, south of the fort, built
for the maharaja of Gwalior
by his architect, Colonel Sir
Michael Filose, in the late
19th century. Still the residence
of the former Scindia rulers,
part of the palace has been
turned into a museum. The
most magnificent room is the
Durbar Hall. Hanging from its
ceiling are two of the world's
largest chandeliers, 13-m
(43-ft) high and weighing
3 tonnes each. Before
they were hung the
strength of the roof
was tested by having
several elephants
stand on it. Also on
view is an extra-
ordinary mechanical
silver toy train that
carried liqueurs around the
maharaja's dining table.
　North of the fort is Gwalior's
old town, which has two
interesting Islamic monuments
– the 16th-century **Tomb of
Mohammed Ghaus**, a Mughal
nobleman, which has
outstanding stone latticework
screens; and the **Tomb of
Tansen**, the famous singer
who was one of the "nine
jewels" of the Mughal emper-
or Akbar's court (*see p180*).

🏛 **Jai Vilas Palace Museum**
⬤ Wed. **Tel** (0751) 232 2390. 📷

Gwalior Fort: Man Mandir Palace

Tile with
parrots

The massive Gwalior fort stretches for
nearly 3 km (2 miles) atop a 100-m (328-ft)
high sandstone and basalt hill. Its
formidable bastioned walls, 10-m (33-ft)
high, enclose exquisite temples and palaces,
the most spectacular of which is the Man
Mandir Palace. Built between 1486
and 1516 by Raja Man Singh of the Tomar
dynasty, this double-storeyed palace is
regarded as one of the finest examples of
Rajput secular architecture, embellished with superb
stone carving and latticework. Brilliant blue, yellow and
green tiles depicting parrots and peacocks, rows of
ducks, elephants, banana trees and crocodiles holding
lotus buds, decorate the Man Mandir's façade.

Courtyard
*The interior court-
yard with its carved
pillars has rooms
around it. Two
subterranean floors,
with fountains and
baths, were later
used as dungeons.*

**The
Bastions**
*Rounded bastions,
topped with cupolas
and decorated with
coloured tilework,
break the severity of
the fort's high walls.*

**Hathia
Paur** is the
magnificent
main gateway.

The lavishly carved and decorated south façade of Man Mandir

Stone Latticework
The oriel window, in the zenana quarters of the palace, is framed against intricately latticed stone battlements. A pair of caparisoned elephants flank the window.

Exploring Gwalior Fort

Described by a 16th-century Persian chronicler as "the pearl in the necklace of castles of Hind", Gwalior Fort has had a turbulent history. Founded in the 8th century AD, it was successively ruled by a series of local Hindu dynasties, followed by the Delhi Sultans, the Mughals and finally the Maratha Scindias *(see p471)*, who became the maharajas of Gwalior in the 18th century. It was also briefly in British hands in the 19th century. The fort is best entered from the **Urwahi Gate** on its western side, where 21 colossal **Jain Sculptures** depicting the *tirthankaras (see p396)* and dating from the 7th to the 15th centuries, are carved into the rock face.

Lying to their left is the richly carved, 25-m (82-ft) high temple, **Teli ka Mandir**, the tallest temple in the fort. Built in the 9th century and dedicated to Vishnu, it has an unusual *shikhara*, rounded at the top. After the Indian Mutiny of 1857 *(see p53)* British soldiers occupied the temple and used it as a soda factory. Situated to its north are a pair of 11th-century Vishnu temples, called the **Saas-Bahu** ("Mother and Daughter-in-Law") **Temples**. They are covered with superb sculptures of dancing girls and deities, though their *shikharas* were destroyed in an attack by Sultan Qutbuddin Aibak *(see p48)* in the 12th century.

North of them is the **Hathia Paur**, entrance gateway to the

Rock-cut Jain sculpture

Man Mandir Palace, its ornate pillars supporting a dome with a richly corbelled arch. At the northeastern edge of the fort is the 15th-century **Gujari Mahal**, built Raja Man Singh for his Gujar (tribal) queen. Now the **Archaeological Museum**, its fine collection of Jain and Hindu sculpture includes the celebrated statue of the *salabhanjika* (wood nymph), originally from the temple at Gyaraspur *(see p243)*.

GWALIOR FORT

1 Urwahi Gate
2 Jain Sculptures
3 Teli ka Mandir
4 Saas-Bahu Temples
5 Hathia Paur Gate
6 Man Mandir Palace
7 Gujari Mahal

0 metres   700
0 yards   700

The 9th-century Teli ka Mandir, the tallest temple in the fort

The strikingly ornamental façade of Gwalior Fort ▷

A Tour of Bundelkhand ❷

Gwalior and the adjoining region of Bundelkhand, named after the Bundela Rajputs, make up a culturally distinctive area in Central India. Countless forts and monuments, situated in a boulder-strewn landscape of great beauty, still echo with stories of the pageantry of the Bundela Rajput courts, and the valour of warriors such as the Rani of Jhansi *(see p195)*. The area's glorious history and refined artistic traditions are reflected in the architectural treasures of Gwalior, the medieval city of Orchha, and the hilltop temples of Sonagiri.

Gwalior ①
The capital of many dynasties since the 8th century AD, Gwalior *(see p228)* is the most splendid of the "gateways" to the Bundelkhand region.

Pawaya ②
The remains of an ancient fort can be seen in this capital of the Nag kings (3rd century AD) from the highway at Dabra.

Sonagiri ③
This impeccably maintained complex of 77 Jain temples is approached through a thriving pilgrim settlement.

Jhansi ⑤
The town is known for its impressive fort and the heroic Rani Lakshmibai, who died leading her troops against the British in 1858.

Datia ④
This erstwhile Bundela capital surrounded by numerous small lakes, has scenically located palaces on hillocks.

KEY

▬ Tour route
= Other roads
≈ River

0 km	20
0 miles	10

Orchha ⑥
The temples, cenotaphs and tiered palaces of Orchha are perfect examples of Bundelkhand architecture.

TIPS FOR DRIVERS

Length: 120 km (75 miles).
Stopping-off points: Gwalior, Sonagiri, Datia, Jhansi, Orchha and Taragram provide convenient stopovers. There is a petrol pump at Dabra, after Gwalior. State tourism hotels and guesthouses are available at Gwalior, Datia, Jhansi and Orchha. Local buses run between the major stops.

Taragram ⑦
A fascinating handmade paper factory here is an interesting experimental centre aimed at upgrading local craftsmanship.

The marble cenotaph of Madhavrao Scindia at Shivpuri

Orchha ❸

See pp234–5.

Shivpuri ❹

Shivpuri district. 117 km (73 miles) SW of Gwalior. 🚶 146,900.
🚉 🚌 ℹ️ *MP Tourism, Railway Station, (0751) 254 0777.*

The summer capital of the Scindia rulers of Gwalior, Shivpuri was once a thickly forested region, and a favourite hunting ground of the Mughals. Most of the elephants in Emperor Akbar's army were taken from these forests. Today, the main attractions are the 19th-century white marble cenotaphs of Madhavrao Scindia and his mother, which stand facing each other in a formal Mughal-style garden. With their mix of *shikharas* (spires), domes and cupolas, they epitomize Indo-Islamic architecture. Madhavrao's cenotaph is decorated with *pietra dura* work in lapis lazuli and onyx. There are life-size statues of the ruler and his mother and, in accordance with family tradition, their favourite foods are brought and left here every day. The colonial-style **Madhav Vilas Palace** has airy terraces overlooking the town. The 156-sq km (60 sq-mile) **Madhav National Park** is a mixed deciduous forest with an artificial lake, surrounded by grasslands. **George Castle**, a hunting lodge, was built by Jiyajirao Scindia in honour of King George V, who stayed here in 1911.

Chanderi ❺

Guna district. 227 km (141 miles) S of Gwalior. 🚶 28,300. 🚌
ℹ️ *MP Tourism, Tanabana, (07547) 25 2222.*

The medieval town of Chanderi is dominated by the **Kirtidurga Fort**, perched 200 m (656 ft) above the Betwa river, and overlooking an artificial lake, Kirtisagar. Built by the Pratihara kings in the 10th century, Chanderi successively fell to the sultans of Delhi and Malwa, the Mughal emperor Babur and finally to the Marathas, becoming part of the Scindia kingdom of Gwalior. The entrance is through the Khuni Darwaza ("Bloody Gateway"), marking the point at which the Mughal emperor Babur broke through the 6-km (4-mile) long granite walls of the fort, when he conquered it in 1528. Cut into the

Minaret detail, Kirtidurga Fort

adjacent rock face are several imposing Jain statues. Most of the structures inside the fort are attributed to Sultan Mahmud of Malwa, and are executed in the graceful provincial Afghan style that distinguishes the buildings of Mandu *(see pp247–9).* The most ambitious edifice here is the **Koshak Mahal**, built in 1445. The sultan originally planned it as a seven-storeyed palace, but only managed to complete two storeys, each with balconies, rows of windows and beautifully vaulted ceilings. Other notable buildings are the domed and arcaded **Jami Masjid** and the **Badal Mahal** with its elegant gateway. Chanderi was once a flourishing centre of trade, and an exploration of the town reveals large sandstone *havelis*, shops raised on plinths and ruined caravanserais lining the winding lanes. The town is also famous for its gossamer muslin saris and brocades.

Environs

Deogarh Fort, the "Fortress of the Gods", is 25 km (16 miles) southeast of Chanderi. Within it are a splendid display of sculptures from a group of 9th- to 10th-century Jain temples. Just below the fort is the 5th-century Vishnu Dasavatara Temple with its fine sculpture and carved pillars topped by celestial musicians. A statue of Vishnu asleep on Ananta, the cosmic serpent *(see pp24–5),* is among the early masterpieces of Indian art.

Chanderi's fort, the scene of many battles

One of the *chhatris* (cenotaphs) of the Bundela kings at Orchha

Orchha ❸

Tikamgarh district. 120 km (75 miles) SE of Gwalior. 🚉 Jhansi, 19 km (12 miles) NW of Orchha, then taxi or bus. ⬛ ℹ️ MP Tourism, Sheesh Mahal, (07680) 25 2624. 🎭 Ramnavami (Apr), Dussehra (Sep/Oct).

Orchha is dramatically positioned on a rocky island, enclosed by a loop of the Betwa river. Founded in 1531, it was the capital of the Bundela kings until 1738, when it was abandoned in favour of Tikamgarh.

Crumbling palaces, pavilions, *hamams*, walls and gates, connected to the town with an impressive 14-arched causeway, are all that remain today. The three main palaces are massed symmetrically together. These are the **Raj Mahal** (1560), **Jahangiri Mahal** (1626) and **Rai Praveen Mahal** (mid-1670s), named after a royal paramour.

The old town is dominated by three beautiful temples – the **Ram Raja**, the **Lakshmi Narayan** and the **Chaturbhuj**. A unique blend of fort and temple styles, the Chaturbhuj Temple is dedicated to Vishnu and has huge arcaded halls for massed singing, and a soaring spire.

Lying along the Kanchana Ghat of the Betwa are the 14 hauntingly beautiful cenotaphs of the Orchha rulers. Along with the many *sati* pillars in Jahangiri Mahal's museum, these serve as reminders of Orchha's feudal past when queens sometimes committed *sati* by jumping into their husband's funeral pyres.

Orchha: Jahangiri Mahal

Flower motif in turquoise stone

An excellent example of Rajput Bundela architecture, this palace was built by the Bundela king Bir Singh Deo and named after the Mughal emperor Jahangir who spent one night here. The many-layered palace has 132 chambers off and above the central courtyard and an almost equal number of subterranean rooms. The square sandstone palace is extravagantly embellished with lapis lazuli tiles, graceful *chhatris* and ornate *jali* screens. It also has a modest museum.

Chhatris
These cupolas give the palace's roofline a delicate and airy feel.

Carved niches line the outer walls.

Entrance

★ **Entrance Gateway**
The impressive entrance gateway, flanked by stone elephants, leads up to the central courtyard.

STAR FEATURES

★ Entrance Gateway

★ Domed Pavilion

★ Domed Pavilion
A domed pavilion, with an apartment beneath, marks the corners as well as the middle of each side of the palace.

VISITORS' CHECKLIST

Palace Complex. ◯ *daily.*
⬤ *public hols.* 🚩 *MP Tourism,
Sheesh Mahal, (07680) 25 2624.*
📷 ✂ 🍴 ⚑⚑ **Museum**
◯ *daily.* ⬤ *public hols.*

Glazed Tilework
Geometric lapis motifs decorate the outer façade at the top.

Jahangir's bedroom

Fortified bastions protect the palace.

The central courtyard can be viewed from each part of the palace and has a small museum in a set of rooms that run along it.

PLAN OF ORCHHA

The fortified town of Orchha encloses three major palaces and ruined ancillary structures.

1 Jahangiri Mahal
2 Sheesh Mahal
3 Raj Mahal
4 Rai Praveen Mahal
5 *Hamam*
6 Stable

KEY

▨ Illustrated area

Khajuraho: Kandariya Mahadev Temple ❻

Amorous couple

The magnificent group of temples at Khajuraho, a UNESCO World Heritage Site, were built between the 9th and 10th centuries by the Chandela dynasty which dominated Central India at that time. The most impressive of the temples is the Kandariya Mahadev, which represents the pinnacle of North Indian temple art and architecture. It is remarkable for its grand dimensions, its complex yet perfectly harmonious composition, and its exquisite sculptural embellishment. Over 800 sculptures cover the temple, depicting gods and goddesses, beasts and warriors, sensuous maidens, dancers, musicians and, of course, the erotic scenes for which the Khajuraho temples are famous.

View of the Kandariya Mahadev temple, built 1025–1050

★ Apsaras
Often carved as support-bracket figures, the celestial nymphs reveal the sculptors' mastery of the female form. Full of natural charm and sensuous grace, they are shown as dancers, attendants of the deities, or simply engaged in everyday activities.

The Maha Mandapa
Carved pillars, nymph-brackets, a corbelled ceiling and balconied windows add to the sumptuousness of the central hall's interior.

The Ardha Mandapa
The east-facing Ardha Mandapa (entrance porch) has an exquisite makara torana (ceremonial arch) flanked by two crocodile heads, and covered with floral tracery.

STAR FEATURES

★ Apsaras

★ Main Shikhara

★ Erotic Panels

VISITORS' CHECKLIST

Chhatarpur district 275 kms (171 miles) SE of Gwalior. ✈ 5 km (3 miles) S of temples. 🚌 ℹ️ MP Tourism, Chandela Cultural Centre (07686) 27 4051. ⬤ Aug–Sep. 📷 🎭 Dance Festival (Feb-Mar). **Son et Lumière** 7.30pm daily. 📷

★ Main Shikhara

The main spire soars to 30m (98ft), while 84 smaller spires rise in a crescendo towards it, to create the impression of a mountain range – more specifically, Mount Kailasa, the abode of Shiva.

★ Erotic Panels

The largest erotic panels are on the northern and southern facades, between the balconies. The erotic sculptures are variously believed to celebrate the marriage of Shiva and Parvati, serve as a love manual, or simply express an exuberant celebration of life and creation.

Garbhagriha

The dark and plain garbhagriha (inner sanctum), *symbolizing a womb, houses a linga, the phallic symbol and principal object of worship in all Shiva temples. The sanctum is entered through a richly carved door frame.*

The first tier above the terrace is carved with processional friezes and goddesses.

Exploring Khajuraho

The 25 temples at Khajuraho represent the brilliant burst of artistic flowering that took place under the generous patronage of the powerful Chandela rulers, who made Khajuraho their peacetime capital. The remoteness of the temples' location saved them from the ravages of Islamic raiders, but also led to their being abandoned after the decline of the Chandelas in the 13th century. Hidden in a dense forest for 700 years, they were "rediscovered" in 1838 by Captain TS Burt of the Bengal Engineers. According to local tradition there were originally 85 temples, and ongoing excavations have unearthed extensive ruins in the area.

The polished stone image of Varaha, Vishnu's boar incarnation

The Khajuraho temples are divided into three groups. The most important are in the **Western Group** which, apart from the Kandariya Mahadev (see pp236–7), includes the **Lakshman** and **Vishwanath Temples**. Both are similar to the Kandariya Mahadev in composition, sculptural embellishments and themes, but they also have outstanding individual features.

The superb ceiling of the entrance porch and the female bracket figures inside the Lakshman Temple (built in AD 930) are worth special notice. The pair of street singers on the south façade are also remarkable, with their expressions of intense absorption. The master architect and his apprentices are exquisitely sculpted on the subsidiary shrine in the temple's eastern corner.

Opposite the Lakshman Temple is a pavilion with a magnificent statue of Varaha, the boar incarnation of Vishnu (see p679), covered with carvings of several deities.

In the Vishwanath Temple, dating to AD 1002, the *apsara* plucking a thorn from her foot (on the south façade) is outstanding, as is the *apsara* playing the flute, which can be seen in the interior chamber.

The **Matangeshwar Temple** (built AD 900), with its plain circular interior, is the only one still in everyday use (see p243).

The **Archaeological Museum**, near the entrance to the Western Group, has a fine

Apsara applying kohl

collection of sculptures found in the area, including a dancing Ganesha, and a fascinating frieze showing the construction of the Khajuraho temples, with scenes of stone being cut and transported.

A short distance away is the **Eastern Group** of temples. The Jain **Parsvanatha Temple**, built in AD 950, is the most remarkable, for the intricately carved ceiling pendants in its entrance porch. Three exquisite sculptures here show *apsaras* applying kohl around their eyes, painting their feet (both on the south façade), and fastening ankle bells (on the north façade).

The last phase of temple-building in Khajuraho is seen in the **Southern Group**. The **Chaturbhuj Temple** (built AD 1090) has a superb, four-armed image of Shiva in the inner sanctum. It is the only

Image of Vishnu in the Lakshman Temple

major temple in Khajuraho without any erotic sculptures.

🏛 **Archaeological Museum**
⊙ Sat–Thu. **Tel** (07686) 27 2320.

Environs
Raneh Falls, 17 km (11 miles) south of the town of Khajuraho, provide a cool retreat. The 19th-century **Rajagarh Palace**, 25 km (16 miles) southeast of Khajuraho, is in the same Bundela style as the palaces at Datia and Orchha (see pp234–5). Situated 32 km (20 miles) southeast of Khajuraho, along the Ken river, the **Panna National Park**, has herds of deer, leopards, crocodiles and the scenic Pandav Falls. A favourite spot for tourists in the park is Gille's Tree House restaurant, perched 20 m (66 ft) above the ground.

Ajaigarh ❼

Panna district. 75 km (45 miles) E of Khajuraho. 🚐 ⊙ daily.

This great Chandela citadel, built in the 9th century AD and perched 500 m (1,640 ft) above the plains, is now a spectacular ruin. The steep path up to the top goes past gigantic sculptures carved into the sheer cliff face, including a particularly enchanting one of a cow and calf. Within the fort lie the ruins of once-magnificent palaces, broken fragments of statues, and several poignant *sati* pillars, marking the self-immolation of countless Rajput widows.

Bandhavgarh National Park ❽

VISITORS' CHECKLIST

Shahdol district. 237 km (147 miles) SE of Khajuraho. 🚉 Umaria, 33 km (21 miles) SW of Tala, the main entry point. 🚌 MP Tourism, White Tiger Lodge, Tala, (07653) 26 5308. ⏱ Oct–Jun. 🎫 📷 extra charges. 🚙 🖼 Jeep safaris available.

Indian tiger

One of India's most important Tiger Reserves, the Bandhavgarh National Park sprawls across an area of 625 sq km (241 sq miles). Apart from some 50 tigers, the park's wildlife includes 250 species of birds, leopards, deer, jungle cats and packs of *dhole* (Indian wild dog). Great rocky hills, lush deciduous forests, marshes and meadows make Bandhavgarh one of India's most scenic areas. A picturesque hilltop fort with fine sculptures is part of the park's attractions.

Sheshasaya Statue
A 11-m (36-ft) long statue of the reclining Vishnu, guarded by a seven-headed snake, is at the base of the fort.

The Fort
The ramparts of Bandhavgarh's fort, whose foundations date back to the 1st century AD, are a good place for birdwatching.

JABALPUR SATNA, PANNA, KHAJURAHO
Manpur
Tala
Charan Ganga
Khatauli
Dorka
Parasi
Hardia
Gohni
UMARIA
Kamarwa
Johilla

Crested Serpent Eagle
This large eagle preys on snakes and lizards.

Dhole
The Indian wild dog has a distinctive whistling call, to assemble the pack. It has a red coat, large upright ears and a bushy tail.

0 km   5
0 miles   5

KEY

▪ ▪ Park boundary
═══ Major road
═══ Minor road
🏛 Temple
ℹ Tourist information
❄ Viewpoint
⌂ Fort

THE WHITE TIGER OF REWA

In 1951, the maharaja of Rewa captured a white tiger in these forests. Named Mohan, he was mated in captivity with several tigresses, and all the white tigers in zoos across the world today are Mohan's descendants. A pair can be seen in the Bhopal zoo *(see p241)*. Since 1951, no other white tiger has been seen in the Bandhavgarh region. The white tiger is an "evolutionary colour aberration" and not an albino, nor a separate sub-species.

The white tiger, very rare in the wild

Bhopal � 9

**Arch detail,
Moti Masjid**

The capital of Madhya Pradesh, Bhopal was founded in the 11th century by Raja Bhoj of the Paramara dynasty. By the 18th century, it was held by a Muslim dynasty whose rulers included several remarkable women, the Begums of Bhopal. The city, ringed by hills, stretches along the shores of two artificial lakes, the Upper and Lower Lakes. The old quarter, north of the Lakes, is a maze of narrow lanes, bazaars and mosques. To the south is the new city, with its leafy suburbs and industrial enclaves. In December 1984, a toxic gas leak from the Union Carbide factory claimed the lives of 5,000 people, in one of the world's worst industrial disasters. With the wounds of this tragedy now healing, Bhopal is a good base for visiting some of the state's fascinating sites.

Fountain and tank inside the 19th-century Moti Masjid

🄲 Taj-ul-Masjid
Hamidia Rd. ⬤ *daily.* ⬤ *to non-Muslims on Fri & on Muslim festivals.*
The most imposing monument in Bhopal, this large, pink-washed mosque was begun by Sultan Jehan Begum in 1878 but was left unfinished for almost a century before being completed in 1971. A progressive ruler, the begum established the city's postal system and hospitals, but virtually bankrupted the royal treasury as a result of her ambitious schemes. The enormous courtyard of the mosque has a *dukka* (water tank) for ritual ablutions, and the vast prayer hall is striking for its rows of pillars. This grandiose mosque is surmounted by three white domes and flanked by two 18-storeyed minarets. Its general ambience is majestic rather than beautiful.

🏛 The Chowk
Bazaar ⬤ *Tue–Sun.* **Jami Masjid** ⬤ *daily.* ⬤ *to non-Muslims on Fri & on Muslim festivals.*
Situated in the centre of the old quarter is the Chowk (literally, main square). Streets radiate out from it, each one specializing in a particular type of goods – the Bhopali *batuas* (elaborately beaded purses) for which Bhopal is famous, tussar silk, caps, drums and spices. *Havelis* line the streets, with wooden fronted shops on the ground floor, and elaborate wrought-iron balconies above. Dominating the area is the **Jami Masjid** with its gold finials, built in 1837 by Qudsia Begum, another of Bhopal's female rulers. It is surrounded by shops selling silver jewellery.
South of the Chowk is another mosque, the **Moti**

Bhopali batua

Masjid ("Pearl Mosque") built in 1860 by Qudsia Begum's daughter and successor. With its striped dome and tapering sandstone minarets, it looks like a smaller version of the Jami Masjid in Delhi (*see p86*).
Also worth visiting in this area is the **Shaukat Mahal**, a 19th-century Indo-Saracenic cum Rococo palace. Built by a French mercenary who claimed to be a descendant of the Bourbons, it now houses government offices, though visitors are usually allowed inside by the guards.

🏛 Bharat Bhavan
Shamla Hills. **Tel** *(0755) 266 0353.* ⬤ *Tue–Sun.* 🄼 🄷
A large cultural complex, Bharat Bhavan was established in 1982 to showcase and promote India's rich tribal and folk art heritage. To the right of the entrance is the Tribal Art Gallery, a superb collection that includes votive objects, terracotta figures, masks, wall paintings, woodcarvings, and the distinctive metal sculptures created by craftsmen from Bastar (*see p253*). A gallery across the courtyard exhibits contemporary Indian art. Bharat Bhavan is also the venue for regular performances of theatre, music and dance in the evenings.

🏛 State Museum
Shamla Hills. **Tel** *(0755) 266 1856.* ⬤ *Tue–Sun.* 🄸 🄼
A collection of 12th-century Jain bronzes, found in Dhar district in western Madhya Pradesh, form the highlight of this museum's collection. It

The Taj-ul-Masjid, Bhopal's most imposing monument

For hotels and restaurants in this region see pp697–9 and pp726–7

Replica of a tribal hut in the Rashtriya Manav Sangrahalaya

VISITORS' CHECKLIST

Bhopal district. 744 km
(462 miles) S of Delhi. 🚂
1,433,900. ✈ 11 km (7 miles)
W of city centre. 🚌 🚋
🛈 MP Tourism, Paryatan
Bhavan, Bhadbhada Rd (0755)
277 4340. 🏛 Tue–Sun.

also has a series of striking stone sculptures, mostly from the 6th to 10th centuries. Older pieces include *yakshis* (female attendants) dating to 200 BC, and a Standing Buddha in black granite. The museum shop has good plaster replicas of some sculptures for sale.

🏛 Rashtriya Manav Sangrahalaya (Museum of Man)

S of Shamla Hills. 🛈 Tue–Sun. 🖭
Set in the hills overlooking the Upper Lake, this museum, which sprawls over a 40-ha (99-acre) site, has authentic replicas of Indian tribal dwell-ings, built by the tribal people themselves. Tribal cultures from all over the country are represented in the museum, through comprehensive displays of utensils, ritual objects, musical instruments, tools, murals, carvings, jewellery and costumes. An Introductory Gallery, in a thatched hut, explains the museum's layout.

🦌 Van Vihar National Park

🛈 Wed–Mon; 6am–10.30am, 3pm–5.30pm. 🖭
The most famous inhabitants of this large park, near the Upper Lake, are the white tigers *(see p239)*. A good time to see these rare creatures is at about 4pm, when they come to the edge of their enclosure for their evening meal. The zoo is also home to lions, leopards and Himalayan bears.

🏛 Birla Museum

Near Lakshmi Narayan Temple. **Tel** (0755) 255 1388. 🛈 Thu–Tue. 🖭
This museum has a well-displayed collection of stone sculptures dating from the 7th to 12th centuries. Shiva, Vishnu and various goddesses are shown in their different incarnations. Particularly impressive are Vishnu in his boar (Varaha) incarnation, Goddess Durga in her ferocious Chamunda form, and Shiva and his consort Parvati in their celestial home on Mount Kailasa. Next to the museum is the large, recently-built and brightly painted Lakshmi Narayan Temple, overlooking the Lower Lake.

BHOPAL CITY CENTRE

Bharat Bhavan ③
State Archaeological Museum ④
Taj-ul-Masjid ①
The Chowk ②

Motia Talab

Baag Munshi
Husain ka Talab

Bhopal Bus Stand

Bhopal Railway Station

SANCHI

HAMIDIA ROAD

INDORE

✈ Airport
6.5 km (4 miles)

NH86

BERASIA ROAD

MARVADI ROAD

① Taj-ul-Masjid

MANGALWARA RD

RAILWAY BRIDGE

PUL BOGDO RD

Jami Masjid

VIP ROAD

Shaukat Mahal

② The Chowk

Moti Masjid

SULTANIA ROAD

Yaadgaar e Shahjahani Park

Upper Lake

Brindaban Garden

Kamala Park

KAMLA ROAD

Lower Lake

Ram Mandir

SULTANIA ROAD

0 metres   500

0 yards   500

Bharat Bhavan ③

SHAMLA HILLS

LAKE DRIVE RD

Rashtriya Manav Sangrahalaya,
Van Vihar National Park

State Museum ④

BHADABHADA RD

Birla Museum

TAIL ROAD

BHOJPUR

Key to Symbols see back flap

Sculpture from the incomplete Bhojeshwar Temple, Bhojpur

Bhojpur ⑩

Bhopal district. 28 km (17 miles) SE of Bhopal. 🚌 🛈 *MP Tourism, Bhopal, (0755) 277 4340.*

Founded by the 11th-century Paramara king, Raja Bhoj, who also established Bhopal *(see p240)*, Bhojpur is dominated by the monumental, though incomplete **Bhojeshwar Temple**. Impressive sculptures cover parts of its unfinished corbelled ceiling and its entrance doorway.

Inside, on a tiered platform, is an enormous stone Shivalinga, 2.3-m (8-ft) high and 5.3 m (17 ft) in circumference. Etched on the paving stones and rocks in the forecourt, are the architect's detailed plans for the finished temple, while on the northeast side are the remains of a massive earthen ramp used to haul stone up to the roof.

Environs
The **Bhimbetka Caves** with their prehistoric paintings, dating back some 12,000 years, are about 17 km (11 miles) south of Bhojpur.

Sanchi ⑪

Raisen district. 46 km (29 miles) NE of Bhopal. 🚉 🚌 🛈 *Traveller's Lodge, (07482) 26 6723.* 📷 *Chaityagiri Vihara Festival (Nov).*

The tranquil hill of Sanchi contains one of India's best preserved and most extensive Buddhist sites. From the 3rd century BC to the 7th century AD, this was a thriving Buddhist establishment of stupas and monasteries. The complex of buildings at Sanchi therefore show the development of Buddhist art across different periods, stretching over more than a 1,000 years.

Founded by Emperor Ashoka *(see p42)* whose wife came from nearby Vidisha, Sanchi grew and prospered under subsequent dynasties, largely through the generous patronage of the rich merchants of Vidisha. By the 14th century, Buddhism was on the wane in India and Sanchi was deserted and half forgotten, until it was "rediscovered" in 1818 by General Taylor of the Bengal Cavalry. Between 1912 and 1919 it was extensively restored by the Archaeological Survey of India

Votive stupa with Buddha image

(ASI) under Sir John Marshall. It was declared a World Heritage Site by UNESCO in 1989. Most of Sanchi's buildings are within an enclosure at the top of the 91-m (299-ft) hill, dominated by the **Great Stupa** and its four superb gateways *(see pp244–5)*. Nearby, to its north, is the smaller **Stupa 3** (built 2nd century BC), with its single gateway, which contained the relics of two of the Buddha's closest disciples, Sariputra and Maudgalayana.

Also within the enclosure are several monasteries, which are located on the eastern, western and southern sides. Of these the 10th-century **Monastery 51** is the most interesting, with its courtyard surrounded by a colonnade, behind which are 22 monks' cells. **Temple 17**, on the eastern side, dates to the 5th century AD. A flat-roofed structure with columns surmounted by double-headed lions, this is the earliest well-preserved example of an Indian stone temple, and its style and features considerably influenced the later development of temple architecture.

Located below the Great Stupa, just outside the enclosure, is **Stupa 2** (2nd century BC), whose railings are carved with lotus medallions and mythical beasts. Also depicted is a horse with stirrups. Near the South Gateway of the Great Stupa lies the broken shaft of an Ashokan Pillar, made of highly

---

THE BHIMBETKA CAVE PAINTINGS

In 1957, the Indian archaeologist VS Wakanker discovered over 1,000 cave shelters in a rocky sandstone ridge near Bhimbetka village, surrounded by thick deciduous forest. More than 500 of these were covered with paintings done in bold, fluent lines, with the same power and energy as the cave paintings in Lascaux, France, or the Kalahari paintings in Africa. The earliest paintings, from the Upper Paleolithic period, are of large animals such as bison and rhino, done in red pigment, with humans drawn in green.

Mesolithic period cave painting from Bhimbetka

The largest number of paintings are from the Mesolithic period (8000 to 5000 BC), and depict vignettes of daily life, hunting scenes and a range of animals including, curiously, a giraffe. Later caves (1st century AD) show battle scenes and Hindu deities. It was declared a UNESCO World Heritage Site in 2003.

Cave shelter at Bhimbetka

Stupa 3, which originally contained the relics of the Buddha's disciples

polished stone. It was used as a sugarcane press by a local landlord in the 19th century. Its four-headed lion capital, similar to the one at Sarnath *(see p208)* but not as fine, can now be seen in the Sanchi **Archaeological Museum**. Some other notable exhibits here include a pair of winged Mauryan lions, sculptural friezes from the gateways and statues of the Buddha and Bodhisattvas.

Environs

Besnagar, situated 10 km (6 miles) northeast of Sanchi, on the confluence of the Beas and Betwa rivers, was once a prosperous centre of trade. A unique relic of its past is the **Heliodorus Column**, with its fluted bell-shaped capital, dating to 113 BC. Dedicated to the god Vasudeva, it was erected by the envoy of the Greek king of Taxila (now in Pakistan), to commemorate his conversion to Hinduism.

Udayagiri, 20 km (12 miles) north of Sanchi, has fine examples of 5th-century AD rock-cut caves, carved into the hillside. Most notable is **Cave 5**, with its impressive sculpture of Varaha, the incarnation of Vishnu as a boar, rescuing the earth goddess from the churning ocean.

Raisen Fort straddles a hilltop 23 km (14 miles) southeast of Sanchi. Its 13th-century gates, palaces, temples and pavilions have lain in ruins ever since a devastating attack in the 16th century by the Sultan of Gujarat, but the site is still hauntingly atmospheric.

Udayapur, 70 km (42 miles) northeast of Sanchi, has the exquisite 11th-century red sandstone **Nilkanteshwar Temple**, dedicated to Shiva. It is comparable in scale and sculptural beauty to the Khajuraho temples *(see pp236–8)*. The symmetry of its graceful *shikhara*, rising in a crescendo of delicately carved stone, is broken by a curious figure that seems to dangle in space. According to local legend, this figure represents the architect, trying to climb to the heavens.

Gyaraspur ⑫

Vidisha district. 64 km (40 miles) NE of Bhopal. 🚌 ℹ️ *MP Tourism, Bhopal, (0755) 277 4340.*

The ornately carved 9th-century **Maladevi Temple** at Gyaraspur is built on a hillside. Partly carved out of a rock, it is now in ruins, and much of its superb sculpture has been pillaged. The exquisite statue of the *salabhanjika*, which is now the pride of the Archaeological Museum at Gwalior Fort *(see p229)*, was salvaged from here.

Sculpture of Varaha, Vishnu's boar incarnation, from Cave 5, Udayagiri

FESTIVALS OF MADHYA PRADESH & CHHATTISGARH

Shivratri *(Feb/Mar)*, Khajuraho. The celestial wedding of Shiva and Parvati is celebrated with colourful processions and an elaborate nightlong re-enactment of the wedding ritual in the Matangeshwar Temple.

Dance Festival *(Feb/Mar)*, Khajuraho. During this week-long festival, India's leading classical dancers perform in front of the Kandariya Mahadeva Temple. The postures and grace of the dancers are echoed in the exquisite stone sculptures of *apsaras* in the temple.

Classical dancer at Khajuraho Dance Festival

Dussehra *(Sep/Oct)* Chhattisgarh. This ten-day festival in honour of Rama is celebrated with great gaiety in the Bastar tribal heartland of Chhattisgarh. Along with lively dramatized episodes from the *Ramayana (see p27)* there are also colourful tribal fairs with dancing, cockfights and spirited bartering of goods.

Chaityagiri Vihara Festival *(Nov)*, Sanchi. Buddhists from all over the subcontinent gather at Sanchi to view the relics of two of the Buddha's closest disciples.

Tansen Music Festival *(Nov/Dec)*, Gwalior. Named after the great musician Tansen, one of the "nine jewels" at the court of Mughal emperor Akbar, this festival brings together the best classical musicians and singers from all over the country.

Sanchi: The Great Stupa

Animals on the torana

India's finest surviving Buddhist monument and World Heritage Site, the Great Stupa at Sanchi, was built in the 2nd century BC. Its hemispherical shape is variously believed to symbolize the upturned alms bowl of a Buddhist monk, or an umbrella of protection for followers of the Buddhist dharma. The stupa's main glory lies in its four stone *toranas* (gateways), added in the 1st century BC. Their sculptures replicate the techniques of wood and ivory carving, and cover a rich variety of Buddhist themes.

West Gateway
This animated scene from the Jataka Tales shows monkeys scrambling across a bridge to escape from soldiers.

Circumambulatory Paths
The paths have balustrades carved with medallions of flowers, birds and animals, and the names of donors who funded them.

South Gateway
The Wheel of Law, being worshipped by devotees, symbolizes the Buddha.

The four gateways show scenes from the Buddha's life, and episodes from the Jataka Tales. The Buddha is not depicted in human form, but only through symbols such as a Bodhi Tree, footprints or a wheel.

Detail of Architrave
The intricate carving on the architraves is believed to be the work of ivory and wood carvers.

★ **North Gateway**
Sujata, the village chief's daughter, offers the Buddha (represented by the Bodhi Tree) kheer (rice pudding), as the demon Mara sends the temptress to seduce him.

The *vedika* (railings) are an impressive recreation in stone of a typical wooden railing design. They were the inspiration for the stone railings around Sansad Bhavan or the Parliament House *(see p74)* in New Delhi.

The Great Stupa and its West Gateway
Enclosing a smaller brick stupa built by Emperor Ashoka in the 3rd century BC, the Great Stupa is capped by a three-tiered stone umbrella, symbolizing the layers of heaven.

Statues of the Buddha meditating, added in the 5th century AD, face each of the gateways.

East Gateway
This scene shows a royal retinue at the palace of Kapilavastu, the Buddha's home before he renounced his princely life.

★ **Salabhanjika**
Supporting the lowest architrave of the East Gateway is this sensuous, voluptuous tree nymph, gracefully positioned under a mango tree.

STAR FEATURES

★ North Gateway

★ Salabhanjika

Indore ⑬

Indore district. 187 km (116 miles) W
of Bhopal. 🚶 1,597,400. ✈ 10 km
(6 miles) W of town. 🚉 🚌 ℹ️ MP
Tourism, behind Ravindra Natyagriha,
(0731) 252 8653. 🛍️ Mon–Sat.
🎭 Ganesha Chaturthi (Aug/Sep).

The bustling commercial
centre of Madhya Pradesh,
Indore was a princely state
until 1947, ruled by the
Maratha Holkar dynasty.
   At the heart of the city,
surrounded by a lively bazaar,
is the **Rajwada Palace**, now
just an imposing façade
following a fire in 1984. A
short walk west of it stands
the **Kanch Mandir** ("Glass
Temple"), an opulent 19th-
century Jain temple, decorated
with mirrors, chandeliers, and
murals on glass.
   On the southwestern edge
of Indore is the opulent
Lalbagh Palace, built by the
rulers of Indore in the early
20th century. Now a museum
called the **Nehru Centre**, its
gilded Rococo interiors house
galleries of miniature paintings, medieval coins and tribal
artifacts. In the garden is a
statue of Queen Victoria,
looking distinctly unamused.

🏛 **Nehru Centre**
Lalbagh Palace. *Tel* (0731) 247
3264. ⏰ Tue–Sun. 📷

Environs
Dewas, 35 km (22 miles)
northeast of Indore, was the
setting for EM Forster's book
The Hill of Devi (1953).

Sacred ghats on the Shipra river in Ujjain

Ujjain ⑭

Ujjain district. 56 km (35 miles) NW
of Indore. 🚶 429,900. 🚉 🚌
ℹ️ MP Tourism, Railway Station,
(0734) 396 9000. 🎭 Kumbh Mela
(every 12 years), Shivratri (Feb/Mar).

On the banks of the Shipra
river, Ujjain is one of
India's seven sacred cities,
and one of the four sites of
the Kumbh Mela *(see p210)*.
In the 4th–5th centuries AD it
was the second capital of the
Gupta Empire *(see p43)*, with
the celebrated Sanskrit poet
Kalidasa as one of its leading
lights. Its glory was, however,
eclipsed in the 13th century
after it was sacked by the
Delhi Sultans *(see p48)*.
   The focal point of the town
is the **Mahakaleshwar
Temple** (an 18th-century
reconstruction on the site of
the original), with its much-
venerated Shivalinga. In the
main square is the **Gopal
Temple**, whose silver doors
are believed to be from the

Somnath Temple in Gujarat,
ransacked by Mahmud of
Ghazni in the 11th century. A
similar pair of doors are at the
Golden Temple in Amritsar
(see pp106–107). **Ram Ghat**,
the largest of sacred ghats on
the banks of the river, is the
site of the Kumbh Mela (the
next Ardh Kumbh here is due
in 2010). On the opposite
bank is the **Chintaman
Ganesha Temple** whose
carved pillars, dating to the
11th century, are the only
relics of the original temple.
At the southwestern edge of
the city is the **Vedh Shala
Observatory**. Built in 1730 by
Sawai Jai Singh II of Jaipur,
the Mughal-appointed
governor of Malwa, it is a
smaller version of the one at
Jaipur *(see pp358–9)*.

Environs
The charming 15th-century
Kaliadeh Palace, 8 km (5 miles)
north of Ujjain, on an island
in the Shipra, was built by
the sultans of Malwa.

THE HILL OF DEVI

The famous British writer Edward
Morgan Forster (1879–1970) spent
several months in the princely state of
Dewas as private secretary to its
eccentric and charming maharaja. *The
Hill of Devi*, based on his letters home,
provides a delightful inside view of life
at a provincial court with its festivities,
intrigues and complicated protocol.
Dewas is dominated by a hill with the
temple of the goddess Chamunda Devi,
hence the title of the book. Curiously,
tiny Dewas was divided and ruled by
two brothers, each with his own palace,
army and anthem. Forster was at the court of the elder
maharaja. The experience also provided Forster with
material for his best-known novel, *A Passage to India* (1924).

Devi image in the
temple at Dewas

The glittering interior of the
Kanch Mandir in Indore

Mandu ⑮

Dhar district. 105 km (65 miles) W of Indore. 🚌 🏨 *Tourist Cottages, (07292) 26 3235.*

Perched on a crest of the Vindhya Mountains is the deserted citadel of Mandu, one of India's most romantic and picturesque sites. Enclosed within its winding parapet walls, and surrounded by steep, wooded ravines, are palaces, mosques, lakes and pleasure pavilions, built between 1401 and 1529, by the sultans of Malwa *(see p49)*, who referred to it as Shadiabad, the "City of Joy". Mandu is spread over a 23-sq km (9-sq mile) area, but its major monuments are clustered in two groups – the Royal Enclave and the Village Group.

A row of lofty arches in the Hindola Mahal or Swinging Palace, Mandu

🏛 Royal Enclave

🕐 *daily.* 🎫
Dominating the Royal Enclave are the **Jahaz Mahal** *(see pp248–9)* and the majestic T-shaped **Hindola Mahal** ("Swinging Palace"), whose massive inward-sloping walls give the impression that the building is swaying. Built in the late 15th century as the royal assembly hall, its austere façade is lightened by delicate tracery work on its arched windows. Next to it is a well, the **Champa Baoli**, connected to a series of subterranean rooms cooled

Detail from Hoshang Shah's tomb

by flowing water, where the ladies of the harem spent hot summer days. To its east are **Gada Shah's House and Shop**, which belonged to an ambitious Rajput chieftain at the court of Mandu. The so-called "Shop" was actually an audience hall, while the house, a luxurious double-storeyed structure with water channels and fountains, still has traces of two fine paintings of the chieftain and his wife. The earliest of the monuments in the Royal Enclave is Dilawar Khan's Mosque, built by the first Malwa sultan in 1405, using the stones and pillars of Hindu and Jain temples that had stood here earlier.

🏛 Village Group

🕐 *daily.*
The first marble tomb to be built in India, **Hoshang**

Shah's Tomb (1440) is a perfectly proportioned structure, where Malwa's most powerful sultan is buried. It has an inscription on the door recording the visit of four of Emperor Shah Jahan's architects in 1659. Opposite it is the magnificent **Jami Masjid** (built in 1454). It is said to have been inspired by the great Mosque at Damascus. Three large domes and 58 smaller ones surmount its colonnades, and the *mihrab* is decorated with beautiful calligraphy. Next to it is the **Ashrafi Mahal** *madrasa* with the ruins of a seven-storeyed Victory Tower, acclaimed in contemporary accounts as Mandu's finest structure. It was built by Sultan Mahmud in 1443, to mark his battle with the maharana of Mewar. Interestingly, the latter also built a Victory Tower at Chittorgarh *(see p402)* after the same battle.

PLAN OF MANDU

1 Delhi Gate
2 Hindola Mahal
3 Champa Baoli
4 Gada Shah's House
5 Jahaz Mahal
6 Hoshang Shah's Tomb
7 Ashrafi Mahal
8 Jami Masjid
9 Malik Mugith's Mosque
10 Dai ka Mahal
11 Baz Bahadur's Palace
12 Rupmati's Pavilion
13 Neelkanth Mahal

| 0 metres | 800 |
| 0 yards | 800 |

Mandu: Jahaz Mahal

The Jahaz Mahal ("Ship Palace") was built by the fifth sultan of Malwa, Ghiyasuddin (r.1469–1500). Lying on a long, narrow strip of land between two of the many man-made lakes, Munja Talao and Kapur Talao, the palace gives the impression of an anchored ship, especially during the monsoon when the lakes are full. This pleasure palace was staffed entirely by the hedonistic sultan's harem of 15,000 women, who also served as his bodyguard.

A pavilion window

The Pavilions
The juxtaposition of conical and domed roofs over the pavilions adds great charm to the Jahaz Mahal's silhouette.

Tilework
Blue and yellow tiles decorated the pavilions.

Entrance

STAR FEATURES

★ Water Channels

★ Bathing Pool

The Terrace
The most spacious part of the palace, the terrace, with its pavilions and kiosks, overlooks the lakes.

Exploring Mandu

Between the Village Group of monuments and Sagar Talao, Mandu's largest lake, are several monuments worth visiting. **Malik Mugith's Mosque**, built in 1432, has carved pillars taken from ruined Hindu temples. To its south are two impressive buildings in a pretty, wooded area – **Dai ki Chhoti Bahen ka Mahal** (the "Nurse's Younger Sister's Palace") and **Dai ka Mahal** (the "Nurse's Palace"). The two women were clearly royal favourites and the pretty, octagonal-domed houses show traces of blue and yellow tilework.

Shivalinga at Neelkanth Mahal

Southeast of Sagar Talao, down a winding road to the edge of a cliff, are the Rewa Kund Group of Monuments, associated with the legendary romance between Sultan Baz Bahadur and the beautiful singer Rupmati. Beside the Rewa Kund Stepwell, fed by an underground stream whose waters are said to be sacred, is **Baz Bahadur's Palace**, constructed between 1508 and 1509. Its most charming feature is an octagonal pavilion overlooking a garden, now covered with weeds. Located just south of the palace is **Rupmati's Pavilion**, with its lovely fluted domes, from where there is a spectacular view of the surrounding countryside.

Baz Bahadur, the last sultan of Malwa, was defeated in battle by the Mughals in 1561. After this, Mandu fell into decline, as the Mughal emperors only used it as a halting place on their journeys to the Deccan. In 1616, Mandu briefly came to life again, when the Mughal emperor Jahangir spent seven months here, renovating the palaces and giving lavish parties at the Jahaz Mahal. Accompanying him was Sir Thomas Roe, the Elizabethan ambassador to the Mughal court. He has left a fascinating account of royal festivities and exciting lion and tiger hunts at Mandu.

For hotels and restaurants in this region see pp697–9 and pp726–7

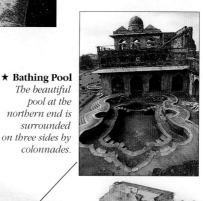

★ Water Channels
The intricate spiral designs of the water channels are characteristic of the simple elegance of Mandu's architecture.

The terrace pool, similar in design to the one on the ground floor, is fed by a water channel.

★ Bathing Pool
The beautiful pool at the northern end is surrounded on three sides by colonnades.

Narrow rooms lie at either end of the ground floor, with its three large halls.

VISITORS' CHECKLIST

Royal Enclave. ☐ *daily.* 📷 🍴
ℹ *Tourist cottages, Mandu, (07292) 26 3235.*

A short distance west of Sagar Talao, a flight of steps leads down a ravine to **Neelkanth Mahal**. This palace, with its many water channels and cascades, was built in 1574 on the site of an ancient Shiva shrine, for the Mughal emperor Akbar's Hindu wife. The main room, overlooking the valley, is once again in use as a Shiva temple, even though its walls are covered with fine Arabic calligraphy.

Environs
The **Bagh Caves**, lying 50 km (31 miles) west of Mandu, date from AD 400–700. Built by Buddhist monks, they have murals similar in style to those at Ajanta *(see pp480–81)*, but unfortunately these are in a very poor state of preservation.

BAZ BAHADUR AND RUPMATI

One day while out hunting, Sultan Baz Bahadur (r.1554–61) spotted a Hindu girl, Rupmati, singing as she bathed in the Narmada river. Bewitched by her beauty and her voice,

Baz Bahadur persuaded her to live with him in Mandu. Thereafter, he spent his time in the pursuit of love and music, leaving his kingdom vulnerable to attack. When Emperor Akbar's general, Adham Khan, attacked Mandu in 1561, he won an easy victory. Baz Bahadur fled the battlefield, deserting Rupmati who was captured. But the courtesan proved more courageous than the king. Even as the Mughal general waited outside her room to claim her, she committed suicide by swallowing poison.

An 18th-century miniature of Rupmati and Baz Bahadur

View of Maheshwar's fort, shrines and ghats, along the Narmada

Maheshwar ⑯

West Nimar district. 90 km (56 miles) SW of Indore. 🚶 *19,600.* 🚌 *Barwaha, 39 km (24 miles) E of town centre, then taxi or bus.* 🚌 ℹ️ *MP Tourism, Narmada Cottages, (07283) 27 3455.* 🏛️ *Panchkosi Yatra (Mar).*

Picturesquely sited on the banks of the Narmada, Maheshwar is an important Hindu pilgrimage centre. It was the site of the ancient city of Mahishmati, mentioned in classical Sanskrit texts. Maheshwar's beautiful temples and ghats were erected by Queen Ahilyabai of the Holkar dynasty *(see p246),* in the mid-18th century.

The 1.5-km (1-mile) long river front is dotted with shrines, ghats and the elegant cenotaphs of the Holkar rulers, and is usually thronged with pilgrims taking a dip. A magnificent fan-shaped stairway leads from the river front to Maheshwar Fort's royal enclosure, and the **Ahilyeshwar Temple**, built in 1798. The richly carved courtyard, leading on to the palace, has an impressive statue of Ahilyabai. This benevolent queen, who also built the Vishwanath Temple *(see p205)* in Varanasi, was described by a British colonial official, Sir John Malcolm, as "one of the purest and most exemplary rulers that ever lived". Also within the fort is the Rehwa Weavers' Society, where the famous gossamerfine Maheshwari cotton and silk textiles are woven.

Statue of Queen Ahilyabai

Omkareshwar ⑰

East Nimar district. 77 km (48 miles) S of Indore. 🚌 🚌 🚌 ℹ️ *MP Tourism, Tourist Bungalow, (07280) 27 1455.* 🏛️ *Shivratri (Feb/Mar).*

The island of Omkareshwar, at the confluence of the Narmada and Kaveri rivers, is one of India's most enchanting pilgrimage towns. Seen from above, it is shaped like the sacred *Om* symbol. The island is 2-km (1.3-mile) long and 1-km (0.6-mile) wide, with jagged cliffs on its southern and eastern sides. It is dotted with temples, sadhus' caves and bathing ghats, and filled with the sound of chanting. A circumambulatory path circles the island, marking out the pilgrim trail.

Omkareshwar is linked to the mainland by a concrete causeway, though visitors can also come on the flat bottomed barges that ply the river. The island is dominated by the towering white *shikhara* of the **Sri Omkar Mandhata** ("Bestower of Desires") **Temple**, within which is a particularly sacred Shivalinga, one of 12 *jyotirlingas* (natural rock lingas said to have miraculously emerged from light) in the country.

At the eastern end of the island is the 10th-century **Siddhnath Temple** which has beautiful sculptures of *apsaras*. The northern end has a cluster of Hindu and Jain temples. Overlooking them is a ruined palace, part of a fortified township that stood here until it was sacked by Muslim invaders in the 11th century.

A pilgrim praying on the banks of the Narmada at Omkareshwar

THE NARMADA DAM CONTROVERSY

Since the mid-1980s, an ambitious scheme to dam the Narmada has been embroiled in controversy. The Narmada Valley Authority claim that the Sardar Sarovar Dam will bring electricity, irrigation and drinking water to millions of people. Environmental activists opposing the dam, who include Medha Patkar, leader of the "Save the Narmada" movement, and Arundhati Roy, the 1997 Booker Prize-winning author, say that the dam will inundate some 37,000 ha (91,429 acres) of forest, and displace more than 200,000 villagers, most of them poor tribal people whose distinctive culture and means of livelihood will be wiped out along with their lands. The Supreme Court of India has now ruled that work on the dam can continue. When completed, it will be the second largest in the world, after the Three Gorges Dam in China.

Anti-dam activists at a protest meeting

The Narmada River

Rising in the Amarkantak Plateau, where the Vindhya and Satpura ranges meet, the Narmada flows westward for 1,247 km (775 miles), across the states of Madhya Pradesh and Gujarat before entering the Arabian Sea. One of India's seven sacred rivers, the Narmada, according to Hindu mythology, was born of Lord Shiva's sweat when he

Image from Chausath Yogini Temple

performed his cosmic dance *(see p566)*. The Narmada is also believed to be the embodiment of purity, and a legend holds that every year the polluted Ganges comes in the guise of a dark woman, and takes a purifying dip in the Narmada. Sugarcane, cotton and bananas grow along the river, whose banks are lined with temples.

Dhuandhar Falls *are a scenic spot, where the river drops 25 m (82 ft) down from the Amarkantak Plateau. The name Dhuandhar means "Stream of Smoke".*

Narmada Kund *at Amarkantak ("Neck of Shiva"), marks the source of the river. It is surrounded by 16th-century temples.*

Maheshwar has beautifully carved river front temples and 28 bathing ghats.

Omkareshwar is an Om-shaped island at the confluence of the Narmada and the Kaveri.

Chausath Yogini Temple which dates to the 10th century, is on a hilltop near the Marble Rocks.

Jabalpur
Bhedaghat • Chausath
Dhuandhar Yogini Temple
Falls
• Hoshangabad Mandla • Amarkantak

GUJARAT Maheshwar •
• Omkareshwar MADHYA PRADESH

• Sardar Sarovar Dam

Arabian Sea MAHARASHTRA

At Mandla, the river takes a sharp turn.

Sethanighat Temple at Hoshangabad has an image of the Goddess Narmada.

The Marble Rocks *at Bhedaghat, where the fast-flowing river has cut a gorge, are especially spectacular on a moonlit night. Boat rides are the best way to experience their beauty.*

The Narmada Parikrama, *undertaken by many sadhus, is a pilgrimage on foot along both banks of the river. It covers 2,600 km (1,616 miles) and takes about three years.*

Pachmarhi's Christ Church, built in 1875, a relic of the Raj

Pachmarhi ⑱

Hoshangabad district. 210 km (130 miles) SE of Bhopal. 🏛 *11,400.* 🚉 *Pipariya, 47 km (29 miles) N of Pachmarhi, then taxi or bus.* ℹ️ *Pipariya, (07576) 22 3499.* 🚌 ℹ️ *MP Tourism, Amaltas Complex Station, (07578) 25 2100.* 🎉 *Shivratri (Feb/Mar).*

This delightful hill station, at an altitude of 1,067 m (3,501 ft), lies in the verdant hills of the Satpura Range. Its attractions include waterfalls and pools, and caves with prehistoric art. In 1857, Captain James Forsyth of the Bengal Lancers spotted this saucer-shaped plateau, and it was quickly developed into a sanatorium and army station by the British.

The town retains a genteel, Raj-era ambience, and among its colonial relics are the **Christ Church**, built in 1875, with beautiful stained-glass windows, and the **Army Music School** which still begins the day with rousing English martial tunes such as the Colonel Bogey March.

Pachmarhi means "Five Houses", and the town takes its name from the five ancient **Pandava Caves**, set in a garden south of the bus stop. From the caves, paths lead to the scenic **Apsara Vihar** ("Fairy Pool") and the **Rajat Prapat Waterfalls**.

The wooded hills around Pachmarhi, home of the Gond and Korku tribes, are dotted with cave shelters, some of them with paintings dating back 10,000 years. The most

accessible of them is the **Mahadeo Cave**, 6 km (4 miles) from the Jai Stambh ("Victory Pillar") in the centre of town. The **Jatashankar Cave Temple**, dedicated to Shiva, is a short excursion, 2 km (1.3 mile) from the main bus stop. At the Shivratri festival, a colourful gathering of pilgrims and sadhus takes place here. En route to it is the **Harper's Cave**, so called because it has a painting of a man playing an instrument that looks like a harp.

Jabalpur ⑲

Jabalpur district. 330 km (205 miles) E of Bhopal. 🏛 *951,500.* ✈️ *14 km (8 miles) W of town centre.* 🚉 🚌 ℹ️ *MP Tourism, Railway Station, (0761) 267 7690.*

The gateway to Bandhavgarh *(see p239)* and Kanha *(see pp254–5)*, two of India's finest wildlife sanctuaries, Jabalpur was from the 12th to 16th centuries the capital of a powerful Gond tribal kingdom, whose most famous ruler was a brave and able woman, Rani Durgavati. In 1817 the British made it an army cantonment and administrative centre, to deal with the growing menace of gangs of highway bandits known as *thuggees*, who would rob travellers. In the 1830s, Colonel William Sleeman launched his famous campaign against the *thuggees*, and in a few years

Detail from a Gond tribal house

had wiped them out. The word thug (from *thuggee*), though, seems to have found a permanent place in the English language. In the bazaar is the **Rani Durgavati Museum** with stone sculptures and Gond tribal artifacts. The ruined **Madan Mahal Fort**, built by a Gond king in 1116, overlooks the town from a hill to the west.

🏛 **Rani Durgavati Museum**
🕐 *Mon–Sat.*

Environs
The **Marble Rocks**, the **Chausath Yogini Temple** and the **Dhuandhar Falls** are 22 km (14 miles) southwest of Jabalpur.

Mandla ⑳

Mandla district. 95 km (59 miles) S of Jabalpur. 🚉 🚌 ⛴️ *daily.*

This sleepy town is situated on a loop in the Narmada river, which provides a natural moat for the 17th-century Gond Fort, now in ruins. Mandla is a sacred city for Gond tribals, whose warrior queen, Durgavati, committed suicide here in 1564 when she was defeated by the Mughal emperor Akbar's army. Temples and ghats line the banks of the river, where the Gonds perform their funeral rites. The main bazaar, near the bus stand, is interesting to explore with its shops selling tribal silver jewellery and bell metal.

The Narmada river at Mandla, lined by temples and ghats

The Folk Art of Bastar

Bastar district, in the newly-created state of Chhattisgarh, is a remote, thickly forested area, predominantly inhabited by tribal people and small communities of craftsmen. They live close to nature, and their arts and crafts have been inspired by the beauty, rhythm and vigour of forest creatures and plants. Animal, bird and plant motifs embellish many of the utilitarian, decorative and ritual objects that they fashion out of clay, wood, metal and cotton yarn. These can be seen at the weekly tribal markets held in Madhya Pradesh and Chhattisgarh, as well as in handicrafts shops in Delhi.

Clay toy on wheels

A newly-wed tribal couple in Bastar

Wooden walking sticks, *toys and ritual objects are carved out of the soft wood of roots and stems. The ingenious walking sticks make an eerie whistling sound, meant to scare away wild animals and evil spirits in the forest.*

Combs *in wood and metal are exchanged between young tribal boys and girls of Bastar as tokens of love. The wooden combs are decorated with simple geometric motifs, while the brass ones are more ornately carved.*

Iron lamps, *embellished with leaf forms and lively animal and bird figures, are a speciality of Bastar's lohars (blacksmiths), who also make agricultural tools.*

A brass comb, carved with the image of a deity

Tribal potters *make fascinating clay ritual figures of mythical animals, horses and elephants. The materials used are the red and black clay from river banks, known for their strength and elasticity.*

Bronze images, *made by the Ghadva community of metalsmiths, using the lost wax technique, include this guardian deity of a Bastar village.*

Textiles *for festive occasions are woven from thick unbleached cotton by the Panka community of weavers. The motifs, always inspired by nature, are woven in red madder-dyed yarn.*

Kanha National Park ㉑

Often described as India's finest game sanctuary and a model for wildlife conservation, Kanha's magnificent landscape combines grassy meadows and flat-topped hills with meandering streams and lush deciduous forests. The setting for Rudyard Kipling's famous *The Jungle Book*, Kanha is today an important Project Tiger *(see p289)* Reserve. Along with Bandhavgarh *(see p239)*, it is one of the best places to spot these elusive creatures. The rich variety of wildlife found within this 1,954-sq km (754-sq mile) park, once the exclusive hunting ground of the British viceroys, includes deer, leopard, hyena, sloth bear, pythons and nearly 300 species of birds.

Common Mongoose
This ferret-like animal is a fierce fighter, particularly known for its masterly combats with snakes.

Dadars and Deer
Grassy meadows, known as dadars, characterize much of Kanha. They provide an ideal habitat for herbivores such as the spotted deer.

0 km   3
0 miles   3

Black Ibis
This elegant bird with glossy plumage is often found at the edges of Kanha's waterholes, looking for small fish, frogs and earthworms.

JABALPUR

Rondha

Sonph

Khatia

Kisli

Kanha

Khapa

Bisanpur

Sonc

Lapsi Kuba

Banjar River

Kipling Camp
This British-run complex (see p698), close to the park entrance at Kisli, has pleasant chalets, surrounded by forest. The camp arranges guided safaris.

Interpretation centres, located at Khatia, Mukki and Kanha, have excellent films, models and books

Shravantal
This tranquil waterhole attracts several water birds, such as the lesser whistling teal and the shoveller. There are viewing platforms located nearby.

Tiger
Kanha's tigers now number about 100. Park guides expertly track them through pug marks and the alarm calls of deer and langurs.

Central Indian Barasingha
Conservation has increased the numbers of this rare species, which was close to extinction 30 years ago.

BILASPUR

• Bahmnidadar

Mukki

KEY

- - Park boundary
= Major road
= Major road
ℹ️ Tourist information
❄️ Viewpoint
🅰️ Accommodation

KIPLING'S JUNGLE BOOK

The English writer Rudyard Kipling (1865–1936) was born in Bombay (Mumbai), and though he spent little time in India, the country provided the setting for many of his books. Among his most enduring works is *The Jungle Books*, delightful stories of animal behaviour and the law of the jungle. Set in the Seonee Forests of Kanha, their endearing hero is the wolf-reared boy Mowgli; and the many enchanting animal characters include Rikki-tikki-tavi, the mongoose, Shere Khan, the tiger, Kaa, the python, and Baloo, the bear.

Jacket for Disney's version of *The Jungle Books*

EASTERN
INDIA

Introducing Eastern India

Kolkata, India's second largest city, is the best known destination for visitors to Eastern India. Apart from this endlessly fascinating metropolis, the region offers an astonishing diversity of landscapes, peoples and cultures. These include the steamy mangrove forests along the Bay of Bengal, habitat of the Royal Bengal tiger, the spectacular mountain vistas of Darjeeling (officially Darjiling) and Sikkim, and Orissa's magnificent temples and beaches. Further east are Assam and the northeastern states, home to many different tribal communities, whose distinct cultures flourish in areas of pristine natural beauty.

An agile Nishi tribesman of Arunachal Pradesh crossing the Siang, a tributary of the Brahmaputra river, on a tightrope

SEE ALSO

- **Where to Stay** pp699–702
- **Where to Eat** pp727–31

GANGTOK

DARJEELING

JALDA

NH34

PANDUA

MURSHIDABAD

Varanasi

SHANTINIKE

NH2

KOL

Hirakud
Reservoir

NH6   NH23   SIMLIPAL

Raipur

NH42   NH5

Bay
of
Bengal

Mahanadi   CUTTACK

BHUBANESWAR

NH5

Chilika
Lake   PURI

GOPALPUR-
ON-SEA

NH43

Hooghly

SUNDE

Visakhapatnam

| 0 km | 80 |
| 0 miles | 80 |

The 10th-century Mukteshwar Temple complex in Bhubaneswar

◁ A woman fishing in Loktak Lake *(see p338)*, Manipur

KEY

▬ National highway

▬ Major road

▬ River

- - State border

Tea gardens in Darjeeling, nestling in the foothills of the Eastern Himalayas

GETTING AROUND

Kolkata, Guwahati and Bhubaneswar, the three major cities in this region, are well connected by air and rail to most parts of India. From Kolkata and Guwahati, there are regular flights to all the northeastern states. The hill station of Darjeeling, and Sikkim's capital, Gangtok, are accessible by air or rail up to Bagdogra-Siliguri, from where buses and taxis complete the journey up to the hills on National Highway 31. The delightful Himalayan Toy Train *(see p294)* also runs from Siliguri to Darjeeling, providing panoramic views of the Himalayas en route. From Kolkata, most destinations in West Bengal are reached on National Highway 34. In Orissa, the major sights are connected by National Highway 5. The gateway to the northeast, Guwahati in Assam, has good road links to the other six states on National Highways 37, 40 and 52. Visitors require travel permits for some destinations in the northeast *(see p758)*.

A PORTRAIT OF EASTERN INDIA

T*he peoples and cultures found in India's eastern states are as varied as the landscape itself. Stretching from the crowded metropolis of Kolkata to the remote tribal settlements of Arunachal Pradesh, which border on China and Myanmar, the region includes mountainous Sikkim, tropical Orissa, and the lush valleys of Assam, watered by the mighty Brahmaputra river.*

West Bengal, the largest and most densely populated of the eastern states, offers the visitor a kaleidoscope of images. These range from the mangrove swamps of the Sunderbans, home of the Royal Bengal tiger, to the misty tea gardens of Darjeeling, and the unique vitality of the state capital Kolkata (formerly Calcutta).

Orchid from Meghalaya

Kolkata is a city that evokes extreme reactions: novelists exhaust metaphors trying to describe it, filmmakers are defeated by it, and even the average non-Bengali agrees that something about the city defines that abstract entity – "culture". As a headquarter of the East India Company, and later, the capital of British India, the city played an early host to crucial Western influences, especially English education. It witnessed the phenomenon popularly described as the Bengal Renaissance, a complex dynamic of socioreligious reform, and literary and artistic efflorescence, with a strong nationalistic undercurrent. Kolkata thus became the first Indian city to have an "intelligentsia". Rabindranath Tagore *(see p292)*, its most famous son, lives on through his stories, poems, plays and songs, loved to this day. Another cultural icon is the famous film director Satyajit Ray, whose work has had a profound impact on Asian art cinema. Since 1977, West Bengal has been under Communist rule. The culture of flag-waving processions, however, blends flawlessly with the

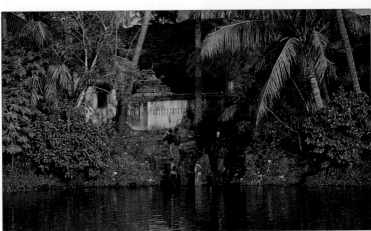

A village pond in Orissa, with a small Hindu temple on its banks

Statues being transported during Durga Puja, Kolkata's biggest festival

typical Kolkata pastime of *adda* – a lively mix of heated political debate, highbrow analyses and lowbrow gossip. This is all played out against a backdrop of crumbling vestiges of some splendid colonial architecture.

From Kolkata, many visitors travel south to the beaches and exquisitely sculpted temples of Orissa. The high-point of Orissa's cultural and religious year is the spectacular annual Rath Yatra, a festival held in the temple town of Puri *(see p312)*. The state pays a price for its scenic location on the Bay of Bengal – it is often hit by devastating cyclones during the monsoon. In recent years, however, Orissa's people, who include many forest-dwelling tribal groups, have enjoyed increasing prosperity, with schemes to develop the state's rich mineral resources and its growing tourism industry.

North of Kolkata lies Sikkim, its skyline dominated by the snow-capped peaks of India's highest mountain, Kanchendzonga *(see p302)*, which soars to a height of 8,598 m (28,209 ft). Sikkim's culture borrows much from neighbouring Tibet and Nepal, and many people practice the Tibetan form of Buddhism, introduced in the 15th century by its former rulers, the Chhogyals, who came from Tibet. Much of Sikkim's cultural and religious

Dancer at monastery festival, Sikkim

life still revolves around its serene and beautiful Buddhist monasteries.

In the extreme eastern corner of India are Assam and the six northeastern states of Arunachal Pradesh, Meghalaya, Manipur, Mizoram, Nagaland and Tripura, connected to the rest of the country only by a thin corridor of land. This region is home to dozens of tribal communities, each with its own language and culture *(see pp336–7)*.

Tea dominates the economy of Assam, which produces more than half the tea grown in India, as well as much of the country's oil. The other six states have rich agricultural and forest resources, and little industry. The isolation of the northeastern states, and their shared borders with Bangladesh, Bhutan, China and Myanmar, has led to violent separatist movements in some areas. Visitors need special permits *(see p759)* for this region whose main attraction is its pristine natural beauty and rare flora and fauna.

An Assamese woman pounding grain

The Story of Indian Tea

Tea leaves

India is the world's largest producer of tea, perhaps the world's most popular drink. The tea plant *(Camellia sinensis)* is indigenous to Northeast India, and though tea was cultivated and drunk for centuries by the Singpho tribe of Arunachal Pradesh as a stimulant and medicinal brew, tea plantations for commercial exploitation were only established in the mid-19th century. Today, the Indian tea industry employs over a million people, half of whom are women, and produces about 850 million kg (1,874 million lb) of tea every year, most of which is grown in Assam, northern Bengal and Darjeeling (Darjiling).

Darjeeling's tea gardens *are a picturesque sight, covering terraced hill slopes upto an altitude of 1,950 m (6,398 ft).*

Fresh tea leaves *are plucked from April to December. A skilled picker can harvest 37 kg (82 lbs) of leaves a day, enough to yield 20 kg (44 lbs) of processed tea.*

Shade trees

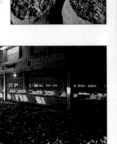

The withering process *blows warm air over the leaves, reducing their moisture content by half. The leaves are then rolled, pressed, fermented, and finally dried again.*

PICKERS IN A TEA GARDEN

The tea bush, with its bright green oval leaves, is regularly pruned to keep its height low, allowing for convenient picking. Left wild, the plant can grow into a tree up to 10 m (33 ft) tall.

Fresh tea leaves　　　Dried tea leaves

The CTC or crush, tear and curl method, *is used to process a more robust, granular Assam tea. The leaves are crushed to release their enzymes, before they are fermented and dried.*

Tea tasters *tell the quality of a tea by breathing on to leaves clutched in their fist, and inhaling the warmed aroma. To fix the base price at auctions, they also sample the brew, swilling the liquid round their tongues, in the manner of wine tasters.*

Darjeeling tea logo

Assam tea logo

SPECIAL TEA

स्पेशल लज्जतदार चहा

A 1950s poster advertising a brand of Indian tea

Darjeeling and Assam teas *are the best known Indian varieties. Darjeeling teas are famous for their delicate muscatel flavour, and the best ones have been sold at auction for up to US$220 for 1 kg (2.2 lbs). Assam tea has a stronger taste and darker colour.*

Women's supple fingers are preferred for the delicate task of plucking just the top two leaves.

Tea bush

Basket for carrying plucked tea leaves

Bronze tea kettles *with dragon-shaped handles and elephant trunk spouts, are typical of the Darjeeling and Sikkim region.*

Masala tea

Herbal tea

Green tea

Darjeeling Golden Tips

Assam Tender Buds

Assam Superior Buds

Different types of Indian tea *include green (unfermented) tea which is drunk in Kashmir, and* masala *tea spiced with cardamom and ginger. Long leaves give a superior brew, while broken leaves and tea dust go into tea bags.*

TEA ESTATES

In the early 19th century, the British began looking for a site in India, suitable for growing tea for the British market. They soon discovered wild tea plants growing in the northeast, and by 1850, vast tracts of tiger-populated jungle had been cleared in Assam, northern Bengal and Darjeeling to establish tea gardens. Today India has over 25,000 tea estates of varying size, each a self-contained world with its own school, shops and medical clinic. At its heart is the plantation manager's gracious bungalow, and a club where the planters used to meet for tennis and sundowners.

A typical tea planter's bungalow in northern Bengal

The Flavours of Eastern India

This region, watered by the rivers of the Gangetic Delta and washed by the sea, is a land of plenty, with an abundance of fresh vegetables, coconut and fish. Rice is the staple food and the region produces a wide variety. Freshwater fish is popular all across this riverine land. Pork and beef are eaten in most of the Northeastern states, while in Sikkim, the food is largely Tibetan with bamboo shoots and steamed dishes featuring on the menu. This region, with its large tea estates in the Himalayan foothills, is also the home of India's finest teas, especially from Darjeeling.

Green chillies and lime

Bay leaves, chillies and other spices on sale at a weekly market

BASIC DISHES

In the delta and coastal areas of Bengal and Orissa, five spices – mustard, aniseed, fenugreek, cumin and black cumin seeds – are used to flavour the food while mustard oil is the preferred cooking fat. The two cuisines are similar, except that the Bengalis pride themselves on having a more sophisticated palate. *Dalma* is Orissa's signature dish and is a combination of vegetables and *arhar dal* (red gram). Vegetables, such as potatoes and aubergines (eggplant), are fried (*bhaja*), mashed (*bharta*) and lightly or heavily spiced as in *dalna*, made with peas and cauliflower. Classic dishes include *shukto* (mixed vegetables with bitter gourd) and *mochar ghonto*, made from the banana flower.

FISH AND SEAFOOD

It is fish that brings out the genius of cooking in this region. Every part is eaten – the head makes a delicious curry (*muri ghonto*) and the roe an excellent cocktail snack (*macher dimer bora*). Popular fish of the region are *rahu* (carp), *betki* and the much-loved *hilsa* or *ilish* fish which floods the rivers during the monsoon. *Hilsa* is

Kalakand   *Kancha gola*   *Peda*   *Jalebi*   *Chumchum*   *Mango sandesh*   *Danadar*

A small selection of the many varieties of sweets from Bengal

LOCAL DISHES AND SPECIALITIES

This region's cuisine is varied. Historically, Calcutta (now Kolkata) has been a melting pot and the tradional Bangla *rana*, which combines the Bengali fish-based, delicately spiced food, the Muslim mutton dishes and the many-layered Dacci *parantha*, was enriched by the flavours of its Jewish, Armenian, Indo-Portuguese and English settlers. Fish is the centrepiece of both the Bengali and Oriya meal, and can be cooked with vegetables, as in *besar maacch*. Often, dried prawns are added to vegetables to enchance the flavour. Rice, a *dal* (lentils), vegetable preparations, sweet and sour chutneys, green chillies and slices of lime accompany the meal. In the Northeast, pork is a favourite. It is cooked with bamboo shoots, wild mushrooms or with ground rice and herbs in a one-pot dish called *onla*.

Tomato chutney

Momos, *Tibetan dumplings, are eaten with a fiery sauce of dried red chillies and a bowl of chicken broth.*

Women working in paddy fields in Orissa

cooked in mustard, fried crisp, smoked to melt its innumerable bones, steamed in a banana leaf *(ilish macher paturi)* or cooked in a light sauce of yoghurt and ginger *(doi maach)*. Other great regional inventions are the delicate *daab chingri*, where prawns are cooked in a tender coconut *(daab)* and *chingri malai* curry (prawns cooked in coconut milk).

OTHER FAVOURITES

Sikkim's distinctive cuisine is influenced also by Nepal and Bhutan. Some popular dishes are the Tibetan-style *thupka* (thick noodle soup), *momos* and the diverse ways of cooking local cottage cheese *(churpi)*. Assamese food combines pungent ingredients with fermented foods, such as the Manipuri *iromba*, made with fermented fish, vegetables and bamboo shoots. Other dishes include *akshi aong* (a delicious pork curry heavily seasoned with chillies) and *anok pongsuem* (steamed fish from Nagaland).

Basket of freshly caught fish being carried to the market

In Kolkata, food from the Raj still reigns supreme among other cuisines. Typical dishes are prawn cocktail, roast lamb with mint sauce and the ever-popular caramel custard.

SWEETS

Both Orissa and Bengal are known for their infinite variety of milk-based sweets. *Sandesh*, made from *chenna* (an Indian ricotta), is by far the most popular. Cottage cheese and syrup are also used to create many varieties of sweets including *kancha gola*, *chumchum* and *danadar*. *Peda* and *kalakand* are made with condensed milk and chopped nuts.

ON THE MENU

Bhapa hilsa *Hilsa* marinated with mustard and chillies and steamed in a banana leaf.

Chholar dal Yellow split peas seasoned with cumin seed and *garam masala*.

Kamla kheer A pudding with oranges and thickened milk.

Kosha mangsho A spicy mutton curry eaten with rice or fluffy fried breads *(luchi)*.

Mishti doi Yoghurt sweetened with molasses and garnished with chopped nuts.

Saag bhaja Stir-fried spinach, garnished with coconut.

Shoshey maachh Fish cooked in a mustard sauce.

Prawn malai curry *has prawns cooked in coconut cream with crushed mustard seeds and red chillies.*

Aloo posto, *common to both Bengal and Orissa, are potatoes cooked with a paste of poppy seeds.*

Caramel custard, *a Raj favourite, is a milk mixture baked in a dish with sweet caramel lining its base.*

KOLKATA

One of the world's great cities, Kolkata or Calcutta as it used to be known, has been through many incarnations. From an obscure village on the banks of the Hooghly river, it evolved into the capital of Great Britain's Indian empire. Today, this vibrant city with its distinct imperial flavour is the capital of the communist state of West Bengal.

In 1690, an English merchant, Job Charnock, established a trading post in the riverside village of Sutanuti which, together with neighbouring Govindapur and Kolikata, grew into the city of Calcutta. Over the next 200 years, the city became a flourishing commercial centre with imposing Victorian Gothic buildings, churches, and boulevards. Simultaneously, intellectual and cultural life bloomed, with a renaissance of Bengali art and literature, and the growth of a strong nationalist reform movement that led to the founding of the Brahmo Samaj, an enlightened off-shoot of Hinduism, and the establishment of Presidency College, then the foremost centre of English education. The decision to shift the capital to New Delhi in 1911 and the urban decay of the 1960s diminished some of the city's affluence, but never quenched its effervescence.

In 2001, Calcutta became Kolkata, the Bengali pronunciation of its name. The city is crowded and dirty in places, but is nevertheless full of character. The teeming life of the waterfront along the Strand, the noisy jumble of bazaars and pavement stalls, the residential streets with their once gracious mansions, all make for an electric, cosmopolitan atmosphere, rarely found in other Indian cities. Kolkata's charms straddle the decaying grandeur of the imperial capital and the smart restaurants and boutiques of Park Street. These coexist with the traditional Bengali world of Rabindranath Tagore's mansion at Jorasanko, the Kalighat temple and the potters' village of Kumartuli, and with the lively politics of the Coffee House and the Maidan, dominated by the Victoria Memorial, a spectacular symbol of imperial high noon.

View of the Hooghly river and the Howrah Bridge, the third longest cantilever bridge in the world

◁ Statue of the young Queen Victoria in the central hall, Victoria Memorial

Exploring Kolkata

The city of Kolkata lies in a long strip, with the river to its west and the wetlands to its east. Along the river front, the Strand, is the city centre with the Maidan, a large 400-ha (988-acre) park where Kolkata's residents play football, hold political rallies or enjoy the cool evenings. On the other side of the park is the city's main thoroughfare, the Chowringhee or Jawaharlal Nehru Road with shops, hotels, offices and residential buildings. The southern part of the city has the middle-class residential areas, while north Kolkata is the older part of the city, its maze of narrow lanes crowded with houses, cheek-by-jowl with shops and offices.

LOCATOR MAP

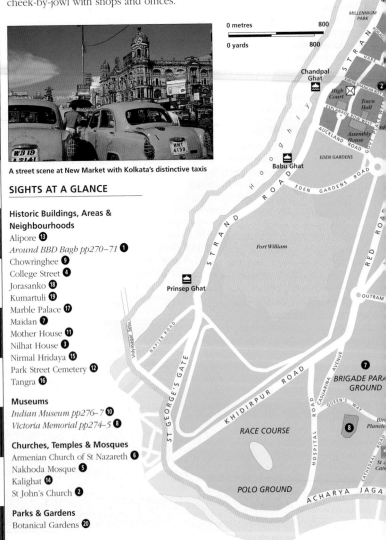

A street scene at New Market with Kolkata's distinctive taxis

SIGHTS AT A GLANCE

Historic Buildings, Areas & Neighbourhoods
Alipore ⑬
Around BBD Bagh pp270–71 ①
Chowringhee ⑨
College Street ④
Jorasanko ⑱
Kumartuli ⑲
Marble Palace ⑰
Maidan ⑦
Mother House ⑪
Nilhat House ③
Nirmal Hridaya ⑮
Park Street Cemetery ⑫
Tangra ⑯

Museums
Indian Museum pp276–7 ⑩
Victoria Memorial pp274–5 ⑧

Churches, Temples & Mosques
Armenian Church of St Nazareth ⑥
Nakhoda Mosque ⑤
Kalighat ⑭
St John's Church ②

Parks & Gardens
Botanical Gardens ⑳

For additional map symbols *see back flap*

GETTING AROUND

Central Kolkata is compact and can easily be covered on foot.
Alternatives include taxis, or the often crowded buses and
mini-buses. Trams and the Metro, linking the southern and
northern parts of the city from Tollygunge to Dum Dum, are
other options. A local mode of transport are cycle-rickshaws
that operate in the congested lanes and side streets.

**A colourful stall in one of Kolkata's
main flower markets**

KEY

▢	Street-by-Street area: *see pp270–71*
🚉	Railway station
🚌	Bus station
⛴	Ferry port
Ⓜ	Metro station
ℹ	Tourist information
➕	Hospital
🚓	Police station
🛕	Temple
🔱	Gurdwara
✝	Church •
⊠	Post office
▬	National highway
▬	Major road
═	Minor road

SEE ALSO

• *Where to Stay* p669–700

• *Where to Eat* pp727–8

GREATER
KOLKATA

Netaji Subhash
Chandra Bose
International
Airport

Howrah

Sealdah

Shibpur

Park Circus

Bhawanipur

0 km   2

0 miles   2

Street-by-Street: Around BBD Bagh ❶

Signage of the Royal Insurance Building

This is the "heart" of Kolkata and was the site of the original Kolikata, one of the villages from which the city grew. The small tank at its core was where three young Indian freedom fighters, Binay, Badal and Dinesh, shot the British inspector-general of police in 1930. The square, now named after them, is ringed by British colonial buildings, dating to the 18th and early 19th centuries. These were once the centres of British administrative and commercial control.

Job Charnock's Tomb
Job Charnock is believed to have laid the foundations of the English settlement in Kolkata.

★ St John's Church
The design of this church (see p272) was based on London's St Martin-in-the-Fields. The constructing engineers wanted the spire to be higher, but desisted fearing the soggy sub-soil.

High Court

Gates of Raj Bhavan
Magnificent Neo-Classical gateways lead to the old Government House, built in the mid-18th century. This is now the residence of the state governor, and can be viewed from across the road.

STRAND ROAD
HARE STREET
KS RAY ROAD
COUNCIL H
ESPLANADE ROW

TRAMS IN KOLKATA

Horse drawn trams first trundled their way from Sealdah station on 24 February 1873. Electric trams were introduced in June 1905 and have survived till today. Riding in them is a pleasant if rattly experience and the tram's slowly clanging bell is one of Kolkata's most characteristic sounds. Though an integral part of the city's transport network *(see p269)* and appreciated for being pollution free, they are under threat for being too slow.

An electric tram plying on the streets of Kolkata

STAR SIGHTS

★ St John's Church

★ GPO

★ Writers' Building

★ GPO
Kolkata's General Post Office is housed in this building with its impressive rotunda. Designed by Walter Granville and built in the 1860s, it stands on the site of the old mud fort.

LOCATOR MAP
See Kolkata Map pp268–9

0 metres   100

0 yards   100

St Andrew's Kirk
Consecrated in 1818, the church has a soaring steeple, a magnificent organ and a beautifully carved pulpit.

FAIRLIE PLACE

SUBASH ROAD

LYONS RANGE

NETAJI

BBD BAGH NORTH

BBD BAGH SOUTH

ROSS PLACE

OLD COURT HOUSE STREET

RN MUKHERJI ROAD

T STREET

WATERLOO STREET

Old Currency House

KEY

– – – Suggested route

★ Writers' Building
The hub of colonial India from 1777, this imposing building with its Corinthian façade derives its name from the "writers" (clerks) of the East India Company who worked here. The state government has its offices here.

View Across Lal Dighi Tank
The East India Company's seat of administration, their courts of justice and the churches for their Sunday services were set up around this small tank, fed by springs.

View of St John's Church with its soaring spire

St John's Church ❷

Council House St. **Tel** (033) 2243 6098.
⬜ daily. 🕐 10am–5pm.

The first parish church in Kolkata, St John's Church was established in 1787. It boasts an impressive stained-glass panel of *The Last Supper*, in which the artist Johann Zoffany gave the 12 disciples the faces of British personalities famous in the city at the time.

St John's has many associations with the history of the English East India Company. Warren Hastings, Governor of Bengal, was married here. In the churchyard is a memorial to Lady Canning, the vicereine who died in 1861. Her name lives on in popular memory because she was much addicted to a fried, syrupy sweetmeat, which was named after her (it is pronounced "leddy-kenny" in Bengali). The mausoleum of Job Charnock (*see p270*) also stands here.

A short distance away is the memorial to the victims of the notorious "Black Hole Tragedy", an event which became one of the favourite horror stories of the Raj. When Siraj-ud-Daula, the Nawab of Bengal, captured the old British fort which stood on the site of the present General Post Office (*see p271*) in 1756, he imprisoned over 100 British inhabitants in a small, airless cell. Only 23 people were found alive the next morning – the rest had died of asphyxiation and thirst.

Nilhat House ❸

Behind Old Mission Church. Auctions held on Mon & Tue at 8:30am. Prior permission required from brokerage houses, J Thomas **Tel** (033) 2248 6201.

A tea auction centre, Nilhat House stands on the site of an indigo trading house (*nil* means indigo, while *hat* is market). It dates to 1861; only the tea auction houses in London are older. Tea has always played an important role in the state's economy, especially in the colonial period. But even today, the bidding for teas from Darjeeling and the Dooars in northern Bengal and Assam (*see pp262–3*) is brisk. The auction prices are determined by the opinions of tea tasters, whose highly trained palates can immediately distinguish the type, plantation and year of each brew. Visitors can view and participate in these animated proceedings with prior permission.

College Street ❹

Bidhan Sarani, North Kolkata.
Ashutosh Museum Tel (033) 2241 0071. ⬜ 10:30am–5pm Mon–Fri; 10:30am–1:30pm Sat. 🖼

As the location of Kolkata's elite educational institutions, College Street is the heart of Bengali intellectual life. The pavements are crowded with stalls selling textbooks, exam guides, classics and second-hand books of all kinds – some people even claim to have discovered valuable first editions. Many of Kolkata's best bookshops are also found here.

The **Presidency College** was established here in 1817 and was then known as the Hindu College. Started as an institution for the city's rich who wanted their sons to receive a Western-style education, it boasts great scholars, scientists and writers such

as film director, Satyajit Ray (1922–92) and economist Amartya Sen, who won the Nobel Prize for Economics in the year 1998.

Across the road is the dark, cavernous **Indian Coffee House**, the favourite haunt of the city's intelligentsia since it opened in 1942. Even today, waiters in shabby cummerbunds serve endless cups of strong coffee to teachers, students, writers and poets.

Down a lane opposite Presidency College is the **Sanskrit College**, founded in 1824 to promote the study of ancient Indian languages, history and culture. Its ground floor has a small display of medieval Hindu sculpture and palm-leaf manuscripts.

Next to Presidency College are the buildings of **Calcutta University**, founded in 1857. Today, the gracious 19th-century main structure is dwarfed by modern high-rise additions, through which the old edifice, with its Ionic pillars and symmetrical proportions, is barely visible.

On the ground floor, the **Ashutosh Museum** specializes in the art of Eastern India. The exhibits include a fine collection of terracottas, bronzes, coins, old manuscripts and some exquisite examples of *kantha* (a quilting technique) and Kalighat paintings, or *pats* (*see p279*).

A second-hand bookstore on College Street

Detail of the ornamental entrance of Nakhoda Mosque

Nakhoda Mosque ❺

Zakaria St. **Tel** (033) 2235 4183.
⬜ daily. ⬛ to non–Muslims during times of prayer. 📷

The city's largest mosque, Nakhoda Mosque is based on the design of Akbar's tomb at Sikandra (*see p178*). Built in 1926, it is surmounted by a dome and faced with red sandstone, with minarets that rise to a height of 46 m (151 ft). It can accommodate over 10,000 people for prayer, but on major religious occasions, people spill out on to the street. Nearby is the **Hotel Royal**, famous for its rich *biryani* and *chaanp* (goat's ribs cooked in spiced gravy). This is a fascinating neighbourhood with 19th-century mansions, old bazaars and temples.

Armenian Church of St Nazareth ❻

Armenian St, near Brabourne Rd. **Tel** (033) 2242 4308. ⬜ daily.

Built by Armenian traders in 1724, the Armenian Church of St Nazareth stands on the site of the original 1707 wooden church, which had burnt down. Immigrants from Isfahan in Persia, the Armenians were among the earliest foreign traders to settle in Kolkata. Once a thriving community, today their numbers have dwindled. The church has a unique rounded spire, and its grounds house several graves with ornate tombstones.

Maidan ❼

Bounded by Strand Rd, AJC Bose Rd, Cathedral Rd & Eden Gardens Rd.
St Paul's Cathedral ⬜ daily.
🏛 7:30am, 8:30am & 6pm Sun.

In the heart of the city, this 400-ha (988-acre) park stretches from the Hooghly river in the west to Chowringhee in the east, and contains several interesting areas and buildings. In the early 18th century, a dense jungle was cut down to build **Fort William**, after the earlier mud fort was destroyed in 1756. The present fort, a squat, irregular octagon, was completed in 1781. Today, it is the headquarters of the Indian Army's Eastern Command and not usually open to the public.

To the north of the fort are the pleasantly laid out **Eden Gardens**, where international cricket matches are held. They were conceived and designed in 1841 by Emily and Fanny Eden, the sisters of the governor general, Lord Auckland. At the northern corner of the Maidan is the **Burmese Pavilion** set in a small lake. This was brought here by Lord Dalhousie from Prome in Myanmar in 1854.

To its east is the **Shahid Minar**, literally "Martyrs' Memorial", originally called Ochterlony Monument. It was

Stained glass, St Paul's Cathedral

named after Sir David Ochterlony, one of the Raj's daredevil soldiers, who had led the British armies to victory in the Anglo-Nepal War in 1816. The monument is a fluted Doric column, 48 m (157 ft) high with a cupola for a roof. To its south is the Maidan's most impressive building, the **Victoria Memorial** (*see pp274–5*).

A short distance from the Memorial is **St Paul's Cathedral**. It was designed by Major WN Forbes in 1847 and its spire, modelled on Britain's Canterbury Cathedral, was added after the earlier one was destroyed in the 1934 earthquake. Its grounds are lined with trees and the interior is notable for a superb stained-glass window, designed by Edward Burne-Jones in memory of the viceroy, Lord Mayo. The **Race Course** is on the southwestern corner of the Maidan. Racing is popular in Kolkata and races are held throughout the year. Polo is played here for a few weeks in the winter season. The city's two famous football clubs, Mohun Bagan and East Bengal, are based in the Maidan.

On Sunday afternoons, a lively fair with acrobats, magicians and jugglers takes place at the northern end of the Maidan. This is also the venue for large political rallies.

Eden Gardens, the site of many cricket matches

Victoria Memorial ⓮

The city's most celebrated landmark, this monument to imperial self-confidence was the brainchild of Lord Curzon (1859–1925), one of British India's most flamboyant viceroys. The domed Classical structure, completed in 1921, was constructed with marble from Makrana, which also supplied marble for the Taj Mahal, and financed by "donations" from princes and ordinary citizens. Now a museum, its 25 galleries are spread over the ground and first floors. The collection, which covers a fascinating selection of Raj memorabilia, includes the Calcutta Gallery, with oil paintings and watercolours of the city's history.

Imperial lion at the entrance

★ Angel of Victory
Surmounting the dome is this 6-m (20-ft) high bronze revolving figure, with a trumpet, made in Italy.

Lord Cornwallis
This 18th-century governor general established the Raj's administration.

Durbar Hall

★ Statue of the Young Queen Victoria
The queen, sculpted in marble by Thomas Brock in 1921, holds an orb and a sceptre.

Entrance

STAR SIGHTS

★ Angel of Victory

★ Statue of the Young Queen Victoria

General View
The impressive marble façade of the Victoria Memorial.

For hotels and restaurants in this region see pp699–700 and pp727–8

Bronze Panel
Two bronze panels depicting a vice-regal procession decorate the bridge at the northern entrance to the Memorial.

Dome
Skylights in the marble rotunda allow light to filter through to illuminate the lobby below.

VISITORS' CHECKLIST

Queen's Way. **Tel** (033) 2223 5142.
◯ Tue–Sun. ◯ public hols.
Ø Son et Lumière (English)
7.15pm, Oct–Feb, 7.45pm, Mar–Jun
www.victoriamemorial-cal.org

Exploring the Victoria Memorial

The foundation stone of this impressive structure was laid by the Prince of Wales, later King George V, during his visit to India in 1906. Designed by William Emerson, President of the British Institute of Architects, the building stands in spacious grounds, dotted with ornamental palms, ponds and statues. The museum contains over 10,000 artifacts that represent various facets of the Raj, such as a desk owned by Queen Victoria, embellished with paintings of Indian birds. Among the fine collection of paintings are works by the 18th-century landscape artists, Thomas Daniell and his nephew William Daniell, whose aquatints and lithographs of Indian scenes virtually determined the way India was perceived in 19th-century Britain. The collection also includes paintings by Johann Zoffany (1733–1810), portraits of imperial stalwarts, records of the East India Company, an exquisite set of Persian manuscripts, and paintings that depict Kolkata's history.

Calcutta Gallery
This gallery has an excellent collection of landscapes painted by 18th-century British artists.

Picture Gallery

A majestic bronze statue of Queen Victoria by Sir George Frampton

Chowringhee ❾

JL Nehru Rd. **The Asiatic Society**
Park St. **Tel** *(033) 2229 2249.* **Library**
⬜ *Mon–Sat.* **Museum** ⬜ *noon–4pm*
Mon–Fri. www.asiaticsocietycal.com

Now called Jawaharlal
Nehru Road, Chowringhee
was a fashionable promenade
during the Raj. This thoroughfare derives its name from a
fakir (holy man), Jungle Giri
Chowringhee, who once lived
here. At its northern end is
the **Oberoi Grand** *(see
p699).* Established in the
1870s, and known as the
Grand Hotel, it was considered "the most Popular,
Fashionable and Attractive
Hotel in India".

Behind the Oberoi Grand is
New Market *(see p282),* built
in 1874. Surmounted by a
clock tower, shops here are
placed along many interconnected corridors. One of the
oldest is the Jewish confectionery and bakery,
Nahoum's, which has a
beguiling variety of cookies,
fudge and spiced cakes.

At its southern end, on Park
Street, is **The Asiatic Society**,
founded in 1784 by Sir
William Jones, a formidable
Oriental scholar. He was the
first to establish the common
origins of Latin and Sanskrit,
and called Sanskrit the
"mother of all languages".
The Society's **Museum** and
Library have a large collection
of over 60,000 old and rare
manuscripts in Sanskrit,
Arabic and Persian, as well as
artifacts such as a 3rd-century
BC stone edict, and 17th-
century folios from the
Padshahnama, Abdul Hamid
Lahori's history of the Mughal
emperor Shah Jahan's rule.

The well-preserved period façade of
Chowringhee building

Indian Museum ❿

Gupta era
gold coin

The oldest and largest museum in India,
the Indian Museum was founded in 1814.
The imposing building, designed by
Walter Granville, also the architect of the
General Post Office *(see p271),* dates to
1878. The museum's impressive collection
is noted for artifacts from the 2,500 BC
Indus Valley Civilization, sculpture from
Gandhara, the superbly sculpted
railings from the 2,000-year-old
Bharhut Stupa, and a fine collection
of 5th-century Gupta coins.

Kalighat Painting
*Painted in the folk style of the 19th-
century Kalighat school, this represents
the Vaishnava saint Chaitanya.*

**Arhat
Vanavasin
Thangka**
*This silk
painting of a
Buddhist sage is
from Tibet.*

Pala Bronze
*This 12th-century
Bodhisattva figure shows
the fluid grace of
Pala sculpture.*

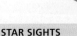

STAR SIGHTS

★ Gandhara Sculpture

★ Bharhut Railings

Nautch Party
This 19th-century Company School Painting of nautch or dancing girls, combines European and Indian techniques of art.

VISITORS' CHECKLIST

JL Nehru Rd. **Tel** *(033) 2286 1702.*
◯ *Tue–Sun.* ◯ *public hols.* 🖼
📷 extra charges 🗝
Note: *Educational film shows daily, and special exhibitions*

KEY

▨ Art and Textile Gallery

▨ Geology Section

▨ Botany Section

☐ Zoological Section

▨ Anthropology Section

☐ Archaeology Gallery

☐ Egyptian Gallery

▨ Numismatics Gallery

▨ Library

Chandela Sculpture
Dating to the 10th–11th century, this sensuous maiden from Khajuraho holds a baby in her arms while two small children cling to her knees.

Second floor

First floor

Ground floor

★ **Gandhara Sculpture**
Dating to the 3rd century, this image of Maitreya, the Future Buddha, shows a strong Greek influence in the way the folds of the robe are sculpted.

Entrance

GALLERY GUIDE
Built around a courtyard are two storeys of galleries. The Archaeology Gallery, to the right of the main entrance, has railings from the Bharhut Stupa as well as displays of ancient and medieval sculpture. The Numismatics Gallery has coins dating from 500 BC to the 17th century. The Zoological Section, exhibits stuffed birds from British zoological expeditions. The second floor has the Art Gallery with paintings and miniatures.

★ **Bharhut Railings**
Episodes from Buddhist scriptures, events from the Buddha's life and scenes from daily life are carved on these railings.

A Sister of Charity outside the Mother House

Mother House ⓫

54A, AJC Bose Rd. **Tel** (033) 2217 2277. ◯ Fri–Wed. **www**.mother teresa.org **Donations** are tax-exempt.

The city of Kolkata is inextricably linked to the name of Mother Teresa. At first a teaching nun at Loreto Convent, the death and devastation she witnessed in the city during the famine of 1943, and Partition of India in 1947 (see p56), made her leave this cloistered world and dedicate her life to the poor. The Missionaries of Charity was a new order she formed in 1950, with the Mother House as its headquarters. This simple building is today also her final resting place. Her grave is on the ground floor in a hall. It has no ornamentation, only a Bible placed on it. On a board on the wall are two words, "I thirst".

Park Street Cemetery ⓬

Bounded by Rawdon St & Park St. ◯ Mon–Fri.

A romantic, overgrown haven of Raj nostalgia in the middle of the city, the Park Street Cemetery was opened in August 1767 to receive the body of John Wood, an official in the Custom House of the East India Company. From that date till the first half of the 19th century, it served as the resting place of many important Europeans who died in Kolkata. It was this graveyard which gave Park Street its original name, Burial Ground Road. Its name Park Street was derived from the park that Elijah Impey, the Chief Justice of the Supreme Court, established in the area. His grave is in this cemetery as well. William Jones, the great scholar and founder of The Asiatic Society, lies under a pyramid-shaped tomb. Henry Vansittart, one of the first governors of Bengal, is also buried here; so too is Henry Louis Vivian Derozio (1809-1831), a Eurasian teacher at Hindu College in the mid-19th century, who died at the young age of 23. Derozio inspired his students to question all established traditions and was one of the pioneers of what has come to be known as the Bengal

Renaissance (see p260). The best known tomb is that of Rose Aylmer, an early love of the poet, Walter Savage Landor. Her tomb, an unpretentious spiralled obelisk, is inscribed with lines by Landor. Also buried here is Colonel Kyd, founder of the Botanical Gardens (see p281).

Alipore ⓭

Bounded by AJC Bose Rd, Belvedere Rd & Alipore Rd. **Alipore Zoological Gardens** ◯ 9am–5pm Fri–Wed. 🈲 **National Library Tel** (033) 2479 1384. ◯ daily. ● public hols. 🈲 **Agri Horticultural Society Tel** (033) 2479 0834. ◯ 7–10am & 2–6pm Mon–Sat. **www**. agrihortcultureindia.com 🈲 Flower Show (Feb).

Best described as the city's most fashionable address, the suburb of Alipore in south Kolkata is a sylvan world of tree-lined avenues, with palatial houses surrounded by well-kept lawns. Kolkata's zoo, the **Alipore Zoological Gardens**, was established here in 1875 and has a large collection of birds and mammals. Situated nearby, the Belvedere Estate has a broad expanse of lawn and also houses the **National Library**. This is the country's largest library with over two million manuscripts and books. The library has now been shifted to the Bhasha Bhawan, a new building on the same

Weathered tombs in the tree-shaded Park Street Cemetery

The National Library in Alipore, with its colonnaded verandah

grounds. Built in the Italian Renaissance style, the original building, Belvedere, was once the residence of the lieutenant governors of Bengal.

Further down are the lush gardens of the **Agri Horticultural Society**, founded in September 1820 by the missionary William Carey *(see p287)*, to develop and promote agriculture and horticulture in India. In the first 40 years of its existence, seeds, bulbs and ornamental plants were imported from England, South Africa and Southeast Asia. Since then the Society has amassed a varied collection of rare flowering trees and herbs. It's also an excellent place to buy winter annuals.

Kalighat ⓴

Ashutosh Mukherjee Rd. ◯ *daily.*

Kolkata's oldest pilgrimage site, Kalighat finds mention in numerous medieval poems and ballads. Legend has it that the god Shiva, in a fury of grief at the death of his

wife, Sati (an incarnation of Parvati), slung her body on his shoulders and danced the terrible *tandava nritya* (dance of death), destroying everything in his path. To stop the carnage, Vishnu flung his magic *chakra* (discus) at Sati's body, and the dismembered pieces scattered across the land. The spot where the little toe fell became Kalighat, and some believe that the name Kolkata is derived from this.

The present Kali Temple dates to the early 19th century, but this has been a sacred spot for much longer. The image of the goddess in the dark inner sanctum is of a wild, untamed figure, with tangled tresses and wide, ferocious eyes. Her extended tongue has a gold covering which is changed every day. The temple is always crowded, especially on Tuesdays and Saturdays.

Kalighat has, over the years, become synonymous with Kalighat *pats*, a distinctive

The brick-and-mortar spire of the Kali Temple at Kalighat

painting style adopted by the scroll-painters of Bengal. They use paper and water-based paints, instead of tempera, to depict contemporary subjects. A good collection of Kalighat *pats* is on display at the Indian Museum *(see pp276–7)*.

Nirmal Hridaya ⓯

251, Kalighat Rd. **Tel** *(033) 2464 4223.* ◯ *8–11am & 3–5pm Mon–Sat, 3–5pm Sun.*

Mother Teresa's home for the destitute, Nirmal Hridaya ("Pure Heart"), is near the Kali Temple. The site was probably chosen as this holy place teems with poor and old people, who come here to die and attain *moksha*. A large, clean hall is full of beds for the sick and dying who are cared for by nuns, in their characteristic white and blue saris. Visitors who want to work as volunteers must first register at Mother House.

Kalighat painting of two wandering mendicants

MOTHER TERESA (1910–1997)

Mother Teresa, born Agnes Gonxa Bojaxhiu in Albania, came to Calcutta in 1929 to begin life as a teacher. The poverty and suffering she saw impelled her to leave the convent. She set up the order of the Missionaries of Charity and her indefatigable work among the lepers, the terminally ill, the unwanted and the poor earned her universal respect and love. To the people of Kolkata she was just "Mother" and their love for her transcended boundaries of religion, class and community. She was awarded the Nobel Peace Prize in 1979.

Mother Teresa on a postage stamp

Kim Li Loi, a family-run Chinese restaurant in Tangra

Tangra ⑯

Off the Eastern Metropolitan Bypass. ⛩ *Chinese New Year (Feb).*

This eastern suburb is the city's new Chinatown. Chinese immigration to Kolkata began in the 18th century, and today large numbers of this still significant community have settled here. Tangra preserves the rich and varied culture of its immigrant population. A Chinese newspaper and journal are published from here, and there are many tiny restaurants, mostly extensions of family kitchens. "Tangra Chinese", with its discernibly Indian taste, is today as distinct a cuisine as Szechwan and Cantonese. Many of the city's leather tanneries are based at Tangra as, traditionally, the Chinese were involved with the very lucrative shoe trade.

Marble Palace ⑰

46, Muktaram Babu St. ◯ *10am–4pm Mon, Thu, & Sat.* 🚫 🎫 **Entry permit** *Contact Tourism Centre, 3/2 BBD Bagh, (033) 2248 8271.*

This opulent mansion was built in 1835 by Raja Rajendra Mullick, a wealthy *zamindar* (landowner). His descendants still live here, but most of the house is open to visitors. Rajendra Mullick, who had travelled extensively in Europe, brought back an eclectic collection of Venetian chandeliers, Ming vases and Egyptian statuary that he housed in his Classical-fronted mansion, built around a colonnaded courtyard. Today, the Marble Palace provides a wonderful glimpse into the life of a rich 19th-century Bengali household. Nearly a 100 varieties of marble have been used on the floors and the dark halls are hung with paintings by European artists. In the courtyard is the family temple, while the grounds have a rock garden and aviary, home to mynahs and peacocks.

Jorasanko ⑱

6/4, Dwarkanath Tagore Lane. **Rabindra Bharati Museum** *Tel* (033) 2269 6610. ◯ *10am–5pm Mon–Fri, 10am–2pm Sat & Sun.* **Son et Lumière** *6 & 7pm (English).* ⬤ *Mon & Thu.* 📷 ⛩ *Rabindranath Tagore's birthday (May).*

A major centre of Bengali art and culture in the 19th century, Jorasanko is the ancestral home of Bengal's favourite son, Rabindranath Tagore *(see p292).* Built in 1785, this simple three-storeyed, red brick structure housed the lively and cultivated Tagore family, many of whose members were prominent intellectuals and social reformers. The lane on which the house is located is named after Dwarkanath Tagore (1784–1846), the poet's father and a wealthy entrepreneur.

Today, the old house has been expanded and turned into **Rabindra Bharati University**, which specializes in the study of Bengali cultural forms. The house itself has been preserved as the **Rabindra Bharati Museum**. Beginning with the room in which Rabindranath Tagore died, it traces the history of the illustrious Tagore family with a large collection of art and memorabilia. There is an entire section devoted to paintings by Rabindranath.

The red brick Rabindra Bharati University, at Jorasanko

Final touches being given to a Durga image

Kumartuli ⑲

North Chitpur Rd.

Literally, the "Area of the Potters", Kumartuli is a maze of alleys, where images of various Hindu gods and goddesses are made. The best time to visit is late August and early September as this is when potters create the idols for the ten-day-long Durga Puja. It is fascinating to watch them at work, moulding the clay, strengthened by straw and pith, to create images of the fish-eyed goddess Durga, her face often modelled on popular Hindi film actresses and her hair long and flowing. Nearby is an ancient temple dedicated to Shiva, known as the **Buro Shiva** or "Old Shiva Temple". This is probably the only extant terracotta temple in the city, embellished with terracotta tablets in the frieze below the roof. Further away is Kolkata's celebrated landmark, the giant **Howrah Bridge** (now called Rabindra Setu), an airy, elegant mesh of steel that appears to float above the turgid Hooghly river *(see p267)*. The sunset behind the bridge is one of the loveliest sights in the city. Built in 1943 to replace the old pontoon bridge, this is the third longest cantilever bridge in the world, measuring 97 m (318 ft) in height and 705 m (2,313 ft) in length. The bridge links Kolkata with Howrah (Haora), the city's main railway station on the opposite bank, and is always clogged with traffic. To its south is the impressive Vidyasagar Setu. This massive cable-stayed suspension bridge was built in 1993 to connect South Kolkata with Shibpur and Howrah station.

Botanical Gardens ⑳

W bank of the Hooghly river, Shibpur. 🚢 *from Babu Ghat.* **Tel** *(033) 2668 9970.* ◯ *daily.* **The Palm House** ◯ *Mon–Fri.* **The National Herbarium** ◯ *Mon–Fri.* ◉ *Weekends and public holidays.*

The Botanical gardens, in the Shibpur suburb of Howrah, were established in 1787 by Colonel Kyd, an official of the East India Company. It has an astonishing array of flora including ferns, cacti and palms, and boasts of plants from every continent. The chief attraction is the magnificent banyan tree *(Ficus bengalensis)*. Claimed to be the largest banyan tree in the world, it is more than 200 years old and its branches, giving rise to nearly 300 aerial roots, spread over 60 m (197 ft). The central trunk was, however, struck by lightning in 1919 and was subsequently removed. The sight of this tree alone is worth the long journey.

The gigantic leaves of the *Victoria amazonica* lily, Botanical Gardens

THE DURGA PUJA

Image of the ten-armed Durga, slaying Mahisha

Durga Puja is West Bengal's favourite annual ritual in which simply everyone participates. Usually held between September and October, it heralds the advent of autumn and the new harvest. Each locality sets up its own *puja*, organized by local clubs and associations, financed through public subscriptions, though some of the old Bengali families perform their own *puja* in their ancestral houses. Brightly illuminated *pandals* (bamboo structures), often shaped like famous monuments such as the White House or the Taj Mahal, are erected on roads and in parks, and an image of the goddess Durga *(see p25)* is installed within. The goddess is elaborately decorated and in traditional Bengali homes, real jewellery is used. Presents are exchanged and great feasts are prepared. On the final day, the images are immersed in the Hooghly, to the frantic beating of drums and cries of "Jai Ma Durga!" ("Hail to Mother Durga!").

Shopping & Entertainment in Kolkata

Kolkata is a delightful place to shop, even though it lacks the fashionable boutiques of Delhi or Mumbai. There are several old-style bazaars and street hawkers, and fewer glitzy shopping malls. Many shops stock a wide variety of goods, such as those in New Market; others cater to special niches. In certain places one needs to drive hard bargains – the shopkeepers both expect and enjoy this process. Kolkata was once famous for its auction houses, but sadly most of these have now shut down. This is also a culturally vibrant city, with regular performances of theatre, music and film shows. Exhibitions by well-known contemporary artists are also held throughout the year.

SHOPS AND MARKETS

Kolkata's **New Market** *(see p276)*, on Lindsay Street, is the city's most famous shopping centre. Officially the Sir Stuart Hogg New Municipal Market, established in 1874, this is still a shopper's paradise, where one can find everything from Chinese sausages and fortune cookies to Tibetan curios and gold jewellery. **Sudder Street**, behind the Indian Museum, is another popular shopping centre. Each locality has its own bazaar; the best known of these are Gariahat, Bhowanipore (or Jadubabu's Bazaar), Bowbazaar and Maniktola. Wandering through bazaars offers a glimpse of street life, but be prepared for touts and beggars.

Shops usually open from 10am to 7pm and remain closed on Sundays and public holidays. New Market and some markets also close after 2pm on Saturday, so do check the timings in advance.

SARIS AND TEXTILES

The best shops for saris unique to West Bengal are **Ananda**, **Meera Bose** and **Kundahar**. Ananda also has an excellent selection of dhotis and *kurtas*. The upmarket boutique **Ritu's** has superb garments designed by Ritu Kumar, one of India's top designers. Exquisite hand-embroidered table linen and children's clothes are available at **Good Companions**. Carpets and *dhurries* are available at **Calcutta Carpets**.

HANDICRAFTS AND GIFTS

Handicrafts special to West Bengal such as the terra-cotta Bankura horse *(see p291)*, are on sale at **Manjusha Emporium**. The **Crafts Council of West Bengal** is another fascinating outlet that sells traditional saris as well as artifacts, while **Sasha** has a wide range of curios and bric-a-brac. Tea of the finest quality is available at **Dolly's Tea Shop** in the Dakshinapan shopping complex. This complex also has numerous other state handicraft emporia.

BOOKS AND MUSIC

This city of intellectuals and Nobel laureates, such as Rabindranath Tagore and Amartya Sen, is heaven for those willing to search for second-hand bargains in the shops that line the pavements of **College Street** *(see p273)* and **Free School Street**. Many of these shops have a good selection of rare and out of print books. **Dasgupta & Co** has a large choice, though there is no place to browse. The **Seagull Bookstore**, on the other hand, encourages browsing and is the best place for serious literature and academic books. **Starmark** too, has a large stock that ranges from thrillers to encyclopedias. The centrally located **Oxford Bookstore**, is also well-stocked and has a good café.

Music aficionados are advised to try **Music World** which has a good selection of Indian and Western CDs and audio cassettes. On Chitpur Road towards Nakhoda Mosque *(see p273)*, are music shops selling sitars, *sarods, veenas,* flutes and violins. Free School Street is about the only place in India where record albums of 1950s Elvis Presley and Jerry Lee Lewis or 1960s Beatles and Rolling Stones are easily available.

SWEETS

West Bengal's sweets are famous. The variety is bewildering, but the two most popular are *sandesh* and *rosogulla (see p264)*. The latter is on sale in every sweetshop, but those in **KC Das & Sons**, the family which invented this delicacy, are the best. *Sandesh*, made of cottage cheese and sugar (molasses or *gur* in the winter months), are of two kinds, those that are soft and those that have a harder outer crust. Both are widely available, but the best are found in **Nakur Nandy & Girish Chandra Dey, Makhan Lal Das & Sons** and **Balaram Mullick**.

ENTERTAINMENT GUIDES, TICKETS AND VENUES

The *Sunday Telegraph* magazine and other English language dailies list the day's entertainment on their engagements page. Other useful sources of information are *Cal Calling* and *Kolkata: This Fortnight*, which is distributed by the West Bengal Tourist office. Information on tickets as well as reviews of plays and concerts also appear with the announcements.

Kolkata's cultural centre is just off the Maidan. The **Rabindra Sadan Complex**, named after Rabindranath Tagore, includes the **Academy of Fine Arts**. Next door is **Nandan**, where retrospectives of films by Satyajit Ray and other renowned directors, are regularly held. Other venues around the city include **89 Cinemas, Gorky Sadan, Fame,** and the well-known **British Council**.

Exhibitions by well-known as well as up and coming artists are held at the city's many art galleries, especially the **Birla Academy of Art and Culture**, **CIMA Gallery** and **Chitrakoot Gallery**. CIMA Gallery also has a gift shop.

MUSIC AND THEATRE

Performances of West Bengal's well-established classical and folk theatre (*jatra*) are staged throughout the year by semi-professional and amateur groups. Bengali theatre is perhaps the most vibrant in the country. Its rich repertoire includes plays with historical and socially relevant themes as well as translations of

Greek, European, Sanskrit and Hindi classics. *Jatra*, on the other hand, was introduced by the Vaishnava saint, Chaitanya Mahaprabhu, in the 16th century, and is based on musical plays that revolve around the Krishna legend (*see p179*). Characterized by dramatic acting interspersed with song and dance, the plays cater to both rural and urban audiences.

Another popular form of entertainment is Rabindra Sangeet. These melodious songs composed by Tagore include folk songs that are traditionally sung by boatmen who ply the Ganges. Regular concerts are held in the city, and attract audiences who continue to revere Tagore.

CLUBS AND NIGHTLIFE

Kolkata is a city of clubs which date to colonial times and are open only to members. Sometimes temporary membership can be arranged, particularly at the **Tollygunge Club** (*see p699*) which has huge grounds with rare trees and birds. Visitors can stay at the club, which has the comfort of a top hotel but at reasonable rates.

Kolkata's once glittering nightlife dwindled during the political upheavals of the 1960s. It is reviving now and affluent youth throng hotels where the city's nightclubs, such as **Shisha**, **Someplace Else**, **Tantra** and **Big Ben**, are situated.

DIRECTORY

SARIS AND TEXTILES

Ananda
13, Russell St.
Tel (033) 2229 2275.

Calcutta Carpets
43, Park St.
Tel (033) 2229 9464.

Good Companions
13 C, Russell St.
Tel (033) 2229 0473.

Kundahar
10, Dr Sarat Banerjee Rd.
Tel (033) 2466 1111.

Meera Bose
8, Dr Sarat Banerjee Rd.
Tel (033) 2466 4043.

Ritu's
111, Park St.
Tel (033) 2226 2792.

HANDICRAFTS AND GIFTS

Manjusha Emporium
Dakshinapan Complex,
Dhakuria
Tel (033) 2423 7099.

Crafts Council of West Bengal
64, Lake Place.
Tel (033) 2465 6792.

Dolly's Tea Shop
G–62, Dakshinapan,
2, Gariahat (S).
Tel (033) 2483 4521.

Sasha
27, Mirza Ghalib St.
Tel (033) 2252 1586.

BOOKS AND MUSIC

Dasgupta & Company
54/3, College St.
Tel (033) 2241 4609.

Music World
18 G, Park St.
Tel (033) 2217 0751.

Oxford Bookstore
17, Park St.
Tel (033) 2229 7662.

Seagull Bookstore
31, SP Mukherjee Rd.
Tel (033) 2476 5869.

Starmark
3, Lord Sinha Rd.
Tel (033) 2282 2617.

SWEETS

Balaram Mullick
2, Puddapukur Rd.
Bhowanipur.
Tel (033) 2475 9490.

KC Das & Sons
11, Esplanade East.
Tel (033) 2248 5920.

Makhan Lal Das & Sons
356, Upper Chitpur Rd.
Tel (033) 2555 8182.

Nakur Nandy & Girish Chandra Dey
56, Ramdulal Sarkar St.
Tel (033) 2241 0048.

ENTERTAINMENT VENUES

89 Cinemas
89 C, Maulana Abdul Kalam Azad Sarani.
Tel (033) 2320 8900.

Academy of Fine Arts
2, Cathedral Rd.
Tel (033) 2223 4302.

Birla Academy of Art and Culture
108, Southern Ave.
Tel (033) 2466 2843.

British Council
16, Camac St.
Tel (033) 2282 5370.

CIMA Gallery
Sunny Towers, Ashutosh Chowdhury Ave.
Tel (033) 2485 8717.

Chitrakoot Gallery
55, Gariahat Rd.
Tel (033) 2461 8812.

Fame
Metropolis Mall, Hiland Park, 925 Chak Garia.
Tel (033) 2436 7744.

Gorky Sadan
3, Gorky Terrace.
Tel (033) 2283 2743.

Nandan
1/1, AJC Bose Rd.
Tel (033) 2223 1210.

Rabindra Sadan
Cathedral Rd.
Tel (033) 2223 9917.

CLUBS AND NIGHTLIFE

Big Ben
The Kenilworth,
Little Russell St.
Tel (033) 2282 3939.

Shisha
22, Camac Street,
Block B, 5th Floor.
Tel (033) 2281 1313.

Someplace Else
The Park Hotel, Park St.
Tel (033) 2249 9000.

Tantra
The Park Hotel, Park St.
Tel (033) 2249 9000.

Tollygunge Club
120, Deshpran Sasmal Rd.
Tel (033) 2473 4741.

WEST BENGAL & SIKKIM

West Bengal has three distinct types of landscape. In the west, the red soil gives its rich colour to the terracotta temples of Bishnupur. The Ganges Delta in lower Bengal has dense, tangled mangrove swamps where Royal Bengal tigers roam, while the charming, Raj-era hill stations of Darjeeling and Kalimpong are located in the foothills of the Himalayas in the northern part of the state. The neighbouring state of Sikkim, which also borders Bhutan, Nepal and China, is ringed by mountains. In its tranquil valleys, richly ornamented Buddhist monasteries stand amidst emerald-green terraced tea fields. The world's third highest mountain, Kanchendzonga (8,603 m/28,209 ft), dominates the skyline and the life of Sikkim's people. The two states have a combined population of 81 million.

SIGHTS AT A GLANCE

Towns & Cities
Barddhaman ❻
Gangtok ❶❻
Murshidabad ❽
Pelling ❶❽
Shantiniketan ❼
Siliguri ❶❶

Historic Sites
Gaur ❾
Pandua ❶❶

Temples, Monasteries & Holy Places
Belur Math ❶
Bishnupur: Shyama Raya Temple ❺
Dakshineshwar ❷
Tashiding Monastery ❷❶

National Parks
Jaldapara Wildlife Sanctuary ❶❷
The Sunderbans ❹

Hill Stations & Areas of Natural Beauty
Darjeeling ❶❹
Kalimpong ❶❺
Kurseong ❶❸
Yuksam ❶❾

Rivers & Valleys
Hooghly River ❸

Tours
A Tour of Northern Sikkim ❶❼

KEY

✈	International airport
✕	Domestic airport
═	National highway
▬	Major road
═	Minor road
—	Major railway
▪-	International border
˙-	State border

0 km   100
0 miles   100

◁ **Image of the ten-armed goddess Durga, elaborately adorned for the Durga Puja festival**

Belur Math

Howrah district. 10 km (6 miles) N of Kolkata. 🚌 🚆 or taxi from Kolkata. ⬜ daily. Conservative dress appreciated.

Just outside Kolkata, on the west bank of the Hooghly river, is Belur Math, the headquarters of the Rama-krishna Mission. The order was established in 1886 by the dynamic, reformist Hindu crusader, Swami Vivekananda (see p615), Ramakrishna Paramhansa's foremost disci-ple. The modern temple within the sprawling complex was built in 1938 and embod-ies Ramakrishna's philosophy, based on the unity of all faiths. The ground plan is in the shape of a cross, the windows have arches reminiscent of Mughal buildings, the gate shows Buddhist influence, and Hindu architectural motifs decorate the façade. Smaller

temples and dormitories for the monks belonging to the order surround it. The place is spotlessly clean, and the atmosphere contemplative and calm. Today, the Mission has centres across the world.

Dakshineshwar ❷

24 Parganas district. 12 km (8 miles) N of Kolkata. 🚌 🚆 or taxi from Kolkata. ⬜ daily. Conservative dress appreciated.

North of Belur Math, on the east bank of the Hooghly river, stands the temple of Dakshineshwar, one of Bengal's most popular pilgrimage spots. The temple, built in 1855 by a rich and pious widow, Rani Rashmoni, was initially opposed by orthodox religious interests as she was not a Brahmin (the highest Indian caste). No Brahmin was therefore willing to be the temple priest. Only Ramakrishna Paramhansa, then still a boy, agreed, and he spent many years there, preaching and developing his

The curved *bangaldar* roof of the Kali temple, Dakshineshwar

philosophy of the essential oneness of all faiths. His room in the temple complex is still preserved in its original state.

The impressive whitewashed temple is set on a high plinth and topped by nine cupolas. The roof, with its line of rounded cornices, stands out impressively against the sky. Inside the sanctum is an image of Bhabatarini, an incarnation of the goddess Kali.

Within the large compound, strung along the river bank, are 12 smaller temples, each dedicated to the god Shiva. Crowds of pilgrims visit the Dakshineshwar temple daily, lending the sprawling temple complex a cheerful, bustling atmosphere.

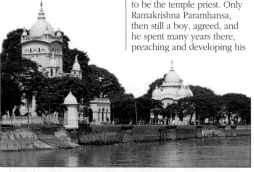

Belur Math, on the west bank of the Hooghly river

Hooghly River ❸

Hooghly district. 24 km (15 miles) N from Kolkata to Shrirampur. 🚆 🚌 🚆 River cruises. ℹ Babu Ghat (near Eden Gardens) or Tourist Office, (033) 2248 7302.

When the Ganges enters the lower Gangetic Plains in West Bengal, the river breaks up into many channels. The main distributary, the Hooghly (now Hugli), flows 260 km (162 miles) from Murshidabad to the Bay of Bengal.

Between the 15th and 19th centuries, this easily navigable river attracted Dutch, French, Portuguese, Danish and British traders. The settlements they established transformed the

---

RAMAKRISHNA PARAMHANSA (1836–86)

Ramakrishna, one of modern India's greatest spiritual teachers, was born into a poor family of priests in 1836. He became a priest at Dakshineshwar, where he began a life of prayer and meditation. His philosophy was lucid – there is an inherent truth in all religions and a simple life is a pure life. A mystic who claimed to speak directly to God, he could explain complex and abstruse theological issues in the simplest language, which appealed to the poor and rich alike. His teachings were carried to the USA and to Britain by his main disciple Swami Vivekananda (1863–1902) who set up many Ramakrishna Mission centres abroad for education and religious studies.

Ramakrishna Paramhansa

Visitors praying at the Church of Our Lady of Bandel

THE HOOGHLY RIVER

KEY

🚉 Railway station

🚌 Bus station

🛕 Temple

⛪ Church

⛴ Jetty

Bansberia

Bandel
Hooghly

Chinsurah

Chandannagar

Barakpur

Shrirampur

0 km 5

0 miles 5

↓ KOLKATA

river banks into a mini Europe – the remnants of which can be best explored today by taking one of the river cruises.

Up river from Kolkata is **Shrirampur** (Serampore), a Danish colony until 1845. Dr William Carey, the first Baptist missionary in India *(see p279)*, set up the earliest printing press here in 1799 and translated the Bible into several Indian languages, including Bengali, marking the beginnings of modern Bengali prose. He also founded the first theological college, today Shrirampur College, in 1805. Its library houses a priceless collection of 18th- and 19th-century books.

On the east bank is **Barakpur** (Barrackpore), the site of the British viceroys' once gracious country house. The mansion, locally referred to as Lat Bagan ("Governor's or Lord's Garden"), was built by Lord Wellesley, the governor general in the early 19th century.

Chandannagar (Chandernagore), a French settlement from 1673 until 1952, still retains a Gallic ambience. The public benches on the waterfront (previously Quai Dupleix) are replicas of those found in Paris parks. The elegant Administrator's Residence, built in the 18th century, is now the Institut de Chandernagore, a library and

Armenian Church, Chinsurah

museum, and contains an interesting collection of French-era documents and artifacts. The Église du Sacré Coeur has a statue of Joan of Arc and a Lourdes grotto.

North of Chandannagar is **Chinsurah** (Chunchura), an Armenian settlement, taken over by the Dutch in 1625 and later by the British. The Armenian Church was built in 1697, though the steeple was added a century later. The town of **Hooghly**, to the north, has an impressive *imambara* (mosque) built in 1836. Further upriver is **Bandel**, founded by the Portuguese in 1580. The Church of Our Lady of Bandel, consecrated

in 1599, is the oldest in Eastern India. After being refaced in granite, it has, however, lost some of its charm. People of all faiths still pray at the statue of Our Lady of Happy Voyages, an icon with an interesting history. In 1632, while the city was being sacked by the Mughal emperor Shah Jahan, the icon was lost in the river, but later reappeared miraculously on the banks in front of the church.

Further north is **Bansberia**, site of several terracotta temples. The Ananta Vasudeva Temple, built in 1679, has a panel of warriors carved above the entrance, while the Hanseshwari Temple, built in 1814, has a fabulous array of Kremlin-like onion domes and an elaborately carved façade.

The French Administrator's Residence in Chandannagar

The Sunderbans ❹

White breasted kingfisher

The vast Ganges-Brahmaputra Delta stretching into Bangladesh, covers 9,630 sq km (3,718 sq miles) and has the world's largest tropical mangrove forest. The Sundarbans Reserve, which spreads across 2,585 sq km (998 sq miles), created within the delta was declared a Tiger Reserve in 1973 to protect the endangered Royal Bengal tiger. A part of the reserve houses the Sundarbans National Park, a UNESCO World Heritage Site covering 1,330 sq km (513 sq miles). The intricate network of waterways, creeks and alluvial islands abounds in a variety of marine life, including crustaceans and dolphins, as well as reptiles such as Olive Ridley turtles and estuarine crocodiles. Birds such as the waterfowl can be seen here. Guided boats are available.

Fiddler Crabs
Male fiddler crabs have a large claw resembling a bow and fiddle, which they use to attract females and deter enemies.

Mangrove Forests
Renowned for their variety of mangroves, the Sunderbans were once dominated by the sundari tree (Heritiera fomes), now nearly extinct due to rampant timber poaching. Mangroves have ingeniously adapted to flooding and salinity, using breathing roots or pneumatophores.

Country Boats
Small rowboats, available from Sajnakhali, take visitors along the reserve's many waterways. These craft are preferable to the noisier motorboats that tend to scare away wildlife, especially the rich variety of waterfowl.

MORE TO SEE

The western boundary of the Sunderbans boasts a number of popular beaches and reserves, all of which can be reached by road or boat. **Ganga Sagar** on Sagar Island, is the spot where millions of pilgrims gather for the annual Ganga Sagar Mela *(see p295)* during Makar Sankranti in January. **Diamond Harbour** is a popular picnic spot, while **Bakkhali** and **Digha** have beautiful beaches and are popular resorts. Bakkhali is also a haven for birdlife.

Estuarine or Saltwater Crocodile
Saltwater crocodiles, known as "salties", grow up to a length of 8 m (26 ft). They feed on small mammals and have occasionally been known to attack humans.

Royal Bengal Tiger
The Indian stretch of the Sunderbans has 245 Royal Bengal tigers. They are the only tigers known to live in mangrove forests and have adapted remarkably to the inhospitable environment. Expert swimmers, they feed on fish, and are even believed to survive on salt water.

0 km 10
0 miles 10

KEY

🚉 Railway station
🚌 Bus station
🚢 Jetty
🛈 Tourist information
🅰 Accommodation
☀ Viewpoint
═ Major road
═ Minor road
- - Park boundary
••• International border

TALE OF THE TIGER

The tiger plays a major role in India's cultural history as a symbol of power and kingship. In Hindu iconography, Shiva wears a tiger skin, while the fearsome Goddess Durga rides a tiger. Tiger images can also be seen in vibrant murals in Buddhist monasteries in Sikkim, Arunachal Pradesh and Ladakh. In the Sunderbans, ritual offerings are made to the forest deity, Banbibi, to seek protection from the tiger. Yet statistics belie the tiger's mythic status. In 1900, India's tiger population was about 40,000; by 1972 it had fallen to 1,800. Alarmed, the Indian government launched Project Tiger. Ever since, numbers have grown substantially and India now has between 2,750 and 3,500 tigers (about 60 per cent of the world's tiger population), protected in 28 Project Tiger Reserves across the country.

A play re-enacting Banbibi protecting a mother and child from the tiger

Bishnupur: Shyama Raya Temple ❺

Creeper motif

Bishnupur, capital of the Mallabhumi kingdom between the 17th and the mid-18th centuries, is renowned for its elaborately adorned terracotta temples, made of the local red clay. The most imposing of these is the Shyama Raya Temple, built in 1643. It is richly decorated with scenes from Lord Krishna's life as well as episodes taken from the epic *Ramayana (see p27)*. Other motifs in the temple include scenes of hunting, boating and military processions.

Front façade of the Shyama Raya Temple

Shikharas
The design of the five spires is inspired by the temple tradition of nearby Orissa (see p306).

The cornice echoes the contours of thatched village huts.

Arched Façade
The arches, supported by squat, ornamented pillars, lead to a vaulted corridor.

The inner chamber, called *thakurbari* (god's house), has a finely decorated altar at one end.

VISITORS' CHECKLIST

Bankura district. 152 km
(94miles) NW of Kolkata.
🚌 128,811. 🚉 🚌 🅿 daily.
🎭 Rasa Festival (Aug).

Terracotta Friezes
*Scenes from the epics
alternate with scenes
from daily life.
Here, Krishna
plays his flute for
the gopis
(milkmaids).*

**The curved
cornice**
deflects rain
water.

The twin hut-like roofs of the Keshta Raya Temple, Bishnupur

Exploring Bishnupur's Temples

The terracotta temples of
Bishnupur are scattered over
a 3-km (2-mile) radius, and
stand out vividly against the
vibrant green and ochre
colours of the landscape.

The **Rasa Mancha Temple**,
built by the ruler Bir Hambir
in the late 16th century, has
108 pillars and a pyramidal
roof. Images of Krishna and
Radha were displayed here
for the Rasa Festival, a tradition that still continues today.

North of the Rasa Mancha
Temple is the large **Keshta
Raya (Jor Bangla) Temple**,
built in 1655. It has joined
twin roofs, literally *jor
bangla*. Floral motifs, scroll work and
scenes from the *Ramayana*
and *Mahabharata* embellish
the friezes on the walls.

The **Madan Mohan Temple**
further north, was built in
1694 and has friezes showing
events from the life of Krishna.
To the northwest, the 19th-
century **Shridhara Temple** has
nine spires or *nav ratna*. The
frieze at the entrance shows
the god Shiva dancing.

Barddhaman ⑥

Barddhaman district. 125 km (78
miles) NW of Kolkata. 🚌
🎭 Barddhaman Festival (Jan).

The Rajas of Barddhaman
(Burdwan) were once
powerful landlords and great
patrons of the arts. Today, the
small, nondescript town is a
gateway to some interesting
sites. The rajas built several
temples at **Kalna**, 50 km
(31 miles) to the east, in the
18th and 19th centuries. The
Shiva temple, with 108 minor
shrines, is the most impressive.
Nabadwip, 20 km (12 miles) to
the north, was the birthplace
of Sri Chaitanya (1486–1533),
founder of the movement that
revived the Krishna cult *(see
p179)*. It is a charming town,
with a few old houses built of
the narrow red brick, unique
to pre-British Bengal. Pilgrims
singing *kirtans* throng the
Gauranga Temple. Nearby, in
Mayapur, is the large and
modern Chandrodaya Temple,
headquarters of ISKCON
(International Society for
Krishna Consciousness).

Interior Arch
*This doorway has rich
carvings of creepers,
foliage and flowers.*

BANKURA HORSES

Bankura district's vibrant tradition of folk
art includes a variety of clay handicrafts.
The district's most famous product is
the Bankura horse, a very stylized
figure with a long neck and elongated
ears, in warm terracotta colours.
Artisans have used the same
techniques of hollow clay moulding
and firing for generations. Sizes vary
from minute, palm-sized toys to gigantic
creations over 1 m (3 ft) high. The horses
are votive figures and are usually placed
in front of local deities.

Bankura clay horse

Students attending open air classes at Visva Bharati University

Shantiniketan ❼

Birbhum district. 213 km (132 miles) NW of Kolkata. 🚉 Bolpur, 3 km (2 miles) S of Shantiniketan, then rickshaw. 🚌 Bolpur. 🎭 Kendulimela (Jan), Paush Mela (Dec).

Rabindranath Tagore founded the serene settle-ment of Shantiniketan in 1921. His aim was to establish an institution that followed the traditional Indian *gurukul* system of instruction where gurus would teach their disciples, while sitting on the grass under shady trees. The university also stressed the importance of community living, and specialized in all branches of the arts and humanities, with a special emphasis on Bengali culture.

Today known as the **Visva Bharati University**, its structure is more conven-tional, but certain traditions, such as open air lessons, remain sacrosanct. The place is still hallowed ground for admirers of Tagore.

In the campus is the Uttarayan Complex, where the poet lived and worked for many years. Other depart-ments include **Kala** (Fine Arts) **Bhavan, Sangeet** (Music) **Bhavan** and **China Bhavan**, specializing in Chinese studies. Shantiniketan's association with contemporary Indian art is evident by the works on display by many of the country's leading artists, such as Binode Bihari Mukherjee (1904–80), Nandalal Bose (1882–1966) and Ram Kinkar

Baij (1910–80). The **Vichitra Museum** has memorabilia from the poet's life, including his paintings, developed from the sketches he made in the margins of his written work. Excellent performances of Rabindra Sangeet (songs written and set to music by Tagore) can be heard at the campus every evening.

The village of **Kenduli**, nearby, is the birthplace of the medieval poet, Jayadeva, who composed the *Gita Govinda*, a paean to Krishna. Every year in January the Bauls, wandering minstrels known for their soulful songs, gather here for Kendulimela, a festival where they sing without pause for three days.

> 🏛 **Visva Bharati University**
> *Tel* (03463) 25 2531. ◯ Thu–Tue.
> 🚫 📷 **Vichitra Museum**
> ◯ daily. 🚫 📷

Murshidabad ❽

Murshidabad district. 200 km (124 miles) N of Kolkata. 🚉 🚌

The former capital of the nawabs of Bengal, Murshidabad lies in the green and gold Bengal countryside. This city, on the banks of the Bhagirathi river, was founded in 1704 by Nawab Murshid Quli Khan, governor of the Mughal emperor Aurangzeb. His grave lies beneath the stairs of the impressive **Katra Mosque**, built in 1724 along the lines of Kartalab Khan's Mosque at Dhaka. The nawab chose this site because he wanted the footsteps of the faithful to pass over him.

Hazarduari ("A Thousand Doors"), the nawabs' palace, was built in the 1830s by General Duncan McLeod of the Bengal Engineers who,

The grand façade of Hazarduari Palace in Murshidabad

RABINDRANATH TAGORE (1861–1941)

Tagore was India's ultimate Renaissance man and his influence is still felt in all branches of the arts, particularly in Bengal. Born in 1861 into the rich and cultivated Tagore family *(see p280)*, he became a poet, lyricist, novelist, short story writer, essayist, painter, choreographer, actor, drama-tist and singer – as well as the author of India's national anthem. Following the translation of his poem *Gitanjali* into English by WB Yeats, he was awarded the Nobel Prize in 1913. He was knighted by the British government, but returned the honour in protest against the massacre at Jallianwala Bagh *(see p56)*. Mahatma Gandhi called him Gurudev ("Great Teacher"). Tagore died in August 1941, but his memory is still deeply revered by Bengalis and his portraits, if not his books, occupy pride of place in nearly all middle-class Bengali homes.

Nobel laureate Tagore, in 1930

For hotels and restaurants in this region see pp700–1 and pp728–9

inspired by Italian Baroque, gave it a banquet hall lined with mirrors and a striking circular Durbar Hall. The palace is now a museum with many fine exhibits, such as a gigantic chandelier, presented by Queen Victoria, which was hung directly over the nawabs' solid silver throne. The library has over 10,000 books, among them some beautiful illuminated Korans. Other items on display are a motley collection of arms and armour, including a cannon which was fired at the crucial Battle of Plassey in 1757 (see p52), when Robert Clive defeated the nawab, Siraj-ud-Daulah – a battle which eventually paved the way for the establishment of the British Empire in India. The town declined after Kolkata grew in importance.

🏛 **Hazarduari Museum**
◯ Sat–Thu. 📷 🚫

The carved terracotta façade of the Eklakhi Mausoleum, Pandua

Gaur ➒

Malda district. 325 km (202 miles) N of Kolkata. 🚉 Malda, 16 km (10 miles) N of Gaur, then taxi or bus. 🚌
Monuments ◯ daily.

The impressive ruins of Gaur are an indication of its former glory, when the city caught the imagination of the second Mughal emperor Humayun who called it Jinnatabad ("Abode of Paradise"). This abandoned city, spread over 52 sq kms (20 sq miles), dates to the 15th and 16th centuries, though the area has a much older history. The Buddhist Pala kings ruled here from the 8th century onwards until they

were ousted by the Senas, Bengal's last Hindu dynasty, in the 12th century. Thereafter, it was ruled by a series of Muslim sultans, including the Ilyas Shahi dynasty. Gaur was sacked by Sher Shah Sur (see p79) in 1539, and ravaged by plague in 1575, after which it became part of the Mughal Empire.

The oldest structure is the **Sagar Dighi**, a large tank built in the 12th century. On the eastern bank of the Bhagirathi river are the ramparts of a fort, within which is a brick wall that once enclosed a palace. The northern gate, the **Dakhil Darwaza**, built in 1459, has a soaring entrance archway and corners embellished with carving. To its north are the remains of **Sona Mosque**, built in 1526, and Gaur's largest mosque. Other interesting buildings include the many-arched **Qadam Rasul Mosque**, built in 1530 to enshrine an impression of the Prophet Mohammad's footprint, the brick **Tantipara Mosque**

The Gumti Darwaza, Gaur

and the **Lattan Mosque** with remnants of blue, green, yellow and white tiles. The **Gumti Darwaza**, the eastern entrance to the city of Gaur, still stands.

Pandua ➓

Malda district. 360 km (224 miles) N of Kolkata. 🚉 Malda, 18 km (11 miles) S of Pandua, then taxi or bus. 🚌

The creeper-covered ruins of Pandua lie on either side of a 10-km (6-mile) stretch of an old paved brick road. In 1353, Pandua replaced Gaur as the capital of Bengal's Muslim rulers. At the northern end, the 14th century **Adina Mosque**, built by Sultan Sikandar Shah, imitates the design of the great mosque at Damascus. Once the largest mosque in India, it contains Sikandar Shah's tomb. Further south is the early 15th-century **Eklakhi Mausoleum** which contains the grave of Sultan Jalal-ud-din. This stucture, built at great cost, was one of the earliest square brick tombs to be constructed in Bengal. The octagonal inner chamber, unusually, has an image of Ganesha, the Hindu elephant god, carved over the entrance archway. The **Qutb Shahi Mosque**, to the south, is sometimes called the "Golden Mosque" as its minarets were once topped with yellow tiles. It was built in 1582 by Sultan Makhdum Shah, whose grave lies adjacent to the mosque.

The Dakhil Darwaza in Gaur, built with small, red bricks

Tea plantations lining the road between Bagdogra and Siliguri

Siliguri ⓫

Darjeeling district. 79 km (49 miles) SE of Darjeeling. 🏠 470,300. ✈ Bagdogra, 12 km (7 miles) W of Siliguri, then taxi or bus. 🚉 New Jalpaiguri, 60 km (37 miles) SE of Siliguri, then taxi or bus. 🚌 ℹ Tourist Office, Siliguri, (0353) 251 1974.

Siliguri, situated in the foothills of the Eastern Himalayas, was once a calm, provincial town, with quiet streets and well-equipped shops, where tea planters would come to stock up on provisions. Today, much of the town is a vast trucking depot, though it has some lively bazaars, such as the one on **Tenzing Norgay Road**. The Tibetan woollens on sale here are good bargains, and cane furniture, a speciality of the area, is widely available. In the winter, Siliguri hosts international Buddhist conferences and also serves as the transit point for travellers to the Jaldapara Wildlife Sanctuary.

Environs
Clustered close to Siliguri are **New Jalpaiguri**, the railhead for the area, and **Bagdogra**, which has the airport. Along with Siliguri, these towns act as gateways to the hill stations of Darjeeling, Kurseong and Kalimpong, as well as to Bhutan and Sikkim. The drive between these towns goes past beautiful green acres of tea plantations.

Jaldapara Wildlife Sanctuary ⓬

Jalpaiguri district. 200 km (78 miles) E of Siliguri. 🚉 Madarihat, the entry point, then taxi. 🚌 Madarihat. ℹ For general enquiries and bookings for the Hollong Forest Lodge contact Tourist Office, Siliguri, (0353) 251 1974. 🕐 Oct–May. 📷 extra charges. 🏨 Hollong.

The region around the Jaldapara Wildlife Sanctuary, in the richly forested Dooars Valley, was once the hunting ground of the kings of Bhutan. Today, it is one of the biggest reserve forests in West Bengal, covering an area of 216 sq km (83 sq miles). Established in 1941,

---

THE DARJEELING HIMALAYAN RAILWAY (DHR)

The most attractive way to travel to Darjeeling from Siliguri is by the "toy train", officially known as the Darjeeling Himalayan Railway (DHR). The narrow gauge train gasps its way up from the railhead at New Jalpaiguri to Darjeeling, 2,128 m (6,982 ft) above sea level. The journey takes nine hours and the track rises a total of 2,088 m (6,850 ft) over its length of 80 km (50 miles). Constructed between 1879 and 1881, the train line was hailed as an engineering masterpiece and is now a UNESCO World Heritage Site. The line makes wide loops as it zigzags up the hill, requiring the train to backtrack for certain stretches. Each of the steam engines, one of which dates to 1892, hauls up three carriages. If nine hours sounds daunting, try journeying to Kurseong by train and taking a bus to Darjeeling, or travelling only the last stretch (from Ghoom to Darjeeling) by train. Tickets for the journey are available at New Jalpaiguri and Darjeeling stations. The train leaves both stations at 9am and 3pm during the peak season. For more details see p777.

The toy train pulled by steam engines

the reserve sprawls over lush, deciduous forests and dense scrubland, with the Torsa river flowing through it. This is one of the few places in India where the great Indian one-horned rhinoceros (see p330) can be easily spotted. About 50 of these magnificent animals live in the sanctuary, protected from poachers who hunt them for their horns, which are believed to be powerful aphrodisiacs. The sanctuary is home to various other rare and endangered species as well, including the leopard, tiger, hispid hare, hogbadger, and sloth bear.

Large numbers of hog deer, spotted deer, barking deer and gaur (Indian bison) can also be seen at Jaldapara. Bird species include the lesser pied horn-bill, and the Bengal florican with its mottled and streaked plumage. In addition, there are eight species of freshwater turtles in Jaldapara's ponds.

The northern part of the sanctuary, known as Totopara, is located along the banks of the Torsa river. It is home to the Toto tribe, now only 950 strong, whose members have consistently refused to succumb to the comforts of civilization.

Jungle fowl, found in large numbers at Jaldapara

A delightful way to explore the Jaldapara Sanctuary is to take an early morning elephant safari through the park. The elephants belong to the forest department and spend their entire lives within the confines of the sanctuary. Quite often, the elephants taking visitors on safaris are accompanied by their calves, which gambol along closely beside them. The many waterholes in the sanctuary, where animals come to drink in the evenings, are excellent spots for wildlife sightings.

The elegant, colonial-style **Hollong Forest Lodge** within the sanctuary offers food and accommodation.

Kurseong ⑬

Darjeeling district. 31 km (19 miles) N of Siliguri. 🚉 🚌

Halfway between Siliguri and Darjeeling, on the Darjeeling Himalayan Railway line, secluded Kurseong has a quiet charm. It is smaller than Darjeeling, with a milder climate because of its lower altitude. Set amid tea gardens, with lush vegetation and a picturesque lake, Kurseong is known for its natural beauty. According to local legend, the place gets its name from *kurson-rip*, a beautiful wild orchid found in the area.

Kurseong is a walkers' paradise. The trek from **Mirik** to Kurseong (see p303), which takes about eight hours, runs through tea estates, orange orchards, cardamom plantations and small villages, and provides spectacular views of the valley. Similarly, the five-hour walk to **Ghoom** is also beautiful, winding along a ridge which runs through a thick, but well-shaded, forest.

Gaur (Indian bison) roaming the scrubland at Jaldapara

Saraswati Puja *pandal*

FESTIVALS OF WEST BENGAL & SIKKIM

Ganga Sagar Mela (mid-Jan), Sagar Island. Thousands of pilgrims assemble for a fair, and a dip at dawn at the point where the Ganges enters the sea.

Saraswati Puja (Jan/Feb). Saraswati is the Goddess of Learning and her image is always dressed in pale yellow. School and college girls dress in yellow too, and place their books at the feet of the goddess during this festival, celebrated all over Bengal.

International Flower Festival (Apr/May), Gangtok. Held at the height of the flowering season, this festival showcases Sikkim's rare orchids, rhododendrons and other beautiful flowers.

Saga Dawa (May), Gangtok. Sacred scriptures are carried from monasteries through the streets by stately processions of lamas during this festival, which celebrates the Buddha's birth, his enlightenment and his attainment of nirvana.

Durga Puja (Sep/Oct) (see p281).

Burra Din (25 Dec), Kolkata. Otherwise known as Christmas, Burra Din is celebrated by Christians and non-Christians alike. Kolkata's main shopping streets are lit up and little plastic pine trees, decorations and thickly-iced fruit cakes are on sale at every local market.

A view of Darjeeling with Mount Kanchendzonga in the background

Darjeeling ⑭

Darjeeling district. 79 km (49 miles) NW of Siliguri. ▨ 107,600. ✕ Bagdogra, 90 km (56 miles) S of city centre, then bus or taxi. 🚃 🚍 ℹ Government Tourist Office, Chowrasta, (0354) 225 4050.

The name Darjeeling derives from the monastery of Dorje Ling (meaning Place of the Thunderbolt) that once stood on Observatory Hill. The British chose this sunny, west-facing ledge of the Himalayan foothills to build a sanatorium in the mid-19th century. Subsequently, it became Bengal's summer capital and the government would move up here when the plains grew too hot. Today, much of Darjeeling's Raj splendour is still in evidence and contrasts with its Tibetan, Nepali and Bengali character.

This picturesque town squats rather precariously on the hillside, and has three main thoroughfares, **Hill Cart Road**, **Laden Road** and **The Mall**. The Mall is the hub of Darjeeling, leading to the crowded **Chowrasta** (cross-roads), lined with bookshops such as the **Oxford Book and Stationery**, which has a wide range of books on India. Other shops sell teas, curios and souvenirs. Vendors offer sets of bright, out-of-focus postcards and guided tours. A rather jolting ten-minute pony ride round the Chowrasta is also available.

Nearby is the **Bhutia Busty Monastery**, built in 1879. The cult text, *The Tibetan Book of the Dead*, was found in the library attached to this shrine, and was translated into English in 1927. The murals in the temple are beautiful – but visitors should ask for permission before entering.

The presence of **Kanchen-dzonga**, (8,598 m/28,209 ft), India's highest peak *(see p302)*, dominates the town. Some of the best views of the entire snow-clad range of the Eastern Himalayan peaks can be enjoyed from the windy, prayer flag-lined **Observatory Hill**.

At **North Point**, in the northwest corner of Darjeeling, is India's first passenger rope-way, a cable car connecting Darjeeling to **Singla Bazaar** in the Little Rangeet Valley. The hour-long journey provides a good view of the mountains and the tea gardens that cling to the sides and bottom of the valley.

The **Himalayan Mountain-eering Institute** is to the south of North Point on Birch Hill. Its Mountaineering Museum has a fascinating contour model of the Himalayan peaks, while the Everest Museum gives a history of the various attempts to climb Everest and other Himalayan peaks. The **Himalayan Zoo** is adjacent, and is famous for its high altitude fauna, including snow leopards, Siberian tigers and red pandas. To the south, the **Lloyds Botanical Gardens** are home to an interesting and varied collection of Himalayan flora – the hundreds of species of orchids in its Orchid House

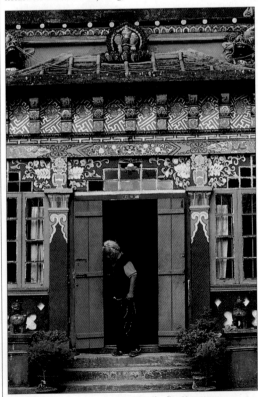

The carved and painted façade of the Yiga Choeling Monastery

are particularly lovely. The town also has some well-preserved colonial churches. **St Andrew's Church**, west of Observatory Hill, was built in 1843, though the clock tower was added later. **St Columba's Kirk**, near the train station, was built in 1894 and is worth a visit for its magnificent stained-glass windows.

Some of the best preserved examples of Raj-era grandeur in India are Darjeeling's hotels and clubs. Just above Observatory Hill is the rattan-and-chintz-decorated **Windamere Hotel** *(see p700)*. Open fires heat the sedate lounge where, to the accompaniment of a string quartet playing genteel tunes, maids in starched aprons serve sandwiches and Darjeeling tea to visitors and guests.

Ghosts of colonial planters can be sensed at the **Planters' Club**. Old hunting prints hang on the walls and visitors can sit in front of coal fires while bearers, who must have been robust young men in 1947, serve drinks in slow motion.

Women tea pickers in northern Bengal's tea gardens, around Darjeeling

Bhutia Busty Monastery
Chowrasta. ⬭ daily.

🏛 **Himalayan Mountaineering Institute**
Birch Hill Park, entrance on Jawahar Rd West. **Tel** (0354) 225 4268. ⬭ daily. ● Thu. 🎟 📷 extra charges.

🐾 **Himalayan Zoo**
⬭ Fri–Wed. 🎟

Environs
Those interested in Buddhism should visit the **Yiga Choeling Monastery**, 10 km (6 miles) south of Darjeeling, established in 1875 by the Gelugpa (Yellow Hat) sect. The monastery has murals of Buddhist deities and beautiful, if faded, frescoes in the prayer hall. Ask for permission before entering the shrine. **Tiger Hill**, 11 km (7 miles) south of Darjeeling, offers spectacular views of the mighty **Everest** (8,848 m/29,029 ft) and other peaks in the Eastern Himalayan Range, including **Makalu** (8,475 m/27,805ft) and **Janu** (7,710 m/25,225 ft), as they catch the first rays of the sun. Early risers can take a pre-dawn drive to Tiger Hill (about 45 minutes in a jeep).

Senchal Lake, 5 km (3 miles) west of Tiger Hill, is a lovely mountain lake, but tends to be crowded with local tourists. For visitors who come to Darjeeling during the plucking season (April to November), the **Happy Valley Tea Estate**, just beyond the town, is a pleasant tea garden to visit.

Mural, Zangdopelri Fo-Brang Monastery

Yiga Choeling Monastery
⬭ daily. Donations welcome.

Kalimpong ⑮

Darjeeling district. 51 km (32 miles) E of Darjeeling. 🚌 43,000. 🚐

Kalimpong was once part of Sikkimese and then Bhutanese territory, before it became part of British India in the 19th century. It was at the head of the ancient trade route to Tibet and still has the feel of a frontier town. Its market sells a mix of the exotic and the mundane, from fern shoots to plastic buckets. Memories of the Raj are recalled by the charming stone cottages and the quaint ambience of the **Himalayan Hotel** *(see p700)*, once a family home. The **Thongsa Monastery** is Kalimpong's oldest monastery. It was built in 1692, and is a brisk hour's walk above the town. To the south of the town, the **Zangdopelri Fo-Brang Monastery**, blessed by the Dalai Lama in 1976, has some interesting three-dimensional mandalas.

The town's many nurseries produce a large number of exotic orchids, gladioli, amaryllis lily and cactii. A good one to visit is the **Udai Mani Pradhan Nursery**.

TENZING NORGAY (1914–86)

Tenzing Norgay and Sir Edmund Hillary were the first two men to stand on top of Mount Everest. Tenzing Norgay was born in Tsa-chu, Nepal, into the Sherpa community, and later made his home in Darjeeling. He undertook his first climb as a porter with a British expedition in 1935 and climbed many mountain peaks, making at least six attempts on Everest before his successful one with Hillary in 1953, when he was the sherpa sirdar (head sherpa). Tenzing won the George Medal and later became the head of Darjeeling's Himalayan Mountaineering Institute. Tenzing's life highlighted the contributions, earlier seldom acknowledged, that sherpas make to Himalayan expeditions.

Statue of Tenzing, Himalayan Mountaineering Institute

Stupa at Gangtok's Namgyal Institute of Tibetology

Gangtok ⑯

East Sikkim district. 110 km (68 miles) N of Siliguri. ⚇ 29,200. ✈ Bagdogra, 117 km (73 miles) S of city centre, then taxi or bus. 🚉 Siliguri, 107 km (66 miles) S of city centre, then taxi or bus. 🚌 ℹ Sikkim Tourism, MG Marg, (03592) 221 634. 🎭 Losar Festival (Feb/Mar), Enchey Monastery Festival (Aug & Dec). **Travel permits** required to enter Sikkim (see p303).

The capital of Sikkim, Gangtok reflects this tiny state's extraordinary ethnic diversity. In the crowded city, which spills precariously down a ridge, Lepchas (the region's original inhabitants) live alongside Tibetans, Bhutias, Nepalis and Indians from the plains. Though now full of modern structures, Gangtok's "Shangrila" aspects can still be experienced in pockets of the city and in its alpine environs.

Until 1975, Sikkim was a kingdom, with the status of an Indian Protectorate. It was ruled by the Chogyals, Buddhists of Tibetan origin, whose dynasty began in the 17th century. However, the British Raj's policies of importing cheap labour from neighbouring Nepal for Sikkim's rice, cardamom and tea plantations drastically changed Sikkim's demography. Soon Nepali Hindus constituted 75 per cent of the state's population. In 1975 the population of Sikkim voted to join the Indian

Republic, ending the rule of Palden Thondup Namgyal, the last Chogyal.

At the town's northern edge is the early 20th-century **Enchey Monastery**, whose large prayer hall is full of murals and images, representing the pantheon of Mahayana Buddhist deities (see p141). Enchey's festivals feature spectacular masked dances. At the southern end is the **Namgyal Institute of Tibetology**. Established in 1958, it has a rare collection of medieval Buddhist scriptures, bronzes and embroidered thangkas.

🏯 **Enchey Monastery**
🕘 daily. 📷 only allowed outside the monastery.

🏛 **Namgyal Institute of Tibetology**
🕘 Mon–Sat. 📷 2nd Sat & public hols. 🌐 www.tibetology.com

Environs

Saramsa Orchidarium, situated 14 km (9 miles) south of Gangtok, displays many of the 450 orchid species found in Sikkim. They flower from April to May, and again in October.

Rumtek Monastery, 24 km (15 miles) southwest of Gangtok, is the headquarters of the Kagyupa (Black Hat) sect, one of the oldest Tibetan Buddhist sects, and the seat of its head, the Gyalwa Karmapa. The 16th Karmapa fled Tibet in 1959 after the Chinese invasion, and built a replica here of his monastery at Tsurphu

Guardian of the East at Rumtek

in Tibet. Rumtek is an impressive complex, its flat-roofed buildings topped with golden finials, and filled with treasures brought from the monastery in Tibet. Especially splendid is the reliquary chorten of the 16th Karmapa, behind the main prayer hall, made of silver and gold and studded with corals, amber and turquoise. Since the 16th Karmapa's death in 1981, however, there have been two claimants to his title (and the monastery's legendary treasures), including one who dramatically escaped from Tibet into India in 2000. Until this dispute is resolved, the armed guards that surround the monastery will remain. Rumtek's main festivals are in February/March and in May/June. **Tshangu Lake**, 40 km (25 miles) northeast of Gangtok, lies at an altitude of 3,780 m (12,402 ft). Visitors to the lake require a special permit from the Sikkim Tourism office in Gangtok.

The drive to Tshangu Lake, close to the border with China, is spectacular. The lake is impressive both in spring and summer, when it is surrounded by alpine flowers, and in winter when it's frozen. Visitors can go for rides on the shaggy black yaks that stand docilely on the lake's shores.

🏯 **Rumtek Monastery**
Tel (03592) 252 329. 🕘 daily. 📷 only allowed outside the monastery. www.rumtek.org

The richly decorated prayer hall of Rumtek Monastery

Flora and Fauna of the Eastern Himalayas

The Eastern Himalayas and their foothills in northern Bengal, Sikkim and the north-eastern states are exceptionally rich in rare flora and fauna. This region receives the brunt of the Southwest Monsoon winds as they rise over the Bay of Bengal and hit the Eastern Himalayas with full force, gradually losing impetus as they travel westward. The resulting high moisture content in the air and soil has helped create a habitat

Primula calderina

of dense virgin forests, fertile hillsides and lush alpine pastures. Among the plants that can be seen in this region are over 50 species of rhodo-dendron, 500 species of orchid and several varieties of primula and bamboo. Typical fauna of the region include yaks, blue sheep and red pandas. Local folklore adds another – the elusive Yeti or Abominable Snowman, glimpsed by many mountaineers.

The blue poppy (Meconopsis roylei), *which attracted famous 19th-century plant hunters such as Joseph Hooker to the Eastern Himalayas, grows above the tree-line, in alpine pastures where yaks graze.*

Orchids, *such as this beautiful yellow* Dendrobium *species, festoon the forests of Arunachal Pradesh, Meghalaya, Manipur, Nagaland and Sikkim.*

The cardiocrinum lily (Cardiocrinum giganteum) *is highly scented. It grows in temperate forests of oak, maple and rhododendron in Sikkim.*

The great pied hornbill , (Buceros bicornis) *with its huge yellow and black beak, is common in the forests of Arunachal Pradesh, where several tribes sport its black and white feathers in their headdress.*

Magnolia campbelli *with its lovely white blossom, blooms profusely in early spring in the temperate forests of the Darjeeling hills and Sikkim.*

The red panda (Ailurus fulgens), *also called the cat-bear, is a bright chestnut colour with white-rimmed ears and a bushy tail. One of its favourite foods is dwarf bamboo which grows in the temperate forests of Arunachal Pradesh and Sikkim.*

The yak *is greatly prized in Sikkim. It serves as a pack animal, and also provides milk, meat and wool from its shaggy coat.*

A Tour of Northern Sikkim ⑰

An area of unspoilt natural beauty, framed by snowcapped Himalayan peaks, northern Sikkim has only recently been opened to visitors. This tour, following the valley of the Teesta river, goes past tranquil monasteries and villages, through forests of rhododendron, to Yumthang where yaks graze in meadows filled with alpine flowers. Along the way there are charming rural markets, and superb views of the world's third highest peak, Mount Kanchendzonga.

TIPS FOR DRIVERS

Length: 149 km (93 miles).
Stopping-off points: The tour can be done in 2–3 days. Phodong, Mangan-Singhik and Lachung are stopping-off points.
Permits: Visitors require special permits for this region, issued by the Department of Tourism in Gangtok, (03592) 221 634. Travel is permitted in groups of two or more persons. For more details see p303.

Yumthang ⑥
The Lachung-Yumthang road crosses rhodo-dendron forests, which bloom bet-ween April and June. Yumthang, at 3,614 m (11,857 ft), also has hot sulphur springs.

Lachung ⑤
Just 15 km (9 miles) from Tibet, with which it used to trade before 1959, Lachung is a pretty village on both banks of the Lachung river.

```
0 km          5
0 miles       5
```

KEY

— Tour route
— National highway
= Minor road

Mangan-Singhik ④
This market centre for northern Sikkim attracts local villagers selling oranges, apples and cardamom. There are breathtaking views of the Kanchendzonga Range from here.

Chungthang

Teesta

Kodyong

Phodong ②
This serene monastery, with 260 resident monks, has beautiful murals, woodcarving and Buddhist images. It was built in 1740.

Dik Chhu

Labrang ③
This monastery (built 1710), 4 km (2.5 miles) from Phodong, has an unusual octagonal shape. On the track below it are the ruins of Tumlong Palace, the seat of the Chogyals in the 19th century.

Gangtok ①
Built on a high ridge above the Ranikhola river, Gangtok (*see p298*) is a bustling town, at an altitude of 1,780 m (5,840 ft).

SILIGURI

Pelling

West Sikkim district. 120 km (75 miles) W of Gangtok. Gezing, 9 km (6 miles) S of city centre, then local bus or taxi. Mount Pandim, Pemayangtse, (03595) 250 573. Pemayangtse Festival (Feb/Mar). **Travel permits** required (see p303).

Situated on a ridge, at an altitude of 2,086 m (6,800 ft), with excellent views of the peaks and glaciers of the Kanchendzonga Range, Pelling is a fast growing town. With plenty of accommodation, it is a convenient base from which to explore western Sikkim and embark on treks (see pp302–303). This is the state's most beautiful and unspoilt region, with expanses of forest, green river valleys, superb trekking trails, and Sikkim's oldest monasteries. Pelling is a day's drive from Gangtok, and is accessible from Darjeeling (72 km/45 miles south).

The main attraction here is the monastic complex of **Pemayangtse**, built in 1705, on a ridge a half-hour's walk from the town. Surrounded by picturesque monks' quarters and outhouses, the austere three-storeyed main monastery is a treasure house of beautiful *thangkas*, murals and images, with a breathtakingly intricate model of Zangdopelri, the seven-storeyed celestial home of Guru Padmasambhava (see p139), on the top floor. Pemayangtse has an annual festival, with spectacular masked dances. Sikkim's second oldest monastery, **Sangachoeling**

Detail of a door, Pemayangste

(built in 1697), is a steep 40-minute hike through thick forests above Pemayangtse. It has exquisite murals. The ruins of Sikkim's 17th-century capital, built by the second Chogyal (see p298), are at **Rabdentse**, 3 km (2 miles) south of Pelling.

Environs
Khecheopalri Lake, 33 km (21 miles) north of Pelling, is an enchanting spot which is sacred to both Buddhists and Hindus, who come here to make a wish. Seen from above, the lake is shaped like the footprint of Buddha. Though surrounded by a forest, it does not have a single leaf floating on its surface, and according to local belief, a holy bird swoops down and removes each leaf as it falls on the water.

Yuksam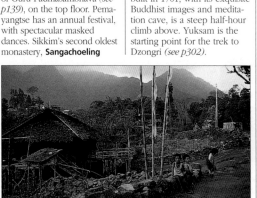

West Sikkim district. 162 km (101 miles) W of Gangtok. Mount Pandim, Pemayangtse, (03595) 250 573. **Travel permits** required (see p303).

Yuksam was the first capital of Sikkim, where the first Chogyal of Sikkim was crowned in 1641 by three learned lamas. A stone throne and some *chortens* mark this historic spot. Below it is **Kathok Lake**, and **Dubdi Monastery**, built in 1701, with its exquisite Buddhist images and meditation cave, is a steep half-hour climb above. Yuksam is the starting point for the trek to Dzongri (see p302).

Prayer flags fluttering near Yuksam, the first capital of Sikkim

Mani stones being carved at Tashiding Monastery

Tashiding Monastery 20

West Sikkim district. 145 km (90 miles) W of Gangtok. daily. Bumchu Festival (Feb/Mar). **Travel permits** required (see p303).

Built in 1716, Tashiding Monastery stands on the summit of a heart-shaped hill, where Guru Padmasambhava is said to have shot an arrow and then meditated on the spot where it fell. Surrounded by *chortens*, *mani* stones, water-driven prayer wheels, and the Ratong and Rangeet rivers, with Mount Kanchendzonga looming behind the hill, this is a magical spot. During the annual Bumchu Festival it attracts large crowds from all over Sikkim.

During this festival, sacred water, said to have been put into a sealed jar by a 17th-century Buddhist saint, is mixed with river water and distributed as a powerful blessing to devotees. Miraculously, the supply of sacred water never runs dry, and each year when the jar is unsealed, oracle priests can predict the future of Sikkim from the water level in it – too much or too little water augurs ill for Sikkim's peace and prosperity. Tashiding also has the **Thongwa Rangdol Chorten**, a mere glimpse of which is supposed to wipe away all sins. The main temple, rebuilt in 1987, has large images of the Buddha and the Bodhisattvas.

Trekking in West Bengal & Sikkim

The eastern Himalayas, spanning Tibet, Nepal, West Bengal and Sikkim, have some of the world's highest peaks such as Kanchendzonga, Everest, Lhotse and Makalu, and offer a variety of trekking options amidst lush hills bursting with orchids and rhododendron blossoms. The region is also alive with legends of the Abominable Snowman or Yeti, a huge, ape-like creature, who allegedly lives above the snowline. West Bengal's most popular trails are centred around the Singalila Ridge near Darjeeling, with views of Nepal's great massifs, while most of Sikkim's trails are dominated by the mighty Kanchendzonga. The best seasons are between October and November, and February and May.

Rhododendron blossoms

LOCATOR MAP

Area shown below

The Singalila Ridge

The Singalila Ridge, which begins near Darjeeling and extends to Kanchendzonga, has several trails. The Sandakphu-Phalut route beginning at Maneybhanjan has spectacular views of Everest, Lhotse, Makalu and Kanchendzonga, with plenty of lodges along the way. The 60-km (37-mile) path ends at the roadhead at Rimbik.

Duration: 6 days
Altitude: 3,636 m (11,929 ft)
Level of difficulty: moderate

MOUNT KANCHENDZONGA

Mount Kanchendzonga, the third highest peak in the world at 8,598 m (28,209 ft), dominates the skyline of Sikkim and West Bengal's Darjeeling district. Its name means "Five Treasures of the Snows", and the Sikkimese believe that the five summits of the Kanchendzonga Range conceal four treasures – gold and gems, grain, silver and holy scriptures. This magnificent mountain is revered as the guardian deity of Sikkim and is worshipped all over the state during the Pang Lhabsol festival, which takes place in the seventh month of the Tibetan calendar (between August and September). Prayers, rituals and masked dances are performed at monasteries – with the massif represented by a red mask crowned with skulls – to ensure that the land is protected in the year to come. Such is the awe in which the Sikkimese hold the peak that in 1999, an Austrian expedition to scale it was cancelled after widespread public protest that this would dishonour the deity and bring catastrophe to Sikkim.

A panoramic view of Mount Kanchendzonga from Dzongri Peak

SIKKIM

Dzo

Tsok

Bak

Rimbi

Denta

Sombare

Phalut   Gorkhe

Sabarkum

Rimb

Sandakphu

Gairib

Jaubari

Meghm

0 km   5

0 miles   5

anchendzonga

The Dzongri Trail

One of Sikkim's most popular treks, the trail from Pemayangtse to Dzongri covers 35 km (22 miles) one way. It leads past Yuksam and Tsokha through forests of rhododendron to Dzongri, with clear views of Kanchendzonga. The return to Yuksam takes two days.

Duration: *6–7 days*
Altitude: *4,030 m (13,222 ft)*
Level of difficulty: *moderate to tough*

•Yuksam
Tashijom
Rathang Chhu
Pemayangtse
• Gezing

Rishi Khola

Rafting and Kayaking

Rafting is very popular on the Teesta and Rangeet rivers, and is possible between October and November. Kayaks can be hired from the West Bengal Tourism office in Darjeeling.

eng
Rangeet
Rangeet
Naya Bazaar
Ramam
GANTOK,
Tsomgo Lake

KEY

- ▪ ▪ The Singalila Ridge
- ▪ ▪ Kurseong to Mirik
- ▪ ▪ The Dzongri Trail
- ▬▬ Major road
- ══ Minor road

• Darjeeling

'anebhanjan

Kurseong to Mirik

A great introduction to the West Bengal hills, this gentle 18-km (11-mile) hike goes past numerous villages and local tea estates.

Duration: *1 day*
Altitude: *1,767 m (5,797 ft)*
Level of difficulty: *easy*

Kurseong

irik

PRACTICAL TIPS

Be prepared: Acclimatization is essential for altitudes over 3,000 m (9,843 ft). See p767 for information on altitude sickness. Guides and porters can be hired in Gangtok and Darjeeling. The region is hit hard by the monsoon and trekking between early June and late September is not advisable. For more details on trekking see p751.

On the trek: Sikkim's trekking trails have suffered deforestation and littering, so ensure that all litter is carried back with you. Drink plenty of water and carry a first aid kit and cooking fuel. Never burn wood, which is a scarce resource. Put out all fires properly, leaving no burning embers. Some trails have leeches (see p767), so carry salt which, when sprinkled on a leech, causes it to fall off.

Permits: Foreign visitors require travel permits for Sikkim, issued for a 15-day period from the District Magistrate's Office in Darjeeling, (0354) 225 4233, or the Sikkim Tourism offices in Delhi, (011) 2611 5346, Kolkata, (033) 2281 5328, and Siliguri, (0353) 221 6502. A 14-day extension is permitted, issued by the Department of Tourism in Gangtok, (03592) 221 634, who also issue special permits for restricted areas such as Dzongri, Yumthang and Tsomgo Lake. Travel to these areas is permitted in groups of two or more persons. Trekking permits for Sikkim are available from the Department of Tourism in Gangtok, and Sikkim Tourism in Delhi. All treks must be arranged by a registered agency. For general information see p758.

Equipment hire & operators: Himalayan Adventures in Darjeeling, (0354) 225 4004, and Sikkim Trekking and Tours in Gangtok, (03592) 203 638, are reputed agencies. For more details see p755.

ORISSA

Bounded on the west by the thickly forested hills of the Eastern Ghats, and on the east by nearly 500 km (311 miles) of coastline on the Bay of Bengal, Orissa covers an area of 156,000 sq km (60,232 sq miles). Its most famous sights are clustered together in a compact triangle on the eastern coast, in the fertile delta of its major river, the Mahanadi. These include the magnificent 13th-century Sun Temple at Konark, a UNESCO World Heritage Site, and other outstanding temples at Bhubaneswar and Puri. To recover from sightseeing fatigue, there are beaches within easy reach at Puri, Konark and Gopalpur-on-Sea, fringed by coconut groves and fishing villages. Just south of this triangle is Chilika Lake, Asia's largest lagoon and a paradise for birdwatchers. The hinterland of the coast is lush with green paddy fields, dotted with ancient Buddhist ruins and tranquil hamlets, where Orissa's beautiful traditional crafts flourish. The spectacular, unspoilt landscape of northern Orissa includes Simlipal National Park, with its wealth of wildlife, and settlements of tribal people who form nearly a quarter of Orissa's population of 35 million.

SIGHTS AT A GLANCE

Towns & Cities
Baleshwar ⑪
Baripada ⑫
Berhampur ⑥
Bhubaneswar ①
Cuttack ⑧
Puri ③

Historic Sites
Konark ②
Ratnagiri ⑨

Areas of Natural Beauty
Chilika Lake ④
Gopalpur-on-Sea ⑤
Taptapani ⑦

National Parks
Bhitarkanika Sanctuary ⑩
Simlipal National Park ⑬

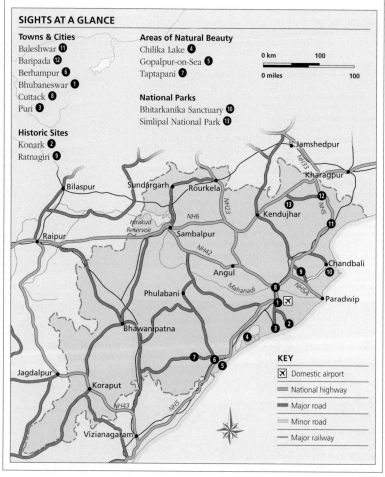

KEY
☒ Domestic airport
National highway
Major road
Minor road
Major railway

◁ Pilgrims swarming around the huge chariot at the Rath Yatra Festival in Puri

Bhubaneswar ❶

Painted dowry box from Orissa

The capital of Orissa, Bhubaneswar is famous for its superb Hindu temples. Most of these are in the older, southern part of the city, while the new town, with its modern administrative buildings and wide tree-lined avenues, is in the north. The temples date from the 7th to the 13th centuries, a period which saw the waning of Buddhism and a revival of Hinduism under the successive dynasties that ruled Orissa: the Shailodbhavas and Bhauma Karas in the 7th–8th centuries; the Somavamshis in the 9th–11th centuries; and the Eastern Gangas in the 12th–13th centuries.

Devotees bathing in the sacred waters of Bindusagar

Exploring the temples

More than 400 temples remain of the 7,000 that are said to have once embellished Bhubaneswar, earning it the title, the "City of Temples". A distinctive version of the North Indian style of temple architecture evolved in Orissa over the centuries *(see p21)*, under the patronage of the different dynasties. As the power and prosperity of these dynasties grew, the temples became bigger and more elaborate. Most of the temples have two main components – a convex curvilinear spire locally known as the *deul* (elsewhere called the *shikhara*), which towers over the inner sanctum where the deity's image is kept; and an entrance porch or assembly hall called the *jagamohan,* with a stepped pyramidal roof. Some of the bigger temples have two or three of these porches. Several smaller shrines and bathing tanks often surround the main temple, which is enclosed in a walled compound.

The magnificent 11th-century **Lingaraj Temple** represents the high point of the Orissan style, where both sculpture and architecture have evolved in perfect harmony. Its grandeur lies in its towering 55-m (180-ft) high *deul* (spire) with dramatic vertical ribs, and in the consummate artistry with which each sculpture and embellishment is executed. The female figures, animals, and friezes of ceremonial processions are full of grace and exuberance. The temple's large courtyard has more than 100 smaller shrines. The main deity here is Shiva as Tribhu-vaneswar ("Lord of the Three Worlds"), from which the city takes its name. The intriguing image of a rampant lion springing on a crouching elephant is a powerful motif in this temple, as in many others in Orissa, and some scholars believe it is a royal emblem. Non-Hindus cannot enter the Lingaraj Temple, but can view it from a platform near its northern gateway. The other temples are open to visitors.

North of the temple is the large **Bindusagar Tank** with a pavilion in the middle. It is believed to contain water from every sacred river in India. The main deity of the Lingaraj Temple is brought here for a ritual bath *(see p309)* every year.

Khangiri & Udaigiri Caves,

UDYAN MARG

JAN PATH

RAJ PA

Airport 4 km (2.5 miles)

Mausima Temple

Ramakrish M

MAHATAB ROAD

ROAD

BARADANDA SAHI ROAD

Vaital Deul Temple ③

Bine

②

Lingaraj Temple

Sari Temple

①

BHUBANESWAR CITY CENTRE

Bindusagar Tank ②
Lingaraj Temple ①
Mukteshwar Temple ⑤
Orissa State Museum ⑦
Parasurameshwar Temple ④
Rajarani Temple ⑥
Vaital Deul Temple ③

The impressive spire of the 11th-century Lingaraj Temple

Key to Symbols *see back flap*

The 8th-century **Vaital Deul Temple**, to the west of Bindusagar, is an unusual temple with eerie interior carvings. These indicate that it was probably used for macabre tantric rites, including human sacrifice. The main deity here is a terrifying, eight-armed Chamunda (a form of Durga), with a garland of skulls, seated on a corpse, flanked by a jackal and an owl.

Built in the 7th-century, the **Parasurameshwar Temple**, on the road to Puri, is the best preserved and most lavishly sculpted of the earliest group of temples. The square-

towered shrine has a rectangular *jagamohan* adjoining it, decorated with wonderfully animated bands of dancers and musicians on its west window. The main entrance to the *jagamohan* also has a fine carving of domestic elephants capturing wild ones, to the left of the lintel. Set into the outer walls of the shrine are images of deities, among them a superb potbellied Ganesha, and his brother Karttikeya sitting on his vehicle, the peacock.

The nearby 10th-century **Mukteshwar Temple**, one of the jewels of Orissan temple architecture, is notable for its exquisite sculptures and elegant proportions. Its beautiful *torana* (gateway) is decorated with langorously reclining female figures. The *jagamohan* is illuminated by diamond-shaped latticed windows on the

Guardian figures, Rajarani Temple

north and south walls, their outermost frames depicting enchanting scenes of frolicking monkeys. A unique feature of the *jagamohan* is the decorated ceiling, carved into a lotus with eight petals. The sculptures of female figures in this temple are remarkable for their expressive faces, with hairstyles and jewellery shown in exquisite detail. The octagonal wall surrounding the temple has a number of niches, each containing a

The beautifully sculpted *torana* of Mukteshwar Temple

wheel, a lotus medallion or a delicate scroll.

Set amidst paddy fields, just off the main road, is the 11th-century **Rajarani Temple**. It has a particularly striking spire decorated with miniature replicas of itself, rising in continuous tiers around the tower. This temple is renowned for its fine sculptures of *dikpals* (the guardians of the eight cardinal directions) perched on lotus flowers. Of these, Agni, the God of Fire on a ram, and Varuna, God of the Oceans seated on a crocodile, are particularly impressive. Also remarkable are the tall and slender female figures, carved in high relief on the walls of the temple.

🏛 Orissa State Museum

BJB Nagar. ⬭ *Tue–Sun.* ⬤ *public hols.* 📷 The highlight of this interesting museum is its rich collection of Buddhist and Jain sculptures, coins, and painted palm-leaf manuscripts. There are also collections of tribal art, traditional jewellery and musical instruments.

Environs

The **Nandan Kanan Zoo** and botanical gardens, 16 km (10 miles) north of Bhubaneswar, is famous for its white tigers (*see p239*). The zoo, surrounded by a thick forest, enables the animals to live in natural surroundings. Panthers and gharials (*Gavialis gangeticus*) have been successfully bred in captivity here.

🦌 Nandan Kanan Zoo

⬭ *Tue–Sun.* 📷 🚻 🛥

0 metres 500
0 yards 500

CUTTACK, Nandan Kanan Zoo
Railway Station
CUTTACK RD
NAGAR
BJB NAGAR
KALPANA SQUARE
⑦
ℹ
Orissa State Museum
PURI CUTTACK ROAD
TANKAPANI RD
...eshwar ...mple
⑤
Rajarani Temple ⑥
...ameshwar
(LEWIS ROAD)
Daya Canal

Chausath Yogini Temple, PURI, KONARAK, DHAULI & PIPLI

Exploring Bhubaneswar's Surroundings

Many sites of historical and architectural significance lie close to Bhubaneswar. They include Jain monastic caves, Hindu temples, Buddhist stupas and ancient rock inscriptions, dotting the lush green landscape around the city. Dating from the 3rd century BC (when the area was part of the great kingdom of Kalinga) to the 13th century AD, these sites bear witness to the region's political and religious importance for a continuous period of over 1,000 years.

Terracotta roof tile

Bagh Gumpha at Udaigiri, shaped like the open mouth of a tiger

♇ Udaigiri and Khandagiri Caves

6 km (4 miles) NW of Bhubaneswar. ☐ daily. 📷 🎫 *Sadhu Convention (Jan).*

The twin hills of Udaigiri ("Sunrise Hill") and Khandagiri ("Broken Hill") were honeycombed to make retreats for Jain monks in the 1st century BC. Located just off the highway that runs from Bhubaneswar to Kolkata, the hills rise suddenly from the flat surrounding plains, and are separated from each other by the highway.

Carvings at Udaigiri Caves

As one approaches from Bhubaneswar, **Udaigiri** is the hill on the right, and is best explored first as it has the more interesting caves. The most impressive of its 18 caves is the double-storeyed **Rani Gumpha** or "Queen's Cave" (Cave 1), which has lavishly sculpted friezes of women dancing and playing music, kings and queens in courtly splendour, elephants, monkeys and foliage. The sculpture is remarkable for its expressive animation, and has

been compared with the famous sculpted gateways at Sanchi (*see pp244–5*).

Other notable caves are **Chhota Hathi Gumpha** or "Small Elephant Cave" (Cave 3), with six superb elephants flanking its entrance; **Ganesh Gumpha** (Cave 10) whose sculptures include an intriguing battle scene with a woman riding an elephant while soldiers in kilts chase her, and **Bagh Gumpha** or "Tiger Cave" (Cave 12), its front ingeniously shaped like a

tiger's head with the mouth open. The most significant cave historically is **Hathi Gumpha** or "Elephant Cave" (Cave 14). On the rock above its entrance is an inscription from the 1st century BC. It records that the caves were built by Kharavela, third king of the powerful Chedi dynasty, whose conquests included large parts of Bihar, the Deccan and South India. The inscription also states that King Kharavela rebuilt his capital, Kalinganagar, after it was destroyed by a cyclone. Even today, Orissa remains vulnerable to cyclones, the last one having devastated the state in October 1999. On the summit of Udaigiri stands a ruined apsidal structure, probably used as a place of worship by the monks.

Across the highway, on **Khandagiri**, are 15 caves with carvings of sacred Jain symbols. The **Ananta Cave** (Cave 3), with its figures of twin serpents on the arches above the doorways, is the most important and has superb ornamentation and lively friezes, including one of boys chasing lions, bulls and other animals. Another enchanting carving in this cave shows the goddess Lakshmi in a lotus pool, being bathed with water from pitchers held by two elephants (*see p24*). Three of the caves – numbers 5, 8 and 9 – have impressive carved figures of the Jain *tirthankaras* in high relief.

Unlike Buddhist caves such as those at Ajanta (*see p479*) and Ellora (*see p478*), most of the Udaigiri and Khandagiri caves are so low that it is impossible to stand upright in

Khandagiri, the site of a Jain monastery with rock-cut chambers

Hirapur's Chausath Yogini Temple, open to the sky

them. This was in keeping with the self-mortification and asceticism that Jain monks were expected to practise. The site still attracts sadhus, who gather here every year in January to meditate in the caves. A lively fair springs up below the hills to entertain the crowds that gather to seek the sadhus' blessings.

Dhauli
8 km (5 miles) S of Bhubaneswar.
A stark white Buddhist stupa in the middle of serene green paddy fields on the banks of the Daya river marks the site of the bloody battle of Kalinga, fought by one of India's greatest rulers, the Mauryan emperor Ashoka *(see p42)* in 260 BC. He won the war but the carnage and misery it inflicted on the people filled the emperor with remorse and brought about a dramatic change of heart. After this battle, he gave up *digvijaya* (military conquest) for *dharmavijaya* (spiritual conquest), embraced Buddhism, and publicized his new maxims in rock edicts, installed in different parts of his empire. One of these is here, at the base of Dhauli Hill, in which the emperor declares, "All men are my children", and enjoins his officials to ensure impartiality, non-violence, justice and compassion in administration. The top of the rock is sculpted into an imposing elephant's head, symbolizing the Buddhist dharma. This is one of the earliest sculptures found in the subcontinent. The huge white **Shanti Stupa** ("Peace Pagoda") at the top of the hill was built by Japanese Buddhists in the early 1970s.

Chausath Yogini Temple
15 km (9 miles) SE of Bhubaneswar.
This 9th-century, circular temple is dedicated to the *chausath yoginis* or 64 manifestations of the goddess Shakti, who symbolizes female creative energy. All the images, each about 0.6 m (2 ft) tall and carved out of black chlorite stone, are placed in niches in the inner enclosure. The presiding deity, a graceful 10-armed *yogini*, is in the 31st niche. The temple is located in the pretty village of Hirapur.

Garden umbrella from Pipli, with appliqué-work

Environs
Pipli, 15 km (9 miles) south of Bhubaneswar, on the highway to Puri, is a village of artisans famous for their colourful appliqué-work fabrics. The craft originated to serve temples, providing intricately stitched awnings and covers for deities, and hangings in vivid hues for festival days. Today, garden umbrellas, cushion covers, wall hangings and bags are made in Pipli using the same techniques, in which cloth is cut into bird, flower, animal and other decorative shapes, and stitched on to fabric of a contrasting colour. Shops selling these line both sides of the highway as it passes through Pipli, enveloping it in a blaze of colour.

FESTIVALS OF ORISSA

Tribal Mela *(Jan)*, Bhubaneswar. Orissa's large and varied tribal population exhibit their dances, music, arts and crafts at this colourful week-long festival

Makar Mela *(14 Jan)*, Chilika Lake. Pilgrims bring offerings to a cave and temple devoted to the goddess Kali on a rocky island called Kalijai in Chilika Lake.

Magha Saptami *(Jan/Feb)*, Konark. To honour Surya, the Sun God, pilgrims come for a purifying dip in the sea before they worship at the temple. A colourful fair is held, with stalls selling food and gifts.

Ashokashtami *(Mar/Apr)*, Bhubaneswar. The image of Shiva, the main deity of the Lingaraj Temple, is taken in procession in a chariot for a ritual bath in the sacred Bindusagar Tank.

Chaitra Parba *(Apr)*, Baripada. This spring festival is marked by displays of the spectacular martial dance known as Mayurbhanj Chhau.

Rath Yatra *(Jun/Jul)*, Puri *(see p313)*.

Konark Dance Festival *(1–5 Dec)*, Konark. Classical dancers perform on an open air stage near the Sun Temple during this five-day festival.

A dancer performing during Rath Yatra celebrations

Konark: The Sun Temple ❷

Colossal elephants in the temple complex

One of India's great architectural marvels, this temple to the Sun God, Surya, was conceived as a gigantic chariot, with 12 pairs of wheels to carry the Sun God on his daily journey across the sky. Built in the 13th century by King Narasimhadeva of the Eastern Ganga dynasty *(see p44)*, the temple is also remarkable for its superb sculptures. Gods and demons, kings and peasants, elephants and horses jostle for space on its walls with dozens of erotic couples. Konark is now a UNESCO World Heritage Site.

Maiden with Bird
Statues of graceful maidens in a variety of poses are carved on the temple's façades.

Amalaka

Court Scene
This enchanting relief of the king being presented with a giraffe indicates the existence of maritime trade between Orissa's Eastern Ganga kings and Africa.

★ Surya
The majestic image of the Sun God stands on a chariot, flanked by his wives, and other deities.

★ Wheels of the Chariot
The 12 pairs of exquisitely carved wheels represent the months in a year, while the eight large spokes mark the division of the day into three-hour sections. The seven horses pulling the chariot represent the days of the week.

The Konark Sun Temple, on the shores of the Bay of Bengal

VISITORS' CHECKLIST

Puri district. 65 km 40 miles) SE
of Bhubaneswar. 🚌 ℹ️ *Orissa
Tourism, Sunvilla, (06758) 236
8202.* ⬜ *daily.* 🎫 📷 📹
*Magha Saptami (Jan/Feb), Konark
Dance Festival (Dec).* **Archaeological Museum** ⬜ *Fri–Wed.* 🎫 📷

The three-tiered roof is
shaped like a stepped pyramid
and crowned with a round fluted stone called an *amalaka*.
The terraces between each tier
are covered with sculptures.

The Cymbal Player
*This sculpture is in a row
of wonderfully animated
dancers, musicians and
drummers on the terrace
of the pyramidal roof.*

Medallion
*Deities and dancers
decorate the medallions
on the hub and the
spokes of the wheels.*

Erotic Sculpture
*A demure snake
goddess provides
a contrast to the
amorous couple
beside her. The
erotic sculptures
at Konark are
a celebration of
the joys of life.*

Bhogmandir

Main entrance

STAR FEATURES

★ Surya

★ Wheels of the
  Chariot

Bhogmandir
*The ruined "Hall of
Offerings" has gigantic
rampant lions on
cowering elephants.*

Exploring Konark

The Sun Temple at Konark originally had a towering *deul* (spire), 70 m (230 ft) high, over its main sanctuary. Visible far out at sea, the temple was an important navigational aid for European sailors headed for Calcutta (Kolkata), who called it the Black Pagoda. Over time, the temple's easily weathered khondalite stone was progressively corroded by seawinds and sand, and by the 19th century the great tower had completely collapsed. Only its base still remains. The temple's Bhogmandir or "Hall of Offerings", is now roofless, but its plinth and pillars remain, carved with figures of dancers, depicting the poses still used in classical Odissi dance *(see p28).*

The chariot-shaped *jaga-mohan* or assembly hall was buried for nearly two centuries under drifting sand. It was only unearthed and restored by the Archaeological Survey of India (ASI) in the early 20th century. Its many remarkable sculptures include no less than 1,700 elephants in animated motion, carved on the plinth; and several enchanting *alasa kanyas* (maidens at leisure), playing with a pet bird, holding a mirror, or leaning against a doorway.

Three life-size images of the Sun God, Surya, made of contrasting coloured chlorite stone, are positioned so that the sun's rays fall on their faces, turn by turn, at dawn, noon and sunset.

In the northeast corner of the compound is the **Shrine of the Nine Planets**, a large stone slab carved with the deities of the nine planets. Colossal sculptures of war horses and elephants stand at the north and south. Near the compound is the **Archaeological Museum** with fine sculptures recovered from the site. The beach is 3 km (2 miles) from the temple, but is unsafe for swimming because of treacherous undercurrents.

Hand-painted *ganjifa* playing card from Puri

Puri's Jagannath Temple, topped with Vishnu's wheel and flag

Puri ❸

Puri district. 60 km (37 miles) S of Bhubaneswar. 🏠 *157,650.* 🚉 🚌 ℹ *Orissa Tourism, Station Rd, (06752) 222 664.* 🛕 *daily.* 🎪 *Rath Yatra (Jun/Jul).* **Jagannath Temple** ⬜ *daily.* 🚫 *to non-Hindus.*

One of India's most important pilgrimage centres, this seaside town is dominated by the towering Jagannath Temple. Early European sailors, for whom its 65-m (213-ft) high spire was an important landmark, called it the White Pagoda, to differentiate it from Konark's Sun Temple which they named Black Pagoda.

The **Jagannath Temple** was built in the 12th century by King Anantavarman of the Eastern Ganga dynasty *(see p44).* Surrounded by a 6-m (20-ft) high wall, its main gate is guarded by a pair of brightly painted stone lions. Non-Hindus are not allowed in, but can get a good view of the complex, with its multitude of small shrines and its courtyard thronged with pilgrims, from the roof of the Raghunandan Library across the street from the main gate.

The temple is similar in design to the Lingaraj Temple in Bhubaneswar *(see p306),* with three smaller shrines adjoining its tall sanctuary tower. The elegant stone column near the entrance, topped with the figure of Arun, charioteer of the Sun God, was brought here from the Sun Temple at Konark in the 18th century.

From the temple, Puri's main street, **Bada Danda**, runs through the town, crammed with pilgrims' rest houses and shops selling food, religious souvenirs and handicrafts. Local specialities are the colourful *pattachitra* paintings and round *ganjifa* playing cards painted with religious themes.

Puri's beach is its other attraction, though not always safe for swimming because of dangerous undercurrents. The long beach front is crowded with stalls and groups of pilgrims along Marine Parade. Sunbathers and swimmers should therefore head to the eastern end, which is cleaner and more secluded, or to the beaches attached to the better hotels. Local fishermen wearing conical hats serve as lifeguards on the beach, and take visitors out to sea in their boats to watch the sunsets.

A family picnic on Puri Beach

The Jagannath Cult

Lord Jagannath

A unique cult has grown around Jagannath (Lord of the Universe), an incarnation of Vishnu. At Puri's Jagannath Temple, 6,000 resident priests perform the elaborate daily rituals of bathing, dressing and worshipping the image of Jagannath, together with those of his brother Balbhadra and sister Subhadra. Sumptuous meals are offered to the three deities five times a day, prepared daily by 400 temple cooks. During the spectacular Rath Yatra (chariot festival) in June/July, the deities are taken out in a procession in mammoth wooden chariots, pulled by thousands of devotees. The word juggernaut (large truck) is derived from the size and unstoppable force of Lord Jagannath's chariot.

Temple offerings *are sold at numerous stalls at the gates of the temple.*

Devotees *try to spend at least three days paying obeisance to Jagannath.*

Balbhadra has a white face and rides in a chariot with 14 wheels and four horses.

Subhadra has a yellow face and rides in a red chariot.

Puri cityscape

Jagannath's chariot is 1,370 m (4,495 ft) tall and has 16 wheels.

Jagannath Temple

Policeman

Musicians and drummers

Temple priests

PATTACHITRA PAINTING OF THE RATH YATRA

The Rath Yatra marks Lord Jagannath's annual journey to his birthplace, the Gundicha Temple, just over 2 km (1.3 miles) away. Over 200,000 people, including priests pilgrims, musicians and drummers, join the procession.

Temple dancers, *young boys known as gotipuas, perform the classical Odissi dance (see p28) before the deities every night. They are accompanied by musicians singing verses from the Gita Govinda, a 12th-century epic poem (see p292).*

Balbhadra, Subhadra and Jagannath, *the three deities, are believed to be of tribal origin, but have been absorbed into the Hindu pantheon. They have huge, all-seeing eyes, and outstretched arms to protect and bless all mankind.*

Fishermen on the beach at Gopalpur-on-Sea *(see p316)* ▷

A view of Chilika Lake, a haven for water birds and dolphins

Chilika Lake ④

Puri, Ganjam & Khordha districts. 50 km (31 miles) SW of Puri. 🚊 Balugaon, then taxi or bus. 🚌 Balugaon & Satpada. 🛈 Orissa Tourism, Barkul, (06758) 220 488. 🗓 Makar Mela (Jan). **Satpada and Nalabana Islands** 🚤 hired from Barkul, Balugaon, Satpada & Rambha.

A great, shallow lagoon covering 1,100 sq km (425 sq miles), Chilika is separated from the Bay of Bengal by a sandy ridge, with just a narrow channel connecting it to the sea. Believed to be the largest brackish water lake in Asia, Chilika is recognized as one of the most important wetlands in the world because of the phenomenal variety of aquatic and birdlife it supports. From November to February, the lake and its reed islands teem with nesting birds, including several winter migrants, such as the golden plover, the flamingo, the purple moorhen and the osprey. A major attraction at Chilika are dolphins, which are often spotted off **Satpada Island**, located at the confluence of the lake and the sea. **Nalabana Island**, at the core of the lake, is the best place for birdwatching. Orissa Tourism arranges boat trips to both the islands. **Kalijai Temple**, built on a small rocky island, is a pilgrimage spot which attracts festive crowds during the Makar Mela in January. The lake also supports the local people who earn their living from Chilika's prawns, crabs and fish.

Gopalpur-on-Sea ⑤

Ganjam district. 172 km (107 miles) SW of Bhubaneswar. 🚊 *Berhampur 18 km (11 miles) E of town centre, then taxi or bus.* 🚌 🛈 *Orissa Tourism, Berhampur Railway Station, (0680) 228 0226.*

This quiet seaside town was, in ancient times, a great seaport for Orissa's maritime trade with Indonesia *(see p318)*. The British later developed it as a beach resort and it now has a sleepy charm, except during the Durga Puja holidays *(see p281)* in October, when it swarms with tourists from Bengal. Swimming in the sea is not safe because of treacherous undercurrents. But the beach, lined with bungalows and dotted with casuarina groves, is a good place to spend the day, watching the fishing boats and the sunset.

Berhampur ⑥

Ganjam district. 170 km (106 miles) SW of Bhubaneswar. 🚊 🚌 🛈 *Orissa Tourism, Railway Station, (0680) 228 0226.*

The main commercial centre in southern Orissa, Berhampur is famous for its beautiful handwoven ikat silk, available in its bustling bazaar where weavers sit at their looms. The railhead for the seaside town of Gopalpur-on-Sea, Berhampur is also a convenient base for visiting **Jaugarh**, 35 km (22 miles) north of the city. Jaugarh has a 3rd-century BC rock edict erected by the Emperor Ashoka following the Battle of Kalinga, after which he had a change of heart. The edict is similar to the one at Dhauli

Painted panel from the 17th-century temple at Buguda

Floral offering to a goddess of fertility at Taptapani's hot springs

(see p309), in which Ashoka declares "All men are my children" and spells out his ethical code. A short distance away, at **Buguda**, is the Biramchinarayan Temple, built in the 17th century, with beautiful murals depicting scenes from the *Ramayana*.

Taptapani ⑦

Ganjam district. 51 km (32 miles) W of Berhampur. 🚌 🛈 *Orissa Tourism, (06816) 255 031.*

Picturesquely located on a forested hill in the Eastern Ghats, this spa is renowned for its hot springs. The boiling, sulphurous water bubbles out of a crevice in the hillside and is piped to a pool in a clearing. Near the pool is a small shrine to a tribal goddess of fertility as, apart from being beneficial for various chronic ailments, the hot springs are also believed to cure infertility. A tree with seed pods overhangs the pool, and women seeking the infertility cure are supposed to pick up seeds from the tree that have fallen to the muddy bottom of the pool – a difficult feat, especially since the water is too hot for more than a quick dip. The Saora tribal women *(see p321)*, whose villages are nearby, can often be seen taking the cure. The most comfortable way to enjoy the hot springs is by renting a room in the Orissa Tourism rest house just below the pool, which has hot water from the springs piped directly into its bathtubs.

The Orissa Weaver's Art

Orissa has a long and rich tradition of handwoven textiles. Over 300,000 people work in the state's textile industry producing a range of materials, from the simple cotton weaves of tribal areas, to the elaborate painted textiles for use in temples. Orissa's forests yield a wealth of wild silk cocoons which, in recent

Eagle motif in ikat fabric

years, have been supplemented by mulberry plantations. The state is famous for its silk ikat weaves, an intricate technique in which warp and weft threads are tie-dyed in such a way as to produce patterns when woven. Typical motifs include birds, animals, fish, seashells, holy *rudraksh* beads and temple spires.

The *bomkai* cotton sari *from Ganjam district was traditionally woven for the local aristocracy. Its distinguishing features are the temple spire pattern on the border, and the rich end piece with its elaborate ikat motifs.*

Vriksha Pattachitra *shows a contemporary minimalist version of the traditional painted textile, used as a temple hanging. The tree is painted on natural-colored wild silk (tussar).*

The *kotpad* sari *from the Koraput tribal region has a simple elegance, with unbleached cotton offset by a rich red madder-dyed border.*

The *ekphulia* (one flower) sari *achieves a striking effect by repeating the one-flower and fish motifs.*

The conch-shell motif *in this silk ikat panel with its delicate, curvilinear pattern, is an example of the fine sense of design and colour that Orissa's weavers have.*

The fish motif *in this tussar silk textile symbolizes prosperity and luck. Below the fish are a row of damroos (hand-held drums).*

The *jotai* ikat sari *is inspired by the finger-painted patterns, called jotai, that adorn the walls of many village homes in Orissa. The rich red colour of the sari, and the rows of stylized trees and temple spires on the borders, add to the sumptuous effect.*

Cuttack ❽

Cuttack district. 35 km (22 miles) N of Bhubaneswar. 🚉 535,150. 🚌 ℹ️ Orissa Tourism, Arunodaya Market Building, Link Rd, (0671) 231 2225. 🎎 Bali Yatra (Oct/Nov).

Situated on the Mahanadi Delta, Cuttack is Orissa's most populous city, and was its capital from the 10th century onwards until 1956, when the capital was moved to Bhubaneswar (see p306). There is little evidence today of the city's historic past. The gateway and moat of the 13th-century **Barabati Fort**, in northwest Cuttack, are all that remain of this great citadel which once had a nine-storeyed palace. The eastern part of town is more interesting, with silversmiths' shops in **Balu Bazaar** and **Nayasarak**, where Cuttack's famous silver filigree jewellery is made. Nearby, in the shops on **Jail Road**, the full range of Orissa's beautiful handicrafts are available, including ikat silk, carved hornware and paintings.

In this area, a cluster of green domes marks the 18th-century **Kadam Rasul Mosque**, where the Prophet Mohammed's footprints are carved on a round stone.

The 18th-century Kadam Rasul Mosque in Cuttack

THE INDONESIAN CONNECTION

From the 4th century BC to the 14th century AD, the power and wealth of successive kingdoms in Orissa derived from their rich maritime trade, especially with Bali, Java and Sumatra. Indeed, ever since the 10th century, the word *kling*, derived from Kalinga which was the ancient name of Orissa, has been used in Indonesia to refer to India and Indians. With the trading links came cultural influences, which are still visible in Orissa's crafts. The state's weavers originally learned the intricate art of ikat weaving (see p317) from Indonesia, and later were especially commissioned to weave all the silks for ceremonial use in the royal courts and temples of Indonesia. Another Orissa craft that originally came from Indonesia was the silver filigree work that is still being done in Cuttack. Today, Orissa's old maritime links with Bali, Java and

The colourful entrance gate to the Bali Yatra fair at Cuttack

Sumatra are commemorated in a festival called Bali Yatra (Bali Journey) held in Cuttack during the full moon of Kartik (October/November). A colourful fair is held on the banks of the Mahanadi river, and tiny boats made of banana bark are lit with clay lamps and floated in the river.

Ratnagiri ❾

Cuttack district. 70 kms (44 miles) NE of Cuttack. 🚌 ℹ️ Orissa Tourism, Link Rd, Cuttack, (0671) 231 2225.

The three Buddhist sites of Ratnagiri, Udaigiri and Lalitgiri, situated close to each other, are most conveniently visited on a day trip from Cuttack or Bhubaneswar, driving through a beautiful landscape of low hills and lush paddy fields. The most impressive of the three sites is Ratnagiri ("Hill of Jewels") which, between the 7th and the 11th centuries, was a major Buddhist university and monastic establishment, described by the 7th-century Chinese traveller Hiuen Tsang (see p219). Located on top of a mound, crowned by a large stupa, the best-preserved structure here is a monastery with a central courtyard and an impressive colonnade around the monks' cells. A beautiful 4-m (13-foot) high image of the seated Buddha can be seen inside, together with other Buddhist divinities, and the entrance doorway is superbly carved. A small **Archaeological Museum** displays other sculptures found at the site.

Udaigiri ("Sunrise Hill"), 10 km (6 miles) south of Ratnagiri, is still being excavated and seems to have better preserved sculptures. The western spur of the hill has a row of rock-cut

The serene 7th-century meditating Buddha image at Ratnagiri

Flocks of waders amidst the mangroves at Bhitarkanika Sanctuary

sculptures, while the northern spur is covered with the ruins of brick stupas. A colossal sculpture of the Buddha here has an inscription dating it to the 8th century.

Lalitgiri ("Hill of Grace"), about 10 km (6 miles) south of Udaigiri (and directly connected by bus to Cuttack), is believed to be the oldest of the sites. The ruins, spread over two adjacent hills, include a terraced stone platform, a gallery of life-size Bodhisattva figures and an apsidal temple. Some of the better-preserved sculptures and a carved doorway have been incorporated into a modern Hindu temple. At the foot of a hill is a village of stone-carvers, who keep alive Orissa's fine tradition of stone sculpture.

🏛 **Ratnagiri Archaeological Museum**
⬜ Sat-Thu. 🖼

Bhitarkanika Sanctuary ❿

Kendrapara district. 106 km (66 miles) NE of Cuttack. Entry points: Chandbali, Rajnagar. ✈ Bhadrakh, 50 km (31 miles) NW of Chandbali, then bus. 🚌 to Rajnagar. 🚤 from Rajnagar or Chandbali to Dangmal, Ekakula & Habalikhati. ℹ For permits and bookings contact Bhubaneswar, (06786) 220 397 or Rajnagar, (06729) 272 460. ⬜ mid-Oct–mid-Apr. 🖼

Famous as the nesting ground of the Olive Ridley turtle, this 170-sq km (66-sq mile) sanctuary is situated on the delta of the Brahmani and Baitarani rivers on the Bay of Bengal. It also has the largest mangrove forests in the country after the Sunderbans in West Bengal *(see pp288–9)*, with 63 of the 72 known mangrove species found here.

Encompassing 12 offshore islands, long sandy beaches and numerous rivulets and creeks, Bhitarkanika is home to an impressive range of fish, more than 170 species of birds such as storks, egrets, ibis and migratory ducks, and the largest number of estuarine crocodiles in the country.

Accommodation is available at a forest rest house at Chandbali, the entry point to the sanctuary, as well as deep within the sanctuary at Dangmal, Habalikhati and Ekakula (all three are accessible by boat). Orissa Tourism in Bhubaneswar and Cuttack organize tours and the necessary Forest Department permits for Bhitarkanika.

THE OLIVE RIDLEY TURTLE

Every year, in an awe-inspiring phenomenon, hundreds of thousands of Olive Ridley turtles arrive from as far away as South America, to nest at Gahirmatha, a 10-km (6-mile) stretch of beach near the mouth of the Brahmani river in Bhitarkanika Sanctuary. The world's largest *arribada* (Spanish for "the great arrival")

An Olive Ridley turtle nesting at Gahirmatha Beach

occurs in February and March, when some 200,000 nesting females congregate here, each laying between 50 and 200 eggs in deep hollows they excavate in the sand. After a two-month incubation with the sun's heat, the hatchlings emerge in millions and scamper out to the sea at night. Sadly, less than 0.1 per cent survive to adulthood, as dogs, seagulls, sharks as well as human poachers take an enormous toll on their numbers. The absence of *arribadas* in 1997 and 1998 caused much alarm among conservationists, until in March 2000 a record 700,000 Olive Ridleys arrived at Gahirmatha. Since the turtles return each year to nest at the spot where they were born, the cycle continues.

Olive Ridley hatchlings heading for the sea

Baleshwar ⑪

Baleshwar district. 214 km (133 miles) NE of Bhubaneswar. 🚉 🚌 ℹ️ Orissa Tourism, SPA Complex, Station Square, (06782) 262 048.

Once a bustling seaport, Baleshwar was established by the British in 1642. It was later in the possession of the French and the Dutch, but had lost its importance by the 18th century, with the silting up of the port. Its colonial past is visible in the ruins of some Dutch tombs, and what are said to be the remnants of old canals which led to the sea. Today Baleshwar is a sleepy town, surrounded by paddy fields and villages, and renowned for the pretty hand-crafted lacquer boxes and brass fish made locally.

Environs

The tranquil seaside village of **Chandipur**, 16 km (10 miles) east of Baleshwar, is easily reached by a short taxi or scooter ride from the town. Here, the sea recedes up to 5 km (3 miles) at low tide, leaving an expanse of clean white sand. Orissa Tourism offers accommodation in a picturesque old bungalow a short distance from the beach, with the day's fresh catch served at dinner. The only blot on this peaceful landscape is the Indian Army's test firing range for rockets, just outside Chandipur village, against which environmentalists and villagers have been campaigning for many years.

Brass fish, Baleshwar

Baripada ⑫

Mayurbhanj district. 295 km (183 miles) NE of Bhubaneswar. 🚉 🚌 🍽️ daily. 🎭 Chaitra Parba (Apr), Rath Yatra (Jun/Jul).

The main market town of northeastern Orissa, Baripada is the headquarters of Mayurbhanj district, which is rich in forests and has a large population of tribal people. Baripada is also the gateway to Simlipal National Park. The town holds a Rath Yatra (chariot festival) in June/July, which takes place around the **Jagannath Temple**.

This festival is a small-scale version of the one that is held in Puri (see p312), but is equally lively and vibrant, as the entire town joins in the procession. A unique feature in Baripada is that the chariot of the female deity, Subhadra, is pulled only by women.

Another colourful festival held here is Chaitra Parba (in April), when tribal groups perform the vigorous Chhau dance wearing fabulous costumes. It was originally performed by warriors just before they went on to the battlefield. In the eastern part of town, **Baripada Museum** has fine sculptures, pottery, and coins found in the area.

🏛️ **Baripada Museum**
⏲️ Tue–Sun. 📷

Environs

Haripur, 16 km (10 miles) southeast of Baripada, has the evocative ruins of palaces and temples built by the rulers of the Bhanja dynasty who made this their capital in the 15th century. The most impressive ruins are of the brick-built Rasikaraya Temple, and the Durbar Hall of the Bhanja kings.

Simlipal National Park ⑬

Mayurbhanj district. 320 km (199 miles) N of Bhubaneswar. **Entry points:** Lulung & Jashipur. 🚉 Baripada, 50 km (30 miles) E of the park, then bus or taxi. 🚌 to Lulung (via Baripada) & Jashipur. ℹ️ For bookings and permits contact Field Director, Simlipal Tiger Reserve, Baripada, (06792) 52 553. ⏲️ Nov–mid-June. 📷 📷 extra charges. 🚙 Jeeps available in the park.

This extraordinarily beautiful park is located amidst the pristine forests and hills of northeast Orissa. Stretching over an area of 2,750 sq km (1,062 sq miles), Simlipal comprises dense sal (Shorea robusta) and rosewood forests, broken by lush grasslands. Numerous rivers and cascading rapids traverse the forest, creating spectacular

Women tending their paddy fields near Baleshwar

A waterfall cascading down the hills at Barehipani, Simlipal National Park

(1,158 m/3,799 ft), one of the highest in the park. Basic food and accommodation are available in forest rest houses at Lulung, Barehipani, Chahala, Joranda and Nawana.

Environs

The capital of the Bhanja kings in the 10th and 11th centuries, **Khiching** has some of the finest examples of temple sculpture to be seen in Orissa. It is 20 km (12 miles) west of Jashipur, the western entry point to Simlipal National Park, and 114 km (71 miles) west of Baripada. The main sight here is the towering Khichakeshwari temple, reconstructed in the early 20th century entirely from the ruins of the original temple that stood here. The temple is adorned with superb images of several deities, including a vibrant dancing Ganesha. A number of other temples, together with the ruins of two forts built by the Bhanja kings, dot this hamlet.

The small **Archaeological Museum** is well worth visiting. Among its highlights are outstanding life-size statues of Shiva and his consort Parvati, and exquisite sculptural panels from now-fallen temples.

🏛 **Archaeological Museum**
◻ Tue–Sun. ⬤ public hols. 📷

waterfalls, such as those at Joranda (150 m/492 ft) and Barehipani (400 m/1,312 ft).

Originally the maharaja of Mayurbhanj's private hunting ground, Simlipal was declared a wildlife sanctuary in 1957. One of the earliest tiger reserves in India, it is home to about 100 tigers, as well as an impressive range of other fauna including elephants, leopards, deer, gaur (Indian bison) and pangolins (or scaly anteaters). These curious-looking animals, covered with large overlapping scales, feed exclusively on termites and ants, tearing open anthills with their powerful claws and scooping up the insects with their long tongues. When threatened, the pangolin rolls up into an impenetrable armoured ball. Over 230 species of birds can also be seen at Simlipal.

Pangolin at Simlipal

The rare *muggers* (marsh crocodiles) can be spotted in rivers or basking on the banks where they dig tunnels to keep cool. At Jashipur, the western entry point to the park, there is a **Crocodile Sanctuary** where the reptiles can be observed at close quarters. One of the park's best spots for viewing wildlife is located in the grasslands at **Bacchuri Chara**, which are a favourite haunt of elephant herds. Another good area for sightings is at **Manghasani Peak**

An 11th-century sculpture of Shiva and Parvati, Khiching

TRIBES OF ORISSA

More than 60 different tribes, descended from the original, pre-Aryan inhabitants of the land, live in Orissa. Many still inhabit hills and forests in the remote interior of the state, relatively untouched by outside influences. The Saoras, who live in the vicinity of Taptapani (*see p316*), are agriculturists whose mud houses are beautifully painted and decorated with carved doors and lintels. Further west live the Koyas, whose customs decree that their women must only marry

Kondh girl in her tribal jewellery

considerably younger men. The dominant tribe in Orissa are the Kondhs, who used to perform human sacrifice to ensure the fertility of their land, until the British stamped out this practice in the mid-19th century. Today the Kondhs are renowned for their knowledge of medicinal herbs, and their beautiful metal jewellery. The Orissa government is now promoting tours of some tribal areas. Interested visitors should contact Orissa Tourism in Bhubaneswar, (0674) 43 2203, for information about the necessary permits, as well as accommodation in areas that have few facilities for travellers. For more details see pp754–55.

ASSAM & THE NORTHEAST

Assam and the six northeastern states, often called the Seven Sisters, make up the most geographically isolated and least visited part of India. This region, which has international borders with China, Myanmar (Burma), Bhutan and Bangladesh, has an unusually rich diversity of ethnic groups, languages, religions, climates and landscapes. The largest of the Seven Sisters is Assam, spread along the valley of the Brahmaputra river, and famous for its tea gardens and for the rare one-horned rhinoceros. The rolling green hills of Meghalaya boast the delightful hill station of Shillong, as well as one of the wettest places on earth, Cherrapunji. Arunachal Pradesh, Nagaland, Manipur, Mizoram and Tripura are home to more than 100 different tribes, with distinct and fascinating cultures. The Northeast is also a naturalist's paradise, with a wealth of rare flora and fauna.

SIGHTS AT A GLANCE

Towns & Cities
Agartala ⑬
Aizawl ⑭
Bomdila ③
Dimapur ⑱
Guwahati ①
Imphal ⑮
Itanagar ⑧
Kohima ⑰
Sibsagar ⑥
Tezpur ②
Ziro ⑨

National Parks
Kaziranga National Park ⑤
Namdapha National Park ⑩

Hill Stations & Areas of Natural Beauty
Loktak Lake ⑯
Majuli River Island ⑦
Shillong ⑪

Tours
Shillong to Cherrapunji Tour ⑫

Monasteries
Tawang Monastery ④

KEY

✕	Domestic airport
	National highway
	Major road
	Minor road
	Major railway
	International border
- -	State border

◁ Lush ferns surrounding a small waterfall in the dense rainforests of Meghalaya, near Shillong

Devotees at Guwahati's Kamakhya Temple, a major centre of pilgrimage for Hindus

Guwahati ❶

Kamrup district. 1,081 km (672 miles) NE of Kolkata. 🚶 808,000. ✈ Borjhar, 25 km (16 miles) W of city centre, then bus or taxi. 🚌 🚈 ℹ Assam Tourism, Station Rd, (0361) 254 4475. 🎭 Rongali Bihu (Apr), Ambubachi (Jun), Assam Tea Festival (Jan).

The capital of Assam, Guwahati is also the gateway to Northeast India. Ringed by the Neelachal Hills, the city stretches along both banks of the broad Brahmaputra river. An ancient seat of tantric Hinduism, with a number of interesting temples in its environs, Guwahati is now a busy commercial centre for Assam's tea and oil industries. Its outer fringes are dotted with the slender, graceful betelnut palm trees from which Guwahati (literally "Betel Nut Market") derives its name.

Brass utensil for serving betel leaf

🛕 Kamakhya Temple
Perched on Nilachal hill, 8 km (5 miles) northwest of the city, this temple is one of India's most important pilgrimage destinations. The present structure with its typically Assamese beehive-shaped *shikhara* dates to the 17th century, after the original temple was destroyed by Muslim invaders. According to legend, as a furious and grieving Shiva carried the corpse of his wife, Sati (also known as Parvati) around the skies, parts of her dismembered body fell to the earth (*see p279*). All these sites have been sanctified by major temples. Kamakhya is believed to mark the place where her vagina fell, and is therefore said to have special powers associated with energy and creation. In accordance with tantric rituals, a goat is sacrificed here every day, and offered to the goddess. The giant turtles in the temple ponds look forward to being fed by visitors. The colourful annual Ambubachi festival, which marks the end of the earth's menstrual cycle, attracts pilgrims here from all over India, to be blessed by the goddess.

🛕 Navagraha Temple
On Chitranchal hill, in northeast Guwahati, is the Navagraha ("Nine Planets") Temple, believed to mark the site of the ancient city of Pragjyotishpur, Guwahati's old name, which was famous as a centre of astronomy. Beneath its red beehive-shaped dome is a dark chamber with nine lingas representing the nine planets.

🛕 Umananda Temple
Peacock Island. 🚤 Umananda Ghat, 1 km (0.6 miles) N of railway station. Enchantingly located on the lush green Peacock Island in the middle of the Brahmaputra, this 16th-century temple is also dedicated to Shiva's wife. The island, swarming with friendly langur monkeys, is an excellent place to stand and watch the river, deceptively slow on the surface but with swift undercurrents.

🏛 State Museum
GN Bordoloi Rd. **Tel** (0361) 254 0651. ◯ Tue–Sun. 📷
This interesting museum, just east of the railway station, has fine reconstructions of tribal villages, a comprehensive

Umananda Temple, on a pretty island in the Brahmaputra

collection of local handicrafts and a gallery of medieval stone and bronze sculptures, which were excavated from Ambari, an archaeological site in the heart of the city.

🦌 Zoo & Botanical Gardens

RG Baruah Rd. ◐ Sat–Thu. 🎫 🅾 extra charges.

The well-maintained zoo is in the eastern part of the city. Clouded leopards, hornbills and, of course, the native one-horned rhinos, can be seen in spacious, moated enclosures. The Botanical Gardens adjoin the zoo.

Vashishtha Temple, on a wooded hill surrounded by streams

Environs

The **Vashishtha Temple**, 12 km (7 miles) southeast of Guwahati, stands in a pretty spot that marks the confluence of three streams, with a waterfall and groves of trees around it. This is said to be the site of the ashram of the sage Vashishtha, a character in the *Ramayana (see p27)*.

Sualkuchi, 32 km (20 miles) west of Guwahati, is a major weaving centre for Assam's famous golden-hued *muga* and *paat* silk. Several houses here have women working at their looms, and they are happy to welcome visitors.

Hajo, 32 km (20 miles) northwest of Guwahati, is a pilgrimage site for Buddhists, Hindus and Muslims. The 16th-century Hayagriva Madhava Temple, on Manikuta Hill, is sacred to Hindus and Buddhists, who believe that the Buddha died here. Fine bas-reliefs of scenes from the *Ramayana* decorate its walls. Below the temple is a pond, home to Hajo's most famous resident – a giant turtle. On another hill is the Poa Mecca ("Quarter of Mecca") Mosque, established by an Iraqi prince who visited Assam in the 12th century. A pilgrimage here is believed to be equivalent to a quarter of the piety attained by a Haj pilgrimage to Mecca.

The spectacular temple ruins at **Madan Kamdev** are 50 km (31 miles) northwest of Guwahati. Exuberantly erotic carvings of deities and celestial nymphs lie strewn on a small hillock here. They date from the 10th to 12th centuries, when the area was ruled by the Pala dynasty *(see p44)*.

THE MIGHTY BRAHMAPUTRA

The Son of Brahma, Creator of the Universe, is the name of this majestic river which dominates life in Assam and much of Arunachal Pradesh. Curiously, it is the only Indian river to have a male name. The Brahmaputra begins its 2,900-km (1,802-mile) course from near the holy mountain of Kailasa in Tibet, where it is known as the Tsang Po. Plunging down from a height of 5,200 m (17,060 ft), it then carves a straight, deep 1,100-km (684-mile) long furrow through the Tibetan Plateau. As it continues, the river makes a great sweeping turn around the eastern end of the Himalayas, before plummeting through the deep gorges of upper Arunachal Pradesh where it is called the Siang. Here, the river is crossed by a group of frighteningly fragile-looking bridges made of rope, including the 367-m (1,204-ft) long suspension bridge at Kamsing, one of the longest in the world.

The Brahmaputra river at dawn

The Brahmaputra enters the plains near the Assam-Arunachal border, and then flows westward through Assam for 724 km (450 miles), broad and tranquil, except during the monsoon when it swells enormously, flooding flat land and forests, and sweeping away homes, crops and animals in an annual ritual of destruction. Just before the end of its course, the Brahmaputra merges with the Ganges to create the huge Bengal delta, before emptying into the Bay of Bengal in Bangladesh.

Sculpture of a goddess from the temple ruins at Madan Kamdev

The ruins of Tezpur's Da Parbatia Temple, dating to the 5th–6th centuries AD

Tezpur ②

Sonitpur district. 180 km (112 miles) NE of Guwahati. 🚶 58,250. ✈ Saloni, 10 km (6 miles) N of town centre, then bus or taxi. 🚊 🚌 ℹ Tourist Office, Zenkins Rd, (03712) 221 016.

A picturesque town on the north bank of the Brahmaputra river, Tezpur is surrounded by undulating green valleys covered with tea gardens. The hills of northern Arunachal provide a scenic backdrop to the town, and for visitors, Tezpur is a convenient stop and a take-off point for trips to parts of Arunachal Pradesh.

Epiphytic orchid

Tezpur means "City of Blood", and this gory name is derived from its legendary past as the capital of the Hindu demon kings, the Asuras, said to have been vanquished here by Lord Krishna in a bloody battle. More recently, in 1962, Tezpur was close to another bloodbath when the invading Chinese army reached its outskirts before suddenly declaring a ceasefire *(see p57)*.

The ruins of the **Da Parbatia Temple**, 5 km (3 miles) west of the city, dating from the 5th to 6th centuries AD, bear testimony to Tezpur's ancient past, and represent the earliest example of sculptural art in Assam. All that is left of the temple are some sculptures and an exquisitely carved door

frame, with images of the river goddesses Ganga and Yamuna on either side. **Cole Park**, close to the Tourist Lodge, is Tezpur's prettiest spot, with a beautifully landscaped garden near a lake. It is embellished with 9th- and 10th-century sculptures unearthed in the city. A charming 19th-century colonial church stands behind the Tourist Lodge.

Environs
Scenic **Bhalukpong**, 58 km (36 miles) northwest of Tezpur, is set in green foothills that mark the border of Assam and Arunachal Pradesh. The Kameng river flows past it. Added attractions are medicinal hot springs, and an Orchid Centre, located 7 km (4 miles) away at **Tipi**, with some 500 varieties of orchids native to Arunachal. **Nameri Sanctuary**, 35 km (22 miles) north of Tezpur, covers 200 sq km (77 sq miles). The Jia Bhoroli river winds through its deciduous forests, which are home to clouded leopards, *mithuns* (Indian bison) and the rare white-winged wood duck. Nameri can be explored on elephant back. The Potasali Eco-Camp on the river, run by the Forest Department, organizes white-water rafting and *mahseer* fishing trips for visitors. **Orang Wildlife Sanctuary**, 65 km (40 miles) northwest of Tezpur, is often described as a mini-

Kaziranga *(see pp330–31)* since it has a similar landscape of marshes, streams and grassland, the favoured habitat of the one-horned rhinoceros. This little sanctuary is also home to the Asiatic wild buffalo and the Hoolock gibbon.

🏇 Nameri Sanctuary
Permits *Divisional Forest Officer, Koloabhomora, (03712) 220 854.* ☀ *Sep–Apr.* 📷 🎥 *extra charges.* 📷 🎣 *Potasali Eco-Camp 09854019932, 09435250025.*

🏇 Orang Wildlife Sanctuary
Permits *Divisional Forest Officer, Mangaldoi, (03712) 22 065.* ☀ *Oct–Apr.* 📷 🎥

Bomdila ③

West Kameng district. 140 km (87 miles) NW of Tezpur. 🚌 🎭 *Losar (Feb/Mar).* **Travel permits** *required (see p758).*

The scenic road from Tezpur winds steeply up through thick forests to this pleasant town, at an altitude of 2,530 m (8,301 ft). The headquarters of Arunachal's West Kameng district, Bomdila has Buddhist monasteries surrounded by apple orchards, with views of snowcapped peaks, terraced paddy fields and waterfalls. The **Crafts Centre** is famous for its carpet weaving. The town's inhabitants belong largely to the Monpa and Sherdukpen tribes, who combine Tibetan Buddhism with some of their original animist rituals and beliefs. They wear a curious black cap with five "tails" projecting from its rim, that serve to drain rainwater away from the face.

Monpas celebrating their New Year with a Yak Dance near Bomdila

Rows of prayer wheels at the 17th-century Tawang Monastery

Tawang Monastery ❹

Tawang district. 325 km (202 miles) NW of Tezpur. 🚌 🎭 *Losar (Feb/Mar)*. **Travel permits** *required* (see p758).

The largest Buddhist monastery in India, Tawang is situated in Arunachal Pradesh at an altitude of 3,050 m (10,007 ft). As the road ascends from Bomdila, the scenery becomes alpine, lush with pine, oak and rhododendron forests, and a short, high-altitude bamboo which is the favourite food of the red panda *(see p299)*. Past the Dirang Valley with its old *dzong* (fort), the road climbs sharply to the **Sela Pass**. At 4,249 m (13,940 ft), this is the second highest motorable pass in the world; the highest is in Ladakh *(see p143)*. This barren, desolate landscape is softened by a serene lake that lies below the Sela Pass.

Beyond a memorial to a valiant Indian soldier who held up the advancing Chinese army during the India-China conflict of 1962, the road descends to a beautiful, wide valley. The monastery, dramatically located on a spur surrounded by snowcapped peaks, dominates the valley. When the Dalai Lama fled Tibet in 1959, his route into India was through Tawang, and he still visits the area regularly to hold special prayers.

Founded in 1645 by a lama from Merak in neighbouring Bhutan, this Gelugpa (Yellow Hat) establishment *(see p139)* has over 500 resident monks. It was also the birthplace of the sixth Dalai Lama. The three-storeyed *dukhang* (assembly hall) has a magnificent 8-m (26-ft) high statue of the Buddha. The ancient library, leading onto the main courtyard, has an excellent collection of *thangkas* and valuable Buddhist manuscripts.

The **Bramdungchung Nunnery**, associated with Tawang Monastery, is located 12 km (7 miles) northwest of Tawang. The road to the monastery, which can be reached by jeep, reveals a stunning alpine landscape of snowpeaks, Monpa hamlets with stone houses, and juniper and dwarf rhododendron bushes. Fluttering prayer flags and a long prayer wall mark the approach to the nunnery, guarded, as are most of the monasteries in this region, by fierce Tibetan mastiffs.

An intricately painted Wheel of Life mural at Tawang Monastery

The Brahmaputra river in full swell, flowing through Assam ▷

Kaziranga National Park ❺

Bar-headed goose in flight

Assam's magnificent Kaziranga National Park, declared a World Heritage Site by UNESCO, is the home of the Indian one-horned rhinoceros. Beautifully situated on the banks of the Brahmaputra, the 430-sq km (166-sq mile) park's landscape is characterized by vast grasslands and swamps, dotted with patches of semi-evergreen forest. The Mikir Hills, where several animals migrate during the monsoon, form its southern boundary. Kaziranga's rich variety of wildlife includes 80 tigers, large numbers of the Asiatic wild buffalo, herds of wild elephants, Hoolock gibbons, pythons and 300 species of birds, including the rare Bengal florican.

Exploring Kaziranga
Visitors on elephant-back are safe from charging rhinos and wild buffaloes.

Asiatic Wild Buffalo
Kaziranga has India's largest population of this mammoth-horned buffalo which likes to wallow in the park's swamps.

Methun

Arimora

Kartika

Holapath

Difolu

Mihimu

Bengal Florican
This rare bird has beautifully streaked plumage.

GUWAHATI   NH37   Gotanga   Deopani   Kuthari   Baguri

THE INDIAN ONE-HORNED RHINOCEROS

Kaziranga is one of the last refuges of the Indian one-horned rhinoceros (*Rhinoceros unicornis*), an endangered species that was close to extinction at the beginning of the 20th century. Successful conservation measures have seen their numbers rise to 2,500 (across Assam and the foothills of Nepal), of which 1,500 are in Kaziranga. Once found extensively across the subcontinent, the rhino population dwindled dramatically because of widespread poaching for its horn, a prized ingredient in Chinese medicine. Actually a mass of closely matted hair, each rhino horn fetches an exorbitant price in Southeast Asia, where it is believed to have great medicinal and aphrodisiac properties.

A rhino mother and her baby in Kaziranga's vast grasslands

Beel (Shallow Lake)

Floods inundate the park every monsoon, leaving behind beels *and marshes as they recede. These attract herds of wild elephants, and many other animals and water birds.*

VISITORS' CHECKLIST

Golaghat district. 215 km (134 miles) NE of Guwahati. ✈ Jorhat, 96 km (60 miles) NE of Kohora, the entry point, then taxi. 🚌 Furkating, 75 km (47 miles) E of Kohora, then taxi. 🏨 🛈 Bonani Tourist Lodge, Kohora, (03776) 26 2423. ⬜ Nov–Apr. 📷 extra charges. 🚙 Jeeps available. 📷

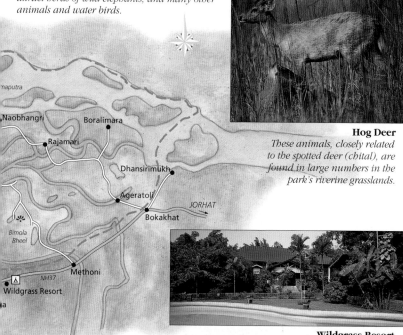

Hog Deer

These animals, closely related to the spotted deer (chital), are found in large numbers in the park's riverine grasslands.

Wildgrass Resort

Located 5 km (3 miles) east of Kohora, just outside the park, this eco-friendly resort (see p702) arranges elephant rides and trips to nearby tea plantations (see pp262–3).

0 km | **8**
0 miles | **8**

KEY

— Park boundary

= National highway

= Minor road

🛈 Tourist information

☀ Viewpoint

Ⓐ Accommodation

Hoolock Gibbon

This 1-m (3.3-ft) ape can be recognized by the distinctive silvery band above its eyebrows, and its loud whooping hoot, which resounds through the forest.

Sibsagar **6**

Sibsagar district. 370 km (230 miles) NE
of Guwahati. ⚥ 54,500. ✈ Jorhat,
60 km (37 miles) S of city centre, then
taxi or bus. 🚗 🚌 ℹ️ Assam Tourism,
near Shivadol Temple, (03772) 222
394. 🎭 Shivratri (Feb/Mar).

At the heart of Assam's tea
and oil-producing region,
Sibsagar is also the state's most
historic city, as the seat of the
Ahom dynasty (see p49) which
ruled Assam for 600 years.
Originally from Myanmar
(Burma), the Ahoms converted
to Hinduism and gradually
indigenized after conquering
Assam in 1228. The Ahoms
were defeated by the Burmese
in 1817, and their kingdom
became part of the British
Indian Empire in 1826.

The Ahoms were great
builders, as is evident from
the ruins in and around
Sibsagar. Dominating
the town is the
enormous 103-ha
(255-acre) man-
made **Sibsagar
Lake**, with three
temples on its
banks. Especially
impressive is the
towering **Shivadol
Temple** with its 33-m (108-ft)
high gilded spire, built by an
Ahom queen in 1734. About
4 km (2 miles) south of the
town are the ruins of two

Vaishnavite mask, Majuli

18th-century brick palaces,
Kareng Ghar and **Talatal
Ghar**. Both are seven storeys
high, and the latter also has
three underground floors and
a warren of secret tunnels.
To its northeast is the elegant
Rang Ghar, the oval, double-
storeyed royal sports pavilion,
constructed in 1746.

Majuli River Island **7**

Jorhat district. 314 km (195 miles)
NE of Guwahati. 🚢 Neamati Ghat,
13 km (8 miles) N of Jorhat. 🚌 from
Neamati Ghat to Majuli, then bus to
Garamur. ℹ️ On arrival, foreigners
must register with the Sub-Divisional
Officer, Majuli, who also handles
bookings.

Perhaps the largest inhabited
river island in the world,
Majuli covers an area of 929
sq km (359 sq miles).
It is easy to forget
that Majuli is an
island, holding
within it hills,
rivulets and
little islands of
its own. This
amorphous land-
mass is constantly
being sculpted into new
dimensions and shapes by the
Brahmaputra. Every year during the monsoon, the river
submerges large tracts of land,
forcing the inhabitants to
move to higher ground. After
the floods recede, leaving
behind fertile, freshly silted
land, the people return to
cultivate the area.

As interesting as Majuli's
distinctive landscape are its
satras, unique monasteries
founded in the 15th century
by the Vaishnavite reformer-
philosopher, Shankardeva.
The satras are rich repositories of traditional Assamese
arts and crafts, and regularly
stage dance-dramas in praise
of Vishnu. Majuli's main
settlement is at **Garamur**
which has two satras. About
20 others are scattered across
the island. Visitors can stay in
the satras, and should offer to
make a donation towards
overnight stays or meals.

Itanagar **8**

Papum Pare district. 420 km (261
miles) N of Guwahati. ⚥ 35,000.
✈ Lakhimpur, 60 km (37 miles) NE
of town centre, then taxi or bus. 🚌
ℹ️ Directorate of Tourism, Itanagar,
(0360) 221 4745. **Travel permits
required** (see p758).

Until it became the capital of
Arunachal Pradesh in 1971,
Itanagar was a settlement of
the Nishi tribe, one of the
largest among the 26 major
tribes that inhabit the state. A

Bamboo forests in the vicinity of Itanagar, in Arunachal Pradesh

Apatani woman in the rice fields near Ziro

few traditional Nishi long-houses still remain, now all but swamped by Itanagar's newly-constructed government buildings. The Nishis are easily recognizable – they sport black and white hornbill feathers in their cane headgear, wear their hair in a bun on their foreheads and often carry bearskin bags.

The **Nehru Museum**, near the Secretariat, offers a comprehensive look at the arts and crafts of all the tribes of Arunachal Pradesh. Cane and bamboo artifacts, textiles, jewellery, and totem objects are on display here. A pretty but bumpy 6-km (4-mile) drive north from Itanagar leads to the lovely, emerald-green **Gyakar Sinyi Lake**, surrounded by dense forests. Many of the tall trees are festooned with orchids.

🏛 **Nehru Museum**
Siddharth Vihar. **Tel** (0360) 221 2276. ☐ Sun–Thu. 🖼 🗿

Ziro ❾

Lower Subansiri district. 150 km (93 miles) NE of Itanagar. 🚶 12,300. 🚌 🛈 Deputy Commissioner's Office, (03788) 224 255. **Travel permits** required (see p758).

The picturesque town of Ziro in central Arunachal Pradesh, lies in a large, flat valley, surrounded by low pine-covered hills. This area, better known as the Apatani Plateau, is the home of the prosperous Apatani tribe who

Adi longhouse near Along

practise a unique system of cultivation that combines rice-growing with pisciculture. The flooded paddy fields are stocked with fingerlings, the two staples of Apatani diet thus coming from the same plot of land. Like the Nishis, the Apatanis wear their hair in a bun on their foreheads, held with a brass skewer. Both the men and women are tattooed and the women sport huge bamboo noseplugs.

Northeast of Ziro, three other areas, **Daporijo**, **Along** and **Pasighat**, are now open to foreigners (with permits). The latter two are situated on the Brahmaputra river and are inhabited by the Adi tribe *(see p336)*. The drive from Ziro to Pasighat (300 km/186 miles) is wonderfully scenic, through dense virgin forest and tribal villages with thatched longhouses.

Namdapha National Park ❿

Changlang district. 380 km (236 miles) NE of Itanagar. 🚉 Margherita, 64 km (40 miles) SW of Miao, the entry point. 🚌 🛈 Director, Project Tiger, Miao, (03807) 222 249. ☐ Oct–Mar. 🖼 **Travel permits** required (see p758).

This superb park in remote eastern Arunachal Pradesh, bordering Myanmar, covers 1,985 sq km (766 sq miles). Rising from the plains to 4,500 m (14,764 ft) in the Himalayas, it covers a variety of habitats, and is the only reserve in India where all the four big cats of the Himalayas – tiger, leopard, clouded leopard and the rare snow leopard are found. It was declared a Tiger Reserve in 1983. Other wildlife includes the great Indian hornbill, the red panda *(see p299)*, and the Hoolock gibbon *(see p331)*.

Environs
The legendary Burma Road (or Stilwell Road) begins at **Ledo**, 60 km (37 miles) southwest of Miao. This 1,700-km (1,056-mile) road, of great strategic importance in World War II, connected Ledo, via the forbidding jungles and mountains of Arunachal Pradesh and Northern Myanmar, to Kunming in China's Yunnan province. Supervised by the American General Joseph Stilwell and built in two years at enormous human cost, it has now fallen into disrepair, but is still used by locals travelling on foot.

Tribal people of eastern Arunachal Pradesh on the Burma Road

Locally made bamboo baskets on sale in Shillong's Bara Bazaar

Shillong ⓫

East Khasi Hills district. 127 km (79 miles) S of Guwahati. 👥 *132,900.* 🚌 ℹ️ *Meghalaya Tourism, 3rd Secretariat, Lower Lachumiere, (0364) 250 0736.* 📷 *Weiking Dance (Apr/May).*

Capital of the tiny state of Meghalaya, Shillong, with its mist-shrouded hills, pine forests, lakes and waterfalls, is sometimes described as the "Scotland of the East". Lying at an altitude of 1,496 m (4,908 ft), it was chosen as the headquarters of the British administration in Assam in 1874. It soon developed into a popular hill station, providing refuge from the searing heat of the plains.

The town still retains a distinctly colonial ambience, with its mock-Tudor bungalows, churches, polo ground and beautiful 18-hole golf course. It is also the home of the matrilineal Khasi tribe. The idyllic countryside around the town can be easily explored in short excursions.

🏯 Bara Bazaar

Bara Bazaar Rd. ⏺ *Mon–Sat.*
This sprawling market offers a vivid glimpse of Khasi tribal society. The stalls are piled high with produce from the surrounding villages – honey, pineapples, piglets, dried fish, wild mushrooms, raw betel nut and bamboo baskets. The market is dominated by Khasi women, who run most of the stalls. Dressed in their traditional tunic-like *jainsems* and tartan-checked shawls, these cheerful matriarchs can drive a hard bargain.

🏛 Museum of Entomology

Umsohsun Rd. **Tel** *(09863) 021965.*
⏺ *Mon–Sat.* 📷
This small private museum, situated north of Bara Bazaar, was established in the 1930s by the Wankhar family, and boasts a collection of rare butterflies and insects found in Meghalaya. Among them are huge stick insects, iridescent beetles, and the giant yellow and black birdwing butterfly which cloaks itself in a deadly poison to protect itself from predatory birds. The family also runs a breeding centre for rare species.

🏵 Ward Lake & Lady Hydari Park

Park ⏺ *daily.* 📷 📷 *extra charges.*
In the centre of town, the horseshoe-shaped Ward Lake has pleasant promenade paths around it, paddle boats for hire and a café. A short distance to its south is Lady Hydari Park, with a pretty Japanese garden and a mini zoo which includes fauna native to Meghalaya's forests, such as hornbills, leopard cats, and the aptly named slow loris, a ferret-like creature that crawls around as though heavily drugged.

Environs

The beautiful **Bishop** and **Beadon Falls** are 3 km (2 miles) north of Shillong, just off the Guwahati-Shillong Highway. Along the same route, 17 km (11 miles) north of Shillong, is **Umiam Lake**, a large artificial reservoir set among forested hills. It offers facilities for angling, kayaking and water-skiing, and has an orchidarium in the adjacent park. The scenic **Elephant Falls** are 11 km (7 miles) south of Shillong. The road to **Mawphlang**, 24 km (15 miles) southwest of Shillong, is richly forested with pine and oak, and is a good place to see some of Meghalaya's rare species of orchids in their natural habitat.

The Elephant Falls, flowing over ferns and rocks

THE KHASIS

The Khasis are the predominant tribe in the Shillong area. Believed to have originated in Southeast Asia, their language belongs to the Mon-Khmer group. It is not known when they migrated to this region. Today, the majority of Khasis are Christians, their ancestors converted by British missionaries in the 19th century. Nevertheless, they retain many of their tribal customs. Chief among these is their matrilineal social structure, which dictates that landed property can only be inherited by females, with the youngest daughter given a special position as custodian of the family house and the clan's traditional rituals.

Khasi matriarch at her stall in Shillong's main market

Shillong to Cherrapunji Tour ⑫

The road to Cherrapunji through the East Khasi Hills winds through dense pine and oak forests, full of ferns and orchids. En route are dramatic gorges and ravines, waterfalls and limestone caves. Cherrapunji is one of the wettest places on earth, and established a world record of an incredible 2,621 cm (1,032 in) of rain in 1861. It continues to record an average rainfall of 1,143 cm (450 in) in the monsoon months of July to September.

Cherrapunji's famous oranges

Shillong Peak ②
The highest point in Meghalaya at 1,965 m (6,447 ft), this peak is named after the Khasi deity, Ushyllong.

Shillong ①
Ward Lake marks the centre of the town.

Cherrapunji ④
Surrounded by groves of orange and banana trees, this little town has a lively weekly market and is famed for its delicious orange-flower honey.

Mylliem ③
A number of rare species of orchids grow around this traditional Khasi blacksmiths' village, where agricultural tools are made.

0 km   5
0 miles   5

Nohkalikai Falls ⑤
These are the second highest falls in India. Tall Khasi memorial stones dot the area around them.

TIPS FOR DRIVERS

Length: 120 km (75 miles).
Stopping-off points: The tour takes between 6–7 hours. Shillong Peak, Cherrapunji (meals, toilets available), Nohsngithiang Falls, Nohkalikai Falls and Mawsmai Caves are the best places to stop.
Getting around: Meghalaya Tourism, (0364) 222 6054, and several travel agencies run daily tours from Shillong to Cherrapunji. Take a torch to explore the caves.

Mawsmai Caves ⑥
Some of these limestone caves run more than 4 km (2 miles) deep.

KEY

▬▬ Tour route
══ Other roads
▬▬ National highway

Nohsngithiang Falls ⑦
On a clear day, there is a fine view of the plains of Bangladesh from these impressive falls, also known as the Seven Sisters Falls.

GUWAHATI

SILCHAR

Mawphlang

Laitlyngkot

MAWSYNRAM

DAUKI

Tribal Peoples of the Northeast

Naga tribal basket

Northeast India is home to an extraordinary diversity of tribal peoples. Arunachal Pradesh alone has 26 major tribes, while Nagaland has 16. Dozens of others inhabit Assam, Manipur, Mizoram, Meghalaya and Tripura. Though living in the same region, they have been geographically isolated from each other by steep mountain ridges, rivers and gorges, and have therefore retained their distinct cultural identities and languages.

Gigantic stone megaliths *can be seen all over the state of Meghalaya. They were erected by the Khasi tribe as memorials to the dead.*

Pipes *of wood and metal are smoked by tribes in Arunachal Pradesh.*

Intricate beadwork, crafted by the Wanchos of Arunachal

The Adis of Arunachal Pradesh *are famous for their engineering skills and construct superb bridges, such as this tube of canework over the Brahmaputra river.*

The Konyaks of Nagaland, *who perform spirited martial dances, wear colourful costumes, with hornbill feathers, wild boar tusks and painted canework caps.*

The Thankuls of Manipur *are skilled at weaving, producing a distinctive red and white textile with a silken sheen.*

A chief's house *in Nagaland has crossed gables and is decorated with his tribe's symbols. The* mithun *(bison species) skull in the foreground symbolizes power and prosperity.*

This Naga chief *used to be a headhunter. The wooden heads on his basket indicate how many heads he took.*

The Cheraw dance *is performed at tribal festivals in Mizoram. The Mizos love music and dancing, and the Cheraw dance requires women to step agilely between rapidly moving bamboo poles.*

Ujjayanta Palace in Agartala, built in 1901

Agartala ⓭

West Tripura district. 600 km (373 miles) S of Guwahati. 👥 189,300. ✈ 12 km (7 miles) N of town centre, then bus or taxi. 🚌 ℹ *Tripura Tourism, Swet Mahal, Palace Compound, (0381) 222 3893.*

The capital of Tripura, a former princely state bordered by Bangladesh, Agartala is a pleasant little town, its lush tropical greenery dotted with red-brick civic buildings. Dominating the town is the sprawling white **Ujjayanta Palace**, built in 1901 in Indo-Saracenic style. Now the State Legislature, the palace's opulent interior includes a tiled Chinese Room with a magnificent ceiling crafted by

Cane basket from Tripura

Chinese artisans. It is open to visitors when the Assembly is not in session. Tripura is renowned for its exceptionally fine cane and bamboo work, freely available in the market.

Environs

Neermahal Water Palace, 55 km (34 miles) south of Agartala, on an island in Rudrasagar Lake, was the summer home of the former maharajas of Tripura. Built in white marble and red sandstone, this fairy-tale palace has a profusion of pavilions, balconies, turrets and bridges, and part of it is open to the public. **Udaipur**, 58 km (36 miles) south of Agartala, is renowned for the 16th century **Tripurasundari Temple** with its distinctive Bengal-style roof.

Aizawl ⓮

Aizawl district. 480 km (298 miles) SE of Guwahati. 👥 229,700. ✈ 35 km (22 miles) W of town centre, then bus or taxi. 🚌 ℹ *Mizoram Tourism, Bungkawn, (0389) 233 3475.*
Travel permits *required (see p758).*

Perched along a ridge, its houses and churches standing out against the green hillside, Aizawl is Mizoram's capital, and home of the Mizo tribes, said to have migrated here from Myanmar's Chin Hills 300 years ago. In the centre of town is the lively **Main Market**, where local farmers congregate. Almost the entire population of Mizoram (as of Nagaland and Meghalaya) is now Christian, converted by missionaries who first came here in 1891. As a result of the schools they started, Mizoram has the second highest literacy rate in India. Blue jeans are more commonly seen today than tribal dress among the men, but the women still wear their elegant *puans* (long, narrow skirts). Visitors can see these being woven at the **Weaving Centre** in Luangmual, 7 km (4 miles) away.

Aizawl, stretching across a ridge

Fish sellers at Imphal's Ima Keithel

Imphal ⓯

Imphal district. 484 km (301) miles
SE of Guwahati. 🏙 217,300.
✈ 6 km (4 miles) S of city centre. 🚌
ℹ Manipur Tourism, (0385) 232 1285. 🎭 Yaosang
(Feb/Mar), Lai Haraoba (Apr/May).
Travel permits required (see p758).

The capital of Manipur
(the "Jewelled Land"),
Imphal lies in a broad
oval valley enclosed
by forested hills. Its
inhabitants mostly
belong to the Meitei
tribe. The liveliest part of
the town is the **Ima
Keithel** ("Mothers' Market")
where more than
3,000 women congre-
gate daily to sell fresh
produce, fish, grain,
canework and handicrafts,
including the elegant striped

textiles worn by the
Meitei women. These
formidable Imas, who
sport *tikas* of sandal-
wood paste on their
noses, have formed a
powerful union and
pride themselves on
charging fair prices.
Imphal's main temple,
the **Govindaji Temple**,
stands east of the
Bazaar, and on fes-
tivals associated with
Lord Krishna
the graceful Manipuri
dance *(see p29)* is
performed here. Sagol
Kangjei, Manipuri polo,
is a favourite sport in
Imphal (they claim to
have invented the
game), and an opportunity to
see a match should not be
missed – the Polo Ground is in
the centre of the town. It is a
fast and furious game, with the
players dressed in dhotis and
often riding bareback on the
agile Manipuri horses. Two
well-tended **Commonwealth
War Graves Cemeteries** are on
the northern and eastern
outskirts of town.
Buried here are the
men who died fight-
ing the Japanese during
the invasion of Manipur
in World War II. Also
worth visiting is an impressive **Orchidarium** displaying
various indigenous species. It
is 12 km (7 miles)
north of the town.

Manipuri dancer

Environs
Moirang, 45 km (28 miles)
south of Imphal, with its

ancient temple to the pre-
Hindu god, Thangjing, is the
spiritual home of the Meiteis,
who celebrate Lai Haraoba
(see p327). During World War
II, Moirang was the head-
quarters of the Indian
National Army (INA), led by
Subhash Chandra Bose, which
fought against the Allies.

Loktak Lake ⓰

Bishnupur district. 48 km (30 miles)
S of Imphal. 🚌 ℹ For bookings on
Sendra Island contact Manipur
Tourism, (0385) 232 1285. 🛥
Travel permits required (see p758).

Loktak Lake is one of the
most enchanting places in
the northeast. Almost two-
thirds of this huge expanse
of freshwater is covered by
unique floating saucer-shaped
islands of reed and humus,
locally called *phumdi*, which
are home to a community of
fishermen. The southern part
of the lake forms the **Keibul
Lamjao National Park** where
contiguous masses of *phumdi*
form the very special habitat of
the endangered Manipur brow-
antlered deer called *sangai*.
These deer have divided
hooves, specially adapted to
their floating habitat, and
elegantly curved antlers. Only
a 100 or so of these graceful
animals are now left, found in
the wild only in an area of 6
sq km (2 sq miles) within the
park. **Sendra Island**, at the
heart of the park, provides a
magnificent view of the lake,
its islands and its rich birdlife.

Floating islands of reed and humus with fishermen's houses and moored boats, on Loktak Lake

For hotels and restaurants in this region see pp701–2 and pp730–31

The Baptist Church in Kohima, one of many churches in the area

Boat rides are also offered. However, due to current political instability, only day-trips to Loktak Lake are possible.

Kohima ⓱

Kohima district. 339 km (211 miles) E of Guwahati. 🚶 78,600. 🚆 Dimapur, 74 km (46 miles) NW of Kohima, then taxi or bus. 🚌 🚐 ℹ️ Nagaland Tourism, (0370) 224 3124. **Travel permits** required (see p758).

The capital of Nagaland, Kohima, at an altitude of 1,500 m (4,921 ft), is a small, pleasant town surrounded by hills which are dotted with villages. Kohima is famous in World War II history for the decisive battle, fought on the tennis court of the British deputy commissioner's house, that finally stopped the Japanese advance into India in April 1944.

War Cemetery, Kohima

Those who fell in the battle are buried in the beautifully kept **War Cemetery** covering a terraced hillside. A poignant inscription at the base of one of the two large crosses here reads: "When you go home tell them of us and say, For your tomorrow we gave our today". The **Cathedral of Reconciliation**, which overlooks the cemetery, was built in 1995, partly funded by the Japanese government.

Kohima's main bazaar is a good place to encounter the handsome Naga people (see pp336–7) in their colourful woven shawls, who come from surrounding villages to sell their produce. The market also offers visitors a glimpse of the diet that supposedly made the Nagas such formidable warriors – bees' larvae and dog meat are favourites.

The **State Museum**, 2 km (1.2 miles) north of the bazaar, has an excellent anthropological collection of Naga masks, textiles, jewellery and totem pillars from all the 16 Naga tribes. Particularly intriguing is a large ceremonial drum that looks like a dugout canoe, kept in a shed outside the museum. The drum is engraved with stylized waves, and has gongs that look like paddles. This and other factors, such as the use of seashells in their costumes, has led some anthropologists to conjecture that the Nagas were originally a seafaring people, possibly from Sumatra. Today, a high percentage of Nagas are Christians and a church can be found in almost every corner of the state.

The original village of Kohima, **Bara Basti**, is a settlement of the Angami Naga tribe, located on a hill overlooking the town. Though now considerably modernized, it still has its ceremonial gateway, and a large traditional community house, the *morung*, with crossed horns surmounting its gable. A less modernized Angami Naga village is **Khonoma**, 20 km (12 miles) southwest of Kohima, with its wooden houses, carved gateway and surrounding stone wall. The villagers are known for their agricultural skills – terraced paddy fields cover the hillside, growing 20 varieties of rice, and a system of bamboo pipes irrigates the fields.

🏛 **State Museum**
Tel (0370) 226 0133 ◯ Mon–Sat. ◉ public hols. 🈲

Dimapur ⓲

Kohima district. 74 km (46 miles) NW of Kohima. 🚶 107,400. 🚆 🚌 ℹ️ Tourist Office, near Nagaland State Transport Office. **Travel permits** required (see p758).

This bustling town in the plains functions as a gateway to the rest of Nagaland. It was founded by the Kachari rulers, a Tibeto-Burmese people who were displaced from their territories in Assam in the 13th century by the invading Ahoms (see p332). Some of the ruins of their old capital can be seen in the heart of the town. Most notable are 30 carved megaliths, believed to be fertility symbols. About 5 km (3 miles) from the city centre, on the road to Kohima, is the **Ruzaphema Bazaar** which displays a fascinating range of tribal handicrafts.

Carved monoliths in Dimapur erected by the Kachari kings

WESTERN INDIA

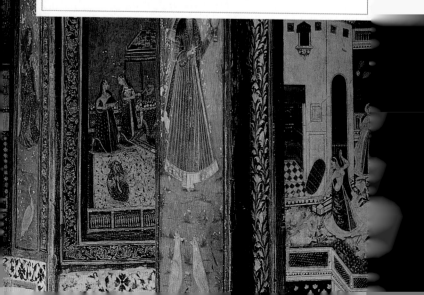

Introducing Western India

This region has some of India's most popular destinations. In Rajasthan, the desert forts of Jaisalmer and Jodhpur, the palaces and lakes of Udaipur, and the Ranthambhore National Park evoke all the romance and splendour of the state's princely past. Gujarat's Jain temples and intricately designed stepwells are architectural marvels, while its natural wonders can be enjoyed on the beaches of Diu and at the lion sanctuary at Gir. The landscapes in this region range from the sand dunes of Rajasthan to the vast salt flats of Kutch, to the urban bustle of the two state capitals, Jaipur and Ahmedabad.

Rajasthani women in festive dress at the Pushkar Fair

Chillies drying in the desert sun near Osian, Rajasthan

0 km 50

0 miles 50

GETTING AROUND

Jaipur, Jodhpur, Udaipur and Ahmedabad are well-connected by air to Delhi and Mumbai as well as to each other. Trains travel between all the major cities, with fast trains connecting Delhi and Jaipur. Two luxury trains, the Palace on Wheels and the Royal Orient (see p777), offer a more romantic way to explore Rajasthan and Gujarat. Within Rajasthan, a network of national highways links most major destinations by road, while National Highways 8, 14 and 15 continue on to Gujarat.

JAISALMER

BARMER

MOUNT

NH15

RANN OF KUTCH

DHOLAVIRA

PATAN

BHUJ

NH8A

NH8A

GANDHINAGAR
AHMEDABAD

JAMNAGAR

NH8A

DWARKA

RAJKOT

Sabarmati

NH8B

BHAVNAGAR

PORBANDAR

JUNAGADH

SURAT

SASAN GIR

DIU

Arabian
Sea

DAMAN

Mumbai

◁ Murals in glowing colours inside the Garh Palace in Bundi (see p404), Rajasthan

Amritsar

RAJASTHAN

GUJARAT

NH15

BIKANER

NH11

NAGAUR

SIKAR

NH8 / *Delhi*

AMBER
JAIPUR

NH11A

NH11

BHARATPUR

PUSHKAR

ODHPUR

AJMER

NH8

RANTHAMBHORE

NH12

BUNDI

KPUR

CHITTORGARH

NH8

UDAIPUR

JHALAWAR

Indore

ODARA

mada

SEE ALSO

- **Where to Stay** pp702–706
- **Where to Eat** pp731–3

KEY

    National highway

    Major road

    River

– – State border

A Rabari nomadic shepherd with his flock in Gujarat

A PORTRAIT OF WESTERN INDIA

The Great Thar Desert and the Arabian Sea have been two dominating influences in the history and culture of Rajasthan and Gujarat. Both these states have boundaries with Pakistan and, before 1947, contained a number of princely states. In most other respects, however, the two states are a study in contrasts.

A many-splendoured land of fairy-tale palaces and vibrant fairs and festivals, Rajasthan fulfills everyone's favourite fantasies about India. Until Independence in 1947 Rajasthan, literally "the Land of Kings", was indeed just that. It was made up of more than 20 princely states, bastions of royal opulence and feudal pageantry. They were ruled by Rajput clans such as the Kachhawahas of Jaipur, the Rathores of Jodhpur and the Sisodias of Udaipur. Their legacy has helped make the state one of the country's most popular tourist destinations.

A desert nomad's shelter in Rajasthan

Today, Rajasthan's once-impregnable forts are open to visitors, and many of the old princely palaces and feudal castles have been converted into delightful hotels, often run by the erstwhile ruling families. Tourism has helped restore these historic buildings, and breathed new life into them. Apart from becoming successful hoteliers, many former princes have found new roles for themselves in politics, representing their constituencies in India's parliament. Rajasthan's traditional arts and crafts have also been revived, with tourists replacing maharajas as the new patrons.

Eighty per cent of Rajasthan's population still lives in rural areas, engaged in agriculture and livestock herding. The rhythm of life in the villages continues much as it has for hundreds of years, the drudgery of the daily grind broken every few weeks by religious festivals and cattle fairs, such as those at Pushkar *(see pp374–5)* and Nagaur *(see p376)*. These wonderfully colourful events provide Rajasthani villagers with an occasion for feasting, socializing, trading, and enjoying traditional entertainments such as camel races and puppet shows. The fairs have become a major attraction for visitors as well, offering a close and memorable encounter with the people and culture of rural Rajasthan.

Rajasthani society is still socially very conservative, with great value placed on

Camels for sale at the Pushkar Fair

ancient feudal codes of conduct and honour. As recently as 1987, an incident of *sati* took place here, when a young widow burnt herself on her husband's funeral pyre, while the whole village watched in admiration. But things are changing: female literacy in Rajasthan, which was just 20 per cent in the early 1990s has increased at a

The Tarnetar Fair in Gujarat

massive growth rate, and women now head many village government councils. Rural development schemes have brought schools, hospitals and water to remote desert villages. What has still not changed, however, is the old-world courtesy and hospitality encountered everywhere in Rajasthan, be it in a princely palace or a mud hut in the desert.

In sharp contrast with Rajasthan, Gujarat is one of the most industrially advanced and urbanized states in the country – nearly 60 per cent of its population lives in cities. The Gujaratis' legendary business acumen has helped make the state one of the most prosperous in India.

While the forbidding expanses of the Thar Desert had for centuries effectively insulated Rajasthani society, Gujarat's 1,600 km (992 miles) of coastline on the Arabian Sea have helped foster contacts with other lands and cultures, and bred an adventurous spirit in the people. Since ancient times, Gujarat has traded with Arabs and Persians, East Africa, China, and Indonesia, through its ports at Surat *(see p420)* and Mandvi *(see p429)*, while from the 15th century onwards European

traders established their bases along the coastline. In the late 19th and early 20th centuries, many Gujaratis sailed to far off lands in search of new opportunities, and today their descendants (many of them with the surnames Patel and Shah) are flourishing – be it as hoteliers in America, retail traders in Britain, industrialists in Nigeria or lawyers in South Africa.

Gujaratis have been deeply influenced by Jainism *(see p396)*, which took hold in the region in the 11th century, during the reign of the Solanki kings. Jainism's emphasis on non-violence, community service, simple living and high thinking was an integral part of the philosophy of Gujarat's most famous son, Mahatma Gandhi, who led India's struggle for independence *(see p56)*. Ordinary mortals too try to follow this creed in their daily lives. Most Gujaratis, whether at home or abroad, are strict vegetarians, known for their toughness and self reliance, and for their thrift and philanthropy. These qualities were especially evident after the devastating earthquake that hit Gujarat in January 2001 *(see p428)*, from which the state has made a remarkable recovery.

Rajasthani women preparing lunch

Forts and Palaces

Fort gate with spikes

The spectacular forts of Rajasthan were originally forbidding, defensive citadels, but by the mid-16th century, when most Rajput states had made peace with the Mughals, luxurious palaces, pleasure pavilions and gardens were added to them, displaying many Mughal-inspired features. In the early 20th century there was another spate of palace-building in both Rajasthan and Gujarat. As a result of increasing contact between the British Raj and the princely states, a marked European influence in both architecture and decor is visible in these palaces.

Cannons *to defend the fort are mounted on the bastions, which tower high above the surrounding area.*

Sileh Khanas *(armouries) store a variety of weapons, from ceremonial jewelled swords to sharp knuckle-dusters, and even special armour for war elephants.*

Ramparts follow the contours of the hill.

Rana Kumbha's Palace

Entrance gates *are high enough for elephants to pass through. Their doors have huge spikes to prevent enemy elephants from storming them.*

Water reservoirs, *often fed by underground springs, are found in forts in the arid areas of Rajasthan and Gujarat.*

TYPES OF FORTS

Ancient Indian treatises list six types of forts for good defences. While *giri durgs* (hill forts) such as Chittorgarh are the most impregnable, other effective types are *dhanva durg*, protected by desert, such as Jaisalmer *(see pp388–9)*; *vana durg*, protected by forest, such as Ranthambhore *(see p406)*; *mahi durg*, protected by thick mud walls, such as Bharatpur's Lohagarh *(see p367)*; *jala durg*, protected by water, such as Ghagron *(see p403)*; and *nara durg*, a city fort such as Nagaur *(see p376)*, protected mainly by trusted men.

Ghagron Fort in Rajasthan, an example of a fort protected by water

PALACES

Palaces built by maharajas during the Raj, unlike those in the old forts, had modern plumbing, drawing rooms and dining halls suitable for entertaining British dignitaries.

Lalgarh Palace *in Bikaner (see p379) was built in 1902. It beautifully combines Rajput decorative features with European elements, such as banquet halls and billiard rooms.*

Wankaner Palace (see p427) *was built in 1907. The ruler's travels in Europe gave him a taste for Italianate pillars and Gothic arches, crowned here with Mughal pavilions.*

Corridors *and staircases, that connect the private chambers in Rajput palaces, are often narrow and twisting to confuse enemy invaders.*

The Victory Tower was built in 1458 after a successful battle. Each of its nine storeys is a temple.

Temples were built by rulers and merchants, who believed their deities protected the fort.

FORTS

Chittorgarh *(see p402)*, founded in AD 728 but added to at various times until the 16th century is, like many Rajput forts, built on a commanding height above the plains. Its massive ramparts encircle palaces, temples, stables and reservoirs.

Sheesh Mahals *("Halls of Mirrors") are ceremonial halls inlaid with mirror mosaic. One candle, reflected in the myriad mirrors, makes the whole room glitter.*

Zenanas *(women's quarters) have secluded courtyards and exquisite stone latticework (jali) screens. These let in light and air, yet maintain privacy. Most zenanas are large, because they also housed the rulers' many concubines.*

The Flavours of Western India

Rajasthan, largely scrub and desert and dominated by hill forts of stone, has a simple cuisine dictated by the landscape and climate. As a result, the food here is more robust and strength-giving, as is evident by the creative use of cereals and lentils. The varied palate of Gujarat has emerged from its contact with the different communities who have settled in this state. What is commonly called Gujarati food is vegetarian with the regional variations of North and South Gujarat, Kathiawar and Kutch. It is a delicate balance of the spicy and sweet and its infinite variety of dishes can be sampled in the Gujarati *thali* (platter).

Bunch of fenugreek

An array of tangy savouries, very popular among Rajasthanis

In the desert districts, milk, *ghee* (clarified butter) and buttermilk are used to make up for the water scarcity. Other substitutes are *amchur* or dried mango powder, used instead of tomatoes, and asafetida to enhance taste. Desert plants such as *sangri (Prosopsis cineraria)* beans and *khair (Capparis decidua)* have great nutritional value. These are dried and cooked with oil and spices to make *khair-sangri*. Mint, turmeric, mango and garlic chutneys are popular accompaniments.

The cuisine of the martial Rajput clans includes highly seasoned meat dishes. The most famous is *lal maas*, a lamb dish cooked with *ghee* and red chillies. A variation is the *safed maas*, a "white" curry with yoghurt and nuts. *Khud khargosh*, is a summer special where rabbit is stuffed with spices, sealed in dough and roasted in cloth.

Spicy lentils, split peas, peanuts and puffed rice are used in crunchy savoury snacks, such as *bhujia*, *dalmoth* and *khatta-meetha sev*.

RAJASTHAN

The best-known dish here is *dal-baati*, a lentil curry with wheat-dough balls which can be buried in the sand to bake. The same *baati*, when crumbled and garnished with raisins and almonds, is transformed into a rich sweet called *chorma*. This food can be carried for days through the parched landscape.

Khakra (wheat wafer)   **Naan**   **Puri** (deep-fried bread)   **Missi roti** (spicy wheat wafer)   **Lachha paratha** (layered bread)   **Pudina para** (layered bre with mint)

A selection of breads from Rajasthan and Gujarat

LOCAL DISHES AND SPECIALITIES

Vegetarian food dominates the cuisine of Rajasthan and Gujarat, both states having been strongly influenced by Jainism and Vaishnavism, which forbid animal slaughter. Rajasthan's cereal-based diet includes *kadhi* (lentil and yoghurt soup), types of *khichdi* (rich rice preparations) and breads made from *bajra* (millet) and *jowar* (sorghum maize). Gujarati cuisine uses a wide range of protein-rich lentils, cereals and vegetables, distinguished by wonderfully subtle seasoning. Pickles, often made of *kairi* (green mango), are a basic part of it. Sweets include the seasonal *aamras* (mango fool) and *doodh pak*, made with thick sweetened milk, dried fruit and nuts.

Khandvi and dhokla

Undhiyo, *a Gujarati thali dish, consists of potatoes and aubergines (eggplant) roasted in an earthenware pot.*

Women selling fresh vegetables in a Rajasthan village

GUJARAT

Gujarat has a large Jain community who, as practitioners of non-violence, have developed an extremely refined vegetarian cuisine, rated as one of India's most sophisticated. A typical *thali* contains innumerable small bowls *(katoris)*, filled with vegetables, lentils, *farsaans* (savoury snacks), pickles, chutneys, breads and sweets. This meal allows a person to savour the delicate balance of flavours – sweet and sour, salty and spicy, crisp and soft, low fat and deep-fried.

Bajra (millet) is the staple grain of Gujarat and is used to make the *rotlis* (baked bread) that are eaten with most meals. Another bread is *thepla*, a savoury griddled bread made from chickpea flour. Rice specialities, such as *khichdi* (a nourishing mixture of rice and five kinds of lentils), *vangi bhat*, (rice with aubergines and coriander) and *masala bhat* (spicy rice) are made more tempting by the addition of a dollop of *ghee* at the end.

Young girls gathering red chillies that have been sun-dried

Jaggery or sugar is used to sweeten every dish and the food is usually seasoned with mustard, asafetida and fenugreek, used both for flavour and digestion.

Integral to a meal are crisp *farsaans*, particularly *dhokla* (steamed spongy cakes of chickpea flour and yoghurt), *khandvi* (chickpea flour rolls filled with coconut), *mirchi pakora* (green chilly fritters) and *khakra* (wafers).

Saurashtra is famous for pickles and *methia masala*, made from powdered fenugreek, chillies and salt and used as a salad dressing, while from the bakeries of Surat come wonderful local biscuits, *nankhatais*.

ON THE MENU

Batata nu shak A dry spicy potato preparation.

Besan halwa A sweet made from chickpea flour.

Dahi pakora Lentil dumplings in yoghurt.

Kadhi A light curry made with chickpeas and lentils.

Makki soyta Corn kernels in a spicy sauce.

Mattar ki kachori Fried bread stuffed with peas.

Mula ni kadi Yoghurt curry with white radish.

Paunk Mixed vegetables seasoned with lime and jaggery, a winter dish.

Gatta curry *has steamed dumplings made from chickpea flour cooked in a spiced yoghurt sauce.*

Sulas, *a speciality of Rajput clans, is barbecued meat softened with a paste made from a melon-type fruit.*

Shrikhand *is a dessert made from yoghurt flavoured with saffron, cardamom, nuts and dried fruits.*

RAJASTHAN

No state in India is as rich in magnificent palaces and forts, colourful festivals and bazaars, as Rajasthan. Stretching over 342,000 sq km (132,047 sq miles), the state is bisected by the Aravalli Range, which runs diagonally from the northeast to the southwest. Its main river is the Chambal. The Thar Desert, which covers western Rajasthan, was once ruled by three great kingdoms – Jaisalmer, Jodhpur and Bikaner. Shekhawati, with its painted *havelis,* is in the semi-arid north while the eastern plains have the bustling state capital, Jaipur, and the Ranthambhore National Park, famous for its tigers. In the hilly, wooded south are the fairy-tale palaces, lakes and forts of Udaipur, and the spectacular Jain temples at Ranakpur, and Dilwara in Mount Abu.

SIGHTS AT A GLANCE

Towns, Cities & Districts
Ajmer ⑪
Alwar ⑥
Barmer ⑲
Bharatpur ③
Bikaner ⑬
Bundi ㉘
Dungarpur ㉔
Jaipur ①
Jaisalmer ⑰
Jhalawar ㉖
Jodhpur ⑮
Kota ㉗
Nagaur ⑫
Phalodi ⑭
Shekhawati ⑧
Udaipur ㉓

Forts & Palaces
Amber Fort ②
Chittorgarh ㉕
Deeg ⑤
Kumbhalgarh ㉒

Temples & Holy Places
Pushkar ⑩
Ranakpur ㉑

Hill Stations
Mount Abu ⑳

National Parks
Keoladeo Ghana National
Park ④
Ranthambhore National Park ㉙
Sariska National Park ⑦

Tours
A Tour of Shekhawati ⑨
Camel Safari around
Jaisalmer ⑱
Tour of Marwar Crafts
Villages ⑯

0 km   100

0 miles   100

KEY

✕	Domestic airport
═	National highway
▬	Major road
—	Major railway
—	International border

◁ **Detail of the exquisitely carved stone façade of the 19th-century Patwon ki Haveli, Jaisalmer**

Jaipur ❶

A labyrinth of fascinating bazaars, opulent palaces and historic sights, Jaipur is often called the "Pink City" because its prominent buildings are washed in this colour. Tradition and modernity exist side by side here. On its colourful streets, motorbikes jostle for space with camels, and turbaned village elders rub shoulders with youngsters in jeans. Jaipur's old walled area has the City Palace, an astronomical observatory and bazaars that sell everything from shoes to jewellery. Recent additions include a multi-arts centre, but the focal point remains the Hawa Mahal.

Stone guardian at Hawa Mahal

Govind Dev Temple, dedicated to Krishna

🏛 City Palace Museum

See pp356–7.

🗿 Govind Dev Temple

Jaleb Chowk (behind City Palace).
◯ *daily.* 🎉 *Holi (Mar), Janmashtami (Aug/Sep), Annakut (Oct/Nov).*
The presiding deity of this unusual temple is the flute-playing Lord Krishna (also known as Govind Dev). The image of this god originally came from the Govindeoji Temple in Brindavan *(see p179)*. It was brought to Amber *(see pp364–5)*, then the capital of Jaipur's ruling family, in the late 17th century to save it from the iconoclastic zeal of the Mughal emperor Aurangzeb.

It is believed that this temple was once a garden pavilion called Suraj Mahal where Sawai Jai Singh II lived while his dream-city, Jaipur, was being built. Legend has it that one night the king awoke from his sleep to find himself in the presence of Krishna who demanded that his *devasthan* ("divine residence")

be returned to him. Jai Singh then moved to the Chandra Mahal, at the opposite end of the garden, and installed the image as the guardian deity of Jaipur's rulers.

Just behind the temple is the 18th-century **Jai Niwas Bagh**, a Mughal-style garden with fountains and water channels. Towards the north is the Badal Mahal, an enchanting hunting pavilion.

🏛 Chaugan Stadium

Brahmpuri. ◯ *daily.*
This large open area near the City Palace derives its name from *chaugan*, an ancient Persian form of polo played with a curved stick. The area was once used for festival processions and wrestling matches, as well as elephant and lion fights. Today the stadium, with its viewing pavilions,

is the venue for the famous Elephant Festival *(see p371)* held at the same time as the Holi celebrations.

🏛 Hawa Mahal

Sireh Deori Bazaar. **Tel** *(0141) 266 8862.* ◯ *daily.* ◐ *public hols.* 📷 *extra charges.*
A whimsical addition to Rajasthan's rich architectural vocabulary, the fanciful Hawa

For hotels and restaurants in this region see pp702–5 and pp731–2

A view of the walled city of Jaipur

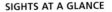

SIGHTS AT A GLANCE

Chaugan Stadium ③
City Palace Museum ①
Government Central Museum ⑤
Govind Dev Temple ②
Hawa Mahal ④
Jantar Mantar ⑥

Mahal or "Palace of Winds" was erected in 1799 by the aesthete Sawai Pratap Singh (r.1778–1803). Its ornate pink façade has become an icon for the city. The tiered Baroque-like composition of projecting windows and balconies with perforated screens is five storeys high but just one room deep, its walls not more than 20 cm (8 inches) thick. Built of lime and mortar, the structure was designed in this way to enable the veiled ladies of the harem to observe unnoticed the lively street scenes below. Dedicated to Lord Krishna, the Hawa Mahal, seen from afar, looks like the *mukut* (crown) that often adorns the god's head. Visitors can climb up the winding ramp to the top, and a gateway towards the west leads into the complex. Within are administrative offices and the **Archaeological Museum**, which houses a small collection of sculptures and local handicrafts, including some utensils dating back to the 2nd century BC.

VISITORS' CHECKLIST

Jaipur district. 261 km (162 miles) SW of Delhi. 🚆 2,324,500. ✈ 15 km (9 miles) S of city centre. 🚌 🚏 ℹ Paryatan Bhavan, Mirza Ismail Rd, (0141) 511 0598. 🏛 Mon–Sat. 🎆 Kite Flying Festival (14 Jan), Elephant Festival (Mar), Gangaur (Mar/Apr), Teej (Jul/Aug).

🏛 Government Central Museum

Ram Niwas Bagh. **Tel** (0141) 256 5124. ☐ Sat–Thu. ⬤ public hols. 🎫 free on Mon.

Also known as Albert Hall, this grand, multi-layered museum was designed by Sir Samuel Swinton Jacob, a master of the Indo-Saracenic style *(see p22)*.

The museum's ground floor displays decorative shields, embossed salvers and local glazed pottery. A 9-m (30-ft) long *phad* (painted cloth scroll), depicts the life of Pabuji, a 14th-century folk hero *(see p381)*. The museum's greatest treasure, however, is one of the world's largest Persian garden carpets (dating from 1632). It can be viewed on request in the Durbar Hall. Presently the museum is closed for renovation. Contact the curator on the exact date of opening.

KEY

🟦 Street-by-Street area: see pp354–5

Key to Symbols see back flap

0 metres 500
0 yards 500

Jai Mahal, GAITOR

Jaigarh & Amber Fort

RAMGARH

Chaugan Stadium ③
Talkatora
Jai Niwas Bagh
Joriwar Singh Gate
Govind Dev Temple ②
MOTI KATRA BAZAAR
City Palace Museum ①
Jantar Mantar ⑥
Hawa Mahal ④
THE PINK CITY
Jami Masjid ⓒ
RAM GANJ BAZAAR
GALTA
Ajmeri Gate
New Gate
Sanganeri Gate
Sisodia Rani ka Bagh, AGRA
Government Central Museum ⑤
Ram Niwas Gardens
SMS Hospital
Jawahar Kala Kendra & Moti Doongri Palace

Caparisoned elephant at a festival

🎵 Jantar Mantar
See pp358–9.

THE BUILDING OF JAIPUR

Sawai Jai Singh II (r.1700–43)

Sawai Jai Singh II was a keen scholar, statesman and patron of the arts. He was awarded the title of "Sawai" ("one-and-a-quarter"), a metaphor for one who is extraordinary, by the Mughal emperor Aurangzeb when he was just 11 years old. With the help of a gifted Bengali engineer, Vidyadhar Chakravarty, Jai Singh built a new capital south of Amber and named it Jaipur ("City of Victory"). Work began in 1727 and took six years to complete. Surrounded by a crenellated wall pierced by seven gates, Jaipur is laid out in a geometric grid of streets and squares and is one of India's finest examples of a planned city.

Street-by-Street: Around Badi Chaupar

The Badi Chaupar ("Large Square") is at one end of the colourful Tripolia Bazaar. Few changes have been made to the original 18th-century plan of streets and squares. Branching out of the main streets are narrow pedestrian lanes where artisans fashion puppets, silver jewellery, and other local handicrafts in tiny workshops. Behind are the *havelis* of eminent citizens, some used as schools, shops and offices. The area is a hub of activity, rich with pungent smells and vibrant colours, with temple bells adding to the cacophony of street sounds.

★ Jantar Mantar
Jai Singh II's observatory of astronomical instruments looks like a series of futuristic sculptures (see pp358–9).

Tripolia Gate
Constructed in 1734, this impressive gate was once the main entrance to the palace.

Ishwar Lat
Ishwari Singh built this tower in 1749 to commemorate his victory over his stepbrother, Madho Singh I.

City Palace

TRIPOLIA

MANIHARON KA RASTA

Chandpol

Chhoti Chaupar ("Small Square") leads to Kishanpol Bazaar, famous for its shops selling rose-, saffron-, almond- and vetiver-flavoured sherbets.

NATANIYON KA RASTA

KISHANPOL BAZAAR

Maharaja Arts College

Flower Sellers
Marigolds and other flowers are made into garlands and used as offerings to beloved deities in temples and roadside shrines.

Lac Bangles
Maniharon ka Rasta is full of tiny workshops of lac bangle makers.

★ Hawa Mahal
A view of Hawa Mahal's unusual rear
façade can be seen from the City Palace.

Badi
Chaupar

Surajpol

★ Johari Bazaar
Vegetable sellers sit at one end
of this street where many big
gem dealers also have
their offices and
shops.

JOHARI BAZAAR

GOPALJI KA RASTA

RASTA

0 metres 100
0 yards 100

KEY

– – – Suggested route

rkeshwar
mple

Jami Masjid
Tall minarets define the "Friday
Mosque", its three storeys
fronted by arched screens.

Pottery Shop
Large terracotta urns, pots of all sizes, bells,
statues, foot-scrapers and oil lamps made by
traditional craftsmen are sold here.

STAR SIGHTS

★ Jantar Mantar

★ Hawa Mahal

★ Johari Bazaar

Jaipur: City Palace Museum

Jaipur's coat of arms

Occupying the heart of Jai Singh II's city, the City Palace has been home to the rulers of Jaipur since the first half of the 18th century. The sprawling complex is a superb blend of Rajput and Mughal architecture, with open, airy Mughal-style public buildings leading to private apartments. Today, part of the complex is open to the public as the Maharaja Sawai Man Singh II Museum, popularly known as the City Palace Museum. Its treasures, which include miniature paintings, manuscripts, Mughal carpets, musical instruments, royal costumes and weaponry, provide a splendid introduction to Jaipur's princely past, and its fascinating arts and crafts.

★ Pritam Chowk
The "Court of the Beloved" has four delicately painted doorways representing the seasons.

Sileh Khana
The erstwhile armoury houses the museum's collection of weapons, among the finest in India. Some pieces, such as this shield, are lavishly decorated.

Crafts demonstration area

★ Mubarak Mahal
The first floor of this sandstone palace houses a dazzling collection of royal costumes and textiles, such as this gossamer-fine gold-embroidered skirt.

STAR FEATURES

- ★ Pritam Chowk
- ★ Mubarak Mahal
- ★ Rajendra Pol
- ★ Silver Urns

★ Rajendra Pol
Flanking this gateway are two large elephants, each carved from single blocks of marble.

Chandra Mahal

Each floor of this seven-storeyed palace is extravagantly decorated and has a specific name according to its function. The palace is closed to the public.

VISITORS' CHECKLIST

City Palace Complex. **Tel** (0141) 260 8055. ☐ daily. ● public hols. ☒ Museum and Jaigarh Palace only. ☒ façades only, extra charges for video photography. ☑ 🖽 **Crafts demonstration area** ☐ daily. ● public hols.

★ Silver Urns

The two giant silver urns in the Diwan-i-Khas, listed in the Guinness Book of Records as the world's largest silver objects, carried sacred Ganges water for Madho Singh II's visit to London in 1901.

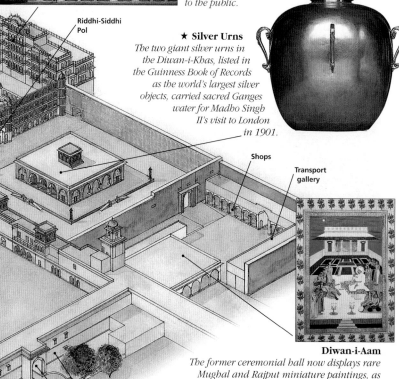

Riddhi-Siddhi Pol

Shops

Transport gallery

Entrance

Ticket counter

Diwan-i-Aam

The former ceremonial hall now displays rare Mughal and Rajput miniature paintings, as well as carpets, manuscripts, a superbly crafted silver throne and an ivory elephant howdah.

THE CITY PALACE

1 Mubarak Mahal
2 Crafts Demonstration Area
3 Sileh Khana
4 Rajendra Pol
5 Diwan-i-Khas
6 Riddhi-Siddhi Pol
7 Pritam Chowk
8 Chandra Mahal
9 Shops
10 Transport Gallery
11 Diwan-i-Aam

KEY

☐ Area illustrated

0 metres 200
0 yards 200

Jaipur: Jantar Mantar

Kantivrita Yantra

Of the five observatories built by Sawai Jai Singh II, the one in Jaipur is the largest and best preserved; the others are in Delhi *(see p78)*, Ujjain, Mathura and Varanasi. A keen astronomer himself, Jai Singh kept abreast of the latest astronomical studies in the world, and was most inspired by the work of Mirza Ulugh Beg, the astronomer-king of Samarkand. Built between 1728 and 1734, the observatory has been described as "the most realistic and logical landscape in stone", its 16 instruments resembling a giant sculptural composition. Some of the instruments are still used to forecast how hot the summer months will be, the expected date of arrival, duration and intensity of the monsoon, and the possibility of floods and famine.

Narivalaya Yantra
Inclined at 27 degrees, these sundials represent the two hemispheres and calculate time by following the solar cycle.

Unnatansha Yantra
was used to determine the positions of stars and planets at any time of day or night.

Laghu Samrat Yantra
This "small sundial" is constructed on Latitude 27° North (Jaipur's latitude) and calculates Jaipur's local time up to an accuracy of 20 seconds.

City Palace Museum

Entrance

Chakra Yantra
A brass tube passes through the centre of these two circular metal instruments. They can be used to calculate the angles of stars and planets from the equator.

★ Ram Yantra
Vertical columns support an equal number of horizontal slabs in the two identical stone structures that comprise this instrument. Its readings determine the celestial arc from horizon to zenith, as well as the altitude of the sun.

A view of Jantar Mantar
The complex of stone and metal instruments was repaired with the addition of marble inlay comissioned by Madho Singh II in 1901.

VISITORS' CHECKLIST

Chandni Chowk, outside City Palace. **Tel** (0141) 261 0494. ☐ daily. ● public hols. 🎫 free on Mon. 📷 extra charges. 🗺 🕍

★ Samrat Yantra
Jai Singh believed that gigantic instruments would give more accurate results. This 23-m (75-ft) high sundial forecasts the crop prospects for the year.

Hawa Mahal

Rashivalaya Yantra
This is composed of 12 pieces, each of which represents a sign of the zodiac and therefore faces a different constellation. This yantra (instrument), used by astrologers to draw up horoscopes, is the only one of its kind.

★ Jai Prakash Yantra
These two sunken hemispheres map out the heavens. Some historians believe that Jai Singh invented this instrument himself, to verify the accuracy of all the other instruments in the observatory.

STAR FEATURES

★ Ram Yantra

★ Samrat Yantra

★ Jai Prakash Yantra

Jaipur: South of the Walled City

By the end of the 19th century, Jaipur had expanded far beyond the boundaries of the walled city established by Sawai Jai Singh II. Many new pleasure palaces, hunting lodges and mansions came up on its outskirts, making the city a harmonious blend of old and new.

Lakshmi Narayan Temple, a white marble addition to the Pink City

🛕 Moti Doongri Palace

Jawaharlal Nehru Marg.
⬤ to the public.

Moti Doongri palace, perched on a low hillock, owes its florid exterior to Sawai Man Singh II, who converted the old fort of Shankargarh into a palace, and added turrets in the style of a Scottish castle. In 1940 he married the beautiful Princess Gayatri Devi of Cooch Behar, and this palace with its modernized interior became the venue for glittering parties hosted by the glamorous couple.

At the foot of Moti Doongri is the white marble **Lakshmi Narayan Temple**, a popular place of worship, admired for its elaborate carvings.

🛕 Rambagh Palace

Bhawani Singh Rd. *Tel (0141) 221 1919.* 🍴 *open to non-residents.*

The Rambagh Palace, now a splendid hotel *(see p703)*, has a colourful past. Built in 1835, it was originally a small garden pavilion for Ram Singh II's wet nurse, but was used as a hunting lodge after she died in 1856. Later, on his return from England, Ram Singh II's son Madho Singh II transformed it into a royal playground with squash and tennis courts, a polo field and an indoor swimming pool. In 1933, it became the official residence of Madho Singh's adopted heir, Man Singh II,

who hired Hammonds of London to redo the interiors. New additions included an exotic red and gold Chinese room, black marble bathrooms, Lalique crystal chandeliers and an illuminated dining table. Surrounded by fairy-tale gardens, it became a hotel in 1957, when Man Singh II moved to the smaller Raj Mahal Palace.

Jawahar Kala Kendra

🛕 Raj Mahal Palace

Sardar Patel Marg. *Tel (0141) 510 5665.* 🍴 *open to non-residents.*

Now a grand heritage hotel, this pleasant 18th-century palace, less opulent than the Rambagh Palace, occupies a special place in the history of Jaipur. Built in 1739 for Sawai Jai Singh II's favourite queen, Chandra Kumari Ranawatji, it was used as a summer resort by the ladies of the court. In 1821, it was declared the official home of the British Resident in Jaipur. However, the most memorable phase of its history dates to the time when Man Singh II and Gayatri Devi moved here from Rambagh Palace in 1956. Among the celebrities they entertained were Prince Philip, the polo player like Man Singh II, and Jackie Kennedy.

🏛 Jawahar Kala Kendra

Jawaharlal Nehru Marg. *Tel (0141) 270 5879.* ◯ *daily.* 📷 🏃

Designed by the Indian architect Charles Correa in 1993, this remarkable building pays vivid tribute to contemporary Indian design. Imaginatively patterned after the famous grid system of the city, each of its nine squares or courts houses a small *mahal,* or palace, named after a planet. Each one displays selected exhibits of textiles, handicrafts and weaponry, while in the centre there is a wonderfully conceived open-air plaza where performances of traditional Rajasthani music and dance are held.

The luxurious interior of Rambagh Palace, now a hotel

For hotels and restaurants in this region see pp702–5 and pp731–2

Jaipur Jewellery

Be it the fabulous rubies and emeralds sported by former maharajas and their queens or the splendid silver and bone ornaments worn by peasants, jewellery is an integral part of Rajasthani culture. Even camels, horses and elephants have specially designed anklets and necklaces. Jaipur is one of the largest ornament-making centres in India, and *meenakari* (enamel work) and *kundankari* (inlay work with gems) are the two traditional

techniques for which it is most famous. In the 16th century, Man Singh I *(see p364)*, influenced by the prevailing fashions of the Mughal court, brought five Sikh enamel workers from Lahore to his state. Since then, generations of highly skilled jewellers have lived and worked here. Jaipur caters to every taste, from chunky silver ornaments to more sophisticated designs intricately set in gold with precious stones.

A kundankari pendant

A jewelled trinket box *with a* kundankari *lid; the lower portion of this box is worked in fine* meenakari *and has traditional floral patterns in red, blue, green and white.*

Sarpech, *the cypress-shaped turban ornament, was a fashion statement introduced by the Mughal emperors in the early 17th century to display their finest gems. Rajput rulers, impressed by Mughal flamboyance, sported similar dazzling ornaments such as this piece of enamelled gold set with emeralds, rubies, diamonds and sapphires, finished with a pearl drop.*

The skill of stone-setting *can be seen in the crowded alleys of Haldiyon ka Rasta, Jadiyon ka Rasta and Gopalji ka Rasta. An inherited art, the jewellery trade is in the hands of artisans' guilds.*

Meenakari *embellishes the obverse side of* kundan *jewellery, for the Rajasthani love of adornment decrees that even the back of a piece of jewellery (left) must be as beautiful as the front (right).*

Kundankari *uses highly refined gold as a base, which is then inlaid with lac and set with precious and semi-precious stones to provide colour and design. Purified gold wire outlines the design and also conceals the lac background.*

Jaipur *is now a centre of lapidary, specializing in cutting emeralds and diamonds from Africa, South America and various regions of India. Gem-cutters learn their skill by cutting garnets.*

Exploring Jaipur: Outer Sites

A parallel range of hills runs along Jaipur's eastern periphery, from Sanganer in the south up to Amber and beyond, enclosing a narrow valley. Consisting of thickly wooded slopes and rocky terrain, this was the area where the nobility built temples, gardens, pavilions and palaces. Perched high above the city are the dramatic fortresses of Nahargarh and Jaigarh that guarded the approach to both Amber and the new capital of Jaipur. The surrounding region also has the remains of fortified walls, temples, *havelis* and the marble cenotaphs of the Kachhawaha kings of Amber and Jaipur.

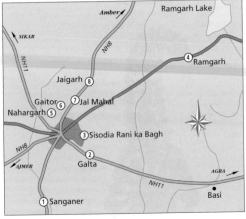

SIGHTS AT A GLANCE

Gaitor ⑥
Galta ②
Jaigarh ⑧
Jal Mahal ⑦
Nahargarh ⑤
Ramgarh ④
Sanganer ①
Sisodia Rani ka Bagh ③

KEY

◼ Jaipur city centre
▭ National highway
▬ Major road

0 kms   25
0 miles   25

Marble statue of a Jain *tirthankara* at Sanganer's Sanghiji Temple

For hotels and restaurants in this region see pp702–5 and pp731–2

Sanganer

Jaipur district, 15 km (9 miles) SW of Jaipur.

This colourful town is famous for its blockprinted cotton. Today most of its printers and dyers belong to a guild, with retail outlets selling reasonably priced fabrics. Sanganer owes its success as a printing centre to a rivulet whose waters have a mineral content that fixes dyes. Sanganer is also a centre of handmade paper, and of Jaipur's renowned, hand-painted Blue Pottery, of which vases and tiles with delicate Persian, Turkish and Indian designs are made. Tucked away in the old walled town is the impressive 11th-century Jain **Sanghiji Temple**, lavishly decorated with carvings. Sanganer is now a busy suburb of Jaipur city and houses the city's airport.

A sacred tank in Galta

🏛 Galta

Jaipur district. 10 km (6 miles) E of Jaipur.

This picturesque gorge cradles Galta Kund, an 18th-century religious site with two main temples and a number of smaller shrines. Its seven sacred tanks, fed by natural spring water, are said to have curative powers. Two pavilions on either side of the complex have well-preserved frescoes. The Surya Temple, high on the ridge, provides spectacular views of Jaipur.

🌿 Sisodia Rani ka Bagh

Jaipur district. Purana Ghat. 6 km (4 miles) E of Jaipur. **Tel** (0141) 264 0594. ⬜ *daily.* 📷
This terraced garden was laid out in the 18th century for Sawai Jai Singh II's second

The picturesque Jal Mahal, seemingly afloat during the monsoon

wife, who married him on the condition that her son would succeed to the throne. To escape the inevitable palace intrigues, the queen moved to a more private home outside the walled city. Her little double-storeyed palace, decorated with lively murals, is surrounded by beautiful gardens. It is today a popular location for Indian films.

🏯 Ramgarh

Jaipur district. 40 km (25 miles) E of Jaipur.

Ramgarh is the site of one of the earliest Kachhawaha fortresses. The fort was built by the dynasty's founder, Duleh Rai (r.1093–1135), who also built a temple dedicated to the goddess Jamvai Mata, now visited by thousands of devotees. Ramgarh Lodge, on the northern bank of a man-made lake, is an elegant French villa-style hunting lodge built in 1931 for the Jaipur royal family. It is now a pleasant heritage hotel with one of the best polo grounds in the country.

🏯 Nahargarh

Jaipur district. 9 km (6 miles) NW of Jaipur. *Tel* (0141) 253 0293. ☐ daily. ● public hols. 🖼 🔲 🏯

The forbidding hill-top fort of Nahargarh ("Tiger Fort") stands in what was once a densely forested area. The fierce Meena tribe ruled this region until they were defeated by the Kachhawahas. Its fortifications, strengthened by Sawai Jai Singh II, were subsequently expanded by successive rulers. Madho Singh II added a lavish palace called Madhavendra Bhavan for his nine queens. Laid out in a maze of terraces and

courtyards, it has a cool, airy upper chamber from which the ladies of the court could view the city. Its walls and pillars are an outstanding example of *arayish*, a form of plaster work that is hand-polished with a piece of agate to produce a marble finish.

🏯 Gaitor

Jaipur district. 8 km (5 miles) N of Jaipur. ☐ daily. ● public hols.

The marble cenotaphs of the Kachhawaha kings are enclosed in a walled garden just off the Amber road. This area was chosen by Sawai Jai Singh II as the new cremation site after Amber (*see pp364–5*) was abandoned. Ornate carved pillars support the marble *chhatris* erected over the platforms where the maharajas were cremated. One of the most impressive cenotaphs in the complex is that of Jai Singh II himself. It has 20 marble pillars carved with religious and mythological scenes and is topped by a white marble

dome. The most recent cenotaph was erected in 1997 in memory of Jagat Singh, the only son of Sawai Man Singh II and Gayatri Devi.

🏯 Jal Mahal

Jaipur district. 8 km (5 miles) N of Jaipur. ☐ daily.

During the monsoon, water fills the Man Sagar lake, and the Jal Mahal ("Water Palace") seems to rise from it like a mirage. Built in the mid-18th century by Madho Singh I, it is inspired by the Lake Palace at Udaipur, where the king spent his childhood. It was later used for royal duck-shooting parties, and a variety of water birds are still seen here. The terraced garden, enclosed by arched passages, has elegant semi-octagonal towers capped by cupolas in each corner.

🏯 Jaigarh

Jaipur district. 12 km (8 miles) NW of Jaipur. *Tel* (0141) 267 1848. ☐ 9am–4:30pm. ● public hols. 🖼

Legendary Jaigarh, the "Victory Fort", watches over the old capital of Amber. One of the few surviving cannon foundries is located here. Its most prized possession is the monumental 50-tonne Jai Van, cast in 1726 and said to be the world's largest cannon on wheels. Ironically, despite its impressive size, the cannon has never been fired.

The famous Jai Van

Other interesting sights are the Diva Burj, a seven-storeyed tower where a huge oil lamp was lit on the king's birthday, two temples and a palace built over 200 years ago.

The ramparts of Jaigarh Fort, a feat of military engineering

Amber Fort ❷

Detail of door at Shila Devi

The fort palace of Amber was the Kachhawaha citadel until 1727, when their capital moved to Jaipur. Successive rulers continued to come here on important occasions to seek the blessings of the family deity, Shila Devi. The citadel was established in 1592 by Man Singh I on the remains of an old 11th-century fort, but the various buildings added by Jai Singh I (r.1621–67) are what constitute its magnificent centrepiece.

Elephant ride on the cobbled pathway to the fort

★ Sheesh Mahal
The flame of a single candle, reflected in the tiny mirrors embedded in this chamber, transforms it into a starlit sky.

Aram Bagh, the pleasure garden.

Jas Mandir
This Hall of Private Audience has latticed windows, a floral ceiling of elegant alabaster relief work and glass inlay. A marble screen here overlooks the Maota Lake and allows in cool air.

Jai Mandir

A view of Amber Fort
Protected by Jaigarh Fort, the massive ramparts of Amber Fort follow the contours of a natural ridge.

STAR FEATURES

★ Sheesh Mahal

★ Ganesh Pol

★ Shila Devi Temple

★ **Ganesh Pol**
This shimmering three-storeyed gateway, built in 1640, is connected to the private apartments by the screened uppermost level, meant for ladies in purdah.

Sukh Niwas

VISITORS' CHECKLIST

Jaipur district. 11 km (7 miles) N of Jaipur. *Tel* (0141) 253 0293.
8am–5:30pm daily. *public hols.*

★ **Shila Devi Temple**
This ornately carved silver door is the entrance to the Shila Devi Temple.

Shila Devi Temple

Sattais Katcheri

Diwan-i-Aam

PLAN OF AMBER FORT

KEY
Area illustrated
Man Singh's Palace
Jaleb Chowk

0 metres 100
0 yards 100

1 Suraj Pol
2 Chand Pol
3 Shila Devi Temple
4 Diwan-i-Aam
5 Ganesh Pol
6 Jai Mandir
6 Jas Mandir
6 Sheesh Mahal
7 Sukh Niwas
8 Baradari
9 Zenana

Exploring Amber (the Old Capital)

Detail of painting on Ganesh Pol

Crowning the crest of a hill, Amber Fort offers a panoramic view of Maota Lake and the historic old town at the base of the hill, which was the early seat of the Amber kings before they made the fort their capital. Several havelis, stepwells, and temples can be seen below the fort, pointing to the existence of a self-sufficient township, where the Mughal emperor Akbar used to stop on his annual pilgrimage to Ajmer (see p376).

Sattais Katcheri, where the revenue records were written

The Fort Complex

The main entrance to the historic Amber Fort is through the imposing **Suraj Pol** ("Sun Gate"), so called because it faces the direction of the rising sun, the Kachhawaha family emblem. The gate leads into a huge courtyard, **Jaleb Chowk**, lined on three sides with souvenir and refreshment shops. A flight of steps leads to the **Shila Devi Temple**, which has silver doors, silver oil lamps, grand pillars carved to look like banana trees, and contains the Kachhawaha family deity, a stone (shila) image of the goddess Kali. The next courtyard is the

Diwan-i-Aam, the space for public audience. Near it is the **Sattais Katcheri**, a colonnade of 27 (sattais) pillars, where scribes once sat to record revenue petitions.

The magnificent **Ganesh Pol** is the gateway to three pleasure palaces, each with special features, built around a Mughal-style garden, **Aram Bagh**. Maota Lake, which provided water to the fort, is surrounded by two exquisite gardens. The **Kesar Kyari Bagh** has star-shaped flower beds once planted with

Marble carving of a Hindu deity

saffron (kesar) flowers, while **Dilaram Bagh**, built in 1568 as a resting place for Akbar on his way to Ajmer, is a clever pun on the name of its architect, Dilaram ("Heart's Ease"). A small Archaeological Museum is located nearby. The farthest and oldest end of the fort was converted into the zenana (women's quarters), with screens and covered balconies for the seclusion of the royal ladies in purdah. Faint traces of frescoes are still visible on the walls. In the centre of the courtyard is a pavilion with 12 pillars, the **Baradari**.

The Township

The **Chand Pol** ("Moon Gate"), directly opposite Suraj Pol, leads to the old town outside the fort. The beautiful **Jagat Shiromani Temple** with its remarkable torana (gateway) is one of the many temples that lies along this route. It also has a water tank, **Panna Mian ka Kund**. To the east lies **Sagar**, a popular picnic spot with two terraced lakes. The Jaipur-Delhi Highway cuts across the town, and Amber's main market and bus stand are located on this road. Further north stands the **Akbari Mosque**, built by Emperor Akbar in 1569, and towards the east is **Bharmal ki Chhatri**, a walled enclosure containing a group of memorials. This was the old cremation site for the rulers of Amber until a new spot was chosen at Gaitor (see p363), near Jaipur.

Kesar Kyari Bagh, named after the rare saffron flowers once planted in its star-shaped flower beds

For hotels and restaurants in this region see pp702–5 and pp731–2

Bharatpur ❸

Bharatpur district. 181 km (112 miles) E of Jaipur. 🚂 204,500. 🚌
ℹ️ RTDC Hotel Saras, (05644) 22 2542. 🎪 Jaswant Mela (Oct).

Most famous for its bird sanctuary, the kingdom of Bharatpur was founded by the fearless Jats, a community of landowners. Their

The moat and ramparts of Lohagarh

most remarkable leader, Raja Suraj Mal (r.1724–63), fortified the city of Bharatpur in 1733 and used the loot from Mughal buildings to embellish the forts and palaces of his kingdom.

In the centre of the town is **Lohagarh** ("Iron Fort"), a masterpiece of construction. Its massive double ramparts of packed mud and rubble surrounded by impressive moats withstood repeated attacks by the Marathas and the British until it was finally captured by Lord Lake in 1805. Three palaces built in the fort display a fine mix of Mughal and Rajput stylistic detail. One is now the site of a pharmaceutical

college, while the other two, around the Katcheri Bagh, house the **State Museum**. Its artifacts include a rare collection of 1st- and 2nd-century stone carvings. An interesting sunken *hamam* (bath) is close by. In 1818, Bharatpur became the region's first princely state to sign a treaty with the East India Company.

🏛️ **State Museum**
Tel (05644) 22 8185. ⬜ Fri–Wed.
🔴 public hols. 🎫 free on Mon.
📷 extra charges.

Keoladeo Ghana National Park ❹

See pp368–9.

Deeg ❺

Bharatpur district. 36 km (22 miles) N of Bharatpur. 🚌 ℹ️ RTDC Hotel Saras, Bharatpur, (05644) 22 3700.
🎪 Holi (Mar), Jawahar Mela (Aug).
Water Palace ⬜ daily. 🔴 the day after Holi (Mar). 🎫

Once the capital of the Jat kings of Bharatpur, Deeg rose to prominence after the decline of the Mughal empire in the 18th century. Its square fort and fortified town, once filled with grand mansions and gardens, now lie unkempt

and forlorn. Deeg's Raja Suraj Mal and his son, Jawahar Singh, were keen builders of lavish pleasure palaces and the most remarkable of these is the **Deeg Water Palace**, a romantic summer retreat for the Jat kings. The magic of the monsoon inspired a lyrical composition of sandstone and marble pavilions replete with gardens and pools. A skilful cooling system drew water from a huge reservoir and used a number of innovative special effects to simulate monsoon showers and even

Sawan Pavilion, Deeg Water Palace

produce rainbows. The coloured fountains are now used only during the Jawahar Mela.

DEEG WATER PALACE

Sawan Pavilion is shaped like an upturned boat. Its ingenious water system created a semi-circle of falling water.

Nand Bhavan

Keshav Bhavan had heavy lithic balls placed on its roof, that rolled and produced "thunder" when water gushed up the hollow pillars and pipes inside the arches.

Entrance

Gopal Bhavan's numerous overhanging kiosks and balconies are reflected in Gopal Sagar from which it seems to rise. The interior still retains the original furnishings and objets d'art.

The roof-top reservoir had water drawn to it from four wells. Pipes leading from its sides supplied water to the chutes and fountains.

Keoladeo Ghana National Park ❹

A UNESCO World Heritage Site regarded as one of the world's most important bird sanctuaries, Keoladeo Ghana derives its name from a Shiva temple (Keoladeo) within a dense forest *(ghana)*. This once-arid scrubland was first developed by Bharatpur's rulers in the mid-18th century by diverting the waters of a nearby irrigation canal to create a private duck reserve. Extravagant shooting parties for British viceroys and other royal guests were held here, and horrifying numbers of birds were shot in a single day. Today, the park spreads over 29 sq km (11 sq miles) of wetlands, and attracts a wide variety of migrant and water birds who fly in each winter from places as distant as Siberia. Keoladeo's dry area has mixed deciduous and scrub vegetation and is home to many animals, including the famed nilgai.

Shallow wetlands, one of the world's finest heronries

Getting Around the Park
Expert boatmen navigate the wetlands and point out bird colonies. Bicycles and cycle-rickshaws are also available for touring the forest paths.

Dry scrubland provides good grazing for nilgai and other species of deer.

BIRDS, RESIDENT AND MIGRANT

The male Sarus crane dances to attract his mate

The park attracts over 375 bird species belonging to 56 families. Egrets, darters, cormorants, grey herons and storks hatch nearly 30,000 chicks every year. The park's most eagerly awaited visitor is the Siberian crane, now an endangered species. Other birds include the peregrine falcon, steppe eagle, garganery teal, snake bird and white ibis. Among the large variety of storks are the open-bill stork, the painted stork and the black-necked stork, considered to be the world's tallest stork. Standing on coral-coloured legs, the bird is 2 m (7 ft) tall, with a wingspan of 2.5 m (8 ft). The Sarus crane, a symbol of fidelity in Indian mythology, woos its partner for life with an elaborate mating dance.

Baby cormorants

KEY

— Main road

= Minor road

-- Park boundary

•• Foot path/cycle trail

▢ Marshland

☼ Viewpoint

🛳 Jetty

⛵ Boating

🏠 Police station

🛕 Temple

Ⓐ Accommodation

BHARATPUR CITY

VISITORS' CHECKLIST

Bharatpur district. 185 km (115 miles) E of Jaipur. Bharatpur, 5 km (3 miles) N of entry point, then taxi. Bharatpur. RTDC Hotel Saras, Bharatpur, (05644) 22 3700. Deputy Chief Wildlife Warden, (05644) 22 2777. extra charges. Bicycles & cycle-rickshaws available.

Painted Storks
Between July and October, the trees become nesting sites for nearly 5,000 pairs of these birds, named after their colourful beaks and their plumage which is "painted" with black bands.

A stone plaque near the temple records figures of past bird shoots.

Indian Soft-Shell Turtle
The park's wetlands provide an ideal habitat for this endangered species.

Nilgai (Blue Bull)
The largest of all Asiatic antelopes, these avid crop grazers are protected against hunting because of their resemblance to the holy cow. Their broad backs offer comfortable resting places for birds.

White-Throated Kingfisher
One of the most commonly sighted birds in the park, the vividly-coloured kingfisher is usually found near the ponds, lakes and marshlands, perched on branches of trees, waiting for its prey.

Nesting
With the arrival of the monsoon, thousands of birds, such as these greater cormorants, set up nesting colonies. As many as 60 noisy nests on one tree may be seen during this season.

Jatoli

AGRA

NH11

Ghasola

Kadam Kunj

oladeo mple

Hans Sarovar

Koladahar

Bahnera

Chiksana Canal

aswaria

Darapur

0 kilometres 1

0 miles 1

Alwar ⬤

Alwar district. 150 km (93 miles)
NE of Jaipur. 🚏 260,300. 🚃 ▦
ℹ️ *RTDC, Nehru Marg, opp railway
station, (0144) 234 7348.*
🎪 *Jagannathji Fair (Mar/Apr).*

The former princely state
of Alwar is now a dusty,
provincial town, visited by
few tourists except those on
their way to the Sariska
National Park. Nevertheless it
has some remarkable monu-
ments, built by its wealthy
rulers in the 18th century, that
are worth seeing. The most
significant of these is the **City
Palace**, whose architectural
features include a profusion
of curved *bangaldar* roofs
and *chhatris* (pavilions) as

Gate of the Tomb of Fateh Jang

well as delicate Mughal floral
tracery and *jalis*. The palace,
built in 1793, now houses the
District Collectorate and
Police Headquarters, and is
best viewed from the central
courtyard with its lovely
marble pavilions. The lavishly
decorated Durbar Hall and
the Sheesh Mahal, on the first
floor, can only be viewed
with special permission.

A door to the right of the
courtyard leads to the **City
Palace Museum**, spread over
three halls on the palace's
upper storey. Its treasures,

which bear witness to the
opulent lifestyles of Alwar's
maharajas, include rare and
exquisite copies of the Persian
poet Sa'adi's *Gulistan* (written
in 1258) and the *Babur Nama*
or "Memoirs of Babur" (1530),
superb Mughal and Rajput
miniatures and an awesome
armoury. Particularly
intriguing is a macabre coil
called *nagphas*, used for
strangling enemies. Another
unique exhibit is a silver
dining table with dividers,
through which shoals of metal
fish can be seen swimming.

The cenotaph of Maharaja
Bakhtawar Singh (r.1790–1815)
lies behind the palace, across a
magnificent *kund* (tank). It is
locally known as **Moosi
Maharani ki Chhatri**, after his
mistress who committed *sati*
here after he died. An elegant
monument that blends brown
sandstone with white marble,
its ceilings are adorned with
gold leaf paintings.

On a steep hill above the
city is the rugged **Bala Qila**, a
fort with extensive ramparts,
massive gateways and some
spectacular views from the
top. Originally a 10th-century
mud fort, it was added to by
the Mughals and Jats, and
captured by Pratap Singh of
Alwar in 1775. Within the fort
is a pretty frescoed palace, the
Nikumbh Mahal, in the
courtyard of which a police
wireless station is, rather
inappropriately, sited. Also
visible are the ruins of the

A page from the *Gulistan*

Salim Mahal, named after
Jahangir (Salim), Mughal
emperor Akbar's heir who was
exiled here after he plotted to
kill Abu'l Fazl, the emperor's
official historian. Near Alwar's
railway station is another fine
monument, the **Tomb of Fateh
Jang**, one of Emperor Shah
Jahan's ministers, built in
1647. Dominated by an enormous dome, the walls and
ceiling of this magnificent five-
storeyed structure have raised
plaster reliefs.

Alwar's green lung,
Company Bagh, is a lovely
garden with a greenhouse.

🏨 **City Palace**
Near Collectorate. ⬜ *daily.* 🎟️

🏛️ **City Palace Museum**
⬜ *Sat–Thu.* ⬛ *public hols.* 🎟️ 📷

⛩️ **Moosi Maharani ki
Chhatri**
⬜ *Sat–Thu.* ⬛ *public hols.* 🎟️

⛩️ **Bala Qila**
⬜ *daily. Written permission not
required anymore. The visitor's
name is entered in a register at the
office of the Superintendent of
Police, City Palace.*

⛩️ **Tomb of Fateh Jang**
Near railway station. ⬜ *daily.*

The elegant marble pavilion at Moosi Maharani ki Chhatri

Sariska Palace, a luxury hotel just outside the Tiger Reserve

Sariska National Park ❼

Alwar district. 37 km (23 miles) NE of Alwar. 🚐 ⓘ *Field Director, Project Tiger Sanctuary, Sariska (0144) 284 1333.* ◻ *Sep–Jun.* 🔁 *extra for personal vehicles or jeeps.* 🎫 🍴

Designated a Tiger Reserve under Project Tiger *(see p289)* in 1979, Sariska National Park, formerly the private hunting ground of the princely state of Alwar, sprawls over 800 sq km (309 sq miles), with a core area of 480 sq km (185 sq miles). The Aravalli Range branches out at Sariska, forming low plateaux and valleys that harbour a wide spectrum of wildlife.

The tiger population at Sariska is now believed to be between 20 and 30. However, spotting one is a rarity. It was reported by the media that not a single tiger survived in the reserve. Nevertheless, forest guides keep track of where a tiger was last seen and can sometimes lead visitors to spot this elusive predator.

There are a series of watering holes in Sariska, at Pandupol, Bandipol, Slopka, Kalighati and Talvriksha, that make good vantage points to view wildlife, especially at sunset when hoards of animals flock to them to quench their thirst. The gentle chital or spotted deer is commonly sighted at the park's watering holes, while the *chausingha* (four-horned antelope), unique to Sariska, can be spotted around Pandupol. Other

Silk cotton in bloom

species that can be seen here are panthers and black-faced langur monkeys, jackals and hyenas, nilgai or blue bulls, wild boars and porcupines.

Among the birds that can be spotted are the crested serpent eagle, the great Indian horned owl, woodpeckers, kingfishers and partridges.

The dry deciduous forests of Sariska come to life during the brief spring and early summer when the flowering *dhak (Butea monosperma)* and laburnum bloom. The date palm begins to bear fruit, while berries known locally as *kair (Capparis decidua)* appear on the bushes.

The **Kankwari Fort**, dating to the 17th-century, and temple ruins, such as those of the **Pandupol Temple**, lie within the park. The **Sariska Palace**, built at the end of the 19th century as a hunting lodge for Alwar's rulers, is now a luxury hotel *(see p705)*, with a collection of vintage *shikar* photographs.

Black-faced Hanuman langurs, a common sight at Sariska

Shekhawati

Sikar & Jhunjhunu districts. 115 km
(72 miles) NW from Jaipur to Sikar.
🚌 🎭 *Gangaur Festival (Mar/Apr),
Dussehra (Sept/Oct).*

A view of the impressive Char-Chowk Haveli, Lachhmangarh

This region, named after its
15th-century ruler Rao
Shekha, has a number of
fascinating small towns with
well-preserved painted
havelis, forts and temples.
Among the most interesting
are **Lachhmangarh** and
Fatehpur with their grand
havelis, and **Dundlod**, with its
well-restored fort. Especially
worth visiting is **Ramgarh**, 20
km (12 miles) north of
Fatehpur. Famous for its Shani
Temple which has an ornate
interior of mirrorwork and
gilt, the town also has the
Ram Gopal Poddar Chhatri,
covered with more than 400
paintings. The main bazaar is
crowded with "antique" dealers, who sell carved doors
and windows from derelict
havelis. Many of these are
extremely skilful new copies
of the originals.

Mahansar, 15 km (9 miles)
northeast of Ramgarh, has the
splendid Sone ki Dukan
Haveli, abundantly worked in
gold leaf. The paintings on its
vaulted ceiling, depicting the
incarnations of Vishnu, are
perhaps the finest in the area.

Bissau, 10 km (6 miles) northwest of Mahansar, has the
18th-century Keshargarh Fort,
which provides an excellent
view of the sand dunes to the

Inside Dundlod Fort

north and west. It also has ten
richly painted *havelis*. During
Dussehra, Ramlila performances take place every evening, with the actors wearing
masks and costumes made by
local *sadhvis* (female ascetics)
who started this tradition in
the 19th century.

Churu, 12 km (8 miles)
northwest of Bissau, is in the
desert. Though not actually
part of the Shekhawati region,
it is included in the painted
haveli circuit, as many merchants had homes here too.
The Surana Double Haveli,
with its imposing proportions
and 1,111 windows, is the
main attraction. The Banthia
Haveli, east of the vegetable
market, has interesting if
bizarre frescoes, including
one of Jesus smoking a cigar.

THE PAINTED HAVELIS OF SHEKHAWATI

The ancestral homes of some of India's leading industrialist
families, such as the Birlas and Goenkas, can be seen in the
many little towns of Shekhawati. These sprawling old *havelis*
with their exuberantly frescoed walls were built between the
late 18th and early 20th centuries by local Marwari merchants

who had migrated to the port-
cities of Bombay (Mumbai) and
Calcutta (Kolkata) to seek their
fortunes. Their interaction with the
British and exposure to modern
urban and industrial trends

Fresco of a group of turbaned
Rajput chieftains

influenced their lifestyles. Consequently, their homes grew
increasingly grand, reflecting the new ideas they brought back
with them, as well as their new-found wealth and social status.

The style and content of the Shekhawati frescoes are a telling
comment on the urbanization of a traditional genre. The local
artists still followed the one-dimensional realism of traditional
Rajput painting *(see p405)*, but juxtaposed among the gods,
goddesses and martial heroes are images from a changing world.
In their celebration of contemporary "pop" themes, the frescoes
of British ladies, top-hatted gentlemen, brass bands and soldiers,
trains, motor cars, aeroplanes, gramophones and telephones,
symbolize the industrial society emerging in the late 19th century.

The entrance to Biyani
Haveli, Sikar

A Tour of Shekhawati ⑨

Situated along the old camel caravan trade route, northwest of Jaipur, the Shekhawati ("Garden of Shekha") region resembles an open-air museum. A network of excellent roads through semi-arid scrubland connects numerous towns and villages, known for minor forts, *baolis* and the painted *havelis* of India's leading merchant families, still standing in all their evocative splendour.

A wall in the Poddar School, Nawalgarh, depicting gods and goddesses flying kites

Mandawa ④
This fort-palace is now a charming hotel and a convenient base from which to visit neighbouring towns.

Dundlod ⑤
Its fort-palace and two splendid Goenka *havelis* are worth a visit.

Fatehpur ③
This picturesque mid-15th century town is best known for the Singhania, Goenka and Jalan *havelis*.

KEY

▦ Tour route

═ Road

▧ River

BIKANER

JHUNJHUNU

Mukundgarh

0 km   20

0 miles   10

NH11

Lachhmangarh ②
An old fort towers above this 19th-century town. The Char Chowk ("Four Courtyards") Haveli, owned by the Ganeriwala family, is said to be the grandest in the region.

Nawalgarh ⑥
The Poddar and the Aath ("eight") *havelis* are renowned for their frescoes.

NAGAUR

JAIPUR

TIPS FOR DRIVERS

Length: 111 km (69 miles).
Stopping-off points: Mandawa, Dundlod, Mukundgarh, Fatehpur and Nawalgarh have good hotels.
Getting around: Petrol pumps are at regular intervals on the main road. A number of lesser roads lead off from NH11 towards Jhunjhunu. All of them have roadside eateries which sell mineral water, hot and cold drinks and snacks.

Sikar ①
Sikar's charm lies in its colourfully painted *havelis*, bazaars and rural ambience.

Street-by-Street: Pushkar ⑩

A turtle shrine

A peaceful pilgrim town of lakes and 400 temples, Pushkar derives its name from *pushpa* (flower) and *kar* (hand) after a legend that claims its lakes were created from the petals that fell from the divine hands of Brahma the Creator. Today, life revolves around its lakeside ghats, temples and vibrant, colourful bazaars, and it is this harmonious mix of the spiritual and commercial that draws people to Pushkar.

Villagers at the Fair
Hundreds of thousands of people, camels and cattle attend the annual fair, said to be one of the largest in Asia.

Residential area

Dhanna Bhagat Temple

SADAR BAZAAR

| 0 metres | 100 |
| 0 yards | 100 |

Fairground

Savitri Temple

PARIKRAMA MARG

★ Brahma Temple
This is one of the few temples in India dedicated to Brahma who, according to myth, was cursed by his wife Savitri when, in her absence, he invited Gayatri, a tribal girl, to take her place in an important ritual.

Badi Ganeshji Temple

Parasurama Temple

KEY

– – – Suggested route

STAR SIGHTS

★ Brahma Temple

★ Ghats

Pushkar Lake
On top of a hill, by the sacred lake of Pushkar, is the temple of Savitri. Across the lake, on another hill, is the Gayatri Temple.

Rangji Temple

*This temple is conspicuous
for its South Indian style of
architecture (see p20). Its
gopura (gateway), carved
with over 360 images of
deities, towers over the area.*

Camel at the Pushkar Fair

Women at Sadar Bazaar

The Pushkar Fair

In the Hindu month of Kartik
(October/November), ten days
after Diwali, this peaceful
town and its environs come
alive as the much anticipated
annual cattle fair begins. Tents
and campsites suddenly spring
up to accommodate the
thousands of pilgrims, tourists
and villagers with herds of
cattle, horses and camels who
come here to participate in
this spectacular event.

Pushkar has always been
the region's central cattle market for local herdsmen and
farmers who buy and sell
camels and indigenous breeds
of cattle. Over the years, this
trade in livestock has greatly
increased in volume. The
Pushkar Fair is now one of
Asia's largest cattle fairs, and
it transforms the quiet little
village into a bustling market.

In the vast, specially-built
amphitheatre on the outskirts
of the town, numerous camel,
horse and donkey races and
contests take place amid lusty
cheers from the spectators. A
festive, carnival atmosphere
prevails in Pushkar during the
fair's two-week duration.
Giant Ferris wheels and open
air theatres offer amusement,
while food stalls do a brisk
trade, as do the shops that
sell a fascinating variety of
goods. In the evenings, people huddle round campfires,
listening to the haunting
strains of Rajasthani folk
ballads. The fair reaches a
crescendo on the night of the
full moon (*purnima*), when
pilgrims take a dip in the holy
lake. At dusk, during the
beautiful *deepdan* ceremony,
hundreds of clay lamps on
leaf boats are lit and set afloat
in a magical tableau.

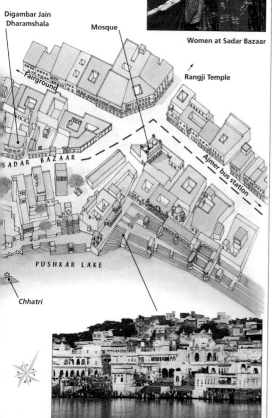

Digambar Jain
Dharamshala

Mosque

Fairground

Rangji Temple

Ajmer bus station

SADAR　BAZAAR

PUSHKAR LAKE

Chhatri

★ Ghats

*Pushkar has 52 ghats. Devout Hindus make
at least one pilgrimage to Pushkar and bathe at
the holy ghats to wash away their sins, thereby
earning themselves a place in heaven.*

Ajmer ⓫

Ajmer district. 135 km (84 miles)
SW of Jaipur. 🏯 485,200. 🚉 🚌
🛈 Rajasthan Tourism, near Khadim
Hotel, (0145) 262 7426. 🎪 Urs (Oct).

Ajmer is famous throughout
the subcontinent for the holy
Muslim shrine, **Dargah Sharif**,
the tomb of the great Sufi
saint, Khwaja Moinuddin
Chishti (1143–1235). Located
in the southwest corner of the
city, the saint's marble-domed
tomb is at the heart of the
Dargah complex, which is
virtually a township in itself.
It includes a bazaar and two
marble mosques, built by the
Mughal emperors Akbar and
Shah Jahan in the 16th and
17th centuries. Akbar was
Chishti's most famous devotee,
and once walked barefoot all
the way from Agra to Ajmer, a
distance of 363 km (226
miles), as thanksgiving after
the birth of his son Salim, the
future Emperor Jahangir.

Millions of pilgrims come
to Ajmer for the saint's annual
Urs (death anniversary) in
October, when
spirited Sufi musi-
cians sing the saint's
praises in front of his
tomb. A special rice
pudding, cooked in
giant iron cauldrons
in the Dargah's
courtyard, is offered
to devotees.

West of the Dargah
Sharif is Ajmer's
architectural gem, the **Adhai-
Din-ka-Jhonpra**, or "Hut of
Two-and-a-Half Days". This
strange name is said to derive
from the duration of a
religious fair that used to be
held here. Though in ruins,
the early 13th-century
mosque complex, built into
a hillside, is most impressive.
Its main glory is its exquisite
seven-arched screen in front
of the colonnaded hall. Each

**Pilgrims at Ajmer's Dargah Sharif,
India's holiest Muslim shrine**

arch is different, and the
numerous columns have
elaborate carvings.

In the southeast corner of
Ajmer is **Mayo College**, one of
India's best public schools. An
excellent example of Indo-
Saracenic architecture, it was
set up in 1875 by the viceroy,
Lord Mayo, as an "Eton of the
East" for Rajput princes. Its
early students came accompanied by family retainers and
private tutors, and
some, like the prince
of Alwar, even
brought along their
own elephants.
Behind the 19th-
century **Nasiyan
Temple**, in the heart
of the old city, is the
Svarna Nagari Hall,
vividly decorated
with coloured-glass

**Calligraphy, Adhai-
Din-ka-Jhonpra**

mosaics and large gilded
wooden figures, recreating
scenes from Jain mythology.

The **Rajputana Museum**,
also in the old city, is located
in Emperor Akbar's fort and
palace. Its exhibits include
impressive sculptures

dating from the 4th to the
12th centuries.

Around **Anasagar Lake**, to
the northwest of the city, are
elegant marble pavilions built
by Emperor Shah Jahan in the
17th century. They are set on
the lake's banks, in a pretty
garden called Daulat Bagh.
North of the city, on the
summit of Beetli Hill, is the
ruined 12th-century **Taragarh
Fort**, which affords spectacular views of Ajmer and
the surrounding countryside.

🏯 **Nasiyan Temple**
SM Soni Marg. ◯ daily. 📷

🏛 **Rajputana Museum**
Near bus stand. ◯ daily. 📷

Nagaur ⓬

Nagaur district. 137 km (85 miles)
NE of Jodhpur. 🏯 83,400. 🚌
🎪 Cattle Fair (Jan/Feb).

This little desert town,
midway between Jodhpur
and Bikaner, is dominated by
Ahichhatragarh Fort, dating
to the 12th century. In the
mid-18th century, the ruler of
Jodhpur received the fort as a
gift from the Mughals and
embellished it with a charming
pleasure palace. Several of its
chambers have exquisite
frescoes, now being carefully
restored. The palace also has
lovely water channels decorated with fish-scale patterns
and ornamental spouts, as
well as an ingenious system of
airducts that used to supply
the inner rooms with cool air.

The Nagaur Cattle Fair rivals
the Pushkar Fair *(see p375)*,
and is a dazzling kaleidoscope of animals, crafts and
people, including Nagaur's
famous puppeteers whose
dramatic shows bring alive
popular Rajasthani legends
and folklore.

The exuberantly decorated seven-arched screen at the Adhai-Din-ka-Jhonpra, Ajmer

Ships of the Thar Desert

The desert dwellers of Rajasthan could not survive without their camels. In the sandy, inhospitable expanse of the Thar Desert, it is their only means of transport, their beast of burden, as well as an

Mural of camels

important source of nourishment (camel's milk, slightly salty in taste, is drunk throughout Rajasthan's deserts). The hardy camel demands little in

return. It can do without food and water for up to a month in winter, and a week in summer, tanking up on 70 litres (148 pints) of water at one go. The Rajasthani's affection for his camel is evident at all the desert fairs, where camels are given pride of place, resplendent in their colourful tassels and jewellery.

VARIETIES OF CAMEL

Three varieties of camel inhabit Rajasthan. All of them have two rows of eyelashes which help keep the sand out of their eyes. Their humps contain a thick layer of fat, which shields their bodies from the scorching desert sun.

Gujarati camels *are darker-haired and adept at traversing marshy areas such as the Rann of Kutch.*

Bikaneri camels *have hairy ears, and great load-bearing capacity and stamina.*

Jaisalmeri camels, *with longer legs, can cover up to 22 km (14 miles) an hour.*

Camel carts, *ingeniously equipped with old aircraft wheels, are a common sight in Rajasthan's cities.*

Dhola and Maru, *star-crossed lovers in Rajasthani folklore who eloped on their trusty camel, are a favourite theme in paintings.*

Camelskin handicrafts *include beautiful embossed water bottles. Bags, slippers, and lacquer-painted lampshades are other camelskin products.*

Camel races *at fairs test the even-ness of a camel's gait by seeing how far it can carry a pot of milk without spilling any.*

Camel cavalry regiments *of the Indian Army have their origin in the camel regiments of the maharaja of Bikaner, which fought in Egypt in World War I. Today they patrol the desert borders.*

Bikaner ⑬

Bikaner district. 361 km (224 miles) NW of Jaipur. 🚗 529,000. 🚉 ✈ 🛈 Dhola Maru Hotel, Pooran Singh Circle, (0151) 222 6701. 🐪 Camel Festival (Jan), Jambeshwar Festival (Feb/Mar), Kolayat Fair (Nov).

Along with Jodhpur and Jaisalmer, Bikaner was one of the three great Desert Kingdoms of Rajasthan and, like them, prospered because of its strategic location on the overland caravan trade route to Central Asia and China. It was founded in 1486 by Rao Bika, the disgruntled younger son of Rao Jodha, the ruler of Jodhpur (see pp380–81), who left home in search of new territory to conquer.

Somewhat over-shadowed by the splendours of Jodhpur and Jaisalmer, Bikaner nevertheless has a great deal to offer visitors, with its old walled town where camels saunter past colourful stalls, its many temples and palaces, and the magnificent Junagarh Fort, perhaps the best preserved and most ornately decorated of all the forts in Rajasthan.

The imposing ramparts of the 16th-century Junagarh Fort

Maharaja's swing at Junagarh Fort

🏛 Junagarh Fort

⬜ Sat–Thu. 📷 🎥 📷 extra charges. **Museum** ⬜ daily. 🎥
Constructed between 1587 and 1593 by the third ruler of Bikaner, Rai Singh, Junagarh Fort is protected by a 986-m (3,235-ft) long sandstone wall with 37 bastions, a moat and, most effectively of all, by the forbidding expanse of the Thar Desert. Not surprisingly, the fort has never been conquered, a fact which explains its excellent state of preservation. Within the fort's austere stone walls are no less than 37 profusely decorated palaces, temples and pavilions, built by its successive rulers over the centuries, though in a harmonious continuity of

style. The most outstanding is the **Anup Mahal**, built by Maharaja Anup Singh in 1690 as his Hall of Private Audience. It was sumptuously decorated between 1787 and 1800 by Maharaja Surat Singh. In an ingenious imitation of Mughal *pietra dura* work at a fraction of the cost, the lime-plaster walls of the Anup Mahal have been polished to a high lustre. They are covered with red and gold lacquer patterns, further embellished with mirrors and gold leaf. The **Karan Mahal** (built between 1631 and 1669) is the Hall of Public Audience and is ornamented in a similar if somewhat less lavish style.

The luxurious interior of Anup Mahal with ornamental lacquer work

Two other gorgeous, heavily decorated palaces are the 17th-century **Chandra Mahal** ("Moon Palace") and **Phool Mahal** ("Flower Palace"). The latter contains Rao Bika's small, low bed with curved silver legs, on which he slept with his feet touching the ground. The bed was so designed to enable Rao Bika to jump quickly to his feet and fight off murderous intruders. The Chandra Mahal, which was the queens' palace, has carved marble panels depicting the Radha-Krishna legend, and both palaces have superb stone carving and *jalis*. The blue-and-gold **Badal Mahal** ("Cloud Palace") is covered with paintings of clouds, yellow streaks of lightning and rain showers – a favourite fantasy in this arid land. The **Hawa Mahal** ("Palace of Winds") has a huge mirror posi-tioned over the maharaja's bed, which apparently enabled him to view the courtyard below, thus alerting him to approach-ing danger. The oldest palace in the fort is **Lal Niwas**, dating to 1595, and decorated with floral motifs in red and gold. The newest palace is the huge **Durbar Niwas** ("Coronation Palace"), built in the early 20th century by Bikaner's most progressive ruler Sir Ganga Singh (r.1887–1943), who gave Bikaner its railway link and built the Ganga Canal which brought precious irrigation water to his kingdom. He was also

For hotels and restaurants in this region see pp702–5 and pp731–2

famous for hosting elaborate *shikars* (hunting expeditions) for visiting British dignitaries. The Durbar Niwas now houses the fort museum, whose armoury section includes such fascinating exhibits as a 56-kg (124-lb) suit of armour, a dagger with a pistol built into it, and swords with lion-shaped handles. Other exhibits include the fragrant sandalwood throne of the rulers, said to date back to their 5th-century ancestors who were the kings of Kannauj (Uttar Pradesh), and a curious half-spoon for soup, used by the maharaja to ensure that his luxuriant moustache remained pristine during mealtimes.

Coat of arms of Bikaner's rulers

🏛 Walled City

West end of MG Rd. **Shops** ⬜ *daily.*
In the old walled city, entered through Kote Gate, is the bazaar, where excellent local handicrafts can be found, such as rugs and carpets, painted lampshades made of camel hide, and beautiful miniatures in the Bikaneri style. Savoury snacks (*bhujias*) are another local speciality, and Bikaneri *bhujias* are renowned throughout India, as are the sweets made of camel's milk. The grand 17th- and 18th-century *havelis* of Bikaner's wealthy merchants line the narrow lanes in the vicinity around Rampuria Street. Two of the most ornate are the **Rampuria** and

One of the two cannons flanking the entrance to Lalgarh Palace

Kothari Havelis. The former is now a delightful heritage hotel. In the southwestern corner of the walled town are two Jain temples, dating from the early 16th century, the **Bhandeshwar** and **Sandeshwar Temples**. Both are ornately carved and are embellished with frescoes, mirror-work and gold leaf scrollwork inside. They were built by two brothers who, having no children, constructed these masterpieces for posterity.

🏛 Lalgarh Palace

N of city centre. **Tel** *(0151) 254 0201.*
Museum ⬜ *Thu–Tue.* 📷 📹
Lalgarh Palace, outside the walled town, is a sprawling extravaganza of carved friezes, *jalis*, pillars and arches in the distinctive reddish-pink local sandstone (which resulted in Bikaner being dubbed the "Red City"). Constructed between 1902 and 1926, it was designed by Sir Samuel Swinton Jacob (*see p353*) in a style that combines traditional Rajput and Renaissance European features with Art Nouveau decor inside. Part of it has been converted into a hotel (*see p702*), and another section into a museum with vintage photographs and wildlife trophies. Lalgarh Palace's museum and beautiful gardens are open to visitors.

Environs

The **Camel Breeding Farm**, 9 km (6 miles) southeast of Bikaner, is best visited in the late afternoon when the camels return from grazing. Set up in 1975, the farm breeds nearly half the camels found in India, including those for the camel regiment of the Indian Army. **Gajner**, 30 km (19 miles) northwest of Bikaner, has the red sandstone Summer Palace of the maharajas, now a luxury hotel (*see p702*), and the Gajner National Park, home to blackbucks, wild boars, desert foxes and a large number of migratory birds. The 17th-century **Karni Mata Temple** at

Deshnok, 30 km (19 miles) southeast of Bikaner, is also known as the Rat Temple, because of the hundreds of rats that swarm around the temple and its precincts. The rats are considered sacred and are fed sweets and milk by the priests and visitors, who believe that they are reincarnated holy men. The temple is dedicated to Karni Mata, an incarnation of Durga, and is entered through intricately carved silver doors, presented by Sir Ganga Singh.

🐫 **Camel Breeding Farm**
⬜ *Mon–Sat.* 📷 📹
🛕 **Karni Mata Temple**
⬜ *daily.* 🎭 *Karni Mata Festival (Mar/Apr & Sep/Oct).*

Devotee feeding milk to rats at Karni Mata Temple, Deshnok

Phalodi ⑭

Jodhpur district. 150 km (93 miles) SW of Bikaner. 🚌

This large town attracts visitors because of the lovely hamlet of Khichan, 4 km (2.5 miles) to its east. Khichan is famous for the demoiselle cranes that gather around its lake between September and March. The birds migrate here from the Mongolian steppes for the winter. Every day, the villagers spread grain on the fields for the birds, and as a result the number of cranes that come here has increased substantially over the years. At last count, 7,000 cranes spent the winter at Khichan.

Jodhpur ⑮

Blue-washed houses around Jodhpur's Mehrangarh Fort

With the majestic Mehrangarh Fort towering over opulent palaces, colourful bazaars and the sands of the Thar Desert, Jodhpur epitomizes all the romance and feudal splendour of Rajasthan. Now the second largest city in the state, Jodhpur was founded in 1459 by Rao Jodha, the Rathore ruler of the kingdom of Marwar. Strategically located on the overland trade route, it soon became a flourishing trade centre. Its merchant class, known as the Marwaris (see pp372), have retained their entrepreneurial skills and continue to run many of India's leading business houses. The special riding breeches, known the world over as jodhpurs, were designed here.

Clock, Umaid Bhavan Palace

🏰 Mehrangarh Fort
See pp382–3.

🏛 Sardar Bazaar
⏱ daily.

Jodhpur's bazaar lies in the heart of the old city, which is surrounded by a 10-km (6-mile) wall, pierced by eight gates. Clustered around a clock tower (built in 1912), the bazaar is a fascinating area to explore, with its little shops selling silver jewellery, lacquer bangles, tie-dyed fabrics, soft camel leather shoes, puppets, clay figurines and colourful heaps of sweets and spices. The pavements are lined with henna artists who decorate women's palms with intricate, lacy patterns.

An interesting building in this area is the early 17th-century **Taleti Mahal**, its carved balconies supported by temple pillars. Built for a favourite royal concubine, it now houses a school. There are several other beautiful houses in the bazaar area, mostly made of red sandstone and heavily carved.

🏰 Jaswant Thada
⏱ daily. 📷

This elegant pillared marble memorial with fine lattice carving is the *chhatri* (cenotaph) of Maharaja Jaswant Singh II (r.1878–95), whose innovative irrigation schemes brought water and prosperity to this parched land. Local people, who

JODHPUR CITY CENTRE

0 metres 500
0 yards 500

MANDORE, OSIAN & Balsamand

OLD CITY

Padamsar Talab
Ranisar Talab
NOVECHOKIA ROAD

① Mehrangarh Fort
Clock Tower
Sardar ② Bazaar
Mertia Gate
MERTIA GATE

Jaswant ③ Thada
Nagauri Gate
MANDORE ROAD

JAIPUR

Paota Bus Stand
Raika Bagh Station

Umaid Gardens

RAIKA BAGH

NAI SARAK

Sojati Gate

Jalori Gate
M.G. HOSPITAL ROAD
STATION RD
Jodhpur Station

Sardar Samand Lake

GAUSALA ROAD
NAYANDA ROAD
AIRPORT ROAD

UMAID BHAVAN ROAD

④ Umaid Bhavan Palace

Airport 4 km (2.5 miles)

Key to Symbols see back flap

Umaid Bhavan Palace, a fusion of Rajput, Jain and Art Deco styles

believe the maharaja has retained his healing touch, come regularly to offer prayer and flowers at his shrine. Cenotaphs of subsequent rulers and members of the royal families are also located here, though earlier rulers have their memorials at Mandore.

Umaid Bhavan Palace

daily.

This immense palace, built of creamy-pink sandstone and marble, is a prime example of princely India's opulence. Its 347 rooms include eight dining halls, two theatres, a ballroom, several lavishly decorated reception halls and a vast underground swimming pool. A 60-m (197-ft) dome covers the cavernous central hall which, at its inauguration, seated 1,000 people for dinner.

The palace was commissioned by Maharaja Umaid Singh, apparently to create jobs for his famine-stricken subjects. Begun in 1929, it took 3,000 men 15 years to complete; 19 km (12 miles) of railway tracks were also laid to bring the sandstone from the quarry. HV Lanchester, the architect of the Central Hall of Westminster in London, created a pleasing fusion of Rajput, Jain and European Art Deco styles for his royal patron.

Umaid Singh's grandson, Gaj Singh, still lives in a section of the palace, while the rest has been turned into a luxury hotel. The palace museum is open to visitors and has an impressive collection of decorated weapons, watches and fantastically-shaped clocks, paintings, French furniture and porcelain.

The road in front of it, leading to the smaller Ajit Bhavan Palace, is lined with antique shops.

Environs

Mandore, 9 km (6 miles) north of Jodhpur, was the capital of the Rathore kings of Marwar until the 15th century, when Rao Jodha built a new capital at Jodhpur. Set around terraced garden on a hillside are the red sandstone *chhatris* of Jodhpur's earlier rulers. The most imposing is that of Ajit Singh with its towering temple-like spire. When he died in 1724, his six wives and 58 concubines committed *sati* on his funeral pyre. The Hall of Heroes has 15 life-size statues of religious deities and folk heroes. Further up the hill are the queens' cenotaphs (Raniyon ki Chhatri) and the tall and narrow 17th-century Ek Thamba Mahal Palace.

Balsamand, 6 km (4 miles) north of Jodhpur, has the 19th-century red sandstone water palace of the maharajas beside a large artificial lake. The **Sardar Samand Lake**, 55 km (34 miles) south of Jodhpur, attracts several water birds including egrets, ibis and pelicans. On its shores are the maharajas' Art Deco-style hunting lodge. The drive here passes through interesting Bishnoi villages *(see p385)*.

Jaswant Thada, the 19th-century cenotaph of Maharaja Jaswant Singh II

BHOPA BALLADEERS

Like the troubadours of medieval Europe, the nomadic Bhopa tribe of western Rajasthan enjoys a lively tradition of storytelling through song and dance. A long painted scroll (known as a *phad*) is, rather like a comic strip, crammed with paintings depicting dramatic events in the life of a Marwar hero, the brave warrior Pabuji. The Bhopa unrolls his scroll, and narrates the story through songs, highlighting relevant pictures on the scroll with a lantern, while his wife brings the tale to life with animated dance sequences. The Bhopas' performances draw enthusiastic crowds at fairs and festivals across the Marwar region.

Painted scroll used by Bhopas

Jodhpur: Mehrangarh Fort

Sati handprints on Loha Pol

Rising sheer out of a 125-m (410-ft) high rock, Mehrangarh is perhaps the most majestic of Rajasthan's forts. Described by an awe-struck Rudyard Kipling as "the creation of angels, fairies and giants", Mehrangarh's forbidding ramparts are in sharp contrast to the flamboyantly decorated palaces within. Founded by Rao Jodha in 1459, the sandstone fort was added to by later rulers, mostly between the mid-17th and mid-19th centuries. The royal apartments within the fort now form part of an outstanding museum.

Chamundi Devi Mandir is dedicated to the goddess Durga in her wrathful aspect.

The Ramparts
The bastioned walls, parts of which are hewn out of the rock itself, are in places 24-m (79-ft) thick and 40-m (131-ft) high. Perched on them are old cannons.

Nagnechiaji Mandir has a 14th-century image of the goddess Kuldevi, the family deity of the rulers.

Zenana Chowk

★ Phool Mahal
Built between 1730 and 1750, this is the fort's most opulent chamber, richly gilded and painted. It was used for royal celebrations.

Suraj Pol is the entrance to the museum.

Palki Khana

Shringar Chowk

Carved balconies crown the towering bastions.

Shringar Chowk
This courtyard has the coronation throne of the Jodhpur rulers, made of white marble. Every ruler after Rao Jodha was crowned on it.

STAR SIGHTS

★ Phool Mahal

★ Moti Mahal

The blue-washed houses of Brahmapuri village, clustered below the ramparts of Mehrangarh Fort

VISITORS' CHECKLIST

Mehrangarh Fort and Museum ☐ daily. **i** Museum Trust, (0291) 254 8790. 🖼 📷 extra charges. 🍴 🛍 🚻 ♿

Chokelao Palace, now under restoration, was a pleasure palace built around a sunken garden.

★ Moti Mahal

Built between 1581 and 1595, this magnificent room was the Hall of Private Audience. Its ceiling is decorated with mirrors and gold leaf, and crushed seashells were mixed with plaster to give its walls a lustrous sheen.

Takhat Mahal

This exuberantly painted room with a wooden ceiling was the favourite retreat of Maharaja Takhat Singh (r.1843–73), who had 30 queens and numerous concubines.

Jhanki Mahal is a long gallery with exquisite latticed stone screens.

Phool Mahal

Sileh Khana's exceptional collection of weapons includes damascened Mughal daggers, gem-studded shields, and special armour for war elephants.

Jai Pol

One of the seven fortified gates to the fort, it is now the main entrance. It was built in 1806 by Maharaja Man Singh to commemorate a victory in battle.

For hotels and restaurants in this region see pp702–5 and pp731–2

Exploring Mehrangarh Fort Museum

The Mehrangarh Fort Museum is justly regarded as the best of the many palace museums in Rajasthan. Its rich and varied collection includes a golden throne, fine miniature paintings, traditional costumes and fascinating weapons. Particularly magnificent are the skilfully restored royal chambers, which present a vivid picture of princely life and culture in Rajasthan.

Maharaja's cradle with a mechanical rocking system, in Jhanki Mahal

The entrance to the museum is through the Suraj Pol on the fort's southeastern side. Inside, to the right, is the **Palki Khana** with a collection of richly gilded palanquins. Along with the impressive elephant howdahs on display in the **Howdah Gallery** next door, these reflect the importance of grand processions in courtly life. Particularly impressive is a 17th-century howdah made of solid silver, a gift from the Mughal emperor Shah Jahan. Another treasure is a spectacular palanquin covered in gold leaf, dating to 1730. This stands in the **Daulat Khana** (Treasury Hall), just before the **Sileh Khana** with its superb collection of weapons.

From here, steps lead up to the **Umaid Mahal**, which exhibits miniature paintings of the Jodhpur School. Heavily influenced by the Mughal style, these paintings provide fascinating vignettes of life at court – the rulers riding camels with their courtesans, playing polo and leading ceremonial processions. Here too is a grand silk canopy, that was used by the rulers for outdoor camps.

A gem-studded rhino-hide shield

The next chamber, on the floor above, is the splendidly gilded, 18th-century **Phool Mahal** ("Flower Palace"), the Hall of Public Audience. It also has superb miniatures, including a set of 36 *Ragamala* paintings that depict the moods of various musical ragas.

The 19th-century **Takhat Mahal**, the chamber of a pleasure-loving ruler, is exuberantly painted with murals of Radha and Krishna and dancing maidens. The glass Christmas tree balls hanging from the ceiling were added in the 1930s. **Sardar Vilas**, just below Takhat Mahal, showcases Jodhpur's fine woodwork. Particularly striking is a door inlaid with ivory.

The next chamber is **Jhanki Mahal** or "Peeping Palace", so called because the women of the royal zenana could peep through its latticed stone screens to observe the ceremonies and festivities in the courtyards below. It now has a collection of royal cradles, including one with an ingenious mechanical rocking system, surmounted by guardian angels. From here a courtyard leads to the 16th-century **Moti Mahal** or "Pearl Palace". A palmist sits in the courtyard to foretell the futures of visitors.

The museum also has a fine collection of Rajasthani turbans and folk music instruments. Rooms displaying costumes, royal tents and special treasures are under preparation.

Environs

Osian, 64 km (40 miles) northwest of Jodhpur, is the site of 16 outstanding Jain and Hindu temples. Built by wealthy traders between the 8th and 12th centuries, when Osian was an important stop on the caravan trade route to Central Asia, they represent the earliest phase of temple architecture in Rajasthan.

Famous for the rich variety and exuberance of their sculptural decoration are the 11 temples at the southern and western edge of Osian village. Of these, the most impressive is the 8th-century **Mahavira Temple** with a superb ceiling and 20 carved pillars holding up the main portico. Equally beautiful are the classically elegant 10th-century **Sun Temple** and the profusely sculpted **Vishnu** and **Harihara Temples**, from the 8th–9th centuries.

The other temples are on a hill east of the village, dominated by the 12th-century **Sachiya Mata Temple**, approached through a series of beautifully carved arches. This temple is particularly popular with infertile women who believe that Sachiya Mata, an incarnation of Durga, has special powers to help them bear children.

Sachiya Mata Temple, Osian

For hotels and restaurants in this region see pp702–5 and pp731–2

Tour of Marwar Crafts Villages ⑯

The arid countryside south of Jodhpur is dotted with villages, their mud and thatch huts inhabited by the Bishnois and communities of potters and weavers. A daylong tour of this area provides a memorable opportunity to observe the rhythm of daily life in these hamlets, experience the warm hospitality of the villagers, and see beautiful traditional crafts being practised.

TIPS FOR DRIVERS

Length: 55 km (34 miles).
Getting around: Allow 6–7 hours for the trip. Refreshments are available at Gudda Bishnoi, Salawas and Kakuni. The heritage hotels at Rohet and Luni (Fort Chanwa) offer good food and are pleasant places for a break. Hotels and travel agencies in Jodhpur can arrange taxis. A four-wheel drive is recommended.

JAISALMER

Jodhpur ①
This historic and beautiful city is on the edge of the Thar Desert.

AJMER

Salawas ③
The villagers here are skilled weavers of *dhurries* (rugs) in traditional geometric patterns and vegetable colours. They are made of cotton or camel hair.

Gudda Bishnoi ②
The Bishnois in this hamlet tend camels and goats. The men wear only white, but the women wear vivid colours and silver jewellery.

KHEJARLI

Mogra

Kakuni ④
This village, 26 km (16 miles) south of Jodhpur, is famous for its pottery, made of the fine local clay.

Luni

Rohet ⑤
The 17th-century palace-fort here is now a heritage hotel (*see p704*), surrounded by villages of leather craftsmen.

THE BISHNOIS

The Bishnois, passionate environmentalists, are followers of a 15th-century sage, Jambeshwar, whose creed is contained in 29 (*bis noi*) principles. Most of these focus on environmental protection, and the Bishnois' faith bids them to protect every living being, if necessary with their lives. Thus, the otherwise timid blackbuck can be seen roaming freely near Bishnoi villages, confident that it will be unharmed. Bishnois believe they will be reborn as deer.

Bishnoi woman

KEY

▬▬ Tour route

══ Other roads

═══ River

⑤

PALI,
RANAKPUR,
KUMBHALGARH

0 km 3
0 miles 3

Jaisalmer ⑰

Today a remote outpost in the Thar Desert, Jaisalmer was founded in the 12th century by Maharawal Jaisal of the Bhatti Rajput clan. It was once a flourishing trade centre, strategically located on the busy caravan trade route to Afghanistan and Central Asia. Its earlier rulers grew rich by looting gems, silk and opium from the caravans, but by the 16th century Jaisalmer had become a peaceful town, whose wealthy traders and rulers vied with each other to beautify their austere desert surroundings with splendid palaces and *havelis*. Made of the local golden-yellow sandstone, they are the most spectacular examples of the Rajasthani stonemason's art. In the 18th century, with the growth of sea ports at Surat and Bombay (Mumbai), Jaisalmer's importance dwindled. But the buildings from its golden age still stand, clustered around a magnificent fort *(see pp388–9)*.

VISITORS' CHECKLIST

Jaisalmer district. 285 kms (177 miles) W of Jodhpur. 🚂 58,300. 🚉 🚌 🛈 *Tourist Reception Centre, Station Rd, (02992) 25 2406.* 🎪 *Desert Festival (Feb), Gangaur Festival (Mar/Apr).*

🏛 Manik Chowk

Located at the entrance to the fort, this is the main marketplace, where caravans used to halt in the past. The tiny shops sell camel hair blankets and gorgeous embroidered textiles. Desert nomads and their camels add to the bazaars' colour.

⛩ Badal Vilas

Near Amar Sagar Gate. ⬜ *daily.*
This late 19th-century palace is distinguished by its multi-tiered tower in the shape of a *tazia* – the ornately decorated tower of wood, metal and coloured paper, carried by Shia Muslims at Muharram *(see p669)*. The Tazia Tower of Badal Vilas, built in the mid-20th century, was a parting gift to the maharawal

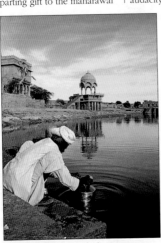
Gadisagar Lake, lined with ghats

from the town's Shia stone-carvers, many of whom moved to Pakistan after Independence.

🏞 Gadisagar Lake

SE of the city walls.
This rainwater reservoir, built in 1367, was once the city's sole source of water. Lined with ghats and temples, it comes alive during the Gangaur festival (March/April), when the maharawal leads a procession here. The beautiful gateway leading to the tank was built by a royal courtesan, Telia, whose audacity so enraged the queens that they demanded its instant demolition. The quick-witted Telia immediately had a statue of Krishna installed on top, thereby ensuring not only that the gateway would stand, but that everyone would bow before passing through it.

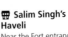
Jaisalmeri smoking a hookah

⛩ Salim Singh's Haveli

Near the Fort entrance. *Local guides can arrange visits for a fee.*
This *haveli* was built in 1815 by a powerful prime minister of Jaisalmer. Narrow at the base, its six storeys grow wider at each level, and all its 38 balconies have different designs. Peacocks dance between the arches on the topmost balcony, and blue cupolas cap the roof. The rear portion of this *haveli* was, sadly, damaged during the Gujarat earthquake in January 2001, but visitors are still allowed in.

⛩ Nathmalji's Haveli

Near Gandhi Chowk. *Local guides can arrange visits for a fee.*
Built in 1855 by another prime minister of Jaisalmer, the particular charm of this five-storeyed mansion is that the two sides of its façade were carved by two craftsman-brothers, Hathu and Lallu. Though at first glance they seem identical, the details on each side are actually quite different. Besides the usual floral, geometric and animal patterns, this *haveli's* motifs also reflect new influences – a European-style horse and carriage, bicycles and steam engines.

⛩ Patwon ki Haveli

E of Nathmalji's Haveli. ⬜ *daily.*
This enormous and very elaborate *haveli* was built between 1805 and 1855 by Guman Chand Patwa, one of Jaisalmer's richest merchants and bankers, who dealt in silk, brocade and opium, and had a chain of trading stations stretching from Afghanistan to China. This six-storeyed mansion has five adjoining apartments for each of his sons, and 66 balconies. The curved eaves on the balconies suggest a fleet of sailing boats, and the numerous latticed windows are carved with breathtaking intricacy.

The Jaisalmer Haveli

After the fort, Jaisalmer's *havelis* are its greatest attraction. Built in the 19th century by the town's merchants and ministers, these mansions dominate its labyrinthine lanes. The *havelis* of Salim Singh, Nathmalji and Patwon are the finest examples of this type of architecture, their golden stone façades so finely carved that they could be made of lace. Several generations of an extended family lived together in these huge mansions, which usually contained secluded women's quarters that outsiders could not enter. Jaisalmer's stonemasons still practise their art, doing restoration work in the fort, and working abroad for wealthy new patrons in the Gulf and Saudi Arabia.

Carved elephant

The entrance *of most* havelis *is on a plinth, raised high above street level, to prevent the desert sand from blowing into the rooms. The ground floor had no living rooms, and was usually used as a warehouse or storeroom.*

The inner courtyard, *found in all* havelis, *was a protected place for children to play in, and for women to attend to their daily chores in privacy.*

Jharokhas, *or projecting balconies, have curved* bangaldar *eaves. Their purpose was more decorative than functional, and they gave the stonemasons an opportunity to display the full range of their creativity and skill.*

Jalis, *or latticed stone screens, display a rich variety of patterns. They keep out the harsh desert sun but let in fresh air. They also enabled women to observe street life without being seen.*

Yellow sandstone *lends itself particularly well to fine carving. Soft when newly quarried, the stone gradually becomes harder with exposure.*

Narrow streets *in the neighbourhood of Patwon ki Haveli, lined with intricately carved façades, retain their traditional ambience.*

Jaisalmer Fort

Detail from Jaisalmer Fort

Jaisalmer Fort rises like a fabulous mirage out of the sands of the Thar Desert, the awesome contours of its 99 bastions softened by the golden hue of the stone. Built in 1156 by Maharawal Jaisal, and added to by his successors, this citadel stands on the peak of the 80-m (263-ft) high Trikuta Hill. In medieval times, Jaisalmer's entire population lived within the fort and even now, thousands of people reside here, making it India's only living fort. Royal palaces, a cluster of Jain temples, mansions and shops are all contained within its walls.

The southern ramparts, built of stone without any mortar

Gyan Bhandar, in the basement of the Sambhavnatha Temple, is a library of illustrated Jain palm-leaf manuscripts, some of them dating to the 11th century.

Intricate sandstone carvings are found in these seven temples dedicated to the Jain *tirthankaras*, including Rishabdeo, Sambhavnatha Parsvanatha and others.

★ **Jain Temples**
Exquisitely carved Jain temples were built in the 15th and 16th centuries by the town's wealthy traders.

The ramparts, with an inner parallel wall, have huge cannonballs perched on top, ready to crush invaders.

JAISALMER IN JEOPARDY

The growth of tourism together with recent efforts to green the nearby desert have, ironically, posed a threat to the fort. Built for an arid climate that hardly ever experienced rainfall, the fort had no provision for water supply or drainage. Now, with rising ground water levels in the area, and the introduction of piped water in the fort, seepage has made the golden stone crumble in places. Conservation efforts by Indian and international organizations are now under way to save this unique fort and town.

The 12th-century Jaisalmer Fort, threatened by rising damp

STAR SIGHTS

★ Jain Temples

★ Moti Mahal

★ Dussehra Chowk

For hotels and restaurants in this region see pp702–5 and pp731–2

Royal Complex
The seven-storeyed palace complex consists of several interconnected palaces, built between the 16th and 19th centuries.

VISITORS' CHECKLIST

Jaisalmer Fort. 🛈 *Rajasthan Tourism, Station Rd, (02992) 25 2406.* ◯ *daily.* 📷 ◎ *extra charges.* 🚻 👖 🎫
Jain Temples ◯ *daily.* 📷 *extra charges.* **Gyan Bhandar** ◯ *daily.*

Annapurna Bhandar was originally the fort's granary. Its ground floor has a temple.

Moti Mahal

Sarvottam Vilas
Brilliant blue tiles and glass mosaic work decorate this mid-18th century palace.

Naqqar Khana, or "Drummers' Gallery", has a richly carved octagonal balcony.

★ **Moti Mahal**
Floral paintings and carved doors embellish this 18th-century palace.

Rani Mahal

★ **Dussehra Chowk**
Festivals, royal performances and parades took place in this open plaza, framed by the palace complex. The rulers' marble throne overlooks the plaza.

Exploring Jaisalmer's Outer Sights

The environs of Jaisalmer are dotted with sites of both architectural and natural beauty. These include beautiful temples, the haunting ruins of the old capital, a fascinating desert village, rolling sand dunes, and the habitat of a rare desert bird, the great Indian bustard.

Manganiyar musicians, whose ballads recount Jaisalmer's history

🏛 Bhattiani Rani Temple

2 km (1.3 miles) S of fort. ◻ daily.
This secluded Hindu shrine was built in honour of a 19th-century Jaisalmer princess who, surprisingly, committed *sati* on her brother-in-law's funeral pyre. A clan of Muslim musicians, the Manganiyars, are the caretakers of the temple, and recount this story, with its intriguing undertones, in their soulful ballads about Jaisalmer's history.

🏛 Bada Bagh

7 km (4 miles) N of fort. 📷
The royal cenotaphs, with elaborately carved ceilings and fine equestrian statues of the rulers, are set in a green oasis. Next to them is the Bhaironji Temple, frequented by childless women who offer their silver girdles to the deity, in the hope that he will cure their infertility.

🏛 Lodurva

15 km (9 miles) NW of Jaisalmer.
The capital of the Bhatti Rajputs before they built the fort at Jaisalmer, Lodurva was abandoned after it was sacked by Muslim invaders in the 11th century. A group of Jain temples dominates this site, where the remains of many other fine buildings lie concealed beneath the desert sands. A beautiful *torana*

leads to the main temple, which houses a metal sculpture of the Kalpavriksha ("Celestial Tree"). It is believed to have wish-fulfilling powers.

🌿 Akal Fossil Park

17 km (11 miles) SE of Jaisalmer.
◻ daily. 📷 📷
Extraordinary fossilized tree trunks, some of them 180 million years old, can be seen in this park. They bear witness to the fact that this arid area was once covered with dense forest.

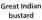

Great Indian bustard

🌿 Khuri

40 km (25 miles) SW of Jaisalmer.
Set among sand dunes, this little village is a superb example of desert architecture. Functional as well as beautiful, the village houses have thick mud walls that provide protection against the fierce desert heat and winds, while

the paintings that decorate their exteriors bring colour and beauty to the brown, parched environs.

🦅 Desert National Park

43 km (27 miles) W of Jaisalmer. *For permission, contact Collector's Office, Jaisalmer, (02992) 25 2201.* 📷 📷 *Jeep & Camel safaris.*
This fascinating park is spread over 3,162 sq km (1,221 sq miles) of scrub and sandy wasteland, close to the border with Pakistan. Its star attraction is the great Indian bustard (*Choriotis nigriceps*), a large bird with a height of 1.2 m (4 ft). The bustard had been hunted almost to extinction, and only about 1,000 remain now, but sightings are likely here. Other wildlife includes sand grouse, several species of falcon and vulture, desert fox, and *chinkara* (Indian gazelle).

Barmer ⑲

Barmer district. 160 km (99 miles) SE of Jaisalmer. 🚉 🚌 ℹ *Rajasthan Tourism, Khartal, (02982) 22 2956.* ☒ *Tilwara Cattle Fair (Jan/Feb), Thar Desert Festival (Mar).*

This remote desert town, whose arid soil cannot support agriculture, has become a major centre for desert handicrafts. Wood-carving, blockprinted textiles, embroidery and carpet weaving are the main source of livelihood for its people. They also lavish their skills on their mud huts, which are beautifully decorated with geometric and floral patterns. Barmer buzzes with activity during the annual Tilwara Fair (January/February), one of the many large cattle fairs in Rajasthan.

Visitors on a camel safari near Jaisalmer

Camel Safari around Jaisalmer ⑱

Window of a desert mud house

The fascinating desertscape around Jaisalmer is best explored on a camel safari. A two-day excursion takes in historic sights and villages of sheep and camel herders. Overnight stays in tents offer magical dawns and sunsets amid the dunes. Cushions are provided, but riders are advised to carry an extra one, to help soften the effects of the camel's lurching gait.

TIPS FOR RIDERS

Duration: Two days and two nights. **Day 1:** Jaisalmer to Lodurva via Bada Bagh and Ramkunda, 18 km (11 miles). **Day 2:** Lodurva to Sam via Kahala and Kanoi, 20 km (12 miles); Sam to Jaisalmer (by jeep), 45 km (28 miles). **Overnight stays:** Camps at Lodurva and Sam. For more details on safaris see p751; for tour operators see p755.

Jaisalmer ①
The camels set off from the First Gate of Jaisalmer's magnificent 12th-century fort.

Bada Bagh ②
The cenotaphs of the maharawals (rulers) of Jaisalmer are surrounded by green mango groves and thorny *khejri (Prosopis cineraria)* trees.

KISHANGARH

Baramsar

Ramkunda ③
A picnic lunch is served at this little village with a 15th-century Shiva temple.

Damodara

NH15

BIKANER

NH15

BARMER

Kuldhera

Kanoi ⑥
The older houses in this village are painted with flowers, animals and birds. The village craftsmen make elaborately carved camel saddles inlaid with brass.

Kahala ⑤
This hamlet of mud houses is inhabited by herders of goats and sheep. They also weave attractive blankets.

Lodurva ④
The night is spent at the old capital of the maharawals, which has lovely Jain temples. Dinner is served under a star-studded sky.

| 0 km | 5 |
| 0 miles | 5 |

KEY

▬ Tour route

═ Other roads

▬ National highway

Sam ⑦
Rippling sand dunes stretch as far as the eye can see. The 45-km (28-mile) journey back to Jaisalmer the next morning is by jeep.

The City Palace, Udaipur *(see pp400–401)*, reflected in the waters of Lake Pichola ▷

The intricately carved Vimala Vasahi Temple

Mount Abu ⑳

Sirohi district. 185 km (115 miles) W of Udaipur. 🏔 22,100. 🚉 Abu Rd, 20 km (12 miles) SE of town centre, then bus. 🚌 ℹ️ opp main bus station, (02974) 23 5151. 🎪 Summer Festival (Jun).

Rajasthan's only hill station, Mount Abu has one of India's most spectacular sights – the **Dilwara Jain Temples**. This group of five marble temples is situated on a hill 3 km (2 miles) northeast of the town. The two most outstanding are the **Vimala Vasahi Temple** and the **Luna Vasahi Temple** which have incredibly intricate and delicate carvings. The sculptural details on the various doorways, archways, pillars and ceilings of both these temples are simply breathtaking, the marble worked so finely that in places it is almost translucent.

The Vimala Vasahi Temple, dedicated to the first Jain *tirthankara*, Adinath, was built in 1031 by Vimala Shah, a wealthy prime minister of the Solanki kings of Gujarat. A statue of him seated on an elephant is in a pavilion to the right of the entrance. Inside, graceful nymphs and musicians, spirited horses and elephants adorn the arches and pillars, and the superb 11-tiered domed ceiling in the main hall. The inner sanctum has a statue of Adinath in tranquil meditation, while 52 carved niches contain images of the other *tirthankaras*.

The Luna Vasahi Temple, dedicated to Neminath, the 22nd Jain tirthankara, dates to 1231 and is even more ornately carved. Its most glorious feature, the main hall, has a magnificent lotus-shaped, tiered pendant carved from a single block of marble, descending from its domed ceiling. Behind the main shrine is the fascinating Hall of Donors, with a series of figures mounted on elephants, some in black marble. There are also life-size statues of the donors and their wives, with every detail of their dress and jewellery exquisitely and painstakingly carved.

The focal point of Mount Abu town is **Nakki Lake**, ringed by colonial mansions dating to the late 19th century, and the summer palaces of Rajput rulers. The curiously shaped **Toad's Rock** overlooks the lake, and **Sunset Point**, southwest of the lake, offers some spectacular views from a stone terrace.

About 4 km (2.5 miles) below Mount Abu, just off the main highway leading to the town, is the historic **Gaumukh** ("Cow's Mouth") **Temple** with a natural spring flowing from the mouth of a marble cow.

Dancer, Luna Vasahi Temple

> 🏛 **Dilwara Jain Temples**
> ◯ daily. ⬤ to menstruating women.
> Leather articles are not allowed inside.

Environs

Achalgarh, 8 km (5 miles) beyond Dilwara, has the ruins of a 15th-century fort, and a Shiva temple. The latter has a statue of Nandi made with over 4,000 kg (8,819 lbs) of gold, silver, brass and copper. A five-minute walk from the temple is **Guru Shikhar**, Rajasthan's highest point at 1,721 m (5,646 ft). It is marked by a small but exquisite Vishnu temple.

Ranakpur ㉑

Rajsamand district. 90 km (56 miles) NW of Udaipur. 🚌 **Temple Complex** ◯ daily. ⬤ to menstruating women. Leather articles are not allowed inside.

Set in a secluded, wooded valley of the Aravalli Hills, the 15th-century Ranakpur temple complex, dominated by the great **Adinath Temple**, is one of the five great holy places of the Jain faith. The grand scale and sheer architectural complexity of the white marble temple distinguish it as perhaps the single most impressive example of Western Indian temple architecture *(see pp396–7)*. The temple has an unusual four-sided plan, with four separate entrances. Each entrance leads through a veritable forest of columns, and a number of beautifully ornamented halls and chapels, to the central sanctum containing a four-faced image of Adinath.

Each of the temple's 1,444 pillars is carved with different patterns of floral motifs, and the play of light and shadow

View of the Jain temple complex at Ranakpur

The winding ramparts of the indomitable Kumbhalgarh Fort

on the pillars, as the sun moves from east to west each day, is one of the glories of this monument. Equally stunning is the superb filigree carving on the concentric ceiling pendants, and the exuberant grace of the goddesses who form the support brackets. On one of the columns facing the sanctum, a carved panel with two figures on it depicts Dharna Shah, the builder of the temple, who was a minister of the maharana of Mewar, and his architect, Depa.

A wall topped with spires surrounds this serene temple complex, which also has a Hindu Sun Temple, and two other Jain temples. Of these, the 15th-century Parsvanatha Temple is distinguished by the exceptionally fine pierced stonework on its windows.

Kumbhalgarh ㉒

Rajsamand district. 63 km (39 miles) N of Udaipur. 🚉 *Kankroli, 35 km (21 miles) SE of Kumbhalgarh, then bus.* 🚌 📷

Like a gigantic brown snake, the great ramparts of Kumbhalgarh Fort wind along the rugged contours of the Aravalli Hills for 36 km (22 miles). This massive 15th-century fort, strategically located at a height of 1,050 m (3,445 ft) along the border between Marwar (Jodhpur) and Mewar (Udaipur), was

known as "The Eye of Mewar", because it offered a commanding view of the countryside for miles around. Built by Maharana Kumbha (r.1433–68), who also built the great fort of Chittorgarh (see p330), Kumbhalgarh was justly reputed to be the most impregnable fort in Rajasthan. Its ramparts are wide enough for six horsemen to ride abreast, and seven fortified gates, studded with threatening spikes, lead to its entrance.

The crenellated walls of the fort enclose the smaller fortress of Kartargarh, several palaces and temples now in ruins, fields, water reservoirs and stables. Standing at the highest point of the fort is the **Badal Mahal**, a 19th-century addition with airy chambers and fine wall paintings of hunting scenes. The 15th-century **Neelkantha Temple**,

A deity on the fort wall, believed to prevent evil happenings

which also lies within the fort, has a huge Shivalinga and is still in use.

Another interesting temple, the **Navachoki Mamdeva Temple**, is in a gorge to the east of Kartargarh. It contains several slabs of black granite inscribed with the history of Mewar, the earliest slab dating to 1491. Next to it is the cenotaph of Maharana Kumbha.

Kumbhalgarh was also the birthplace of Maharana Pratap (1540–97), a great warrior king famous for his heroic stand against the armies of the Mughal emperor Akbar.

Environs

The **Kumbhalgarh Wildlife Sanctuary** covers 578 sq km (223 sq miles) of the Aravalli Hills, west of the fort, on the leeward side. Panther, flying squirrel, wolf and many bird species can be seen here.

Kankroli, 35 km (21 miles) southeast of Kumbhalgarh, has the 17th-century Dwarkadhish Temple on the southern shore of Rajsamand Lake. The western shore is lined with lovely marble pavilions and ghats.

The charming little town of **Deogarh**, 55 km (34 miles) north of Kumbhalgarh, set among lakes and hills, has the 17th-century Rajmahal Palace with exquisite wall murals, and the Anjaneshwar Mahadev Temple in a cave in the hillside. Deogarh is also a popular base for horse safaris which explore this picturesque part of Mewar.

Marblework in Jain Temples

Detail from Ranakpur

Rajasthan's most outstanding Jain temples, at Ranakpur and at Dilwara in Mount Abu *(see p394)*, are breathtaking in the wealth and variety of their sculptural ornamentation. Made of white marble quarried at Makrana, which also provided the marble for the Taj Mahal, the Ranakpur and Dilwara temples are architectual marvels. Above all, they are testimony to the incredible artistry of the marble carvers who created these masterpieces. Visitors should use binoculars to fully appreciate the astounding work on the ceilings and pillars.

This four-faced image of Adinath, *the first* tirthankara, *stands in Ranakpur's main sanctum. It faces the four cardinal directions.*

THE JAIN RELIGION

Jain nuns with covered mouths

Jainism, founded in the 6th century BC, is based on a doctrine of non-violence towards all living beings. Jains are strict vegetarians, and the more orthodox ones cover their mouths to avoid inadvertently swallowing living organisms. Jains believe in 24 *tirthankaras* or crossing-makers, enlightened beings who guide others across the "river of transmigration" (the journey of the soul from one life to the next). The first of the *tirthankaras* was Adinath, also known as Rishabdeo, and the last was Mahavira (born in 540 BC). Regarded as the religion's founder, his 2,600th birth anniversary was celebrated in 2001. Jainism attracted many followers among the wealthy traders and merchants of Western India, who were also politically powerful as financiers and ministers in Rajput princely states. As acts of devotion and penance, they financed the building of several elaborately carved temples in Gujarat and Rajasthan.

HALL OF PILLARS

A forest of carved columns connected by wavy arches leads to the main sanctum at Dilwara's Vimala Vasahi Temple. It was built in the 11th century.

EXTERIOR

The uncarved exterior of Ranakpur's 15th-century Adinath Temple contrasts sharply with the profuse decoration inside. This symbolizes the Jain belief in the insignificance of outward forms, and the importance of a rich inner life.

CORBELLED CEILINGS

The ceilings are carved in concentric tiers to symbolize the Jain view of the universe as a series of cosmic cycles. Marble carvers were paid in gold according to the weight of the marble shavings they presented at the end of each day's work.

Dancers and deities, *gracefully sculpted, are the struts that support the ceiling.*

This Ranakpur ceiling *is a typical example of the Rajasthani marble carvers' art. It is so finely worked that the marble is translucent in places.*

Sculptured panels *at Ranakpur show dancers full of grace and movement.*

Pillars *in Dilwara are densely carved with floral motifs and figures in niches. No two pillars are identical in their ornamentation.*

Kalpavalli medallions, *with their exquisite patterns of foliage, tendrils and flowers, feature at both Dilwara and Ranakpur.*

The Parsvanatha plaque *shows the 23rd tirthankara protected by a multi-headed cobra. It is set into the southern wall of the Adinath Temple at Ranakpur.*

Udaipur ㉓

This fairy-tale city, with its marble palaces and lakes surrounded by a ring of hills, was founded by Maharana Udai Singh in 1559, and became the capital of Mewar after the fall of Chittorgarh in 1567 *(see p402)*. The rulers of Mewar, who belonged to the Sisodia clan of Rajputs, traced their dynasty back to AD 566. Fiercely independent, they refused matrimonial alliances with the Mughals, and took great pride in their reputation as the prime defenders of Rajput honour. The city is dominated by the massive City Palace, which overlooks Lake Pichola with its romantic island palaces. Picturesque *havelis*, ghats and temples line the lake front, with the lively bazaars of the old walled city stretching behind them.

A view of Lake Pichola, with the Jag Mandir Palace on an island

Jag Niwas, or the Lake Palace, in its magical setting on Lake Pichola

City Palace
See pp400–401.

Jag Mandir
Lake Pichola. ◯ *daily.* ▭ *City Palace Jetty.* ▨ **Jag Niwas** *Tel* (0294) 252 8016. ⑪ *open to non-residents.*

Jag Mandir, with its lush gardens and marble chambers exquisitely inlaid with coloured stone, was built in 1620. Eight stone elephants stand solemn guard at its entrance. Between 1623 and 1624, this island palace provided refuge to Prince Khurram (who would later become the Mughal emperor Shah Jahan) while he rebelled against his father. It is believed to have inspired some of his ideas for the Taj Mahal.

Jag Niwas, or the Lake Palace, built between 1734 and 1751, was once a royal summer retreat and is now one of the world's great hotels *(see p705)*. It is also a popular location for film shoots (including James Bond's *Octopussy*). Both palaces can be seen on a boat tour of Lake Pichola.

Jagdish Mandir
Moti Chhohta Rd. ◯ *daily.*
Bagore ki Haveli Gangaur Ghat.
Tel (0294) 25 3858 ▨

This 17th-century temple, just north of the City Palace's main gate, has an enormous black stone image of Vishnu in its profusely carved main shrine. The entrance is flanked by stone elephants, and a superb bronze image of Garuda (the mythical bird who is Vishnu's vehicle) stands in front of the temple. Nearby, at Gangaur Ghat, is the 18th-century **Bagore ki Haveli**, now a museum exhibiting Udaipur's traditional arts and crafts, costumes, musical instruments and marblework. Folk music and dance performances are held here every evening at 7pm.

Pichhwai painting

The old walled city, a jumble of shops and houses, many with beautifully painted façades, lies east of the Jagdish Mandir. In its narrow, lanes are the **Bapu** and **Bara Bazaars**, selling wooden toys, puppets, textiles, jewels and *pichhwais*.

🎣 Fateh Sagar Lake
Fateh Sagar Rd.
North of Lake Pichola is Fateh Sagar Lake, with a garden café on its island. Overlooking it is Moti Magri Hill with a statue of Udaipur's great 16th-century warrior, Maharana Pratap, and his valiant steed, Chetak.

🌺 Saheliyon ki Bari
Saheli Marg. ◯ *daily.* ▨
This delightful 18th-century retreat in the north of the city (its name means "Garden of the Maids of Honour") has ornamental fountains, a lotus pool and a rose garden. It was built for a queen of Udaipur, whose dowry included 48 maids.

Ahar
Ashok Nagar Rd. **Museum**
◯ *Sat–Thu.* ● *public hols.* ▨
Located 3 km (2 miles) east of Udaipur, Ahar has the impressive cenotaphs of 19 Mewar rulers, and a small archaeological museum.

Environs
Shilpgram, 8 km (5 miles) northwest of Udaipur, is a lively ethnographic crafts village, with artisans, folk performers, and replicas of traditional houses. Camel rides are also available.

Pavilion in the Saheliyon ki Bari, an 18th-century queen's garden

Nagda's Saas-Bahu Temples, seen through the finely-carved *torana*

VISITORS' CHECKLIST

Udaipur district. 269 km (167 miles) S of Jodhpur. 389,400. 25 km (16 miles) E of city centre. Rajasthan Tourism, Suraj Pol, (0294) 241 1535. Gangaur Festival (Mar/Apr), Mewar Festival (Apr).

Eklingji, 22 km (14 miles) northeast of Udaipur, is a complex of 108 temples and shrines, dedicated to Lord Shiva. It marks the site where the founder of the Mewar ruling dynasty, Bappa Rawal, received special blessings from a sage who lived here. The main temple dates to the 16th century. Built of marble and granite, it includes an impressive pillared hall and a four-faced image of Shiva crafted in black marble, with a silver Nandi facing it.

Nagda, a short distance away from Eklingji, is worth a visit for the Saas-Bahu Temples ("Mother and Daughter-in-law Temples"), twin structures dedicated to Vishnu. The 11th-century temples are entered through a finely carved *torana* and are renowned for their elaborate sculptures depicting amorous couples and scenes from the epic *Ramayana*.

One of Rajasthan's main pilgrimage sites is the 18th-century Shrinathji Temple at **Nathdwara**, 48 km (30 miles) northeast of Udaipur. The main deity is Lord Krishna, known locally as Shrinathji. His black stone image was brought here from Mathura *(see p152)* to save it from destruction by the Mughal emperor Aurangzeb in the 17th century. Beautiful painted cloth hangings known as *pichhwais* are hung behind it. Non-Hindus cannot enter the temple, but Nathdwara town's picturesque bazaar, with its pichhwai painters at work, is worth a visit. *Pichhwais*, one of the most vibrant forms of Indian painting, are done on stiff cloth in vegetable and mineral colours. They depict 24 scenes from the Krishna legend, each linked with a particular festival or holy day. At the centre of each painting is a stylised image of Lord Krishna, with dusky skin, slanting eyes and intricate jewellery, set against a background of verdant foliage, birds, animals and skyscapes. Around the deity are cows, milkmaids and devotees.

UDAIPUR CITY CENTRE

City Palace ①
Fateh Sagar Lake ⑤
Jag Mandir ②
Jag Niwas ③
Jagdish Mandir ④
Saheliyon ki Bari ⑥

0 metres 800
0 yards 800

Key to Symbols *see back flap*

Udaipur: City Palace

Royal sun symbol

Stretching along the eastern shore of Lake Pichola, Udaipur's City Palace is a fascinating combination of Rajput military architecture and Mughal-style decorative techniques. Its stern, fortress-like façade, topped by a profusion of graceful balconies, cupolas and turrets, has been aptly described by one writer as a massive plain cake topped with fabulous icing. The largest palace in Rajasthan, covering an area of 2 ha (5 acres), the City Palace is actually a complex of several palaces, built or added to by 22 different maharanas between the 16th and 20th centuries. Much of it is now a museum, and parts of it are luxury hotels.

Fateh Prakash
This early 20th-century palace, now a hotel, has a magnificent Durbar Hall and a gallery of crystal furniture.

City Palace Museum

Rajya Angan Chowk, with a temple to the goddess Dhuni Mata

Exploring the City Palace

The older section of the City Palace complex dates from 1568. Behind its fortified walls is a maze of royal apartments, reception halls and courtyards. They are linked to each other by narrow passages and steep staircases – a feature typical of Rajput palaces of that period, designed to confuse invaders. The superb **City Palace Museum** is spread out through several palaces in this section, and is entered through the imposing **Tripolia Gate** (built in 1713). Above the entrance is the Mewar crest – a large Sun face (reinforcing the Sisodia clan's claim to be descended from the Sun), flanked by Rajput and Bhil warriors (the tribal Bhils, skilled archers, played a heroic role in Mewar's great battles). Beyond this is the **Ganesh Deorhi Gate** where entrance tickets for the museum are checked. It leads into a courtyard decorated with frescoes of horses and elephants, and a marble relief of the god Ganesha surrounded by dazzling mirror and glass inlay.

The next courtyard is the **Rajya Angan Chowk**, from where steps lead to the **Chandra Mahal** (built in 1620). One of the loveliest palaces in the complex, it has beautiful columns, fretwork windows and striking marble reliefs of Rajput women, one of whom carries a shield. There is a magical view of Lake Pichola and its island palaces from here.

Another flight of steps from here leads to the charming **Bari Mahal** (built in 1699). Perched 27 m (89 ft) above the ground, it is built on a terraced hillside that is com-

A view of the City Palace, on the eastern shore of Lake Pichola

VISITORS' CHECKLIST

City Palace Complex
Tel (0294) 252 8016. ◯ *daily.*
📷 📷 *restricted.* 🏛 **Museum**
📷 *extra charges.* ✦ ▢
Fateh Prakash 🍴 *open to non-residents.* **Shiv Niwas** 🍴 *open to non-residents.*

Shambhu Niwas
is now home to
the maharana's
descendants.

Shiv Niwas
*This sumptuously
decorated crescent-shaped
palace was the royal
guesthouse and is now a
luxury hotel (see p705).*

Fateh Prakash

Shiv Niwas

Kanch Burj, with its dazzling
decoration of red and silver glass

pletely enclosed within the palace walls. Deep halls with receding rows of carved arches open into an enchanting courtyard with a marble pool in the middle. Tall *neem* trees stand around it, providing dappled shade.

The Bari Mahal leads to the **Dilkhushal Mahal** (built in 1620) with two remarkable chambers – the Kanch Burj ("Glass Turret") inlaid with red and silver glass, and the Krishna Niwas which exhibits outstanding Mewar miniature paintings *(see p405)*. This was the room of 16-year-old Princess Krishna Kumari, who committed suicide in 1807 when rival suitors from Jodhpur and Jaipur threatened to go to war over her hand.

To the left of this palace is the ornate **Moti Mahal**, the chamber of the dissolute Maharana Jawan Singh (r.1828–38), who once promised a dancing girl half his kingdom if she could walk a tightrope across Lake Pichola. The girl had almost reached when the maharana's alarmed courtiers cut the rope, and the dancer drowned. Still

Mosaic of dancing peacock in the Mor Chowk

further left is the **Mor Chowk** ("Peacock Courtyard") with its brilliantly coloured 19th-century mosaics of three dancing peacocks.

The southern end of the City Palace complex has three other opulent palaces built in the late 19th and early 20th centuries – **Shambhu Niwas** where the descendants of the rulers now live; **Fateh Prakash** with its magnificent Durbar Hall, fine portraits and gallery of crystal furniture; and the semi-circular **Shiv Niwas** built as the royal guesthouse (Queen Elizabeth II once stayed here). Fateh Prakash and Shiv Niwas are now luxury hotels, but are open to non-residents for tours and meals.

A colourfully painted chamber in Juna Mahal, Dungarpur

Dungarpur ㉔

Dungarpur district. 110 km (68 miles) S of Udaipur. 🚕 42,550. 🚌
📷 Vagad Festival (Jan/Feb), Baneshwar Festival (Feb).

This remote, relatively un-known town boasts some unexpected artistic treasures. Dominating Dungarpur is the seven-storeyed **Juna Mahal**, built in the 13th century on a large rock. The interior of this palace-fort, in contrast to its rather battered exterior, glows with exuberant ornamentation, and contains some of the most beautiful frescoes to be seen in Rajasthan. Remarkably well-preserved, these include a series of erotic paintings from the *Kama Sutra* in the erstwhile ruler's bedroom, on the top floor of the palace.

The 19th-century **Udai Vilas Palace** beside a lake, is built of local grey-green granite in a blend of Rajput and Mughal styles. Rising from the centre of its courtyard is a fantastic four-storeyed pavilion with cusped arches, densely carved friezes, and a profusion of canopies and balconies. The large room on its top storey is inlaid with a variety of semi-precious stones.

Chittorgarh ㉕

Chittorgarh district. 115 km (72 miles) NE of Udaipur. 🚉 🚌 ℹ️
Janta Avas Graha, Station Rd, (01472) 24 1089. 📷 Meera Utsav (Oct).

The great, battle-scarred Chittorgarh Fort epitomizes in its tragic history the valour, romance, chivalry and strict death-before-dishonour code glorified in Rajput myths and legends. Sprawling across 280 ha (692 acres), atop a steep 180-m (591-ft) high rocky hill, Chittorgarh's ruined palaces, temples and towers bear witness to its illustrious and turbulent past, when it was the capital of the Sisodia rulers of Mewar, between the 12th and 16th centuries.

As Rajasthan's mightiest fort, it was the target of successive invaders. The first siege, in 1303, was by Sultan Alauddin Khilji *(see p48)*, whose goal was to capture not only the fort but also the queen, Rani Padmini, whose legendary beauty the sultan had glimpsed reflected in a mirror. When defeat seemed inevitable, Rani Padmini along with 13,000 women committed *jauhar* – a ritual form of mass suicide by immolation, practised by Rajput women to escape dishonour at the hands of their enemies. It is said that 50,000 Rajput warriors died in the ensuing battle. Alauddin's army then proceeded to sack the fort and destroyed many of its buildings. Within a few years, however, the ruler's grandson had regained it for the Sisodia dynasty.

The next great battle, this time against Sultan Bahadur Shah of Gujarat in 1535, saw the Queen Mother, Rani Jawaharbai, lead a cavalry charge and die on the battle-field along with the flower of Rajput youth. Once again, thousands of women inside the fort committed *jauhar*. The third and final assault on Chittorgarh was led by the Mughal emperor Akbar, who was able to capture it in 1567. Chittorgarh was abandoned thereafter, and the Sisodias moved their capital to Udaipur *(see pp398–9)*.

Seven massive spiked gates lead to the fort. The first building to the right is **Rana Kumbha's Palace** (built between 1433 and 1468), probably the earliest surviving example of a Rajput palace. Its northern side has a profusion of richly carved balconies,

A view of the impressive Chittorgarh Fort, spread over a rocky hill

and a unique stepped wall.
Elephant stables and a
council chamber comprise its
public areas, while the private
apartments are a maze of
small rooms, including a
zenana section. Near it are
the 20th-century **Fateh
Prakash Palace**, which now
houses a museum of sculpture
found on the site; the
Kumbha Shyam Temple,
dating to the 15th-century,
with a fine sculpture of Vishnu
in his Varaha (boar) incarnation; and the **Meerabai
Temple**, built in 1440 by
Meerabai, *(see p49)* another
remarkable Mewar queen. A
mystic and a poetess, she
defied Rajput convention and
devoted her life to the worship
of Lord Krishna.

The main street runs south
of this temple towards the
nine-storeyed **Vijay Stambh**
("Victory Tower"), built by
Maharana Kumbha
between 1458 and
1468, to commem-
orate his victory
over Sultan
Mahmud of Malwa
(see p247). The
view from the top
of this extraordinary
36-m (118-ft) high
sandstone structure,
richly carved with
gods and goddess-
es, is magnificent.
The main street
continues further
south past noble-
men's mansions
to the **Gaumukh
Reservoir**, fed by
an underground
spring, and the 16th-century
Kalika Mata Temple, built over
the original Sun Temple which
was destroyed during the
devastating siege of 1303.

Opposite this temple stands
the 19th-century reconstruction of **Padmini's Palace** with a
lake pavilion adjacent to it.
The palace contains the mirror
in which Alauddin Khilji supposedly saw her reflection.
Standing further south, past
some Jain temples, is the **Kirti
Stambh**. This seven-storeyed
tower is dedicated to the first
Jain *tirthankara*, Adinath.

**Vijay
Stambh**

🏛 **Fateh Prakash Museum**
⭕ *Sat–Thu.* 🎫 *free on Mon.*

**The 11th-century temple of the Sun
God, in Jhalrapatan**

Jhalawar ㉖

Jhalawar district. 323 km (201 miles)
S of Jaipur. 🚂 48,100. 🚌 🛈 *Hotel
Chandrawati, (07432) 23 0081.* 🎪
Chandrabhaga Cattle Fair (Oct/Nov).

This delightful little town,
surrounded by orange
groves and poppy fields, is
dominated by a 19th-century
fort, the seat of the erstwhile
princes of Jhalawar. It now
houses government offices.
An incongruous yet charming
part of the fort is the **Bhavani
Natya Shala Theatre** (built in
1921), which was modelled
on the grand opera houses
the maharaja had seen on his
European tours. The old
walled town of **Jhalrapatan**
("City of Bells"), 6 km
(4 miles) south of the fort,
has a splendid cluster of 11th-
century temples. Of these the
most impressive is the **Surya
Temple** with its stunning
image of the Sun God. About
1.5 km (1 mile) south of this
temple, on the banks of the
Chandrabhaga river, stands
the superbly carved 7th-
century **Chandra
Mauleshwar Temple**.

Environs
The 14th-century **Ghagron
Fort**, 10 km (6 miles) west of
Jhalawar, is situated amid a
landscape of hills, woods and
fields, and surrounded on
three sides by the Kali, Sindh
and Ahu rivers.

The lush forests, cliffs and
grasslands of **Darrah Wild-life
Sanctuary**, 70 km (44 miles)
west of Jhalawar, look just as
they do in the famous Kota
paintings *(see p405)* of hunting
scenes – only the tigers and
princes are now missing.

Kota ㉗

Kota district. 261 km (162 miles) S
of Jaipur. 🚂 696,000. 🚌 🛈
🛈 *Hotel Chambal, (0744) 232 7695.*
🎪 🎫 *Dussehra Mela (Sep/Oct).*

The imposing façade of Kota's
fortified **City Palace**, which
dates back to 1625, stretches
along the banks of the
Chambal river, recalling the
princely past of this now
heavily industrialized city.
Kota's artistic heritage is well-
represented in the palace
apartments – every available
surface is covered with miniature paintings, mirrorwork,
murals and mosaics.
Particularly resplendent is the
Durbar Hall, with its ebony-
and-ivory doors, and paintings
depicting Kota's history. Many
of the royal apartments now
form part of the excellent **Rao
Madho Singh Museum**, which
has a fine collection of weapons and royal regalia.

On Kishorsagar Lake, in the
middle of the town, is the
charming island palace
known as **Jag Mandir** *(see
front cover)*, built in the 18th
century by a Kota queen who
yearned for her childhood
home in Udaipur *(see p398)*.

🏛 **Rao Madho Singh
Museum**
⭕ *Sat–Thu.* 🎫

Environs
Bardoli, 55 km (34 miles)
southwest of Kota, has one of
Rajasthan's most beautiful
temple complexes. The 9th-
century Ghateshwar Mahadev
temple has an outstanding
sculpture of Nataraja (the
dancing Shiva) on the door of
its sanctum.

**Ebony-and-ivory door in the 17th-
century City Palace, Kota**

View of Bundi, nestled in a narrow valley of the Aravalli Hills

Bundi ㉘

Bundi district. 215 km (134 miles) S
of Jaipur. 88,350. 🚉 🚌
ℹ Rajasthan Tourism, Circuit House,
(0747) 244 3697. 🗓 daily.
🎭 Gangaur (Mar/Apr).

Bundi is often described as
the undiscovered jewel of
Rajasthan. Surrounded on
three sides by the
rugged, thickly
forested Aravalli
Hills, this walled
town has retained
much of its historic
character. The
Taragarh Fort
crowns the crest of a
steep hill overlook-
ing the town, while
the **Garh Palace**
spills picturesquely
down the hillside.
This palace is Bundi's
– and Rajasthan's –
jewel. Lieutenant
Colonel James Tod,
(1782–1835), the British
Political Agent and author of
the authoritative *Annals and
Antiquities of Rajasthan*, wrote that "the *coup d'oeil* of
the castellated palace of
Boondi, from whichever side
you approach it, is the most
striking in India".

The state of Bundi was
founded in 1341 by Rao Deva
of the "fire-born" Hada
Chauhan Rajput clan, and the
massive, square Taragarh Fort
dates to his reign. Work on
the palace began in the 16th
century, and it was added to
by successive rulers over the
next 200 years, at different
levels on the hillside. Unlike
most other palaces in Rajasthan, there is very little Mughal
influence in its architecture.

Painting from the
Chitrashala

The Garh Palace represents a
rare example of the pure
Rajput style, with curved
roofs topping pavilions and
kiosks, a profusion of temple
columns and ornamental
brackets, and typically Rajput
motifs such as elephants and
lotus flowers. Unusually, the
palace is not built of the
sandstone favoured by most
other Rajput king-
doms, but of a hard,
green-tinged serpen-
tine stone, quarried
locally. This stone,
unlike sandstone,
does not lend itself
to fine carving.
Instead, Garh Palace
was embellished by
superb paintings.
The palace is
entered through the
imposing **Hathia Pol**
("Elephant Gate-
way"), flanked by
two towers and
topped by a pair of
huge painted elephants. The
most spectacular parts of the
palace are the **Chattar Mahal**
(built in 1660), and the
Chitrashala, an arcaded
gallery (built between 1748
and 1770) overlooking a
hanging garden. The murals
in these are regarded as
among the finest examples of
Rajput painting. The
themes they cover
include scenes from
religious cere-
monies, hunting
scenes and other
princely amuse-
ments. The colours
are predominantly
blue and green, with
touches of deep red
and yellow. In the
middle of the town

is the **Naval Sagar Lake**, with
a little temple on an island in
its centre. The fort and palace
reflected in the lake make a
pretty sight.

Bundi has over 50 stepwells,
of which the most beautiful is
the 46-m (151-ft) deep **Rani-ki-
Baori**, also in the centre of
town. Built in the 17th century,
it is strikingly similar to Adalaj
Vav in Gujarat *(see pp414–15)*,
with richly decorated archways
and sculptures of Vishnu's ten
avatars *(see p679)*.

Situated at the northern
edge of the town is the 18th-
century **Sukh Niwas Mahal**, a
romantic summer palace
overlooking **Jait Sagar Lake**.
Standing at the opposite end
of the lake are the royal
cenotaphs, and at its western
edge is an elegant hunting
tower, the **Shikar Burj**.

Environs
Bijolia, 50 km (31 miles)
southwest of Bundi, on the
road to Chittorgarh, has a
group of three beautiful 13th-
century temples, dedicated to
Shiva. **Menal**, lying 20 km (12
miles) further along the same
road is a delightful wooded
spot with 11th-century temples
standing near a gorge.

Tonk, 113 km (70 miles)
north of Bundi, was once the
capital of the only Muslim
princely state in Rajasthan.
Founded in the early 19th-
century, its main attraction is
the splendid Sunehri Kothi
("Golden Mansion") within the
palace complex, every inch of
its interior covered with gold
leaf, lacquerwork, moulded
stucco and striking mirrorwork.
Stained-glass windows bathe
this opulent hall in glowing
colours. Tonk's Arabic and
Persian Research Institute has
rare, illuminated medieval
Islamic manuscripts.

The gilded interior of Sunehri Kothi in Tonk

Rajasthani Miniature Painting

The intricate and vivid paintings of Rajasthan's princely states grew out of illustrated Jain and Hindu sacred texts. Originally, they depicted mainly religious themes, in bold lines and bright primary colours. After the 17th century, however, the influence of the more sophisticated Mughal-Persian art tradition brought greater delicacy of line, and a wider range of colours and themes into

Radha and Krishna, Bundi

Rajasthani art. By the 18th century, many princely states such as Kishangarh, Mewar, Bundi and Kota had developed their own distinctive styles. In most schools of Rajasthani painting, however, human figures are shown in profile, and different colours, seasons, flowers and animals are used symbolically to express a variety of moods. These various schools of miniature painting continue to flourish in Rajasthan today.

The Maharana Celebrating Gangaur (1715)

Jain religious text, early 17th century

MEWAR PAINTINGS

Large, detailed compositions, showing scenes from the lives of the maharanas of Udaipur, are characteristic of the Mewar School. The paintings depict festivals, grand processions, historic battles and religious ceremonies. The intricate detail was achieved by using just a single squirrel hair as a brush.

BUNDI AND KOTA PAINTINGS

The neighbouring princely states of Bundi and Kota produced outstanding miniatures. Bundi specialized in depicting palace life and scenes from Krishna's life, executed in soft blues and greens. Kota is renowned for its superb hunting scenes, set in dramatic forested landscapes, with wonderful depictions of animals and foliage. An 18th-century court painter named Sheikh Taju created many of them.

Bundi miniature depicting a palace scene

Bani Thani Radha, often called the Indian Mona Lisa

KISHANGARH PAINTINGS

Famous for his fine portraits, the 18th-century Kishangarh artist, Nihal Chand, found a favourite model in the royal courtesan, Bani Thani Radha, with her elegantly elongated features and enigmatic expression. He was also known for his lyrical depictions of skyscapes and seasons.

Maharao Durjan in the Kota Forest (1730)

Ranthambhore National Park

Park sign

This park lies in the shadow of the Aravalli and Vindhya mountain ranges and covers a core area of 275 sq km (106 sq miles). Its razor-sharp ridges, deep boulder-filled gorges, lakes and jungles are the habitat of carnivores such as the caracal, panther, jackal and hyena, numerous species of deer, and a rich variety of resident and migratory birds. The most famous resident, however, is the endangered tiger, and it is a unique experience to catch glimpses of this majestic animal. Like other parks in the region, this was originally the hunting ground of Jaipur's maha-rajas and it only became a Project Tiger Reserve in 1973.

Rajbagh Talao
Ruined pavilions stand on the banks of Rajbagh Talao, one of the three lakes in the park.

Ranthambhore Fort
The park derives its name from this great Rajput forest fort that is 1,000 years old and stands at a height of 215 m (705 ft).

Sambar
Large herds of sambar (Cervus unicolor) are seen around the lakes, wallowing in the water and feeding on aquatic plants, unperturbed by jeeps and visitors.

JAIPUR

TONK

Sawai Madhopur

MUMBAI

Padam Talao

Ranthambhore Fort

Rajbagh Talao

Jogi Mahal

Nalghati Valley

Lahpur

Man Sarovar

Banyan Tree
This enormous banyan tree (Ficus bengalensis) lies in the grounds of Jogi Mahal. Its many spreading branches are all supported by roots.

0 km   5

0 miles   2

For hotels and restaurants in this region see pp702–5 and pp731–2

DELHI

Banas

Tiger
Sighting the park's main predator is a matter of chance, but one can often find traces of its activities.

Semli Valley

arda

Gilai Sagar

Khandar Fort

Khatola

Indian Roller Bird
This is one of the many species of birds found in the park. The others include birds of prey such as the crested serpent eagle and Bonelli's eagle, and many species of pigeons, flycatchers, storks and water birds.

Marsh Crocodile
Muggers, or marsh crocodiles, are commonly seen submerged in water or basking on the shores of the lakes. Ungulate species are their main prey, and sometimes a crocodile can be glimpsed dragging the carcass of a deer into the water. Monitor lizards and pythons are some of the other reptiles found in the park.

Sloth Bear
This shaggy bear with short hind legs and a long muzzle emerges at dusk to feed. During the day it shelters in the rocky outcrops and is difficult to sight.

KEY

= Major road

— Railway

▬ Park border

☼ Viewpoint

˙ ˙ Trails

∩ Archaeological site

ℹ Tourist information

GUJARAT

The state of Gujarat has three distinct regions – a corridor running north to south which is the industrial mainland, a peninsula known as Saurashtra, and Kutch, which is partly desert and partly marshland. The state's 1,600-km (994-mile) coastline has attracted seafarers through the ages, lured by the rich prospects of trade. The Arabs, Portuguese, Dutch, Mughals and British, as well as Parsis fleeing their native Iran, have all left their mark on Gujarat's culture. Fascinating archaeological sites, superb Jain, Hindu and Islamic architecture, exquisite crafts and rare wildlife, including the Asiatic lion, are among Gujarat's attractions, as are its hardworking, enterprising people. In January 2001, an earthquake hit Gujarat and devastated the region of Kutch. But with their legendary capacity to overcome hardship and disaster, the people lost no time in rebuilding their lives out of the debris around them.

SIGHTS AT A GLANCE

Towns & Cities
Ahmedabad ❶
Bhavnagar ❿
Bhuj ㉒
Daman ⓫
Diu ⓮
Jamnagar ⓴
Junagadh ⓱
Mandvi ㉓
Patan ❻
Porbandar ⓲
Rajkot ㉑

Siddhpur ❼
Surat ❿
Vadodara ❽

Historic Sites
Adalaj Vav ❷
Champaner ❾
Dholavira ㉔
Lothal ❸
Modhera Sun Temple ❺

Temples & Holy Places
Dwarka ⓳
Palitana ⓭
Somnath ⓯

National Parks & Areas of Natural Beauty
The Little Rann of Kutch Sanctuary ㉕
Nal Sarovar Sanctuary ❹
Sasan Gir National Park ⓰

KEY

🛬 International airport
✖ Domestic airport
━ National highway
━ Major road
═ Minor road
━ Major railway
▪ ▪ International border

0 km   100
0 miles   100

◁ **Kutchi woman from the Meghwal tribe, in embroidered mirrorwork garments and heavy silver jewellery**

Ahmedabad ❶

Gujarat's leading city, Ahmedabad was the state capital until 1970. This bustling industrial and commercial centre also has a fascinating old quarter, redolent with Gujarat's traditional culture and history. Legend has it that the city owes its foundation to Sultan Ahmed Shah (r.1411–42), who, while out hunting, encountered a warren of rabbits on the banks of the Sabarmati river. Astonishingly, the rabbits turned fiercely on his hounds and defended their territory. Viewing this as an auspicious sign, the sultan built his new capital at this site and named it after himself – Ahmedabad.

A view of the crowded banks of the Sabarmati river

🏛 The Old City

Bounded by Lady Vidyagauri Rd, Sardar Patel Rd & Kasturba Gandhi Rd. **Heritage Walking Tours** *Tel* (079) 2657 4335.

A maze of crowded bazaars, *pols* (large gateways, leading to residential quarters), exquisitely carved façades, temples, mosques and subterranean stepwells *(vavs)* mark the 3-km (2-mile) square that makes up the Old City. This area is best explored on foot, and the Ahmedabad Municipal Corporation organizes a daily Heritage Walking Tour through the atmospheric bylanes.

Built at the site of the original city, **Bhadra Fort** has panoramic views of the surrounding streets. Southwest of the fort is **Ahmed Shah's Mosque**, a simple place of worship, built in 1414 on the site of an early 13th-century Hindu temple.

Perhaps Ahmedabad's most photographed monument, **Siddi Saiyad's Mosque** in the northeast corner of Bhadra Fort, is renowned for its superb yellow stone latticework. Made by a slave of Ahmed Shah in 1572, the twin *jalis* on the western wall depict the intertwining branches of a tree, carved with extraordinary delicacy.

Southeast of the fort, the **Teen Darwaza** ("Triple Gateway") straddles the road, which is lined with shops selling block-prints, silverware and assorted bric-à-brac. Close by, along Mahatma Gandhi Road, is the **Jami Masjid**, which Sultan Ahmed Shah built in 1423, to enable the faithful to

Tree of Life *jali* in Siddi Saiyad's Mosque

congregate for Friday prayers. The masons who constructed this yellow sandstone structure, ingeniously used pieces retrieved from demolished Hindu and Jain temples – the black slab close to the main arch is said to be the base of an inverted Jain idol. The mosque's 15 domes are supported by 260 pillars covered with intricate carvings. The interior is illuminated by natural light filtered through latticework screens.

Outside the east entrance of the Jami Masjid, close to the jewellery bazaar in Manek Chowk, is the **Tomb of Ahmed Shah**, with elegant pillared verandahs, where the sultan, his son and grandson are buried. In the heart of the market, echoing the plan and layout of the sultan's tomb, lies **Rani-ka-Hazira**, the mausoleum of his many queens.

To the southeast of Manek Chowk is **Rani Sipri's Mosque**, also known as Masjid-e-Nagina ("Jewel of a Mosque") because of its elegant proportions and slender minarets. Northwest of Manek Chowk is **Rani Rupmati's Mosque**, dedicated to the sultan's Hindu wife. Built in the mid-15th century, the mosque incorporates elements of Hindu and Islamic design, with perforated stone screens to provide privacy for women. The city's famous Shaking Minarets, which are located next to the railway station, are closed to visitors.

Traffic moving through the Teen Darwaza thoroughfare

Outside the Old City

N of the Old City.

Situated outside the Delhi
Gate, the **Hatheesing Temple**
was built in 1850 by Huthising
Kesarising, a Jain merchant.
This intricately carved marble
temple is dedicated to
Dharmanath, the 15th Jain
tirthankara. A paved courtyard has 52 cubicles, housing
shrines dedicated to different
tirthankaras.

A fine example of Gujarat's
stepwells is the **Dada Harir
Vav** lying to the northeast of
the old city. Built in 1500 for
Bai Harir Sultani, a lady from
the sultan's harem, its walls
and pillars are beautifully decorated with elaborate carvings.

New Ahmedabad

W of Sabarmati river.

Across the Sabarmati river,
modern Ahmedabad has some
fine examples of contemporary architecture designed by
Le Corbusier *(see p93)* and the
American architect, Louis
Kahn. The **Sanskar Kendra**,
designed by Le Corbusier, has
a rare collection of miniature
paintings. The Indian Institute
of Management (IIM), India's
top college for business studies, is in a campus designed
by Louis Kahn. Close by, the
LD Institute of Indology
houses ancient manuscripts

and paintings, and the **Calico
Museum** *(see pp338–9)* displays an outstanding collection
of textiles. The prestigious
National Institute of Design is
on the south bank of the river.

Sabarmati Ashram

◻ 8:30am–7pm daily.
● mid-Jun–mid-Oct.

A spartan colony of tiled
houses, the **Sabarmati Ashram**
was a second home to
Mahatma Gandhi. It was from
here that he orchestrated the
final struggle for India's freedom. His cottage, Hriday Kunj,
has been maintained much as
he left it, and contains some
personal items such as his
round eyeglasses, wooden
slippers, books and letters.

**Gandhi's room in the Sabarmati
Ashram, with his spinning wheel**

VISITORS' CHECKLIST

Ahmedabad district. 545 km (338
miles) NW of Mumbai.
🚶 3,515,400. ✈ 10 km (6
miles) N of city centre. 🚃 🚆
ℹ HK House, Ashram Rd,
(079) 2657 8046. ⏰ Mon–Sat.
🎉 Uttarayan (14 Jan),
Navratri (Sep/Oct).

Environs

About 4 km (2.5 miles) south
of the city is the **Vishala
Complex** with a museum
displaying traditional utensils.
It also has an excellent outdoor restaurant for Gujarati
cuisine, set in an attractive
rural ambience *(see p611)*.
A short distance to the southwest is the **Sarkhej Roja**, a
beautiful complex of tombs
and pavilions around an
artificial lake, built as a retreat
for Gujarat's rulers between
1445 and 1461. Its tombs
include that of Ahmed Shah's
spiritual advisor, Sheikh Ahmed Khattu. Finely carved
brass latticework is a unique
feature of this site. Built in the
late 1960s, the state capital,
Gandhinagar, is 25 km (16
miles) north of Ahmedabad.
Spread over 60 sq km (23 sq
miles), this planned township
has the state's administrative
complex at its centre.

AHMEDABAD OLD CITY CENTRE

Ahmed Shah's Mosque ②
Bhadra Fort ①
Jami Masjid ⑤
Rani-ka-Hazira ⑦
Rani Rupmati's
   Mosque ⑨
Rani Sipri's Mosque ⑧
Siddi Saiyad's Mosque ③
Teen Darwaza ④
Tomb of Ahmed Shah ⑥

0 metres 500
0 yards 500

Key to Symbols *see back flap*

Ahmedabad: The Calico Museum

A major centre of India's textile trade and industry since the 15th century, Ahmedabad is an appropriate location for this outstanding museum. Its collection of rare textiles includes royal tents, carpets and costumes; religious paintings on cloth; embroideries, brocades and silk weaves; and Kashmir shawls. The exhibits, most of which date to the 17th and 18th centuries, are displayed in a beautiful old *haveli*. The museum was established in 1949 by the Sarabhai family, textile mill owners and leading philanthropists of Gujarat.

Detail from kalamkari fabric

Brocade Patka
This 18th-century gold brocade waist band, patterned with pink poppies, was part of a royal costume.

★ **Mughal Tent**
This sumptuous 17th-century tent is made up of intricately hand-painted cotton panels in the kalamkari technique (see p680). Mughal kings used these tents during military campaigns, on hunting expeditions and while touring their kingdom.

Ground floor

★ **Sharad Utsav Pichhwai**
Lord Krishna plays the flute in this exquisite 18th-century pichhwai from Nathdwara (see p399). It was hung in the temple on the autumn full moon, when nectar is believed to fall from heaven. Note the delightful cow licking Krishna's leg.

GALLERY GUIDE
The museum, set in the verdant Shahi Bagh gardens, is spread over 12 rooms on two floors of the haveli. The exhibits are displayed with great imagination, and each gallery presents the craft of a region, a tribal group or a religious sect. Within the museum compound, housed in another fine haveli, are the Sarabhai Foundation Galleries, with a fine collection of bronze icons and paintings.

A view of the Calico Museum, showing the richly carved wooden façade of the old *haveli* in which it is housed

First floor

Entrance

★ **Phulkari**
Elaborately embroidered with cotton thread and floss silk, this 19th-century piece from Punjab was part of a bride's dowry.

Telia Rumal
This cotton kerchief from Andhra Pradesh is made by a unique technique, where the yarn is oiled before being dyed and woven.

0 metres 2
0 yards 2

The *haveli* façade had been taken to the British Museum in the 19th century, but was brought back and painstakingly reconstructed here in the 1950s.

Outer gate

STAR EXHIBITS

★ Mughal Tent

★ Sharad Utsav Pichhwai

★ Phulkari

KEY

☐	Export textile galleries
☐	Court textiles
☐	Gallery of shawls
☐	Mughal costumes
☐	Jain and Vaishnav textiles
☐	Kutch and Sindh embroidery
☐	Kathiawar embroidery
☐	Textiles of Orissa
☐	Madhubani quilts
☐	Phulkari from Punjab, Kantha from Bengal
☐	Tie-and-dye gallery

Adalaj Vav ②

Detail of carving on a wall niche

The stepwells *(vavs)* of Gujarat are an ingenious answer to the water scarcity in this arid region. Many of these elaborately ornamented, underground wells are dedicated to deities, acknowledging the hand of God in providing life-sustaining water. Adalaj Vav, perhaps Gujarat's finest stepwell, was built in 1499 by Rudabai, the wife of a local chieftain, to conserve water and provide a cool and pleasant ambience for social interaction. A series of beautiful platforms and galleries are built into the sides of the stepwell, all the way down to its subterranean depths.

Local women at the stepwell, which is still used for rest and recreation

The Stepped Corridor
The main corridor leads down five storeys to a depth of 30 m (98 ft), through pavilions whose walls, pillars and niches are covered with sculptures.

★ The First Well
Adalaj has an intermediate tank, 7 m (23 ft) in diameter, just before the main well. The octagonal well-shaft is entirely covered with fine carvings.

Ramp for drawing water

Stringed courses

The main well is no longer in use, but the ramp at the top, used for drawing water, still exists.

The steps surrounding the first well were used by people taking ritual baths.

STAR FEATURES

★ The First Well
★ The First Landing
★ Wall Niches

Ornamental Detail
*The well-shafts are pro-
fusely carved with intricate
floral and geometric motifs,
interspersed with figurines.*

VISITORS' CHECKLIST

Gandhinagar district. 17 km (11
miles) N of Ahmedabad. 🚌 *Taxis
and autos are the best options
from Ahmedabad.* 🔲 *daily.* 📷
flash photography is prohibited.

One of the three
main entrances

★ **The First Landing**
*Balconies, windows,
doors and shrines line
the first landing – a
large underground
platform. Adalaj is
best viewed at noon,
when sunlight filters
down to the bottom.*

Stringed courses,
or horizontal
detailing, break
the monotony of
plain walls.

The Pavilions
*The pavilions, supported by rows of carved
pillars, are flooded with diffused light and
provide ideal resting places.*

★ **Wall Niches**
*Niches feature in all the
pavilions, carved with
motifs of pots, horses,
flowers and leaves.*

OTHER STEPWELLS IN GUJARAT

The 11th-century **Rani ni Vav** in Patan *(see p417)*
is among the most elaborately carved stepwells,
with some 800 sculptures. Built in 1499, **Dada
Harir Vav** *(see p411)* in Ahmedabad, is one of the
finest examples of a *vav* from the Muslim period
in Gujarat. The 15th-century **Ambarpur Vav**, 18
km (11 miles) from Ahmedabad, is one of the
few *vavs* still in use.

Rani ni Vav in Patan, one of India's largest *vavs*

The dry dock at Lothal, dating to 2500 BC

Lothal ❸

Ahmedabad district. 75 km (47 miles) SW of Ahmedabad. 🚊 Lothal–Burkhi station, 6 km (4 miles) SW of Lothal, then local transport. 🚌 to Burkhi. ⬜ Sat–Thu. 🎫 🚫

Excavations at Lothal have unearthed the remains of a remarkable city of the Indus Valley Civilization *(see p41)* that existed 4,500 years ago. Located 6 km (4 miles) northwest of the confluence of the Sabarmati and Bhogavo rivers, Lothal (literally, "Mound of the Dead") had a navigable estuary to the sea through the Gulf of Cambay (now Gulf of Khambat), which made it a flourishing port that once traded with Egypt, Persia and Mesopotamia.

The site reveals the foundations of a well-planned city with blocks of houses, paved drains, channels and wells, and 12 public baths. Other finds include beautifully made beads and pottery decorated with bird and animal motifs. Seals with intriguing, pictographic writing (as yet undeciphered), and weights and measures were also found here. The city was surrounded by a mud brick embankment, to protect it from the perennial floods which, in all probability, caused the city's destruction around 1,900 BC.

Among the prize exhibits in the **Archaeological Museum** are a copper figurine and a gold-bead necklace.

In 2001, Indian oceanographers carrying out water pollution tests in the Gulf of Cambay nearby, made an astonishing discovery. They found the foundations of two cities under the sea, complete with streets, houses, staircases and temples. Objects recovered from the seabed, such as a stone slab covered with mysterious markings (which could be the earliest form of writing yet discovered), and carved wooden logs, have been carbon-dated to 7500 BC. The discovery of this site, which has been dubbed "Asia's Atlantis", has excited historians and archaeologists all over the world, as it suggests that civilization may have started 5,000 years earlier than previously believed. They surmise that the city may have been submerged as sea levels rose at the end of the Ice Age in about 8000 BC.

🏛 **Archaeological Museum**
⬜ Sat–Thu. 🎫 🚫

Nal Sarovar Sanctuary ❹

Ahmedabad district. 60 km (37 miles) SW of Ahmedabad. 🚊 *Viramgam, 35 km (22 miles) N of entry point, then taxi.* 🚌 *Viramgam.* 🛈 *Conservator of Forests (Wildlife), Gandhinagar, (079) 952717–223 500.* 🎫 🚭 **permit** *needed from Forest Department to enter sanctuary.*

Nal Sarovar sanctuary is one of the largest bird sanctuaries in the country. The 115-sq km (44-sq mile) Nal Lake and the surrounding swamp forests are best visited between November and February, when they attract as many as 250 species of waterfowl, including flamingoes, geese, cranes, pelicans, storks, cormorants, ibis and spoonbills. Winter migrants from as far as Siberia, such as the elegant bluish-grey

Reed beds on Nal Lake

demoiselle crane, also congregate here in hundreds, and can be observed at fairly close quarters. A perennial resident is the Sarus crane, the largest species of crane in the world. Believed to pair for life, Sarus cranes enact a spectacular courtship ritual, performing a synchronized dance that involves bowing with outstretched wings. Unfortunately, pressures on the habitat from the resident fishing communities, and from growing numbers of tourists, are slowly depleting the Nal Lake's rich variety of birdlife.

Graceful flamingoes, a regular sight at the Nal Sarovar Sanctuary

Exquisitely carved images of Hindu deities at Rani ni Vav, Patan

Modhera Sun Temple ❺

See pp418–19.

Patan ❻

Mehsana district. 140 km (87 miles) from Ahmedabad. 🚐 *112,050.* 🚉 🚌 🎪 *Jatar Fair (Sep/Oct).*

The town of Patan was the capital of this region between the 8th and 15th centuries, before Sultan Ahmed Shah moved base to Ahmedabad *(see pp410–11)* in 1411. The ruins of the old capital, Anhilwada, lie 2 km (1.3 miles) northwest of Patan, and include an impressive stepwell, **Rani ni Vav**, and a water tank. The seven-storeyed stepwell ranks with Adalaj Vav *(see pp414–15)* as the finest in Gujarat. This splendid piece of architecture from the Solanki period (10th–14th centuries), now painstakingly restored, boasts some 800 individual, elaborately carved sculptures. Constructed in the 11th century by Queen Udaymati as a memorial to her husband, Bhimdeva, its unique feature is its direct as well as lateral series of steps leading to the water's edge. At the base are 37 niches, with the elephant god Ganesha carved into them. Nearby, the **Sahastralinga Talav**, a water tank with 1,000 shrines dedicated to the god Shiva, stands on the banks of the Saraswati river.

Patan also boasts more than 100 beautifully carved Jain temples, of which the **Panchasara Parsvanatha Temple** is the most striking. The town also has numerous traditional *havelis* with intricately carved façades.

Another attraction for many visitors is the beautiful *patola* sari. This lavish fabric is woven in Patan by a single family who have passed the craft down from one generation to the next. They are available locally and in major cities.

Siddhpur ❼

Mehsana district. 128 km (80 miles) N of Ahmedabad. 🚐 *53,600.* 🚉 🚌

Lying along the Anjuni river, Siddhpur was once famous for the Rudra Mala Complex of Shiva temples, dating from the 10th century. It was later destroyed by Muslim invaders in the 13th century. Historical accounts describe a three-storeyed complex, profusely carved in stone and supported by 1,600 pillars, with 11 smaller shrines and three 40-m (131-ft) tall gateways. Two porches and four columns from the main shrine are all that remain today, together with a well-preserved, carved gateway with two high columns. An exploration of the town reveals interesting wooden *havelis* and pillared mansions, built by Muslim traders in the 19th century.

Environs
This region has the popular temple towns of **Ambaji**, 88 km (55 miles) north of Siddhpur, and **Bahucharaji**, 55 km (34 miles) southwest of Siddhpur. Both temples are dedicated to the goddess Amba (a reincarnation of Shiva's consort, Parvati) and they attract large crowds of devotees during the four main full-moon festivals each year in March, June, September and November. The pilgrims have their heads shaved *en masse* at both temples.

Traditional houses in Siddhpur with finely carved façades

PATOLA WEAVING

Detail of a typical *patola* sari

Patola is an intricate silk weaving technique practised in Patan. The warp and weft threads are coloured in parts by tie-dyeing, and then woven to form clear designs in a method called double ikat *(see p668)*. Typical motifs include jewels, flowers, animals and dancing women, interspersed with geometric forms. The craft is laborious – a month's work goes into weaving one sari length (5.5 m/6 yards) – and its product is highly prized, especially in a bridal trousseau. This exquisite fabric was exported to Indonesia where it became the cloth of the royal court.

Modhera Sun Temple ❺

Surya, the Sun God

The Sun Temple at Modhera was built in 1026 by King Bhima I of the Solanki dynasty. It is so precisely laid out in an east-west direction that the sun's rays course through its chambers and strike the centre of the inner sanctum at high noon every day. The carvings, both inside and on the exterior, are extraordinarily detailed, depicting a pantheon of Hindu deities as well as scenes from everyday life. An impressive tank dominates the forecourt. The juxtaposition of a tank with a Sun Temple is inspired by Vedic scriptures, which say that the sun was born from the depths of a primordial ocean.

The Entrance Hall
This hall has 12 representations of Surya, that depict the phases of the sun in each month of the year.

Shrines
The tank is surrounded by miniature shrines, topped by curved shikharas.

The Kund
Flights of stairs create a ripple effect down to the base of the tank (kund), which is shaped like an inverted pyramid.

Vadodara ❽

Vadodara district. 113 km (70 miles) SE of Ahmedabad. ▩ 1,306,100. ✈ 8 km (5 miles) NE of town centre. 🚉 🚌 ℹ Gujarat Tourism, (0265) 242 7489. ✉ Vadodara Municipal Corporation, (0265) 243 3116.

Situated on the banks of the Vishwamitri river, Vadodara owes much of its splendour to Sayajirao Gaekwad III (1875–1939), a former ruler who transformed his principality into a progressive centre of culture, education and industry. Today Vadodara, also known as Baroda, is a vibrant city with many interesting buildings, museums and parks. The **Laxmi Vilas Palace**, an Indo-Saracenic pile, was designed by the English architect, Major Charles Mant (*see p468*). It took 12 years to build and was finally completed in 1890. It is still the residence of the erstwhile ruling family, though there are plans to convert parts of it into a luxury hotel. The **Maharaja Fateh Singh Museum**, within the palace grounds, has a rare

The magnificent façade of the Laxmi Vilas Palace

The Torana
All that survives of the torana *or arched gateway are these two intricately carved columns leading into the temple.*

Garbhagriha
The walls and pillars of the inner sanctum are richly carved with images of deities, in strict order of their celestial hierarchy.

Sabha Mandapa, the assembly hall, was reserved for religious discourses and socio-cultural ceremonies.

Nritya Mandapa
This hall, which leads from the assembly hall towards the inner sanctum, was used for dance performances.

collection of paintings by the famous Indian artist, Raja Ravi Varma (1848–1906). **Sayaji Bagh**, a beautiful park in the heart of the city, houses a zoo, a planetarium and the **Vadodara Museum and Picture Gallery** which exhibits an eclectic collection of Mughal miniatures, European oil paintings and royal artifacts. Pride of place goes to its collection of 68 striking bronzes from Akota, a centre of Jain culture in the 5th century. Other notable sights

Radha and Madhava by Raja Ravi Varma

are the **Kirti Mandir**, the *samadhi* (memorial) of Vadodara's royal family; and the **Nyaya Mandir**, an Indo-Saracenic building which is now a law court. The city also has the Maharaja Sayajirao University's **College of Fine Art**, an institute of national eminence.

🏛 **Laxmi Vilas Palace**
Tel (0265) 243 1819. ☐ *Tue–Sun. Visits by prior appointment only.* 🎫

🏛 **Maharaja Fateh Singh Museum**
Tel (0265) 242 6372. ☐ *Tue–Sun.* 🎫

🏛 **Vadodara Museum and Picture Gallery**
Tel (0265) 279 3801. ☐ *10:30am–5:30pm Tue–Sun.* 🎫

Environs
The famous Amul Dairy is located in **Anand**, 38 km (24 miles) northwest of Vadodara. Synonymous with the "White Revolution" that made India self-sufficient in milk, it helped pioneer India's dairy cooperative movement, and now procures one million litres of milk every day from 1,000 milk cooperative societies. It is open daily to visitors from 3 to 5pm.

Jain Temple in Pavagadh Fort, near Champaner

Champaner ❾

Vadodara district. 52 km (32 miles) NE of Vadodara. 🚌 🎭 *Mahakali Festival (Mar/Apr).*

The deserted city of Champaner, a UNESCO World Heritage Site, is situated at the foot of Pavagadh Hill. Originally the seat of a Rajput Chauhan dynasty, Champaner was conquered by the Muslim ruler Mahmud Begada in 1484. He spent 23 years rebuilding the citadel, adding mosques, palaces and tombs within its massive walls, guarded by huge gateways. Champaner remained the capital of Gujarat until 1535, when it was conquered by the Mughal emperor Humayun. Thereafter, it fell into gradual decline.

Much of Champaner lies in ruins today, with the remains of many old mosques and palaces reflecting a blend of Islamic and Jain traditions. The **Jami Masjid**, built in 1523, is a large, symmetrical structure with a perfectly pro-portioned dome. Its richly ornamented exterior with 172 pillars and 30-m (98-ft) high minarets, makes it one of the finest Islamic monuments in western India. Another ele-gant mosque here is the 16th-century **Nagina Masjid**.

The **Pavagadh Fort**, at the crest of the 820-m (2,690-ft) high Pavagadh Hill, is 4 km (2.5 miles) to the southwest of Champaner. It has a cluster of Muslim, Hindu and Jain shrines, and the ruins of an ancient fortification, reflecting

its chequered past. On the way up the hill are the ruins of the **Sat Mahal**, the seven-storeyed palace of the Chauhan kings. The kings were slain when they refused to embrace Islam after the Muslim conquest, and their women and children committed *jauhar*. There are also two domed granaries, the Makai Kothar and the Naulakha Kothar.

Environs
Dabhoi Fort, 75 km (47 miles) south of Champaner, was constructed in the 13th century by the Solanki Rajputs (10th–14th centuries). It is an interesting example of Rajput military architecture, with four gates, a water tank fed by an aque-duct and fields within the fort to provide food during a siege.

Detail from the Jami Masjid

Ruins of the 16th-century Jami Masjid in Champaner

Surat ❿

Surat district. 234 km (145 miles) S of Ahmedabad. 🚶 *2,433,800.* 🚉 🚌 🛈 *1/847 Athugar St, Nanpura, (0261) 247 8586.* 🏛 *Mon–Sat.*

Strategically located on the coast, Surat was once a pros-perous port and many powers battled to control it between the 16th and 18th centuries. At various times the Portuguese, Dutch, Mughals, Marathas and British held sway here, but its importance began to wane after 1837, when it was rav-aged by flood and fire. Many of Surat's Hindu and Parsi merchants *(see p447)* left for Bombay (Mumbai), which then gradually overtook Surat as the premier port on the western coast. Though no longer a port of any consequence, Surat is today a major industrial centre. The 16th-century **Surat Castle**, beside the Tapti Bridge, is the town's oldest structure. Built by Khudawan Khan, an Albanian Christian who embraced Islam, the castle has 12-m (39-ft) high battle-ments and 4-m (13-ft) thick walls. Iron strips were used to bind its various elements and all its joints were filled with molten lead, to make it as impenetrable as possible. Especially note-worthy is the imposing gateway in its eastern wing, with a menacingly spiked exterior, and a delicately carved interior. Sadly, sundry offices now housed within the castle have robbed it of its historic ambience.

Northeast of the castle, just beyond Kataragama Gate, are the English, Dutch and Armenian cemeteries, that bear witness to the city's cosmopolitan past. Though now overgrown, they are worth exploring for the intriguing personal histories recounted on the tombs' epitaphs. Particularly impres-sive is the mausoleum of Sir George Oxinden, a governor of the Surat Port, and his brother, in the British cemetery. The tomb of Baron

Adriaan van Reede, built in the 17th century, in the Dutch cemetery has an enormous double cupola.

Modern Surat is known for its flourishing textile industry which produces the famous *tanchoi* (brocade) silk. It also specializes in jewellery and is a major diamond-cutting centre for suppliers from all over the world. During the 1980s, the city had, unfortunately, become a byword for urban squalor, and in 1994 suffered an outbreak of plague. This galvanized the city's administration into a massive clean-up drive, which has resulted in the revival of Surat as a prosperous commercial centre.

Daman ⓫

Daman Union Territory. 390 km (242 miles) S of Ahmedabad. 🏠 35,750. 🚇 Vapi, 10 km (6 miles) SE of Daman, then taxi or bus. 🚌 🛈 Nani Daman, (0260) 225 5104.

Tucked away in the southern tip of Gujarat, adjoining Maharashtra, is the tiny enclave of Daman which was a Portuguese colony until 1961. The Damanganga river, which flows into the Arabian Sea, divides the town into two distinct parts – Nani Daman (Little Daman) which is dotted with hotels and bars, and Moti Daman (Big Daman), the old Portuguese township.

Moti Daman is enclosed within the massive **Daman Fort**. Its ten bastions and two gateways date to 1559, and it is ringed by a moat linked to the river. Daman's well preserved churches include the large **Bom Jesus Cathedral**,

The gateway to St Jerome's Fort in Nani Daman

built in 1603, which has a richly carved portal and an ornamental altar. The smaller **Rosario Chapel**, outside the fort walls, has exquisitely carved wooden panels, depicting scenes from the life of Jesus. The lighthouse, to the north of the fort, affords fine views of the Gulf of Cambay.

St Jerome's Fort, in Nani Daman, is less grand than Daman Fort but houses the lovely chapel of Our Lady of the Sea. The chapel has a delicate, classical façade of 12 columns crowned with a cross.

Liquor flows freely in Nani Daman's dingy bars, attracting crowds of tipplers from the rest of Gujarat where alcohol is prohibited. Those who want to take in local colour would be well advised to avoid the bars and explore the farmers' market or the riverside fish market instead.

The Devka and Jampore beaches, 5 km (3 miles) north and south of Daman respectively, are not spectacular, but offer tranquil retreats among casuarina groves.

FESTIVALS OF GUJARAT

Uttarayan (*14 Jan*). Coinciding with Makar Sankranti which marks the height of winter, this colourful festival fills the sky all over Gujarat with thousands of beautifully crafted kites.

Modhera Dance Festival (*Jan*), Modhera Sun Temple. This three-day festival of Indian classical dance is a unique opportuniy to enjoy these dance forms in the setting in which they were originally performed.

Bangles on sale at Tarnetar Fair

Tarnetar Fair (*Aug/Sep*), Tarnetar. This unique matchmaking *mela* sees prospective grooms promenading the fairgrounds, holding colourful umbrellas, as young women wearing multi-pleated skirts swirl around in dance. A girl indicates her preference by approaching a youth for a chat, leaving it to the elders to settle matrimonial details.

Navratri (*Sep/Oct*). Navratri or "nine nights" is celebrated throughout Gujarat and is marked by nine nights of dancing in honour of the mother goddess. Women perform the *garba* dance, whirling around in a circle, clapping their hands. The exhilarating *dandia ras* is the highlight, when men and women strike small lacquered batons to a beat that gets faster and faster till it finally breaks in a frenzied crescendo.

View of the harbour below St Jerome's fort in Nani Daman, Daman

Bhavnagar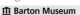

Bhavnagar district. 200 km (124 miles)
SW of Ahmedabad. 🏘 511,000. ✈
8 km (5 miles) SE of city centre. 🚇 🚌

For most visitors, Bhavnagar
is little more than a convenient base for exploring the
magnificent temple town of
Palitana. Yet Bhavnagar itself
is not without charm – its old
bazaar, dotted with merchants'
havelis, has shops specializing
in tie-dye textiles and gold
and silver jewellery. In the
southeast corner of the city,
on the road to the airport, is
the semi-circular **Barton
Museum** (built in 1895). It
houses the private collection
of coins, weapons and *objets
d'art* of a British officer,
Colonel Barton, who
served here in the
19th century.
   The **Nilambagh
Palace**, once the for-
mer rulers' residence,
was built in 1859 and
is now a luxury hotel
(see p706) with a
great banquet hall
and peacocks in
the garden.

**Detail from the door of
a temple in Palitana**

🏛 **Barton Museum**
Tel (0278) 242 4516.
◐ 10am–6:30pm Mon–Sat.
⬤ *public hols.* 📷 📹

🏨 **Nilambagh Palace**
Ahmedabad Rd. *Tel (0278) 242 4241.*

Environs
The flat grasslands of the 36 sq-
km (14 sq-mile) **Velavadar
National Park** (65 km/40 miles
north of Bhavnagar) are home
to over 1,000 blackbucks.
Blackbucks were protected by
the Bishnoi community *(see
p385)* until the state took over
this role. A walk
through the

park at dusk provides a glimpse
of the wolves that hunt this
Indian antelope, and of the
nilgai that congregate at the
park's watering holes.

🦌 **Velavadar National Park**
ℹ Forest Dept, Bhavnagar, (0278)
288 0222. ◐ mid-Oct–May. 📷
⬤ extra charges. 📹

Palitana ⑬

Bhavnagar district. 52 km (32 miles) SW
of Bhavnagar. ℹ (02848) 25 2327.
🚇 🚌 📷 Falgun Suth Tera (Feb/Mar).

An extraordinary cluster of
1008 Jain temples crowns the
twin summits of Palitana's
Shatrunjaya Hill and covers the
saddle linking them. The first
Jain *tirthankara*, Adinath
(*see p396*), is said to
have visited this hill,
while his chief disciple,
Pundarika, is believed
to have attained
enlightenment here.
Most of the temples
date to the 16th
century – earlier
temples on this site
were destroyed by
Muslim invaders in
the 14th and 15th centuries.
The temples are grouped into
nine fortified clusters called
tuks, and named after the
wealthy devotees who paid for
their construction. Each *tuk*
has a main shrine surrounded
by several smaller ones. The
most impressive of the main
shrines is the 17th-century
Adinath Temple, on the hill's
northern ridge. Its ceilings,
walls and supporting brackets
are covered with carvings of
saints, dancers, musicians and
lotus blossoms. Many images
of Adinath are enshrined

**Sculptures of Jain *tirthankaras*
along a temple corridor, Palitana**

inside. The southern ridge is
dominated by the 16th-century
Adishvara Temple, with its
richly ornamented spire. The
main image within portrays
Rishabhnath. It has eyes made
of crystal and is adorned with
necklaces and a magnificent
gold crown.
   The 4-km (2.5-mile) ascent
to the summit of the hill takes
about two hours, a task made
lighter by the spectacular silhouette of hundreds of temple
spires and domes against the
sky. From the top, there is a
panoramic view of the Gulf of
Cambay and the countryside.

Diu ⑭

Diu Union Territory. 418 km (260
miles) S of Ahmedabad. 🏘 21,600.
🚇 Delwada, 8 km (5 miles) N of
town centre. 🚌 ℹ Diu Jetty,
(02875) 225 2653.

The little island of Diu covers
an area of just 39 sq km (15
sq miles). Once known as the
"Gibraltar of the East", it was

The 19th-century Nilambagh Palace in Bhavnagar, set in a huge garden

The abandoned seaside fort at Diu, dating to the 16th century

a flourishing Portuguese colony from the 16th century onwards. It was ceded to India in 1961 and is today a Union Territory administered by the Central Government. The majestic **Diu Fort** on the eastern end of the island dominates the town. Built in 1535 when the Portuguese took control of Diu, it is worth a visit for its impressive double moat, its old cannons and for the superb views of the sunset it offers.

Diu town, sandwiched between the fort to the east and the city wall to the west, retains a distinctly Portuguese atmosphere in its churches and its many mansions. The **Nagar Seth Haveli** is particularly outstanding, with carved balconies and stone lions. The **Church of St Paul** (built in 1610) has a lovely, carved wooden altar, statues of the saints and a sonorous old organ. Its impressive Gothic façade was rebuilt in 1807. Nearby, the **St Thomas Church** (built in 1598) houses a museum of religious artifacts and stone inscriptions linked to the island's history.

The beach at **Nagoa**, 7 km (4 miles) from the town, has a long stretch of sand fringed with palm trees. Other beaches within easy reach of Diu are Jallandhar and Chakratirth which has a sunset viewpoint. As a Union Territory, Diu is not subject to Gujarat's prohibition laws. This explains the profusion of bars in the town, and the invasion, on weekends, by thirsty Gujaratis.

Somnath **⑮**

Junagadh district. 406 km (252 miles) SW of Ahmedabad. 🚌 🖉

Situated on the coast with a commanding view of the Arabian Sea, the **Somnath Temple** is revered as one of the 12 most sacred sites dedicated to Lord Shiva. The temple's legendary wealth made it the target of successive plundering armies, beginning with Mahmud of Ghazni in 1026, who is said to have made off with camel-loads of gold and precious gems, leaving the edifice in ruins. The cycle of pillage

and reconstruction at Somnath continued over the next seven centuries. The present temple, made of stone, was built in 1950.

East of the temple, at the confluence of three rivers, is **Triveni Tirth**. The ghats going down to the sea at this spot are said to mark the place where Lord Krishna's funeral rites were performed, after a hunter mistook him for a deer and killed him.

Sasan Gir National Park **⑯**

Junagadh district. 368 km (229 miles) SW of Ahmedabad. **Entry point:** *Sasan Gir.* 🚗 🚌 🚹 *For permits contact Field Director, Sinh Sadan, Sasan Gir (02877) 28 5541.* ⏰ *mid-Oct–mid-Jun.* 💰 📷 *extra charges.* 🚙 *Jeeps available.*

Until a century ago, the Asiatic lion roamed vast areas of India, from Gujarat all the way to Bihar in the east. Now, the Sasan Gir National Park is the only habitat left of the lion outside Africa. Asiatic lions are smaller than African lions, with a fold of skin along the belly. The males have shorter manes. About 320 lions live in Gir's 259 sq km (100 sq miles) of dry scrub forest. By the early 1900s, the Asiatic lion had been hunted and poached almost to the point of extinction. Their remarkable resurgence in Gir is attributed to the conservation efforts of the erstwhile nawab of Junagadh *(see p426)* and, subsequently, the Gujarat government.

A number of rivers wind through Gir, making it a haven for a range of wildlife, including the caracal, the *chausingha* (four-horned antelope), the blackbuck and a substantial leopard population.

THE MOON GOD AND SOMNATH

Legend weaves an interesting tale around the origins of the temple at Somnath. Som, the Moon God, was wedded to the 27 daughters of Daksha, a son of Brahma, but he loved only one of them, Rohini, causing great frustration to the other sisters. An infuriated Daksha cursed his son-in-law, causing him to lose his lustre. In despair, Som turned to Shiva and served him with such zealous devotion that Shiva gave him respite from the curse – he would wax for half the month and wane for the rest. In gratitude the Moon God built a Shiva temple at Somnath.

The Somnath Temple, visited by devotees of Shiva

An Asiatic lioness basking in the sun in Sasan Gir Sanctuary

A view of Palitana's 1,008 Jain temples, clustered on top of Shatrunjaya Hill ▷

The impressive Jain temple complex on Girnar Hill, just outside Junagadh

Junagadh ⑰

Junagadh district. 393 km (244 miles) SW of Ahmedabad. 🚶 168,700. 🚉 🚌 🛈 Majwadi Darwaza, (0285) 262 1201. 🕿 Mon–Sat. 🎭 Bhavnath Fair (Feb/Mar), Kartik Mela (Oct/Nov).

Junagadh, which means "Old Fort", takes its name from the ancient fort of Uparkot, built in the 4th century on a plateau at the eastern edge of the town. The fort is surrounded by massive walls, over 20 m (66 ft) high in places, and a 90-m (295-ft) deep moat inside the walls. This once teemed with crocodiles that were fed on criminals and political enemies. An ornate, triple-arched gateway marks the entrance to the fort. Inside, a cobbled path leads past Hindu temples to the now deserted **Jami Masjid** at the top of the plateau. Its carved stonework and pillars show that it was constructed on the remains of a destroyed Hindu temple. Nearby are a cluster of Buddhist caves dating to the 2nd century. The fort also has two fine 11th-century stepwells, the Navghan Kuan and the Adi Charan Vav.

In the mid-19th century, the nawabs of Junagadh moved down from the old fort into new colonial-style palaces in the city. The **Durbar Hall** of the City Palace, built in 1870, houses a museum with the typical trappings of royalty – palanquins, silver thrones and old armour. A complex of royal mausoleums can be seen

Intricate carving on Mahabat Maqbara

near the city's railway station, the most notable of which is the **Mahabat Maqbara** with splendid silver doors.

Junagadh's main attraction, however, is **Girnar Hill**, 6 km (4 miles) east of the city. An extinct volcano, this has been a holy site for Buddhists, Jains and Hindus since the 3rd century BC. Over 4,000 steps lead to the top of the 1,080-m (3,543-ft) high hill. En route is an **Ashokan Rock Edict**, dating to 250 BC (see p42), that conveys Emperor Ashoka's message of non-violence and peace. Halfway up the hill are a cluster of beautiful Jain temples. Most notable among them is the **Neminath Temple**, enshrining a black marble image of the 22nd Jain *tirthankara* (see p396) who

is believed to have died here. The 12th-century **Amba Mata Temple**, at the summit, is very popular with newlyweds, who come seeking blessings for conjugal bliss.

🏛 **Durbar Hall Museum**
Tel (0285) 262 1685. ☐ Thu–Tue. ⚫ 2nd & 4th Sat. 📷

Porbandar ⑱

Porbandar district. 404 km (251 miles) SW of Ahmedabad. 🚶 133,100. 🚉 🚌 🕿 Mon–Sat. 🛈 (0286) 221 085. 📷 extra charges.

Once a major port on the Arabian Sea, Porbandar is today famous as Mahatma Gandhi's birthplace. The house where Gandhi was born in 1869 still stands in a small alley, in the western part of the city. Next door is the **Kirti Mandir Museum** with photographs from the Mahatma's life, and extracts

THE NAWAB OF JUNAGADH AND HIS DOGS

The 11th Nawab of Junagadh (1900–59), like his forebears, had a passion for breeding dogs, and these pedigreed pooches, 800 of them, were housed in luxury with separate rooms and personal attendants. The Nawab even held elaborate banquets to celebrate their "nuptials". On the eve of India's Independence, when the princely states were given the option of either remaining in India or becoming a part of Pakistan, the Nawab's decision to accede to Pakistan was thwarted by popular protest. The Nawab, however, decided to leave Junagadh. When the time for departure came, the Nawab, true to form, boarded the aircraft with his dogs, leaving behind his entire harem of concubines.

Portrait of the Nawab with his favourite dog

from his speeches and writings. The city has little else to attract visitors and in recent years it has gained the dubious distinction of housing local mafia dons. Interestingly, large sections of Gujarat's diasporic population originated from this district.

Entrance to the Kirti Mandir Museum, Porbandar

Dwarka ⑲

Jamnagar district. 453 km (282 miles) W of Ahmedabad. 🚉 🚌 🪔 *Janmashtami (Jul/Aug).* 🛈 *(02892) 23 4013.*

Legend has it that about 5,000 years ago, Lord Krishna *(see p679)* forsook his kingdom at Mathura *(see p178)* and came to live on the seafront at Dwarka, where he founded a glittering new city. It is believed that the city was subsequently submerged under the sea. Whether or not this is myth or fact, recent excavations of the seabed have indeed established the existence of a submerged city in the vicinity of Dwarka.

Hindu pilgrims flock to Dwarka throughout the year. The city's main temple is the towering **Dwarkadhish Temple**, dating to the 16th century. Built of granite and sandstone on a plinth area of 540 m (1,772 ft), it is supported by 60 pillars and rises seven storeys to an impressive height of 51 m (167 ft).

Situated a short distance to its east is the small, lavishly carved **Rukmini Temple**. Built in the 12th century, it is dedicated to Krishna's wife.

Jamnagar ⑳

Jamnagar district. 308 km (191 miles) SW of Ahmedabad. 🏚 *447,800.* ✈ *10 km (6 miles) W of city.* 🚉 🚌 🛇 *Mon–Sat.*

Founded by a local prince, Jam Rawal, in 1540, Jamnagar's old walled city is dominated by the **Lakhota Fort**, the original seat of its rulers, and the **Ranmal Lake** which surrounds it. The fort was badly damaged during the earthquake in January 2001, though visitors are still allowed inside. The museum in the fort has fine sculptures from nearby excavation sites, dating from the 9th to 18th centuries. Close by is the Kotha Bastion which once stored the rulers' arsenal.

In the heart of the old town is the circular **Darbar Gadh** where the Jamsahebs (as the rulers were called) held public audiences. This structure was also damaged heavily in the 2001 earthquake, but the ground floor is safe for visitors. The lanes leading off from here are worth exploring as the city is famous for its tie-dye fabric and silver jewellery. In this area are two Jain temples, the **Shantinath** and **Adinath Temples**, entirely covered with mirrorwork, gold leaf, murals and mosaics. Close to them is the 19th-century **Ratanbai Mosque**, its doors inlaid with mother-of-pearl. In the early 20th century, Jamnagar was ruled by the famous cricketer KS Ranjit Sinhji (r.1907–33). The city acquired several elegant public buildings and parks under his able administration.

🏛 **Lakhota Fort Museum**
🕐 *Thu–Tue.* ● *2nd & 4th Sat.*
🈯 🚫

Environs
The **Marine National Park**, in the Gulf of Kutch, is 30 km (19 miles) from Jamnagar. An archipelago of 42 islands, the park's marine life is best viewed from the island of Pirotan.

🐾 **Marine National Park**
🚤 *Jamnagar jetty. For permits contact the Park Director, Jamnagar, (0288) 255 2077.* 🈯

Rajkot ㉑

Rajkot district. 216 km (134 miles) W of Ahmedabad. 🏚 *966,700.* ✈ *1 km (0.6 miles) NW of city centre.* 🚉 🚌 🛈 *Bhavnagar House, (0281) 223 4507.* 🛇 *Mon–Sat.*

The headquarters of the Saurashtra region (southwest Gujarat) during the British Raj, modern Rajkot is a commercial and industrial town. The centre of the region's groundnut trade, it is also reputed for its handicrafts.

Rajkot's many 19th-century buildings give it a distinctly colonial flavour. The **Watson Museum** in Jubilee Bagh, named after a British Political Agent, has a fine collection of portraits of local rulers, tribal artifacts, archaeological finds from Harappan sites and a large statue of Queen Victoria. The impressive **Rajkumar College**, established by the British for the sons of the Gujarat nobility, remains a prestigious public school.

🏛 **Watson Museum**
Tel (0281) 222 3065. 🕐 *9am–1pm, 3–6pm Thu–Tue.* ● *2nd & 4th Sat.* 🈯 📷 *extra charges.*

Environs
Wankaner Palace, 39 km (24 miles) northeast of Rajkot, is an eclectic mix of Mughal, Italian and Victorian-Gothic styles. Though still inhabited by the former royal family, a portion is now a luxury hotel. **Halvad**, 125 km (78 miles) north of Rajkot, has a 17th-century lakeside palace.

Statue of the first principal, Rajkumar College, Rajkot

Rabari women near Bhuj, bringing water home

Bhuj ㉒

Kutch district. 217 km (135 miles) W of Ahmedabad. ⫘ 121,100. ✈ 7 km (4 miles) N of city centre. 🚌 🚉 ℹ Gujarat Tourism, Toran Rann Resort, Mirzapur Bhuj, (02832) 22 4950. 🛕 Ashadhi Bij (Jul/Aug).

Until the earthquake of January 2001 reduced much of Bhuj to rubble, this was a fascinating walled city, with beautiful palaces and *havelis*, and a bazaar famous for its rich handicrafts and jewellery. Bhuj was the capital of the prosperous princely state of Kutch, whose wealth derived from its sea trade with East Africa and the Persian Gulf ports. African slaves were an important part of Kutch's maritime trade, and their many descendants still live in the city. The town's main attraction was the **Darbargadh Palace** complex, which houses the fabulous **Aina Mahal** or "Palace of Mirrors". Built in 1752, it was damaged in the 2001 earthquake and was temporarily closed down but has now been re-opened after extensive renovation. The palace and its contents are linked to the remarkable life of its Gujarati architect, Ramsinh Malam. Shipwrecked off the East African coast as a 12-year-old, he was rescued by a Dutch ship and taken to the Netherlands, where he spent the next 17 years. There, he blossomed as a craftsman, mastering Delft tile-making, glass-blowing, enamelling and clock-making. When he returned home, the ruler of Kutch, Rao Lakha, gave him an opportunity to display these skills. The Aina Mahal was thus decorated with Venetian-style chandeliers, Delft blue tiles, enamelled silver objects and chiming clocks – all made locally under Ramsinh's supervision. At the same time, local crafts of the highest quality were also displayed, such as a superb ivory-inlaid door, jewelled shields and swords, and a marvellously detailed 15-m (49-ft) long scroll painting of a royal procession, complete with African pageboys. All these form a part of the palace museum.

The royal cenotaphs, the Swaminarayan Temple and the bazaar are now unfortunately in ruins, but the excellent **Folk Arts Museum** still stands. It has a choice collection of Kutch textiles and local crafts, and a reconstructed village of Rabari *bhoongas (see p430)*.

🛕 **Folk Arts Museum**
Mandvi Rd. **Tel** (02832) 220 541.
⭘ Mon–Sat. 🛕 🖼 📷

EARTHQUAKE IN GUJARAT

On 26 January 2001, at 8:46am, as India celebrated its Republic Day, a devastating earthquake struck Gujarat. Its epicentre was in Kutch. Measuring 7.7 on the Richter Scale, it destroyed most of Bhuj, the headquarters of Kutch district, as well as Anjar, the second largest town in Kutch, and razed 450 villages in the district to the ground. Among the 20,000 people killed in the earthquake were 400 schoolchildren of Anjar, who were crushed under the rubble of falling buildings in a narrow street as they marched jauntily through town in the Republic Day Parade. In the state capital, Ahmedabad, most of those killed were trapped in recently-built highrise apartment buildings, which collapsed like houses of cards while, ironically, centuries-old historic monuments throughout the state suffered relatively little damage. An exception was the spectacular 18th-century Darbargadh Palace in Bhuj, with its richly decorated interiors showcasing the finest Gujarati craftsmanship. Much of the damage it suffered is irreparable, however, after some necessary renovation it is open to visitors yet again. In contrast, the traditional, round mud *bhoongas* of the semi-nomadic Rabaris of Kutch withstood the earthquake remarkably well. Gujarat, and in particular Kutch, has always been an area of seismic activity, and some historians believe this is one reason that cities of the Indus Valley Civilization *(see p41)*, such as Dholavira and Lothal, declined around 1900 BC. In more recent times, 1,100 people died in the 1819 earthquake and 7,000 in the 1956 earthquake. The disaster of 2001 made more than 250,000 people homeless. A massive rehabilitation effort began almost immediately. Besides the Gujarat government and the Indian Union, over 150 countries readily came forward to provide assistance. Above all, it was the resilience of the residents that brought life back to normal.

Labourers at an earthquake relocation center, Bhuj

The tranquil seafront at Mandvi, once a busy port

Mandvi ㉓

Bhuj district. 60 km (37 miles) SW of Bhuj. 14,300.

This old port town has fine beaches, good swimming, and camel and horse rides along the shore. Close to the beach is the **Vijay Vilas Palace**, an impressive Indo-Edwardian pile built in the 1940s as a royal summer retreat. Its lovely garden, drawing room and rooftop terrace are open to visitors and provide beautiful views of the sea. In the town is the curious 18th-century **Old Palace** of the Kutch rulers (now a girls' school). Architecturally a blend of local and European styles, its façade is decorated with cherubic Dutch boys holding wine goblets – architect Ramsinh Malam's touching salute to his adopted country.

🏛 **Vijay Vilas Palace**
◐ Thu–Tue. extra charges.

Dholavira ㉔

Bhuj district. 250 km (155 miles) NE of Bhuj. For permission contact the Superintendent of Police, Bhuj, (02832) 25 0444. daily.

Dholavira is a small village where archaeologists have unearthed extensive remains of a city that dates back to about 3000 BC. Lying on Khadir island in the Rann of Kutch it is, along with Lothal (see p416), the largest known Indus Valley settlement in India. The site reveals evidence of a remarkable, planned city with broad roads, containing a central citadel, a middle town with spacious dwellings, a lower town with open spaces for markets and festivities, and two stadia. An intriguing ten-character inscription (which is still to be deciphered) is on the citadel's northern gate. The presence of large reservoirs and a dam reflect the existence of sophisticated systems for harvesting water.

The Little Rann of Kutch Sanctuary ㉕

Kutch district. **Entry points:** Dhrangadhra, 130 km (81 miles) W of Ahmedabad, & Dasada, 117 km (73 miles) NW of Ahmedabad. Dhrangadhra, 20 km (12 miles) S of park. Dhrangadhra & Dasada, then bus or jeep. Gujarat Tourism, Ashram Rd, Ahmedabad, (079) 2657 8046. For permits & tours contact Forest Office, Dhrangadhra. extra charges.

An expanse of salt flats and grasslands in northwest Gujarat, the Little Rann of Kutch has a stark and unforgettable beauty – in sunlight, the salt crystals in the sand glitter like diamonds, while at night they bathe the landscape in an eerie blue haze. Every year, during the monsoon, when the sea and rivers flood the region, the salt flats are transformed into great marshy swamps, with patches of higher ground forming grassy islands known as *bets*. Some 4,841 sq km (1,869 sq miles) of this unique ecosystem, which supports a variety of rare fauna, form a wildlife sanctuary which is one of the last refuges of the Asiatic wild ass *(Equus hemionus khur)*, known locally as *ghorkhur*. Akin to the Tibetan *kiang*, the *ghorkhur* is distinguished by a dark stripe along its back. Only about 1,000 of them now remain. Known for its speed (up to 60 km or 37 miles per hour), the wild ass lives in herds led by a stallion, and survives by migrating between the grassy *bets* through the seasons, in search of food.

The sanctuary also has a large population of nilgai (blue bull), blackbuck, *chinkara* (Indian gazelle), wolves, and the rare caracal. Birdlife includes migratory demoiselle cranes, pelicans and flamingoes who come to the salt marshes during the winter months.

The Asiatic wild ass, found in Kutch

Dhrangadhra and Dasada are both interesting bases from which to visit the Little Rann of Kutch Sanctuary. Dasada has a 15th-century fort and a village where potters and textile printers practise their craft. The family of Dasada's former feudal chiefs arrange accommodation and guided tours of the Rann. Dhrangadhra, capital of a former princely state, has a fine 18th-century palace, and a bazaar with interesting colonial buildings. Tours of the sanctuary can be arranged through the Forest office here. Accommodation is available in the government rest house.

Salt pans in the Rann, a major source of livelihood in Kutch

Rural Life and Art in Kutch

Clay storage niche

Kutch is home to several pastoral communities, many of them semi-nomadic herders of camels and sheep. Among them are the Rabaris, whose round houses (*bhoongas*) with conical roofs are a distinctive feature of the Kutch landscape. These communities are skilled in a variety of crafts, the vibrant hues and forms of their creations adding beauty to their stark surroundings. Anjar, which used to be the crafts centre of Kutch, was tragically destroyed in the January 2001 earthquake, as were many of the crafts villages near Bhuj. Despite this, the intrepid craftspeople continue to work and sell their creations at shops in Mumbai, Ahmedabad and Delhi.

A typical toadstool-shaped Rabari house in Kutch

THE RABARI BHOONGA

The *bhoongas* of the Rabaris, superbly designed for the hot, arid climate of Kutch, are also structurally solid. Most of them withstood the 2001 earthquake. A typical cluster of *bhoongas*, their beautifully decorated interiors displaying the artistic skills of the Rabaris, can be seen at Tunda Vandh, 15 km (9 miles) east of Mandvi.

Bhoongas are built of hard, packed mud and thatch.

Shed for livestock

The **otla** is a platform surrounding the house, shaded by the thatched roof. Women do embroidery and meet their neighbours here.

The roof *is conical, with a deep overhang to keep the walls cool. The parasol-shaped roof frame is made of wood, covered with tightly woven thatch.*

Central courtyard

Small windows, set into the thick walls, are beautifully embellished with brass appliqué patterns.

Entrance

The thick walls, tiny windows and thatched roofs provide excellent insulation against the harsh desert climate. The circular shape helps the smooth circulation of air inside.

Storage jars *and chests, for grain, milk or clothes, are made of clay, and decorated by the women with fine bird, animal and geometric motifs.*

The circular living space *is plastered with white clay, covered with relief patterns and studded with tiny mirrors to provide more light to its dark, cool interior. Niches and shelves built into the walls provide storage for items of everyday use.*

PEOPLE

The pastoral communities of Kutch include Jaths, Ahirs, Meghwals, Bharwads and Sodhas, as well as Rabaris. While the men wander with their flocks, the women, children and elders stay at home, adding to the family income with their crafts skills.

Rabari women *dress in black wool, dramatically offset with silver jewellery. They also sport tattoos of peacocks and camels, as well as small crosses to keep away the evil eye.*

Rabari men, *in contrast to the women, wear only white, with fine embroidery at the back of their pleated* kediyans *(jackets). White and red woven shawls and voluminous turbans complete their attire.*

Rabari girls *wear the family's finest heirlooms. They begin embroidering their trousseau dresses as soon as they can hold a needle.*

CRAFT

Crafts are not just a means of earning and employment for the rural people of Kutch. They are also a proud and creative expression of each community's distinct culture and identity, through which utilitarian objects like cupboards, quilts, shoes, cowbells or clay dishes are transformed into art forms.

Embroidery *is done by most semi-nomadic communities. This section of a large wall hanging shows the work of a Rabari woman.*

Rogan, *a speciality of Niruna village near Bhuj, is a unique technique by which cloth is decorated with intricate, embossed lacquer-work patterns.*

Leather *objects are made by Meghwal men. They are embellished with bright tassels and embroidery.*

Pottery *dishes such as this large platter are used at village feasts. They are made by the men of the Kumbhar (potter) community.*

Patchwork *in vivid colours, using scraps and waste material, is done by Bharwad women to make items such as quilts, awnings and camel saddle covers.*

Silverwork *is crafted by the Sodha community, who also make jewellery to order in traditional designs, for the other pastoral communities.*

SOUTHWESTERN INDIA

Introducing Southwestern India

Encompassing the three states of Maharashtra, Goa and Karnataka, Southwestern India contains the central Deccan Plateau, the narrow Konkan coastline and the craggy Western Ghats that run parallel to the coast. Its major city is Mumbai (Bombay), India's vibrant commercial capital. The region's varied attractions include Goa's idyllic beaches and Portuguese churches, the ancient caves and temples of Ajanta and Ellora, and the magnificent ruins of Hampi. Further south are Bangalore, often described as Asia's Silicon Valley, the former princely state of Mysore, and the great Hoysala temples of Belur and Halebid.

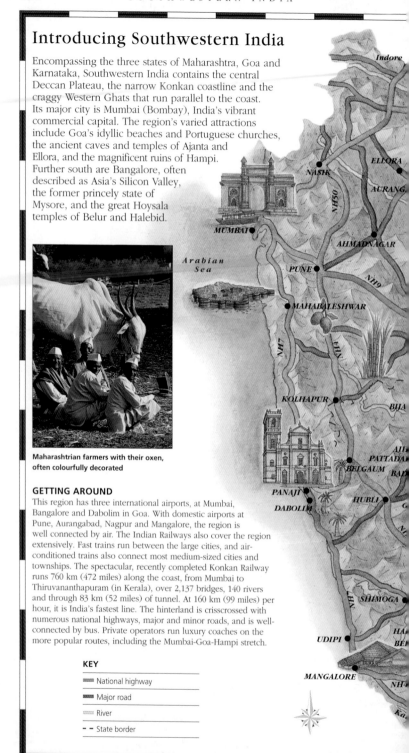

Maharashtrian farmers with their oxen, often colourfully decorated

GETTING AROUND

This region has three international airports, at Mumbai, Bangalore and Dabolim in Goa. With domestic airports at Pune, Aurangabad, Nagpur and Mangalore, the region is well connected by air. The Indian Railways also cover the region extensively. Fast trains run between the large cities, and air-conditioned trains also connect most medium-sized cities and townships. The spectacular, recently completed Konkan Railway runs 760 km (472 miles) along the coast, from Mumbai to Thiruvananthapuram (in Kerala), over 2,137 bridges, 140 rivers and through 83 km (52 miles) of tunnel. At 160 km (99 miles) per hour, it is India's fastest line. The hinterland is crisscrossed with numerous national highways, major and minor roads, and is well-connected by bus. Private operators run luxury coaches on the more popular routes, including the Mumbai-Goa-Hampi stretch.

KEY

▭	National highway
▭	Major road
▭	River
--	State border

◁ Banyan trees forming a canopy over a stretch of road in Maharashtra

Colourful floats on parade, during Goa's annual Carnival

SEE ALSO

- **Where to Stay** pp706–12
- **Where to Eat** pp734–39

0 km   100

0 miles   100

A view of the King's Bathing Ghat surrounded by verdant paddy fields, Srirangapattana, Karnataka

A PORTRAIT OF SOUTHWESTERN INDIA

The southwest is a region of many and varied splendours. Its three states, Maharashtra, Goa and Karnataka, contain golden beaches, wooded hills, serene villages along the picturesque Arabian Sea coastline, and two of India's most cosmopolitan and dynamic cities – Mumbai (formerly Bombay) and Bangalore.

Mumbai, capital of Maharashtra, is India's largest and most populous city, as well as its commercial and financial capital. It is also home to the world's largest cinema industry, popularly known as Bollywood. The city presents extraordinary and sometimes shocking contrasts – the glamorous world of film stars and business tycoons exists side by side with the squalor of slums and shantytowns, where over three million people (nearly one-third of Mumbai's population) live. The dominant image, however, is that of an upbeat, street-smart city full of dynamism and *joie de vivre*.

Green coconut

Mumbai's population includes Marathi-speaking Hindus, a sizeable number of Muslims and Christians, as well as Jews, Parsis and other communities from different parts of India, drawn by its vibrant entrepreneurial culture, and often, by dreams of making it big in films. While this makes Mumbai remarkably cosmopolitan, it has on occasion led to sectarian strife, especially over the past decade, since the rise of the militant Hindu rightwing Shiv Sena Party.

Maharashtra is a vast state, its population of over 96 million making it politically important, and major industries based on cotton, sugar, engineering goods and processed foods lending it economic vitality. In recent years, strawberry fields and

Little fishing boats in Mumbai's harbour, against a backdrop of the city's skyscrapers

Goan women on their way to Sunday Mass

grape vineyards have made their appearance in its rich agricultural hinterland, but the most prized crop remains the Alfonso mango, a particularly sweet and luscious variety, which is exported across the world. Central Maharashtra has two World Heritage sites to its credit, at Ajanta and Ellora *(see pp476–81)*. The murals and sculptures found here testify to the common, ancient roots of Hinduism and Buddhism.

Many visitors travel by train from Mumbai to the tiny neighbouring state of Goa. The Konkan Railway which connects the two, and continues southwards to Karnataka, is a wonderful way to see the lush coastal scenery of coconut groves, spice plantations and fishing villages. Goa was a Portuguese colony from 1510 until 1961, when it was liberated by the Indian Army. The Portuguese departed peacefully, leaving behind a rich cultural legacy in cathedrals and mansions, music, dance, and in its distinctive cuisine. Another legacy of 450 years of Portuguese rule is in religion – almost one-third of Goa's population is Roman Catholic. Tourism and related industries are today a major source of livelihood here. Visitors from all over the world throng the beautiful beaches, which offer secluded palm-fringed retreats, as well as lively resorts buzzing with bars, cafés and discos.

A Hanuman statue in Nasik, Maharashtra

Karnataka is often described as the geographical and cultural meeting point between India's Dravidian south and its Indo-Aryan north. The state's varied landscape and architecture both reflect this unique melange. Karnataka's narrow strip of fertile coastland is backed by the green hills of the Western Ghats, covered with forests of fragrant sandalwood and teak. These slope down to a vast plateau, watered by the Kaveri and Krishna rivers. This is the state's historic and cultural heartland, dotted with architectural treasures in an extraordinary variety of styles. They were built by local Hindu and Muslim dynasties, as well as by ambitious rulers from the north, Maratha warriors and medieval Islamic chieftains, all of whom had once established kingdoms here.

Bangalore, the state capital, presents a sharp contrast to Karnataka's historic sites. As the ebullient centre of India's burgeoning computer software industry, this once laid-back town has been transformed into a globalized, high-tech showcase for contemporary India. Several multinational corporations have opened offices here, while pubs and shopping malls line its streets, catering to a young, cosmopolitan population.

The lush landscape along Karnataka's coastline

The Konkan Coast

All along the Konkan Coast, from Mumbai to the south of Mangalore, are villages where, for over 2,000 years, fishing communities have harvested the fruits of the sea. A distinctive culture has developed in this area, protected by the forested hills of the Western Ghats. Beyond the coastline are fertile paddy fields, and plantations of coconut, cashew, betel nut, rubber, pepper and other spices. This is also India's monsoon land, where the Southwest Monsoon is at its heaviest, and where Arab merchants, drawn by the monsoon winds, came to trade long before the Europeans.

A Konkani fisherwoman

LOCATOR MAP

▢ *Extent of Area*

Harvesting *ripe paddy is a full-time occupation for the entire village.*

PADDY CULTIVATION
In wet paddy cultivation, seedlings are raised in a nursery and then transplanted in waterlogged fields when they are 30 cm (12 in) high.

Pepper, cashew and betel nut *are some of the major cash crops that this region grows in abundance.*

A rubber plantation *bungalow is festooned with strips of cured rubber hanging out to dry.*

FISHERFOLK OF THE COAST
Coastal people belong to different communities, speak their own dialects and celebrate local festivals. Strong and hard-working, their lives are ruled by natural forces.

Fishermen prepare their boats *before they cast off just before dawn. The boats return by late morning.*

A basket of freshly caught fish *is carried to the shore to be sold directly to waiting customers.*

These women *from Mumbai's small Koli fishing community are dressed in bright festival finery.*

Coastal dwellings *have sloping roofs made of tiles to deflect the heavy rains during the monsoon.*

Flowers *are a common form of adornment and are picked each morning by girls and women for their hair.*

Small boats moored in the Konkan backwaters

KONKAN COAST

The narrow coastal strip that runs along the Arabian Sea is sheltered by the verdant slopes of the Western Ghats. This region can be explored either by road or on the Konkan Railway (see p434).

Monsoon clouds *herald the onset of the monsoon, when the coast is lashed by torrential rain from June to early September.*

The Western Ghats, *or the Sahyadri Range, run in an unbroken line along the coast.*

Dried fish *is eaten during the monsoon when heavy rains prevent fishing.*

Local fish markets *sell a large variety of freshly caught produce.*

Boat building *is done by expert artisans who repair old boats using traditional methods, as well as build new ones from locally procured wood.*

The Flavours of Southwestern India

A large part of this region lies on the shores of the Arabian Sea and consequently fish, coconut and rice are the dominant ingredients. Mumbai is a metropolis, home to many groups of people, and the city's cuisine reflects its myriad influences. Further south, along the Konkan Coast to Goa and Mangalore, the fish and rice diet has regional variations. Interior Maharashtra has a large number of vegetarian communities especially around Pune, although spicy mutton curries are a speciality of the state. Karnataka's food is a mosaic of distinct communities such as the coastal Udipi vegetarian fare and the meat-based food of Kodagu.

Custard apple

A local woman selling bananas, coconuts and other fruit

BASIC DISHES

In Maharashtra, rice, wheat, lentils and *jowar* (sorghum maize) form the backbone of the people's diet. This accompanies the *bhaji* (a vegetable dish) or *rassa*, (curried vegetables cooked in groundnut oil). The food is distinguished by a blend of spices, coriander, sesame, cumin seeds and dried coconut (*goda*) and *kalaa masalas*. *Koshimbirs* (relishes freshly made with cucumber or carrots) perk up the meal.

In Karnataka, the three staples are rice, *jowar* and *ragi* (finger millet). In rural areas, *ragi* is steam-cooked, rolled into balls and served with hot chutney or *huli* (a spicy lentil dish). Variations of the *dosa* (see pp554–5) are also eaten here with coconut chutney and potatoes.

COASTAL FARE

Along the Konkan Coast, coconuts, cashew nuts and fresh vegetables are in abundance. However, seafood predominates and the types of fish available range from the flat pomfret, salmon (*rawas*) and mackerel to prawns, lobsters and clams. Fish is grilled, fried or cooked as curries with fresh coconut and spices. *Kokum*

Prawns · Mackerel · Lobster · Squid · Pomfret · Mussels · Sardines

Selection of seafood available along the Arabian Sea coastline

LOCAL DISHES AND SPECIALITIES

The culinary choices in this region are varied and range from stalls selling spicy savouries, such as *bhelpuri, pani-puri* and *pav-bhaji*, to beach shacks and specialist restaurants. Tastes are eclectic and reflect flavours imported from as far off as Iran (Parsi) and Portugal (Goa). Karnataka's and Maharashtra's vegetarian food is complemented by the fish, pork and chicken dishes from the Konkan Coast, Goa, Mangalore and Coorg. This fertile region yields fruits, such as *chikoo* (sapodilla plum) custard apple, mango, papaya and grapes, as well as crops such as sugarcane and cashew, and spices, particularly pepper. During the mild winters in south Maharashtra, jaggery is made, and with it, a peanut or sesame toffee (*chikki*).

Cashew nuts

Akuri, *spicy scrambled eggs cooked with tomatoes and onions and garnished with coriander, is a Parsi delicacy.*

Fishermen unloading the catch of the day, Goa

leaf), *jardaloo sali boti* (mutton with apricots), and the popular *dhan sak* (a meat and lentil casserole).

The Kodavas of Coorg have a distinct culture and cuisine and are the only Hindu community that allows non-vegetarian food and alcohol to be served at weddings. *Pandi* (pork) curry is a favourite and is eaten with steamed rice balls *(kadumbuttu)*. *Koli* curry, a chicken curry, and *bembla* curry, made from bamboo shoots, are other specialities, as are their wonderful rice preparations, such as *noolputtu* (rice noodles) or *oduputtu* (rice pancakes), enjoyed by other communities too.

(a dried sour plum), tamarind, raw mango or the local Goan vinegar are used as souring agents. *Kokum* and coconut milk are also used to make a drink, *sol kadhi.*

Although the coastal area has several culinary features in common, particularly in the preparation of seafood, Goa's cuisine is different as it combines Portuguese and local flavours. Some typical dishes include *peixe a Portuguese* (a fish curry with olive oil) and *ambot-tik* (a tangy fish curry with tamarind). Goan chillies are famed for their colour and are used to make the *recheio masala,* which is added to fish, pork and mutton curries.

Malvan fish dishes are equally tasty, especially the *mori chi aamti* (a spicy shark curry) and *bangda* (whole mackerel fried with spices).

OTHER FAVOURITES

The cuisine of the Parsis of Mumbai reflects their Persian ancestory. Their food is mainly non-vegetarian and includes *patra ni machhi* (fish steamed in a banana

Coffee berries from a plantation in Coorg, Karnataka

ON THE MENU

Amti Sweet and sour lentils.

Balachão Prawns or chicken cooked with pickling spices.

Bebinca A multi-layered cake.

Kesari bhath Sweet made of semolina, sugar and saffron.

Kolhapuri mutton Mutton with chillies, coconut, aniseed and poppy seed.

Moru kolumbu Vegetables in a yoghurt sauce.

Patra ni macchi Fish with a coriander-coconut chutney, steamed in banana leaves.

Suran Steamed yam garnished with dry red chillies and curry leaves.

Vindaloo *a dish of pork cooked in a marinade of vinegar, red chillies and other spices, is Goa's signature dish.*

Fugad *is finely sliced, stir fried cabbage garnished with coconut and chillies. Beans can also be used.*

Bisibele huliyana, *a preparation of lentils, rice and vegetables, is a one-dish meal from Karnataka.*

MUMBAI

Mumbai (formerly Bombay), capital of Maharashtra, is India's most dynamic, cosmopolitan and crowded city. The country's financial centre and its busiest port, Mumbai is also home to the world's biggest cinema industry, popularly known as Bollywood. Some 15 million people, from billionaire tycoons to homeless pavement dwellers, live in this teeming megalopolis.

Consisting of seven swampy islands when the Portuguese acquired it in 1534, Bombay (from the Portuguese Bom Bahia or "Good Bay") came to the British Crown in 1661 as part of the dowry of Catherine of Braganza when she married Charles II. Finding little use for the islands, the British then leased them for a pittance to the East India Company, which quickly realized their potential as an excellent natural harbour in the Arabian Sea. By the 18th century, Bombay had become the major city and shipbuilding yard on the western coast, and by the 19th century land reclamations had joined the islands into the narrow promontory that it is today. The promise of commercial opportunities lured communities of Gujaratis, Parsis *(see p447)* and Baghdadi or Sephardic Jews to settle in Bombay, giving the city its vibrant multicultural identity.

The city has now reverted to its local name, Mumbai, from Mumba Devi, the eight-armed goddess worshipped by the Koli fishermen who were the islands' original inhabitants.

Mumbai is a city of striking contrasts. Here skyscrapers stand next to stately Victorian buildings, noisy traditional bazaars adjoin glittering new shopping malls, and opulent neighbourhoods are surrounded by sprawling slums. Swelling Mumbai's population and stretching its suburban environs are migrants from all over the country who continue to flock to this "city of gold", in search of fame, fortune, or just a bit part in a Bollywood movie.

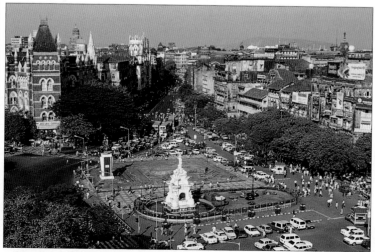

Swirling traffic around Flora Fountain in the heart of Mumbai

◁ The Gateway of India, Mumbai's signature landmark, on the shores of the Arabian Sea

Exploring Mumbai

Mumbai is a long, narrow promontory covering 430 sq km (166 sq miles), which juts into the Arabian Sea. Its downtown is the historic Fort area in South Mumbai, that derives its name from earlier colonial fortifications. This is the city's nerve centre, with the best known sights, hotels and restaurants. The posh residential area of Malabar Hill lies along the western coastline, just north of Marine Drive. Suburban Mumbai, with its sprawling new developments, stretches northwards from Bandra.

SEE ALSO

• **Where to Stay** pp706–08

• **Where to Eat** pp734–5

Fishing boats, decorated for Holi, at the seafront in South Mumbai

SIGHTS AT A GLANCE

Historic Buildings, Streets & Neighbourhoods
Ballard Estate ⑬
Bandra ㉑
Colaba Causeway ❸
Flora Fountain ❾
Gateway of India ❶
General Post Office ⑭
Horniman Circle ❼
Kala Ghoda pp448–9 ❹
Khotachiwadi ⑱
Malabar Hill ⑯
Marine Drive ⑮
Mumbai Stock Exchange ❽
Shahid Bhagat Singh Marg ⑫
Town Hall ❻
Victoria Terminus pp454–5 ❿
Wellington Fountain ❷

Historic Sites
Elephanta Island ㉕

Museums
The Prince of Wales Museum pp450–51 ❺

Temples & Mosques
Banganga ⑰
Haji Ali Mosque ⑳
Mahalaxmi Temple ⑲

Beaches & Parks
Juhu Beach ㉒
Sanjay Gandhi National Park ㉔

Shops & Markets
Crawford Market ⑪

Entertainment
Film City ㉓

LOCATOR MAP

KEY

▪	Street-by-Street area: see pp448–9
✈	International airport
✈	Domestic airport
🚆	Railway station
🚌	Bus station
⛴	Ferry port
ℹ	Tourist information
✚	Hospital
👮	Police station
✉	Post office
✝	Church
━	National highway
━	Major road

GETTING AROUND

Three punctual, if crowded, suburban railway lines link the northern suburbs to the city centre and the southern tip. A private car, taxi, or the red BEST buses are all convenient and reasonably priced ways to get around within the city.

Doubledecker bus at Victoria Terminus *(see pp454–5)*

0 metres 400
0 yards 400

GREATER MUMBAI

Thane
Malad
Andheri
New Mumbai
Sahar
Santa Cruz
Arabian Sea
Trombay
Nhave

0 km 1
0 miles 1

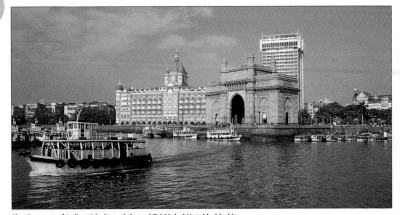

The Gateway of India with the red-domed Taj Mahal Hotel behind it

Gateway of India ❶

Apollo Bunder, Chhatrapati Shivaji
Marg & PJ Ramchandani Marg.

Mumbai's most famous
landmark, the Gateway
of India, was the first sight
to greet travellers to Indian
shores during the heyday of
the British Raj. Ironically, it
also became the exit
point for British
troops after India
gained independence in 1947. It
was built to commemorate the visit
of King George V
and Queen Mary
in 1911, en route
to the Delhi Durbar,
but in fact, the
King and Queen
were met with a
mock cardboard
and pastiche
structure – the
actual Triumphal Arch, built
in honey coloured basalt, was
only completed in 1924, years
after the royal visit. This monumental structure with two
large reception halls, arches
and minarets, and embellishments inspired by medieval
Gujarati architecture, was
designed by the Scottish
architect George Wittet, and
commands a spectacular view
of the sea. The Gateway
looks particularly impressive
at night when it is illuminated, with the inky black sea
stretching into the horizon
beyond it. This is the heart of
Mumbai's tourist district, the

**Statue of Chhatrapati Shivaji
opposite the Gateway**

city's most popular gathering
place, and always teems with
locals, visitors, vendors and
boatmen. Boats and barges
moored here provide regular
services across the bay and to
islands such as Elephanta *(see
p461)*. They can also be hired
for leisurely trips down the
Mumbai coastline.

North of the Gateway of
India, towards Wellington
Fountain, is Chhatrapati
Shivaji Road. Formerly
Apollo Pier Road, it has now
been renamed after
Shivaji *(see p471)*,
Maharashtra's great
warrior-hero.
Shivaji's equestrian statue is
placed here in a
pleasant garden,
in line with the
Gateway. Standing nearby is
another statue,
that of the great
19th-century Hindu philosopher and reformist, Swami
Vivekananda *(see p615)*.

Around the Gateway are
some majestic buildings
dating from the colonial era.
These include the old **Yacht
Club** which now houses the
offices of the Atomic Energy
Commission (entry restricted),
the **Royal Bombay Yacht Club**,
originally built as a residential
annexe to the Old Yacht Club,
and the **Taj Mahal Hotel** *(see
p708)*, behind which lies the
busy Colaba Causeway.

The stately, red-domed Taj
Mahal Hotel was built in 1903
by a prominent Parsi industrialist, Jamshedji Tata *(see
p225)* who, it is said, decided
to construct this magnificent
hotel when he was barred
from entering the "Whites
Only" Watsons Hotel. The
Taj, with its splendid Moorish
arches and columns, majestic
stairways and galleries,
remains one of Asia's grandest hotels, while Watsons is
now a dilapidated building,
the hotel having closed down
long ago.

The eastern sea face stretching in front of the Gateway of
India is Mumbai's favourite
promenade. Called **Apollo
Bunder**, it was once the
traditional dockyard of the
local Koli fishermen, the
islands' original inhabitants.
Today, snake charmers and
performing monkeys, astrologers and ear-cleaners hustle
for business among the
strollers. Dozens of yachts,
fishing boats and ferries are
moored in the waters beyond.

**The Royal Bombay Yacht Club, a
relic of the British Raj**

The entrance to Cusrow Baug, a Parsi enclave along Colaba

Wellington Fountain ❷

Bounded by MG Rd, Shahid Bhagat Singh Marg, Chhatrapati Shivaji Marg & Madame Cama Rd.

Built to commemorate the Duke of Wellington's visit to Bombay in 1801, Wellington Fountain (now renamed Shyama Prasad Mukherjee Chowk) is encircled by some magnificent colonial buildings. These include the old **Majestic Hotel** (now the government-owned Sahakari Bhandar) with its mock minarets and Gujarati balconies, and the elegant Art Deco **Regal Cinema**, designed by Charles Stevens and completed in 1934. His father, Frederick William Stevens, designed the imposing grey stone Indo-Gothic **Sailors' Home**, with a bas-relief of Neptune on its front gable, in 1876; it is now the Police Headquarters. Equally impressive are the Edwardian Cowasjee Jehangir Hall, now the **National Gallery of Modern Art** (see p449), and

the Indo-Saracenic **Prince of Wales Museum** (see pp450–51). Adjoining it is Hornbill House, the headquarters of the Bombay Natural History Society (BNHS), a prestigious institution established in 1883.

Colaba Causeway ❸

Shahid Bhagat Singh Marg. **Afghan Memorial Church** ☐ daily. 🛉 7am & 4:30pm, Sun.

Constructed by the British in 1838, Colaba Causeway helped integrate the main city with Colaba, its southernmost spur. Today, the Causeway, also known as Shahid Bhagat Singh Road (see p456), is a lively mix of shops, restaurants and residential enclaves. Among them is the charming Parsi housing colony of **Cusrow Baug**, built in the 1930s, where the distinct culture and lifestyle of this dwindling community is preserved. Of the Causeway's many restaurants is one that has become an institution, the **Leopold Café and Bar** (see

p735), established in 1871, and a popular meeting place ever since. Further south are the **Sassoon Docks**, worth visiting early in the morning when they are buzzing with activity. This is when the fishermen bring in their catch and a wholesale fish market is set up by the lively, sharp-tongued Koli fishwives.

At the southern end of Colaba is the **Afghan Memorial Church of St John the Evangelist**, built between 1847 and 1858 (see p21). This grand Neo-Gothic structure with its tall spire and imposing front porch in buff basalt stone, was built in memory of the soldiers who died in the First Afghan War (1843), and the church is full of poignant memorial stones. It has superb stained glass, especially on its west windows, where an outstanding panel depicts the Crucifixion. A memorial to the martyrs stands in the garden.

Fishermen bringing in the day's catch at Sassoon Docks

THE PARSI COMMUNITY IN MUMBAI

Conductor Zubin Mehta, a Mumbai-born Parsi

Mumbai's cosmopolitan, progressive culture owes a great deal to the contribution of the Parsi community. Originally from Iran, where they followed the ancient Zoroastrian faith, they migrated to India in the 9th century AD when the advent of Islam brought with it the religious persecution of Zoroastrians. They settled along the west coast of Gujarat, absorbing many local traditions, and later moved to Mumbai where they made their name as brilliant financiers and traders. Often, they adopted the name of their trade, and so one finds Parsi surnames such as Mistry (mason) and Vakil (lawyer), or even Readymoney! A wealthy and talented community that has produced several leading industrial houses, such as the Tatas and the Godrejs, Parsis are also renowned for their philanthropy and have founded several cultural, educational and medical institutions in Mumbai.

Street-by-Street: Kala Ghoda ❹

Kala Ghoda, or "Black Horse", takes its name from an equestrian statue of King Edward VII that once stood at the intersection of Mahatma Gandhi Road and K Dubash Marg. The statue has long since been removed, but the name persists in public memory. Stretching from Wellington Fountain at the southern end of Mahatma Gandhi Road, to Bombay University at the north, and flanked by the Oval Maidan and the naval base at Lion Gate, this historic area is a hub of cultural

Detail, Clock Tower

activity. It also houses a number of art galleries, cafés, restaurants and fine shops and boutiques.

David Sassoon Library
The garden behind the library serves as a reading area.

Flora Fountain

Victoria Terminus

★ Rajabai Clock Tower
This 78-m (256-ft) high tower in Bombay University is adorned with figures representing different Indian communities.

Bombay University complex

★ High Court
This fortress-like building, the second largest public building in the city, has a grand central staircase, well-appointed court rooms, and a large library.

Esplanade Mansion, formerly Watsons Hotel, witnessed the city's first motion picture in 1896.

Old Secretariat

STAR SIGHTS
★ Rajabai Clock Tower
★ High Court
★ Prince of Wales Museum

Army & Navy Building
The Neo-Classical Army & Navy Building, a departmental store in the early 1900s, is home to several offices of the Tata Group.

Kenneseth Eliyahoo Synagogue

This is the oldest Sephardic synagogue in the city, donated by the Sassoon family. It is used for prayer by Mumbai's Baghdadi and Bene Israeli Jewish community.

0 metres 50

0 yards 50

LOCATOR MAP
See Mumbai Map pp444–5

KEY

– – Suggested route

Elphinstone College
Part of this delightful Venetian Gothic building houses the State Archives.

Kenneseth Eliyahoo Synagogue

K DUBASH MARG

Lion Gate

Hornbill House

Police Headquarters

Wellington Fountain

Gateway of India

Regal Cinema

David Sassoon Library

★ Prince of Wales Museum
Mumbai's most prestigious museum has a good collection of Rajput miniatures and sculptures (see pp450–51).

The National Gallery of Modern Art, an Edwardian building, has the most impressive exhibition space in Mumbai.

Jehangir Art Gallery
This gallery exhibits paintings by leading contemporary Indian artists, and also has a popular café.

The Prince of Wales Museum ❺

Especially renowned for its superb sculptures and miniature paintings, the Prince of Wales Museum's exhibits are housed in a grand Indo-Saracenic building, designed by George Wittet. Its foundation stone was laid by the Prince of Wales (the future George V) in 1905. During World War I, it served as a military hospital, and was formally inaugurated in 1923. Generous gifts from discerning private collectors have enabled the museum to build a collection of rare quality.

Damascened sword, Mysore, 1732

Japanese Cloisonné
This 19th-century vase forms part of an impressive collection of Far Eastern art.

Second floor

Ivory Statuette
A Parsi girl, Bai Aimai Wadia, is depicted in traditional dress in this 19th-century piece from the Decorative Arts gallery.

Arms and Armour include the finely decorated swords and shields of the Mughal emperors.

★ Jahangir Giving Alms
This early 17th-century Mughal miniature shows Jahangir giving alms to Sufi mendicants at the Dargah Sharif in Ajmer. The gallery has over 200 miniatures.

The Coomaraswamy Hall hosts seminars and temporary exhibitions.

KEY TO FLOORPLAN

- ▢ Pre- and Proto-History Gallery
- ▢ Key Gallery
- ▢ Indian Sculpture
- ▢ Natural History Section
- ▢ Decorative Arts
- ▢ Miniature Paintings
- ▢ Bronzes
- ▢ Nepalese and Tibetan Art
- ▢ Maritime History
- ▢ European Paintings
- ▢ Far Eastern Art
- ▢ Arms and Armour
- ▨ Premchand Roychand Gallery

STAR EXHIBITS

- ★ Jahangir Giving Alms
- ★ Maitreya Buddha
- ★ Gandhara Sculpture

GALLERY GUIDE

The museum, now re-named the Chhatrapati Shivaji Maharaj Vastu-Sangrahalaya, has galleries on three floors. The ground floor houses sculpture (including Gandhara masterpieces), the Pre- and Proto-History Gallery, and the Natural History Section. On the first floor are miniature paintings, decorative arts, Nepalese and Tibetan Art, and the newly opened Premchand Roychand Galleries. The second floor has European paintings, arms and armour.

VISITORS' CHECKLIST

MG Rd, Fort Area. *Tel (022) 2284 4519.* 🅾 Tue–Sun. 🎫 *Students with an International ID card get a discount.* 📷 ♿ 🏪

Key Gallery

The central hall on the ground floor offers a sampling of the museum's treasures, with prize exhibits from different galleries.

First floor

Karl Khandalvala Gallery

★ Maitreya Buddha

An outstanding example of Nepalese art, this 12th-century gilt bronze statue of the Future Buddha was, like most of the museum's prized pieces, a gift from a private collector.

Ground floor

★ Gandhara Sculpture

This 3rd-century AD sculpture of the Buddha meeting an ascetic shows strong Greek influence.

Entrance

The Town Hall, Mumbai's most elegant public building

Town Hall ❻

Shahid Bhagat Singh Marg, Fort Area.
Tel (022) 2266 0956. ⬤ Mon–Sat.
⬤ public hols. **The Asiatic Society**
Tel (022) 2266 0956. ⬤ Mon–Sat.

In recognition of Mumbai's importance as a burgeoning commercial centre in the 19th century, the city was bestowed with a Town Hall, facing the vast open space of Cotton Green (now Horniman Circle). Designed by Colonel Thomas Cowper and completed in 1833, the Town Hall is considered to be among the finest Neo-Classical buildings in India, and is one of the earliest surviving colonial buildings in Mumbai. Its impressive façade of pedimented porticoes surmounts a row of fluted Doric columns, which were shipped out from England. A grand flight of steps leads into a magnificent Assembly Hall, the venue for public meetings during the Raj.

The Town Hall's north wing houses **The Asiatic Society**, founded in 1804, with its imposing high ceiling, teak-panelled walls, and elegant cast iron balustrades. This institution's extensive library has a priceless collection of 800,000 volumes, including a first edition of Dante's *Divine Comedy*, ancient Sanskrit manuscripts and old Bombay gazetteers. On the first floor are marble statues of Mumbai's founding fathers, among them two governors, Mountstuart Elphinstone and Sir Bartle Frere, and the Parsi philanthropist, Sir Jamsetjee Jeejeebhoy.

Horniman Circle ❼

Veer Nariman Rd, Fort Area.
St Thomas' Cathedral Tel (022)
2202 0121. ⬤ daily. ✝ 8am &
4:30pm, Sun.

The central green, the old Cotton Green where traders used to buy and sell bales of cotton, was laid out as a public garden in 1869. Later known as Elphinstone Circle, it was renamed after Independence in honour of Benjamin Guy Horniman, a former editor of the *Bombay Chronicle* who was an active supporter of India's Freedom Movement. Today, the garden remains a delightful spot, much frequented by students and office workers who relax here before the long commute back to their homes in the distant suburbs. The garden is also the venue for

Greek-inspired keystone at
Horniman Circle

open-air theatrical performances and cultural events in the winter.

The elegant circle of Neo-Classical buildings around the garden was built in the 1860s, and fashioned after acclaimed English examples such as Bath Crescent and Tunbridge Wells. Designed by James Scott, the buildings around the garden share a uniform façade with pedestrian arcades and decorative terracotta keystones from England, and represent the earliest planned urban compositions in Mumbai.

Anchoring the western edge of the flower-filled green patch of Horniman Circle is **St Thomas' Cathedral**, the city's oldest church, which was consecrated in 1718. Like many of Mumbai's great edifices, this too was funded by public donations, collected in large part by a young East India Company chaplain named Richard Cobbe. The church has an imposing bell tower and flying buttresses, and some fine 19th-century stained glass. The cathedral's spacious interior is especially remarkable for its splendid marble memorials to heroes of the Raj. An exceptionally fine one is the monument to Governor Duncan, which depicts him being blessed by Hindus for his efforts to stop infanticide. In front of the entrance porch is a charming Neo-Gothic fountain. Designed by Sir Gilbert Scott, it was donated by the Parsi financier, Sir Cowasjee Readymoney.

Opposite the Cathedral are some lovely buildings – the Neo-Gothic **Elphinstone Building**, built in the late 19th century, and the Neo-Classical **British Bank of the Middle East**. Across the road is the **Readymoney Mansion** with its detailed timberwork, carved balconies, and Mughal arches. Reminiscent of a Rajasthani *haveli*, it was also designed by George Wittet *(see p450)*.

Stained glass,
St Thomas'
Cathedral

The Mumbai Stock Exchange, India's financial epicentre

Mumbai Stock Exchange **8**

Dalal Street, Fort Area. ◑ to public.

India's financial epicentre, the **Mumbai Stock Exchange** towers above Dalal Street. This is Mumbai's Wall Street and derives its name from the many stockbrokers (*dalals*) in the area. The presence of close to 50 banks on a short stretch underlines the frenetic pace of its commercial activity. Just before lunchtime, the area swarms with *dabbawallahs (see p457)* who bring home-made lunchboxes to the thousands of office workers in the area.

Flora Fountain **9**

Junction of Veer Nariman Rd, MG Rd & Dr Dadabhai Naoroji Rd, Fort Area.

Standing at the intersection of three major streets is **Flora Fountain**, the quintessential icon of Mumbai. Crafted out of Portland stone and shipped out from England, the fountain is surmounted by the Roman goddess Flora who stands above exuberantly carved seashells, dolphins and mythical beasts. Erected in 1869 in what was then a spacious open plaza, Flora Fountain is now swamped in a sea of traffic, and over-shadowed by a **Martyrs' Memorial** put up by the Maharashtra state government in 1960. The area has now been renamed Hutatma

Chowk ("Martyrs' Square"). This area marks the western ramparts of the now-vanished old Fort, built by the East India Company in 1716, which covered the southern part of the city. The Fort was demolished in the 1860s by the governor, Sir Bartle Frere, to allow the city to expand, and to accommodate the grandiose new civic and commercial buildings he had planned. All these buildings were designed with pedes-trian arcades, which today are crowded with hawkers selling a wide range of goods, from old books to clothes and electronic gadgets.

North of Flora Fountain, leading towards Victoria Ter-minus, is Dadabhai Naoroji (DN) Road, lined with some magnificent Victorian and later colonial structures such as the **Capitol Cinema** with its classical detailing, the **JN Petit Institute and Library** (1898) with its Venetian Neo-Gothic façade, and the Art Deco **Watcha Agiary** (Parsi Fire Temple) with its Assyrian-style carvings, built in 1881. Other interesting struc-tures include the **Times of India Building** and the fanciful **Municipal Corporation Building**, with its Islamic minarets, Gothic towers and onion domes.

Victoria Terminus **10**

See pp454–5.

Flora Fountain, a favourite Mumbai landmark

Crawford Market **11**

Dr Dadabhai Naoroji Rd & Lokmanya Tilak Rd. **Shops** ◐ daily.

One of Mumbai's most fascinating and lively areas, Crawford Market, now renamed Mahatma Jyotiba Phule Market, lies to the north of Victoria Terminus. Designed by William Emerson and completed in 1869, this architectural extravaganza of Moorish arches and half-timbered gables, topped by a clocktower, consists of a large central hall with two wings. Tiers of wooden stalls display nearly 3,000 tonnes of fresh produce daily, from fruit and flowers to fish and exotic birds. The floor is paved with stone from Caithness in Scotland, which remains cool through the day. The lamps are shaped like winged dragons. Above the entrance doors, the charming marble bas-reliefs depict scenes from market life. They were carved by Lockwood Kipling (*see p110*), father of the writer Rudyard Kipling, as was the fountain in the courtyard exuberantly decorated with Hindu river goddesses and animals.

Just west of Crawford Mar-ket is **Zaveri Bazaar**, where diamond, gold and silver merchants have their opulent stores. Northwest of Crawford Market, on Mutton Street, is **Chor Bazaar** ("Thieves' Market"), with its fascinating antique and bric-a-brac shops.

Vegetable stall at Crawford Market

Victoria Terminus ⑩

Central Railway emblem on the gate

The most impressive example of Victorian Gothic architecture in India, Victoria Terminus Railway Station (now renamed Chhatrapati Shivaji Terminus) is a rich extravaganza of domes, spires and arches. Designed by Frederick William Stevens and decorated by local art students and craftsmen, it was completed in 1888 and named to commemorate Queen Victoria's Golden Jubilee. Now the headquarters of the Central Railway, over 1,000 trains and two million passengers, including crowds of suburban commuters, pass through the station daily. In 2004, it was declared a UNESCO World Heritage Site.

Victoria Terminus, often mistaken for a grand palace or cathedral

The Gables
The gables are crowned by sculptures representing Engineering, Agriculture and Commerce.

★ Booking Hall
A Neo-Gothic vaulted roof with wooden ribs covers the hall. Stained glass, colourful tiles and decorative iron grilles add to its beauty.

Entrance
The entrance gate piers are topped by stone sculptures of a lion and a tiger, symbolizing Britain and India, respectively.

STAR SIGHTS

★ Booking Hall

★ Stone Carvings and Sculptures

The Central Dome
A 4-m (13-ft) high statue of "Progress", holding a torch, crowns the colossal dome, which has eight decorated ribs.

A majestic staircase of blue stone, with beautiful iron railings, sweeps up beneath the dome.

Water spouts shaped like animal heads jut out from the base of the dome.

VISITORS' CHECKLIST

Dr Dadabhai Naoroji Rd, Fort Area. **Tel** (022) 2264 6464
☒ of the interiors. 🍴 ♿ 🏠

Stained Glass
Set into the octagonal tower below the dome are brilliantly coloured stained-glass windows, decorated with a locomotive and foliage.

Portrait Medallion
Studded into the façade are busts of Raj-era personalities, such as Sir Bartle Frere (see p452).

★ Stone Carvings and Sculptures
An exquisite peacock carving decorates this window. Other carved screens and friezes feature elephants, monkeys and snakes.

The Ruttonsee Mulji fountain, elaborately carved and embellished

Shahid Bhagat Singh Marg ⑫

Fort Area.

This busy street, also known as Colaba Causeway *(see p447)* towards its southern end, is the bustling commercial and administrative hub of the so-called Fort area *(see p453)*. Virtually no traces of this historic structure remain, but the area still offers a fascinating glimpse into the continuities between colonial and present-day Mumbai.

The **Reserve Bank of India**, which stands on the site of an old military barracks, is India's leading banking institution. Built in 1939 and designed by JA Ritchie, its grand Art Deco entrance, flanked by two impressive columns, enhances its air of respectable solidity. There are attractive cast iron grilles in the window panels. The new highrise offices of the Reserve Bank, across the road, stand in the grounds of the old **Mint**. This is a majestic Classical-fronted building, built in 1817 by Major John Hawkins, a member of the Bombay Engineers' Regiment. Entry into the Mint is restricted, but visible from its compound is a stone gateway erected by the Portuguese, now inside the naval establishment, INS Angre.

West of the Mint, occupying a corner site at the intersection of Pherozeshah Mehta and Shahid Bhagat Singh roads, is

the imposing **Gresham Assurance Building**. This Art Deco structure has an impressive basalt façade, with two grand pillars and a dome.

The **Marshall Building**, directly opposite, has a Florentine dome, and was constructed in 1898 to accommodate the warehouse and offices of a British engineering firm. Its façade, embellished with a medley of angels, portholes and pediments, is a wonderful example of how contemporary European architecture was successfully transplanted to eastern settings.

Drinking water fountains or *pyavs* were set up across the city by local philanthropists to provide respite from the hot Indian summer. At the point where Shahid Bhagat Singh Marg meets Mint Road is the **Ruttonsee Mulji Drinking Water Fountain** designed by FW Stevens, the leading architect of Victorian Bombay, who also designed the Municipal Corporation Building and the Victoria Terminus *(see pp454–5)*. This fountain was erected in 1894 by a local trader, in memory of his only son, whose statue stands beneath the dome. Made of limestone and red and blue granite, it is decorated with projecting elephant heads, whose trunks spout water. The dome, supported by columns made of blue granite, is crowned by the figure of a young boy. The fountain also has a special trough from which animals can drink.

Further down Mint Road, just before its junction with Walchand Hirachand Marg, is another *pyav* and the **Kothari Kabutarkhana**. Literally "Pigeon House", the Kabutarkhana is an ornate

stone structure, constructed in the 18th century by a Jain merchant, Purushottamdas Kothari, and added to in the 19th and early 20th centuries. Jains, like Buddhists, believe that all living beings have souls, and that kind acts towards all life forms will earn the giver merit in the next life.

At the western end of Walchand Hirachand Marg is **Nagar Chowk**, an oasis of green in the midst of swirling traffic. It has an impressive statue of Sir Dinshaw Manekji Petit, a baronet, captain of industry and leading Parsi philanthropist of the early 20th century. The statue was sculpted by Sir Thomas Brock and the surrounding garden is a good place from which to view some of Mumbai's grand Victorian buildings – among them Victoria Terminus, the Bombay Municipal Corporation building and the General Post Office. Shahid Bhagat Singh Marg eventually runs into D'Mello Road, formerly known as Frere Road. This area lay under water until the 1860s, when it was reclaimed by the Port Trust. Today the road is lined with popular eateries.

Gresham Assurance Building

Pigeons at the Kothari Kabutarkhana pecking at their daily supply of grain

Ballard Estate ⑬

Bounded by Shahid Bhagat Singh Marg, Walchand Hirachand Marg & Shoorji Vallabhdas Marg.

This entire area was once part of the sea until it was reclaimed by the Bombay Port Trust and converted into a business district. Planned between 1908 and 1914 by George Wittet, architect of the Gateway of India, the area was developed according to the strict guidelines he set, maintaining a restrained elegance in contrast to the over-ornamentation of the Victorian edifices in the Fort area. The district's broad pavements and neat tree-lined avenues are lined with stone buildings of uniform height and style, giving the Estate an atmosphere of calm tranquillity, unusual in a business quarter.

A convenient point of entry into Ballard Estate is from Shoorji Vallabhdas Marg, near the imposing Marshall Building. Among the most impressive buildings on this street is the **Customs House**. Designed by Wittet himself, it has a grand entrance portico in stately Renaissance style, framed by two columns rising to the height of the building. Next to it is the **Bombay Port Trust** also designed by George

The General Post Office, combining European and Indian styles

Wittet. Two striking ships in full sail are sculpted on its basalt façade. Further down the road, to the east, is the **Port Trust War Memorial**, honouring the memory of port officers who died in World War I. The memorial has a single, fluted column shaft in stone, surmounted by a lantern. The **Grand Hotel** dominates the corner of Walchand Hirachand Marg and Ram Gulam Marg. Another of George Wittet's designs, it has a striking central atrium. The grandiose **Mackinnon & Mackenzie Building** has an impressive portico, columns and statues. This, and other beautiful Edwardian buildings, such as **Darabshaw House** and **Neville House**, make Ballard Estate a uniquely elegant business district.

Port Trust Memorial

General Post Office ⑭

Walchand Hirachand Marg.
⬜ *Mon–Sat.*

Completed in 1911, this fantastic composition of minarets, domes and arches was designed by John Begg and supervised by George Wittet. A prime example of the Indo-Saracenic style, the General Post Office (GPO) building combines elements of Indian architecture, most notably an Islamic dome inspired by the Gol Gumbad in Bijapur *(see p543)*, with classical European traditions. Mumbai's main post office, the GPO has a lofty three-storeyed rotunda inside, which leads to its various departments. Business is transacted from behind delightful old-fashioned wooden counters.

THE DABBAWALLAHS OF MUMBAI

Among Mumbai's most characteristic sights are the *dabbawallahs*, men who pick up freshly cooked lunches from over 100,000 suburban homes and deliver them to offices all over the city. Most office workers spend an average of two hours travelling to work. Hot, home-cooked lunches therefore would normally be an impossible luxury – if it weren't for the *dabbawallas*. They pick up the meals, usually *rotis*, vegetables and *dal*, packed in three or four round stainless steel containers, known as tiffin boxes or *dabbas* (hence the name

Dabbawallahs delivering home-cooked lunch to office workers

dabbawallah) from each house, colourcode the office addresses onto the lids, thread the *dabbas* onto long poles and cycle off to the nearest station. Here the *dabbas* are handed over to other *dabbawallas*, who deliver them to the right offices. Lunches rarely go astray, and empty *dabbas* are delivered back home by late afternoon. *Dabbawallahs*, traditionally migrants from the neighbouring city of Pune, are organized under the Mumbai Tiffin Box Suppliers Association. They provide one of Mumbai's most efficient services.

Marine Drive, sweeping in an arc along the sea, connecting the northern and southern ends of Mumbai

Marine Drive ⑮

Netaji Subhash Chandra Rd.

Known as the "Queen's Necklace" after the glittering string of streetlights lining the road, Marine Drive (renamed Netaji Subhash Chandra Road) sweeps along a sea-facing promenade which runs from **Nariman Point** to **Malabar Hill**. Built on land reclaimed from the sea in the 1920s, it is also the main arterial link between the suburbs and the city's prime commercial and administrative centres, Nariman Point and the Fort area *(see p453)*. Situated at its eastern periphery is the **Oval Maidan**, nursery of such modern-day Indian cricketing heroes as Sachin Tendulkar (b.1973) and Sunil Gavaskar (b.1949).

The buildings of Marine Drive are characterized by a strong Art Deco flavour, popular in Mumbai during the 1930s and 1940s. With the advent of electric elevators, and with concrete replacing the earlier stone and brick, the apartment blocks on the seafront were built to a uniform height of five floors, making this the most fashionable residential area of the time.

The best way to enjoy Marine Drive during the day is from the upper floor of a red double-decker bus, which provides panoramic views of the sea and the city's skyline. In the evening, it swarms with people taking their daily walks, couples meeting after work and families gathering around the vendors selling coconut water and *bhelpuri*

(see p441). **Chowpatty Beach** is the city's most popular promenade and the southernmost of Mumbai's beaches. Earlier cluttered with food stalls and hawkers, the area has now been substantially cleaned up in a drive by the civic authorities. An inexpensive evening destination for the city's residents, it remains lively till late at night. It is also the venue for Mumbai's largest festival, Ganesha Chaturthi *(see p467)*, when huge crowds gather at Chowpatty Beach to immerse images of Ganesha, the elephant-headed god, in the Arabian Sea.

The **National Centre for Performing Arts (NCPA)**, at the southern tip of Marine Drive, is the city's most active venue for music, dance and theatre performances. Its Tata Theatre and Experimental Theatre stage works by international and Indian playwrights with the best of local talent, while India's finest musicians and dancers perform regularly in its other auditoriums *(see pp462–3)*.

Malabar Hill ⑯

Bounded by Napean Sea Rd, Ridge Rd & Walkeshwar Rd.

This leafy residential area, once dotted with bungalows set in large, forested compounds, is today crowded with highrise apartment blocks, home to Mumbai's rich and famous. The Parsi **Towers of Silence** are also located in this area. Parsis *(see p447)*, who believe that the elements of earth, water, air and fire are sacred and should not be defiled, place their dead in these tall, cylindrical stone towers to be picked clean by vultures. This, they believe, is one of the most environmentally friendly ways of disposing of the dead. A fall in Mumbai's vulture population, however, remains a cause of worry. A high wall and a thick belt of trees surround the Towers, which are closed to visitors.

The **Hanging Gardens** provide a pleasant open space in the vicinity, with good views of the city.

The Hanging Gardens, rising in tiers on Malabar Hill

For hotels and restaurants in this region see pp706–8 and pp734–5

Banganga ⓱

Walkeshwar, Malabar Hill.

Hidden amidst the soaring skyscrapers of Malabar Hill is the small settlement of Banganga, set around a sacred tank. According to legend, Rama, hero of the *Ramayana* (*see p27*), pausing here while on his way to rescue his abducted wife Sita, shot an arrow into the ground and a spring gushed forth. This is the origin of the tank, and devotees take regular ritual dips in it. The site has several temples – the **Jabreshwar Mahadeo**, at the tank's corner, is the prettiest, while the **Walkeshwar Temple**, built in the 18th century, has a linga said to have been built by Rama himself. Around the tank and temples are rest houses (*dharamsalas*) for pilgrims.

Khotachiwadi's narrow lanes and balconied houses

Khotachiwadi ⓲

Bounded by Jagannath Shankarsheth Rd & Raja Ram Mohan Roy Rd, Girgaum.

In the narrow bylanes of Girgaum in central Mumbai is the old-fashioned neighbourhood of Khotachiwadi (literally, "Headman's Orchard"). Khotachiwadi grew as a suburban settlement, north of the Fort, in the 19th century, and retains the sleepy quality of a coastal village. The low, tile-roofed cottages have timber eaves and open verandahs with cast-iron balconies, the focal point for most daytime activities. The inhabitants were converted to Christianity by Portuguese missionaries and adopted names such as Fernandes, D'Costa and D'Lima. Anant Ashram, a tiny eatery in Khotachiwadi's bylanes, serves excellent prawn curry and rice.

Mahalaxmi Temple ⓳

Mahalaxmi Temple Lane, off Bhulabhai Desai Rd.

Devotees, both rich and poor, throng this temple dedicated to Lakshmi, the Goddess of Wealth and Prosperity, who is also known as Laxmi in Maharashtra and in parts of Gujarat (*see p419*). The approach is lined with stalls selling religious offerings, such as coconuts, flowers and small plastic icons. The temple's history dates to the 18th century, when an embankment being constructed along the bay was repeatedly washed away. The contractor dreamt that if a temple was built to Laxmi, the wall would hold. And this actually happened. Nearby is the **Mahalaxmi Race Course**, next to Mahalaxmi Station, which has horse races every weekend from November to April. In its crowded stands the city's fashionable set rub shoulders with the poor and hopeful.

The Mahalaxmi Temple, dedicated to Lakshmi, the Goddess of Wealth

Haji Ali Mosque ⓴

Off Lala Lajpat Rai Marg.

Approached by a long causeway which gets submerged at high tide, is the *dargah* (tomb) of a rich merchant, Haji Ali Shah Bukhari, who gave up his wealth after a pilgrimage to Mecca. The *dargah* dates to the 15th century, but the dazzling white mosque was built in the 1940s and seems to float on its small island in the Arabian Sea. The causeway, usually lined with beggars, leads to a huge marble courtyard. The tomb lies at its centre and devotees touch their heads to the heavily embroidered *chador* (ceremonial cloth) covering it. Female devotees sit behind a *jali* (stone screen).

Haji Ali Mosque, built on an island linked to the shore by a causeway

Bandra ㉑

N of Mahim Bay. **Mount St Mary Basilica** Mount Mary Rd. *Tel* (022) 2642 3152. ◻ daily. 🎪 Bandra fête (Sep).

The prosperous suburb of Bandra, in the north of Mumbai, is connected to the city by the Mahim Causeway. Amidst its new apartment blocks, swanky boutiques and restaurants, are vestiges of its past as a small Portuguese enclave. The quiet lanes with tile-roofed bungalows are inhabited by a community of local East Indian Christians, whose ancestors were converted by the Portuguese. A number of Roman Catholic churches, too, were built by the Portuguese, who retained Bandra until the late 18th century. The most important of these is the **Mount St Mary Basilica**, which attracts devotees of all faiths. Outside the church is a bizarre market selling wax models of various body parts. Devotees with ailing limbs buy the appropriate model and solemnly place it on the altar before the Virgin Mary in the belief that she will effect a miraculous cure. A deserted Portuguese fort, **Castella de Aguada**, on a hill, offers spectacular views of the sea and the hinterland.

Bandra's plush **Pali Hill** locality, which has the villas of several Bollywood stars, draws crowds of star-struck Indian tourists. Its other attractions are the seafront promenades at **Bandstand** and **Carter Road**, especially popular with the local youth. Also situated here is a small Koli fishing village.

A green coconut vendor on Mumbai's crowded Juhu Beach

Juhu Beach ㉒

N of Bandra.

The sandy coastline of Juhu Beach lies north of the city centre. This is not a beach for leisurely sunbathing, though, since it is always crowded. On weekends, especially, it is packed with families of picnickers playing cricket on the beach, paddling tentatively in the water and enjoying the sea breeze. Crowds of vendors offering snacks, toys and fairground rides add to the *mela* (fair) atmosphere. Juhu also has several luxury hotels that serve as weekend retreats for Mumbai's tycoons and Bollywood film stars.

The **Prithvi Theatre**, on Juhu Church Road, was founded in 1978 by one of Bollywood's leading families, the Kapoors. It stages plays in Hindi, Gujarati and English, and has a lively café, popular with Mumbai's arty crowd. A theatre festival is held in November *(see p462)*.

Film City ㉓

Goregaon East. 🛈 Contact Film City's Public Relations Office (022) 2840 1533.

Built in 1978 to meet the needs of Mumbai's booming Hindi film industry, better known as Bollywood *(see pp32–3)*, Film City sprawls over 140 ha (346 acres) in the city's northern outskirts. Bollywood produces some 120 feature films a year, making it the world's largest film industry, rivalled only by South India's Telugu and Tamil film industries. Film City is where many Bollywood blockbusters are shot, as are most TV soaps and serials. Song-and-dance routines, scenes of tear-jerking melodrama and action-packed fight sequences take place simultaneously on Film City's dozen shooting stages, against outsize backdrops of medieval forts, dense jungles and opulent cardboard palaces. In between takes, mythological heroes rub shoulders with rifle-toting bandits and skimpily clad vamps.

Sanjay Gandhi National Park ㉔

Borivili. 🛈 Conservation Education Centre, near elephant gate Goregaon, (022) 2842 1174. ◻ Tue–Sun. 🎫 **Kanheri Caves** ◻ Tue–Sun. 🎫

An hour's train ride north of Mumbai, this national park is one of the few in India within the limits of a city. Surrounded by rolling hills, its deciduous forests harbour a wealth of birdlife and fauna, wild boar, cobras, as well as the occasional tiger. Tiger and Lion Safaris are offered in fenced-off sections of the park.

In a picturesque wooded area of the park is an extraordinary complex of 109 Buddhist caves, the **Kanheri Caves**, dating from the 2nd to the 9th centuries AD. The 6th-century **Cave 3** is the most impressive, with its colossal Buddhas, richly carved pillars and brackets and hemispherical stupa. The caves are best approached through the Park's northern entrance.

A film shoot in progress at Film City, Goregaon

For hotels and restaurants in this region see pp706–8 and pp734–5

Elephanta Island ㉕

Located on an island off Mumbai's eastern shore, the 6th-century AD Elephanta cave temples, chiselled into a rocky cliff and dedicated to Shiva, contain some great masterpieces of Indian sculpture. Originally called Gharapuri or "Fort-City", the island was renamed Elephanta by the Portuguese after a huge stone elephant that once

Shiva and Parvati, carved in stone

stood here. This is now in the garden of the Bhau Daji Lad Museum in Mumbai's Byculla area. A UNESCO World Heritage Site, the Elephanta cave temples can be visited on a day trip by boat from Mumbai.

VISITORS' CHECKLIST

9 km (6 miles) NE of Mumbai. 🚢 from Gateway of India at 9am. 📞 for ferries, (022) 2202 6364. ◷ Wed–Mon. 📷 ✔ 🎭 Elephanta Music & Dance Festival (Feb).

The Elephanta caves, cut into the cliff high above the water

PLAN OF ELEPHANTA CAVES

1 Northern Entrance
2 Mahesamurti
3 Ardhanarishvara
4 Gangadhara
5 Western Entrance
6 Marriage of Shiva-Parvati
7 Shiva spearing Andhaka
8 Eastern Entrance
9 Shiva and Parvati Playing Dice

Exploring Elephanta

The origins of the cave temples at Elephanta are lost in obscurity, but in all probability they date to the 6th century AD and represent the period of Brahmanical revival after Buddhism began to decline. From the pier, where visitors disembark from the boats, a long flight of 125 steps leads to the temple's main **Northern Entrance**. This is a huge square hall with sides measuring 40 m (131 ft), supported by two dozen massive pillars. Here, in a deep recess against the rear (south) wall, is the huge triple-headed Shiva statue, the **Mahesamurti**. This is the glory of Elephanta, and few visitors can fail to be moved by this powerful, compelling image, hailed by art historian Percy Brown as "the creation of a genius". The three faces represent Shiva in his different manifestations. The central

face with its towering, elaborate crown depicts Shiva the Preserver, sublimely serene and introspective. The one facing west represents Shiva the Creator, gentle, solicitous and graceful. The head facing east, with its cruel mouth, fiercely hooked nose and serpents adorning the hair, shows Shiva as the Destroyer. On either side of the statue are other superb sculptures.

The one on the east shows Shiva as **Ardhanarishvara** – the Lord who is Both Male and Female, and thus symbolizes the Divine Unity in which all opposites are resolved. The image on the west is of Shiva as **Gangadhara**, helping the river goddess Ganga descend to earth (see p163) while his consort Parvati and other deities look on.

Contrasting images of peace and violence, joy and fury, can be seen in exquisite sculptures throughout the temple. Thus, one sculpture near the **Western Entrance** lyrically depicts the marriage of Shiva and Parvati, while opposite it is a powerful panel showing Shiva brutally impaling the demon Andhaka. The **Eastern Entrance** has Shiva and Parvati contentedly playing dice in their mountain abode, as the demon-king Ravana tries to destroy their home by shaking the mountain.

The 5.5-m (18-ft) high Mahesamurti, dominating the cave temple

Shopping & Entertainment in Mumbai

Mumbai is one of India's best shopping destinations. Large malls, department stores and exclusive boutiques stocking international brand names, coexist with traditional bazaars and pavement stalls selling everything from diamonds to dentures. Mumbai also has a vibrant nightlife, with more discotheques and pubs than any other Indian city. As the home of the Hindi film industry, Bollywood, Mumbai often holds gala premiere nights at its many cinema halls. The city's crowded cultural calendar also includes several concerts, exhibitions, theatre shows and festivals. But perhaps the best entertainment the city offers is the non-stop circus on its bustling streets and sidewalks.

SHOPS AND MARKETS

South Mumbai's main shopping areas include Colaba Causeway, Kemp's Corner, and the shopping arcade in the Oberoi Hotel at Nariman Point. The traditional market for fresh produce is Crawford Market (see p453), while Bhuleshwar and Kalbadevi, north of the Fort area, are popular haunts for textiles and jewellery. Crossroads, a large new shopping mall, has come up in central Mumbai, close to the Haji Ali Mosque.

ANTIQUES AND JEWELLRY

A fascinating place for antiques is Chor Bazaar or "Thieves' Market" near Crawford Market. This warren of shops is crammed with colonial furniture, Victorian bric-a-brac and Chinese porcelain, along with a lot of junk and fakes. Very good bargains can still be found here. **Phillips Antiques**, on Shyama Prasad Mukherjee Chowk, stocks a fine collection of old postcards, prints and Raj-era lithographs. There are strict rules, however, regarding the export of antiques (see p758).

Central Mumbai's Zaveri Bazaar is lined with jewellers' shops, **Tribhovandas Bhimji Zaveri** being the most famous. **Palazzo** at the Crossroads Mall has dozens of jewellery stores under one roof, offering elegant, exclusive designs. The shopping arcades at the **Oberoi** and **Taj Hotels** (see p707 & p708) are also good places to shop for jewellery.

TEXTILES AND FASHION

Mumbai is a highly fashion-conscious city and most Indian designers have outlets here. Exclusive boutiques include **Ensemble**, **Melange** and **Abraham & Thakore**, while casual ready-made garments are available at **Cotton World. Fantasia** and **Indian Textiles** specialize in a wide range of traditional Indian textiles and weaves, including silk saris, home furnishings and accessories. For good quality handwoven home furnishings and floor-coverings, the best shop is **Shyam Ahuja**.

HANDICRAFTS AND GIFTS

Handicrafts from all over India are available in Mumbai. The widest range and best quality can be found at the **Cottage Industries Emporium**, **Contemporary Arts and Crafts** and **Bombay Store** in the Fort area. **Chimanlal's** has a good selection of handmade paper, while **Inshallah Maashallah** stocks pure perfume essence (attar) in tiny glass bottles capturing the fragrances of rose, vetiver and jasmine.

Mumbai is renowned for its high quality leather goods at reasonable prices. **Rasulbhai Adamji** at Colaba, and many shops in the Oberoi Shopping Centre have a good range of jackets, handbags, wallets and luggage, some of it "inspired" by Gucci, Prada and Louis Vuitton. **Joy Shoes** at the Taj Hotel has high quality shoes and leather accessories. Books, CDs and audio cassettes of both Indian and Western music, are available at various outlets throughout the city, including hotel book-shops. However, one of the best shops for music is **Rhythm House**.

ENTERTAINMENT GUIDES, TICKETS AND VENUES

Daily newspapers list the day's entertainment and events on their engagements page. Another good source of information is the magazine *Discover Mumbai*. A useful website which offers online information on cultural events and entertainment is *www.explocity.com* Tickets for most concerts and plays can be bought at **Rhythm House** or at the venue itself. The major venues for Mumbai's cultural events are the **NCPA** or the National Centre for the Performing Arts (see p458), the **Nehru Centre** auditorium and **Shanmukhananda Hall. Prithvi Theatre** in Juhu (see p460) is a lively centre for stage productions. Other active exhibition venues include the **Jehangir Art Gallery**, the **NGMA** (National Gallery of Modern Art) and the Artists' Centre, located at Kala Ghoda (see pp448-9).

PERFORMING ARTS

Mumbai is a great centre of classical Indian music, and many well-known performers can be heard here. This cosmopolitan city also has many enthusiasts of jazz and Western classical music (conductor Zubin Mehta received his early training in Mumbai) and frequent concerts are held by both local and visiting international groups. Classical and folk dance performances from different parts of the country also feature regularly on the cultural calendar. Mumbai has a vibrant theatre tradition, with productions in English as well as Marathi, Gujarati and Hindi. These are often staged in the open at **Horniman Circle Gardens** (see *p452)*. The cultural high season is from November to April, though performances take place through the year.

CINEMA

As the capital of the Hindi film industry, Mumbai hosts a number of film-related events. Most of the film studios are located in the suburbs as are the private residences of most screen celebrities. Great fanfare precedes the release of big-budget blockbusters, and glittering premieres are held at popular cinema halls such as **Sterling**, **Regal** and **Metro**. These draw star-struck fans who spend hours standing outside, waiting for a glimpse of their favourite stars. Film festivals, documentary film screenings, lectures, talks and exhibitions are also held throughout the year at various venues, such as the **British Council**.

HERITAGE TOURS

The Maharashtra Tourism Development Corporation (MTDC), offers guided tours of Mumbai on double-decker buses. **Bombay Heritage Walks**, organized by a group of young architects, take visitors through historical districts such as Banganga, Khotachi-wadi and the Fort area, on weekends, except during the monsoon (June to September). Prior booking is necessary.

NIGHTCLUBS AND BARS

Mumbai's nightlife is more active than that of any other Indian city. While nightclubs and bars open and close at regular intervals, some have remained consistently popular. One of the liveliest is **Fire & Ice**, ingeniously housed in a mill compound in Parel. In south Mumbai, **Not Just Jazz by the Bay** has live music Wednesday through Saturday. Most hotels have their own bars and nightclubs such as **Insomnia** at the Taj and Opium Den in the Oberoi, both of which attract Bollywood's A-list stars. Another favourite haunt of Mumbai's jetset is **Athena**, one of the city's trendiest new nightspots.

DIRECTORY

ANTIQUES AND JEWELLERY

Palazzo
Crossroads Mall.
Tel (022) 2351 5890.

Phillips Antiques
SP Mukherjee Chowk.
Tel (022) 2202 0564.

Tribhovandas Bhimji Zaveri
Zaveri Bazaar.
Tel (022) 2342 5001.

TEXTILES AND FASHION

Abraham & Thakore
The Courtyard, Colaba.
Tel (022) 5638 5486.

Cotton World
Mandlik Rd, Colaba.
Tel (022) 2283 3294.

Ensemble
Great Western Bldg, Shahid Bhagat Singh Marg.
Tel (022) 2287 2883.

Fantasia
Oberoi Shopping Centre.
Tel (022) 2284 6369.

Indian Textiles
Taj Hotel, Apollo Bunder.
Tel (022) 2202 8783.

Melange
Altamount Rd.
Tel (022) 2385 4492.

Shyam Ahuja
Crossroads Mall.
Tel (022) 2351 5890.

HANDICRAFTS AND GIFTS

Bombay Store
Western India House, PM Rd, Fort Area.
Tel (022) 2288 5048.

Chimanlal's
Fort Area.
Tel (022) 2207 7717.

Cottage Industries Emporium
Chhatrapati Shivaji M Rd.
Tel (022) 2202 6564.

Contemporary Arts and Crafts
Napean Sea Rd.
Tel (022) 2363 1979.

Inshallah Maashallah
Colaba.
Tel (022) 2204 9495.

Joy Shoes
Taj Hotel, Apollo Bunder.
Tel (022) 5665 3366.

Rasulbhai Adamji
Colaba.
Tel (022) 2202 1267.

Rhythm House
Kala Ghoda.
Tel (022) 2284 2835.

ENTERTAINMENT INFORMATION

www.explocity.com

ENTERTAINMENT VENUES

British Council
Nariman Point.
Tel (022) 2282 3530.

Jehangir Art Gallery
Fort Area.
Tel (022) 2284 3989.

NGMA
Kala Ghoda.
Tel (022) 2285 2457.

NCPA
Nariman Point.
Tel (022) 2283 4500.

Nehru Centre
Worli.
Tel (022) 2496 4676.

Prithvi Theatre
Janaki Kutir,
Juhu.
Tel (022) 2614 9546.

Shanmukhananda Hall
King's Circle.
Tel (022) 2401 5164.

CINEMA

Metro
MG Rd,
Dhobi Talao.
Tel (022) 2203 0303.

Regal
Shyama Prasad Mukherjee Chowk.
Tel (022) 2202 1017.

Sterling
Hazarimal Somani Marg.
Tel (022) 2207 5187.

HERITAGE TOURS

Bombay Heritage Walks
Tel (022) 2834 4622.

NIGHTCLUBS AND BARS

Athena
Minoo Desai Marg,
Colaba.
Tel (022) 2280 5155.

Fire & Ice
Parel.
Tel (022) 2498 0555.

Insomnia
Taj Hotel, Apollo Bunder.
Tel (022) 5665 3366.

Not Just Jazz by The Bay
Marine Drive.
Tel (022) 2285 1876.

MAHARASHTRA

Verdant hills, scenic coastal plains and busy industrial centres make up the varied landscape of Maharashtra, which covers an area of 300,000 sq km (115,831 sq miles). The hills of the Western Ghats, source of many rivers, run parallel to the narrow Konkan Coast, while cradled in the centre is the Deccan Plateau, formed from black volcanic lava 70 million years ago. This area saw a great flowering of art and architecture from the 2nd century BC onwards, and two famous UNESCO World Heritage sites are located here – the Buddhist caves

at Ajanta and the rock-cut temples at Ellora. The rocky terrain around Pune is dotted with the massive forts built by the 17th-century Maratha leader, Shivaji, who launched successful guerrilla campaigns against the Mughals. His cult-like status is today perpetuated by the Shiv Sena, a nationalist political party.

Modern Maharashtra is a prosperous, highly industrialized region, with a strong agrarian base. Cotton and tobacco are widely cultivated, as are a variety of fruits including oranges, *chikoos* (sapodilla) and mangoes.

SIGHTS AT A GLANCE

Towns & Cities
Ahmadnagar **9**
Aurangabad **11**
Kolhapur **4**
Nagpur **17**
Pune **6**
Wardha **18**

Temple Towns & Holy Places
Nasik **10**
Pandharpur **19**

Historic Sites
Ajanta **14**
Daulatabad **12**
Ellora **13**
Murud-Janjira **2**

National Parks & Geographical Sites
Lonar **15**
Melghat Tiger Reserve **16**

Hill Stations
Lonavla **7**
Mahabaleshwar **5**
Matheran **8**

Beaches
Alibag **1**
Ganapatipule **3**

KEY

✈ International airport
✖ Domestic airport
━ National highway
━ Major road
━ Minor road
━ Major railway

0 km 50
0 miles 50

◁ **View of the votive stupa in the late 5th-century *chaitya* hall, Cave 19, at Ajanta**

View of the imposing Janjira Fort, built on an island

Alibag ❶

Raigarh district. 108 km (67 miles) S of Mumbai. 🚋 🚤 *from Gateway of India, Mumbai, to Mandve, 18 km (11 miles) N of Alibag, then bus.*

The port of Alibag was developed by the Marathas in the 17th century to protect their kingdom from the Dutch, Portuguese and the increasingly powerful British. Alibag is today a quiet town, just across the bay from Mumbai. Its most impressive sight is its beach, a 5-km (3-mile) stretch of soft silver sand, lined by a stand of coconut and casuarina trees.

Kolaba Fort, constructed on an island in 1680 by the Maratha ruler Chhatrapati Shivaji *(see p471)*, looms over the skyline. It is a forbidding grey mass of lead, steel and stone, built on a rock jutting from the sea, and can be reached on foot during low tide. Within its high ramparts are enclosed a temple dedicated to Lord Ganesha, and next to it a sweet-water well that must have been useful during sieges. There are two main entrances to the fort, one from the shore and another from the sea. The enormous shore-side doorway is decorated with sculptures of tigers, elephants and peacocks.

Environs

Kihim Beach, 9 km (6 miles) north of Alibag, is a tranquil getaway, with woods brimming with birds and wild flowers. It was the favourite haunt of the famous Indian ornithologist Salim Ali (1896–1987), author of the finest book on Indian birds.

Murud–Janjira ❷

Raigarh district. 185 km (115 miles) S of Mumbai. 🚤 *from Gateway of India, Mumbai to Mandve, 120 km (74 miles) N of Murud, then bus.* 🚤 *from Rajpuri to Janjira Fort.*

A sleepy coastal town with Indo-Gothic houses and meandering pathways, Murud has a picture-perfect beach that promises lazy, sunny afternoons and cool dips in the clean sea. The little village of Rajpuri, 4 km (2.5 miles) south of the main Murud town, is the gateway to the Janjira Fort, the strongest island-fort in the Konkan, still enduring the surge and retreat of the Arabian Sea. Boats are available at Rajpuri to take visitors to the fort.

Also evocatively known as the Jazira-Mehruba or "Moon Fort", it was built in 1511 by the Siddis, who originally arrived in the Deccan from Abyssinia as slave-traders. The fortress, with its high ramparts, 22 bastions and granite walls jointed with lead to withstand the onslaught of the sea, proved invincible against attacks by the Portuguese and British, and even against the great Maratha leader, Shivaji. Steps lead to a sturdy stone gate, where a stone engraving of a lion holding six diminutive elephants in captivity, represents six successive Siddi victories. Rusty cannons point outwards through niches in the ramparts. The palaces, gardens and mosques lie in silent ruin, and luxurious vegetation grows around the palace of the Siddi ruler, Sirul Khan.

Ganapatipule ❸

Ratnagiri district. 365 km (227 miles) S of Mumbai. 🚉 *Ratnagiri, 22 km (14 miles) S of Ganapatipule, then bus.* 🚌 🛕 *Gauri Ganapati (Sep/Oct).*

The small coastal village of Ganapatipule derives its name from the 400-year-old temple of Swayambhu Ganapati, where the naturally occurring idol of Ganapati (the local name of Lord Ganesha), is revered by Hindus as one of the eight sacred sites, or "Ashtha Ganapatis", in India. Despite attracting the usual smattering of holy men and mendicants, its beach has long stretches of pristine white sands and clear waters. Beyond the coast lie groves of fruit trees, including mango, banana, jackfruit, coconut and betel nut.

Alphonso mango

Environs

Ratnagiri, 19 km (12 miles) south of Ganapatipule, is famous for its groves of delicious Alphonso mangoes, locally known as *hapus*. Ratnagiri's fortress, Bala Qila, is situated along the coast, and is intact, with a notable Bhagavati temple within its walls.

The Swayambhu Ganapati Temple, at the base of a hill in Ganapatipule

Ganesha, the Remover of Obstacles

Lord Ganesha, the elephant-headed son of Shiva and Parvati, is the most auspicious and popular deity in India, and especially beloved in Maharashtra. Images of the endearing, potbellied god are found in every household, on temple doorways and shop entrances, on letterheads and wedding invitations. No task or enterprise is ever begun

Lord Ganesha imitating the dance of Shiva

without invoking him, as he is the Lord of New Beginnings. Worshipped in many guises, he is Vighneshvara, the Remover of Obstacles, and Siddhidata, the God of Prosperity and Success. Ganesha is above all a friend, lovable and benign, and his festival, Ganesha Chaturthi, crosses all social boundaries uniting the people of Maharashtra in a frenzied ten-day celebration.

LORD GANESHA

Lord Ganesha's four arms hold his various attributes. Two of these, his broken tusk and a round sweetmeat called *modaka*, appear consistently. In the other two hands, he sometimes holds a lotus blossom, an elephant goad, an axe or prayer beads. According to legend, Ganesha gained his elephant head after Shiva, in a state of fury, cut his son's head off and then, in remorse, stuck on the head of a passing elephant.

Elephant goad

A half halo indicates his divinity.

Modaka

The broken tusk, used as a pen to write the *Mahabharata*, was the result of an encounter with Parasuram *(see p679)*.

A rat is the vehicle of Ganesha

Intricate clay images *of Ganesha are made and consecrated on the first day of Ganesha Chaturthi (see p473). These are then enshrined in pandals or decorated stages, and worshipped continuously for ten days amidst Hindi and Marathi recitations and musical performances.*

Colourful floats, *accompanied by folk dancers, lead the serpentine processions that fill the streets, amidst chants and drumbeats. The processions end at the water's edge, where hundreds of idols are immersed in rivers, lakes or the sea. This final immersion on the tenth day marks the deity's return to his abode.*

See also features on Hindu Mythology *(see pp24–5)*, Shiva *(see p566)* and Vishnu *(see p679)*.

Colourful fishing boats docked off the Malvan coast

Kolhapur **4**

Kolhapur district. 225 km (140 miles) S of Pune. 485,500. Maharashtra Tourism, (0231) 265 2935.

Situated on the banks of the Panchganga river, the city of Kolhapur is a thriving commercial centre, noted today for its flourishing dairy industry. It is also one of Maharashtra's most important pilgrimage sites, associated from early times with the worship of Shakti (the Mother Goddess). Ruled by the Hindu Yadava dynasty between the 10th and 13th centuries, it was later occupied by the Mughals. In 1675, Kolhapur was finally seized by the Maratha chief Shivaji *(see p471)*, and was later inherited

by his younger son. The state remained with the Bhonsles (one of the four Maratha princely families) until Independence.

Of the numerous temples in Kolhapur, the **Shri Mahalakshmi** or Amba Bai Temple, dedicated to the Mother Goddess, is the most venerated. Built in the 7th century by the Chalukya king Karnadeva, the temple's idol, said to be a *swayambhu*, or naturally occurring monolith, is encrusted with diamonds and other precious stones. The *mandapa* has a finely carved ceiling. Behind the temple are the

Kolhapuri *chappals*

remains of the **Old Palace** or Rajwada, where members of the former maharaja's family still live.

Its huge entrance hall was once used for large public wedding ceremonies. Situated near the palace gates are the town's wrestling grounds, where young men practise traditional Indian wrestling, known as *kushti*. The **New Palace**, 2 km (1.3 miles) north of the city centre, was completed in 1881 and designed by Major Charles Mant *(see p418)*, who merged European, Jain, Hindu and Islamic elements to create a style which widely became

THE MALVAN COAST

Fishing boat, Malvan coast

The Southern Konkan coastline in the Sindhudurg district, known as the Malvan Coast, is dotted with marine forts and pretty fishing villages which, though off the beaten track, are worth visiting. **Vijaydurg Fort**, 505 km (314 miles) south of Mumbai, stands on the site of an 11th-century fort, rebuilt by the Bijapur sultans *(see pp542–3)* in the 16th century. In 1654, it was further renovated by Shivaji, who added three layers of fortifications, 27 bastions and 300 guns. It became the main naval base for the great Maratha admiral, Kanhoji Angre, who used the fort to plunder European ships in 1698. It fell to the British in 1756; a platform stands within the grounds, where British astronomers set up their telescopes to study a solar eclipse. About 74 km (46 miles) south of Vijaydurg, **Sindhudurg Fort**, built by Shivaji in 1664, lies deserted on an island known as Kurte. With its 10-m (33-ft) high ramparts, it was a Maratha stronghold until power shifted to Vijaydurg. It is the only place in Maharashtra where a statue of Shivaji depicts him without a beard. His palm and feet impressions are preserved in mortar near the entrance. The small port of **Malvan**, 4 km (2.5 miles) north of Sindhudurg, lends its name to this stretch of coast. It is being developed into a beach resort, as is **Vengurla**, 52 km (32 miles) south of Malvan.

Savantwadi, 23 km (14 miles) east of Vengurla, was the capital of the Bhonsle kings. The art of making *ganjifa* cards (painted, circular playing cards) was developed here. The town is also known for its wooden toys and lacquer work. **Amboli**, 25 km (16 miles) northeast of Savantwadi, is a pretty hill station.

A view of Vijaydurg Fort, overlooking fishing boats in the bay known as the Indo-Saracenic style of architecture. The palace is today the Shahji Chhatrapati Museum and displays a collection of royal memorabilia, including garments, hunting photographs and one of Mughal emperor Aurangzeb's swords.

The **Town Hall**, another structure designed by Mant, has a small museum with a number of artifacts from nearby excavation sites. Kolhapur is also famous for its handcrafted leather slippers, known as Kolhapuri *chappals*.

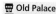

🏛 **Old Palace**
◯ *daily.*

🏛 **New Palace**
◯ *daily.* 📷

Environs

One of the most important forts in the Deccan is at **Panhala**, a hill station 19 km (12 miles) northwest of Kolhapur. Situated on a steep hillside, the fortress is well protected by three impressive double walled gates, and 7-km (4-mile) long ramparts. Within its walls stand two temples, one dedicated to Amba Bai and the other to Maruti, the Wind God. The most interesting monuments are the huge stone granaries, the largest of which, Ganga Kothi, covers 948 sq m (10,204 sq ft). Established in the 12th century by Raja Bhoja II, the fortress fell successively to the Yadavas, the Adil Shahis of Bijapur, Shivaji, Emperor Aurangzeb and the British. There are

Panhala Fort in the picturesque Sahyadri Hills, after the monsoon

Panchgani, with spectacular views of the Krishna river

many private homes in Panhala as well, including that of the famous Indian singer Lata Mangeshkar *(see p503)*.

Mahabaleshwar ❺

Satara district. 115 km (72 miles) SW of Pune. 🚶 *12,800.* 🚲 *Cycles available.*

The largest hill station in Maharashtra, Mahabaleshwar is situated 1,372 m (4,501 ft) above sea level. In 1828, Sir John Malcolm, Governor of Bombay, chose this beautiful spot as the site for the official sanatorium. Soon after, the wooded slopes were covered with typical colonial structures, among them **Christ Church**, **Frere Hall**, **Government House** (which was the grand residence of the governor), the **Mahabaleshwar Club**, and the ever-popular polo grounds and race course.

Due to its high altitude, the town has a cool climate and offers many pleasant walks. There are also several lookout points such as **Bombay Point**, from where the sea can be seen on a clear day, and **Arthur's Seat**, which affords panoramic views of the Konkan Coast. **Venna Lake** has facilities for boating.

In the old town is the sacred **Krishna Temple**, supposedly built on the legendary site of the Panchganga, or source of five rivers – the Koyna, Savitri, Venna, Gayatri and the mighty Krishna. The latter covers

Water spout, Krishna Temple

1,400 km (870 miles), stretching from this spot to the Bay of Bengal on the east coast. The temple has a much venerated, naturally occurring Shivalinga, and a small tank. There are two other temples here, dedicated to Hanuman and Rama. There are also several berry farms close by, where visitors can help to pick strawberries, raspberries and mulberries.

Environs

The hill station of **Panchgani**, 18 km (11 miles) east of Mahabaleshwar, is surrounded by five hills. The town is the starting point for many scenic trekking trails *(see p473)*. It is also dotted with some charming old British and Parsi bungalows, some of which can be visited. The majestic hilltop forts of **Pratapgarh** and **Raigad**, 18 km (11 miles) west and 70 km (44 miles) northwest of Mahabaleshwar respectively, were both Maratha strongholds. They offer commanding views of the surrounding countryside.

About 111 km (69 miles) south of Mahabaleshwar is **Chiplun**, lying on the banks of the Vashishti river, whose waters supply Koyna Lake, a large man-made reservoir. The town is well-known for its irrigation scheme, developed in the 1980s, that provides water to the coastal fringe between the Sahyadri Hills and the sea. This quiet place offers splendid views of the Vashishti river as it winds through the hills.

The sprawling campus of Pune University

Pune ❻

Pune district. 170 km (106 miles) SE of
Mumbai. 🏠 2,540,500. ✈ 12 km (7
miles) NE of city centre, then taxi or
auto. 🚉 🚌 ℹ Maharashtra Tourism,
I Block, Central Bldg, (020) 2612 6867.
🎉 Ganesha Chaturthi (Aug/Sep).

The fast-growing, industrial
city of Pune is situated on the
Deccan Plateau, at the confluence of the Mutha and Mula
rivers, and is bounded by the
Sahyadris in the west. Its
pleasant climate and proximity to Mumbai made it the
perfect monsoon capital for
the British in the 19th century. Then called Poona, it
became an important administrative centre and military
cantonment. Even today, the
Indian army's Southern
Command is based here.

Pune was also the child-
hood home of the Maratha
leader, Shivaji. From 1750
until 1817, it was the capital
of the Maratha Confederacy
and was ruled by the
Peshwas. The remains of their
Shaniwar Wada Palace is in
the old city. Built in 1736, the
palace was razed in a fire in
1828. Only its outer walls and
the main entrance with large
spikes, designed to deter the
enemy's elephants, survive.
Further south is **Vishram Bagh
Wada**, a beautiful Peshwa
palace with an elaborate
wooden façade.

For many visitors, Pune is
synonymous with the famous
Osho International Commune
founded by Bhagwan

Rajneesh or Osho, and
situated at Koregaon
Park in the north of the
city. The flamboyant pop
mystic, or "sex guru" as
he was called, had a
meteoric rise in the West.
Even after his demise in
1990, his well-appointed
ashram continues to
attract devotees from
Europe and America.
Housed in a traditional
Maratha house or *wada*,
is the charming privately-
owned **Raja Kelkar
Museum**. On display are
a collection of beautiful
everyday objects such
as pots, lamps, pens,
ink stands, collection of
nutcrackers, and other
utilitarian items. An interesting
piece is a Maharashtrian
Chitrakathi scroll painting,
used in folk theatre
performances.

The **Tribal
Museum**, east of
the railway
station, show-
cases the state's
tribal cultures,
especially from
the Sahyadri and
Gondwana regions.

A Warli painting from
Raja Kelkar Museum

The **Aga Khan
Palace**, across the Mula river
to the north of the city, was
where Mahatma Gandhi was
imprisoned by the British for
two years; today, it is the
Gandhi National Memorial.
Gandhi's wife, Kasturba,
died here and her ashes have
been interred in a memorial
in the gardens.

Other places of interest in
the city include St Mary's
Church, a fine garrison structure consecrated in 1825; the

rock-cut Pataleshwar Temple,
dating from the 8th century;
the Parvati Temple perched on
a hilltop; and fine gardens,
such as Empress Botanical
Gardens and Bund Gardens.

Pune is the centre of
Maratha culture, with a lively
tradition of theatre, classical
music and dance. It is also
an important university town
and is home to the prestigious
government-run Film and
Television Institute and the
National Film Archives.

Environs

About 6 km (4 miles)
southwest is the **National
Defence Academy**, the training
school for army, navy and air
force cadets, at Khadakvasla.
Further southwest are the
forts of **Rajgad** and **Sinhgad**
(the "Lion Fort"). The latter is
associated with Shivaji's
general, Tanaji Malasure.
According to
legend, he tied
strong ropes to
monitor lizards,
made the crea-
tures stick to the
fort walls with
their adhesive
foot pads, and
thus scaled the
walls and captured the fort.

🏛 **Osho International
Commune**
Tel (020) 401 9999. ⬜ daily. 🎦 🎫
🏛 **Raja Kelkar Museum**
1378, Shukrawar Peth. ⬜ daily.
⬤ public hols. 🎦
🏛 **Tribal Museum**
Off Koregaon Rd. ⬜ daily.
🏛 **Aga Khan Palace**
Ahmadnagar Rd. ⬜ Mon–Sat.
⬤ 2nd & 4th Sat, public hols. 🎦

Vishram Bagh Wada, a Peshwa palace in the heart of the old city

Shivaji and the Marathas

Maharashtra's greatest hero, Shivaji, was born in 1627 to Shahji Bhonsle, a chieftain from Pune who served the sultans of Bijapur *(see pp542–5)*. Daring, ambitious and restless since his boyhood, by the age of 19 he had become the head of a band of intrepid fighters. Soon, Shivaji's brilliant guerrilla tactics against Emperor Aurangzeb and the powerful Mughal army, and his swift conquests of mountain and sea forts, enabled him to establish a separate Maratha kingdom. In 1674, he was crowned Chhatrapati, the traditional title of a Hindu monarch, at his capital, Raigad. When he died in 1680, at the age of 53, he left behind a powerful Maratha state, which continued to play an important role in Indian history for the next 100 years.

Coronation Canopy at Raigad

Waghnakh ("tiger's claw"), a deadly hand weapon, was used by Shivaji to overcome and kill Afzal Khan, the Bijapur general, in a "friendly" meeting at Pratapgad.

Maratha horsemen were feared for their lightning raids which wrought havoc on enemy territory. The Deccan Plateau's hilly terrain aided their guerrilla tactics against the Mughals.

Shivaji is revered all over Maharashtra as a god-like hero. A fearless soldier and charismatic leader, he united the Marathas into a formidable force that defied the mighty Mughals. Today, he has become a symbol for the Hindu revivalist movement.

Fortresses, such as Rajgad and Raigad (see p469) and the sea forts (see p468) along the west coast, were the key to Maratha strategy and success. Shivaji's conquest of the crucial Purandhar Fort in 1649 compelled the sultan of Bijapur to condemn him as a rebel.

Shaniwar Wada was the former residence of the Peshwas, who came to power after Shivaji's grandson's death. The other main clans of the Maratha Confederacy – which was a significant power in the 18th century – were Holkars (see p246), Scindias (see pp228–9), Gaekwads (see p419) and Bhonsles (see p468).

The Buddhist *chaitya griha* at Karla Cave, near Lonavla

Lonavla ❼

Pune district. 62 km (39 miles) NW of Pune. 🚶 *55,700.* 🚉 🚌 **Karla Cave** ℹ *Maharashtra Tourism, Karla, (02114) 282 230.* ⭕ *daily.* 📷 **Bhaja Caves** 📷

Situated on the main train line from Mumbai to Pune, Lonavla was once a sleepy hill station famous for its *chikki*, a type of caramelized sweet. It has now become an extremely popular weekend getaway for city-dwellers from nearby Mumbai. Spread around the bustling main street, lined with souvenir shops, the town offers pleasant walks and is a convenient base for exploring the surrounding hills.

Environs
About 8 km (5 miles) northwest of Lonavla is **Khandala**, another pretty town with panoramic views of the scenic Western Ghats. The famous Buddhist rock-cut

Statue of a divine couple, Karla Cave

Karla Cave, 11 km (7 miles) east of Lonavla, dates from the 2nd to 1st centuries BC. The splendid *chaitya griha (see p20)*, the largest and best preserved of the early Buddhist caves in the Deccan, is the most significant sight here. It has a magnificently sculpted courtyard, a towering 14-m (46-ft) high façade with a horseshoe shaped window, and a large pillared hall with a monolithic stupa. The 20-odd **Bhaja Caves**, located 3 km (2 miles) off the Karla road, are the oldest in the region, dating from the 2nd century BC. Cave 12, a *chaitya griha*, still contains the remains of wooden beams on its ceiling. On either side of the façade are carvings of multistoreyed structures with windows and balconies. The **Bedsa Caves**, situated 9 km (6 miles) southeast of Bhaja, date to the 1st century AD. The roof of the main cave bears faint traces of paintings.

Matheran ❽

Raigarh district. 118 km (73 miles) NW of Pune. 🚶 *5,200.* 🚉 *From Neral Junction, take the toy train to Matheran (2 hrs).* 🚌 ℹ *Opp railway station.*

The closest hill station to Mumbai, Matheran (which means "Mother Forest") lies at a height of 803 m (2,635 ft) above sea level. This picturesque town is situated in the forested Sahyadri Hills. In 1855, Lord Elphinstone, the governor of Bombay, visited Matheran, and the town soon became fashionable. The stately **Elphinstone Lodge** that he built became his weekend retreat. A railway line was laid in 1907, and a quaint toy train *(see p777)* still winds its way slowly through hills and forests from the junction at Neral. All motor vehicles are completely banned within the limits of the town, making it uniquely peaceful, despite the burgeoning crowds of visitors, particularly on weekends.

Matheran has as many as 33 lookout points. **Porcupine Point** or Sunset Point, a favourite with sightseers, is known for its spectacular sunsets. **Louisa Point** has views of the ruined Prabal Fort and a mountain trail called Shivaji's Ladder. By far the most impressive viewpoint is **Hart Point**, from where it is possible, on a clear day, to see Mumbai in the distance. St Paul's Anglican Church, the pretty Lord's Hotel and the Roman Catholic Church are among the many Raj-era buildings in Matheran.

Splendid views at Porcupine Point, also known as Sunset Point, Matheran

Carved stonework, Damri Mosque

Ahmadnagar ❾

Ahmadnagar district. 140 km (87 miles) NE of Pune. 🚉 307,500. 🚉 🚌

The seat of a powerful Muslim kingdom in the 16th century, Ahmadnagar was founded in 1490 by Ahmad Nizam Shah Bahri, the son of a Hindu convert. In 1599, the Mughals, led by Akbar, invaded the city after his favourite commander Abu'l Fazl murdered the ruling sultan. However, the sultan's sister, Chand Bibi, ably defended the kingdom. The succeeding years saw the rise of Malik Ambar, a former African slave who fought

successful battles against neighbouring Bidar (*see p545*) and Golconda (*see pp666–7*). In 1636, the kingdom finally submitted to Mughal rule.

The rulers of the Nizam Shahi dynasty were great builders, and their style of architecture shows an unmistakeable Persian influence. The **Ahmadnagar Fort**, 4 km (2.5 miles) northeast of the station, was built in 1490, though the impressive stone walls were added in 1563. Its palace, the only surviving structure, consists of a large hall with a series of domes. In 1942 it housed an important political prisoner, Jawaharlal Nehru, who wrote his famous book, *The Discovery of India*, here. The **Jami Masjid** dates to the same period. Nearby is the ornate **Damri Mosque**. Built in 1568, it has a cut-out trefoil parapet and finials topped by miniature pavilions.

Emperor Aurangzeb died in Ahmadnagar in 1707, and his body rested briefly at the small **Alamgir Dargah,** near the cantonment, before being interred at Khuldabad (*see 475*).

To the west of the town lies **Bagh Rauza**, a walled garden complex. It contains the mausoleum of Ahmad Nizam Shah Bahri, which has a lavishly decorated interior.

HIKING IN THE SAHYADRIS

The Western Ghats, also known in Maharashtra as the Sahyadris, run parallel to India's west coast and stretch across the states of Maharashtra, Karnataka, Tamil Nadu and Kerala. Formed from volcanic rock, the hills are a maze of ridges and valleys. In Maharashtra, the many popular hill stations serve as excellent starting points for a number of scenic walking trails. **Mahabaleshwar** and **Panchgani** are particularly well-marked with hiking routes that lead through lush forests and valleys. These hills also have a wealth of craggy rock-faces perfect for climbing and **Lonavla** is a favourite base for rock climbing enthusiasts. **Matheran** has a much-trodden path known as Shivaji's Ladder, which

leads from One Tree Hill down to the valley below. The Sahyadri Hills are particularly beautiful in September after the rains, when the hills are carpeted with wild flowers and cascading waterfalls seem to appear at every turn.

The rugged ranges of the Sahyadri Hills

FESTIVALS OF MAHARASHTRA

Janmashtami *(Jul/Aug)*. The birth of Lord Krishna is celebrated enthusiastically all over the state. Pots of butter are strung high in the streets and human pyramids attempt to reach them, imitating the god's childhood pranks.

Janmashtami in Mumbai

Naga Panchami *(Aug/Sep)*. Snakes, considered powerful creatures and revered across India, are worshipped during this festival. After being fed cupfuls of milk, they are taken out in colourful processions and later released into the fields.

Ganesha Chaturthi *(Aug/Sep)*. This is the most significant festival in Maharashtra, celebrated with particular fervour in Pune and Mumbai. Clay idols of Lord Ganesha (*see p467*) are made and then worshipped over 10 days, amidst lively festivities. After this they are led in colourful processions to the closest water body and immersed.

Kalidasa Festival *(Nov)*, Nagpur. Some of the most renowned exponents of classical music and dance gather at this festival, organized to honour the 4th-century Sanskrit dramatist and poet, Kalidasa.

Ellora Festival *(Dec)*, Ellora. This festival presents a variety of classical performing arts against the evocative setting of the Kailasanatha Temple.

The holy tank of Ramkund, Nasik

Nasik ⑩

Nasik district. 187 km (116 miles) NE of Mumbai. 🚶 *1,077,000.* 🚉 🚌
ℹ️ *Maharashtra Tourism, (0253) 257 0059.* 📅 *Kumbh Mela (every 12 years).*

The town of Nasik is one of India's most holy sites. A bustling temple town, built on both banks of the Godavari river, it has almost 200 shrines. The ghats that line the river front are the venue for the spectacular Kumbh Mela *(see p211)*. Legend says that Rama, hero of the *Ramayana (see p27)*, lived here during his 14-year exile. **Ramkund**, the centrally located tank and the town's focal point, is believed to mark the spot where Rama and his wife Sita bathed. The ashes of the dead are also immersed here.

Most of Nasik's temples date to the 18th century. The **Kala Rama Temple**, east of Ramkund, is built in black stone with a 25-m (82-ft) high *shikhara*. It supposedly marks the spot where Sita was abducted by Ravana. The **Rameshwar Temple** has carvings on the roof of its hall, while the **Muktidham Temple**, close to the station, carries inscriptions from the *Bhagavad Gita* on its walls.

Environs
Pandu Lena, 8 km (5 miles) south of Nasik, has 24 Buddhist caves dating to the 1st and 2nd centuries BC. The oldest is Cave 10, a *vihara* (monastery)

which has splendid sculptures and inscriptions above its entrance. Cave 18, an early *chaitya griha*, has a beautifully carved exterior. Other fine caves include Caves 3 and 20. The sacred **Trimbakeshwar Temple**, 33 km (21 miles) west of Nasik, is built on the site of one of Shiva's 12 naturally-occurring *jyotirlingas* (lingas of light). It is surrounded by a large paved platform and has a carved *shikhara*. Though closed to non-Hindus, visitors can still get a good view of the courtyard and the shrine leading off it. About 65 km (40 miles) south of Nasik is **Shirdi**, the temple complex of the first Sai Baba, Maharashtra's most popular saint, who died in 1918.

Aurangabad ⑪

Aurangabad district. 404 km (251 miles) NE of Mumbai. 🚶 *873,000.* ✈️ *10 km (6 miles) E of town centre, then taxi.* 🚉 🚌 ℹ️ *Maharashtra Tourism, Station Rd East, (0240) 233 1513.*

The largest city in northern Maharashtra, Aurangabad is the nearest air-link to the splendid caves at Ellora and Ajanta *(see pp476–81)*. It was founded in 1610 by Malik Ambar, prime minister of the Nizam Shahi rulers of Ahmadnagar *(see p473)*. In 1653 it became the head-quarters of Aurangzeb, the last great Mughal emperor. It was

Detail of the entrance door, Bibi ka Maqbara

from this city – which he renamed after himself – that he conquered the Deccan states.

The city's most famous monument is the **Bibi ka Maqbara**. Located outside the walled city, this imitation of the Taj was built in 1678 by Aurangzeb's son, Azam Shah, in memory of his mother Rabia Durrani. Standing in the middle of a large Mughal garden, it has four disproportionately large minarets at the ends of its raised platform. Like the Taj, it uses white marble and stucco, but there is none of the fine *pietra dura* work that distinguishes Shah Jahan's creation *(see pp172–3)*.

Aurangzeb's walled city makes up the central part of the town, although a few structures from Malik Ambar's older city remain, including the **Naukonda Palace** (largely in ruins) and the **Jami Masjid**. On the left bank of the Khan river is the **Dargah of Baba Shah Musafir**, a Sufi saint who was Aurangzeb's spiritual guide. The complex contains a small mosque, a *madrasa* (theological college), a law court, the zenana (women's quarters) and a water mill (Panchakki), fed by a rectangular tank. Also within the old city, close to Zafar Gate, is the **Himroo Factory**. Aurangabad is famed for its ancient art of weaving brocade, using silk and gold threads, known as *kamkhab*. When the city's prosperity declined, the weavers began

Bibi ka Maqbara in Aurangabad, an imitation of Agra's Taj Mahal

An ornately carved pillared hall in Cave 3, Aurangabad Caves

using less expensive cotton and silver threads, producing *himroo,* which literally means similar. A variety of such shawls and saris are available in showrooms across town. The factory also produces rich Paithani saris, intricately woven with gold thread.

Environs

About 3 km (2 miles) north are the **Aurangabad Caves**. Mainly excavated during the Vakataka and Kalachuri periods (6th and 7th centuries), these caves can be divided into two groups. Of the five caves in the western group, the oldest is Cave 4, dating to the 1st century AD. It is a fine *chaitya griha* with a monolithic stupa. Carved on the rock face outside is a superb image of the Buddha, seated on a lion throne. Cave 3 (5th century) has an ingeniously designed pillared hall that is acoustically sensitive and amplifies sound. Inside the inner sanctum, a Seated Buddha is flanked by devotees with floral offerings.

The eastern group, nearby, comprises four caves. Cave 6 has delicately sculpted Bodhisattvas, surrounded by flying figures. The most splendid of the caves is Cave 7, a sumptuous shrine with large sculptures of Tara and Avalokitesvara *(see p141).* Its inner sanctum has a superb frieze of a female dancer accompanied by seven musicians.

Daulatabad ⑫

Aurangabad district. 13 km (8 miles) E of Aurangabad. 🚌 *Bus tours are offered by Maharashtra Tourism, Aurangabad, (0240) 233 1513. Taxis & jeeps also available from Aurangabad.* ☐ *daily.* 🎥

Perched on a granite outcrop of the Deccan Plateau, this formidable fort has witnessed some of the greatest carnage in the region. Originally known as Deogiri, it was captured in 1296 by Alauddin Khilji, the Deccan's first Muslim invader from Delhi. He was followed by Muhammad bin Tughluq, who annexed the fort in 1328 and renamed the town Daulatabad ("City of Fortune"). In a fit of misguided reasoning, he decided to shift his capital here, and compelled Delhi's entire population to march across 1,127 km (700 miles). Thousands died of starvation or disease along the way, and when the move failed, the sultan and his court marched back to Delhi. Daulatabad was successively conquered by the Deccani Bahmani sultans, the Nizam Shahis, the Mughals, the Marathas and finally the Nizam of Hyderabad – each conquest proving more bloody and savage than the last.

Himroo fabric, Aurangabad

The pyramid-shaped hill, on which the imposing fort is built, stands apart from the surrounding ranges, and towers to a height of 183 m (600 ft). This made Mughal emperor Shah Jahan's chronicler note that "neither ant nor snake could scale it". Four solid concentric walls protect the fort. The first of its three zones is **Ambarkot**, the outer fort. Within, stands the 60-m (197-ft) high victory tower, **Chand Minar**, built in 1435 by Alauddin Bahmani to celebrate his conquest of the fort. In the nearby **Jami Masjid**, 106 pillars from Jain and Hindu temples separate the main hall into 25 aisles. A triple gateway studded with iron spikes provides access into **Kataka**,

the inner fort. Gateways lead through fortified walls into the base of the citadel, known as **Balakot**, separated by a moat once infested with crocodiles.

Near the innermost gate lies the blue and white tiled **Chini Mahal**, where the last sultan of Golconda was imprisoned by Aurangzeb in 1687. On a nearby bastion is the enormous bronze cannon, the **Qila Shikhan** or "Fort Breaker". This 6-m (20-ft) long cannon has a splendid ram's head, and Persian inscriptions along its length refer to it as the "Creator of Storms". A series of dark tunnels lead to the heart of the citadel and end near a pillared pavilion, **Baradari**, a late Mughal building. The fort's ramparts offer sweeping views.

Environs

The walled village of **Khuldabad** ("Heavenly Abode") is 10 km (6 miles) north of Daulatabad. The Alamgir Dargah, dedicated to the Muslim saint, Sayeed Zain-ud-din, (d.1370), is its most famous monument. Also known as Rauza, this religious complex, established by Sufi saints in the 14th century, was considered so sacred that several Deccani sultans chose to be buried here. Emperor Aurangzeb, who died in the Deccan in 1707, is buried in a simple tomb in the courtyard. The beautiful tomb of Malik Ambar *(see p473),* is a short distance to the north.

The Chand Minar, once covered in glazed Persian tiles, Daulatabad

Ellora: Kailasanatha Temple ⑬

Detail, roof of the entrance gateway

The finest of the Ellora group of rock-cut caves is the magnificent Kailasanatha Temple (Cave 16), a UNESCO World Heritage Site. Commissioned by the Rashtrakuta king Krishna I in the 8th century, this mammoth complex, spanning 81 m (266 ft) by 47 m (154 ft), was carved out of a huge rocky cliff face. Sculptors chiselled through 85,000 cubic metres (approximately 3 million cubic ft) of rock, beginning at the top of the cliff and working their way down. The resulting marvel, embellished with huge sculptural panels, was meant to depict Mount Kailasa, the sacred abode of Lord Shiva.

★ The Roof
The mandapa (assembly hall) roof is embellished by a lotus carved in concentric rings, topped by four stone lions.

The Nandi Pavilion

Courtyard
On either side of the courtyard are two life-size elephants.

Obelisks
Flanking the Nandi Pavilion are two monolithic pillars, 17 m (56 ft) high, with carvings of lotus friezes and garlands.

★ Lakshmi with Elephants
Facing the entrance, the ornate Gaja-lakshmi panel in the Nandi Pavilion depicts Lakshmi seated in a lotus pond and being bathed by elephants bearing upturned pots in their trunks.

The tower rises 32.6 m (107 ft), and was once covered in white plaster, to replicate Mount Kailasa's snowy peaks.

VISITORS' CHECKLIST

Aurangabad district. 30 km (19) miles) NW of Aurangabad. Jeeps are also available at Aurangabad & tour operators also organize trips. Tue–Sun, (all caves). Flash photography is prohibited. Light is best in the afternoon. Take packed lunch, a torch, wear comfortable shoes and a sun hat. Ellora Festival (Dec).

Supporting Elephants
Elephants with lotuses in their trunks are carved all along the lower storey, and appear to support the structure.

| 0 metres | 10 |
| 0 yards | 10 |

Rock-cut monasteries

★ Ravana Shaking Mount Kailasa
A large panel depicts Ravana (the demon king in the Ramayana*) shaking Mount Kailasa in order to disturb Shiva and Parvati in their mountain home.*

Ramayana panels flank the south wall, while the north wall has *Mahabharata* and Krishna legends.

STAR FEATURES

- ★ The Roof
- ★ Lakshmi with Elephants
- ★ Ravana Shaking Mount Kailasa

Three Goddesses
The Hall of Sacrifice contains life-size images of Durga, Chamunda and Kali, as well as of Ganesha, Parvati and the seven mother goddesses.

Exploring Ellora

The 34 caves at Ellora, hewn from a 2-km (1.3-mile) long escarpment, are among the most splendid examples of rock-cut architecture in India.

The emergence and growing importance of Ellora coincided with the decline of Buddhism, and a Hindu renaissance under the Chalukya and Rashtrakuta dynasties (7th–9th centuries AD). Ellora was situated on an important trade route that ran between Ujjain in Madhya Pradesh and the west coast. It was the revenue from this very lucrative trade that sustained 500 years of excavation at Ellora, as the older Ajanta caves began to be abandoned.

View of the dramatic Ellora escarpment with its seasonal waterfall

The caves at Ellora fall into three distinct groups – Buddhist, Hindu and Jain – and they are numbered from the southern end. The **Buddhist Caves** (1 to 12) date from the Chalukya period, between the 7th and 8th centuries. The first nine are variations of *viharas* or monasteries, and are filled with fine Buddha figures, Bodhisattvas and scenes from Buddhist mythology. The most splendid is **Cave 10**, or Vishwakarma, named after the celestial carpenter. A striking *chaitya griha (see p20)*, it is dominated by a figure of the Teaching Buddha carved in front of a

votive stupa, placed under a vaulted roof. It is so intricately carved that it seems to be made of wood. Other important caves are **Cave 11**, or Do Thal (two-storeyed), and **Cave 12**, or Tin Thal (three-storeyed). The upper hall of Cave 12 has large Bodhisattvas carved on its walls, while rows of seven Buddha figures flank the entrance to the antechamber.

The **Hindu Caves** (13 to 29), were carved out between the 7th and 9th centuries, and represent the peak of Ellora's development. **Cave 14**, or Ravana ki Khai, contains impressive sculptures of deities from the Hindu pantheon, such as Durga slaying the buffalo demon, and Vishnu as the boar-headed Varaha. **Cave 15**, or Dashavatara, also has superb sculptural depictions.

Cave 21, or Rameshvara, and **Cave 29**, or Dhumar Lena, are other impressive caves.

The **Jain Caves** (30 to 34) date from Ellora's last stage, in the 9th century, and are simpler than the Hindu ones. **Cave 32**, or Indra Sabha, is the finest of the group. A monolithic shrine, it has carvings of elephants, lions and *tirthankaras (see p396)* on the courtyard walls. **Cave 30**, or Chhota Kailasa, is a small, incomplete replica of the Kailasanatha Temple *(see pp476–7)* and has sculptures of various *tirthankaras* and Mahavira on a lion-throne.

Environs

The 18th-century **Grishneshvara Temple**, nearby, is one of the 12 *jyotirlinga* shrines dedicated to Shiva, built by Rani Ahilyabai of Indore *(see p250)*.

The upper-storey hall, Vishwakarma (Cave 10)

ELLORA CAVES

30-34
29 Dhumar Lena
28
27
26
25
24
23
22
21 Rameshvara
20
19
18
17
Girija
● Ghrishneshvara Temple
16 Kailasanatha Temple
15 Dashavatara
14 Ravana ki Khai
13
12 Tin Thal
11 Do Thal
10 Vishwakarma
6-9
5
4
3
2
1

0 metres   300
0 yards   300

Façade of Cave 19, Ajanta, with a large horseshoe-shaped window

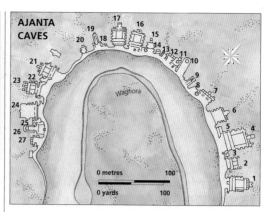

AJANTA CAVES

Waghora

0 metres 100

0 yards 100

Ajanta ⑭

Aurangabad district. 110 km (68 miles) NE of Aurangabad. *from Aurangabad.* ○ *Tue–Sun.* *flash photography is prohibited.* *Organized tours & taxis are also available from Aurangabad. Take a packed lunch, bottled water, torch, and wear comfortable shoes and a sun hat.*

A UNESCO World Heritage Site, the 30 extraordinary rock-cut caves at Ajanta lie within a horseshoe-shaped escarpment, overlooking the narrow Waghora river gorge. At its head is a waterfall that drops into the Saptakunda pool. The caves were occupied for only a short period and, over time, the surrounding jungle concealed their existence. They were "rediscovered" quite accidentally in 1819, when John Smith, of the 28th Madras Cavalry, suddenly saw the top of the façade of Cave 10 while on a tiger hunt.

Ajanta's caves fall into two groups. The early group belongs to the more austere Hinayana phase of Buddhism (2nd–1st century BC), during which the Buddha was not represented in human form but only by symbols such as a Wheel of Law or a Bodhi Tree. The second group dates from the Mahayana period (5th–6th centuries AD), carved out during the rule of the Vakataka dynasty, when artistic expression was more exuberant. The caves were inhabited by monks, artists and craftsmen, who used them as *varsh-vatikas* or monsoon shrines. Stylistically they are of two

types – *chaitya grihas* (prayer halls) and *viharas* (monasteries). The *chaityas* have vaulted ceilings and octagonal columns that divide the space into a central hall with a votive stupa, the object of veneration. The side aisles that run around the hall were used for ritual circumambulation. The Mahayana *chaityas* also have Buddha images. *Viharas* typically have a verandah, a hall surrounded by cells, and an inner shrine with enormous Buddha figures.

Of the seven Mahayana caves, dating from the 5th century AD, **Cave 1** is famous for its splendid murals *(see pp480–81)*. Above its verandah are friezes of scenes from the Buddha's life, while its ceiling is supported by 20 carved and painted pillars. **Cave 2** has a superb façade carved with images of Naga kings, and their attendants *(ganas)*, while its main shrine has a magnificent painted ceiling.

Caves 8, 9, 10, 12, 13 and 15 are Hinayana caves. **Cave 9**, a *chaitya griha*, has a façade adorned with windows and lattice-work. The large Buddha figures along the sides were a later addition (5th century) and its murals are from both periods. **Cave 10** is thought to be Ajanta's oldest cave and is one of its finest *chaitya grihas*.

Caves 15 to 20 are late 5th-century Mahayana caves. **Cave 16** has sculptures of beautiful maidens flanking the doorway, while in **Cave 17** the entrance to the inner shrine is ornamented with Buddha figures, goddesses and lotuses.

Caves 21 to 27 (7th century), make up the final group. **Cave 26** displays the full magnificence of Ajanta's sculptural art. Especially remarkable are two splendid panels – one depicts the Temptation of the Buddha by the Demon Mara, while the **Parinirvana** is a 7-m (23-ft) image of the reclining Buddha, with his eyes closed as if in sleep. His disciples mourn his passing, while above, celestial beings rejoice in his salvation.

The moving Parinirvana, depicting the passing of the Buddha, Cave 26

The Ajanta Murals

The earliest and finest examples of Buddhist painting in India can be seen at the Ajanta caves. Executed between the 2nd century BC and the 5th century AD, the murals show scenes from the Buddha's life, and from the Jataka Tales, which recount stories of the Buddha's previous incarnations as an enlightened being or Bodhisattva. Magnificent, detailed compositions, the murals include depictions of court scenes, princes and musicians, and offer fascinating glimpses of daily life in the 5th century. The colours, derived from plants and minerals, are in rich shades of ochre, lime, black, green and lapis lazuli.

Avalokitesvara, *also identified as Vajrapani, is the most venerated Bodhisattva in the Mahayana pantheon, and can be seen to the right of the antechamber doorway.*

CAVE 1
This late 5th-century *vihara* (monastery) contains some of Ajanta's most evocative murals.

The Miracle of Sravasti, *on the antechamber's right wall, depicts a famous miracle when the Buddha multiplied himself a thousand-fold.*

Padmapani *(Lotus-Holder), the Bodhisattva of Compassion, can be seen on the wall to the left of the antechamber doorway. He is surrounded by celestial beings and air-borne figures.*

The *Mahajanaka Jataka*, *to the left of the antechamber, recounts the life of Prince Mahajanaka, who renounced the world to become an ascetic. Here, the prince is surrounded by female attendants.*

A scene depicting a king, possibly the Vakataka ruler Harisena, greeting a Persian embassy

Scenes from the *Mahajanaka Jataka*, *from left to right, depict Prince Mahajanaka, Queen Shivali enticing the prince, palace maids, and a dancing girl.*

CAVE 2

Similar in design to Cave 1, this 5th-century *vihara* is profusely painted in lustrous colours. The walls, columns, capitals and ceiling are covered in scrollwork, geometric and floral patterns, and numerous Jataka panels, including stories connected with the Buddha's birth.

The large mandala *(circular diagram) dominates the elaborately painted ceiling of this remarkable cave. A depiction of the cosmos, its outer ring is filled with lotus motifs.*

CAVE 10

Considered to be Ajanta's oldest cave, this *chaitya griha* dates to the 2nd century BC. The left wall has its oldest mural, a frieze depicting a prince worshipping a Bodhi Tree.

Numerous figures of the Buddha *embellish some of the octagonal pillars (39 in all), that separate the aisles from the central nave in Cave 10.*

CAVE 16

Outstanding paintings in this cave depict the conversion of Nanda, the Buddha's half-brother, and show his wife swooning when she hears the news of his becoming a monk.

Nanda's wife, Sundari, fainting upon hearing of his conversion

CAVE 17

This cave has the largest number of paintings. Among the finest are a vast panel depicting Simhala's shipwreck and encounter with a man-eating ogress; and a lady at her toilet, gazing intently into a mirror.

Eight seated Buddha figures *are depicted above the doorway in the verandah, with a row of amorous couples directly below them.*

A panel from the *Visvantara Jataka*, *to the left of the doorway, depicts Prince Visvantara and his wife drinking wine. They then move to the city gate and give alms to the needy.*

This detail of an *apsara* *(celestial maiden) adoring the Buddha, is part of a larger mural on the verandah to the right of the door. The Ajanta murals are renowned for their exquisite portrayal of women.*

The enormous meteorite crater at Lonar, partially filled by a lake

Lonar ⓯

Buldana district. 130 km (81 miles)
E of Aurangabad. 🚉 Jalna, 83 km
(52 miles) W of Lonar, then bus. 🚌
from Aurangabad, taxis also available.

The tiny village of Lonar, is
famous for its remarkable
meteorite crater. Thought to be
the only hyper-velocity impact
crater in basaltic rock in the
world, the mammoth crater,
2 km (1.3 miles) in diameter
and 700 m (2,297 ft) deep, is
estimated to be about 50,000
years old. Scientists believe
that the meteorite is still buried
beneath the southeastern edge
of the crater. A lake fills the
bottom and the ruins of some
Hindu temples stand on its
shores. The crater is rich in
birdlife, and monkeys and
herds of deer can also be seen.
There are a few rest houses
that offer rooms and the village has some eateries as well.

Melghat Tiger Reserve ⓰

Amravati district. 400 km (249 miles)
NE of Aurangabad. 🚉 Amravati,
100 km (62 miles) SE of entry point.
Maharashtra Tourism, organizes buses
or jeeps from Amravati to the park. ℹ
For bookings contact the Field Director,
(0721) 266 2792. ◯ Dec–May. 🎫

The Project Tiger Reserve of
Melghat, which means
"Meeting Place of the Ghats",
spreads across the Gawilgarh
Hills in the southern part of
the Satpura Mountains. Its
highest altitudes are approximately 1,178 m (3,865 ft)
above sea level. These hills
have a dense canopy of the
country's finest deciduous

teak and bamboo forests,
which are now threatened by
rampant commercial exploitation for timber. Along with its
elusive 73 tigers, the reserve
is home to about 80 leopards,
chausingha (four-horned
antelope), *dhole* (Indian wild
dog), jungle cats, hyenas and
a rich variety of birds. The
sanctuary also supports the
state's largest concentration
of *gaur*, the endangered
Indian bison.
  The best time to visit is
between January and April,
when the park is pleasantly
cool. Its five rivers, the
Khandu, Khapra, Sipna, Garga
and Dolar, dry out in summer,
and the few remaining pools
of rainwater are highly prized
as watering holes.

Environs
Chikhaldhara, lying 25 km
(16 miles) northeast of
Melghat, is a quaint hill
station established by the
British in 1839.

A tiger resting in a tree at the
Melghat Tiger Reserve

Nagpur ⓱

Nagpur district. 520 km (323 miles) NE
of Aurangabad. 🏠 2,051,500. ✈
10 km (6 miles) S of city centre, then
bus or taxi. 🚉 🚌 ℹ Maharashtra
Tourism, (0712) 253 3325. 🎫 Pola
(Jun/Jul), Kalidasa Festival (Nov).

Situated on the banks of the
Nag river, Nagpur was the
capital of the Central Provinces
until it became part of
Maharashtra state after
Independence. It is a fast
developing industrial city lying
on India's main north-south
railway line and is also the
country's orange-growing
capital. Historically, it was the
capital of the aboriginal Gond
tribals until it was captured by
the Maratha Bhonsles (see
p468) in 1740, and finally by
the British in 1861.
  In October 1956, the city
witnessed an event of great
social importance, when Dr BR
Ambedkar, writer of the Indian
Constitution and a freedom
fighter born into a lower caste
Hindu family, converted to
Buddhism in a stand against
the rigid Hindu caste system.
Nearly 200,000 people
followed him, and the
movement gathered great
momentum, resulting in about
three million conversions.
  Nagpur town is built around
Sitabaldi Fort, which is
encircled by a deep moat. It is
open to the public only on
26 January and 15 August. In
the eastern part of the city are
the remains of the **Bhonsle
Palace**, which was destroyed
by fire in 1864. South of the
old city lie the **Chhatris**, or
memorials of the Bhonsle
kings, while a number of
colonial buildings are situated
in the western part of Nagpur.
Among the most noteworthy
are the High Court (1737–42)
and the Anglican Cathedral
of All Saints (1851).

Environs
Ramtek, 40 km (25 miles)
northeast of Nagpur, is associated with the 14-year exile of
Rama, Sita and Lakshman, as
told in the epic *Ramayana*
(see p27). It was the capital of
the Vakataka dynasty between
the 4th and the 6th centuries,
and the fort on the Hill of

Baskets of juicy oranges on sale in Nagpur's thriving market

Rama dates to this period. Its walls, however, were built in 1740, by the founder of Nagpur's Bhonsle dynasty, Raghoji I. There are also temples dedicated to Rama and Sita, dating to the 5th century.

Wardha ⑱

Wardha district. 493 km (306 miles) NW of Aurangabad. 🚃 ➡ *from Nagpur to Wardha, then bus or auto to Sevagram.* **Tel** *(07152) 284 753.*

Most visitors to Wardha are en route to Mahatma Gandhi's historic **Sevagram Ashram**, now a national institution, 8 km (5 miles) northwest of Wardha town. Established by Gandhi in 1933, Sevagram ("Village of Service") was based on Gandhi's philosophy of rural economic development. It became the headquarters of India's National Movement, where Gandhi lived and worked for more than 15 years. Spread over 40 ha (99 acres) of farmland, the ashram has numerous *kutirs* or rural dwellings and several research centres. Gandhi's personal effects, such as his spinning wheel and spectacles, are on display, and khadi, the coarse home-spun cotton that Gandhi made famous as the symbol of India's freedom struggle, is also on sale. A photo exhibit opposite the main entrance depicts scenes from Gandhi's life, while a hospital catering to the needs of local villagers, is located on the main road. Prayers are held daily at 4.30am and 6pm under a pipal tree planted by Gandhi, which visitors can attend.

An oil lamp in a niche, Sevagram

Environs

The ashram of Gandhi's disciple, Vinobha Bhave, is 10 km (6 miles) north of Sevagram at **Paunar**. Bhave started the successful Bhoodan Movement (which literally means "land donation") that sought to persuade wealthy landowners to give portions of their holdings to the poor.

Pandharpur ⑲

Sholapur district. 250 km (155 miles) SE of Pune. 🏃 *91,500.* 🚃 ➡ 🚲 *Ashadh Ekadashi Fair (Jul).*

The spiritual capital of Maharashtra, Pandharpur is situated on the banks of the Chandrabhaga river and is the site of the sacred shrine of Vithoba, an incarnation of Lord Vishnu. The temple was built in 1228 and is the focal point of a sacred pilgrimage which draws thousands of Varakaris (members of one of the state's most popular religious sects) here every July to attend the Ashadh Ekadashi fair. *Dindis* or group processions travel to Pandharpur from every village in the area, accompanied by devotional singing. The river front, lined with numerous bathing ghats, comes alive with crowds of people, who gather here for their ritual dip.

The spartan interior of Mahatma Gandhi's ashram at Sevagram, near Wardha

GOA

This tiny state, along the Konkan Coast, covers 3,702 sq km (1,429 sq miles) and consists of just two districts, North and South Goa. Goa's distinct culture is a legacy of its colonial past. In 1510, Alfonso de Albuquerque established a small but powerful Portuguese enclave here. Though Goa became a part of the Indian Union in 1961, evidence of the 400-odd years of Portuguese rule is still apparent in the people's dress, language, religion and cuisine, and in their music, a fusion of the plaintive *fado* with the lilting rhythms of local Konkani folk songs. Today, Goa is one of India's most popular holiday destinations, with its idyllic beaches, lush paddy fields, coconut plantations and villages dotted with pretty whitewashed churches and grand mansions. Its other attractions include the Hindu temples around Ponda, built between the 15th and 18th centuries, and the magnificent cathedrals of Old Goa. Goa's friendly, easy-going people go out of their way to make visitors feel at home.

SIGHTS AT A GLANCE

Towns & Cities
Mapusa ⑤
Margao ⑮
Panaji ①
Pernem ⑦

Churches, Seminaries & Temples
Pilar ⑪
Ponda ⑫
Rachol ⑭
Reis Magos ②
Tambdi Surla ⑬

Historic Sites
A Walk through Old Goa ⑩
Terekhol Fort ⑨
Braganza House ⑯

Beaches & Beach Towns
Anjuna ④
Arambol ⑧
Calangute ③
Cavelossim ⑱
Colva ⑰
Palolem ⑲
Vagator ⑥

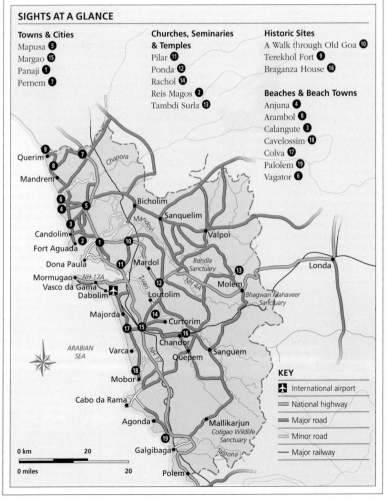

◁ Coconut groves and rice fields surrounding a village chapel in Goa

Panaji ❶

Goa's capital, Panaji, situated at the mouth of the Mandovi river, is reminiscent of a provincial Mediterranean town. Earlier a port of the Adil Shahi kings of Bijapur *(see p542)*, it became a military landing stage and warehouse after the arrival of the Portuguese in 1510. In 1759, after a series of epidemics in Old Goa, the viceroy was forced to move his residence to Panaji, or Panjim as it was then called. However, it was only in 1843 that the town became the official capital of Portuguese territories in India. Today, Panaji has a relaxed and friendly ambience, especially along the leafy avenues of the old town *(see pp488–9)*. The newer commercial hub, laid out on a grid, has concrete structures interspersed with colonial buildings and churches.

The Church of Our Lady of the Immaculate Conception

🏛 Secretariat

Avenida Dom Joao Crasto. *Tel (0832) 222 2701.* ◯ Mon–Fri.

The river front Secretariat housing the State Legislative Assembly, is one of Panaji's oldest buildings. It was once the summer palace of Yusuf Adil Shah, Goa's 16th-century Muslim ruler, and fell to the Portuguese in 1510, despite a formidable battery of 55 cannons and a salt-water moat that protected it.

The 19th-century statue of Abbé de Faria

Rebuilt in 1615, its strategic location made it a point of entry for ships and a stopover for viceroys and governors en route to Old Goa *(see p501)*. In 1760, after Old Goa was abandoned in favour of Panaji, the Idalcaon's Palace (a corruption of Adil Shah's or Khan's Palace), as it was then known, became the official residence of the viceroys – until 1918, when the residence moved to the Cabo Palace, southwest of Panaji. Extensive renovations have transformed the original Islamic structure into the colonial building it is today, with a sloping tiled roof, wide wooden verandahs and cast-iron pillars. The Ashoka Chakra and the Buddhist Wheel of Law, the emblems of the Indian government, have replaced the Portuguese viceroys' coat of arms, above the entrance to the building.

Standing west of the Secretariat is the arresting statue of Abbé de Faria. This Goan priest, who was born in Candolim in 1756, underwent theological training in Rome. After his ordination, he moved to Paris, where he won acclaim as the father of modern hypnosis.

⛪ Church of Our Lady of the Immaculate Conception

Church Square. *Tel (0832) 242 6939.* ◯ daily. ✝ (English) 8am, Mon–Sat; 8.30am, Sun.

Overlooking Largo da Igreja or "Church Square", Panaji's main square, is the Church of Our Lady of the Immaculate Conception, the town's most important landmark. Portuguese sailors used to come to the original chapel, consecrated in 1541, to offer thanksgiving prayers after their long and treacherous voyage from Lisbon.

The present church, with its Baroque façade framed by twin towers, was built in 1619. Its most striking feature, the double flight of stairs leading up to the church, was added in 1871. The central pediment was built at the same

View of the the riverside Secretariat at Panaji, with its tiled roof and colonial façade

For hotels and restaurants in this region see pp709–11 and pp737–8

time, as was the belfry to accommodate the huge bell brought from Old Goa's Augustinian monastery *(see p496)*. The chapel in the south transept has fine reredos (altar panels) retrieved from the viceroy's chapel in the Secretariat. The Baroque splendour of the main altar and the two transept altars is in sharp contrast to the otherwise simple interior.

🏛 Menezes Braganza Institute

Malaca Rd. **Tel** *(0832) 222 4143.* ◯ *Mon–Fri.*

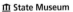

The central pavilion, Azad Maidan

An excellent example of 19th-century Portuguese civic architecture, the Institute Vasco da Gama was built to impart knowledge in the arts and sciences. It was later renamed after the philanthropist Luis de Menezes Braganza (1878–1938), whose family home is in Chandor *(see p508)*.

Today, this is Goa's Central Library, with a good collection of rare books. The superb mural in blue painted ceramic tiles *(azulezos)* was added to the entrance lobby in 1935, and depicts scenes from the epic *Os Lusiadas* (Lusiada, meaning the "people of Portugal", is derived from Lusitania, Portugal's old name). Written by the 16th-century Portuguese poet, Luis Vaz de Camões, this recounts the history of the Portuguese presence in Goa. The institute used to have an art gallery with works by late 19th- and early 20th-century European artists. These exhibits are now housed in the State Museum.

The grassy square in front of the Institute, **Azad Maidan**, is lined on one side by the Police Headquarters, built in 1832 with stones from Old Goa's abandoned buildings. The pavilion in the centre was made in 1847, using Corinthian pillars taken from a Dominican church, dating to the mid-16th century. Inside, a memorial to the freedom fighter, Dr Tristao de Braganza Cunha, has replaced an earlier statue of the first viceroy, Alfonso de Albuquerque, now in the Archaeological Museum in Old Goa *(see p500)*.

🏛 State Museum

Patto. **Tel** *(0832) 243 8006.* ◯ *Mon–Fri.* ◑ *public hols.*

This museum houses a rather modest collection of pre-colonial artifacts, including statues, *sati* stones, antique furniture and carvings from

VISITORS' CHECKLIST

North Goa district (Tiswadi taluka). 588 km (365 miles) S of Mumbai 🚂 58,800. ✈ Dabolim, 30 km (19 miles) S of town centre, then bus or taxi. 🚉 Margao, 33 km (21 miles) SE of town centre. 🛈 GTDC Trionora Apartments, (0832) 222 6515. 🎭 Feast of Our Lady (Dec); Carnival (Feb).

ravaged Hindu temples, as well as some Christian icons.

Environs
Panaji's nearest beach, **Miramar**, is 3 km (2 miles) west. **Dona Paula**, 7 km (4 miles) southwest of Panaji, is near the headland dividing the estuaries of the Zuari and Mandovi rivers. It is named after a viceroy's daughter who, the story goes, jumped into the sea when she wasn't allowed to marry a local fisherman. The jetty offers fine views of Fort Aguada across the bay. Jet skis are available for rent and visitors can also take a ferry-ride to Vasco da Gama harbour.

A scene from *Os Lusiadas*, depicting Vasco da Gama's arrival in Goa

GOAN RIVER CRUISES

A delightful way to spend an evening in Goa is to take one of the many sunset cruises along the Mandovi river, organized by the Goa Tourism Development Corporation, (0832) 222 6728, and also by private operators. Most of the cruises begin from the jetty at the foot of Mandovi bridge, every day between 6 and 7pm (tickets are available at the jetty). Entertainment is provided by troupes of Goan dancers and musicians. On full moon nights, an excellent dinner is also provided on board. Some operators, such as Sea Adventure, (0832) 255 0705, organize specialized tours through the backwaters, a vibrant mangrove habitat and home to marsh crocodiles and migratory birds. Focussing on culture and food, Spice Villages, (0832) 234 4268, takes visitors to the sylvan settings of spice plantations, which attract flocks of beautiful birds.

An evening cruise down the Mandovi river

Street-by-Street: Panaji Old Town

Terracotta medallion

Tucked away between Ourem Creek and Altinho Hill in Panaji are the old residential quarters of Fontainhas and São Tomé, built on reclaimed land in the 19th century. Fontainhas was named after the fountain of Phoenix, a spring that provided the quarter's only source of water, while São Tomé takes its name from the São Tomé Church. This old-world precinct, characterized by a jumble of painted, tile-roofed houses, has streets lined with taverns offering authentic Goan cuisine and *feni* (cashewnut liqueur), and bakeries serving *bebinca*, the delicious local cake. Many of the residents still speak Portuguese.

A priest in the doorway of St Sebastian's Chapel

Panjim Inn

Velha Goa Galeria

FILIPE NERI XAVIER ROAD

GOVERNADOR TEXEIRA DA SILVA ROAD

RUA DE NATALE

31ST JANUARY ROAD

RUA DE NATA

CORTE DE OI

RUA DE OURE

Dr Arminio Ribeiro de Santana Mansion

★ **Fundação de Oriente**
Originally a family home, it now houses a Portuguese foundation that promotes artistic, cultural and scientific work. Its library is open to the public.

STAR SIGHTS

- ★ Fundação de Oriente
- ★ St Sebastian's Chapel
- ★ Rua de Natale

★ **St Sebastian's Chapel**
The chapel, built in 1888, has a life-size crucifix that used to hang in the Palace of the Inquisition in Old Goa.

★ **Rua de Natale**
This road snakes up Altinho Hill and has steps laid out to help pedestrians negotiate the gentle climb.

VISITORS' CHECKLIST

Fontainhas & São Tomé. **St
Sebastian's Chapel** ◻ *am only.*
São Tomé Church ◻ *am only.*
**Fundação de Oriente Library
Tel** *(0832) 243 6108.* ◻ *Sun–Fri.*
Velha Goa Galeria Tel *(0832)
242 6628.* ◻ *Mon–Sat.*

Ourem Creek
The picturesque Rua de Ourem faces Ourem Creek. Behind it, colourful houses dot the slopes all the way up Altinho Hill.

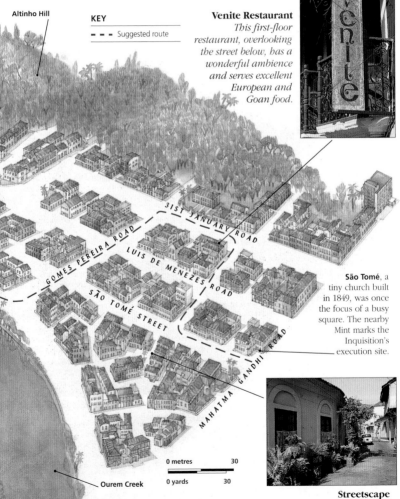

Altinho Hill

KEY

- - - Suggested route

Venite Restaurant
This first-floor restaurant, overlooking the street below, has a wonderful ambience and serves excellent European and Goan food.

31ST JANUARY ROAD

GOMES PEREIRA ROAD

LUIS DE MENEZES ROAD

SÃO TOMÉ STREET

MAHATMA GANDHI ROAD

São Tomé, a tiny church built in 1849, was once the focus of a busy square. The nearby Mint marks the Inquisition's execution site.

Ourem Creek

0 metres   30
0 yards   30

Pato Bridge

Streetscape
Most houses are painted yellow, ochre, green or indigo with a white trim – in keeping with the old Portuguese building code.

Reredos behind the main altar, Reis Magos Church

Reis Magos ❷

North Goa district (Bardez taluka).
3 km (2 miles) NW of Panaji. 🚌
📷 *Feast of Three Kings (Jan).*

The fort at Reis Magos as built in 1551 by Don Alfonso de Noronha, the fifth viceroy, as a second line of defence after the forts at Aguada and Cabo (the tip of Dona Paula). It once housed a prison, which was moved to Mormugao in 1996. Adjacent to the fort is the Reis Magos Church. Constructed in 1555, this is one of Goa's earliest churches, and has the royal Portuguese coat of arms on its façade.

Environs
Fort Aguada, 4 km (2.5 miles) west of Reis Magos, was built in 1612 as a defence against the Marathas and the Dutch. Its church, dedicated to St Lawrence, the patron saint of sailors, was built in 1630, while the huge lighthouse dates to 1864. Some buildings within the fort now house the state prison. The local beach, Sinquerim, is known for its luxury resorts.

Calangute ❸

North Goa district (Bardez taluka). 16 km (10 miles) NW of Panaji. 🚌 ℹ
GTDC Tourist Resort, (0832) 227 6024.

The centre of the hippie scene in the 1960s and 1970s, Calangute is Goa's most popular beach. During the

day, it is packed with sun-bathers, hawkers, masseurs, hair-braiders and ear-cleaners. The entire stretch of sand right up to the adjacent Baga Beach is lined with resorts, trinket stalls, bars and beach shacks such as Reggie's Bar and Souza Lobo *(see p738)*, which serve excellent Goan food. **Atlantis Water Sports**, offers a diverse range of water sports. Rides on fishing boats are also available at bargain prices. Calangute's church, **St Alex**, topped by a large dome, is on the road to Mapusa. Its Rococo-style white-and-gold interior has pretty, shell-shaped niches.

Soccer game in progress, Calangute

🏄 Atlantis Water Sports
Calangute. **Tel** 09890–47272.

Environs
Extending north of Calangute, **Baga Beach** is far less crowded, although its expanse of soft, white sand has its share of

guesthouses and bars. It hosts the leisurely Saturday Night Ingo's Bazaar – a great alternative to the Wednesday market at nearby Anjuna. Tito's Bar, which has the only dance floor on the entire beach, is the hub of Baga's nightlife. **Candolim Beach**, 2.5 km (2 miles) south of Calangute, stretches all the way to Fort Aguada. Popular with large tour groups, the once peaceful waters now resound with the whir of speedboats and jet skis. **Saligao**, 2 km (1.3 miles) east of Calangute, has the pretty Church of Mae de Deus, in Neo-Gothic style, as well as a seminary which prepares boys for theological studies at Rachol Seminary *(see p504).*

Anjuna ❹

North Goa district (Bardez taluka).
18 km (11 miles) NW of Panaji. 🚌
🛍 *Flea Market (Wed).*

Anjuna has now replaced Calangute as a haven for backpackers. It is better known for its full-moon rave parties and sprawling flea market than for its beach. The popular market, held every Wednesday, is crowded with hawkers from all over India selling everything from Bali-nese batik, silver jewellery and papier-mâché boxes, to Tibetan prayer wheels, Rajas-thani mirrorwork and Kerala woodcarvings. Fluorescent rave gear and trendy beach-wear round off the selection, while added attractions are performing monkeys and fortune-telling Nandi bulls.

A woman selling sarongs at the Anjuna flea market

For hotels and restaurants in this region see pp709–11 and pp737–8

Beaches and Beach Life

Goa's splendid beaches stretch over 106 km (66 miles), from Querim in the north to Mobor in the south. Each beach has its distinct character, though in general, South Goa's beaches are far less developed than those in North Goa, and have only recently become popular as tourist destinations. To cater to the growing number of visitors, many beaches now have shacks serving beer, snacks and seafood, lively flea markets, and vendors offering a variety of services from head massages to dolphin-watching trips.

Visitor under a beach umbrella

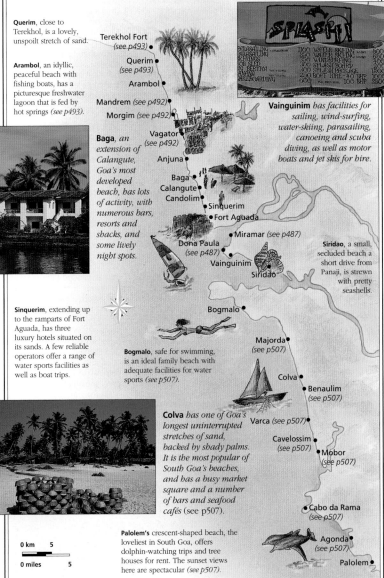

Querim, close to Terekhol, is a lovely, unspoilt stretch of sand.

Arambol, an idyllic, peaceful beach with fishing boats, has a picturesque freshwater lagoon that is fed by hot springs *(see p493)*.

Baga, *an extension of Calangute, Goa's most developed beach, has lots of activity, with numerous bars, resorts and shacks, and some lively night spots.*

Sinquerim, extending up to the ramparts of Fort Aguada, has three luxury hotels situated on its sands. A few reliable operators offer a range of water sports facilities as well as boat trips.

Terekhol Fort *(see p493)*
Querim *(see p493)*
Arambol
Mandrem *(see p492)*
Morgim *(see p492)*
Vagator *(see p492)*
Anjuna
Baga
Calangute
Candolim
Sinquerim
Fort Aguada
Miramar *(see p487)*
Dona Paula *(see p487)*
Vainguinim
Siridao
Bogmalo

Vainguinim *has facilities for sailing, wind-surfing, water-skiing, parasailing, canoeing and scuba diving, as well as motor boats and jet skis for hire.*

Siridao, a small, secluded beach a short drive from Panaji, is strewn with pretty seashells.

Bogmalo, safe for swimming, is an ideal family beach with adequate facilities for water sports *(see p507)*.

Colva *has one of Goa's longest uninterrupted stretches of sand, backed by shady palms. It is the most popular of South Goa's beaches, and has a busy market square and a number of bars and seafood cafés* (see p507).

Majorda *(see p507)*
Colva
Benaulim *(see p507)*
Varca *(see p507)*
Cavelossim *(see p507)*
Mobor *(see p507)*
Cabo da Rama *(see p507)*
Agonda *(see p507)*
Palolem

Palolem's crescent-shaped beach, the loveliest in South Goa, offers dolphin-watching trips and tree houses for rent. The sunset views here are spectacular *(see p507)*.

0 km 5
0 miles 5

The façade of St Jerome's Church (Our Lady of Miracles), Mapusa

Mapusa ❺

North Goa district (Bardez taluka).
13 km (8 miles) N of Panaji.
🏛 40,150. 🅿 🚌 ℹ GTDC Hotel, (0832) 226 2794. 🛒 Fri. 🎭 Feast of Our Lady of Miracles (Apr).

The largest town in northern Goa, Mapusa's main point of interest is the colourful Friday market, with its tantalizing aromas of dried fish, spices, chillies, vinegar, local toddy and the spicy Goan sausages, *chouriça*. The region's famous cashewnuts are also much in demand. Hawkers peddle a range of beachwear, including cheap T-shirts and summer dresses, in the covered colonnades in front of the rows of shops. In the lanes leading off from the main market are stalls selling handicrafts and souvenirs from all over the country.

St Jerome's Church, also known as the Church of Our Lady of Miracles, was rebuilt twice, first in 1719 and again in 1838, after it was destroyed by fire. Its main altar, with the image of Nossa Senhora de Milagres, has some grand ornamental screens, salvaged from a church in Old Goa.

Interestingly, both Hindus and Catholics celebrate the Feast of Our Lady (held 16 days after Easter) with equal fervour. At the end of the festival Hindu devotees, accompanied by Catholics, take the holy oil from St

Jerome's church back to the nearby Shanteri Temple.

Environs
Mayem Lake, 14 km (9 miles) southeast of Mapusa, is an ideal picnic spot, with boating facilities and a good resort.

Vagator ❻

North Goa district (Bardez taluka).
17 km (11 miles) N of Panaji.
🚌 Chapora village.

A beautiful bay sheltered by rocky outcrops at both ends, Vagator consists of a number of small beaches fringed by shady coconut palms. Rarely crowded, it is the perfect place to discover Goa's unspoilt beauty.

The southernmost cove of **Ozran** lies below a steep cliff, where a freshwater stream empties into a clear pool, ideal for swimming. **Little Vagator**, to the north, is a secluded stretch of sand popular with more discerning visitors. **Big Vagator Beach** is dominated by the red laterite **Chapora Fort** situated on top of a hill at its northern tip. Now in ruins, this fort was built by the Portuguese in 1717 on the remains of an older bastion erected by the Adil Shahi sultans. Its name, Chapora, is derived from "Shahpura", or "Town of the Shah", as the village was once known. In 1739, Sambhaji, the son of the Maratha chief Shivaji (see p471), occupied the fort for a short time until it was returned to the Portuguese

Brightly coloured fishing nets

in exchange for Bassein, near Mumbai. Its ramparts, now desolate, offer sweeping views of the coast. Chapora village, below the fort, has many pleasant cafés.

Environs
The many fishing villages along the northern coastline can only be reached by taking a ferry across the Chapora river from Siolim, 10 km (6 miles) from Chapora village. The area around the village of **Morgim**, 5 km (3 miles) north of Chapora village, is ideal for birdwatching. **Mandrem** is another quiet village with a beautiful location and glorious beach, 12 km (7 miles) north of Chapora village.

Pernem ❼

North Goa district (Pernem taluka).
29 km (18 miles) N of Panaji.
🚌 🚌 every half hour from Siolim.

The headquarters of Goa's northern most *taluka*, or sub-district, Pernem was occupied by the Portuguese in the mid-18th century. It was one of the last conquests they made between 1764 and 1788 – a period during which they expanded their territory to include Pernem, Bicholim and Satari in the north, and Ponda (see p502), Sanquem, Quepem and Canacona in the south. By this time, the fevour for conversions that existed during the period of the early conquests had waned, and these areas remained predominantly Hindu.

The brightly painted **Bhagavati Temple**, in the bazaar, stands on a 500-year-old site, although the present

Shack restaurant on Morgim Beach, a common sight in Goa

A fisherman casting his net at Querim Beach

and skirts. Unlike in central Goa, the Hindu influence is apparent here; the numerous cafés and guesthouses are called Ganesha or Namaste instead of Pete's or Johnny's.

At the northern end, a rocky footpath leads to a second beach, entirely surrounded by cliffs. This sandy cove has a freshwater lagoon fed by hot springs and lined with sulphurous mud. A 5-km (3-mile) long path, heading north, leads to **Querim Beach** (pronounced "keri") – a pristine strip of white sand, backed by casuarina trees.

Terekhol Fort ➒

North Goa district (Pernem taluka). 42 km (26 miles) N of Panaji. 🚌 every half hour from Querim.

Across the Terekhol river from Querim is the little hamlet of Terekhol, with Terekhol (Tiracol) Fort situated on a plateau above it. The early 18th-century fort was captured by the Portuguese in 1776 from the Bhonsles, a Maratha clan. It was the scene of an uprising in 1954, when a group of *satyagrahis* (freedom fighters) hoisted the Indian flag on its ramparts in an act of civil disobedience against colonial rule. The fort's high battlements face the sea, looking across the waters to Fort Aguada, Arambol and Chapora. The tiny chapel within the fort, with a statue of Christ in the courtyard, is usually closed but the atmospheric Terekhol Fort Heritage Hotel *(see p711)* offers some excellent views.

structure dates to the 18th century. It is dedicated to the eight-armed Bhagavati, an incarnation of Shiva's consort Parvati. Its elaborate gateway is framed by two life-size elephants. A short distance from the bazaar is the palatial **Deshprabhu House**, the 19th-century mansion of the wealthy Hindu Deshprabhu family, who fought for Goa's liberation in 1961. This sprawling property, built around 16 courtyards, has a private temple and a museum displaying family portraits and antiques.

🏯 **Deshaprabhu House**
Tel (0832) 220 1234 to arrange a visit.

Arambol ➑

North Goa district (Pernem taluka). 50 km (31 miles) N of Panaji. 🚌 🚌 every half hour from Siolim.

Also known as Harmal, Arambol is the only fishing village in North Goa that has some basic facilities for visitors. Situated along one of Goa's less commercial beaches, it still retains all the charm of a traditional fishing village, except for the occasional gypsy selling bright scarves

FESTIVALS OF GOA

Jatra *(Jan)*, Quepem. A colourful festival *(jatra)* honouring local temple deities is celebrated at the Shantadurga Temple *(see p502)*. Other such festivals take place through the year at various temples in Ponda.
Carnival *(Feb)*, Panaji. Goa's grandest festival marks the beginning of Lent. "King Momo", who personifies fun and frolic, orders his subjects to forget their troubles, and leads a colourful parade through the streets. Three days and nights of non-stop revelry follow.

Masked dancers, Carnival

Shigmotsav (Shigmo) *(Mar)*. This joyous Hindu spring festival is celebrated acoss the state. Festivities continue for five days and include colourful street floats (in the larger towns), local folk theatre, sword dances and the lively spraying of coloured powder.
All Saints Procession *(Apr)*, Goa Velha, Pilar. Large crowds of devotees carry statues of 26 saints in procession from St Andrew's Church, in this small village near Pilar.
Feast of St Francis Xavier *(3 Dec)*, Old Goa. The feast of Goa's patron saint is held on the anniversary of his death (1552). Attended by Catholic pilgrims from all over the world, the feast is preceeded by novenas (nine days of prayer).

A holy cross on top of a knoll, Arambol Beach

Seagulls flocking around the day's catch at Arambol Beach ▷

A Walk through Old Goa ❿

Portrait of
Vasco da Gama

A magnificent complex of cathedrals, churches and monasteries, spread along a 1.5-km (1-mile) stretch, marks the site of Old Goa, the Portuguese capital until the mid-18th century. The walk through this area, now a UNESCO World Heritage Site, takes in two of Goa's most important religious monuments, the Basilica de Bom Jesus and the grand Sé Cathedral, and ends on Holy Hill, where some of Goa's oldest churches are located. Most of these buildings, designed by Italian or Portuguese architects, encompass a range of European styles, from sober Renaissance to exuberant Baroque and Portuguese Manueline *(see p501)*.

④ **Sé Cathedral**
This is thought to be Asia's largest church. The gilded high altar has six splendid panels depicting the life of St Catherine of Alexandria.

⑬ **Our Lady of the Rosary**
was built on top of Holy Hill in 1526 by Alfonso de Albuquerque. He had watched Yusuf Adil Shah's defeat in 1510 from this very spot and vowed to build a church here.

⑦ **The Chapel of St Catherine**, like Our Lady of the Rosary, was built to celebrate Albuquerque's victory in 1510, and served as Goa's only cathedral until the Sé Cathedral was built.

⑫ **Royal Chapel of St Anthony**
St Anthony, Portugal's national saint, was also considered the Captain of the army.

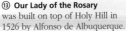

PANAJI

RUA DAS NAUS DE ORMUZ

Holy Hill

⑬ ⑫ ⑪ ⑩ ⑨ ⑦

⑩ **Convent of St Monica**, dating to the mid-17th century, will house Asia's first Museum of Christian Art, currently being relocated from Rachol *(see p504).*

⑨ **Church and Convent of St John of God**
This convent was built in 1685 by the Order of the Hospitallers of St John of God, to tend to the sick. It was rebuilt in 1953.

⑪ **Church and Monastery of St Augustine**
The 46-m (151-ft) high laterite belfry dominates the remains of what was once India's largest church.

② Gateway of Adil Shah's Palace
The gate, comprising a lintel and basalt pillars, is all that survives of Adil Shah's palace, also used as the viceroys' residence from 1554 to 1695.

① Viceroy's Arch
Over 1,000 ships a year brought new arrivals to Goa in the 17th century. They passed under this laterite archway, built by Francisco da Gama (viceroy 1597–1600).

dovi River

Quay

① ② ③

④

OUR LADY OF THE MOUNT

RUA DIREITA

⑧ Basilica de Bom Jesus *(see pp498–9).*

COLLEGE OF ST PAUL

PILLORY

| 0 metres | 200 |
| 0 yards | 200 |

③ Church of St Cajetan
Built by Italian friars in 1651, this church is renowned for the exuberant woodcarvings on its high altar and pulpit.

⑥ Archaeological Museum
A bronze statue of the poet Luis Vaz de Camões, holding his epic Os Lusiadas (see p487), stands in the museum, now housed in the converted convent of St Francis of Assisi, adjoining the church.

⑤ Church of St Francis of Assisi
Built by the Franciscan friars in 1521, this is one of Old Goa's most important churches. Its carved and gilded main altar depicts the crucified Jesus, four Evangelists, St Francis, and Our Lady with the baby Jesus.

Old Goa: Basilica de Bom Jesus

The Basilica de Bom Jesus is revered by Roman Catholics all over the world since it houses the mortal remains of Goa's patron saint, Francis Xavier. It was the first church in South Asia to be granted the status of Minor Basilica, by Pope Pius XII in 1946. Built by the Jesuits in 1594, this grand Baroque structure blends Corinthian, Doric, Ionic and composite styles in its magnificent three-tiered façade. The Duke of Tuscany, Cosimo III, donated the elaborate tomb of St Francis in exchange for the pillow that lay under the saint's head. The tomb took the Florentine sculptor Giovanni Foggini ten years to build; it was finally assembled in 1698. The adjoining Professed House (1589) was used as the priests' quarters until it was damaged by a fire in 1633.

Doorway to Sacristy
An exquisitely carved wooden door leads to the sacristy.

★ Main Altar
The gilded reredos has a statue of St Ignatius of Loyola and another of the Infant Jesus. Local craftsmen, used to decorating temples, made plump, typically Hindu looking cherubs on the altar.

Altar of Our Lady of Hope

Chapel of the Blessed Sacrament

Altar of St Michael

ST FRANCIS XAVIER (1506–1552)

Francis Xavier was sent to Goa by the Portuguese king, Dom Joao III. He arrived in May 1542, aged 36, and worked tirelessly over the next few years, converting nearly 30,000 people. He died while on voyage off the coast of China in 1552, and was temporarily buried on an island. When his body was dug up three months later to transfer his bones, it showed no signs of decay. A year later, when his remains were enshrined in the Basilica in Goa, his body was still in pristine condition. This was declared a miracle, and in 1622 he was canonized. Expositions of his relics take place every ten years or so, the last one was in 2004–2005.

St Francis Xavier, Art Gallery

STAR FEATURES

★ Main Altar

★ Tomb of St Francis Xavier

★ Wooden Pulpit

For hotels and restaurants in this region see pp709–11 and pp737–8

★ Tomb of St Francis Xavier
The marble and jasper tomb has four bronze plaques depicting scenes from the saint's life. Built in a mixture of Italian and Indian styles, the silver reliquary containing the sacred relics is surmounted by a cross with two angels.

★ Wooden Pulpit
The figures of Jesus and several Evangelists are beautifully carved on the pulpit.

Sacristy

Basalt Stone Tablet
The Jesuit motto, IHS or Iaeus Hominum Salvator, *means "Jesus the Saviour" in Greek.*

Catholic nuns at the entrance to the Basilica

Façade
This is the only Goan church not covered in lime plaster. Its original coat was removed in 1956, exposing the soft red laterite beneath. Each of the three doorways and six windows is flanked by elegant pillars and basalt detailing.

Exploring Old Goa

Portugal's Goa Dourada ("Golden Goa") was once a vast city, inhabited by more than 30,000 people. In the 16th century, it attracted missionaries and soldiers, merchants and horse-traders, and its elegant palaces and mansions were much praised by contemporary visitors. However, by the mid-18th century, a series of epidemics and the silting up of the Mandovi river forced the viceroy to move his residence downstream to Panaji *(see p486)*. Thereafter, decline set in and, by the 19th century, the city was finally abandoned and its houses demolished. Today, Old Goa is a mere shadow of its former self, but the few churches and cathedrals that remain are considered to be among Goa's most significant monuments.

Rows of pillars on either side of the central nave, Sé Cathedral

🔒 Church of St Cajetan

E of Viceroy's Arch. ⬜ *daily.*

In the 17th century, Pope Urban III sent Italian priests from the Theatine Order to Golconda *(see pp666–7).* When refused entry, they settled in Old Goa. Here, in 1651, they erected a church dedicated to their founder, St Cajetan, and designed along the lines of St Peter's in Rome. The distinctive dome and interior, laid out in the shape of a Greek cross, embody the majesty of Italian Baroque. The adjacent monastery is today a college of theology.

Detail of altar, Churh of St Cajetan

🔒 Sé Cathedral

Senate Square. **Tel** *(0832) 228 4710.* ⬜ *daily.* ✝ *(Konkani) 7.30am & 6pm, Mon–Sat; 7.20am & 4pm, Sun.*

When ordered by the government in Portugal to build a church worthy of their mighty empire, Francis Coutinho (viceroy, 1561–4) envisaged a magnificent cathedral that would be the largest in Asia. The result is the Renaissance-style Sé Cathedral, designed in the 16th century by Julio Simao and Ambrosio Argueiro, and built over 80 years. Its 30-m (98-ft) high Tuscan-style façade was flanked by two square bell towers, only one of which survives. In it hangs the Golden Bell, known for its melodic tones, which rang out during the dreaded *auto da fé* trials, held in the cathedral's front square.

The interior, with intricate Corinthian detailing, has a 76-m (249-ft) long central nave. As many as 15 altars grace the interior, but the *pièce de résistance* is the gilded high altar, dedicated to St Catherine of Alexandria, with panel paintings depicting scenes from her life. Two of the eight chapels, the Blessed Sacrament and the Cross of Miracles, have delicate filigree work on their screens. The font, used by St Francis Xavier to baptize converts, is near the entrance. The sacred relics of his body, kept in the Basilica de Bom Jesus *(see pp498–9),* are brought to the cathedral during the expositions held every ten years.

🏛 Archaeological Museum

Convent of St Francis of Assisi. **Tel** *(0832) 228 5333.* ⬜ *Sat–Thu.* 📷

Once Goa's largest monastery, the Convent of St Francis of Assisi (built in 1517) now houses the Archaeological Museum, established in 1964. A huge bronze statue of Alfonso de Albuquerque, moved from Panaji, dominates the entrance hall. Among the objects of interest are a finely carved image of Vishnu and a Surya statue, dating to the Kadamba period (11th–12th centuries), and stone inscriptions in Marathi and Persian,

From right to left, Sé Cathedral, Church of St Francis of Assisi and Church of Our Lady of the Rosary in Old Goa

relics of earlier ruling dynasties. Other exhibits include Hindu *sati* stones, a model of *São Gabriel* (the ship in which Vasco da Gama sailed to India in 1498), and a bronze statue of St Catherine in the courtyard. The Portrait Gallery on the first floor has 60 paintings of Goa's viceroys and governors.

Detail of memorial, St Augustine's ruins

⚜ Church of St Francis of Assisi

W of Sé Cathedral. ☐ *daily.*

Built by the Franciscan friars in 1521, and rebuilt in 1661, this church has a beautifully carved doorway (taken from the original building). This is a rare example of the Portuguese Manueline style, which uses many nautical motifs, and was developed during the reign of King Dom Manuel (r.1469–1521). A pair of navigator's globes and a Greek cross (the emblem of all Portuguese ships) embellish the door. The superb Baroque interior has floral frescoes on the walls and ceiling, and the floor is paved with the sculpted tombstones of Portuguese nobility. The gilded altar has figures of St Francis and Christ. Other noteworthy features are the pulpit, which is carved in floral designs and the painted panels in the chancel, which depict various scenes from the saint's life.

Façade with two octagonal towers, Church of St Francis of Assisi

⚜ Church and Monastery of St Augustine

Holy Hill.

Once the largest church in India, with a grand five-storeyed façade, St Augustine's now lies in ruins. Erected by the Augustinian order in 1512, the Gothic-style church was abandoned in 1835, and its roof caved in seven years later. Excavations begun in 1989 revealed eight chapels, four altars, wall sculptures and more than 100 splendid granite tombstones. According to contemporary descriptions, the church also had grand staircases and galleries, and a library that rivalled the one at Oxford (England), in the 17th century. Today, all that remains of St Augustine's is its soaring bell tower *(see p496).*

⚜ Church of Our Lady of the Rosary

Holy Hill. ☐ *daily.*

With its castle-like turrets and simple altar painted with baskets of flowers, this is one of Goa's earliest Manueline-style churches. The tomb of Dona Catarina, wife of Garcia de Sá (viceroy from 1548–9) and the first Portuguese woman to migrate to Goa, also lies here.

Further Afield

A few buildings of interest lie in Old Goa's southeastern corner. Marking the end of the Rua Direita, Old Goa's main street, is a desolate basalt pillar on a raised platform, the remains of the terrible **Pillory**. Criminals and heretics were strung up here as punishment, in the centre of the city square. Close by, on the road to Ponda, lies the **College of St Paul**. Founded by the Jesuits in 1541, it had 3,000 students, making it the largest Jesuit school in Asia. It also housed Asia's first printing press. St Francis Xavier stayed and preached here; the chapel further up the road was also used by him, and was later dedicated to his memory.

The Church of Our Lady of the Mount, built in 1510, sits on top of a hill and is reached by a lane that leads off the Cumbarjua Road. Built by Alfonso de Albuquerque after his victory over Yusuf Adil Shah, the church has recently been restored. The views over Old Goa's towers and turrets are magnificent.

Altar in the Church of Our Lady of the Rosary, on Holy Hill

THE GOA INQUISITION

At the request of Francis Xavier *(see p498)*, a tribunal of Jesuits arrived in 1560 and took over Adil Shah's secondary palace (of which few traces now remain), to the south of Sé Cathedral. Their mission was to curb the libertine ways of the Portuguese settlers and convert "infidels". During the Inquisition in 1567, all Hindu ceremonies were banned,

Mural of a prose-lytizing priest

temples were destroyed and Hindus forcibly converted. Those who refused were locked away in the dungeons of the "Palace of the Inquisition" (as Adil Shah's palace was known) to await the *auto da fé* (acts of faith) trial. The condemned were burnt alive in front of a congregation of dignitaries. Over the next 200 years, 16,000 trials were held and thousands killed, and it was not until 1812 that the Inquisition was finally dissolved.

17th-century painting of St Cecilia, patroness of church choirs, Pilar

Pilar ⓫

North Goa district (Tiswadi taluka). 12 km (7 miles) SE of Panaji. 🚍

Set on a hilltop, **Pilar Seminary** was originally built by the Capuchins (a Franciscan order) in 1613, on the site of an old Hindu temple. Abandoned in 1835, when all religious orders were disbanded, it was reopened by the Carmelites in 1858. In 1890, the Society of Pilar set up a mission college here, and classes are still held in the old seminary building.

The adjoining **Church of Our Lady of Pilar** has an elaborately carved stone doorway with a figure of St Francis of Assisi above it. Inside is a statue of Our Lady of Pilar, brought here from Spain. The tomb of Agnelo D'Souza (seminary director, 1918–27) lies adjacent to the church. The **New Seminary**, built in 1946, stands close by. Its museum displays fragments from the original temple, Christian art, Portuguese coins and a stone lion, the symbol of the Kadamba dynasty.

🏛 **Museum**
Tel (0832) 221 8521. ☐ *daily.*

Environs
Goa Velha, 2 km (1.3 miles) southwest of Pilar, marks the site of Govapuri, the port-capital of the Kadamba rulers between the 11th and 13th centuries, of which few traces now remain.

Ponda ⓬

South Goa district (Ponda taluka). 28 km (17 miles) SE of Panaji. 🚶 17,700. 🚍 🎪 Urs of Shah Abdullah (Feb).

The town of Ponda is a busy commercial centre, and its main sight is the **Safa Shahouri Mosque**, 2 km (1.3 miles) to the west. Built by Ibrahim Adil Shah (a successor of Yusuf Adil Shah) in 1560, it is a rectangular structure, with window arches, topped by a slanting tiled roof. A ritual tank to the south has the same designs as those on the *mihrabs* (arched niches).

Ponda also lends its name to the *taluka* (sub-district) of the same name, which is renowned for its numerous Hindu temples, tucked away in thick forests. As the Portuguese expanded their territory in central Goa, they destroyed over 550 temples. Hindu priests fled with their religious artifacts to regions that lay outside Portuguese control, especially the area around Ponda town, where they built new temples in the 17th and 18th centuries.

More than half of Goa's population is Hindu, and Goan temples, unlike those elsewhere in India, are a fascinating blend of European Baroque, Muslim and Hindu architectural styles. Their basic plan remains Hindu, but often Muslim domes replace the usual

Brass lamp tower, Shri Mahalsa Temple

shikharas (spires) over the main sanctum, and the prayer halls are decorated with ornate European chandeliers.

The **Shantadurga Temple**, 3 km (2 miles) southwest of Ponda at Quela, is Goa's most popular shrine. Built by Shahu, the grandson of the Maratha chief Shivaji *(see p471)*, the russet and cream coloured temple has an unusual pagoda-style roof, dominated by a five-storeyed octagonal lamp tower, unique to Goa. Grand chandeliers hang from the gilded roof in the huge central hall, and embossed silver screens shield the main sanctuary, which holds the silver deity of Shantadurga (a form of Shiva's consort Parvati), brought from Mormugao *taluka*. Also of interest are the huge *rathas* (chariots) that are used during the Jatra in January *(see p493)*. The **Shri Ramnath Temple**, a short walk away, is noted for the grand silver screen embossed with animal and floral motifs, in front of its sanctum. Its linga, originally from Loutolim, is worshipped by devotees of both Shiva and Vishnu.

The **Shri Nagueshi Temple**, 4 km (2.5 miles) west of Ponda at Bandora, dates to 1780, though a temple may have stood here earlier. Built for the worship of Nagesh (Shiva as Lord of the Serpents), it is one of the oldest temples in this region. Its entrance hall

The large 18th-century water tank at the Shri Mangesh Temple

has carved wooden friezes depicting scenes from the epics *Ramayana* and *Mahabharata (see pp26–7).*

The 18th-century **Shri Lakshmi Narasimha Temple** is situated in Velinga village, 5 km (3 miles) northwest of Ponda. Its majestic image of Narasimha, Vishnu's man-lion incarnation *(see p679),* was brought here from Mormugao in the 1560s. Surrounded by forest, it is one of Goa's most attractive temples, with a sacred tank and an elaborate gateway. A tower standing close by houses the temple's musicians during the annual Jatra festival, held here in May.

Dedicated to Vishnu, the **Shri Mahalsa Temple** is 7 km (4 miles) northwest of Ponda, in Mardol village. The main deity (either a female form of Vishnu or his consort Lakshmi) was taken from Verna. The temple's distinguishing feature is an exceptionally tall brass pillar, 21 tiers in all, rising from a figure of Kurma (Vishnu's incarnation as a turtle), with Garuda (his vehicle) perched on top. The pillar symbolizes Mount Kailasa which, according to Hindu mythology, was placed on Kurma's back and was used to churn the primordial ocean. The original shrine is a wooden structure with a sloping roof, and the entrance porches have carvings of musicians and warriors. Its main hall has

A procession during the Shigmo Jatra, at the Shri Mahalsa Temple

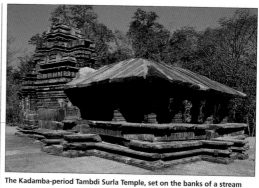

The Kadamba-period Tambdi Surla Temple, set on the banks of a stream

intricately carved pillars, while the central part of the ceiling is raised, with painted images of gods set in niches.

A short distance to the northwest, at Priol, lies Goa's wealthiest temple, the 18th-century **Shri Mangesh Temple**, dedicated to Shiva. The courtyard has a sacred *tulsi* (basil) plant growing in a bright green urn, a characteristic Goan feature. There is a large sacred tank and a seven-storeyed lamp tower. Dance-dramas are performed here during the Jatra festivities in April and May. A vividly painted elephant on wheels stands at the entrance to the white and yellow temple. Inside, 19th-century Belgian chandeliers hang from the ceiling, while the main sanctum has a linga transferred from Mormugao. The childhood home of Lata Mangeshkar (b.1929), India's most famous singer of film songs, was near the temple.

About 4 km (2.5 miles) northeast of Ponda town, near the village of Khandepar, is a cluster of **Hindu Rock-cut Caves** from the 10th–13th centuries, with carved lotus decorations on the ceiling, simple door frames and niches for oil lamps.

A few spice gardens that grow aromatic spices such as cardamom, nutmeg and cinnamon, make interesting day trips from Ponda. The Pascoal Plantation, 8 km (5 miles) east, and the Savoi Spice Garden at Savoi Verem, 12 km (7 miles) north, are easy to reach.

Detail, Tamdi Surla Temple

Tambdi Surla ⑬

South Goa district (Sanguem taluka). 73 km (45 miles) E of Panaji. *Taxis from Panaji or Ponda are the best option.*

Hidden away in the forests of Tambdi Surla, stands the oldest existing Hindu temple in Goa, dating from the Kadamba period (between the 11th and 13th centuries). Built in black basalt and dedicated to Shri Mahadeva (Shiva), the temple probably survived because of its remote location. The symmetrical structure is made of stone slabs fitted neatly into each other, without using mortar. Set on a low plinth, the entrance hall has ten pillars, and the *shikhara* (spire) above the sanctum has a miniature relief and fine carvings of Brahma, Vishnu, Shiva and his consort, Parvati.

Environs
The **Bhagwan Mahaveer Sanctuary**, 20 km (12 miles) southeast of Tamdi Sura, covers an area of 240 sq km (93 sq miles) and is home to leopards, deer and the Indian bison. The 600-m (1,969-ft) high **Dudhsagar Waterfalls** on the Goa-Karnataka border are its main attraction. The small **Bondla Sanctuary**, 30 km (19 miles) east of Tambdi Surla, is known for its variety of birds.

Bhagwan Mahaveer Sanctuary
daily.

Bondla Sanctuary
Sep–Jun: Fri–Wed.

Altar, Church of St Ignatius Loyola, Rachol

Rachol ⑭

South Goa district (Salcete taluka).
52 km (32 miles) SE of Panaji. 🚌

The small hamlet of Rachol occupies the site of an old fortress built by the Bijapur sultans *(see p542)*, which was ceded to the Portuguese in 1520. A laterite archway and a dry moat are the only remnants of the bastion – once fortified with 100 cannons – that used to guard the southern borders of the Portuguese territories. The pretty **Church of Nossa Senhora das Neves** (Our Lady of the Snows), in the village, was built in 1576.

Today, **Rachol Seminary**, built in 1606, is probably the most important of Goa's seminaries. First established in Margao in 1574, and known as the College of All Saints, the earlier seminary included a hospital, a school for the poor and a printing press. It was relocated here after the Margao institution was destroyed in a Muslim raid in 1579. For generations, this was Goa's most prestigious educational institution, both for secular and religious studies, offering a seven-year course in theology and philosophy, to prepare young seminarians for the priesthood.

Spectacularly located on the summit of a hill, the building has a grand fort-like façade, flanked by imposing watch-towers. The seminary's vast entrance hall is covered with impressive murals and opens on to a central courtyard, surrounded by cloistered rooms made of solid teak, each one with an adjoining wood-panelled study. The grand staircase is adorned with Hindu sculptures, excavated from the ancient Hindu temple on the site of which the seminary was constructed. This leads to the first floor and the library, which has a rare collection of Latin and Portuguese books, and portraits of Goa's archbishops.

Attached to the seminary is the **Church of St Ignatius Loyola**, dedicated to the eponymous saint. It has an ornately carved and gilded altar with a painting of St Constantine, the first Roman emperor to convert to Christianity. According to legend, a few bone fragments and a vial of his blood were brought to Rachol in 1782, and are supposedly enshrined near the entrance. The choir stall has delicate murals of the founding saints of various religious orders. On the first floor balcony is a beautiful 16th-century pipe-organ from Lisbon.

Silver reliquary, museum collection

Until mid-2001, Rachol Seminary also housed the renowned Museum of Christian Art, established in 1991 by the Indian National Trust for Art and Cultural Heritage (INTACH) and the Gulbenkian Foundation of Portugal. The entire collection is currently being shifted to the Convent of St Monica in Old Goa *(see p496)*, and will be set up in the Chapel of the Weeping Cross, adjacent to the convent. Its impressive collection of 17th- and 18th-century religious objects includes silver and ivory ornaments, ornate clerical robes, processional crosses and holy water sprinklers. Particularly charming is a portable altar for travelling missionaries, complete with candle stands and a mass kit.

Margao ⑮

South Goa district (Salcete taluka).
33 km (21 miles) S of Panaji.
🏛 78,500. 🚉 🚌 ℹ Margao Residency, (0832) 271 5528. 🎉 *Feast of the Holy Spirit (Dec).*

Margao (Madgaon), Goa's second most important city after Panaji, is the administrative and commercial capital of the South Goa district. This bustling town also serves as the area's main trading centre for local fish and farm produce.

The town square, **Praça Jorge Barreto**, has the large, colonial Municipal Building, which houses the library on its southern side, and a popular café called Longinhos

A view of the hilltop Seminary and Church at Rachol

nearby. Just behind the Municipal Building, to the south, are Margao's lively bazaars, selling the day's catch of fish and fresh fruit and vegetables. The **Covered Market**, close by, sells just about everything, including piles of soap flakes, pulses, dried fish, pickles, spicy pork sausages, tamarind, flower garlands, jaggery and crockery. A row of shops to the north sells locally brewed wines, and the lane just outside the market has a number of cloth merchants.

Abbé de Faria Street, winding north from the town square, is lined with some well-preserved colonial mansions, and leads to Margao's old Latin Quarter. Its central square, **Largo de Igreja**, is also surrounded by colourful 18th- and 19th-century town houses, with tiled roofs, wrought-iron balconies and balustrades. In the centre of the square is a monumental, 16th-century cross, overlooked by the towering Baroque **Church of the Holy Spirit**. Built in 1565 on the site of a ravaged Hindu temple, the church and the adjoining Jesuit College of All Saints were ransacked numerous times by Muslim raiders. While the seminary was moved to Rachol, the church was rebuilt in 1675. Its whitewashed façade is flanked by two towers topped by domes and embellished with lanterns, though its side

The red and white Municipal Building, Praça Jorge Barreto, Margao

walls have been left unusually bare of lime-plaster. The grand interior has a stucco ceiling, a gilded pulpit decorated with carvings of the apostles, a Rococo altar, and elegant Baroque altar-pieces in the transepts.

Just behind the church, Agostinho Lorenço Street leads east to the imposing mansion called **Sat Burnzam Gor**, or "Seven Gables" *(see p506)*, named after the original seven gables or pyramidal crests on its roof. It is the only surviving example

Monumental cross in Largo de Igreja

of a house with pyramidal roofs in Goa. Built in 1790 by Ignacio da Silva from his earnings as the viceroy's secretary, the huge, impressive salons are filled with richly carved rosewood furniture and priceless porcelain, and its private chapel was the first that was permitted in Goa. From the intersection lying east of the church, a road winds up to

Monte Hill. Although one cannot enter the tiny chapel at the top, the views across Margao's rooftops of the entire southern coast are spectacular.

🏛 **Sat Burnzam Gor**
📋 *Only by prior appointment; contact Mrs de Silva.*

Environs
The pretty villages around Margao have a number of colonial country mansions, dating from the prosperous period from the 18th to the 19th centuries, when local landlords began to profit from Portugal's control over the maritime trade routes from Africa to Malacca (in Malaysia). Many of these homes were also owned by Goans, who held high posts in the Portuguese government and were granted land in exchange for their services.

Loutolim, 10 km (6 miles) to the northeast, was once an important Portuguese administrative centre, and has a cluster of stately homes, all situated fairly close to the main church square. The Goa Tourism office, and the Houses of Goa museum, (0832) 241 0711, located at Salvador do Mundo, can organize visits to these buildings. **Chandor**, 13 km (8 miles) east of Margao, has the palatial Braganza house, Goa's largest private dwelling *(see pp508–9)*. **Chinchinim**, 10 km (6 miles) south of Margao, and **Benaulim**, 6 km (4 miles) southwest of Margao, also have fine mansions, with typical Goan *balcaos* (porches) and terracotta-tiled sloping roofs.

Fresh prawns, sardines, mackerel and salmon, Margao bazaar

Goa's Colonial Mansions

Goa's countryside is dotted with grand colonial mansions, built by the wealthy land-owning Goan gentry, who prospered in the 18th and 19th centuries. The homes of these local aristocrats were built in the traditional style of the region, with central courtyards, deep porches and window shutters made of oyster-

Chinese vase

shell. The furniture and interior decor, however, were largely European. Today, the Belgian chandeliers, Venetian cut-glass and gilded mirrors, Baroque-style rosewood furniture and Chinese porcelain, displayed inside, provide a fascinating picture of the tastes and lifestyles of a vanished era.

Oyster-shell window shutters *line the façade of Sat Burnzam Gor ("Seven Gables") in Margao. A unique feature of 16th- and 17th-century Goan architecture, oyster shells were used in place of glass panes and effectively kept out the heat and glare.*

A typical pyramidal balcao, *or porch, graces the entrance of the Figueredo House in Loutolim. Chairs were often placed under the balcao, as it was customary to socialize at the front door.*

This antique rosewood carving *from Goa's grandest mansion, Braganza House in Chandor (see pp508–9), is a typical example of Indo-Portuguese Baroque.*

European-style salons, *such as the regal ballroom in the Dr Alvaro Loyola Furtado Mansion in Chinchinim, built in 1833, have crystal chandeliers and elegant furniture.*

Carved antique furniture at the Casa dos Mirandos

WHERE TO SEE GOAN HOUSES

Loutolim has four houses of interest – Salvador da Costa House, Roque Caetan Miranda House, Figueredo House and Casa dos Mirandos, which is the finest. **Margao** has the Sat Burnzam Gor, **Chinchinim** has the Loyola Furtado Mansion, and **Chandor** has the Braganza House. For more details see page 505.

Colva

South Goa district (Salcete taluka). 6 km (4 miles) W of Margao. GTDC Tourist Cottage, (0832) 278 8047. Fama de Menino Jesus (Oct).

Colva's proximity to Margao makes it an ideal summer retreat for Margao's residents. It is one of South Goa's oldest and most developed beach resorts, and its 25-km (16-mile) long sandy beach, from the Mormugao peninsula in the north to Mobor in the south, is the longest uninterrupted stretch in the state.

Today, Colva draws vast numbers of visitors, who spend the day enjoying the lively atmosphere of its many beach shacks, set high on stilts and backed by shady palms. These serve delicious grilled lobster and other seafood specialities. Numerous top-end and mid-range hotels stand on the main beach road, while the southern extremities have more pristine stretches. Fisherfolk haul in their catch on the beach front, which also plays host to full-moon rave parties.

A cheerful waiter, Mobor

Standing a short distance from the sea, Colva's **Church of Our Lady of Mercy**, built in 1630, has an attractive Baroque interior and houses the famous statue of Menino (baby) Jesus, holding an orb and a flag, revered for its miraculous healing powers.

Environs
Majorda, 7 km (4 miles) north of Colva, has a wide beach

dotted with luxury hotels. **Bogmalo Beach**, 20 km (12 miles) northwest of Colva, is a popular venue for wind-surfing.

Tourism has spilled over from Colva to the quiet fishing village of **Benaulim**, 2 km (1.3 miles) south, whose roads are lined with small guesthouses, restaurants and bars. **Varca Beach**, 5 km (3 miles) further south, has many plush hotels, as well as a parish church with an imposing façade.

Cavelossim ⑱

South Goa district (Salcete taluka). 15 km (9 miles) S of Margao.

A favourite with Indian celebrities, Cavelossim has an enchanting 2-km (1.3-mile) stretch of sand. It also has a golf course, luxury resorts and excellent seafood restaurants, such as the Seaways Bar. The ornate **Church of the Holy Cross**, is situated in a pretty square.

Environs
Mobor, 5 km (3 miles) south of Colva, is an idyllic spot, with its backdrop of hills and the pretty fishing village of **Betul** nestling near the Sal river. The Leela Beach Resort is located here. **Cabo da Rama** ("Cape Rama"), the promontory just south of Betul, is named after Rama, hero of the *Ramayana*, who supposedly hid here during his 14-year exile *(see p27)*. It has the ruins of a Hindu fortress that fell to the Portuguese in 1763.

A thatch-roofed beach shack, Palolem Beach

Palolem ⑲

South Goa district (Salcete taluka). 37 km (23 miles) S of Margao.

Famous for its spectacular sunsets, this bay is enclosed by a rocky outcrop at one end, and Canacona Island, a good camping site, at the other. Palolem's remote location, away from the crowded beaches of central Goa, makes it an ideal for a quiet holiday. A special attraction are the boat rides offered by fishermen, who take visitors out to sea for dolphin-watching trips.

Environs
Southern Goa is for the most part isolated and unspoilt by tourism. **Agonda**, 7 km (4 miles) north of Palolem, is even quieter than its neighbour. **Galgibaga**, 8 km (5 miles) south of Palolem, has a beautiful stretch of virgin sand, shaded by eucalyptus trees rather than palms. The remote **Cotigao Wildlife Sanctuary**, 18 km (11 miles) west of Palolem, is worth visiting for its tranquil beauty.

Visitors cycling on the sands at Colva, Goa's longest beach

Braganza House ⑯

Chinese blue porcelain dish

The awesome scale of Braganza House, and the magnificence of its interior, make it Goa's grandest colonial mansion. This 17th-century building is still occupied by two branches of the Braganza family. The descendants of Antonio Elzario Sant'Anna Pereira occupy the east wing, while Francisco Xavier de Menezes Braganza's descendants live in the west wing. Both men received royal titles and a coat of arms from the king of Portugal in the late 19th century. The top floors of their private apartments have the splendid ballroom, library and chapel, and fine collections of 18th-century furniture and Chinese porcelain.

Dining Hall
A long table fills the first floor dining hall of this sprawling mansion.

★ The Chapel
The Baroque-style chapel has a diamond-encrusted fingernail of St Francis Xavier on its altar.

Guest Bedroom
A large rosewood four-poster bed dominates the bedroom. At its foot is a rosewood two-seater.

The East Wing
is owned by the Braganza Pereiras.

★ The Ballroom
A rosewood armchair with the Braganza coat of arms, and a gilded mirror are in the mansion's grandest room. The walls as well as the floors are of marble, and chandeliers hang from its floral-patterned zinc ceiling.

STAR FEATURES

★ The Chapel

★ The Ballroom

★ The Hallway

For hotels and restaurants in this region see pp709–11 and pp737–8

Menezes Braganza Salon
A collection of exquisite Chinese porcelain is displayed in one of the salons, where a large vase takes pride of place.

VISITORS' CHECKLIST

Church Square, Chandor (Salcete taluka). 20 km (12 miles) E of Margao. **Menezes Braganza Wing** *Tel* (0832) 278 4201; **Braganza Pereira Wing** *Tel* (0832) 278 4227. Admission to both wings only by prior appointment. 🚻 🎫 *Donations appreciated.*

Portrait of Francisco Xavier de Menezes Braganza
A portrait of the grandfather of renowned journalist, Luis de Menezes Braganza (see p487), hangs in the ballroom of the west wing.

The West Wing is occupied by the Menezes Braganzas.

The Library has Goa's finest private collection, with over 5,000 leather-bound books.

Entrance

0 metres 10
0 yards 10

★ The Hallway
A long and elegantly furnished hallway lies just behind the façade of the house. It is lined with 28 bay windows and overlooks a well-maintained garden.

Stairway
The monumental double staircase forms the core of the house, connecting the lower entrance level to the furnished top floors.

KARNATAKA

Extending from the Arabian Sea and the fertile forested ridges of the Western Ghats, with their thriving plantations of coffee, spices and fruit, to the drier, boulder-strewn region of the Deccan Plateau, Karnataka's scenic diversity is striking. Equally varied are its historical monuments. These range from the 6th–8th century Hindu temples at Badami, Pattadakal and Aihole, the earliest to be found in South India, to Tipu Sultan's 18th-century, European-style island fort at Srirangapattana, and the extravagantly turreted, early 20th-century palace in Mysore. Other sights include the superb temples at Halebid and Belur, the colossal Gommateshvara monolith at Sravana Belgola and the magnificent ruins of Hampi, the site of the great citadel of Vijayanagar. In northern Karnataka are the medieval citadels of the Deccan sultans at Bijapur, Gulbarga and Bidar, their walls enclosing mosques, audience halls and royal tombs.

SIGHTS AT A GLANCE

Towns, Cities & Districts
Bangalore **1**
Barkur **13**
Belgaum **20**
Bhatkal **14**
Bidar **26**
Bijapur **24**
Gadag **19**
Gokarna **15**
Gulbarga **25**

Kodagu **6**
Mangalore **11**
Mysore **5**

Historic Sites
Aihole **23**
Badami **21**
Belur **10**
Chitradurga **17**
Halebid **9**
Hampi **18**
Pattadakal **22**
Srirangapattana **4**
Talakad **2**

Temples & Holy Places
Melkote **7**
Somnathpur **3**
Sravana Belgola **8**
Sringeri **16**
Udipi **12**

KEY

✈ International airport
✕ Domestic airport
═ National highway
▬ Major road
═ Minor road
— Major railway

0 km   50
0 miles   50

◁ **A mendicant at a shrine beside the Tungabhadra river, Hampi**

Bangalore ❶

Stone carving, Museum

Often described as Asia's Silicon Valley because of its thriving information technology industry, Bangalore is India's fifth-largest and fastest-growing city. Until its high-tech boom began in the late 1980s, it was known as the Garden City, with greenery flourishing in its pleasant, temperate climate. Today, with a growing population of young professionals, it has acquired a vibrant, cosmopolitan air.

Bangalore was founded in the 16th century by a local chieftain, Kempe Gowda, but derives its name from the Kannada word *benda kaluru*, or "boiled beans", which an old woman gave a 10th-century Hoysala king when he turned up hungry at her doorstep.

🏛 Vidhana Soudha

Dr Ambedkar Rd. ● *to the public.*

Built of granite and porphyry, this imposing building houses the Secretariat and the State Legislature of Karnataka. Constructed in 1956 after the transfer of power from the ruling Wodeyar dynasty to the central government, it was designed by Kengal Hanumanthaiah, the then chief minister, who intended it to "reflect the power and dignity of the people". It is capped by a 20-m (66-ft) dome, which is surmounted by the four-headed Ashokan lion, symbol of the Indian state. With Rajasthani *jharokhas*, Indo-Saracenic pillars and other decorative elements, the Vidhana Soudha exemplifies the Neo-Dravidian style of post-Independence Bangalore. The woodwork inside is noteworthy,

especially the sandalwood door to the Cabinet Room, and the Speaker's Chair made of rosewood from Mysore. The building looks spectacular on Sunday evenings when it is beautifully illuminated.

🏛 Attara Kacheri

E Vidhana Vidhi.
● *Mon–Fri.*

This graceful, two-storeyed building with Corinthian columns, was completed in 1864 and housed the Public Offices from 1868 until 1956. These were later moved to the Vidhana Soudha, and this building became the High Court. On the ceiling of its Central Hall is a portrait of Sir

Mark Cubbon, commissioner of Mysore from 1834 to 1861. Behind the building is an equestrian statue of him by Baron Marochetti.

🌿 Cubbon Park

Cantonment. ○ *daily.* 🔢

Laid out in 1864 by Richard Sankey, the chief engineer of Mysore, and named in honour of the commissioner, Cubbon Park extends over 135 ha (334 acres). Its partly formal landscaping imaginatively integrates natural rock outcroppings with groves of trees and giant bamboos.

The park is liberally dotted with statues, such as that of the 19th-century ruler Chamarajendra Wodeyar (1868–94), overlooking the pond near an octagonal, cast-iron bandstand. There are also marble statues of Queen Victoria and Edward VII. In the middle of the park, a red-painted, Neo-Classical building known as the **Sheshadri Iyer Memorial**, houses a public library.

Chamarajendra Wodeyar

🏛 Government Museum

Kasturba Gandhi Rd.
Tel (080) 2360 5033.
○ *Tue–Sun.* 🏷
Venkatappa Art Gallery *Tel* (080) 2286 4483. ○ *Tue–Sun.* 🏷
Established in 1866, this is one of the oldest museums in the country. Housed in a

The magnificent Vidhana Soudha, housing the Karnataka Secretariat

GARDEN CITY

The Cantonment in Bangalore was established in 1809, to house British troops quartered here during the 19th century. With its orderly streets, houses with characteristic "monkey top" eaves, and its lawns, trees, flowers and shrubbery, Bangalore was eventually christened the "Garden City of India". Two large parks, Cubbon Park and Lalbagh, along with numerous smaller ones such as the Kensington Gardens, act as the lungs of this verdant city. These gardens provide a welcome retreat from Bangalore's crowded streets and give a refreshing sense of space. The city is particularly charming in January and August when dahlias, marigolds and roses bloom in abundance.

A corner of Cubbon Park

red stucco Neo-Classical building with Corinthian columns, it has 18 sections, with a fine collection of jewellery, miniature paintings, sculpture, artifacts from Mohenjodaro, and 5,000-year-old neolithic relics.

The **Venkatappa Art Gallery**, named after an early 20th-century artist patronized by the Wodeyar rulers of Mysore, forms one wing of this museum. It has watercolours and paintings made in the Mysore style.

Mysore painting from Venkatappa Art Gallery

These works still retain a greenish coating, imparted by a finishing rub with jade. The gallery also has a collection of leather puppets made of deer- and goat-skin, and fine sculptures from the Satvahana, Hoysala and Vijayanagar periods.

🔒 St Mark's Cathedral

Mahatma Gandhi Rd. ⏺ *Tue–Sun.*
This simple, Neo-Classical cathedral was completed in 1812 and consecrated by the Bishop of Calcutta in 1816. An elegant, cream-coloured structure, it has an imposing portico in front and an apsidal recess at the rear. A shallow dome marks the internal crossing.

🏛 Bangalore Palace

N of Vidhana Soudha.
Tel *(080) 2336 0818*
for permission to visit.
Built in 1880 at the exorbitant cost of one million rupees, the Bangalore Palace was modelled on Windsor Castle, complete with fortified towers and turreted parapets. It stands amid undulating lawns, partly converted into a formal garden with axial paths.

VISITORS' CHECKLIST

Bangalore district. 1,033 km (642 miles) S of Mumbai. 🏢 *4,292,500.* ✈ *9 km (6 miles) E of city centre, then bus or taxi.* 🚇 🚌 ℹ *Govt of India Tourist Office, 48 Church St, (080) 2558 5417; Karnataka Tourism, Badami House, NRS Square, (080) 2227 5869.* 🎭 *Karaga (Apr), Kadalekaye Parishe (Nov/Dec).*

Spread over 13,700 sq m (147,466 sq ft), the palace fell into disrepair after 1949 when it was at the centre of an ownership dispute between the government and the ruling Wodeyars. It has since been restored to the Wodeyars and is now rented out as a popular venue for functions such as weddings and music concerts, and film shoots. No Kannada movie is considered complete if a scene is not shot here.

BANGALORE CITY CENTRE

0 metres 800
0 yards 800

Bangalore Palace

SHIVAJI NAGAR

Ulsoor Lake

INFANTRY ROAD

General Post Office

Vidhana Soudha ①

CUBBON ROAD

Attara Kacheri ②

Cricket Stadium

St Andrews Church

Cubbon Park ③

St Mark's Cathedral ⑤

Parade Ground

Bus Station 2 km (1 mile)

Railway Station 3.5 km (2 miles)

Government Museum ④

Sheshadri Iyer Memorial

GRANT RD

CHURCH STREET

MAHATMA GANDHI ROAD

ULSOOR RD

St Patricks Church

RAJARAM MOHAN ROY RD

GEN THIMMAIAH ROAD

All Saints Church

VICTORIA RD

Airport 7 km (4.5 miles)

Tipu Sultan's Palace, Gavi Gangadhareshvara Temple

Lalbagh

Key to Symbols *see back flap*

Exploring Old Bangalore

In spite of rapid development, vestiges of the city's historic past are still found in the streets of Old Bangalore, south of the city centre. In contrast to the relentless modernization of the rest of Bangalore, this area contains monuments from the period of the Gowdas to that of Haider Ali and Tipu Sultan, and bears witness to the city's history from the 16th to the 19th centuries.

▦ Tipu Sultan's Palace

Albert Victor Rd.
Tel (080) 2670 6836
◻ Mon–Sat. ▨

Within the original citadel, a mud-brick fort built by Kempe Gowda in 1537, lies Tipu Sultan's Palace, dating from about 1790. Made mostly out of wood with finely embellished balconies, pillars and arches, this two-storeyed structure, a replica of the Daria Daulat Bagh in Srirangapattana *(see p516),* served as a summer retreat of Tipu Sultan. He endearingly called it Rashk-e-Jannat, or the "Envy of Heaven". Although now dilapidated, it is still a hauntingly atmospheric place retaining the original elegant teak pillars.

The palace housed the public administrative offices from 1831, until they were shifted to the Attara Kacheri in 1868 *(see p512).* It now has a museum with artifacts from the Haider Ali–Tipu regime.

Dahlia bloom, Lalbagh

The **Venkataramana-swamy Temple**, nearby, dates from the early 18th century and was built by the Wodeyar kings.

♣ Lalbagh

Lalbagh Fort Rd.
Tel (080) 2657 0181
◻ daily. ▨ ⑪ ▨ Flower Show (Jan & Aug).

Regarded as one of the most richly diverse botanical gardens in South Asia, Lalbagh, in the southern part of the city, was laid out by Haider Ali in 1740. Spread over 97 ha (240 acres) of parkland, many of its tropical and subtropical plants were brought here by Haider Ali's son, Tipu Sultan. Later, John Cameron, the Gardens' Superintendent in the 1870s, imported several more rare species from Kew Gardens in London. Cameron was also responsible for initiating work on Lalbagh's famous Glass House, modelled on London's Crystal Palace and conceived as a

venue for horticultural shows. Surrounded by *champaka* trees and pencil cedars, the Glass House has played host to several visiting dignitaries. An Annual Flower Show is still held here.

The entrance to the park is marked by an equestrian statue of Chamaraja Wodeyar of Mysore. Another popular attraction is the surreal Floral Clock, surrounded by Snow White and the seven dwarfs; this was a gift from Hindustan Machine Tools, leading Indian manufacturers of watches.

▤ Gavi Gangadhareshvara Temple

W of Lalbagh. ◻ daily. ▨ Makar Sankranti (Jan).

One of Bangalore's oldest temples, the Gavi Gangadhareshvara Temple was built inside a natural cave in Gavipuram by Kempe Gowda in the 16th century. Legend has it that Kempe Gowda built this temple in gratitude after being released from his five-year imprisonment by Rama Raya.

Highlights include granite pillars, two of which support huge discs representing the sun and the moon, while the other two are topped by a Nandi and a trident. Devotees gather here during the Makar Sankranti festival to witness a unique phenomenon – the evening sun's rays passing between Nandi's horns and falling on the linga inside the cave.

The spacious, 19th-century Glass House at Lalbagh, with its intricate cast-iron frame

For hotels and restaurants in this region see pp711–12 and pp738–9

The Glitter of Gold

The ancient seers of India referred to gold by many names – synonyms for life, longevity, and beauty. Indians considered this metal auspicious and believed that wearing gold ornaments would ensure a long life. Craftsmen traditionally drew inspiration for their designs and motifs from nature, and also from the splendid temples with their ornately carved façades. The Kolar and Hatti mines in Karnataka were the repositories of the largest deposits of gold in ancient India. Due to the high price of gold, craftsmen mastered the technique of beating a minuscule quantity of gold into thin sheets and then transforming them into exquisite jewellery.

A gold *tali* pendant

Bangles

Hair ornament

Earrings

DECORATIVE ORNAMENTS
Gold ornaments were designed to be worn on practically every part of the body, from the crown of the head to the tips of the toes, to decorate and protect the wearer. Plants, animals and astral bodies inspired many of the shapes.

A Lady, late 19th-century painting by Raja Ravi Varma showing a woman in her finery

A large cobra head, *set with rubies, emeralds and diamonds and edged with emerald beads, is tied to a plait to prevent it from unravelling. The snake form, as a symbol of fertility, occurs in many ornaments.*

Temple deities *are often adorned with ritual ornaments. These pieces display some of the forms and techniques used by ancient Indian jewellers, and show the evolution of their craft.*

Pavan Sara, *a necklace made of coins, is a piece of jewellery found all over the country. As an instrument of savings, the coins were redeemed for cash when the need arose.*

Devotees congregating at the Vaidyeshvara Temple, Talakad

Talakad ②

Mysore district. 50 km (30 miles) SE of Mysore. ☷ ⚑ *Panchalinga Darshana (at intervals of 4–12 years).*

The historic city of Talakad, situated on the north bank of the Kaveri river, now lies partly buried under shifting sand dunes. From the 5th to the 10th centuries it was the capital of the Ganga dynasty *(see p522)*, but only two modest temples survive from that period. The largest edifice at this site is the 12th-century **Vaidyeshvara Temple**, dedicated to Shiva. Nearby is the more modest Kirti Narayana Temple, where the 3-m (10-ft) high image of Vishnu is still worshipped. A festival, the Panchalinga Darshana, is celebrated here at intervals ranging from four to 12 years.

Somnathpur ③

Mysore district. 36 km (22 miles) E of Mysore. ☷

One of the finest representations of Hoysala architecture *(see p524)*, the **Keshava Temple** is the highlight of this obscure little village. Built in 1268 by Somnatha, a general of King Narasimha III, its design is attributed to the celebrated sculptor and architect,

Janakacharya. The temple is accessed from the east, through a doorway with an open portico, where a slab records Somnatha's generous donations. Unlike the other Hoysala temples at Halebid and Belur *(see p523)*, this is well preserved and has complete towers. The temple has three star-shaped shrines that lead off a pillared hall; both the shrines and the hall stand on a high plinth. The basements of the inner sanctums and hall are profusely carved with animal and floral patterns, while images of deities under foliage canopies occupy the walls above. The interior of the hall is remarkable for its splendid columns and the elaborate ceilings which display lobed motifs, pendant buds and looped bands. The three shrines house fully-modelled, life-size images of Krishna playing the flute (south) and Janardana,

Insignia engraved on a horse-cart, Srirangapattana

a form of Vishnu (north). The Krishna image in the western shrine is a recent replacement of the original.

Also in Somnathpur is the ruined granite **Panchalinga Temple**, built in 1268 as a memorial in honour of Somnatha's family.

🏛 **Keshava Temple**
⃝ *daily.*

Srirangapattana ④

Mandya district. 16 km (10 miles) N of Mysore. **Tel** *(08232) 238 377.* ☐ *from Mysore.* ☷ *from Mysore. Autos and cycles available.*

Known to the British as Seringapatam, this island fortress in the Kaveri river enjoys historical significance as the site of the battles between the British and Tipu Sultan, the "Tiger of Mysore". The British finally stormed the citadel in 1799, killing Tipu and consolidating their power in South India. Today, none of the structures within the fort survive, barring the bridges across the two arms of the Kaveri river, from which the bathing ghats and the ramparts can be seen.

To the east and the south, a broad moat surrounds the polygonal bastions and turreted parapets constructed by the French engineers employed by Tipu. The Mysore Gate and Elephant Gate, to the south, are flanked by guardrooms. Sultan Battery, the dungeons where Tipu used to keep British prisoners, is to the north; nearby is the Water Gate, where Tipu was killed.

The **Sri Ranganatha Temple**, after which the island is named, is a large complex that was substantially restored in the 19th century. The inner sanctum enshrines an image

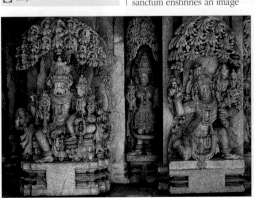

Representations of Hindu deities at the Keshava Temple

Mural depicting a battle at the Daria Daulat Bagh, Srirangapattana

of the reclining Vishnu and is approached through pillared halls and an open courtyard with a gilded lamp column.

The fort's eastern end has the **Jami Masjid**, erected by Tipu in 1787. It has an elevated prayer chamber.

The **Daria Daulat Bagh**, Tipu Sultan's summer palace, built in 1787, stands in the middle of a beautiful garden near the river, a short distance south of the fort. Each of its sides has three arched openings in the centre and the whole palace is surrounded by a pillared verandah. The east and west walls of the verandah are both covered with murals, restored in 1855. On the west wall are scenes of battle, one of which illustrates Haidar Ali's victory over the British at Pollilur (1780), while the east wall depicts courtly scenes. The carved woodwork and the

Snake shrine, Srirangapattana

elegant painted floral designs on the wall reveal Mughal influence. The palace is now a museum, with paintings, maps and Tipu memorabilia on display. Further south, past the Church of the Abbé Dubois (where the learned French Jesuit priest and author lived between 1799 and 1823) and the British Cemetery, is the **Gumbaz** – the tombs of Haidar Ali and Tipu Sultan. The walls of the chambers are decorated with the tiger-stripes motif (*bubri*) favoured by Tipu. The ebony and ivory doors were a gift from the viceroy, Lord Dalhousie, in 1855. The *sangam* (confluence) of the two arms of the Kaveri river is further south.

🏛 **Daria Daulat Bagh Museum**
Tel (08326) 252 045. ⬚ *Sat–Thu.*
📷

TIPU SULTAN: "TIGER OF MYSORE"

Portrait of Tipu Sultan (1750–99)

Tipu Sultan, the ruler of Mysore, stands head and shoulders above the many Indian rulers who were his contemporaries. He was a shrewd diplomat, expert soldier, excellent scholar and accomplished poet, and his military and administrative skills were complemented by his dream of a modern industrial state. The latter found expression in his cultivation of European contacts and employment of French engineers. The Sultan's main adversaries were the British who had conquered part of his father Haider Ali's territory and wealth in the first two Mysore Wars (1767–9 and 1780–84). Tipu waged two further wars against them, culminating in the fall of Srirangapattana in May 1799, where he died fighting.

FESTIVALS IN KARNATAKA

Banashankari Temple Fair *(Jan/Feb)*, Badami. This 20-day festival com-bines religious rites with the excitement of a funfair. An annual cattle fair, specializing in white bulls, is held at the same time.

Hoysala Mahotsava *(Mar)*, Belur and Halebid. A festival of dance and music unfolds against the spectacular backdrop of these historic temples.

Royal Dasara *(Sep/Oct)*, Mysore. This grand, 10-day festival, known as Dussehra in North India, celebrates the victory of the goddess Chamundeshvari (Durga) over the buffalo demon, Mahisha-sura; it owes its origin to the Mahanavami festival *(see p531)*. A royal elephant carrying an image of the goddess leads a splendid display of military bands, sports and parades, while religious ceremonies worship the elephant, the horse and weapons such as the State sword. Firework displays, concerts and wrestling matches liven up the evenings. A descendant of the former ruling Wodeyars plays a pivotal part and the famous golden throne, generally not on display, is used for the rituals.

Hampi Festival *(Nov)*, Hampi. Well-known dancers and musicians from around the country participate in this lively event.

Caparisoned elephant at the Dasara celebrations, Mysore

Mysore: Amba Vilas Palace

The magnificent Amba Vilas Palace, a treasure house of exquisite carvings and works of art from all over the world, was built by the Wodeyar rulers. The main block of this Indo-Saracenic building, with domes, turrets, arches and colonnades, was designed by Henry Irving in 1897. It replaced an earlier structure that was destroyed by a fire. During weekends and festivals, thousands of light bulbs enliven the palace's stern grey exterior.

Public Durbar Hall
The richly decorated gold-and-turquoise Durbar Hall, on the second floor, exudes royal splendour. On its rear wall are a series of paintings by Raja Ravi Varma.

Amba Vilas Hall
The Private Durbar Hall is smaller than, but as sumptuous as, the Public Hall. It is roofed with stained glass imported from Glasgow. The central part of its ceiling is supported by cast-iron columns and arches.

Mysore ❺

Mysore district. 140 km (87 miles) SW of Bangalore. 🚶 742,500. 🚉 🚌 ℹ️ KSTDC Transport Wing, Hotel Maurya Yatri Niwas, 2 Jhansi Laxmi Bai Rd, (0821) 242 3652. 🎭 Vairamudi Festival (Mar/Apr), Feast of St Philomena (Aug), Royal Dasara (Sep/Oct).

Situated among fertile fields, and skirted by wooded hills, Mysore was the capital of the Wodeyar rulers, who were governors of southern Karnataka under the Vijaya-nagar kings. The Wodeyar dynasty ruled almost uninterrupted from 1399 until Independence, except for the 38-year rule of the Muslim warlord Haider Ali and his son, Tipu Sultan, in the 18th century (*see p517*). Modern Mysore is the creation of Tipu Sultan who, in 1793, levelled the old city and built the present town. Today, Mysore is an important cultural centre, with the largest university in Karnataka. It is also renowned for its ivory work, silk-weaving, sandalwood incense and carvings.

Several elegant public buildings, erected under the Wodeyars, enhance the wide, tree-lined streets. In the heart of the city is the **Amba Vilas Palace**. To its west is **Jagan-mohan Palace**, built in 1902 to mark the coronation ceremony of Krishnaraja III. It partly obscures a Neo-Classical structure, now the **Chama-rajendra Art Gallery**, which houses an interesting collection of disparate objects including antique furniture, musical instruments, ceramics and ivory. On its top floor is a splendid collection of musical instruments, as well as magnificent paintings by the renowned 19th-century artist from Kerala, Raja Ravi Verma.

Near the northwestern corner of Amba Vilas Palace is **Krishnaraja Circle**, where a

The crouching Nandi on Chamundi Hill

For hotels and restaurants in this region see pp711–12 and pp738–9

View of the Amba Vilas Palace, Mysore

VISITORS' CHECKLIST

Ramvilas Rd. **Tel** (0821) 242 2620. ⬚ daily, 10am–5pm. 🖼 🎫 🍴 📷 🎪 Royal Dasara (Sep/Oct).

Golden Throne
Originally made of fig-wood overlaid with ivory, this jewelled throne was later plated with gold and silver. It is now brought out only during the Dasara celebrations.

Seating gallery for viewing the annual Mysore Dasara procession *(see p517).*

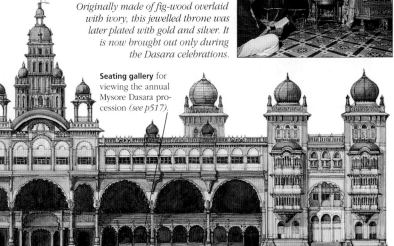

statue of Krishnaraja Wodeyar stands beneath a pavilion. The **Sayyaji Rao Road** that leads out from this circle is the principal shopping centre of the town. A short distance away is the Government House, the seat of the British Residents from 1805. Nearby, the **Cathedral of St Philomena**, with a stained-glass interior, is a new Neo-Gothic structure, which was completed in 1959.

In the western part of the city is the Neo-Classical **Manasa Gangotri**, the campus of Mysore University. The **Oriental Research Institute** here houses a collection of Sanskrit manuscripts, while the **Folklore Museum** has one of the most important ethnographic collections of South Indian toys, puppets and household objects, as well as two wooden chariots.

On the way to **Chamundi Hill**, 3 km (2 miles) southeast of Mysore, is **Lalitha Mahal Palace**, built in 1930. Formerly a private royal guest house, it is now a hotel *(see p712).* About halfway up the hill is the Nandi monolith, dating to 1659. Carved out of a single boulder, it is 7.5 m (25 ft) long and 5 m (16 ft) high. The richly decorated bull is depicted crouching. The **Chamundeshvari Temple**, at the summit of the hill, was built in the 17th century by the Wodeyars and was later refurbished. It houses a beautifully decorated idol of Chamundeshvari, the family deity of the Wodeyar kings.

Environs
The picturesque **Brindavan Gardens** are 16 km (10 miles) to the north of the city. This popular picnic spot was laid

out below the Krishnarajasagar Dam by Krishnaraja Wodeyar. The numerous fountains are illuminated every evening with beautiful multi-coloured lights.

Cathedral of St Philomena

Wildlife Sanctuaries of Karnataka

The Nilgiri Biosphere Reserve, encompassing six contiguous wildlife sanctuaries, spans the states of Karnataka, Kerala and Tamil Nadu. Created to protect the extraordinary biodiversity of the last surviving tracts of tropical evergreen and deciduous forests of the Western Ghats, it includes the area over which the notorious sandalwood smuggler and bandit, Veerappan, once held sway. This reserve, along with the adjacent Mudumalai Sanctuary *(see p604)*, forms one of the most important migratory corridors for animals such as the Asian elephant and the Indian bison. These parks are within convenient reach of Bangalore *(see pp512–3)* and Mysore *(see pp518–9)*.

Heron

The Ranganthittoo Bird Sanctuary *covers 540 sq km (209 sq miles) of riverine islands in the middle of the Kaveri river and attracts a large number of water birds during the nesting season, especially from June to November.*

Bandipur, *declared a wildlife sanctuary in 1931 by the then Maharaja of Mysore, has many chausingha (four horned antelope), and is also a Project Tiger Reserve (see p289). It spreads over 875 sq km (338 sq miles).*

The BRT Wildlife Sanctuary, *east of the Nilgiri Biosphere Reserve, is a corridor between the Western and Eastern Ghats. Covering an area of 540 sq km (209 sq miles), it supports a variety of birdlife, including storks.*

The Nagarhole Wildlife Sanctuary's *profusion of rivers and swampy grasslands keep it green all year. Established in 1983, the park has 645 sq km (249 sq miles) of deciduous vegetation. Its wildlife includes the bonnet macaque.*

The Kabini Reservoir, *separating Bandipur from Nagarhole, offers fine views. The Kabini River Lodge nearby is an excellent place for sighting wildlife, and a good place to stay (see p712).*

LOCATOR MAP

☐ *Wildlife Sanctuaries*

Coffee plantation in Madikeri

Kodagu ❻

Kodagu district. 120 km (75 miles) S of
Mysore. 🚌 ℹ️ Department of
Tourism, Madikeri, (08272) 228 580.
🎭 Keil Poldu (Sep), Huthri (Nov).

Picturesquely set amid the
forested mountains of the
Western Ghats, the district of
Kodagu (or Coorg) was an
independent state until it was
incorporated into the newly
formed state of Karnataka in
1956. **Madikeri**, the district
headquarters, situated 1,500
m (4,921 ft) above sea level
and surrounded by rolling
coffee and orange plantations,
is a charming hill town, and a
convenient base from which
to explore Kodagu.

Madikeri (or Mercara) was
once the capital of the Hindu
Lingayat kings, who ruled for
over 200 years from 1600,
except for a brief period
when Tipu Sultan seized
power. The **Fort**, at the centre
of the town, was built by the
third Lingayat king in 1812.
Within its stone ramparts,
it contains the simple,
unpretentious palace of the
Lingayat rulers, along with a
temple, an old church, a
museum and the local prison.

The famous **Omkareshvara
Shiva Temple**, situated in a
hollow east of the Fort, was
built by Linga Raja II in 1820
and dedicated to Vishnu and
Shiva. The temple complex
consists of brick buildings in
the Indo-Saracenic style set in

courtyards surrounded by
pillared verandahs. Other
notable monuments in
Madikeri are the **Royal
Tombs** of Raja Dodda Vira,
his wife and his son, Linga
Raja II. Curiously, these
display a distinct Islamic
influence, with onion-
shaped domes, minarets
and trellis work.
Kodagu remains pleasantly
cool all year round, and
the hills are at their most
lush after the heavy mon-
soon showers when they
make for delightful hikes.
The walk up to **Abbey
Falls**, 8 km (5 miles) from
Madikeri, is popular and
takes trekkers through
forests and coffee
plantations. Kodagu is
renowned for its sprawling
coffee plantations, first introduced in the mid-19th century
by the British. The Kodava
people bought back their land
after Independence, but
several estates still retain their
British names. Kodagu
produces some of the world's
finest varieties of mild coffee;
in fact, it is Karnataka's
richest district because it
accounts for the majority of
coffee exports from the state.
Coffee bushes are grown in
the benevolent shade of large
trees such as oak and rosewood, and in mixed plan-
tations with crops of oranges,
pepper vines and cardamom.

Nisargadhama, 27 km
(17 miles) from Madikeri, is a
beautiful forest retreat on a
riverine island on the Kaveri.
The bamboo cottages built
here by the forest department
are ideal for viewing wildlife.
Talakaveri, 45 km (28 miles)
southwest of Madikeri, at an
altitude of 1,276 m (4,186 ft), is
the source of the Kaveri, one
of India's seven sacred rivers
(see p600); there is a small
shrine built around the spring.
At **Bhagamandala**, 36 km (22
miles) southwest of Madikeri,
the Kaveri meets its two tributaries, Kanike and Sujoythi.
Several shrines dot the area
near the confluence – also the
site of the striking Bhandesh-
vara temple, built in the Kerala
style (see p21).

**The Talakaveri shrine, a place of
great religious significance**

THE KODAVAS

The people of Kodagu, known as Kodavas, are a distinct
ethnic group, and have their own language, Coorgi. The
Kodavas are proud of their martial origins and the country's armed forces have had a fair number of generals from
this community. They may no
longer live in the huge four-winged
homes called *ain mane*, but their
many traditional festivals, celebrated with great elan, still bring
them together. Coorgi weddings
are unique, in that there are no
priests and they are solemnized
by elders. The men dress in
traditional *kupyas*, or long black
coats tied at the waist by a gold-
and red-tasseled sash, while
women wear Coorgi-style saris
with pleats at the back. Their
distinctive cuisine includes
tangy pork curry served
with rice dumplings.

**A Kodava couple in
traditional dress**

Melkote ❼

Mandya district. 54 km (34 miles) N of Mysore. ℹ️ *Tourist Office, (08232) 238 377.* 🚌 *Vairamudi (Mar/Apr).*

A picturesque hill town of shrines and monasteries, Melkote is a major pilgrimage centre for devotees of Vishnu; it is also associated with Ramanuja, the renowned Hindu philosopher and social reformer who died in 1137. Ramanuja is worshipped along with Vishnu in the **Narayana Temple**, in the southern part of town. South of the temple stands a solitary gopura, while perched on the summit of a hill to the northeast of the town, is the small **Narasimha Shrine**, overlooking the large Kalyani Tank.

Daily life in Melkote revolves around temple rituals, and the tradition of religious learning introduced by Ramanuja survives in its many institutions, of which the Academy of Sanskrit Research is most famous.

Narasimha Shrine overlooking the Kalyani Tank at Melkote

Sravana Belgola ❽

Hassan district. 145 km (90 miles) W of Bangalore. 🚌 ℹ️ *Tourist Office, (08176) 257 254.* 🎭 *Mahamastaka-bhisheka (every 12 years; last one was in 2005).*

This small town, situated between two granite hills, Indragiri and Chandragiri, is the most important Jain site in South India. It is dominated by the colossal 17.7-m (58-ft) high monolithic **Statue of Gommateshvara**, also known as Bahubali, son of the first Jain tirthankara *(see p396).* On the summit of the 143-m (469-ft) high

The head-anointing ceremony at Sravana Belgola

Indragiri Hill, the north-facing statue of the naked saviour stands on an anthill staring impassively ahead. Entwined around his legs and arms are creepers, indicating the length of time he stood immobile in meditation. An inscription at the base records its consecration in AD 981 by Chamundaraya, the powerful minister of Rajamalla IV, one of the Ganga kings.

The town, which lies at the base of the hill, has a large tank as well as a number of Jain temples *(bastis)*. Perhaps the most interesting of these is the *matha*, near the steps leading to Indragiri Hill. The walls of its courtyard have a series of vivid 18th-century murals illustrating the past and present births of Parsvanatha, the 23rd *tirthankara*, as well as scenes from the annual fair held here. Some fine Jain bronzes are displayed in the sanctuary that opens off the courtyard.

On Chandragiri Hill, to the north of the town, is another cluster of *bastis* established by the 10th–12th century Ganga kings and their powerful ministers. The **Neminatha Basti**, commissioned by Chamundaraya, enshrines an image of Neminatha, the 22nd *tirthankara*. The adjoining **Chandragupta Basti** has miniature panels carved on perforated stone screens depicting episodes from the life of Bahubali and his royal disciple, Chandragupta. A 5-m (16-ft) high sculpture of Parsvanatha, the 23rd *tirthankara*, is enshrined in another nearby *basti*.

Every 12 years, Jainism's most important festival, the spectacular Mahamastaka-bhisheka (head-anointing ceremony) is held here. The festival commemorates the consecration of the Bahubali monolith, and attracts thousands of monks, priests and pilgrims. A special scaffold is erected behind the statue so that priests can ritually bathe the god with milk, water from the holy rivers, ghee, saffron, sandalwood paste, vermilion and flower petals. At the last ceremony, held in 1993, a specially-hired helicopter flew overhead, showering the statue with 20 kg (44 pounds) of gold leaf, 200 litres (423 pints) of milk, marigolds and jewels, to the delight of the assembled crowds.

Environs

The village of **Kambadahalli**, 15 km (9 miles) east of Sravana Belgola, is another Jain settlement. The 10th-century Panchakuta Basti houses a trio of *tirthankaras* in three separate shrines.

A view of Chandragiri Hill above Sravana Belgola

A columned Nandi pavilion in the Hoysaleshvara Temple, Halebid

Halebid 9

Hassan district. 213 km (132 miles) W of Bangalore. Hassan, 27 km (17 miles) S of town centre, then bus or taxi. Cycles available on hire. Tourist Office, (08177) 273 224.

Set amid a lush agricultural landscape ringed by distant hills, this isolated site was the Hoysala capital in the 12th and 13th centuries. While the palace has yet to be excavated, the stone ramparts that once surrounded the city can still be seen. Outside the ramparts, to the east, is the vast tank known as Dorasamudra, which was also the city's original name.

Today, the principal attraction of Halebid is the **Hoysaleshvara Temple**, begun in 1121 by King Vishnuvardhana, but never finished. This structure comprises a pair of identical temples, each with its own east-facing linga sanctuary opening on to a hall and a screened porch. Each temple is also preceded by a pavilion with a huge statue of Nandi, the bull-vehicle of Shiva. As the two halls are joined together to create a spacious columned interior, the temples function as a single monument. The outer walls are elevated on friezes of naturalistic and fanciful animals, interspersed with animated carvings of scenes from the *Ramayana* and *Mahabharata* (see pp26–7). Among the finest wall panels here are those of Shiva dancing on the

A magnificent seated Nandi at Halebid

outstretched skin of the elephant demon he had slain, Krishna playing the flute and Krishna holding up Mount Govardhan, on the south face of the southern sanctuary. On the north face of the northern sanctuary is a a splendid Nataraja (Shiva as the Lord of Dance) and a panel depicting a crouching multi-armed and -headed Ravana creeping up on Shiva and Parvati seated on Mount Kailasa. Set on the plinth on which the temple is raised is a three-dimensional composition of a warrior plunging his sword into a leonine beast with a ferocious head, interpreted as the dynastic symbol of the martial Hoysala rulers. The landscaped garden in front of the Hoysaleshvara Temple serves as an **Archaeological Museum**. A panel here shows a majestic seated Ganesha. A short distance south of the complex is a group of 12th-century Jain *bastis*.

🏛 **Archaeological Museum**
Tel (08177) 263 067. 10am–5pm Sat–Thu.

Belur 10

Hassan district. 17 km (11 miles) SW of Halebid. Hassan, 34 km (21 miles) SE of town centre, then bus or taxi. Tourist Office, (08177) 222 209.

One of the jewels of South Indian architecture, Belur's **Chennakeshava Temple** was built in 1117 by Vishnuvardhan to commemorate the Hoysala triumph over the Cholas (see pp46–7). At the end of the town's main street, a towered *gopura*, erected by the kings of Vijayanagar (see p530) in the 16th century, marks the entrance to the temple. Inside is a spacious paved courtyard, surrounded by subsidiary shrines and colonnades. In the centre is the main temple, a single star-shaped sanctuary opening onto a columned hall fronted by a screened porch.

The entire surface of the grey-green schist structure is covered with richly textured relief carvings. The lintels have foliate frames running between open-mouthed aquatic monsters (*makaras*) with exuberantly foliated tails. The stone grilles that filter light into the porch are raised on friezes of elephants, lotus stems, garlands and amorous couples. Brackets fashioned as female dancers, musicians and huntresses, standing gracefully under perforated trees, support the sloping eaves above the grilles. Many bear the artists' signatures, a sign of their elevated status under the Hoysalas. Even finer bracket figures can be seen inside the temple.

🛕 **Chennakeshava Temple**
Tel (08177) 222 218 daily. to non-Hindus

Belur's Chennakeshava Temple, in the centre of a large courtyard

Hoysala Art and Architecture

Frieze with mythological scene

The temples of the Hoysala kings (12th–13th centuries) and their powerful ministers are among the wonders of South Indian art and architecture. They embody a fusion of the curving towers (*shikharas*) of North India with the columned *mandapas* of the south, and are characterized by their unique star-shaped plan and their rich surface decoration. The dense imagery of the basement friezes and wall panels, sculpted with religious and mythological scenes, as well as the exquisite bracket figures, are fashioned out of grey-green schist, a material that permits beautifully intricate carving.

Gods *seated with their consorts, such as this remarkable rendering of the Lakshmi-Narayana theme from Belur, are carved in full detail and set into the outer walls of Hoysala temples.*

Flowing foliate patterns, *derived from lotus stems and leaves, run continuously around the basements of Hoysala temples.*

Bracket figures, *fashioned as beautiful female dancers, are the highlights of Hoysala temples. This sculpture of a female drummer from Belur has an engraving of the artist's signature.*

Mandapa interiors *have spacious aisles lined with massive, highly polished lathe-turned columns, with undulating profiles and sharp ridges. A good example is this magnificent Nandi pavilion opposite the main shrine at Halebid.*

THE SOMNATHPUR TEMPLE

The perfectly proportioned triple-sanctuaried Keshava Temple at Somnathpur (*see p516*), built in 1268, was the last of the great Hoysala temples.

Towers over Hoysala sanctuaries have small spires arranged in tiers.

The stepped outlines of the plinth echo the complex star-shaped plan of the sanctuary.

Miniature shrines flank the entrance steps.

Terracotta-tiled rooftops in Mangalore

Mangalore ⓫

South Kanara district. 357 km (222 miles) W of Bangalore. 399,000. 20 km (12 miles) N of city centre, then taxi or bus. Karnataka Tourism, Hotel Indraprastha, (0824) 242 1692.

This thriving port on the estuary of the Netavati and Gurpur rivers is the largest city in Dakshina (South) Kanara, the coastal district famous for its coffee, cashewnut and pepper plantations. Rich harvests of these crops have attracted traders through the ages. Arab merchants first came here in the 13th and 14th centuries, and were later followed by the Portuguese and the British.

Mangalore today, presents a panorama of terracotta-roofed houses, whitewashed churches, temples and mosques, nestling amid groves of coconut palms. Among its historic monuments is the old watchtower, known as **Sultan's Battery**, built of laterite in 1763 by Haider Ali of Mysore (see p518).

Mangalore's 19th-century churches include the domed Church of the Most Holy Rosary and the Jesuit College of St Aloysius. Situated at the foot of Kadiri Hill, 3 km (2 miles) north of the city, is the 17th-century **Manjunath Temple**, with some superb bronze images of the Buddha, dating to the 10th–11th centuries, installed in the porch.

Environs
The pleasant beach resort at **Ullal** is just 12 km (7 miles) south of the city. Numerous Jain temples and monasteries dot the villages around Mangalore. The finest is the elaborate 15th-century Chandranatha Basti at **Mudabidri**, 35 km (22 miles) to the northwest. Dominating the summit of a hill at **Karkala**, 18 km (11 miles) further north, is the 13-m (43-ft) high Gommateshvara monolith (1432), an obvious imitation of the larger and earlier one at Sravana Belgola (see p522). The 16th-century Chaturmukha Basti, a perfectly symmetrical temple with a central chamber enshrining 12 tirthankaras, stands at the base of the hill. The pilgrimage town of **Dharmasthala**, 75 km (47 miles) to the east, is well-known for its Shiva temple. Its Gommateshvara statue was installed in 1973.

Udipi ⓬

Udipi district. 58 km (36 miles) N of Mangalore. 113,100. Tourist Office, Krishna Building, Car Street, (0820) 252 9718. Pargaya (Jan), Chariot Festival (Aug).

All roads in Udipi lead to the large open square in the city centre where the **Krishna Temple** is located. This is the focal point of all activity, spiritual and commercial, in this bustling pilgrim town. The famous 13th-century Vaishnava teacher, Madhava, is believed to have founded the temple by installing an image of Krishna he had rescued from a shipwreck. Parked outside the temple are the festival chariots with dome-like towers made of bamboo and covered with colourful textiles. After passing through the entrance gate, pilgrims bathe in the tank before entering the main sanctuary with its silver doors and viewing window. Surrounding the square are other temples and the eight mathas associated with the Krishna Temple, built in the typical Kanara style with wooden verandahs and sloping roofs.

Udipi also lends its name to the inexpensive eateries that originated here. Catering to a local clientele, the menu concentrated on traditional South Indian vegetarian food, such as the masala dosa and idli (see pp554–5). These restaurants, with their affordable rates, quick turnover and simple but good food, are now found all over India.

Environs
About 5 km (3 miles) west of Udipi is **Malpe Beach**, where fishing boats can be hired for excursions. **Manipal**, 4 km (2.5 miles) to the east, is an industrial and educational centre. The **House of Vijayanath Shennoy** in Manipal, now a museum, is an example of a traditional home, with a fine collection of everyday objects.

🏛 **House of Vijayanath Shennoy**
◯ Mon–Sat.

Priests performing rituals during the Chariot Festival at Udipi

Shop selling religious paraphernalia at Barkur

Barkur ⑬

Udipi district. 71 km (44 miles) N of Mangalore. 🚉 🎉 *Navaratri (Sep/Oct).*

The coastal town of Barkur was a flourishing port in the 15th and 16th centuries until its river silted up. Today, the town's main attractions are its many temples with their typical sloping terracotta-tiled roofs. The largest is the **Panchalin-geshvara Temple**, situated at the southern end of the town. Devotees gather at the stepped tank near the temple for a ritual bath before worshipping at the two east-facing linga shrines. The other temples include one dedicated to both Shiva and Ganesha, and the smaller Someshvara and Somanatheshvara temples.

Environs
The little hamlet of **Mekkekattu**, 8 km (5 miles) north of Barkur, has shrine of painted *bhuta* figures (local spirits). These are copies of the originals, which were removed to New Delhi's Crafts Museum (*see pp80–81*) and the Folklore Museum in Mysore (*see p519*), after the shrine's renovation in the 1960s. The vividly painted deity Nandikeshvara, (the winged bull) stands in the lower shrine while his consort occupies the upper one. Fierce guardian deities crowd a side chamber.

Bhatkal ⑭

North Kanara district. 165 km (102 miles) N of Mangalore. 🎉 *31,800.* 🚉 🎉 *Navaratri (Sep/Oct).*

Located along a picturesque highway that follows the coastline, this town was an important port during the 16th and 17th centuries. The many beautiful Jain and Hindu stone temples found here date from those days of prosperity. Standing in the town's main street are the Chandranath-eshvara and Parsvanatha *bastis*. Situated 2 km (1.3 miles) to the east, on the other side of the highway, is the **Khetapai Narayan Temple**, built in 1540. Its sanctuary and hall are enclosed within stone screens fashioned to imitate wood. Finely sculpted guardian figures flank the doorway.

Detail of a stone panel, Bhatkal

Environs
Tucked away in the forested hills at **Kollur**, 35 km (22 miles) southeast of Bhatkal, is a shrine dedicated to the goddess Mukambika. This is a very popular pilgrimage.

India's highest waterfalls, the **Jog Falls**, lie 60 km (37 miles) northeast of Bhatkal. They can be seen at the head of the Sharavati river, framed by jagged pinnacles of rock.

Gokarna ⑮

North Kanara district. 200 km (124 miles) N of Mangalore. 🚉 🛈 *Tourist Office, Main Rd, Karwar, (08382) 221 172.* 🎉 *Shivratri (Feb/Mar).*

Spectacularly situated by the Arabian Sea, Gokarna is a favourite with visitors in search of sun, sea and sand. A charming little town with two principal streets and clusters of traditional tile-roofed brick houses, Gokarna is also an important centre of Sanskrit learning.

The **Mahabaleshvara Temple**, at the western end of the main street, was destroyed by the Portuguese in 1714 and then rebuilt later in the 18th century. In the sanctuary is a stone linga, encased in brass, placed on a coiled stone serpent. The floor of the hall in front has an intricate engraving of a giant tortoise. Shiva's birthday (Feb/Mar) is celebrated here with great fanfare. The two great temple chariots lead a procession through the town's narrow streets, while priests chant hymns in praise of Shiva.

BEACHES AROUND GOKARNA
Long stretches of beautiful, unspoilt beaches extend along the western coast from Gokarna to Karwar, a seaside town 60 km (37 miles) to the north. South of Gokarna are the Half Moon and Paradise beaches, while nearer Karwar are the lovely Binaga and Araga beaches. The gently curving bays, fringed by palms, are still occupied by small fishing villages where life revolves around the sea and the daily catch. Tourism remains unknown and only a few simple shacks offer basic food and shelter.

Waves breaking against rocks at a beach near Karwar

The two-storeyed Vidyashankara Temple at Sringeri

Sringeri ⑯

Chikmagalur district. 100 km (62 miles) NE of Mangalore. 🚉 🚌 🎭 Navaratri (Sep/Oct).

The small settlement of Sringeri, tucked away in the forested ranges of the Western Ghats, is today an important pilgrimage centre and one of the most powerful seats of orthodox Hinduism in South India. This was where Shankaracharya, *(see p648)*, the great 9th-century philosopher and social reformer, established the first of his four *mathas*; the other three are at Joshimath in the Himalayas *(see p187)*, Puri *(see p312)* to the east and Dwarka *(see p427)* to the west. Today, his successors (also known as Shankaracharyas) wield tremendous influence in both

Floral offerings at Sringeri's temple

religious and temporal matters, while the *mathas* still function as centres of spiritual learning.

Standing on a paved terrace are two temples overlooking the Tunga river, crammed with sacred fish. The smaller temple, dedicated to Sharada, a popular form of the goddess Saraswati, is the principal destination for local pilgrims. Next to it is the 16th-century **Vidyashankara Temple**, where the Shankaracharya is worshipped in the form of a linga. This stone structure, which stands raised on a high platform, is laid out on an almost circular star-shaped plan. Friezes depicting the many forms of Shiva and Vishnu embellish the faceted walls. The hall that precedes the inner sanctum has massive piers carved as rearing *yalis* (mythical leonine beasts).

Chitradurga ⑰

Chitradurga district. 200 km (124 miles) N of Bangalore. 🛈 Kamana Bhavi Extension, 8th Ward Fort Rd; *(08194) 234 466.* 🚉 🚌

Located at the base of a rugged chain of hills, this town was a prominent outpost of the Vijayanagar Empire *(see pp530–31)*. Later, in the 17th–18th centuries, it became the headquarters of a line of local chiefs known as Bedas, until it was occupied by Haider Ali *(see p517)* in 1799 and then by the British.

The **Fort**, defined by walls of huge granite blocks, rises above the town. A series of three gates leads to the irregular inner zone, strewn with striking granite boulders. There are several small temples here, as well as a number of ceremonial gateways erected by the Bedas. The platforms and pavilions within the compound of the Sampige Siddheshvara Temple mark the spot where the Bedas were crowned. The remains of rubble and mud-built granaries and residences, and a large circular well can be seen nearby.

In the town below, the local **Government Museum** displays artifacts from surrounding sites. The 17th-century Ucchalingamma Temple is on the main street and should not be missed.

🏰 **Fort**
◻ *daily.* 📷

🏛 **Government Museum**
Tel (08194) 224 202. ◻ Mon–Sat.

The fort at Chitradurga, with gateways and shrines dotting the boulder-strewn landscape

A view of Hampi, with a ruined bridge over the Tungabhadra river in the foreground ▷

Hampi ⑱

Sculpted staircase, Mahanavami platform

A UNESCO World Heritage Site on the south bank of the Tungabhadra river, Hampi boasts the evocative ruins of Vijayanagar or the "City of Victory". The capital of three generations of Hindu rulers for more than 200 years, Hampi reached its zenith under Krishnadeva Raya (r.1510–29) and Achyuta Raya (r.1529–42). The site, which comprises the Sacred and Royal Centres, has a superb location, with rocky ridges and granite boulders acting as natural defences. The urban core of the city was fortified and separated from the Sacred Centre by an irrigated valley, through which ancient canals and waterways still run.

King's Balance
Ruling kings were weighed on this balance against gold or grain, for distribution to the poor.

Vitthala Temple
(see pp532–3)

Krishna Temple
Krishnadeva Raya erected this temple in 1516 to commemorate his victory over Orissa. It is no longer a place of worship.

Tiruvengalanatha Temple

Matanga Hill

★ Virupaksha Temple
The ancient temple of Virupaksha, dedicated to the goddess Pampa and her consort Shiva, is dominated by a 50-m (164-ft) high gopura. This is the principal place of worship in Hampi.

Tungabhadra

Hemakuta Hill

★ Narasimha Monolith
Carved out of a single boulder in 1528, this awe-inspiring image of Vishnu shows him in his half man-half lion incarnaton (see p679).

STAR SIGHTS

★ Virupaksha Temple

★ Narasimha Monolith

★ Lotus Mahal

Chariot Festival
The bustling Bazaar Street is the main centre of activity and the venue for the colourful Chariot Festival. The temple chariot carries the main deity through the streets so it can be publicly honoured.

VISITORS' CHECKLIST

Bellary district. 315 km (196 miles) NW of Bangalore. ☐ Hospet, 13 km (8 miles) W of site. ☐ ℹ Bazaar St, (08394) 228 537. ☐ **Virupaksha Temple** ☐ daily. **Lotus Mahal** 🗺 also covers the Vitthala Temple. 🎏 Chariot Festival (Feb), Hampi Festival (Nov). Foreigners must register at Virupaksha Temple Police Station.

Elephant Stables
An imposing structure of 11 chambers, this once housed the royal elephants. Especially noteworthy are the polygonal roofs, alternating with smooth or ribbed domes.

| 0 metres | 500 |
| 0 yards | 500 |

★ Lotus Mahal
A skilful blend of Hindu and Islamic architecture, this building may have served as a council chamber for the king.

Tiruvengalanatha Temple

Hospet

Hazara Ramachandra Temple

Ruined Palaces

Great Bath

Archaeological Museum

The Queen's Bath, an open-air structure, seems to have been designed for royal recreation.

The Mahanavami Platform was used by kings during the Mahanavami festival *(see p517)*, and for pre-war ceremonies.

Stepped Tank
This small, square tank with multiple steps was fed by a water chute, part of an extensive "hydraulic system" that brought water to the Royal Centre.

Hampi: Vitthala Temple

The grandest of all the religious monuments in the Sacred Centre, the Vitthala Temple represents the high point of Vijayanagar art and architecture. Though its founder remains unknown, it was enlarged in the 16th century by two of Vijaynagar's greatest rulers, Krishnadeva Raya and Achyuta Raya. Preceding the main shrine is the great open hall, or *mahamandapa*, built on a low platform and supported by intricately carved pillars. This was the gift of a military commander in 1554, just 11 years before the city was sacked and abandoned.

★ Yalis
Leaping yalis (mythical leonine beasts), many with riders, adorn the outer piers of the temple.

RECONSTRUCTION OF THE TOWER
This shows the pyramidal vimana (tower), over the main sanctuary of the Vitthala Temple, as it looked when it was built in the 16th century.

Relief
A niche in a stone pillar has a superb rendering of Garuda, the eagle mount of Vishnu.

STAR FEATURES

★ Yalis
★ Chariot

Exploring Hampi

The fabled city of the Vijaya-nagar kings (see pp530–31), covering an area of around 20 sq km (8 sq miles), sprawls across a spectacular barren and boulder-strewn landscape.

The **Sacred Centre**, on the southern bank of the Tungabhadra river, is dominated by the impressive **Virupaksha Temple**. It is dedicated to a form of Shiva (Virupaksha), known here as Pampapati (the "Lord of Pampa"), and commemorates his wedding to Pampa, the goddesss of the Tungabhadra. In front is the colonnaded **Bazaar Street** that dates mainly from the 16th to the mid-17th centuries, when it teemed with pilgrims and travellers in search of exotic wares. A path beside the river leads past the **Kodandarama Temple**, with its figures of Rama, Sita and Lakshman carved on to a boulder inside the sanctuary. The bathing ghats here are considered to be the holiest at the site.

Beyond lies the **Temple of Achyuta Raya**, one of the major Hindu complexes at Hampi, dating from 1534 and dedicated to Tiruvengalanatha, the form of Vishnu that is venerated at Tirupati (see p678). Its perfect plan of two concentric enclosures, each entered by a towering gopura to the north, is clearly visible from the summit of **Matanga Hill**. The riverside path continues to the Vitthala Temple, from where a road proceeds to the village of **Kamalapuram**, where the **Archaeological Museum** is located. En route is a gateway with a damaged façade with windows and battlements.

The road that runs south from Hampi village, through the Sacred Centre, leads up **Hemakuta Hill**, scattered with numerous pre- and early Vijayanagar shrines, many with small pyramidal towers. A large image of the elephant god, Ganesha, carved on a

A view of Matanga Hill

Vitthala Temple
This striking temple with its elaborate mandapas *(columned halls) is dedicated to Vitthala, an incarnation of Vishnu the Preserver, the second god in the Hindu Trinity.*

Musical Columns
Small hollow columns emit different tones when lightly tapped.

→ Chariot

★ **Chariot**
This shrine in front of the temple is dedicated to Garuda and is fashioned as a stone chariot.

Frieze Detail
This panel depicts a trio of celestial nymphs riding on parrots.

boulder, marks the top of the ridge. Further south is the **Krishna Temple**, erected in the early 16th century during the reign of Krishnadeva Raya. It is entered through a massive, though partly ruined gopura. The colonnaded street to the east now runs through fields of sugarcane, while the square tank nearby still stores water. As it continues south, the road travels past the tremendous Narasimha Stone Monolith, a representation of Vishnu's man-lion incarnation (see p679).

Fortified walls enclose the **Royal Centre**. At the latter's core is the superb **Hazara Rama Temple**, built by Deva Raya I, a Vijayanagar king of the 15th century. Its outer walls are covered with friezes that depict ceremonies of the Mahanavami festival. Reliefs of episodes from the Ramayana can be seen here. Around

A coracle ferrying people across the Tungabhadra river

the temple are excavated remains of palaces, baths and a hundred-columned audience hall, while to its north are the Elephant Stables and the **Lotus Mahal**.

🏛 **Archaeological Museum**
Kamalapuram, (08394) 241 237.
☐ 10am–5pm Sat–Thu.

Environs
The historic village of **Anegondi** lies on the opposite bank of the Tungabhadra river. Until a bridge under construction becomes operational, it can be reached only on the coracles that have plied the river for centuries.

An important settlement before the establishment of Vijayanagar, Anegondi's now dilapidated palaces, temples and bathing ghats still preserve vestiges of their former glory. The Kalyan Mahal, a palace-like building reminiscent of Hampi's Lotus Mahal (see p531), stands in the central square. Nearby are a temple and a 14th-century gateway. The massive walls and rounded bastions of Anegondi's citadel enclose the rocky hills lying west of the main town. Anegondi is also of interest for its traditional mud-clad houses.

An outer wall of Gadag's Someshvara Temple, with temple towers in relief

Gadag ⑲

Gadag district. 450 km (280 miles) NW of Bangalore. 🚉 🚌 ℹ️ *Hotel Durga, Vihar Complex.* 🛍️ *daily.*

An important cotton collection centre, the sleepy little town of Gadag comes to life during the cotton season in May and June. During these months, the cotton market hums with activity and is well worth a visit.

A number of late Chalukyan monuments (11th–12th centuries) in the city indicate its historic past. Standing to the south is the **Trikuteshvara Temple**, remarkable for its three sanctuaries facing a common, partly open hall. Inclined slabs that serve as balcony seats are decorated with figurative panels, and are overhung by steeply angled eaves. Inside the hall, the columns have figures arranged in shallow niches. The east sanctuary accommodates three lingas, while the one to the south is dedicated to the goddess Saraswati.

In the middle of the city stands the **Someshvara Temple**. Though abandoned and now in a dilapidated state, its intricate carvings are fairly well preserved. Look for the doorways to the hall, which have densely carved figures and foliation.

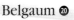

Sculpted figures

Environs

The small village of **Lakkundi**, 11 km (7 miles) southeast of Gadag, has temples dating from the 11th–12th centuries, built of grey-green chloritic schist. Surrounded by mud houses, a number of such temples are tucked away down narrow streets. Jain Basti, the largest temple, has a five-storeyed tower. Its basement is adorned with friezes of elephants and lotus petals. Lathe-turned columns are seen on the porch. The nearby Kashi Vishvanatha Temple has a pair of sanctuaries facing each other across a common porch. Relief carvings of a pair of *makaras* or aquatic monsters, sitting on the walls, are typical motifs of late Chalukyan art.

Belgaum ⑳

Belgaum district. 502 km (312 miles) NW of Bangalore. 🚉 🚌 ℹ️ *Tourist Office, Ashoka Nagar, (0831) 247 0879.*

This bustling city, on the border with Maharashtra, was an important garrison town under the British. Even today, the cantonment, with its bungalows and barracks, has a significant military presence. Earlier, in the 16th and 17th centuries, Belgaum was a provincial centre under the Adil Shahi rulers of Bijapur *(see p542)*, the Marathas of Pune *(see p471)*, as well as the Mughals when they occupied this part of Karnataka. The **Fort** to the east is unusually elliptical in layout and its stone walls incorporate many reused temple blocks. The **Safa Mosque** nearby was built in the first half of the 16th century by Asad Khan, the governor of Belgaum. The town also has three temples that date to the late Chalukyan period.

The elliptical fort at Belgaum

Performing Arts of Karnataka

Karnataka has a rich and vibrant performing arts tradition. Story telling, with the help of media such as paintings and leather puppets, was among the most popular folk entertainments in the northern and northeastern part of the state, and in neighbouring Andhra Pradesh, before the advent of the cinema. Itinerant folk performers would delight rural audiences with

String puppet

stirring tales of good and evil, based on mythological episodes. A number of dance-dramas, such as the Yakshagana, developed in South Kanara, the region of Karnataka that borders Kerala. As in Kathakali *(see p657)*, Yakshagana actors dress in awe-inspiring costumes to perform a heavily mimetic dance, while the singer recites the story to the accompaniment of music.

KARNATAKA'S LEATHER PUPPETS

Huge figures made of goatskin are punched with holes of various shapes to allow light to filter through, thus creating the interplay of light and coloured shadow, so essential to shadow theatre. The chief puppeteer recites the story, while his assistants provide musical accompaniment.

Figures *are etched on the prepared skin with a sharp instrument, then cut along the outline and coloured.*

The chief puppeteer *manipulates the puppet with the help of an attached stick.*

Performances *take place at night. A light is placed behind a thin cotton screen, so that the audience, sitting in front, sees the moving shadows.*

Perforations on the figure allow light to pass through.

Bright colours and outlines are combined to create striking effects.

A stick is attached for manipulation.

Hanuman, the Monkey God, a major character in the *Ramayana*

YAKSHAGANA

This folk dance-drama originated in the early 16th century. An all-male cast consisting of about 20 actors and musicians act out a repertoire that is inspired mainly by episodes from the great epics *(see pp26–7)*, especially the *Mahabharata*. All-night performances, organized at the behest of a wealthy patron on special occasions, take place in the open, and no particular props are needed. Yakshagana's spectacular costumes are enhanced by tall headgear, a profusion of ornaments and elaborate make-up.

A man creating the elaborate headgear

Actors performing a scene from the *Mahabharata*

Badami ㉑

Coiled Serpent, Ceiling, Cave 1

Dramatically situated within a horseshoe of red sandstone cliffs, overlooking the green waters of a large lake, this historic town was the capital of the powerful early Chalukya kings, who ruled the Deccan during the 6th–7th centuries AD. These rulers also held sway at Pattadakal *(see pp538–9)* and Aihole *(see pp540–41).*

Among the rock-cut and structural monuments, the most richly decorated are the cave temples, which are carved into the cliff on the southern side. Of these, Cave 1 is dedicated to Shiva, Caves 2 and 3 to Vishnu, and Cave 4 to the Jain saints.

Columned verandah, Cave 3

A linga sanctuary is carved into the rear wall.

CAVE 1

A flight of steps in this cave leads up to a pillared verandah, behind which is a square, columned hall with a small sanctuary carved into the rear wall. The highlights here are the Nataraja panel and the carved panels on the ceiling.

Cave 2
This Vaishnava cave has a superb frieze of Varaha, the boar incarnation of Vishnu, on one end of the porch. A row of dwarfs is carved below it.

Cave 3
The verandah of this large and beautiful cave has an enormous four-armed figure of Vishnu seated on Adisesha, the serpent whose five hoods spread protectively over his crown. At his feet is the bird Garuda, his mount. This is the only cave with an inscription, dated AD 578.

Nataraja Panel
This 12-armed dancing Shiva is one of the earliest and finest depictions of the Nataraja in Karnataka.

Exploring Badami

Most of Badami's temples are situated on the imposing cliff that lies north of the man-made Agastya Lake. The boulder-strewn landscape and the large lake acted as natural defences of the site. Standing on the embankment is the 11th-century **Yellamma Temple**, with its multi-storeyed tower. Further away, inside the village, is the **Jambulinga Temple**, dating to AD 699, with triple shrines dedicated to Brahma, Vishnu and Shiva opening off a common *mandapa*. The **Bhutanatha Temple** is scenically located at the end of the lake and was built in several phases. The core shrine, with a pyramidal tower, is from the 6th–7th centuries, while the porch, embellished with angled eaves and overlooking the water, dates to the 11th century. Several boulders lying around the temple have reliefs of a sleeping Vishnu, and a seated Jain figure. Lesser shrines nearby show the pyramidal layered towers that are typical of the late Chalukya style.

The **Archaeological Museum**, on the north side of the lake, displays a magnificent triangular panel depicting Brahma surrounded by elaborate foliage; this piece must have once surmounted a free-standing portal. Other items of interest include a squatting female divinity with a lotus head, and two panels showing Shiva – spearing a demon and shooting arrows as he rides in a chariot.

Steps ascend through a rugged gorge to the 7th-century **Upper Shivalaya Temple** that crowns the cliffs rising to the north of the town. Only the walls of the passageway and the multi-storeyed tower capped with a square-domed

The tower of the Upper Shivalaya Temple

VISITORS' CHECKLIST

Bagalkot district. 480 km (298 miles) NW of Bangalore. 🚊 🚌 ℹ️ *Karnataka Tourism, Hotel Mayura Chalukya, (08357) 220 117.* **Caves** ⬜ *daily.* 🎫 📷 **Archaeological Museum** *Tel* (08352) 220 047. ⬜ *10am–5pm, Sat–Thu.* 📷

roof still stand; the *mandapa* in front has been dismantled. Its simple basement mouldings and wall pilasters are typical of early structural architecture under the Chalukyas. Diminutive scenes of Krishna holding up Mount Govardhana, and Narasimha disembowelling his victim, are carved intricately on the walls. Perched on top of an isolated boulder near the main road north of the town, is the **Mallegitti Shivalaya Temple**, a well-preserved 7th-century structure. Perforated stone windows flank sculptured panels of Vishnu and Shiva, topped with garlands.

Environs

A popular Devi shrine, facing a large tank dating from the 18th century, is situated at **Banashankari**, 5 km (3 miles) east of Badami. At **Mahakuta**, 14 km (9 miles) to the east, a group of 7th-century temples built in contrasting North- and South-Indian styles *(see p20)*, are clustered around a small tank.

Cave 4
Standing and seated Jain tirthankaras *cover the walls and columns in Cave 4, on top of a cliff. Some of these were added in the 11th and 12th centuries, when this part of Karnataka was governed by a later line of Chalukya rulers.*

The Bhutanatha Temple overlooking the tank

Pattadakal ②

The sacred complex at Pattadakal is picturesquely situated on the banks of the Malprabha river. A UNESCO World Heritage Site, its superb 8th-century temples are a fitting climax to the artistic achievements of the Chalukya kings, as seen in neighbouring Badami *(see pp536–7)* and Aihole *(see pp540–41)*. While these towns were important ancient settlements, Pattadakal, with only a small resident population, was mainly used for royal festivities and coronation ceremonies.

Shiva appearing out of the fiery linga, Virupaksha Temple

Exploring Pattadakal

The main temple complex is situated in landscaped gardens next to the small village. Built in a combination of the North Indian and South Indian temple styles *(see p20)*, these striking structures reveal a great deal about the evolution of temple architecture in South India.

The modest Galaganatha Temple, built of sandstone

North Indian-style Temples

Characterized by their curved towers *(shikharas)* over the inner sanctum, North Indian-style temples are exemplified in the **Kadasiddeshvara** and **Jambulinga Temples**, which are situated near the entrance. These are unassuming sandstone structures with damaged wall sculptures and curving tiered towers. The larger but incomplete **Galaganatha Temple** nearby has a well-preserved tower with sharply cut tiers of horseshoe-shaped motifs and a ribbed finial. The **Kashi Vishvanatha Temple**, which lies to the west, dates from the mid-8th century and further illustrates the developments in the North Indian temple style. Its faceted tower is entirely covered with a mesh design of interlocking horseshoe-arched motifs. The columns inside the small vestibule preceding the sanctum are carved with a variety of mythological scenes.

South Indian-style Temples

South Indian temple towers *(vimanas)* rise in a stepped pyramidal formation, as in the **Sangameshvara Temple**, the earliest in the complex. It was erected by the Chalukya king, Vijayaditya, who died in AD 733 before the structure was completed. Its multistoreyed tower is capped with a square domed roof. The incomplete hall in front has been restored.

The largest temples are the twin **Virupaksha** and **Mallikarjuna Temples** to the south. Both are dedicated to Shiva and were constructed in AD 745 by two sister queens of the powerful Chalukya king, Vikramaditya II, to commemorate his victory over the Pallava rulers of Tamil Nadu. These temples represent the climax of early Chalukya architecture and are said to be based on the Kailasanatha Temple in Kanchipuram *(see p582)*. They also served as the inspiration for the colossal Kailasanatha monolith at Ellora *(see pp476–8)*.

Today, the Virupaksha Temple is the only functioning shrine in this complex. In

View of the twin Virupaksha and Mallikarjuna Temples, Pattadakal

Nataraja, ceiling panel from the Papanatha Temple

front is a Nandi pavilion with a magnificently carved bull covered by a cloth. The temple itself consists of a spacious, columned hall with triple porches leading to the linga sanctum, surrounded by a passageway. The ornately carved pillars and ceilings portray mythological and religious stories. The finest reliefs are on either side of the east porch and include one of Shiva as *lingodbhavamurti*, appearing out of a fiery linga, and a depiction of Vishnu as Trivikrama, traversing the Universe in three steps.

The Mallikarjuna Temple, though identical, is smaller and more compact. The carvings on the columns of

the interior hall show scenes from the *Panchatantra*, a collection of fables with bird and animal heroes. The walls surrounding the temple, and the Nandi pavilion in front of it, are incomplete.

A path from the Virupaksha Temple gateway along the river leads to the **Papanatha Temple**. This early 8th-century temple was extended several times, as can be seen in the unusual arrangement of double halls leading to the sanctuary, and in the later addition of passageway walls with porches on three sides. The interesting exterior combines South Indian-style pilastered wall niches with North Indian-style mesh patterns and curvilinear towers. Battle scenes from the *Ramayana (see p27)*, carved on the east wall, conclude with Rama's coronation, shown on the column of the main porch. Both the halls have central aisles, with pot

Battle between Arjuna and Shiva, Virupaksha Temple

and foliage motifs carved on the capitals. Ornate brackets and beams support ceiling panels, the finest of which show a coiled *naga* (snake) deity and a Dancing Shiva (Nataraja), in the inner hall.

Jain Temple

To the west of the village, is a 9th-century Jain Temple built by the Rashtrakuta rulers, who succeeded the Chalukyas in the middle of the 8th century. A spacious open porch with peripheral lathe-turned columns is overhung with angled eaves. Some remarkable carvings of life-size elephant torsos are placed beside the doorway that leads into the inner hall.

PLAN OF PATTADAKAL

1	Entrance	7	Virupaksha
2	Jambulinga	8	Nandi Pavilion
3	Galaganatha	9	Museum
4	Sangameshvara	10	Village
5	Kashi Vishvanatha	11	Papanatha
6	Mallikarjuna		

KEY

🅿 Parking

🚌 Bus station

0 metres　　　100

0 yards　　　100

A view of the Gaudar Gudi with the Ladkhan Temple behind it, Aihole

Aihole ㉓

Bagalkote district. 44 km (27 miles) NE of Badami. 🚉 *Badami, 44 km (27 miles) SW of town, then bus or taxi.* 🚌 🎪 *Ramalinga Temple Chariot Festival (Feb/Mar).*

Time seems to have stood still in this small, dusty town, situated on the Malprabha river, about 17 km (11 miles) downstream from Pattadakal *(see pp538–9)*. Fortifications encircle much of the town. Within are ancient sandstone temples of varying types, some of which were used as dwellings and are named after their former inhabitants. The temples are associated with both the early and later Chalukya rulers of Badami *(see pp536–7)*, and date from the 6th–11th centuries.

Most visitors begin their tour of Aihole at the **Durga Temple**. Nearby is a small complex with the **Ladkhan Temple**. This building is recognizable by the tiers of sloping slabs that roof the spacious hall as well as the adjoining entrance porch. River goddesses and amorous couples are carved on the columns of the porch, while images of deities can be seen on the side walls of a small chamber at the rooftop level. The adjacent **Gaudar Gudi** comprises a small sanctuary set within an open *mandapa*, with balcony seating on four sides. The ruined Chakra Gudi is near the stepped tank. The **Kunti Group**, a quartet of

temples conceived as open columned halls with interior sanctuaries, lies to the south. The temple to the southeast, probably the first to be built, has superbly carved ceiling panels portraying the Hindu Trinity of Brahma, Vishnu and Shiva. A similar trio of ceiling panels can be seen in the Hucchapayya Math, lying a short distance beyond.

A stepped path leads to the top of the hill southeast of the town, passing by a two-storeyed Buddhist temple. At the summit of the hill stands the serene **Meguti Temple** built in AD 634, the earliest dated structural monument in Karnataka. The temple's clearly articulated basement, plastered walls and eaves show the South Indian style of temple architecture *(see p20)* in its earliest phase. An impressive seated Jain figure is installed in the sanctuary. Prehistoric megalithic tombs are located to the rear of the

temple. The road, going downhill, follows the curving fortifications and passes the Jyotirlinga Group, until it ends at the Durga Temple. To the north of the Durga Temple is the **Chikki Gudi**, with exquisitely carved columns, beams and ceiling panels. A path to the right, leads to the small **Hucchimalli Gudi**, with a North Indian style tower, and an unusual icon of Karttikeya, Shiva's son, carved on the ceiling of the front porch.

Nearby lies the rock-cut **Ravala Phadi Cave**, dating to the late 6th century. Its interior is enhanced with splendid carvings of Hindu divinities. These include a Dancing Shiva in a subshrine; Ardhanarishvara, Harihara and Shiva with Ganga, on the walls of the main hall; and Varaha and Durga in the antechamber preceding the small linga sanctuary. Tiny shrines and a fluted column stand in front.

The exuberant Dancing Shiva relief in Ravala Phadi Cave

Aihole: Durga Temple

Medallion on porch pillar

The largest and finest monument at Aihole, the Durga Temple is also the most unusual because of its apsidal sanctuary surrounded by an open colonnade. The temple is elevated on a lofty plinth, with steps at one end leading to a porch with elaborate carvings of sensuous couples and guardians on its columns. Other sculptural masterpieces, of Shiva with Nandi, Narasimha, Vishnu with Garuda, Durga and Harihara, are placed in the niches lining the colonnade. The interior of the hall is plain by contrast and the circular plinth within the sanctuary empty. The temple's name is a misnomer, as the identity of the image that was once worshipped here remains unknown.

VISITORS' CHECKLIST

N of Archaeological Museum. ◯ daily. 🎟 covers all main temples.

A view of the semi-circular sanctuary of the Durga Temple

Naga Ceiling
A ceiling panel in the mandapa *depicts a* naga *with a coiled serpent body.*

The entrance porch has columns embellished with intricate carvings.

The capstone *(amalaka),* a ribbed disc, has fallen down from the tower.

Durga
This niche shows a multi-armed Durga slaying the buffalo demon.

Shikhara
Little remains of the tower that once rose above the inner sanctum.

Column Carving
This depiction of an amorous couple, carved on one of the columns in the porch, is a masterpiece of Chalukyan art.

Bijapur

Bijapur district. 570 km (354 miles) NW of Bangalore. 246,000. Karnataka Tourism, Station Rd, (08352) 250 359. Bijapur Music Festival (Jan), Asar Mahal Urs Festival (Sep).

After the fall of the Bahmanis (see p544), the Adil Shahi sultans emerged as the principal rulers of the Deccan in the 16th and 17th centuries. Their capital, the fortified city of Bijapur, was protected by ramparts with prominent bastions; many of the original cannons are still in place. The Malik-i-Maidan ("Lord of the Plain"), reputedly the largest cannon of the period in India, still guards the western entrance. Within the fort's walls are splendid mosques, palaces and tombs built by a succession of enlightened rulers.

The Citadel

The Citadel, in the heart of the city, is defined by its own fortified walls and surrounded by a wide moat. The south gate, the only one surviving, leads into what was once the palace complex. This ceremonial centre of Bijapur, surrounded by arcades, is known as the **Quadrangle**, and is today occupied by municipal offices. To its northwest stands the **Sat Manzil**, the seven-storeyed pleasure palace from the top of which the whole city could once be seen. Of this, only five storeys now remain. It overlooks an

Medallion at Jami Masjid

The arcaded prayer hall of the Jami Masjid

exquisitely ornamented miniature pavilion called the **Jal Mandir**. A short distance to the north are the **Gagan Mahal**, the audience hall of Ali Adil Shah I, with an arched façade facing an open space, and the **Anand Mahal**, or the "Palace of Joy", where the ladies of the seraglio lived. Other fine structures include the **Mecca Masjid**, a charming little mosque to the east of the Citadel, and **Karimuddin's Mosque** near the south gate, built with temple materials pillaged in 1310 by Alauddin Khilji (see p48).

Outside the Citadel

The walled city, outside the Citadel, is scattered with monuments built by the Adil Shahi sultans. To the east of the Citadel is the double-storeyed **Asar Mahal**, built in 1646 as the hall of justice, and later converted into a sacred reliquary to house two hairs of the Prophet. Chambers on the upper level are decorated with murals depicting floral themes and courtly scenes with European-style figures. A short distance away is the elegant **Mihtar Mahal**, belonging to the period of Ibrahim II (1580–1626) and entered through a triple-storeyed gateway. Balconies projecting over the street are supported on angled struts carved as if they were made of wood. The gateway leads to a small mosque.

The grandly conceived **Jami Masjid**, to the southeast, was begun by Ali Adil Shah I in 1576, but never finished. The marble floor of the capacious prayer hall has been divided into some 2,250 rectangular bays to resemble prayer mats. Even today, the mosque attracts more than 2,000 worshippers during Friday prayers. To the north and west are more tombs and mosques, including the Taj Baoli, a large square tank surrounded by steps.

Ibrahim Rauza

daily. extra charges. This exquisite mausoleum, often described as the finest Islamic building in the Deccan, was built by Ibrahim II for his wife. In fact, he predeceased her and is buried here too. The funerary complex consists of a tomb and a mosque, raised on a plinth in the middle of a formal garden. A huge tank nearby is named after his wife, Taj Sultana. The walls of the tomb, as seen within an arcaded verandah, are embellished with superb calligraphic and geometric designs. The tomb chamber is roofed by a flat vault with curving sides.

Ibrahim Rauza, the beautifully proportioned tomb of Ibrahim II

Bijapur: Gol Gumbad

Bijapur's most celebrated building, the
monumental tomb of Muhammad Adil Shah
(1627–56), second son and successor of
Ibrahim II, is commonly known
as the "Round Dome", or Gol Gumbad.
The slightly bulbous dome, the largest
in the world after St Peter's in Rome,
rises on a base of petals to
form a fitting climax to
the whole composition. Completed in
1656, the tomb stands in the middle
of a formal garden. On the
west side is a small mosque
with five arches flanked
by slender minarets.

**Detail of a
medallion**

VISITORS' CHECKLIST

Mahatma Gandhi Rd. **Tel** (08352)
250 728 ☐ daily. 🎫 free on Fri.
Autos & cycles available.

The dome is nearly 44 m
(133 ft) in diameter. It is
carried on eight over-
lapping arches with
intervening pendentives.
The circular Whispering
Gallery, over which the
dome is raised, has
remarkable acoustics.

**Circular
gallery**

A bulbous dome
on a petalled
base tops the
minaret.

Minaret

The *mihrab* bay is
within a part-octagonal
projection, to the west. The
walls are overhung by richly
carved stone brackets with
tiers of lotus buds.

Tomb of
Muhammad
Adil Shah.

Entrance Arch
*The entrance façade
has a wide, lofty arch
in the centre, pierced
with small windows
on either side.*

DECCANI PAINTING

The Muslim rulers of the Deccan, especially of Golconda *(see pp666–7)* and
Bijapur, during the 14th and 15th centuries, encouraged art and established a
Deccani School of Painting. This was
influenced first by direct contact with
Central Asia and Persia, and later by
the Mughals. At the court of Bijapur,
elements of European Renaissance and
Persian art were assimilated into the
classical Indian tradition, to create a
distinctive Deccani style.

Chand Bibi Playing Polo,
a Deccani painting

The vaulted hall of the Jami Masjid at Gulbarga

Gulbarga ㉕

Gulbarga district. 160 km (99 miles) NE of Bijapur. 🚉 428,000. 🚏 🚌 🛈 Gulbarga Tourist Office, (08472) 240 947. 🗓 Urs (Mar).

This small provincial town contains some of the earliest examples of Islamic architecture in Karnataka. These date to the 14th and 15th centuries, when Gulbarga flourished as the capital of the Bahmani sultans *(see p49)*, the first of the great Muslim kingdoms to dominate the Deccan.

The **Dargah of Gesu Daraz** (d.1422), to the northeast of the present town, is one of South India's holiest Muslim shrines. Khwaja Gesu Daraz, or Bande Nawaz as he was

Devotees at the gateway to the Dargah of Gesu Daraz, Gulbarga

affectionately known, was a Sufi mystic from the Chishti sect *(see p376)*. He fled from North India and sought refuge here at the court of Firuz Shah Bahmani, a pious and enlightened ruler. His simple tomb stands in the middle of a large, sprawling complex comprising a group of lesser tombs, mosques and *madrasas*, and is a major pilgrimage centre. The Dargah of Shah Kamal Mujarrad, another saint who lived in Gulbarga, lies further south.

A complex of seven royal tombs, known as the **Haft Gumbad**, lies to the west of the *dargah*. Firuz Shah Bahmani, who also died in 1422, is buried here in the largest and most elaborate of all the mausoleums. Immediately west of the city are the desolate ruins of the forbidding fort, almost circular and protected by a wide moat. Little of the royal centre remains intact today. Near the entrance gateway is the Bala Hisar, a solid keep dating from the 17th century, when the Adil Shahis *(see pp542–3)* occupied the city. The most interesting structure, however, is the large **Jami Masjid** nearby. Built in 1367, to commemorate Gulbarga's status as the capital, this is one of the earliest mosques in South India, and the only one without an open courtyard. To its

rear is the 14th-century Bazaar Street, lined with small chambers now converted into dwellings. This leads to a series of gateways shielded by walls that protrude outwards from the fort walls. To the west of the fort are the derelict tombs of the early Bahmani sultans.

Another 14th-century monument is the **Shah Bazaar Mosque**, to the north of the fort. Its domed entrance chamber leads into a courtyard with a prayer hall beyond. A street from here proceeds westwards to an arcaded portal flanked by lofty minarets. Behind this portal lies the Dargah of Sheikh Sirajuddin Junaydi, a simple tomb with arcaded recesses and a flattish dome.

Environs
The picturesque ruins of **Firuzabad**, the palace city founded in 1400 by Firuz Shah Bahmani on the east bank of the Bhima river, are located 28 km (17 miles) south of Gulbarga. The massive stone walls with quadrangular bastions and arched gateways define an approximately square zone, almost 1,000 m (3,281 ft) wide. The best-preserved structures are the Jami Masjid and a two-storeyed audience hall. Among the remains are the royal baths *(hamams)*, with pyramidal vaults and fluted domes, said to be the oldest in the Deccan.

Bidar ㉖

Bidar district. 120 km (75 miles) NE of Gulbarga. 🚌 Autos & cycles available.

Bidar became the Bahmani capital in 1424, when Firuz Shah's brother and successor, Ahmad Shah, moved his court here. With the collapse of the Bahmani dynasty at the end of the 15th century, control of the region passed into the hands of the Baridis.

Bidar's **Fort**, built in 1428 by Ahmed Shah Bahmani, occupies a promontory that is defended by double rings of walls and a moat partly carved out of the bedrock. A trio of arched gates, one with polychrome tilework, another with

The walled road leading to the entrance gateway of Bidar's fort

a prominent dome, leads into what was once the royal enclave. To the left is the Rangin Mahal, an exquisite palace built by Ali Shah Barid in the 16th century. The hall, with its original wooden columns displaying ornate brackets and beams, and the rear chamber adorned with magnificent tile mosaics and inlaid mother-of-pearl decoration, are especially striking. Nearby is the unusual Solah Khamba Mosque, with massive circular columns, built by the Tughluqs *(see p48)* in 1327. In front is the Lal Bagh, a walled garden with a central lobe-fringed pool. A short distance to the south is the ruined Diwan-i-Am, the Public Audience Hall, and the Takht Mahal, a monumental portal with traces of hexagonal tiles decorated with tiger and sun emblems in the spandrels.

The old walled town sprawls beneath the ramparts of the fort. On one side of the main north-south street is the **Takhti-i-Kirmani**, a 15th-century gateway embellished with bands of foliate and arabesque designs. Further south is the magnificent late 15th-century **Madrasa of Mahmud Gawan**, named after the erudite prime minister who was the virtual ruler of the Bahmani kingdom. This used to be a famous theological college, and at one time boasted a huge library, well-stocked with scholarly

Tile mosaic at Bidar's madrasa

manuscripts. A superb example of Central Asian-style architecture, it has four arched portals that stand against a background of domes facing a central court. A pair of minarets flanks its façade. Tile mosaics on the exterior still survive, including a finely worked calligraphic band in rich blue and white. Still further south, the **Chaubara** marks the intersection of the two principal streets running through Bidar.

The **Mausolea of the Baridi rulers** lie west of Bidar. The largest is the Tomb of Ali Shah Barid (1577). This lofty, domed chamber, open on four sides, stands in the middle of a symmetrical four-square garden. Blank panels above the arches once contained tile mosaic, examples of which are preserved inside. The black polished basalt sarcophagus is still *in situ*.

Bidar is also known for a special type of encrusted metalware, often mistaken for damascening, known as *bidri (see p665)*. Introduced in the mid-17th century by artisans from Iran, the craft flourished under court patronage. The style, characterized by intricate floral and geometric designs, inlaid in gold, silver or brass onto a matt black surface, was used to embellish various objects, including platters, boxes, *huqqa* bases and trays. Today, the finest

pieces are housed in museums, and only a handful of artisan families still practise this craft in the town of its origin.

Environs
The Bahmani necropolis stands in the open countryside near **Ashtur**, a small village 3 km (2 miles) northeast of Bidar. The oldest and grandest of the tombs is the early 15th-century Tomb of Ahmad Shah. Splendid murals embellish the interior walls as well as the huge dome. The adjacent tomb of Alauddin Ahmad II, his successor, has coloured tile mosaics. Just outside is the Chaukhandi, the modest tomb of the saint Khalil Allah (d.1460), which has superb calligraphic panels over the doorways.

Façade of the Madrasa of Mahmud Gawan in Bidar

SOUTH INDIA

Introducing South India

South of the Vindhya range, India's Dravidian heartland has all that a visitor could look for. Dramatic coastlines, both on the Arabian Sea and the Bay of Bengal, meet at Kanniyakumari on the Indian Ocean. Isolated beaches, dense forests and game reserves are among its natural wonders. Tamil Nadu has some of India's most magnificent ancient temples, still active centres of religious practice. A different culture prevails in Pondicherry, which retains a strong French influence. Kerala is rich in beautiful scenery as well as in cultural heritage, while Andhra Pradesh has some of the region's most fascinating historic sites.

Fisherman at a sluice gate on the Kaveri river

A class in progress in a traditional Vedic school, Tamil Nadu

↑ Panaji

Bangalore

Hogenakkal Falls

PUTTAPAR

LEPAKSHI

KANNUR

KOZHIKODE

THRISSUR

Arabian Sea

KOCHI

NH49 MUNNAR

ALAPPUZHA

COIMBATORE

KODAIKANAL

SALI

MADUR

TIRUNELVELI

THIRUVANANTHAPURAM

KANNIYAKUMA Indian Ocean

LAKSHADWEEP ISLANDS

AGATTI

KAVARATTI

0 km   100

0 miles   100

◁ The spectacular Hogenakkal Falls on the Kaveri river *(see p600)*

Bhopal

avari

0 km   100

0 miles   100

Bhubaneswar

RANGAL ● *PALAMPET*

● *BHADRACHALAM*

DERABAD NH9

VISAKHAPATNAM ●

NH5

ARJUNA *NDA*

● *RAJAHMUNDRY*

● *VIJAYAWADA*

● *MACHILIPATNAM*

Krishna

Bay of Bengal

NH5

ANDHRA PRADESH

CHENNAI

ANDAMAN ISLANDS

KERALA   TAMIL NADU

LAKSHADWEEP

● *TIRUMALA*

TIRUPATI

LLORE

● *CHENNAI*

● *MAMALLAPURAM*

NGEE

● *PONDICHERRY*

● *CHIDAMBARAM*

● *THANJAVUR*

● *RAMESHVARAM*

ANDAMAN ISLANDS

● *PORT BLAIR*

0 km   200

0 miles   200

SEE ALSO

- *Where to Stay* pp712–17
- *Where to Eat* pp739–43

KEY

▨▨▨	National highway
▬▬▬	Major road
═══	River
– –	State border

GETTING AROUND

The three state capitals, Chennai, Thiruvanantha-puram and Hyderabad are serviced by domestic and international airlines. The extensive road and railway network connects the smaller towns. For a special rail journey, take the Blue Mountain Train from Coimbatore to Ooty *(see pp604–605)*. There are regular flights from Kolkata and Chennai to the Andaman Islands, and from Kochi (Kerala) to Agatti (Lakshadweep). Cruises to Lakshadweep are available from Kochi, and to the Andamans from Chennai, Kolkata and Visakhapatnam.

A PORTRAIT OF SOUTH INDIA

*T*he term "South India", though it conveys a sense of geographical unity, also encompasses a multitude of differences. While the three states – Tamil Nadu, Kerala and Andhra Pradesh – share, to some extent, an ancient heritage, they speak different languages, and each has its distinct artistic, cultural and political tradition.

A popular view holds that while the history of North India is one of wars and invasions, the south remained cocooned in peaceful stagnation. In actual fact, the three states witnessed bloody conflicts between Jainism and Buddhism on the one hand, and Brahminical Hinduism on the other. They saw the rise and fall of powerful kingdoms, who fought many wars to establish their dominance. In the beginning of the colonial period, South India was also a battleground between the Europeans and the regional kingdoms. All these upheavals have left their mark on the region.

Tamil Nadu, the heartland of Dravidian India has, for over three decades, been ruled by two regional

Wooden effigy, Thiruvananthapuram

parties. Though arch-rivals, they share a common platform, based on a strong advocacy of Tamil language and culture. Tamil is the oldest surviving Dravidian language, with a literature that goes back to AD 300. This period, known as the Sangam era, derives its name from the Tamil Sangams, gatherings of poets and writers, which produced countless poems, remarkably secular in nature, of which over 2,000 have survived. Another enduring expression of Tamil culture is visible in Tamil Nadu's Hindu temples – it has no less than 30,000 of them.

A more modern face of Tamil Nadu can be seen in the state capital, Chennai, a vibrant commercial and

A 16th-century Catholic church, overlooking a little fishing village at Kanniyakumari

A portrait of film star-turned-politician Jayalalitha

exceptional among Indian states – the country's highest literacy rate (the language spoken here is Malayalam), a low population growth rate, the lowest infant mortality rate, and a near-perfect record in communal harmony. Culturally, Kerala boasts spectacular dance forms such as Kathakali *(see p657)*, and the martial *kalaripayattu (see p626)*. Today, its renowned Ayurvedic health resorts *(see p629)* are also a major draw for international travellers.

Telugu-speaking Andhra Pradesh is South India's largest state, with its capital, Hyderabad, located in the heart of the Deccan Plateau. This city was once the seat of the powerful Nizams *(see p660)* whose wealth was legendary. Their legacy has given Hyderabad a unique flavour, rich in manifestations of an Islamic culture – in its architecture and cuisine, and in the widespread use of Urdu.

political centre that still retains its traditional values. Here, classical Carnatic music concerts draw as large and enthusiastic crowds as raucous political rallies. Many coastal areas in Tamil Nadu were devastated by the December 2004 tsunami, which took a toll of over 10,000 lives. Kerala and Andhra Pradesh were also affected, though to a much lesser extent.

A truck overloaded with hay

Andhra Pradesh shares with Tamil Nadu a penchant for film stars-turned-politicians. For many years it was ruled by Telugu cinema's most loved actor, NT Rama Rao, who specialized in playing mythological heroes. His son-in-law, Chandrababu Naidu, as chief minister, chose a more down-to-earth way of winning popular support, with his schemes to modernize the state. As a result, Hyderabad now vies with Bangalore for the title of India's information technology capital.

In Kerala, separated from Tamil Nadu by the magnificent forested hills of the Western Ghats, the main attraction is not temples (though it has those too), but natural beauty. It is easy to understand why this narrow strip of land between the Arabian Sea and the Western Ghats, with its verdant landscape of palm trees, paddy fields and coffee plantations, criss-crossed by enchanting waterways, has been dubbed "God's own country".

Modern-day Kerala, with a strong leftist political tradition, boasts of development indices that are

Tamil Brahmin boys performing a religious ritual

Temple Towns

Religious symbol

Srirangam *(see p601)* is typical of many towns in South India, especially in Tamil Nadu, that are dominated by sanctuaries dedicated to Hindu deities who protect the city and its population. Conceived as a vast religious complex, the town is enclosed by high fortress-like walls, and entered through towering gateways *(gopuras)*. The temple itself consists of multiple walled enclosures, often in concentric arrangements, surrounded by streets that echo the temple's layout. Though Srirangam is the largest and most perfect in layout, other such towns include Chidambaram *(see p590)* and Madurai *(see pp608–11)*.

Puja items being sold outside the temple enclosure

Kalyana Mandapas *(marriage balls) have raised platforms in the middle. Portable images of the deities are placed here during the ritual marriage ceremonies and festivals that are conducted annually, in the presence of thousands of devotees.*

Kitchens produce food for priests and thousands of pilgrims during festivals that take place in the complex. Nearby are stores and granaries.

Subsidiary shrines *of other deities, such as Garuda and Hanuman in Vishnu temples, and Ganesha, Nandi and Subrahmanya or Murugan in Shiva temples, are also venerated within the complex.*

Banners are hoisted on slender, brass-clad wooden columns in the middle of the enclosure. Here, too, are small altars.

The outer enclosures *of temple complexes are packed with houses to accommodate the priestly community, which presides over the religious life of temple towns.*

The main sanctum, *where the principal deity is enshrined, forms the nucleus of the whole complex. This is the* garbhagriha, *or womb chamber. The main doorway into the sanctuary is opened only during prayer time, to allow worshippers to make offerings to the deity within.*

Wooden chariots covered with carved panels are parked outside the main gates. During festivals they are pulled by devotees through the streets of the town.

Tanks and wells *provide water for ritual bathing, cooking and general washing. Temple tanks have steps on four sides for bathers to descend to the water. Small pavilions in the middle are used for special festivals.*

The inner enclosures, constituting the most sacred precincts, are filled with subsidiary shrines, pillared halls, flag columns, altars, kitchens, rest houses, tanks and wells.

Axial *mandapas* **and corridors** direct worshippers from the outer *gopuras* towards the main sanctuary. Sculptures on columns embellish these passageways. Bronze images are also displayed here.

Mandapas *are columned halls which sometimes take on vast proportions, especially the so-called thousand-pillared halls. These can accommodate large numbers of visitors who come to listen to sermons or to enjoy performances of classical music and dance.*

Gopuras, *or ceremonial gateways, with soaring, pyramidal towers, are set into four sides of each of the concentric sets of walls that define the sacred complex. Their hollow brick towers are covered with brightly painted plaster sculptures. Barrel-vaulted roofs at the tops of the towers are crowned by gilded pot finials, visible from all over the town.*

The Flavours of South India

Rice preparations dominate South Indian cuisine, of which the best known are *dosas* (rice pancakes served with spiced potatoes), *idli* (steamed rice dumplings), *vada* (deep-fried lentil doughnuts) and *uttapam* (a spicy pancake). All are eaten with *sambhar* (lentil broth) and chutneys made with coconut, garlic and chillies. These are "tiffin" or breakfast foods, and specialist restaurants can be found all over India and abroad. Despite the commonalities, each state's cuisine has its own flavour, dictated by regional tastes and locally grown ingredients, as is evident in Hyderabad's sophisticated Muslim cuisine.

Sprig of curry leaves

Fresh green coconuts, providing a refreshing drink on a hot day

KERALA

Kerala, the land of spices, particularly pepper, inspired the European race for an empire in the East. An abundance of spices, such as cloves, mace, cardamoms and cinnamon, have infused the cuisine with a range of exotic aromas. Added to this are coconuts, used in the preparation of almost all dishes.

The different communities have distinctive cuisines. The Hindus specialize in vegetarian food, while the Muslims and Christians excel in mutton and poultry dishes. Foreign influences are apparent and the classic *moilee*, a term used for fish or vegetable curries, is a corruption of the Portuguese *molho* or sauce.

The staple food is rice and the best-known dish is the *appam,* a steamed rice pancake. A typical middle-class meal comprises boiled rice accompanied by pulses, a vegetable curry, a dry vegetable, pickles, poppadams, and a meat or fish dish for non-vegetarians. The *sadya,* a festive meal eaten at Onam, is always served on a banana leaf.

TAMIL NADU

Six tastes – sweet, sour, salty, bitter, peppery and astringent – define Tamilian food. A traditional meal includes

Spiced potatoes   Vada   Rava dosa   Uttapam   Plain dosa

Chilli chutney   Coconut chutney   Sambhar   Idli

Selection of South Indian rice preparations and other accompaniments

LOCAL DISHES AND SPECIALITIES

The common culinary heritage leans heavily on rice, lentils, coconut and spices. Vegetable preparations are diverse and range from the steamed or stir-fried *poriyal*, which is tempered with spices and curry leaves, to *avial* (mixed vegetables in thick coconut sauce) and *mirchi ka salan* (a curry with whole green chillies). Interestingly, the word curry is a derivative of *kari*, a spicy dish from Kerala and Tamil Nadu, while *rasam*, integral to a meal as an appetizer and digestive, was the base of the Anglo-Indian mulligatawny soup. Chicken, lamb and fish also feature on the menu, particularly the seafood curries from Kerala and Andhra Pradesh and the delicious *biryanis* and wide range of *kebabs* from Hyderabad.

Coconuts

Appams and stew, *a popular dish, consists of fermented rice dumplings served with a vegetable or chicken stew.*

Chinese fishing nets, an iconic sight in Fort Cochin, Kerala

all six to balance nutrition, the appetite and digestion. The special flavour of the food comes from a combination of curry leaves, ginger, coconut, garlic, coriander, asafetida, tamarind, pepper, chillies, cloves, cumin, cinnamon and cardamom.

Meals consist of cooked rice served with an array of vegetable dishes, *sambhar*, *rasam* (pepper water) and chutneys. Crisp poppadams or *appalam* (rice wafer) complete a meal. Desserts include the warm milky rice *payasam* or sweet *pongal*, also made from rice.

Non-Brahmin communities, such as the Chettiars from Chettinad, are meat eaters. Their hot and spicy cuisine has several interesting fish, mutton and chicken dishes, of which pepper chicken is considered the best.

ANDHRA PRADESH

The liberal use of red chilli and tamarind make Andhra food one of the country's spiciest. Rice and vegetables form the basis of a meal. Some common dishes

View of a street vegetable market in rural Tamil Nadu

include *pulihora* (a vegetable *pulao*), *pessarattu*, (a variation of the *dosa*), *dhapalam* (a vegetable curry) and *pachidi* (a curd-based relish).

In contrast is the cuisine of Hyderabad with its distinct Muslim influences. Savoury mutton or chicken *biryanis* are accompanied by *kebabs*, lamb, chicken or vegetable curries *(salans)*, vegetables and breads. Some specialities include *pathar gosh* (lamb cooked on a stone), *haleem* (a pounded wheat and lamb dish eaten during the fasting months of Ramzan or Ramadan) and desserts such as *shahi tukra* and *kubani ka meetha*, made with dried apricots and cream.

ON THE MENU

Aadu olathiayathu Fried cubes of lamb garnished with coconut and curry leaves.

Meen varuval *Masala* fried fish from Chettinad, served with sliced onions and lime.

Sambhar A spicy lentil broth with mixed vegetables, a must for all meals.

Tahari A rice and mincemeat *pulao*, a Hyderabad special.

Tamatar pappu A spicy tomato and lentil curry.

Thengai saadham Coconut rice, seasoned with red chillies and curry leaves.

Upma A savoury semolina breakfast dish.

Bagharey baingan, *whole aubergines stuffed with spices, are Hyderabad's most famous vegetarian dish.*

Meen moilee, *a speciality of the Christian community of Kerala, is a lightly spiced coconut fish curry.*

Pasayam *is a creamy dessert made from rice and milk and garnished with cashew nuts and raisins.*

CHENNAI

*C*hennai, formerly known as Madras, is the state capital of
Tamil Nadu and the gateway to the rich and varied culture of
the South Indian peninsula. Originally a cluster of fishing
hamlets along the Coromandel Coast, the city developed its cohesive
shape under the British. Today, it is South India's commercial and
cultural capital, and the fourth largest metropolis in India.

A modern capital, with the appearance of a gracious garden city, Chennai was once a group of villages set amidst palm-fringed paddy fields, until two English East India Company merchants, Francis Day and Andrew Cogan, established a factory-cum-trading post here. Completed on St George's Day, 23 April 1640, this fortified settlement came to be known as Fort St George. Outside its walls was George Town, the so-called "native town", whose crowded lanes, each devoted to a particular trade, serviced the British colonists. Colonial rule linked the various villages, including the settlement founded in the 16th century by the Portuguese at San Thomé, the sacred site associated with St Thomas the Apostle. Several centuries before the Europeans arrived, the great 7th-century Pallava port was at Mylapore; its Kapalesvara Temple, along with the Parthasarathi Temple at Triplicane, bear testimony to the city's antiquity.

Colonial rule marked the beginning of the city's growth as a major commercial centre. Today, most of the large business houses have their offices in George Town, while Fort St George is the power centre of the Tamil Nadu state government. Extending across 172 sq km (66 sq miles), Chennai today is a dynamic mix of the old and the new, its stately colonial structures juxtaposed with modern high-rises. Its rich cultural heritage of Tamil literature, music and dance is perpetuated in universities and performing arts centres. It is also a highly political city, as can be seen from the many grandiose memorials to politicians that line Marina Beach.

A huge hoarding depicting Jayalalitha, a Tamil Nadu political leader, looming above Marina promenade

◁ **Flower seller with fragrant garlands near the Kapalesvara Temple, Mylapore**

Exploring Chennai

A conglomeration of several overgrown villages, Chennai has no single centre, but can be divided into a numerous urban districts, connected by four main roads. George Town is to the northeast of Periyar EVR High Road (Poonamallee High Road), while Egmore, Triplicane and Mylapore are to the south. The city's main thoroughfare, Anna Salai (Mount Road), links Fort St George with Mount St Thomas, to the south. Chennai's other main roads, Rajaji Salai (North Beach Road) and Kamarajar Salai (South Beach Road), run along the seafront, along the popular Marina promenade towards Kalakshetra.

LOCATOR MAP

An early morning scene at a flower shop at Parry's Corner

SIGHTS AT A GLANCE

Historic Buildings, Areas & Neighbourhoods
Adyar ⑩
Anna Salai ⑥
Egmore ④
Fort St George ①
George Town ②
Triplicane ⑧

Churches & Holy Places
Little Mount & Mount of
St Thomas ⑭
Mylapore & San Thomé ⑨
St Andrew's Kirk pp562–3 ③

Walk
A Walk along the Marina
pp568–9 ⑦

Museums
The Pantheon Complex ⑤

Parks & Gardens
Guindy National Park ⑬

Entertainment
Kalakshetra ⑪
MGR Film City ⑫

For additional map symbols *see back flap*

GETTING AROUND
Public buses and private cars or taxis are the most convenient means of getting around within the city. The local (above-ground) trains of Chennai's Mass Rapid Transit System (MRTS) and the suburban railway together cover large sections of the city and its outskirts. Private tour operators have organized coach tours to most sites of interest.

SEE ALSO

• **Where to Stay** pp712–13

• **Where to Eat** pp739–40

Traffic on Anna Salai, Chennai's main thoroughfare

KEY

✈	International airport
✈	Domestic airport
🚉	Railway station
🚌	Bus station
Ⓜ	MRTS station
ℹ	Tourist information
✚	Hospital
🔲	Police station
卍	Temple
C	Mosque
🔲	Gurdwara
✝	Church
⊠	Post office
=	National highway
—	Major road

GREATER CHENNAI

The Secretariat at Fort St George, the seat of Tamil Nadu's government

Fort St George ❶

Bounded by Sir Muthuswamy Iyer Rd, Flag Staff Rd & Kamarajar Salai (South Beach Rd). **Fort Museum Tel** *(044) 2538 4510.* ⬜ *Sat–Thu.* 🌑 *public hols.* 📷

Britain's first bastion in India, the nucleus from which an empire grew, was established in a banana grove owned by a farmer called Madrasan. The official grant for the land, however, was given by Venkatadri Nayak, the deputy of the Raja of Chandragiri *(see p680)*. The first factory within the fortified enclosure was completed on St George's Day, 23 April 1640, and named Fort St George. This was the East India Company's principal settlement until 1774, when Calcutta, now Kolkata, was declared the seat of the government.

The sloping ramparts, with battlements for gun emplacement that can still be seen today, were designed and constructed by Bartholomew Robins in 1750, after the original walls were destroyed by the French army in 1749. These ramparts form an irregular pentagon, further reinforced by a ring of earthen walls that slope down to a moat surrounding the entire complex. The drawbridges that once led to the Fort's five main gates have now been replaced by roads.

The first building to be seen on entering the Fort through the Sea Gate is the Neo-Classical **Secretariat**, which is today the seat of the government of Tamil Nadu. Behind it lie the **Legislative Council Chambers**. With their handsome classical lines and façades embellished with gleaming black pillars, these impressive buildings, built between 1694 and 1732, are said to be among the oldest surviving British constructions in India. The 45-m (148-ft) tall flagstaff was erected by Governor Elihu Yale in 1687 to hoist the Union Jack for the first time in India. Today, the Indian tricolour flies in its stead. Yale began his career as a clerk with the East India Company and later founded Yale University in the USA, with his considerable fortune.

Standing to the south of the Legislature building is **St Mary's Church**, the oldest Anglican church in Asia. It was built between 1678 and 1680 by Streynsham Master, then the governor of Madras. Memorials, paintings, antique Bibles (including one printed in 1660) and silver are displayed in the church, and speak of its vibrant history. Both Elihu Yale and Robert Clive were married in this church, and the three daughters of Job Charnock *(see p267)* were baptized here before the family moved to Bengal. Arthur Wellesley, who later became the Duke of Wellington and triumphed at Waterloo, and Robert Clive, both lived in Fort St George. Their residences, Wellesley House and Clive House, still stand, albeit in a somewhat dilapidated condition, across from the church.

To the north is the **Parade Ground**, formerly Cornwallis Square, which was laid out in 1715. Magnificent parades and rallies were held here. To its east are ministerial offices, and barracks for regiments. Near the southeast corner of

The altar in St Mary's Church with a painting of the Last Supper

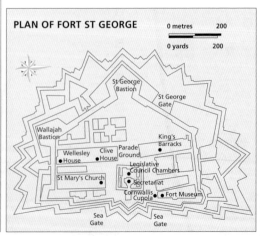

PLAN OF FORT ST GEORGE

| 0 metres | 200 |
| 0 yards | 200 |

St George Bastion
St George Gate
Wallajah Bastion
King's Barracks
Wellesley House
Clive House
Parade Ground
Legislative Council Chambers
St Mary's Church
Secretariat
Cornwallis Cupola
Fort Museum
Sea Gate
Sea Gate

the Parade Ground is the **Fort Museum**, built in the 1780s. A treasure trove of colonial memorabilia, the museum is housed in what was built to be the Public Exchange. It has paintings of British royalty, 18th-century weaponry, emblems and other relics from the British era. Among its prized possessions are a scale model of the Fort and a painting of King George III and Queen Charlotte. There are lithographs on the second and third floors that provide fascinating perspectives of old Madras and other parts of South India.

Near the museum's southern end, and overlooking its cannon, is the **Cornwallis Cupola**, which originally stood in the Parade Ground. It is the largest one built to house the statue of the governor-general, Lord Cornwallis, sculpted in 1800. It shows him accepting the two young sons of Tipu Sultan (see p517) as hostages.

George Town ❷

Bounded by Rajaji Salai (North Beach Rd) & NSC Bose Rd.

In the 1640s, weavers and dyers from Andhra Pradesh were settled in this enclave to manufacture cloth for the East India Company's textile trade. The British referred to the settlement as "Black Town",

The General Post Office, George Town

while its inhabitants called it Chennapatnam, from where Chennai gets it name. After the entire area was rebuilt 100 years later, it was renamed George Town. During this period, most of the city's commercial activity was concentrated within this 5-sq km (2-sq mile) area. It still remains a busy hive of activity with public institutions in the south, trade and commercial premises in the centre, and residential quarters in the north.

The first feature of interest is the 38-m (125-ft) high

Fruit vendors on the pavements of George Town

Lighthouse on Rajaji Salai, whose beacon was visible 25 km (16 miles) out at sea. The adjacent red-brick **High Court**, designed by Chisholm in the Indo-Saracenic style, with stained glass and carved furniture, was opened in 1892, while the nearby **General Post Office** with its archways and square towers, is another fine Indo-Saracenic building. **Parry's Corner**, at the junction of NSC Bose Road and Rajaji Salai, is named after Parry and Company. Founded by Thomas Parry in 1790, it is the oldest British mercantile company still operating in Chennai. **Dare House**, the present headquarters of this 200-year-old company, now stands at the site.

The area's longest street, **Mint Street**, gets its name from the authorized mint that was set up here in 1841 to produce gold coins for the British as well as for various local rulers. The mint buildings are now part of the government printing press. The 17th-century houses lining George Town were once the residences and business centres of Indian as well as Portuguese, Armenian and other foreign traders. **Armenian Street** is named after the many Armenians who lived here, while **Coral Merchant Street** housed a small Jewish community that traded in corals. Today, each street in George Town is dominated by a particular trade. Anderson Street specializes in paper, grain merchants operate from Audiappa Naicken Street, while textile wholesalers have their warehouses on Govindappa Naicken Street and Godown Street. Some streets, such as Kasi Chetty Street and Narayanamudali Street, are lined with shops selling fancy goods and imported bric-a-brac.

ROBERT CLIVE (1725–74)

A portrait of Robert Clive by Nathaniel Dance (1773)

One of the most flamboyant personalities in the history of British India, Robert Clive was only 19 when he began his career as a clerk for the East India Company at Fort St George. Soon tiring of paperwork, he became a soldier and fought many successful battles (see p52), including the Carnatic Wars, which established the Company's rule in South India. Clive was given the stewardship of Fort St George and later become Governor of Bengal. The wealth he amassed in India led to his trial, in England, on charges of corruption. Clive committed suicide in 1774.

St Andrew's Kirk ❸

A memorial plaque

A magnificent example of Neo-Classical architecture, St Andrew's Kirk was consecrated in 1821. Inspired by St Martin-in-the-Fields in London, it was designed and executed by Major Thomas de Havilland and Colonel James Caldwell of the Madras Engineers, at a cost of £20,000. The body of the church is a circle, with rectangular compartments to the east and west. The circular part, 24.5 m (80 ft) in diameter, is crowned by a shallow masonry dome coloured a deep blue. This is painted with golden stars and supported by 16 fluted pillars with Corinthian capitals.

A view of St Andrew's Kirk with its towering steeple

★ Dome
An architectural marvel, the dome has a framework of brick supported by an annular arch and is filled in by pottery cones. Its blue interior is formed by crushed sea shells mixed with lapis lazuli.

Stained glass
The stained-glass windows above the altar, in warm, rich colours, are among the glories of the church.

Pews
Superb mahogany pews and a pulpit furnish the interior. From 1839, the pews were let out to prominent citizens; the brass fittings that once held their name cards can still be seen.

Sixteen fluted Corinthian columns support the dome, lending beauty and balance to the design.

The steeple is 50 m (164 ft) high, 4 m (13 ft) taller than its inspiration, St Martin-in-the-Fields in London. On top of the slim pyramidal spire is a bronze weathercock.

VISITORS' CHECKLIST

Egmore. **Tel** (044) 2561 2608.
☐ daily. ✝ 9am & 6pm Sun.
St Andrew's Day (Nov).

THE WELLS OF ST ANDREW'S KIRK

Because of sandy soil and a site prone to flooding during the monsoon, the church's foundations are actually a series of wells sunk to depths ranging from 4 m to 15 m (13 ft to 49 ft) below ground level. This example of engineering ingenuity is based on a structural practice followed by most indigenous buildings in the area. The wells are constructed either of specially made curved bricks, or pottery cylinders. These are placed so as to ensure maximum compaction of the soil, allowing the water to rise within them and thus protecting the main structure. The 150 wells were dug by a group of itinerant well-sinkers, the Mumvutties.

0 metres   10
0 yards   10

★ Pipe Organ
Dominating the altar is the handsome pipe organ in dull green and burnished gold. Installed in 1883, this instrument was built in Yorkshire, England.

STAR FEATURES

★ Dome

★ Pipe Organ

Entrance

A double colonnade of 12 polished Ionic columns is surmounted by a pediment.

A view of Egmore Railway Station, one of the city's major landmarks

Egmore ❹

Bounded by Periyar EVR High Rd & Pantheon Rd. ▮ *Egmore Railway Station, (044) 2819 4579.*

The entire area south of Periyar EVR High Road (earlier known as Poonamallee High Road) and the curve of the Cooum river is known as Egmore. This was originally a small village that the East India Company acquired in the late 17th century, as it began to expand its territories. Egmore was also one of the earliest residential localities, where wealthy Company merchants built palatial homes surrounded by luxuriant gardens – the so-called "garden houses" that were extremely popular in colonial Chennai.

The **Government College of Arts and Crafts**, founded in 1850, stands on EVK Sampath Salai. This striking Gothic building and its art gallery were built by Robert Fellowes Chisholm (*see p569*), who was also appointed its superintendent (principal) in 1877. Its first Indian principal, Debi Prasad Roy Chowdhary, was a renowned painter and sculptor in the 1950s. The artists' village at Cholamandal (*see p578*) was established by his successor, Dr KCS Panicker. Today the prestigious Government College is one of India's foremost art schools. Its gallery has regular exhibitions of contemporary painting and sculpture by artists and students.

To its west is the **Egmore Railway Station**, another of Chisholm's architectural gems. This is a handsome building, constructed in Indo-Saracenic style, with unconventional flattish domes and pointed arches. The station, operational since the early 20th century, connects Chennai with the rest of Tamil Nadu and the south.

Today Egmore is the up-market commercial heart of Chennai, a concrete jungle of offices, department stores, boutiques and hotels. On Pantheon Road are the largest showrooms of Co-Optex (*see p574*), a unit of the Tamil Nadu Handloom Textiles Cooperative, which sells handwoven silk and cotton saris and fabrics from the state.

Standing Buddhas from Amravati

The Pantheon Complex ❺

Pantheon Rd. ***Tel** (044) 2819 3778.* ◯ *Sat–Thu.* ◯ *public hols.* 🖼 📷
Connemara Public Library ***Tel** (044) 2819 1842.* ◯ *daily.*

This complex of cultural institutions derives its name from The Pantheon, where the Public Assembly Rooms were housed in the 18th century. At the time, its spacious tree-lined grounds were the venue for all public entertainment in the city.

The Indo-Saracenic **Government Museum**, with its faded red walls and labyrinth of staircases and

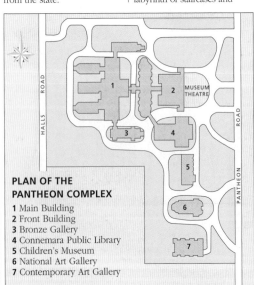

PLAN OF THE PANTHEON COMPLEX

1 Main Building
2 Front Building
3 Bronze Gallery
4 Connemara Public Library
5 Children's Museum
6 National Art Gallery
7 Contemporary Art Gallery

The façade of the National Art Gallery, built in Neo-Mughal style

interconnecting galleries, is spread over five sections of a large complex, each with a specific collection of objects. The 30,000-odd exhibits range from rocks and fossils to books and sculptures.

The Archaeological Section, in the main building, is noted for its exceptional collection of South Indian antiquities. The exhibits include stone and metal sculpture, woodcarvings and manuscripts. Its rare collection of Buddhist antiquities numbers over 1,500 pieces. A major section comprises artifacts from Amravati *(see p675)*, that were brought here in the early 1800s by an intrepid Englishman, Colonel Colin Mackenzie. On display are sculptural reliefs, panels and free-standing statues. Objects include a 2nd-century votive slab with a rendering of a stupa, and numerous stone panels with episodes from the Buddha's life depicted in low relief.

The Numismatics Section has a large collection of coins, particularly South Indian and Mughal coins. There are also some gold Gupta coins with Sanskrit inscriptions.

The Government Museum was one of the earliest institutions in India where ethnology and prehistoric archaeology were represented as museum subjects. The Anthropology Section, in the front building, has a good collection of prehistoric antiquities, including

Parvati, 9th century, Chola period

cooking utensils and hunting tools, among them the first palaeolith in India, discovered in 1863 by Bruce Foote. The Zoological Section, in the main building, is one of the largest sections of the Museum. Although its scope is limited to South Indian fauna, a few non-indigenous animals and birds, such as the macaw, mandarin duck, and golden pheasant, have been added to enrich the collection. There is also an 18.5-m (60-ft) long whale skeleton on display. The adjoining 19th-century Museum Theatre, a semi-circular structure also built in Indo-Saracenic style, was initially used as a lecture hall. It is now a venue for public performances.

Some of the finest examples of South Indian bronze casting are on display in the **Bronze Gallery**. Its superb collection of almost 700 bronzes, specifically from the Pallava and Chola periods (between the 9th and 13th centuries) have been retrieved from temples and sites in the region. There are many impressive sculptures of the Nataraja – the depiction of Shiva performing his cosmic dance of creation *(see p566)*. Another outstanding piece

is an 11th-century Chola Ardhanarisvara, a composite figure where Shiva and his consort Parvati are joined together to form a holistic entity. Bronzes of other gods and goddesses in the Hindu pantheon, include Rama, Sita and Ganesha. The panorama of images also includes various Buddhist bronzes from Amravati, a Chola Tara and Maitreya Avalokitesvara, and 11th century images of various Jain *tirthankaras.*

Opposite is the imposing **Connemara Public Library**, inaugurated in 1896. This structure, with its profuse stucco decoration, woodwork and stained-glass windows, was named after a dissolute brother of the viceroy, Lord Mayo. It is one of India's four national libraries and contains every book published in the country. Its oldest and most prized possession is a Bible, dated 1608.

The **National Art Gallery**, the former Victoria Memorial Hall and Technical Institute, is perhaps the finest building in the complex. Designed by Henry Irwin, one of the city's most celebrated architects, it was constructed in 1909 in Neo-Mughal style with a pink sandstone finish. Its immense door echoes the monumental gateways of Fatehpur Sikri *(see pp180–83)*. On display are more Chola bronzes, including two fine images of Rama and Sita, and a superb 11th-century Nataraja. Nearby, the **Contemporary Art Gallery** has a collection of contemporary Indian art, with works by renowned South Indian artists, among them Raja Ravi Varma *(see p626).*

A 2nd-century stupa panel from Amravati

Shiva, the Cosmic Dancer

Bronze sculptures depicting gods and goddesses, are the glory of South Indian art. Strict iconographic guidelines determine the proportions of each image and the symbolic meaning of every stance, hand gesture, weapon, and adornment. Master sculptors working within these rules were able, nevertheless,

A slender bronze image of Parvati

to create images of extraordinary individuality, power and grace. Among the most remarkable bronze sculptures are those of Shiva as Nataraja, the Cosmic Dancer, and his wife Parvati. Richly symbolic in their iconography, they were made during the Chola period, from the 9th to the 13th centuries.

NATARAJA

The Nataraja figure of Shiva as the Cosmic Dancer symbolizes nature's cycle of evolution and transmutation, and displays the Chola artists' mastery of form and expression.

A tiny crescent moon, a symbol of the passage of time, balances in his hair.

The fire in the left hand symbolizes destruction.

Goddess Ganga is shown among Shiva's flying locks since it was Shiva who eased her descent to earth *(see p163).*

The drum in his right hand symbolizes the rhythm of creation.

An open palm grants freedom from fear.

The left palm pointing to the foot symbolizes salvation from ignorance.

The left leg is lifted up in an animated dance movement.

The ring of flames symbolizes the cosmos.

The right leg tramples Apasmara, a dwarfish figure representing ignorance.

Bronze images *representing the main temple deity are taken out in processions on festive occasions. These images are clad in silk and decked with sandalwood paste and floral garlands.*

The marriage of Shiva and Parvati *is a beautiful example of Chola art. It shows Shiva, standing regal and tall, tenderly holding his bashful bride Parvati's hand. Vishnu, as the brother of Parvati, is shown as an onlooker.*

See also features on Hindu Mythology *(see pp24–5)*, Ganesha *(see p467)* and Vishnu *(see p679).*

The multi-arched façade of the Thousand Lights Mosque

Anna Salai ❻

From Cooum Island to Little Mount.
Rajaji Hall *Tel* (044) 2536 5635.
◻ *daily.*

A long arterial road leading from north Chennai to Little Mount at its southern end *(see p573)*, Anna Salai (or Mount Road) is the city's main thoroughfare. The "garden houses" that belonged to Chennai's elite stood on either side of it until well into the early years of the 20th century. Today, it is a modern commercial road, lined with hoardings depicting film stars, and the expansive homes of the past have been replaced by multistoreyed buildings.

Anna Salai begins on an island in Cooum Creek, just south of Fort St George. The site is watched over by the statue of Sir Thomas Munro, the governor of the Madras Presidency from 1819 to 1826. Nearby, set in an expanse of greenery, is the prestigious **Gymkhana Club**. Sited close to the army headquarters, this was an exclusive facility for military officers. Until 1920, its membership was restricted to garrison officers only and, even today, the club grounds belong to the armed services.

The **Old Government Estate**, southwest of the Gymkhana Club, houses the mansion where the governors of Madras once lived in regal splendour. Though the main building is falling apart, the banqueting hall, built in 1802 by the second Lord Clive, the eldest son of Robert Clive, retains its grandeur. It was named **Rajaji Hall** after the first Indian governor-general, C Rajagopalachari, popularly known as Rajaji. Inside this elegant Neo-Classical building, an impressive broad staircase leads up to the vast banqueting hall, which has beautiful panelling and chandeliers. Anna Salai then enters its commercial stretch. Along this length of the road are some of the city's oldest commercial landmarks, including one of India's largest bookshops, **Higginbotham's** *(see p574)*, **Spencer's**, an international department store, and the **Taj Connemara**, one of the city's finest hotels *(see p713)*.

Across the road is the **Old Madras Club**, now somewhat dilapidated. Established in 1832, it was known in its heyday as the "Ace of Clubs". The 19th-century **Thousand Lights Mosque** further down, gets its name from the tradition of lighting 1,000 oil lamps to illuminate the Assembly Hall that once occupied the site. Standing further south is **St George's Cathedral**, planned by James Lillyman Caldwell and built by Thomas de Havilland in 1814. Its 42 m (138 ft) tall spire is one of Chennai's major landmarks.

Main altar in St George's Cathedral, built in the early 19th century

---

FILM STARS AND POLITICS

The South Indian film industry, particularly Tamil and Telugu cinema, is credited with having been the breeding ground of many politicians. The first chief minister from the Dravidian Party (then called DMK), the late Dr CN Annadurai, as well as his immediate successor, M Karunanidhi, were both scriptwriters with large followings. However, the most remarkable actor-turned-politican was Marudur Gopalamenon Ramachandran, whose portrayal of a swashbuckling hero made him the embodiment of righteousness. Popularly known as MGR, he acquired a cult status in the region and was chief minister of Tamil Nadu from 1977 to 1987. His co-star and protégée, Jayalalitha, another charismatic chief minister, was ousted on charges of corruption in 2001, but was reinstated later that year. Current heroes, such as Rajnikant and Chiranjeevi, have more macho images that depend heavily on daredevil stunts. They, too, have fans throughout South India.

Hoardings depicting popular South Indian heroes

A Walk along the Marina **❼**

Chennai's seashore hosts one of India's largest urban beaches, stretching for 13 km (8 miles) along the city's eastern flank. The Marina, connecting Fort St George with San Thomé Basilica almost 5 km (3 miles) away, was built by Mounstuart Elphinstone Grant-Duff, the governor between 1881 and 1886. Described by architectural historian Philip Davies as "one of the most beautiful marine promenades in the world", it is a favourite place for Chennai's citizens to escape the humid heat of the city and enjoy the sea breezes. The walk along Kamarajar Salai (earlier known as South Beach Road) takes in parks, tree-lined cobbled streets and spectacular colonial and Indo-Saracenic buildings.

The Indo-Saracenic Presidency College, nucleus of Madras University

Anna Park

The walk starts from the Victory War Memorial ① which marks the north end of Kamarajar Salai. This memorial originally commemorated the victory of the Allied armies during World War I, and was later dedicated to the memory of those soldiers from the Madras Presidency who lost their lives in World War II. To its south, in Anna Park, is the Anna Samadhi ②, a memorial erected in honour of CN Annadurai, the former chief minister of Tamil Nadu, who introduced significant political and social reforms in the state. Further south is the MGR Samadhi ③, a commemorative garden with gateways and pathways, built in honour of the popular Tamil film icon and chief minister, MG Ramachandran (*see p567*). An array of souvenir shops and eateries can be found along this stretch of the beach, attracting tourists from the rest of the state. Particularly interesting is the Sunday market, with its curious jumble of goods.

Victory War Memorial, Kamarajar Salai

North Marina

Across Kamarajar Salai is a series of imposing red brick buildings, built in a combination of architectural styles, which include Indian and Moorish features. The Indo-Saracenic Madras University ④ was founded in 1857, making it one of the oldest universities in India. An architectural marvel, the Senate House ⑤ was designed by Robert Chisholm in a mixture of Byzantine and Saracenic styles. This became the headquarters of Madras University in 1879. These buildings now stand in what was once the sprawling estate of the old Chepauk Palace ⑥. This splendid Indo-Saracenic structure, on Wallajah Road, was once the home of the Nawab of Arcot. Though the palace was built in 1768, Chisholm added the extensions, including the tower that once connected the two wings. It now houses government offices. Chepauk Stadium, Chennai's famous cricket ground, lies behind the palace. Further down the road is Presidency College ⑦, the first institution in South India for higher education, founded in 1840. This rather austere structure has a ribbed dome with four clocks on its surface. Among the famous alumni of the college are the first Indian governor-general, C Rajagopalachari, and the Nobel Prize-winning physicists, CV Raman and his nephew, S Chandrasekhar.

South Marina

Further south, an impressive landmark on Kamarajar Salai is the statue *Triumph of Labour* ⑧.

A busy evening scene on the Marina Beach

TIPS FOR WALKERS

Starting point: *Victory War Memorial.*
Length: *5 km (3 miles).*
Getting there: *MRTS train station (Fort), bus or taxi.*
Stopping-off points: *A range of eateries and cafés line the beachfront.*

KEY

• • • Suggested route

🚌 Bus

Ⓜ MRTS train station

This sculpture was created by Debi Prasad Roy Chowdhary *(see p564)*, who became the first Indian principal of the Madras School of Arts and Crafts in 1929.

West of the main road, off Annie Besant Road, is the Ice House ⑨, till recently a women's hostel known as Vivekananda House. In the 1840s, this circular building, with a stone pineapple perched on its roof, was a storehouse for ice, which was imported all the way from New England (USA). It was also the site from which Swami Vivekananda *(see p615)* delivered his speeches when he visited the city. It has now been handed over to the Ramakrishna Mission which has plans to restore it. Further south is Queen Mary's College ⑩, today the Madras College for Women. Opened in July 1914, this was Chennai's first women's college. A bust of the queen still graces the entrance of the building. An imposing lighthouse ⑪ marks the southern end of the Marina.

Triumph of Labour **by Debi Prasad Roy Chowdhary, 1959**

ROBERT CHISHOLM'S LEGACY

Robert Fellowes Chisholm (1845–84) was among the most talented architects in India in the mid-19th century. In 1864, Chisholm's designs for the proposed Presidency College and Senate House won a competition, and he was appointed the consulting architect to the Madras government. The next 15 years saw considerable building activity along the Marina, where many innovative buildings were erected. Chisholm's designs blended Italian and Saracenic features so that the new structures would harmonize with the existing Chepauk Palace. For many years he was the head of the School of Industrial Art, founded in 1855 and now known as the Government College of Fine Arts.

Senate House, Robert Chisholm's signature building, completed in 1873

Fruits on sale at Triplicane Market

Triplicane ❽

Off Kamarajar Salai (South Beach Rd). **Parthasarathi Temple** ◯ daily. 🎭 *Neeratu Utsavam* (Dec).

The crowded suburb of Triplicane was among the first villages to be acquired by the East India Company in the 1670s. It derives its name from the sacred lily tank *(tiru-alli-keni)* that once stood here. One of the oldest temples in the city, the historic **Parthasarathi Temple**, is situated in Triplicane. Built in the 9th century, the temple is dedicated to Krishna (or Partha) in his role as Arjuna's divine charioteer *(sarathi)* in the epic, the *Mahabharata* *(see p26)*. The temple festival, in December, attracts thousands of devotees. At one time, the residences of the priestly Brahmin caste were clustered in the narrow lanes around the temple. Among them were the homes of the mathematical genius, Srinivasa Ramanujan (1887–1920), and the early 20th-century nationalist poet, Subramania Bharati.

Triplicane was once part of the kingdom of Golconda *(see pp666–7)*, and as a result this quarter has the largest concentration of Muslims in the city. The Nawab of Arcot, Muhammad Ali Wallajah (1749–95), an ally of the British in their struggle for power against the French, contributed generously to the construction of a large mosque here in 1795. Known as the **Wallajah (Big) Mosque**, this beautiful grey granite structure with slender minarets is situated on Triplicane High Road. The adjoining graveyard contains the tombs of various Muslim saints. The nawab's descendants still live in Triplicane, in a stately mansion known as **Amir Mahal**. Constructed in 1798, it became their residence after the Chepauk Palace *(see p568)* was taken over by the British.

The graceful façade of Wallajah Mosque, with its flanking minarets

For hotels and restaurants in this region see pp712–13 and pp739–40

Mylapore & San Thomé ❾

S of Triplicane. **Kapaleshvara Temple** ◯ daily. **Basilica of San Thomé** ◯ daily. **Luz Church** ◯ daily.

The site of a great Pallava port in the 7th and 8th centuries, Mylapore is today one of the busiest parts of the city. This traditional quarter, with its religious organizations, tiny houses and lively bazaars, is dominated by the **Kapaleshvara Temple**, the largest in Chennai. The main deity, Shiva, is symbolized as a peacock *(mayil)*, thus giving the area its original name, Mayilapura, the "Town of the Peacocks". According to legend, Shiva's consort, Parvati, assumed the form of a peahen to worship Shiva, represented here by his linga. A sculptural panel in a small

The Gothic-style Basilica of San Thomé

shrine in the courtyard depicts the legend. The present temple was built after the original was destroyed by the Portuguese in the 16th century. Mylapore's links with Christianity date to the 1st century AD, to the time of St Thomas *(see p573)*. In the 10th century, a group of Nestorian Christians from Persia (Iran) discovered the saint's burial site and built a church and tomb. The Portuguese, following the trail of the saint, established the settlement of San Thomé in the early 16th century. The present **Basilica of San Thomé**, over the tomb of the saint, is an impressive Gothic-style structure built in 1898. It has an ornate interior with magnificent stained-glass windows and a towering steeple. The crypt is said to contain a small bone from the saint's hand and the weapon that killed him.

Nearby is the **Luz Church**, which was built by a Franciscan monk in 1516, making it the oldest Catholic church in Chennai.

Adyar ⑩

S of San Thomé, across Adyar river.
Theosophical Society *Tel* (044)
2491 2474. ☐ *Mon–Fri & (Sat morn).* **Brodie Castle** ☐ *daily.*

The 400-year-old banyan tree in the gardens of the Theosophical Society

Few places in Chennai offer greater serenity than the sprawling gardens of the **Theosophical Society**, situated in the city's Adyar neighbourhood, on the banks of the Adyar river. Founded in New York in 1875, the Society moved here seven years later when it acquired Huddlestone Gardens. Built in 1776 by John Huddlestone, a wealthy civilian, this large mansion is today the world headquarters of the Society. Its magnificent 108-ha (270-acre) estate comprises several 19th-century buildings, one of which is the former home of its founder Colonel Henry S Olcott.

The main building houses the Great Hall, almost spartan in its simplicity, where prayer meetings are held. Bas-reliefs, representing the different faiths, and engravings of verses taken from the holy books of all world religions can be seen here. There are also marble statues of the founders, Colonel Olcott and Helena Petrovna Blavatsky, as well as one of Annie Besant, who became president in 1907.

The Adyar Library and Research Centre, founded by Olcott in 1886, is one of the finest libraries in India. Its collection of 165,000 books and 20,000 palm-leaf and parchment manuscripts has made it a valuable repository for Indological research. The surrounding tranquil gardens have shrines dedicated to

various faiths. The greatest attraction here, however, is the 400-year-old banyan tree, whose spreading branches cover an immense area of 4,180 sq m (44,993 sq ft). Over the decades, many of the Society's meetings and spiritual discourses were held under its canopy. Unfortunately, a terrible storm in 1989 destroyed its main trunk.

Brodie Castle, north of the Theosophical Society, is an imposing white structure on the banks of the Adyar. Now known as Thenral, it houses the prestigious College of Carnatic Music. Built in 1796 by James Brodie, an employee of the East India Company, it is said to be among the first "garden-houses" built in the city. These spacious, airy

houses with broad pillared verandahs, set in sprawling wooded gardens, were characteristic of colonial Chennai. This house later became the home of the first Chief Justice of the Madras Supreme Court.

Further north of Brodie Castle is the **Madras Club**, built by George Moubray, who came to India as an accountant in 1771. He acquired 42 ha (104 acres) of land on the banks of the Adyar, and built a house with a central cupola, surrounded by a beautiful garden. Known as Moubray's Cupola, this was once the exclusive preserve of the city's European population. Indians were only allowed membership in 1964, after it merged with the Adyar Club.

The pillared entrance of Brodie Castle in Adyar

THE THEOSOPHICAL SOCIETY

In the 1870s, Colonel Henry S Olcott, a veteran of the American Civil War, met the Russian aristocrat and clairvoyant, Madame Helena Petrovna Blavatsky in Vermont (USA) at the farm of the Christian Scientist, Mary Baker Eddy. Soon after, they launched a movement to foster the spirit of universal brotherhood, aiming to create a Utopian society in which people of all castes, creeds and colour could live in harmony. The movement attracted great thinkers and intellec-

Theosophical Society

tuals, among them Dr Annie Besant, president of the Indian National Congress in 1917. The idea of forming a national political party was, in fact, first voiced in the 1890s at the Society's headquarters in Adyar, under the banyan tree, by the British civil servant AO Hume. The famous philosopher Jiddu Krishnamurti was also associated with the Society.

A Bharat Natyam dance lesson in progress at Kalakshetra

Kalakshetra ⑪

Thiruvanmiyur, East Coast Rd. 🚌 or taxi. **Tel** (044) 2452 1844. ◯ daily. 🎭 Kalakshetra Arts Festival (Dec/Jan).

This pioneering institution for classical dance, music and the fine arts, established in 1936, was the brainchild of Rukmini Devi. A protégée of Annie Besant, she was deeply influenced by the progressive views of the Theosophical Society (see p571). At 16, she scandalized conservative society by marrying George Sydney Arundale, the 40-year-old Australian principal of the Society's school. The couple's extensive travels around the world exposed Rukmini to the world of Western culture, specially dance, inspiring her to study ballet under the great Russian ballerina, Anna Pavlova. Back in Chennai, she again defied tradition by learning and performing the classical dasi attam, hitherto the domain of devadasis (temple dancers). The International Centre for the Arts, which she set up for the revival of this dance form, now called Bharat Natyam, (see p29), is today Kalakshetra, the "Temple of Art".

The school is set in a vast 40-ha (99-acre) campus, where classical music and dance are taught according to the traditional methods, by which a guru imparts knowledge to a small group of students. Some of India's best known dancers, including Yamini Krishnamurti, and the institute's current director, Leela Samson, were trained

here. At the end of each year, a festival is held and performances are staged in an auditorium designed like a koottambulam, the traditional theatre of Kerala temples (see p639).

MGR Film City ⑫

Near Indira Nagar. 🚌 **Tel** (044) 2254 2424. ◯ daily 🎫 📷 extra charges.

One of Chennai's newest attractions is a film city, dedicated to the memory of the hugely popular matinée idol, MG Ramachandran (see p567). This is now the most popular location for Chennai's flourishing Tamil film industry, which is second only to Mumbai (see pp32–3) in film production. A fantasy world of extravagant sets and hi-tech equipment, Film City attracts starstruck fans from all over Tamil Nadu, who come here to catch a glimpse of their favourite film stars.

A film set in MGR Film City

Guindy National Park ⑬

S Chennai. Sardar Vallabhbhai Patel Rd. 🚆 Guindy station. 🚌 ◯ Wed–Mon. 🏛 **Raj Bhavan** ◯ to public.

Once a distant suburb which was nearly twice its current size, Guindy has now been engulfed by the fast growing metropolis of Greater Chennai. Originally part of the private forest surrounding Guindy Lodge, a portion was officially declared the Guindy National Park in 1977. This predominantly dry deciduous scrub jungle of acacia is interspersed with larger trees such as sandalwood (Santalam album), banyan (Ficus bengalensis) and jamun (Syzygium cumini). Its most famous residents are the herds of endangered blackbuck (Antelope cervicapra), introduced in 1924. Among its 130 species of birds are raptors such as the honey buzzard and the whitebellied sea eagle. Winter is the best time for birdwatching, when migrant birds visit the region.

Also located within the park is the **Madras Snake Park**, established in the 1970s by Romulus Whitaker, the American zoologist, who also set up the Crocodile Bank outside Chennai (see p578). Today, the well-maintained Snake Park houses numerous species of snakes, among them king cobras, vipersand pythons. Other reptiles include crocodiles,

A song-and-dance sequence being shot on location for a Tamil movie

turtles and lizards. Large information boards, strategically placed, provide interesting details on the habitat and behaviour of the various species. For those who are interested, there are live demonstrations of venom extraction; the venom is used as an antidote for snake bites.

The historic 300-year-old Guindy Lodge, to the west of the Park, is now the **Raj Bhavan**, the residence of the governor of Tamil Nadu. Built as a weekend retreat for the city's British rulers, this handsome white building was renovated and expanded in the mid-1800s by the then governor, Grant-Duff.

Today, Guindy has some of the city's most prestigious institutions. The area also has many impressive memorials to modern India's leaders, Mahatma Gandhi, K Kamaraj and C Rajagopalachari.

Façade of the Church of Our Lady of Expectations, Mount of St Thomas

The Masonry Cross, engraved on a rock in the cave, Little Mount

Little Mount & Mount of St Thomas ⓮

SW Chennai. Near Marmalog Bridge. 🚉 St Thomas Mount station. 🚌

A rock-hewn cave on Little Mount is believed to be the place where, in AD 72, the mortally wounded St Thomas sought refuge. Near the modern **Church of Our Lady of Good Health** is the older **Blessed Sacrament Chapel** built by the Portuguese over the cave. Inside the cave is the opening through which the fleeing saint is said to have retreated, leaving behind a still visible imprint of his hand near the entrance. At the rear end of the cave is the Masonry Cross before which St Thomas is said to have prayed. By the **Church of the Resurrection** is a perennial spring with curative powers. Legend claims that the spring originated when St Thomas struck the rock with his staff to provide water for his thirsty congregation.

About 3 km (2 miles) southwest of Little Mount is the 95-m (312-ft) high Mount of St Thomas or Great Mount. A flight of 132 steps leads to the summit and the **Church of Our Lady of Expectations**, built by the Portuguese in the 16th century. The most important relic here is the ancient stone cross embedded into the wall of the altar. Said to have been engraved by the saint himself, this is the legendary "bleeding cross" that miraculously bled between 1558 and 1704.

Below the eastern flank of the Mount is the **Cantonment** area, with its shady streets lined with 18th-century Neo-Classical bungalows.

ST THOMAS IN INDIA

Portrait of St Thomas

According to legend, St Thomas or Doubting Thomas, one of the 12 apostles, came to South India soon after Jesus Christ died. He is said to have arrived in Cranganore (see p649) in AD 52 and spent the next 12 years along the Malabar Coast, spreading the Gospel and converting the local population. He gradually moved eastwards and finally settled in Mylapore (see p570). He spent the last years of his life in a cave on Little Mount, from where he would walk every day to the beach, resting for a while and preaching in the groves. It is said that one day in AD 72, while praying on the Mount of St Thomas, he was mortally wounded by a lance, and fled to Little Mount, where he died. His body was carried by his converts to San Thomé, where he was buried in the crypt of the small chapel he had built. This is today the Basilica of San Thomé, and the large stained-glass window depicts his story. The Portuguese colonized Mylapore in the early 16th century, lured by accounts left by the 13th-century Venetian traveller, Marco Polo, who had visited the early Nestorian chapel here. The saint holds a special place in the hearts of Indians, and was decreed the Apostle of India in 1972.

Shopping & Entertainment in Chennai

As the capital of Tamil Nadu, Chennai has an excellent selection of handicrafts and handwoven textiles from the state. From shimmering silks in glowing colours and finely woven cottons to jewellery and replicas of Chola bronzes, the choice is enormous. The city's shopping centres include up-market department stores, malls and trendy boutiques, as well as the vibrant local bazaars which sell a wide range of merchandise. Chennai is also the cultural capital of South India, where performances of classical dance and music take place throughout the year. The height of the cultural season is from mid-December to mid-January, when the city hosts the prestigious Chennai Festival.

SHOPS AND MARKETS

The best shopping in Chennai can be found in the more traditional areas, such as Panagal Park, Pondy and Burma bazaars, and the lanes around the temple at Mylapore. These were small street markets that have now grown into mini shopping malls, where everything is available at bargain prices. Chennai's oldest department store, Spencer's, partially burned down in the 1980s, and has now been rebuilt as a modern mall. It houses shops selling merchandise as varied as groceries and imported Swiss watches. Next door is the city's oldest landmark, **VTI** (Victoria Technical Institute), where handicrafts and a range of good quality linen are sold. This charitable organization supports South Indian Christian missions that specialize in exquisite hand-embroidery.

Most shops are open Monday to Friday, from 9:30am to 7pm. Bazaars, however, keep more flexible hours.

JEWELLERY AND ANTIQUES

The best place for high quality traditional South Indian gold jewellery is **Vummidi Bangaru Jewellers**. They also stock excellent reproductions of the gem-encrusted costume jewellery worn by classical dancers. **Prince Jewellery**, in Panagal Park, has jewellery from Kerala and also specializes in light weight gold ornaments.

Modern and traditional silverware and jewellery are available at **Sukhra** and **Amethyst**.

Genuine antiques are hard to find. However, **Rani Arts & Crafts** stocks copies of old artifacts, including brass and metal images and objects, Tanjore (Thanjavur) paintings *(see p597)* and lacquerware.

TEXTILES AND SARIS

Tamil Nadu is renowned for the richness and variety of its silk and cotton textiles, a good selection of which is available in Chennai. **Radha Silks**, **Kumaran Silks** and **Sundari Silks** are famous all over India for their wonderful range of fabrics and silk saris from Kanchipuram *(see p583)*. **Nalli's**, a huge multistoreyed shop, has the widest range of Kanchipuram saris, and is always packed with local shoppers, particularly during the festival and wedding seasons. Other outlets are **Man Mandir** and **Shilpi**, a small boutique that sells saris and home furnishings. **Fabindia** too, stocks furnishings and ready-made garments. A good variety of textiles can be found at **Co-optex**, the large Tamil Nadu Cooperative of Textiles showroom. This pioneering society has encouraged the revival of handlooms.

HANDICRAFTS AND GIFTS

A fine selection of handicrafts can be found at **Poompuhar**, the Tamil Nadu State Emporium. VTI also sells handicrafts, though hand-embroidered linen and nightwear are their main specialities. **Cane and Bamboo** is another interesting little shop with an assortment of gift items and souvenirs.

Apparao Galleries not only stocks paintings by contemporary Indian artists, but also has an accessory shop for gifts and home products. Their boutique sells trendy designer-wear.

Naturally Auroville specializes in natural products made in the Pondicherry Ashram and Auroville *(see pp586–8)*. The merchandise includes pottery, handmade paper, perfumed candles, incense sticks and aromatherapy oils and lotions.

Chennai is also a good place to shop for handcrafted musical instruments, such as the violin, *mridangam* and *veena*. While these are found at many outlets in the city, the best selections are available at **Musee Musicals** and **Sapthaswara Music Store**. **Music World** stocks a wide range of CDs and audio cassettes by well-known Carnatic musicians. The city also has a number of excellent bookshops. Of these, the oldest and most well-stocked is **Higginbotham's**, established in 1844.

ENTERTAINMENT GUIDES, TICKETS AND VENUES

Announcements of performances of Carnatic music *(see p595)* and classical dance such as Bharat Natyam *(see p28)*, appear regularly in the entertainment columns of local newspapers. The city guides *Hallo! Madras and Chennai This Fortnight* list entertainment venues and information on tickets.

Performances of music and dance are held throughout the year. However, the peak season is from 15 December to 15 January, when the Chennai Festival, organized by the city's *sabhas* (cultural societies), takes place. During this period more than 500 concerts are held. The most prestigious cultural centre is the **Music Academy**. Other venues are **Narada Gana Sabha**, **Sri Krishna Gana Sabha** and **Karthik Fine Arts**. Classical dance and music performances are also held at the **Museum Theatre** in the Pantheon Complex *(see p564)* and the auditorium at **Kalakshetra** *(see p572)*.

MUSIC AND DANCE

Since the 1920s, Chennai has been the leading centre of Carnatic music and classical dance. The first music festival took place in December 1927 during the Madras session of the Indian National Congress. A year later, the Music Academy was established to promote Carnatic music, and in 1936, Rukmini Devi set up Kalakshetra to popularize Bharat Natyam, the dance form once performed only in temples. Today, these two institutions along with the many *sabhas* are the major sponsors of music and dance events in the city.

During the season, music lovers gather in Chennai to hear India's top performers as well as promising new talent. Concerts of Carnatic music, both vocal and instrumental, begin in the morning and often last till midnight. Dance recitals are also held. Recently, some dancers have experimented with the traditional repertoire to create a contemporary form that is a fusion of Indian folk and classical forms with Western themes.

CINEMA

The choice of films that show at Chennai's many cinemas, such as **Devi**, **Ega**, **Gaiety** (founded in 1919), and the **Sathyam Cineplex**, ranges from Bollywood and Tamil blockbusters to the latest Hollywood releases. Tamil films are very similar to those produced in Mumbai's Bollywood, with song and dance sequences and a great deal of melodrama. But they play a role far beyond mere entertainment – their themes often have a social message and their charismatic actors, with their political links *(see p567)*, make them a potent medium of communication, especially among rural audiences.

DIRECTORY

JEWELLERY AND ANTIQUES

Amethyst
14 Padmavathi Rd,
Jeyapore Colony,
Gopalapuram.
Tel (044) 2835 1627.

Prince Jewellery
13 Nagaeswara Rao Rd,
Panagal Park.
Tel (044) 2436 3137.
769 Spencer Plaza,
Anna Salai.
Tel (044) 2849 5817.

Rani Arts & Crafts
8 Nowrojee Rd, Chetpet.
Tel (044) 2642 2948.
73 Gangadareswar Koil St.
Tel (044) 2642 2948.

Sukhra
42 North Mada St,
Mylapore.
Tel (044) 2461 0193.

Vummidi Bangaru Jewellers
Rani Seethai Hall,
603 Anna Salai.
Tel (044) 2849 3056.

TEXTILES AND SARIS

Co-optex
Pantheon Rd, Egmore.
Tel (044) 2819 2394.

Fabindia
Illford House, 3 Woods Rd,
off Anna Salai.
Tel (044) 2851 0395.

Kumaran Silks
12 Nageswaran Rd,
T Nagar.
Tel (044) 2434 3544.

Man Mandir
15 Khader Nawaz Khan
Rd, Nungamabakkam.
Tel (044) 2823 9474.

Nalli's
9 Nageswaran Rd,
T Nagar.
Tel (044) 2434 4115.

Radha Silks
Sannathi St, Mylapore.
Tel (044) 2494 1906.

Shilpi
1 GG Minar, 23 College
Rd, Nungambakkam.
Tel (044) 2828 2603.
29, CP Ramaswamy Rd.
Tel (044) 2499 7526.

Sundari Silks
54–55 North Usman Rd,
T Nagar.
Tel (044) 2814 3093.

HANDICRAFTS AND GIFTS

Apparao Galleries
7 Wallace Garden, 3rd St.
Tel (044) 2833 4955.

Cane and Bamboo
20 C-in-C Rd, Ethiraj Lane.
Tel (044) 2827 5180.

Higginbotham's
116 Anna Salai.
Tel (044) 2841 3146.

Musee Musicals
67 Anna Salai.
Tel (044) 2852 2780.

Music World
Spencer's Plaza.
Tel (044) 2849 3232.

Naturally Auroville
30 Khader Nawaz Khan
Rd, Nungambakkam.
Tel (044) 2821 7517.

Poompuhar
818 Anna Salai.
Tel (044) 2852 0624.

Sapthaswara Music Store
165 Royapetta H Rd,
Mylapore.
Tel (044) 2499 3294.

VTI
New 180, Anna Salai.
Tel (044) 2858 6779.

ENTERTAINMENT VENUES

Kalakshetra
Kalakshetra Foundation,
Thiruvanmiyur.
Tel (044) 2491 1844.

Karthik Fine Arts
New 39, Bhimanna
Garden St, Alwarpet.
Tel (044) 2499 7788.

Museum Theatre
Pantheon Rd, Egmore.
Tel (044) 2819 3778.

Music Academy
306 TTK Rd, Alwarpet.
Tel (044) 2811 5162.

Narada Gana Sabha
314 TTK Rd, Alwarpet.
Tel (044) 2499 3201.

Sri Krishna Gana Sabha
8 Maharajapuram
Santhanam Salai,
T Nagar.
Tel (044) 2814 0806.

CINEMA

Devi
47 Anna Salai.
Tel (044) 2855 5660.

Ega
435 Poonamallee High Rd.
Tel (044) 2641 1666.

Gaiety
Anna Salai.
Tel (044) 2841 5154.

Sathyam Cineplex
Sathyam Theatre Complex,
8, Thiru Vi Ka Rd.
Tel (044) 2852 3813.

TAMIL NADU

The cradle of ancient Dravidian culture, Tamil Nadu extends from the Coromandel Coast in the east to the forested Western Ghats in the west. At its heart is the fertile Kaveri valley, a land of rice fields and spectacular temples. This is the site of ancient Cholamandalam, where the Chola kings built magnificent temples at Thanjavur and elsewhere. Great temples also stand at Madurai and Chidambaram, which witnessed an efflorescence of dance, music and literature under their enlightened rulers. The 7th-century port-city of Mamallapuram with its spectacular rock-cut temples is now a World Heritage Site, while the former French enclave of Pondicherry, and British forts and churches reflect the state's colonial history. Many towns in Tamil Nadu have the prefix "Tiru", which means sacred, and indicates the presence of a major religious site.

SIGHTS AT A GLANCE

Towns, Cities & Districts
Chettinad ㉓
Coimbatore ⑲
Pondicherry ⑦
Ramanathapuram ㉔
Tiruchirapalli ⑭
Tuticorin ㉖
Vellore ④

Historic Sites
Dakshina Chitra ①
Gingee Fort ⑥
Mamallapuram ②

Temples & Temple Towns
Chidambaram ⑧
Gangaikondacholapuram ⑩
Kanchipuram ③

Kanniyakumari ㉚
Kumbakonam ⑪
Madurai ㉒
Palani ⑳
Rameshvaram ㉕
Srirangam ⑮
Suchindram ㉙
Thanjavur ⑬
Tiruchendur ㉗
Tirunelvelli ㉘
Tiruvaiyaru ⑫
Tiruvannamalai ⑤

Tours
Coromandel Driving Tour ⑨
Tour of the Nilgiris ⑱

National Parks
Mudumalai Wildlife
  Sanctuary ⑰

Hill Stations
Kodaikanal ㉑
Yercaud ⑯

KEY

🛫	International airport
☒	Domestic airport
▬	National highway
▭	Major road
═	Minor road
—	Major railway
▪▪▪	International border

⊲ **Detail from a temple *gopura* with colourful stucco figures, Sarangapani Temple, Kumbakonam**

Dakshina Chitra ❶

Chingleput district. 26 km (16 miles) S of Chennai. 🚌🚆 *Tel* (04114) 272 603. ⏰ *Wed–Mon.* 🏛️🎫🍴🛍️

This heritage village, on the Coromandel Coast, provides a fascinating glimpse into the homes and lifestyles of the people of South India. The village features reconstructions of traditional houses, including, so far, six from Tamil Nadu, three from Kerala and one from Karnataka. The handsome Chettiar mansion *(see p612)* on view, with its elaborately carved wooden door, reflects the wealth of the Chettiar merchant community, while the homes of priests, farmers, weavers and potters are simple, utilitarian yet elegant structures. Within the complex is an Ayyanar shrine *(see p605)* and an open courtyard, where folk and classical dance performances and craft demonstrations are held.

Environs
Cholamandal Village, 12 km (7 miles) north of Dakshina Chitra, is an artists' village established in 1966 and the first of its kind in India. For nature lovers, the **Crocodile Bank**, founded by an American zoologist, Romulus Whitaker, is 15 km (9 miles) south of the village. It includes a snake farm and a cooperative of Irulas, a community of rat-catchers.

🏛️ **Cholamandal Village**
Tel (044) 2449 0092. ⏰ *daily.*

🏛️ **Crocodile Bank**
⏰ *Wed–Mon.* 🎫 📷 *extra charges.*

A colourful sign announcing the entrance to the Crocodile Bank

The sculpted relief at Mamallapuram, depicting Bhagiratha's Penance

Mamallapuram ❷

Kanchipuram district. 58 km (36 miles) S of Chennai. 🚌 ℹ️ *Covelong Rd, (04114) 242 232.* ⏰ *daily.* 🏛️🍴🎭 *Dance Festival (Jan/Feb).*

The Unesco World Heritage Site of Mamallapuram (or Mahabalipuram) was once a major port-city, built in the 7th century by the Pallava king, Narasimha Varman I, also known as Mamalla, the "Great Wrestler". This spectacular site, situated on the Bay of Bengal, extends across a boulder-strewn landscape and comprises rock-cut caves and monolithic shrines *(see pp580–81)*, structural temples and huge bas-reliefs that are considered the greatest examples of Pallava art. The stone-carving tradition that created these wonders is still alive in the many workshops scattered around the village.

Krishna's Butter Ball, a natural boulder

The spectacular **Shore Temple**, perched dramatically on a promontory by the sea, has survived the ravages of time and erosion. It was built by Mamalla for Vishnu, while the two Shiva shrines were added by Mamalla's successor Narasimha Varman II. The temple has a low boundary wall, with rows of seated Nandis surrounding it. Placed inside are a reclining Vishnu, a 16-faceted polished linga and reliefs of Somaskanda – a composite form of Shiva with his consort, Parvati and sons, Skanda and Ganesha.

Inland from the Shore Temple, in the village centre, is the celebrated bas-relief **Bhagiratha's Penance**, also known as Arjuna's Penance or the Descent of the Ganges. Carved on an immense rock with a natural vertical cleft, symbolizing the Ganges, the panel depicts in great detail the story of the sacred river's descent from the sky *(see p163)*. This divine act, made possible by the penance of the sage Bhagiratha, is witnessed on the panel by celestial and semi-celestial beings, ascetics, and animals. The symbolism is best understood during the monsoon, when rainwater flows down the cleft and collects in the tank below. Nearby are the unfinished **Panch Pandava Cave Temple**, and **Krishna's Butter Ball**, a natural boulder perched precariously on a slope.

South of Bhagiratha's Penance is the **Krishna Mandapa**, a huge bas-relief showing the god lifting Mount Govardhan to protect the people from torrential rains, as well as performing his tasks as a cowherd. The **Olakkanatha Temple**, above the *mandapa*, was once used as a lighthouse.

On the ridge southwest of Bhagiratha's Penance are three cave temples. The **Mahishasuramardini Cave**

Temple has a graceful portrayal of Goddess Durga on her lion mount, subduing the buffalo-headed demon, Mahisha, on the northern wall. This panel seems to emanate life and motion, in contrast to the one on the southern wall, where Vishnu reclines in deep meditation before creating the earth.

Nearby, the **Adivaraha Cave Temple** has interesting panels of Pallava rulers with their consorts. The Lion Throne, on top of a hill further west, is a raised platform with a seated lion, discovered near the piles of brick rubble thought to be the remains of the palace of the Pallavas.

The **Trimurti Cave Temple**, northwest of Bhagiratha's Penance, is dedicated to three gods – Shiva, Vishnu and Somaskanda. The shrines are guarded by statues of graceful doorkeepers. A sculpture of Durga standing on Mahisha's head is on an outer wall. To its south, the **Varaha Cave Temple** has beautifully moulded lion pillars, while the relief sculptures of Lakshmi, Durga

and Varaha, the boar incarnation of Vishnu, are among the masterpieces of Pallava art. The two-storeyed, rectangular **Ganesha Ratha**, further south, is attributed to Parameshvara Varman I (r.669–90). The temple, originally dedicated to Shiva, has beautifully carved inscriptions listing the royal titles of Parameshvara Varman.

A small **Archaeological Museum**, with sculptures and fragments excavated from the site, lies to its east.

🏛 **Archaeological Museum**
West Raja St. ◯ daily. 🎟 **Shore Temple** 🎟 also covers Panch Rathas.

Environs

The **Tiger's Cave**, 4 km (2.5 miles) north, is a shallow cave framed by a large boulder, with heads of *yalis* (mythical leonine beasts). It was probably a stage for outdoor performances.

The **Vedagirisvara Temple**, dedicated to Shiva, at the top of a hill in the village of **Thirukkazhukunran**, 17 km (11 miles) west, is famous for the two eagles that swoop down at noon to be fed by the temple priests. According to legend, these birds are saints who fly from Varanasi (*see pp202–208*) to Rameshvaram, stopping here to rest.

Fishermen with their boats on the beach at Mamallapuram

PLAN OF MAMALLAPURAM

Tiger's Cave

COVELONG ROAD

TIRUKKULA ROAD
OTHAVADAI RD
CONERI ROAD

WEST RAJA STREET
EAST RAJA STREET

Trimurti Cave Temple

Varaha Cave Temple

Vedagirisvara Temple

Ganesha Ratha

BAY OF BENGAL

Archaeological Museum

Bhagiratha's Penance
Panch Pandava Cave Temple

Krishna's Butter Ball

Koneri Tank

Olakkanatha Temple

Krishna Mandapa

Shore Temple

BEACH ROAD

Adivaraha Cave Temple

Lighthouse

Mahishasuramardini Cave Temple

0 metres   300

0 yards   300

Panch Rathas

Mamallapuram: Panch Rathas

Sculpture of Subramanya

This 7th-century complex of mono-lithic rock-cut shrines called the Panch (five) Rathas (processional temple chariots) is named after the five Pandava brothers, heroes of the epic *Mahabharata (see p26)*, and their queen Draupadi. Although unfinished, these impressive temples are a tribute to the genius of the stone-cutters who carved these large boulders *in situ*. In an ambitious experiment, the styles and techniques of wooden architecture were imitated in stone, to create a variety of forms that later came to influence South Indian temple design.

Arjuna Ratha, Draupadi Ratha and Nandi

Arjuna Ratha

This two-storeyed temple has a graceful portrayal of Shiva leaning on his mount, the bull Nandi. Royal couples and other elegantly carved figures in the niches embellish the outer walls.

Nandi, carved out of a single rock, faces the Arjuna Ratha.

★ Durga Panel

A four-armed Durga is carved on the rear wall of the Draupadi Ratha's sanctum, with kneeling devotees in front. One of these is shown in the process of cutting his head off, as a supreme act of self-sacrifice.

STAR FEATURES

* ★ Durga Panel
* ★ Standing Lion
* ★ Harihara

Draupadi Ratha, a stone replica of a thatched tribal shrine, is the smallest *ratha* of the group, and is dedicated to the goddess Durga.

★ Standing Lion

The mount of Durga is placed in front of the Draupadi Ratha.

King Narasimha
The Pallava king Narasimha Varman I, the patron of this complex and after whose title, Mamalla, the site is named, is shown wearing a crown, a silk garment and jewellery.

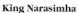

Dharmaraja Ratha, an imposing three-storeyed *ratha,* is crowned by an octagonal domed roof. Sculpted panels are carved on the upper storeys.

Bhima Ratha, a gigantic, rectangular *ratha* with a barrel-vaulted roof and unfinished lower level, is named after the Pandava brother famed for his strength.

★ Harihara
Niche figures on the lower level include beautiful sculptures of Harihara, a composite form of Vishnu and Shiva (see p47). The right side of the body with matted locks of hair is Shiva, and the left is Vishnu, with a smooth, tapering cylindrical crown.

Nakul Sahdeva Ratha
Named jointly after the Pandava twins, this ratha *is unique for its apsidal form, known in architectural terms as gajaprishta (back of an elephant). As if to emphasize this, a perfectly sculpted elephant, carved from a single stone, stands next to it.*

Vaishnavite priests, Varadaraja Temple

Kanchipuram ❸

Kanchipuram district. 76 km (47 miles) SW of Chennai. 🚊 153,000. 🚌 🚉 ℹ Hotel Tamil Nadu, 78, Kamakshi Amman Sannathi St, (04112) 222 552. 🎭 Shivratri (Feb/Mar), Panguni Uthiram Festival (Mar/Apr), Brahmotsava (May/Jun).

The small temple town of Kanchipuram, or Kanchi, as it is popularly known, is one of the seven sacred cities of the Hindus. From the 6th to the 8th centuries, it was the capital of the Pallavas (see p578), who built numerous temples here and founded universities for higher learning. Royal patronage from the succeeding Chola, Pandya and Vijayanagar dynasties further consolidated the city's reputation as a religious and commercial centre.

Kanchipuram is sacred to Shaivites (devotees of Shiva) as well as to Vaishnavites (worshippers of Vishnu). The town is thus divided into two distinct zones, with the Shaivite temples to the north and the Vaishnavite temples to the southeast.

It also has an important Devi (goddess) temple, the **Kamakshi Temple**, situated northeast of the bus stand. Dedicated to Kamakshi, or the "loving-eyed" Parvati, the temple was rebuilt in the 14th century, during the Vijayanagar period. It has four colourful *gopuras* and the main sanctum

has a gold-plated roof. The **Kailasanatha Temple**, to the west of the bus stand, is the oldest and grandest structure in the town. Built in the early 8th century by Rajasimha, the last great Pallava king, this Shiva temple is surrounded by 58 smaller shrines, each with splendid carvings of the various representations of Shiva. The recently discovered frescoes here are the earliest in South India. The sanctum has a circumambulatory passage with great symbolic meaning – seven steps (indicating seven births) lead to a dark passage (indicating the journey of life) and a narrow outlet (indicating death).

The great **Ekambareshvara Temple** on Car Street, constructed originally by the Pallavas, has a 16-pillared *mandapa* in front of it, that was added later by the Vijayanagar kings. This is one of the five *panchalinga* shrines (see p584) and houses a linga made of earth (*prithvi*). Legend says that the goddess Kamakshi, as part of her penance for disturbing Shiva's meditation, created this linga with earth taken from under a mango tree. Lingas abound in the corridors of the temple complex, while on the western side of the shrine stands the sacred mango tree, said to be 3,000 years old. The **Vaikuntha Perumal Temple**, near the railway station, is one of the 18

temples dedicated to Vishnu. Erected by the Pallava king Nandi Varman II (r.731–96), this unique structure has three main sanctums, built one on top of the other. Each of them enshrines an image of Vishnu in a different form – standing, sitting and reclining. The hall in the lower shrine has panels depicting the genealogy, coronations and martial conquests of the Pallava kings.

The **Varadaraja Temple**, on Gandhi Road, is the town's main Vishnu temple. The chief deity is a form of Vishnu known as Varadaraja (the "King who Bestows Benediction"). It is believed that the temple stands on the site where Brahma performed a *yagna* (sacrifice) to invoke Vishnu's presence. Among the temple's jewels is a valuable gold necklace, said to have been presented by Robert Clive (see p561).

Kanchipuram, famous for its silk, is also the seat of one of the four Shankaracharyas. They belong to the long line of head priests of the *matha* (religious centre) founded by the much-respected 9th-century philosopher-saint Adi Shankaracharya (see p648).

Environs
The bird sanctuary of **Vedanthangal**, 30 km (19 miles) southeast, attracts more than 30,000 migratory birds. Species such as cormorants, egrets, white ibis, and grey wagtails can be seen between October and February. The sanctuary has been looked after by locals for well over 250 years.

View of Kailasanatha, Kanchipuram's oldest temple

Kanchipuram Silk

Initially, Kanchipuram was a weaving and trade centre for cotton textiles. But from the 19th century, with the increase in availability of mulberry silk from neighbouring Karnataka, the craftsmen turned entirely to silk weaving. Today, the silk fabric and saris created by the

Kanchipuram sari patterns

city's weavers and dyers are ritually offered to the gods before being sold. Kanchipuram silks, an essential part of every Indian bride's trousseau, are renowned for their lustre, and for their elegant combination of contrasting colours on the borders and end pieces (*pallavs*).

Cocoons *of the silkworm* (Bombyx mori) *are reared on bamboo frames before being dropped into boiling water to preserve the length of the fibre.*

Yarn being sorted and graded before dyeing

Dyeing *is done by a special community which is skilled in this technique. The dyer first dips the yarn into a cauldron of colour and then dries the hanks in the sun.*

Warp and weft yarns *are prepared by family members. More than 5,000 families are involved in this very lucrative handloom industry.*

Classic Kanchipuram saris *are woven from twisted yarn, which makes them extremely durable. They are embellished with motifs such as temple spires, holy* rudraksha *beads, lotus flowers and peacocks, often woven in gold thread.*

Weavers' dwellings *are simple structures built around a courtyard, and serve as both a home and a work place. The loom is the main feature and occupies a large portion of the living area. Weaving skills are passed from generation to generation within families.*

Vellore

Vellore district. 145 km (90 miles)
W of Chennai. 🏠 *177,500.* 🚉
*Katpadi, 5 km (3 miles) N of town
centre, then bus or auto.* 🚌 🚐 *daily.*

Surrounded by a deep
artificial moat, the 16th-
century **Vellore Fort** dominates the heart of this town.
An impressive example of
military architecture, the fort
has a turbulent history. This
formidable structure has withstood many battles, including
an ill-fated mutiny led by the
son of Tipu Sultan *(see p517)*
in 1806 against the British
East India Company. Today,
part of the fort houses some
government offices, including
the Archaeological Survey of
India (ASI), district courts
and a prison. A museum
within has a small but good
collection of historical objects
found in the area.

The only major structure
to survive in the fort is the
magnificent **Jalakanteshvara
Temple**, constructed by the
Nayakas, governors of the
region under the Vijayanagar
kings, in the mid-16th century. This Shiva temple is
located near the fort's northern wall. It is surrounded by
a low-lying boundary wall
and contains a tank and
subsidiary shrines. In the
early 20th century, the temple
was used as a garrison and its
linga was removed from the
sanctum. This was reinstated

The broad moat surrounding the quadrangular Vellore Fort

in 1981, after which worship
recommenced. In the outer
courtyard is the ornate
Kalyana Mandapa. Its pillars
are carved with magnificent
horses and *yali* riders.

Vellore is renowned for its
prestigious Christian Medical
College, set up in 1900 by the
American Dr Ida Scudder.
This instiution specializes in
research on tropical diseases.

> **🏛 Vellore Fort**
> 🔲 *daily.* **Museum** 🔲 *Sat–Thu.*
> ⬤ 2nd Sat of every month.
> **Jalakanteshvara Temple** 🔲 *daily.*
> 📷 *inside the sanctum.*

Environs
Arcot, 27 km (17 miles) east of
Vellore, is best known for its
flamboyant nawabs *(see p570)*
and their resistance to the
British and French forces in the
late 18th century. Some derelict
tombs and a Jami Masjid are all
that remain from that period.

Tiruvannamalai ❺

Tiruvannamalai district. 85 km (53
miles) S of Vellore. 🚉 ▨
🎫 *Karthigai Deepam (Nov/Dec).*

One of the most sacred
cities of Tamil Nadu, this
pilgrim town is the place
where Shiva is believed to
have appeared as a column
of fire *(sthavara* linga*)* in
order to assert his supremacy
over Brahma and Vishnu.
Arunachala Hill (the "Red
Mountain"), which forms
a backdrop to the town, is
said to be the site where the
fire manifested itself, and is
thus perceived as the light of
god himself. On the day of
the Karthigai Deepam festival
(see p589), an enormous
deepa (lamp), using 2,000
litres (528 gallons) of ghee
and a 30-m (98-ft) wide wick,
is lit on the hill, and burns for
days. On a full moon night,

THE FIVE ELEMENTAL LINGAS

Hindu belief holds that five essential elements – air,
water, fire, earth and ether – created man and the universe. Shiva, one of the three main gods of the Hindu
Trinity, is represented as the embodiment of these five
elements in five different places. At Sri Kalahasti in
Andhra Pradesh *(see p680)*, he is represented as air; in
Tiruvanaikka *(see p603)* he takes the form of water, so
the linga (phallic symbol) in the main sanctum is partly
immersed in water. At
Tiruvannamalai, Shiva
represents fire, while in
the Ekambareshvara
Temple at Kanchipuram
(see p582), the linga is
made of earth. Finally, at
Chidambaram *(see p590)*
Shiva represents ether,
the most sacred of the
five elements.

Nataraja Temple, Chidambaram,
housing the ether linga

The 16th-century Arunachaleshvara
Temple at Tiruvannamalai

pilgrims perform a 14-km (9-mile) long circumambulation on foot around the hill.

Arunachaleshvara Temple, the town's most important structure, is one of the five elemental shrines of Shiva, where the linga, encased in gold, represents fire. Covering a vast area of 10 ha (25 acres), this is also one of the largest temple complexes in India, parts of it dating to the 11th century. It has nine imposing towers, huge *prakaras* (walled and cloistered enclosures), the large Shivaganga Tank and a vast thousand-pillared hall.

Tiruvannamalai is also where Sri Ramana Maharishi, the famed 20th-century saint, spent 23 years in meditation. The **Sri Ramana Maharishi Ashram**, near Arunachala Hill, is an internationally renowned spiritual centre that attracts devotees from all walks of life.

🔲 **Arunachaleshvara Temple**
🔲 *daily.* 🔲 *to non-Hindus.*
🔲 *inside the sanctum.*

Kalyana Mahal with Rajagiri Hill in the background, Gingee

Gingee Fort ❻

Viluppuram district. 37 km (23 miles) E of Tiruvannamalai. 🚌 🔲 *daily.* 📷

Gingee (locally called Senji) Fort, is a remarkable example of military engineering. Its three citadels, dramatically perched atop three hills – Krishnagiri to the north, Rajagiri to the west and Chandrayandurg to the south-

The Krishna Temple and Durbar Hall on Krishnagiri Hill, Gingee Fort

east – are enclosed by solid stone walls to form a vast triangular-shaped area extending more than 1.5 km (1 mile) from north to south.

Built by the local Nayaka governors, feudatories of the Vijayanagar kings, in the 15th and 16th centuries, the fort was occupied by Bijapur's Adil Shahi Sultans *(see p542)*, the Marathas *(see p471)*, the French and finally the British.

This once-great fortress city is dotted with dilapidated arcaded chambers, mosques, *mandapas*, small shrines, tanks and granaries. Many temples, mostly dedicated to Vishnu, survive as well. These include the deserted temple in the main citadel on the 242-m (794-ft) high Rajagiri Hill. The most prominent, however, is the great **Venkataramana Temple**, in the foothills of the outer fort, near Pondicherry Gate. This was constructed by Muthialu Nayaka in the 17th century. Its original pillars were removed by the French and used in the Government Square at Pondicherry *(see p586)*. Near the gateway are

panels depicting scenes from the *Ramayana (see p27)* and the *Vishnu Purana*.

A Ranganatha Temple and a Krishna Temple, both smaller than the Venkataramana Temple, are located on Krishnagiri Hill, as is the **Durbar Hall**. The Durbar Hall has balconies extending to the edge of the hill which provide good views of the surrounding countryside.

The fort's finest monument is the **Kalyana Mahal**, a square hall built for the ladies of the court. The building has a central eight-storeyed pyramidal tower with a single large room on each floor.

There are also traces of a network of natural springs and tanks that provided an excellent supply of water to the citadel. One of the tanks, Chettikulam, has a platform where Raja Thej Singh, a courageous 18th-century Rajput chief and vassal of the Mughal emperor, was cremated. Tamil folk songs glorify Gingee and Raja Thej Singh, who was killed in a heroic battle against the Nawab of Arcot.

Gingee Fort sprawling across three hills

Street-by-Street: Pondicherry **❼**

The former capital of French territories in India, Pondicherry was established in 1674 by François Martin, the first director of the French East India Company. The town is laid out in a grid pattern, with parallel streets cutting across each other at right angles. Its main promenade, the 3-km (2-mile) long Goubert Salai running along the Bay of Bengal, formed part of the French Quarter, with its elegant colonial mansions, tree-lined boulevards, parks, bars and cafés. Beyond this was a canal, now dry, that demarcated the Tamil Town, where the local populace once lived.

Statue of Jeanne d'Arc

Government Square
A pavilion stands in the centre of this tree-lined square.

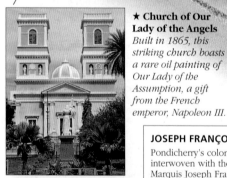

VICTOR SIMONEL STREET

CASERNE STREET

MAHE DE LABOURDONNAIS STREET

GOUBERT SALAI (BEACH ROAD)

A Statue of Mahatma Gandhi, 4 m (13 ft) high, stands on a pedestal surrounded by eight stone pillars.

★ Church of Our Lady of the Angels
Built in 1865, this striking church boasts a rare oil painting of Our Lady of the Assumption, a gift from the French emperor, Napoleon III.

Le Café, a popular restaurant on Goubert Salai.

JOSEPH FRANÇOIS DUPLEIX

Pondicherry's colonial past is intricately interwoven with the life of the redoubtable Marquis Joseph François Dupleix, governor between 1742 and 1754. This energetic statesman tried valiantly to prevent British supremacy by forming alliances with local princes. This power struggle was aggravated by the War of Austrian Succession in Europe between England and France. With the final defeat of the French in the Second Carnatic War, Dupleix relinquished his governorship and returned in disgrace to Paris. His memorial statue is on Goubert Salai.

Dupleix (1697–1764)

STAR SIGHTS

★ Church of Our Lady of the Angels

★ Aurobindo Ashram

★ View of the Seafront

Raj Nivas
*A harmonious
fusion of French
and Indian styles
of architecture,
Dupleix's palatial
home is now
the Lieutenant
Governor's official
residence.*

VISITORS' CHECKLIST

Union Territory of Pondicherry.
160 km (99 miles) S of Chennai.
🚶 220,800. 🚉 🚌 🛈
Pondicherry Tourism, Goubert
Salai, (0413) 233 9497. 📷
🏛 Mon–Sat. 🎭 Masimagam
(Feb/Mar), Ganesha Chaturthi
(Aug/Sep).

**Manakula
Vinayakar Temple**
*Dedicated to
Ganesha, this temple
has a golden spire,
and walls portraying
40 different forms
of Ganesha.*

KEY

– – – – Suggested route

★ Aurobindo Ashram
*Named after Sri Aurobindo (see p588), this
serene ashram organizes regular meditation sessions to which all are welcome.*

Pondicherry
Museum's collection
ranges from ancient Roman
artifacts and Chola bronzes
to beautiful snail shells.

★ View of the Seafront
*Goubert Salai, the boulevard
along the Bay of Bengal, is lined
with grand colonial buildings.*

0 metres   80

0 yards   80

General Hospital

MANAKULA VINAYAKAR

KOIL STREET

FRANCOIS MARTIN STREET

LAW DE LAURISTON STREET

CAMPAGNIE ST

MARINE STREET

Exploring Pondicherry

Often described as a sleepy French provincial town, Pondicherry retains a distinct Gallic flavour. French is still spoken among the older residents, while stately colonial mansions stand in tree-lined streets that are still known by their colonial names. Even the policemen continue to wear the military-style caps, known as kepis. Today, Pondicherry, has been renamed Puduchcheri. Located on the east coast of Tamil Nadu, it is the administrative capital of a Union Territory that includes the former French enclaves of Mahe in Kerala (see p655), Yanam in Andhra Pradesh and Karaikkal in Tamil Nadu.

A policeman wearing a kepi

🏛 Pondicherry Museum

49, Rue St Louis. **Tel** Director Art & Culture (0413) 233 6236. ⬤ Tue–Sun.

Located in the lovely old Law Building, near Government Park, the Pondicherry Museum has an outstanding collection of artifacts from the French colonial period. The rooms in one section are furnished in French style, and are decorated with marble statuary, paintings, mirrors and clocks. Prized exhibits include the bed that Dupleix slept in when he was the governor, and a pousse-pousse, an earlier version of the rickshaw.

The museum also displays rare bronzes and stone sculptures from the Pallava and Chola periods. Among the artifacts excavated from nearby Arikamedu, an ancient port that had trade links with Imperial Rome, are beads, amphorae, coins, ornamented oil lamps, funerary urns and fragments of pottery and china.

Inside the same compound is the **Romain Rolland Library**. Established in 1872, the library now has a rich collection of more than 300,000 volumes, including many rare editions in both French and English. Its mobile library service takes more than 8,000 books in a bus to nearby villages. The reference section, on the second floor, is open to the public.

🏛 Romain Rolland Library
Tel (0413) 233 6426. ⬤ Mon–Sat.

Stained glass, Church of the Sacred Heart

🔒 Church of the Sacred Heart of Jesus
South Boulevard. ⬤ daily.

A serene atmosphere cloaks this brown and white Neo-Gothic church, built in the 1700s. Its most interesting features are its large stained-glass panels depicting incidents from the life of Jesus Christ, and the handsome arches that span the nave. Further along the southern boulevard is the cemetery, which has tombs with ornate marble decorations.

🌿 Botanical Gardens
S of City Bus Stand. 🖼

Lying at the far western end of the old Tamil Town, the Botanical Gardens, laid out in 1826, were designed in the formal French style with clipped trees, flower beds, gravel walks and fountains. The French introduced many unusual and exotic trees and shrubs from all over India and the world, many of which are still here. With its 1,500 species of plants, this is one of the best botanical gardens in South India. An interesting little aquarium displays some of the more spectacular marine species from the Coromandel Coast.

🏛 House of Ananda Rangapillai
Ananda Rangapillai St. **Tel** (0413) 233 5756 for permission to visit.

This lavishly furnished house, once the home of an 18th-century Indian nobleman, offers fascinating glimpses into a vanished lifestyle. Now a museum, the house is owned by Ananda Rangapillai, Dupleix's favourite courtier and dubash (trade agent). A perceptive observer and commentator, he maintained a series of diaries between 1736 and 1760, recording his views of the fluctuating fortunes of the French in India. However, he displeased Madame Dupleix, who eventually ousted him from his post.

SRI AUROBINDO GHOSE

The firebrand Bengali poet-philosopher, Aurobindo Ghose, who joined the struggle for freedom in the early 1900s, was known for his extremist views. To escape from the British, he took refuge in the French territory of Pondicherry, where he was drawn into the spiritual realm. It was here that he studied, wrote about and popularized the principles of yoga. His disciple, Mirra Alfassa, known later as "The Mother", was a Parisian mystic, painter and musician, who first came to Pondicherry with her husband during World War I. Sri Aurobindo's philosophy so inspired her that she stayed on, and was later instrumental in the establishment of the Aurobindo Ashram.

Sri Aurobindo (1872–1950)

The verdant courtyard of the École Française d'Extrême-Orient

🏛 École Française d'Extrême-Orient

16 & 19, Rue Dumas. *Tel (0413) 233 2504.*

An internationally renowned research institution, the 19th-century École Française d'Extrême-Orient is noted for its research in archaeology, history and sociology.

🏛 French Institute of Indology

11, St Louis St. *Tel (0413) 233 4539.*

The prestigious French Institute of Indology was established in the mid-1950s by an eminent French Indologist, Dr Jean Fillozet. Originally set up for the study of local language and culture, this institute now has links with many French universities and research organizations.

🏛 Aurobindo Ashram

Rue de la Marine. *Tel (0413) 223 3604.* ⬜ *daily.*

Pondicherry's best-known landmark, the Aurobindo Ashram dominates life in this town. Founded by Sri Aurobindo in 1926, the Ashram is a peaceful retreat with tree-shaded courtyards. The flower-festooned *samadhi* (memorial) of Sri Aurobindo and The Mother lies under a frangipani tree in the main courtyard. This memorial, with two chambers, one above the other, is the focal point for all disciples and followers.

Environs

Auroville, or the "City of Dawn", 8 km (5 miles) northwest of Pondicherry, was designed by French architect Roger Anger in 1968. Conceived as a utopian paradise by The Mother, Mirra Alfassa, it was planned as a futuristic international city, where people of goodwill would live together in peace. The International Commune, with 40 settlements with names like Grace, Serenity and Certitude, and 550 permanent residents, was meant to bring people from different castes, religions and nations under one roof, where they could live in harmony. Two important settlements, Fraternité and Harmonie, sell handicrafts made by local artisans. The Matri Mandir, a meditation centre set in an area of 25 ha (62 acres), reflects The Mother's spiritual beliefs. This spherical marble chamber has a crystal placed inside it, reflecting the sun's rays. The concentrated light acts as a focal point to aid meditation.

Matri Mandir, the spiritual and physical centre of Auroville

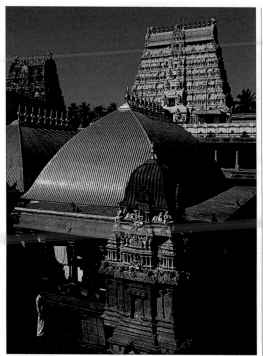

The gold-plated roof of the main sanctum, Nataraja Temple, Chidambaram

Chidambaram ❽

Thanjavur district. 60 km (37 miles) S of Pondicherry. 🚍 59,000. 🚉 🚌 🏨 Hotel Tamil Nadu, Railway Feeder Rd, (04144) 238 739. 🎭 Dance Festival (Feb/Mar), Arudhra (Dec/Jan).

Sacred Chidambaram, where Shiva is believed to have performed his cosmic dance, the *tandava nritya*, is a traditional temple town where history merges with mythology to create a deeply religious ambience. All ancient Hindu beliefs and practices are zealously observed here, manifested in an endless cycle of rites and rituals.

The focal point of the town is the awe-inspiring **Nataraja Temple**, built by the Cholas (*see pp46–7*) in the 9th century to honour their patron deity, Shiva as Nataraja, the "Lord of Dance" (*see p566*). The temple has an unusual hut-like sanctum with a gold-plated roof, the huge, colonnaded Shivaganga Tank, and four colourful *gopuras*. The most interesting is the eastern *gopura* which

features detailed sculptures of the 108 hand and feet movements of Bharat Natyam (*see p29*), and is considered a veritable encyclopaedia of this classical temple dance.

Within the temple's three enormous enclosures are five major halls (*sabhas*), each conceived for a special purpose. In the outer enclosure, next to the Shivaganga Tank, is the Raja Sabha ("Royal Hall"), a beautiful thousand-pillared hall, built as a venue for temple rituals and festivals. Many Chola kings were crowned here in the presence of the deity. In the central enclosure is the Deva Sabha ("Divine Hall"), where temple bronzes are housed, and administrative functions performed. The adjacent Nritya Sabha ("Dance Hall") has a superb collection of sculptures, the finest being the **Urdhava Tandava**. The

Urdhava Tandava, Nataraja Temple

innermost enclosure, the holiest part of the complex, contains the Chit Sabha or Chitambalam ("Hall of Bliss"), from which the town derives its name. This is the main sanctum, housing one of the five elemental lingas of Shiva (*see p584*), the *akasha* linga, which represents ether, the all-pervading element central to human existence. The inner sanctum containing the linga is hidden behind a black curtain, symbolizing ignorance, which is removed only during prayer time. There is a certain aura of mystery to this veiled sanctum and it is often called the Sacred Secret of Chidambaram (Chidambara Rahasyam). Finally, the fifth hall, in front of the Chit Sabha, is the Kanaka Sabha ("Golden Hall"), where Shiva is supposed to have performed his cosmic dance.

Other areas of interest in the complex are the **Govindarajaswamy Shrine**, housing the reclining Vishnu, the **Shivakamasundari Shrine**, dedicated to Shiva's consort, Parvati, and the **Subramanyam Shrine**, in which Murugan is worshipped.

Religious traditions in the temple are preserved by a group of hereditary priests whose ancestors came to Chidambaram 3,000 years ago. Known as the *dikshitars*, they are easily recognized by their top-knots. Chidambaram's other claim to fame is the modern **Annamalai University**, which is located to the east. Founded by a philanthropist over 50 years ago, it is Tamil Nadu's first residential university, specializing in South Indian studies.

🏛 **Nataraja Temple**
Near bus stand. ◯ daily. 🎭 🎫

Environs
Located 16 km (10 miles) east of Chidambaram, **Pichavaram's** maze of picturesque backwaters, with mangrove forests and 1,700 islands in 4,000 canals, can be explored in rowboats.

Coromandel Driving Tour ❾

Named after Cholamandalam ("the Realm of the Cholas"), the Coromandel Coast extends from the Godavari Delta in Andhra Pradesh in the north, to Point Calimere in the south. This spectacularly beautiful strip of land played a significant role in the maritime history of India. Its great ports have, through the ages, attracted traders and merchants in search of textiles and spices.

Dansborg Fort at Tarangambadi

Tirumullaivasal ①
A magnificent shrine to Shiva dominates this small, coastal town.

Poompuhar ②
This historic port city once had trade links with ancient Greece and Rome. An interesting museum here recreates stories of its past glory in bas-reliefs.

Tarangambadi ③
More popularly known as Tranquebar, this little town was a Danish settlement in the 17th century. It has an impressive fort, churches and a beautiful brick gateway, the Town Gate.

KEY

— Tour route

— Other roads

Bay of Bengal

Karaikal ④
This former French town has many 19th-century mansions and a Neo-Gothic church.

Nagapattinam ⑥
An old Chola port, this was also a major Buddhist centre till the 13th century. It was later occupied by the Portuguese, the Dutch and finally the British.

Nagore ⑤
The 16th-century tomb of Hazrat Sayyid Shahul, a Muslim saint who died in Nagore, attracts devotees of all religions, castes and creeds.

Velanganni ⑦
People of all religions seek cures at the Neo-Gothic Basilica of Our Lady of Good Health.

Point Calimere ⑧
This wildlife sanctuary spread over 20,000 ha (49,421 acres) of saline marshland is a haven for migratory birds.

TIPS FOR DRIVERS

Length: 90 km (56 miles).
Stopping-off points: Hotel Tamil Nadu at both Poompuhar and Nagapattinam are convenient stopping-off points. The route is well connected by government and private buses.

Map labels: CHIDAMBARAM, Sirkazhi, Kaveri, Mayiladuthurai, Thiruvarur, Vettar, Vellar, Tiruthuraippundi

0 km 10
0 miles 10

The superb Nataraja sculpture at Gangaikondacholapuram

Gangaikondacholapuram ⑩

Tiruchirapalli district. 40 km (25 miles) SW of Chidambaram. 🚌 *from Chidambaram or Kumbakonam.*

Grandly titled Gangaikondacholapuram, "The City of the Chola who Took the Ganges", this now modest village was the capital of the powerful Chola dynasty *(see pp46–7)* during the reign of Rajendra I (r.1012–44). A great military commander like his father Rajaraja I, Rajendra I was the first Tamil ruler to venture northwards. He built this city to commemorate his successful campaign across the Ganges. According to an inscription, he then ordered the defeated rulers to carry back pots of sacred Ganges water on their heads to fill the Chola-Ganga tank, a victory memorial.

Except for the magnificent **Brihadishvara Temple**, little remains of his capital city. Built as a replica of Thanjavur's Brihadishvara Temple *(see pp598–9)*, the towered sanctum of this granite Shiva temple is shorter than the one at Thanjavur. Adorning the lower walls, columns and niches are many remarkable sculptural friezes. One of the most outstanding is the panel depicting Shiva blessing Chandesha, a pious devotee sculpted to resemble Rajendra I himself. The sculptures of the *dikpalas* (guardians of the eight directions), *ekadasas* (the 11 forms of Shiva), Saraswati, Kalyanasundara and Nataraja *(see p566)* are also splendid examples of Chola art. Steps near the small Durga shrine in the courtyard lead past a sculpture of a seated lion to a well, believed to have been filled with Ganges water for daily rituals.

The small **Archaeological Museum**, near the temple, exhibits Chola artifacts from neighbouring sites.

🏛 **Brihadishvara Temple**
◯ *daily.* **Museum** ◯ *Sat–Thu.*

Kumbakonam ⑪

Thanjavur district. 74 km (46 miles) SW of Chidambaram. 🚶 *140,100.*
🚉 🚌 ℹ *Thanjavur tourist office, (04362) 231 325.* 🎭 *Nageshvara Temple Festival (Apr/May), Mahamaham Festival (every 12 years).*

Like Kanchipuram *(see p582)*, Kumbakonam is one of the most sacred cities in Tamil Nadu. Located on the southern bank of the Kaveri river, this is an ancient city that, as legend says, Shiva's arrow shattered the cosmic pot *(kumbh)* containing the divine nectar of creation *(amrit)*. This myth has given Kumbakonam both its name and sanctity. Today, the city represents the traditional cultural values of the Tamil heartland. It is also the region's main commercial and craft centre, famous for its textiles, jewellery, bronze casting and the superior quality of its locally grown betel leaves.

It is believed that when the divine nectar emerged from the pot, it filled the huge **Mahamaham Tank**. This is Kumbakonam's sacred centre and the site of the great Mahamaham Festival, held every 12 years (the last one was held in 2004). At the

The 17th-century Adikumbheshvara Temple, Kumbakonam

auspicious time, thousands of devotees enter the tank for their holy dip. This is when the purifying power of the water is said to be at its height. The devout believe that all of India's nine sacred rivers (Ganges, Yamuna, Saraswati, Sarayu, Godavari, Narmada, Kaveri, Payokshini and Kanniyakumari) also bathe in the tank to cleanse themselves of the sins of humanity accumulated in their waters.

The tank, renovated by the Nayakas in the 17th century, has steps at the four cardinal points, and 16 ornate pavilions in honour of the 16 *mahadanas* (great gifts bestowed by a ruler on a spiritual centre). A fine example of Nayaka art is a relief depicting a king being weighed on a balance against gold (a ceremony known as *tulapurushadeva*), carved on the roof of a 16-pillared *mandapa* that stands at the northwest corner of the tank. To the north is the **Kashivishvanatha Temple**, which has a small shrine facing the water; this is dedicated to the nine sacred rivers, personified as goddesses. The shrine representing the Kaveri river occupies the central position.

To the east of the tank is the 17th-century **Adikumbheshvara Temple**, built on the legendary spot where Shiva shattered the pot. A unique feature here is the depiction of 27 stars and the 12 zodiac signs carved on a large block of stone in the Navaratri Mandapa. It also has a superb collection of silver *vahanas* (vehicles) which are used during festivals to carry the temple deities. The grand, 12-storeyed **Sarangapani Temple**, to the east, is the most important Vaishnavite shrine in the city.

Nearby is the 9th-century **Nageshvara Temple**, a fine example of early Chola architecture. The town's oldest temple, this is the site of an annual festival that celebrates the worship of the linga by the sun. Niches on the sanctum walls contain exquisitely carved figures depicting the forms of Shiva, and scenes from the *Ramayana*.

Temple chariots at Kumbakonam's Adikumbheshvara Temple

Environs

The spectacular Airavateshvara Temple at **Darasuram**, 4 km (2.5 miles) west of Kumbakonam, was built by the Chola king, Rajaraja II (r.1146–73). This temple is dedicated to Shiva, who is known here as Airavateshvara, the "Lord of Airavata". Legend claims that after Airavata, the white elephant of Indra, the God of the Heavens, regained his lost colour, he worshipped Shiva at this spot.

Shiva's wedding procession, Darasuram

The four-tiered temple has a sanctum and three halls, of which the finest is the Rajagambira Mandapa, conceived as a stone chariot drawn by caparisoned horses, with Brahma as its driver. The outer walls have fine friezes and carvings of musicians, dancers and acrobats as well as depictions from the *Periya Puranam*, a Tamil treatise on the 63 Shaivite poet-saints, the Nayannars *(see p45)*.

The late Chola temple at **Tirubhuvanam**, 8 km (5 miles) northeast of Kumbakonam, is dedicated to Kumbheshvara, the "God who Removes Fear". This is also an old silk weaving centre. About 8 km (5 miles) west of Kumbakonam is **Swamimalai**, one of the six sacred shrines devoted to Lord Murugan *(see p25)*, who, legend says, propounded the meaning of "Om", the sacred mantra, to his father Shiva, and thus assumed the title Swaminatha ("Lord of Lords"). The temple, situated on a hill, has an impressive statue of Murugan in the sanctum; interestingly, he has an elephant as his vehicle instead of the typical peacock. This small village is also an important centre for bronze casting, where artisans still use traditional methods to create beautiful images for temples *(see p594)*.

Small votive shrines outside the Airavateshvara Temple, Darasuram

The College of Music at Tiruvaiyaru, on the Kaveri river

Tiruvaiyaru ⓬

Thanjavur district. 13 km (8 miles) N of Thanjavur. 🏛 14,500. 📷 Thyagaraja Music Festival (Jan).

The fertile region watered by the Kaveri river and its four tributaries is known as Tiruvaiyaru, the sacred *(tiru)* land of five *(i)* rivers *(aru)*. For nearly 2,000 years the Tamil people have regarded the Kaveri as the sacred source of life, religion and culture. As a result, many scholars, artists, poets and musicians settled in this region, under the enlightened patronage of the rulers of Thanjavur *(see pp596–7)*. Among these was Thyagaraja (1767–1847), the greatest composer-saint of Carnatic music. The history of this small town is thus deeply linked with the growth and development of South Indian classical music.

The little **Thyagaraja Temple**, in the town, was built to commemorate the last resting place of the celebrated composer-saint. A musical festival is held here every year on the anniversary of his death, which falls, according to the Tamil calendar, in January. Hundreds of musicians and students of Carnatic music gather in the town and sing Thyagaraja's songs from morning till midnight for a whole week.

As dawn breaks over the river, a procession of musicians makes the short journey from Thyagaraja's house to the temple, singing continuously all the way. Music lovers wait eagerly at the shrine, seated on the mud floor of the thatch-roofed auditorium. To the sacred chants of priests, the stone image of Thyagaraja is ritually bathed with milk, rosewater, sandalwood and honey. The five songs known as the *pancha ratna* ("five gems") of Thyagaraja, which are considered unequalled masterpieces of Carnatic music, are sung in a grand chorus by all the assembled musicians. This ceremony is an annual reaffirmation of devotion to the composer and to a great tradition of music. For music lovers from all over India, it can be a magical experience.

Also in the town is the 9th-century **Panchanandishvara Temple** ("Lord of the Five Rivers"), built by the Cholas. Dedicated to Shiva, the shrines of Uttara (north) Kailasha and Dakshina (south) Kailasha, on either side of the main temple, were built by the wives of Rajaraja I and Rajendra I *(see pp46–7)*. The temple's huge *prakara* (boundary) walls, pillared *mandapas* and the Mukti Mandapa are immortalized in the songs of the Nayannars, a sect of 7th-century poet-saints *(see p45)*.

Environs
Pullamangai village, 12 kms (7 miles) northeast of Tiruvaiyaru, is noted for the **Brahmapurishvara Temple**, dating to the 10th century. The temple features elegant depictions of various gods and goddesses.

Children frolicking in the waters of the Kaveri, Tiruvaiyaru

THANJAVUR BRONZES

Artisan fashioning bronze idols

The Thanjavur region's wealth of artistic traditions includes the creation of exquisite bronze images through a process known as *cire perdue* or the "lost wax" technique. A model of the image is first made in wax and then coated with layers of clay to create a mould, which is heated to allow the melting wax to flow out through a hole at the base. A molten alloy of five metals *(panch loha)* is poured into the hollow. When it cools, the mould is broken and the image is finished and polished. Finally, the image's eyes are sealed with a mixture of honey and ghee and then ritually "opened" by a priest, using a golden needle. Even today, traditional artisans, known as *sthapathis*, create these images according to a fixed set of rules and guidelines laid down in the *Shilpa Shastra*, an ancient treatise on art. The main centre for bronze casting in Tamil Nadu is Swamimalai *(see p593)*.

Carnatic Music

The classical music of South India is known as Carnatic music. Though based on the general concepts of raga (melody) and *tala* (rhythm) found in Hindustani music *(see pp28–9)*, Carnatic music differs in many respects. It is almost exclusively devotional in character, uses different percussion and musical instruments, and develops the melody in a more

Thyagaraja, father of Carnatic music

structured manner. It also lays more emphasis on rhythm. Some of the greatest Carnatic music was composed between 1750 and 1850, by the musical trinity of Thyagaraja, Syama Sastri, and Muthuswami Dikshitar who, between them, wrote over 2,500 songs in Sanskrit and Telegu, modifying and refining features that are now essential to the genre.

ACCOMPANYING INSTRUMENTS

Traditional South Indian instruments such as the *veena*, the *nadasvaram*, the flute and the *thavil* are used for accompaniment, along with Western instruments such as the violin and saxophone.

MS Subbulakshmi is a leading vocalist.

The violin, *a bow-string instrument of Western origin, is played in a seated position.*

The ghatam, *a mere clay pot, can produce fabulous rhythms in the hands of an accomplished performer.*

Mridangam (two-headed drum)

Saraswati veena

Flute

Tanpura

Ghatam

Mridangam

Violin

Music festivals *are often held in large cities, where concerts take place in small auditoriums, called* sabhas. *Most performers are accompanied by a violinist and two percussionists. A typical concert lasts for about three hours, during which a series of songs, usually in Telugu, are sung. The lyrics are as important as the melody, and many are devotional in nature.*

The nadasvaram, *which is a wind instrument, is a must at temple festivals, weddings and auspicious occasions. The thavil (drum) player performs complex rythmic improvisations to accompany the melody.*

The veena, *which resembles the more widely seen sitar, is a beautifully hand-crafted string instrument.*

Thanjavur

The city of Thanjavur, or Tanjore, lies in the fertile Kaveri Delta, a region often referred to as the "rice bowl of Tamil Nadu". For nearly a thousand years, this great town dominated the political history of the region as the capital of three powerful dynasties – the Cholas (9th–13th centuries), the Nayakas (1535–1676) and the Marathas (1676–1855). The magnificent Brihadishvara Temple *(see pp598–9)*, is the most important Chola monument, while the Royal Palace dates to the Nayaka and Maratha periods. Today, Thanjavur's culture extends beyond temples and palaces, to encompass classical music and dance. It is also a flourishing centre for bronze sculpture and painting.

Seven-storeyed observation tower of the Royal Palace, Thanjavur

🏯 Shivaganga Fort
Off Hospital Rd. ☐ *daily.*
The quadrangular Shivaganga Fort, southwest of the old city, was built by the Nayaka ruler, Sevappa Nayaka, in the mid-16th century. Its battlemented stone walls, which enclose an area of 14 ha (35 acres), are surrounded by a partly rock-cut moat. The square **Shivaganga Tank** in the fort was excavated by Rajaraja I, and later renovated to provide drinking water for the city. The fort also contains the great Brihadishvara Temple, Schwartz Church, and a public amusement park.

Maratha ruler Serfoji II (r.1798–1832)

🛕 Brihadishvara Temple
See pp598–9.

⛪ Schwartz Church
Off West Main Rd. ☐ *daily.*
The 18th-century Christ Church or Schwartz Church, a legacy of Thanjavur's colonial past, stands to the east of the Shivaganga Tank. This church was founded by the Danish missionary, Reverend Frederik Christian Schwartz, in 1779. When he died in 1798, the enlightened Maratha ruler, Serfoji II, donated a striking marble tablet to the church. This tablet, made by John Flaxman, has been placed at the western end of the church. It depicts the dying missionary blessing his royal patron, surrounded by ministers and pupils from the school that he established.

🏛 Royal Palace
East Main Rd. ☐ *daily.* 🎥 ☐ *extra charges.*
Resembling the shape of a flying eagle, this palace was built originally by the Nayaka rulers as their royal residence, and was subsequently remodelled by the Marathas. A large quadrangular courtyard leads into the palace complex, at one end of which is a pyramidal, temple-like tower. Outside the palace complex stands the seven storeyed, arcaded observation tower, now without its capping pavilion.

The splendid Maratha Durbar Hall, built by Shahji II in 1684, has elaborately painted and decorated pillars, walls and ceiling. A wooden canopy embellished with glittering glass pieces and supported by four wooden pillars stands above a green granite slab on which the royal Maratha throne once stood. The other buildings include the Sadir Mahal, which is still the residence of the erstwhile royal family, and the Puja Mahal.

The **Rajaraja Museum and Art Gallery**, in the Nayaka Durbar Hall, was established in 1951 and has an impressive collection of bronze and stone idols dating from the 7th to the 20th centuries. Particularly noteworthy are the images of Shiva, such as the Kalyanasundaramurti, which depicts the wedding of Shiva and Parvati *(see p566)*, and the Bhikshatanamurti, which shows Shiva as a wandering mendicant, carrying a begging bowl and accompanied by a dog.

Next to the Rajaraja Museum is the **Saraswati Mahal Library**, constructed by the Maratha rulers. This is one of the most important reference libraries in India, with a fine collection of rare palm-leaf manuscripts and books collected by the versa-

Mural at the entrance of Saraswati Mahal, Royal Palace, Thanjavur

tile and scholarly Serfoji II. An adjoining **Museum** displays some of these valuable works.

The **Royal Museum** occupies part of the private quarters of the Maratha Palace, and exhibits the personal collection of Serfoji II.

Nearby is the Sangeeta Mahal (Music Hall), built by the Nayakas, and specially designed with acoustic features for musical gatherings.

Vithoba fresco in the Art Gallery, Royal Palace, Thanjavur

🏛 Rajaraja Museum and Art Gallery
○ daily.
● public hols. 📷

🏛 Saraswati Mahal Library
◐ to public. **Museum** ○ Thu–Tue.

🏛 Royal Museum
○ daily. 📷

Environs
Lying 55 km (34 miles) east of Thanjavur, Thiruvarur is famous for its Thyagaraja Temple dedicated to the

---

VISITORS' CHECKLIST

Thanjavur district. 350 km (218 miles) SW of Chennai.
🚉 215,800. 🚌 🚆 ℹ Jawan Bhavan, (04362) 230 984.
📧 Mon–Sat. 📷 Rajaraja Chola's Birth Anniversary (Oct).

Somaskanda form of Shiva (see p578). The temple has four gopuras. Its ceiling is covered with 17th-century paintings of scenes from the Shiva legend.

THANJAVUR PAINTINGS

A distinctive school of painting emerged during the rule of the Marathas, patronized by Serfoji II. This highly ornamental style was characterized by vibrant colours as well as decoration with gold leaf and precious and semi-precious stones. The themes are mostly religious, and the symbolic colour palette of red, black, blue and white depicts each deity in a specific colour. The subjects usually have rotund bodies and almond-shaped eyes. A favourite image is Krishna portrayed as a chubby infant.

Baby Krishna with his mother, Yashodhara

THANJAVUR CITY CENTRE

Brihadishvara Temple ②
Royal Palace ④
Schwartz Church ③
Shivaganga Fort ①

NORTH REHANI STREET
NORTH MAIN STREET
Food Market
NORTH MAIN STREET
EAST MAIN STREET
MARKET ROAD
D KULAM RD
Royal Palace Compound
④ Entrance
Rajaraja Museum & Art Gallery
Saraswati Mahal Library & Museums
WEST MAIN STREET
WEST RAMPART STREET
SOUTH MAIN STREET
SOUTH RAMPART STREET
MARKET ROAD

0 metres 250
0 yards 250

City Bus Stand
③ Schwartz Church
HOSPITAL ROAD
Shivaganga Tank
① Shivaganga Fort
Seppu Naikkan Tank
Brihadishvara Temple ②
GANDHIJI ROAD
ABRAHAM PANDITHER RD
GRAND ANICUT CANAL RD
Grand Anicut Canal
KUTCHERY RD
Railway Station
200 m (220 yards)
THIRUVARUR

Key to Symbols see back flap

Thanjavur: Brihadishvara Temple

A Shiva sculpture

This monumental granite temple, the finest example of Chola architecture, is now a UNESCO World Heritage Site. Completed in AD 1010 and dedicated to Shiva, it was built by Rajaraja Chola I *(see pp46–7)* as a symbol of the unrivalled power and might of the Cholas. The temple basement is covered with inscriptions that give details of the temple's administration and revenue, and provide valuable historical information on Chola society and government.

An octagonal cupola, beautifully carved out of a massive block of granite weighing 80 tonnes, crowns the *vimana*.

The passageway is circumambulatory and built on two levels, owing to the colossal height of the 4-m (13-ft) linga.

★ **Vimana**
The 66-m (217-ft) high pyramid-shaped vimana, over the sanctum, is a 13-storeyed structure. Its gilded finial was presented by the king.

★ **Dvarapala**
Two gigantic dvarapalas, or doorkeepers, at the eastern entrance, direct devotees to the sanctum with their pointed fingers.

Linga shrine

STAR FEATURES

★ Vimana

★ Dvarapala

★ Nandi Mandapa

Frescoes
Chola frescoes adorn the passage around the sanctum. They were discovered when the 17-century Maratha paintings covering them began to disintegrate.

General View of the Temple
*The Brihadishvara Temple stands
in the middle of a rectangular
court, surrounded by subsidiary
shrines. On the southern side of
the courtyard is an Archaeological Museum which displays,
among other things, photographs
of the temple before restoration.*

★ **Nandi Mandapa**
*Carved out of a single
block of granite weighing
25 tonnes, this huge
Nandi figure is 6 m
(20 ft) long, and faces
the inner sanctum.*

**Priests Outside the
Temple**
*Although under the
jurisdiction of the
Archaeological Survey
of India, the temple has
recently been opened
for worship.*

Nandi
Mandapa

Shiva-Parvati
*Granite divinities occupy the
wall niches of the sanctum.*

Tiruchirapalli's Rock Fort looming above the city

Tiruchirapalli ⑭

Tiruchirapalli district. 60 km (37 miles) W of Thanjavur. ▥ 746,100. ✈ 7 km (4 miles) S of town centre, then bus or taxi. ▤ ▭ ⓘ Hotel Tamil Nadu, 1 Williams Rd, (0431) 241 4346. ◪ Teppakulam Float Festival (Mar).

Situated at the head of the fertile Kaveri Delta, this city is named after the fierce three-headed demon *(tirusira)* who attained salvation after being slain by Shiva. The town's history is interwoven with the political fortunes of the Pallavas, Cholas, Nayakas and finally the British, who shortened its name to Trichy. Today, Tiruchirapalli is Tamil Nadu's second largest city.

Dominating the town is the massive **Rock Fort**, perched dramatically on a rocky outcrop that rises 83 m (272 ft) above the flat plains. This impregnable fortress was constructed by the Nayakas of neighbouring Madurai, who made Tiruchirapalli their

second capital in the 16th and 17th centuries. They also expanded the Shiva temple, where the god is worshipped as Thayumanavar (the "God who Became a Mother"). Legend says that when a flash flood prevented a mother from coming to her pregnant daughter's aid, Shiva assumed her form and helped in the childbirth. Further up, on the summit, is a small Ganesha Temple from where there are spectacular views of verdant rice fields and the sacred island of Srirangam.

At the base of the southern rock face is the first of the two cave temples. The lower one dates to the 8th century, and the upper one to the reign of the great Pallava ruler, Mahendra Varman (r.600–630). This contains one of the great wonders of Pallava art, the Gangadhara Panel, depicting Shiva holding a lock of his matted hair to receive the River Ganga as she descends from the heavens *(see p163)*.

Much of the present town dates to the 18th and 19th centuries, when the British constructed the cantonment and numerous civic buildings and churches. Many of these buildings are located around the large Teppakulam Tank at the base of the fort – a busy area surrounded by fruit, vegetable and flower markets.

Among the town's earliest churches are Christ Church (1766), founded by Reverend Frederick Christian Schwartz *(see p596)*, to the north of the tank; the Neo-Gothic **Cathedral of Our Lady of Lourdes** (1840), to the west of the tank; and the Jesuit St Joseph's College, also to the west of the tank. In the cantonment, which lies to the southwest of the fort, is the Church of St John (1816).

⚑ **Rock Fort**
◯ daily. 📷 extra charges.

The Cathedral of Our Lady of Lourdes at Tiruchirapalli

THE KAVERI RIVER

Shrine depicting the legend of Goddess Kaveri

One of the nine sacred rivers of India, the Kaveri covers a length of 785 km (488 miles) from its source at Talakaveri in Karnataka *(see p521)* to Poompuhar on the Bay of Bengal. Myths glorify the Kaveri as the personification of a female deity (in some versions, Brahma's daughter), who erupted from the sage Agasthya's *kamandala* (water pot). From the early centuries of the Christian era, the Kaveri has been central to Tamil culture, especially under the Cholas, who ruled the region between the 9th and 13th centuries. The great temple cities that developed along its course became centres of religion, dance, music and the arts. Farsighted water management schemes in the delta, instigated by the Cholas, transformed the Thanjavur region into the "rice bowl" of Tamil Nadu, and even today, devotees offer rice to the river goddess on the 18th day of the Tamil month Adi (July/August). Unfortunately, the river has now become the subject of a bitter dispute over water distribution between the Tamil Nadu and Karnataka governments.

Environs

At **Kallanai**, 24 km (15 miles) northeast of Tiruchirapalli, is a 300-m (984-ft) long earthen dam across the Kaveri river, the Grand Anicut. This formed part of the huge hydraulic system created by the Cholas *(see pp46–7)* to divert water from the river into a vast network of irrigation canals. The original no longer exists and the dam in operation today was rebuilt by British engineers in the 19th century.

Other places of interest are the 7th-century Shiva temple at **Narthamalai**, 17 km (11 miles) to the south, and the 9th-century Jain cave temples at **Sittanavasal**, 58 km (36 miles) to the southeast. Faded paintings here portray dancing girls, and a lotus tank with swans and fishes.

Srirangam ⓑ

Tiruchirapalli district. 9 km (6 miles) N of Tiruchirapalli. *Vaikuntha Eka-dashi (Dec/Jan), Chariot Festival (Jan).*

The sacred 3-km (2-mile) long island of Srirangam, formed by the Kaveri and Kollidam rivers, is one of the most revered pilgrimage sites in South India. At its core is the majestic **Ranganatha Temple** *(see pp552–3).* Dedicated to Vishnu, this is one of the largest temple complexes in Tamil Nadu and covers an enormous area of 60 ha (148 acres).

The complex as it exists today has evolved over a period of four centuries.

Extensive reconstruction first took place in 1371, after the original 10th-century temple was destroyed by the Delhi Sultan, Alauddin Khilji *(see p48).* Its present form, however, includes extensions added in the 17th century by the Nayaka rulers, whose second capital was in neighbouring Tiruchirapalli. Interestingly, the last addition was as recent as 1987, when the unfinished southern gateway was finally completed.

Dominated by 21 impressive *gopuras* (gateways), the complex has seven *prakara* (boundary) walls defining its seven enclosures. The outer three comprise residences for priests, hostels for pilgrims, and small restaurants and shops selling religious books, pictures and sundry temple offerings. The sacred precinct begins from the fourth enclosure, beyond which non-Hindus are not allowed. This is where the temple's most important shrines are located. Among these are the spacious Thousand-Columned Mandapa, where images of Ranganatha and his consort are enthroned and worshipped during one of the temple's many festivals, and the magnificent **Seshagirirayar Mandapa**, with its rearing

A coracle ride on the Kaveri, Srirangam

stone horses with mounted warriors attacking fierce animals and *yalis* (mythical leonine beasts). A small museum close by has a good collection of stone and bronze sculptures.

The core of the complex is the sanctum, with its gold-plated *vimana*, where an image of Vishnu as Ranganatha, reclining on the cosmic serpent, Adisesha, is enshrined. This temple is also the place where the great 11th-century philosopher, Ramanuja *(see p522)*, developed the *bhakti* cult of personal devotion into a formalized mode of worship. Today, a constant cycle of festivals glorifying Vishnu are celebrated throughout the year.

Horse, Sesha-girirayar Mandapa

East of the Ranganatha Temple is the mid-17th-century **Jambukeshvara Temple** in the village of Tiruvanaikka. The main sanctum contains one of the five elemental lingas *(see p584)*, representing Shiva as the manifestation of water. Legend says that the linga was created by Shiva's consort, Parvati, and in homage to her, the priest wears a sari when performing the *puja*. Non-Hindus can view the outer shrines in the complex, but not the main sanctum.

🏛 **Sri Ranganatha Temple**
🕐 daily. 🎫 for viewpoint on top. 📷 extra charges. **Museum** 🕐 daily.

🏛 **Jambukeshvara Temple**
🕐 daily. 🎫 📷 extra charges.

One of the impressive gateways at the Ranganatha Temple, Srirangam

▷ **The verdant Marthanda Valley, with the misty Nilgiri Hills in the background**

Yerikadu Lake, from which Yercaud derives its name

Yercaud ⑯

Salem district. 32 km (20 miles) NE of Salem. 🚩 *Salem, then bus.* 🚌 *Hotel Tamil Nadu, Yercaud Ghat Rd, (04281) 223 334.* 🎭 *Shevaroyan Temple Festival (May).*

This attractive hill station, situated in the Shevaroy Hills, was established in the early 1800s by the British, who introduced the coffee plant here. Today, this is one of the state's most productive areas, and its surrounding slopes are entirely covered with plantations of coffee, tea, jackfruit and plantains.

The man-made **Yerikadu Lake** and the **Killiyur Falls** are two of the area's most scenic spots, while **Lady's Seat**, near the lake, offers delightful views of the surrounding countryside. The town and its environs have several apiaries that produce delicious honey. The **Horticultural Research Station** has an interesting collection of rare plants.

Mudumalai Wildlife Sanctuary ⑰

Nilgiris district. 64 km (40 miles) W of Udhagamandalam. 🚌 *Theppakadu, the main entry point.* 🛈 *Tourist Office, Theppakadu, (0423) 244 3977. For bookings contact Wildlife Warden's Office, Ooty, (0423) 244 4098.* ◯ *daily (may be closed during Feb–Mar).* 🎫 📷 *Jeeps available.* 🏕

Mudumalai or "Ancient Hill Range", situated at the base of the Nilgiri Hills, is separated from Karnataka's Bandipur National Park *(see p520)* by the Moyar river.

This sanctuary is an important constituent of the 5,500-sq km (2,124-sq mile) Nilgiri Biosphere Reserve of the Western Ghats. Along with adjacent Bandipur and Nagarhole, it provides one of the most important refuges for the elephant and the bison in India. The park encompasses 322 sq km (124 sq miles) of undulating terrain, and rises to 1,250 m (4,101 ft) at Moyar

Tour of the Nilgiris ⑱

The picturesque *nila Giri* or "Blue Mountains", at the junction of the Eastern and Western Ghats, are so named because the shrub *kurunji (Strobilanthes kunthianus)* turns the hills blue with its blossoms every 12 years. Covered with high altitude grasslands and *sholas* (montane evergreen forests), they are of special interest to botanists and entomologists. This tour offers enchanting glimpses of lush green valleys, hill stations and hamlets inhabited by tribal people.

Jacaranda in full bloom in the Nilgiris

Pykara ⑥
Dams, fenced *sholas*, green meadows and conical-shaped Toda houses can be seen here.

MUDUMALAI

Pykara Reservoir

TIPS FOR DRIVERS

Length: 90 km (56 miles).
Getting around: Avalanche and Pykara can only be reached from Ooty, as there are no road links from Coonoor. The route is well covered by public & private buses. An exciting alternative is the *Nilgiri Blue Mountain Train*, which runs from Mettupalayam to Ooty, via Coonoor (see p777).

Avalanche ⑤
This natural paradise has dense forests and a beautiful lake.

| 0 km | 3 |
| 0 miles | 3 |

KEY

—— Tour route

══ Other roads

Makurti Lake

⑤

Betta. The lowest point of the sanctuary is at the picturesque **Moyar Waterfalls**. Its topography is as varied as the vegetation, which ranges from dense deciduous forests of teak, laurel and rosewood in the west, to scrub jungle towards the east, interspersed with grassland, swamps and bamboo brakes.

The sanctuary provides a habitat for a rich diversity of wildlife, including the Nilgiri tahr *(see p19)*, sambar, tiger, leopard, spotted deer, flying squirrel, Malabar civet and Nilgiri langur. Over 120 species of birds, resident and migratory, can be seen here as well. These include the scops owl and the crested hawk eagle.

GUARDIAN DEITIES

Huge figures made of burnt clay can be seen on the outskirts of villages in the southern districts of Tamil Nadu. They are worshipped as the guardians of the villages. The most prominent folk deity is Ayyanar, the son of Shiva and Vishnu. This mustachioed god, with prominent eyes, wears short trousers and carries a sword. His horse stands by his side so that he can ride through the night, keeping evil spirits at bay. Other deities are Munisami, who holds a trident and shield and rides a lion, and the black-hued Karuppusami, the nocturnal avenger who punishes thieves.

Guardian deities outside a village shrine

Coimbatore ⑲

Coimbatore district. 96 km (60 miles) NE of Chennai. 🏠 924,000. ✈ 10 km (6 miles) NE of city centre, then bus. 🚌 🚃 ℹ Tamil Nadu Tourism, Railway Station, (0422) 230 2176. 🏛 Mon–Sat. 🎎 Thaipoosam (Jan/Feb), Karthigai (Nov/Dec).

Tamil Nadu's third largest city, Coimbatore is a major industrial centre and the state's commercial capital, with huge textile mills and engineering units. It is also a convenient base for visiting the Nilgiri hill stations. The city has a reputed Agricultural College, and two famous temples. The **Perur Temple** on the Noyyal river and the popular **Muruga Maruthamalai Temple**, on top of a hillock, are dedicated to Lord Shiva and his son, Murugan, respectively. They are visited by thousands of devotees during temple festivals.

The **Siruvani Waterfalls** are beautiful, and Siruvani water famed for its purity and taste.

Ooty ①
Officially known as Udhagamandalam, this Queen of Hill Stations was originally inhabited by the Todas *(see p607)*. The century-old Blue Mountain Train terminates here.

Dodda Betta ②
The highest peak in the Nilgiris (2,623 m/8,606 ft) has fantastic views of the hills, valleys and plateaus.

Kotagiri ③
Known for its salubrious climate, this hill station is situated in the shadow of Dodda Betta Peak.

Nadubatti

METTUPALAYAM

Coonoor ④
A pretty town surrounded by hills and tea and coffee plantations, Coonoor hosts an annual fruit and vegetable show in May, at Sim's Park.

Tree-lined avenue in Kodaikanal

Palani ⑳

Madurai district. 100 km (62 miles)
NW of Madurai. ✈ *Madurai, 119
km (74 miles) SE of town centre, then
bus or taxi.* 🚌 🚐 🎪 *Thaipoosam
(Jan/Feb), Karthigai (Nov/Dec).*

A major pilgrimage centre,
Palani is situated on the
edge of the great Vyapuri
Tank. Its hilltop **Subrahman-
yam Temple** is the most
famous of the six abodes of
Murugan, the son of Shiva,
who is said to have come
here disguised as a mendicant
after quarreling over a fruit
with his brother, Ganesha.
Popularly known as Danda-
yutha Pani ("Bearer of the
Staff"), Murugan is depicted
with a clean shaven head,
holding a stick. His image is
made of medicinal herbs,
mixed together to create a
wax-like substance. During
the Thaipoosam festival, the
temple attracts thousands of
pilgrims, many of whom
shave their heads as an act of
worship. An electric cable car
takes devotees up the 600
steps to the hill shrine.

Palani is also a base for
hikes in the surrounding hills.

Kodaikanal ㉑

Madurai district. 120 km (75 miles)
NW of Madurai. 🚌 *Palani, 65 km (
40 miles) N of town centre, then bus
or taxi.* 🚐 ℹ️ *Tamil Nadu Tourism,
(04542) 241 675.* 🏠 *Mon–Sat.* 🎪
*Summer Festival (May), Flower Show
(May), Winter Festival (Dec).* 🛶

Lush green valleys, terraced
plantations and a pleasant
climate make Kodaikanal one
of Tamil Nadu's most popular
hill stations. Kodaikanal, or
Kodai as it is commonly called,
was first "discovered" by
American missionaries in the
1840s. Drawn by its bracing
climate and clean environs,
they created a sanatorium-
cum-retreat here. They also
established Kodai's International School in 1901.

This picturesque town is
today spread out around the
man-made, star-shaped **Kodai
Lake**, created by the dam built
by Sir Vere Henry Levinge in
1863. The 3-km (2-mile) long
trail around the lake makes for
a pleasant walk. On the shore
is a Boat House, built in 1910.
East of the lake is **Bryant Park**,
famous for its plant collection
and its annual flower show,
held in May.

Beyond the city centre are a
number of scenic areas, such
as Pillar Rocks, Silver Cascade
and Green Valley View (originally known as Suicide Point),
which offer enchanting picnic
spots and views of the deep
valley. Kodai also has many
opportunities for cycling, riding and long, rambling walks.
A trail following the hillside,
called **Coaker's Walk**, provides
a panoramic view of the hill
station. The walk ends at the
Church of St Peter, built in
1884, which has fine stained-
glass windows. Nearby is a
small **Telescope House**.

Some 3 km (2 miles) northeast of the lake is the **Kurunji
Andavar Temple**, dedicated to
Murugan. It is named after
the amazing *kurunji* flowers
(see p649), associated with the
god. The Chettiar Park nearby,
laid out along the hillside, is
where the *kurunji* blooms
every 12 years.

Religious offerings for sale in Palani

HIKING IN THE NILGIRIS

Short excursions around
Ooty offer many oppor-
tunities to explore the
Nilgiris *(see pp604–605)*
on foot. There are scenic
trails in the grasslands
around Mukurthi, an
extinct volcano known
to the Todas as the
"Gateway to the Dead",
and in the windswept

Waterfall in the Nilgiris

Avalanche region, which consists of rolling, grassy
downs, *shola* trees and rhododendrons. The western
edge of this region falls away into the dense
tropical jungles of Kerala. The eastern half of the
range, largely deprived of the Southwest Monsoon,
is dominated by dry scrub and volcanic rock.

The Todas

The Nilgiris are home to 18 tribal groups, among whom the Todas are the most remarkable. A pastoral community, the Todas are fair-skinned and curly haired, and are strict vegetarians. Their language, though of Dravidian origin, has no script. According to their creation myth, Goddess Teikirshy and her brother On first created the buffalo by waving a magic wand, and then created the Toda man. The first Toda woman was created from the right rib of the man. The Todas' first contact with civilization occurred when the East India Company annexed the Nilgiris in 1799. In 1823, John Sullivan, the then Collector of Coimbatore, built the first stone house in Ooty on land purchased from the Todas. Today, there are only about 1,100 Todas left.

Traditional silver jewellery

Toda buffaloes, *pale brown with long horns, are deeply revered. A buffalo is often sacrificed after a funeral to accompany the deceased's soul in the afterlife.*

Homespun cotton shawls *called* puthikuzhi *have black-and-red embroidered motifs. Worn by both Toda men and women, they are tied around the waist, with one end thrown over the shoulder, almost like a Roman toga.*

The dairy temple, *conical in shape, is decorated with sun, moon, serpent and buffalo head motifs. Only men are allowed to go inside.*

Elders *are treated with great respect, and greeted by lifting their right foot and putting it on one's head for their blessings.*

Dairy ceremonies *are festive occasions, generally celebrated with dance and music. The lively songs consist of simple stanzas, describing important events from the Todas' past.*

The barrel-shaped huts, *made of bamboo, grass and cane, consist of a single room. Entry is through a carved wooden door, so small that one has to crawl through it to enter. Several of these windowless bamboo huts make up a Toda village, which is called a* mund.

Madurai ㉒

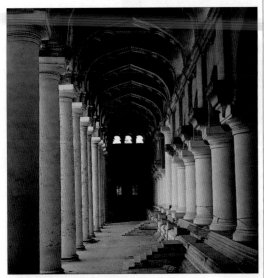

One of South India's great temple towns, Madurai is synonymous with the celebrated Minakshi Temple *(see pp610–11)*. This ancient city on the banks of the Vaigai river has, over the centuries, been a rich repository of Tamil culture. Some 2,000 years ago, it hosted the famous Sangams (gatherings of writers and poets), which were to provide Tamil literature with some of its most enduring works. From the 7th to 13th centuries, as the capital of the Pandyas, it saw art and trade with Rome and China flourish. It later became part of the Vijayanagar Empire, and was the Nayaka capital in the 16th–17th centuries. Today, religion and culture remain a vibrant part of the city's daily life.

Sculpted image

The grand pillared hall in the Thirumalai Nayaka Palace

Minakshi Sundareshvara Temple
See pp610–11.

Thirumalai Nayaka Palace
1.5 km (1 mile) SE of Minakshi Temple. ☐ *daily.* 🎞 **Son et Lumière** *(English):* 6.45pm, *daily.* 🎞

The power and wealth of the Nayakas is evident from the remains of this once grand palace, built by Thirumalai Nayaka in 1636. The building, with its interesting Islamic influences, was partially restored in the 19th century by Lord Napier, governor of Madras between 1866 and 1872. Today, only the spacious rectangular courtyard called the Swarga Vilasam ("Heavenly Pavilion") and a few adjoining buildings survive, their awesome scale evoking the grandeur of a vanished era. The courtyard measures 3,900 sq m (41,979 sq ft), and is surrounded by massive circular pillars. To its west lies the Throne Chamber, a vast room with a raised, octagonal dome. This room leads to the Dance Hall, which now houses a display of archaeological objects.

Theppakulam
E of Minakshi Temple. ☐ *daily.* 🛥

Madurai's great tank is another marvel attributed to Thirumalai Nayaka. The square tank has steps, flanked by animal- and bird-shaped balustrades, leading down to the rippling waters. This is the venue of the annual Theppam (Float) festival, celebrating the marriage of Shiva and Minakshi, when their images are taken in illuminated boats to the small pavilion in the centre of the tank.

Kadal Alagar Temple
1 km (0.6 miles) SW of Minakshi Temple. ☐ *daily.* ● *to non-Hindus.*

One of the 108 sacred Vaishnavite shrines, this glorious temple has three superimposed sanctuaries, of diminishing size, housing Lord Vishnu. From bottom to top, the images show Vishnu in the seated, standing and reclining position. The outer wall has beautiful sculptures and stone screens.

Anglican Cathedral
Off W Masi St. ☐ *daily.*

A fine example of Neo-Gothic architecture, this church was designed by Robert Fellowes Chisholm *(see p569)*, and consecrated in 1881.

Tombs of the Madurai Sultans
N of the Vaigai river. ☐ *daily.*

The sultans of Madurai ruled the city after the invasion in 1310 by Malik Kafur, a general of Alauddin Khilji *(see p48)*. They lie buried to the north of the city. The complex includes Alauddin's Mosque, with its flat-roofed prayer hall and tapering octagonal towers, and the tomb of a local Sufi saint, Bara Mastan Sada, built in the 16th century.

Entrance to the Anglican Cathedral at Madurai

A mural depicting a scene from the *Ramayana*, Alagarkoil Temple

<h3>VISITORS' CHECKLIST</h3>

Madurai district. 498 km (309 miles) SW of Chennai. 923,000. 12 km (7 miles) S of city centre. Hotel Tamil Nadu, (0452) 273 3757. Mon–Sat. Theppam Festival (Jan/Feb), Navaratri (Sep/Oct), Avanimoolam (Aug/Sep).

The temple at **Alagarkoil**, 12 km (7 miles) north of Madurai, is dedicated to Kallalagar, a form of Vishnu who is regarded as Minakshi's brother. According to legend, when Kallalagar went to give his sister in marriage to Sundareshvara, he stayed on the banks of the Vaigai river during the ceremony. This event is celebrated every year, in April/May. On the summit of the hill is Palamudircholai, the last of the six abodes of Murugan, marked by a shrine, while further away is Nupura Ganga, a perennial spring, used for all rituals in the temple, and believed to have emerged from Vishnu's ankle.

Environs

Thiruparankunram, 6 km (4 miles) southwest of Madurai, is a small town known for its sacred granite hill. Regarded as one of the six sacred abodes of Murugan, the son of Shiva, the hill was the site of his marriage to Devayani, the daughter of Indra. There is a rock-cut temple here, built by the Pandyas in the 8th century. The temple is approached through a series of 17th- and 18th-century *mandapas*, at ascending levels, linked by stone steps. The entrance *mandapa* has typical Nayaka period pillars with horse and *yali* riders, while portraits of Nayaka rulers are carved on the columns. The temple's main sanctum contains five shrines.

The 14-day temple festival, in March/April, celebrates the victory of Murugan over the demon Suran, his coronation, and his subsequent marriage to Devayani.

MADURAI CITY CENTRE

Anglican Cathedral ④
Kadal Alagar Temple ③
Minakshi Sundareshvara Temple ①
Thirumalai Nayaka Palace ②

Madurai: Minakshi Sundareshvara Temple

This enormous temple complex is dedicated to Shiva, known here as Sundareshvara (the "Handsome God"), and his consort Parvati or Minakshi (the "Fish-eyed Goddess"). Originally built by the early Pandyas (7th–10th centuries), it was extensively added to by succeeding dynasties, especially between the 14th and 18th centuries. The temple complex is within a high-walled enclosure, at the core of which are the two sanctums for Minakshi and Sundareshvara, surrounded by a number of smaller shrines and grand pillared halls. Especially impressive are the 12 *gopuras*. Their soaring towers rise from solid granite bases, and are covered with stucco figures of deities, mythical animals and monsters, painted in vivid colours.

Guardian Deities
Fierce monster images, with protruding eyes and horns, mark the arched ends of the vaulted roofs, and serve as guardian deities.

GOPURA

Pyramidal gates *(gopuras)* rise to a height of more than 50 m (164 ft). These towering gateways indicate the entrance to the temple complex at the four cardinal points, while lesser *gopuras* lead to the sanctums of the main deities.

Stucco Work
The figures of deities on the tower are repaired, repainted and ritually reconsecrated every 12 years.

Openings in the middle of the long sides allow light to enter the hollow chambers at each level.

The profusely carved pillars of the Thousand-Pillared Hall

Exploring the Minakshi Temple

The temple is entered from the eastern side through the **Ashta Shakti Mandapa** or the "Hall of Eight Goddesses", with sculpted pillars representing the various aspects of the Goddess Shakti. Next to this hall is the **Minakshi Nayaka Mandapa**, a spacious columned hall used for shops and stores. This hall has a votive lamp-holder with 1,008

lamps, which are lit on festive occasions and present a spectacular sight.

The adjacent seven-storeyed **Chitra Gopura**, is the tallest tower in the complex. Next to it is the **Potramarai Kulam**, or "Golden Lotus" Tank, with steps leading down to the water. It is surrounded by pillared corridors that once bore paintings from the Vijayanagar period. To the west of this tank is the **Minakshi Shrine**,

Kalyana Sundara, Vishnu giving Minakshi to Shiva

one of the two main shrines, comprising two concentric corridors and many halls and galleries. Here lies the bed to which Minakshi's "husband", in the form of Sundareshvara's image, is brought every night from his own shrine, the **Sundareshvara Shrine**, which stands to the north. The god resides in this, the second

main shrine, amid columns that bear the fish motifs emblematic of his wife.

The 16th-century "Flagpole Hall" or **Kambattadi Man-dapa**, in front of this shrine, has a pavilion with a seated Nandi, a gilded flagpole and ornately carved pillars depicting the 24 forms of Shiva.

To its east is the **Thousand-Pillared Hall** with 985 beautifully decorated columns. Dating to the 16th century, this hall is now a museum, which displays bronze and stone images. A set of pillars, a marvel in stone, produce the seven notes of Carnatic music. The **Kalyana Mandapa**, to the south of the pillared hall, is where the marriage of Shiva and Parvati is celebrated every year during the Chitirai Festival in mid-April.

Pudumandapa, the 100-m (328-ft) long "New Hall" with portrait sculptures of the Nayaka rulers, is outside the main temple complex. Built by Tirumalai Nayaka in 1635, it now houses a market selling saris, jewellery and spices.

MINAKSHI SUNDARESHVARA TEMPLE COMPLEX

1 Ashta Shakti Mandapa
2 Minakshi Nayaka Mandapa
3 Chitra Gopura
4 Potramarai Kulam
5 Minakshi Shrine
6 Sundareshvara Shrine
7 Kambattadi Mandapa
8 Thousand-Pillared Hall
9 Kalyana Mandapa

0 metres 100
0 yards 100

The Potramarai Kulam, surrounded by a colonnade

Chettiar Mansions

The arid region encompassing the towns of Karaikudi, Deva-kottai and their neighbouring villages, collectively known as Chettinad, is distinguished by large ornate mansions which are the ancestral homes of the Chettiars, Tamil Nadu's rich merchant community. Like the Marwaris of Shekhavati

An arched passageway

(see pp372–3), the Chettiars were astute businessmen who travelled far to make their fortunes. The wealth they acquired in Burma, Sri Lanka, Malaysia, and Vietnam was used to build these elaborate mansions. Today, the Chettiars are prominent bankers and industrialists based in Chennai and Bangalore.

CHETTIAR HOUSES

Built in the early 20th century, these houses reflect the social, ritual and kinship needs of the community, as well as its economic status. Though now unoccupied for most of the year, they are still used for family celebrations.

The splendid Chettinad Palace, Karaikudi

A long verandah *with wooden pillars leads to a series of open courtyards, surrounded by rooms to accommodate the growing family.*

The first pillared hall, *where each pillar is made from an entire tree trunk of Burma teak, is reserved for the men of the house to receive guests and conduct business.*

The formal reception room *has marble floors, stained-glass windows, painted cornices, teak and rosewood furniture and ornate chandeliers.*

Elaborate marble floors, *well-polished doorways, carved wooden beams, granite pillars, and other decorative elements in a Chettiar house display the skills of the Tamil craftsmen.*

Intricately carved wooden doorway

Chettinad ㉓

Chettinad district. 82 km (51 miles)
NE of Madurai. 🚉 🚌 🛕 daily.
🎎 Bullock Races (Jan/Feb).

Karaikudi, the heart of the
Chettinad area, has several
temples, including the 7th-
century **Pillaiyarpati Temple**
dedicated to Lord Ganesha.
It also has fine Chettiar mansions, and antique shops
stocked with treasures from
these mansions. Chettinad is
famous for its hot, spicy, non-
vegetarian cuisine – pepper
chicken is one of the most
popular dishes. The food is
prepared in copper vessels
and served on plantain leaves.

The longest corridor at Ramanathaswamy Temple, with sculpted pillars

Ramanathapuram ㉔

Ramanathapuram district. 117 km
(73 miles) SE of Madurai. 🚉
62,000. 🚉 🚌 🛕 daily. 🎎 Urs at
Erwadi Dargah (Dec).

This ancient town is
associated with the Setupatis,
local rulers who rose to
prominence in the late 17th
century under the Madurai
Nayakas. They derived pres-
tige and income by cont-
rolling the isthmus that led to
Rameshvaram island. A
century later, their rule came
to an end when they surrendered to the East India
Company in 1792.

To the west of the present
town is the palace complex
of the Setupatis. Though little
remains, the 17th-century
Ramalinga Vilas, on the north
side of the palace complex,
still has well-preserved wall
paintings. These depict the
epics as well as battle scenes,
business transactions and
royal ceremonies. The upper
chambers depict more private
royal scenes, such as family
gatherings, music and dance
recitals, and hunting expeditions. A small shrine, facing
north, is dedicated to the
family goddess of the
Setupatis, Rajarajeshvari. It
stands immediately south of
the Ramalinga Vilas.

On the outskirts of the town
is the 800-year-old **Erwadi
Dargah**, housing the tomb of
Ibrahim Syed Aulia, a Muslim

saint. It attracts devotees from
all over India, as well as from
Sri Lanka, Malaysia and
Singapore during its annual
festival in December.

Rameshvaram ㉕

Ramanathapuram district. 163 km
(101 miles) SE of Madurai.
🚉 38,050. 🚉 🚌 ℹ️ Tourist office,
East Car Street, (04573) 221 064.
🎎 Ramalinga (Jun/Jul).

A major pilgrimage site, the
sacred island of Rameshvaram
juts out into the Gulf of
Mannar, the narrow body of
water separating Tamil Nadu
from Sri Lanka.

The **Ramanathaswamy
Temple**, in the middle of the
island, is dedicated to Shiva.
It houses the linga that Lord
Rama, the hero of the epic
Ramayana (see p27), is
said to have installed and
worshipped after his victory
against Ravana in Lanka.
Founded by the Chola rulers
but expanded extensively

Devotees taking a dip in the holy
waters of the Agni Tirtha

during the Nayaka period, in
the 16th to 18th centuries, this
massive temple is enclosed
within a high wall with five
gopuras. The most remarkable feature of this temple
is the **Sokkattan Mandapa**, so
called because it resembles a
sokkattan (dice) in shape.
It surrounds the core of the
temple on four sides in a
continuous corridor, and is
the largest and most elaborate
of its kind, with 1,212 pillars
extending 197 m (646 ft) from
east to west and 133 m (436
ft) from north to south. The
complex also has a staggering
22 *tirthas* (tanks) for ritual
ablutions; it is believed that a
dip in the Agni Tirtha, in front
of the temple, removes all
sins. The installation ceremony of the linga by Rama and
Sita is celebrated every year.

Standing on **Gandamadana
Hill**, the highest point of the
island, 3 km (2 miles) northwest of the Ramanathaswamy
Temple, is a two-storeyed
mandapa that is said to
shelter the footprint of Rama.

Dhanushkodi ("Rama's
Bow"), the southern-most tip
of Rameshvaram, about 18
km (11 miles) from the main
temple, has a spectacular
beach. From here, a series of
boulders, known as Adam's
Bridge, can be seen extending
far into the horizon. These
are believed to have been
used by Hanuman when he
crossed the ocean in search
of Sita. The Kodandarama
Temple, on the shore, is said
to be where Ravana's brother
surrendered to Rama. Miraculously, the temple survived a
devastating cyclone in 1964.

Tuticorin ㉖

Tuticorin district. 135 km (84 miles)
S of Madurai. 🚶 216,100. �"🚌
🎪 Golden Chariot Festival (Aug).

This is Tamil Nadu's second
largest natural harbour, and
the main port of call for ships
from Southeast Asia, Australia
and New Zealand. Tuticorin is
also a major industrial centre
with thermal power stations,
spinning mills and salt
extraction units.

The city's other important
commercial activity is pearl
fishing. Since the early centuries of the Christian era, this
region's pearls have been in
demand throughout the
world. Ancient Tamil literature mentions a flourishing
trade with the Romans, who
bought Tuticorin pearls in
exchange for gold and wine.

Today the government,
which has set up a society of
divers, strictly regulates pearl
fishing, in order to protect the
oyster beds – sometimes pearl
fishing is allowed only once
in ten years. The pearl fishers
still use traditional methods,
diving to a depth of up to
70 m (230 ft) without oxygen
to extricate the pearls. Most
divers can remain underwater
for more than a minute; their
only safeguard against accidents or natural danger is
to dive in pairs.

Tuticorin was occupied by
the Portuguese in the 17th
century and later by the Dutch
and the British. Its colonial
past is visible in two elegant
churches, the Dutch **Sacred
Heart Cathedral**, built in the
mid-18th century, and the
beautiful 17th-century **Church
of the Lady of the Snows**,
built by the Portuguese.

Corridor of the Kanthimathi Nellaiyappar Temple, Tirunelvelli

Tiruchendur ㉗

Tuticorin district. 223 km (139 miles)
S of Madurai. 🚂 🚌 from Madurai,
Tirunelvelli, Tuticorin & Nagercoil.
🎪 Annual Temple Festival (Jun/Jul).

This beautiful coastal town,
one of the six sacred abodes
of Shiva's son, Murugan (see
p606), has the impressive
Subramanyam Temple.
Dating to the 9th century, it
was renovated in the 20th
century. The temple, entered
through the towering Mela
gopura, is built on a rocky
promontory overlooking the
Gulf of Mannar, and provides
lovely views. On the seashore
there are many caves and
rock-cut sculptures.

Environs
Manapad, 18 km (11 miles)
south, has one of the oldest
churches in India, the Church
of the Holy Cross. Built in 1581,
it preserves a fragment of the
"True Cross", brought from
Jerusalem. An annual festival
held every September attracts
pilgrims from all over the region.
St Francis Xavier visited this
coastal village in 1542.

Tirunelvelli ㉘

Tirunelvelli district. 154 km (96
miles) SW of Madurai. 🚂 🚌 ℹ️
Tamil Nadu Tourism, Tirunelvelli
Junction, (0462) 250 0104. 🎪
Chariot Festival (Jun/Jul).

Situated in the fertile tract
by the Tamaraparani river,
Tirunelvelli is dominated by
the **Kanthimathi Nellaiyappar
Temple**, parts of which date
to the 13th century. This
complex of twin temples,
dedicated to Shiva and
Parvati, has two huge
rectangular enclosures connected by a long corridor.
The Shiva temple is to the
north, while the Parvati
temple is to the south. The
elaborate mandapas here
include the Somavara Man-
dapa, which contains two
pillars carved like gopuras;
the Rishaba Mandapa, with
exquisitely carved sculptures
of Manmatha, the God of
Love, and his consort Rathi;
and the Mani Mandapa, with
a set of stone pillars that
produce the melodic notes
of Carnatic music (see p595)
when tapped.

Every summer, the temple's
wooden chariots are led in
procession through the town
during the annual Chariot
Festival, which attracts
thousands of devotees.

Environs
Courtallam (Kuttalam) Falls,
at an elevation of 170 m (558
ft), are 59 km (37 miles)
northwest of Tirunelvelli. This
picturesque spot is famed for
its exotic flora and the medicinal properties of its waters.

The Church of the Holy Cross in Manapad

Sthanumalaya Temple at Suchindram, overlooking the temple tank

Suchindram ㉙

Kanniyakumari district. 247 km (154 miles) S of Madurai. ⊠ Nagarcoil, 5 km (3 miles) NW of town centre, then bus. ▦ ◳ Arudhra Festival (Dec/Jan).

This small temple town is closely linked with the legend of Kumari, the Virgin Goddess (an incarnation of Parvati). It is believed that Shiva rested at this quiet spot by the banks of the Pelayar river, while the goddess Kumari performed her penance at Kanniyakumari.

Suchindram's unique **Sthanumalaya Temple** is dedicated to the Hindu Trinity of Brahma, Vishnu and Shiva. The rectangular complex has enormous, brightly coloured *gopuras* dating from the 17th–18th centuries, which depict stories from the great epics *(see pp26–7)*. One of the two main shrines, built in the 13th century, contains the Sthanumalaya linga, which symbolizes Brahma, Vishnu and Shiva. The other is dedicated to Vishnu, whose image is made of a special kind of jaggery and mustard.

The temple also boasts a set of musical pillars made from single blocks of granite. When tapped, each pillar produces a different musical note. Other highlights are a 5-m (16-ft) high statue of Hanuman placed opposite the Rama shrine, and the exquisite sculptures in the Vasantha Mandapa. A special *puja* is held here every Friday evening, with music and a procession. In the complex is an ancient banyan tree, and a sculpture of Shiva's bull, Nandi, which locals believe actually continues to grow.

Kanniyakumari ㉚

Kanniyakumari district. 235 km (146 miles) S of Madurai. 🚶 19,700. ⊠ ▦ ⓘ Tamil Nadu Tourism, Beach Rd, (04652) 246 257. ◳ Chaitra Purnima (Apr), Navaratri (Sep/Oct).

The southernmost tip of the Indian subcontinent, where the Indian Ocean, the Arabian Sea and the Bay of Bengal meet, Kanniyakumari enchants visitors with its spectacular views, especially at sunrise and sunset. The most breathtaking of these occurs on Chaitra Purnima (the full moon night in April) when both sunset and moonrise occur at the same time.

Kanniyakumari is believed to be the abode of Kumari, the Virgin Goddess, who is supposed to have done penance here so that she could marry Shiva. The marriage, however, did not take place, since it was deemed that she remain a virgin in order to save the world. Her temple, the **Kumari Amman Temple**, a popular pilgrimage centre on the seashore, was built by the Pandya kings in the 8th century and was extensively

renovated by the Chola, Vijayanagar and Nayaka rulers.

A magnificent structure, the temple has a Navaratri Mandapa with a beautifully painted panel of Mahishasuramardini (Durga killing the demon Mahisha). An 18th-century shrine within the temple contains the footprints *(sripadaparai)* of the goddess Kumari, who performed her penance at this spot.

The **Gandhi Memorial**, near the temple, is where Mahatma Gandhi's ashes were kept before immersion. The building is designed so that every year on October 2nd (Gandhi's birthday), at midday, the rays of the sun fall on the exact spot where his ashes were placed.

Just off the coast, on a rocky island, the **Vivekananda Memorial** marks the spot where the great Indian philosopher, Swami Vivekananda *(see p286)* meditated before attending the World Religious Conference in Chicago in 1893. Near the memorial is the imposing 40-m (131-ft) high statue of Tiruvalluvar, the 1st-century BC Tamil poet, who wrote the epic *Tirukural*, often referred to as one of the greatest classics of Tamil literature.

The **Church of Our Lady of Joy**, which was founded by St Francis Xavier in the 1540s, is located at the southern edge of the town. Other attractions include the sandy beaches and the multicoloured granite rocks.

🏯 **Kumari Amman Temple**
◯ daily. ● Sanctum closed to non-Hindus.

🏛 **Vivekananda Memorial**
◯ Wed–Mon. 🎟 ▦ every 30 min.

A statue of the poet Tiruvalluvar, on the beach at Kanniyakumari

ANDAMAN ISLANDS

An archipelago of 572 idyllic islands in the Bay of Bengal, about 1,000 km (620 miles) from the mainland, the Andamans and the neighbouring Nicobar Islands are actually the peaks of a submerged mountain range which extends from Myanmar to Indonesia. They encompass three distinct ecosystems – tropical forests, mangroves and coral reefs, which support a staggering variety of plant and animal life. Foreign visitors require a permit *(see p758)*, and are not allowed on the Nicobar Islands. Many parts of the Andamans, too, are off-limits, to preserve their rare biodiversity and protect the six tribal groups, some of whom are fiercely independent. Their hostility was probably the reason why Marco Polo described the islands as being inhabited by cannibals. The Andamans acquired the sinister name Kala Pani ("Black Waters") in the 19th century, when the British established a penal colony here. The islands were severely hit by the tsunami waves in December 2004. Their permanent population includes migrant Indians, Bangladeshis, Sri Lankans and Karens from Myanmar. The surrounding reefs are ideal for water sports.

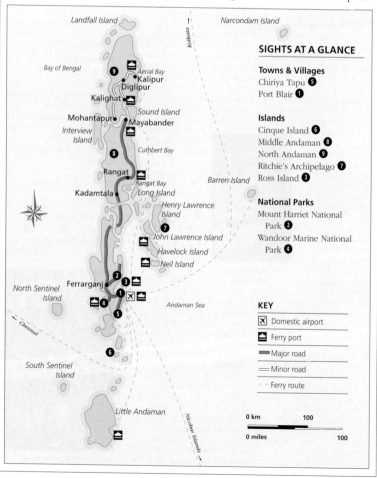

SIGHTS AT A GLANCE

Towns & Villages
Chiriya Tapu **5**
Port Blair **1**

Islands
Cinque Island **6**
Middle Andaman **8**
North Andaman **9**
Ritchie's Archipelago **7**
Ross Island **3**

National Parks
Mount Harriet National Park **2**
Wandoor Marine National Park **4**

KEY

✕	Domestic airport
⛴	Ferry port
▬	Major road
═	Minor road
- -	Ferry route

0 km _____ 100

0 miles _____ 100

◁ **An island in the Andamans covered by a dense, evergreen canopy of trees, surrounded by crystal waters**

An aerial view of the capital, Port Blair

Port Blair ❶

South Andaman Island. 1,190 km
(739 miles) E of Chennai. 🏠
100,200. ✈ 3 km (2 miles) S of town
centre, then bus or taxi. 🚌
ℹ️ Govt of India Tourist Office,
Junglighat Rd, (03192) 233 006;
Andaman & Nicobar Tourism, (03192)
230 933. **Travel permits** are required
for the Andaman Islands (see p758).
🎭 Island Tourism Festival (Dec/Jan).

The capital, Port Blair, is
located to the southeast of
South Andaman Island. The
town is a base from
which to travel
around the archi-
pelago, and is well
equipped with
hotels, banks,
tour operators and
sports complexes.
The town's
tumultuous history
began in 1789,
when Lieutenant
Archibald Blair of
the British East
India Company
conducted a survey
to identify a safe harbour for
the Company's vessels. He
chose the site of what is now
Port Blair. Fifty years later
the islands became a penal
colony. Those incarcerated
were political activists involved
in the Indian Mutiny of 1857
(see p53); by 1864, the number
of prisoners had grown from
773 to 3,000. In 1896, the
construction of the **Cellular Jail**
began; it soon became an
infamous symbol of colonial
oppression. Designed
specifically for solitary
confinement, it earned the

A row of tiny cells,
Cellular Jail

Islands the dreaded name of
Kala Pani or "Black Waters",
reflecting the atrocities that
awaited the prisoners. It
remains Port Blair's most
prominent landmark.
Of the original seven wings
laid out around a central
watchtower, only four remain;
three have been converted into
a hospital and are lined with
cells, each 3 by 3.5 m (10 by
11 ft) in size. Daily rations consisted of two cups of drinking
water and two cups of rice.
Executions were frequent and
many were made to
undergo hard
labour. Japanese
troops, who occu-
pied the Islands
during World War
II, destroyed part of
the prison. In 1945,
the British moved
back, re-established
their headquarters
at Port Blair and
closed the jail. It is
now a memorial to
the political pris-
oners; a moving
sound and light show is held
here every evening. The
town's other places of interest
are scattered around Aberdeen
Bazaar, on the east side of
town. The **Anthropological
Museum**, west of the bazaar,
sheds light on the islands'
tribal inhabitants and has a
collection of rare photographs
taken in the 1960s. The
Aquarium, also known as the
Fisheries Museum, at the
eastern end of MG Road,
displays hundreds of species of
unusual fish, corals and shells.
Next door, the **Andaman Water**

Sports Complex offers a range
of activities, including wind-
surfing and parasailing, and
also hires out row boats and
rubber dinghies. The
Samudrika Marine Museum,
run by the Indian Navy, has
five galleries devoted to the
history, geography and
anthropology of the Islands,
and has a superb display on
marine life. The tiny zoo at
Haddo has successfully bred
saltwater crocodiles and
returned them to the wild. At
the **Forest Museum** nearby,
different varieties of local
wood are on display.
Chatham Sawmills on
Chatham Island, 5 km (3 miles)
north, is one of the oldest and
largest saw mills in Asia.
Established by the British in
1836, this is where many of the
Islands' fast disappearing
species of trees, including the
towering *padauk* (Andaman
redwood), are processed.

🏛 **Cellular Jail**
Son et Lumière 6–7pm (Hindi),
daily. 7–8pm (English), daily. 📷

🏛 **Anthropological Museum**
◯ Tue–Sun. ● public hols.

🏛 **Fisheries Museum**
Tel (03192) 232 291. ◯ Tue–Sun.
● public hols. 📷

🏊 **Andaman Water Sports
Complex**
Tel (03192) 230 799. ◯ daily.

🏛 **Samudrika Marine
Museum**
Tel (03192) 232 871. ◯ Tue–Sun. 📷

🏛 **Forest Museum**
◯ Tue–Sun. ● public hols.

Chatham Sawmills
◯ Mon–Sat, mornings are best. 📷

**The day's catch, a boatful of
fresh crayfish**

Environs

The nearest beach from Port Blair is the crescent shaped **Corbyn's Cove**, 7 km (4 miles) south of the capital. **Viper Island**, named after a 19th-century British shipping vessel that was wrecked off its shore, can be reached via a cruise from Port Blair. Its sinister history involves the local prison, built in 1867, whose macabre gallows and torture posts can still be seen. Only daytime visits are allowed as the island has no inhabitants. About 15 km (9 miles) from Port Blair lies **Sippyghat Farm**, where many varieties of spices and indigenous plants and shrubs are grown.

Mount Harriet National Park **②**

South Andaman Island. 10 km (6 miles) N of Port Blair. 🚢 *From Chatham Wharf or Phoenix Bay Jetty (Fisheries Jetty) in Port Blair to Bamboo Flats Jetty, then taxi to park entry point. Tickets for day visits are available at entrance.*

Some of the Andamans' highest peaks are in Mount Harriet National Park, lying across the inlet from Phoenix Jetty in Port Blair. Mount Harriet, at 365 m (1,198 ft), is surrounded by evergreen forests that support a remarkable biodiversity, predominantly birds such as the great black woodpecker and the green imperial pigeon. Well-marked hiking trails include the 2-km (1-mile) walk to Kalapathar, and the 16-km (10-mile) trail to Madhuban Beach, where elephants are trained for lumbering. Beware of leeches during the monsoon.

The **Forest Guest House**, on top of Mount Harriet, offers fine views of Port Blair and Ross Island. Visits and overnight stays are possible with permission from the Wildlife Warden (*see p621*).

Ross Island **③**

Ross Island. 2 km (1 mile) E of Port Blair. 🚢 *from Phoenix Jetty.* **Travel permits** *required for the Andamans* (see p758). *Only day trips allowed.*

A short ferry ride from Port Blair leads to Ross Island, which served as the administrative capital for most of the Andaman Islands from 1858 until 1941. Ross Island's history, however, is much older, for it was the home of the indigenous Great Andamanese (*see p623*). Within 20 years of British occupation, diseases such as syphilis and measles virtually wiped out the tribe, whose numbers dropped from 5,000 to just 28. Ross Island was also the base for the British administrators of the penal colony in Port Blair, and was equipped with swimming pools and bungalows. In 1941, the Japanese converted the site into a POW camp, and built war installations, remnants of which can still be seen. It now lies deserted, and the few signs of its colonial glory, such as the chief commissioner's house and the Anglican church, are dilapidated and overgrown. The area is now under the control of the Indian Navy, whose museum, Smritika, records the lives of its political prisoners.

Orchid

The rare Narcondam hornbill

Snorkelling, a popular way to explore marine life

Snorkelling

Snorkels can be hired out for around Rs 70 per day from numerous tour operators including the Andaman Water Sports Complex in Port Blair. Popular venues are Corbyn's Cove, Wandoor, Chiriya Tapu, Neil and Havelock Islands.

Scuba Diving

There are two registered dive centres in Port Blair. Samudra, (03192) 227 824, in Hotel Sinclair Bay View, is well established, and charges Rs 2,500 for a couple of dives near Port Blair, Rs 3,500 for areas further than Wandoor. It also runs diving courses. Port Blair Underwater, (03192) 229 312, at Peerless Resort in Corbyn's Cove also offers diving courses. The recently opened Andaman Scuba Club on Havelock Island, is a pretty resort on the beach. www.andamanscubaclub.com

Eco-friendly Diving

Coral reefs are sensitive and even the gentlest touch can kill them. So avoid touching or treading on them, and be careful with your flippers. Practise descending into the sea before the actual dive, as descent is often too fast, leading to collision with reefs. Do not use anchors near reefs.

Wandoor Marine National Park ❹

Created in 1983 to preserve the tropical ecosystems of 15 uninhabited islands in the Andamans, the Mahatma Gandhi Marine National Park at Wandoor stretches over 280 sq km (108 sq miles). It encompasses myriad bays, coral reefs, lagoons, rainforests and mangrove creeks. Ferries from Wandoor village skirt lagoons with kaleidoscopic sea beds, and are often chased by schools of playful dolphins. Most of the islands are protected and are therefore inaccessible; however, their coasts reveal a fascinating transition from towering tropical canopies to stilted mangroves. The only islands that allow visits are Jolly Buoy Island, which is ideal for snorkelling, and Redskin Island, with a well-marked nature trail. Unfortunately, the December 2004 tsunami caused widespread destruction of coral reefs in Jolly Buoy.

Types of Coral
Corals are of two broad types – either hard or soft. The colourful soft coral has no outer skeleton.

Angelfish
The angelfish is one of the reef's most vividly coloured fish. Its bright hues help to camouflage it as well as to advertise its territory.

Lion or Scorpion Fish
Measuring up to 40 cm (16 in), this ornate fish has deadly venom in its rays, which can be fatal for humans.

Giant Robber Crab
One of the largest and rarest crabs in the world, its powerful claws help it to climb trees such as the coconut palm, and break the hard shell of its fruit.

THE CORAL REEF
Referred to as rainforests of the sea, the multi-coloured reefs are delicate ecosystems that support an amazing variety of marine life *(see p647)*, and over 200 species of coral.

Grouper Fish
Among the most commonly found species, groupers can change their colour to match the rocks and surrounding reefs.

Sea sponges are the simplest of the marine animals that live attached to the sea bed.

Giant clams can measure up to 1 m (3 ft).

Brain coral

Sea fan

Staghorn coral

Mushroom coral

Plate coral

Clown fish

Sea anemone

Green Tree Snake
One of the 40-odd species found here, this harmless snake has no fangs and eats reptiles and frogs.

Gurjan trees make up the emergent layer, which towers above the canopy at 60 m (197 ft).

The second layer, known as the canopy, with trees such as the *padauk*, absorbs most of the sunlight.

Padauk, or Andaman redwood, grows up to 36 m (118 ft).

Orchids

Toung Pienne tree

TROPICAL RAINFOREST
The multi-layered tropical rainforests include giant trees such as the *gurjan* and *padauk*, a rich undergrowth of epiphytes and climbers, and over 120 species of ferns.

Bamboo

Pandanus forms part of the understorey layer.

Ferns

Mushrooms

Mangroves
Dense mangrove forests grow along the waterlogged creeks of Wandoor's islands, and support a variety of fauna such as snakes, crabs, crocodiles and waterfowl.

A boat gliding across the glass-like surface of a lagoon, Andamans

Chiriya Tapu ❺

South Andaman Island. 28 km (17 miles) S of Port Blair. 🚌 🚢 from Port Blair. Taxis available from Port Blair.

The fishing village of Chiriya Tapu ("Bird Island"), at the southernmost tip of South Andaman Island, is an hour's drive from Port Blair. Its white beaches, skirting a large bay, make it a popular day trip with visitors.

Forest trails through the surrounding tropical under-growth are a birdwatcher's delight, as they teem with a vast variety of species, including rare sunbirds, kingfishers, woodpeckers and eagles. Its beaches, especially the picturesque **Munde Pahar Beach**, are excellent for snorkelling, and there are good camping facilities as well. The forest department is setting up a biological park, to house the animals from Port Blair's zoo (see p618).

Cinque Island ❻

Cinque Island. 39 km (24 miles) S of Port Blair. 🚢 motor boats from Port Blair & Wandoor, ferries from Chiriya Tapu. Travel permits required for the Andamans (see p758). Only day visits are allowed.

The volcanic Cinque Island is perhaps the most beautiful of the entire Andamans group, as it has had little human interference over the years and is mostly uninhab-ited. Comprising two islands, North and South Cinque, connected by a sand bar, it was declared a sanctuary in 1987. The surrounding reefs of rare coral and varied marine life offer some of the best snorkelling and scuba diving in the Andamans. The sandy shores are also among the last refuges of the hawks-bill and green sea turtles, which nest here annually in their hundreds.

Environs
Tiny groups of islands known as the **Sisters** and the **Brothers**, lying 12 km (7 miles) and 32 km (20 miles) south of Cinque respectively, can be visited only with a professional diving group.

A hermit crab digging a temporary home

Large tracts of the remote southern island of **Little Andaman**, 70 km (44 miles) and eight hours by ferry from Port Blair, are a reserve for the 100-odd surviving members of the Onge tribe. It is not advisable to try and make contact with them. Part of northern Little Andaman is open to visitors.

Little Andaman
🚢 twice a week from Port Blair.

Ritchie's Archipelago ❼

The group of islands lies between 20 km (12 miles) & 40 km (25 miles) E of South Andaman. 🚢 from Port Blair & Rangat Bay (Middle Andaman). **Travel permits** required for the Andamans (see p758).

This cluster of tiny islands, collectively known as Ritchie's Archipelago, are for the most part protected as national parks to preserve their remarkable biodiversity. Only three islands are open to visitors and are connected to Port Blair by ferry on specific days of the week.

Neil Island, 36 km (22 miles) northeast, is the closest to the capital and is inhabited by settlers from Bengal. The interior is lush with paddy fields and plantations; the island is the region's main producer of fresh fruit and vegeta-bles. The relatively untouched beaches offer superb snorkelling opportunities.

Havelock Island, 54 km (34 miles) northeast of Port Blair, is the most popular among visitors as it is well equipped, with government and private guesthouses, and also has a well-stocked main bazaar. It is worth trying out the tented accommodation on Radhanagar Beach, at the western tip of the island, where dolphins and turtles can be spotted from the long stretches of white sand. The elephants found on the island

A colourful sea fan and a grouper fish

Elephants, indispensable to the islands' lumber trade

were originally brought here to work the timber trade. Bikes and scooters are available and are the best way to explore.

The northernmost island in the archipelago, **Long Island**, 82 km (51 miles) north of Port Blair, attracts few visitors, perhaps because of the eight-hour journey to get there. It nevertheless has attractive beaches. There is just one rest house and virtually no public transport available, although bicycles can be hired. North Passage Island, 55 km (34 miles) S of Port Blair, has a beautiful white sandy beach at Merk Bay.

A vividly coloured local pineapple

Environs
Barren Island, 132 km (82 miles) northeast of Port Blair, has the only active volcano in India. It erupted twice in recent years, first in 1991 and then in 1994, after lying dormant for nearly two centuries. Rising sharply from the sea, its enormous crater continues to spew smoke. The island is now a wildlife sanctuary. There is no public ferry service and only chartered ferries make the long, 20-hour journey from Port Blair. Since landing on the island is not permitted, divers are the only visitors, drawn here by the rich marine life.

INDIGENOUS TRIBES

Until the 18th century, the Andaman and Nicobar Islands were inhabited by 12 distinct groups of aboriginal tribes. Now, overwhelmed by the immigrant population and threatened by disease and loss of land, their numbers have fallen from 5,000 to just 400. The Mongoloid Nicobarese and Shompen tribes of the Nicobars probably migrated from Myanmar, while the origins of the four Negrito tribes, the Jarawas, Great Andamanese, Onges and Sentinelese, continue to baffle anthropologists. Of these, only the largest – the Nicobarese – have partially integrated into the mainstream, while the Onges and the Great Andamanese, now increasingly dependent on subsidies, live in tribal "reserves". The Sentinelese from

A Jarawa tribesman

North Sentinel Island, are still hostile, fending off strangers with showers of arrows. The Shompens of Great Nicobar are wary of outsiders. Most tribal groups survived the December 2004 tsunami, by following their own early warning systems. As the last representatives of truly independent indigenous peoples, perhaps their only chance of survival remains in self-imposed isolation.

Middle Andaman 8

Middle Andaman Island. 170 km (106 miles) N from Port Blair to Rangat. from Port Blair. **Travel permits** required for the Andamans (see p758).

This is literally the middle island among the Andamans trio. Large tracts of its interior are a part of the highly protected Jarawa Tribal Reserve. The Jarawas, traditional hunter-gatherers, are probably the last racially pure tribe left in India. The Andaman Trunk Road winds along the island's spine, running from Port Blair through Bharatrang Island to Middle Andaman. But with the welfare of the Jarawas in mind, only restricted public transport is encouraged. The area around **Rangat** is lush with tropical forests; the town itself has only a few provision stores. **Rangat Bay** is the point of departure for ferries to Port Blair and Havelock and Long Islands. Just 15 km (9 miles) away, **Cuthbert Bay** is a sanctuary for hundreds of marine turtles, which arrive here annually to nest. **Mayabander**, at the northern tip, 71 km (44 miles) from Rangat, is a beautiful spot. Some of its beaches, such as **Karmatang**, are famous for their spectacular sunrises, and are also nesting grounds for marine turtles.

North Andaman 9

North Andaman Island. 290 km (180 miles) N from Port Blair to Diglipur. from Port Blair. **Travel permits** required for the Andamans (see p758).

North Andaman is the least populated of the three large islands. **Diglipur**, in the northeast, is one of the few places with accommodation. It is known for its beaches – in particular, Ram Nagar and Kalipur – and also has the islands' highest peak, **Saddle Peak** (737 m/2,418 ft), which was recently declared a national park. A scenic trail leads to the peak's summit.

From **Aerial Bay**, 9 km (6 miles) northeast of Diglipur, one can visit Smith and Ross Islands (see p619).

KERALA

Nestling between the Western Ghats and the Arabian Sea, Kerala is an enchanting mosaic of coconut groves and paddy fields, wide beaches and labyrinthine backwaters, verdant hills and rainforests. Its diverse culture is enriched by the three great religions that have ancient roots here. Hinduism is the religion of the majority, practised here with a rare rigour that prohibits non-Hindus from entering most temples. Christianity, followed by a quarter of the population, was brought here by the Apostle St Thomas, while Islam was introduced by Arab traders in the 7th century. The architectural treasures of the state include the beautiful wooden palace at Padmanabhapuram, stately colonial buildings and a 16th-century synagogue in Kochi. This politically conscious state, where power alternates between Left and Centrist parties, boasts the highest literacy rate in India. Many of its people work in the Middle East, their remittances home adding greatly to Kerala's prosperity.

SIGHTS AT A GLANCE

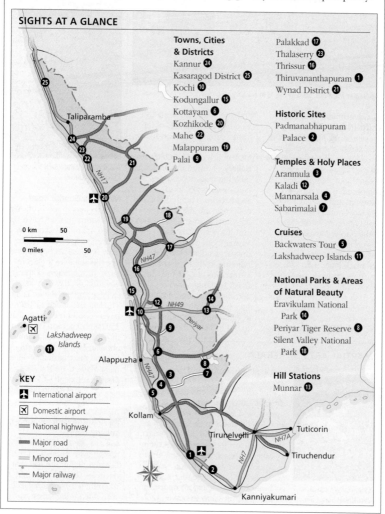

Towns, Cities & Districts
Kannur ㉔
Kasaragod District ㉕
Kochi ⑩
Kodungallur ⑮
Kottayam ⑥
Kozhikode ⑳
Mahe ㉒
Malappuram ⑲
Palai ⑨
Palakkad ⑰
Thalaserry ㉓
Thrissur ⑯
Thiruvananthapuram ①
Wynad District ㉑

Historic Sites
Padmanabhapuram Palace ②

Temples & Holy Places
Aranmula ③
Kaladi ⑫
Mannarsala ④
Sabarimalai ⑦

Cruises
Backwaters Tour ⑤
Lakshadweep Islands ⑪

National Parks & Areas of Natural Beauty
Eravikulam National Park ⑭
Periyar Tiger Reserve ⑧
Silent Valley National Park ⑱

Hill Stations
Munnar ⑬

KEY

🛧 International airport
☒ Domestic airport
═ National highway
▬ Major road
═ Minor road
— Major railway

0 km   50
0 miles   50

Taliparamba
Agatti
Lakshadweep Islands
Alappuzha
Kollam
Tirunelvelli
Tuticorin
Tiruchendur
Kanniyakumari

NH7
NH47
NH49
NH7A
Periyar

◁ **Wooden canoes resting in the backwaters near Alleppey (Alappuzha)**

Thiruvananthapuram ❶

Vishnu in wood

Kerala's capital, known until recently as Trivandrum, was the seat of the former royal family of Travancore from 1750 to 1956. The magnificent Anantha Padmanabhaswamy Temple has given the city its name, Thiruvananthapuram – literally the "Holy City of Anantha", the sacred thousand-headed serpent on whom Vishnu reclines. Built across seven hills, the city's old quarter clusters around the temple, while along busy Mahatma Gandhi Road are colonial mansions, churches and modern high-rises.

The Napier Museum, built in the 19th century

🏛 Government Arts and Crafts (Napier) Museum

Museum Rd. ⬤ Mon, (Wed am) & public hols for all museums. 📷 covers all museums. **Kanakakunnu Palace Tel** (0471) 231 8294 for permission. Located in a well-planned compound is a complex of museums and the city's zoo. The Government Arts and Crafts Museum, earlier known as the Napier Museum after John Napier, a former governor of Madras, is in a red and black brick Indo-Saracenic structure, designed by Robert Fellows Chisholm (see p569) in the 19th century. It exhibits a rare collection of bronzes, stone sculptures, exquisite gold ornaments, ivory carvings

and a temple chariot, all fashioned in the territories of the former kingdom of Travancore.

To the north of the Museum, is the **Shri Chitra Art Gallery**, housed in a beautiful building that incorporates the best elements of local architecture. The pride of its collection are the works of Raja Ravi Varma (1848–1906) and his uncle Raja Raja Varma, both pioneers of a unique academy style of painting in India. Raja Ravi Varma was considered the finest Indian artist of his time, and his mythological paintings have inspired the popular religious prints found in many Indian homes.

The **Natural History Museum**, to the east, has a fine replica of a typical Kerala Nair wooden house, *naluketu*, detailing the principles of its construction.

The **Kanakakunnu Palace**, where the Travancore royal family once entertained their guests, is adjacent to the complex, on top of a hill.

A short drive down the road from the complex leads to Kowdiar Junction, a roundabout of walls and ornate railings facing the Kowdiar Palace, the former maharaja's official residence.

A painting by Raja Ravi Varma in Sri Chitra Art Gallery

Mahatma Gandhi Road

The city's main road runs from the Victoria Jubilee Town Hall to the Anantha Padmanabhaswamy Temple. Among the many impressive buildings that line this road are the Secretariat, headquarters of the state government, the University College and the Public Library. The latter, founded in 1829, has a collection of more than 250,000 books and documents in Malayalam, Hindi, Tamil and Sanskrit. To the north, beyond the charming Connemara Market, are the Jami Masjid, St Joseph's Cathedral and the Neo-Gothic building of Christ Church.

🛕 Anantha Padmanabhaswamy Temple

Fort area. ⬤ to non-Hindus. Special rules for clothing apply (see p762). Located within the fort that encircles the old town, this is the only temple in the state with a towering seven-storeyed *gopura*, commonly

---

MARTIAL ARTS OF KERALA

Kalarippayat practice, CVN Kalari Sangham

Constant warfare in the 11th century gave rise to *kalaripayattu*, Kerala's martial arts. From it emerged two streams – the *chavverpada*, suicide squads, and the *chekavan*, warriors who fought duels to the death, in order to settle the nobility's disputes. Students learn to use weapons such as swords, spears, daggers, the *urumi*, (a flexible metal sword) and wooden poles. In the final stage, the student is taught how to defeat an opponent by applying pressure to nerve points.

The imposing *gopura* of the Anantha Padmanabhaswamy Temple

seen in Tamil Nadu's temple architecture. The restrained ornamentation, however, is typical of Kerala. A flagstaff encased in gold stands in the huge courtyard. The main corridor, which runs around four sides of the courtyard, has 324 columns and two rows of granite pillars, each embellished with a woman bearing a lamp (*deepalakshmi*). The hall also has mythological animals, sculpted with rotating stone balls in their jaws. Rich murals adorn the outer walls of the inner shrine, where the 6-m (20-ft) long reclining Vishnu resides, with his head towards the south and feet towards the north.

Kuthiramalika Palace Museum

Fort area. Tue–Sun. extra charges. Carnatic Music Festival (Jan/Feb).

This interesting museum (also known as Puthen Malika) is housed in an 18th-century palace, built by Raja Swathi Thirunal Balarama Varma, a statesman, poet, musician and social reformer. A fine example of Kerala architecture, this wooden palace has polished floors and a sloping tiled roof. The wood carvings are particularly noteworthy, especially the 122 horses lining the eaves of the building. On display are various artifacts from the royal collection,

including a solid crystal throne given by the Dutch, and another carved out of the tusks of 50 elephants.

CVN Kalari Sangham

East Fort area. Mon–Sat. This training centre for *kalaripayattu* was established in 1956 to revive Kerala's martial arts tradition. Each morning, students collect at the gymnasium (*kalari*) to perform a series of exercises that will help them develop the necessary combat skills. The centre also has a shrine to the deity of martial arts, Kalari Paradevata, and an Ayurvedic clinic where students are given oil massages.

THIRUVANANTHAPURAM CITY CENTRE

Anantha Padmanabhaswamy
  Temple ③
CVN Kalari Sangham ⑤
Government Arts and Crafts
  (Napier) Museum ①
Kuthiramalika Palace Museum ④
Mahatma Gandhi Road ②

0 metres 500
0 yards 500

Key to Symbols *see back flap*

Exploring Thiruvananthapuram's Environs

Thiruvananthapuram is the gateway to the southern tip of India. South of the city, along the Lakshadweep Sea, are many beach resorts, the most famous of which is Kovalam. The Padmanabhapuram Palace *(see pp630–31)*, the former residence of the Travancore kings, is to the southeast, while to its north and east are tranquil hill stations located picturesquely in the densely forested Cardamom (Ponmudi) Hills. Thiruvananthapuram also houses many important institutions, including the meteorological station, which performs the task of plotting the arrival of the Southwest Monsoon. The city is also one of Kerala's main centres of Ayurveda.

A young boy flaunts his catch, Kovalam Beach

Lighthouse Beach, one of the many idyllic beaches in Kovalam

🚉 Kovalam

Thiruvananthapuram district.16 km (10 miles) S of Thiruvananthapuram. 🚌 ℹ️ *Tourism Office, (0471) 248 0085.*

Until the 1960s, Kovalam was just a sleepy fishing village with narrow lanes and thatched dwellings with wide courtyards for drying fish. However, once its spectacular beach and shallow, crystal-clear waters were discovered, it became a favourite with hippies and backpackers, and over the years acquired the reputation of being a shabby, downmarket resort. Today, however, it also attracts the rich and famous, who come here in private planes. As a result, the beaches are dotted with both luxury and budget resorts, as well as cafés and several government-approved Ayurveda centres that offer anything from a simple massage to three-week treatments. Hawkers, too, have set up stalls selling handicrafts and inexpensive beachwear. Despite

the onslaughts of mass tourism, Kovalam retains an inherent charm that makes it one of India's finest and most popular beach resorts.

Kovalam's sheltered natural bay is ringed by two rocky headlands. Its four beaches – Samudra Beach, Ashok Beach, Eve's Beach and Lighthouse Beach – all within short walking distance of each other, – provide visitors with their fill of sun, sea and sand. While the beaches to the south of the promontory are more crowded, the ones to the north offer ample secluded space for sunbathing, safe swimming in the placid blue waters, catamaran trips, and water sports.

Bananas and other fruit on sale, Varkala

🚉 Varkala

Thiruvananthapuram district. 40 km (25 miles) N of Thiruvananthapuram. 🚌 ℹ️ *Tourist Information Centre, near the helipad.*

This beautiful little beach town is better known among locals as a major pilgrimage centre. According to legend, the sage Narada flung a cloth made from the bark of a tree into the air, and it landed at the spot where the small town of Varkala now stands. Narada then directed his disciples to pray for salvation at the newly created beach, which came to be known as Papanasham Beach or the "Beach of Redemption". Since then, this beach has been associated with ancestor worship, as Hindus immerse the ashes of their dead here.

At the heart of the town is the sacred **Janardhana Swamy Temple**, believed to be more than 2,000 years old. This temple, dedicated to Krishna, attracts many pilgrims. One of the bells in the temple is said to have been given in gratitude by the captain of a 17th-century Dutch sailing ship, after his prayers were answered.

Varkala's other pilgrimage centre is the hilltop **Memorial of Sree Narayana Guru** (1855–1928) at Sivagiri, 3 km (2 miles) east of the temple. Every day, countless devotees flock to the memorial of this great saint and social reformer who advocated "one caste, one religion, one god for mankind".

With its backdrop of red laterite cliffs overlooking the beach, Varkala has now emerged as a popular resort

A view of the long sandy beach at Varkala

and spa. The town is famous for its natural springs with therapeutic qualities, and is also a centre for Ayurvedic treatment and yoga. To the south is the desolate Anjengo Fort, the main garrison of the Dutch East India Company in the 17th and 18th centuries.

Ponmudi

Thiruvananthapuram district. 61 km (38 miles) NE of Thiruvananthapuram. *Government Guest House, (0472) 280 230.*

Ponmudi, literally "Golden Crown", rises to a height of 915 m (3,002 ft) from the base of a thick tropical forest. Surrounded by tea estates and forested hills, this hill station is still unspoilt, refreshingly cool and mist-shrouded for most of the year. Its narrow winding paths and verdant environs offer pleasant walks. Wild flowers grow in abundance on the banks of gurgling brooks, adding to the charm of this peaceful place.

Agasthyarkoodam

Thiruvananthapuram district. 60 km (37 miles) NE of Thiruvananthapuram. **Trekking permits** *Contact the Office of the Wildlife Warden, Thiruvananthapuram, (0471) 232 9925.*

At an elevation of 1,890 m (6,201 ft), Agasthyarkoodam is the highest peak in southern Kerala. It forms part of the Western Ghats and the Agasthyavanam Forest, designated a sanctuary in 1992.

The mountain is revered by both Buddhists and Hindus, as it is believed to be the abode of the Bodhisattva Avalokitesvara *(see p141)*, as well as of the sage Agastya, a disciple of Shiva. Women are not allowed here. The hills are rich in medicinal herbs, and harbour many species of birds and wildlife. Trekking to the top – a distance of 28 km (17 miles) – takes two days and is permitted only between December and April. The summit provides fine views of the lake created by the Neyyar Dam.

FESTIVALS OF KERALA

Vishu *(Apr)*. The first day of the Malayali New Year is celebrated with zest throughout the state. It is believed that looking upon a group of auspicious objects at dawn ensures a year of peace and prosperity.

Thrissur Pooram *(Apr/May)*, Thrissur. The highlight of this festival is the ceremonial procession of two *devis* (goddesses) on caparisoned elephants to the Vadakunnathan Temple. The parasols held above the elephants are changed in an exciting synchronized ritual, accompanied by *chendamelam*, an orchestra of percussion instruments. A display of fireworks marks the climax.

Onam *(Aug/Sep)*. The most popular of Kerala's festivals. It honours Mahabali, a selfless ruler whose subjects were so content that envious gods tricked him into losing his life and kingdom. His last wish was to visit his people once a year to ensure that they were happy. During Onam, an aura of plenty is created to gladden Mahabali's heart. Great feasts are prepared, new clothes worn, and courtyards are decorated with floral patterns *(athapookkalam)*. The Nehru Trophy Boat Race *(see p36)* is held at this time.

AYURVEDA THERAPY

Ayurvedic treatment in progress

A classical text on medicine, the *Ashtangahridaya*, is the foundation of Ayurveda in Kerala. Its author, Vagbhata, was the disciple of a Buddhist physician, and received little recognition in the rest of India. It is believed that a few Nampoothiri (Brahmin) families were the original Ayurvedic physicians, and their descendants still carry the honorific title of *ashtavaidyan*. Today, this holistic science of healing is practised throughout India. However, the Kerala method is famous for its five-pronged treatment, *panchakarma*, in which medicated oils, herbs, milk, massage and a special diet are used to cure all types of ailments.

Caparisoned elephants and musicians, Thrissur Pooram

Padmanabhapuram Palace ❷

Set amid lush hills, verdant paddy fields and perennial rivers, Padmanabhapuram Palace is the finest example of Kerala's distinctive wooden architecture. Laid out in a sequence of four adjoining walled compounds, comprising public and private zones, the palace has richly carved wooden ceilings, sculpted pillars, slatted windows, and pagoda-like tiled roofs. From 1590 to 1790, Padmanabhapuram was the home of the the former princely state of Travancore, which straddled parts of present-day Tamil Nadu as well as Kerala. By some quirk of fate, this beautifully kept palace now falls in Tamil Nadu but is maintained by the government of Kerala.

Detail from a carved rosewood door

The Lady's Chamber houses two large swings, a pair of enormous Belgian mirrors and a royal bed.

★ Prayer Hall

The prayer hall, on the third floor of the King's Palace, has exquisite murals on its walls. A medicinal bed here, carved from 64 different types of wood, was a gift from the Dutch.

The clock tower's chimes could be heard from a distance of 3 km (2 miles).

Entrance Hall

The entrance hall has a profusely carved wooden ceiling with 90 different inverted flowers, a polished granite bed and an ornate Chinese throne.

Main Gate

The main entrance to the palace complex is reached after crossing a large courtyard. This gate has a decorated gabled roof.

Entrance

| 0 metres | 20 |
| 0 yards | 20 |

Carved bay window for watching processions

Guest house

The Bath House is a small airy room, where the male members of the royal family were given a massage before they descended, down covered steps, to a private tank to bathe.

VISITORS' CHECKLIST

Tamil Nadu state. Kanniyakumari district. 52 km (32 miles) SE of Thiruvananthapuram. *Tel* (04651) 250 255. Tue–Sun. extra charges.

★ Mother's Palace
Built in 1550, this is the oldest building in the complex. It contains intricately carved wooden pillars fashioned from the wood of the jackfruit tree. The floor was polished to a red gloss with hibiscus flowers.

Lamp
A horse lamp (the horse is a symbol of valour) in the entrance hall, hangs suspended from a special chain that keeps the lamp perfectly balanced.

The dining hall, laid out over two storeys, could seat 2,000 guests.

The palace museum houses artifacts including furniture, wooden and granite statues, coins, weapons and utensils.

STAR SIGHTS

★ Prayer Hall

★ Mother's Palace

★ Council Chamber

★ Council Chamber
The king's council chamber has wooden louvres to let in light and air. The gloss on the floor was achieved with a mixture of lime, sand, egg white, coconut water, charcoal and jaggery.

An elephant being led down the steps of Aranmula's Parthasarthy Temple

Aranmula ❸

Pathanamthitta district. 125 km (78 miles) NW of Thiruvananthapuram. 🚌 🚂 from Alappuzha. 🏹 Onam Boat Regatta (Aug/Sep).

The picturesque village of Aranmula, situated on the banks of the Pampa river, is famous as the venue for Kerala's magnificent snake boat races. The boat race festival has its origins in the legend of a devotee who once gave food to a Brahmin, believed to be Vishnu in disguise. However, the Brahmin, before disappearing, advised him to send his offering to Aranmula instead. Since then, during the festival, a ceremonial boat, carved out of a single block of wood, carries a consignment of food from a nearby village to the temple at Aranmula. On the last day of Onam (see p629), this ceremonial boat leads a procession of about 30 snake boats to the temple. On this day, there is no racing and all the boats arrive together, as Krishna is said to be present on each boat at the same time.

The **Parthasarathy Temple**, one of the state's five most important temples, is dedicated to Krishna, and has an image of the god as Parthasarathy, the Divine Charioteer in the great epic, the *Mahabharata*. The image was brought here on a raft made of six bamboos, and this is what the town's name signifies – in Malayalam *aaru* means six and *mula*, bamboo.

Aranmula is also known for its unique metal mirrors made from an alloy of silver, bronze copper and lead. These mirrors were traditionally used as part of the arrangement of auspicious objects during Vishu, the Malayali New Year, in April (see p629).

Environs
The 14th-century **Thiruvamundur Temple**, near Chengannur, 7 km (4 miles) of Aranmula is dedicated to Krishna and attributed to Nakul, one of the five Pandava brothers (see p26). Near Chengannacherry, 27 km (17 miles) northwest of Aranmula, is the **Tirukkodittanam Temple**. This 11th-century temple is dedicated to Sahadev, Nakul's twin brother, and has lovely murals adorning its walls. It is a temple vibrant in traditional art and music.

Metal mirror, Aranmula

Mannarsala ❹

Alappuzha district. 132 km (82 miles) NW of Thiruvananthapuram, (0479) 241 3214. 🚌 🏹 Thulam (Oct/Nov).

The custom of worshipping snakes in Kerala reaches a climax at Mannarsala, the best known of the four main Naga temples in the state. According to legend, a woman from a family of great Naga devotees gave birth to two sons, one of whom was a serpent-child, who asked his family to worship him and vanished. The temples at Mannarsala, dedicated to the King of Snakes, Nagaraja, and his consort, Sarpayakshini, are situated in a thick grove of tall trees and dense bushes, surrounded by thousands of hooded stone serpents of various styles and sizes.

In Kerala, the ancestral home (tharavad) of every upper-class Namboothiri and Nair family is supposed to have a *sarpa-kavu* or snake-grove, housing a *nagakal* or snake stone. If a *tharavad* cannot afford to maintain its own shrine, the snake stones are offered to this temple.

The holy rites at Mannarsala are conducted by a priestess (*amma*), a vestal virgin, who lives on the premises and is supported in her religious duties by her family.

Childless couples place a bell metal vessel (*uruli*) face down in front of the deities, to seek their blessings.

SACRED SERPENT SHRINES

In Kerala, the sacred serpent plays a significant role in belief and ritual. Malayali folklore speaks of a wooded, rural land inhabited mainly by Nagas (snakes) – the Lords of the Underworld – who were overthrown by the Brahmin settlers brought here by Parasurama (see p679), the sixth incarnation of Vishnu. This mythological incident is the origin of snake worship in Kerala since, after their defeat, Parasurama ordered that snakes be accorded divine status. Most temples thus have a niche for a snake god, amid dense sacred groves of ancient trees. The old ancestral homes (*tharavads*) also have private temples or groves for a snake deity.

Sacred grove with snake (naga) images, Mannarsala Temple

Boats of Kerala

Kerala's ancient boat-building industry is a specialized part of its rich wood-working tradition, that also includes architecture *(see p638)*. Boats built at Beypore *(see p653)* were highly prized and used by Arab merchants. The construction of a boat is always begun on an auspicious day in the Malayalam

Dugouts with carved sterns

calendar, and is marked by an invocation to the gods. The most sought-after wood is *anjili (Artocarpus hirsuta)*, though teak is also used. Racing boats of various sizes and shapes participate in the annual Onam regatta at Aranmula. Of these, the most magnificent is the long, narrow *chundanvallam*, or snake boat.

BOAT BUILDING

A master craftsman, assisted by a team traditionally drawn from different religions, builds the boat. No nails or metal pieces are used; only wooden pegs and joints hold the parts together.

SNAKE BOAT RACES

Snake boats *(chundanvallam)*, once used to carry warriors, now participate in what is believed to be the world's largest team sport. The Nehru Trophy Boat Race *(see p36)*, introduced in 1952, is the most famous.

Rowing *is perfectly synchronized to the pulsating rhythm of vanchipattu (boatmen's songs). Their themes are devotional, mythological, or related to rural life.*

The prow of the boat is normally manned by four boatmen.

Oarsmen

Singers

Amaram, the stern, is decorated with brass studs and inlay work.

Kettuvallams *are now often converted into houseboats. Kettu means a bundle, while vallam is a big boat. Originally, these were used as ferries or to carry rice.*

Canoes, *usually made from a single log of wood, can carry no more than one or two people. They are commonly used to transport light cargo, such as coir fibre.*

Backwaters Tour ❺

A cruise along the backwaters is one of the most enchanting experiences that Kerala offers. Exploring this labyrinthine network of waterways, which weave through villages set amidst lush vegetation, offers glimpses of Kerala's unique rural lifestyle, where land and water are inseparable. The most popular backwaters tour is from Kollam (Quilon), situated between Ashtamudi Lake and the Arabian Sea, to Alappuzha (Alleppey) on the edge of Vembanad Lake. The choice of transport ranges from local ferries and speedboats to *kettuvallams (see p633)*.

LOCATOR MAP

Water hyacinths *are the cause of a serious ecological problem since untamed growth has clogged the waterways of Kuttanad, the rice bowl of Kerala.*

Children going to school *by boat are a common sight. Various types of boats are used as transport along the backwaters, connecting the small villages with the mainland.*

Coconut palms fringe the waterways. In addition to coconuts, rice is cultivated extensively in Kuttanad, the area between Kottayam and Alappuzha.

Houses along a canal *have jetties with moored boats. The ground and water levels are often equal, which makes flooding a problem during the monsoon.*

Coconut Lagoon (see p715) *is a wonderful resort on Vembanad Lake, near the bird sanctuary in Kumarakom.*

Toddy tappers *are expert at scaling coconut palms. The local brew, made from fermented coconut palm sap, is sold in shacks along the waterways. The first brew is light and delicious – however, potency levels rise with subsequent fermentation.*

TIPS FOR PASSENGERS

Route 1: Kollam to Alappuzha
Dep: 10:30am. Maximum duration: 8 hrs. 🛈 *District Tourism Promotion Council (DTPC), Kollam, (0474) 274 5625.*
Route 2: Alappuzha to Kollam
Dep: 10:30am. Maximum duration: 8 hrs. 🛈 *DTPC, Alappuzha, (0477) 225 3308. For more details see p781.*

Chinese fishing nets *along the backwaters are used to trap fish. A popular fish in Kerala, karimeen (pearl spot), is found in these waters.*

Children with banana trunks playing in the water

BACKWATERS

According to legend, Parasurama, the sixth incarnation of Vishnu, created Kerala by throwing his battle axe into the sea. The abundance of canals, lagoons and lakes in the state seem to reinforce this legend of a land born from the sea.

In this coir-producing village, *women beat the husk and spin the fibre to make ropes or floor coverings. The fibre is often dyed to create brightly coloured mats with geometric designs.*

Coconut husks *soak in the shallow waters near the banks. This softens the husks before they are beaten to produce the fine fibre that is turned into coir. The flesh is converted into oil, or used in cooking.*

Tea gardens surrounding the Mattupetty Reservoir, Munnar *(see p648)* ▷

Kottayam ⑥

Kottayam district. 160 km (99 miles)
N of Thiruvananthapuram.
60,750. *District Tourist
Promotion Council, (0481) 256 0479.*
Drama Festival (Jan).

Enclosed by the blue waters
of Vembanad Lake and the
paddy fields of Kuttanad to its
west, and by the lush hills of
the Western Ghats to its east,
Kottayam is one of Kerala's
most beautiful districts. Its
climate and landscape have
combined to make the region
prosperous. Kottayam town is
surrounded by extensive
plantations of rubber, and
other valuable cash crops
such as tea, coffee, cardamom
and pepper. The first town in
India to attain 100 per cent
literacy, it is also the birthplace of Kerala's publishing
industry and home to many
Malayalam newspapers and
magazines. A writers' co-
operative society, the Sahitya
Pravarthaka Sahakarana
Sangham, which was set up
here more than 50 years ago,
has played a cardinal role in
fostering the growth of
Malayalam literature.

Kottayam also has an old
Christian tradition that has
been preserved by its large
Syrian Christian population. It
was one of the first towns to
be patronized by St Thomas
(see p573) in the 1st century
AD. Of the many fine
churches and seminaries that
dot the landscape, the best
known are the two Syrian
Orthodox churches, **Valia Palli**
and **Cheria Palli**, both dating to
the mid-16th century. The

Mural from the stately Shiva temple at Ettumanur

churches stand on a hillock,
about 2 km (1.2 miles) north
of the city centre, and have
colourful frescoes adorning
their walls. The Nestorian
cross at Valia Palli is said to
have come from Kerala's first
church, founded by St Thomas
at Kodungallur *(see p649)*.
Cheria Palli has painted panels
behind its main altar, depicting
scenes from the life of the
Virgin Mary.

Nestorian cross at Valia Palli Church, Kottayam

Environs
Mannanam, 8 km (5 miles)
north of Kottayam, is a
pilgrimage centre for Syrian
Christians, who gather in their
thousands each January to
attend a religious convention,
one of the largest in Asia.

Kumarakom, a bird
sanctuary on the banks of
Vembanad Lake, is 12 km (7
miles) west of Kottayam. A
great variety of birds can be
observed from vantage points.

A large temple dedicated to
Shiva at **Ettumanur**, 12 km (7
miles) north of Kottayam, has
beautiful murals, similar to
those found at Mattancherry
Palace in Kochi *(see p642)*.
The 11th-century Mahadeva
Temple at **Vaikom**, 40 km (25
miles) northwest of Kottayam,
is famous for its elephant
pageants and traditional dance
performances, which take
place between Nove-mber and
December each year. It is also
the site where Mahatma
Gandhi led an important
satyagraha (civil disobedience
movement) to make temples
accessible to untouchables.

WOODEN ARCHITECTURE IN KERALA

The importance of wooden architecture in
Kerala is evident in legends that glorify
the master carpenter, Perunthachhan.
Palaces, temples, mosques and homes all
have characteristic sloping tiled roofs
to drain away the heavy rains
during the monsoon. Roofs are
generally hipped, often with
decorated gables, topped by brass
pot finials. To achieve height,
they rise in two or more superimposed
tiers to create steeply pyramidal
profiles. Joints and wooden pegs,
instead of nails, are used.

Brackets are often
carved as *yalis* or figures
of gods and goddesses.

Wooden pillars
are ornate. These
are decorative as
well as functional,
as they support
the roof.

Temple with pyramidal roof

The Baroque façade of St Thomas Church, at Palai

Sabarimalai **7**

Pattanamthitta district. 191 km (119 miles) N of Thiruvananthapuram. to Pamba, then by foot. *Mandalam (Dec/Jan), Makaravilakku (mid-Jan).*

One of the most famous pilgrimage centres in India, Sabarimalai lies in the Western Ghats at an altitude of 914 m (2,999 ft). The final 14-km (9-mile) approach from Pamba, through dense forest, is made on foot.

The focus of devotion here is the temple dedicated to the popular deity, Ayyappa. The temple stays open from November to mid-January, in April and during the first five days of each month of the Malayalam calendar. People of all religions can worship here, but women between the ages of 10 and 50 are restricted from entering. The final 18 sacred steps (each representing a sin that a devotee renounces on setting foot on it) are sheathed in *panchaloha*, an alloy of five metals, and lead to the sanctum. Only those who have observed 41 days of penance (celibacy, wearing black and and not shaving) are entitled to undertake the pilgrimage.

Periyar Tiger Reserve **8**

See pp640–41.

Palai **9**

Kottayam district. 175 km (109 miles) N of Thiruvananthapuram. *Epiphany (6 Jan).* **St Thomas Church** *(Malayalam)* 6am daily.

The prosperous town of Palai is surrounded by thick rubber plantations. The small but beautiful, 16th-century **St Thomas Church**, is its principal attraction. Constructed in the traditional style of early Christian churches in Kerala, It has a quaint wooden pulpit with a fish-like base, an elaborately carved main altar and two simpler side altars. A stone slab carries inscriptions in Syriac. Attractive glass candelabra are suspended from wall brackets, while a chandelier hangs from the ceiling. There is a wooden balcony at the rear. Services are still held in the church. Adjoining this building is a modern church, also dedicated to St Thomas.

THE AYYAPPA CULT

A Dravidian deity worshipped throughout Kerala, Ayyappa (or Sastha), was born out of the union between Shiva and Vishnu (who had transformed himself into a woman, Mohini). The baby, found on the banks of the Pamba river, was adopted by the childless king of Pandalam.

Ayyappa devotees, Sabarimalai

Ayyappa later revealed his divine status when he destroyed a demon. Before returning to his heavenly abode, however, the god shot an arrow into the air which landed near the ashram of the sage Sabari, where a temple was built. Ayyappa's warrior friend, Vavar, is a Muslim saint whose *dargah* nearby is visited by both Muslims and Hindus.

Ceilings are divided into panels carved with lotus designs or Hindu deities, such as Brahma, surrounded by *dikpalas* (guardian figures).

Koottambulams, traditional theatres, are usually situated in the precincts of large temples and palaces. They serve as the venue for staging Koodiyattam (dance-drama) performances.

Interiors of *koottambulams* have tall wooden pillars and *jalis* on three sides for ventilation. The roof is specially designed to provide excellent acoustic quality.

Periyar Tiger Reserve 🕗

Visitors viewing wildlife from a boat on Periyar Lake

Common kingfisher

The construction of the Mullaperiyar Dam across the Periyar river at Thekkady, in 1895, submerged large tracts of land and created a huge lake, covering an area of 26 sq km (10 sq miles). Years later, in 1935, the then Maharaja of Travancore declared 600 sq km (232 sq miles) of forest surrounding the lake a wildlife sanctuary. The Periyar Lake now forms the nucleus of the ecosystem of the sanctuary which, over the years, has been expanded to 777 sq km (300 sq miles). Declared a Tiger Reserve in 1978, the sanctuary is a rare example of human interference having enhanced rather than damaged an ecosystem.

Lake Palace
The former hunting lodge of the Maharaja of Travancore is now a delightful hotel inside the sanctuary (see p716).

Birdlife
The petrified tree trunks that jut out from the lake make convenient perches for birds looking out for fish.

IDUKKI ↑   MADURAI

Kumily

NH 49

KOTTAYAM

Thekk.

Edapalayam

Manakarala

Periyar   ▪ Dam   Periyar Lake

0 km   1

0 miles   1

Wildlife
The deciduous forests, grasslands and tropical evergreen interiors of Periyar are the habitat of the endangered lion-tailed macaque (left), as well as Indian bison (gaur), sloth bears and the slender loris.

For hotels and restaurants in this region see pp714–17 and pp742–3

Herds of Elephants
The lake, a year-round source of water, and the abundant grassland make the sanctuary an ideal habitat for elephants, which now number approximately 800.

VISITORS' CHECKLIST

Idukki district. 190 km (118 miles) N of Kochi. ⛴ ℹ️ *Forest Divisional Office, Kumily (04869) 22 2028, Tourist Information Centre, Kumily (04869) 22 2620.*

Indian Giant Squirrel
This agile squirrel can make amazing leaps that cover about 6 m (20 ft). It is found in Periyar's deciduous and evergreen forests.

Mangaladevi Temple 🛕☀️

The Mangaladevi Temple, 15 km (9 miles) east of Thekkady, lies at a height of 1,337 m (4,387 ft), and offers excellent panoramic views of the forested hills of the Ghats.

Periyar Lake
Two-hour boat cruises on the mist-shrouded lake offer excellent opportunities for spotting wildlife, especially herds of elephants.

☀️ 🅰️ Mullakady

Thannikudi ☀️🅰️

Periyar

KEY

▬▬	National highway
▬▬	Major road
▬▬	Minor road
⛴	Jetty
ℹ️	Tourist information
☀️	Viewpoint
🛕	Temple
🅰️	Accommodation

Orchids
Periyar is known for its many species of flowering plants, including nearly 150 species of orchids. The rare orchid Habeneria periyarancis, named after the region, is found only here.

Kochi ❿

Antique mask

Kochi, better known as Cochin, is Kerala's most cosmopolitan city. It is also its main trading centre for spices and seafood. Built around a saltwater lagoon of the Arabian Sea, Kochi is in fact a collection of narrow islands and peninsulas. While mainland Ernakulam boasts of concrete shopping malls and glitzy apartment buildings, Mattancherry and Fort Kochi have an old world charm, with their blend of Dutch, Portuguese and English bungalows and quaint narrow streets *(see pp644–5)*. The scenic location of Kochi's natural harbour, surrounded by palm groves, green fields, inland lakes and backwaters, has enchanted visitors from across the globe for centuries.

Brahma emerging from Vishnu's navel, mural, Mattancherry Palace

🏛 Mattancherry Palace

Jew Town. **Tel** *(0484) 222 6085.*
◯ *Sat–Thu.*
The Mattancherry Palace, constructed by the Portuguese in the mid-1550s, was given to the ruler of Cochin as a token of goodwill in exchange for trading rights. It was later renovated by the Dutch, and so gained the misnomer, Dutch Palace. The two-storeyed structure, built around a courtyard with a small shrine to the goddess Bhagavati, is today a museum with a rare collection of murals and royal artifacts.
 In the central Durbar Hall, where coronation ceremonies were once held, is the portrait

gallery of the Kochi rulers; it also displays palanquins and textiles. The adjacent bedrooms and chambers are renowned for their fine 17th-century murals, representative of Kerala's temple art. Painted in rich, warm shades of red, yellow, black and white, they depict religious and mythological themes as well as episodes from the *Ramayana*.

✡ Paradesi Synagogue

Jew Town. ◯ *Sun–Fri.* 🖼
Nestling in a cul-de-sac at the end of a narrow lane, in the heart of Jew Town, is India's oldest synagogue. The first Jewish settlers are said to have reached Kodungallur *(see p649)* in the 1st century AD. Their settlement, then known as Shingly, prospered over the centuries.
 However, persecution by the Portuguese in the early 16th century forced them to migrate to Cochin, where they settled on land given by the raja, and built a synagogue in 1568. Cochin's Jewish community was divided into two distinct groups – the so-called Black or Malabari Jews who claimed to be descendants of the original settlers, and the White or Paradesim Jews who came here from the Middle East, and after whom

KOCHI CITY CENTRE

Bolghatty Island ⑥
Kochi International
 Pepper Exchange ③
Mattancherry Palace ①
Paradesi Synagogue ②

St Francis Church ④
Willingdon Island ⑤

KEY

Street-by-Street area: see pp644–5

Key to Symbols see back flap

0 metres 500
0 yards 500

Main hall with brass pulpit and blue-tiled floor, Paradesi Synagogue

the synagogue is named. A third, smaller group was the Brown or Meshuhurarum Jews, descended from converted slaves, many of whom were in the spice trade. In 1940, there were 2,500 Jews in Kerala, but today only a dozen families remain, the rest having migrated to Israel.

The present synagogue, with its tiled roof and clock tower, was rebuilt in 1664 with Dutch help, after the Portuguese destroyed it in 1662. The synagogue's treasures include beautiful silver and gold Torah scrolls, a multitude of hanging oil lamps and crystal chandeliers, and a superbly crafted brass pulpit. The floor is covered with exquisite hand-painted blue willow-pattern tiles, which were brought from Canton in the mid-18th century by a powerful merchant, Ezekiel Rahabi.

The narrow lanes around the synagogue are crammed with Dutch-style residences. Today, most of these house antique shops.

Antique shops lining the narrow lanes in Jew Town

Kochi International Pepper Exchange

Jew Town. **Tel** (0484) 222 4263. Passes required to enter hall. ☐ Mon–Sat.
This unique establishment reverberates with voices, seemingly raised in anger, as one ascends the stairs. However, nothing prepares the visitor for what lies within – the small hall is lined with tiny cubicles, each with a man talking animatedly on a telephone. Theatrical gestures accompanied by a loud cacophony of sounds mark the drama of each day's pepper auction.

St Francis Church

Fort Kochi. ☐ Mon–Sat.
(English) 8am, daily.
Established in the early 1500s by the Portuguese (who called it Santo Antonio) this is one of India's earliest European churches, with a simple façade that became the model for later churches. Taken over by the Dutch and then the British, it is today affiliated to the Church of South India.

Within are numerous gravestones with inscriptions, the earliest a Portuguese epitaph, dated 1562. Vasco da Gama *(see p653)* was buried here in 1524 until his body was taken to Portugal 14 years later.

Willingdon Island

This man-made island, named after the viceroy, Lord Willingdon, was created in the 1920s out of silt dredged to deepen Kochi port. Situated between Fort Kochi, Mattancherry and Ernakulam, it has some good hotels, as well as the main harbour, the Port Trust building, the customs house and the railway station. It is also an important naval base.

The gracious façade of Bolghatty Palace, now a hotel

Bolghatty Island

Bolghatty Palace Hotel Tel (0484) 275 0500. open to non-residents.
A narrow strip of land, this beautiful island with breathtaking views of the bay, is the location of Bolghatty Palace. Set in 6 ha (15 acres) of lush green lawns, this palatial structure was originally built by the Dutch in 1744 and later became the home of the British Resident. It has now been converted into a hotel run by the Kerala Tourism Development Corporation *(see p714)*.

Environs

Kochi's bustling business centre, **Ernakulam**, is 10 km (6 miles) east of Fort Kochi. The Hill Palace at **Thripunithura**, 10 km (6 miles) southeast of Ernakulam, was built in 1895 and was the official residence of the former rulers of Cochin. The palace, set in spacious grounds, is now a museum with a fairly good collection of paintings, manuscripts and royal memorabilia. The exquisite floor tiles differ from room to room, and the sweeping wooden staircases have a grandeur all of their own. The 10th-century **Chottanikkara Temple**, dedicated to the mother goddess Bhagavati, one of Kerala's most popular deities, is 16 km (10 miles) northeast of Ernakulam.

Thripunithura Museum

Tel (0484) 278 1113. ☐ Tue–Sun.

Street-by-Street: Fort Kochi

Kochi's natural harbour, created by a massive flood in 1341, attracted imperialists and merchants from all over the world. In the 16th century, the Portuguese built a fort here, which was later occupied by the Dutch and then the British. Today, this quarter, with its mixture of architectural styles, encapsulates Fort Kochi's tumultuous history. The most important building here is St Francis Church, erected by the Portuguese in 1502 and considered to be among the oldest churches built by Europeans in India. This area has now been declared a Heritage Zone to preserve its many historic buildings.

★ Santa Cruz Cathedral
Built in 1887, this cathedral has impressive murals on its ceiling.

Kashi Art Café
This charming restaurant, in an old Dutch building, houses an art gallery.

Mattancherry

Koder House
The residence of Satu Koder, patriarch of Kochi's Jews, was built by his ancestors in 1808. It has now been converted into a boutique hotel.

★ Chinese Fishing Nets
First erected between 1350 and 1450, these cantilevered fishing nets indicate trade links with China.

For hotels and restaurants in this region see pp714–17 and pp742–3

Peter Celli Street
*Many hotels and shops
are located here.*

Bishop's House
*Once the Portuguese governor's
house, this 16th-century structure
is now home to Kochi's bishop.*

United Club, once a British
club, now houses a school.

Bishop's
House

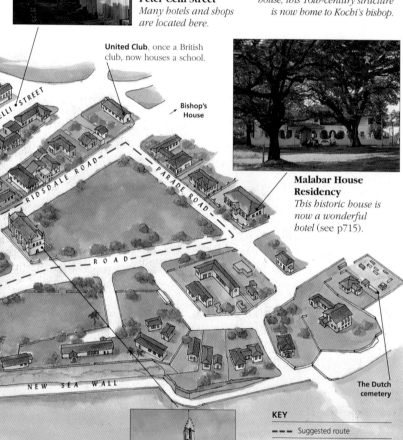

**Malabar House
Residency**
*This historic house is
now a wonderful
hotel (see p715).*

ELLI STREET

RIDSDALE ROAD

PARADE ROAD

ROAD

NEW SEA WALL

The Dutch
cemetery

KEY

--- Suggested route

STAR SIGHTS

★ Santa Cruz
  Cathedral

★ Chinese Fishing
  Nets

★ St Francis Church

★ **St Francis Church**
*Vasco da Gama was
buried here in 1524,
before his body was
taken to Portugal.*

Lakshadweep Islands

Formerly the Laccadives, the Lakshadweep Islands are an archipelago of 36 exquisite coral islands, with untouched beaches and verdant coconut groves, scattered off the Kerala coast in the Arabian Sea. With a total land area of only 32 sq km (12 sq miles), Lakshadweep (which means 100,000 islands) is the smallest Union Territory in India. The atolls enclose shallow lagoons harbouring India's richest diversity of coral varieties, and a multitude of colourful reef fish. Only two islands, Bangaram and Kadmat, are open to foreign visitors, while Indian visitors have a choice of six; all offer superb snorkelling and scuba-diving.

Bird of paradise

Cherbaniani Reef

Byramgore Reef

Bitra Island

Chetlat Island

Kiltan Island

Perumulappara

Kadmat Island

Amindivi Island

Bangaram Island

Agatti Island

Pitti Island   Androth Island

Kavaratti Island

Suheli Island

Kalpeni Island

Wind-surfing in the Lakshadweep Islands

Minicoy Island

0 km   50
0 miles   50

Kavaratti Island

450 km (280 miles) W of Kochi. ▣ ○ *to Indian passport holders only.* 🔺

Lakshadweep's administrative headquarters, Kavaratti is the busiest island, and home to a large number of mainlanders, most of whom work for the government. It has beautiful white beaches and its crystal-clear lagoon is popular with water sports enthusiasts.

There are 52 mosques on the island that cater to the predominantly Muslim population. The **Ujra Mosque** has an ornate ceiling, carved from driftwood. The island also has a **Marine Aquarium**, which displays a variety of tropical fish and corals.

Huts at Bangaram Island Resort

Agatti Island

55 km (34 miles) NW of Kavaratti Island. ✕ ▣ ○ *to Indian passport holders only.* 🔺

Lakshadweep's only airport is on Agatti Island. It has a fine lagoon and offers easy access for day visits to the uninhabited islands of Bangaram, Tinnakara and Parali I and II. Although all visitors arriving by plane must go through Agatti, the island itself is not open to foreign visitors.

Bangaram Island

58 km (36 miles) NW of Kavaratti. ▣ 🔺

The uninhabited Bangaram Island is covered with dense groves of coconut palms and has lovely sandy beaches.

The **Bangaram Island Resort** *(see p715)*, run by Casino Hotels of Kochi, has about 30 rooms as well as a restaurant and bar. Its lagoon, rich with corals and tropical fish, is excellent for scuba diving and snorkelling. Visitors can also choose from the variety of water sports available,

including sailing. A health certificate from a doctor is required for diving.

Kadmat Island

70 km (44 miles) N of Kavaratti Island. ▣ 🔺

Thickly covered with palm trees, Kadmat Island has two fine lagoons, to the east and west. The **Water Sports Institute** offers canoeing,

Snorkelling in Lakshadweep Islands' crystal-clear waters

Fisherfolk picking mussels among reefs in the shallows

kayaking and glass-bottomed boat rides, and the **Lacadives Dive School**, on the same premises, offers snorkelling and scuba diving and has qualified instructors.

Water Sports Institute
SPORTS Office, Kochi.
Tel (0484) 266 8387.

Lacadives Dive School
Tel Mumbai, (022) 5662 7381; Kochi, (0484) 236 7752.
www.lacadives.com

Kalpeni Island

125 km (78 miles) SE of Kavaratti Island. to Indian passport holders only.
The clear, shallow lagoon of Kalpeni Island is the largest in Lakshadweep. With excellent reefs, Kalpeni is ideal for diving and

A hermit crab coming out of a shell

snorkelling. Coral debris, deposited by a storm in 1847, has formed raised banks on the eastern and southern shores. Kalpeni's inhabitants were among the earliest islanders to send girls to school, paving the way for other islanders who had traditionally kept their girls and women confined to the home.

Minicoy Island

250 km (155 miles) S of Kavaratti Island. to Indian passport holders only.
Lakshadweep's southernmost island, Minicoy has a unique culture influenced by the neighbouring Maldives. Mahl, spoken here, is a dialect of the Maldivian Dhivehi, which is related to the Indo-Persian languages with a script written from right to left. Minicoy is often referred to as "Women's Island", as its ten villages are matrilineal. It is also rich in the performing arts; the traditional Lava dance is performed on festive occasions. Tuna fishing has become an important activity, with the establishment of a tuna canning factory.

Minicoy has a grand lagoon, and is the only island in the archipelago with a stretch of mangroves along its shores. A large lighthouse, built by the British in 1885, commands an impressive view of the sea.

MARINE LIFE IN THE CORAL REEFS

The Lakshadweep Islands are a conglomeration of atolls – ring-shaped coral reef formations – that are the richest coral reefs found in India. Formed over thousands of years, they are made up of billions of minute organisms called polyps. Related to sea anemones, polyps build their skeletons outside their body. As they grow, their limestone skeletons become elaborate coral formations, with new colonies spreading over dead ones, and eventually turn into formidable reefs. The complex and fragile reef ecosystem is alive with an extraordinary range of plants and marine life. Over 600 species of reef fish, such as clown fish and parrot fish in a dazzling array of colours, giant clams with purple lips, delicate sea fans and sea anemones, ink-blue starfish, dolphins, harmless sharks and marine turtles, make up the spectacular diversity of the underwater world. (For tips on eco-friendly diving, see p619.)

Parali Island, one of Lakshadweep's many atolls

Corals of a 100-odd varieties, including the boulder-like porites, the ridged brain (right), and the branched staghorn, can be seen here. The myriad colours are produced by the variety of algae that grow on them.

The nine-tiered tower dedicated to Shankaracharya, Kaladi

Kaladi ⑫

Ernakulam district. 35 km (22 miles) NE of Kochi.

This quiet town on the banks of the beautiful Periyar river is celebrated as the birthplace of the great philosopher, Shankaracharya. Two shrines, built in 1910 on the river bank, honour his memory. One is dedicated to him and the other to the goddess Sharada, and both are maintained by the Sringeri Matha *(see p527)*.

Nearby is a spot known as Brindavan, where the Shankaracharya's mother, Aryamba, was cremated. The old Shri Krishna Temple, near the Sharada Temple, has an image of the deity, said to have been installed by Shankaracharya himself. On the road to the Krishna Temple is a 46-m (151-ft) tall, nine-tiered octagonal tower, the Shri Adi Shankaracharya Kirti Stambha Mandapa. Each of its floors commemorates the life and works of Shankaracharya.

Environs

The **Malayattor Church**, 8 km (5 miles) east of Kaladi, is said to be where St Thomas erected a cross. The 1,000-year old rock-cut **Kalill Temple**, 22 km (14 miles) southeast of Kaladi, was originally a Jain temple. It is now dedicated to the mother goddess. Unlike at other temples, a female elephant is used in all ceremonial rituals.

Munnar ⑬

Idukki district. 130 km (81 miles) N of Kochi. *Tourist Information Centre, Munnar, (04865) 23 1516. daily.*

The picturesque little town of Munnar lies at a height of about 1,800 m (5,906 ft), in a part of the Western Ghats known as the High Ranges. The name Munnar (which means "Three Rivers" in Tamil) is derived from its location at the confluence of three mountain streams – Kundala, Mudrapuzha and Nallathanni.

Located in 24,000 ha (59,305 acres) of sprawling tea estates, first established by the British in 1878, Munnar was once a summer resort for the British government in South India. The most important plantation in the High Ranges today belongs to Tata Tea, which oversees almost every public facility in the vicinity. The quaint High Range Club, made of wicker and teak, still serves as a social centre for Munnar's planters and, with its customary "gentlemen's bar", retains an old-world atmosphere.

Munnar remains a popular destination for visitors from Tamil Nadu and Kerala. Because of this, the town and its environs have witnessed a proliferation of hotels, restaurants and shopping centres. However, areas further away from the city centre remain relatively unspoilt, and the gentle hills offer excellent cycle rides and walks.

Environs

Mattupetty Lake, 13 km (8 miles) north of Munnar, is surrounded by lovely semi-alpine scenery. A specialized cattle-breeding centre is located nearby.

A view of the tea plantations around Munnar

ADI SHANKARACHARYA (AD 788–820)

Adi Shankaracharya, only 32 when he died, travelled the length and breadth of India, wrote erudite commentaries on Hindu scriptures, and composed devotional poems and prayers. The core of his monist philosophy is that there is only one reality and that is Brahman, the all-pervading cosmic force of which the human soul is a part, while all material objects are mere illusions *(maya)*. The Buddhist elements in his philosophy provoked, during his lifetime, the orthodox Brahminical charge that he was a "Buddha in disguise". His historical importance lies in the fact that he provided an intellectual basis to Hinduism.

The philosopher Adi Shankaracharya

The captivating landscape of Eravikulam National Park

Eravikulam National Park ⑭

Idukki district. 16 km (10 miles) NE of Munnar. ☐ or auto-rickshaw from Munnar to Rajamalai, the entry point. ☐ For information contact Divisional Forest Officer, Munnar, (04865) 23 1587. ☐ Aug–May. ☑

The rolling high-altitude grasslands, a striking contrast to the dense *sholas* or tropical montane forests of the valleys, are unique to the mountain landscape of the Western Ghats. Easily the best preserved stretch of this extra-ordinarily beautiful landscape is the Eravikulam National Park, spread across an area of 97 sq km (38 sq miles) at the base of the **Anaimudi Mountain**. With a height of 2,695 m (8,842 ft), this has the distinction of being the highest peak south of the Himalayas. Anaimudi, which means "Elephant Head", not surprisingly resembles one. The peak and its environs provide good hiking territory.

The park, on the border of Kerala and Tamil Nadu, was established in 1978 with the specific aim of conserving the endangered Nilgiri tahr, a rare breed of mountain goat (see p19). Today, the park is home to about 3,000 tahr, the single largest population of this slate-grey goat in the world. Extremely agile, it inhabits the rocky slopes, and can be observed at surprisingly close quarters. The park is also home to macaques, leopards,

and packs of *dhole*, the rare Indian wild dog. Its streams contain trout, and there are also more than 90 species of birds, including song birds such as the laughing thrush.

Eravikulam is regarded as one of the best managed national parks in the country. The Muduvan tribals, who live at the periphery of the park, are employed to assist in its conservation. Their traditional method of selectively burning parts of the grassland prevents large forest fires, and also helps regenerate the tender grass on which young tahr feed. Eravikulam is also famous for the *kurunji (Strobilanthes kunthianus)*, the blue flowers that suddenly bloom en masse every 12 years and transform the rocky landscape into a sea of blue. The *kurunji* is next expected to bloom here in 2006.

Kurunji flower in full bloom

Kodungallur ⑮

Thrissur district. 32 km (20 miles) N of Kochi. ☐ ☑ Id (Feb/Mar), Bharani Festival (Mar/Apr).

Known as Muziris to the Greeks, and Cranganore to the Europeans, Kodungallur was the historic capital of the Cheraman Perumals, monarchs of the Chera empire (see p43). Situated at the mouth of the Periyar river, this was the Malabar Coast's main port until a flood tide in 1341 silted up the harbour. After this catastrophe, Kochi (see p642) became the main port.

The town is today a major destination for Hindus, Christians and Muslims alike. The **Bhagavati Temple**, in the city centre, is the venue of a three-day festival of erotic song and dance. This temple was originally the shrine of a Dravidian goddess. It was then taken over by either the Buddhists or the Jains. The festival marks the reclaiming of the site for the goddess.

St Thomas (see p573) is said to have landed here in AD 52. The **Mar Thoma Pontifical Shrine** houses a sacred relic that was brought from the Vatican in 1953 to celebrate the anniversary of the saint's arrival 1,900 years earlier.

The **Cheraman Mosque**, 2 km (1.3 miles) from the city centre, was built in AD 629 by Malik Bin Dinar, who introduced Islam to Kerala. Perhaps the first mosque in India, it resembles a Hindu temple.

KERALA'S MATRILINEAL FAMILY SYSTEM

Called *marumakkathayam* in Kerala, the matrilineal family system, whereby inheritance is determined through the female line, is believed to have evolved in the late 10th century. This was a period of internecine warfare, and by placing women at the core of the inheritance, men could go to battle, knowing that their children's material well-being was protected. Children thus bear their mother's family name, and are identified as members of her family, with her brothers performing the role of the father figure. The Nairs are best known for this system, since warriors traditionally came from this community. Anthropologists, however, have traced its origin to the cult of the mother goddess widely prevalent in Kerala.

A Nair matriarch from Kerala

The Asian Elephant

Literature, art and culture in India celebrate the elephant. Ganesha, the elephant-headed son of Shiva and Parvati, is the Remover of Obstacles, and his name is invoked before any important task is undertaken *(see p467)*. Unlike in the rest of India, Ganesha is a minor deity in Kerala. Yet, elephants play a major role in the daily life and festivals of the people

Ganesha, the elephant god

of Kerala, who have a uniquely close and affectionate relationship with elephants. Though mainly used as draught animals, elephants also participate in temple rituals, where they carry the deity in sacred processions. For such occasions, elephants are splendidly caparisoned with ornaments of gold. The wealthier temples have their own elephants.

ASIAN ELEPHANT
Denizen of the forests and floodplains of the Himalayan foothills, Central India and the southern highlands, the Asian elephant *(Elephas maximus)* is not as tall as the African elephant, and has smaller ears.

The tusker *(a male with large tusks) faces great danger from poaching, despite the ban on ivory.*

This 19th-century print *shows how trained elephants were used to capture wild ones by driving them into* khedas *(corrals).*

Temple elephants *are usually bought at the Sonepur Mela in Bihar (see p216). The mahout devotes hours every day to grooming and training them for temple festivals. All commands are given in Malayalam.*

In Kerala, *elephants are often seen carrying their own feed. Most people allow mahouts to cut as many fronds of palm as the animal needs – up to 200 kg (441 lb) a day.*

Icons and motifs *depicting the elephant are common in Indian art, as they are an integral part of Hindu mythology and pageantry.*

View of the Catholic Lourdes Cathedral in Thrissur

Thrissur ⑯

Thrissur district. 80 km (50 miles) N of Kochi. 🚶 317,500. 🚃 🚌 ℹ️ Tourist Office, Govt Guest House, (0487) 232 0800. 🎭 Thrissur Pooram (Apr/May), Kamdassamkadavu Boat Races (Aug/Sep).

This town, built around an elevated area called The Round, was planned during the reign of Raja Rama Varma, the ruler of Cochin (Kochi) in the 18th century. In the heart of The Round is the multi-roofed **Vadakkunnathan Temple**. This great Shiva temple was built in the 9th century, and has superb wood-carvings and rich decorative murals. The splendid Pooram festival is held here each year, with the main activities taking place outside the temple walls (non-Hindus are not permitted inside the shrine).

Northeast of the temple is the State Museum, displaying a good collection of murals, wood-carvings, sculpture and antique ornaments. The Archaeological Museum nearby is currently undergoing renovation.

Entrance, Shri Krishna Temple

Thrissur is often dubbed Kerala's cultural capital as the town is home to two prestigious state-run cultural institutions. These are the Kerala Sangeetha Nataka Academy (for music and theatre) and the Kerala Sahitya Academy (for literature).

The town suffered political upheavals for centuries, having been successively ruled by the Zamorins of Kozhikode (see p653), Tipu Sultan of Mysore and the rulers of Kochi. The Dutch and the British have also made their presence felt in the history of this district, as is evident from the many impressive churches, such as the late 19th-century **Lourdes Cathedral**, around the town.

Environs

Guruvayur, 29 km (18 miles) north of Thrissur, has Kerala's most popular temple. Legend has it that the 16th-century Shri Krishna Temple was created by Guru ("Instructor of the Gods"), and Vayu ("God of the Winds"). The temple's elephant sanctuary is within the compound of an old palace nearby. It houses more than 40 elephants that belong to the deity – it is customary to present an elephant as an offering here.

The renowned performing arts and teaching centre, the **Kerala Kala Mandalam**, is 32 km (20 miles) northeast of Thrissur. Founded in 1930 by the famous Malayali poet, Vallathol Narayan Menon, at Cheruthuruthy, it offers intensive training in Kathakali, Mohiniattam and Koodiyattam dance forms. Instrumental and vocal music forms are taught here as well. The complex also has a large *natyagriha* (dance hall) for performances.

🏛 **Kerala Kala Mandalam**
Tel (04884) 26 2305 for permission.
⭕ Mon–Fri. ⬤ public hols, Apr/May.

Vadakkunnathan Temple in Thrissur

THE POORAM FESTIVAL

A *pooram* (meeting) is a temple festival marked by the ceremonious congregation, at a particular temple, of deities from various other temples. Though a number of *poorams* are held throughout Kerala, Thrissur's Pooram is the most spectacular. Held between April and May, it celebrates the processional arrival of two goddesses before Shiva, after whom the town is named. Through a sea of devotees and the hypnotic beat of percussion instruments, two rows of elephants, with the central ones carrying the deities, move majestically towards each other. A firework display ends the celebrations.

Elephants at the Pooram festival

Palakkad ⑰

Palakkad district. 99 km (62 miles) N of Kochi. 🚷 130,750. 🚉 🚌 *Tourist Information Centre, near Children's Park, (0491) 253 8996.* 📷 *Chariot Festival (Oct/Nov).*

Situated at the base of the Western Ghats, Palakkad (Palghat) derives its name from the dense forests *(kadu)* of *pala (Alsteria scholaris)* trees that once covered the land. Today, however, paddy fields and tobacco plantations have taken their place.

Tipu's Fort, in the heart of the town, was built by Haider Ali of Mysore in 1766; it was subsequently occupied by the British after they defeated his son and successor, Tipu Sultan *(see p517)*, some 30 years later. This sombre, granite structure now houses various government offices.

The large **Vishwanatha Temple**, on the banks of the Kalpathy river, is famous for its chariot procession.

On the outskirts of town are the extensive **Malampuzha Gardens**, laid out above a huge irrigation dam built across the Malampuzha river. Pleasant boat cruises are possible on a large lake, nestling in the foothills.

Environs
The town of **Kollengode** is 19 km (12 miles) south of Palakkad and is set in pastoral surroundings. The Vishnu Temple and Kollengode Palace are worth a visit. **Thrithala**, 75 km (47 miles) west of Palakkad, has a Shiva temple and the ruins of a mud fort. Its most important sight, the Kattilmadam Temple, is a granite Buddhist monument dating from the 9th–10th centuries.

Silent Valley, a haven of rare plants and herbs

Silent Valley National Park ⑱

Palakkad district. 88 km (55 miles) NW of Kochi. 🚌 *Mannarkkad, the entry point. Jeeps available to Mukkali.* 🛈 *For permits contact the Wildlife Warden, Mannarkkad, (04924) 25 3225.*

The Silent Valley National Park, spread over an area of 90 sq km (35 sq miles), preserves what is perhaps the country's last substantial stretch of virgin tropical evergreen forest. An important part of the Nilgiri Biosphere Reserve *(see p520)*, it represents some of the spectacular biodiversity of the Western Ghats. The park is renowned for its rare plants and herbs, which include over 100 species of orchids. Wildlife includes tigers, elephants, the Nilgiri langur, the sloth bear, the shy nocturnal slender loris, and the endangered lion-tailed macaque. A variety of birds, as well as a remarkable 100 species of butter-

Slender loris

flies and 400 species of moths, are also found here. Visitors can trek to the source of the Kunthipuzha river which flows through this valley. Accommodation is available at the forest lodge in Mukkali, just outside the park.

Malappuram ⑲

Malappuram district. 153 km (95 miles) N of Kochi. 🚌 🛈 *(0483) 2733 1504.* 🏠 *daily.* 📷 *Valiya Nercha (Feb/Mar), Shivratri (Feb/Mar).*

This "land atop hills" stands at the entrance to the Malabar region, and is crossed by three major rivers – the Chaliyar, the Kadalundi and the Bharatapuzha. A military centre of the Zamorins of Calicut, it was the scene of fierce fighting between British forces and the Mopplahs (Muslim peasants), known as the Mopplah Revolt. The most serious uprising occurred in 1921, after which many rebels were exiled to the Andamans *(see pp618-19)*. The old British barracks, on a hilltop overlooking the Kadalundi river, now houses the district administration. Malappuram is also an important seat of both Hindu and Islamic learning.

Environs
Kerala's pioneering Ayurvedic institution *(see p629)* is at **Kottakkal**, 12 km (7 miles) southwest of Malappuram. Started in 1902, the Kottakkal Arya Vaidyasala is based in a splendid building, and has a

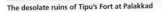
The desolate ruins of Tipu's Fort at Palakkad

For hotels and restaurants in this region see pp714–17 and pp742–3

Arya Vaidyasala, at Kottakkal

research centre and hospital. **Tirur**, 32 km (20 miles) southwest of Malappuram, was the 16th-century birthplace of the father of Malayalam literature, Tunchat Ramanuja Ezhuthachan. He also taught the Malayalam alphabet to children, a practice that continues at a shrine dedicated to him.

One of the earliest Portuguese settlements on the Malabar Coast was at **Tanur**, 34 km (21 miles) southwest of Malappuram. St Francis Xavier *(see p498)* is said to have come here in 1546.

Kozhikode ⑳

Kozhikode district. 254 km (158 miles) N of Kochi. 🏠 436,600. ✈ Karipur, 25 km (16 miles) S of city centre. 🚌 🚂 ℹ District Tourism Promotion Council, (0495) 273 4355. 📷 *Shivratri Utsavam (Feb/Mar).*

This busy commercial town, better known throughout the world as Calicut, was the capital of the kingdom of the powerful Zamorins (a Portuguese corruption of their title, Samoothiri). Under them the town prospered as a major centre of the Malabar trade in spices and textiles, and it was from Calicut that the word calico originated as the term for white, unbleached cotton.

It was in Calicut, too, that Vasco da Gama, the intrepid Portuguese explorer who discovered the sea route to India, was first received by the Zamorin in his palace in May 1498.

Dominating the city centre is the large Manamchira Tank, flanked by the Town Hall and the Public Library, both fine examples of traditional architecture. A striking Roman Catholic cathedral also stands near the Manamchira Tank.

The town's Muslim heritage is indicated by its numerous mosques, remarkable for their massive size and elaborate wood carvings. Among these, the Mishqal Palli, near the port, is the most impressive, with a five-tiered tiled roof.

The **Pazhassirajah Museum** exhibits wood and metal sculptures, models of temples and reconstructions of megalithic monuments. The Art Gallery next door has paintings by Raja Ravi Varma, the 19th-century painter who belonged to a princely family from Travancore *(see p626)*. Kozhikode's busy shopping area, the quaintly-named **Sweetmeats Street**, was once lined with shops selling the famous Calicut *halwa*, a brightly coloured sweet made of flour and sugar. Today, SM Street, as it is popularly known, has only a few shops that sell *halwa*. Court Road, leading off SM Street, houses the bustling Spice Market. Kozhikode is today the storage and trading centre for hill produce from Wynad *(see p654)*; spices such as cloves,

cardamom, pepper, turmeric and coffee are sorted and packaged in the old warehouses along the waterfront.

🏛 Pazhassirajah Museum
East Hill. ***Tel** (0495) 238 1253.*
🕐 *Tue–Sun.*

Environs
A short 16-km (10-mile) drive north of the city leads to the small village of **Kappad**, where a stone plaque on the beach commemorates the spot where Vasco da Gama is supposed to have landed in 1498.

The historic village of **Beypore**, 10 km (6 miles) south of Kozhikode, is believed to be the fabled Ophir, referred to in ancient Greek and Roman texts. Artisans still follow the traditional methods of their forefathers at this ancient shipbuilding centre *(see p633)*. The type of dhows that were built here for Arab merchants more than 1,500 years ago are still in demand in West Asia. Old vessels are also brought here to be repaired.

Thusharagiri, 50 km (31 miles) away from Kozhikode, is a plantation town that abounds in rubber, arecanut, pepper, ginger and spices. It is also a trekking and rock climbing destination. The surrounding hills offer some exciting trails. One of the most popular is a 12-km (7.5-mile) long trek that crosses three lovely waterfalls, one of which falls from a height of 75 m (246 ft), and climbs up through dense evergreen forests where a variety of birds and animals can be spotted. The nearest airport is at Karipur, about 23 km (14 miles) from Kozhikode.

Fishermen with colorful nets in the harbor of Beypore.

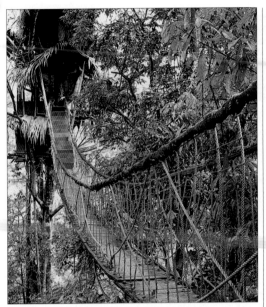

The Tree House in Wynad, blending into the sylvan landscape

Wynad District ㉑

280 km (174 miles) NE from Kochi to Kalpetta. 🚌 🛈 *Tourist Information centre, Kalpetta, (04936) 20 4441.*

A remote region of virgin rainforests and mist-clad mountain ranges, Wynad provides the ideal climatic conditions for Kerala's extensive plantations of cardamom, pepper, coffee and rubber. Relatively untouched by modernization, this is the homeland of large groups of indigenous tribal communities, such as the cave-dwelling Cholanaikens, and the downtrodden Paniyas, who until 50 years ago were sold as bonded labour to plantation owners. It is also the favoured habitat of animals such as the, Nilgiri langur, wild elephants and the giant Malabar squirrel.

The gateway to Wynad is **Lakkidi**, at its southern end. An ancient tree on the main highway, ominously draped with a heavy iron chain, presents a curious sight. Local legend claims that it binds the angry spirit of a Paniya tribal who showed a group of British surveyors the path through the dense forest. Instead of being rewarded, he was killed here and his spirit apparently haunted the highway until it was exorcised.

Kalpetta, the district headquarters, is 15 km (9 miles) to the north. Once a major Jain centre *(see p396)* this has two Jain temples situated nearby. The Anantanathaswami Temple is at Puliyarmala, 6 km (4 miles) away, while the Glass Temple of Koottamunda, dedicated to the third Jain *tirthankara*, Parsvanatha, is on the slope of Vallarimal Hill, 20 km (12 miles) to the south. The area's tallest peak, Chembara Peak

Coffee blossoms in a Wynad plantation

(2,100 m/6,890 ft) is 14 km (9 miles) southwest of Kalpetta, and is excellent for trekking and birdwatching.

Sulthan's Bathery (Sultan's Battery), 10 km (6 miles) east of Kalpetta, derives its name from Tipu Sultan of Mysore *(see p517)*, who built a fort here in the 18th century. The **Edakkal Caves** are 12 km (7 miles) away. Their inscriptions and carvings of human and animal figures are said to date to prehistoric times; some believe that these caves were the refuge of Jain monks. The caves' environs abound in megaliths. The **Wynad (Muthanga) Wildlife Sanctuary**, 16 km (10 miles) east of Sulthan's Battery, was established in 1973 and is part of the Nilgiri Biosphere Reserve *(see p520)*.

Mananthavady, 35 km (22 miles) north of Kalpetta, was the scene of a long guerrilla war between the local king, Pazhassi Raja, and British troops, led by Lord Arthur Wellesley, the future Duke of Wellington who defeated Napoleon at Waterloo. About 32 km (20 miles) to the north is the Vishnu Temple at Thirunelli, built beside the Paapanassini river. This is a major pilgrimage site, where Hindus perform funeral rites.

🪔 **Edakkal Caves**
⭘ *daily.* 📷 📹

🦌 **Wynad Sanctuary**
📹 📷 *extra charges. Permits from Wildlife Warden, Sulthan Bathery, (04936) 22 0454.*

The remains of Tipu's fort, Sulthan's Battery

Mahe ②

Union Territory of Pondicherry. Mahe district. 48 km (30 miles) N of Kozhikode. 🚌 📧 ℹ Govt Tourist Home, (0495) 270 2304. 📷 St Theresa's Feast (Oct).

Situated on the Mayyazhi river, this former French enclave is named after the French admiral, Mahe de La Bourdonnais, who landed here in November 1741. A French colony until 1954, it is today part of the Union Territory of Pondicherry *(see p586)*. Only some traces of Mahe's colonial heritage remain, among them the beautiful old residence of the French administrator, at the mouth of the river. It is now the office-cum-residence of the Indian government's administrator. Mahe's main church, the whitewashed, Baroque St Theresa's Church, is situated on the highway. The town's main "industry" seems to centre around the supply of cheap alcohol, attracting truck drivers and motorists who come here from nearby areas to stock up.

Thalaserry ②

Kannur district. 255 km (158 miles) N of Kochi. 🚌 📧

Fishing is a major occupation in Thalaserry (once known as Tellicherry), and observing the bartering of the day's catch can be an enjoyable experience. The British East India Company established

Fishmongers awaiting the daily catch at Thalaserry

one of their first trading posts at Thalaserry at the end of the 17th century. In 1708, they built the enormous laterite fort on the coast. An old lighthouse still stands on its ramparts, and there are also two secret tunnels, one of which leads into the sea.

The Thalaserry Cricket Club, founded in 1860, is one of the oldest in India, as cricket was introduced here in the late 18th century.

This region is one of the main centres of *kalaripayattu (see p626)*, a fact that has made it a training ground for circus artistes as well. It is a common sight to see young men in the *kalari* (gymnasium), exercising to tone their muscles and practising with wooden weapons. Many images of deities adorn the *kalari*, giving it a sacred character.

Façade of the fort, Thalassery

Kannur ②

Kannur district. 66 km (41 miles) N of Kochi. 🚉 📧 ℹ District Tourism Promotion Council, Taluk Office Campus, (0497) 270 6336. 📷 daily.

This scenic coastal town, called Cannanore by European settlers, was an important maritime centre in the 14th and 15th centuries. The Portuguese built **St Angelo Fort**, 5 km (3 miles) south of the city, in 1505. This enormous laterite structure overlooks the fishing harbour and is protected by the sea on three sides. It was later occupied by the British, who established a large military garrison here.

Muzhapilangad Beach, 15 km (9 miles) south of Kannur, is a serene spot with a 4-km (2.5-mile) long sandy beach, safe for swimmers.

THEYYAM, KERALA'S SPECTACULAR DANCE-RITUAL

This dance-ritual, particular to the north Malabar region, was originally aimed at appeasing ancient village deities, the mother goddess, folk heroes, ancestors and spirits. With the advent of Brahminism, Hindu divinities replaced many of the earlier ones, and the Theyyam pantheon shrank from 300 to around 40. The Theyyam presentation begins with the singing of the *thottam* (song) in praise of the deity relevant to that particular ritual. This is followed by the dance, the steps and postures of which show the strong influence of Kerala's martial arts tradition, *kalaripayattu*. Drums, pipes and cymbals provide the accompaniment. The performers, all male, wear masks, body paint, colourful costumes and imposing headgear *(mudi)*, which often rises to a staggering height of more than 2 m (7 ft). The tender leaves of the coconut palm are cut to various designs and shapes to form part of the elaborate costume of the dancer. Theyyams, usually annual rituals, are held between December and May. However, at the Parassinikadavu Temple, 20 km (12 miles) north of Kannur, Theyyam is performed every day.

A Theyyam dancer clad in a colourful costume

The laterite ramparts of Bekal Fort, outside Kasaragod town

Kasaragod District ㉕

400 km (249 miles) S from Kochi to Kasaragod. 🚌 🚐 🛈 *Tourism Promotion Council (04994) 25 6450.*

Kerala's northernmost district, flanked by the Western Ghats to the east and the Arabian Sea to the west, is a fertile region of thickly forested hills and meandering rivers. The district is named after its main town, Kasaragod, a bustling centre of the coir and handloom industries. About 8 km (5 miles) north of Kasaragod, is the **Madhur Temple**. This beautiful temple, with its copper-plate roofing, has a commanding location overlooking the Madhuvahini river.

Situated 16 km (10 miles) south of Kasaragod is **Bekal Fort**, the largest and best-preserved fort in Kerala. This enormous, circular structure is built with large blocks of laterite, and its outer wall rises majestically from the sea to a height of 39 m (128 feet). Inside is a cunningly concealed tunnel that leads directly to the sea. The fort's origins are shrouded in mystery, though it is generally thought to have been built in the mid-1600s by a local chieftain Shivappa Nayak, whose fiefdom was in neighbouring Karnataka. The scene of much conflict, the

fort was eventually occupied by the British after the defeat of Tipu Sultan *(see p517)*.

Many beautiful beaches lie to the north and south of the fort. The closest, **Pallikere Beach**, provides a spectacular view of the fort. The Kerala government, along with the Bekal Resorts Development Corporation, have plans to develop this area as a major tourist complex. About 6 km (4 miles) north of Bekal, **Kappil Beach** is a secluded area, ideal for swimming. Kodi Cliff, at one end of the beach, is a scenic spot with wonderful views of the sunset on the Arabian Sea.

The **Chandragiri Fort**, on the banks of the Chandragiri river, is 10 km (6 miles) north of Bekal. This 17th-century fort is also attributed to Shivappa Nayak, who built it to defend his kingdom against the Vijayanagar rulers *(see pp530–31)*. The imposing Malik Dinar Mosque, nearby, is said to have been

A typical temple lamp

founded by Malik Ibn Dinar, a disciple of the Prophet Muhammad, who introduced Islam to Kerala in about AD 664. The grave of Malik Ibn Muhammed, a descendant of Malik Ibn Dinar, lies here. The 9th-century **Ananthapura Temple**, 30 km (19 miles) north of Bekal, is the only temple in Kerala erected in the centre of a lake. It is said to be the original abode of Ananthapadmanabha, the presiding deity of the Anantha Padmanabhaswamy Temple in Thiruvananthapuram, the state capital *(see p627)*.

The small hill station of **Ranipuram** is situated 85 km (53 miles) east of Kasaragod. Set amid acres of rubber and spice plantations, it offers good opportunities for trekking.

This region is also the centre for a number of performing arts, such as Theyyam *(see p655)* and Yakshagana, the elaborate folk art form from Karnataka *(see p535)*.

Ananthapura Temple, built in the middle of a lake

For hotels and restaurants in this region see pp714–17 and pp742–3

Kathakali: Kerala's Classical Dance-Drama

Literally meaning "story-play", Kathakali is a highly evolved classical form of dance, drama and music (both vocal and instrumental), that is almost 400 years old. Male actor-dancers, in voluminous colourful skirts, elaborate headdresses and jewellery, enact stories from the Puranas and epics, mainly the *Mahabharata (see p26)*. The story unfolds simply at first, before building to a dramatic climax. The frenetic drumming, the emotive singing and the rhythmic movements of the dancers reach a crescendo, as the many scenes of love and valour culminate in the triumph of good over evil. These are traditionally all-night performances, held in temple courtyards during religious festivals. Modern performances are shorter.

A noble *paccha* character

Make-up, *a complex four-hour process, helps identify characters and define their roles. Mineral pigments and lamp black are the main ingredients. A paper frill defines the jaw line.*

Facial movements *are used to convey emotions, and to conduct dialogues.*

***Tadi* characters wear red, white or black beards.**

Mythical bird

Bejewelled crowns are worn by *kathi* characters.

Paccha character

Fingernails are long and painted silver.

The female character (minukku)

Voluminous skirts

KATHAKALI CHARACTERS

Costumes and facial make-up use symbolic colours. Green (*paccha*) signifies divine and heroic characters, such as Krishna and Arjuna, while royal though arrogant personalities, such as Ravana, are distinguished by the red (*kathi*) patch applied over the bridge of the nose on a green background. Black (*kari*) is used for demons.

Actor-dancers, *all male, do not speak but instead use symbolic mudras (hand gestures) and facial expressions, with immense eloquence.*

Percussion *is provided by two drums, chenda and madalam. The lead singer marks the beat with a chengila (gong), and his assistant plays the cymbals.*

ANDHRA PRADESH

From the unspoilt beaches of Visakhapatnam along the Coromandel Coast, to the emerald green paddy fields of Nellore district, much of Andhra Pradesh is occupied by the rocky Deccan Plateau which rises 1,000 m (3,281 ft) above the fertile coastal plains. This is South India's largest state, covering an area of 275,000 sq km (106,178 sq miles). The main language spoken by its 78 million people is Telugu, though Urdu is also spoken in the state capital, Hyderabad. This vibrant city was until 1947, the seat of the fabulously wealthy royal family, the Asaf Jahi Nizams. Andhra Pradesh's varied cultural heritage is visible in its monuments. These include the ancient Buddhist site at Nagarjunakonda, the great Islamic fort of Golconda and the hilltop Hindu temple at Tirupati, which attracts more pilgrims than any other temple in India. The state's distinctive handicrafts include superb woven ikat textiles, pearl jewellery and inlaid metal *bidri* work.

SIGHTS AT A GLANCE

Towns, Cities & Districts
East Godavari District ⑩
Hyderabad ①
Kondapalli ⑬
Machilipatnam ⑪
Pochampalli ③
Srikakulam District ⑨
Vijayawada ⑫
Visakhapatnam ⑥
Warangal ④

Historic Sites
Amravati ⑭
Chandragiri ⑲
Golconda ②
Nagarjunakonda ⑮
Penukonda ㉒
Ramatirtham ⑧

Temples & Holy Places
Alampur ⑰
Lepakshi ㉓
Palampet ⑤
Puttaparthi ㉑
Sri Kalahasti ⑳
Srisailam & Krishna Gorge ⑯
Tirupati ⑱

Areas of Natural Beauty
Borra Caves ⑦

KEY

- ✈ International airport
- ☒ Domestic airport
- ═ National highway
- ═ Major road
- ═ Minor road
- ─ Major railway

◁ **Sunflowers, grown for their oil, in a field near Alampur in western Andhra Pradesh**

Hyderabad ❶

Enamel tiles, Badshahi Ashurkhana

The sixth largest city in India, Hyderabad was founded in 1591 and planned as a grid with the Charminar *(see pp662–3)* at its centre. It has now grown well beyond the confines of the original walled city, to include a new town north of the Musi river, the military cantonment at Secunderabad, and a burgeoning high-tech estate, nicknamed "Cyberabad". The city's sights include the grand palaces of its erstwhile rulers, the Nizams, and the colourful bazaars and mosques of the old city.

Portraits of Salarjung III and his son, painted on ivory

The Neo-Classical façade of the 19th-century Purani Haveli

🏛 Purani Haveli (Nizam's Museum)

Near Mir Alam Mandi Rd. *Tel* (040) 2452 1029. ◯ Sat–Thu. 📷

This sprawling complex of mid-19th-century Neo-Classical buildings was the main residence of the sixth Nizam, Mahbub Ali Pasha. A glimpse of his lavish lifestyle can be seen in the eastern wing of the main building, in the Massarat Mahal. This has the Nizam's gigantic wooden wardrobe, a 73-sq m (786-sq ft) room with closets on two levels, and a mechanical elevator affording access to the upper tier. Its contents once included 75 identical tweed suits – the Nizam liked the pattern so much that he bought the Scottish factory's entire stock of it.

Purani Haveli also houses the Nizam's Museum, which displays china, silver objets d'art, and several fascinating photographs that capture the legendary opulence of the Nizam and his court.

🏛 Salarjung Museum

Near Naya Pul. *Tel* (040) 2452 3211. ◯ Sat–Thu. ● public hols. 📷 📹

This eclectic collection of over 40,000 objects once belonged to Salarjung III, Prime Minister of Hyderabad between 1899 and 1949. Salarjung's highly individual taste ranged from objects of sublime beauty to some bordering on kitsch, which is what makes this museum so fascinating.

The pride of the museum is the outstanding Mughal jade collection, which includes an exquisite, translucent leaf-shaped cup. Miniature paintings are also well-represented, including those of the local Deccani School *(see p543)*, as are Indian stone and bronze sculpture, inlaid ivory objects and medieval Islamic manuscripts. A prized 13th-century Koran

has the signatures of three Mughal emperors.

Salarjung's rather florid taste in European art is represented by some 19th-century statuary, while the collection of oil paintings include a Canaletto, a Guardi and a Landseer.

🏥 Osmania General Hospital

Afzalganj. *Tel* (040) 2460 0121. ◯ daily.

A spectacular stone building with soaring domes, Osmania General Hospital was built in 1925 as part of the seventh Nizam's modernization plan after a catastrophic flood in 1908. Opposite it, across the river, are the **Boys' High School** and the **High Court**, built in pink granite and red sandstone. An imaginative blend of Islamic decorative detail and Western interior layouts, all three buildings, as

THE NIZAMS OF HYDERABAD

Hyderabad was India's biggest and richest princely state, as large as England and Scotland together. Its rulers, known as the Nizams, belonged to the Asaf Jahi dynasty, founded in 1724 by Nizam-ul-Mulk who first came to Hyderabad as the Mughal governor of the Deccan, and then established his independence as Mughal power in Delhi waned. The Nizams' fabulous wealth derived largely from their leg-

Portrait of the last Nizam (r.1911–48)

endary hoard of emeralds and their diamond mines near Golconda, and many tales are told of their extravagance and eccentricities. The seventh and last Nizam, Osman Ali Khan, was the richest man in India but, unlike his ancestors, he was a notorious miser who smoked cigarette butts and wore the same set of shabby, patched clothes for weeks on end. After Independence in 1947, the Nizam resisted joining the Indian Union. However, riots broke out and Indian Army action to restore order finally led to the state's accession.

well as the city's Railway Station, were constructed between 1914 and 1936, and are the work of the British architect Vincent Esch.

⛩ Badshahi Ashurkhana

Patthergatti Rd. ◯ *daily, with permission of the caretaker.*
This historic building, the Ashurkhana or "Royal House of Mourning", was built in 1595 by Muhammad Quli Qutb Shah, the fifth Qutb Shahi ruler *(see p667)*, as a congregation hall for Shias during the month of Muharram. It houses beautiful silver and gold *alams* (cere-monial standards) studded with precious stones, which are carried in procession during Muharram *(see p669)*, and are on display here through the year, on Thursdays.

Exquisite enamel-tiled mosaics adorn the central niche and the western wall, in glowing yellow, orange and turquoise. The outer hall with wooden colonnades was added later.

∩ Charminar
See pp662–3.

☾ Mecca Masjid
See pp662–3.

Splendid 17th-century tiled mosaics in the Badshahi Ashurkhana

VISITORS' CHECKLIST

Ranga Reddy district. 688 km (428 miles) N of Chennai. 🏯 3,449,900. ✈ 16 km (10 miles) N of city centre, then bus or taxi. 🚊 🚌 🛈 AP Tourism, (040) 2329 8456. 🏛 *daily.* 🌙 *Muharram (Mar/Apr), Mrigasira (Jun).*

⛩ Falaknuma Palace

Near Naya Pul. ◯ *Closed for renovation, check for opening dates.*
The most opulent of the Nizams' many palaces, Falaknuma Palace was built in 1872. The front façade is in Palladian style, while the rear is a jumble of Indo-Saracenic domes and cupolas, added on to house the zenana. A huge amount of money was lavished on the interior, with tooled leather ceilings created by Florentine craftsmen, furniture and tapes-tries ordered from France, and marble imported from Italy.

The Nizams' most important guests, including King George V, stayed at Falaknuma, but after the death of the sixth Nizam here in 1911 (after a heavy bout of drinking), it was rarely used again. The palace is now being converted into a luxurious hotel.

HYDERABAD CITY CENTRE

Badshahi Ashurkhana ④
Charminar ⑤
Mecca Masjid ⑥
Osmania General Hospital ③
Purani Haveli (Nizam's Museum) ①
Salarjung Museum ②

Hussain Sagar, State Archaeological Museum

Railway Station 1.5 km (1 mile)
Airport 10km (6 miles)

The Residency, SECUNDERABAD

GOSHAMAHAL

Imlibun Bus Station

NH-9

Birla Archaeological Museum

Osmania Hospital ③

Golconda Fort

AFZALGANJ ROAD

River Musi

Naya Pul

Salarjung Museum ②

High Court

RAZEN ROAD

BANGALORE

Badshahi Ashurkhana ④

Purani Haveli (Nizam's Museum) ①

0 metres 500
0 yards 500

PATTHERGATTI

LAD BAZAAR ROAD

Charminar ⑤

Mecca Masjid ⑥

Falaknuma Palace

KEY

▬▬ Street-by-Street *see pp662–3*

Key to Symbols *see back flap*

Hyderabad Street-by-Street: Charminar

Detail from arch, Charminar

In the heart of the Old City, Charminar ("Four Towers") is Hyderabad's signature landmark. It was built in 1591 by King Muhammad Quli Qutb Shah of the Qutb Shahi dynasty *(see p666)* and, according to legend, marks the spot where he first saw his lover, the beautiful Hindu dancer Bhagmati. Another story says he built it as thanksgiving at the end of a deadly plague epidemic. Today, Charminar is the hub of a busy commercial area, where the grand mosques and palaces of the erstwhile rulers are surrounded by lively bazaars selling everything from pearls and perfumes to cabbages and computers.

Caps on sale on the pavement outside Mecca Masjid

Chowmahalla Palace

SHAH ALI DANDA ROAD

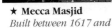

★ Mecca Masjid
Built between 1617 and 1694, this huge mosque has bricks from Mecca embedded in its central arch. Several Nizams are buried here.

Unani Hospital was built by the last Nizam in the 1920s for the practice of traditional Graeco-Arab medicine.

| 0 metres | 50 |
| 0 yards | 50 |

KEY

– – – Suggested route

Silver-leaf is beaten into wafer-thin sheets in the shops in this street, and used to decorate sweets.

SARDAR MAHAL ROAD

★ Charminar
Grand arches frame Charminar's four sides. On the top floor is the city's oldest mosque. The minarets soar to 54 m (177 ft).

STAR SIGHTS

★ Mecca Masjid

★ Charminar

★ Lad Bazaar

For hotels and restaurants in this region see p717 and p743

★ Lad Bazaar
Bangles, tinsel, embroidery, brocade turbans for bridegrooms, henna, herbal potions, and everything else needed for a bride's trousseau, are sold in this colourful bazaar.

Attar Shop
Perfume oils, sold in tiny bottles, include a local speciality called gil, which captures the scent of wet earth after the first rainfall of a scorching summer.

Charminar Kamaan served as the entrance to the royal mosque inside Charminar. Nearby are shops selling pearls.

Sher-e-dil Kamaan leads to shops selling gorgeous brocades and antique silk saris.

Machhli Kamaan
This is one of four ceremonial arches, built in 1594, around an open area where parades were held. It is carved with the auspicious fish symbol denoting prosperity.

GULZAR HAUZ ROAD

MITTI KA SHER ROAD

PANJERSHAH ROAD

PATTHERGATTI ROAD

Naya Pul

Jami Masjid
This simple whitewashed mosque, built in 1597, is the second oldest in Hyderabad.

Exploring Hyderabad & Secunderabad

By the 19th century, Hyderabad had begun to expand beyond the crowded confines of the old quarter, clustered on both banks of the Musi river. New palaces, and the British military cantonment of Secunderabad, were now built on the city's outskirts.

🏛 Birla Archaeological Museum

Opposite Ravindra Bharathi, Saifabad.
Tel (040) 2323 4336. ⬜ Mon–Sat.
🌑 public hols. 🚫

Located in the 19th-century hunting lodge of the sixth Nizam, Asmangarh Palace is the Birla Archaeological Museum. Its exhibits include sculptures and metal artifacts found at excavation sites in Andhra Pradesh, among them some beautiful bronzes of Shiva and Vishnu.

A short distance to the south is an obelisk which marks the Tomb of Michel Raymond. A French mercenary who fought in the Nizam's army from 1785 till his death in 1798, Raymond became a local hero, revered by both Muslims and Hindus.

🏛 The Residency

Koti. ⬜ Mon–Sat.

This elegant Palladian mansion, now the University College for Women, was built in 1805 by the third Nizam as a gift for the British Resident at his court, James Kirkpatrick. It was decorated in style, with a painted ceiling, and mirrors and chandeliers from Brighton Pavilion in England. The pediment above the portico still bears the East India Company's lion-and-unicorn coat of arms.

In the grounds is a small replica of the main building, which Kirkpatrick built for his aristocratic Hyderabadi wife, Khairunissa Begum – a liaison that created a great scandal at the time. There is a small British cemetery in a corner of the grounds.

🏛 State Archaeological Museum

Assembly Rd, N of Railway Station.
Tel (040) 2323 2267. ⬜ Sat–Thu.
🌑 Fri & public hols. 📷

Two large Norman-style gateways mark the entrance to the Nampally Public Gardens, which contain the State Archaeological Museum. It has a large collection of Buddhist art, some fine Chola bronzes, Roman coins, and even an Egyptian mummy. There are also replicas of murals and sculptures from the Ajanta and Ellora caves (see pp476–81). Nearby is the **State Legislative Assembly** (built in 1913), a domed complex modelled on a Rajasthani palace.

Hussain Sagar, with a gigantic statue of the Buddha

🪷 Hussain Sagar

This huge lake, created in the 17th century, lies off Mahatma Gandhi Road, which bisects Hyderabad and Secunderabad. The 3-km (2-mile) stretch of road along its southern boundary is Hyderabad's most popular promenade; it is lined with statues of eminent figures from Andhra Pradesh's history. At the centre of the lake is a rock, on which stands a 17-m (56-ft) high monolithic statue of the Buddha, weighing 350 tonnes. Completed in 1986, it sank to the bottom of the lake when the ferry carrying it capsized. It was finally salvaged (intact) seven years later and installed on the rock in 1994.

🏚 Secunderabad

Northeast of Hussain Sagar along the Tank Bund Road, Secunderabad was established in 1806 as a cantonment to house British troops. It has since grown into a teeming city which is an extension of Hyderabad. At its centre is the **Parade Ground**, overlooked by **St Andrew's Church** and the imposing colonial-style **Secunderabad Club**. The Neo-Gothic **Holy Trinity Church** (built in 1848) is 6 km (4 miles) north of the Parade Ground, and has beautiful stained-glass windows, elegant steeples on its square tower and a British cemetery.

The walled compound of the **Paigah Palaces**, where the Hyderabadi aristocracy lived, is 2 km (1.3 miles) west of the Parade Ground, opposite Begumpet Airport. The most imposing palace is Vicar Manzil, built by the leading nobleman at the sixth Nizam's court, Sir Vicar-ul-Umra; he had built the magnificent Falaknuma Palace (see p661) for himself but had to move out when the Nizam decided to acquire it. At its entrance is the **Spanish Mosque** (built in 1906), with Moorish arches and octagonal spires.

The Spanish Mosque at the entrance of Vicar Manzil, Secunderabad

Hyderabadi Culture

Sultan Muhammad Quli Qutb Shah, who founded Hyderabad in 1591, was an enlightened ruler, and a poet, scholar and patron of the arts. His kingdom was also a flourishing centre of trade, especially in pearls, diamonds and horses. At his court and in his bazaars, Hyderabadis rubbed shoulders with traders, scholars and artisans from different lands. This cosmopolitan

Golden lunch box

tradition, and the culture of courtly elegance and etiquette, continued with the next dynasty – that of the Asaf Jahi Nizams, which ruled from 1724 until 1947. As a result, Hyderabad has a uniquely composite culture, a mélange of Hindu and Muslim customs, mingled with Arab, Persian and Turkish influences, evident in its language, food, manners and arts.

Bidriware *uses a technique introduced by Persians in the 16th century, by which black gunmetal is intricately inlaid with silver in floral and geometric patterns.*

Hyderabad's distinctive cuisine *includes dishes of Persian and Turkish origin such as* haleem *(minced meat cooked with wheat) and* lukmi *(puff pastry squares filled with meat).*

Falaknuma Palace, *photographed towards the end of the 19th century by the court photographer Lala Deen Dayal, captures the opulence of the Nizam of Hyderabad's lifestyle.*

The Nizams' jewels *were legendary, and included fabulous pieces such as this 19th-century turban ornament, set with rubies from Burma and diamonds from their mines at Golconda (see p666).*

Muharram (see p669) *is observed by processions of Shia Muslims carrying decorated* tazias *through the city. Hyderabad's Shia population is mostly descended from Persians who settled here several generations ago.*

Golconda miniatures *often depict the city's sophisticated, cosmopolitan culture. This 18th-century painting shows merchants from many lands calling on a lady.*

Golconda ❷

Detail of a carving, Bala Hisar gate wall

Sprawling across a boulder-strewn plateau, Golconda ("Shepherd's Hill") Fort was the citadel of the Qutb Shahi dynasty, which ruled the Hyderabad region from 1507 to 1687. The earlier 12th-century mud fort that stood here was transformed between 1518 and 1580 into a splendid fortified city of grand palaces, mosques and gardens by successive Qutb Shahi rulers. Golconda Fort was also famous for its great hoard of diamonds, mined nearby, which included the celebrated Kohinoor diamond, now part of the British Crown jewels. The colossal ruins of Golconda cover an area of 40 sq km (15 sq miles).

Bala Hisar Gate, entrance to the royal complex at Golconda Fort

🏰 Golconda Fort

This great fortress is protected by three formidable lines of defence. The first, an outer fortification made of enormous blocks of granite, encircles the citadel and its entire township. The middle wall surrounds the base of the hill, while the innermost one follows the contours of the highest ridge. Visitors enter through the **Fateh Darwaza** ("Victory Gate"), on the east side, which has a Hindu deity carved above its arch. Huge iron spikes are studded into the gate to prevent it from being stormed by elephant cavalries.

From the Fateh Darwaza, the road curves past the **Archaeological Museum** (the old Treasury), and through the bazaar, once a famous centre for cutting and polishing diamonds. Beyond are the two massive arches of the **Habshi Kaman Gate**, with rooms on top. These used to house a drummers' gallery and the sultans' Abyssinian guards. This gate leads to the middle fortification wall.

To its north is the austere, domed **Jami Masjid**, built in 1518 by Sultan Quli Qutb Shah, the founder of the dynasty; he was murdered here while at prayer by his son Jamshed in 1543. Beyond is the ceremonial arch, the **Bala Hisar Gate**, decorated with various Hindu motifs, including *yalis* (fantastic leonine beasts). This is the entrance to the inner citadel, known as the **Bala Hisar Complex**, where the royal palaces, assembly halls, workshops and an armoury are located. North of the Bala Hisar is a walled enclosure, begun in 1652, and planned as an extension to the inner fort. Within it is **Hathion ka Jhaad** ("Elephant Tree"), an extraordinary 700-year-old Baobab tree

PLAN OF GOLCONDA FORT

Qutb Sbabi Tombs

Sikkalam Cheruvu

- Premamati's Mosque
- Banjara Gate
- Naya Qila
- Taramati's Pavilion
- Hathion ka Jhaad
- Bala Hisar Gate
- Mahakali Temple
- Jami Masjid
- Durbar Hall
- Habshi Kaman Gate
- Rani Mahal
- Langarhouse Cheruvu
- Mecca Gate
- Archaeological Museum
- Fateh Darwaza

Nau Mabal

0 metres   200
0 yards   200

The royal bath near Rani Mahal, Golconda Fort

(*Adansonia digitata*), said to have been brought to Golconda by the sultans' Abyssinian guards.

The large-domed **Grand Portico** behind the Bala Hisar Gate is a good place to test the remarkable acoustics that were an important feature of the fort's defences. A soft handclap here can be heard in the king's chambers at the summit of the hill.

West of the Grand Portico are the ruins of the Qutb Shahi palaces. The most impressive of these is the **Rani Mahal**, a vaulted hall on a raised terrace, decorated with lovely floral arabesques. Hollows in these carvings were once inlaid with Golconda's famous diamonds and other precious stones. To the west of the Rani Mahal, a steep flight of 200 steps winds past royal baths, granaries, treasuries, water tanks and the remains of gardens, to the summit of the hill. Traces of the elaborate water supply system which carried water to the top of the citadel are visible along the route.

Just below the summit is a graceful mosque built by Sultan Ibrahim Qutb Shah, the third sultan, and the ancient Hindu **Mahakali Temple**, built into a cave.

At the summit of the hill is the three-storeyed **Durbar Hall** ("Throne Room"), with a rooftop pavilion. From here there are wonderful views of the entire fort and its surroundings, which include two pretty structures on hillocks – **Taramati Baradari** and **Premamati's Mosque**. These

are named after the two dancers who were royal favourites, and said to be so lightfooted that they could dance all the way from the pavilion to the Bala Hisar on a tightrope.

Standing outside the fort, east of the Fateh Darwaza, is the **Nau Mahal** ("Nine Palaces"), where the Nizams of Hyderabad held court whenever they came to Golconda.

Qutb Shahi Tombs

1 km (0.6 miles) NW of Golconda Fort. This royal necropolis, where seven of the nine Qutb Shahi rulers are buried, is laid out in gardens with water channels, pools and tree-lined pathways. The tombs, built by each king in his lifetime, display a distinct and eclectic architectural style – they have large onion domes, Persian arches, Turkish columns and Hindu brackets and motifs.

Built of grey granite and plaster, each tomb's dome is set on a petalled base, with a richly ornamented gallery and small minarets surrounding it. The **Tomb of Muhammad Quli Qutb Shah**, the founder of the city of Hyderabad, is the most impressive. It is surrounded by a spacious terrace, where poetry and music festivals and Hyderabadi food festivals are occasionally held. Traces of brilliant turquoise and green enamelled tiles, which once

Ceiling decoration, Bala Hisar Gate

VISITORS' CHECKLIST

Hyderabad district. 9 km (6 miles) W of Hyderabad. ⊟ ☐ *daily.* ☑ ☒ **Son et Lumière** *(English) Mar–Oct: 7pm daily; Nov–Feb: 6:30pm daily.* ☒

Archaeological Museum and **Qutb Shahi Tombs** ☐ *Sat–Thu.* ☒

The elegant tomb of Muhammad Quli Qutb Shah, Golconda

covered the façades of all the tombs, still remain. Other remarkable monuments are the **Tomb of Queen Hayat Baksh Begum**, the wife of Mohammed Quli Qutb Shah, and the mosque behind it (both mid-17th century), decorated with exquisite floral designs and calligraphy.

At the centre of the complex is the simple but beautifully proportioned **Royal Mortuary Bath**. The bodies of the deceased kings were ritually bathed before burial on the inlaid, 12-sided platform; the surrounding 12 water tanks symbolize the 12 Shia Imams.

A panoramic view of Golconda Fort

Pochampalli ❸

Nalgonda district. 50 km (31 miles)
E of Hyderabad. 🚌 🚆 *daily.*

Andhra Pradesh's ikat belt,
where intricate tie-and-dye
textiles *(see p317)* are woven,
borders Hyderabad.
Pochampalli, the name by
which most of the state's ikat
fabric is known, is the largest
centre for this craft. The technique in its present form was
first introduced in the 19th
century in Chirala, in Guntur
district, from where the fabric
was exported to Africa.

Pochampalli's main street is
lined with busy workshops
where the various stages of
production take place. Ikat
weavers first tie the yarn
according to the pattern and
then dye them in great vats. A
special oil-based technique is
used to restrict the dye to
those parts of the yarn that
need to be coloured. The
dyed yarn is then dried in the
sun and finally woven on
large hand-operated looms, to
produce a cloth called *telia
rumal (see p413).* The state
cooperative warehouses, as
well as several shops, sell a
wide range of beautiful silk
saris and fabrics.

Environs
The neighbouring villages of
and **Choutuppal** produce
mainly cotton ikat fabrics.
Narayanpur, another major
weaving centre, is about 20
km (16 miles) further down
the Vijaywada Highway.

**Khush Mahal, the audience hall
at Warangal Fort**

Warangal ❹

Warangal district. 140 km (87 miles)
SW of Hyderabad. 🚉 🚌 ℹ️ *APTDC,
Kazipet, (0870) 244 6606.*

A major *dhurrie*-weaving
centre today, Warangal was
described by the 13th-century
Venetian traveller, Marco Polo,
as one of the principal cities of
South India. It was the capital
of the Hindu Kakatiya kings,
who dominated this region
until the beginning of the
14th century.

An ancient fort at the edge
of the modern town is all that
remains of this once grand
city. Built during the reign of
the Kakatiya queen Rudrama-
devi (r.1262–89), its striking
circular plan, with three concentric rings of walls, is still
intact. The outer two rings,
both of mud, define a circle
1.2 km (1 mile) in diameter.
The innermost ring is made

of stone, with four massive
gateways at the cardinal
points. At its geometric
centre, four ornate *toranas*
(gateways), marking the sacred
precinct, are the only remains
of a great Shiva temple that
once stood here. The *toranas*
themselves are remarkable for
their size and beauty.

A short distance to the west
is the **Khush Mahal**, an
audience hall that was built by
Muslim invaders in the 14th
century. Massive angled walls
with slit windows define a
lofty interior with vaulted
arches, though the roof is quite
damaged. It is remarkably
similar to the Hindola Mahal in
Mandu *(see p247).*

Environs
Hanamkonda, the site of the
first Kakatiya capital before it
moved to Warangal, is 3 km (2
miles) northwest of Warangal.
A magnificent thousand-
pillared temple here, dedicated
to Shiva, was erected in 1163
by Rudradeva (r.1158–95), the
first great Kakatiya king.

This grey-green basalt
temple, known as the *trikuta*
or triple shrine, consists of a
trio of shrines dedicated to
Shiva, Vishnu and Surya. They
are connected to a *mandapa*,
now roofless, by a platform
with a magnificently polished
Nandi bull. The columns have
sharply cut, lathe-turned shafts.
A ceiling panel carved with an
image of Nataraja *(see p566)*
covers the central bay. The
temple's gardens contain
several small linga shrines, and
an ancient well.

The magnificent thousand-pillared temple at Hanamkonda, near Warangal

The 13th-century Ramappa Temple at Palampet

Palampet ❺

Palampet district. 70 km (44 miles) SW of Hyderabad.

This village is dominated by the **Ramappa Temple**, the best preserved example of Kakatiya architecture. Dedicated to Shiva, it was built in 1234 by Recherla Rudra, a general of the ruler Ganapatideva (r.1199–1262). Like the temple at Hanamkonda, it too has a spacious *mandapa* with beautifully sculpted black basalt columns. This *mandapa*, cruciform in plan, also has porches with balcony seats on three sides. The eaves sheltering the peripheral

Carving, Ghanpur

columns are supported by angled struts, many of which are fashioned as three-dimensional maidens with graceful bodies in dancing poses. Other similar but smaller relief figures, as well as scenes from the epics, are seen in the central ceiling panel within the *mandapa*.

The exterior of the sanctuary, in contrast, is devoid of any carvings. The restrained ornamentation and simple modelling are typical of the elegance of Kakatiya art. A stone pavilion sheltering a Nandi, smaller in size than the one at Hanamkonda, but as exquisitely carved, stands in front of the temple.

South of the Ramappa Temple is **Ramappa Cheruvu**, a vast artificial lake created by Recherla Rudra, and surrounded by picturesque hills.

Environs
More Kakatiya temples can be seen at **Ghanpur**, a little village 13 km (8 miles) northwest of Palampet. The largest consists of a pair of Shiva shrines, both with *mandapas* and balcony seats. The main shrine has delightful female *dvarapalas* (doorkeepers), dancing maidens and finely carved brackets. Other minor shrines dot the walled compound.

FESTIVALS OF ANDHRA PRADESH

Ugadi *(Mar)*. Homes are spring-cleaned throughout the state and special food is prepared to celebrate the Telugu New Year.

Mrigasira *(Jun)*, Hyderabad. On this day a unique cure for asthma is administered to patients from all over India, who swallow live a small, freshwater fish called *maral*. Many sufferers claim miraculous cures.

Batkamma Festival, Warangal

Batkamma *(Sep/Oct)*, Warangal. This festival in honour of the goddess of wealth, Lakshmi, begins just before Dussehra and continues for nine days. Flowers are arranged over a turmeric representation of the goddess and carried on a bamboo tray to a lake or river, where the women dance in a circle around the floral offering before immersing it in the water.

Festival of Andhra Pradesh *(Nov)*, Hyderabad. This ten-day cultural festival marks the anniversary of Andhra Pradesh's statehood. The state's best musicians and dancers perform.

Muharram *(Feb/Mar)*, Hyderabad. The Shia Muslim community commemorates the martyrdom of the Prophet's grandson, Hussain, at the battle of Karbala, with 40 days of mourning. On the final day, gem-studded *alams* and colourful *tazias* (replicas of his tomb) are carried in procession through the Old City.

TRADITIONAL ANDHRA DHURRIES

Although lustrous silk and wool carpets from Persia and Turkey embellished the palaces of the Nizams of Hyderabad, Andhra Pradesh has long had a local tradition of carpet weaving in Warangal and Eluru. Commonly known as *dhurries*, the rugs are made in both cotton and wool, in a variety of designs and colours. The cotton *dhurries* from Warangal are usually woven into geometric patterns, while the woollen carpets of Eluru (314 km/195 miles southeast of Warangal) sport floral designs that hint at a Western

A *dhurrie* with geometric patterns

influence. The more expensive *shatranjis* (a chessboard-like pattern) are made with heavy cotton thread and produced on horizontal looms. The *kalamkari* craftsmen of Sri Kalahasti *(see p680)* make rugs in traditional designs on a jute base, using vegetable dyes.

A view of the Visakhapatnam harbour on the Bay of Bengal

Visakhapatnam ➏

Visakhapatnam district. 350 km (218 miles) N of Vijayawada. 🏢 969,600. ✈ 12 km (7 miles) W of town centre, then bus or taxi. 🚉 🚌 ℹ️ APTDC, RTC Complex, (0891) 278 8820. 🛍️ daily.

The second busiest port in India after Mumbai, Visakhapatnam, also known as Vizag, is rapidly becoming the largest shipyard in the country. It is an important industrial town and naval base as well. The town makes a convenient point from which to visit some of the beautiful beaches along the Bay of Bengal and the many picturesque temple towns of the northern coastal districts of Andhra Pradesh.

Named after Visakha, the Hindu God of Valour, Visakhapatnam was once part of the Mauryan emperor Ashoka's vast empire *(see p42)*. Later, it was ruled by the Andhra kings of Vengi, and other South Indian dynasties, including the Pallavas, Cholas and Gangas. In the 15th century, it became part of the Vijayanagar Empire *(see pp530–31)*. It finally came into British hands in the 17th century, after which it was developed into a major port.

Looming above the port is a hilly ridge with three crests, each with a religious shrine. On the southernmost one, **Venkateshvara Konda**, is a temple dedicated to Balaji (Krishna); in the middle is **Ross Hill**, with a mid-19th-century church; the third, **Dargah Konda**, has a shrine

dedicated to a Muslim saint, Ishaque Madina.

Along the southern coastline is **Dolphin's Nose**, a 358-m (1,175-ft) long rocky outcrop that rises 175 m (574 ft) above the sea. On it stands a lighthouse with a beam that can be seen 64 km (40 miles) out at sea. Vestiges of the city's colonial past are visible here in an old Protestant church, a fort, barracks and an arsenal, all dating to the 18th century.

Dutch heraldry, Bheemunipatnam

Idyllic beaches, set on the fringes of the Eastern Ghats and bounded by forested hills and rocky cliffs, include the **Ramakrishna Mission Beach**, now being developed as a tourist resort by Andhra Pradesh Tourism, **Rishikonda Beach** and **Lawson's Bay**.

Towards the north of the town, beyond Lawson's Bay, is **Kailasagiri**, a forested hill which has several lookout points for a panoramic view

of the city and harbour. The twin town of **Waltair**, once a health resort for British officers, is north of the bay. Andhra University, one of the largest campuses in the state, is also situated here, along with a number of pretty 19th-century churches.

Environs

Simhachalam, the "Lion's Hill" Temple, dedicated to Lord Varaha Narasimha, an incarnation of Vishnu *(see p679)*, stands at the summit of the thickly forested Ratnagiri Hill, 16 km (10 miles) northwest of Visakhapatnam. A flight of steps leads to the northern gateway, an elaborately decorated *gopura* that is the main entrance to the temple. Inside the compound is a tall *dvajast-hambha* (flagpole). Similar in style to Konark's Sun Temple *(see pp310–11)*, the temple was constructed in the 9th or 10th century, and was extensively re-built during the 13th century. It is believed that the presiding deity was originally Shiva, but he was replaced by this incarnation of Vishnu after the reformer-saint, Ramanuja *(see p522)*, visited the site in the 11th century.

Bheemunipatnam is a 24-km (15-mile) drive north from Visakhapatnam, along one of the longest stretches of beach road in the country. This quiet fishing village, situated at the mouth of the Gosthani river, was a Dutch settlement in the early 17th century.

Obelisk-shaped Dutch tombs at Bheemunipatnam

Bimlipatam, as it was then known (locally referred to as Bhimli), was the site of Maratha attacks and Anglo-Dutch wars throughout the 17th and 18th centuries. Its Dutch legacy can be seen in some of the old colonnaded houses, the ruined fort, and the Dutch cemetery, which has unusual, obelisk-shaped tombstones.

A fascinating stalactite formation inside the Borra Caves

Borra Caves ❼

Visakhapatnam district. 100 km (62 miles) N of Visakhapatnam. 🚌 daily. 📷

Close to the northern border of Visakhapatnam district are these magnificent limestone caves, discovered in 1807 by William King of the the Geological Survey of India. The extensive underground chambers, lined by stalactites and stalagmites, are now being developed by the state tourism department as a major attraction for visitors. Some smaller stalagmites are worshipped as lingas, with Nandi bulls placed in front of them. The local people believe that the water trickling from the roof of the caves is from a mountain spring which is the source of the Gosthani river.

Environs
About 22 km (14 miles) northeast of Borra is the **Araku Valley**, home of several tribal communities, the state's original inhabitants. The road to Araku goes past forests and coffee plantations, and the valley, with its woods, waterfalls and bracing climate, offers pleasant walks.

Tribal women from Araku Valley

Ramatirtham ❽

Visakhapatnam district. 72 km (45 miles) NE of Visakhapatnam. 🚌

Ruins from the Ikshvaku period (3rd to 4th centuries AD), when Buddhism flourished in this area, can be seen at Ramatirtham. Just outside the village is a group of structures on a hill known as Gurubhaktakonda ("Hill of the Devoted Disciple"). On a narrow rocky ledge about 165 m (541 ft) above the surrounding plains are the ruins of a stupa, monasteries, and prayer halls enclosing smaller stupas. Close by, on another hill called Durgakonda, is a similar set of ruins, along with carvings of Jain *tirthankaras* (*see p396*) that date from the 8th and 9th centuries.

Srikakulam District ❾

108 km (67 miles) N from Visakhapatnam to Srikakulam. 🚌

The headquarters of Andhra Pradesh's northernmost district, Srikakulam is located on the banks of the Swarnamukhi river. On the outskirts of the town, at **Arasavalli**, is a sun temple, ingeniously constructed at such an angle that the sun's rays fall directly on the deity's feet twice a year. The **Srikurmanatha Temple** at Srikurman, 13 km (8 miles) east of Srikakulam, is dedicated to Kurma, the tortoise incarnation of Vishnu. It was built by the Chalukya kings in the 10th century but was substantially rebuilt by the Cholas in the 12th and 13th centuries. The colonnade around the main shrine has 19th century murals of Krishna and Vishnu.

Mukhalingam, 46 km (29 miles) north of Srikakulam, was the first capital of the Eastern Ganga kings, before they moved to Orissa (*see p44*). The temples here date to their reign, between the 9th and 13th centuries. The best preserved is the 9th-century Madhukeshvara Temple, with magnificent sculptures of Shiva and friezes of scenes from the Krishna legend. The 10th-century Someshvara Temple, at the entrance to the town, has beautiful statues of river goddesses and other deities, flanking the main doorway.

Mural showing Krishna surrounded by *gopis*, at Srikurmanatha Temple in Srikakulam district

Ripening fields of paddy with the Eastern Ghats in the background, near Rajahmundry

East Godavari District ⑩

380 km (236 miles) E from Hyderabad to Rajahmundry. 🚂 *Rajahmundry.* 🚌

The Godavari, one of South India's most sacred rivers, swells to a wide torrent (at places 6 km/4 miles across), just north of **Rajahmundry** town. Lush paddy fields and sugarcane plantations characterize the countryside.

Rajahmundry, the largest town in East Godavari district, is best known for the many Chalukya temples in its vicinity, and for the 2,743-m (8,999 -ft) long bridge that spans the river. The lookout points on **Dowleshvaram Dam** (built 1848–52), 10 km (6 miles) downstream, offer spectacular views of the river. Every 12 years, the Dakshina Pushkaram festival – the Kumbh Mela (*see p211*) of the South – takes place here.

Peddapuram, famous for its fine handwoven silk and cotton, is 30 km (19 miles) northeast of Rajahmundry, on the road to Visakhapatnam.

Annavaram, 70 km (44 miles) to the northeast of Rajahmundry, is the site of the Satyanarayana Temple, on Ratnagiri Hill, renowned for its 4-m (13 ft)-high statue of the Hindu Trinity, and its ancient sundial.

The **Godavari Gorge** begins 80 km (50 miles) north of Rajahmundry. A drive or boat ride along the Gorge, which cuts through the hilly Eastern Ghats, offers views of spectacular scenery, with a series of beautiful lakes that many visitors have found reminiscent of Italy and Scotland.

Ryali, 24 km (15 miles) south of Rajahmundry, has a Chalukya temple dedicated to Vishnu. It houses a stone image of the Goddess Ganga (*see p163*), from which flows a continuous trickle of water.

Draksharamam, 40 km (25 miles) southeast of Rajahmundry, is famed for its 10th-century Bhimesvara Temple, which combines the Chalukya and Chola styles of architecture, and houses a 5-m (16-ft) high linga. The Godavari is said to have been split into seven streams by the Saptarishis (seven great sages) of Hindu mythology and three of these streams are believed to have gone underground here. Close to the town is an old Dutch cemetery, locally known as Ollandu Dibba ("Holland Mound"), with gravestones dated between 1675 and 1728, some with very elaborate designs.

Antarvedi, on the banks of the Vashishta river, a branch of the Godavari, is 112 km (70 miles) south of Rajahmundry. It is best reached by boat from Narsapur on the south bank. The Lakshminarayana Temple (built in 1823), with its brightly painted tower stands on the river bank, and is usually thronged with pilgrims who come for a dip in the holy river.

Machilipatnam ⑪

Krishna district. 340 km (211 miles) E of Hyderabad. 🚂 🚌 🚢 *daily.*

One of the first European settlements on India's eastern coast, Machilipatnam ("City of Fish") was a thriving port and textile centre in the 17th and 18th centuries. It was also the headquarters of the English East India Company on the Coromandel Coast. The French and the Dutch briefly established themselves here as well. The Dutch cemetery, with its ornate tombstones, are all that remain from that period.

Machilipatnam was hit by a giant tidal wave in 1864, which drowned more than 30,000 people. It was caused by a volcanic eruption at Mount Krakatoa, 5,000 km (3,107 miles) away. After that it lost its importance as a port, but it remains famous for its *kalamkari* textiles (*see p680*).

A *kalamkari* blockprinter at work in Machilipatnam

Trade Textiles: Tree of Life

Between the 17th and 18th centuries, the Coromandel Coast, with Machilipatnam as its trade centre and port, was one of the main producers and exporters of cotton textiles to Western Europe. At first just items of barter, they soon became fashionable in Europe, increasing the demand for the region's dye-painted cotton

Detail of flowers and foliage

kalamkari (see p680) fabric, known in Europe as chintz. Special designs were commissioned, among them the Tree of Life, which absorbed techniques and aesthetics from India, Persia, China and Europe. Valued for their richness of colour and design, they were widely used as hangings and spreads in European homes.

TREE OF LIFE

The Tree of Life was a very popular motif in textiles from the Coromandel Coast. Based on ancient nature myths that deified plants and trees, and inspired largely by Persian miniatures, its central flowering tree, rising from a rocky mound, linked earth to heaven and symbolized creation.

Birds, *real and mythical, inhabit the thickly foliated upper branches of the tree. Standing on the mound are two stylized peacocks holding snakes in their beaks.*

Aquatic creatures, *such as fish and tortoise, are depicted to show marine life in the holy waters below the Sacred Mound. Shades of indigo have been used to create the effect of rippling waves and flowing water.*

A bamboo thicket, *composed as a single Tree of Life, rises from the Sacred Mound. The painted and printed flowers and feathery leaves suggest nature's exuberance.*

A view of the Prakasam Barrage, built over the Krishna river at Vijayawada

Vijayawada ⑫

Krishna district. 267 km (166 miles) SE of Hyderabad. 825,400. APTDC, (0866) 257 1393. daily.

The third largest city in the state, Vijayawada is a busy commercial town with one of the largest railway junctions in the country. In a picturesque spot on the northern bank of the Krishna river, it is bounded on three sides by the Indrakiladri Hills. The area around the river banks is a pleasant contrast to the noisy, crowded town.

Within the city limits, on a low hill to the east, is the **Kanakadurga Temple**, dedicated to the goddess Lakshmi. The **Victoria Jubilee Museum**, on Bunder Road, houses a fine collection of Buddhist and Hindu relics from the 2nd and 3rd centuries. Especially impressive are the white limestone Standing Buddha from the nearby Buddhist site of Alluru (3rd or 4th century), and the powerful depiction of Durga slaying the buffalo demon Mahisa (2nd century).

On the outskirts of town is the 1-km (0.6-mile) long **Prakasam Barrage**, first built in 1855 and extensively reconstructed in 1955. It irrigates nearly 1.2 million ha (3 million acres) of land, turning the Krishna Delta into the richest granary in Andhra Pradesh. **Bhavani Island**, a scenic picnic spot, is just upstream, reached by launch from the river bank.

🏛 **Victoria Jubilee Museum**
Sat–Thu. extra charges.

Environs
Mogalrajapuram, 3 km (2 miles) east of Vijayawada, and **Undavalli**, 4 km (2.5 miles) to the south, on the other side of the river, are famous for their rock-cuttemples (5th–7th centuries).

Mangalgiri, 12 km (7 miles) south of Vijayawada, is a textile village, specializing in fine cotton saris and striped and checked fabrics. It also has the impressive 14th-century Lakshmi Narasimha Temple complex, with a small Garuda shrine in front of it.

Kondapalli ⑬

Krishna district. 14 km (9 miles) W of Vijayawada.

This pretty village, famous for its painted wooden toys, is dominated by the 8th-century Hill Fort built by the Eastern Chalukya dynasty. Encircled by ramparts and towers, the fort was an important stronghold in the Krishna Valley under the Qutb Shahis of Hyderabad (see p666), in the 16th century. At the crest of the hill, a steep climb up, is the ruined Tanisha Mahal palace. The path descends past a deep tank, the granary and the armoury, to the Golconda Gate, which faces northwest towards Hyderabad.

KONDAPALLI TOYS

The craft of toy-making has been passed down for many generations in Kondapalli. In the hands of the deft artisans, the light yet strong and flexible *poniki* wood is fashioned into distinctive figures of gods and goddesses, fruits and vegetables, which adorn many Andhra homes during festivals. Each part of the toy is whittled into shape, and then glued together using a special tamarind-seed glue. The piece is then covered with lime glue, which gives it a smooth finish. It is allowed to dry before being brightly painted in vivid blues, greens, reds and yellows, with touches of black.

Lord Krishna

A toy being painted in bright colours

The Maha Chaitya at Amravati, now only a low earthen mound

Amravati ⑭

Guntur district. 30 km (19 miles) W of Vijayawada. 🚌 from Guntur. 🚌 from Hotel Krishnaveni, Vijayawada. 🚗 run by AP Tourism, Vijayawada. ℹ️ Haritha Hotel, (08645) 255 332.

Renowned for its **Maha Chaitya**, or "Great Stupa", Amravati was once the most impressive of the many Buddhist religious settlements along the Krishna Valley. Today, nothing remains of this stupa except a low earthen mound, but in its day it was reputed to be the largest and most elaborate stupa in South India. It was built by the Satavahanas, the great Andhra dynasty, in the 3rd and 2nd centuries BC (*see p43*).

The Maha Chaitya was enlarged several times by the Ikshvaku kings, who succeeded the Satavahanas, reaching its final form between the 3rd and 4th centuries AD. Clad in the local white limestone, the Maha Chaitya was an earthen hemispherical mound about 45 m (148 ft) in diameter and more than 30 m (98 ft) in height, including its supporting drum and capping finial. It was surrounded by a 6-m (20-ft) high railing with posts and cross pieces, and lofty entrance gateways at the cardinal points, all exuberantly carved.

In the 5th century, when South India saw a revival of Hinduism, the stupa was

Amravati limestone carving with a scene from the Jataka Tales

abandoned, and remained so until a British official, Colonel Colin Mackenzie, began excavating the site in 1796. Unfortunately, by the time a thorough investigation of the ruins began in the mid-19th century, most of the limestone portions had been pillaged, many fine pieces having been shipped to Britain.

Nevertheless, a great deal of fine sculpture remains at the site, and is on display at the **Archaeological Museum**, next to the Maha Chaitya. Unlike the stupa at Sanchi (*see pp244–5*), where the Buddha is represented through symbols such as the Bodhi Tree or footprints, the Amravati sculptures show him in human form. The museum's display includes large Standing Buddha images, some more than 2 m (7 ft) high, whose natural poses and elegantly fluted robes suggest the influence of late Roman classical art. The second gallery has a remarkable life-sized ceremonial bull,

reconstructed from fragments discovered in 1980. A part of the stupa's railing, decorated with scenes from the Buddha's life, is reconstructed in the courtyard. Other exhibits include an instructive model of the original monument and superb sculptures of the Bodhi Tree, under which the Buddha is said to have meditated.

🏛 **Archaeological Museum**
◯ Sat–Thu. 📷 extra charges.

Environs
Overlooking the Krishna river, just north of the museum, is the **Amareshvara Temple**. Built during the 10th and 11th centuries, it was renovated in the 18th century by a local chief whose statue stands in the outer hall. The sanctuary and the open-columned hall are in a walled compound. A basement, reached by a flight of stairs, is believed to conceal the remains of a stupa, suggested by the pillar-shaped linga in the sanctuary, which was probably part of the stupa dome.

Ceremonial bull, Amravati Museum

THE AMRAVATI SCULPTURES

The surviving limestone carvings from the Maha Chaitya are now divided between the Archaeological Museum at Amravati, the Government Museum in Chennai (*see p565*) and the British Museum in London. These reliefs testify to the vitality of early Buddhist art traditions in South India. Posts and railings show ornate lotus medallions, friezes of garlands carried by dwarfs, and Jataka Tales (*see p480*) illustrated with vivid scenes of crowds, horse riders and courtiers. Drum panels are adorned with pots filled with lotuses, model stupas with serpents wrapped around the drums, and flying celestials above the umbrella-like finials.

Limestone carving, Amravati Museum

Nagarjunakonda ⑮

Guntur district. 175 km (109 miles)
W of Vijayawada. 🚉 *Macherla,
22 km (14 miles) SE of site, then bus
to Vijayapuri.* 🚌 🚲 *daily from
Vijayapuri, except Fri.* ℹ️ *Vijay
Vihar, (08680) 277 362.* 📷
from Hyderabad.

View of the hemispherical stupa, Bodhishri Chaitya, Nagarjunakonda

Nagarjunakonda or
"Nagarjuna's Hill", on the
banks of the Krishna river, was
named after Nagarjuna Acha-
rya, the 2nd-century Buddhist
theologian and founder of an
influential school of philosophy. Once a sophisticated
Buddhist settlement, with large
monasteries and stupas, wide
roads and public baths, it was
established in the 3rd and 4th
centuries, when the area flourished under the rule of the
powerful Ikshvaku kings.

Thereafter, Nagarjunakonda
was ruled by a succession of
dynasties, culminating with the
Vijayanagar rulers, who built a
fort around the Buddhist ruins.
When the Vijayanagar Empire
declined, the area was abandoned. It was rediscovered
only between 1954 and 1961.

In the early 1960s, when the
huge Nagarjuna Sagar Dam
was being constructed across
the Krishna, a number of these
rediscovered ancient Buddhist
settlements were threatened
with submersion. However, the
Archaeological Survey of India
salvaged and reconstructed
many of them, brick by brick,
on top of the hill where the
citadel once used to stand.

Today, most of the hill, and
the secluded valley in which

these settlements once stood,
have been submerged by the
waters of the Nagarjuna Sagar
lake. Only the top of the hill,
where the rescued remains
have been reassembled, juts
out like an island. The island
is accessible by launches,
which leave regularly from
the small village of Vijayapuri,
on the banks of the lake.

On the island, the path from
the jetty leads first to
the **Simha Vihara 4**. This
comprises a stupa built
on a high platform
with a pair of *chaitya
grihas* (prayer halls)
adjoining it. While
one of the *chaitya
grihas* houses a
second stupa, the
other enshrines a
monumental sculp-
ture of the Standing Buddha.
The **Bodhishri Chaitya**,
opposite it, has a raised stupa
contained within a semi-
circular-ended brick structure.
To its west is the **Maha
Chaitya** stupa which, with a

Detail of a carving,
Nagarjunakonda

diameter of 27.5 m (90 ft),
was one of the largest at
Nagarjunakonda. Its internal
rubble walls radiate outwards
like the spokes of a wheel,
and are filled with earth. Just
ahead of it is the **Swastika
Chaitya**, named after the
Indian swastika emblem formed by its rubble walls.

Near the citadel walls is a
stone megalith, some 2,000
years old. It conceals a simple
burial chamber that once
contained four skulls.
To its east is the
**Archaeological
Museum**, which
houses superb
Buddhist sculptures
from the ruins of
Nagarjunakonda.
They include lime-
stone reliefs and
panels carved with seated
Buddhas, flying celestial
beings and miniature replicas
of stupas. Friezes from the
railings which surrounded the
stupas depict scenes from the
Buddha's life. Among the free-
standing sculptures are digni-
fied Buddha figures dressed in
elegant robes.

🏛 **Archaeological Museum**
⭕ *Sat–Thu.* 📷 📷

Environs
More structures from the
Ikshvaku period are
reassembled at a site 15 km
(9 miles) south of Vijayapuri.
These include a Stadium, with
tiered galleries around a central
court, possibly used for musical
and theatrical performances and
sporting events. The adjacent
Monastic Complex has shrines
and *chaitya grihas* as well as a
refectory, store and baths.

A giant-sized statue of the Standing Buddha in Nagarjunakonda

Srisailam & Krishna Gorge ⑯

Kurnool district. 225 km (140 miles) S of Hyderabad. 🚌 *daily from Hyderabad.* 🏨 *Haritha Hotel, APTDC, (08524) 287 411; Punnami Hotel, Srisailam, (08524) 288 311.* ⛪ *Shivaratri (Feb/Mar).*

The pretty temple town of Srisailam, situated in the thickly wooded Nallamalai Hills, overlooking the deep Krishna Gorge, is a popular pilgrimage spot. Dominating the town is the **Mallikarjuna-swamy Temple**, whose white tiered *gopuras*, standing atop fortress-like walls, are visible from a great distance. The temple, which houses one of the 12 *jyotirlingas* (naturally formed lingas said to contain the light of Shiva), is believed to date to pre-Vedic times, though the present structure was built in the 15th century. The carvings on the walls represent Shiva in his many forms. A pillared hallway leads to the inner shrine, guarded by a monolithic Nandi bull.

Further up the hill is the **Hatakesvaram Temple**, said to be the spot where the philosopher-saint Shankaracharya (*see p648*) wrote one of his celebrated treatises. A small Shiva temple at the summit, **Sikharam**, offers breathtaking views of the valley.

The dammed waters of the Krishna power a huge hydroelectric project at Srisailam. When the waters are high enough, a luxury launch, the *Zaria*, ferries visitors from the reservoir at Nagarjuna Sagar to Srisailam Dam. For almost half the distance between the reservoir and Srisailam Dam, the river passes through a thick forest reserve, habitat of the tiger, panther and hyena. The river, which runs very deep at Srisailam, is known here as the Patal Ganga ("Underground Ganges") – according to legend, it springs from an underground tributary of the Ganges. On the ghats close to the dam, boatmen offer enchanting rides on their basin-shaped reed and bamboo boats.

The Sangameshvara Temple outside Alampur village

Alampur ⑰

Mahboobnagar district. 200 km (124 miles) S of Hyderabad. 📷 🚌

This village, on the northern bank of the Tungabhadra river, is the site of the earliest Hindu temples in Andhra Pradesh. Constructed by the Chalukyas of Badami (*see pp536–7*) in the 7th and 8th centuries, the nine red sandstone shrines are collectively known as the **Nava Brahma Temples**, and are dedicated to Shiva. The layout conforms to a standard scheme – each temple faces east, has an inner sanctum, a pillared *mandapa*, and is surrounded by a passage. The tower over the inner sanctum, capped by an *amalaka* (circular ribbed stone), shows the distinct influence of North Indian temple architecture (*see p20*).

The later temples in the group have porches with perforated stone screens on three sides of the passageways, as in the **Svarga Brahma Temple**,

Detail from the Padma Brahma Temple

built in AD 689. This beautiful temple has outstanding sculptures, including a complete set of *dikpalas* (guardian figures) in the corner niches, and icons of Shiva in various forms. Some columns in the interior have been elaborately carved, such as those in the **Padma Brahma Temple**. The pillars here have seated lions at the base, fluted shafts and ribbed pot-shaped capitals.

The **Bala Brahma Temple** is the only one of the group, still in use. The **Archaeological Museum**, next to the complex, has a fine collection of early Chalukya sculptures. Just outside the village is the reconstructed **Sangameshvara Temple**, removed from a site that was submerged by the damming of the Krishna, 15 km (9 miles) to the north. Standing on a high terrace, it is similar to the Nava Brahma group, except that the sculptural details have eroded.

Just southwest of the Nava Brahma Temple complex are the **Papanashanam Temples** (9th–10th centuries). These temples have imposing multitiered pyramidal roofs but little external decoration, though the interior columns are ornately carved. One of the temples has a fine ceiling panel of Vishnu's incarnations (*see p679*), and another has a powerful image of Durga.

🏛 **Archaeological Museum**
◯ *Sat–Thu.* 📷

Naga (Snake deity) from the Archaeological Museum, Alampur

View of Tirupati, with the gold-gilded *vimana* of the temple

Tirupati ⑱

Chittoor district. 585 km (364 miles)
S of Hyderabad. ⛩ 227,700. ✈
12 km (7 miles) S of the city centre,
then taxi. 🚉 🚌 ℹ *Andhra
Pradesh Tourism, Sridevi Complex
(0877) 228 9120.* 🎭 *Brahmotsavam
(Sep/Oct).*

The most popular destination
for Hindu pilgrims in India,
Tirupati is the site of the **Shri
Venkateshvara Temple**,
situated in the Tirumala
Hills, 700 m (2,297 ft)
above the town. The
seven "sacred hills" of
Tirumala are believed
to symbolize the
seven-headed serpent
god Adisesha, on
whose coils Vishnu
sleeps. The temple
dates to the 9th
century, although it
has often been
expanded and
renovated from
the 15th century
onwards.

Lord Venkateshvara, the
presiding deity at Tirupati

The aura that surrounds Lord
Venkateshvara (a form of Lord
Vishnu, who is also known as
Balaji) as the "Bestower of
Boons" has made his temple
the most visited and the richest
in India. It eclipses Jerusalem
and Rome in the number of
pilgrims it attracts – around
25,000 a day, and up to
100,000 on festival days. The
gold *vimana* and flagpole,
and the gold-plated doorway
into the inner sanctum,
proclaim the temple's wealth.
The jet-black stone image,
2-m (7-ft) high, stands on a
lotus and is adorned with
rubies, diamonds and gold.
The deity also wears a
diamond crown, believed to

be the singlemost precious
ornament in the world. He is
flanked by his consorts, Sridevi
and Bhudevi. The entrance
portico has superb life-size
images of the Vijayanagara
king and queens (*see
pp530–33*), who worshipped
Venkateshvara as their
protective deity.

The entire complex is built
to accommodate the huge
influx of pilgrims, who come
to seek favours from Lord
Venkateshvara. This is
one of the few
temples in South
India where non-
Hindus are allowed
into the inner sanc-
tum. Devotees wait
patiently in long
queues for a special
darshan, and make
offerings of money,
gold and jewellery
that net the
temple an annual
income of nearly
1.5 billion rupees.
The Tirumala Tirupati Deva-
sthanam (TTD), which runs
the temple, employs a staff
of 6,000 to see to the pilgrims'
needs and maintain the
temple premises.

The temple complex in-
cludes a ritual bathing tank,
and a small **Art Museum** with
images of deities, musical
instruments and votive
objects. Surrounding it are
green valleys and the Akash
Ganga waterfall, which is the
source of the holy water used
for bathing the deity.

A unique feature at Tirupati
is that many devotees offer
their hair to the deity, and
there are separate enclosures
for this purpose. It is believed
that since hair enhances a

person's appearance, shaving
it off sheds vanity as well.
This offering is usually made
after the fulfilment of a wish.
The hair-offerings are later
exported to the United States
and Japan where they are
made into wigs.

Most pilgrims stop at the
small Ganesha shrine in the
foothills, and at the **Govindarajaswamy Temple** in Tirupati
town, before driving up the
hill to the Tirumala shrine.
This temple, which dates to
the 16th–17th century, is
dedicated to both Krishna and
Vishnu. Built by the Nayakas,
the successors to the
Vijayanagar rulers, it is
approached through a
massive, grey outer *gopura*
that dominates Tirupati's
skyline, and is carved with
scenes from the *Ramayana*
(*see p27*). An exquisite
pavilion in the inner
courtyard has carved granite
pillars, an ornate wooden
roof, and impressive sculptures of crouching lions. The
temple has a magnificent
image of the reclining Vishnu,
called Ranganatha, coated
with bronze armour. A short
distance north of the temple
is the **Venkateshvara Museum
of Temple Arts**, with temple
models, photographs and
ritual objects.

🏛 **Shri Venkateshvara
Temple**
⭕ *daily. Darshan: 6–11am. Extra
charges to join the shorter queue for
special darshan of the deity.*

**The main gateway to
Govindarajaswamy Temple**

Avatars of Vishnu

Vishnu, the second god in the Hindu Trinity, personifies the preserving power of nature. Seen as the most "human" of the gods and the redeemer of humanity, he is said to have appeared on Earth in several avatars or incarnations, whenever the cosmic order was disturbed. From the 2nd century, a

Krishna, the eighth avatar of Vishnu

new devotional worship of Vishnu's incarnation as Krishna developed in South India, and, by AD 1000, Vaishnavism had become widespread. At his most famous temple, in Tirupati, Vishnu is worshipped as Venkateshvara, the God who Fulfills Desires. Lakshmi, the Goddess of Wealth, is his consort.

THE TEN INCARNATIONS

Vishnu descends to earth periodically, in order to redress the balance between good and evil. He is said to have ten main avatars, of which nine have already appeared; the tenth is yet to come.

Kavad is a portable wooden shrine, which shows Vishnu in his Krishna avatar, protected by the serpent Adisesha, and with his brother Balrama.

Main image of Vishnu

Krishna, who came to free the world from oppression.

Matsya, the fish and first avatar, rescued Manu (the first man) and the Vedas from a flood.

Rama, the seventh avatar, is the embodiment of goodness.

Buddha, is the ninth avatar *(see p221).*

Kurma, the tortoise and second avatar, churned the ocean to produce *amrita*, the divine nectar.

Krishna

Vamana, the dwarf priest and the fifth avatar, saved the world from a demon.

Parasurama, the sixth avatar, came to subdue the Kshatriyas who were overpowering the Brahmins.

Varaha, *the boar and third avatar, saved the earth from drowning in the ocean by lifting it up on his tusks.*

Narasimha, *the half-man, half-lion fourth avatar, killed the demon Hiranyakshipu and delivered the earth from his evil deeds.*

Kalki, *the tenth avatar, is still to come. Vishnu will then appear for the final destruction and will recreate the world in perfect purity.*

See also features on Hindu Mythology *(see pp24–5)*, Ganesha *(see p467)* and Shiva *(see p566)*.

Rani Mahal, roofed by stepped pyramidal towers, at Chandragiri

Chandragiri ⑲

Tirupati district. 12 km (7 miles) W of Tirupati. 🚌 *from Tirupati*.

This small village was once an important outpost of the Vijayanagar kings. It later became the capital of the Aravidu ruler, Venkatapatideva (r.1586–1614), whose reign saw the decline of the Vijayanagar Empire.

Chandragiri's once glorious past is reflected in the massive walls of its late 16th-century fortress and some abandoned palaces. The most important of these is the **Raja Mahal**, which has an arcaded Durbar Hall and a domed pleasure pavilion. It was here that Sir Francis Day of the East India Company was granted land in 1639, in order to set up a factory in what later came to be known as Madras (*see p557*). Nearby is the **Rani Mahal**, with its striking pyramidal towers, and its façade decorated with foliate and geometric motifs.

A temple next to the ruined palaces at Chandragiri

Sri Kalahasti ⑳

Chittoor district. 36 km (22 miles) E of Tirupati. 🚌 *from Tirupati*. 🎎 *Temple Festival (Sep/Oct)*.

Located between two steep hills, on the southern bank of the Svarnamukhi river, this town is one of the most important pilgrimage centres in Andhra Pradesh. Dominating one end of the crowded main street is a 36.5-m (120-ft) high freestanding *gopura*, erected in 1516 by Emperor Krishnadeva Raya of Vijayanagar (*see pp530–33*). The royal emblems of

Flower seller at Sri Kalahasti

the dynasty, depicting the boar and the sword together with the sun and the moon, are intricately carved on to the walls of this seven-storeyed towered gateway.

Nearby, similar but smaller *gopuras* provide access to the **Kalahastishvara Temple**, the town's main attraction, surrounded by a paved rectangular compound. A doorway to the south leads into a crowded enclosure of columned halls, pavilions, lamp columns and altars, connected by a maze of colonnades and corridors. Some of the columns are carved as rearing animal figures. In the north corridor are a set of bronzes of the 63 Shaivite saints called Nayannars (*see p45*). The inner sanctum, opening to the west, enshrines the *vayu* (air) linga, one of the five elemental lingas of Shiva (*see p586*) in South India. It is a curiously elongated linga protected by a cobra hood, made of brass. According to a local legend, a spider, a cobra and an elephant worshipped the linga in their own special way. The spider first spun a web around it to protect it from the sun's

---

KALAMKARI FABRICS

Deriving their name from the word *kalam* for pen and *kari* for work, these brightly coloured cotton fabrics are produced at Machilipatnam (*see p672*) and Sri Kalahasti. Using a mixture of painting and dyeing techniques, figures of gods, goddesses, trees and birds are first drawn on the fabric, and then painted with a "pen" made of a bamboo stick padded at one end with cotton cloth. The traditional natural colours of ochre, soft pink, indigo, madder red and iron black are characteristic of *kalamkari* textiles. *Kalamkaris* from Sri Kalahasti were part of temple ritual and, like temple murals, depict mythological themes, with gods, goddesses and other celestial beings. The ones from Machilipatnam display a distinct Persian influence (*see p673*) and once formed part of a lucrative trade with Europe, dating back to the 17th century.

Kalamkari depicting Shiva and Parvati

View of Sri Kalahasti town, with its towering *gopuras* and the Kannappa Temple on a hillock

rays. The cobra, when he reached the shrine, was so upset to see the linga covered with dirty cobwebs that he cleaned and covered it with little stones. The last to arrive was the elephant, who removed the stones and decorated the linga with flowers. This continued for some time until the three devotees, each sure that his way of worship was the purest and that the others had committed sacrilege, decided to confront each other. In the fight that ensued, they collapsed and Lord Shiva, pleased by their devotion, blessed them and named the shrine after them – Sri (spider), Kala (cobra) and Hasti (elephant).

Sri Kalahasti is also linked to the legend of Kannappa, the hunter, through its **Kannappa Temple**. One of the 63 Nayannars, Kannappa plucked out his eye in a frenzy of devotion and offered it to Shiva. A shrine commemorating him stands on the summit of the hillock that rises to the east.

Worshippers have thronged to this temple for generations to seek relief from the "evil effects" of Saturn. Some pilgrims also come here with their unmarried daughters in the hope that a special *puja* at the temple will help them find good husbands.

Puttaparthi ㉑

Ananthapur district. 437 km (272 miles) S of Hyderabad. ✈ 6 km (4 miles) S of ashram, then taxi. 🚉 Dharmavaram, 40 km (25 miles) N of Puttaparthi, then bus. 🚌 ℹ APTDC, (08555) 289 565. 🎉 Sai Baba's Birthday (23 Nov).

As the birthplace of Sri Satya Sai Baba, the "godman" who preaches religious tolerance, universal love and service to others, Puttaparthi has a very special significance for his vast number of devotees from all over the world. Sai Baba's ability to produce *vibhuti* (sacred ash), seemingly miraculously out of thin air, is considered by his devotees to be an important symbol of his godlike status and powers.

Sri Satya Sai Baba, a popular godman

From a very young age, Sai Baba, born as Satyanarayana Raju in this village on 23 November 1926, claimed divine powers. When he was only 14, he declared that he was the reincarnation of a celebrated saint, Sai Baba from Shirdi in Maharashtra, who died in 1918. It is believed that he will return after his death as another saint called Prem Sai Baba. In 1950 Satya Sai Baba established an ashram for his followers, whose numbers had swollen to gigantic figures. Known as **Prasanthi Nilayam** or the "Abode of Highest Peace", it is today a large complex with guesthouses, dormitories, kitchens and dining halls. Over the years, several buildings have appeared around the ashram – schools, colleges, residential complexes, hospitals, a planetarium, a museum and recreation centres, transforming this tiny village into a cosmopolitan township. Outside the ashram, at the lower end of the village, rural life continues, seemingly unaffected by the ashram's activities. The countryside around is very fertile, with stretches of well-irrigated fields.

Women working in the fields, Puttaparthi

The ornate *mihrab* of the Sher Shah Mosque, Penukonda

Penukonda ㉒

Anantapur district. 425 km (264 miles) S of Hyderabad. 🚌 🚉
Babayya Fair (Dec).

A rocky hill dominates Penukonda, or the "Big Hill", with walls rising up its steep sides to form an almost triangular fort. A strategic Vijayanagar citadel from the 14th and to 16th centuries, Penukonda was the capital of the succeeding Aravidu rulers until it was captured, first by the Qutb Shahis, and then by the Mughals followed by the Marathas. Today, gateways, watchtowers, dilapidated halls and shrines skirt the path to the summit.

At the foot of the hill is the walled city, with its main gateways in the northern and eastern sides. To the south is a large tank. The main monuments are situated along the city's north-south road. The **Parsvanatha Jain Temple** here contains a remarkable sculpture, dating from the Hoysala period (12th–13th centuries), of the Jain saint Parsvanatha *(see p396)* standing in front of an undulating serpent. The 16th-century **Sher Shah Mosque**, nearby, has an arcaded façade and a bulbous dome.

Further south, standing next to each other, are two granite temples dedicated to Rama and Shiva. The pilastered façade walls of the **Rama Temple** are brought to life by

carvings depicting episodes from the *Ramayana (see p27)* and the Krishna legend, while scenes from the Shiva mythology are sculpted on the walls of the **Shiva Temple**.

The adjacent **Gagan Mahal** is a palatial structure dating to the Vijayanagar period. An arcaded verandah leads to a vaulted hall with rear chambers. The domed pavilion above is topped by a pyramidal octagonal tower. A similar, smaller tower tops the adjoining staircase. To its east is a square pavilion with curving eaves, a pierced parapet and an octagonal pyramidal tower. The interior has traces of intricate plasterwork. Nearby is a well with an ornate entrance shaped like a lion.

A short distance north of the walled city is the **Dargah of Babayya**, the shrine of a 16th-century Muslim saint. A popular pilgrimage place which was much patronized by Tipu Sultan *(see p517)*, it holds a big fair in December.

Lepakshi ㉓

Anantapur district. 460 km (286 miles) S of Hyderabad. 🚌 🚉 *daily.*
🛕 *Shivratri (Feb/Mar).*

An enormous monolith of Nandi, Shiva's bull, stands 1 km (0.6 miles) east of Lepakshi, welcoming visitors to this important pilgrimage town.

Lepakshi's top attraction is the **Virabhadra Temple**, which stands on a rocky outcrop. It was built in the mid-16th century, under the patronage of two brothers, Virupanna and Viranna, governors of Penukonda under the Vijayanagar empire.

The temple is an important repository of the styles of sculpture and painting that evolved during this period. Dedicated to Virabhadra (Shiva in his

Monolithic *naga*, Virabhadra Temple

ferocious form), the temple stands in the middle of two concentric enclosures, built on three levels. It is entered through a *gopura* on the north side. On either side of the inner entrance are figures of the river goddesses Ganga and Yamuna, with a background of foliage. Among the other notable sculptures here are the carvings on the massive pillars that define the central space in the open hall; the deities, guardians and sages carved on to the piers of the unfinished Kalyana Mandapa; and the imposing monolithic seven-headed *naga* (serpent) sheltering a granite linga, to the southeast of the main shrine. Paintings in vibrant vegetable and mineral colours cover the ceilings of the two adjoining *mandapas* (one open and the other walled in), the walls of the Ardha Mandapa and some subsidiary shrines. Gods and goddesses, groups of donors and worshippers, and scenes from myths and legends, bear witness to the superb pictorial art of the Vijayanagar empire.

A gory legend connected to the Virabhadra Temple says that Virupanna misused state funds to build this shrine, and then forestalled royal punishment by blinding himself. The two dark reddish spots on the western wall of the inner enclosure are said to be the marks left by his eyes.

Carved pillars at the Virabhadra Temple

Lepakshi Paintings

The glory of Lepakshi lies in the magnificent frescoed ceilings of the Virabhadra Temple, where a series of exquisite paintings illustrate in lively fashion episodes from the epics and the *Puranas*. The figures are shown in profile, with prominent eyes and sharply chiselled noses and chins. The frescoes are characterized by elegant black linework, set out against an orange-red background. Particularly

Lord Shiva as a mendicant

striking are the beautiful costumes and the detailed rendering of hairstyles, textile patterns, and jewellery. The palette of colours is limited to white, green, black and various shades of ochre and brown, applied to a stucco surface specially treated with lime. Some of the most beautiful paintings are on the ceiling of the open *mandapa*, arranged in long strips along the surrounding bays.

Ravana   Nandi   Shiva   Parvati   Brahma officiating as the priest   Garuda, Vishnu's bird-vehicle

THE MARRIAGE OF SHIVA AND PARVATI
This is Lepakshi's most spectacular fresco, and echoes the murals at Ajanta *(see pp480–81)* in its colours, detailed depiction of costumes and jewellery, and graceful female figures.

Dakshinamurti *(Shiva as a Divine Teacher) is shown seated on a hillock, expounding on mysticism and philosophy to sages gathered at his feet.*

Parvati, *with her maids, is shown getting ready for the wedding. Flat figures in stylized poses, often arranged in rows, characterize these paintings.*

The Boar Hunt *shows a wild boar charging at Arjuna and Shiva, who are preparing to shoot him.*

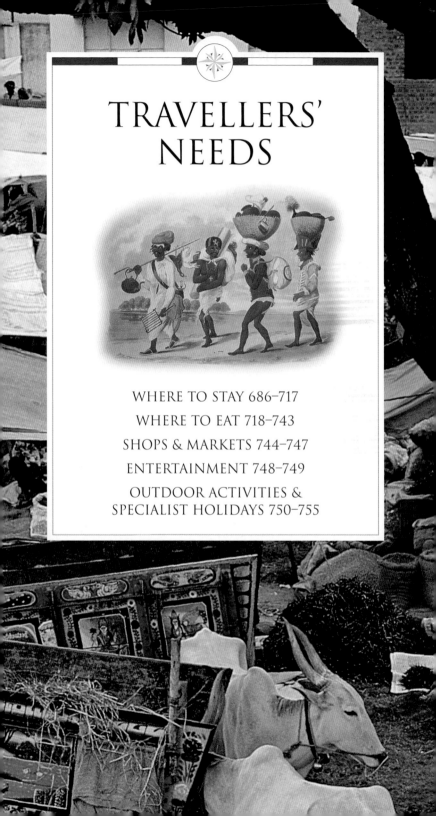

TRAVELLERS' NEEDS

WHERE TO STAY

A wide choice of accommodation is on offer for the rising number of visitors to India – from modern Western-style deluxe hotels and grand old palaces to budget hotels and tourist bungalows. Prices vary accordingly, depending on the quality of services offered, and the location. Star-rated luxury hotels, speciality hotels, health spas and heritage hotels are expensive, but the amenities they offer more than justify the high room rates. The moderately-priced budget hotels, often managed by state tourism departments, may lack the glamour of a five-star, but they are clean and excellent value for money. Cheaper accommodation is available at guesthouses, youth hostels and even spartan pilgrim abodes, such as *dharamshalas* and ashrams. Hotel rates fluctuate with the season and are usually cheaper during the off-season from April to September. The hotel listings on pages 690–717 provide a selection of some of the best hotels throughout India, to suit every taste and budget.

RAJVILĀS

Logo of an Oberoi
luxury hotel

GRADING AND FACILITIES

At the top end of the scale are the five-star deluxe hotels. Most of these are part of international and Indian hotel chains, such as **Welcomgroup, Oberoi, Taj**, and the national India Tourism Development Corporation's (ITDC) **Ashok Group**. Many of the Ashok Group's properties, however, are now in the process of being sold to private operators. Next, are the four- and three-star hotels, many of them run by the state governments, followed by the cheaper guesthouses. The heritage hotels offer visitors a chance to stay in atmospheric, beautifully restored forts, palaces and stately homes.

PRICING AND BOOKING

The most expensive establishments are the five-star and five-star deluxe hotels as well as the exclusive heritage hotels, although the smaller properties among the latter can be cheaper. Accommodation in the bigger cities is generally more expensive. Rates can differ among the state-run hotels, which have a good nationwide network. Prices vary at guesthouses, and seasonal discounts mean that prices can go down by almost 50 per cent.

Tariffs are based on the European system of room rent only, although in some places breakfast is included. Flexible prices dominate the market during the off-season and it is worth negotiating for a good discount.

Foreigners have to pay the dollar room rate in some hotels which have a policy of dual tariff (for foreigners and Indians), plus any additional taxes on the listed price. This is payable in foreign currency or in Indian rupees. Hotel rates are usually revised every October, at the start of the tourist season. Many hotels, however, maintain the same rates as the previous year. Book well in advance during the peak tourist season (Oct–Mar). Since the classifications of hotels can be bewildering, it's best to get a complete description of what to expect in terms of both room and service quality. Getting a reservation confirmed in writing is a sensible precaution. While making reservations, especially for mid-range and budget hotels, do also check which credit cards are accepted. Note that some hotels demand payment in advance and will refund only part of it if the booking is cancelled.

Check-out time is usually 12 noon, though some hotels are more flexible and allow a 24-hour departure, or accept a small fee for a few hours' extension. Sometimes, some of the smaller hotels allow a later check out, for free. When paying, scrutinize the bill thoroughly and retain all receipts on departure.

TAXES

The hotel bill includes taxes levied by the federal and state governments. The federal government charges a uniform 10 per cent hotel expenditure tax (on room rent only), which is imposed on all hotels with a tariff of Rs 3,000 and above. States levy a luxury tax on room rent as well, and this varies from 5 to

The charming Raj-style Fernhill Palace Hotel in Ooty

◁ **Weekly market at Srirangapattana, Karnataka** *(see pp516–17)*

Udaipur's opulent Lake Palace Hotel in the middle of Lake Pichola

25 per cent. There may also be local taxes such as sales tax, service tax and special taxes on alcohol, which vary from state to state. Some hotels also levy a service charge.

HIDDEN COSTS

Be prepared to pay extra for breakfast, the mini bar, mineral water, telephone calls, laundry, room service (if this is not a regular sevice), extra bedding, business centre usage, e-mails and faxes, concierge services and even pay channels on television. Transfers to and from the hotel are complimentary only for up-market package tours.

For non-local and international telephone calls, check if there's an in-house ISD/STD facility, though it's cheaper to use an STD booth *(see p770)* outside the hotel. Smaller hotels, with no running hot water, often charge extra for buckets of hot water.

LUXURY HOTELS

India's luxury hotels are comparable with the best anywhere in the world. They offer spacious suites and rooms, excellent service and a host of amenities. These usually include a travel desk, state-of-the-art conference facilities, shopping arcades, swimming pools, modern fitness centres, and multi-cuisine restaurants. The staff are very polite and attentive and can help plan itineraries and make arrangements for activities such as tennis, golf or riding. Reservations should be made in advance, especially during the peak season.

HERITAGE HOTELS

Several palaces, forts and *havelis*, particularly in Rajasthan, Madhya Pradesh, Himachal Pradesh and Gujarat, have been restored, modernized and converted into plush, luxury hotels. These establishments have a gracious, old-world charm, and many are still run by former princely families, who treat visitors like honoured guests.

Classified as Grand, Classic and Ordinary under the umbrella of the **Indian Heritage Hotels Association of India**, some can be booked through private agencies, such as **HRH Group of Hotels, Neemrana Hotels** and **WelcomHeritage**. Bookings at these hotels can also be made through well-known travel agents.

MIDDLE-RANGE HOTELS

The four- and three-star hotels offer a scaled-down version of five-star luxury and are less expensive. Levels of comfort, cleanliness and professional services are, however, high. Rooms are air conditioned and have attached bathrooms. In addition, there are restaurants, gift shops, business centres and sometimes extensive gardens for dining outdoors.

BUDGET HOTELS AND TOURIST LODGES

Budget hotels are often found around bus stands and railway stations. They are inexpensive, with simple decor, Indian or Western-style toilets, ceiling fans and basic food options in a dining hall. Enterprising proprietors sometimes offer e-mail services for a fee. The tariff in major cities is higher than in smaller towns.

An excellent option, particularly in lesser known tourist destinations, is the country-wide network of tourist bungalows and lodges run by the state tourism departments or the Ashok Group. Moderately priced, they offer both independent rooms with attached baths as well as dormitory accommodation.

DAK BUNGALOWS

Government-run dak bungalows (inns with very basic facilities) are cheap, clean, and conveniently located. Although not easily available for public use, visitors can contact the local or district authorities for help in making reservations. Book in advance as priority usually goes to visiting officials.

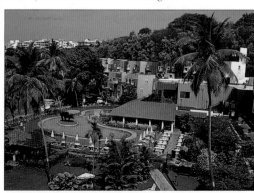

Cidade de Goa Beach Resort, designed by architect Charles Correa

GUESTHOUSES, PAYING GUESTS AND HOME STAYS

In certain states, such as Goa, Tamil Nadu, Rajasthan and Madhya Pradesh, family cottages and old mansions have been converted (though sometimes only partially) into guesthouses. While these usually fall into the mid-range or budget categories, the number of amenities, quality of service and price can be erratic. Look at rooms before checking in, as the difference between one room and another for the same price can be substantial. The better ones have air-conditioned rooms, with attached baths and Western-style toilets.

Home stays with local families are becoming a popular option, especially in Kerala. It is best to check with the state tourism offices (*see p761*) for a list of establishments under their Paying Guest Scheme. Rajasthan Tourism has a comprehensive list, as does Madhya Pradesh Tourism. In Kerala, **Sundale Vacations** specializes in home stays. The UK-based **Munjeeta Travels** also organizes home stay tours across India.

DHARAMSHALAS AND ASHRAMS

Religious centres, among them *dharamshalas*, ashrams and monasteries, offer clean but basic accommodation all over the country. For most, prior booking is not essential and stay is often free, although donations are appreciated. It is wise to abide by the rules of the house and not offend

Luxury campsite at Pushkar during the annual cattle fair

any sentiments. Some ashrams in the older sections of town may provide only a mattress on the floor, which should suffice if the stay is just for a night. But be prepared to share rooms and bathrooms with others.

Popular ashrams such as the **Sri Aurobindo Ashram**, the **Ramakrishna Mission** and the **Sivananda Ashram**, have branches spread across the country, and bookings must be made in advance. Their head offices can be contacted for details.

In Ladakh, many monasteries run hotels fairly close to their premises. One of the best is the **Lamayuru Monastery Hotel** which has a great setting within the compound (*see p138*).

NATIONAL PARKS AND CAMPING SITES

Most National Parks and wildlife sanctuaries have forest rest houses with basic facilities. Since most of these are often reserved for forest officials, many of the larger parks now have plush

private resorts located on their periphery. The most popular among these are in Ranthambhore (Sher Bagh), Corbett (Infinity Resorts), Kaziranga (Wildgrass) and Nagarhole (Kabini River Lodge). Reservations can be made through **Wild World India**, or through travel agencies. Camping is not allowed inside wildlife sanctuaries, and as a rule, it is not even safe to venture out for unguided walks.

Tented camps are provided by operators who organize adventure tours, such as river rafting along the Ganges (*see p185*), or those that specialize in camping holidays (*see p752*). Check the arrangements in advance, as some may not provide mosquito nets or mineral water. In Rajasthan, some hotels offer guests the option of staying in luxury tents set in spacious gardens. During the Pushkar and Kumbh *melas* (fairs), the state governments provide tented accommodation.

SPECIAL HOTELS

The rising interest in holistic health and well-being has spawned a number of exclusive health spas and specialized resorts. The most popular are those that offer herbal treatments, such as Ayurveda, and yoga. Other services include massage therapies, such as aromatherapy and reflexology, and meditation. Usually, a strict diet is part of the spartan regime, although rules at the top-end resorts are flexible. Raj Vilas and Amar Vilas of the **Oberoi** Group and

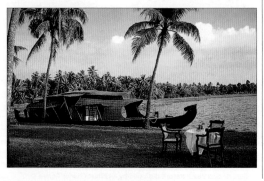

Ananda are world class spas. Kerala's *kettuvallams* (converted rice boats) are luxurious and have good services. Trips can be organized by **Tourindia**.

YOUTH HOSTELS

India has an excellent network of youth hostels. Although these are available at very low rates, they also tend to be packed. Members of the **Youth Hostel Association of India** and Youth Hostel International get priority bookings, but non-members can get a room for a higher fee. Both room and dorm-style accommodation is available. The **YMCA** is better equipped, though more expensive and located in fewer towns.

TOUTS

Visitors with no prior bookings should contact tourist counters at the airport, railway station or bus stand to avoid being harassed by touts, who also operate as taxi and auto-rickshaw drivers. Many are very persuasive and offer incredible discounts, all for a commission. Some, however, are genuinely helpful, and if there is no other option, keep the driver waiting until sure about the lodgings. Speak to a policeman if they become too persistent.

FACILITIES FOR THE DISABLED AND CHILDREN

Though facilities for the disabled are few, hotel staff are generally considerate. The government has recently initiated a move to add wheelchair ramps, special lifts and bathrooms wherever possible, although older properties, even the five-star hotels, may find it difficult to accommodate them.

Most hotels have no special amenities for children. However, Indian hotel staff are usually good with children and provisions can be made for extra beds. Only a few hotels offer baby-sitting services.

The impressive entrance foyer, Cecil Hotel, Shimla

TIPPING

Despite the inclusion of service charges in the bill, tips are expected in most places. The amount is discretionary. A tip of Rs10 is fine for parking attendants, room service and porters, but waiters expect ten per cent of the bill. Taxi drivers don't need to be tipped. However, tipping is a great way to get things done quickly.

DIRECTORY

HOTEL CHAINS

Ashok Group
ITDC, 7 Lodhi Rd, Delhi.
Tel (011) 2436 0303.
www.theashokgroup.com

Oberoi Group
Oberoi Maidens, Delhi.
Tel (011) 2392 5464.
www.oberoihotels.com

Taj Group
Taj Intercontinental,
Mumbai.
Tel (022) 2202 5515.
www.tajhotels.com

Welcomgroup
Maurya Sheraton, Delhi.
Tel (011) 2611 2233.
www.welcomgroup.com

HERITAGE HOTELS

Indian Heritage Hotels Association
Sansar Chandra Rd, Jaipur.
Tel (0141) 237 1194.
www.indianheritagehotels
.com

HRH Group of Hotels

City Palace, Udaipur.
Tel (0294) 252 8016.
www.hrhhotels.com

Neemrana Hotels
A-58, Nizammudin East, Delhi.
Tel (011) 2435 8348.
www.neemranahotels.com

WelcomHeritage
31, Siri Fort Rd, New Delhi.
Tel (011) 2626 6650.
www.welcomheritagehotels.
com

GUESTHOUSES, PAYING GUESTS & HOME STAYS

Munjeeta Travels
12 Cavendish Rd,
Woking, Surrey,
GU22 OEP, UK.
Tel (01483) 773 331.

Sundale Vacations
39/5955–A, Atlantis
Junction, MG Rd, Kochi.
Tel (0484) 235 9127.
www.sundale.com

DHARAMSHALAS & ASHRAMS

Lamayuru Monastery Hotel
Lamayuru Monastery,
Ladakh district,
Jammu & Kashmir.
Tel No telephone.

Ramakrishna Mission
Belur Math, Howrah
district, West Bengal.
Tel (033) 2654 1144.
www.sriramakrishna.org

Sivananda Ashram
Divine Life Society, PO
Shivanandanagar, 249192,
Tehri Garhwal District
Uttaranchal.
Tel (0135) 243 0040.
www.divinelifesociety.org

Sri Aurobindo Ashram
1 Goubert Salai
(Beach Road), Pondicherry.
Tel (0413) 233 4836.
www.sriaurobindoashram.
org

NATIONAL PARKS & CAMPING SITES

Wild World India
21, Kailash Hills,
New Delhi 110 065.
Tel (011) 2691 4417.
www.wildworldindia.com

SPECIAL HOTELS

Tourindia
PO Box 163,
Thiruvananthapuram.
Tel (0471) 233 1507.
www.tourindiakerala.com

YOUTH HOSTELS

YMCA
YMCA Hostel, 1 Jaisingh
Rd, PO Box 612, Delhi.
Tel (011) 2336 1915.
www.ymca.int

Youth Hostels Association of India
Vishwa Yuvak Kendra,
5, Nyaya Marg, Delhi.
Tel (011) 2687 1969.
www.yhaindia.org

Choosing a Hotel

Hotels have been selected across a wide price range for their facilities, good value and location. Most have Internet access, and in some cases, fitness facilities may be off-site. The prices listed are those charged by the hotel, although discounts may be available through agencies. The hotels are listed by region.

PRICE CATEGORIES
Price ranges are for a standard double room per night, including taxes and service charge but not breakfast.

(Rs) Under 550 rupees
(Rs)(Rs) 550–1,200 rupees
(Rs)(Rs)(Rs) 1,200–3,000 rupees
(Rs)(Rs)(Rs)(Rs) 3,000–6,000 rupees
(Rs)(Rs)(Rs)(Rs)(Rs) Over 6,000 rupees

DELHI

DELHI Hotel Broadway
4/15A Asaf Ali Rd (Near Delhi Gate), 110 002 **Tel** *(011) 2327 3821* **Fax** *(011) 2327 9966* **Rooms** *26*

This is one of the city's oldest budget hotels and the first skyscraper built 50 years ago. Rooms overlook the busy Asaf Ali Road and also offer a view of the spectacular Mughal area of Old Delhi. Comfortable rooms, friendly staff and two good restaurants make this a popular tourist refuge. **www.oldworldhospitality.com**

DELHI Jor Bagh '27' Guesthouse
27 Jor Bagh, 110 003 **Tel** *(011) 2469 4430* **Fax** *(011) 2469 8647* **Rooms** *18*

This guesthouse is modest yet capable of providing the kind of comfort and facilities that other budget hotels fail to offer. Strategically located and connected to the bustle of the city, it is nonetheless surprisingly calm and peaceful with cosy, neatly furnished rooms. The staff provide a friendly service. **www.jorbagh27.com**

DELHI YWCA International Guest House
10 Parliament Street (Sansad Marg), 110 001 **Tel** *(011) 2336 1662* **Fax** *(011) 2334 1763* **Rooms** *24*

Popular among female students and women travelling alone or with children, the YWCA offers good services at a low cost. With a prime location near Delhi's main business and shopping area, the rooms are simple yet comfortable. Free breakfast served from 8 to 10am. Beverages are available around the clock. **www.ywcaindia.org**

DELHI Hotel Centre Point
13 Kasturba Gandhi Marg, 110 001 **Tel** *(011) 2335 4304* **Fax** *(011) 2332 9138* **Rooms** *55*

This is a former Colonial residence, which has been converted into a hotel. Services are excellent for the price range. The rooms have an air of luxury of days gone by. Centre Point is strategically located near important business, shopping and media centres. One of the best low budget hotels for the travelling businessman or tourist.

DELHI Oberoi Maiden's
7 Sham Nath Marg, 110 054 **Tel** *(011) 2397 5464* **Fax** *(011) 2398 0771* **Rooms** *53*

One of the oldest hotels in the city, the classic architecture of this building could have been the inspiration for Lutyens who stayed here on his first visit to India more than a century ago. With spectacular views of the lush green Delhi Ridge, this heritage hotel exudes an air of serenity and quiet beauty. **www.maidenshotel.com**

DELHI The Ashok
50-B Chanakyapuri, 110 021 **Tel** *(011) 2611 0101* **Fax** *(011) 2687 3216* **Rooms** *550*

The Ashok's dramatic and palatial Mughal architecture along with sweeping views and impeccable staff make it a grand holiday treat. The rooms are lavish, spacious and luxurious. Visitors can spend their days lazing by the sun-drenched poolside or in the spa, Amatra City. The hotel bar, Soho, hosts regular music events. **www.theashok.com**

DELHI Claridges
12 Aurangzeb Rd, 110 011 **Tel** *(011) 4133 5133* **Fax** *(011) 2301 0625* **Rooms** *138*

Situated in the quiet leafy avenues of Central Delhi, this stylish hotel blends the classic and contemporary to perfection. The rooms are luxurious and tastefully furnished, with most having lovely views of the pool or the surrounding greenery. Good facilities ensure a relaxed and peaceful stay. **www.claridges-hotels.com**

DELHI Hyatt Regency
Bhikaji Cama Place, 110 029 **Tel** *(011) 2679 1234* **Fax** *(011) 2679 1122* **Rooms** *508*

Majestic and grand, the rooms here exude sheer luxury. Modern furnishing, wooden floors and exquisite glasswork portray a chic, avant-garde look. Of the hotel's two restaurants, La Piazza undoubtedly serves the city's best Italian cuisine, while TK's Oriental Grill offers an interactive dining experience. **www.delhi.regency.hyatt.com**

DELHI The Imperial
Janpath, 110 001 **Tel** *(011) 2334 1234* **Fax** *(011) 2334 225* **Rooms** *263*

Considered to be one of Asia's finest hotels, The Imperial offers visitors a unique Colonial experience. Luxurious rooms have a vintage feel, yet are equipped with all modern facilities. Next to Janpath, the location is ideal for exploring the city. **www.theimperialindia.com**

Key to Symbols *see back cover flap*

DELHI InterContinental Eros

Nehru Place, 110 019 **Tel** *(011) 4122 3344* **Fax** *(011) 2622 4288* **Rooms** *224*

Luxurious in every aspect, from the elegant rooms and luxury spa to the great location next to Nehru Place, with many popular restaurants and shops just minutes away. The in-house restaurant, the Empress of China, is worth trying for its authentic Oriental cuisine. **www.ichotelsgroup.com**

DELHI Intercontinental The Grand

Barakhamba Avenue, Connaught Place **Tel** *(011) 2341 1001* **Fax** *(011) 2341 2233* **Rooms** *444*

A popular choice for the travelling business executive, this hotel provides a mix of sophistication, comfort and style. Rooms are stately, spacious and contemporary in their decor. The Law Club, the first of its kind, is a popular place for the city's top legal fraternity. Its in-house restaruants and bars are superb. **www.thegrandhotels.net**

DELHI Le Meridien

Windsor Place, 110 001 **Tel** *(011) 2371 0101* **Fax** *(011) 2371 4545* **Rooms** *355*

Situated at the heart of Central Delhi, this is a lovely atrium hotel with the added appeal of having the highest rooftop nightclub in the city, among other popular bars and speciality restaurants. The luxurious rooms are well-equipped to ensure the highest comfort. **www.lemeridien-newdelhi.com**

DELHI The Manor

77 Friends Colony (West), 110 065 **Tel** *(011) 2692 5151* **Fax** *(011) 2692 7510* **Rooms** *10*

Built in the late 1950s, The Manor is set against a lovely residential backdrop. The rooms have stately queen-sized beds and other modest facilities which make for a delightful stay. For a relaxing experience, lounge on the roof terrace, which overlooks a pretty garden. **www.themanordelhi.com**

DELHI The Metropolitan Hotel Nikko

Bangla Sahib Rd, 110 001 **Tel** *(011) 4250 0200* **Fax** *(011) 4250 0300* **Rooms** *176*

This hotel houses world-class facilities and is a perfect blend of the Orient and the West. Lavish, spacious rooms have a classic, elegant decor. Their beautifully designed craft shop is great for souvenirs and the hotel's Zen Health Club, offers relaxing spas and therapeutic massages. **www.hotelnikkodelhi.com**

DELHI Maurya Sheraton

Diplomatic Enclave, Sardar Patel Marg, 110 001 **Tel** *(011) 2611 2233* **Fax** *(011) 2611 3333* **Rooms** *484*

This exclusive hotel offers luxury, privacy and style along with a range of world-class facilities. Its list of leisure activities extends from tarot readings to a round of golf at a 27-hole Jack Nicklaus signature course. It also houses Bukhara and Dum Pukht, two of the city's top restaurants. **www.itcwelcomgroup.in**

DELHI The Oberoi

Dr Zakir Hussain Marg, 110 003 **Tel** *(011) 2436 3030* **Fax** *(011) 2436 0484* **Rooms** *300*

Awarded "Best Five-Star Hotel In India" recently, The Oberoi ensures a comfortable, luxurious and exciting stay. The rooms are the finest in the city, with glamorous and stylish interiors. A must-try for lovers of quality and excellence. Be sure to check out Travertino, their speciality Italian restaurant. **www.oberoidelhi.com**

DELHI The Park

15 Parliament Street, 110 001 **Tel** *(011) 237 43000* **Fax** *(011) 2374 4000* **Rooms** *224*

Stay in this hotel for unadulterated luxury and privacy. The rooms have a progressive, avant-garde look and offer state-of-the-art services. A popular gift shop in the shopping arcade, The Box, offers unique handicrafts and accessories. Restaurants provide world-class cuisine. **www.theparkhotels.com**

DELHI Radisson Hotel

Sikandarpur, National Highway No 8, 110 037 **Tel** *(011) 2677 9191* **Fax** *(011) 2677 9090* **Rooms** *256*

Part of the worldwide chain of 350 hotels, the Radisson is conveniently located close to the airport. The hotel endeavours to exceed their guests' expectations by providing world-class rooms and sheer luxury. It houses many popular restaurants and bars, although be wary of unexpectedly steep taxes. **www.radisson.com**

DELHI Shangri-La

19 Ashok Rd, Connaught Place, 110 001 **Tel** *(011) 4119 1919* **Fax** *(011) 4119 1988* **Rooms** *323*

The hotel lobby is adorned with paintings by world-renowned painter, MF Husain. Rooms are lavishly furnished and offer a spectacular view of the city. Janpath, the popular shopping street, is just a walk away. Overall, this newly-built luxury hotel is popular with the travelling businessman and tourist alike. **www.shangri-la.com**

DELHI The Taj Ambassador

Sujan Singh Park, Cornwallis Rd., 110 003 **Tel** *(011) 2463 2600* **Fax** *(011) 2463 2252* **Rooms** *88*

Ideal for the connoisseur of art, the hotel's colonnaded building exudes a certain old-world charm. If you are looking for a peaceful and relaxed stay, then their simple yet elegant rooms are the right choice. Take a walk to Lodi Gardens or shop at Khan Market, a treasure trove of boutiques and restaurants. **www.tajhotels.com**

DELHI The Taj Mahal Hotel

1 Mansingh Rd, 110 001 **Tel** *(011) 2302 6162* **Fax** *(011) 2302 6070* **Rooms** *296*

The Taj offers lavish rooms, created specially for the discerning traveller who appreciates quality and sophistication. The Mughal decor and hospitable service are truly royal. The Taj Mahal hotel boasts Machan, their ever popular coffee shop, Ricks, a lively lounge bar, and the House of Ming for classic Chinese food. **www.tajhotels.com**

HARYANA & PUNJAB

AMRITSAR Hotel Mohan International
*Albert Rd, 143 001 **Tel** (0183) 222 7802 **Fax** (0183) 222 6520 **Rooms** 76*

This four-star hotel is located near the Wagah border on the outskirts of Amritsar. Offering excellent facilities, it is a very convenient place to stay being just 1 km (half a mile) away from the railway station and 3 km (2 miles) from the bus station. Even the airport is only 15 km (9 miles) away. **www.nivalink.com/mohan/index.html**

CHANDIGARH Shivalik View
*Sec 17, 160 017 **Tel** (0172) 464 4450 **Fax** (0172) 270 1094 **Rooms** 108*

Whether on a business or pleasure trip, savour the excellent facilities and services of this modern hotel located in the heart of the city. The second biggest hotel in Chandigarh, it is well-known for its impeccable standards of service and luxury. **www.citcochandigarh.com/shivalikview/index.php**

CHANDIGARH Hotel Mountview
*Sector 10, 160 011 **Tel** (0172) 274 0544 **Fax** (0172) 274 2220 **Rooms** 145*

This is one of the few five-star hotels in the region north of Delhi. Surrounded by lush green lawns with the Shivalik Hills in the background, the hotel has a pleasant ambience and is famous for the tranquility of its Rock Garden. **www.citcochandigarh.com/mountview/index.php**

CHANDIGARH Taj Chandigarh
*Block 9a, Sector 17, 160 017 **Tel** (0172) 551 3000 **Fax** (0172) 551 4000 **Rooms** 152*

This newly built hotel, located in the city's prime business and shopping area, is a comfortable 30-minute drive from the airport and a 15-minute drive from the railway station. The rooms are equipped with the latest technology, ergonomic furniture and modern amenities. **www.tajhotels.com**

GURGAON Tikli Bottom
*Manender Farm, Gairatpur Bas, PO Tikli, 122 001 **Tel** (0124) 2766556 **Rooms** 4*

The beauty and traditions of Colonial India come alive at Tikli Bottom. This lovely Lutyens-style building offers four luxurious rooms with breathtaking views of the surrounding Aravalli Hills. Room tariffs include all meals and drinks. Indulge in a stay at this mansion for complete and sublime relaxation. **www.tiklibottom.com**

GURGAON Trident-Hilton
*443 Udyog Vihar, Phase V **Tel** (0124) 245 0505 **Fax** (0124) 245 0606 **Rooms** 136*

An award-winning business hotel, the Trident-Hilton is the latest buzzword among the swanky hotels that have sprung up around Delhi. Their lavish rooms are equipped with ultra-modern facilities to suit every travellers' comfort and needs. Cilantro, their multi-cuisine restaurant, is popular. **www.trident-hilton.com**

HIMACHAL PRADESH

CHAIL Palace Hotel
*Palace Hotel, Chail, 173 217 **Tel** (01792) 248 141 **Fax** (01792) 248 334 **Rooms** 54*

Once the summer palace of the erstwhile royal family of Patiala, this beautiful property, set in 30 ha (75 acres) of gardens and deodar cedar forests, offers a range of accommodation, including nine cottages. There is also a pleasant outdoor café and a billiards room. **palace@hptc.in**

DALHOUSIE Grand View Hotel
*Dalhousie, 176 304 **Tel** (01899) 240 760 **Fax** (01899) 240 609 **Rooms** 26*

True to its name, this clean, comfortable hotel offers spectacular views of the Pir Panjal Range from its well-tended front lawn. Travellers will find all basic comforts such as round-the-clock room service, TV and activities for children. Their restaurant serves delicious food. **grandview@rediffmail.com**

DHARAMSALA Chonor House
*Thekchen Choeling Rd, McLeodganj, 176 219 **Tel** (01892) 221 006 **Fax** (01892) 221 077 **Rooms** 11*

Traditional Tibetan wall paintings, teak and rosewood furniture and hand-knotted carpets adorn the elegant rooms of Chonor House, which have been decorated by the artists of the Norbulingka Institute. It is centrally located, overlooking Tsuglagkhang, the main Buddhist temple. The perfect peaceful getaway. **www.norbulingka.org**

DHARAMSALA Glenmoor Cottages
*McLeodganj, 176 219 **Tel** (01892) 221 010 **Fax** (01892) 221 021 **Rooms** 7*

Five pleasant cottages, situated in idyllic and peaceful surroundings, provide comfortable and clean accommodation. Each has an attached bathroom, kitchenette and a small glazed verandah. Sightseeing, trekking and pony rides are arranged on request. Simple and hearty meals are available. **www.glenmoorcottages.com**

Key to Price Guide *see p690* **Key to Symbols** *see back cover flap*

KALPA Kinner Villa

Village & PO Kalpa Distt, Kinnaur, 172 108 **Tel** *(01786) 226 006* **Rooms** *11*

This secluded hotel, built in stone and conifer wood, has comfortable rooms with balconies offering splendid views of the snow-clad peaks of Kinner Kailash. Children can play in the well-manicured garden or lounge in the recreation room.

KEYLONG Hotel Dekyid

Town End Upper Keylong, Lahaul & Spiti District, 175 114 **Tel** *(01900) 222 217* **Rooms** *23*

Spacious rooms are available at this budget hotel, which has an amiable staff and a decent restaurant. Set against the backdrop of snowy peaks, Hotel Dekyid offers a family suite comprising three rooms and 22 double rooms with regular hot water supply. A good base for visiting Kardang.

KULLU Span Resorts

Kullu-Manali Highway, Kullu District, 175 101 **Tel** *(01902) 240 138* **Fax** *(01902) 240 140* **Rooms** *30*

The Beas river runs right past this superbly located resort with pretty cottages set in a sprawling garden. Each cottage has a patio with splendid views of the river and the mountains. The friendly staff can arrange for adventure activities such as rafting, sailing, horse-riding and angling. **www.spanresorts.com**

MANALI John Banon's Hotel

Near Circuit House, 175 131 **Tel** *(01902) 252 335* **Fax** *(01902) 252 392* **Rooms** *14*

This atmospheric Raj-era hotel is located in a pretty apple and cherry orchard. With round-the-clock room service and a TV in every room, this place has a modern ambience. A good base for hiking trips and during the winter, if weather permits, skiing is a also an option.

MANALI Snowcrest Manor

Beyond Log Huts area, 175 131 **Tel** *(01902) 253 351* **Fax** *(01902) 253 188* **Rooms** *32*

Situated near the market, Snowcrest Manor has luxury written all over it. Large windows with splendid views across the valley to Rohtang Pass grace every room in this plush modern hotel built on a hillside. This is also a good base for adventure sports. **snowcrest@hotmail.com**

NALAGARH The Nalagarh Fort Resort

The Fort, Nalagarh, 174 101 **Tel** *(01795) 223 009* **Fax** *(01795) 223 021* **Rooms** *31*

Housed in a fortress built by Raja Ajai Chand in AD 1100, this comfortably refurbished hotel has a medieval ambience. It also has a gift shop and provides facilities such as wheelchair access and parking. The extensive grounds include orchards and forests. **fortresort@satyam.net.in**

PRAGPUR Judge's Court

Jai Bhawan, Tehsil Dehra, Kangra District, 177 107 **Tel** *(01970) 245 035* **Rooms** *12*

Built in the early 20th century by an eminent judge, Justice Jai Lal, this stately country manor in Indo-European style is surrounded by fruit orchards and has been tastefully restored. The latest additions are a swimming pool, conference hall, gift shop and golf course. **www.judgescourt.com**

SARAHAN Shrikhand

Village & PO Sarahan, Rampur District, 172 102 **Tel** *(01782) 274 234* **Rooms** *31*

This hilltop HPTDC deluxe hotel commands great views of the Shrikhand peaks and the mountains that divide the Satluj and Beas valleys. It is an excellent stopover for sightseeing, leisure and pilgrimage. A range of accommodation is available – dormitory-style, standard and deluxe rooms, as well as cottages. **booking@himachalhotels.in**

SHIMLA Hotel Combermere

The Mall, 171 001 **Tel** *(0177) 265 1246* **Fax** *(0177) 265 2251* **Rooms** *41*

Centrally located, this hotel offers well-furnished rooms with all basic amenities such as a mini fridge, colour TV, Jacuzzi, personal safe and round-the-clock room service. It also houses The Seventh Heaven restaurant that serves a variety of cuisines. **www.hotelcombermere.com**

SHIMLA Oberoi Cecil

Chaura Maidan, 171 001 **Tel** *(0177) 280 4848* **Fax** *(0177) 281 1024* **Rooms** *79*

Part of the Oberoi Group, this elegant hotel stands at the quiet end of Shimla's Mall. A cozy atrium bar, log fires, parquet floors and a heated pool add to the feeling of luxurious comfort. It also has state-of-the-art audio and video equipment. **www.oberoicecil.com**

SHIMLA Woodville Palace Hotel

Raj Bhawan Rd, 171 001 **Tel** *(0177) 262 3919* **Fax** *(0177) 262 2156* **Rooms** *28*

This well-maintained palace-turned-hotel, built in 1938 by the Raja of Jubbal, has a private forest perfect for walks. It offers all modern luxuries while maintaining the charm of a bygone era with characteristic wrought-iron beds and huge drapes decorating the bedrooms. **www.woodvillepalacehotel.com**

SHIMLA Radisson Jass Hotel

Good Wood Estate, Lower Bharari Rd, 171 001 **Tel** *(0177) 265 9012* **Fax** *(0177) 280 6902* **Rooms** *59*

Built to the most exacting international standards, this hotel combines the charm and beauty of the local area with modern comforts. The well-appointed rooms overlook the mountains and dense pine forests. Facilities include the Pulse Terrasse Bar and Deck, and the multi-cuisine restaurant, Café Valley Vue. **www.radisson.com**

SHIMLA Wildflower Hall
Chharabra, Dalli PO, Mashobra, 171 012 **Tel** *(0177) 264 8585* **Fax** *(0177) 264 8686* **Rooms** *87*

The former residence of Lord Kitchener, this stately stone and slate building is set amid cedar and pine forests. It offers splendid mountain views, restaurants, outdoor Jacuzzi and a heated swimming pool. Rooms have personalised service and spacious bathrooms with walk-in closets. **www.oberoiwildflowerhall.com**

LADAKH, JAMMU & KASHMIR

ALCHI Alchi Resort
Alchi **Tel** *(01982) 25 2631, 9419 218636* **Fax** *(01982) 25 2520* **Rooms** *15*

These clean, comfortably furnished huts in a tranquil setting are located a stone's throw from the historic Alchi Monastery, with the Indus river flowing close by. The architecture and decor are on traditional lines. Excursions to other monasteries in the vicinity can be organised. **alchi_resort@hotmail.com**

KARGIL Hotel D'zoji-La
Baru **Tel** *(01985) 23 2227* **Rooms** *41*

Situated 2 km (1.3 miles) out of town on the banks of the Suru river, this popular hotel has room service, direct dialling and fax facilities. A beautiful garden adds to the aesthetics of this budget hotel. Guests can enjoy meals in the garden or on the terrace – both are good options.

LEH Dragon
Old Rd, 194 101 **Tel** *(01982) 25 2139* **Fax** *(01982) 25 2720* **Rooms** *30*

This hotel is a fine example of traditional Ladakhi architecture. It is a short walk from the main market and offers most modern facilities. The restaurant provides simple, wholesome and tasty food, and has a well-stocked cellar for chilly evenings. Try the local Tibetan fare and the different kinds of teas. **advnorth@sancharnet.in**

LEH Hotel Shambhala
Skara, 194 101 **Tel** *(01982) 25 1100, 941917 7900* **Fax** *(01982) 25 2607* **Rooms** *24*

Located in a grove of poplars, surrounded by a large meadow, this hotel has clean, cheerful rooms and bright wall murals. Arrangements for excursions and treks throughout Ladakh can be made on request. The hotel is open from May 1 until the end of October. **www.hotelshambhala.com**

LEH Oriental Guest House
Changspa, 194 101 **Tel** *(01982) 25 3153* **Fax** *(01982) 25 0516* **Rooms** *25*

A favourite with budget travellers, this family-owned guesthouse on the road to Shanti Stupa exudes great warmth and hospitality. Heating and water are run by eco-friendly solar systems, so your stay will have a minimal impact on Leh's fragile ecosystem. **www.oriental-ladakh.com**

LEH Yak Tail
Fort Rd, 194 101 **Tel** *(01982) 25 2118* **Fax** *(01982) 25 2735* **Rooms** *23*

Centrally located in Leh, this hotel has balconies and a pleasant garden restaurant, and remains open through the winter. It is a block or two from the central square and just a block from the Tibetan market. It is also within a stone's throw of great restaurants, bakeries and Internet cafés.

LEH Omasila
Changspa, 194 101 **Tel** *(01982) 25 2119* **Rooms** *35*

Situated near barley fields on the outskirts of Leh, this quiet family hotel provides hygienically prepared food, with vegetables from its own garden. It is only a 15-minute drive from Leh airport and a few minutes away from the market. Omasila also offers a panoramic view of the Himalayan mountains. **info@omasila.com**

NUBRA Hotel Yarab Tso
Tegar Village, PO Sumur **Tel** *(01982) 220 008, 25 2480* **Rooms** *16*

This hotel offers a charming rural, almost farmhouse ambience. It has large, clean rooms with all basic amenities, including well-equipped bathrooms. The room service is also surprisingly good for the price. The tariff includes meals. Ample parking space available.

PADUM Hotel Ibex
Padum **Tel** *(01903) 24 5012* **Rooms** *15*

This is the best hotel in the sparsely populated valley of Padum. It offers clean rooms with attached baths and a laundry service. The hotel also has its own restaurant, which provides tasty food. A pleasant garden with outdoor seating and a sundeck adds to the beauty of the place. You can be assured of an undisturbed stay here.

SRINAGAR Grand Palace Intercontinental
Gupkar Rd, 190 001 **Tel** *(0194) 247 0101* **Fax** *(0194) 245 3794* **Rooms** *125*

Built in 1910 as the Maharaja of Kashmir's palace, this hotel has sumptuous walnut wood interiors and a lovely garden shaded by *chinar* trees, overlooking Dal Lake. The palace is located 15 km (9 miles) from the airport and just minutes away from the city's key historic attractions. **www.thegrandhotels.net**

Key to Price Guide *see p690* **Key to Symbols** *see back cover flap*

ULEY-TOKPOI Ule Ethnic Resort

PO Box 268 **Tel** *(01982) 25 3640* **Fax** *(01982) 25 3144* **Rooms** *43*

Close to Alchi, this delightful resort set amid apricot orchards on the banks of the Indus, offers clean thatched huts and tents. The hotel has no shops, and hawkers are not allowed inside so you are left to yourself to enjoy the peace and tranquillity of the Himalayan mountains. **ulecamp@sancharnet.in**

UTTAR PRADESH & UTTARANCHAL

AGRA Hotel Agra Deluxe

Fatehabad Rd, 282 001 **Tel** *(0562) 33 0110, 33 0384* **Fax** *(0562) 33 1330* **Rooms** *30*

This clean and fairly basic budget hotel has simple rooms with attached baths, and a multi-cuisine restaurant. You can choose your favourite drink from the well-stocked bar. Round-the-clock room service and business facilities make it a popular choice. **hotelad@agr.dot.net.in**

AGRA Taj View Hotel

Taj Ganj, Fatehabad Rd, 282 001 **Tel** *(0562) 2232 400/418* **Fax** *(0562) 2232 420* **Rooms** *100*

Distant views of the Taj can be had from this multi-storeyed hotel with landscaped gardens and Mughal-style interiors. The hotel is also conveniently located just 6 km (4 miles) from Agra Cantonment railway station. Guests can look forward to personalised service and a memorable stay. **www.tajhotels.com**

AGRA The Trident

Taj Nagari Scheme, Fatehabad Rd, 282 001 **Tel** *(0562) 233 1818* **Fax** *(0562) 233 1827* **Rooms** *140*

The Trident in Agra is set amid beautiful gardens and is only a few minutes walk from the Taj Mahal. The hotel is built of red stone reminiscent of the Mughal era, designed around a landscaped central courtyard with a swimming pool and fountains. **www.trident-hilton.com**

AGRA Amar Vilas

Taj East Gate Rd, Taj Nagri Scheme, 282 001 **Tel** *(0562) 223 1515* **Fax** *(0562) 223 1516* **Rooms** *102*

Set in elegant Mughal-style gardens with pavilions and pools, every room in this luxurious spa-hotel, run by the Oberoi Group, offers views of the Taj Mahal, which is just a short distance away. The hotel also provides golf cars for trips to the monument. **www.oberoihotels.com**

AGRA Welcomgroup Maurya Sheraton

Fatehbad Rd, Taj Ganj, 282 001 **Tel** *(0562) 33 1701* **Fax** *(0562) 33* **Rooms** *285*

Recipient of the Agha Khan award for architecture, this imaginatively designed hotel has a modern exterior, Mughal-style decor and immaculate rooms. A luxury business hotel, there is an impressive range of facilities, including two bars, three restaurants (one 24-hour) and even a private butler service for some suites. **www.itcwelcomgroup.in**

ALMORA Kalmatia Sangam Himalaya Resort

Kalimat Estate, PO 002, 263 601 **Tel** *(05962) 23 1572* **Fax** *(05962) 23 1572* **Rooms** *9*

This resort offers nine cottages set on a pretty hillside. Designed in Colonial style with Kumaoni touches, the cottages are constructed with an eye for comfort, elegance and taste. The tariff includes meals. During winter, the restaurant and all cottages are well heated. Yoga and meditation courses offered. **www.kalmatia-sangam.com**

ALLAHABAD Hotel Kanha Shyam

Civil Lines, 211 001 **Tel** *(0532) 560 123* **Fax** *(0532) 560 123* **Rooms** *85*

Located in the Raj-era Civil Lines area with its broad avenues, this modern, well-run hotel is Allahabad's finest. Built in 1997 by the Government of India, it has redefined luxury by renovating rooms to suit discriminating tastes. Situated in the hub of the city, a stay at Kanha Shyam is a memorable experience. **www.kanhashyam.com**

DEHRA DUN Best Western Hotel Madhuban

97 Rajpur Rd, 248 001 **Tel** *(0135) 274 9990* **Fax** *(0135) 274 6496* **Rooms** *60*

One of Dehra Dun's best, this centrally air-conditioned hotel has well-appointed, spacious rooms with modern amenities, a mini golf course and a pretty garden. It is located near the market place and provides good parking space. The restaurant is very popular. **www.hotelmadhuban.com**

KANPUR The Landmark

10 Somdatt Plaza, The Mall, 208 002 **Tel** *(0512) 230 5305* **Fax** *(0512) 230 6291* **Rooms** *125*

Hotel Landmark is a picture of modern elegance with especially beautiful ceilings. The views of the holy Ganges river are breathtaking. The atmosphere is warm and relaxed, embracing the uniqueness of the local culture. **www.thehotellandmark.com**

LUCKNOW Clarks Avadh

8 MG Marg, 226001 **Tel** *(0522) 262 0131* **Fax** *(0522) 261 6507* **Rooms** *98*

Amid the grandeur of the erstwhile City of Nawabs, Hotel Clarks Avadh offers you more than just a room. The royal kitchen with its speciality Avadhi cuisine invites you to experience the varied delights of Nawabi culture. Hotel rooms provide spectacular views of the city. **www.hotelclarks.com**

LUCKNOW Piccadily

Alambagh, Kanpur Rd, 226 001 **Tel** *(0522) 409 6000* **Fax** *(0522) 409 6029* **Rooms** *110*

Piccadily, one of the biggest five-star hotels in Lucknow, is conveniently located near the airport and is just 8 km (5 miles) from Hazratganj, the heart of the town. Seven unique meeting spaces that can accommodate up to 1,000 guests make Piccadily a perfect place for meetings and conferences. **www.piccadilylucknow.com**

LUCKNOW Taj Residency

Vipin Khand, Gomti Nagar, 226 010 **Tel** *(0522) 239 3939* **Fax** *(0522) 239 2282* **Rooms** *110*

Lucknow's top hotel is housed in a gracious Colonial-style building topped by a large dome. It has luxurious rooms, sprawling lawns and a restaurant serving superb Avadhi cuisine. The bar, Mehfil, with live ghazal sung performances in the evenings, is a great place to relax with friends. **www.tajhotels.com**

MUSSOORIE Kasmanda Palace Hotel

The Mall Rd, 248 179 **Tel** *(0135) 263 2424* **Fax** *(0135) 263 0007* **Rooms** *24*

This large white bungalow, built in 1836 as a summer retreat for the royal family of Kasmanda, has cosy interiors decorated with family photographs and curios. Antique furniture adorns the large rooms, reminding guests of the hotel's regal past. **www.welcomeheritagehotel.com**

NAINITAL The Palace Belvedere

Awagarh Estate, Mallital, 263 001 **Tel** *(05942) 23 5082* **Fax** *(05942) 23 7434* **Rooms** *22*

Formerly the palace of the Raja of Awagarh, this resplendent hotel boasts spacious rooms and suites that have an old-world charm. Guests are also treated to panoramic views of the famous Naini lake, which is popular as a place of meditation. Good service. **www.welcomheritage.com**

NAUKUCHIATAL The Lake Resort

Naukuchiatal, 263 601 **Tel** *(05942) 24 7415* **Rooms** *24*

This secluded lakeside resort with large lawns has clean, comfortable and tastefully decorated rooms. Great for bird-watching. The resort has its own boats, which guests can use for fishing expeditions. Horse riding is also available for the adventurous. **lakeresort@sancharnet.in**

RISHIKESH High Banks Peasant Cottage

Tapovan, 249 201 **Tel** *(0135) 243 3478* **Fax** *(0135) 43 1654* **Rooms** *3*

Situated on the outskirts of Rishikesh, this is the best choice for budget tourists. The guest house has clean rooms with attached baths and hot water. Each room has a balcony overlooking the gardens and forest, the Ganges and the town. Nature walks are a good option. **himalayas@vsnl.com**

RISHIKESH Hotel Ganga Kinare

16 Veerbhadra Rd, 249 201 **Tel** *(0135) 243 1658* **Rooms** *38*

At the riverside Hotel Ganga Kinare guests can view the evening *aarti* (worship) or take a dip in the sacred Ganges. This modern multi-storeyed hotel offers great views of the river. The 24-hour coffee shop is well-stocked with numerous blends and varieties of coffee that are served with style. **hotelgangakinare@hotmail.com**

TEHRI GARHWAL The Glass House on the Ganges

23rd Milestone, Rishikesh-Badrinath Rd, 249 303 **Tel** *(01378) 26 9224, 26 9218* **Rooms** *12*

Located beside a secluded sandy beach on the banks of the Ganges, this delightful hotel offers spectacular views, log fires and riverside barbecues. Set in a litchi and mango orchard, with a garden full of tropical plants, rare birds and butterflies, this is one of the most idyllic hotels in the region. **www.nemranahotels.com**

TEHRI GARHWAL Ananda – in the Himalayas

Narendra Nagar, 249 175 **Tel** *(01378) 22 7500* **Fax** *(01378) 22 7550* **Rooms** *75*

This is a luxurious spa-resort set in a tranquil 40-ha (100-acre) estate that once belonged to the Maharaja of Tehri Garhwal. It offers meditation, yogic and Ayurvedic treatments and other forms of holistic healing. Its restaurant serves modern and organic Indian, Asian and Western cuisine. **www.anandaspa.com**

VARANASI Scindia Guest House

Scindia Ghat, Chowk, 221 001 **Tel** *(0542) 242 0319* **Rooms** *21*

Located right on the riverfront, this guesthouse has small and simple but clean rooms, helpful, friendly staff and great views from its terrace and balconies. The food is home-cooked and excellent. The guesthouse undoubtedly offers a comfortable stay at a reasonable price. **www.scindiahouse.com**

VARANASI Hotel Ganges View

Asi Ghat, 221 005 **Tel** *(0542) 231 3218* **Rooms** *11*

Guests are required to take off their shoes upon entering this lovely Colonial lodge at the edge of the Ganges. This hotel has attractively furnished rooms and a large terrace. Straw mats and colourful Indian throws add character to the bedrooms. The vegetarian food is excellent. The top-floor rooms are best.

VARANASI Clarks Varanasi

The Mall, Cantonment, 221 002 **Tel** *(0542) 250 1011* **Fax** *(0542) 250 2736* **Rooms** *113*

Varanasi's oldest hotel has spacious rooms, inviting verandahs and a tree-shaded swimming pool. It also organises cultural shows and yoga lessons at the Amrit Rao Haveli by the river. All rooms have individually controlled air conditioning, attached bathrooms, satellite television and free in-house movies. **www.clarkshotels.com**

Key to Price Guide *see p690* **Key to Symbols** *see back cover flap*

VARANASI Taj Ganges

Nadesar Palace Ground, 221 002 **Tel** *(0542) 250 3001* **Fax** *(0542) 250 1343* **Rooms** *130*

Taj Ganges is a luxury hotel with all modern facilities, including tennis courts, yoga classes and massage. The Indian restaurant hosts classical music and dance performances in the evenings. The hotel is popular with travellers visiting the Buddhist pilgrimage centre and the famous temples of Varanasi. **www.tajhotels.com**

BIHAR & JHARKHAND

BODH GAYA Mahayana Guest House

PO Box 04, 824 231 **Tel** *(0631) 220 0756* **Fax** *(0631) 220 0676* **Rooms** *73*

Run by a Tibetan monastery, this hotel has pleasant rooms, airy courtyards and a spacious lobby where monks often hold court. The Dalai Lama stayed here during his 1998 visit. Facilities such as a non-smoking room, women's guest room, coffee shop, gift shop, restaurant and meeting rooms are also provided. **mahayanag@yahoo.com**

BODH GAYA Hotel Lotus Nikko

Near Archeological Museum, 824 231 **Tel** *(0631) 220 0700* **Fax** *(0631) 220 0788* **Rooms** *32*

At walking distance from the Mahabodhi Temple, this pleasant hotel has comfortable rooms and an attractive garden. Hotel Lotus Nikko also has all amenities, facilities and levels of comfort guests would expect from a hotel of this class, which makes it popular with international travellers. **lotus.nikk.hotels@vsnl.net**

PATNA Republic

Lauriya Bagh, Exhibition Rd, 800 001 **Tel** *(0612) 232 0021* **Fax** *(0612) 232 1024* **Rooms** *35*

The attractions of this modest hotel include a multi-cuisine restaurant, friendly service, conference facilities and a roof garden. The vegetarian food is particularly good. The hotel offers a special discount for group bookings. Authorised money-changing facilities are also available. **www.biharonline.com**

PATNA Hotel Chanakya & Towers

R-Block, Beerchand Patel Marg, 800 001 **Tel** *(0612) 222 3141* **Fax** *(0612) 222 0598* **Rooms** *90*

This hotel has tastefully furnished rooms and suites, a multi-cuisine restaurant and conference facilities. Situated in the centre of the city, within 1 km (half a mile) of the railway station, this is a convenient place to stay. Patna airport is only ten minutes away. **www.hotelchanakyapatna.com**

PATNA Maurya Patna

South Gandhi Maidan, 800 001 **Tel** *(0612) 220 3040* **Fax** *(0612) 220 3060* **Rooms** *75*

The city's best hotel, this establishment offers all standard modern facilities, and has a very helpful information desk. It is located on prime property in the heart of commercial Patna, giving it a definitive advantage over other choices in Patna. **maurya@maurya.com**

RAJGIR Indo Hokke Hotel

Nalanda Distt, 803 116 **Tel** *(06119) 255 245* **Fax** *(06119) 255 231* **Rooms** *26*

Built to attract well-heeled Buddhist pilgrim-tourists, this hotel's special features include Japanese- and Western-style prayer rooms, a bathhouse, a prayer hall, a restaurant that serves Japanese food and an imposing tower reminiscent of ancient Buddhist stupas. **www.theroyalresidency.com**

RANCHI Hotel Yuvraj Palace

Doranda, 834 002 **Tel** *(0651) 248 0326* **Fax** *(0651) 248 0328* **Rooms** *35*

This comfortable hotel, with efficient, friendly staff, is located in the leafy Doranda quarter of this industrial town. It has a multi-cuisine restaurant and conference facilities. The lobby is elegant, with marble flooring, comfortable sofas, and walls adorned with beautiful Jaisalmer paintings. **www.hotelyuvrajpalace.com**

MADHYA PRADESH & CHHATTISGARH

BANDHAVGARH NATIONAL PARK White Tiger Forest Lodge

Village Tala, Distt Umaria, 484 661 **Tel** *(07627) 265 308* **Fax** *(07627) 265 366* **Rooms** *38*

Located in the vicinity of the world famous Bandhavgarh National Park, this hotel-lodge is a dream abode for wildlife enthusiasts. Tiger safaris and elephant rides are offered. Tired adventurers can dine at the multi-cuisine restaurant and enjoy the offerings of a well-stocked bar. **www.mptourism.com**

BANDHAVGARH NATIONAL PARK Mahua Kothi

Village Tala, Distt Umaria, 484 661 **Tel** *(07627) 265 402* **Rooms** *12*

Owned by Taj Hotels and CC Africa, this safari lodge is built in the vernacular style of central India. Its 12 luxurious cottage suites have stone flooring, local textile furnishings and handmade sroof tiles. Service is impeccable. Ancestral cooking and dining customs add to make your stay a charming experience. **www.tajhotels.com**

BHOPAL Jehan Numa Palace

157 Shamla Hills, 462 013 **Tel** *(0755) 266 1100* **Fax** *(0755) 266 1720* **Rooms** *98*

Located on the slopes of Shamla hills, this heritage hotel is a fusion of Colonial and Classical European architecture. Service is discreet and excellent, and guests can expect to be thoroughly pampered. Attractions include a garden barbecue and traditional massage. **www.hoteljehanumapalace.com**

BHOPAL Welcomheritage Noor-us-Sabah Palace

VIP Rd, Koh-e-Fiza, 462 001 **Tel** *(0755) 422 3333* **Fax** *(0755) 422 7777* **Rooms** *67*

Literally, "The Light of the Day", this elegant palace is now a heritage hotel with modern facilities. It has well-appointed suites and rooms, with separate balconies offering majestic views of the famous Bhopal Lake. Dynasty, its specialty Chinese restaurant, is a must-visit. **www.noorussabahpalace.com**

GWALIOR Taj Usha Kiran Palace

Jayendraganj, Lashkar, 474 009 **Tel** *(0751) 244 4000* **Fax** *(0751) 244 4018* **Rooms** *28*

A government approved heritage hotel, Taj Usha Kiran Palace was the palace of the erstwhile Scindia rulers and has now been converted into one of the finest hotels in Gwalior. It is an architectural jewel with an enchanting ambience, intricate stone carvings and sprawling lawns. **www.tajhotels.com**

INDORE Sayaji Hotel

H–1 Scheme 54, Vijay Nagar, 452 010 **Tel** *(0731) 400 6666* **Fax** *(0731) 400 3131* **Rooms** *194*

Sayaji Hotel reflects the city's spirit in a harmonious blend of tradition and contemporary sophistication. With exquisite interiors and fine cuisine, what truly sets it apart from other business hotels are its warm service, attention to detail and ability to cater to all kinds of business needs. **www.sayajihotels.com**

KANHA NATIONAL PARK Baghira Log Huts

Kisli, Kanha, 481661 **Tel** *(07649) 277 227* **Rooms** *16*

A jungle lodge, Baghira Log Huts in Kisli, located on the fringes of Kanha National Park, is a lively group of cottages with an attached bar and restaurant. Perfect for weekend getaways, it is a popular tourist attraction, drawing many tourists visiting Kanha National Park. **www.mptourism.com**

KANHA NATIONAL PARK Kipling Camp

Mocha Village, Mandla, 481768 **Tel** *(07649) 277 218* **Fax** *(07649) 277 219* **Rooms** *20*

Blending in with the surrounding sanctuary, the cottages at Kipling Camp have two to four rooms each, with tiled roofs, whitewashed walls and verandahs. Attractions include a well-stocked library, excellent home-cooked food and guided tours around the park. **www.kiplingcamp.com**

KHAJURAHO Taj Chandela

Khajuraho, District Chatarpur, 471606 **Tel** *(07686) 272 355* **Fax** *(07686) 272 365* **Rooms** *94*

A haven of peace and tranquillity, Taj Chandela offers easy access to the world-famous Khajuraho temples, Panna National Park and Tiger Reserve. Tucked snugly amid 4 ha (11 acres) of beautifully landscaped gardens, this hotel offers an array of modern comforts. **www.tajhotels.com**

MAHESHWAR Ahilya

Ahilya Fort, Maheshwar, 451 224 **Tel** *(07283) 27 3329* **Fax** *(07283) 27 3203* **Rooms** *14*

A stay at Ahilya Fort is an experience straight out of the 18th century. Situated near the banks of the sacred Narmada river, Ahilya Fort was the capital of one of India's celebrated women rulers, Ahilya Bai Holkar. Her fortress, virtually unchanged, has been converted into a guest residence. **www.ahilyafort.com**

ORCHHA Sheesh Mahal

Orchha, Tikamgarh Distt, 472 246 **Tel** *(07680) 25 2624* **Fax** *(07680) 25 2624* **Rooms** *8*

One of Orchha's most appealing palaces, the Sheesh Mahal has spacious rooms with good views. It is located next to Jahangiri Mahal and Raj Mahal, which is famous for its paintings. The MP State Tourism Development Corporation (MPSTDC) has recently refurbished the resort making it a tourist hot spot. **www.mptourism.com**

PACHMARHI Glen View

Near Raj Bhavan, 461 881 **Tel** *(07578) 252 533* **Fax** *(07578) 252 434* **Rooms** *21*

This is the MP State Tourism Development Corporation's (MPSTDC) star property in Pachmarhi. Located within 2 km (1 mile) of the marketplace, it is by far the best-looking hotel in this hill station, with beautiful heritage-style interiors and lush green lawns. **www.mptourism.com**

ORCHHA Betwa Cottages

Kanchanghat, Tikamgarh, 470 046 **Tel** *(07680) 252 618* **Rooms** *18*

A government approved accommodation, these charming cottages stand on the banks of the Betwa river and face some of Orchha's loveliest monuments. Each cottage has its own garden. The restaurant offers good Indian, Continental and Chinese cuisine. There is also a well-stocked bar. **mpstdc@vsnl.com**.

RAIPUR Babylon International

VIP Rd, Rajiv Gandhi Marg,, 492 006 **Tel** *(0771) 409 3101* **Fax** *(0771) 409 3100* **Rooms** *80*

A lavish hotel, Babylon International is located on the outskirts of Raipur. Check in and discover a world of luxury, style and comfort. It combines traditional hospitality and modern sophistication. The best part is that it is located just ten minutes away from Raipur airport. **www.hotelbabylon.com**

Key to Price Guide *see p690* **Key to Symbols** *see back cover flap*

UJJAIN Surana Palace
23 GDC Rd, Dussehra Maidan, 456 001 **Tel** *(0734) 253 0045* **Rooms** *22*

This well-managed hotel offers large, comfortable rooms as well as luxury suites. It is set in a well-tended garden with all modern amenities. A very cost effective option that caters to both business and pleasure. It is also easily accessible from the railway station. **suranaujn@satyam.net.in**

KOLKATA

KOLKATA Fairlawn Hotel Pvt Ltd
13/A Sudder Street, 700 016 **Tel** *(033) 2252 1510* **Fax** *(033) 2252 1835* **Rooms** *20*

Located in the most cosmopolitan and vibrant part of the city, the Fairlawn is a Colonial mansion converted by its owners into a charming hotel. Though it lacks many modern conveniences, most of the guests come here for its relaxed old-world ambience and warm hospitality. A full English breakfast is served. **www.fairlawnhotel.com**

KOLKATA Hotel Victerrace International
1B Gorky Terrace, 700 017 **Tel** *(033) 2280 0713* **Fax** *(033) 2283 2753* **Rooms** *53*

Hotel Victerrace International is an impressive four-storey building. The hotel has a noise-free zone even though it is situated in the heart of the city's business and cultural centre. There is plenty of parking space within the premises. Currently under renovation. **www.hotelvicterrace.com**

KOLKATA The Astor Hotel
15 Shakespeare Sarani, 700 071 **Tel** *(033) 2282 9957* **Fax** *(033) 2282 7430* **Rooms** *32*

This hotel, located in the heart of the city, is housed in a 100-year-old building that has been given heritage status. Its red and white brick exterior is typical of Kolkata's Victorian architecture. The Colonial ambience extends to the rooms. Well-known for its warmth and hospitality. **www.astorkolkata.com**

KOLKATA Lytton Hotel
14 Sudder Street, 700 016 **Tel** *(033) 2249 1875* **Fax** *(033) 2249 1747* **Rooms** *80*

Located in the heart of the city, this tastefully decorated hotel has comfortable rooms and also offers business facilities. Lytton Hotel's main attraction is its proximity to the business district and to tourist destinations such as the Victoria Memorial, Indian Museum and New Market. **www.lyttonhotelindia.com**

KOLKATA Tollygunge Club
120 Deshapran Sasmal Rd, 700 033 **Tel** *(033) 2473 4539* **Fax** *(033) 2473 1903* **Rooms** *66*

Spread over 40 ha (100 acres) on the outskirts of Kolkata, the club boasts an 18-hole golf course, spacious rooms and guest cottages with courteous, if somewhat slow service. The hotel is currently going through a programme of renovation with many rooms newly appointed. **www.tollygungeclub.org**

KOLKATA Hyatt Regency
JA-1 Sector 3, Salt Lake City, 700 098 **Tel** *(033) 2335 1234* **Fax** *(033) 2335 1235* **Rooms** *235*

Hyatt Regency Kolkata is a premium business hotel, contemporary in design with innovative hospitality concepts and classic standards of service and excellence. This modern hotel's 235 technologically equipped guest rooms and suites are amongst the largest in Kolkata. Bathrooms are luxurious. **www.kolkata.regency.hyatt.com**

KOLKATA The Kenilworth
1 & 2 Little Russell Street, 700 021 **Tel** *(033) 2282 3939* **Fax** *(033) 2282 5136* **Rooms** *105*

This quiet hotel has an elegant charm and comfortable rooms. It has excellent breakfast and lunch buffets, and a cosy English-style pub, complete with a red London phone booth. As a hotel with a history, The Kenilworth retains its Colonial standards of good service and friendly staff. **www.kenilworthhotels.com**

KOLKATA Oberoi Grand
15 Jawaharlal Nehru Rd, 700 013 **Tel** *(033) 2249 2323* **Fax** *(033) 2249 9427* **Rooms** *213*

This 125-year old *Grand Dame* of Kolkata is an institution in the city. Housed in an elegant Victorian building, the Oberoi Grand remains a class apart with its charming interiors, rooms with four-poster beds, an inviting tea lounge and outstanding restaurants. **www.oberoihotels.com**

KOLKATA The Park
17 Park Street, 700 016 **Tel** *(033) 2249 9000* **Fax** *(033) 2249 4000* **Rooms** *174*

The Park Kolkata has 150 luxurious rooms and 24 lavishly furnished deluxe rooms and suites. Service is efficient and of global standards. The high-energy nightclub, Tantra, is a popular place for Kolkata's younger set. Extensive facilities at the gym and the luxury spa are added attractions. **www.parkhotels.com**

KOLKATA Sonar Bangla Sheraton
1 JBS Halden Avenue, 700 046 **Tel** *(033) 2345 4545* **Fax** *(033) 2345 4455* **Rooms** *238*

Although the Sonar Bangla Sheraton has a sleek, modern design, it maintains its traditional and cultural values. This five-star hotel's speciality is its serene and tranquil ambience that is a rarity in any city hotel. Committed to eco-tourism, the hotel maintains lush green lawns with over 1,200 trees. **www.itcwelcomgroup.in**

KOLKATA Taj Bengal

34-B Belvedere Rd, Alipore, 700 027 **Tel** *(033) 2223 3939* **Fax** *(033) 2223 1766* **Rooms** *229*

Winner of the Best Luxury Hotel, Eastern Region 1998 National Award, the Taj Bengal is decorated with local and contemporary furnishings. An imposing palatial-style atrium lobby and a vertical garden make this the most beautiful hotel in this part of the world. **www.tajhotels.com**

WEST BENGAL & SIKKIM

DARJEELING Glenburn Tea Estate

Glenburn Tea Estate, 734 101 **Tel** *(033) 2288 5630* **Fax** *(033) 2288 3581* **Rooms** *4*

Nature walks and tours of tea plantations are some of the services offered by this estate. Price includes food and treks. With acres of beautiful forests to explore and numerous in-house activities, a week-long stay at the Glenburn Tea State is a rejuvenating experience. **www.glenburnteaestate.com**

DARJEELING Cedar Inn

Jalapahar Rd, 734 101 **Tel** *(0354) 225 4446* **Fax** *(0354) 225 6764* **Rooms** *29*

There are great views of Mount Kanchenzonga from this Victorian Gothic-style hotel. The cosy wood-panelled interiors reflect a commitment to a level of service reminiscent of an age more gracious and less hurried than today's. Houses a well-stocked library on this region's colourful culture. **www.cedarinnindia.com**

DARJEELING Windamere Hotel

Observatory Hill, 734 101 **Tel** *(0354) 225 4041* **Fax** *(0354) 225 4043* **Rooms** *38*

A relic of the Raj, this delightful family-run hotel, established in the 19th century, is furnished in elegant Colonial style, with coal fires and hot-water bottles in the rooms. It serves wholesome food and a string quartet serenades guests during dinner. **www.windamerehotel.com**

GANGTOK Hotel Tashi Delek

MG Marg, 737 101 **Tel** *(03592) 20 2991* **Fax** *(03592) 20 2362* **Rooms** *46*

Located near Mount Kanchendzonga in Gangtok, Hotel Tashi Delek has grand, royal surroundings with spectacular sunrises and sunsets. It offers clean, comfortable and beautifully decorated rooms, with modern facilities. A multi-cuisine restaurant, café and bar add to its appeal. **www.hoteltashidelek.com**

GANGTOK Hotel Tibet

Paljor Stadium Rd, 737 101 **Tel** *(03592) 20 2523* **Fax** *(03592) 22 6233* **Rooms** *40*

With its colourful Tibetan decor, excellent restaurant and bar and friendly atmosphere, this hotel is deservedly popular. The staff are very helpful in planning local itineraries for their guests. It also boasts a currency exchange counter. Baths are attached, with running hot and cold water. **www.sikkiminfo.net/hoteltibet**

GANGTOK Netuk House

Tibet Rd, 737 101 **Tel** *(03592) 22 6778* **Fax** *(03592) 22 6778* **Rooms** *12*

Buddhist prayer flags flutter above this gorgeously situated and well-run family guesthouse with a genuine Sikkimese flavour. Guest rooms are simple but pleasing. Carefully prepared traditional four-course Sikkimese meals are served in the dining room. There is also a good bar. **slg_netuk@sancharnet.in**

GANGTOK The Chumbi Residency

Tibet Rd, 737 101 **Tel** *(03592) 22 6618* **Fax** *(03592) 22 6620* **Rooms** *26*

Situated in the heart of Gangtok, this is a modern four-storey hotel located on the historic Silk Route to Tibet. The Chumbi Residency offers very comfortable accommodation. The high standards of traditional Sikkimese hospitality are reflected in the warmth and care shown to guests. **www.chumbiresidency.com**

GANGTOK Nor-Khill Hotel

Paljior Stadium Rd, 737 101 **Tel** *(03592) 20 5637* **Fax** *(03592) 20 5639* **Rooms** *32*

This "Mansion of Jewels" (*Nor*: jewel, *Khill*: mansion) was once the royal guesthouse of the Chogyal dynasty, the former rulers of Sikkim. The hotel is set in a lovely garden and has spacious rooms with views of Mount Kanchendzonga. Welcoming staff add to the gracious atmosphere. **www.elginhotels.com**

KALIMPONG Himalayan Hotel

Upper Cart Rd, 734 301 **Tel** *(03552) 25 5248* **Fax** *(03552) 25 5122* **Rooms** *16*

This heritage hotel is filled with fascinating photographs and Tibetan and Bhutanese art, and has a garden displaying Himalayan flora. It also offers excellent views of Kanchendzonga. Ideal base for a trek in the eastern Himalayas, or for a relaxed holiday in this beautiful region. **www.himalayanhotel.biz**

SHANTINIKETAN Mark & Meadows

Sriniketan Rd, Distt Birbhum, 731 204 **Tel** *(03463) 26 4870* **Fax** *(03463) 26 4870* **Rooms** *32*

Spread over landscaped grounds, the little red-tiled cottages that make up the Mark and Meadows accommodation are all well-appointed and air-conditioned. The multi-cuisine restaurant offers a delectable array of authentic Bengali, North Indian, delicious Tandoori and exquisite Chinese and Continental cuisine. **www.markandmeadows.com**

Key to Price Guide *see p690* **Key to Symbols** *see back cover flap*

SILIGURI Hotel Cindrella

Sevoke Rd, 3rd Mile, 734 401 **Tel** *(0353) 254 7136* **Fax** *(0353) 243 0615* **Rooms** *42*

Comfortable rooms, efficient service and Internet facilities make this Siliguri's best hotel. The in-house restaurant serves only vegetarian food and will make up packed lunches for guests. The hotel's billiards room and health club are added attractions. **www.cindrellahotels.com**

SUNDERBANS Sajnekhali Tourist Lodge

PO Pakhiralay, PS Gosaba, 743 379 **Tel** *(03218) 236560* **Rooms** *30*

This lodge, which runs on solar energy, has basic accommodation, with meals served in a dining hall. It also has a watchtower and a crocodile pool. The standard rooms are non air-conditioned. Guests can visit the dense forests and verdant green stretches and enjoy the wildlife.

ORISSA

BHUBANESWAR Mayfair Lagoon

8-B Jayadev Vihar, 751 013 **Tel** *(0674) 236 0101* **Fax** *(0674) 236 0236* **Rooms** *70*

This elegant low-rise hotel has a lovely landscaped garden, a lake and clean tile-roofed cottages for guests. It also has excellent restaurants, a pool and a shopping arcade. Located in the heart of Bhubaneswar, it is only a short walk from the best of the city's entertainment centres. **www.mayfairhotels.com**

BHUBANESWAR The Oberoi

CB-1 Nayapalli, 751 013 **Tel** *(0674) 30 1010* **Fax** *(0674) 30 1302* **Rooms** *70*

The Oberoi is a part of the internationally recognised Oberoi Group. The classic ambience of Orissa's rich culture is recreated in this hotel. Everything here, from the temple-inspired architecture to its restaurants, has a touch of class. It also has tennis courts and a swimming pool. **www.oberoihotels.com**

CHILIKA LAKE Barkul Panthnivas

Barkul, Balugaon, 752 030 **Tel** *(06756) 20 488* **Rooms** *25*

Situated on the banks of Chilika Lake, this modest hotel offers its guests fresh seafood, yatching and speed boat excursions. Despite offering only basic facilities in the rooms, Barkul Panthnivas is a hot favourite amongst travel enthusiasts. Guided tours are also available. **www.orissa-tourism.com**

GOPALPUR-ON-SEA The Oberoi Palm Beach

Gopalpur-on-Sea, Ganjam, 761 002 **Tel** *(0680) 28 2021, 28 2023* **Fax** *(0680) 28 2300* **Rooms** *18*

The Oberoi Palm Beach is situated on one of the finest beaches in India with most of its rooms overlooking the Bay of Bengal. It is only 17 km (11 miles) from the railway station and downtown area, and a little more from the airport. It has beautifully kept gardens, with a mini zoo for children. **www.oberoihotels.com**

KONARK Yatri Nivas

AT/PO Konark, 752 111 **Tel** *(06758) 23 6820* **Fax** *(06758) 23 6821* **Rooms** *18*

The best accommodation available at Konark is run by the state tourism department. It is clean, safe and moderately priced. A great bargain for a short stay as it is situated right next to the Sun Temple. Cottages available for rent are dotted over a lush garden. Both air-conditioned and cheaper non air-conditioned rooms are available.

PURI Toshali Sands

Ethnic Village Resort, Konark Marin Drive, 752 002 **Tel** *(06752) 23 571* **Fax** *(06752) 23 899* **Rooms** *104*

Overlooking the Balukhanda reserve forest, and sprawling across 12 ha (30 acres) of lush grounds, this hotel offers cottages with modern amenities and a soothing ambience. Enjoy a rejuvenating massage at the in-house parlour. There is also a host of indoor and outdoor activities. **tsands@sancharnet.in**

PURI Mayfair Beach Resort

Chakratirtha Rd, 752 002 **Tel** *(06752) 22 7800* **Fax** *(06752) 22 4242* **Rooms** *33*

This imaginatively designed resort has comfortable rooms, each with its own patio. Many of the rooms have sea views. Other attractions include a good pool and fresh seafood on offer in the restaurant. A relaxing spot to enjoy the untamed beauty of the nearby beach. **www.mayfairhotels.com**

ASSAM & THE NORTH EAST

AGARTALA Hotel Rajarshi

Governor's House, near Circuit House, 799 006 **Tel** *(0381) 220 1034* **Fax** *(0381) 220 7050* **Rooms** *17*

The Hotel Rajarshi is ideally located close to the main market and the forest park. The hotel is spacious and has good security arrangements. The lush lawn is an ideal retreat in the evening. The exquisitely designed rooms come equipped with modern amenities, although only some are air-conditioned. **http://tripura.nic.in/accommo.htm**

AGARTALA Royal Guest House

Palace Compound, West Gate,799 001 **Tel** *(0381) 22 5652* **Fax** *(0381) 22 4958* **Rooms** *34*

Tucked away in one of the streets leading to the former maharaja's palace, this guesthouse has large rooms, and serves good Indian and Chinese food. The nearest airport is a mere 8 km (5 miles) away. The verdant, natural surroundings offer a rejuvenating experience. **http://westtripura.gov.in/tripuratourism.htm**

AIZAWL Tourist Lodge

Chaltlang, Aizawl, 796 017 **Tel** *(0389) 234 1083* **Rooms** *41*

Clean and reasonably priced, this lodge is run by the state tourism department and offers pleasing views and a good restaurant. It has basic facilities like TV, phone and room service and is conveniently located close to the markets. Situated on a high ridge surrounded by deep valleys, it is also a good retreat for those looking for fresh air and tranquility.

GUWAHATI Hotel Brahmaputra Ashok

MG Rd, 781 001 **Tel** *(0361) 260 2281* **Fax** *(0361) 260 2289* **Rooms** *31*

Situated on the banks of the Brahmaputra river, overlooking the Umananda riverine island, Hotel Brahmaputra Ashok has a peaceful ambience. Built in traditional Assamese style with bamboo and cane furnishings, it offers all modern amenities. The restaurant and coffee shop are good. **www.hoteldynastyindia.com**

GUWAHATI Hotel Dynasty

Lakhotia, Guwahati-1, 781 001 **Tel** *(0361) 251 6021* **Fax** *(0361) 251 4112* **Rooms** *76*

Located close to the city market, this hotel has clean and comfortable rooms, with pleasant decor and great ambience. It stands out because of the greenery in and around the area. This is often the preferred choice for visiting dignitaries and important guests to the city. **www.hoteldynastyindia.com**

IMPHAL Hotel Anand Continental

Khoyathong Rd, Imphal **Tel** *(0385) 244 9422* **Fax** *(0385) 224 0107* **Rooms** *30*

This hotel situated in the heart of town has easy access to public modes of transport and market areas. It is a modern building with comfortable rooms. The multi-cuisine restaurant serves sumptuous Manipuri food on special request. **http://manipur.nic.in/tourism.htm**

ITANAGAR Hotel Donyi Polo Ashok

C- Sector, 791 111 **Tel** *(0360) 221 2626* **Fax** *(0360) 221 2611* **Rooms** *20*

Despite its location close to the city centre, this hotel is a tranquil spot with a hillside location. Hotel Donyi Polo Ashok has comfortable rooms, some air conditioned. Guides are available for sightseeing and local folk dances can be arranged on request. **www.ashokgroup.com**

KAZIRANGA NATIONAL PARK Wild Grass Resort

Bochagaon, 785 109 **Tel** *(03776) 262 085* **Rooms** *19*

This attractive resort at the edge of the Kaziranga National Park gives guests plenty of opportunity to enjoy elephant safaris, bird-watching, walks in the forest and visits to the nearby tribal villages with specially trained local guides. Cultural programmes are also organised by local troupes. **www.oldassam.com**

KOHIMA Hotel Japhu

PR Hills, 797 001 **Tel** *(0370) 224 0211* **Fax** *0370) 224 3439* **Rooms** *26*

Located on a hilltop, this hotel provides great views of the hills around Kohima. Rooms are large and spacious and come with heaters during the winter. The building has wood panelling and Naga artifacts. Boutiques and craft shops are close by. **www.northeastindiatravel.com**

SHILLONG Hotel Pinewood

Rits Rd, European ward, 793 001 **Tel** *(0364) 222 3116* **Fax** *(0364) 222 4176* **Rooms** *40*

This delightful Raj-era hotel, with mock-Tudor gables and fireplaces in each room, is located close to the centre of town and Ward Lake. The rooms and cottages are spacious and comfortable. The lovely garden is a great place to sit and enjoy the green surroundings. **www.meghalayatourism.in**

SHILLONG Hotel Polo Towers

Polo Grounds, 793 001 **Tel** *(0364) 222 2341* **Fax** *(0364) 222 0090* **Rooms** *50*

A 5-minute walk from the picturesque Golf Course, Hotel Polo Towers is also close to the main market. A modern and efficient hotel, it has the added advantage of a weekend discotheque, Platinum. During the week, guests can enjoy the services of the bar and the multi-cuisine restaurant, Ginger. **www.hotelpolotowers.com**

RAJASTHAN

ALWAR Amanbagh

Village Ajabgarh, Thanagaji, 301 027 **Tel** *(065) 223 3001* **Fax** *(065) 22 3335* **Rooms** *40*

The former hunting preserve of the Alwar kings, bordered by the hilly terrain of the Aravallis and set in a walled compound, Amanbagh is now a super-luxury resort. It offers easy access to local palaces and various other places of interest. **www.amanresorts.com**

Key to Price Guide *see p690* **Key to Symbols** *see back cover flap*

AJMER Mansingh Palace

Vaishali Nagar, 305 001 Tel (0145) 242 5956 Fax (0145) 24 5858 Rooms 54

The ambience of the Mansingh Palace is greatly influenced by the holy and festive environment of the fascinating town of Ajmer. The restaurant, Shesh Mahal, overlooks Ana Sagar Lake. The rooms are decorated with traditional artifacts and yet are very modern. **www.mansinghhotels.com**

BHARATPUR Laxmi Vilas Place

Kakaji Ki Kothi, Old Agra-Jaipur Rd, 321 001 Tel (05644) 22 3523 Fax (05644) 22 5259 Rooms 38

Laxmi Vilas Palace was built in 1887 and converted into a hotel in 1994. Come here to relive the history of Bharatpur and experience the warm hospitality extended by the present generation of royalty living in the palace. Its location offers a variety of daytime sightseeing excursions, which can be arranged in-house. **www.laxmivilas.com**

BIKANER Lallgarh Palace

Lallgarh Complex, 334 001 Tel (0151) 254 0201 Rooms 38

Lallgarh Palace is a genuine example of Indo-Saracenic architecture. Forty elegantly appointed rooms with all modern day comforts and facilities await the traveller. Guests will find exquisite period furniture, magnificent chandeliers and intricate filigree work. **www.lallgarh.com**

BIKANER Gajner Palace Hotel

PO Gajner, Tehsil Kolayat, 334 001 Tel (01534) 25 5064 Rooms 44

This enchanting hotel, with a fairy-tale setting beside a lake, used to be the maharaja of Bikaner's hunting lodge. Surrounded by a forest, it offers comfortable rooms with period flavour, excellent bird-watching opportunities, jeep safaris and friendly service. **www.gajkesri.com**

BUNDI Royal Retreat

Garh Palace, 323 001 Tel (0747) 244 4426 Fax (0747) 244 3263 Rooms 5

Situated in the compounds of Bundi's fort, this resort offers beautiful views of the Aravallis. The ambience is calm and its rooftop restaurant has good vegetarian food. As the name suggets, comfortable accommodation and fine dining are guaranteed here. **royalretreatbundi@yahoo.com**

CHITTORGARH Hotel Castle Bijaipur

Village Post Bijaipur, 311 001 Tel (01472) 24 0099 Rooms 23

This atmospheric feudal castle is located in picturesque, rural Mewar. It organises jeep safaris to nearby villages and forts, fishing trips and folk entertainment in the evenings. The castle offers breathtaking views of the lake and the village around it. **www.castlebijaipur.com**

DEOGARH Deogarh Mahal

PO Deogarh, Rajsamand Distt, 313 331 Tel (02904) 25 2777 Fax (02904) 25 2555 Rooms 46

Deogarh Mahal is a benchmark in heritage hospitality. The comforts of the past and the present are offered with such panache that guests keep coming back for more. The home-grown fruits and vegetables used in the food is another strong point. **www.deogarhmahal.com**

DUNGARPUR Udai Bilas Palace

Udai Bilas Palace, 314 001 Tel (02964) 23 0808 Fax (02964) 23 1008 Rooms 20

Run by the former ruling family who are attentive hosts, this hotel is near a lake and private forest. The Art Deco furniture blends harmoniously with the traditional murals and decorative inlay work. Spacious rooms and suites have modern comforts as well. **www.udaibilaspalace.com**

JAIPUR Raj Vilas

Babaji Mod, Goner Rd, 302 016 Tel (0141) 268 0101 Fax (0141) 268 0202 Rooms 71

A luxury spa-resort run by the Oberoi Group, Raj Vilas has lovely gardens with pools and pavilions, tasteful decor, excellent cuisine and faultless service. Air-conditioned luxury tents with a private garden are intimate and romantic. Round-the-clock butler service is available. **www.oberoihotels.com**

JAIPUR Rambagh Palace

Bhawani Singh Place, 302 005 Tel (0141) 221 1919 Fax (0141) 238 1098 Rooms 95

The "Jewel of Jaipur" as it is fondly called, Rambagh Palace offers rooms including restored suites which were personal chambers of the former maharaja. It is set amid lush gardens and combines princely Rajput decor with modern amenities. Horse-riding is on offer, and the grounds include a polo field. **www.tajhotels.com**

JAIPUR Samode Haveli

Ganga Pole, 302 002 Tel (0141) 263 2370 Fax (0141) 263 1397 Rooms 42

Built over 200 years ago, this gracious mansion has some stunning rooms with original wall paintings and mirrorwork. Jacqueline Kennedy Onasis was probably the first world-renowned dignitary to visit this hotel and there have been many more since. **www.samode.com**

JAISALMER Killa Bhawan

Jaisalmer Fort, 445 Katari Para, 354 001 Tel (02992) 25 1204 Fax (02992) 25 4518 Rooms 7

Expect the epitome of Rajasthani hospitality in this small, well-run hotel. Other attractions include camel and jeep safaris to explore the surrounding countryside. Bright rooms are decorated in vivid shades of crimson and orange. Fine views of the city from the terrace. **www.killabhawan.com**

JAISALMER Narayan Niwas Palace

Malka Prol, 345 001 **Tel** *(02992) 25 2408* **Fax** *(02992) 25 2101* **Rooms** *43*

This hotel is housed in a beautifully carved stone mansion with traditional Rajasthani decor throughout. The rooftop restaurant has wonderful views of Jaisalmer Fort and the surrounding desert. Other attractions include a beauty parlour and folk music peformances. **www.narayanniwas.com**

JAISALMER Gorbandh Palace

1 Tourist Complex, Sam Rd, 345 001 **Tel** *(02992) 25 3801* **Fax** *(02992) 25 3811* **Rooms** *67*

A new hotel with all modern conveniences, Gorbandh Palace is built in the traditional style using carved golden Jaisalmer stone. It has an inviting central courtyard and a good craft and book shop. Enjoy the offerings of the in-house restaurant, which provides traditional Rajasthani and European cuisine. **www.hrhindia.com**

JODHPUR Devi Bhawan

1 Defence Lab Rd, Ratanada Circle, 342 001 **Tel** *(0291) 251 1067* **Fax** *(0291) 251 2215* **Rooms** *14*

Devi Bhawan is one of the most moderately priced hotels in Jodhpur and is run by a friendly young couple. The hotel is in a pleasant garden, and the homely rooms here are spotless and tastefully furnished. A small restaurant serves *thalis* to visitors staying at the hotel. **www.devibhawan.com**

JODHPUR Ajit Bhawan Palace

Near Circuit House, 342 001 **Tel** *(0291) 251 0674* **Fax** *(0291) 261 4451* **Rooms** *60*

This palace hotel has a vintage feel and is decorated with sepia photographs and antiques. Guests can also stay in the rustic cottages set out in the grounds. Some of the best traditional Rajasthani specialities or a wide range of Indian and European delicacies are available in any of the several restaurants. **www.ajitbhawan.com**

JODHPUR Taj Hari Mahal

5 Residency Rd, 342 001 **Tel** *(0291) 243 9700* **Fax** *(0291) 261 4451* **Rooms** *93*

Truly a romantic haven, Taj Hari Mahal is in harmony with Rajasthan's grandeur. Skillfully designed and decorated, the hotel weaves tradition with modern day elegance. On special requests, dinner can be arranged on the sand dunes with wine and Rajasthani musicians to entertain you. **www.tajhotels.com**

KOTA Brijraj Bhawan Place

Civil Lines, 324 001 **Tel** *(0744) 245 0529* **Fax** *(0744) 245 0057* **Rooms** *7*

The erudite former ruler of Kota still lives in a part of this mansion which was once the British Residency. The food is excellent and the ambience regal yet friendly, with royal memorabilia, family souvenirs and wildlife trophies decorating the rooms. **brijraj@datainfosys.net**

KUMBHALGARH Aodhi Hotel

PO. Kelwara, Rajsamand Distt, 313 301 **Tel** *(02954) 24 2341* **Fax** *(02945) 24 2349* **Rooms** *26*

Located just below the great fort, this comfortable hotel, with superb views of the hilly countryside, organises safaris on horseback to view wildlife in the region, and visit tribal villages. Rooms with stone walls give the place a rustic feel. **crs@udaipur.hrhindia.com**

MOUNT ABU Palace Hotel

Bikaner House, Dilwara Rd, 307 501 **Tel** *(02974) 23 8673* **Fax** *(02974) 23 8674* **Rooms** *33*

Built as the summer palace of the ruler of Bikaner in 1894, this comfortably refurbished stately pile has a large garden, grand banquet hall and great period flavour. The hotel has a multi-cuisine restaurant. Services offered include 24-hour room service, a travel desk, outdoor games, and nature walks. **www.rajasthaninfo.org**

NEEMRANA Neemrana Fort Palace

Jaipur-Delhi Highway, Alwar Distt, 301 705 **Tel** *(01494) 24 6006* **Fax** *(01494) 24 6005* **Rooms** *44*

This superbly renovated 15th-century Rajput fort has a series of charming courtyards and a swimming pool on the top floor, as well as a good shop. It is one of India's oldest heritage resorts and has been sensitively restored and reconstructed. The village below has an impressive stepwell. **www.neemranahotels.com**

PUSHKAR Pushkar Palace

Chhoti Basti, Pushkar Lake, 305 022 **Tel** *(0145) 277 3001* **Fax** *(0145) 277 3001* **Rooms** *36*

Stylishly furnished with family antiques, this heritage property's main attraction is its superb location by the lake. It has well-appointed deluxe rooms and suites which overlook the water. Pure vegetarian food is served. Experience the breathtaking views of the sun rising and setting behind the Aravallis range. **www.pushkarpalace.com**

PUSHKAR Pushkar Resorts

Village Ganhera, Motisar Rd, 305 022 **Tel** *(0145) 277 2944* **Fax** *(0145) 277 2946* **Rooms** *44*

With luxurious cottages set amid orchards, this resort offers a golf putting range and camel and jeep safaris. Every room has a mini bar, television with satellite links and telephone with direct dialling facilities. It is family managed and the warm welcome will make your stay an occasion to remember. **www.pushkarresorts.com**

ROHET Rohet Garh

Pali Distt, 346 421 **Tel** *(02936) 26 8231* **Fax** *(02936) 264 9368* **Rooms** *30*

This tranquil fort-hotel, a favourite with authors Bruce Chatwin and William Dalrymple, has delightful owners who help guests explore the nearby villages and their crafts. The hotel is set around a tranquil garden courtyard where tea is served in the afternoon. **www.rohetgarh.com**

Key to Price Guide *see p690* **Key to Symbols** *see back cover flap*

SAMODE Samode Palace

Village Samode, 303 806 **Tel** *(01423) 24 0023* **Fax** *(01423) 24 0013* **Rooms** *42*

This glittering palace, where scenes for the 1984 film *The Far Pavilions* were shot, boasts a spectacular setting and interiors. It also runs a tented camp a short distance from the palace. A fine hotel with consummate standards of modern hospitality, accommodation, services, cuisine and amenities. **www.samode.com**

SARISKA Hotel Sariska Palace

Sariska, 301 022 **Tel** *(0144) 284 1322* **Fax** *(0144) 284 1323* **Rooms** *101*

A former royal hunting lodge, this comfortable hotel also has an Ayurvedic and yoga centre. Each room is furnished in period Victorian style with wood floors. The huge garden overlooks the surrounding hills. Decent food, especially breakfast. **www.sariska.com**

SAWAI MADHOPUR Aman-I-Khas Resort

Sherpur Khilji Village, 322 001 **Tel** *(07462) 25 2052* **Fax** *(07462) 25 2178* **Rooms** *12*

This is a super-luxury jungle resort run by the internationally renowned Aman Resorts. The tents are air-conditioned. The resort operates only when the Ranthambore National Park is open. Jeep safaris are on offer for those keen to look around the wildlife reserve. **www.amanresorts.com**

SAWAI MADHOPUR Sher Bagh

Sherpur Khilji Village, 322 001 **Tel** *(07462) 25 2120* **Fax** *(07462) 25 2119* **Rooms** *12*

All 12 tents in this exclusive camp are stylishly furnished and have attached bathrooms with running hot and cold water. Great food and service. The camp, open from October to March, organizes excursions to the nearby Ranthambore National Park. The boutique, Pugmark, has a range of specially-commissioned merchandise. **www.sherbagh.com**

SHEKHAVATI Hotel Castle Mandawa

Jhunjhunu Distt, 333 704 **Tel** *(01592) 22 3124* **Fax** *(01592) 22 3171* **Rooms** *70*

No two rooms are alike in this pleasant 18th-century fort-hotel. Its simple pleasures leave a lasting impression, whether it is a quiet breakfast on the terrace or the views of distant temples. Dinners are candle-lit with folk dances and music. **www.castlemandawa.com**

UDAIPUR Jagat Niwas Palace

24/25 Lal Ghat, City Place, 313 001 **Tel** *(0294) 242 2860* **Fax** *(0294) 241 8512* **Rooms** *29*

Famous for its superb views of Lake Pichola, this delightful 17th-century *haveli* has comfortable, palatial rooms and an inviting ambience. Horse-riding can be arranged. The in-house restaurant provides guests with an array of delectable dishes. **www.jagatniwaspalace.com**

UDAIPUR Shiv Niwas Palace

City Palace, Haridas Ji Ki Magri, 313 001 **Tel** *(0294) 252 8016* **Fax** *(0294) 252 8006* **Rooms** *36*

Located next to the City Palace, this elegant crescent-shaped former royal guesthouse is decorated with superb antique art and furniture, and is rated among the finest heritage hotels in the world. It also offers a holistic health centre. The famous 1983 James Bond film *Octopussy* was shot here. **crs@udaipur.hrhindia.com**

UDAIPUR Udai Vilas

Haridasji Ki Nagri, 313 001 **Tel** *(0294) 243 3300* **Fax** *(0294) 243 3200* **Rooms** *90*

This new luxury hotel is scenically located near Lake Pichola. The landscaped gardens, fountains, pavilions and decor are inspired by traditional Udaipur decorative arts. Dining options include an all-day restaurant and a speciality Indian restaurant, serving traditional Rajasthani food. **www.oberoihotels.com**

UDAIPUR Devi Garh

Village Delwara, Rajsamand Distt, 313 001 **Tel** *(02953) 28 9211* **Fax** *(02953) 28 9357* **Rooms** *30*

Minimalist, chic interiors combine with magnificent architecture in this beautifully restored hill-fort. A special effort has been made to ensure that the food served has an authentic home cooked flavour with an emphasis on fresh ingredients. A range of Ayurvedic therapies is also on offer. **www.deviresorts.com**

UDAIPUR Taj Lake Palace Hotel

PO No 144 Lake Pichola, 313 001 **Tel** *(0294) 25 2880* **Fax** *(0294) 28 9357* **Rooms** *85*

This fairy-tale island palace is among India's most romantic hotels. An experience not to be missed, if you can afford it. Magnificent bedrooms and bathrooms are decorated in Rajasthani style with marble and rich fabrics. The butlers, descendants of the original palace retainers, ensure all guests are treated like royalty. **www.tajhotels.com**

GUJARAT

AHMEDABAD Cama Hotel

Khanpur, 380 001 **Tel** *(079) 2560 1234* **Fax** *(079) 2560 2000* **Rooms** *50*

Recently renovated, this elegant and comfortable hotel has pretty gardens, a swimming pool, a coffee shop, and a good handicrafts boutique. It overlooks the Sabarmati river. Cama Hotel is as Ahmedabad's first boutique luxury hotel. **www.camahotelsindia.com**

AHMEDABAD The House of Mangaladas Girdhardas

Opp Siddi Sayyed Mosque, Lal Darwaza, 380 001 **Tel** *(079) 2550 6946* **Fax** *(079) 2550 6535* **Rooms** *12*

The House of Mangaladas Girdhardas offers an old-world experience in a contemporary setting. Located in the middle of the city, it offers heritage tours as well as sumptuous food. The hotel also screens films and is a dream come true for culture lovers. **www.houseofmg.com**

AHMEDABAD Taj Residency Ummed

International Airport Circle, Hansol, 382 475 **Tel** *(079) 6666 1234* **Fax** *(079) 6666 4444* **Rooms** *91*

Located near the airport, the hotel is a quiet retreat from the main city. Imaginatively constructed around a central court-yard, the decor showcases Gujarati crafts and antiques. It offers fine dining and helps organise heritage tours within Ahmedabad. Baby-sitting facilities also available. **www.tajhotels.com**

BHAVNAGAR Nilambagh Palace Hotel

Nilambagh, 364 002 **Tel** *(0278) 242 4241* **Fax** *(0278) 242 8072* **Rooms** *28*

This grand 19th-century palace has richly carved pillars, glittering hallways, antique teak furniture and an enormous garden. Excursions to neighbouring tourist spots are also organised. This beautiful khaki stoned structure is surrounded by verdant lawns creating a secluded ambience. **www.heritagehotelsofindia.com**

DIU Hotel Radhika Beach Resort

Nagoa, 362 520 **Tel** *(02875) 25 2553* **Fax** *(02875) 252 552* **Rooms** *42*

Located near a quiet, sandy beach, this clean and well-maintained resort has comfortable rooms, excellent service and good food. Every room is built with a view. You can choose between the sea or the beautifully landscaped greenery. **www.gujaratholiday.com**

JAMNAGAR Orbit Park Inn International

PO Baid, 361 006 **Tel** *(0288) 234 4484* **Fax** *(0288) 234 4486* **Rooms** *60*

Well-appointed rooms and excellent service characterise this tranquil hotel. Ideal for the business traveller as well. A full range of audiovisual equipment and well-trained staff make this the perfect place for conferences, workshops and parties. Enjoy the soothing views of the lagoon from the tea lounge.

SASAN GIR The Gir Lodge

Sasangir, Junagarh Distt, 362 135 **Tel** *(02877) 285 521* **Fax** *(02877) 285 528* **Rooms** *29*

Overlooking the river and hills, this lodge has comfortable rooms and friendly staff. Books and videos of wildlife films are available, as are jeeps for hire. The Gir Lodge offers easy access to Sasan Gir National Park, habitat of the Asian Lion as well as several bird species. **www.tajhotels.com**

VADODARA WelcomHotel Vadodara

RC Dutt Rd, Alkapuri, 390 007 **Tel** *(0265) 233 0033* **Fax** *(0265) 2330050* **Rooms** *134*

Located at the city's main shopping hub, Alkapuri, WelcomHotel Vadodara has a large corporate clientele. Corridors serve as art galleries and the ambience is soothing. Special facilities include golf and a splash pool for children. Its signature restaurant, Peshawari, is very popular. **www.itcwelcomgroup.in**

WANKANER Royal Oasis & Residency

The Wankaner Palace, 363 621 **Tel** *(02828) 22 0000* **Fax** *(02828) 22 0002* **Rooms** *12*

The renovated guesthouse of the Wankaner Palace is on the banks of the Machhu river, amid fruit orchards. An outstanding feature is its exquisite stepwell, three storeys deep. It is one of the finest heritage hotels in Wankaner and is situated 53 km (33 miles) from Rajkot. **www.colorsofgujarat.com**

MUMBAI

MUMBAI YMCA International House

18, YMCA Rd, near Mumbai Central, 400 008 **Tel** *(022) 2309 1191* **Fax** *(022) 2309 1101* **Rooms** *71*

This hotel is a great favourite with budget travellers, mainly because it offers secure, reliable services and a casual, relaxed atmosphere. The rooms are clean and spacious and the staff are courteous. Book well in advance as the rooms are much in demand. **www.ymcabombay.org**

MUMBAI Chateau Windsor Guest House

86 Vir Nariman Rd, 400 001 **Tel** *(022) 2204 3376* **Fax** *(022) 2202 6459* **Rooms** *60*

One of South Mumbai's leading budget hotels, Chateau Windsor Guest House is just walking distance from Mumbai's business district. The service is friendly, and the 60 rooms are comfortable and decorated with Italian and Spanish tiles. Rooms have electronic safes. **www.chateauwindsor.com**

MUMBAI Garden Hotel

42 Garden Rd, Colaba, 400 039 **Tel** *(022) 2283 4823* **Fax** *(022) 2204 4290* **Rooms** *33*

Situated near Electric House, and the colourful shopping area of Colaba Causeway, this hotel has 33 clean and well-furnished rooms. Round-the-clock room service and an efficient and polite staff make your stay even more memorable. Guests can relax on the terrace. **www.gardenhotel.com**

Key to Price Guide *see p690* **Key to Symbols** *see back cover flap*

MUMBAI Hotel Harbour View

25 PJ Ramchandani Marg, 400 001 **Tel** *(022) 2282 1089* **Fax** *(022) 2284 3020* **Rooms** *21*

A short walk from the Gateway of India, this hotel offers a beautiful view of the Arabian Sea. Spotlessly clean, the rooms are well-furnished. All rooms have a fridge, TV, air-conditioning and plenty of open space. They offer cots for children at an extra charge. **www.viewhotelsinc.com**

MUMBAI Hotel Suba Palace

Near Gateway of India, Apollo Bunder, 400 039 **Tel** *(022) 2288 5444* **Fax** *(022) 2202 0812* **Rooms** *51*

Close to the sea and the city's most famous landmark, the Gateway of India, Hotel Suba Palace is a comfortable hotel and ideal for both business and leisure. Room service is excellent. The coffee shop, Café Lounge, is exclusive to hotel residents. **www.hotelsubapalace.com**

MUMBAI Sea Green Hotel

145 A, Marine Drive, 400 020 **Tel** *(022) 2282 2294* **Fax** *(022) 6633 6530* **Rooms** *34*

Convenient location, spacious and clean rooms, friendly and attentive staff and reasonable rates have made this hotel a Mumbai favourite for over 50 years. Many of the rooms have views of busy Marine Drive, while others overlook a stadium. **www.seagreenhotel.com**

MUMBAI West End Hotel

45 New Marine Lines, 400 020 **Tel** *(022) 2203 9121* **Fax** *(022) 2205 7506* **Rooms** *85*

A leading economy hotel, West End, built in 1948, is a popular choice. It is just a stone's throw from the city's shopping and entertainment districts. Its large suites are well-suited for families. The hotel has a charming, old-fashioned ambience. **www.westendhotelmumbai.com**

MUMBAI The Fariyas Hotel

Off Arthur Bunder Rd, Colaba, 400 005 **Tel** *(022) 2204 2911* **Fax** *(022) 2283 4992* **Rooms** *87*

Located just off Colaba Causeway, near the Gateway of India, The Fariyas Hotel has comfortable rooms and a rooftop garden, from where there are spectacular views of the harbour. The hotel is just 10 minutes from the business districts of Nariman Point, Ballard Estate and the World Trade Centre. **www.fariyas.com**

MUMBAI Gordon House

5 Battery Street, Apollo Bunder, Colaba, 400 039 **Tel** *(022) 2287 1122* **Fax** *(022) 2287 2026* **Rooms** *29*

This charming little hotel behind Regal Cinema is perfect for those who appreciate style. Each of its three floors is themed differently – Mediterranean, Country and Scandinavian. The American buffet breakfast is popular. Service is warm and efficient. **www.ghotel.com**

MUMBAI Grand Hyatt Mumbai

Santa Cruz (East), 400 055 **Tel** *(022) 6676 1234* **Fax** *(022) 6676 1235* **Rooms** *547*

Off the Western Express highway and next door to the prime Bandra-Kurla business complex, this five-star hotel impresses you with its contemporary decor and its collection of commissioned art – the largest in the country. Its new speciality restaurant, China House, is one of the city's most popular. **www.mumbai.grandhyatt.com**

MUMBAI The Hilton Towers

Nariman Point, 400 021 **Tel** *(022) 5632 4343* **Fax** *(022) 2204 3133* **Rooms** *547*

This enormous luxury hotel dominates Mumbai's shoreline. The Hilton has non-smoking floors and rooms specially designed for the disabled traveller. Rooms have wireless Internet access, while the granite bathrooms are well-stocked with herbal toiletries. It is just 27 km (17 miles) from the airport. **www.tridenthotels.com**

MUMBAI Hotel Grand Maratha Sheraton

Sahar, 400 099 **Tel** *(022) 2830 3030* **Fax** *(022) 2830 3131* **Rooms** *386*

Close to the airport, the Grand Maratha Sheraton is one of the leading five-star deluxe hotels in Mumbai. It is the only hotel in the city to have a typical Indian look, reminiscent of an ancient Indian palace. The many award-winning restaurants serve Indian as well as international cuisine. **www.itcwelcomgroup.in**

MUMBAI InterContinental Marine Drive

135 Marine Drive, 400 020 **Tel** *(022) 5639 9999* **Fax** *(022) 5639 9600* **Rooms** *58*

Great views of the Arabian Sea and Marine Drive add to this boutique hotel's considerable charms. Rooms are fitted with noise-protection windows. Guests at InterContinental Marine Drive can choose from a variety of fine cuisines. **www.mumbai.intercontinental.com**

MUMBAI The Oberoi

Nariman Point, 400 021 **Tel** *(022) 5632 5757* **Fax** *(022) 5632 4142* **Rooms** *331*

Michael Jackson stayed at this plush hotel overlooking the Arabian Sea. There are separate floors for non-smokers and women travellers. Round the clock butler service and limousine transfers are other services. Rooms have 2-line speaker phone, fax machine, mini-bar, hairdryer, colour TV and Internet. **www.oberoihotels.com**

MUMBAI The Orchid

79-C Nehru Rd, Near Domestic Airport, 400 099 **Tel** *(022) 2616 4040* **Fax** *(022) 2616 4141* **Rooms** *245*

Asia's first certified eco-friendly five-star hotel, The Orchid is conveniently located near the domestic airport. A 21-m (70-ft) indoor waterfall complete with planted orchids make for a soothing ambience. Guests can dine at Vindhyas or the Boulevard. Karaoke nights at Merlins are very popular. **www.orchidhotel.com**

MUMBAI Ramada Hotel Palmgrove

Juhu Beach, 400 049 **Tel** *((022) 2611 2323* **Fax** *(022) 2611 3682* **Rooms** *114*

This hotel's best feature is its proximity to Juhu Beach. Besides other five-star facilities, it has a swimming pool, a well-equipped fitness centre, a book store and a beauty salon. Restaurants Oriental Bowl and the Tangerine Café are hot favourites. The Shooters Bar is worth a visit. **www.ramada.com**

MUMBAI Ramee Guestline

462, A B Nair Rd, Juhu, 400 049 **Tel** *(022) 6570 5555* **Fax** *(022) 2670 3344* **Rooms** *84*

Part of the Ramee group, this hotel is a short distance from Bandra beach. Ramee Guestline is simple and modern and boasts of a rooftop pool and excellent fitness facilities. Guests can dine at the in-house Indian restaurant, It's Mirchi, or lounge at the coffee shop. The night club is open Thursday to Saturday. **www.ramee-group.com**

MUMBAI Taj Lands End

Band Stand, Bandra (West), 400 050 **Tel** *(022) 6668 1234* **Fax** *(022) 6699 4488* **Rooms** *368*

This attractive hotel in the lively suburb of Bandra has an impressive three-storeyed marble lobby, tropical landscaping, and a separate swimming pool for women. All rooms have sea views. Taj Lands End's location, decor, attentive staff and excellent restaurants make it an excellent choice. **www.tajhotels.com**

MUMBAI The Taj Mahal Palace & Tower

Apollo Bunder, 400 001 **Tel** *(022) 6665 3366* **Fax** *(022) 6665 0323* **Rooms** *565*

This is certainly Mumbai's grandest and most beautiful hotel. Built in 1903, its architecture is a blend of classical and contemporary. No wonder, everyone from presidents to kings and actors have stayed here. Pierce Brosnan did, as did Bill Clinton. The hotel has several award-winning restaurants. **www.tajhotels.com**

MUMBAI The Taj President

90 Cuffe Parade, 400 005 **Tel** *(022) 6665 0808* **Fax** *(022) 6665 0303* **Rooms** *292*

Convenient for business travellers, this recently renovated hotel has panoramic views of the harbour and the city. The Konkan Café serves delicious regional food. The newest addition, Wink, a bar complete with a British DJ, is a huge hit with guests. **www.tajhotels.com**

MAHARASHTRA

AURANGABAD Welcomgroup Rama International

R-3 Chikalthana, 431 210 **Tel** *(0240) 663 4141* **Fax** *(0240) 662 8720* **Rooms** *90*

Verdant gardens covering 5 ha (13 acres) surround this luxurious hotel. Special features include yoga and massage therapy, mini-golf and a poolside barbecue. Tastefully furnished rooms overlook sprawling lawns and the pool. **www.itcwelcomgroup.in/hotels**

AURANGABAD Taj Residency

8-N-12 CIDCO, Rauza Bagh, 431 003 **Tel** *(0240) 238 1106* **Fax** *(0240) 238 1053* **Rooms** *66*

Set amid lovely gardens, this elegant hotel has spacious rooms leading onto private verandahs. Styled along the lines of an Indian palace, this hotel is located close to the World Heritage Sites of Ellora and Ajanta. The landscaped gardens are relaxing, and the service is excellent. **www.tajhotels.com**

CHIPLUN Quality Resort, The Riverview

Dhamandivi Taluka Khed, Distt Ratnagiri, 415 707 **Tel** *(02355) 39 5081* **Fax** *(02356) 72 059* **Rooms** *37*

Perched atop a hill in the Western Ghats overlooking the Vashishti river, this is an ideal place for a holiday. Its convenient location on the Mumbai-Goa highway makes it the perfect stopover on the long drive to Goa. The rooms are clean and comfortable. **www.chiplunhotels.com**

GANAPATIPULE MTDC Holiday Resort

Beach, Distt Ratnagiri, 415 622 **Tel** *(02357) 23 5248* **Fax** *(02357) 235328* **Rooms** *80*

This resort is located on a beach and offers accommodation varying from suites to tents. Some rooms have views of the sea. Cottages are in Konkani style with little balconies to lounge in. Water sports and other adventure activities are available. Tents are not available during the monsoon. **www.beachresortsindia.com**

LONAVLA Fariyas Holidays Resort

PO 8, Frichley Hill, Tungarli, 410 401 **Tel** *(02114) 73 852* **Fax** *(02114) 72 080* **Rooms** *90*

A five-star deluxe resort in the hills of Lonavla and Khandala, this hotel matches the destination. A warm welcome and good service is guaranteed. An added advantage is the express check-in and check-out. The luxurious resort also has a solar-heated pool, a health club, and a discotheque. **www.fariyas.com**

MAHABALESHWAR Brightland Holiday Village

Kates Point Rd, Distt Satara, 412 806 **Tel** *(02168) 26 0700* **Fax** *(02168) 26 0707* **Rooms** *60*

This clifftop resort, with fine views of the Krishna river, has clean cottages and apartments. An Ayurvedic health centre, a children's park and a discotheque are among its facilities. Rooms offer panoramic views of the Sahyadris. Even the bathrooms, with their glass doors, bring the outdoors inside. **www.brightlandholiday.com**

Key to Price Guide *see p690* **Key to Symbols** *see back cover flap*

MATHERAN The Rugby

Vithal Rao, Katwal Rd, 410 102 **Tel** *(02148) 30 291* **Fax** *(02148) 30 259* **Rooms** *60*

This hotel has a serene ambience and a pretty rock garden. The spotless rooms have private balconies with good views. Other attractions include an open-air theatre and a discotheque. The hotel conducts various entertainment programmes including bonfires, treasure hunts and magic shows. **www.tajhotels.com**

NAGPUR The Pride Hotel

Wardha Rd, Opp Airport, 422 010 **Tel** *(0253) 660 4499* **Fax** *(0253) 660 3366* **Rooms** *102*

Conveniently located, this hotel has well-furnished rooms, modern comforts and courteous staff. Beautifully landscaped gardens, a swimming pool, modern gymnasium, and plush multi-cuisine restaurants, enhance its charms. **www.pridegroup.com**

NASIK Taj Residency

P-17 MIDC Ambad, 422 010 **Tel** *(0253) 660 4499* **Fax** *(0253) 660 3366* **Rooms** *68*

Located on a small hillock amid an expanse of greenery, the decor of Taj Residency is inspired by Maratha palaces. There are views of the Satpura hills from some rooms. The staff are very efficient. The hotel's main clientele are business travellers. **www.tajhotels.com**

PUNE Sun N Sand

Bund Garden Rd, 411 001 **Tel** *(020) 2613 7777* **Fax** *(020) 2613 4747* **Rooms** *137*

A luxurious hotel, special attractions here include a full American breakfast, a pool with a sun-deck and a shopping arcade. Golf and tennis can be arranged on request. The contemporary decor in the atrium lobby offers a preview of the tastefully decorated, Wi-Fi equipped rooms and special suites. **www.sunnsandpune.com**

PUNE Taj Blue Diamond

11 Koregaon Rd, 411 001 **Tel** *(020) 6602 5555* **Fax** *(020) 6602 7755* **Rooms** *109*

Located in the swish and green residential Koregaon Park, Taj Blue Diamond is a stone's throw away from the Osho Ashram. Among the celebrities it has housed are Brad Pitt and Angelina Jolie. Elegant decor, a well-designed golf course, a poolside restaurant and warm hospitable service mark this hotel. **www.tajhotels.com**

SEVAGRAM Ashram Yatri Niwas

Sevagram Ashram, 442 001 **Tel** *(07512) 28 4753* **Rooms** *12*

This spartan but clean establishment, which can accommodate up to 70 people, has a bookshop stocked with Mahatma Gandhi's works. Smoking and consumption of alcohol and non-vegetarian food are not allowed. **http://wardha.nic.in/htmldocs/sevagram.asp**

GOA

ANJUNA BEACH Laguna Anjuna

Sorantto Vaddo, 403 509 **Tel** *(0832) 227 4305* **Fax** *(0832) 227 4305* **Rooms** *30*

Simple yet tastefully designed beach cottages, excellent service and a pleasant garden and swimming pool, have made this resort deservedly popular with foreign visitors. Designed by famous architect Dean D'Cruz, the spacious cottages are built around an intimate central courtyard. **www.lagunaanjuna.com**

ARPORA Sun Village Resort

Baga Beach, 403 518 **Tel** *(0832) 227 9409* **Fax** *(0832) 227 9409* **Rooms** *135*

An imposing statue of Helios, the Sun God, welcomes guests to this resort. The rooms are well-equipped with modern conveniences. Other attractions include a large swimming pool and a range of cuisines at the indoor and outdoor restaurants. An hourly shuttle takes guests to the nearby Baga beach. **www.desouzahotels.com**

BAGA Captain Lobo's Beach Hideaway

Calangute, 403 516 **Tel** *(0832) 227 6103* **Fax** *(0832) 227 6917* **Rooms** *21*

This friendly, family-run resort has comfortable suites in whitewashed villas, with attached verandahs and kitchenettes. The location, on Baga Beach, is ideal and the staff are friendly and helpful. The swimming pool offers respite to those who have had enough of the sea. **www.captloboshideawaygoa.com**

BAGA Hotel Baia Do Sol

Baga Beach, 403 516 **Tel** *(0832) 227 6084* **Fax** *(0832) 227 6085* **Rooms** *23*

An idyllic location with awesome views of the sea, and a lively bar with large bay windows, are the main attractions here. Music and barbecues create a special ambience in the evenings. The room service is excellent and guests are treated warmly by the hotel staff. **www.ndnaik.com**

BAGA Ronil Beach Resort

Baga Bardez, Calangute Beach, 403 516 **Tel** *(0832) 227 6101* **Fax** *(0832) 227 6068* **Rooms** *126*

Offering guests a slice of traditional Goan life, this resort boasts excellent Goan cuisine, rooms with fine views attractively decorated with local artifacts, and Ayurvedic massage therapy. It is just a stroll away from the beach. The service is friendly and the comforts are first-class. **www.alcongoa.com**

BARDEZ Nilaya Hermitage

House No 60, Bhatti Arporo Bardez, 403 518 **Tel** *(0832) 227 6793* **Fax** *(0832) 227 6792* **Rooms** *11*

Situated on a hilltop and surrounded by acres of banana, papaya and palm trees, this boutique hotel is a delight. Discreet luxury and delicious food are special features here. The resourceful and obliging staff can rustle up moonlit beach picnics or classical dance performances. **www.nilaya.com**

BARDEZ The Taj Holiday Village

Sinquerim, 403 519 **Tel** *(0832) 664 5858* **Fax** *(0832) 664 5868* **Rooms** *142*

The Taj Holiday Village has been described as a "a picture-postcard hamlet fringing the beach". Charming terracotta-roofed cottages built in typical Goa-Portuguese style and painted in bright colour are scattered around the landscaped garden. The rooms are luxurious and the ambience warm and welcoming. **www.tajhotels.com**

BARDEZ Whispering Palms Beach Resort

Fort Aguada Rd, Candolim, 403 515 **Tel** *(0832) 247 9140* **Fax** *(0832) 247 9142* **Rooms** *106*

This boutique beach resort lies ensconced between the Aguada foothills and Candolim. The poolside, brimming with colourful bougainvillaea creepers is the focal point of the sun-kissed resort. Live music is played on most evenings, making dining a truly delightful experience. **www.whisperingpalms.com**

BENAULIM Taj Exotica

Calwaddo, Benaulim Salcette, 403 716 **Tel** *(0832) 668 3333* **Fax** *(0832) 277 1515* **Rooms** *140*

This five-star resort is definitely one of the best in Goa. Sprawling across a lush garden, the resort overlooks the Arabian Sea. Every room has a view of the sea; some even have private plunge pools. Excellent restaurants, water sports facilities and a recreated fishing village are other attractions here. **www.tajhotels.com**

CALANGUTE Paradise Village Beach Resort

Tivai Vado, 403 516 **Tel** *(0832) 227 6351* **Fax** *(0832) 227 6155* **Rooms** *81*

Winding pathways lead from this aesthetically designed resort to the beach. Well-furnished studio apartments and one-bedroom suites are available. The restaurant offers both vegetarian and non-vegetarian cuisine. The hotel also organises cultural nights featuring Goan folk dances. **www.paradisevillage.org**

CALANGUTE Vila Goesa Beach Resort

Cobrawaddo, Calangute Beach, Bardez, 403 516 **Tel** *(0832) 227 7535* **Fax** *(0832) 227 6182* **Rooms** *79*

A stone's throw from Calangute Beach, this attractively designed, well-maintained resort has clean, comfortable rooms surrounded by extensive gardens. The restaurant serves good Goan seafood. Facilities include a Jacuzzi and sun-loungers. **www.vilagoesa.com**

CALANGUTE Pousada Tauma

Porba Vaddo, Calangute, 403 516 **Tel** *(0832) 227 9061* **Fax** *(0832) 227 9064* **Rooms** *13*

A quaint, charming place with an earthy feel, Pousada Tauma is refreshingly different in its architecture. It's the only boutique hotel in Goa that uses the traditional architecture of exposed masonry to create eco-friendly rooms. The resort's main attraction is the Ayurvedic centre. **www.pousada-tauma.com**

MAJORDA Majorda Beach Resort

Salcette, 403 713 **Tel** *(0832) 668 1111* **Fax** *(0832) 288 1124* **Rooms** *120*

This large, plush resort has spacious and well-furnished rooms and suites, an enormous swimming pool and a covered street inspired by a Mediterranean village. Amongst lush greenery, by the outdoor pool, the Garden Café serves buffet breakfasts and moonlit dinners (seasonal). **www.majordabeachresort.com**

PANAJI Panjim Inn

31st January Rd, Fontainhas, 403 001 **Tel** *(0832) 222 6523* **Fax** *(0832) 243 5220* **Rooms** *37*

This 150-year old heritage hotel has been renovated and restored to recapture the romance of Goa's past. Each room is unique with massive Burma teak beams, four-poster beds, carved rosewood *almirahs*, period furniture and paintings. A favourite with many visitors to Goa's capital. **www.panjiminn.com**

PANAJI Hotel Mandovi

PO Box 164, Panjim, 403 501 **Tel** *(0832) 222 4405* **Fax** *(0832) 222 5451* **Rooms** *65*

Perched on the banks of the Mandovi, this three-star hotel offers scenic views of the meandering river and the verdant hills beyond. The spacious, clean and luxurious rooms overlook the promenade leading to the beach. Its restaurants offer authentic Goan and Portuguese cuisine. **www.hotelmandovigoa.com**

SALCETTE Dona Sylvia Beach Resort

Cavelossim Beach, Mobor Salcette, 403 731 **Tel** *(0832) 287 1888* **Fax** *(0832) 287 1320* **Rooms** *181*

Pink bougainvilleas, whitewashed villas with typical Goan roofs and winding pathways distinguish this lovely resort. Perfectly suited for couples who need privacy, families looking to relax and unwind and even corporate employees looking to recharge. **www.donasylvia.com**

SINQUERIM The Aguada Hermitage

Bardez, 403 519 **Tel** *(0832) 564 5858* **Fax** *(0832) 247 9300* **Rooms** *15*

Built on a verdant hillock, each of these secluded, luxurious villas, run by the renowned Taj Group, has its own lovely garden. For food and facilities such as the pool, guests must use the Fort Aguada Beach Resort, situated at the foot of the hillock. **www.tajhotels.com**

Key to Price Guide *see p690* **Key to Symbols** *see back cover flap*

SIOLIM Siolim House

Opp Vaddi Chapel, Siolim Bardez, 403 517 **Tel** *(0832) 227 2138* **Rooms** *14*

This magnificent 300-year old Portuguese-style manor house, which once belonged to a governor of Macau, has been restored beautifully. Now a boutique heritage hotel, its two sprawling floors have only seven suites all with curtained four poster beds and shaded patios and gigantic bathrooms. **www.siolimhouse.com**

TEREKHOL Hotel Tiracol Fort Heritage

Querim, Pernem, 403 705 **Tel** *(02366) 227 631* **Fax** *(0832) 227 6792* **Rooms** *7*

Located at the mouth of the Tiracol river, this hotel offers glorious views of the estuary and surrounding countryside. Rooms in this romantic, atmospheric old fort have been restored and furnished with charm. The German chef creates mostly European dishes but specialises in Goan and Portuguese cuisine.

VAINGUINIM BEACH Cidade de Goa Beach Resort

Vainguinim Beach, South District, 403 004 **Tel** *(0832) 245 4545* **Fax** *(0832) 245 4543* **Rooms** *210*

Located at Vainguinim Beach, this resort is marked by its contemporary orange and white architecture designed by famous Indian architect Charles Correa. Pristine white furnishings and minimalistic design create a tranquil atmosphere. Guests have a choice of live folk dances or intimate candlelight dinner. **www.cidadegoa.com**

VARCA Club Mahindra Varca Beach Resort

Varca Beach, Salcete Taluka, 403 721 **Tel** *(0832) 274 4555* **Fax** *(0832) 274 4666* **Rooms** *206*

Located right on Varca Beach, the resort, with its huge marble lobby built in authentic Goan architectural style, welcomes you. Well-furnished, comfortable rooms offer modern amenities including a kitchenette. Guests have leisure options such as a three-level swimming pool, health club and gymnasium. **www.clubmahindra.com**

VARCA Ramada Caravela Beach Resort

Varca Beach Fatrade, 403 721 **Tel** *(0832) 274 5200* **Fax** *(0832) 274 5200* **Rooms** *202*

Sea-facing rooms with private balconies, attractive architecture, a pristine beach, water sports facilities and impeccable service make this a truly luxurious resort. This hotel is among Goa's finest international hotels. The lagoon-shaped swimming pool is a piece of art. **www.caravelabeachresort.com**

KARNATAKA

BADAMI Hotel Badami Court

Station Rd, 587 201 **Tel** *(08357) 22 0230* **Fax** *(08357) 22 0207* **Rooms** *27*

Situated in a scenic location, Hotel Badami Court offers a breathtaking view of sandstone cliffs and is close to the major tourist sites. It offers modern accommodation with all basic amenities. There is a swimming pool as well as a gym. Service is friendly. **www.hotelbadamicourt.com**

BANGALORE The Capitol Hotel

3 Raj Bhavan Rd, 560 001 **Tel** *(080) 2228 1925* **Fax** *(080) 2225 9922* **Rooms** *140*

The perfect place to stay when you have more than business on your mind. Awarded the best First Class Business Hotel in India for its superb service. This hotel provides complimentary one-way pick up from the airport. An exclusive hospitality desk on every floor ensures personalised attention. **www.thecapitolhotel.com**

BANGALORE Le Meridien

28 Sankey Rd, PO 174, 560 052 **Tel** *(080) 2228 6197* **Fax** *(080) 2226 7676* **Rooms** *196*

Luxurious and elegant, Le Meridien offers panoramic views of the soaring cityscape. A stone's throw from prominent shopping areas, this hotel towers over a lush golf course, offering both leisure and business travellers the ultimate in comfort and recreation. **www.starwoodhotels.com/lemeridien/index.html**

BANGALORE The Oberoi

37 MG Rd, 560 001 **Tel** *(080) 2558 5858* **Fax** *(080) 2558 5960* **Rooms** *160*

This luxury hotel has an abundance of greenery that is characteristic of the Garden City. The rooms, with elegant interiors and wooden flooring, overlook the pool and landscaped gardens. The hotel offers understated luxury, efficient service, fine cuisine and ultra modern facilities. **www.oberoihotels.com**

BANGALORE The Park

14/7 MG Rd, 560 001 **Tel** *(080) 2559 4666* **Fax** *(080) 2559 4029* **Rooms** *109*

The first contemporary Indian boutique hotel in the city, the Park has been designed by the UK-based Conran and Partners as a perfect urban retreat. Small, luxurious and intimate, the rooms provide complete relaxation. Bangalore's first lounge bar, I-bar, is a current favourite. **www.theparkhotels.com**

BANGALORE Royal Orchid Hotel

1 Gold Avenue, Airport Rd, 560 008 **Tel** *(080) 2520 5566* **Fax** *(080) 2520 3566* **Rooms** *195*

Each time guests enter the Royal Orchid Hotel, they can be sure of one thing – they are in elite company. Each room has unique decor with beautiful lighting and wood work. Impeccable service. The hotel is just 3 km (2 miles) away from the commercial hub of the city. **www.royalorchidhotels.com**

BIJAPUR Hotel Madhuvan International

Station Rd, 586 101 **Tel** *(08352) 25 5571* **Fax** *(08352) 25 6201* **Rooms** *36*

Views of the monumental Gol Gumbaz are the special features of this comfortable hotel. There is a pleasant garden restaurant serving regional specialities. The hotel organises excursions to nearby sites. A good place to stay in Bijapur. **www.hotelmadhuvan.com**

CHIKMAGALUR Taj Garden Retreat

Opp Pavitravana, KM Rd, 577 102 **Tel** *(08262) 22 0202* **Fax** *(08262) 22 0222* **Rooms** *29*

Perched on the gentle slopes of the Sahayadri Range, the Taj Garden Retreat is a well-run hotel comprising small cottages with spacious, well-designed rooms. The restaurant serves excellent regional cuisine. The hotel also organises excursions to the nearby Hoysala temples. Great for a relaxed holiday. **www.tajhotels.com**

COORG Orange County Resort

Karadigodu Post, Siddapur, 571 253 **Tel** *(08274) 45 8481* **Fax** *(08274) 45 8485* **Rooms** *48*

Set amid coffee and spice plantations, this hotel has 48 thatched cottages in mock-Tudor style. Excursions to surrounding forests, fishing in the Kaveri and herbal massages are just some of the activities on offer at this exclusive and tranquil place. **www.trailsindia.com**

HOSPET Malligi Tourist Home

6/143 Jambunath Rd, 571 253 **Tel** *(08274) 45 8481* **Fax** *(08274) 45 8485* **Rooms** *48*

Close to Hampi, this well-managed hotel also runs an efficient travel agency. Its most attractive feature is the swimming pool, which is inspired by the royal Pushkarni pool at Hampi. Everything the hotel does is centred around its guests to ensure that they have a relaxed and comfortable stay. **malligi@hotmail.com**

KARAPUR Kabini River Lodge

Nagarhole National Park, 571 114 **Tel** *(08228) 26 4402* **Fax** *(08228) 26 4405* **Rooms** *30*

Nestled on the southern fringes of the Nagarhole National Park, the Kabini River Lodge is a perfect getaway for nature-lovers. Once the hunting lodge of the erstwhile Maharaja of Mysore, the lodge is today rated as one of the top five wildlife resorts in the world. **www.junglelodges.com**

MANGALORE Taj Manjarun Hotel

Near DC Office, Old Port Rd, 567 001 **Tel** *(0824) 666 0420* **Fax** *(0824) 666 0585* **Rooms** *88*

A picturesque view of the sea on one side and of tranquil rivers on the other, this hotel is sure to take your breath away. Taj Manjarun Hotel provides warm hospitable service with distinctly personal touches. Good facilities for business travellers and a decent restaurant. **www.tajhotels.com**

MYSORE The Green Hotel

Chittaranjan Palace, 2270 VA Rd, 570 012 **Tel** *(0821) 425 5000* **Fax** *(0821) 251 6139* **Rooms** *31*

Originally built for the princesses of Mysore, this delightful palace-hotel has lovely gardens and elegant decor. Set up as a model of sustainable tourism by a UK charity, all profits go to worthy local projects. The Western Ghats, coffee plantations, game reserves and Ooty are all within a few hours' drive. **thegreenhotel@airtelbroadband.in**

CHENNAI

CHENNAI Breeze Hotel

850 Poonamallee High Rd, 600 010 **Tel** *(044) 2641 3334* **Fax** *(044) 2641 3301* **Rooms** *90*

This hotel is well-known for its quality service and the diverse menu served at its delightful restaurant. It is located within close proximity to the railway station and most of the city's shopping centres. A beauty parlour and choice of indoor games are some of the facilities offered. **www.breezehotel.com**

CHENNAI New Woodlands Hotel

72-75 Dr Radhakrishnan Rd, 600 004 **Tel** *(044) 2811 3111* **Fax** *(044) 2811 0460* **Rooms** *175*

The New Woodlands Hotel is a pure vegetarian establishment run by an orthodox southern Indian family. Clean rooms and hospitable service are the hallmarks here. Air-conditioned and non air-conditioned rooms available. Located in the heart of the city. **www.newwoodlands.com**

CHENNAI Hotel Residency

49 GN Chetty Rd, 600 017 **Tel** *(044) 2825 3434* **Fax** *(044) 2825 0085* **Rooms** *110*

The comfortable rooms on the upper floors offer good views of the city. Facilities include a bar with a Mexican theme. It is conveniently located in the heart of the business centre. Great for sports-lovers as premier sporting events are shown on a giant screen. **www.theresidency.com**

CHENNAI MGM Beach Resort

1/74 East Coast Rd, Muttukadu, 603 112 **Tel** *(044) 2747 2435* **Fax** *(044) 27472408* **Rooms** *52*

This beachside property offers some great views of the rising sun. The resort has well-designed cottages with spacious rooms. Some of the activities on offer are turtle-watching, camping, bonfires and Ayurvedic massages. There is also a gym. **www.mgm-hotels.com**

Key to Price Guide *see p690* **Key to Symbols** *see back cover flap*

CHENNAI ITC Park Sheraton & Towers

132, TTK Rd, 600 018 **Tel** *(044) 2499 4101* **Fax** *(044) 2499 7101* **Rooms** *283*

Elegant rooms, fountains in the lobby, a shopping plaza and health club add to the luxurious feel of this hotel, located in an exclusive quarter. Suites in the attached tower block have fine views. Conference rooms and banquet halls are spacious and beautifully carpeted. **www.welcomgroup.com**

CHENNAI Le Royal Meridien

1 GST Rd, St Thomas Mount, 600 016 **Tel** *(044) 2231 4343* **Fax** *(044) 2231 4344* **Rooms** *240*

Set in well-landscaped gardens, Le Royal Meridien caters to the business as well as the leisure traveller. Its lavish interior draws on local traditions. The six restaurants serve a variety of cuisines. Massages and relaxation therapies are also offered. **www.leroyalmeridien-chennai.com**

CHENNAI The Park

61 Anna Salai, 600 002 **Tel** *(044) 4214 4000* **Fax** *(044) 4214 4100* **Rooms** *214*

A stylish business hotel located in the former premises of the famous Gemini Film Studios. A dramatic entrance leads to an atrium that is breathtaking in its simplicity. The Park is centrally located and is popular with the business traveller. **www.theparkhotels.com**

CHENNAI Radisson

531 GST Rd, St Thomas Mount, 600 016 **Tel** *(044) 2231 0101* **Fax** *(044) 2231 0202* **Rooms** *101*

Radisson Hotel Chennai is a deluxe business hotel just 3 km (2 miles) away from Chennai airport. They offer high-speed Wi-Fi Internet, round-the-clock access to the swimming pool, gymnasium and other modern facilities along with speciality restaurants and bar. **www.radisson.com**

CHENNAI Taj Connemara

2 Binny Rd, 600 002 **Tel** *(044) 6600 0000* **Fax** *(044) 6600 0550* **Rooms** *150*

A charming heritage hotel with Art Deco interiors, serene courtyard and a beautiful pool. Authentic Chettinad cuisine is served at dinner in the open-air restaurant, accompanied by a cultural show. The hotel reflects the traditions of South India. **www.tajhotels.com**

CHENNAI Trident Hilton

1/24 GST Rd, 600 027 **Tel** *(044) 2234 4747* **Fax** *(044) 2234 6699* **Rooms** *167*

This elegant low-rise hotel, located close to the airport, is surrounded by gardens with luxuriant tropical foliage. There is a well-equipped gymnasium, a conference hall and an excellent restaurant. With Marina Beach a short drive away and an on-site outdoor pool, sun-seekers will be in their element here. **www.trident-hilton.com**

TAMIL NADU

COVELONG Fisherman's Cove

Covelong Beach, Kanchipuram Distt, 603 112 **Tel** *(044) 67413 333* **Fax** *(044) 6741 3332* **Rooms** *88*

This beach resort on the site of an old Dutch fort has charming rooms and cottages, many of them facing the sea, and excellent seafood. Water sports can be arranged on request and there is a private Jacuzzi for guests to relax in. Facilities are of an international standard. **www.tajhotels.com**

KARAIKUDI The Bangala

Devakottai Rd, Senjai, 630 001 **Tel** *(04565) 220 221 (reservations)* **Rooms** *12*

This heritage hotel is a complex of old bungalows renovated to showcase Chettinad's distinct architecture and decor, with teakwood fittings, colonnaded verandahs and airy rooms. Chettinad food is prepared on request. **www.thebangala.com**

KODAIKANAL The Carlton

Lake Rd, 624 101 **Tel** *(04542) 240 056* **Fax** *(04542) 241 170* **Rooms** *91*

A blend of vintage Raj and modern comforts, this superb hotel is set in sprawling, landscaped grounds overlooking Kodai Lake. This property scores high on ambience, food and service. One of the most picturesque, unspoilt and idyllic hill resorts in India. **www.krahejahospitality.com/carlton**

MADURAI Taj Garden Retreat

40 TPK Rd, Pasumalai Hill, 643 001 **Tel** *(0452) 237 1601* **Fax** *(0452) 237 1636* **Rooms** *63*

Built on a hillock overlooking the Meenakshi Temple, this retreat has beautiful terraced gardens. Some rooms are in a 19th-century Colonial house while others are in cottages with private terraces. The hotel provides ample scope for leisure activities such as tennis and badminton. There is also a swimming pool. **www.tajhotels.com**

MUDUMULAI WILDLIFE SANCTUARY Jungle Hut

Near Bokkapuram **Tel** *(0423) 252 6240* **Fax** *(0423) 252 6240* **Rooms** *12*

The rooms in this attractive resort are set in three stone cottages located on a large estate. The 30 resident elephants are a special attraction. They take part in an enchanting ritual every evening, when they perform a *puja* (prayer) to the elephant-headed god, Ganesha.

OOTACAMUND Fernhills Palace Nilgiris

Fernhill Rd, 643004 **Tel** *(0423) 244 3910* **Fax** *(0423) 244 3318*

Located in the heart of the city, close to Mudumulai and Bandipur wildlife sanctuaries, Fernhills Palace is set amid sprawling lawns overlooking dense forests and tea gardens. Caters to both business and leisure travellers. All guest rooms have fireplaces with provisions for a log fire. Attractions include golf and horse-riding.

OOTACAMUND Savoy Hotel

77 Sylks Rd, 643001 **Tel** *(0423) 244 4142* **Fax** *(0423) 244 3318* **Rooms** *40*

Nestled in the Nilgiri Hills amid lovely gardens, the Savoy Hotel has cosy rooms with fireplaces. This graceful 150-year old building was once a school. The massive wooden beams that support the roof were dragged all the way from Tipu Sultan's palace in Srirangapattanam. **www.tajhotels.com**

PONDICHERRY Anandha Inn

154 SV Patel Rd, 605 001 **Tel** *(0413) 233 0711* **Fax** *(0413) 233 1241* **Rooms** *70*

Within easy reach of the city's picturesque beach boulevard, temples and churches, this establishment has clean, well-equipped rooms, a business centre, bar and a boutique. Rooms are centrally air-conditioned with temperature control facilities, 24-hour room service and TV. There is a doctor on call. **www.anandhainn.com**

PONDICHERRY Hotel De L'Orient

17 Rue Romain Rolland, 605 001 **Tel** *(0413) 234 3067* **Fax** *(0413) 222 7829* **Rooms** *14*

This is an enchanting hotel, filled with fine Colonial furniture, old maps and prints and furnishings made to 18th-century French Colonial designs. The rooms are fitted with modern conveniences for guests to enjoy a comfortable sojourn. The restaurant serves excellent Indo-French fusion cuisine. **www.neemrana.com**

THANJAVUR Hotel Parisutham

55 GA Canal Rd, 613 001 **Tel** *(04362) 231 801* **Fax** *(04362) 230 318* **Rooms** *52*

Friendly and helpful staff, a beautiful pool, comfortable rooms and wholesome and tasty food make this small, modern hotel a good choice. Cultural programmes by the poolside in the evenings and excursions to nearby coconut plantations can be organised on request. **www.hotelparisutham.com**

TIRUCHIRAPALLI Jenneys Residency

3/14 McDonald's Rd, 246 1301 **Tel** *(0431) 241 4414* **Fax** *(0431) 246 1451* **Rooms** *93*

This spacious hotel has rooms with character, shops, a health club and efficient services. The promise of warm hospitality and impeccable service makes it a favourite among business as well as leisure travellers. The surrounding lawns and pool offer a welcome respite from the bustle of the city. **jennys@satyam.net.in**

TIRUCHIRAPALLI Femina Hotel

14-C Williams Rd, Cantonment, 246 1301 **Tel** *(0431) 241 4501* **Fax** *(0431) 246 1451* **Rooms** *178*

This is one of the finest hotels in the city, located a 15-minute drive from the airport and 5-minute drive from the rail and road junction. It also offers state-of-the-art banquet facilities. The lounge bar is well-stocked with Indian and foreign liquor. **femina@tr.dot.net.in**

ANDAMAN ISLANDS

PORT BLAIR Hotel Sinclairs Bay View

South Point, 744 106 **Tel** *(03192) 22 7824/ 227937* **Rooms** *30*

Located on the Bay of Bengal, overlooking Ross Island, the rooms here offer spectacular views of the sea. The hotel runs a diving centre that arranges scuba diving, snorkelling and water sports. It has beautifully appointed rooms with satellite TV channels, attached baths, telephones and room service. **www.sinclairshotels.com**

PORT BLAIR Fortune Resort Bay Island

Marine Hill, 744 101 **Tel** *(03192) 23 4101* **Fax** *(03192) 23 1555* **Rooms** *45*

Built almost entirely of the fabulous local *padauk* wood, this resort has lovely, imaginatively furnished rooms built into a hillside. The swimming pool here is filled with sea water. Fortune Resort Bay Island is situated on one of the world's last outposts of virgin rainforest overlooking the Bay of Bengal. **www.fortunehotels.in**

KERALA

ALAPPUZHA Kayaloram Lake Resort

Punnamada, 688 006 **Tel** *(0477) 223 2040* **Fax** *(0477) 225 2918* **Rooms** *12*

Built in the style of a traditional *tharavad* (ancestral home), rooms here have tranquil courtyards with bathrooms open to the sky. Kerala cuisine, Ayurvedic treatments and backwater cruises are on offer. Kayaloram is 15 minutes away from Alleppey town and is accessible by road and water. **www.kayaloram.com**

Key to Price Guide *see p690* **Key to Symbols** *see back cover flap*

ALAPPUZHA Lake Palace Resort

Thirumala, Chungam, 688 011 **Tel** *(0477) 223 9701* **Fax** *(0477) 223 9705* **Rooms** *38*

Modern luxury merges with traditional Kerala architecture at Lake Palace Resort, which is located on the banks of Vembanad Lake. This is an ideal place to enjoy the beauty of the backwaters. Water sports and cruises are on offer. There is a mini swimming pool for children too. **www.lakepalaceresort.com**

ALAPPUZHA Raheem Residency

Beach Rd, Alleppey, 688 012 **Tel** *(0477) 223 9767* **Fax** *(0477) 223 0767* **Rooms** *10*

An 1868 Colonial villa, this private residence was converted into a boutique hotel two years ago. A spacious courtyard with a velvet apple tree adds a special touch. The restaurant offers a mesmerising view of the surrounding waters. An unexpected bonus is the well-stocked library. **www.raheemresidency.com**

ERNAKULAM Taj Residency

Marine Drive, 682 011 **Tel** *(0484) 237 1471* **Fax** *(0484) 237 1481* **Rooms** *108*

Right in the heart of the city, this hotel has all the modern facilities associated with the Taj Group of Hotels. Great service combined with stunning views of the sea, the sunset and Cochin harbour. Facilities to shop for everything from footwear to spices are close by. Don't miss the Bubble Café. **www.tajhotels.com**

KOCHI Bolgatty Palace

Mulavukadu, 682 504 **Tel** *(0484) 275 0003* **Fax** *(0484) 275 0457* **Rooms** *26*

Its spectacular location on the tip of Bolgatty Island adds to the ambience of this hotel, housed in a lovingly restored 18th-century Dutch palace that was once also the British Residency. Guests can play golf and cool off in the pleasant beer parlour. Cottages close to the lake are also available to stay in. **www.ktdc.com**

KOCHI Koder House

Tower Road, 682 001 **Tel** *(0484) 221 8485* **Fax** *(0484) 221 7988* **Rooms** *6*

A three-storeyed heritage boutique hotel opposite the beach at Fort Kochi, Koder House has six luxury suites. Its multi-cuisine resturant, Menorah, is the only one in the country to offer Indo-Jewish cuisine. Added attractions include a plunge pool, a spa and a library. **www.koderhouse.com**

KOCHI The Malabar House Residency

1/269 Parade Rd, Fort Kochi, 682 001 **Tel** *(0484) 221 6666* **Fax** *(0484) 221 7777* **Rooms** *17*

Part of Fort Cochin's historic fabric, The Malabar House Residency was originally a Dutch mansion built in 1755. The rooms in this boutique hotel are elegant. The food is excellent and there is a pool and a stage for cultural events. Full of character and charm. **www.malabarhouse.com**

KOCHI Taj Malabar

Willingdon Island, 682 009 **Tel** *(0484) 266 811* **Fax** *(0484) 266 8297* **Rooms** *96*

Built in 1935, the Taj Malabar has a heritage wing with Victorian interiors. The newly renovated guest room suites in the tower wing look modern with a touch of classical elegance. Worth a special mention is the spa which is housed in a villa with a pool that merges with the sea. Exotic food in all three restaurants. **www.tajhotels.com**

KOCHI Trident Hilton

Bristow Rd, Willingdon Island, 682 003 **Tel** *(0484) 266 9595* **Fax** *(0484) 266 9393* **Rooms** *85*

Comfortable, modern and luxurious rooms and good service are the strong points of Trident Hilton. A hot favourite with travellers, it is ideally located, within a few minutes' drive to the city. It is away from traffic and blaring horns, yet close enough to reach city hot spots easily. **www.trident-hilton.com**

KOLLAM Aquaserene

South Paravoor, 691 301 **Tel** *(0474) 251 2410* **Fax** *(0474) 251 2104* **Rooms** *28*

Aquaserene offers elegantly designed cottages surrounded by water. This luxury resort has all modern facilities required for a comfortable stay but the enchanting views and complete privacy are the main attractions for visitors here. The resort's private beach is a 15-minute boat ride away. **www.aquasereneindia.com**

KOTTAYAM Chamundi Hill Palace Ayurvedic Resort

Rajkumar Estate, Nadukani, Edakkunnam PO, 686 512 **Tel** *(04828) 251 246* **Rooms** *13*

A 60-year old family house has been converted into this resort, while keeping its original character intact. Located on a mist-shrouded hill, the surroundings are scenic and tranquil. The accommodation, which includes a treehouse, is spacious, with palatial and comfortable rooms. **www.chamundihillpalace.org**

KOTTAYAM Taj Garden Retreat

1/104 Kumarakom, 686 563 **Tel** *(0481) 2524377* **Fax** *(0481) 2524371* **Rooms** *22*

On the banks of the Vembanad Lake, this hotel has rooms in an atmospheric Colonial bungalow and in cottages. Martial arts demonstrations, bird-watching and backwater cruises are arranged. Other facilities include a swimming pool, speed boats, row boats and waterskiing. **www.tajhotels.org**

KOVALAM Surya Samudra

Surya Samudra Beach Garden, Pulinkudi, 695 521 **Tel** *(0471) 226 7333* **Rooms** *21*

Traditional wooden architecture, coconut groves, bathrooms open to the sky and a superb beach are the highlights of this resort. It also has two private wells with good water. The swimming pool is a natural untiled rock pool. **suryasamudra@kovalamhotels.com**

KOZHIKODE The Renaissance Cochin Kappad Beach Resort

Thuvapara, Chemanchery, 673 304 **Tel** *(0496) 268 8777* **Fax** *(0496) 268 9194* **Rooms** *16*

This resort is located near the village of Kappad, where Vasco Da Gama landed in 1498. Bright, clean rooms and chalets are situated right on the beach. The seafood restaurant and Ayurvedic treatments are also a big appeal. The restort also organises barbecues and beach campfires. **www.renaissancekappadbeach.com**

KUMARAKOM Coconut Lagoon

Kumarakom, 686 563 **Tel** *(0481) 252 4373* **Fax** *(0481) 242 4495* **Rooms** *50*

The Coconut Lagoon is located hidden among the palm trees on the eastern shore of Vembanad Lake. Comprising heritage cottages and open-air bathrooms, it can only be reached by boat. A ferry leaves from one of several embarkation points, the closest being Kumarakom, at scheduled times throughout the day. **www.cghearth.com**

LAKSHADWEEP Bangaram Island Resort

Lakshadweep **Tel** *(0484) 266 8221* **Fax** *(0484) 266 8001* **Rooms** *29*

A pristine island paradise, this imaginatively-designed resort consists of clean attractively furnished beach huts and bungalows. There is a multi-cuisine restaurant as well as a well-stocked bar. Snorkelling, scuba diving and fishing are arranged. **www.somatheeram.in**

MUNNAR Tea County Hill Resort

KTDC Hill Resort, Munnar, 685 612 **Tel** *(04865) 230 460* **Fax** *(04865) 230 970* **Rooms** *43*

These plantation bungalow-type cottages have all modern facilities including a dance floor at the restaurant and an Ayurveda centre. Breakfast and dinner for two are included in your stay. Paragliding is one the activities offered here. **www.ktdc.com**

MUNNAR Windermere Estate

Pothamedu, PO.Box 21, Munnar, 685 612 **Tel** *(04865) 230 512* **Fax** *(04865) 230 978* **Rooms** *15*

Built in Colonial style, Windermere Estate has a special charm that makes for a memorable stay. Set amid tea and cardamom plantations, this establishment offers comfort, friendly service and enchanting surroundings and views. It is only 5 km (3 miles) from Munnar town. **www.windermeremunnar.com**

POOVAR Poovar Island Resort

KP VII/911, Pozhiyoor, 695 513 **Tel** *(0471) 212 070* **Fax** *(04869) 222 282* **Rooms** *28*

Close to Thiruvanathapuram, this island resort offers the option to stay in floating cottages. Ayurvedic massages are also available. The multi-cuisine restaurant at the resort offers a choice of Western, Asian and Indian cuisines to its guests. **www.hotelskerala.com**

THEKKADY Lake Palace

Thekkady, Idukki, 685 536 **Tel** *(04869) 222 023* **Fax** *(04869) 222 282* **Rooms** *6*

Feel like royalty at this erstwhile summer palace, built on a peninsula jutting into Periyar Lake. The surrounding forests offer plenty of opportunities for spotting wildlife. Lake Palace only has six rooms, so book well in advance to enjoy the wonders of nature. **www.ktdc.com**

THIRUVANANTHAPURAM The South Park

MG Rd, 695 034 **Tel** *(0471) 233 3333* **Fax** *(0471) 233 1861* **Rooms** *83*

In the heart of Thiruvanathapuram, this comfortable, recently-renovated hotel boasts a live band, a leafy garden where barbecue dinners are held and Ayurvedic massage therapy. The newly renovated multi-cuisine restaurant offers lavish and elaborate buffet spreads for lunch and dinner. **www.thesouthpark.com**

THIRUVANANTHAPURAM The Muthoot Plaza

Punnen Rd, 695 039 **Tel** *(0471) 233 7733* **Fax** *(0471) 233 7734* **Rooms** *57*

Located in the city's commercial hub, this hotel has comfortable rooms, good business facilities and efficient service. The high-end rooms even have laptops for the guests to use. It follows international standards and is a 20-minute drive from the airport. **www.themuthootplaza.com**

THIRUVANANTHAPURAM The Leela Kempinski Kovalam Beach

Kovalam, 695 527 **Tel** *(0471) 248 0101* **Fax** *(0471) 248 1522* **Rooms** *182*

This hotel is the epitome of luxury. Perched on a rockface with panoramic views of Kovalam Beach, the hotel's modern facilities include an exclusive beach and wellness spa. The rooms are well equipped and provide all the comforts a guest can expect. Efficient staff. **www.theleela.com**

VARKALA Taj Garden Retreat

Janardana Puram, 695 141 **Tel** *(0470) 260 3000* **Fax** *(0470) 260 2296* **Rooms** *30*

Surrounded by green paddy fields and overlooking the sea, the Taj Garden Retreat offers spectacular views. The 30 spacious guest rooms have private balconies. A library, tennis court, freshwater pool and a long pristine beach are some of the other attractions. Excellent food is served in this restaurant. **www.tourindiakerala.com**

WAYANAD Green Magic Nature Resort

Meppadi, 673 577 **Tel** *(0471) 232 8070* **Fax** *(0471) 233 1407* **Rooms** *6*

Located right in the middle of a tropical rainforest, this is a nature resort with basic amenities. There are no TVs or air-conditioning, but then these modern conveniences are not missed. The eco-lodges and ethnic houses, built on trees 26 m (86 ft) above the ground, are unique. Organic food is served. **www.tourindiakerala.com**

Key to Price Guide *see p690* **Key to Symbols** *see back cover flap*

WAYANAD Tranquil Resort

Kuppamudi Estate, Kolagappara PO., 673 591 **Tel** *(04936) 220 244* **Fax** *(04936) 222 358* **Rooms** *8*

The perfect place to forget everything and be absorbed by the beauty of the surroundings. Added advantages are enchanting views and great food. The traditional ambience is soothing. Do not miss the tree villas, which provide a world of beauty and comfort. **www.tranquilresort.com**

ANDHRA PRADESH

HYDERABAD Green Park

Begumpet, 500 016 **Tel** *(040) 2375 7570* **Fax** *(040) 2404 2242* **Rooms** *148*

The most centrally located hotel in Hyderabad with state-of-the-art facilities, offering world class standards at great prices, Green Park hotel is the first choice of the discerning business traveller. Well-furnished and comfortable rooms equipped with baths and direct dial telephones. **www.hotelgreenpark.com**

HYDERABAD ITC Kakatiya Sheraton Towers

6-3-1187 Begumpet, 500 016 **Tel** *(040) 2340 0132* **Fax** *(040) 2340 1045* **Rooms** *188*

This elegant hotel's special feature is a unique pool that is built from a natural rock formation. It is reputed for its excellent service and its cuisine, offered in three speciality restaurants. Complimentary airport transfers in luxury limousines are another highlight. It is just 3 km (2 miles) away from the airport. **www.welcomgroup.com**

HYDERABAD Quality Inn Residency

Public Garden Rd, Nampally, 500 001 **Tel** *(040) 3061 6161* **Fax** *(040) 2320 4040*

A central location makes this hotel a good choice. It provides clean, comfortable rooms, as well as a pub. The public garden opposite the hotel is one of the green lungs of this city, and is ideal for a quick walk or an early morning jog. **www.theresidency-hyd.com**

HYDERABAD Taj Banjara

Rd No 1, Banjara Hills, 500 034 **Tel** *(040) 6666 9999* **Fax** *(040) 6666 1919* **Rooms** *118*

Situated on Banjara Hills, Taj Banjara overlooks its own private lake and is a 10-minute drive from the business and shopping district. The hotel offers five meeting and banquet rooms with a capacity of 15 to 400 people. Facilities include a swimming pool and fitness centre. **www.tajhotels.com**

HYDERABAD Taj Deccan

Rd No 1, Banjara Hills, 500 034 **Tel** *(040) 6666 3939* **Fax** *(040) 6666 4848* **Rooms** *140*

A five-star business hotel, the Taj Deccan has excellent views of Hussain Sagar Lake, just a 20-minute drive from the airport and a 15-minute drive from all major business and shopping centres. All rooms are well-appointed with large size beds, individual temperature control, direct dialling and a refrigerator with a mini bar. **www.tajhotels.com**

TIRUPATI Hotel Guestline Days

14-37, Karakambadi Rd, 517 507 **Tel** *(0877) 228 0800* **Fax** *(0877) 228 1774* **Rooms** *140*

Overlooking the picturesque Tirumala Hills, this comfortable hotel has good food. Pilgrims hard-pressed for time can make use of the hotel's special service (for a fee) and bypass the long queues to enter the main sanctum of the Sri Venkateshvara Temple. **guestlinetirupati@rediffmail.com**

VIJAYAWADA Quality Inn D V Manor

40-47 MG Rd, 520 010 **Tel** *(0866) 247 4455* **Fax** *(0866) 248 3170* **Rooms** *94*

Centrally located, this modern, comfortable hotel has a central atrium with capsule lifts, a multi-cuisine restaurant and a bar. It is just minutes away from points of interest such as Indrakila Hill, Undavalli Caves, Kanaka Durga Temple and Gandhi Hill, the first Gandhi memorial in India. **www.dvmanno.com**

VISAKHAPATNAM The Park

Beach Rd, 530 023 **Tel** *(0891) 275 4488* **Fax** *(0891) 275 4181* **Rooms** *61*

Conveniently located near the beach, this modern hotel's facilities include a crafts court, where local artisans can be seen at work, and a bookshop. The air-conditioned rooms have sea views. Guests' dining choices include the Bamboo Bay or Vista restaurants, which are ideally placed for breathtaking tropical sunsets. **www.theparkhotels.com**

VISAKHAPATNAM Taj Residency

Beach Rd, 530 002 **Tel** *(0891) 256 7756* **Fax** *(0891) 256 4370* **Rooms** *93*

With the usual standards of comfort and service associated with the Taj Group, this hotel also boasts panoramic views of the Bay of Bengal. Also available is a fully equipped business centre with secretarial service and a meeting room accommodating 12 people. **www.tajhotels.com**

WARANGAL Ashoka Hotel

6-1-242 Main Rd, Hanamkonda, 506 314 **Tel** *(08712) 57 8491* **Fax** *(08712) 57 9260* **Rooms** *57*

A popular choice, the Ashoka Hotel sits in a large area providing spacious and clean rooms to the guests. The staff are efficient, warm and friendly. Excellent food is offered at the in-house restaurant. There is also a well-stocked bar. **www.dvmanno.com**

WHERE TO EAT

Indian cuisine is as rich in variety as the country itself. The delicate flavours of the classical cuisine that developed in the imperial courts of Delhi, Kashmir, Hyderabad and Lucknow are complemented by a vast range of regional specialities, made with a variety of exotic ingredients. From the arid deserts of Rajasthan come chilli-hot robust curries, whereas fish dominates in the cuisine of the lush, coastal areas of West Bengal, Goa and, to some extent, Kerala. Gujarat and Tamil Nadu are mostly vegetarian.

Red chilli

Eating habits in urban India have undergone considerable change in recent years, triggered off by rapidly changing lifestyles and the introduction of Western fast food chains. Though most Indians relish food cooked at home, eating out is becoming increasingly popular in the larger cities. Restaurants now offer anything from pizzas to sophisticated multi-course meals accompanied by local and imported wines. The restaurants on pages 720–43 have been selected for their quality, variety, service and price range.

ETIQUETTE

Indians are overwhelmingly hospitable and treat a guest as they would a favourite deity. In keeping with this tradition, many hotels and restaurants strive to follow a similar ethos. While it is customary for Indians to eat with their fingers, eateries do provide cutlery. There is usually a wash basin on the premises for washing hands before and after a meal, and restaurants often provide finger bowls with warm water and lemon for this purpose. Eating beef is taboo among Hindus, as is pork for Muslims.

RESTAURANTS

Changing lifestyles have been widely responsible for the proliferation of eating places, not just in large cities, but in smaller towns as well. These

Visitors savour a meal at one of Mumbai's many restaurants

range from luxurious gourmet restaurants to small cafés and roadside stalls, offering an eclectic choice of food, from Indian to Italian and Japanese. Most urban restaurants are air conditioned and the more expensive ones offer decor and service that is comparable with international standards. Traditional eating places, especially those that cater to a local clientele, are large, noisy halls, with special "family rooms", where parents can eat with their children. Simple and wholesome, mainly vegetarian, meals, are served here.

International chains, such as Pizza Hut and McDonalds, now have outlets in most big towns. They are becoming increasingly popular, particularly among the young. Special menus have been introduced to suit local tastes.

Most restaurants open by about 11am and close by midnight. In larger cities, it is best to book a table in

advance for weekends and holidays, especially at the more popular restaurants.

SPECIALITY RESTAURANTS

The growing appreciation for international cuisine has led to a rise in up-market speciality restaurants in most major cities. Authentic Thai, Chinese, Mexican, Japanese and Italian dishes, prepared by expert chefs using choice imported ingredients, are enthusiastically patronized by discerning gourmands.

Regional Indian specialities, too, are equally in demand. Restaurants specializing in barbecued *tandoori* kebabs and breads, as well as cuisine from Goa, Kerala, Tamil Nadu, Kashmir, Lucknow, Hyderabad, West Bengal, Gujarat and Rajasthan, now offer a wide range of dishes derived from traditional family recipes. Certain select restaurants offering fusion

A cook deftly prepares a paper-thin, plate-sized *rumali roti*

An improvised eatery in Rajasthan's Thar Desert

food have begun to attract diners in search of unusual tastes and flavours. Here, inspired chefs experiment with recipes and ingredients from India and abroad, to create exciting new menus.

COFFEE SHOPS

Luxury hotels have 24-hour coffee shops, which allow diners to grab a late dinner or early breakfast. Many local cafés and restaurants serving beverages and light snacks, however, also keep flexible hours. A recent addition is the small, bistro-type establishment in many shopping malls and at tourist sites. These are convenient places to relax and people-watch over sandwiches and a cup of tea.

ROADSIDE AND MARKET FOOD STALLS

For a glimpse of the original Indian fast food industry, there is nothing better than a journey through the country's roadside and market food stalls. Improvised stalls, vans or carts, equipped with stoves and other cooking appliances, dish out tasty meals with speed and efficiency. The choice ranges from vegetarian snacks, such as spicy, deep-fried samosas, *dosas* and *idlis*, to *tandoori* chicken, kebabs, "fish fry" and Indian-style Chinese chow mein and spring rolls. If tempted to sample some of the fare, ask for a minimum of chillies. Indian sweets, fruit, ice cream and a variety of drinks, including mineral water, colas and juices, are also available. Unpretentious eateries also serve good food fast. These

include the North Indian *dhaba*s (which serve both non-vegetarian and vegetarian food), the Goan beach shacks (which specialize in fish curries with rice) and the South Indian Udipi restaurants (which serve only vegetarian meals). For health precautions, see pages 764–67.

VEGETARIAN FOOD

India's excellent vegetarian food emanates from the country's largely vegetarian population. A simple but delicious meal of fresh seasonal vegetables, *dal* (lentil curry) and a wide choice of *rotis* and rice preparations can be had anywhere. Often these are served all together on a *thali* (platter) and are great value for money. The food's quality is endorsed by the displayed signs "Cooked in pure ghee" or "Cooked in ghee made from cow's milk".

ALCOHOL

The serving of alcohol is restricted, and some states, such as Gujarat, are officially "dry". Liquor is sold through

government-approved shops and licensed restaurants and prices vary across the country, because of the fluctuations in taxes from state to state. Luxury hotels are permitted to import wines and liquor, though they also serve Indian Made Foreign Liquor (IMFL), such as rum, beer, whisky and vodka. The quality of Indian wines and champagne is fast improving and some brands are even exported. Carrying alcohol for consumption in a restaurant is not permitted, nor is drinking in public places. National holidays and notified election days are "dry days" when no alcohol is served in hotels, bars and restaurants.

PRICES AND TIPPING

Prices are fixed everywhere, be it in a luxury hotel or at a market stall. Luxury hotels also levy a Food and Beverage Tax (though the amount varies) which can escalate costs considerably.

Check your bill before paying. Even though a service charge is usually included, waiters do expect to be tipped – ten per cent of the bill is acceptable. Roadside eateries and street vendors are extremely cheap.

PAYING

Credit cards are usually accepted in up-market restaurants and bars, particularly if these are in luxury hotels. However, always keep cash (Indian rupees) on hand to pay for meals at eateries in small towns or roadside stalls and cafés.

Afternoon tea in a resort in the backwaters of Kerala

Choosing a Restaurant

The restaurants in this guide have been selected across
a wide price range and many are in recommended
hotels (for hotel listings *see pp690–717*). Chosen for
their good food, good value, and convenient or interesting location, they are listed by region. Individual
entries are listed alphabetically within price category.

PRICE CATEGORIES
The price ranges are for a meal for one,
including tax and service charges but
not alcohol.

(Rs) Under 100 rupees
(Rs)(Rs) 100–200 rupees
(Rs)(Rs)(Rs) 200–400 rupees
(Rs)(Rs)(Rs)(Rs) 400–700 rupees
(Rs)(Rs)(Rs)(Rs)(Rs) Over 700 rupees

DELHI

DELHI Sagar Ratna
*The Ashok, 50-B Chanakyapuri, 110 021 **Tel** (011) 2687 8885*

The Sagar Ratna name is synonymous with perhaps the best South Indian food served in the city. The deluxe *thali*
platter is popular as a an economical but hearty meal. The onion *rava masala dosa* and *idli (see pp554–5)* are also
highly recommended. Another branch, the Sagar Ratna at Defence Colony in New Delhi, has lower rates.

DELHI Triveni Tea Terrace
*Triveni Kala Sangam, 205 Tansen Marg, 110 001 **Tel** (011) 2371 8833*

Tucked away in a quiet corner of the famous art gallery, this dining room is discreet and homely. They offer a simple
main course of *shami kebabs*, vegetarian *pulao* (rice dish) and *aloo parathas (see p67)* with refreshing *chai* or tea.
Owing to its proximity to the courts, the restaurant is patronised largely by artists and lawyers.

DELHI Karim's
*16 Jami Masjid, 110 006 **Tel** (011) 2326 9880*

Located near the beautiful Jami Masjid, India's largest mosque, Karim's is famous throughout the country for serving
the best Mughlai cuisine. A meat-eater's paradise, their Jehangiri chicken, lamb *burra* (marinated) and tandoori *raan*
(leg of lamb) are much sought-after. Try their *phirni* (sweet rice pudding) for dessert.

DELHI Basil and Thyme
*Santusthi Shopping Complex, New Wellington Camp, 110 003 **Tel** (011) 2467 4933*

A small eating joint with a peaceful ambience, this is the perfect place to relax after a hectic shopping spree at the
popular Santusthi complex. Basil and Thyme serves both Italian as well as other European cuisine. Try the chicken
liver paté, quiche Lorraine and pasta bolognese.

DELHI Chor Bizzare
*Hotel Broadway, 4/15 Asaf Ali Rd, 110 002 **Tel** (011) 2327 3821*

Best known for its Kashmiri cuisine, Chor Bizarre is based on the concept of a thieves' market. Try the *yakhni (see
p67)* or *gushtaba* (meat balls cooked in yoghurt). The *thali*, an assortment of various dishes, is especially good.
Vegetarians must also try the Kashmiri *dam aloo* (spicy fried potatoes). The decor is imaginative.

DELHI Kwality
*67 Regal Building, Connaught Place, 110 001 **Tel** (011) 2374 2310*

Delhi's first ice-cream parlour later converted into a popular restaurant. The *chhola bhaturas* (spicy chickpeas eaten
with deep fried fluffy bread) remains eternally popular among other Punjabi dishes served. Also worth trying are the
kebabs, especially the lamb *gilafi* (with peppers). Leave some space for the ice creams.

DELHI Swagath
*14 Defence Colony Market, 110 024 **Tel** (011) 2433 0930*

Its serene, stylish atmosphere, hearty meals and affordable rates make Swagath a popular restaurant. Offers South
Indian, Mughlai and Chinese cuisine and specializes in seafood. Among its most delectable preparations are the
Chettinad chicken, butter chicken, grilled prawns and garlic butter crabs.

DELHI The Big Chill
*68A Khan Market, 110 003 **Tel** (011) 4175 7588*

Decorated with film posters and very popular with a young crowd, The Big Chill serves Italian and other European
food. The bistro's best dishes include prawn and courgette salad, chicken in spicy *piri piri* sauce and crisp pizzas. Their
squidgy cakes and frozen yoghurts are the most popular desserts.

DELHI Dhaba
*The Claridges, 12 Aurangzeb Rd, 110 011 **Tel** (011) 2301 0211*

Dhaba is a recreation of numerous little eateries lining North India's highways that serve authentic Punjabi cuisine.
Splurge on *balti* meat and tandoori prawns, amongst other fresh, spicy food that will tantalise your taste buds. A
recommended eating experience.

Key to Symbols *see back cover flap*

DELHI Flavors

52-C Flyover Complex, Next to Moolchand Flyover, Defence Colony, 110 024 **Tel** *(011) 2464 5644*

Tarsilo Nataloni is the affable chef-owner of this Italian restaurant. The pizzas, chorizo pasta and *sole mio* are some of the best dishes on the menu. For vegetarians, the spinach and ricotta cheese ravioli is a must. For dessert, both the mango cheesecake and crème brûlée are recommended.

DELHI Nanking

Opp. Delhi Public School, Vasant Kunj, 110 070 **Tel** *(011) 2613 8936*

A Chinese speciality restaurant that is rated as one of the city's best. Offers fabulous duck along with crab and other seafood, all served within the restaurant's spacious interiors by friendly and helpful staff. Nanking is also popular for its special dimsum lunches, which offer an extensive array of vegetarian and meat-based delicacies.

DELHI Park Baluchi

Inside Deer Park, Hauz Khas, 110 016 **Tel** *(011) 2696 9829*

Strategically located amid the lush greenery of the Deer Park and near the shopper's paradise that is Hauz Khas Village, the Park Baluchi serves fine Northwest Frontier cuisine, especially for meat lovers. The *murgh potli* (stuffed chicken breast) and the *haryali choosa* (special chicken dish) are the house specialities.

DELHI The Great Kebab Factory

Hotel Radisson, National Highway-8, Mahipalpur, 110 037 **Tel** *(011) 2677 9191*

A speciality restaurant serving sumptuous *kebabs* among other things. The *kebab* platters are popular and include the *galouti* and *gosht babri seekh* kebabs. The *malai* broccoli and *pudina paneer tikka* (cottage cheese with mint) are recommended for vegetarians. There is also an "eat as much as you like" offer.

DELHI Aqua

The Park,15 Parliament Street, 110 001 **Tel** *(011) 2374 3000*

Aqua is a cool, poolside lounge, which attracts a VIP crowd for the intimacy of its tent-like alcoves. Mediterranean and barbecued cuisine is served here and the grilled mushroom with basil and falafel platter are particularly good. The desserts are also scrumptious.

DELHI Bukhara

ITC Maurya Sheraton Hotel and Towers, Diplomatic Enclave, 110 021 **Tel** *(011) 2611 2233*

Featured on the cover of *Time* magazine, Bukhara counts numerous international politicos among its fans. This is a cozy venue with lovely stone walls, crossed by dark wooden beams. Famous for its appetising *kebabs* and mouth-watering *tikkas*, but try the *sikandari raan* (marinated lamb) or the chicken *malai kebabs*.

DELHI Dum Pukht

ITC Maurya Sheraton Hotel and Towers, Diplomatic Enclave, 110 021 **Tel** *(011) 2611 2233*

Serving the best Avadhi and Hyderabadi cuisine in the city, this critically acclaimed restaurant has an excellent menu. Try the *kakori kebabs* (minced lamb) and the grilled king prawns. Their famous *dum pukht (see p164)* or *biryanis* are delicious. Excellent food and a majestic ambience make for an unforgettable experience.

DELHI House of Ming

Hotel Taj Mahal, 1 Mansingh Rd, 110 011 **Tel** *(011) 2302 6162*

Arguably Delhi's premier Chinese restaurant, House of Ming serves the best of spicy Schezwan and Cantonese flavours. The shark fin soup and crispy thousand corner king prawns, Chef Wang's signature dish, are not to be missed. The crispy fried spinach is one of several vegetarian delicacies. Finish with the "fried" ice cream.

DELHI La Piazza

Hyatt Regency, Bhikaji Cama Place, Ring Rd, 110 066 **Tel** *(011) 2679 1234*

An extensive wine list, exquisite cuisine prepared by their Italian chef and an attractive bistro-like decor make La Piazza the best Italian restaurant in town. The Antorio Gavi wine, Pizza La Piazza, and grilled salmon are winners on the menu. Special fixed-price brunches are served every Sunday.

DELHI Lodi – The Garden Restaurant

Lodi Garden, Opp. Mausam Bhavan, Lodi Rd, 110 003 **Tel** *(011) 2465 5054*

Set amidst beautiful trees and lanterns, this garden restaurant assures a fine dining experience. Start with *salata dijaj* (chicken salad) or Moroccan lamb, their chef's speciality. For vegetarians, the vegetable platter is a good choice. Recommended international wine list.

DELHI The Spice Route

The Imperial, Janpath, 110 001 **Tel** *(011) 2334 1234*

Decorated to reflect the art and culture along the historical spice route that brought the spices of Southeast Asian countries to Europe, this restaurant is a visual and culinary delight. The establishment's exotic meals, which include the Sri Lankan *marris* curry and *phad phak ruam mitr* (stir-friend mixed vegetables) complete the experience.

DELHI Threesixty°

The Oberoi, Dr. Zakir Hussain Marg, 110 003 **Tel** *(011) 2436 3030*

This recently opened, popular restaurant offers a variety of cuisines. The Japanese fare is highly recommended and the wood-fired pizzas come with toppings such as chorizo and jalapenos. The buffet options provide good choices for a quick meal. Good range of European and New World wines.

HARYANA & PUNJAB

AMRITSAR Crystal Restaurant
Crystal Chowk, Queen's Road, 143 001 **Tel** *(0183) 222 5555*

This restaurant offers Chinese, Indian and Italian cuisine but diners are advised to stick to the delicious, meat-heavy Punjabi dishes, which include great tandooris and curries. Service can be slow, especially in the evenings and over the weekend, when the restaurant gets very crowded.

CHANDIGARH Chop Sticks
SCO 1085, Adjacent Hotel Piccadily, Sector 22-B, 160 022 **Tel** *(0172) 277 4181*

The ambience and decor of the restaurant are obviously oriental, with pictures of dragons painted on the walls. Food is prepared in the original Chinese style by dicing vegetables and meat pieces into small cubes. Do try the vegetable basket. Open for lunch and dinner only.

CHANDIGARH Khyber Restaurant
SCO 333-34, Sector 35-B, 160 022 **Tel** *(0172) 260 7728*

Efficient service and top quality food. The *dal* (lentils), *kebabs* and tandoori preparations are delicious. Food is served in copper bowls by staff who wear *pathani* suits, all in-keeping with the general Afghani ambience. The most striking feature, however, is the tree growing right in the middle of the restaurant.

CHANDIGARH Kwality
SCO 40, Punjab University Sector 14, 160 014 **Tel** *(0172) 254 1427*

Built in 1955, Kwality is part of the well-known North Indian restaurant chain of the same name. One of the Chandigarh's original restaurants, it was also the first to introduce ice cream cones in the city. A perfect family restaurant, visit Kwality to enjoy good food in a relaxed atmosphere.

CHANDIGARH Mehfil
SCO 183-185, Sector 17-C, 160 017 **Tel** *(0172) 270 3539*

Mehfil, one of the oldest restaurants in the city, is a multi-cuisine restaurant, famous for its vibrant ambience. Authentic Punjabi cuisine is served with traditional warmth and the curries are particularly recommended. The decor, which includes bright lighting, is a little overpowering.

CHANDIGARH Black Lotus
Taj Hotel, Block 9A, Sector 17, 160 017 **Tel** *(0172) 551 3000*

This restaurant serves the choicest Schezwan fare for lunch and dinner. Sectioned into a private dining room and bar, a high ceiling, fabric panelled walls and oriental artifacts create a contemporary oriental ambience. The menu features a wide range of vegetarian and meat-based delicacies including fresh seafood.

HIMACHAL PRADESH

CHAIL Palace Hotel's Restaurant
Palace Hotel, 173 217 **Tel** *(01792) 248 141*

This delightful restaurant specializes in Himachali regional cuisine such as *sepu badi* (fried purée of chickpea and lentil) and *kadi* (chickpea and lentil curry) but Chinese and European dishes are also available. Enjoy your tea or coffee in the open air café. The bar serves Indian as well as imported brands of alcohol.

CHAMBA Iravati Hotel
Near Main Sehgal, 176 310 **Tel** *(01899) 222 671*

Great mountain views add to the dining experience at this restaurant which serves good Himachali food. Chamba *guchi madara* (spicy mushroom and pea dish) is a must-have. For those who enjoy hearty meat-based dishes try the *daruwala* lamb and *achari* chicken. The Ravi View café serves South Indian food as well as light snacks.

DHARAMSALA Nick's Italian Kitchen
Kunga Guesthouse, 176 215 **Tel** *(01892) 221 180*

This rooftop, vegetarian restaurant offers excellent views of the Vasu Temple dedicated to Lord Shiva. They serve sumptuous Italian dishes, and the Tibetan noodle soup and *momos (see p264)* are hot favourites here. The restaurant is closed for three days during Tibetan New Year and on July 6 to mark the Dalai Lama's birthday.

KALPA Kinner Villa Restaurant
Hotel Kinner Villa, 172 108 **Tel** *(01786) 226 606*

Although the restaurant serves Chinese and Continental food, it specializes in Indian cuisines. However, it is best to stick to basic fare such as the *dal-roti* (lentils and bread). If weather permits, ask to be served in the garden, which has pleasant views of the mountains.

Key to Price Guide *see p720* **Key to Symbols** *see back cover flap*

KULLU Silhouette

Hotel Le Grand, National Highway 21, Kullu Manali Rd, 175 101 **Tel** *(01902) 251414*

Chinese, European and Indian cuisines are all on offer at Silhouette. A large number of tandoori dishes are served as well. Pure vegetarian food is available on request. Their special *kadhai paneer* (cottage cheese dish with peppers) with oven hot *rotis* (bread) are a favourite with guests. Food can be served in the garden on request.

MANALI Chopsticks

The Mall, Opp. Bus Stand, 175 131 **Tel** *(01902) 252 639*

Generous helpings of Japanese, Chinese and Tibetan food are served at this friendly restaurant. Try their *gyakok*, a delicious Tibetan hotpot which serves five and must be ordered well in advance. Also sample other specialities that include yoghurt and pancakes.

MANALI Johnson's Café

The Mall, 175 131 **Tel** *(01902) 252 316*

Best known for its Italian fare, Johnson's Café offers excellent homemade pastas, cakes, juices and ice creams. The butter garlic trout and butter lemon trout, prepared with special herbs for extra flavour, are not to be missed. Finish off with a slice of their excellent chocolate cake for dessert.

SHIMLA Baljees

The Mall, Opp. Town Hall, 171 001 **Tel** *(0177) 265 2313*

One of Shimla's oldest eateries, this restaurant offers delicious Indian and Western food. Vegetarians should try the *rava masala dosa (see p554)* and *chhola bhatura (see p67)*, while meat lovers shouldn't miss the butter chicken and lamb *rarha*. They have a whole range of sweets for dessert, but the *gulab jamun (see p67)* is outstanding.

SHIMLA Davicos

The Mall, Near Telegraph Office, 171 001 **Tel** *(0177) 280 6335*

An institution in Shimla, the basement restaurant serves mouthwatering appetisers and good *kebabs*. Continental as well as Chinese dishes are well prepared. The ground floor has a nice café which offers delicious snacks and coffee shakes. The first floor houses the well-stocked bar.

SHIMLA Cecil Restaurant

Oberoi Cecil, Chaura Maidan, 171 001 **Tel** *(0177) 280 4848*

Impeccable service and excellent food can be found at this elegant Oberoi-owned restaurant. It serves delicious Asian and European cuisine. The salads and pastas are particularly good and the chicken steak sizzler plate is a must-have. Finish off with the delectable pastries or fruit salad.

LADAKH, JAMMU & KASHMIR

JAMMU Falak

KC Residency, Residency Rd, 180 001 **Tel** *(0191) 252 0770*

Falak is a revolving rooftop restaurant that offers a wide variety of Indian, Mughlai, Continental, Chinese and regional food. The coffee parlour, called Café Sea Side, and the bar, Baron, are great places to relax with a cup of steaming hot coffee or a glass of beer. Closed November and March.

LEH Amdo Cafeteria

Main Market, 194 101 **Tel** *(01982) 253 114*

Good Tibetan, Chinese and Kashmiri food is served at the rooftop Amdo Cafeteria, which offers great views of Leh Palace and the old fort. Try the spring rolls, which can be filled with ingredients of your choice. The fried noodles are a hit with diners. Open for breakfast, lunch and dinner.

LEH Budshah Inn Restaurant

Main Bazaar, 194 101 **Tel** *(01982) 252 813*

Try this restaurant's *wazawan*, a Kashmiri feast traditionally comprising lamb, lotus roots and other delicacies. The prices are reasonable and the portions generous. The ambience could be slightly better but the food is ample compensation. Closed November to March.

LEH Ibex Hotel Restaurant

Fort Rd, 194101 **Tel** *(01982) 252 281*

This small eatery serves Indian and Chinese food, though Western food is also available on request. Guests enjoy ordering beer with their meals. The *seekh* (lamb) *kebabs* are served with a delicious *pudina* (mint) chutney. The lamb and chicken curries also also exceptional – perfect with steaming-hot *naan* bread. Closed November to March.

LEH Summer Harvest Restaurant

Fort Rd, 194 101 **Tel** *(01982) 252 226*

A modest eatery, run by a Tibetan lady, Summer Harvest Restaurant serves a selection of Tibetan, Ladakhi and Kashmiri dishes. Western food is also served here. Do try the *momos (see p264)* prepared with the choicest of vegetables and served generously. Closed November to March.

LEH Café World Peace

Near New Gas Service, 194 101 **Tel** *(01982) 252 988*

The menu includes mouthwatering Indian, Chinese, Western and Kashmiri food, but the baked goods are by far the most popular items at the café, especially the cinnamon rolls and pies. The outdoor dining area, surrounded by the green mountainside, is spectacular. Open for lunch and dinner.

LEH Omasila Restaurant

Hotel Omasila, Changspa, 194 101 **Tel** *(01982) 252 119*

This pleasant garden restaurant prides itself on its organically grown fresh garden vegetables, and its quiet, scenic location. The dining experience is enjoyable mainly because of the picturesque surroundings. Both regional specialities and their Western delicacies are recommended.

LEH Penguin Bar and Restaurant

Fort Rd, 194 101 **Tel** *(01982) 251 523, 09469049658*

The German bakery is the highlight at this laid-back hangout set in a large leafy courtyard. Cool lounge tunes resonate in the background. Serves breakfast, lunch and dinner. On request, Penguin staff will prepare special meals for road journeys or trekking trips. Closed from October to May.

LEH Mentokling Garden Restaurant

Zansti, 194 101 **Tel** *(01982) 252 992*

Located far from the hustle and bustle of city traffic, this pretty garden restaurant is set in idyllic surroundings with dining tables under apple trees. Offers local and Western dishes and serves breakfast, lunch and dinner. Closed from November to February.

LEH High Life

Fort Rd, 194 101 **Tel** *(01982) 251 013*

This restaurant has a Tibetan decor, and serves Italian, Chinese, Tibetan and Indian cuisine. Offers breakfast, lunch and dinner. Slightly expensive when compared to other restaurants in this area, but the dining experience is worth the money spent. Closed from October to April.

UTTAR PRADESH & UTTARANCHAL

AGRA Only Restaurant

45 Taj Rd, 282 001 **Tel** *(0562) 222 6834*

A traditional multi-cuisine restaurant, ideal for families. Also a getaway for those seeking to unwind in a quiet place. The food offered can be plain and simple but of reliable quality. Performances of Indian music liven up the evenings. The bar is well-stocked and the staff are friendly and eager.

AGRA Olive Garden

Sanjay Palace, MG Rd, 282 002 **Tel** *(0562) 252 3460*

Situated in the heart of the city, Olive Garden is easily accessible to Agra visitors. The restaurant offers an interesting blend of various international cuisines. It is best known for its sumptuous buffets served for breakfast, lunch and dinner. Also on offer are a fine selection of wines. Live music sets the mood.

AGRA Mughal

54 Taj Rd, Hotel Clarks Shiraz, 282 001 **Tel** *(0562) 222 6121*

True to its name, the restaurant seems to be straight out of the Mughal period. The setting is grand, the service impeccable and the food delicious. The establishment owns two bars that both serve fine blends of alcohol from across the world. Mughal is situated quite close to the Taj Mahal.

ALLAHABAD Elchico

24 MG Rd, Civil Lines, 211 001 **Tel** *(0532) 242 0753*

One of the oldest in the city, this restaurant serves good Indian and Western dishes. Popular with youngsters and grown-ups alike, Elchico also serves light snacks, such as pastries, accompanied by steaming cups of coffee. It has a warm and friendly ambience.

DEHRA DUN Kwality

19 B Rajpur Rd, 248 009 **Tel** *(0135) 265 7001*

As with other branches of the Kwality restaurant chain, this one offers wholesome and tasty Punjabi dishes. It is also known for its Chinese and Continental cuisine. Alcohol is served here. The restaurant is located close to the marketplace and its fare is reasonably priced. Service is quick and efficient.

FATEHPUR SIKRI Navratan Restaurant

Gulistan Tourist Complex, 283 110 **Tel** *(0561) 328 2490*

Open throughout the day, Navratan Restaurant is located close to the famous historical monuments of Fatehpur Sikri and offers impressive views. Popular as a stopover point, it offers snacks and meals in a cheerful garden setting. Specializes in Western cuisine. Alcohol is served.

Key to Price Guide *see p720* **Key to Symbols** *see back cover flap*

HARIDWAR Bestee Restaurant
Jassa Ram Rd, 247 667 **Tel** *(0133) 427 210*

Built in 1988, Bestee Restaurant is most famous for its views of the city; then for its savoury snacks, fresh fruit milkshakes and *lassis* (buttermilk). Good breakfasts are available here. The eatery also serves tasty South Indian and Chinese dishes. Live music creates a soothing background ambience. Smoking not allowed.

KANPUR Kwality
16/97 The Mall, 208 016 **Tel** *(0512) 231 2290*

Part of the Kwality chain of restaurants, this is a popular eatery offering wholesome and tasty Punjabi food at reasonable prices. Western cuisine is available and the bar is also popular with guests. Breakfast is not served. The staff are friendly and efficient.

LUCKNOW Tunde Ke Kebab
Aminabad Chowk, 226 001

People travel long distances to eat the melt-in-the-mouth *kebabs* perfected by the legendary one-armed cook, Tunda at Tunde Ke Kebab. Indian film actors like Shah Rukh Khan and Dilip Kumar are among his clientele. It is a must-visit for those keen on savouring the best *kebabs* in the city.

LUCKNOW Vyanjan Restaurant
Vinay Palace, 10 Ashok Marg, 226 002 **Tel** *(0522) 228 0537*

The vegetarian food is excellent, and the effective air-conditioning adds to the pleasure of eating at this restaurant. The menu, which focuses on regional specialities, is served by efficient staff. The atmosphere of Vyanjan captures the laid-back attitude that the city of Lucknow is famous for.

LUCKNOW Zaika
10 Rani Laxmi Bai, Hazratganj, 226 004 **Tel** *(0522) 400 4040*

Avadhi dishes such as *biryani* and mutton *korma* are the specialities of this restaurant, which also serves other types of cuisine. Prices are reasonable and the quality of service is good. Zaika is a great place for a simple and hearty meal that you will always remember.

LUCKNOW Falaknuma
8 MG Marg, 226 001 **Tel** *(0522) 262 0131*

This rooftop restaurant offers great views of the city and the river; serving delicious, traditionally prepared *dum pukht* cuisine. The service is efficient and the ambience pleasing. Performances by live musicians is an added attraction. Open for lunch and dinner only.

LUCKNOW La Pavilion
6 Shahnajaf Rd, Hazratganj, 226 001 **Tel** *(0522) 400 4040*

Located at Park Inn Hotel, the multi-cuisine La Pavilion is known for serving good Indian as well as Continental dishes. It has a well-equipped executive bar with soft lighting, that creates a soothing ambience. Fine wines are available here.

LUCKNOW Oudhyana Restaurant
Vipin Khand, Gomti Nagar, 226 010 **Tel** *(0522) 239 3939*

The luxurious ambience perfectly complements the regal Avadhi cuisine served at Oudhyana. The restaurant's specialities include *kebabs* and *pulao* (rice dish). Mehfil, the bar, is known for serving rare wines. *Ghazals* (see p748) are usually played here. The quality of service is consistent and very impressive.

MATHURA Best Western Radha Ashok
Masani Bypass Rd, PO Chhatikara, 281 001 **Tel** *(0135) 263 2020*

Conveniently located off the Delhi-Agra highway, Best Western Radha Ashok serves good multi-cuisine food at reasonable prices. The piety of the city, the birthplace of Lord Krishna, is part of the restaurant's ambience. Smoking is not permitted. Plush gardens surround the eatery.

MUSSOORIE Whispering Windows
Library Bazaar, The Mall, 248 179 **Tel** *(0135) 263 2020*

This popular eatery, with views of The Mall, serves delicious Punjabi-style butter chicken as well as some Western dishes. Live music is played only when requested. Wines are also served but only on special request. Credit cards are not accepted here. Open for breakfast, lunch and dinner.

NAINITAL Kumaon Retreat
Grasmere Estate, Mallital, 262 402 **Tel** *(05942) 23 7341*

With wholesome food and fine views of the surrounding town, eating at this multi-cuisine restaurant is a pleasant experience. Regional specialities or Western dishes would be the best choice. The popular bar is well stocked and has an extensive list wine list. Open for breakfast, lunch and dinner.

RISHIKESH Chotiwala
Swarg Ashram, Across Shivanand Jhula, 249 201 **Tel** *(0135) 243 0070*

One of the most famous and popular restaurants in Rishikesh, Chotiwala has been offering delectable South Indian vegetarian delicacies for over four decades. Food is served quickly and efficiently by cheerful waiters. Try the *aloo poori* (potatoes and fried bread). Crowded at most times.

VARANASI Keshari Restaurant

D 14/90 Dasashvamedha, 221 001 **Tel** *(0542) 240 1472*

Well-known for serving pure vegetarian dishes, which are specialities of Varanasi. The menu boasts more than 80 different types of vegetables. Serves breakfast, lunch and dinner. Outdoor seating is available, with special wheelchair access. Service is good. The restaurant has a no-smoking policy.

VARANASI Chowk

Nadesar Palace Ground, 221 002 **Tel** *(0542) 250 3001*

A variety of international favourites are on offer at this lavish multi-cuisine restaurant. Both meat and vegetarian dishes are served. Regular buffets are held. Chowk is also known for organising food festivals that are very popular. Fine wines are available at the bar.

BIHAR & JHARKHAND

BODH GAYA Café Om

Near Bank of India, 824 231

This popular eatery serves excellent breakfasts and delicious cakes. It is also well-known for its Tibetan and Japanese food. Open daily during the pilgrimage season, but closed from May to October. The notice board here carries information that is useful for exploring the city.

BODH GAYA Uruvelya Garden Restaurant

Hotel Niranjana, 824 231 **Tel** *(0631) 240 0475*

A pleasant restaurant offering standard multi-cuisine fare, with soothing music in the background. Pure vegetarian and regional food is also served on request. Breakfast, lunch and dinner available. Alcohol is not served. Major credit cards accepted. Unlike most city-based restaurants, Uruvelya has a quiet, chaos-free ambience.

PATNA Darpan Restaurant cum Coffee Shop

Beer Chand Patel Marg, 800 001 **Tel** *(0612) 222 6270*

A choice of Indian, Chinese and Western cuisines as well as tasty snacks are available here. Inside, the rich aroma of coffee fills the air but dining outdoors is also an attractive option. The Diwana Bar is a nice place to relax with your favourite drink.

PATNA Samrat

Hotel Chanakya, 800 001 **Tel** *(0612) 222 0590*

Quiet and efficient service accompanies the wide choice of Indian, Chinese and Western food served at the Samrat. The restaurant is open for breakfast, lunch and dinner. All meals are freshly prepared. The bar serves excellent beverages and select cocktails.

RAJGIR Centaur Hokke Restaurant

Centaur Hokke Hotel, 803 116 **Tel** *(06119) 25 5245*

This establishment prides itself on its authentic Japanese food, prepared by chefs trained in Japan. Try their fresh shrimps and *tempura* (deep-fried, battered vegetables or seafood). Indian food is also available. The interior has a cosy look with green mats, teak furniture and exotic lamp shades that create the ambience of a Japanese household.

RANCHI Kaveri Restaurant

11 GEL Church Complex, Main Rd, 834 001 **Tel** *(0651) 233 0330*

The best-known vegetarian restaurant in town, Kaveri serves generous portions of simple, wholesome food at reasonable prices. Located in the heart of the city, the restaurant is very popular with businessmen. Separate smoking and non-smoking areas.

MADHYA PRADESH & CHHATTISGARH

BANDHAVGARH Bandhavgarh Jungle Camp Restaurant

Bandhavgarh National Park, 484 661 **Tel** *(07627) 265 303*

English breakfast, Indian lunch and Continental dinner are served in a delightful thatched roundhouse location. Special theme-dinners can be arranged on request. Enjoy your favourite wine while listening to the animals in the national park, a small walk from here.

BHOPAL Jharokha Restaurant

Hotel Amer Palace, 209 Zone I, Maharana Pratap Nagar, 462 011 **Tel** *(0755) 2527 2110*

A well-stocked bar and decent multi-cuisine fare make this one of Bhopal's most popular restaurants. The bakery house just outside the restaurant offers scrumptious pastries, cakes, cookies, cream rolls and pizzas. Open for breakfast, lunch and dinner. Strict no-smoking zones.

Key to Price Guide *see p720* **Key to Symbols** *see back cover flap*

BHOPAL La Kuchina

*157 Shamla Hills, Hotel Jehan Numa Palace, 462 013 **Tel** (0755) 266 1100*

A gastronomic delight for those fond of Italian food and other international cuisines. The only restaurant in the city to serve great pasta. Elegantly decorated the Italian way, La Kuchina has an impressive stock of wine and alcohol. Open for breakfast, lunch and dinner. The service is courteous.

GWALIOR Daawat Restaurant

*Hotel Gwalior Regency, Link Rd, 474 002 **Tel** (0751) 234 0670*

A popular venue for business lunches and family outings, this restaurant serves very good Mughlai and Punjabi fare. Quick service adds to the pleasure of eating here. The quality and taste of the food has remained consistent over the years. Open for breakfast, lunch and dinner.

INDORE Ambrosia

*Hotel Fortune Landmark, Near Meghdoot Gardens, Vijay Nagar, 452 010 **Tel** (0731) 2398 8444*

One of Indore's most exclusive multi-cuisine restaurants, Ambrosia offers an extensive range of Chinese, Indian and Continental food. The menu offers a delicious and fairly priced buffet for lunch. A perfect place to relax over à la carte dinner. All major credit cards are accepted.

JABALPUR Vatika

*Hotel Samdariya, Russel Chowk, 482 001 **Tel** (0761) 241 3400*

A multi-cuisine restaurant with the usual mix of Indian, Chinese and Western food. The South Indian dishes are specially recommended. Serves only lunch and dinner, though breakfast is available for guests staying at the hotel. Reasonably priced. All major credit cards are accepted.

KHAJURAHO Raja Café

*Opp entrance to Western Group of temples, 471 606 **Tel** (07686) 272 307*

Located near the temples, Raja Café is a popular rendezvous point in Khajuraho run by a formidable Indo-Swiss lady. It is great on atmosphere, with tables set out in a large tree-shaded courtyard. The juices, pasta dishes and chocolate cake are recommended.

ORCHHA Hotel Sheesh Mahal Restaurant

*Hotel Sheesh Mahal, 472 246 **Tel** (07680) 252 624*

This atmospheric restaurant located inside the 17th-century palace Sheesh Mahal offers freshly prepared multi-cuisine meals, including lavish lunch and dinner buffets. The restaurant has been recently refurbished and decorated in an attractive manner.

PANNA Machaan Restaurant

*Ken River Lodge, Village Mandla, 488 001 **Tel** (07732) 27 5235*

Built on stilts, this imaginatively designed tree house (*machaan*) has an enchanting ambience and great views of the surrounding countryside. On offer are regional specialities and Western dishes. The food is simple but wholesome and the bar boasts many popular brands of wine.

UJJAIN White House

*Hotel Surana Palace, 23 GDC Rd, Dusshera Maidan, 456 001 **Tel** (0734) 253 0046*

Considered by many to be the best restaurant in Ujjain, White House serves good Indian and Chinese cuisine at reasonable rates. Wonderful views of the surrounding area make outdoor dining an agreeable option here. The staff are friendly. Open for breakfast, lunch and dinner.

KOLKATA

KOLKATA Chung Wah

*13A&B Chittaranjan Avenue, 700 072 **Tel** (033) 2237 7003*

Established in 1920, Chung Wah offers excellent Indian-style Chinese food. Try the chilli chicken, special fried rice and *chop suey* (meat and vegetable stir-fry). Prices are reasonable and portions generous, although the service could be improved. Still recommended for a quick and affordable meal.

KOLKATA Suruchi

*89 Elliott Rd, 700 016 **Tel** (033) 2229 1763*

This little restaurant is run by a women's group that provide help for destitute women. It caters largely for the office-going crowd. The food is simple, wholesome and reasonably priced. Guests claim never to have tasted better prawn *malai* curry, *dal (see p67)* and *mangsho* (lamb in mustard oil). Lunch only.

KOLKATA Kewpie's Kitchen

*2 Elgin Lane, 700 020 **Tel** (033) 2486 9929*

Housed in a 100-year-old Bengali mansion that has been tastefully refurbished.The mouthwatering dishes served at this "food boutique" are very popular, especially the Kewpie *thali* (platter). The restaurant remains crowded throughout the day and serves the best Bengali food in town. It also sells its own well-regarded recipe book and pickles.

KOLKATA Mainland China

3A Gurusaday Rd, 700 019 **Tel** *(033) 2283 7964*

Another of Kolkata's famous Chinese restaurants that attracts discerning palates, especially those with a taste for seafood. The specialities here include skewered jumbo prawns, peking duck with traditional condiments and *drunken chicken* in shaoxing wine.

KOLKATA Silver Grill

18E Park Street, 700 071 **Tel** *(033) 2229 4549*

A popular restaurant, Silver Grill serves reasonably priced Indian-Chinese food. Their fried chicken *wonton* (noodle dumpling) is heartily recommended. Other tasty dishes include the crispy chicken and the Singapore-Thai fish. The bar here is also popular. Open for lunch and dinner.

KOLKATA Tangerine

2/1 Outram Street, 700 017 **Tel** *(033) 2281 5450*

This Chinese restaurant specializes in lobster thermidor and grilled *bhetki* (fish). The prawns are also very good. Fine wine is also available. Service is very quick and the staff are efficient. The ideal place for a business lunch. Tangerine does not serve breakfasts.

KOLKATA Aheli

The Peerless Inn, 12 Jawaharlal Nehru Rd, 700 013 **Tel** *(033) 2228 0301*

One of Calcutta's first upscale Bengali restaurants, Aheli still draws a crowd for its traditional Bengali delicacies, such as steamed *hilsa* (fish), *macher sorse paturi* (fish cooked with mustard paste) and *chingri malai* curry (prawns and coconut milk curry). Food is served in an intimate terra-cotta coloured dining room by courteous staff.

KOLKATA Charnock's

KB-26, Sector 3, Salt Lake City, 700 098 **Tel** *(033) 2335 1349*

Located in the busy IT hub of the city, Charnock's offers a wide variety of options from fast food to multi-cuisine meals to fresh fruit juice and ice cream. The restaurant also serves a selection of wines. Pleasant ambience and efficient service. Open for lunch and dinner.

KOLKATA Fire and Ice

41 Chowringhee, 700 071 **Tel** *(033) 2288 4073*

A new restaurant, Fire and Ice has already established a reputation for serving the best pizzas in town. Decorated with posters of Hollywood and Bollywood films, this eatery has a real pizzeria atmosphere. The menu also features other classic Italian fare and diners appreciate the authentic taste.

KOLKATA Kwality

17 Park Street, 700 016 **Tel** *(033) 2229 7681*

This well-established restaurant is famous for its North Indian food, although their Western dishes are equally popular. Specialities include fish *masala kebab*, *sangam kebab* (a combination of mutton and chicken) and chicken tetrazzini. Also recommended are the ice cream sundaes and iced coffee.

KOLKATA Baan Thai

The Oberoi Grand Hotel, 15 Jawaharlal Nehru Rd, 700 013 **Tel** *(033) 2249 2323*

For those in a hurry, Baan Thai undertakes to serve lunch in no longer than 45 minutes. Others are welcome to linger over the wide variety of excellent Thai dishes on offer. The restaurant decor imitates the traditional Thai seating arrangement known as "Khuntok". Open for lunch and dinner.

KOLKATA Zaranj and Jong's

26 Jawaharlal Nehru Rd, 700 087 **Tel** *(033) 2249 0369*

Zarjang and Jong's are two separate upmarket restaurants that share an entrance. Zaranj is renowned for its Punjabi cuisine, especially the Zaranj *raan* (marinated lamb). Jong's specializes in Chinese, Japanese, Thai and Burmese food – try their coconut prawns with bamboo shoots. Closed on Tuesdays.

WEST BENGAL & SIKKIM

DARJEELING Glenary's

Nehru Rd, 734 101 **Tel** *(0354) 225 4122*

This multi-cuisine restaurant is a popular meeting place for travellers. It has an attached bakery that serves great breads and pastry, fine Darjeeling tea, and dishes made with Kalimpong cheese. It also offers beautiful views of Kanchendzonga on clear days.

DARJEELING The Park Restaurant

41 Laden La Rd, 734 101 **Tel** *(0354) 225 4989*

The Park Restaurant serves some of the best Indian cuisine in town. The tempting buffet lunches and the mutton *biryani* are hot favourites. Their Thai food is also worth trying, especially the Thai red curry. Packed lunches are provided for travellers on request. The restaurant is closed from mid-January to mid-February.

Key to Price Guide *see p720* **Key to Symbols** *see back cover flap*

DARJEELING Windamere Hotel Restaurant
Windamere Hotel, Observatory Hill, Mall Rd, 734 101 **Tel** *(0354) 225 4041*

The main dining room at Windamere seats up to 80 people, but there are also three smaller rooms for intimate dining. The cuisine is Continental, Indian, Nepalese and Tibetan. Beautiful views and the excellent Darjeeling tea and cakes at this Raj-era establishment make up for the rather stodgy meals.

GANGTOK Dragon Hall
Hotel Tashi Delek, 737 101 **Tel** *(03592) 202 991*

Beautifully decorated with traditional Sikkimese art, Dragon Hall serves buffet spreads that offer a choice of Tibetan, Sikkimese, Indian and Chinese fare. Western dishes are also available. The Yak Bar serves a popular selection of beverages and wine. Open for breakfast, lunch and dinner.

GANGTOK Snow Lion Restaurant
Hotel Tibet, Paljor Stadium Rd, 737 101 **Tel** *(03592) 203 468*

Snow Lion Restaurant is an excellent place to sample Sikkimese and Tibetan food. The *momos* (dumplings) and mandarin fish are specially recommended. Also on offer are Indian, Japanese and Continental cuisines. The well-stocked bar adds to the dining experience. The decor is tasteful and very Tibetan.

GANGTOK The Tea House Bar and Restaurant
Hotel Chumbi Residency, Tibet Rd, 737 101 **Tel** *(03592) 226 618*

Watch the twinkling lights of Rumtek Hill as you dine at The Tea House Restaurant. Good Tibetan, Chinese and Indian fare is served here and the authentic taste of the North Indian tandoor is a special draw for most visitors. The bar is the ideal place for an informal meal and a refreshing drink.

GANGTOK Wild Orchid Restaurant
Central Hotel, 31-A National Highway, 737 101 **Tel** *(03592) 202 105*

Furbished in the traditional Sikkimese style, Wild Orchid offers Chinese, Western and South Indian fare. Alcohol is served here and banquet facilities are also available. The staff are courteous and prompt. Open for breakfast, lunch and dinner, with last orders taken at 8pm. Smoking is prohibited.

GANGTOK The Oyster Restaurant
Hotel Sonam Delek, Tibet Rd, 737 101 **Tel** *(03592) 202 566*

The French toast and banana pancake at The Oyster are justly popular. The magnificent views of Kanchendzonga from the restaurant is an added attraction. The cuisine comprises of Indian, Chinese, Continental and local Sikkimese dishes. The restaurant serves breakfast, lunch and dinner.

KALIMPONG Kalimpong Park Hotel
Rinkingpong Rd, 734 301 **Tel** *(03552) 255 304*

On offer here is the usual variety of Sikkimese and Chinese food as well as a selection of wines. Some Nepali and Tibetan dishes are also available on request. The restaurant serves breakfast, lunch and dinner. It has large dining areas and is well-equipped to deal with business guests.

SILIGURI Amrapali
Hotel Cindrella, 3rd Mile, Sevoke Rd, 734 401 **Tel** *(0353) 254 7136*

This is a vegetarian restaurant that serves excellent breakfasts and lunches. Outdoor dining facilities and a well-stocked bar add appeal to a visit to Amrapali. Packed meals are available for travellers who are in a hurry. The staff are courteous and eager to please.

ORISSA

BHUBANESWAR Fish & Prawn Restaurant
P-1 Jaydev Vihar, 751 015 **Tel** *(0674) 253 5771*

As the name suggests, this restaurant is famous for its fresh seafood cooked in a variety of styles. The portions are generous and local specialities can be ordered in advance. Tai Pai prawn, *samadri khazana*, fish florentine, seafood sizzler plate, schezwan crab, and pomfret in red Thai curry are popular.

BHUBANESWAR Nakli Dhaba
Mayfair Lagoon Hotel, 8-B Jaydev Vihar, 751 015 **Tel** *(0674) 255 9533*

Decorated to look like a *dhaba* (roadside eatery), this restaurant serves good *tandoori* and vegetarian food. The Western fast food and confectionery are also popular. Specializes in Northwest Frontier cuisine. The ambience is warm and inviting. Open for lunch and dinner.

BHUBANESWAR Pushpanjali
CB-1 Nayapali, 751 013 **Tel** *(0674) 230 1010*

With all-day dining, this multi-cuisine restaurant offers an appetising buffet and a special dish of the day. The decor, with its rich earthy tones and ethnic atmosphere, is inspired by temple interiors in Orissa. The bar, Madhushala, serves both domestic and international drinks. Ample parking space available.

CHILIKA LAKE Panthanivas
Barkul, PO Balgaun, 752 030 **Tel** *(06756) 220 488*

With lovely views of the lake and a constant cool breeze, Panthanivas is a beautiful place to dine at. The best thing to sample here is the fresh seafood prepared in the local style. The menu also features some Western and Chinese dishes. The restaurant is open for breakfast, lunch and dinner.

CUTTACK Sagun
Hotel Akbari Continental, Haripur Rd, 753 001 **Tel** *(0671) 262 3264*

Regional and vegetarian food may be had here on request, but the restaurant is best known for its rich Mughlai dishes. Outdoor barbecue is provided when the weather is favourable. Live music is also played but only on special occasions. Open for breakfast, lunch and dinner.

GOPALPUR-ON-SEA Chilika – Swosti Palm Resort Restaurant
Beach Rd, 761 002 **Tel** *(0680) 224 2453*

Situated on one of the best beaches in India, Chilika – Swosti Palm Resort Restaurant serves multi-cuisine fare. The fresh seafood specialities on the menu are much recommended. Views from the restaurant are spectacular and the atmosphere is relaxed. Facilites include a bar and outdoor dining space.

KONARK Gitanjali Restaurant
Panthnivas, OTDC Ltd, 752 111 **Tel** *(06578) 235 831*

This good-value restaurant is conveniently situated close to the Sun Temple and is a popular choice for visitors to the area. Gitanjali offers Chinese, Indian and Western food, but seafood dishes are the restaurant's speciality. Outdoor seating available.

PURI The Legend
SE Railways Hotel, CT Rd, 752 001 **Tel** *(06752) 222 063*

The food here is a good example of Raj cuisine which traces its ancestry to the railway catering of colonial times. Multi-course meals are served at fixed times and offer fantastic value for money. The restaurant is open for breakfast, lunch and dinner. Western dishes are also available.

ASSAM & THE NORTH EAST

AGARTALA Rajdarbar
Hotel Rajdhani, BK Rd, 799 001 **Tel** *(0381) 222 3387*

The restaurant has cane and bamboo interiors inspired by traditional Tripura craftsmanship. The menu offers tasty Indian, Chinese and *tandoori* items. Rajdarbar is also a good place to savour Tripura's tribal cuisine, such as *vhanghui* (a rice dish). Hosts food festivals in October and November.

DIMAPUR Hotel Tragopan
Circular Rd, 797 112 **Tel** *(03862) 230 351*

Hotel Tragopan is conveniently located near the airport as well as the railway station. Apart from the usual Indian and Chinese fare, the menu also features the Tragopan Special – a fish or chicken curry. Also known for its traditional Naga food, where the pork or fish is cooked in a bamboo shoot.

GUWAHATI Tandoor
Dynasty Hotel, Lakhotia, 781 001 **Tel** *(0361) 251 6021*

As the name suggests, this restaurant is renowned for its *tandoori* delicacies. The chef whips up *goshth pasandas* (lamb in rich onion gravy), *raan-e-gulmarg* (stuffed mutton leg) and *tandoori* prawns among others specialities. The ambience is pleasant with potted plants and a fountain. Live music is also performed. Open for lunch and dinner.

GUWAHATI Ushaban Restaurant and Coffee Shop
Hotel Brahmaputra Ashok, MG Rd, 784 001 **Tel** *(0361) 260 2281*

The restaurant has traditional Assamese decor and the menu features Chinese, Indian, Continental and Assamese cuisine. The *masor tenga* (a kind of fish curry) and papaya *khar* are worth trying, as is the excellant coffee. Outdoor seating is available. Open for breakfast, lunch and dinner.

IMPHAL The Host
Hotel Anand Continental, Khoyathong Rd, 795 001 **Tel** *(0385) 244 9422*

A simple yet modern restaurant, serving Continental, Mughlai and Indian cuisines. This is also a good place to try some regional specialities such as *iromba* (dry fish) and *nga thomba* (fish curry). Service is efficient and friendly. Credit cards are not accepted.

ITANAGAR Bhismak Restaurant and Coffee Shop
Hotel Donyi Polo Ashok, C-Sector, 791 111 **Tel** *(0360) 221 2626*

Located on a hill, this restaurant provides panoramic views and sumptuous food. The menu comprises of Indian, Chinese and Continental dishes. *Tandoori* items are the specialities here. Local cuisine is prepared but only on special request. A good place for snacks as well as meals.

Key to Price Guide *see p720* **Key to Symbols** *see back cover flap*

KOHIMA Shilloi

Hotel Japhu, PR Hills, 797 001 **Tel** *(0370) 224 0211*

A hilltop location and a charming garden dining area make Shilloi a popular restaurant. The menu varies and offers standard but well-made Indian, Chinese and Continental food. Traditional Naga cuisine, such as pork cooked in bamboo shoots, is also served here.

SHILLONG Pinecone

Hotel Pinewood, European Ward, Rita Rd, 793 001 **Tel** *(0364) 222 3116*

Set in tranquil surroundings close to Ward Lake, the Pinecone restaurant offers popular Indian and Western buffet meals. Open for breakfast, lunch and dinner. The coffee shop here is known for its fine snacks and beverages. The bar lounge, The Cellar, serves a wide range of alcoholic drinks.

TEZPUR Gabharu

Hotel Luit, Ranu Singh Rd, 784 001 **Tel** *(03712) 224 708*

Friendly staff, attractive surroundings and reasonably priced Indian, Western and Chinese food make eating at the Gabharu a pleasant experience. Despite its location in the middle of the town, it has a serene and quiet air about it. Open for breakfast, lunch and dinner.

RAJASTHAN

AJMER Sheesh Mahal

Hotel Mansingh Palace, Vaishali Nagar., 305 001 **Tel** *(0145) 242 5956*

Meals at the Sheesh Mahal are complemented by stunning views of the Ana Sagar lake. The restaurant specializes in a variety of cuisines including Continental, Chinese, mughlai and Rajasthani fare. The bar, Sipehsalar, is well-stocked with variety of drinks. Puppet-shows and folk songs are presented in the evenings.

BHARATPUR Laxmi Vilas Palace

Kakaji-Ki-Kothi, Civil Lines, 321 001 **Tel** *(05644) 223 523*

Farm-fresh vegetables from the palace gardens are used here and the cottage cheese is made in the palace dairy. The authentic Rajasthani dishes include the famous *churma*, a sweet dish. Personal supervision by the royal family that owns the palace ensures high standards of service.

BIKANER Hotel Bhanwar Niwas

Rampuria Street, 334 005 **Tel** *(0151) 252 9323*

Endless waves of sand dunes form the backdrop to this splendid restaurant, located in a *haveli* (mansion). The menu offers tasty vegetarian food and includes both Western and regional specialities. There is a concert in the courtyard every evening. Good business and banquet facilities are also available.

BIKANER Manwar

Hotel Karni Bhawan, Gandhinagar, 334 001 **Tel** *(0151) 252 4701*

Authentic Marwari cusine and simple Continental dishes are served in this Art Deco heritage hotel and restaurant. Rajasthani food is also served here in the traditional style. Its Maikada Bar has a great selection of Indian and foreign alcohol. Open for breakfast, lunch and dinner.

JAIPUR Four Seasons

D-43/A Subash Marg, C-Scheme, 302 001 **Tel** *(0141) 237 5221*

A favourite with locals for family outings, this multi-cuisine restaurant is particularly known for its vegetarian dishes. Take-away food, free home delivery and ample parking space are also available. Due to its popularity expect to wait for a table at the weekend.

JAIPUR Laxmi Mishthan Bhandar (LMB)

Johari Bazaar, 302 003 **Tel** *(0141) 256 5844*

This vegetarian restaurant, in the centre of the old city, is an institution in Jaipur. Try their *paneer tikka* (marinated cheese and vegetables) and creamy *kulfi* (milk dessert). The *thali* offers 15 items from Marwari cuisine. Select Continental dishes are also served. LMB is perhaps best known for its delicious range of *mithais* (sweets).

JAIPUR Niros

MI Rd, 302 001 **Tel** *(0141) 221 8520*

Reservations are needed to eat at this popular restaurant, which serves excellent Chinese food, *reshmi* (chicken) *kebabs* and *paneer tikka*. The iced coffee with a scoop of ice cream is another favourite. Niros has been serving quality food since 1947 and is recommended by most visitors.

JAIPUR Surabhi

Old Amber Rd, Subash Chowk, 302 016 **Tel** *(0141) 263 5954*

Authentic Rajasthani cuisine is served in this atmospheric restaurant housed in an old *haveli* (see p22). Take a look at the fascinating collection of turbans here (200 styles are displayed). You can even try your hand at tying one while you wait for your meal.

JAISALMER Miraj

Hotel Narayan Niwas, 345 001 **Tel** *(02992) 252 408*

Majestic views of the desert are on display at this rooftop restaurant. The food and dining services are excellent and the menu offers a variety of cuisines. The atmosphere lightens up during the evening with exotic food and folk performances. All major credit cards are accepted.

JAISALMER Trio

Gandhi Chowk, Near Amar Sagar Gate, 345 001 **Tel** *(02992) 252 738*

Located near the Amar Singh Gate, this restaurant serves delicious local cuisine of the desert areas. The chef also brings interesting variations to signature Rajasthani dishes. The service here is excellent. Open for breakfast, lunch and dinner. All major credit cards are accepted.

JODHPUR Kalinga Resturant

Opp Sakar Bazaar, Station Rd, 342 001 **Tel** *(0291) 262 4066*

The speciality of Kalinga Restaurant is traditional Rajasthani and Gujarati food. There is a special menu for children. Also available are fine wines and tasty desserts. The items are very reasonably priced and the establishment is open for breakfast, lunch and dinner. The interior is bright and lively.

JODHPUR Ranbanka Bagh Restaurant

Near Circuit House, 342 006 **Tel** *(0291) 251 2801*

An open-air restaurant by a swimming pool, Ranbanka Bagh Restaurant offers a wide range of international dishes. Ask for the popular *murgh lahsuni tikka* (garlic chicken) and *murgh malai kebab (barbecue chicken)*. The staff are quick and attentive and the place is ideal for large banquets and receptions. Open for breakfast, lunch and dinner.

JODHPUR On the Rocks

Hotel Ajit Bhawan, Opp Circuit House, 342 006 **Tel** *(0291) 251 0410*

This garden restaurant, with lovely landscaping, has an enchanting ambience. It serves tasty Indian and Continental dishes. Guests have a choice between large buffets and à la carte meals. Traditional Rajasthani dances bring the evenings alive. Open for lunch and dinner.

MOUNT ABU Palace Hotel Restaurant

Palace Hotel, Bikaner House, Dilwara Rd, 307 501 **Tel** *(02974) 238 673*

The spacious, stately dining room of the Palace Hotel offers an excellent variety of meals from around the world. The Rajasthani dishes are particularly tasty. The restaurant provides breakfast, lunch and dinner, and also prepares picnic hampers. All major credit cards are accepted.

PUSHKAR Shiva

RTDC, Sarovar Hotel, 305 022 **Tel** *(0145) 277 2040*

Located in a government-run tourist hotel, Shiva serves pure vegetarian meals. Reasonably priced all-you-can-eat breakfast options are available. This includes cereal, fruit and brown bread with a choice of butter, jam or cheese. No alcohol is served in this holy city.

PUSHKAR Sunset Café

Next to Pushkar Palace, 305 022 **Tel** *(0145) 277 2010*

Try breakfast or tea here and watch the sunrise or sunset, as the sound of temple bells and the view of the tranquil lake soothe your senses. The *dosas (see p554)* and cakes are good. The restaurant serves breakfast, lunch and dinner, and is a popular hangout with most travellers. All major credit cards accepted.

UDAIPUR Jagat Niwas Palace

Lal Ghat, Jagdish Mandir, 313 001 **Tel** *(0294) 242 2860*

This open-air restaurant offers spectacular views of the Lake Palace. Tables are well-arranged and the cushions are elevated to create alcoves, so you can sit comfortably and eat your meal at leisure. The Indian food here is very tasty and the ambience spellbinding.

UDAIPUR Ambrai

Amit-Ki-Haveli, Outside Chandpol, 313 001 **Tel** *(0294) 243 1085*

A superb lakeside location, good multi-cuisine fare and a lovely garden make Ambrai a popular restaurant. Its North Indian food is characterized by meat-based delicacies, with gravy made of poppy seeds and cashew. The *gulab jamun (see p67)* and *peda* (biscuits) are delicious. There is live Indian music in the evenings.

UDAIPUR Gallery Restaurant

Fateh Prakash Palace, City Palace, 313 001 **Tel** *(0294) 252 8016*

The Gallery Restaurant at Fateh Prakash Palace is a speciality restaurant serving Continental cuisine. It offers breathtaking views of Lake Pichola and the island palaces of Jagmandir and Jagniwas. A good choice of alcohol is available at the bar. Open for breakfast, lunch and dinner.

UDAIPUR Jharokha

Lake Palace Hotel, Lake Pichola, 313 001 **Tel** *(0294) 252 7961*

The buffet meals served in the fabulous interiors of Jharokha are accompanied by enchanting views of the lake. Reservations are essential. This 24-hour restaurant offers a wide choice of contemporary cuisines from various parts of the world, and includes traditional Rajasthani cuisine.

Key to Price Guide *see p720* **Key to Symbols** *see back cover flap*

GUJARAT

AHMEDABAD Swati Snacks

13 Gandhi Baug Society, Opp Nirman Bhavan, Law Garden, 380 009 **Tel** *(079) 2640 5900*

Swati is the place to go for traditional Indian snacks and wood-fired pizzas. Be sure to try the *moong khichdi* (lentils and rice) and *kadhi* (chickpea and lentil curry) combo or the *dhan-shak* (meat and lentil casserole) with rice. Handmade ice cream is available in a variety of flavours. Drinks like coconut punch and sugarcane juice are also served.

AHMEDABAD RK Egg Eatery

Vision Complex, Panjarpole Char Rasta, 380 009 **Tel** *(079) 2415 3787*

With over 150 different egg-based dishes on its menu, RK Egg Eatery is a popular establishment, especially with youngsters. The outlet's unique egg-shaped design and unusual dishes, such as Abhijit Omlette or Varsha Fry (named after students of the design institute where Egg Eatery began), give this restaurant lots of character.

AHMEDABAD Tomato's

Mardia Plaza, CG Rd, Navrangpura, 380 006 **Tel** *(079) 2646 1198*

Mexican food is the speciality at this American-style diner, which also offers free popcorn. The decor is vintage American, with part of the restaurant dedicated to Charlie Chaplin and Elvis Presley. Guests can request their favourite songs to be played. Only lunch and dinner are served.

AHMEDABAD Rajwadu

Near Jivaraj Park, 380 055 **Tel** *(079) 2664 3845*

An open-air eatery located on the outskirts of the city, Rajwadu has a traditional and enchantingly rustic atmosphere. It offers excellent Gujarati cuisine with specialities such as *bajri rotlas* (millet bread) and sweet *malpuas* (deep-fried pancakes). The service here is excellent. The restaurant serves pure vegetarian food and is only open for dinner.

AHMEDABAD Vishalla

Opp Vasna Tolnaka, 380 055 **Tel** *(079) 2660 2422*

This unique open-air restaurant recreates the atmosphere of rural Gujarat, with authentic Gujarati food served in traditional village huts. It also has a superb museum of antique kitchen utensils. Do not miss the performances by folk artists in the evenings.

AHMEDABAD Fortune Landmark

Usmanpura Crossroads, Ashram Rd, 380 008 **Tel** *(079) 3988 4444*

Consisting of three restaurants, Fortune Landmark is a food-lover's paradise. Khyber, the barbecue restaurant, serves delicious Indian and Continental cuisine, while Orchid, a multi-cuisine restaurant offers mouthwatering buffets from breakfast to dinner. Pastries and coffee can be enjoyed at the in-house café.

BHAVNAGAR Nilambagh Dining Hall

Nilambagh Palace Hotel, 364 002 **Tel** *(0278) 242 4241*

Part of a heritage hotel, the Nilambagh Dining Hall is regal, with chandeliers and gleaming silver. Try the regional dishes and *tandoori* food. During summer, garden chairs, swings and wrought-iron chairs are laid out on the lawns where guests can dine.

DIU Apana Restaurant

Apana Guesthouse, Old Fort Rd, 362 520 **Tel** *(02875) 252 112*

A pleasant rooftop restaurant with sea views, Aparna offers an excellent choice of meals from a menu of 263 different dishes. It gives good value for money and is popular with most travellers. The generous seafood platter with lobster and crab is a must-have.

DIU Rivera Restaurant and Bar

Radhika Beach Resort, Nagoa Beach, 362 520 **Tel** *(02875) 251 553*

This excellent restaurant offers a wide choice of cuisines and specializes in seafood. Staff are attentive and the surroundings idyllic. The well-stocked bar serves Indian and imported alcohol. The coffee shop is also a popular hangout. Ideal for both business and leisure travellers.

JAMNAGAR The Orion Restaurant

Hotel Orbit Park Inn, Khambalia Highway, 361 006 **Tel** *(0288) 223 4484*

Modestly-priced multi-cuisine food is offered at the pleasant Orion Restaurant. Lavish buffets are laid out on request for groups. The decor uses the natural colours and hues of its surroundings to make the restaurant a truly soothing and relaxing place. Open for breakfast, lunch and dinner.

VADODARA Mandap

Hotel Express Towers, RC Dutt Rd, 123 303 **Tel** *(0265) 305 5000*

The traditional decor of Mandap goes well with the authentic Gujarati meals for which this restaurant is famous. The food is pure vegetarian. There is also an excellent cake shop. The staff are cooperative and the restaurant is ideal for holding business lunches. Smoking is prohibited.

MUMBAI

MUMBAI Rajdhani Restaurant

361 Sheikh Memon Street, Near Crawford Market, 400 002 **Tel** *(022) 2342 6919*

Situated close to the famous Crawford Market, Rajdhani Restaurant is the ideal retreat for tired shoppers. The establishment specializes in regional Indian cuisine and offers *thalis* (platters) from Gujarat, Rajasthan, Maharashtra and Kathiawar. Open for lunch and dinner.

MUMBAI The Bharat Bar & Restaurant Excellensea

317 Bharat House, SBS Rd, Fort, 400 001 **Tel** *(022) 2267 2677*

Customers can choose from live seafood at this excellent establishment. A great favourite with most visitors is the crab curry. The restaurant also serves delicious South Indian breads as accompaniments to their gravies. Select Western dishes are also available. The restaurant has a strict no-smoking zone. Open for lunch and dinner.

MUMBAI Ankur

Meadows House, Tamarind House, Fort, 400 001 **Tel** *(022) 2263 0393*

An old restaurant that has reinvented itself, Ankur now serves both vegetarian and meat dishes. The prawn *gassi* (coconut curry) and chicken *aadajina* are highly recommended. Located close to Bombay House, this busy seafood eatery is a favourite with the office-going crowd. Service is prompt and unintrusive.

MUMBAI Khyber

145 Mahatma Gandhi Rd, Fort, 400 001 **Tel** *(022) 2267 3227*

An atmospheric restaurant with murals by renowned Indian artist, Anjolie Ela Menon. The waiters, dressed as Pathans, serve delicious grilled meats including *kebabs* and Khyber *raan* (leg of lamb). The menu offers exclusively North Indian dishes, predominantly from Punjab.

MUMBAI Leopold Café

Colaba Causeway, 400 001 **Tel** *(022) 2287 3362*

A longtime favourite with travellers, this restaurant, established in 1971, has a large selection of well-made multi-cuisine dishes. The fruit drinks and milk shakes are legendary. The ambience is unique, with street café style tables and Hollywood film posters adorning the walls. The staff are helpful and efficient.

MUMBAI Ling's Pavilion

19/21 Mahakavi Bhushan Marg, behind Regal Cinema, 400 039 **Tel** *(022) 2285 0023*

Ling's Pavilion has a rather overpowering interior, decorated in loud reds and greens, but the food, including the hugely popular baby lobsters, is excellent. Reservations are essential at this family-run restaurant and the staff are helpful in recommending dishes. Open for lunch and dinner.

MUMBAI Mahesh Lunch Home

8B Cawasji Patel Street, 400 001 **Tel** *(022) 2287 0938*

This restaurant specializes in delicious, fresh seafood and is credited with having made the seafood dishes of the Konkan Coast popular. Giant portions of crab and *rawas* (salmon) are among the most popular items here. Also try the *surmai* (fish) fry, pomfret in green masala, *koliwada (marinated fish)*, crab *tandoori* and *sol kadi (kokum* and coconut drink).

MUMBAI Not Just Jazz By The Bay

Marine Drive, 400 020 **Tel** *(022) 2285 1876*

Great lunch buffets with a variety of salads and pastas are offered at this music-themed restaurant. The place comes to life in the evenings, with live jazz from Wednesday to Saturday. The piano shaped steps at the entrance, softly-lit interiors, the guitar-shaped bar and stylised music notes on crockery make dining here a unique experience.

MUMBAI Bayview

29 Marine Plaza, Marine Drive, 400 020 **Tel** *(022) 2285 1212*

A palm-fringed view of the sea adds to the great multi-cuisine lunch and dinner buffets served here. On offer are regional specialities as well as Western dishes. As the evening sets in, the large glass windows offer fine views of the beautifully lit Queen's Necklace. The restaurant is open for breakfast, lunch and dinner.

MUMBAI Café Royal

166 Mahatma Gandhi Rd, Opp Regal Cinema, 400 001 **Tel** *(022) 2288 3982*

Catering mainly to meat-eaters, this restaurant's sizzling meat and vegetable plates, grilled sandwiches and burgers are especially popular. Originally an Iranian eatery, this softly-lit restaurant made news when Bill Clinton had a meal here; which can be seen by the many pictures on the wall. Open for lunch and dinner.

MUMBAI Fountain Restaurant

57 Mahatma Gandhi Rd, 400 001 **Tel** *(022) 2267 5315*

Despite its slightly faded air, you can be assured of a good meal here. The plates of sizzling meat and vegetables are highly recommended. Guests can choose from chicken steak, chicken *shashlik* (kebab) and the popular fountain veggies. Portions are generous. There is a non-smoking area on the ground floor. Open for lunch and dinner.

Key to Price Guide *see p720* **Key to Symbols** *see back cover flap*

MUMBAI Indigo

4 Mandlik Rd, Colaba, 400 001 Tel (022) 6636 8999

All the big names in showbiz frequent this establishment. Situated in a pleasant old mansion, Indigo has elegant surroundings which complement its *nouvelle* Indo-English cuisine. Its signature dish is the risotto with lobster and tuna. Try also the *rawas* (Indian salmon), *filet mignon* and the tempting desserts.

MUMBAI Little Italy

18-B Hotel Atlantic, Juhu Tara Rd, 400 049 Tel (022) 2660 8815

Run by a native Italian, Little Italy offers pure vegetarian Italian food. The *fettucine primavera* pasta, with capsicum, capers and olives and the *risotto alla milanese* (saffron-infused rice) are delicious and few guests notice the absence of meat. The restaurant also has a fine selection of wines to accompany meals.

MUMBAI O Calcutta

Hotel Rosewood, Tulsiwadi Lane, Tardeo, 400 034 Tel (022) 2496 3114

This small, stylish restaurant offers a choice of regional Indian fish dishes. Try its Bengali-style *machher jhol* and the banana flower with *luchis* (fried bread). Its mouthwatering *rasmalai* (milk and cottage cheese) makes a great dessert. The well-stocked bar is a hit with guests. Open for lunch and dinner.

MUMBAI Soul Fry Casa

Currimjee Building, Opp Mumbai University, MG Rd, 400 001 Tel (022) 2267 1421

The best thing about Soul Fry Casa is that it has music gigs almost every night. On the food front, the restaurant boasts Goan delicacies such as *vindaloo* (marinated pork curry), *balchao* (see p441) and *sorpotel* (spiced pork), but it is Soul Fry Casa's signature dish – fried bombay duck – that draws most visitors.

MUMBAI Vong Wong

Express Towers, First Floor, Nariman Point, 400 021 Tel (022) 2287 5633

Located in the business district of Mumbai, this Oriental eatery probably has the best interior in southern Mumbai. A wooden stairway, huge windows and semi-circular arches make you want to stay and enjoy the surroundings. About 300 Chinese and Thai dishes are on the menu.

MUMBAI Apoorva

Noble Chambers, SA Brelvi Marg, Near Horniman Circle, Fort, 400 001 Tel (022) 2287 0335

This excellent restaurant specializes in Konkan seafood. Try the fried *surmai* fish, crab and prawns with feather-light *neer dosas* (rice and water pancakes). The seafood cooked in Keralite style is particularly delicious here. The bar has an impressive collection of both Indian and imported wines. Open for lunch and dinner.

MUMBAI Busaba

4 Mandlik Rd, Off Colaba Causeway, 400 001 Tel (022) 2204 3779

Recently renovated, Busaba's new interiors are decorated with exotic lamps, chic sofas, scented candles and orchids. Try the steamed tiger prawns, *ghimbap* (Korean sushi) or the mustard *goop* with the *carpaccio*. The bartender is famous for his creative cocktail mixing. Open for lunch and dinner.

MUMBAI Olive Bar and Kitchen

14 Union Park, Pali Hill Tourist Hotels Pvt Ltd, Bandra (W), 400 052 Tel (022) 2605 8228

A trendy new restaurant serving pricey gourmet delicacies such as oysters, caviar and salmon. More down-to-earth treats are also available, including a velvety cocoa fudge. Lamps hanging from the frangipani trees, as well as candles and pebbled pathways, give the establishment a distinct identity.

MUMBAI Tetsuma

41/44 Minoo Desai Marg, Colaba., 400 005 Tel (022) 2287 6578

Tetsuma is located in the member's only club Athena. You will find everyone here – from industrial tycoons to top film stars. Soft lighting, Buddha statues and even decorative ponds give this up-market restaurant a Japanese look. The cuisine is essentially Oriental and Japanese.

MUMBAI The Pearl of The Orient

The Ambassador, Churchgate, 400 020 Tel (022) 2204 1131

This revolving restaurant is open 24 hours and offers superb views of the Arabian Sea. The cuisine is predominently Thai, Chinese and Japanese. Specialities include the sushi platter, Korean noodles, tom yum soup, Thai red and green curry, crispy corn chilli and cheese ginger chilli. Open for lunch and dinner.

MUMBAI Trishna Bar and Restaurant

7 Ropewalk Lane, Sai Baba Marg, Fort Rd, 400 024 Tel (022) 2270 3213

Another of Mumbai's great seafood restaurants, Trishna attracts many celebrities. The Konkan-style lobster, king crab and *tandoori* pomfret are outstanding. Chinese cuisine is also served. The decor is a bit dull and the service can be slow, but the food more than makes up for it. The service takes time. Reservations are recommended.

MUMBAI Wasabi by Morimoto

Taj Mahal Palace and Tower, Apollo Bunder, 400 001 Tel (022) 6665 3366

Mumbai's first contemporary Japanese restaurant features a sake and sushi bar. The menu offers a diverse selection of seafood and vegetarian dishes. Try the Kumamoto oysters and the tofu cheesecake. Views of the Arabian Sea help make the meal truly memorable.

MAHARASHTRA

AURANGABAD Foodwalas Tandoor
*Shyam Chambers, Bansidal Nagar, 431 001 **Tel** (0240) 232 8481*

Located near the railway station, this restaurant has been serving Indian, Chinese and Continental cuisines for almost 20 years. The succulent and tender chicken dishes are recommended. The decor is dominated by Egyptian statues. The establishment is open during lunch and dinner hours.

AURANGABAD Chinatown Restaurant
*Hotel Amarpreet, Jalna Rd, 431 001 **Tel** (0240) 233 2521*

Located in the heart of the city, Chinatown Restaurant serves Indian, Thai, Italian, Continental and Chinese cuisines. The establishment is most popular for its rice and fish dishes. This Chinese-motifed place has a bar and good outdoor seating and dining arrangements.

AURANGABAD Residency Restaurant
*Taj Residency, 8-N-12 CIDCO, Rauza Bagh, 431 003 **Tel** (0240) 238 1106*

Set inside the palace-styled Taj Residency hotel overlooking beautiful gardens, the Residency Restaurant serves a wide variety of Indian, Chinese and Western food. This is a good place to sample regional food specialities. A themed dinner or food festival is organised once a month. Open for breakfast, lunch and dinner.

CHIPLUN Riverview Restaurant
*Gateway Riverview Lodge, Dhamandivi Taluka Khed, Distt Ratnagiri, 415 707 **Tel** (02355) 259 081*

Though a wide selection of cuisines is offered here, Marwari and Konkani dishes are the Riverview Restaurant's specialities. Its stylish bar also attracts a lot of attention. Scenic views from large windows of this cozy dining place add to the wonderful dining experience.

LONAVLA Kailash Parbat Restaurant
*Kaliash Parbat, Pune–Mumbai Rd, Valvan, 410 401 **Tel** (02114) 273 086*

On offer here is a wide variety of vegetarian food, with the emphasis on regional specialities. Even simple paneer dishes like *paneer tikka* (marinated cheese and vegetables) and *paneer Hyderabadi* (marinated cheese and spices) taste out of this world. Mushrooms cooked *tandoori* style are also a hit. Also on offer is a 24-hour coffee shop.

MAHABALESHWAR Brightland Holiday Village
*Kates Point Rd, Distt Satara, 412 806 **Tel** (2168) 260 700*

The Brightland Holiday Village has a cluster of eateries that cater to many palates. There is a choice of Indian, mughlai, *tandoori* and barbecued food. The Village Pub offers a tempting array of cocktails and mocktails, while the nightclub, The Electric Mist, has a lively atmosphere.

NAGPUR Ashoka Bar and Restaurant
*Mount Rd, Sadar, 440 001 **Tel** (0712) 253 1141*

Established in 1955, Ashoka is the oldest restaurant in this city. It has, however, kept up with the times and even uses palmtops to take orders. These communicate directly with the kitchen, so the service is truly quick. The restaurant overlooks a pool and green lawns and its menu offers multi-cuisine fare.

NAGPUR Lahoree Deluxe Bar and Restaurant
*Lahoree Deluxe Building, WHC Rd, Dharampeth, 440 010 **Tel** (0712) 253 3808*

Hearty *tandoori* food is the speciality here, but select Chinese and Western dishes are also on offer. Besides the modern air-conditioned interior, there are 25 tables set outdoors in a small garden, and a lively, well-stocked bar. Recorded music and a television set also available.

NASIK Panchratna
*Taj Residency, P-17, MIDC Ambad, Mumbai–Agra Rd, 422 010 **Tel** (0253) 660 4499*

Overlooking the picturesque Satpura hills, the Panchratna serves excellent food. Dim lighting with candles creates a romantic atmosphere. On offer are Indian and Chinese dishes, the most popular of these being *murgh tikka lababdar* (chicken curry) and *methi makai* (fenugreek, peas and corn). Closed for lunch during summer and monsoon season.

PUNE Hotel Vaishali
*1218/1 Shivajinagar, Fergusson College Rd, 411 004 **Tel** (020) 2553 1244*

This is a pleasant garden restaurant serving good South Indian food. Reasonable prices make it popular with local residents. Located opposite Fergusson College, the restaurant is popular with students. Simple dishes such as *chaat* (see p66) and *sev batata puri* (potato and chickpea fried bread) are enough to make your mouth water for more.

PUNE Arthur's Theme
*No 2 Vrindavan Apartments, North Main Rd, Koregaon Park, 411 001 **Tel** (020) 613 2710*

This small and cozy restaurant prides itself on its French cuisine and both vegetarian and meat dishes are served. Delicate flavours and fine presentation define the quality of service here. The imaginative menu adds excitement to your meal. Book in advance.

Key to Price Guide *see p720* **Key to Symbols** *see back cover flap*

PUNE The Place
Clover Centre, Moledina Rd, 411 001 **Tel** *(020) 2613 2710*

Best known for its plates of sizzling chicken and lamb, this restaurant also offers delicious homemade ice cream. The portions are generous, with a sizzler plate becoming a whole meal in itself. The service is good and unintrusive and the bar is well-stocked with wine. Open for lunch and dinner.

GOA

ASSAGO Axirwaad
483 Rue De Boa Vista, 403 107 **Tel** *(0832) 227 7331*

This is an interesting combination of restaurant and private club, with an art gallery as well. The food is mainly Western with a few Middle Eastern dishes prepared by the husband and wife team who run it. Dining here is truly an experience as tables are placed on the sand, under the palm trees and the open sky. Open for lunch and dinner.

BAGA Britto's
End of Baga Beach, Near St Anthony's, 403 511 **Tel** *(0832) 227 7331*

Located at the end of Baga beach, Britto's tables are placed right next to the sea. The seafood is fresh and excellent. Try any of the fish curries (depending on the catch of the day) with rice. The *vindaloo (marinated pork curry)* is also recommended followed by alpine chocolate mousse.

BENAULIM Miguel Arcanjo
Taj Exotica, Colwaddo, Benaulim, Salcette, 403 716 **Tel** *(0832) 668 3333*

Facing the Arabian Sea and set within the landscaped environs of Taj Exotica hotel, the Miguel Arcanjo is full of old-world charm. This restaurant serves delicious Italian, Moroccan and Spanish fare. House specialties include Lebanese *mezze* such as *falafel, babaghanouj* (papika and eggplant dip), *tabbouleh* (bulgar and herb salad) and vine-leaf *dolmas.*

CALANGUTE Valerio's
Hotel Baia Do Sol, Baga Beach, Calangute Bardez, 403 516 **Tel** *(0832) 227 6084*

This restaurant, with an upbeat contemporary decor, serves Continental and Goan cuisines. Some of the best-loved dishes here include vegetable pie with bell pepper sauce, grilled kingfish with beetroot puree and sautéed spinach. The Saturday night barbecue with live music is especially popular.

CALANGUTE O' Pescador Restaurant and Pub
Cobra Vaddo, Calangute Vardez, 403 516 **Tel** *(0832) 227 9447*

The menu at this multi-cuisine restaurant is predominantly Continental and Chinese. The seafood platter, *tandoori* grilled platter, chicken *tikka* and mutton are highly recommended. The spare ribs in plum sauce is also very popular. Karaoke nights are on Sundays. The restaurant is closed from May to September.

CALANGUTE Bernard's Place
Cobra Vaddo, Baga Rd, Calangute, 403 511 **Tel** *(0832) 227 6712*

Popular cuisines served here include *tandoori*, Chinese and Continental, but it is the seafood dishes which are by far the most appreciated items on the menu. Sunday roast (from a choice of beef, chicken and pork) is served everyday. The pineapple crumble with hot custard makes for a delectable dessert.

CALANGUTE Cavala Seaside Resort Restaurant
Sauntavado, Baga Calangute, 403 516 **Tel** *(0832) 227 6090*

A stone's throw from Calangute Baga beach, this garden restaurant at Cavala comes highly recommended for its mouthwatering seafood. The well-stocked bar, live music and barbecue nights have made this a popular establishment and the service is excellent. Wheelchair access.

CALANGUTE Fiesta Restaurant
Sauntavado, Baga Calangute, Bardez, 403 516 **Tel** *(0832) 227 9894*

The stunning decor and an open area with beautiful views of the sea, make for a relaxing ambience. The menu of this multi-cuisine restaurant includes Mediterranean, Italian, Indian and Continental items. Prawns steamed in red wine is one of the best dishes served here.

CALANGUTE Golden Nest
The Ronil Beach Resort, Sauntavado, Baga Calagute, 403 516 **Tel** *(0832) 227 6101*

Located near Baga beach, the Golden Nest's menu offers Indian, Continental and Chinese cuisines. Tables are arranged over a stone-tiled patio and palm trees dot the surroundings. Live music (during high season) and friendly staff making dining here a memorable experience.

CALANGUTE Souza Lobo Bar and Restaurant
Umta Vaddo, Calangute Beach, Baga Bardez, 403 516 **Tel** *(0832) 227 6463*

A favourite since 1932, Souza Lobo Restaurant looks out to the sea, with tables set on a tiled verandah. The eatery is known for its excellent seafood, especially the stuffed crabs, *vindaloo, sorpotel*, the stuffed pomfret and the *tandoori* kingfish. Try the *bebinka*, a Goan sweet made of coconut pancakes, for dessert.

CALANGUTE Copper Bowl

Pousada Tauma, Porba Vaddo, Calangute, 403 516 **Tel** *(0832) 227 9061*

An open pavilion with an intricate stone colonnade, broad benches and a green marble floor; Copper Bowl serves authentic Goan food in quaint copper pots. Coconut-based chicken *xacuti* (curry), prawn *balchao (see p441)*, crispy prawns and baby lobster are some of the delicious dishes served here. Konkani cuisine is a recent addition to the menu.

CANDOLIM Palm and Sand

Dando, Candolim, 403 515 **Tel** *(0832) 247 9171*

Situated right on the beach, this intimate restaurant offers beautiful views of the sea. A great place to sample fresh and well-made seafood. Specialities include the crab *bisque*, crab spring rolls and crab *xacuti* (curry). The pork spare ribs and stuffed suckling pig are also popular. Try the apple pie and date pancake for dessert.

DONA PAULA Alfama Restaurant

Cidade de Goa Beach Resort, Vainguinim Beach, 403 004 **Tel** *(0832) 245 4545*

This is probably the only restaurant in Goa that serves cuisines from more exotic former Portuguese colonies such as Brazil and Mozambique. Continental food is also served. The bar has an extensive wine list. A Goan band performs in the evenings, with the Arabian Sea forming the backdrop.

PANJIM Rio Rico Restaurant

Hotel Mandovi, DB Marg, Panjim, 403 501 **Tel** *(0832) 242 6270*

Located in northern Goa, this well-respected establishment offers Goan, Indian, Continental and Portuguese cuisines. Its speciality lies in seafood preparations. A wide range of dishes, live music, and breezy outdoor dining facilities make it a popular place with families. Smoking is not allowed.

PANJIM Hotel Venite

31st January Rd, Sao Tome, 403 001 **Tel** *(0832) 242 5537*

This lovely restaurant, housed in a 200-year-old building, serves Goan, Portuguese and Mediterranean food. Among their most delicious dishes are the stuffed crab, sizzling fish fillet, pork chops in barbecue sauce and beef steaks stuffed with ham and cheese. Credit cards are not accepted.

PANJIM Simply Fish

Marriot Hotel, PO Box 64, Miramar, 403 001 **Tel** *(0832) 246 3333*

This is the in-house restaurant at the Marriot Hotel. Tables are arranged outdoors so guest can enjoy the scenic views of the bay. The menu offers excellent seafood items including lobster *bisque* and stews. Simply Fish is open for dinner only and is closed between May and October.

SALCETTE Martin's Corner

Binvaddo, Betalbatim, 403 731 **Tel** *(0832) 288 0061*

A homely restaurant with fish *caldin* (cooked with coconut and spices), fresh lobster and red snapper as the highlights on the menu. The goan sausage *pulao* is also worth trying. The staff here are chatty and warm. The outdoor seating arrangements provide a good dining venue. Live music fills the air.

SALCETTE Riverside

The Leela, Goa-GHM Mobor, Cavelossim, 403 731 **Tel** *(0832) 287 1234*

True to its name, this open air, canopied restaurant at The Leela hotel is located on a grassy terrace by the Sal river. There are a variety of authentic Italian and Mediterranean items on the menu. The ambience is intimate and warm and the staff are pleasant.

SALIGAO Florentine

Pequeno Morod, 403 511 **Tel** *(0832) 240 9664*

This restaurant is a little out of the way for most travellers, but the food here is worth the journey. Florentine is a small friendly establishment known for its Goan and *tandoori* cuisine. Try their excellent chicken *cafreal* (spiced and marinated), which is eaten with bread. The generous portions make this restaurant an ideal place for a hearty meal.

SINQUERIM BARDEZ Banyan Tree

Taj Holiday Village, 403 519 **Tel** *(0832) 664 5858*

Located behind a 320-year-old banyan tree, this upmarket Asian eatery specializes in Thai food. Right from the appetiser *som tham* (papaya salad), all dishes have an authentic Thai flavour. Try the *tab tim grob* (water chestnuts with sugar syrup and coconut milk) for dessert. The outdoor seating and live music make dining memorable.

KARNATAKA

BADAMI The Pulakeshi Dining Hall

Station Road, 587 201 **Tel** *(08357) 220 230*

This multi-cuisine restaurant is named for the great Chaulakyan king, Pulkesin. The regional Karnataka specialities are recommended but Continental dishes are also served. The outdoor seating provides an alternative to the air-conditioned interiors. Open for breakfast, lunch and dinner. Smoking is also not allowed.

Key to Price Guide *see p720* **Key to Symbols** *see back cover flap*

BANGALORE Three Quarter Chinese

22 Church Street, 560 001 **Tel** *(080) 4112 1937*

The decor at this restaurant gives the impression of being underwater, with waves all around. A popular restaurant, Three Quarter Chinese serves Indian and Chinese dishes. Try the lobster in Schezwan sauce, the flaming prawns, or the grape clustered fish.

BANGALORE 24/7

The Grand Ashok, Kumara Krupa High Grounds, 560 020 **Tel** *(080) 3052 7777*

The Grand Ashok's signature multi-cuisine restaurant, 24/7 offers an array of world cuisines ranging from Indian to Continental to Pan Asian. Overlooking the pool and lawns, this 24-hour coffee shop serves buffet breakfast, lunch and dinner. The staff are welcoming and attentive.

BANGALORE Bay Leaf

123 Raheja Arcade, Kormangala, 560 029 **Tel** *(080) 2553 5050*

With huge bay windows, smart wooden furniture and abstract glass art, the cosmopolitan Bay Leaf is well-known for its excellent Punjabi food and extensive wine list. Try their *kebabs* and stuffed *rotis*. For a traditional taste the *zaffrani chawal* (basmati rice with saffron and spices) and *murgh adraki* (chicken and ginger curry) are good options.

BANGALORE I-Talia

The Park Hotel, 14/7 Mahatma Gandhi Rd, 560 001 **Tel** *(080) 2559 4666*

Relish authentic Italian cuisine at this speciality restaurant that is a hot favourite with young and old alike. Run by a passionate gourmet, I-Talia offers a variety of dishes including wood-oven pizzas, homemade pastas, salads and the special mango and Campari sorbet. All this in a boutique-styled interior with a pool side view.

BIJAPUR Hotel Madhuvan International Restaurant

G-37 Brigade Garden, St Marks Rd, 586 101 **Tel** *(08352) 225 571*

Generous portions of wholesome vegetarian food are served here on a traditional *thali* (platter). The surrounding gardens are pleasant. The restaurant is open for breakfast, lunch and dinner, and provides outdoor dining facilities. The staff are courteous and efficient. Ample parking space available.

CHIKMAGALUR The Peaberry

Taj Garden Retreat, KM Rd, Jyothi Nagar, 577 101 **Tel** *(08262) 220 202*

This attractive multi-cuisine restaurant offers good coastal cuisine as well as standard North Indian favourites. The Mukhwada bar serves superb drinks. Located by the beautiful Sahyadri mountains, The Peaberry is ideal for both business and leisure travellers. Open for breakfast, lunch and dinner.

HAMPI Mango Tree Restaurant

400 m (1,300 ft) west of the ghats, on the south bank, 583 201

Situated on the banks of the river, under the shade of a mango tree, this restaurant serves its food on banana leaves. The fare is simple, wholesome and includes delicious *dosas (see p554)*, honey pancakes and *lassi* (buttermilk). The staff are friendly and helpful. A big swing hung from a branch of the mango tree is a fun feature.

HUBLI Lake Palace

Hotel Naveen, Unkel, 580 025 **Tel** *(0836) 237 2939*

A homely restaurant with round tables, Lake Palace offers Continental, Chinese, North Indian and South Indian cuisine. Their best dishes, however, are traditional ones from northern Karnataka, such as *jawar roti* (wheat wafers*)*, *brinjal* (eggplant dish), pickles and gravy. There is also a well-stocked bar on the premises. Open for lunch and dinner.

MANGALORE Cardamom

Taj Manjarun Hotel, Near. DC Office, Old Port Rd, 567 001 **Tel** *(0824) 666 0420*

Cardamom offers a wide choice of Continental, Chinese and Indian delicacies, including traditional Manglorean food. A recommended signature dishes is the *neitha kori* (marinated fried fish). The restaurant also offers a fine selection of wine and cigars.

MYSORE The Green Hotel Restaurant

2270 Vinoba Rd, Jl. Puram, 570 002 **Tel** *(0824) 666 0420*

Delicious, subtly spiced food made from fresh ingredients is served at The Green Hotel Restaurant. Their outdoor seating arrangements, on a charming verandah and in the garden, provide a pleasant ambience. The establishment excels in regional specialities and also provides a good choice of wines. Open for breakfast, lunch and dinner.

CHENNAI

CHENNAI Amaravathi

1 Cathedral Rd, 600 086 **Tel** *(044) 2811 6416*

Reasonably priced Andhra cuisine is the highlight at Amaravathi. The *biryani* is particularly good. The restaurant is pleasant and clean and though it mainly serves meat-based meals the smell of fish and meat is not overpowering. Ample parking space is provided inside the compound for both cars and bikes.

CHENNAI Annalakshmi

804 Anna Salai, 600 006 **Tel** *(044) 2852 5109*

Run entirely by volunteers, this restaurant is named after the goddess of food – Annalakshmi. It serves sumptuous vegetarian fare, elegantly presented on silver and gold *thalis* (platters). The profits go to charity. Advance reservations and orders are a must for speciality cuisines. Closed on Mondays.

CHENNAI Karaikudi Chettinad Restaurant

84 Dr Radhakrishnan Salai, Mylapore, 600 004 **Tel** *(044) 2811 1893*

Recreating a traditional Chettinad ambience, including with the waiters' uniforms, this restaurant's specialities include *Pallathur* chicken, *Chettiar* pepper chicken roast and pigeon *varuval*. Hot and cold non-alcoholic beverages are served here. Beer is also served. Open for lunch and dinner only.

CHENNAI Ponnuswamy Hotel

24-C IN Rd, Egmore, 600 012 **Tel** *(044) 2827 0784*

Authentic Chettinad food is served at Ponnuswamy Hotel. This includes a variety of spicy dishes featuring quail, crab and rabbit. The *biryani* is excellent and the garlic pickles taste out of this world. Continental and Chinese food are also served. Do try the soups and salads. Services include door-to-door delivery.

CHENNAI Benjarong

148 TTK Rd, Alwarpet, 600 018 **Tel** *(044) 2432 2640*

Orchids decorate the tables at this Thai restaurant, which has fresh ingredients flown in daily from Bangkok. Signature dishes include the spicy *tom yam* soup, made using *goong* (prawn brains) tempered with ginger, and the chargrilled duck cooked to perfection. Benjarong also offers some unusual and tempting desserts.

CHENNAI Coastline

84 Dr Radhakrishnan Rd, Mylapore, 600 004 **Tel** *(044) 2811 1893*

A relatively new restaurant, Coastline's cool interior invites you to linger over your meal. On offer are fresh seafood delicacies. Smoking is not permitted here. The restaurant is open for lunch and dinner only. Major credit cards are accepted. Ample parking space is available.

CHENNAI Copper Chimney

74 Ground Floor, Cathedral Rd, 600 086 **Tel** *(044) 2811 5770*

This spotlessly clean restaurant is known for its North Indian *tandoori* cuisine. Its *kebabs* and soups are highly recommended. Also on offer is an extensive selection of wines. Separate smoking and non-smoking areas are available. All major credit cards are accepted here. Open for breakfast, lunch and dinner.

CHENNAI Dhaba Express

9 Cenotaph Rd, 600 004 **Tel** *(044) 2432 8212*

Dhaba Express offers a unique dining experience. The chairs make way for *charpoys* (string cots) and outdoor seating is the option to take here. On offer are dishes typical of North Indian roadside eateries. Try the robust *dal makhani* (see p67). The restaurant is open for lunch and dinner only.

CHENNAI Rice and Spice

3 Kodambakkam High Rd, Nungambakkam, 600 034 **Tel** *(044) 2822 2211*

The decor at Rice and Spice is pleasingly artistic. A wide variety of cuisines is offered here, but the authentic Andhra food is the best and what makes it so popular. The *bisibelabath* (curried rice and vegetables) and *pudina parathas* (flatbread with dried mint) are highly recommended. Book a table in advance at weekends. Open for lunch and dinner.

CHENNAI The Rain Tree

Taj Connemara Hotel, 1 Binny Rd, 600 002 **Tel** *(044) 6600 1543*

This is an atmospheric outdoor restaurant with seating arrangements under a huge raintree. The menu offers a variety of Chettinad dishes. Cultural shows in the evening add to the charm of dining here. An ideal place to hold business meals. The retro-bar is a cool hangout. Open for dinner only.

TAMIL NADU

KANCHIPURAM Kanchi Kudil

53-A Sangeetha Vidwan, Nainar Pillai Street, 600 088 **Tel** *(04112) 2827 1100*

One of the most popular sites in Kanchipuram, Kanchi Kudil was born of a desire to turn ancestral property into a place of public interest. Visitors to this beautifully restored house get to experience the traditional ways of Kanchipuram. Open for breakfast, lunch and dinner. Serves vegetarian South Indian snacks. Fine handicrafts are also available.

MADURAI Temple View Rooftop Restaurant

Hotel Park Plaza, 114-5 West Perumal Mistry Street, 625 001 **Tel** *(0452) 234 2112*

One of the best eateries in Madurai, with superb views of the temple. The chefs at Temple View Rooftop Restaurant offer traditionally cooked dishes from Indian, Continental and Chinese cuisines. Try the delicious chicken garlic fry. Open for dinner only. All major credit cards are accepted.

Key to Price Guide *see p720* **Key to Symbols** *see back cover flap*

MADURAI The View

Taj Garden Retreat, 40 TPK Rd, Pasumalai Hill, 625 003   **Tel** *(0452) 237 1601*

A tranquil ambience and efficient staff make The View an ideal place to take a break from sightseeing in this temple town. The menu here offers a variety of Indian, Continental and Chinese dishes. There is also a good selection of wines. Open for breakfast, lunch and dinner.

MAMALLAPURAM Moonrakers

34 Othavadai Street, 603 104

Well-known for its *kebabs*, *koftas*, pasta and chicken. Moonrakers is a cheerful and friendly place to visit. Seafood is the speciality here, but also try also the salads and snacks. Finish off your meal with a generous helping of pancakes or tropical salad. The items are very reasonably priced. Open for breakfast, lunch and dinner.

OOTACAMUND Tandoori Mahal

Commercial Rd, 643 101

Chilled beer with good *tandoori* vegetarian and meat dishes can be had at this well-run eatery. Regional specialities are also available. The staff are welcoming and the service is good. The restaurant is open for lunch and dinner only. Ample parking space is available.

OOTACAMUND The Nilgiri Woodlands Restaurant

Ettines Rd, Opp Race Course, 643 001   **Tel** *(0423) 244 2551*

Set in a colonial mansion, The Niligiri Woodlands Restaurant has preserved all its old flair and charm. Set amid sprawling lawns, the surroundings are pleasant and soothing. This is a value-for-money vegetarian restaurant that serves satisfying South Indian *thali* (platter) meals. Smoking is strictly prohibited.

PONDICHERRY Le Club

Hotel de Pondicherry, 38 Rue Dumas Street, 605 001   **Tel** *(0413) 222 7409*

This classy French restaurant serves refreshing cocktails along with good *coq au vin*, grilled prawns with basil, and *chateaubriand* steak. Its *fondant* chocolate is also recommended. The walls are covered with paintings and photographs of celebrities who have visited the restaurant.

PONDICHERRY Rendezvous Café

30 Rue Suffren, 605 001   **Tel** *(0413) 233 9132*

Along with French food, Rendezvous Café also offers Italian and Indian-style Chinese dishes. Try its steak *de capitaine* and grilled prawns. The breakfasts here are also very good. With advance booking, a wide choice of menus can be had for private parties, cocktail parties and elaborate buffets.

PONDICHERRY Carte Blanche

Hotel de L'Orient, 17 Rue Romain Rolland, 605 007   **Tel** *(0413) 234 3067*

The atmospheric decor in this outstanding restaurant includes antique maps of Pondicherry. The Carte Blanche takes you back to a period when *punkhawallas* (servants) gently fanned the air and Tamil spices blended with French restraint to give rise to the famous Creole cuisine. The dishes are imaginative and superb.

THANJAVUR Geetham

Hotel Parisutham, 613 001   **Tel** *(04362) 231 801*

Its moderately priced items, friendly staff and superb service make Geetham a very popular restaurant. Vegetarian food is served here on traditional *thalis* (platters) and the menu features a repertoire of no less than 72 curries. Alcohol is also served. Open for lunch and dinner.

ANDAMAN ISLANDS

PORT BLAIR Mandalay Restaurant

Bay Island Hotel, Marine Hill, 744 101   **Tel** *(03192) 234 101*

Located at the entry to Port Blair harbour, this multi-cuisine restaurant offers superb views of Ross and Havelock islands. Savour the regional specialities along with Indian, Chinese and Continental platters. The lounge, Look Out, is the place to enjoy an assortment of snacks while observing the serene sea.

PORT BLAIR Waves

Corbyn's Cove, 744 101   **Tel** *(03192) 245 110*

This multi-cuisine restaurant, situated in a pleasant garden just across the Carbyus Cove beach, provides a kaleidoscopic view of the beautiful blue water front. On offer are regional specialities, Western dishes and fine wine. Its outdoor seating provides the ideal place to relax and unwind. Open for dinner only.

PORT BLAIR The Wild Orchid Havelock Island

Vijaynagar, Havelock Island, 744 103   **Tel** *(03192) 282 472*

The Wild Orchid Havelock Island is both a restaurant and a bar. At the Red Snapper Restaurant guests are offered international dishes in authentic flavours. The local fresh seafood preparations are excellent. The Emerald Gecko Bar is well-stocked with Indian as well as imported alcoholic beverages.

KERALA

ALAPPUZHA Chakara

Raheem Residency, Beach Rd, 688 012   **Tel** *(0477) 223 9767*

Situated facing the sea, Chakara has a serene air about it. The restaurant offers Continental dishes such as chicken in orange and mint sauce. *Kuttanadan* fish curry, *nadan* fish curry and mint fish are also favourites here. The signature dish is Alappuzha fish curry made with local spices.

KOCHI The Fort House

Calvathy Rd, Fort Cochin, 682 001   **Tel** *(0484) 221 7103*

Set in a quiet backwater, The Fort House is a peaceful place to dine. This is a family-run restaurant serving home-cooked Keralite food, including excellent vegetable curries and fresh seafood dishes. Cocktails are also on offer. The staff are efficient.

KOCHI The Malabar Junction Restaurant

The Malabar House, Fort Kochi, 682 018   **Tel** *(0484) 221 6666*

The Malabar Junction offers sophisticated, alfresco dining. An awning made from traditional Keralite woodwork covers the small seating area. An adjacent stage plays host to live music performances in the evening. Excellent Western food is on offer here. The seafood and Mediterranean dishes are particularly good.

KOCHI Bubble Café

Taj Residency, Ernakulam, 682 011   **Tel** *(0484) 237 1471*

A must-visit during the monsoon as the transparent roof gives you the feeling of being in the middle of the rain. Regular buffets are organised here, with a range of cuisines from across the globe. The salads and desserts are particularly good. The restaurant also serves some of the best wines available in Kochi.

KOTTAYAM Vembanad Restaurant

Vembanad Lake Resort, Kodimatha, 686 039   **Tel** *(0481) 236 0866*

A wide range of culinary delicacies, both Indian and international, are offered at Vembanad Restaurant. It is also one of the best places in Kottayam to sample regional specialities and its seafood is especially fresh and tasty. The eatery has splendid views of the nearby lake. There is also little shack that sells ornate jewellery.

KOTTAYAM Coconut Lagoon Restaurant

Coconut Lagoon, PB No 2, Kumarakoram, 686 563   **Tel** *(0481) 252 5834*

Cited in Arundhati Roy's Booker Prize winning best-seller *The God of Small Things*, this restaurant is renowned as much for its superb Keralite cuisine as for its enchanting setting in a beautifully restored old *tharavad* (ancestral home). It is not accessible by road and must be reached by boat.

KOVALAM Rockholm

Hotel Rockholm, Lighthouse Rd, 695 521   **Tel** *(0471) 2481 0306*

This is a terrace restaurant with breathtaking views of the sea. The outdoor seating area is a comfortable place to dine. The establishment serves some fine Indian, Chinese and Continental delicacies. The seafood and local dishes are fresh and very well-prepared.

KOVALAM Octopus

Surya Samudra Beach Garden, Pulinkudi, 695 521   **Tel** *(0471) 248 0413*

Housed in reassembled old wooden Kerala houses, this multi-cuisine resort-restaurant has a magical atmosphere. It is famous for excellent seafood, fresh vegetables, genuine Kerala dishes and homemade cakes and ice creams. Guests usually take trips around the place to view the beautiful backwaters and local temples.

KOZHIKODE Coral Reef Restaurant

Hotel Taj Residency, PT Usha Rd, 673 101   **Tel** *(0484) 266 9595*

A wide variety of cuisines, including Chinese, Continental, North Indian, seafood and local dishes, is served at this pleasant restaurant. Health food based on Ayurvedic principles is also on offer. Magnificent views of the pool and the landscaped garden are an added attraction. Coral Reef Restaurant is open for lunch and dinner only.

LAKSHADWEEP Restaurant Hut

Bangaram Island Resort, 682 552

Made of bamboo and palm fronds, Restaurant Hut is an architectural marvel and has a cheerful atmosphere. Meals along the beach are extremely memorable and the evening barbecues delightful. On offer are regional specialities and Western dishes. There is also a well-stocked bar. Open for breakfast, lunch and dinner.

THEKKADY Shalimar Spice Garden Resort Restaurant

Murikkady PO, 685 536   **Tel** *(0486) 232 2132*

Decorated in the traditional style of Kerala, this restaurant serves authentic Indian and Keralite cuisine on banana leaves. The chef can also produce some of the best Italian and Continental dishes and there is a good choice of wines to go with them. Staff are attentive and friendly.

Key to Price Guide *see p720*   **Key to Symbols** *see back cover flap*

THIRUVANANTHAPURAM The Regency

The South Park, 695 001 **Tel** *(0471) 233 0377*

Recently renovated, this restaurant offers a lavish buffet spread for dinner. For those who like to dine under the stars, there is a roof garden for alfresco dining. The Regency's menu offers a variety of regional specialities as well as select Western dishes. Business facilities are also available.

THIRUVANANTHAPURAM Zodiac

Hotel Saj Lucia, East Fort, 695 023 **Tel** *(0471) 246 3443*

The authentic flavour of Kerala can be tasted both in the food and the ambience of this restaurant. The menu lists Continental, Indian and Chinese delicacies. A popular place for family outings. Listen to *ghazals (see p748)* over some delicious food. Smoking prohibited.

VARKALA Café Comorin

Taj Garden Retreat, Varkala, 695 141 **Tel** *(0470) 260 2296*

As with other Taj-run restaurants, it is the vibrant setting of Café Comorin that attracts attention. This is a cosy eatery, overlooking lawns and a swimming pool, with excellent views of the sea. On offer is a wide variety of cuisines including Chinese, Indian and Continental. The bar lounge offers fine wines.

ANDHRA PRADESH

HYDERABAD Minerva Coffee Shop

6-3-1110 Amrutha Mall Somajiguda, 500 016 **Tel** *(040) 2340 4635*

Minerva is a comfortable place that is great for light snacks in the evening. Fluffy *idlis* (rice and lentil batter), super-crisp paper *dosas (see p554)* and rice pongal with coconut chutney are a few of them. But as the name suggests, steaming hot coffee is the speciality here.

HYDERABAD Dakhni

Taj Banjara, 500 034 **Tel** *(040) 2330 5762*

This restaurant serves authentic Hyderabadi and Andhra cuisine. Try the Bijapuri *usli*, a dry lentil curry with *bajra* bread, and the *gosht gulbarga* (mutton dish) cooked in a delicious coconut sauce. Live music and a good wine list makes Dakhni well worth the visit. Smoking is not allowed. Open for lunch and dinner.

HYDERABAD Dum Pukht

Grand Kakatiya Sheraton, 6-3-1187, 500 016 **Tel** *(040) 2340 0132*

A connoisseur's delight, Dum Pukht offers the authentic taste of a 200-year-old culinary tradition. It is characterised by the subtle flavours and aromas of dishes simmered over a low flame in sealed *deghs*. Try the *khwams*, which offers three different curries, *sheermal* bread, skewered mutton *kebabs* and creamy curd.

TIRUPATI Bhima's Deluxe Restaurant

Bhima's Deluxe Hotel, 38 Govind Raja Car Street, 517 501 **Tel** *(08754) 222 5521*

In keeping with the aura of piety that envelops Tirupati, Bhima's Deluxe Restaurant serves wholesome, pure vegetarian Indian food. They also serve refreshing drinks and healthy fruit juices. The food, service and the general ambience will ensure your return. Open for breakfast, lunch and dinner.

VIJAYWADA Aromas

Quality Inn DV Manor, MG Rd, 520 010 **Tel** *(0866) 247 4455*

A small but cosy restaurant run by a friendly couple, Aromas is popular with both residents and visitors in this city. The menu offers a wide choice of Indian, Mughlai and South Asian food, but its best known items are the Punjabi dishes. Open for lunch and dinner.

VISHAKHAPATNAM Dakshin Restaurant

Hotel Daspalla, 28-2-48 Suryabagh, 530 020 **Tel** *(0891) 256 4825*

This speciality restaurant serves authentic hot and spicy Andhra cuisine. Try their *gongura* mutton dish. The restaurant has good business facilities, with separate smoking and non-smoking areas. Recorded music fills the air. Open for lunch and dinner.

VISHAKHAPATNAM Bamboo Bay

The Park, Beach Rd, 530 022 **Tel** *(0891) 275 4488*

The only open-air beach restaurant in the city, Bamboo Bay serves mainly coastal cuisine – a combination of Andhra and Chettinad dishes, with some *tandoori* food thrown in. Try their *tandoori* pomfret, *gongura mamasam* and *yaar varuval*, all on one platter. Open for dinner only.

WARANGAL Kadambari Restaurant

Hotel Ashoka, 6-1-242 Main Rd, Hanamkonda, 506 250 **Tel** *(08712) 257 8491*

This friendly restaurant specializes in Keralite cuisine, though it also also offers tasty Chinese and *tandoori* food. The staff are very efficient and help guests choose from the menu. The atmosphere is relaxed and friendly. Open for lunch and dinner.

SHOPS & MARKETS

India's superb tradition of textiles, arts and crafts makes shopping in this country tremendous fun. The range and quality is diverse – finely crafted bronzes and metalware, lustrous silks, jewellery, miniature paintings and handwoven carpets, as well as delightful, inexpensive tribal artifacts and souvenirs. The kaleidoscope of hues, textures and scents at local bazaars and markets, where flowers, fresh produce and spices are sold, is fascinating, as are the rows of pavement sellers hawking clothes and accessories. Though often a noisy and chaotic experience, browsing through the stalls can often lead to exciting bargains. Traditional bazaars co-exist with the multi-storeyed department stores and shopping malls of urban India, where all manner of goods, both local and imported, are sold under one roof. These are a favourite with local shoppers. For details on shopping in Delhi, see pages 96–7; for Kolkata, see pages 282–3; for Mumbai, see pages 462–3; and for Chennai, see pages 574–5.

Puppet

OPENING HOURS

Most shops in the principal shopping areas in urban India are open from about 10am to 7.30pm. Local stores keep longer hours, while markets selling fresh produce are open for business from dawn until late at night. Government emporia have fixed shopping hours, from 10am to 6pm with a lunch break between 1pm and 2pm. Shop timings vary from city to city, as do holidays. Republic Day (January 26th), Independence Day (August 15th) and Mahatma Gandhi's Birthday (October 2nd) are national holidays, and by law all shops and markets in the country remain closed.

HOW TO PAY

The rupee is accepted everywhere. All the larger stores now accept major international credit cards,

A shopping mall in Gurgaon

such as MasterCard and Visa, but it is wise to carry some cash for purchases in bazaars and smaller shops. Some stores accept traveller's cheques as well, though a passport will be required for identification. International currency, too, can be used in certain places. If paying by credit card, ensure that the voucher is filled out in front of you, to avoid fraud. A Value Added Tax (VAT), between 4 to 12.5 per cent, is charged on some items, unless the bill has been paid in foreign currency or with a foreign-based credit card.

RIGHTS AND REFUNDS

When buying expensive items, such as carpets, jewellery or antiques, always insist on a receipt or cash memo. This is important in case damaged goods need to be returned or exchanged, though often in India this is less easy than it sounds. Refunds, too, are difficult.

Take particular care when purchases need to be shipped out. Check what costs are involved, including insurance, and ensure that all the paperwork is done correctly. International courier services (see p771) can also be approached to ship out large purchases.

BARGAINING

A good way to get the best results when bargaining, is to check out costs and quality at a number of outlets. Usually, the big stores have fixed prices with no scope for bargaining, but haggling in bazaars and smaller shops can be quite rewarding. Try not to quote unrealistically low prices and miss out on a good deal in the process.

Flower-seller displaying garlands on a pavement, Kolkata

TOUTS

Handle touts firmly and try not to succumb to offers of genuine antiques or fantastic bargains. They all operate on a commission basis, and taking visitors to shops of their choice is just a means of acquiring extra cash. Tourist coaches often stop at selected stores, but it is not obligatory to purchase anything. Don't be taken in by shops that say "government approved"; these are private enterprises not to be confused with government-run outlets.

DEPARTMENT STORES AND BOUTIQUES

Plush, air-conditioned department stores, malls and plazas, and up-market boutiques are now a regular feature in most large towns. They stock a variety of goods, ranging from clothes and leather items to kitchenware. International brands of cosmetics, perfume, fashion accessories, home appliances, glassware and more, are also available here. Boutiques specialize in popular Indian designer labels, including high-fashion Western-style and traditional Indian apparel.

GOVERNMENT EMPORIA

All state governments have special outlets, with fixed prices, selling textiles and handicrafts from that particular region. These emporia have large premises in all state capitals, and although the range and quality of the items vary, they are good places to shop for gifts and souvenirs. Some of the well-stocked ones that also have branches in most larger cities are Poompuhar (Tamil Nadu), Rajasthali (Rajasthan), Khadi (Delhi) and Gurjari (Gujarat).

CRAFT CENTRES AND BAZAARS

The diversity of traditional Indian crafts is one of the attractions of travelling in this country. Each region, town and village specializes in a particular skill, be it pottery,

Colourful paper kites on sale in a Rajasthan village

weaving, metalware or painting. In some smaller villages it is possible to observe artisans at work and buy directly from them. If a craft centre is not on your itinerary, many cities have arts and craft shops that sell handicrafts made in the region.

Shopping in local bazaars, with their noise and colour, is a unique experience. Located in the heart of old cities, bazaars are typically a maze of tiny shops and pavement stalls, selling a variety of merchandise, from flowers, vegetables and other fresh produce, to cooking utensils, textiles and jewellery.

SPECIALIST STORES

Specialist stores have built their reputation on the quality of merchandise they sell. The passion for antiques has led to a proliferation of shops selling bronzes, stone sculpture and metal artifacts.

If buying antiques, check with the Archaeological Survey of India *(see p759)* as objects over 100 years old cannot be taken out of the country. However, excellent reproductions can always be found. Exquisite gold and silver jewellery is readily available, though it is best to visit established jewellers. Jaipur is an excellent place to shop for precious stones, while Hyderabad is known for good-quality pearls.

Rajasthan, particularly Jaipur, Udaipur and Jodhpur, specializes in good quality miniatures, folk paintings and religious *pichhwais* on cloth. Other types of painting, such as Tibetan *thangkas* and the jewel-encrusted Tanjore paintings, are available in Ladakh, Himachal Pradesh and Tamil Nadu.

India's renowned textile tradition ranges from South India's glorious silk saris and Varanasi brocades to fine handwoven cottons, in a wide range of designs and colours. Inexpensive casual wear can be bought at pavement stalls. Boutiques are good places for designer clothes. Carpets and woollen goods, especially the pricey pashmina and *jamavar* shawls, should be bought only from reliable shops.

Tea, spices, herbal products and incense are also popular items. Kerala's spices are famous, while tea can be purchased all over the country. Herbal cosmetics and incense are usually sold in general stores, while *attar* (traditional perfume) can be found in most bazaars.

Mumbai's Chor Bazaar, a treasure trove of antiques

What to Buy in India

Shopping in India is a fascinating experience, since the bazaars and boutiques showcase a wide range of the country's decorative arts and crafts. The quality can vary, but the choice is enormous. Superb jewellery, colourful textiles, handicrafts and artifacts, as well as aromatic spices and herbal products, are all available. There are also elegant contemporary interpretations of traditional designs. In many places visitors can watch artisans at work and buy directly from them.

Wooden peacock head

Lacquerware
Bowls and platters in red and black lacquer were originally imported from Burma. Many of these can still be found in Chennai and on Kochi's Jew Street (see p643).

Brassware
A wide variety of perfectly proportioned ritual and utilitarian objects, such as boxes and lotas (water pots) were once an essential part of every household. They are now freely available in antique shops all over India.

Silverware
The choice of intricately carved and embossed silver artifacts includes salvers, candlesticks, nut bowls and decorative objects. Different parts of India usually specialize in a particular craft. Orissa is well known for its delicate filigree, while in Gujarat and Rajasthan, silversmiths carve elaborate designs on a solid base.

Stoneware
Stoneware is strongly influenced by the pietra dura *motifs on the Taj Mahal (see pp174–5). Designers have now created a select range of tableware for the modern home that uses white marble as a base with delicate patterns printed in silver and gold foil.*

Jewellery
Exquisite gem-encrusted kundan *and enamelled* meena-kari *jewellery from North India (see p361), as well as gold ornaments from the south, are available in jewellery shops. Tribal or rural-style silver jewellery is also sold.*

Gold necklaces and bangle

Silver anklets, bracelet and armband

Navratna necklace and emerald earring

Textiles

A dazzling choice of blockprints, silk and cotton woven textiles and gold brocade can be bought by the metre or as ready-made garments, scarves, saris and home accessories. Good-quality paisley jamavar *and pashmina shawls are also available in select stores.*

Printed and silk tissue cushion covers

Light-weight cotton quilts

Paisley *jamavar* **shawl**

Brocade textile and scarf

Bamboo and Cane Products

The northeastern states are famous for their fine bamboo and cane work. Besides objects of everyday use, such as large baskets for tea-pluckers, hats and utensils, artisans have now created a variety of trays, baskets, boxes and containers for the contemporary market. Good-quality furniture is also made for local and international buyers.

Bronze image

Tribal elephant

Paintings

Many places, especially Jaipur, Jodhpur and Udaipur in Rajasthan, have shops and ateliers where painters skilfully recreate old miniatures (see p405). Poster colours are now used instead of natural pigments, but the themes are still traditional. These range from court scenes to depictions of religious and mythological stories.

A miniature painting

Artifacts

Excellent reproductions of antique bronzes (see p594) are available in many shops. These include images of Hindu deities, such as Krishna and Ganesha, as well as objects made by tribal artisans.

Herbal and Beauty Products

Traditional herbal remedies have been re-invented to suit the modern-day need for eco-friendly soaps and cosmetics, soothing oils and lotions. Aromatherapy is highly popular, and Auroville (see p589) has developed a wide range of scented candles and joss sticks.

Aromatherapy candles from Auroville

Joss sticks (agarbatti)

Soaps

Ayurvedic cosmetics

ENTERTAINMENT

Entertainment in India offers fascinating insights into the religious, cultural and social diversity of the country. The vast and complex tradition of performing arts is an ancient one, inextricably linked to religion and mythology. Initially, classical music and dance were performed as part of temple ritual, while the rich repertoire of folk forms

Kathakali dancer

emerged as a response to local conditions, the land and community. Today, the choice of entertainment includes classical dance and music, religious dance-dramas, contemporary theatre and colourful temple festivals. There are popular alternatives as well, especially cinemas, where the latest Bollywood blockbusters are shown.

SOURCES OF INFORMATION

Local newspapers and magazines are good sources of information, as they carry regular listings and advertisements of events. Often, hotels have in-house publications highlighting the city's sights as well as its entertainment venues and programmes. If not, the travel desk can usually provide the necessary information. In addition, the India Tourism offices and website *(see p759)* publish an annual calendar of events. Good travel agents can also let visitors know what is happening where, and can help prepare an itinerary of cultural events. For details on entertainment in Delhi, see pages 96–7; for Kolkata, see pages 282–3; for Mumbai, see pages 462–3; and for Chennai, see pages 574–5.

BOOKING TICKETS

For cultural programmes and the cinema, it is best to book tickets in advance at the venue itself. Tele-booking,

especially for the more popular shows, is not always reliable. Some stores in the larger cities also have ticket counters; event organizers will indicate where these are in the local newspapers. Hotels or tour operators can often arrange tickets as well.

CLASSICAL MUSIC AND DANCE

Classical music and dance are a dynamic reflection of India's rich cultural heritage *(see pp28–9)*. Regular performances of Odissi, Bharat Natyam, Kuchipudi and Kathakali, the dance-drama from Kerala, are organized by state tourism departments and private cultural organizations at auditoriums and hotels. In recent years, dance festivals against the backdrop of historic sites have become popular. Such events are now held at Ajanta and Ellora *(see pp476–81)*, Konark *(see pp310–12)*, Mamallapuram *(see pp578–81)*

Folk musicians from Rajasthan playing *sarangis* **(string instruments)**

as well as Khajuraho *(see pp236–8)*, and offer a unique way to enjoy India's many famed dance forms.

Concerts of Indian classical music, in the North Indian (Hindustani) and South Indian (Carnatic) styles, draw crowds of music lovers. Concerts by soloists as well as groups are held regularly in the larger cities. There is often a lively interaction between the artistes and the audience, who express their appreciation by exclaiming or clapping several times during a concert.

Devotional music, such as Sufi qawwalis and Hindu *bhajans*, also attracts large audiences. Other forms include *ghazals*, lyrical poems in Urdu, and Rabindra Sangeet, songs composed by the great Bengali poet, Rabindranath Tagore *(see p292)*.

FOLK THEATRE, MUSIC AND DANCE

The traditions of folk and tribal theatre, music and dance are as vibrant as those of the classical forms. At one time,

A classical dancer performing at the dance festival at Mamallapuram

A movie theatre in Mumbai, with large posters of Bollywood releases

these indigenous forms were restricted to the region of their birth. Today, promotion by various cultural organizations has given folk artistes greater exposure. As a result urban audiences can watch Chhau, a masked dance performed by men from Orissa, Bihar and West Bengal; balladeers *(bhopas)* and *manganiyars* from Rajasthan; the *garba* from Gujarat; the exuberant Punjabi *bhangra*; street theatre *(jatra)* from West Bengal; traditional martial arts from Kerala; and *tamasha*, a theatre troupe with dancers and musicians from Maharashtra. During the Dussehra festival, Ramlilas – exuberant dramatizations of the epic *Ramayana (see p27)* – are held all over North India. The most elaborate of these take place by the banks of the Ganges in Varanasi *(see p203)*.

CONTEMPORARY THEATRE

In the larger cities, good quality performances of Western shows are staged. However there is also a very strong tradition of Indian-language theatre in Marathi, Gujarati, Hindi and Bengali. The range covers adaptations of contemporary works by well-known Indian authors, musicals and political satires. Many of these productions, draw their inspiration from India's rich repertoire of classical and folk forms.

PUPPET SHOWS

Puppetry in India is an ancient tradition, especially in Orissa, Karnataka *(see p535)*, Rajasthan, Tamil Nadu, Andhra Pradesh and West Bengal, where itinerant folk performers use string, rod, glove and shadow puppets to tell mythological tales to a primarily rural audience. Today, many hotels organize cultural programmes for their foreign guests, which often include a traditional puppet show. A contemporary puppet theatre movement dealing with socially relevant themes related to education, health and gender and sexuality, is also becoming popular.

CINEMA

The most popular form of entertainment is cinema, especially the extravagant blockbusters from Bollywood *(see pp32–3)*. Some excellent regional-language films, which touch on socially or politically relevant themes, are also made in Kerala, West Bengal, Tamil Nadu and Andhra Pradesh. Select theatres hold special screenings of avante-garde films, or New Wave Cinema, but these lack popular appeal. There are cinema halls in almost every town and large village, whereas the larger cities have multiplexes (with fast food eateries) that offer a mix of both Bollywood and Hollywood films. Tickets are more expensive here.

BARS AND DISCOS

Nightlife in India is definitely getting livelier. While Mumbai's night spots *(see p463)*, Bangalore's pub culture and Goa's night-long beach parties and moonlight raves have been much publicized, more conservative towns elsewhere in the country now have at least a few bars, pubs, pool lounges or discotheques.

INDIPOP

International music channels such as MTV have given a tremendous boost to the Indian pop scene. Known as Indipop, the music of groups such as Indian Ocean and Euphoria, and singers such as Lucky Ali and Alisha Chinai has made pop stars as popular as film stars. The styles range from fusion music and folk-inspired *bhangra* pop to re-mixes of popular Hindi film hits. Some classical singers, such as Shubha Mudgal, have begun to experiment with popular music in order to reach a wider audience, particularly the MTV generation.

FAIRS AND FESTIVALS

The constant cycle of fairs and festivals is intrinsic to the Indian way of life, *(see pp34–7)*. From Holi, the festival of colour in spring, to Diwali, the festival of lights at the onset of winter, there are a series of colourful celebrations that mark the changing seasons or mythological events, as well as countless temple festivals. Visitors will usually have ample opportunity to witness these vignettes of the country's cultural and religious heritage, during their travels. Being invited to a home during a festival or a traditional celebration can also be an enjoyable experience.

Each chapter in this book has a column highlighting the main regional festivals.

Polo Lounge, a popular bar in the Hyatt Regency Hotel, Delhi

OUTDOOR ACTIVITIES & SPECIALIST HOLIDAYS

India offers a wide range of sporting and outdoor activities. The larger cities have facilities for golf, tennis, swimming and riding. Winter (Oct–Feb) is the main season for sports, such as polo and cricket. For the more adventurous, there are treks in the Himalayas, tiger tracking in India's many wildlife parks, and a choice of rivers for white-water rafting. Camel or horse

Batsman at the crease

safaris offer a memorable way to explore the Rajasthan desert. For the more spiritually inclined, there are yoga and meditation centres, and opportunities to spend time with renowned gurus at their ashrams. An increasing number of visitors are attracted by India's Ayurvedic health spas, and other holistic healing centres, which emphasize nature-based treatments.

SPECTATOR SPORTS

Indians are cricket-crazy and grab at any chance to watch or play the game. Winter is the main season, when world-class teams tour the country and test matches and one-day internationals are held in cities such as Delhi, Kolkata, Mumbai, Chennai, Bangalore and Kanpur. During these matches, fans of all age-groups crowd the stands, where a picnic atmosphere prevails. Announcements of match schedules and ticket details appear in the national and local newspapers.

Soccer does not have the high profile that cricket enjoys, but in certain places, such as Kolkata, Goa and Kerala, it is as popular. The game creates great hysteria in Kolkata, and professional clubs such as Mohun Bagan and its rival team East Bengal have mass followings. Check the local press for matches on in the city. Hockey, although a national passion, is not yet big enough to attract international events.

SWIMMING AND TENNIS

All five-star hotels have excellent swimming pools with attached fitness centres. Non-residents are allowed to use hotel pools for a fee. In North India, outdoor pools close in winter. Beach resorts have pools as well as access to beaches. Before swimming in the sea, check with the lifeguard that it is safe. Swimming and sunbathing in the

nude are strictly prohibited.

Hotels offer grass or hard court tennis facilities and can also arrange games at certain local clubs, especially in the larger cities. India joined the Davis Cup fraternity in 1921, and has hosted the current numerous times. The **All India Tennis Association** also organizes tournaments. Currently among India's pride are the young Doubles team, Leander Paes and Mahesh Bhupathi, who won the French Open Men's Doubles title for the second time in June 2001.

GOLF

A vast network of clubs with well-maintained courses has made India a popular destination for golfers. The Royal Calcutta Golf Club was set up as early as 1829, and was followed by others in Raj-era hill stations, tea estates and cantonments. Exclusive golf resorts such as the ITC Classic Resort near Manesar,

designed by the international golfer Jack Nicklaus, are much frequented, especially by top executives who like to combine a round of golf with negotiating business deals.

The **Indian Golf Union** in Kolkata organizes a choice of activities, ranging from international events to leisurely games. It can also arrange temporary membership at the Royal Calcutta Golf Club and the Delhi Golf Club.

Many towns in India, such as Jaipur, Agra and Ranikhet, have well-maintained, army-run golf courses located in cantonment areas, which are open to foreigners for a fee. It is therefore worthwhile to enquire about facilities when in a new town.

POLO AND RIDING

Still very much an elitist sport, polo is enjoying a pleasant revival thanks to corporate sponsorships. The **Army Polo and Riding Club** in Delhi is the main centre, and can be

A golfer beneath the ramparts of Jaipur's Moti Doongri Fort

contacted for match schedules and other information. The season is in winter when regular matches are held in Delhi, Kolkata, Jaipur, Jodhpur and Mumbai.

Two of India's leading teams still play under the banners of the erstwhile princely houses of Jodhpur and Kashmir, while the Indian Army continues its long association with polo and fields its own team. Polo is extremely popular in Jaipur, and matches are held at the Rajasthan Polo Club near the Rambagh Palace Hotel. In some hotels in Rajasthan's Shekhawati district, visitors are taught how to play the game. Some variations are elephant and camel polo (both played in Jaipur), while in Ladakh, a rough and ready form of polo is played, with ponies instead of horses.

As for riding, thoroughbred horses can be hired at clubs in Delhi and Kolkata, as well as at the **Royal Equestrian Polo Centre** in Jaipur, after applying for a temporary membership. For joyrides there are always the hack ponies, found in most hill stations or on beaches.

HELI TOURISM

For short but delightful package tours, **Deccan Aviation** organizes helicopter trips to many exotic destinations, such as the mountain ranges of the north and north-east, and around Bangalore and Mumbai. The cost includes food and lodging While expensive, these are perfect for tourists with plenty of cash but limited time. The government-run **Pawan Hans Helicopters Ltd** also offers heli-trips in collaboration with hotels or tour operators.

JEEP, CAMEL AND HORSE SAFARIS

Often, the best way to explore places that are off the beaten track is to take one of the many safaris on offer. Jeep safaris are popular in Ladakh, especially to the Nubra Valley *(see p143)* and to the lakes of Tso Moriri and Pangong Tso.

Horse safaris, a delightful way of exploring Rajasthan

Jeep safaris are also popular in Lahaul, Spiti and Kinnaur in Himachal Pradesh. A good base is Manali which has a large number of adventure tour operators. Among them, **Himalayan Adventurers** is a reputable agency that organizes off road jeep safaris as well as other adventure activities such as trekking and rafting. The two-day route from Manali to Leh is a very popular one.

Camel-owners in the Thar Desert in Rajasthan, around Jaisalmer, specialize in camel safaris between October and February. Most safaris last about four days, and the minimum charge is around Rs400 per day (inclusive of meals and blankets, with extra charges for tents). Among the many operators, is the **Desert Resort and Camp** at Manvar, which offers top-end safaris in luxury tents. A pleasant alternative is horse safaris around Jodhpur, Shekhawati, Kumbhalgarh and Udaipur. These offer unique glimpses

Trekking over the spectacular Shingo-la pass in Zanskar, Ladakh

of rural life, taking in forts, palaces and remote villages. **Ghanerao Safari Tours** in Jaipur specializes in horse safaris and offers both easy and challenging trips. Many hotels in Rajasthan organize horse safaris. Elephant safaris are also available *(see p753)*.

TREKKING

India has a fantastic range of trekking options. Besides the Himalayas, the Nilgiris *(see p606)* in South India, and the Sahyadris *(see p473)* in Maharashtra, have many trails for short hikes.

The great Himalayas are a trekker's paradise. **Ibex Expeditions**, a reputable agency, organizes expeditions all over the Himalayas. For more detailed information on trekking and local adventure tour operators in Himachal Pradesh, see pages 114–15; in Ladakh and Zanskar, see pages 152–3; in Garhwal and Kumaon, see pages 188–9; and in West Bengal and Sikkim, see pages 302–303.

This guide divides trails into three types, based on levels of difficulty. "Easy" ones, which involve mildly strenuous walking at mid-high altitudes, are a good introduction. "Moderate" routes cover various terrains and should not be attempted by people with heart problems and serious ailments. Only experienced climbers should attempt "tough" treks, since these go to very high altitudes and require high levels of fitness. It is mandatory to carry a permit *(see p758)* near international border areas.

Parasailing, popular in Himachal Pradesh and Uttaranchal

CAMPING AND ADVENTURE SPORTS

Holidays that combine camping and trekking can be particularly enjoyable. **Banjara Camps** specializes in tented holidays in the scenic Sangla Valley in Himachal Pradesh, while **Jungle Lodges and Resorts** organizes well-run luxury camps in Karnataka.

India also provides opportunities to pursue a range of adventure sports. However, it is advisable to take out extra cover on your insurance if you plan on trying any of these activities.

Hang-gliding and parasailing are offered in Himachal Pradesh, especially in Manali and Dharamsala, and near Billing in Kangra. Ooty in Tamil Nadu is another great hang-gliding site, while the Western Ghats in Maharashtra and Goa offer idyllic conditions for parasailing. Local tourism offices in each state organize these sports and can be contacted for bookings and equipment hire.

For mountaineering and rock climbing enthusiasts, the Himalayas offer a number of challenging peaks, many rising above 7,000 m (22,966 ft). Uttaranchal and Himachal Pradesh are India's main mountaineering regions, and Sikkim also offers climbing in the Himalayas. The **Indian Mountaineering Foundation** in Delhi is the central agency; it organizes expeditions and has an active rock climbing fraternity, too. It also provides information on the country's

other institutes, such as the Himalayan Mountaineering Institute in Darjeeling *(see p296)*, and the Nehru Intitute of Mountaineering in Uttarkashi *(see p187)*, both of which offer courses.

Auli in Uttaranchal is the best-equipped ski-centre in India, and is open between January and March. For bookings and skiing information, contact the **GMVN Office** in Dehra Dun, or the **GMVN Tourist Rest House** in Auli, which also hires out gear. Solang Nala, 13 km (8 miles) northwest of Manali, also has ski slopes that are open between February and March. The **Institute of Mountaineering and Allied Sports** in Manali rents out skiing equipment, offers mountaineering courses, and also organizes kayaking on the Beas river.

KAYAKING AND RIVER RAFTING

The challenge of the fast-flowing rivers of the Himalayas makes India a popular destination for kayaking and white-water rafting. Rivers are graded from levels I to VI, and only professionals should attempt rapids that are graded IV and above. The main destinations are the Indus and Zanskar in Ladakh, the Beas and Satluj in Himachal Pradesh, the Ganges, Bhagirathi and Tons in Uttar Pradesh, and the Teesta in Sikkim. The best seasons are between September and December, and again between February and April.

Numerous agencies run organized trips and provide tents, rafts, life jackets and meals. The Ganges near

Rishikesh is a popular site *(see p185)*, as it is just a few hours drive from Delhi. Many companies have set up rafting camps and provide equipment during the season. **Himalayan River Runners**, and **Aquaterra Adventures** are two of the reputable agencies that run various rafting camps in Uttaranchal and Ladakh.

WATER SPORTS

Goa is a popular destination for water sports, where yachting competitions and wind-surfing regattas are attended by enthusiasts from all over the world. Sports such as water-skiing, sailing, wind-surfing and parasailing are offered by local agencies, on beaches such as Baga, Vainguinim, Sinquerim, Anjuna and Bogmalo. The **National Institute of Watersports**, located in Panaji, also offers training courses in wind-surfing, water-skiing, sailing and scuba diving, and hires out boats and equipment as well.

The **Royal Bombay Yacht Club** in Mumbai organizes sailing excursions for visitors every Saturday, while Kerala's popular Kovalam Beach has some facilities for surfing and snorkelling. In Tamil Nadu, a few water sports centres and hotels have recently opened, offering water sports facilities along the coast between Chennai and Mamallapuram.

The Lakshadweep Islands, off the Kerala coast, have excellent centres for wind-surfing, parasailing and water-skiing, as well as snorkelling and scuba diving. **Lacadives** on Kadmat Island has the best

White-water rafting on the Ganges

Colourful wind-surfing sails, Goa

equipped centre *(see p647)*. An equally exciting destination for snorkelling, scuba diving and other water sports is the tropical Andaman Islands in the Bay of Bengal. It is best to check in advance however as some water sports may not be available because of the 2004 tsunami. Quality equipment, including glass-bottomed boats and scuba gear, is on offer at the **Andaman Water Sports Complex** *(see p618)* in Port Blair.

FISHING

India's network of rivers and lakes provides ample opportunity for fishing enthusiasts. All fishing in India requires a permit, which can be obtained from the Fisheries Officer at the various state Fisheries Departments. However, it is simpler to let an agency organize the permits for you. Himalayan River Runners organizes exciting *mahseer* fishing expeditions in the Ganges in February and March.

The best spots in North India are the Ramganga river, outside Corbett National Park; Gangalehri, off the Haridwar-Rishikesh road on the Ganges; and Pong Dam, on the Beas in Himachal Pradesh. This state also offers superb trout-fishing on the Beas river at Katrain, and in the scenic Sangla Valley on the Baspa river. In South India, **Jungle Lodges and Resorts** *(see p755)* run the Kali River Camp at Dandeli and the Cauvery Fishing and Nature Camp, in Karnataka. These are luxury camps for discerning visitors who wish to combine a fishing holiday with modern comforts.

WILDLIFE TOURISM

A relatively new concept in tourism, combining nature study with conservation activities, is becoming increasingly popular in India. The country has an extraordinary diversity of habitats that support a vast variety of plant and animal life, including many rare and endangered species.

Today, India has 70 protected national parks and over 400 wildlife sanctuaries that cover 4.15 per cent of its total area. Numerous societies are actively involved in environmental issues. The **World Wide Fund for Nature, India (WWF)**, with its headquarters in Delhi, has a regular programme of activities such as camping trips, film shows and seminars on wildlife. The **Bombay Natural History Society (BNHS)** is one of the foremost nature institutions in India. Its first Indian president was the renowned ornithologist, Dr Salim Ali *(see p466)*. The Society, dedicated to conservation, with special emphasis on bird studies, also organizes workshops. Another eminent institution is the **Madras Naturalists' Society**.

India's many wildlife reserves and game sanctuaries are the best places to see endangered species in the wild. **Ibex Expeditions** organizes eco-friendly trips to parks all over India; **Exotic Journeys** is another reputable agency *(see p689)*. Jungle Lodges and Resorts in Karnataka runs numerous luxury camps, spread across the Nagarhole and BRT Wildlife Sanctuaries *(see p520)*, with coracle boat rides, elephant safaris and film screenings on offer for visitors.

Corbett Park in Uttaranchal *(see pp192–3)*, Kanha in Madhya Pradesh *(see pp254–5)* and the Sunderbans in West Bengal *(see pp288–9)*, are among India's largest Tiger Reserves. Rajasthan's Keoladeo Ghana National Park *(see pp368–9)* attracts a large variety of migratory birds in winter and is a birdwatcher's paradise, while Kaziranga in Assam *(see pp330–31)* is one of the few places in the world where the Indian rhino can be found in the wild. The best park for observing Asian elephants is Periyar in Kerala *(see pp640–41)*, which has the largest population of wild elephants in the country.

A few practical tips should be followed while visiting wildlife reserves. Do not litter, and be especially careful not to drop any plastic and synthetic materials. Carry a pair of binoculars, wear sturdy boots, and never wander off on your own, as this could be dangerous. Do not play loud music or blow horns within park limits since this disturbs the animals. Also, talk softly on safaris to improve the chances of spotting wildlife.

An elephant safari in Kaziranga National Park, habitat of the Indian rhino

A traditional head massage with Ayurvedic oils, Kovalam Beach

YOGA AND HEALING

Yoga, meditation and Hindu philosophy are taught at ashrams and spiritual centres in most Indian cities. Some of the best are in Rishikesh, where courses are conducted by learned gurus, renowned in their fields.

Of these, the **Sivananda Ashram** (see p689) is the most famous. Pune's **Osho International Commune** (see p470), started in the 1960s by the charismatic guru Bhagwan Rajneesh, offers residential courses in meditation and philosophy. The **Ramamani Iyengar Memorial Yoga Institute**, run by the well-known Yogacharya BKS Iyengar is also in Pune, and offers a choice of *hatha* yoga courses. Among India's other reputed yoga and meditation centres are the **Sri Aurobindo Ashram** in Pondicherry (see p689), the **Chinmaya Mission** at Mumbai and the **Ramakrishna Mission** at Belur Math (see p689). Hotels and travel agencies can find out about local branches of many of these centres.

India also has numerous institutes that conduct courses in Buddhist meditation and *vipassana*. Dharamsala and McLeodganj, the home of the Dalai Lama, have some of the best centres. Residential courses are held at the **Tushita Meditation Centre**. Ayurveda and naturopathy

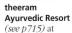

Logo of a yoga centre in Rishikesh

rely on the healing powers of herbs and natural foods, and are widely practised in India. Ayurvedic treatment using special herbal oils, is thought to have originated in Kerala (see p629), and is widely practised there today. Almost all hotels in the state have Ayurvedic centres, especially around Kovalam and Thiruvananthapuram. The **Kairali Ayurvedic Health Resort** at Palakkad (with branches in Delhi and Khajuraho), and the **Somatheeram Ayurvedic Resort** (see p715) at Kovalam are among the best centres. For visitors in search of medical advice and treatment, the **Arya Vaidyasala** in Kottakal (see p652) is a pioneer institute.

India also has a handful of luxury spas, which emphasize holistic healing (see p688). The **Institute of Naturopathy and Yogic Sciences** in Bangalore, also known as Jindal's Farm, admits patients for specialized treatments for respiratory and stomach disorders, ulcers, migraines and diabetes.

Other healing practices such as Reiki and Pranic healing (methods that channel positive forces through the body's *chakras* or energy centres), are practised in many larger cities, and it is best to check local city magazines for details. A magazine, published every month, called *Life Positive*, focuses on new-age healing techniques.

CULTURAL ACTIVITIES

Indian classical dance and music are taught at renowned institutes all over the country. **Triveni Kala Sangam** (see p75) in Delhi holds courses in classical singing, dance and painting. Dharamsala's **Norbulingka Institute** teaches Tibetan arts and crafts, including *thangka* painting and embroidery. The dance village of **Nrityagram**, near Bangalore, offers long-term courses in classical dance, choreography, music and painting. **Kalakshetra** in Chennai (see p572) is a premier institute for teaching Carnatic music and classical dance, and the **Kerala Kala Mandalam** (see p651) near Thrissur, is another renowned centre for the performing arts.

A few travel agencies offer special interest tours on subjects such as architecture, rural and tribal culture, traditional arts and crafts, and cuisine. They make itineraries to suit individual tastes. **Incent Tours** focuses on textiles, architecture and food, while **Travel Link** specializes in tribal tours in Orissa.

Various institutions all over the country promote traditional crafts and artisans. The **Crafts Museum** (see pp80–81) in Delhi, and the **Dastkar Craft Centre**, which is near Ranthambhore in Rajasthan, are two places where visitors can observe artisans at work and learn more about their skills and way of life.

Gujarati musicians at the Crafts Museum, New Delhi

DIRECTORY

SPORTS

All India Tennis Association
Tennis Stadium, Africa Avenue, Delhi.
Tel (011) 2617 6280.

Indian Golf Union
Room 1138–B, Jawaharlal Nehru Stadium, Gate 27, Lodi Rd, Delhi.
Tel (011) 2436 7161.

POLO & RIDING

Army Polo & Riding Club
C/o B Squadron, 61 Cavalry, Cariappa Marg, Delhi.
Tel (011) 2569 9444.
www.indianpolo.com

Royal Equestrian Polo Centre
Dundlod House, Civil lines, Jaipur.
Tel (0141) 221 1276.

HELI-TOURISM

Deccan Aviation
E–17 Anand Niketan, Delhi.
Tel (011) 2410 3521.
Fax (011) 2410 3522.
www.deccanair.com

Pawan Hans Helicopters Ltd.
Safdarjung Airport, Delhi.
Tel (011) 2461 5711.
Fax (011) 2461 1801.
www.pawanhans.com

JEEP, CAMEL & HORSE SAFARIS

Desert Resort & Camp, Manvar
646 Hanuwant Nagar, 'A', BJS, Jodhpur.
Tel (0291) 254 6188.
Fax (0291) 254 6188.
www.manwar.com

Ghanerao Safari Tours
B–II/302 Kamal Apts, Bani Park, Jaipur.
Tel (0141) 220 1209.
Fax (0141) 220 1209.
www.horsesafari.com

Himalayan Adventurers
The Mall, Manali.
Tel (01902) 252 365.
Fax (01902) 252 182.
www.himalayanadventurersindia.com

TREKKING

Ibex Expeditions
G-66 East of Kailash, Delhi.
Tel (011) 2691 2641.
www.ibexexpeditions.com

CAMPING & ADVENTURE SPORTS

Banjara Camps
1 A Haus Khas Village, Delhi.
Tel (011) 2686 1397.
Fax (011) 2685 5152.

GMVN
74/1 Rajpur Rd, Dehradun.
Tel (0135) 274 6817.
Fax (0135) 274 6847.

GMVN Tourist Rest House, Auli
Tel (01389) 223 208.

Indian Mountaineering Foundation
6 Benito Juarez Marg, Delhi.
Tel (011) 2467 7935.
www.indmount.org

Institute of Mountaineering & Allied Sports
Manali.
Tel (01902) 252 342.

Jungle Lodges & Resorts
Shrungar Shopping Centre, MG Rd, Bangalore.
Tel (080) 2559 7021.
Fax (080) 2558 6163.
www.junglelodges.com

KAYAKING & RIVER RAFTING

Aquaterra Adventures
S–507 Greater Kailash II, New Delhi.
Tel (011) 2921 2760.
Fax (011) 2921 2641.
www.treknraft.com

Himalayan River Runners
N–8 Green Park, Delhi.
Tel (011) 2685 2602.
Fax (011) 2686 5604.
www.hrrindia.com

WATER SPORTS

National Institute of Watersports
Sundial Apts, AS Rd, Altinho, Panaji, Goa.
Tel (0832) 243 6550.
Fax (0832) 243 6400.

Royal Bombay Yacht Club
Apollo Bunder, Mumbai.
Tel (022) 2285 4259.

WILDLIFE TOURISM

Bombay Natural History Society
Hornbill House, Shaheed Bhagat Singh Marg, Mumbai.
Tel (022) 2282 1811.
www.bnhs.org

Madras Naturalists' Society
8 Janaki Avenue, Abhiramapuram, Chennai.
Tel (044) 2499 5833.
www.blackbuck.org

World Wide Fund for Nature, India
172–B Lodi Estate, Delhi.
Tel (011) 5150 4791.
Fax (011) 5150 4817.
www.wwfindia.org

YOGA & HEALING

Arya Vaidyasala
Kottakkal.
Tel (0423) 274 2216.
Fax (0423) 274 2210.
www.aryavaidyasala.com

Chinmaya Mission
Central Chinmaya Mission Trust, Mumbai.
Tel (022) 2857 2367.
Fax (022) 2857 3065.
www.chinmayamission.com

Tushita Meditation Centre
McLeodganj.
Tel (01892) 221 866.

Institute of Naturopathy & Yogic Sciences
Jindal Nagar, Bangalore.
Tel (080) 2371 7777.
Fax (080) 2371 7785.
www.naturecure-inys.org

Kairali Ayurvedic Health Resort
Olassery, Post Kodumbu, Palakkad District.
Tel (0492) 232 2553.
Fax (0492) 232 2732.
www.kairali.com

Osho International Commune
17 Koregaon Park, Pune.
Tel (020) 401 9999.
www.osho.com

Ramamani Iyengar Memorial Yoga Institute
1107 B/1 Hare Krishna Mandir Rd, Model Colony, Shivaji Nagar, Pune.
Tel (020) 565 6134.
www.bksiyengar.com

CULTURAL ACTIVITIES

Dastkar Craft Centre
Kutalpura Village.
Tel (07462) 252 049.

Incent Tours
C-4/41 Safdarjung Developmental Area, Delhi.
Tel (011) 5165 7576.
Fax (011) 5165 7205.
www.incent–tours.com

Norbulingka Institute
Dharamsala.
Tel (01892) 246 402.
Fax (01892) 246 404.

Nrityagram
The Dance Village, Hessaraghatta, Bangalore.
Tel (080) 2846 6313.
Fax (080) 2846 6312.

Travel Link
Metro House, Vani Vihar Square, Bhubaneswar.
Tel (0674) 254 6591.
Fax (0674) 254 6595.
www.travellink-india.com

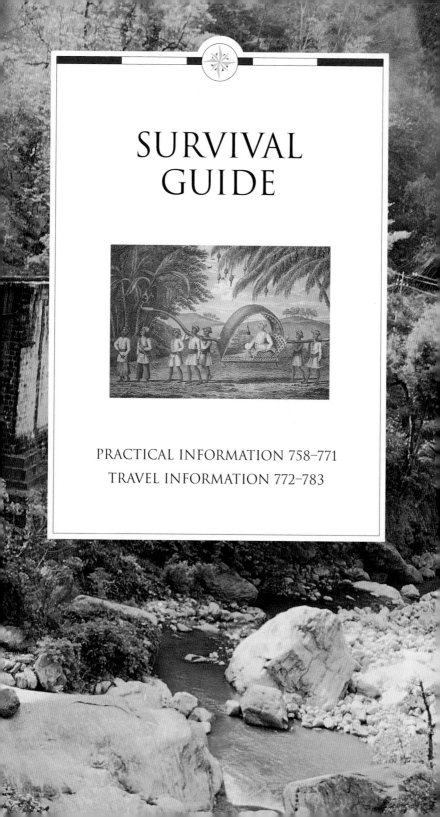

SURVIVAL
GUIDE

PRACTICAL INFORMATION

India receives over 4.4 million visitors each year. The peak season is in winter (Oct–Mar), and it is wise to book ahead during this time. English is widely spoken in most parts of the country, so communication is rarely a problem. Tourist infrastructure (transportation, accommodation and restaurants) are of international standard in the larger cities; the remoter areas offer fairly basic accommodation

Logo of the Ministry of Tourism & Culture

and some areas are still not equipped to cater to the international tourist, who may seek better banking services or prefer to pay by credit card. The Department of Tourism has offices across the country (see p781) as well as overseas, which provide brochures, itineraries and guided tours. There are many travel agencies in India, but it is wise to approach a reputable one for accommodation, tickets and tours.

WHEN TO GO

India's weather is, for most, the key facor in deciding when to visit. The best time is between October and March, when conditions are pleasant across the country. Try to avoid the summer (Apr–Jun), which is unbearably hot in the north, and very sultry in the south. The rainy season (Jul–Sep) is also best avoided, as frequent heavy rainfall can make travel difficult, especially in the southwestern states of Goa, Maharashtra and Kerala. The Himalayan region can be very cold from November to January. The foothills, which provide a welcome escape from the heat of the plains, are at their best between March and June, and again in September (after the rains). Climate and rainfall charts can be found on pages 38–39.

WHAT TO TAKE

The clothes you need will depend on the time of year that you visit. In northern India, from November until

February, you will need a warm jacket, sweater and socks, especially after sundown, whereas in the south, the weather is balmy at that time. In February and March, and again in October, bring light woollens. During the summer and monsoon season (Apr–Sep) only loose-fitting cotton clothes are comfortable. Bring footwear that is easy to remove, as you will have to take off your shoes in places of worship. A first aid kit is a must (see p766). A raincoat or umbrella, a hat to protect against the strong sun, and a torch are also useful.

ADVANCE BOOKING

It is advisable to have confirmed advance bookings for accommodation and travel, especially during the peak season (Oct–Mar). Airline tickets are available at short notice, but as trains are always crowded, bookings should be made ahead – ticket reservations can be made two months in advance. Insist on written confirmations.

VISAS AND PASSPORT

Everyone needs a passport and visa to enter India. The Indian consular offices around the world issue a standard six-month multiple-entry visa for tourists, which is convenient for visiting neighbouring countries such as Nepal and Sri Lanka. Foreigners who arrive in India on this visa do not need to register themselves with a local authority and can travel freely in all areas except the so-called "Restricted Areas", which require special permits.

Visa extensions are sometimes granted for 15 days or, in exceptional cases, for a longer period. The application process is complicated. In Delhi, collect an extension form from the **Ministry of Home Affairs** office; then submit it to the **Foreigners Regional Regisration Office (FRRO)**; it will finally be issued by the Ministry of Home Affairs. In Mumbai, Chennai or Kolkata, contact the local FRRO.

Obtaining a visa extension, whether for 15 days or longer, is extremely difficult and extensions are only granted, if at all, in special circumstances.

PERMITS

In addition to a visa, you may need special travel permits to visit what are known as "Restricted Areas". Obtaining a permit can be complicated, so it is best to ask a reliable travel agent, at home or in India, to arrange it for you.

A Goa café doing brisk business in winter, when the weather is balmy

◁ The Blue Mountain Train on its scenic journey to Ooty (see p605)

This can take up to four weeks, so plan in advance. Permits are also issued by Indian embassies and consular offices abroad; from the FRRO in Delhi, Kolkata, Mumbai and Chennai; and from the Resident Commissioner's offices in Delhi. You will be asked to show these permits when travelling in restricted areas. You will also need trekking permits for the Himalayan regions bordering Pakistan, Tibet and China, and for treks in Uttaranchal *(see pp188–9)*, Himachal Pradesh *(see p115)*, Ladakh *(see p142, p143 & p153)* and West Bengal and Sikkim *(see p303)*. All visitors to Sikkim require 15-day travel permits, because of its proximity to a sensitive border with China.

Among the seven northeastern states, no permits are required for Assam, Meghalaya and Tripura. However, permits are required for Arunachal Pradesh, Mizoram, Manipur and Nagaland, and can be acquired from any of the state tourist offices. In some areas, permits are issued only to groups of four or more – these are best organised by a travel agent.

Foreign nationals require a permit, valid for 30 days, for the Andaman Islands, but this excludes tribal areas and some islands, including Nicobar. Permits can be obtained on arrival at the immigration counter at Port Blair airport, or at Kolkata and Chennai airports. If travelling by ship, a permit can be obtained on arrival at Port Blair, as well as from the FRRO offices in the four main cities. For permits to travel to the Lakshadweep Islands, see page 647.

EMBASSIES AND CONSULATES

Most countries have embassies in Delhi, as well as consulates in Mumbai, Kolkata and Chennai. Consular offices can re-issue passports and assist in case of emergencies, such as theft,

imprisonment and hospitalization. All city telephone directories and information guides carry detailed listings of embassies and consulates, as does the Indian Ministry of Tourism's website. (www.tourindia.com)

CUSTOMS INFORMATION

When entering India, visitors have a duty-free allowance of 950 ml of alcohol and 200 cigarettes. For articles such as jewellery, video cameras, music systems or laptop computers, they must fill in the tourist baggage re-export form, undertaking to take these items back or else pay a fairly heavy duty on them on departure. They must also fill in the currency declaration form at the airport for more than US$2,500 in cash or traveller's cheques.

There is a duty of 60 per cent if the baggage value limit is exceeded. Antiques over 100 years old cannot be exported. Neither can wildlife products, such as animal pelts, *shahtoosh* shawls or ivory. Consult the **Archaeological Survey of India (ASI)** and the **Ministry of Environment and Forests** for details of these rules.

Visa Stamp

IMMUNIZATION

Only visitors travelling from certain countries in Africa, South America and Papua New Guinea require a valid vaccination certificate for yellow fever. However, visitors should get vaccinated against tetanus, typhoid and hepatitis A and B. It is also advisable to start a course of anti-malarial tablets before leaving for India, after consulting a doctor *(see p767)*.

INSURANCE

It is advisable to take out an insurance policy for medical emergencies as well as theft before leaving home. Travel insurance is also essential to cover any adventure activity or sport that you may undertake on your trip.

DIRECTORY

FRRO

www.nic.in

Delhi
East Block 8, Level 2,
Sector 1, RK Puram.
Tel (011) 2671 1348.

Mumbai
Annexe Building,
Sayed Badruddin Rd.
Tel (022) 2262 1169.

Chennai
Shastri Bhavan Annexe,
26 Haddow Rd.
Tel (044) 2354 4970.

Kolkata
237 AJC Bose Rd.
Tel (033) 2247 0549.

MINISTRY OF HOME AFFAIRS

Delhi
Loknayak Bhawan,
Khan Market.
Tel (011) 2469 2731.

TRAVEL AGENTS

Abercrombie & Kent
Tel (011) 2617 8418 (India).
Tel (0044) 207-190 7710 (UK).
www.abercrombiekent.co.uk

Cox & Kings
Tel (011) 4129 7922 (India).
Tel (0044) 207-873 5000 (UK).
www.coxandkings.com

Kuoni Travel India
Tel (011) 2612 1110 (India).
Tel (0044) 1306-74 4115 (UK).
www.sitaindia.com

Mercury Travels
Tel (011) 2389 0505 (India).
www.mercury-india.com

ASI

Janpath, Delhi.
Tel (011) 2301 3574.

MINISTRY OF ENVIRONMENT & FORESTS

Paryavaran Bhavan,
CGO Complex, Lodhi Rd,
New Delhi.
Tel (011) 2436 0861.

GENERAL INFORMATION

www.outlooktraveller.com
www.travel.indiamart.com
www.tourindia.com

TOURIST INFORMATION

Tourist information offices run by the **Government of India Department of Tourism** *(see p781)* can be found across the country and abroad. Each state also has its own tourism department, providing reliable and detailed advice and practical information on sightseeing, travel and stay. Tourist brochures and maps are readily available. A number of travel sites on the Internet also provide up-to-date information. There are information counters in the arrival halls of international and domestic airports, as well as information booths at railway and bus stations.

Tourist brochures

ADMISSION CHARGES

Most museums, historical monuments and wildlife parks charge an entry fee. This is often a modest amount, though admission to UNESCO World Heritage Sites costs more – foreigners pay a fee of 970 rupees for the Taj Mahal. Note that payment in US dollars may incur a surcharge or not be accepted at all.

There are often additional fees for cameras, video cameras, and for special shows such as the Son et Lumières. Most places of worship do not have any admission fee, but often have a donation box. If you are of a different religious denomination, it is advisable to ask if you may enter *(see p762)*.

HOLIDAYS AND OPENING HOURS

Each year, the government issues a new holiday list *(see p35)* that includes all major religious festivals, whose exact dates may change from year to year. Some are known as "restricted holidays", which means that though the office may be open, the staff may be on leave. Banks, offices and most markets remain closed on the three national holidays: Republic Day (26 January) Independence Day (15 August) and Mahatma Gandhi's birthday (2 October). Monuments and museums are normally open from 10am to 6pm with an hour's lunch break, and generally close on Mondays and government holidays. Markets and shops stay open until at least 7pm in most places. Temples tend to close between 1pm and 4pm when the deity is "at rest". Government offices work from Monday to Friday, from 9:30am to 6pm with, supposedly, a half-hour lunch break.

GUIDES

All tourist offices, travel agents and hotels can arrange a certified guide for fixed hourly rates. At popular monuments amateur guides can be a nuisance. Look instead for English-speaking guides who wear a metal badge certifying government tourist department approval. French, Italian, Spanish, German, Russian and Japanese-speaking guides are also available at many popular destinations.

BACKPACKERS

For students and young travellers, most of the larger cities have branches of the **Youth Hostels Association of India** or **YHAI** *(see p689)*. Though it is not necessary to be a member of the International Association to stay, members do get priority and lower rates. **YMCA** hostels in larger cities also provide cheap lodgings for backpackers. Apart from these, plenty of cheap options are also available across the country, including the smaller towns. It is a good idea to buy a strong padlock as some of the budget hotels have flimsy locks. Many of these are not air conditioned, nor do they have mosquito nets – the latter are essential, and available locally. Do not leave money and important documents in your hotel; keep them with you at all times. Be wary of conmen enticing you with the promise of cheap accommodation and bargain shopping.

FACILITIES FOR THE DISABLED

Facilities for the disabled are still relatively basic across the country and public buildings and places of interest seldom have ramps or rails. However, airports and all main railway stations do have wheelchairs and ramps, and porters are always available to carry luggage. Pavements are difficult to negotiate in a wheelchair as they are often uneven. Few hotels are equipped for the needs of the disabled visitor. The staff, however, will go out of their way to help.

FACILITIES FOR CHILDREN

Although some luxury hotels do have baby-sitting facilities, these services are not commonly available. However, Indians are generally tolerant of children, who are warmly

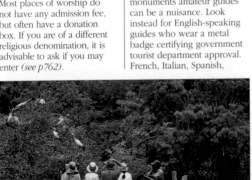
Visitors on a guided tour of the lake at Ranganthittoo Bird Sanctuary

welcomed in most places. If travelling with young infants, it is advisable to bring your own supplies of baby food and formula milk. Disposable nappies are now widely available in the larger towns.

LANGUAGE

Though Hindi is the official language of India, there are several regional languages as well. Bengali is spoken in Kolkata and West Bengal, Marathi in Mumbai and Maharashtra, Tamil in Tamil Nadu, Telugu in Andhra Pradesh and Malayalam in Kerala. English has become the most convenient link language and is widely spoken in most Indian cities. It is also the language of commerce, and most people who deal with tourists, such as taxi drivers, guides, hotel staff, shop assistants and officials, speak English. Road signs and numbers are usually in English as well as in the regional language of the particular state.

ELECTRICITY

The electrical current in India is 220–240 volts, 50 Hz. The power supply can be very erratic during the summer months, with low voltage, fluctuations and fairly long power cuts.

Triple round-pin sockets are the norm, but adaptors and transformers are easily available at the larger stores. It is advisable to carry a power surge cable to protect laptop computers against voltage fluctuations.

INDIAN STANDARD TIME AND CALENDAR

In spite of its size, India has only one standard time. India is 5.5 hours ahead of Greenwich Mean Time (GMT) 4.5 hours behind Australian Eastern Standard Time, and 10.5 hours ahead of US Eastern Standard Time. The Western Gregorian calendar is used for all official work as this avoids the confusion of traditional calendars, which vary between religions and

regions. For example, in 2009, the official Indian calendar (Saka era) reads 1931, whereas the old Hindu calendar (Vikram era) reads 2066.

MEASUREMENTS AND CONVERSION CHART

The metric system is most commonly used all over the country.

Imperial to Metric
1 inch = 2.5 centimetres
1 foot = 30 centimetres
1 mile = 1.6 kilometres
1 ounce = 28 grams
1 pound = 454 grams
1 pint = 0.6 litres
1 gallon = 4.5 litres

Metric to Imperial
1 centimetre = 0.4 inches
1 metre = 3 feet 3 inches
1 kilometre = 0.6 miles
1 gram = 0.04 ounces
1 kilogram = 2.2 pounds
1 litre = 1.8 pints

A range of plugs

PHOTOGRAPHY

Sophisticated film and colour-processing facilities are readily available, even in smaller towns. Remember to check expiry dates when buying batteries and film. Larger photo shops also have excellent developing and printing facilities and offer quick services.

Taking pictures of women, tribal communities, and places of worship can be sensitive issues and it is best to ask before using your camera. Photographing security-sensitive areas, such as railway stations, dams, airports and military installations, is prohibited. Notice boards indicate where photography is not allowed.

DIRECTORY

STATE GOVERNMENT TOURIST OFFICES IN INDIA

Delhi
N–36, Connaught Place.
Tel (011) 2331 5322.
www.delhitourism.com

Goa
Dr Alvarez Costa Rd, Panaji.
Tel (0832) 222 6728.
www.goa-tourism.com

Himachal Pradesh
Near Victory Tunnel, Shimla.
Tel (0177) 265 4589.
www.hptdc.nic.in

Karnataka
49, Khanija Bhavan,
Race Course Rd, Bangalore.
Tel (080) 2235 2901.
www.kstdc.nic.in

Kerala
Parkview Building,
Thiruvanthanapuram.
Tel (0471) 232 1132.
www.keralatourism.org

Madhya Pradesh
Paryatan Bhavan, Bhadbhada Rd,
Bhopal.
Tel (0755) 277 8383.
www.mptourism.com

Maharashtra
CDO Hutments, Madame Cama
Rd, Nariman Point, Mumbai.
Tel (022) 2202 6713.
www.mtdcindia.com

Rajasthan
Paryatan Bhavan, MI Rd, Jaipur.
Tel (0141) 511 0595.
www.rajasthantourism.gov.in

Tamil Nadu
TN Tourism Complex,
Omandurar Govt Estate,
Wallajah Rd, Chennai.
Tel (044) 2536 8358.
www.tamilnadutourism.org

Uttar Pradesh
C-13, Vipin Khand, Lucknow.
Tel (0522) 230 8017.
www.up-tourism.com

West Bengal
4, Shakespeare Sarai, Kolkata.
Tel (033) 2282 5813.
www.wbtourism.com

Etiquette

India is still a traditional society, governed by strong family values. Though in cities and larger towns you will find youngsters in Western dress with a modern, cosmopolitan outlook, they remain traditional in many ways. And though the diverse social, religious and caste groups have their own distinct customs, they share certain common values. Respect for elders is deeply ingrained, so it is important to treat older people with special courtesy. Indians are extremely hospitable and helpful to visitors – sometimes to an almost embarassing degree. It is a good idea to respond to this by bringing your hosts flowers, or a small gift, even though this is not an Indian custom. If you find yourself facing delays and inefficient services, or grappling with bureaucracy, it is far more effective to be firm and polite than to lose your temper.

Eating off banana leaves at a ceremonial temple feast

GREETING PEOPLE

The traditional greeting in India is the *namaskar* or *namaste* (pronounced "namastay") when meeting or parting. The palms are pressed together, raised towards the face, and the head is bent slightly forward. Greetings and gestures vary somewhat according to religion or regional group. Muslims raise their right hand towards the forehead with the words *adaab* or *salaam aleikum* (to which you reply *walekum salaam*). The Western handshake is also widely used, though more conservative women still prefer to greet visitors with a *namaskar*.

The suffix "*ji*" after someone's name is a mark of respect. Using first names only can be taken as overly familiar, so it's best to address new acquaintances as Mr, Miss or Mrs, or simply "*ji*".

Older people, particularly grandparents, are treated with great respect, and younger relatives often greet them by touching their feet. Your host will not expect you to do the same, but a courteous greeting in any form is important.

Indians will think nothing of asking you apparently very personal questions within minutes of first meeting you, so don't take offence if a relative stranger asks you how much you earn or whether you are married. Such questions are seen as nothing more than taking a normal friendly interest in a new acquaintance.

Namaskar, the traditional greeting

BODY LANGUAGE

The feet are considered to be the lowliest part of the body, and shoes are treated as unclean. People will usually take their shoes off before entering a house. Putting your feet up on the furniture is considered bad manners, as is touching someone inadvertently with your feet. If you are sitting on the floor, as is often the case, try to keep your feet tucked underneath rather than stretched out, and avoid stepping over people.

The head, on the other hand, is thought to be a person's spiritual centre. An older person may bless someone younger by touching his or her head.

Living in close quarters with family and neighbours gives Indians a different sense of "personal space" than many Westerners are used to. If you find yourself crowded or jostled, particularly while travelling, be as tolerant as you can, since space is often at a premium.

You should also be aware that public displays of affection between couples is frowned on in Indian society.

SUITABLE DRESS

Indians tend to dress conservatively and keep the body well covered. In small towns, most women wear saris or *salwar-kameez (see p30)*. In cities, jeans, skirts, and t-shirts are common, particularly among the younger generation. However, men do tend to stare at skimpily-clad women, so try to avoid short skirts, halter-neck tops, or anything that might attract unwanted attention.

It is best to dress formally when visiting Indian homes. In fact, wearing an Indian outfit for the occasion will probably delight your hosts. Inexpensive, ready-made Indian clothes for men and women are widely available.

It is acceptable for men to go shirtless on the beach. Nude sunbathing is never allowed, and women are advised to wear full swimsuits, or sarongs over their bikinis. If you are going out for the evening, remember that most nightclubs have a dress code, and you may not get in if you are wearing shorts or sneakers.

PLACES OF WORSHIP

Whether you are visiting a Hindu temple, Buddhist monastery, Islamic mosque or Sikh gurdwara, make sure that you behave and dress appropriately. You should, for example, always ask permission to take photographs. Women should wear dresses that cover the upper arms, and are at least mid-calf length, and and take a scarf along to cover their head. It is acceptable for women to wear long trousers. Men should avoid shorts and may be asked to cover their heads with a handkerchief or scarf (rather than a hat).

Jain temples have strict rules, and will not allow leather items, even wallets or watch straps, inside. In some South Indian temples, men

Sign for removing footwear

are expected to remove their shirts and wear a *dhoti* instead of trousers. These are often provided at the temple entrance. At most places of worship, shoes are taken off at the door, and you should sit with your feet facing away from the main shrine. In a temple or monastery, walk around in a clockwise direction. You may be offered *prasad* (sacred food) in most temples and gurdwaras, which must be taken only in the right hand. The segregation of men and women is common.

In Hindu temples, it is usual for devotees and visitors to offer flowers and incense. Do not sit on or lean against temple walls or shrines. Even those in ruins, as well as simple roadside graves are considered holy. Some Hindu temples, (especially in Kerala and a few in Orissa) are out of bounds for non-Hindus. If you are barred from entering,

do not take offence. Avoid entering a mosque during Friday prayers, and men should stay away from the women's enclosure.

BARGAINING

Bargaining is a way of life in India. Exchanges can be heated, but it is not necessary to be aggressive. Firmly state what you would like to pay and walk away if the shopkeeper does not agree. If you are buying in bulk, you may ask for an extra discount. The prices in larger shops and government emporia are usually fixed (*see p744*).

EATING INDIAN STYLE

Eating with your fingers can take a bit of getting used to, but it is the best way to enjoy traditional Indian food. If in doubt about how to eat a particular dish, don't be embarrassed to ask. It is considered impolite to use your left hand for eating. Sitting on the floor for meals is common and, in the south, banana leaves are often used instead of plates.

TIPPING

There are no norms for tipping, or *baksheesh*, as it is called. Porters and doormen at hotels are usually happy with a 5 or 10 rupee tip. In restaurants, check the bill before you decide on the tip, since the larger ones usually include a service charge. If

not, ten per cent of the total amount is usually fine. Tipping taxi or auto-rickshaw drivers is optional, and not generally expected. If you hire a car with a driver, however, you are expected to give him a *baksheesh*. The same goes for hairdressers, masseurs or anyone offering you a personal service.

SMOKING AND ALCOHOL

Although smoking in public places is officially banned in some states (such as Delhi and Kerala), this rule is widely flouted. Smoking is banned on domestic flights, and in some hotels, restaurants and offices. Smoking or drinking within the precincts of a temple, gurdwara or mosque is strictly taboo, and in Amritsar, no smoking is permitted within the city limits.

Alcohol is available all over India, though the state of Gujarat is "dry", as are some religious sites and temple towns, such as Haridwar, Rishikesh and Pushkar. In addition, there are certain designated "dry days" all over the country, such as Mahatma Gandhi's birthday (2 October) and Independence Day (15 August). Only some restaurants are licensed to serve alchohol, and you are not allowed to drink alcohol in parks, buses or trains.

BEGGARS

As a foreign visitor in India, you will get more than your share of harassment from beggars at city traffic lights, markets and outside places of worship. Beggars can be extremely persistent. Although it's very difficult to refuse, visitors who give money to one, will soon find themselves surrounded by a throng. Be especially careful of being pickpocketed in the confusion. The best strategy is to ignore them, and walk on until they leave you alone. If necessary, complain to a nearby policeman. If you do wish to help monetarily, the staff at your hotel will be able to suggest deserving charities to whom donations can be made.

Hindu pilgrims outside a temple in Orissa

Personal Security and Health

Police officer's badge

Each state in India has its own police force, which is run from local police stations (*thanas*). If you need to report a crime, such as theft, to the police, try to do so within 24 hours of the incident. Although Indian police are generally helpful, the system itself is extremely bureaucratic and prone to corruption, so it is always best to contact your embassy or consular office for help and advice in the first instance. For a trouble-free visit, a few simple precautions are necessary. Protect your valuables and important documents at all times, stay and eat in places that look clean, and drink only mineral water. If you require medical attention, it is better to opt for a private clinic rather than one of the many government-run hospitals.

Policeman in summer uniform directing traffic in Kolkata

GENERAL PRECAUTIONS

Travelling in India is relatively safe for tourists. Take simple safety measures, such as wearing a money belt under your shirt for cash, traveller's cheques and important documents, such as passports and visas. Protect your camera and avoid wearing jewellery or carrying large amounts of cash in crowded areas. Valuables can be kept in a hotel safe, but do insist on a receipt. While shopping, ensure that shopkeepers make out a bill and process your credit card in front of you. There have been incidents of tourists being drugged and robbed, especially on trains, so it is not advisable to accept food or drink from strangers. Padlock your luggage to your seat

during train journeys. It is a good idea to let your hotel know where you are going. Do not stray into deserted areas alone, especially at night, and avoid hitchhiking.

DANGER AREAS

The border areas are high-security zones, so when trekking or travelling in the Himalayan regions make sure you have an Inner Line Permit *(see p758)*. The state of Jammu and Kashmir has had long-standing militant activity and much of the state is unsafe for visitors *(see p154)*. Bihar too has a law and order problem and there have been incidents where buses and cars have been held up and robbed. Before travelling to such areas, it is a good idea to contact the state tourism department in Patna *(see p215)* for up-to-date information on the law and order situation. In restricted areas always travel in groups rather than on your own. Communal unrest and even riots are usually confined to the crowded older parts of cities. It is best to avoid these areas if the political situation is uneasy, or during important religious festivals which attract large crowds.

A police jeep

A hospital ambulance

SECURITY

Since the attack on New York's World Trade Center in 2001, security has been tightened throughout India, especially at airports and railway stations. Bag-and body-searches are usual when entering cinemas and public auditoria. Never pick up un-attended baggage, and inform the police immediately if you notice anything suspicious.

NARCOTICS

Since the 1960s, India has been part of the "hippy trail" with marijuana easily available. With the arrival of Ecstasy and other harder drugs in the 1990s, particularly in places such as Goa, the law has tightened considerably. Possession, trafficking and use of narcotics (including marijuana) is now banned by law and punishable by tough jail sentences. Drug convictions lead to a minimum sentence of ten years without parole or remission. Never carry anything for strangers or check in their luggage for them at airports. A Narcotic Drugs and Psychotropic Substances Court has been established specifically to try drug-related offences.

WOMEN TRAVELLERS

Women, both Indian and foreign, face a certain amount of unwanted male attention, even though "eve-teasing" is today a punishable offence. When travelling alone, the problems women encounter can range from being stared at to more active harassment such as suggestive comments and body contact in buses and crowded places.

Take your cue from Indian women who continue with their independent lifestyles despite such annoyances. Dress modestly, and avoid wearing clothes that can be thought of as provocative. Ignore men lounging at street corners and, if you find their attention offensive, approach the nearest policeman. Avoid walking about alone in quiet places and in the rougher parts of cities. When hiring a car or taxi, ask the hotel to book it for you and note the licence plate number. Hitch-hiking is not advisable under any circumstances.

When queuing for train or cinema tickets, use the "ladies' lines" which are usually much shorter. On many buses and on some trains there are "ladies only" seats or compartments to make the journey that much safer.

LEGAL ASSISTANCE

Legal problems are rare for travellers, but if you do find yourself in a legal tangle, contact your embassy immediately. Always carry your passport and keep a photocopy handy. Do not hand over your travel papers to anyone until your embassy has been informed. Some insurance policies also cover legal costs for emergencies such as accidents.

PUBLIC TOILETS

Wayside public toilets have poor hygiene and are best avoided. However, although few in number, those known as "Sulabh Shauchalayas" located on city roads are a great civic invention. Attractively designed, they are easy to spot, extremely clean and charge a nominal fee for use. They are, however, of the

Indian "squatting" variety and can be difficult to use if you are not used to them. Some hotels allow non-residents to use their toilets. It is always a good idea to carry your own toilet paper with you, just in case.

HOSPITALS AND MEDICAL FACILITIES

Do take out comprehensive medical insurance before arriving in India. **MASTA** (Medical Advisory Service for Travellers Abroad) in the UK can give a health update for travellers to India. The larger cities have reasonably good government and private hospitals and nursing homes, with 24-hour services equipped to handle casualty and emergency cases. It is always best to contact your embassy for their list of approved hospitals, clinics, doctors and dentists. They may also be able to advise on sourcing safe, screened blood for transfusions. If in doubt, the local **Indian Red Cross Society** is one of the safest options for blood transfusion. Even in the best hospitals, it is imperative to ensure that staff use disposable syringes.

A local pharmacy or chemist shop

PHARMACIES

Most big markets in all cities and towns, have well-stocked pharmacies (or chemist shops, as they are known in India). They stock toiletries, sanitary napkins and tampons, baby food and disposable nappies. Pharmacists can also suggest simple remedies. For special medication, it is advisable to carry a prescription, or show the packaging with the generic name if the brand is unfamiliar, so that the pharmacist can suggest a suitable alternative. Antibiotics are sold only by prescription. Most pharmacies are open between 9am and 7:30pm. Many hospitals have 24-hour pharmacies.

DIRECTORY

ALL INDIA EMERGENCY NUMBERS

Tel Police 100.
Tel Fire Brigade 101.
Tel Ambulance/Emergency 102.

HOSPITALS AND MEDICAL FACILITIES

Delhi
Indraprastha Apollo, Sarita Vihar, Mathura Rd.
Tel (011) 2692 5858.

Indian Red Cross Society
1 Red Cross Rd.
Tel (011) 2371 6424.
www.ifrc.org

Mumbai
Breach Candy Hospital, 60 Bhulabhai Desai Rd.
Tel (022) 2367 1888.

Kolkata
Woodlands Hospital and Medical Centre, 8/5 Alipur Rd.
Tel (033) 2456 7075.

Chennai
Apollo Hospitals, 21 Greams Lane, Off Greams Rd.
Tel (044) 2829 0200.

MASTA (UK)
Tel + 44 (0) 113 238 7575.
www.masta.org

EMBASSIES

Australia
1/50 G Shantipath, New Delhi.
Tel (011) 4141 9900.
www.ausgovindia.com

Canada
7/8 Shantipath, New Delhi.
Tel (011) 4178 2000.
www.canadianembassy.org

Ireland
230 Jor Bagh, New Delhi.
Tel (011) 2460 3335.

United Kingdom
Shantipath, New Delhi.
Tel (011) 2687 2161.
www.ukic.com

USA
Shantipath, New Delhi.
Tel (011) 2419 8000.
www.usembassy.state.gov

HEAT AND HUMIDITY

Northern, central and western India are scorchingly hot *(see pp38–9)* during the summer (Apr–Jun). The east and the south are not as hot but can get oppressively humid during the monsoon.

Take things easy for a few days to get acclimatized. To prevent dehydration, drink plenty of fluids and add an extra pinch of salt to the food. It is wise to stay indoors during the hottest part of the day, and if outdoors wear a wide-brimmed hat and sunglasses, and use sun screen to protect your skin. Prolonged exposure to the sun can cause heat stroke, a serious condition with high body temperature, severe headaches and disorientation.

Polyester clothing and covered shoes and socks trap perspiration and can lead to prickly heat and fungal infections, especially in the scalp, between the toes, (athlete's foot), in the groin and other sensitive parts of the body. Prickly heat powder and anti-fungal ointments are available at most pharmacies. The best prevention is to wear light, loose-fitting cotton clothing and open sandals, and to always dry yourself well after washing.

In winter (Oct–Feb), cities have a lot of smog, as the pollution in the air tends to settle. This aggravates chest infections, and asthmatic travellers should always carry their own medication, although inhalers, such as Asthaline, are readily available on prescription.

Hand fan

FIRST AID KIT

A basic first aid kit for travelling in India should include all personal medication, aspirin or painkillers for fevers and minor aches and pains, tablets for nausea, antiseptic and calamine lotion for cuts and bites, an anti-fungal ointment, plaster and crêpe bandages, a pair of scissors, insect repellent and tweezers. It should also have antihistamines for allergies, anti-diarrhoea tablets, water purification tablets, disposable syringes and a thermometer. Most of these items are also available at Indian pharmacies. They stock effective herbal remedies as well; buy only brands that have been recommended by a reliable practitioner or pharmacist.

STOMACH UPSETS AND DIARRHOEA

Diarrhoea, usually caused by a change of diet, water and climate, is common among visitors. Spicy Indian food often leads to digestive disorders, in which case it is best to eat plain boiled food until the attack subsides. Most importantly, drink plenty of liquids. Avoid raw salad, cut fruit, cold cuts, fresh juice and yogurt. Instead of tap water opt for bottles of sealed mineral water of well-known brands, such as Evian or Himalayan, if available. Most international brands of carbonated drinks are widely

Bottled mineral water

available, and fresh coconut water is also safe. Street food often looks tempting, but it is safer to avoid it unless it is hot and freshly cooked in front of you.

A good pharmacist can suggest standard diarrhoea medication, though if the attack is severe, it is best to consult a doctor. Also, take a course of oral rehydrating salts (ORS), commercially available under the popular Indian brand names of Electral or Electrobion. An effective home-made remedy is half a teaspoon of salt and three teaspoons of sugar mixed in boiled water.

FOOD AND WATER-BORNE DISEASES

Visitors must guard against dysentery. Bacillary dysentery lasts about a week and is accompanied by severe stomach pains, vomiting and fever, whereas amoebic dysentery has similar symptoms but takes longer to manifest. If left untreated, this can become chronic. The same is true of giardiasis, a type of diarrhoea caused by contaminated water. Vaccination against hepatitis A is advisable before travelling to India. The symptoms of this unpleasant disease include fever, fatigue, severe chills and jaundice. The only treatment is rest and a strictly controlled diet. Other waterborne diseases such as cholera (prevalent in flood-hit areas) and typhoid can also be prevented with vaccines.

Intestinal worms, common in most tropical areas, include tapeworms which are found in under-cooked meats and green leafy vegetables. Others, such as hookworms, can be contracted by walking barefoot on contaminated soil. Ensure that all food is well-cooked and always wear sturdy shoes in remote or waterlogged areas. A course of medication can be taken for worm infestation, which normally does not recur.

Green coconut-water, good for soothing an upset stomach

SEXUALLY TRANSMITTED AND OTHER INFECTIOUS DISEASES

Awareness of sexually transmitted diseases such as HIV, which causes Acquired Immune Deficiency Syndrome (AIDS), is high in India. However, screening at blood banks is still unreliable, and for blood transfusions it is best to contact the **Indian Red Cross Society** *(see p765)*. Hepatitis B is also transmitted through infected blood, sexual contact, unsterilized needles, tattoos and shaves from roadside barbers. However, it can be prevented with a vaccine. Using a condom is essential for protection against all sexually transmitted diseases.

General precautions to follow are: before an inoculation, buy a disposable syringe, or insist that a new syringe and needle is unwrapped in front of you. Never have shaves from roadside barbers and stay away from seedy-looking beauty parlours, as you can pick up infections during manicures and pedicures. Any procedure using needles, such as tattooing and ear-piercing, is best avoided in places where hygiene is dubious.

Vaccination against tetanus is essential when travelling. Tuberculosis (TB), though common in India, is not a great risk for visitors. Meningitis, spread through droplet infection, is a more real threat – it needs immediate medical attention. Symptoms include fever, stiff neck and headache.

RABIES

Animal bites, especially from dogs and monkeys, can cause rabies. Clean the bite with an antiseptic solution and seek medical help at once, as treatment involves a course of injections, even if you have been bitten by a pet dog. There is a vaccination which partially protects against rabies, but this is only advised if you are going to high-risk areas. You should only take this vaccine if your doctor advises it.

INSECT-BORNE DISEASES

Malaria is prevalent in most parts of India during the summer and monsoon (Jul–Sep). The parasite is carried by mosquitoes, and symptoms include shivering followed by high fever and sweating. Seek medical help immediately. You should take a preventive course of anti-malarial drugs before, during and after your trip. For information on malaria medication, call a travel clinic or MASTA *(see p765)*.

Another serious mosquito-borne disease is dengue fever, with symptoms similar to malaria, including severe pain in the joints and muscles, and rashes. Seek medical treatment if you think you might be infected. Japanese B Encephalitis is a dangerous viral infection of the brain, and there have been outbreaks in rural areas. It is also mosquito-borne and its symptoms are similar to malaria, often with a loss of consciousness. Though there is a vaccine for this disease abroad, it is not always found in India.

To guard against mosquito bites, use mosquito repellent gadgets and a net over the bed while sleeping. If outdoors in the evenings, wear shoes and clothes that cover the arms and legs, and rub mosquito repellent cream on exposed skin. As a rule, carry mosquito repellent cream with you at all times.

Mosquito repellent coil and cream

CUTS AND BITES

Insect bites are common, especially in areas prone to heavy rainfall, such as the coasts, the Nilgiri Hills, parts of Kerala and the northeastern states. To avoid insect and ant bites, it is best not to sleep on the ground. Ticks, lice and mites are another problem, since they are carriers of typhus and Lyme's disease. Use insect repellents,

avoid staying in places with poor hygiene and, if bitten, apply antiseptic cream. An antihistamine is the best antidote if you get stung by a wasp or bee. Rainforests are usually infested with blood-sucking leeches that attach themselves to the skin. Never try and pull them off since their heads remain embedded in the skin. A very effective way of getting them to drop off is to sprinkle them with salt, or touch them with a lighted cigarette. Clean the bite and apply an antiseptic.

Snake bites are rare, but if bitten, tie a tight crêpe bandage or tourniquet above the bite to prevent the blood flowing. Keep the limb immobile, note the time of the bite, and seek immediate medical help. Scorpion stings can also be serious, and the victim can sometimes go into shock. The treatment is similar to that of snake bite. If you are stung by a jellyfish whilst swimming, vinegar or lemon juice, calamine lotion and antihistamines help reduce the pain and swelling. Clean the area with an antiseptic lotion.

ALTITUDE SICKNESS

A lack of sufficient oxygen at altitudes higher than 2,500 m (8,202 ft), can cause attacks of Acute Mountain Sickness (AMS). This can lead to severe headaches, dizziness and loss of appetite. These often subside within a day or two, but if the symptoms persist, you should immediately seek medical attention. Though some doctors recommend Acetaolamide (Diamox) and dexamethasone, they are controversial drugs and should not be used.

A few tips to avoid AMS are: ascend slowly; once above 3,000 m (9,842 ft), do not increase camping altitude by more than 300 m (984 ft) a day; drink plenty of fluids; and avoid alcohol and sedatives.

Banking and Local Currency

Logo, State Bank of India

India provides a range of accessible banking facilities and money exchange services, with English speaking staff at the counters. These facilities are available in all the larger cities, at international airports, major banks and hotels, travel agencies and registered moneychangers. Touts might offer enticing exchange rates, but they are illegal operators and should be avoided. Traveller's cheques are the safest way to carry money, but always keep some cash for telephones, tips, transport and purchases, especially when travelling in smaller towns or off the beaten track, where credit cards and traveller's cheques are not always accepted.

BANKS AND BANKING HOURS

Most international banks now have branches in all the larger cities across the country. The Indian bank with the largest distribution network is the **State Bank of India**, though there are other major banks with a national presence. The services they offer include international money transfers.

Banking hours are between 9.30/10am–2pm (Mon–Fri), and 9.30/10am–12 noon (Sat). Try to arrive early to avoid the long queues. Banks are always closed on regional and national holidays (*see p35*) and occasionally they shut down without any notice at all in response to public protests or strikes.

CHANGING MONEY

In India, banks offer the best exchange rates, though most good hotels also change money for resident guests. **LKP Forex Limited** is a reliable foreign exchange broker, and there are numerous other brokers who also change money at the official rates for major international currencies. Rates of exchange are subject to

fluctuation, so check any national daily newspaper for the current rate. The "black-market" in India, operating through literally thousands of touts, offers much better rates than the official ones, but it is safer to go to authorized dealers.

TRAVELLER'S CHEQUES

Traveller's cheques are convenient, safer to carry than large amounts of cash, and give better exchange rates than currency. All major brands of traveller's cheques are accepted in India, with **American Express** and **Thomas Cook** being the most widely used, and US dollars and pounds sterling the most widely exchanged currencies. Banks have the lowest surcharge and give the best value. They charge a small fee per cheque so using large denomination cheques is more economical. Traveller's cheques can be encashed easily in large cities and towns. Smaller towns, though not all of them, also have registered dealers. Keep a record of the serial numbers of cheques, as well as the proof of purchase slips, in case of loss or theft. Also, be

---

DIRECTORY

STATE BANK OF INDIA

Delhi
11 Sansad Marg.
Tel (011) 2336 2741.

Mumbai
State Bank Bhavan,
Madame Cama Rd.
Tel (022) 2202 2426.

Kolkata
Middleton Row.
Tel (033) 2229 5811.

Chennai
Circle Top House,
21 Rajaji Salai.
Tel (044) 2522 0141.

CITIBANK

Delhi
Jeevan Bharti Building, 124
Connaught Circus.
Tel (011) 2371 4211.

Mumbai
Bandra Karla Complex.
Tel (022) 2653 5757.

Kolkata
Kanak Building,
Chowringhee Rd.
Tel (033) 2288 2484.

Chennai
2 Clubhouse Rd.
Tel (044) 2846 1151.

HSBC

Delhi
15 Kasturba Gandhi Marg.
Tel (011) 2373 9696.

Mumbai
SK Ahire Marg,
Worli.
Tel (022) 2491 0001.

Kolkata
25-A Shakespeare Sarani.
Tel (033) 2243 8686.

Chennai
30 Rajaji Salai.
Tel (044) 2526 9696.

BUREAUX DE CHANGES

American Express
A Block, Wenger House,
Connaught Place,
Delhi.
Tel (011) 2332 5221.
Oriental Building,
364 Dr Dadabhai Naoroji
Rd, Mumbai.
Tel (022) 2204 3361.
21 Old Court House St,
Kolkata.
Tel (033) 2210 5151.
187 Anna Salai,
Chennai.
Tel (044) 2851 5800.

Thomas Cook
C–33 Connaught Place,
New Delhi.
Tel (011) 2341 6585.
Dr Dadabhai Naoroji Rd,
Fort, Mumbai.
Tel (022) 2204 8556.

19B Shakespeare
Sarani, First Floor,
Kolkata.
Tel (033) 2282 4711.
Ceebros Centre,
45 Monthieth Rd,
Egmore, Chennai.
Tel (044) 2855 4600.

LKP Forex Limited

1101 Hemkunt Tower,
98 Nehru Place,
New Delhi.
Tel (011) 2629 2410.
22/B Cusrow Baug, Colaba
Causeway, Mumbai.
Tel (022) 2288 5586.
Shop 41–A, Park
Mansions, 57A Park St,
Kolkata.
Tel (033) 2216 0055.
G15C & 20 Spencer Plaza,
769 Anna Salai,
Chennai.
Tel (044) 2849 5001.

sure to keep records of encashment, as you will need these should you wish to reconvert rupees to other currencies when leaving the country.

CREDIT CARDS

Credit cards are now widely accepted in most big hotels, restaurants and department stores. The most common are VISA, Master-Card, Diner's Club and American Express. Air and rail tickets can also be paid for by credit card, and cash advances can be made at the parent bank. For example, Citibank account holders can directly access their account with their Citibank Card. However, many smaller establishments, even in the bigger cities, only accept cash.

Credit card-related fraud is on the increase, so keep your cards safe, and insist that receipt vouchers are made out in front of you.

ATM SERVICES

Most foreign, and many Indian, banks in large cities have 24-hour ATMs (automatic teller machines). Instructions are displayed in English, and cash is dispensed in rupees. Check with your bank at home which Indian banks will accept your ATM card, as not all machines are compatible. Some ATMs will dispense cash against credit cards. Cards with a PLUS or CIRRUS symbol are accepted at the following ATMs: Citibank, Standard Chartered, and Hong Kong and Shanghai Bank.

CURRENCY

The Indian rupee (Rs) is divided into 100 paisas. The most commonly used coins are 50 paisa, 1, 2, and 5 rupee coins. Currency notes are available in denominations of Rs5, 10, 20, 50, 100, 500 and 1,000. Be careful not to mix up the 100 and 500 rupee notes as they look very similar. Beware of accepting torn or damaged notes, as shops and even banks are often reluctant to accept or exchange them. Banks often give notes stapled together in large packs. Ask them to remove the staples for you as you will find it difficult to do it yourself without tearing the notes.

Foreign nationals are not permitted to bring or take Indian currency into or out of the country.

Bank Notes
All currency is minted by the Reserve Bank of India. The notes have either Mahatma Gandhi or the Ashoka lion symbol on one side.

10-rupee note

20-rupee note

50-rupee note

100-rupee note

500-rupee note

1000-rupee note

Coins
Visitors should always keep some loose change handy. Some older variations of these silver coins are still in circulation.

50 paisa

1 rupee

Rs2

Rs5

Communications

Public telephone booth sign

The Indian postal system is fairly efficient, with a wide variety of options from registered post to reliable courier services, offered by post offices countrywide. Telecommunications systems are sophisticated even in smaller towns: all main hotels have business centres and most markets have shops or booths from where international calls can be made, e-mails sent and the internet accessed. A range of English-language newspapers and magazines are available, and foreign newspapers and magazines are sold in bookshops, particularly in the main cities.

Postage stamps in 5-rupee denomination

INTERNATIONAL AND LOCAL TELEPHONE CALLS

All major hotels offer subscriber trunk dialling (STD) for calls within India, and international subscriber dialling (ISD) for international calls. Trunk calls can also be booked from private telephones. Calls made from STD/ ISD booths, identified by their yellow signage, are much cheaper than at hotels. Rates are fixed for international calls, but STD rates depend on the distance of the city called and the time of day when the call is made. Calls are cheapest between 11pm and 6am. Medium rate is between 8pm and 11pm. Local calls made from public booths take new 1 rupee coins for every three minutes.

The government-run Mahanagar Telephone Nigam Limited (MTNL) sells phone cards for both STD and ISD calls. For calling within India, you can buy cards for Rs200, Rs500 or Rs1,000. There is a 5 per cent service charge. For more information call 1600 11 1111 or contact the main telephone exchange offices. The service is currently available in Delhi and Mumbai.

MOBILE PHONE RENTALS

Mobile phones can easily be rented from service counters at the international airports, as well as at registered offices located in most large cities. In Delhi, Airtel and Essar are the main service

networks, while in Mumbai, the networks are provided by BPL and Orange. Kolkata has Usha and Modi Telstra, and Chennai has RPG Cellular and Skycell. Hire charges range between Rs100 and Rs300 per day inclusive of a SIM card (rates are higher for roaming cards) and a handset. If hiring a handset, you will pay a fairly sizeable deposit, which is refundable.

FAX, E-MAIL AND INTERNET FACILITIES

Fax and telegraph services are available at main post offices and also at local STD/ISD booths which, though often more accessible, have higher charges. The business centres of all large hotels also have centralized telecommunication services, which only residents can use.

The internet is widely used in India. Most large hotels offer net access to guests in their business centres, while privately operated internet cafés with the latest facilities can be found in markets and shopping areas in most large cities. Even smaller towns

Internet café, Bangalore

usually have enterprising hole-in-the-wall internet outlets. Some main post offices and many STD/ISD phone booths also offer internet facilities. All outlets have fixed hourly or half-hourly rates.

POSTAL SERVICES

There are many different services offered by the Indian Postal Service – general or registered mail, parcel post, poste restante, and a special courier service known as EMS-Speed Post.

Letterboxes are colour coded: local letters, green; metropolitan and other cities, as well as international mail, red; and Quick Mail Service (QMS) yellow. Post offices are open Monday to Friday between 10am and 5pm, and on Saturdays until noon. Some services, such as registered mail, close earlier.

Letters sent poste restante are held at the **General Post Office** for up to one month, and you will need some form of identification – preferably your passport – to retrieve your mail. The same service is also provided by **Foreign Post Offices** in the four main cities, as well as American Express in most major cities. Envelopes should be addressed with the surname underlined and in capitals, c/o Poste Restante, followed by the name and address of the post office.

Parcels sent overseas cannot exceed 20 kg (44 pounds). Check the details at the post office. Book Post is a cheaper option for documents, books and printed material. The maximum weight is 5 kg (11 pounds). Some hotels sell stamps and may offer to post letters and parcels. Always be sure to stick stamps and post postcards and letters yourself.

ADDRESSES

In India, addresses always begin with the house number, followed by the name of the street, and finally the city and its pin code. The newer residential localities are divided into blocks, and the block number usually appears with the house number. Therefore, B4/88 Safdarjung Enclave would be: house number 88 in the B4 block of Safdarjung Enclave Colony. Each state and city has its own variations, which can be confusing and hard to decipher, especially if trying to locate a house number. Often there may not even be a road sign. If you are lost, a passer-by will always help, but the best bet is to get directions from a taxi or rickshaw driver.

COURIER SERVICES

Courier services are available across the country, but less so in rural and remote areas. While it is better to ship larger items such as furniture by regular land, sea or air cargo, letters, documents or smaller parcels

are best sent through a courier agency, even though it may be more expensive. **United Parcel Service (UPS), Federal Express** and **DHL Worldwide Express** are international courier agencies, with a widespread network all over India and the world. Many shops offer to send purchases by courier, but except for the government emporia and well-known establishments, you will be doing so at your own risk.

NEWSPAPERS AND MAGAZINES

India's leading national English language newspapers include *The Times of India, Hindustan Times, The Indian Express, The Hindu* and *The Asian Age.* In the east, *The Statesman* and *The Telegraph* are widely read. There are other regional newspapers as well that provide local news. Many international newspapers, such as the *International Herald Tribune* and the *Financial Times,* are available alongside Indian weekly news magazines, such as *India Today* and *Outlook. Time* and *Newsweek* are available in large cities. For local news and cultural events, the city sections of the newspapers give reasonable coverage.

A typical post box

TELEVISION AND RADIO

The state-run Doordarshan television network has programmes in English and the major regional languages.

DIRECTORY

Foreign Post Office
Kotla Marg, Near ITO, Delhi.
Tel (011) 2323 1281.
Ballard Estate, Mumbai.
Tel (022) 2261 4488.
Church Lane, Kolkata.
Tel (033) 2248 1523.
Anna Salai, Chennai.
Tel (044) 2852 1947.

General Post Offices
Ashok Rd, Delhi.
Tel (011) 2336 4111.
Nagar Chowk, Mumbai.
Tel (022) 2262 0693.
1 Koilaghat St, Kolkata.
Tel (033) 2210 5451.
25 Rajaji Salai, Chennai.
Tel (044) 2521 6766.

UPS Courier Service
Tel (011) 2678 4343, Delhi.
Tel (022) 2685 0202, Mumbai.
Tel (033) 2227 0835, Kolkata.
Tel (044) 2431 4741, Chennai.

Federal Express
Tel (011) 5167 2272, Delhi.
Tel (022) 5679 7777, Mumbai.
Tel (044) 2825 9495, Chennai.

DHL Worldwide Express
Tel (011) 2375 2700, Delhi.
Tel (022) 5678 9001, Mumbai.
Tel (033) 2282 6914, Kolkata.
Tel (044) 2855 3047, Chennai.

With the arrival of satellite TV, the choice has become much wider. Cable TV is now also available everywhere, for international channels, such as the BBC World Service, CNN, Discovery, National Geographic and the Hong Kong-based Star network. Star Sports and ESPN are exclusive sports channels and Channel V and MTV are the main music channels. Most Indian TV channels show popular Hindi films or song and dance sequences; there are many regional Indian language channels as well.

India also has a wide radio network, with programmes in English and local languages. It is still the best form of communication, especially in the rural areas. Radio and television listings and reviews can be found in all major daily newspapers.

USEFUL DIALLING CODES AND NUMBERS

- To make an inter-city call, dial the STD code of that city and the local number. For Delhi, dial 011; Mumbai, 022; Kolkata, 033; Chennai, 044.
- To make an international call (ISD), dial 00, the country code, area code and the local number.
- Country codes: UK 44; France 33; USA & Canada 1; Australia 61; Ireland 353; New Zealand 64; South Africa 27; Japan 81.
- Dial 180 to book a trunk call in the country, and 186 to book an international call.
- Dial 197 to obtain a phone number in Delhi, Mumbai, Kolkata and Chennai.

TRAVEL INFORMATION

The Maharaja, mascot of Air India

Most international visitors to India arrive by air, though road and ferry links also connect India and her neighbours, such as Pakistan, Bangladesh, Nepal and Sri Lanka. Travelling within the country is possible by air, train, road and, in some places, either ferry or boat. Even remote regions are accessible. However, whatever your mode of transport, you should be prepared for delays and unexpected detours that may test your patience. The state-run Indian Airlines has the widest network of air routes. Private airlines, such as Kingfisher and Jet Airways, also cover a number of cities and offer excellent services. Indian Railways is one of the world's largest networks, and travelling first class is a good way to see the country. The long-distance air-conditioned luxury coach is another option.

ARRIVING BY AIR

All major international airlines fly to India, usually as stop-overs on air routes between the East and West. Air India is India's international carrier. North American and European airlines such as British Airways, Lufthansa, KLM/Northwest, Air France, and Swiss have regular flights to either some or all of India's four major cities – Delhi, Mumbai, Chennai and Kolkata. There are also numerous connections to the Far East and Australia, offered by Thai Airways, Singapore Airlines, Malaysian Airlines, Japan Airlines, and Cathay Pacific. Flights to destinations in the Gulf and Central Asia are offered by Emirates, Air Lanka and Gulf Air.

Austrian Airlines and Virgin Atlantic currently fly to Delhi and Mumbai, though they plan to introduce flights to other Indian cities in the near future. Delta, South African Airways and Kenya Airlines fly only to Mumbai. Lufthansa flies to Bangalore, while Emirates flies to Hyderabad; and Malaysian Airlines flies to both these cities. In addition, Air Lanka also flies to Thiruvanathapuram and Tiruchirapalli.

INTERNATIONAL FLIGHTS AND AIRPORTS

India's four main international airports are at Delhi, Mumbai, Kolkata and Chennai. Other international airports offering flights to select destinations are at Hyderabad (Kuwait, Muscat, Sharjah and Kuala Lumpur), Bangalore (Muscat, Sharjah, Singapore, Kuala Lumpur, London, Frankfurt and a few flights via Mumbai to Paris, the Gulf and New York), Goa (UK and Germany), Ahmedabad (UK and the US), Kochi and Thiru-vananthapuram (the Gulf, Singapore, Sri Lanka and the Maldives). A limited number of international flights also operate from Kozhikode, Amritsar, Varanasi, Lucknow, Guwahati, Tiruchirapalli, Jaipur and Agra. These are designated "customs airports" and permit landing of charter planes as well as certain international flights.

AIR FARES

Air fares vary according to the airline and the season. It is best to book tickets well in advance of the peak season (October–March). At this time of year flights to India are overbooked, as apart from tourists, Indian families settled abroad and students at universities abroad, make their annual visit home.

ON ARRIVAL

Before landing, visitors must fill in a disembarkation form that has to be submitted along with their passport at the immigration counter.

International airports offer a range of facilities that include currency exchange counters, left-luggage services, air-conditioned visitors' lounges, duty-free shops, restaurants, business centres and rest rooms with access for the disabled. In addition, there are counters for pre-paid taxis, car rentals and mobile phone rentals. Travel agencies located within the arrival area can help with tour itineraries, hotel reservations and onward bookings. There is also a Tourism Department information counter.

CUSTOMS

The green channel is for those who do not have dutiable goods as listed in the Immigration Certificate. The

Indira Gandhi International Airport, Delhi

Red Channel is for passengers with any goods that are liable to customs duty, including money in excess of US$2,500.

GETTING FROM THE AIRPORT

Coaches connect the airport with the city for a fee. Pre-paid taxis with fixed rates can be booked from counters outside the arrivals area. Metered auto-rickshaws are also available. Make sure you agree on the fare before taking one, and ask an airport policeman to note down its licence plate number. If you have booked accommodation, check if your hotel offers a free pick-up service.

AIRPORT TRANSFERS

Visitors who are travelling onwards to other Indian cities will need to transfer to domestic terminals. Be sure to allow enough time to get between the two terminals. At all major aiports there is a free transit service from one terminal to the other. Delhi's Indira Gandhi (IG) International Airport has two terminals: Terminal I (for domestic flights) is 7 km (4 miles) from Terminal II (the international terminal). In Mumbai, the international terminal at Sahar is 4 km (2.5 miles) from the

DL·1Y 5732
ALL INDIA TOURIST PERMIT

Yellow licence plate of a taxi

domestic terminal. Kolkata's Netaji Subhash Chandra Bose International Airport, has both the international and domestic terminals in the same building. Chennai's Aringar Anna International Airport is next door to the Kamaraj Domestic Airport. In Thiruvananthapuram, both domestic and international flights operate from the same building.

CHECK-IN

For international flights, check-in is usually three hours ahead of departure. Tele-check-in is allowed by some airlines for business and first class passengers. Most airlines allow an economy-class passenger 20 kg (44 pounds) in the hold and one item of hand baggage. Make sure that your luggage is within the weight limit set by your airline, as excess baggage charges can be very high.

DEPARTURE TAX

A foreign travel tax of Rs500–750 (US$10–15) has to be paid when leaving India, unless already included in your ticket. Only Rs150 (US$3) needs to be paid if travelling to neighbouring countries, such as Nepal, Pakistan or Sri Lanka.

DIRECTORY

AIRLINE OFFICES

Air India
Tel (011) 2331 8737, Delhi.
Tel (022) 2202 4142, Mumbai.
Tel (033) 2282 1187, Kolkata.
Tel (044) 2855 4477, Chennai.

British Airways
Tel (011) 2565 2078, Delhi.
Tel (022) 2682 8806, Mumbai.
Tel (033) 2511 8424, Kolkata.
Tel (044) 2256 0952, Chennai.

Cathay Pacific
Tel (011) 2332 1286, Delhi.
Tel (022) 6657 2222, Mumbai.
Tel (044) 4214 0941, Chennai.

KLM/Northwest Airline
Tel (011) 2565 2715, Delhi.
Tel (022) 2682 8607, Mumbai.
Tel (033) 2283 0151, Kolkata.
Tel (044) 2852 4427, Chennai.

Lufthansa
Tel (011) 2565 4000, Delhi.
Tel (022) 2682 9898, Mumbai.
Tel (044) 2256 9393, Chennai.
Tel (080) 2522 9617, Bangalore.

Virgin Atlantic
Tel (011) 4130 3030, Delhi.

Austrian Airlines
Tel (011) 2335 0125, Delhi.

Thai Airways
Tel (011) 4149 7777, Delhi.
Tel (033) 2283 8865, Kolkata.

AIRPORT	INFORMATION	DISTANCE TO CITY CENTRE	AVERAGE JOURNEY TIME
Delhi: IG International (Terminal II)	(011) 2567 5126	20 km (12 miles)	Road: 45–60 minutes
Mumbai: Sahar International	(022) 2615 6600	30 km (19 miles)	Road: 50 minutes
Kolkata: Netaji Subhash Chandra Bose International	(033) 2511 8787	20 km (12 miles)	Road: 30–60 minutes
Chennai: Aringar Anna International	(044) 2256 0551	12 km (8 miles)	Road: 30 minutes
Thiruvananthapuram: International Airport	(0471) 501 312	6 km (4 miles)	Road: 20 minutes
Bangalore: International Airport	(080) 2522 8011	8 km (3 miles)	Road: 20 minutes
Goa: Dabolim International Airport	(0832) 540 806	29 km (18 miles)	Road: 50 minutes
Kochi: Kochi International Airport	(0484) 261 0115	30 km (19 miles)	Road: 45–60 minutes

Domestic Air Travel

Logo of Indian Airlines

Although more expensive than travelling by train, air travel in India is the most comfortable and convenient mode of travel, especially considering the huge distances between the major cities. There are as many as 115 domestic airports in India, many of which have been greatly improved in recent years in terms of technology as well as customer services. The main cities of Chennai, Delhi, Kolkata and Mumbai are very well connected to all domestic airports within the country. The national carrier is the government-run Indian Airlines which, along with its subsidiary Alliance Air, offers the widest choice of routes and the most frequent services. If you have booked internal flights before leaving for India, it is highly recommended to reconfirm on arrival. Erratic flight timetables, flight cancellations and delays due to bad weather conditions in winter (Dec–Jan) are common, so remember to reconfirm not just your ticket but the flight timing as well.

DOMESTIC AIRLINES

The national carrier **Indian Airlines** offers the largest number of routes and the most frequent connections across the country. Two major private airlines, **Jet Airways** and **Kingfisher Airlines**, also connect a number of cities. India's international carrier **Air India**, has domestic flights on the Delhi–Mumbai, Delhi–Kolkata, Mumbai–Kolkata and Mumbai–Chennai routes. A few regional airlines such as Archana Airways, Jagson Airlines and Gujarat Airways with limited operations within India, fly short feeder routes. Baggage allowance is 30 kg (66 pounds) for business class and 20 kg (44 pounds) for economy class.

PRINCIPAL DOMESTIC AIR ROUTES

DOMESTIC AIRPORTS

Airports at the four main cities of Delhi, Mumbai, Kolkata and Chennai, and cities such as Agra, Bhubaneswar, Hyderabad, Kochi and Bangalore have modern terminal buildings with up-to-date facilities. However, less-visited towns, such as Dehra Dun, have tiny airports with almost no facilities.

GETTING TO AND FROM THE AIRPORT

The distance from airports to city centres varies, so it is useful to check the travel time beforehand. Also always allow time for unforeseen delays en route. Airport coaches run regularly for a fee. Pre-paid taxis with fixed rates can usually be booked from counters outside the arrivals area. Metered auto-rickshaws are also available. Make sure the meter is working, or agree on a fixed amount before taking one. If you are booking accommodation, check if your hotel offers a free pick-up service.

Indian Airlines air tickets

CHECK-IN

For most domestic flights, the check-in time is normally one hour before departure. If travelling to politically sensitive places such as Kashmir, Jammu, Leh and some of the northeastern states, security checks are more stringent and can require up to an extra half

hour. Make sure all bags are tagged, and do not carry batteries, lighters or any sharp objects, not even scissors, nail files or tweezers. As part of the security measures on some routes, you may be asked to identify your baggage on the tarmac, before boarding the flight.

RESERVATIONS

All domestic airlines have their own booking offices in the city, as well as a reservation counter at the airport (usually only in larger towns and cities). Tickets can also be booked through travel agents (see p759). Indian Airlines has computerized booking and flight information facilities all over the country, even in smaller towns. Tickets can be paid for in US dollars or sterling, as well as in rupees. Payment can also be made by credit card. All airlines require you to reconfirm your ticket 72 hours before flight departure. There are special fares for infants and children, and students carrying an international student ID card get a 25 per cent discount, Indian nationals aged 65 and above get a 50 per cent discount. All ticket cancellations must be done at least two hours before your flight. Some airlines will waive a cancellation charge if given sufficient notice. If you fail to do so, you may lose the full value of the ticket. If flights are cancelled or delayed you can claim a refund.

(see p759)

DIRECTORY

DOMESTIC AIRLINES

Indian Airlines
Tel (011) 2463 1337, *Delhi.*
Tel (022) 2202 3031, *Mumbai.*
Tel (033) 2211 6869, *Kolkata.*
Tel (044) 2345 3302, *Chennai.*

Air India
Tel (011) 2331 9068, *Delhi.*
Tel (022) 2279 6666, *Mumbai.*
Tel (033) 2282 6014, *Kolkata.*
Tel (044) 2855 4477, *Chennai.*

Jet Airways
Tel (011) 3989 3333, *Delhi.*
Tel (022) 3989 3333, *Mumbai.*
Tel (033) 3989 3333, *Kolkata.*
Tel (044) 3989 3333, *Chennai.*

Kingfisher Airlines
Tel (011) 2373 0238, *Delhi.*
Tel (022) 3021 2656, *Mumbai.*
Tel (033) 2248 6551, *Kolkata.*
Tel (044) 2858 4360, *Chennai.*

Airport Enquiries
Tel (011) 2567 5433, *Delhi.*
Tel (022) 2615 6400, *Mumbai.*
Tel (033) 2511 9721, *Kolkata.*
Tel (044) 2330 289, *Chennai.*

TRAVEL PACKAGES

Indian Airlines offers two travel packages if the payment is in US dollars. The "Discover India Fare" for 15 or 21 days is about US$500– 750, and allows unlimited travel with certain route restrictions. The "India Wonder Fare" for about US$300 is for seven days of travel in one region. This package does not include the Andaman Islands. Private airlines, such as Jet Airways and Kingfisher Airlines, also offer special packages for foreign nationals. The "Visit India" offer by Jet Airways ranges from US$550–800 for economy class travel over a period of 15–20 days. Airlines have started offering discounts on tickets, and value add-ons such as free stays and gourmet dining to beat the competition. It is therefore worth doing a little research before purchasing your ticket.

Passengers waiting in the airport lounge at Delhi

Travelling by Train

Indian Railways logo

For most visitors, train journeys add a fascinating new dimension to their experience of India – there are few better ways of getting to know the people and see the countryside. The Indian Railways network is the fourth largest in the world, with tracks running over 108,513 km (67,427 miles) and connecting 7,150 stations. Over 10,000 trains run daily, transporting an average of 13 million people. Trains are always crowded, so try to book your tickets in advance. There are computerized ticket counters at railway stations, and most travel agents can also get tickets for you.

THE RAILWAY NETWORK

The Indian rail network, established in 1853, runs the length and breadth of the country. The network is divided by region, and there are 16 zonal divisions. Delhi is served by Northern Railways, Mumbai by both Central and Western Railways, Kolkata by Eastern Railways and Chennai by Southern Railways. All four cities have either two or three main train stations, so it is important to confirm from which station your train is leaving. Indian Railways employ over 1.6 million people, making them the world's largest single employer.

TRAINS AND TIMETABLES

Of the three kinds of trains (passenger, express and mail), it is best to take the air-conditioned express trains, as they have fewer stops and offer better facilities and services. They provide fast and punctual connections to some of India's most important cities. The Rajdhani Express links the capital,

Delhi, to most of the large cities such as Mumbai, Kolkata, Chennai, Thiruvananthapuram and others. The superfast inter-city train, the Shatabdi Express, connects main cities with many well-known tourist destinations, with connections such as Chennai–Bangalore, Delhi–Dehra Dun and Delhi–Agra. The recently opened Konkan Railway *(see p437),* on the western coast, offers speedy connections to Maharashtra, Goa, Karnataka and Kerala.

Each train is known by its name and number. When consulting the information board, do check both, since there may be more than one "Shatabdi" for example. Trains have first and second class chair-cars, and two- and three-tiered sleeper coaches. If these are air conditioned, the fares increase. Sleeper coaches have berths that fold back during the daytime to provide seating. Fares for express trains such as the Shatabdi or Rajdhani include meals and mineral water, and the Rajdhani also provides its overnight passengers with

bedding. Food items, such as biscuits, and reading material are sold by vendors en route. Try to get a window seat or the uppermost sleeper. Toilets are of the Indian and Western style. Carry your own toilet paper, soap and towel.

Train timings are subject to change. The printed timetable is available in most station bookshops, or check the very useful official website: www.indianrail.gov.in

TRAIN TICKETS, FARES AND RESERVATIONS

It is important to make train bookings well in advance for a confirmed reservation. Railway stations now have computerized ticket counters, otherwise the hotel travel counter or a travel agent can arrange them for a fee. Never buy tickets from touts, as this is both illegal and unreliable.

Tickets can be booked up to six months in advance, and reservation fees are nominal. You will be asked for your age and gender and these details will appear on your ticket, along with the coach and seat number. Once at the station, find your coach and check for your name and seat number, which are usually posted on a list outside the coach. If wait listed, arrive at the station early to take advantage of any last-minute cancellations. The station-master will help.

If reserved tickets are unavailable, you can get an RAC (Reservation Against Cancellation) ticket. This allows you to board the train and get seating space. You may eventually be given a berth, but there is no guarantee. Reserved tickets can be cancelled, for a fee. If cancellation is more than a day in advance, a nominal fee is charged. Up to four hours before train departure, the charge is 25 per cent of the fare, and less than that, you forfeit 50 per cent of the fare.

Stations at Delhi, Mumbai, Kolkata and Chennai as well as other major cities have special booking counters for foreigners, called "Tourist Bureaus", within the main

Churchgate Station, Mumbai, during rush hour

booking offices. These provide information regarding reservations, itinerary and other inquiries. Payments may be made in US dollars or pounds sterling, or the rupee equivalent, and you must show your passport. You get priority reservation and are exempted from reservation fees. At New Delhi Railway Station, the International Tourist Bureau is located on the first floor of the main hall.

INDRAIL PASS

To travel extensively around India, the Indrail Pass is a convenient option. It offers unlimited travel across the country, and is available for second or first class and for different periods (half-day, 2 days, 4 days and anywhere between 7 and 90 days). It can be bought in India or abroad, but must be paid for in foreign currency. Indrail Passes are available from sales agents abroad, as well as overseas offices of Indian Airlines and Air India. They are also available at tourist counters and Tourist Bureaus at major railway stations, and from travel agents in Delhi, Mumbai, Kolkata and Chennai. Unless you do a lot of travelling, the pass may

work out more expensive than buying individual tickets. Even with a pass you will still need to reserve your seat.

SERVICES

At the station, look for the licensed porters or coolies who wear a red shirt and an armband with a metal tag bearing a licence number on it. Porters are always well-informed about delays and platform changes which may not be announced on the board. Note your porter's number because you could lose sight of him in the crowds. His tariff varies according to weight, although Rs10–20 per item is acceptable. Indian stations are crowded and confusing. Keep your cool and keep an eye out for pickpockets who take advantage of the chaos. Railway waiting rooms (especially first class ones) are good places to spend the night if you are stranded. You need a valid ticket or Indrail Pass to use this facility. There are also waiting rooms only for women travellers. Left luggage facilities, called cloakrooms, are offered at most stations.

Station canteens are reasonably clean and provide mineral water and hygenically-packed meals.

Official porter in red jacket

DIRECTORY

RAILWAY ENQUIRIES

www.indianrail.gov.in

Delhi
Tel (011) 131.

Mumbai
Tel (022) 131, Western Railways.
Tel (022) 134, Central Railways.

Kolkata
Tel (033) 2220 3545.

Chennai
Tel (044) 131, 132, 133.

BOOKING CENTRES FOR SPECIAL TRAINS

Darjeeling Himalayan Railway
West Bengal Tourist Centre,
Baba Kharak Singh Marg, Delhi.
Tel (011) 2374 2840.

Matheran Hill Railway
Govt of India Tourist Office,
123 M Karve Rd, Mumbai.
Tel (022) 2203 3144.

Palace On Wheels
Bikaner House, Delhi.
Tel (011) 2338 1884.

The Shivalik Queen
Divisional Railway, Ambala.
Tel (0171) 645 500.

Blue Mountain Railway
Chennai Central Railway, Chennai.
Tel (044) 2535 3816.

Royal Orient
Tourism Corp of Gujarat Ltd, Baba
Kharak Singh Marg, Delhi.
Tel (011) 2373 4015.

Fairy Queen
Rail Museum, Delhi.
Tel (011) 2688 1816.

SPECIAL TRAINS

You can travel in style on board some of India's luxury trains, particularly the **Palace on Wheels** and the **Royal Orient**. Both operate week-long tours from September to April. The former covers mainly Rajasthan, and includes Jaipur, Udaipur, Jaisalmer and Agra. The latter goes through Rajasthan to Ahmedabad in Gujarat. The **Fairy Queen**, a 150-year old restored steam engine, is the oldest in the world, featuring in the *Guinness Book of Records*. It runs from Delhi to Alwar between October and February. India's quaint "toy trains", connecting numerous hill stations with tracks laid across precariously steep slopes, include the World Heritage **Darjeeling Himalayan Railway** *(see p294)* which goes from New Jalpaiguri to Darjeeling. **The Shivalik Queen** runs between Kalka and Shimla *(see p110–11)*, while the Kangra Valley Railway connects Pathankot and Jogindernagar *(see p120)*. Another toy train, the **Matheran Hill Railway**, runs from Neral Junction to Matheran *(see p472)*, while the luxurious **Blue Mountain Railway**, built in 1898, offers spectacular views of the Nilgiri Hills, up to Ooty *(see p605)*.

Royal service in the Palace on Wheels

Travel by Road

Logo of the Auto-
mobile Association

India has an extensive network of major and minor roads, as well as a number of well-maintained national highways, linking all the major cities. Driving is on the left, with right-hand drive cars. Indian traffic, particularly in the cities, is very chaotic, so visitors are strongly advised to hire a driver along with a car, rather than trying to negotiate the roads themselves. A number of international car rental companies, hotels and taxi stands provide excellent car rental services. In case of breakdowns, the remarkably ingenious roadside mechanics can solve most problems.

DRIVING LICENCES

It is necessary to have an international driving licence to drive in India. If not, the **Automobile Association of India (AAI)** has several branches across the country that will issue a temporary license, provided you have a passport and an ordinary driving licence. This may take a day or two. You must be over 25 years old and there is a refundable insurance deposit of Rs10,000. You may be asked to take a driving test.

ROADS

India has a network of over 3,000,000 km (1,860,000 miles) of roads. The primary arterial roads, the national highways, cover 52,000 km (32,240 miles) and carry 45 per cent of the country's total traffic. State highways run a total length of 128,600 km (79,732 miles). The National Highway Authority of India is in the process of improving links between the country's four major cities: Delhi, Mumbai, Chennai and Kolkata.

The countryside is criss-crossed with numerous major and minor roads of very variable quality. Some village roads are little more than dirt tracks riddled with potholes, so be prepared for a dusty, bumpy ride.

Most highways and major roads are well-equipped with tourist facilities such as motels, petrol pumps and STD/ISD telephone booths. Midway refreshment points and *dhabas (see p179)* are well-marked with hoardings, and provide clean food as well as toilets.

CAR RENTALS

Several reputed car rental companies, such as **Avis, Budget, International Travel House Limited** and **Autoriders International Limited** now operate in India. They offer both chauffeur-driven and self-driven cars, which can be hired at travel desks in larger hotels, tourist offices, travel agencies or directly from the companies themselves. Most of them operate through collaborations with local companies. Avis is in partnership with the Oberoi Group while Budget operates through Sapna Travel Agency. Autoriders International Limited, a reliable Indian company, was earlier a partner of Hertz. Local hire services and private taxis are also available in cities from taxi stands and agencies. These can usually be arranged by your hotel or through a reliable local travel agent *(see p759)*.

HIRING A CHAUFFEUR-DRIVEN CAR

Indian road and traffic conditions can be a trial for anyone unused to these conditions. Hiring a driver is much the safest option, and not all that expensive. All taxis as well as agency-hired cars are distinguished by their yellow number plates with black lettering. Most taxi stands also have private cars for hire, which are usually white with yellow number plates. All car rental companies with "All India Tourist Permits" have licenses for interstate travel.

All drivers are familiar with Indian traffic rules, but insist on getting a driver who knows the area that you plan to visit. Also, do test both the driver and the car before embarking on a long journey.

Chauffeur-driven cars for long-distance travel usually charge per kilometre, with a minimum of 250 km (155 miles) per day plus additional charges per extra kilometre. If you are travelling only one way, additional charges will be levied for the return journey on the assumption that the car will return empty. Costs are also dependent on the car model and the region of hire, with air-conditioned cars being the most expensive. For travelling outside the state or city boundaries, extra charges as well as interstate

Traffic on Marine Drive in Mumbai

taxes are added. If the driver has to stay overnight, you will have to pay for his board and lodging, so it is best to negotiate a flat rate in advance. Car hire is more expensive in hill regions.

In certain areas, shared taxis are available for long journeys, which are cheaper. Certain companies require foreign nationals to pay in foreign currency, though most accept payment in rupees as well.

FUEL

Highways and main roads have well-maintained filling stations (or petrol pumps as they are called) at regular intervals, usually closer to towns. Many pumps in cities as well as on highways are open 24 hours, and carry both leaded and unleaded petrol, as well as diesel, which is cheaper. Most cars run on petrol, though some of the newer models also use diesel, as do most taxis. Unleaded petrol is not available everywhere, especially in remote areas, so ensure that your fuel tank is full when visiting these areas. Many petrol pumps in the main cities are now equipped with utility stores where mineral water, soft drinks, magazines and snacks are sold. Often they also have telephone booths and toilets.

Since 2001, most taxis, autorickshaws and buses in Delhi and Mumbai are being run on CNG (Compressed Natural Gas), in an effort to tackle the severe air pollution caused by vehicular emissions.

MAPS AND ROAD SIGNS

The Automobile Association of India, the Survey of India and the State Tourism offices provide good maps, brochures and information on all cities and regions in India. However, the placement of road signs is often erratic, and at times they are in the regional language rather than English. It is fine to stop and ask for directions, repeatedly if necessary – people are always happy to help.

A typical Indian Oil pump at a filling station in Delhi

RULES OF THE ROAD

If you plan to drive in India, you need to ensure that you are well accustomed to the chaotic traffic conditions. Though there are established traffic rules, such as lane driving and discreet use of high-beam lights, more often than not these are not followed. Vehicles drive on the left-hand side of the road, but often, you will find a stray car – or cow, for that matter – coming at you on the wrong side of the road.

On the highways, beware of trucks, who often use muscle power to force you off the road while overtaking. As a rule, stay clear of buses and trucks.

Few drivers adhere to the rules for overtaking, which is meant to be from the right. Many vehicles often overtake from the left, with no prior warning. Avoid night driving on highways unless absolutely necessary, as a lot of heavy traffic (especially trucks) use them then. Also, never offer lifts to strangers, as this could prove to be very dangerous. It is wise to make liberal use of your horn. If you are unlucky enough to be caught speeding, or jumping a red light, a fine is payable on the spot.

In cities, ensure that your car is parked only in an authorized parking area, otherwise it may be towed away to the nearest police station, and released only on the payment of a heavy fine. Parking attendants should hand you a parking slip, with the parking charges printed on it. Charges are usually between Rs5 and Rs10.

Travelling by Bus, Coach and Ferry

Logo of the India Tourism Development Corporation (ITDC)

India has an extensive bus and coach network, offering excellent connections to most cities as well as to the remotest parts of the country. Buses refer to the ordinary transport corporation-run vehicles, which are cheaper and ply interstate or within cities. Coaches are usually much more comforatble, with air conditioning. These are often hired out for guided tours and also ply between cities. The advantage of travelling by bus or coach rather than by train is that you have a wider choice of timings, stops and itineraries. A busy network of passenger ferries serve places along India's east and west coasts, and luxury cruises link the mainland to the Lakshadweep Islands as well as to the Andamans.

STATE TRANSPORT CORPORATION-RUN BUSES

The various state transport departments in India run extensive interstate bus services. The Interstate Bus Terminus (ISBT) in Delhi is the main point of departure for Punjab, Haryana, Himachal Pradesh, Uttar Pradesh and Rajasthan. Buses for Agra leave from Sarai Kale Khan, near Nizamuddin railway station. Mumbai's Central Bus Stand provides information on the Maharashtra Road Transport Corporation that runs services to all major cities within the state, as well as to Goa, Ahmedabad, Vadodara, Mangalore, Indore and Hyderabad. Kolkata too has an extensive network throughout West Bengal and the neighbouring states of Bihar, Orissa and Sikkim. Guwahati is the main entrance point for visitors to the northeastern states. The Assam State Transport Corporation runs buses within the city and to the neighbouring states. The Paltan Bazaar Bus Stand provides the best information on these services.

Computerized advance bookings can be made at the **Government of India Tourism Offices** in the four metropolitan cities.

Most interstate bus terminals are chaotic places, so do arrive early to book tickets. Then check at the enquiry counter to find the stand from where your bus will depart. Finally, be prepared for a lot of jostling as passengers tend to push to get the best seats.

STATE TOURISM-RUN COACHES AND PACKAGE TOURS

Some of the best guided tours, both within cities and to neighbouring towns, are offered by the Government of India Tourism Department and the various state tourism departments *(see p761)*. The Government of India Tourist Offices in most cities offer the latest information on schedules, routes and pick-up points. It is a good idea to buy tickets in advance though they can also be bought on the spot. Coach operators can also customize itineraries keeping in mind the size of the group and the destination.

Coaches run by the tourism departments are, by and large, clean, uncrowded and comfortable. Coach tours organized by them tend to include a guide, so you are also less likely to be surrounded by "freelance" guides or touts when you reach your destination.

PRIVATE OPERATORS AND PACKAGE TOURS

Private tour operators and travel agencies also offer a wide variety of coach trips for visitors. These are good value for money, especially if you have a tight budget and limited time.

Agencies usually use either 18 seater or 35 seater super deluxe air-conditioned coaches with pushback seats. Tariffs depend on the quality of service and the itinerary. The ticket price will often include a guide as well as an overnight stay at a hotel as part of the package. Most travel agents have a partnership with luxury coach companies who pick up tourists from designated hotels. Reservations can be made either through the hotel's reception desk or from one of their recommended local agencies.

BUS AND COACH TICKETS AND FARES

Bus or coach fares are cheaper than train fares and depend on the kind of transport you opt for. Travel by "ordinary" bus is not advisable for tourists. Deluxe buses are somewhat better, but, if you are travelling in summer, the best option are the deluxe air-conditioned (a/c) coaches. Many deluxe coaches, known as "video coaches" blast loud music and Hindi movies through the

A luxury coach, run by Rajasthan Tourism

Passenger ferry near the Gateway of India, Mumbai

night. If you have an option, it is better to take a deluxe coach that is not a "video coach". If opting for a deluxe or a/c deluxe bus, you can book your ticket in advance and also reserve your seat.

The charges for bus and coach package tours often include airport transfers, road taxes, overnight stays, guides and any monument or museum entry fees en route.

FERRIES AND BOATS

Rajasthani coach ticket

Ferry connections link some of India's more exotic island destinations, as well as cities along the coasts. They are available from Kolkata to Chennai and Mumbai to Goa. There is also a catamaran service between Mumbai and Goa, although it is suspended during the monsoon season from July to September. Passenger liners also operate from both Chennai and Kolkata to the Andaman Islands, as well as from Kochi to Lakshadweep. Many luxury cruise fares include meals on board, ferrying charges between the ship and islands, sightseeing, lagoon cruising and land accommodation. These are very popular, so it is advisable to book at least two months in advance.

Two passenger liners, the *MV Nancowry and MV Akbar*, run by the **Shipping Corporation of India** (SCI), operate between Chennai and Port Blair in the Andaman Islands, once every ten days, and another SCI ship sails to Port Blair once a month from Visakhapatnam. Within the

Andamans, there are four passenger-cum-cargo ferries for transport from Port Blair to the other islands.

Ships also ply between Kochi and Lakshadweep.

S.P.O.R.T.S., the Society for Promotion of Nature Tourism and Sports, the official tourist agency of the Lakshadweep Islands, operates two ships, the *MV Bharatseema and the MV Tipu Sultan*, between Kochi and Lakshadweep. The Goa Tourism Development Corporation *(see p761)* operates river cruises within the state, whereas in Kerala, half- or full-day backwater cruises are organized by the Kollam (Quilon) District Tourism Promotion Council *(see p634–5)*. The Kerala Tourism Development Corporation in Kochi *(see p761)* also organizes cruises through the state's beautiful backwaters, on vessels ranging from luxury houseboats in traditional *kettuvallams* (rice boats) to modern 12-seater safari boats.

In Goa and Kerala, travelling by boat is often quicker than going by car. Ferries connect the mainland to nearby islands, such as Ernakulam to Willingdon Island. In Lakshadweep and the Andamans, they offer the only link for people travelling between the islands. In the northeastern states, ferry rides on the River Brahmaputra are available at Guwahati. In Varanasi, boats can be hired at the ghats on the River Ganges. Mumbai has taxi boats plying between the Gateway of India and Elephanta Island.

Local Transport in Cities

A regular taxi meter

Transport options vary from city to city. Most large cities have reliable bus, taxi and auto-rickshaw services. The main cities also have suburban trains that provide speedy connections to areas within city limits. There is also a wide variety of other transport available, especially in the smaller towns and in the old quarters of cities where it is better to opt for a small, light vehicle to cut through narrow congested lanes. Cycle-rickshaws, auto-rickshaws, vikrams (larger versions of auto-rickshaws), tempos and jeeps can be found in most cities, and in some areas horse-drawn carriages (*tongas*) and camel carts are still in use.

TAXIS AND AUTO-RICKSHAWS

Yellow-topped black taxis operate in most cities except Kolkata, where they are completely yellow, and Bangalore, where they are totally black. These metered taxis can be hailed in the street or hired from the local taxi stand. They are available for point-to-point service or for a fixed rate for half a day, which is four hours or 40 km (28 miles); or a full day which is eight hours or 80 km (50 miles). The Ambassador is the favourite model, though Maruti vans are becoming increasingly popular.

Private cabs (some of which are air conditioned), are usually white in colour, and are also available at some of the regular taxi stands. In some cities, there are no yellow-topped taxis, but private taxis can be hired from agencies or hotels. Recently, Radio Cabs have been introduced in some cities such as Delhi and Mumbai. These are more expensive than the ordinary cabs, because they are air conditioned.

The ubiquitous auto-rickshaws (popularly called autos, scooters, or phat-phats) are the most common mode of transport in most places. Autos are more economical than taxis, but be prepared

An auto-rickshaw, cheap, fast and sometimes hair-raising

for some hair-raising drives – they love squeezing between buses. In Delhi and Mumbai, the anti-pollution drive has seen the introduction of vehicles run on Compressed Natural Gas (CNG). Taxis and autos that have converted to CNG usage have a green band across the usual yellow and black body. All new CNG autos run on CNG and are painted yellow and green, instead of yellow and black.

FARES AND METRES

All taxis and autos have meters, though fares fluctuate according to the prevailing price of fuel. Often, meters are not updated and drivers are required by law to carry a rate (tariff) chart listing both the old and current fare, based on the rate per kilometre. Night charges are higher than day fares and payment is extra for luggage. Drivers are notorious for over-charging passengers. The most common argument is that the meter is not working. It is best to firmly negotiate in advance, and insist on seeing the tariff chart. You can also negotiate a flat rate

before getting in. Carry some small change, as drivers often claim not to have return change. They are also prone to taking you via a long route so, if possible, try to find out the best route to take.

BUSES

Though city bus networks are very extensive, travelling by these buses is not a pleasant experience. Unable to cope with the large numbers of commuters, buses are overcrowded, and you will have to battle your way to even buy your ticket from the conductor. Buses that are full rarely stop at bus stops, which are usually seen full of waiting commuters. Drivers are known for their reckless driving. Even the so-called luxury buses drive at break-neck speed. Unless absolutely necessary, it is best to use some other form of transport.

SUBURBAN TRAINS AND METRO RAILS

Mumbai has the best suburban train network in India, providing efficient and affordable connections. However, it is extremely overcrowded and the rush hour is best avoided. Women should use the "ladies only" compartments. There are

The conductor standing at the door of a crowded city bus, Kolkata

Motorcycle taxis, a convenient way of getting around in Goa

rides. In Rajasthan, camel carts are also available – they offer a novel, if jerky, journey.

Jeeps and vans can be conveniently hired from cities (*see p779*), for short trips to explore the environs and neighbouring towns. They are also the main form of transport in Ladakh. Jeeps are also the best way of exploring the hills. Many areas have shared jeep taxis, which work out cheaper than private jeeps. A flat rate is usually charged, which includes any tolls en route. Private cars are often not allowed in hill towns, where the easiest options are to hire cycle-rickshaws or to explore the area on foot.

ROAD NAMES

In most cities, especially in the four main cities, many roads which were named after Raj-era figures, have been renamed after well-known Indian and international figures. This might cause some confusion, as maps often carry the newer names, while locals usually refer to the road by the old name. When in doubt, it is best to ask two or three people, and cross-check the directions that you are given.

three main lines, the most popular of which leaves from Churchgate and goes past Mumbai Central and Andheri. The others begin at Victoria Terminus (VT).

In Chennai, the surburban trains offer fast connections from Egmore to Central Station or George Town, and to Guindy or the airport.

India's first underground metro railway is in Kolkata. Limited routes in the northern and southern sectors are open, and the lines are still being extended. The service is clean and efficient and trains run between 7am and 10pm everyday. The main stations are situated opposite the Oberoi Grand and near Dr M Ishaque Road. Certain sections of Chennai's local above ground trains, the Mass Rapid Transit System (MRTS), are operational, while Delhi's metro has three lines running through the city, and is expanding to cover the outskirts.

MOTORCYCLES AND BICYCLES

Often the best way to explore smaller towns and cities and their environs, is by motorcycle or bicycle. In Goa, motorcycle taxis are distinguished by their yellow mudguards and white number plates, and are available everywhere. If you prefer to travel independently, motorcycles are also available for

hire on a daily basis. Towns such as Pondicherry, Hampi, Belur and Halebid, can be explored by bicycle, available for rent at reasonable rates.

OTHER MODES OF TRANSPORT

Other transport options include minibuses, cycle-rickshaws and horse-drawn carriages. Cycle-rickshaws are a popular and practical means of transport to traverse the congested pockets of the old quarters of cities. They are more plentiful in smaller towns, where they can easily manoeuvre through narrow bylanes and galis. It is best to negotiate rates in advance, though some of them may have a flat rate for fixed routes. Tempos are battery-powered wagon-like vehicles, equipped with seats in the rear half. Uncomfortable and overcrowded, they charge flat rates for fixed routes. Horse-drawn carriages (tongas or ikkas) are also very common in small towns and around railway stations, and offer leisurely

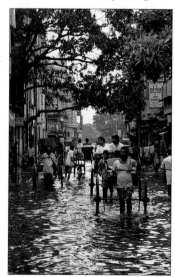

Hand-pulled rickshaws, found only in certain areas of central Kolkata

General Index

Acknowledgments

Dorling Kindersley would like to thank the following people whose contributions and assistance have made this book possible.

Main Contributors
Roshen Dalal has a PhD in Ancient Indian History from the Jawaharlal Nehru University, Delhi, and is the author of *A History of India for Children*.

Partho Datta teaches Indian History at a college in Delhi University.

Divya Gandhi, an environmentalist and geographer, is pursuing a doctorate at the University of Michigan.

Premola Ghose has travelled extensively, especially in Madhya Pradesh and Maharashtra. She is the Programme Officer at the India International Centre, Delhi.

Ashok Koshy is a senior civil servant who has spent many years in Gujarat and Kerala.

Abha Narain Lambah is an architectural conservationist, who is the Director of Bombay Collaborative, a pioneering firm in the field of urban design and conservation in Mumbai.

Annabel Lopez is a practising architect as well as an architectural historian who has co-authored the book *Houses of Goa*.

Sumita Mehta is a journalist and travel writer based in Delhi, who has worked on conservation projects in Rajasthan.

Rudrangshu Mukherji is a leading columnist, journalist and author based in Kolkata

Meenu Nageshwaran runs a travel agency, Incent Tours, in Delhi.

Rushad R Nanavatty is a keen mountaineer who has trekked extensively in northern, central and eastern India.

Ira Pande is the editor of *IIC Quarterly* in Delhi.

Usha Raman is a freelance writer and editor based in Hyderabad.

Janet Rizvi, a PhD from Cambridge, is a leading authority on Ladakh and author of two books, *Ladakh, Crossroads of High Asia* and *Trans-Himalayan Caravans: Merchant Princes and Peasant Traders in Ladakh*.

Ranee Sahaney is a well-known travel writer, and regular contributor to *outlooktraveller.com*.

Deepak Sanan is a senior civil servant who has spent many years working in Himachal Pradesh. He has written extensively on the region.
Darsana Selvakumar has a post-graduate degree in Ancient Indian History and archaeology.
Sankarshan Thakur is a senior journalist and author of a book on Bihar.
Shikha Trivedi is an authority on traditional crafts. She is presently working with India's leading television news channel.

Lakshmi Viswanathan is a Bharat Natyam dancer based in Chennai. She also sits on the governing body of the Music Academy Madras, one of South India's leading cultural organizations.

Consultant
George Michell is an architectural and cultural historian specializing in India. Among his many publications are books on Hindu temples, royal palaces, the Vijayanagar Empire and Deccani art and architecture.

Additional Contributors
John Abraham, Anvar Alikhan, Usha Balakrishnan, Manini Chatterjee, Anuradha Chaturvedi, Rta Kapur Chishti, Anna Dallapiccola, Dharmendar Kanwar, Ranjana Sengupta.

Additional Illustrations
Naveed Ahmed Vali, Ampersand.

Additional Photography
Akhil Bakshi, Benu Joshi, Ian O'Leary, Aditya Patankar, Ram Rahman.

Proof Reader and Indexer
Anita Roy, Ranjana Saklani.

Fact Check
Ranee Sahaney.

Editorial, DTP and Cartographic Assistance (DK London)
Brigitte Arora, Jo Cowen, Fay Franklin, Emily Hatchwell, Jason Little, Juliet Kenny, Carly Madden, Casper Morris, Dave Pugh, Vivien Stone, Janis Utton, Dora Whitaker.

Publishing Manager
Anna Streiffert.

Art Director
Gillian Allan.

Publisher
Douglas Amrine.

Special Assistance
Arundhti Bhanot; Mahesh Buch; Tarun Chhabria; Manosh De; Sharada Dwivedi; Asit Gopal; Sandhya Iyer; GM Kakpori; Vijayan Kannampilly; Kurt Kessler Dias; Sumita Khatwani; Meenal Kshirsagar; Aparajita Kumar; Ritu Kumar; Anna Madhavan; Aditi Mehta; Milan Moudgill; Sunil Philip; Nihar Rao; Anita Roy; KJ Ravinder; Samit Roychoudhury; Shweta Sachdeva; Saba Shaikh; Lalit Sharma; Parvati Sharma; Tara Sharma; Yuthika Sharma; Luiyo Shimray; Dr A Jaya Thilak; Maharao Brijraj Singh of Kotah; Maharaja Gaj Singh II of Jodhpur; Vijay Singh.
American Institute of Indian Studies.
Archaeological Survey of India, New Delhi.
Architecture Autonomous, Goa: Gerard da Cunha and Amit Modi.
Architectural Conservation Cell of the Associated Cement Companies Ltd.
Aurobindo Ashram.
Central Cottage Industries.
Department of Culture, Government of India: Kasturi Gupta Menon, Joint Secretary.
Department of Tourism, New Delhi:

Rekha Khosla, Director; Ashwini Lohani,
Director.
Indian Institute of Public Administration.
Indian Museum, Kolkata: Dr SK Chakravarty,
Director; Chanda Mukherjee.
Indian National Trust for Art and Cultural
Heritage: Martand Singh.
Maharana Mewar Historical Publications Trust,
Mewar: Shriji Arvind Singhji, Chairman and
Managing Trustee.
Mehrangarh Museum Trust, Jodhpur: Trustees;
Mahendra Singh, CEO.
Sangath: BV Doshi.
Tibet House, New Delhi.
Tibetan Institute of Performing Arts, Dharamsala.
Wildlife Trust of India: Vivek Menon.
World Wide Fund: Krishna Kumar.

Special Assistance in Photography
Archaeological Survey of India, New Delhi:
Komal Anand, Director General;
Dr KM Poonacha, Director (Monuments);
Dr RC Aggarwal, Director (Museums);
Mr Bakshi, Assistant Director (Monuments).
Crafts Museum, New Delhi: Dr Jyotindra Jain.
Government Museum, Chennai: R Kannan.
Khuda Baksh Oriental Library, Patna: HR Chigani.
Mathura Museum, Mathura: Jitendra Kumar. Maharaja
Fatehsingh Museum Trust, Baroda. National Museum,
New Delhi:
RD Chowdhourie; U Dass; JC Grover;
Dr Daljeet Kaur.
Prince of Wales Museum of Western India,
Mumbai: Dr Kalpana Desai, Director.
Rampur Raza Library, Rampur: WH Siddiqi. Sarabhai
Foundation, Calico Museum of
Textiles, Ahmedabad:
DS Mehta, Secretary; A Sen Gupta.
Sanskriti Museum, New Delhi: OP Jain.
State Museum, Patna: Naseena Akhtar.

Dorling Kindersley would like to thank all regional
and local tourist offices throughout India for their
valuable help. Particular thanks to Ravi Babu;
Chandana Khan, Secretary, Tourism & Culture
Department, Hyderabad; Victoria Memorial, Kolkata:
CR Panda; Indian Museum, Kolkata: Shyamalkanti
Chakravarti; The Asiatic Society, Kolkata: Ms Sarkar;
Kunjo Tashi; Rajiv Mehrotra; Tenzin Geyche Tethong,
Secretary to His Holiness, the Dalai Lama,
Dharamsala; Chief PRO, Central Railways, Mumbai:
Mukul Marwah; Quila House, Patna: BM Jalan;
Secretary, Department of Cultural Affairs,
Thiruvananthapuram: Prof HV Pradhan; INTACH
(Pune); RK Saini.

Photography Permissions
Dorling Kindersley would like to thank all those at
temples, forts, palaces, museums, restaurants,
shops and other sights, for their cooperation and
contribution to this publication. The Publisher would
also like to thank the following for their assistance and
kind permission to photograph at their establishments:
Brindavan, New Delhi; Crafts Museum, New Delhi;
Good Earth, New Delhi; Annie Kumar, Regalia, India
Tea House, New Delhi; Ramji Bharany, Bharany's, New
Delhi. Particular thanks also to Urmila Dongre and
Vivek Narang for their kind permission to photograph
their products.

Picture Credits
t = top; tl = top left; tlc = top left centre; tc = top
centre; tr = top right; cla = centre left above; ca =
centre above; cra = centre right above; cl = centre
left; c = centre; cr = centre right; clb = centre left
below; cb = centre below; crb = centre right below;
bl = bottom left; b = bottom; bc = bottom centre; bcl
= bottom centre left; br = bottom right; bra = bottom
right above; d = detail.

The publishers are grateful to the following
individuals, picture libraries and companies, for
permission to reproduce their photographs:

Ahmed, Idris 369crb.
Air India 772tc.
Alamy Images Adams Picture Library t/a
apl/Dhanwant Plahay 348cl; Arco Images 10tl; China
Span/Keren Su 67c,265tl; Dinodia Images 9br,10c;
Michele Falzone 67tl; Tim Gainey 555c; Blaine
Harrington III 11t; Indiapicture 12tl,/Ravi Verma 66cl;
Huw Jones 554cl; Michael Juno 165tl; Wolfgang
Kaehler 10br; David Pearson 772bl; Photo Provider
Network 264cl; Simon Reddy 440cl,441tl; Robert
Harding Picture Library Ltd/Jeremy Bright 164cl, 265c;
Dave Thompson 8tc; Andrew H Williams 441c
AMR Vastra Kosh Trust, New Delhi 317bra/bl/c.
Arya, Aditya 214c, 217c, 225cr, 233t/c/b, 239cr,
242bl/br, 246t, 252t, 261c, 338c, 457b, 459t,
748t, 777b.

Bagla, Pallava 19trb, 24-25d, 28tr, 65bl, 162cl, 193b,
221cl, 250b, 371c, 377cb, 641b.
Bahuguna, Manu 34b, 75b, 85c, 328 & 329, 408, 430tr,
445b, 454tr, 471bl, 521b, 543br, 556, 559c, 570t, 572t,
607t, 616, 618b, 619t, 622t, 646c, 750b, 752t, 753t.
Bakshi, Akhil 28b/br, 29bl, 186b, 219br, 391b, 436t,
778b.
Balan, M 18crb, 30br, 369b, 520b, 550t, 624,
626b, 627t, 628tl/tr, 629bl, 630tl/tr, 631tl, 633c/bl, 634-
635c, 635tl/br, 640tl/cb, 641tl/cr, 646br, 647t/c/br,
648c, 649t/c, 650cl, 652b, 654t/c, 656t/c, 657t/cr/c,
688b, 719b.
Barkakoti, Kakoli 324c, 325br, 333t.
Bartholomew, Pablo/Mediaweb India 262cl, 262-263c.
Behl, Benoy 42t, 47tr, 136t/c, 137tr/b, 138tr/cl/cr/br,
139tl/cl/b, 140b, 141bl/b/br, 143cl/clb,
144tl/tr/cl/cr/b, 145tr/c/b, 146c/b, 147cl/b, 151c/b,
476tr/cb, 477t/c, 478t, 479t/b,
480t/cl/c/cr/clb/crb/bl/b/br, 481cr/bl/br, 565b, 566c.
Bhargava, Subhash 23clb, 56bl, 179c, 346br, 358c/bl,
364b, 367t/c, 373t, 377cl/bc/b, 378t, 379t, 380tl, 381b,
386t, 387t, 390b, 398tr, 401bl, 402t/b, 403t, 404t, 407t,
751t.
Bhojani, Namas 442.
Big Screen Entertainment Pvt.Ltd. 33tr, 33cra.
Bihar School of Yoga Ganga Darshan, Munger, 217t.
Brown, Dean K 78b.
Chandola, Ashish 62t, 368b.
Chhabra, Tarun 607cl.
Chishti, Rta Kapur 209t/c/clb/crb/bl/br (a, b, c, d),
583t/c/cb/crb, 673cr (a, b, c, d, e, f).
Chundawat RS 18br, 19cl/bra, 64cla, 136b, 140t, 142c,
143t, 152t, 153b, 186t, 188t, 192c/cb, 194b, 255crb,
295b, 321c, 371b, 423br, 520crb.
Costumes & Textiles of Royal India, Ritu Kumar 30cl.
Corbis Atlantide Phototravel 8cl; Arvind Garg 13br;
Blaine Harrington III 349tl; Lindsay Hebberd 11bc;
Jon Hicks 12br; Bob Krist 9tl; Sergio Pitamitz 13tr;

Steve Raymer 770bc; Robert Harding World
Imagery/Tony Waltham 8br; Leplat Véronique 165c
Crafts Museum 80tr/c/cb, 81tl/tc/crb, 252c.
Crampes, Gilles 123cl.

Das, Tanmoy 318bl.
Das, Vivek 262bl/br.
Dasgupta, Prosenjit 316tl.
Deen Dayal Trust 665clb.
Dharma Productions: 33tl
Dilwali, Ashok 112t, 113c/br, 114b, 115tr, 116c, 117cr,
118c/b, 120t/c/b, 121t/c, 122t, 123tr, 124c, 125c/b,
126t/c, 127bl, 128c/bl, 129t/c/b, 130trb, 131br, 158t,
163c, 170t, 180tl, 182tl, 187t, 189b, 191b, 259b,
299crb, 300t, 301b, 302t/b, 618t/c, 619c, 620clb, 621b,
623t/c/b.
Dix, Thomas 226, 230 & 231, 236tr/c, 237b,
346-347c, 350, 371cr, 392 & 393, 394t, 397tr/bl,
414tr/cl/cr, 415tr/cl/b, 418tl/tr/c/cb, 419tr/c,
422t, 424 & 425, 464, 476tl/c/b, 477b, 478b,
481t/cl/crb, 679br.
DK Classic Cookbook 718t.
DK Picture Library Andy Crawford 27tr/bl, 141cr
(Wimbledon Buddhist Temple, London); Geoff Dann
(Ashmolean Museum, Oxford) 679ca; Gables 21c;
Ellen Howdon (Glasgow Museum, Glasgow) 467c;
Dave King 163b; Linda Whitwam 646tl.
Dongre, Urmila 3 (inset), 24tl/c, 25tl/b, 44t, 597tr,
746tl/cl (a, b, c, d).
Dube, DN 50cla, 172c, 173cr, 180tr, 181tl, 182tr/c.
Dubey, Suman 132 & 133.

Fotomedia Picture Library 55tr, 59(inset), 142t, 152bl,
196b, 284, 286b, 433(inset), 471cl; Jyoti M Banerjee
193t, 334c; Francois Gautier 396cl, 441br, 754t, 783t;
Nihal Mathur 406tr; Sanjiv Mishra 37b; Sundeep
Nayak 368c; Christine Pemberton 22cl, 158b, 195t,
306tr, 308b, 443b, 444t, 454c, 473tr, 718b; Otto Pfister
130bl, 368t/cb, 369tl/c; Sanjay Saxena 185c, 303c,
355bl; Satish Sharma 467t; Mathew Titus 55tl; Henry
Wilson 203br.

Gaur, RK 61b, 258t, 326b, 333b, 336cl.
Getty Images AFP/Emmanuel Dunand 428br,/Prakash
Singh 754br; Aurora/PatitucciPhoto 555tl; National
Geographic/James L. Stanfield 653b; Robert
Nickelsberg 744cr.
Ghose, Premola 221crb.
Ghosh, Ashim 48bl, 183br.
Gruisen, Joanna van 18clb/bl/bla, 19tr, 34t, 64tl, 65tr,
127c, 138clb, 142cl/cr, 193cb, 224c, 254t, 288tr,
319t/c/b, 326c, 330tl, 388tl, 390c, 406cl, 520cr,
640tl/bl, 641tr.
Tradition & Beyond: Handcrafted Indian Textiles, Roli
Books India 2001 by Rta Kapur Chishti & Rahul Jain
317t/cl/cr (a) & (b)/br.
Husain, Fawzan 436b.
Hyatt Regency 749b.
Image Bank/London 64-65c.
India Today Magazine 32cl, 447b, 665cl.
Israni, Prakash 18tr, 36c, 63t, 101b, 183bl, 309c, 467b,
472c/b.

Kaimal, Ravi 124t.
Kapoor, Prem 42c, 56br, 57br, 128t, 195bl, 632t, 639c,
748b.
Kapoor, Kanika 30-31c.
Kasliwal, Sudhir 360b, 361tl/clb/bl/b, 746bl.
Khanna, Dinesh 30bl, 31bl, 105b, 162tl, 163tl, 179b,
202cl/c/cr/b, 203cl/c/bl, 206cl, 207cr/bl, 313tr/br,

345t, 377c, 380tr, 421c, 437c, 438br, 439tl/tc/bc/br,
484, 494 & 495, 506b, 551t, 663tl, 665bl, 746cr.
Khazanchi, BN 34c, 36b, 37c, 327tr.
Khokar, Ashish 28cl, 253br.
Khullar, Rupinder 30t,103b, 104b, 200 & 201, 221clb,
225b, 304, 312b, 318br, 321t/br, 458t, 459b.
Kohli, Bobby 263tl.
Kumar, Krishna 620t/cl/cr/crb, 622b.

Lewis, Karoki 204t, 207tl/cl.
Lonely Planet Images: Dallas Stribley 349c.

Mandhani, Pradeep 750t.
Mehrangarh Fort, Jodhpur 382b, 383b.
Mehta, Dalip 377bl, 299t/cr/c/clb.
Mehta Hemant/Picture India 31cr.
Mishra, Vishwanath 439bl.
Muthuraman, V 2 & 3, 6 & 7, 22b, 24cl, 25cr/br, 36t,
38b, 45bl, 47tl/bl/br, 54br, 204bl/br, 205tl/tr, 206bl,
207tr, 208t/b, 210t, 220t/b, 221b, 222c/br, 237c, 238c,
262tl, 267b, 269t, 271crb, 274tr/b, 275t, 281c, 324t,
334b, 335t/c, 516b, 517t/br, 518b, 519tl/tr,
524cr/crb/b, 535cla/cl/clb, 546 & 547, 548t/c, 551c/b,
554trb, 560t/b, 565t, 566bl/br, 569t/c/b, 571br,
576, 578t, 582t/b, 583cl/ cr/clb/b, 584t/bl/br, 585t/c/b,
586tr, 587tl/tr/c, 588c, 589bl/br, 590b, 591br, 592t,
593t/c/b, 594t/c/b, 595t/bl/br, 596t/c/b, 597tl, 598b,
599t/c, 600t/c, 601t/c/b, 602 & 603, 604t/b,
605t/c/b, 606t/bl/br, 607c/cr/crb/bl/br, 608t/c/b, 609t,
610t/b, 611t/c/b, 612t/cl/cr/clb/crb/bl/br, 613t/b,
614t/b, 615t/b, 628b, 633cb, 636 & 637, 642t, 650t/clb,
652t, 653t, 654b, 655t/c/b, 656b, 657cl/bl/br, 753b,
762t.

Nath, Aman 45br, 50br.
Nath, Ashok 327tl, 332b, 336tc.
National Museum, New Delhi 24br, 26bla, 40, 41t/bl,
43t/br/bc, 48br, 49t, 50tl/c/clb, 51c/crb, 53bl,
76tl/tr/c/clb/bl/br, 77t, 141cl, 249b, 405cr/bl, 665br;
JC Arora 52bl; RC Dutta Gupta 29tl, 42b, 44b, 52t;. P
Roy 361crb (a) & (b)
National School of Drama, New Delhi 26crb.
Nehru Memorial Library, Teen Murti, New Delhi 57t.

Pasricha, Amit 18cr, 31br, 38t, 39t, 44c, 55bl, 60t, 98,
140c, 141t, 162br, 256 & 257, 336bl/b, 337tl, 338t/b,
341(inset), 385t/cr/b, 400tr, 426b, 427t/b, 587b.
Pasricha, Avinash 28c/cr, 29cl/cr/bc/br, 102t, 313bl,
514t, 550b, 557b, 595cl/c/cr/crb/cra/bc, 775b.
Patankar, Aditya 28tl, 228tl/tr/c/b, 229t/cl/cr/b,
346tl/clb/bl, 347cr, 356tr, 372t/c, 390t, 403b, 748c.
Prabhakar, K 663tr/c/b, 665t, 666t, 667c, 669t/cr.
Prince of Wales Museum of Western India, Mumbai
450tl/tr/c/b, 451c/b.
Press Information Bureau 56t.
Rahman, Ram 72bl.
Rajamani, VK 25tr, 46tl/tr/bl/br, 46-47c, 552c/bl,
553tl/bl, 561b, 564c, 565c, 747cb.
Ramamrutham, Bharath 515 t/cl/c/ca/bl/b/br.
Rao, CR Anantha Padmanabha 652c.
Rao, E Hanumantha 19bl, 288tl, 407cb/b, 650cr.
Reshi Maryam 35t, 63b, 154t/c, 155t/c, 400tl, 430tl/c,
431c.
Reuters Sherwin Crasto 32bl; Kieran Doherty 32clb;
Lucas Jackson 33bl.
Rizvi, Janet 147t/cr.
Roli Books 27cl, 31tl, 236tl/b, 388b.

Sahai, Kamal 43bl.
Saith, Sanjeev 60b, 100b, 103t, 116b, 154b, 162tr,

163cb, 187b, 188c, 190t/c/b, 191t, 197c, 207crb, 209cl, 216c, 224t/b, 260t, 288c, 300b, 411c, 752b.
Sanan, Deepak 118t, 119t/c, 327b, 332t, 333c, 337cl.
Sanctuary Features & Photo Library 438cb, 439tr;
Parvish Pandya 622c; Shailendra Yashwant 467cl.
Sanghvi, Hemen 23tr/cl/cr/crb/bl, 261b, 324b, 325t, 334t, 336tl, 337tr/b, 339t/c/b.
Sankaran, R 619b.
Saran Shalini 35b, 48c, 50bl, 51tl/b, 52br, 54bl, 77c/b, 91b, 95t, 160t, 168tl, 170b, 171b, 183tl, 184b, 194t/c, 199br, 207br, 221t/tc, 240tr, 242c, 244tr/c/cb, 245t/bl/br, 248b, 251br, 374tl, 405crb, 429t, 431tl/tc/tr/bc, 685(inset), 757(inset).
Sarabhai Foundation, Calico Museum of Textiles, Ahmedabad 412tl/tr/c/b, 413t/c/b.
Satyan, TS 19br, 26tl, 27cr, 29tr, 165br (a, b), 517bl, 518tr/c, 535bl/br, 590t, 635tr, 762b.
Sekhsaria, Pankaj 369tr.
Seth, Pepita 216b, 649b.
Sethi, Ajay & Mugdha 101t, 164br, 165clb, 174c/bra, 175cl/bl, 203t, 205b, 206br, 281b, 291br, 631tr, 760t, 769bla.
Siddharth 263b.
Sinclair, Toby 7(inset), 18cl/bra, 19tl/clb/crb/b, 20tl, 25bl, 31tr, 113bl, 124b, 139tr, 155b, 157(inset), 159b, 161b, 163tr, 187c, 192t/b, 193c, 211t/b, 237t, 238t/b, 239t/cl/clb/crb/b, 254cl/clb/b, 255t, 257(inset), 261t, 288b, 289t/c/b, 291t, 292t, 298t/c, 299cl, 307t, 309t, 321bl, 322, 325bl, 326t, 330tr/c/b, 331t/cb, 335b, 336tr, 379c, 381t, 384b, 396b, 397cr, 401tr, 404b, 406tl/c/b, 407c, 416t, 423bl, 429c/b, 439bra, 461tl, 520t, 524t, 547(inset), 578b, 580tr, 621c, 631c, 634cl/br, 640c, 643tr, 644tl, 645c, 646bl, 647bl, 650crb, 670c/b, 679bc, 687t, 689t, 756 & 757, 760b, 781t.
Singh, NP 354bl.
Singh, Dhruv 394b, 396tl.
Singh, Hashmat 58 & 59, 62b, 64clb, 108, 114c, 115tl/b, 116tl/tr, 119b, 123clb/bl, 125t, 126b, 127br, 130tr/c/br, 131tl/cl/bl, 139cr, 143cr, 150t, 151t, 152c/cb, 153t, 189t, 262tr/clb, 294t, 296t, 297t/c/b, 298b, 301t, 302c, 303t/b, 345b, 377t, 381c, 395b, 397tl/crb, 688t.
Singh, Thakur Dalip 18tl, 19bc, 65cr/bra/br, 112c, 186c, 191c, 295c, 299bl, 331c, 482b, 520cl/clb.
Stock Transparency Services 460b, 466t/c, 471c, 482t, 483t.

Talwar, Amar 57bl, 65trb, 113t, 114t, 117br, 127t, 161t, 163cra, 182b, 188b, 225t, 248cr, 253cl, 428t, 430br, 431bl.
The Statesman/R De 37t.

UTV Motion pictures 33br.

V & A Museum, London (Courtesy of the Board of Trustees) 50tr, 53b.
Varuni, Ritu 336cr/br, 337cr.
Verma Bimla 23tl, 26tr, 27crb, 102c, 123crb/br, 162cr, 217b, 221cr, 253t/cr/cb/clb, 295t, 306tl, 308t, 309b, 312c, 320t, 398c, 431br, 470c, 679t/bl.

Wadhwa, Rajinder Kumar 313t.
Walia, BPS 101cl/cr, 103c, 104t/c, 105t/c, 106tl/tr/cl/cr/b, 107t/c/b, 121b, 123tl/t/cr (a) & (b), 141c, 199bl, 243c, 244tl/b, 245tr, 247t/c, 248tr/tl/cl, 249tl/tr, 255cr, 306b, 308cb, 310cl, 340 & 341, 396tr, 397br, 423t, 458b, 524cl.
Wedding Affair Magazine 31cl.
Whitaker, Rom 621t.
World Wildlife Fund 330cb, 331b.

Yash Raj Flims 32tr, 32-33c.

Works of art have been reproduced with the permission of the following copyright holders
© National Gallery of Modern Art, New Delhi 55br; Trustees of Rao Madho Singh Trust Museum, Kotah 405br; Courtesy Shriji Arvind Singhji Mewar, Chairman and Managing Trustee, Maharana Mewar Historical Publications Trust 405cl; Ramachandra Maharana, Puri, Orissa 313c; Mundrika Devi, Madhubani, Bihar 27tl;

JACKET:
Front: DK Images: Toby Sinclair clb; Masterfile: Jeremy Woodhouse. Back: Alamy Images: Anders Blomqvist tl; DK Images: Dinesh Khanna cla; Aditya Patankar bl; Bharath Ramamrutham clb. Spine: DK Images: Courtesy of the Indian Museum, Kolkata/Amit Pashricha b; Masterfile: Jeremy Woodhouse t

All other images © Dorling Kindersley. For further information see: www.dkimages.com

SPECIAL EDITIONS OF DK TRAVEL GUIDES

DK Travel Guides can be purchased in bulk quantities at discounted prices for use in promotions or as premiums. We are also able to offer special editions and personalized jackets, corporate imprints, and excerpts from all of our books, tailored specifically to meet your own needs.

To find out more, please contact:
(in the United States) **SpecialSales@dk.com**
(in the UK) **Sarah.Burgess@dk.com**
(in Canada) DK Special Sales at
general@tourmaline.ca
(in Australia)
business.development@pearson.com.au

Further Reading

History

A Discovery of India Jawaharlal Nehru, Oxford University Press, New Delhi, 1997.

A History of India (Vol 1) Romila Thapar, Penguin, New Delhi, 1990.

A History of India (Vol 2) Percival Spear, Penguin, New Delhi, 1990.

A History of South India KA Nilakanta Sastri, Oxford University Press, New Delhi, 1999.

A History of the Sikhs Khushwant Singh, Oxford University Press, New Delhi, 1991.

Alberuni's India Edward C Sachau, Routledge & Kegan Paul, London, 1988.

A New History of India Stanley Wolpert, Oxford University Press, New York, 1990.

Annals and Antiquities of Rajasthan Col James Tod, South Asia Books, Columbia, 1987.

Babur Nama: Memoirs of Babur (trans) Wheeler M Thackston, Oxford University Press, London, 1996.

Delhi Between Two Empires Narayani Gupta, Oxford University Press, New Delhi, 1981.

Freedom at Midnight Dominique Lapierre and Larry Collins, Avon Books, New York, 1955.

India: A History John Keay, HarperCollins, New Delhi, 2000.

India Britannica Geoffrey Moorhouse, Harvill, London, 1983.

India's Struggle for Independence Bipan Chandra et al, Penguin, New Delhi, 1989.

Ladakh: Crossroads of High Asia Janet Rizvi, Oxford University Press, New Delhi, 1996.

Liberty or Death Patrick French, HarperCollins, London, 1997.

Lives of the Indian Princes Charles Allen & Sharada Dwivedi, Century, London, 1985.

Plain Tales from the Raj Charles Allen, Andre Deutsch, London, 1975.

The Great Moghuls Bamber Gascoigne, Dorset Press, London, 1971.

The Last Mughal: The Fall of a Dynasty, Delhi, 1857 William Dalrymple, Bloomsbury, London, 2007.

The Idea of India Sunil Khilnani, Farrar Strauss Giroux, New York, 1997.

The Wonder that was India AL Basham, Rupa, New Delhi, 1967.

The Wonder that was India Part II, SAA Rizvi, Sidgwick & Jackson, London, 1987.

Tuzuk-i-Jahangiri: Memoirs of Jahangir (trans) Alexander Rogers and Henry Beveridge, London, 1909–14.

Xuanzang: A Buddhist Pilgrim on the Silk Road Sally H Wriggins, Boulder Press, Colorado, 1996.

Religion and Philosophy

Buddhism Christmas Humphreys, Penguin, London, 1951.

Hinduism Kshiti Mohan Sen, Penguin, London, 1961.

Hindu Myths Wendy O'Flaherty, Penguin, London, 1974.

Manifestations of Shiva (exhibition catalogue), Stella Kramrisch, Philadelphia Museum of Art, Philadelphia, 1981.

The Bhagwadgita Robert Charles Zaehner, Oxford University Press, London, 1969.

The Ramayana and the Mahabharata Chakravarti Rajagopalachari, Bharati Vidya Bhavan, Mumbai, 1951.

Culture and Society

A Taste of India Madhur Jaffrey, Atheneum Publishers, New York, 1986.

Banaras, City of Light Diana L Eck, Alfred A Knopf, New York, 1982.

Bombay: City of Gold Gillian Tindall, Penguin, London, 1992.

Bombay: The Cities Within Sharada Dwivedi & Rahul Mehrotra, India Book House, Bombay, 1995.

Butter Chicken in Ludhiana Pankaj Mishra, Penguin, New Delhi, 1995.

Calcutta, The City Revealed Geoffrey Moorhouse, Weidenfeld & Nicolson, 1971.

Dance of the Peacock: Jewellery Traditions of India Usha R Bala Krishnan & Meera S Kumar, India Book House, Mumbai, 1999.

Desert Places Robyn Davidson, Viking, London, 1996.

Eyewitness India, Manini Chatterjee & Anita Roy, Dorling Kindersley, London, 1969.

Garden of Life: An Introduction to the Healing Plants of India Naveen Patnaik, Doubleday, New York, 1993.

Hanklyn-Janklin Nigel B Hankin, Banyan Books, New Delhi, 1992.

Historical Dictionary of Indian Food KT Achaya, Oxford University Press, New Delhi, 1998.

India: A Million Mutinies Now VS Naipaul, Heinemann, Oxford, 1990.

India: A Wounded Civilization VS Naipaul, Vintage Books, New York, 1977.

Indian Cinema, Past and Present Feroze Rangoonwala, Clarion Books, New Delhi, 1983.

Madras Rediscovered S Muthiah, EastWest Books, Chennai, 1999.

May You Be the Mother of a Hundred Sons Elizabeth Bumiller, Random House Inc, New York, 1990.

No Fullstops in India Mark Tully, Viking, London, 1991.

The Great Indian Middle Class Pavan K Varma, Penguin, New Delhi, 1998.

The Muslim Community of the Indo-Pakistan Subcontinent Dr Ishtiaq Hussain Qureshi, Oxford University Press, New Delhi, 1977.

The Remembered Village MN Srinivas, Oxford University Press, New Delhi, 1996.

Architecture

Forts Walks: Around Bombay's Fort Areas Sharda Dwivedi & Rahul Mehrotra, Eminence Designs, Bombay, 1999.

Indian Architecture Percy Brown, (2 vols), DB Taraporevala Sons and Co, Bombay, 1964

Mughal Architecture Ebba Koch, PRESTEL-Verlag, Munich, 1991.

Stones of Empire Jan Morris, Oxford University Press, Oxford, 1983.

The Moonlight Garden Elizabeth B Moynihan, Smithsonian Institution, Washington DC, 2000.

The Forts of India Virginia Fass, Collins, London, 1986.

The Hindu Temple George Michell, University of Chicago Press, Chicago, 1988.

The History of Architecture in India Christopher Tadgell, Phaidon, London, 1990.

The Palaces of India Virginia Fass and Maharaja of Baroda, Collins, London, 1980.

The Penguin Guide to the Monuments of India (2 vols) George Michell and Phillip Davies, Viking, London, 1989.

Rajput Palaces GHR Tillotson, Oxford University Press, New Delhi, 1987.

Traditional Buildings of India Ilay Cooper & Barry Dawson, Thames & Hudson, New York, 1998.

Arts and Crafts

Art of the Imperial Cholas Vidya Dehejia, Columbia University Press, New York, 1990.

A Second Paradise Naveen Patnaik, Sidgwick & Jackson, London, 1985.

Company Paintings: Indian Paintings of the British Period Mildred Archer, Victoria and Albert Museum, London in association with Mapin Publishing, Ahmedabad, 1992.

Costumes and Textiles of Royal India Ritu Kumar, Christie's Books, London, 1999.

Himalayan Art Madanjeet Singh, Macmillan, New York, 1963.

India: Art and Culture 1300–1900 (exhibition catalogue), Stuart Cary Welch, The Metropolitan Museum of Art, New York, 1985.

Indian Art Vidya Dehejia, Phaidon, London, 1997.

Indian Interiors Sunil Sethi, Taschen, Cologne, 2000.

Indian Painting MS Randhawa, and John Kenneth Galbraith, Vakils, Feffer and Simon, Mumbai, 1982.

Kalighat Paintings: Images from a Changing World Jyotindra Jain, Mapin Publishing, Ahmedabad, 1999.

Masterpieces from the National Museum Collection SP Gupta, New Delhi, 1985.

Paradise as a Garden Elizabeth B Moynihan, George Braziller Inc, New York, 1979.

Penguin Dictionary of Indian Classical Music Raghava Menon, Penguin, New Delhi, 1995.

South Indian Bronzes C Sivaramamurti, Lalit Kala Akademi, New Delhi, 1963.

The Art of India: Traditions of Indian Sculpture, Painting and Architecture Stella Kramrisch, Phaidon, New York, 1954.

The Essence of Indian Art (exhibition catalogue), Asian Art Museum of San Francisco, 1986.

The New Cambridge History of India: Architecture and Art of the Deccan Sultanates George Michell and Mark Zebrowski, Cambridge University Press, Cambridge, 1999.

The New Cambridge History of India: Mughal and Rajput Painting Milo C Beach, Cambridge University Press, Cambridge, 1992.

Tradition & Beyond: Handcrafted Indian Textiles Rta Kapur Chishti and Rahul Jain, Roli Books, New Delhi, 2000.

Traditions of Indian Classical Dance Mohan Khokar, Clarion Books, New Delhi, 1979.

Nature and Wildlife

Collins Handguide to Birds of the Indian Subcontinent Martin, Williams Woodcock, Collins Sons & Co, London, 1980.

Encyclopaedia of Indian Natural History RE Hawkins (ed), Oxford University Press, Bombay, 1986.

Flowers of the Himalaya Oleg Polunin and Adam Stainton, Oxford University Press, New Delhi, 1984.

Handbook of Birds of India and Pakistan, 2nd edition, Salim Ali and S Dillon Ripley, Oxford University Press, London, 1995.

In Danger Paola Manfredi (ed), Ranthambhore Foundation, New Delhi, 1997.

Indian Wildlife S Israel and T Sinclair (eds), APA Publications, Hong Kong, 1987.

India's Wildlife History: An Introduction Mahesh Rangarajan, Permanent Black, New Delhi, 2001.

Land of the Tiger Valmik Thapar, BBC Consumer Publishing, London, 1997.

Trees of India Pallava Bagla, Timeless, New Delhi, 2000.

Literature

A Passage to India EM Forster, Harcourt, Brace & World, New York, 1924.

A Suitable Boy Vikram Seth, Viking-Penguin, New Delhi, 1993.

Gitanjali Rabindranath Tagore, Chiswick Press, London, 1912.

Heat and Dust Ruth P Jhabvala, John Murray, London, 1975.

In Custody Anita Desai, Heinemann, Oxford, 1984.

Kim Rudyard Kipling, Tuttle Publishing, Boston, 1901.

Malgudi Days RK Narayan, Viking, New York, 1982.

Midnight's Children Salman Rushdie, Penguin, London, 1991.

Such a Long Journey Rohinton Mistry, Faber & Faber, London, 1991.

Sunlight on a Broken Column Attiya Hussain, Virago Press, London, 1988.

The Far Pavilions MM Kaye, St Martin's Press, New York, 1978.

The Glass Palace Amitav Ghosh, Ravi Dayal, New Delhi, 2000.

The God of Small Things Arundhati Roy, IndiaInk, New Delhi, 1999.

The House of Blue Mangoes David Davidar, Viking in association with Weidenfeld & Nicolson, New Delhi, 2002.

The Jungle Books Rudyard Kipling, Lancer Books, New York, 1968.

The Raj Quartet Paul Scott, William Morrow and Company, New York, 1976.

The Shadow Lines Amitav Ghosh, Ravi Dayal, New Delhi, 1988.

Those Days Sunil Gangopadhyaya, Penguin, New Delhi, 1997.

Three Plays: Nagamandala, Hayavadana and Tughlaq, Girish Karnad, Oxford University Press, New Delhi, 1997.

Train to Pakistan Khushwant Singh, Ravi Dayal, New Delhi, 1988.

Memoirs/Biography

A Princess Remembers Gayatri Devi, Rupa, New Delhi, 1995.

India's Bandit Queen: The True Story of Phoolan Devi Mala Sen, Harvill, London, 1991.

Indira Gandhi Katherine Frank, HarperCollins, New Delhi, 2001.

My Experiments with Truth Mohandas Karamchand Gandhi, Navjivan, Ahmedabad, 1927.

The Hill of Devi EM Forster, Harcourt Brace, New York, 1953.

The Life of Mahatma Gandhi Louis Fischer, Harper & Row, New York, 1950.

The Tribal World of Verrier Elwin Ramachandra Guha, Oxford University Press, New Delhi, 1999.

Travelogues

Branch Line to Eternity Bill Aitken, Penguin India, New Delhi 2001.

Chasing the Monsoon Alexander Frater, Alfred Knopf Inc, New York, 1992.

City of Djinns William Dalrymple, Flamingo, London, 1994.

Elsewhere: Unusual Takes on India Kai Friese (ed), Penguin India, New Delhi, 2000.

India By Rail Royston Ellis, Bradt Publications, UK, 1997.

In the Court of the Fish-Eyed Goddess William Dalrymple, HarperCollins, New Delhi, 1998.

Sikkim: A Traveller's Guide Sujoy Das, Permanent Black, New Delhi, 2001.

Slowly Down the Ganges Eric Newby, Lonely Planet Publications, Hawthorn, 1998.

The Goddess in the Stones Norman Lewis, TransAtlantic Publications Inc, Philadelphia, 1995.

The Great Railway Bazaar Paul Theroux, Viking, London, 1995.

Travels on my Elephant Mark Shand, Penguin India, New Delhi, 1993.

Travels through Sacred India Roger Thorsons Housden, HarperCollins, London, 1996.

Travels with a Tangerine: A Journey in the Footnotes of Ibn Battuta Tim Mackintosh Smith, John Murray, London, 2001.

Glossary

ARCHITECTURE

amalaka circular ribbed stone atop a Hindu temple tower

apsara celestial maiden (*p236*)

bagh garden

bangaldar roof curved roof, like those on thatched huts in Bengal (*p290*)

baoli stone-clad stepwell, with galleries on its sides (*see vav*)

baradari 12-pillared pavilion

bhavan house or abode

bhulbhulaiya labyrinth

chaitya rock-cut Buddhist shrine

chaitya griha prayer hall in a rock-cut Buddhist shrine (*p20*)

charbagh formal Mughal garden, divided into four quarters (*p21*)

chhatri, cenotaph small ornamental pavilion or kiosk, topped by a cupola; also pavilion with a canopy, built at the site of a royal cremation

chorten Mahayana Buddhist reliquary shrine or memorial stupa

chowk courtyard in a palace or fort; also main square in a city

dargah shrine of a Muslim saint

darwaza door or gateway

Diwan-i-Aam Hall of Public Audience

Diwan-i-Khas Hall of Private Audience

dukhang assembly hall in a Mahayana Buddhist monastery

dvarapala guardian deities near Hindu temple doorways; literally, doorkeeper (*p24*)

garbhagriha womb chamber or inner sanctum in a Hindu temple

garh fort

ghat steps on river bank; also a hilly range

gompa Mahayana Buddhist monastery in Himachal Pradesh, Ladakh and Arunachal Pradesh

gonkhang temple of the guardian deities in a gompa

gopura towering pyramidal gateway in a South Indian Hindu temple complex (*p610*)

gurdwara Sikh temple (*p21*)

hamam traditional steam bath of the Turkish type

haveli large traditional town house or mansion, with inner courtyards (*p387*)

jali ornamental pierced or latticed stone screen (*p175*)

jharokha decorative projecting balcony (*p387*)

kalasha pot-like finial crowning a Hindu temple spire (*p21*)

khirkee window

kund tank or lake

lhakhang Mahayana Buddhist temple in Ladakh and Himachal Pradesh

mahal palace

mandapa pillared hall leading to a Hindu temple sanctuary

mandir Hindu temple

mani stones/mani walls stones carved with sacred Mahayana Buddhist chants

masjid mosque

mihrab arched niche in a mosque that faces west towards Mecca

pol fortified gateway

prakara wall enclosing South Indian Hindu temple compound

qila fort

salabhanjika tree nymph (*p245*)

shikhara spire of a North Indian Hindu temple (*p20*)

tharavad ancestral home in Kerala; also matrilineal clan

torana ceremonial gateway, usually leading to a religious site

tshog-khang/jokhang secondary assembly hall in a Buddhist monastery in Ladakh or Himachal Pradesh

vav stepwell in Gujarat (*p414*)

vihara Buddhist monastery

vimana multi-staged pyramidal spire above the inner sanctum of a South Indian Hindu temple

yakshi female attendant

yali fierce mythical leonine creature

yogini attendant, or manifestation, of Devi, a form of Parvati

zenana area of a palace or house where women live in seclusion

CRAFTS AND CULTURE

asanas physical postures in Yoga

Ayurveda ancient Indian system of medicine, largely based on plants (*p629*)

Baramasa series of paintings or verses depicting the seasons; literally 12 months

dhurrie woven cotton rug

ganjifa cards painted, circular playing cards (*p26*)

gharana school of classical music or dance (*p28*)

ikat textile pattern where the yarn is resist-dyed or tie-dyed before being woven (*p319*)

jauhar mass suicide by immolation practised by Rajput women, to escape dishonour at the hands of their captors

-ji honorific suffix added to a person's name

kundankari inlay work with gems (*p361*)

kushti Indian style of wrestling

meenakari enamel work (*p361*)

mela fair, fête

Natya Shastra ancient Sanskrit treatise on dance

nautanki vaudeville

pandit learned Sanskrit scholar, wise elder or priest

pattachitra religious paintings from Orissa (*p313*)

phad long painted cloth scroll from Rajasthan (*p381*)

pichhwai a vibrant form of painting on cloth from Rajasthan, depicting 27 scenes from the Krishna legend (*p399*)

qawwals Sufi musicians

raga melodic structure with a fixed sequence of musical notes

rasa mood or emotion; also essence

sati the custom of a widow immolating herself on her husband's funeral pyre

satyagraha a form of non-violent, moral protest started by Mahatma Gandhi

Shilpa Shastra ancient Sanskrit treatise on sculpture

shishya disciple

tala rhythm/rhythmic cycle in classical Indian music

thangka scroll painting framed in silk, depicting Mahayana Buddhist deities (*p123*)

thumri light classical music, sung in North India

DRESS

bindi circular dot on forehead

chappal handcrafted leather slippers; sandals

chikankari finely embroidered cotton textile from Lucknow

choli tight-fitting blouse

ghaghara/lehenga women's gathered skirt (*p31*)

juttis traditional leather shoes with pointed or upturned toes

kurta long stitched shirt (*p31*)

mukut crown

odhni/dupatta women's veil or long scarf (*p30*)

pallav end-piece of a sari (*p30*)

safa/pagri turban (*p30*)

salwar loose pantaloons, tapered at the ankle (*p30*)

sarpech jewelled turban ornament (*p665*)

sherwani long formal coat for men (*p31*)

topi cap (*p31*)

zardozi elaborate gold thread embroidery (*p171*)

zari gold thread

RELIGION

aarti Hindu prayer ritual with oil or butter lamps

ahimsa doctrine of non-violence

alams ceremonial standards used by Shia Muslims during Muharram *(p669)*

amrit divine nectar of immortality

ashram Hindu spiritual centre or religious retreat

avatar incarnation of a Hindu deity *(p679)*

bhajans Hindu devotional songs

bhakti cult of intense personal devotion to God, without going through priests

Bodhisattvas highly enlightened Mahayana Buddhist beings who refuse nirvana so that they can devote themselves to the service of others

chador ceremonial cloth to cover Muslim saint's grave; literally, a sheet

chakra discus or wheel; also Buddhist symbol of eight-spoked wheel, representing the Eightfold Path of Righteousness

darshan an auspicious sighting of a Hindu deity, religious person, temple or holy river; also formal audience given by a ruler or holy man

devadasi Hindu temple dancer

dharamshala rest house for pilgrims

dorje thunderbolt symbol in Mahayana Buddhism

dukka ablution tank in a mosque complex

Gangajal holy water from the Ganges river

gopis Lord Krishna's milkmaid companions

Hinayana "Small Vehicle" school of Buddhism practised in parts of India, Sri Lanka and Thailand, which emphasizes the importance of an ascetic, monastic way of life

imam Muslim religious leader

imambara shrine of a Shia Muslim holy man; ceremonial halls used by Shia Muslims during Muharram *(p197)*

Jataka Tales stories based on legends of the Buddha's previous lives *(p480)*

jyotirlinga linga symbolizing Shiva's energy, believed to have miraculously materialized out of light; found in the 12 most sacred sites linked to Shiva

kumbh cosmic pot holding the nectar of immortality *(amrit)*

linga phallic emblem representing the Hindu god Shiva

madrasa Islamic theological school

Mahayana "Greater Vehicle" school of Buddhism which emphasizes the importance of Bodhisattvas

mandala circular diagram symbolizing the universe, used as an aid to meditation by Buddhists

mantra meditational Hindu or Buddhist chant

matha Hindu or Jain religious centre

maya Hindu concept of illusion

moksha Hindu term for salvation

mudra symbolic hand gestures

namaaz Muslim daily prayers

navaratri nine-day fasting period preceding the Hindu festivals of Ramnavami and Dussehra

Om sacred Buddhist and Hindu syllable, invoking the divine

parikrama clockwise circumambulation of a Hindu or Buddhist holy site

prasad specially consecrated food from a Hindu or Sikh temple

puja Hindu prayer ritual

ratha temple chariot

samadhi memorial platform at Hindu cremation site

sangam holy confluence of rivers

Shaivite devotee of Lord Shiva

Shia a sect of Islam that reveres the Prophet Mohammed's cousin Ali and his successors as the true imams

Sufi mystical Islamic philosophy

Sunni a sect of Islam to which the majority of Indian Muslims belong; Sunnis follow traditional Islamic law, believed to be based on the words and acts of the Prophet Mohammed

takhts principal seats of Sikhism

tandava nritya Shiva's cosmic dance of destruction *(p590)*

tazia ornately decorated tower of wood, metal and paper carried by Shia Muslims at Muharram

thiru/tiru holy

tirtha Hindu holy place, usually near sacred river or tank

tirthankaras the 24 religious teachers worshipped by Jains

trishul trident carried by Hindu god, Lord Shiva

tuk fortified cluster of Jain temples

tulsi the sacred basil plant

Urs festival commemorating a Muslim saint

vahanas vehicles of Hindu gods

Vaishnavite devotee of Hindu god, Lord Vishnu

Vedas the oldest known Indian texts, written in Sanskrit, codifying Aryan beliefs and principles

vibhuti sacred ash

yagna Hindu ritual sacrifice

yatra Hindu pilgrimage

MISCELLANEOUS

adivasi tribal person

akash sky

attar/ittar perfume, usually distilled from flowers

badal cloud

bagh tiger

basti settlement or slum; also Jain temple complex

chaugan ancient Persian form of polo, played with a curved stick

diya oil or butter lamp

dhaba roadside eatery *(p179)*

durbar royal court or royal gathering; audience held by a ruler

dzo cross between yak and cow

gali lane or narrow alleyway

ghee clarified butter

gulal coloured powder used during the Holi festival *(p35)*

haat open-air market, usually held once a week

howdah ceremonial seat on an elephant's back

kettuvallam Kerala rice boat *(p633)*

kheda elephant corral

machaan raised observation platform in a forest

mahout elephant trainer

marg major road

mayil/mayur peacock

nava ratna nine precious jewels

nawab Muslim prince

paan betel leaf, a digestive *(p165)*

pandal marquee or decorated stage made of cloth and bamboo

padma lotus

prithvi earth

purnima full moon

pushpa flower

pyav drinking water fountain

rumal handkerchief or square cloth

sagar large lake or reservoir; also ocean or sea

shikar hunting expedition

shila stone

tal lake

taluka sub-district

thakur Hindu chieftain

thali platter

thuggees highway bandits

vayu air

zamindar landowner

Phrase Book

India has 18 major regional languages, many with their own scripts. While Hindi, spoken by 30 per cent of the people and widely understood throughout India, is the official national language, other languages enjoy predominance in their respective regions. Our phrase book covers five languages, four of them spoken in India's four largest cities and their surrounding regions: Hindi (spoken in Delhi); Bengali (spoken in Kolkata); Marathi (spoken in Mumbai); and Tamil (spoken in Chennai). The fifth language, Malayalam, is spoken in Kerala. While Hindi, Bengali and Marathi are Indo-European languages, descended from Sanskrit, Tamil and Malayalam are Dravidian languages, unrelated to the Indo-European group, though influenced by Sanskrit over the centuries. English is widely spoken and understood throughout the country and serves as a link language between the different regions. One can get by with English almost anywhere in India, but most Indians are delighted and warmly appreciative if a visitor makes an attempt to speak their language.

HINDI

In an Emergency

Help!	Bachao!
Stop!	Roko!
Call a doctor!	Doctor ko bulao!
Where is the nearest telephone?	Yahan phone kahan hai?

Communication Essentials

Yes	Haan
No	Na/Naheen
Thank you	Dhanyavad/Shukria
Please	Kripaya/Meharbani sé
Excuse me/Sorry	Kshama karen/ Maaf karen
Hello/Goodbye	Namasté
Stop	Rook jao
Let's go	Chalo
Straight ahead	Seedha
Big/Small	Bara/Chhota
This/That	Yeh/Voh
Near/Far	Paas/Door
Way	Raasta
Road	Sarak
Yesterday	Beeta hua kal
Today	Aaj
Tomorrow	Aane wala kal
Here	Yahaan
There	Wahaan
What?	Kya?
Where?	Kahaan?
When?	Kab?
Why?	Kyon?
How?	Kaisé?
Up	Upar
Down	Neeché
More	Aur zyada
A little	Thora
Before	Pehlé
Opposite/ Facing	Saamné
Very	Bahut
Less	Kam
Louder/Harder	Zor sé
Softly/Gently	Dheeré sé
Go	Jao
Come	Aao

Useful Phrases

How are you?	Aap kaisé hain?
What is your name?	Aapka naam kya hai?
My name is ...	Mera naam ... hai
Do you speak English?	Angrezi ati hai?
I understand	Samajh gaya (male)/ gayi (female)
I don't understand	Nahin samjha (m)/ samjhi (f)
What is the time?	Kya baja hai?
Where is ...?	... Kahaan hai?

What is this?	Yeh kya hai?
Hurry up	Jaldi karo
How far is ...?	... Kitni door hai?
I don't know	Pata nahin
All right	Achha/Theek hai
Now/Instantly	Abhi/Isi waqt
Well done!	Shabash!
See you	Phir milengé
Go away!	Hat jao/Hato
I don't want it	Mujhe nahin chahiye
Not now	Abhi nahin

Useful Words

Which?	Kaun sa?
Who?	Kaun?
Hot	Garam
Cold	Thanda
Good	Achha
Bad	Kharaab
Enough	Bus/Kafi hai
Open	Khula
Closed	Bundh
Left	Baayan
Right	Daayan
Straight on	Seedha
Near	Paas/Nazdeek
Quickly	Jaldi
Late	Der sé
Later	Baad mein
Entrance	Pravesh
Exit	Nikas
Behind	Peechhé
Full	Bhara
Empty	Khali
Toilet	Shauchaalaya
Free/No charge	Nih shulka/Muft
Direction	Disha
Book	Kitaab
Newspaper	Akhbaar

Shopping

How much does this cost?	Iska kya daam hai?
I would like...	Mujhe ... chahiye
Do you have...?	Kya aap ké paas ... hai?
I am just looking	Abhi dekh rahen hain
Does it come in other colours?	Yeh dooserey rangon main bhi aata hai kya?
This one	Yeh wala
That one	Voh wala
Black	Kaala
Blue	Neela
White	Safed
Red	Lal
Yellow	Peela
Green	Hara
Brown	Bhura
Cheap	Sasta
Expensive	Mehanga
Tailor	Darzi

Bargaining

How much is this?	Yeh kitne ka hai?

How much will you take?	Kya logé?
That's a little expensive	Yeh to mehanga hai
Could you lower the price a bit?	Daam thoda kam kariyé
How about xx rupees?	xx rupeye laingé?
I'll settle for xx rupees	xx rupeye mein dena hai to dijiyé

Staying in a Hotel

Do you have any vacant rooms?	Aapke hotel mein khali kamre hain kya?
What is the charge per night?	Ek raat ka kiraya kya hai?
Can I see the room first?	Kya mein pehle kamra dekh sakta hoon?
Key	Chaabhi
Soap	Sabun
Towel	Tauliya
Hot/Cold water	Garam/Thanda pani

Eating Out

Breakfast	Nashta
Food	Khaana
Water	Pani
Ice	Baraf
Tea	Chai
Coffee	Kaufi
Sugar	Cheeni
Salt	Namak
Milk	Doodh
Yoghurt	Dahi
Egg	Anda
Fruit	Phal
Vegetable	Sabzi
Rice	Chaawal
Pulses (lentil, split peas etc)	Dal
Fixed price menu	Ek daam menu
Is it spicy?	Mirch-masala tez hai kya?
Make it less spicy please	Mirch-masala kam, theek hai?
Knife	Chhuri
Fork	Kanta
Spoon	Chammach
Finished	Khatam

Numbers

1	Ek
2	Do
3	Teen
4	Char
5	Panch
6	Chhé
7	Saat
8	Aath
9	Nau
10	Dus

11	Gyarah
12	Barah
13	Terah
14	Chaudah
15	Pandrah
16	Solah
17	Satrah
18	Atharah
19	Unnees
20	Bees
30	Tees
40	Chalees
50	Pachaas
60	Saath

70	Sattar
80	Assi
90	Nabbé
100	Sau
1,000	Hazar
100,000	Lakh
10,000,000	Karod (crore)

Time

One minute	Ek minit
One hour	Ek ghanta
Half an hour	Aadha ghanta
Quarter hour	Pauna ghanta
Half past one	Derh

Half past two	Dhai
A day	Ek din
A week	Ek haftah
Monday	Somwar
Tuesday	Mangalwar
Wednesday	Budhwar
Thursday	Veerwar
Friday	Shukrawar
Saturday	Shaniwar
Sunday	Raviwar
Morning	Subah
Afternoon	Dopahar
Evening	Shaam
Night	Raat

BENGALI

In an Emergency

Help!	Shahaajjo korun!
Stop!	Thamun!
Call a doctor!	Daktar dakun!
Where is the nearest telephone?	Ekhanay phone kothai?

Communication Essentials

Yes	Haen
No	Na
Thank you	Dhonnobad
Please	Doya koray
Excuse me/ Sorry	Maap korben
Hello/Goodbye	Nomoshkar
Stop	Thamun
Let's go	Cholun
Straight ahead	Shoja
Big/Small	Boro/Chhoto
This/That	Eta/Ota
Near/Far	Kaachhé/Dooré
Way	Raasta
Road	Raasta
Yesterday	Goto kaal
Today	Aaj
Tomorrow	Kaal
Here	Ekhaané
There	Okhaané
What?	Ki?
Where?	Kothayé?
When?	Kokhon?
Why?	Kaeno?
How?	Ki koray?
Up	Opor
Down	Neeché
More	Aaro
A little	Ektu
Before	Aagey
Opposite/ Facing	Shaamney
Very	Khoob
Less	Kom
Louder/Harder	Jorey
Softly/Gently	Aastey
Go	Jao
Come	Esho

Useful Phrases

How are you?	Kaemon aachhen?
What is your name?	Aapnaar naam ki?
My name is …	Aamaar naam …
Do you speak English?	Ingriji bolen?
I understand	Bujhi
I don't understand	Bujhi na
What is the time?	Kota bajé?
Where is …?	… Kothhai?
What is this?	Eta ki?
Hurry up	Taarataari
How far is …?	… Koto door?

I don't know	Jaani na
All right	Theek achhey
Now/Instantly	Ekkhuni
Well done!	Bah!
See you	Aashi
Go away!	Jao
I don't want it	Chai na
Not now	Ekhon na

Useful Words

Which?	Konta?
Who?	Kay?
Hot	Gorom
Cold	Thanda
Good	Bhalo
Bad	Khaaraap
Enough	Bus
Open	Khola
Closed	Bondho
Left	Baayen
Right	Daayiné
Straight on	Shojaa
Near	Kaachhey
Quickly	Taarataari
Late	Deri
Later	Porey
Entrance	Probesh
Exit	Prosthaan
Behind	Pechhoney
Full	Bhora
Empty	Khaali
Toilet	Shauchaalaya
Free/No charge	Bina poisha
Direction	Disha
Book	Boi
Magazine	Potrika
Newspaper	Khoborer kagoj

Shopping

How much does this cost?	Koto?
I would like…	Aami chaai
Do you have…?	Aapnaar kaachhe aachhe?
I am just looking	Shudhu dekhhi
Does it come in other colours?	Aaro rong aachhey?
This one	Eta
That one	Ota
Black	Kaalo
Blue	Neel
White	Shaadaa
Red	Laal
Yellow	Holud
Green	Shobuj
Brown	Khoiri
Cheap	Shostaa
Expensive	Daami
Tailor	Dorji

Bargaining

How much is this?	Eta koto?
How much will you take?	Koto neben?
That's a little expensive	Beshi daam

Could you lower the price a bit?	Ektu komaan
How about xx rupees?	xx taka cholbé?
I'll settle for xx rupees	xx takar beshi debo na

Staying in a Hotel

Do you have any vacant rooms?	Ghor khaali aachhey?
What is the charge per night?	Ek raater bhaara koto?
Can I see the room first?	Aagey ghor dekhte paari?
Key	Chaabi
Soap	Shaabaan
Towel	Towaaley
Hot/Cold water	Gorom/Thanda jol

Eating Out

Breakfast	Jolkhaabaar
Food	Khaabaar
Water	Jol
Ice	Borof
Tea	Chaa
Coffee	Koffee
Sugar	Cheeni
Salt	Noon
Milk	Doodh
Yoghurt	Dohi
Egg	Deem
Fruit	Phol
Vegetable	Shobji
Rice	Bhaat
Pulses (lentils, split peas etc)	Daal
Fixed price menu	Ek daam menu
Is it spicy?	Jhaal ki?
Make it less spicy	Beshi jhaal chaai na
Knife	Chhuri
Fork	Kanta
Spoon	Chaamoch
Finished	Shesh

Numbers

1	Ek
2	Dooi
3	Teen
4	Chaar
5	Paanch
6	Chhoy
7	Shaat
8	Aath
9	Noy
10	Dosh
11	Egaro
12	Baaro
13	Tero
14	Chaudoh
15	Ponero
16	Sholo
17	Shotero
18	Aathero
19	Unneesh
20	Kuri/Beesh

30	**Tirish**
40	**Cholleesh**
50	**Ponchaash**
60	**Shaat**
70	**Shottor**
80	**Aashi**
90	**Nobboi**
100	**Eksho**
1,000	**Haajaar**
100,000	**Lakh**
10,000,000	**Koti**

Time

One minute	**Ek minit**
One hour	**Ek ghonta**
Half an hour	**Aadh ghonta**
Quarter hour	**Pauney ghonta**
Half past one	**Derh**
Half past two	**Aadhai**
A day	**Ek din**
A week	**Ek shopta**

Monday	**Shombar**
Tuesday	**Mongolbar**
Wednesday	**Budhbar**
Thursday	**Bishuttbar**
Friday	**Shukkurbar**
Saturday	**Shonibar**
Sunday	**Robibar**
Morning	**Shokaal**
Afternoon	**Duphur**
Evening	**Bikel**
Night	**Raat**

MARATHI

In an Emergency

Help!	**Vachau!**
Stop!	**Thamba!**
Call a doctor!	**Doctorana bolwaa!**
Where is the nearest telephone?	**Ithé jawal phone kuthé aahé?**

Communication Essentials

Yes	**Ho**
No	**Nahi**
Thank you	**Dhanyavad**
Please	**krupaya**
Excuse me/ Sorry	**Kshama pahijé**
Hello/ Goodbye	**Namaskar**
Stop	**Thamba**
Let's go	**Chala**
Straight ahead	**Saral**
Big/Small	**Mota/Lahan**
This/That	**Hé/Thé**
Near/Far	**Zawal/Laamb**
Way	**Marga**
Road	**Rastha**
Yesterday	**Kaal**
Today	**Aaj**
Tomorrow	**Udya**
Here	**Ithé**
There	**Tithé**
What?	**Kay?**
Where?	**Kuthé?**
When?	**Kenhvah?**
Why?	**Ka?**
How?	**Kasè?**
Up	**Varti**
Down	**Khali**
More	**Aankhi**
A little	**Thodé**
Before	**Aadhi**
Opposite/ Facing	**Samor**
Very	**Khoop**
Less	**Kami**
Louder/Harder	**Mothyané/Zorané**
Softly/Gently	**Haloo**
Go	**Za**
Come	**Ya**

Useful Phrases

How are you?	**Kasa Kain?**
What is your name?	**Apla nao?**
My name is ...	**Maajhe nao ...**
Do you speak English?	**Inglish yeté ka?**
I understand	**Samazté**
I don't understand	**Kalale nahin**
What is the time?	**Kiti vajlé?**
Where is ...?	**Kuthé aahé?**
What is this?	**Hé kay aahé?**
Hurry up	**Aatpa lavkar**
How far is ...?	**Kiti laamb aahé?**
I don't know	**Mahiti nahin**
All right	**Theek aahé**
Now/Instantly	**Aathach**

Well done!	**Chhan!**
See you	**Bhétuya**
Go away!	**Chalta ho**
I don't want it	**Nakoy malaa**
Not now	**Aatha naahin**

Useful Words

Which?	**Konté?**
Who?	**Kon?**
Hot	**Garam**
Cold	**Thanda**
Good	**Changla**
Bad	**Vait**
Enough	**Puré**
Open	**Ughadé**
Closed	**Banda**
Left	**Davikadé**
Right	**Uzavikadé**
Straight on	**Saral**
Near	**Zawal**
Quickly	**Lavkar**
Late	**Ushira**
Later	**Nanthar**
Entrance	**Pravesh**
Exit	**Baaher**
Behind	**Maagé**
Full	**Bharalelé**
Empty	**Rikamé**
Toilet	**Shauchaalaya**
Free/No charge	**Mophat**
Direction	**Disha**
Book	**Pusthak**
Magazine	**Maasik**
Newspaper	**Vartaman patra**

Shopping

How much does this cost?	**Hé kevdyala?**
I would like…	**Mala... hava hotha**
Do you have…?	**Tumechyakadé ... aahé ka?**
I am just looking	**Ajun bagté/Aahé bagto**
Does it come in other colours?	**Aankhi ranga aahetka?**
This one	**Hé**
That one	**Té**
Black	**Kaala**
Blue	**Neelé**
White	**Pandhra**
Red	**Lal**
Yellow	**Piwala**
Green	**Hirvva**
Brown	**Chocoleti**
Cheap	**Svastha**
Expensive	**Mahaag**
Tailor	**Shimpi**

Bargaining

How much is this?	**He kevdhyala?**
How much will you take?	**Kithi dyaché?**
That's a little expensive	**Zara mahaag aahe**
Could you lower the price a bit?	**Zara kami karana ka?**
How about xx rupees?	**Xx rupyé thik aahé?**
I'll settle for xx rupees	**Xx barobar aahé**

Staying in a Hotel

Do you have any vacant rooms?	**Tumchya hotel madhé jagaa aahé ka?**
What is the charge per night?	**Eka ratri ché kiti**
Can I see the room first?	**Mee aadhi kholi baghoon ka?**
Key	**Killi**
Soap	**Saban**
Towel	**Towel**
Hot/Cold water	**Garam/Thanda pani**

Eating Out

Breakfast	**Nasta**
Food	**Jewan**
Water	**Pani**
Ice	**Barpha**
Tea	**Chaha**
Coffee	**Kofi**
Sugar	**Saakhar**
Salt	**Mith**
Milk	**Doodh**
Yoghurt	**Dahi**
Egg	**Andé**
Fruit	**Phal**
Vegetable	**Bhaji**
Rice	**Bhath**
Pulses (lentils, split peas etc)	**Dal**
Fixed price menu	**Ekach bhav**
Is it spicy?	**Tikhat aahé ka?**
Make it less spicy please	**Har tikhat nakon bara ka?**
Knife	**Suri**
Fork	**Kata**
Spoon	**Chammcha**
Finished	**Samplé**

Numbers

1	**Ek**
2	**Don**
3	**Teen**
4	**Char**
5	**Pach**
6	**Saha**
7	**Sath**
8	**Aath**
9	**Nou**
10	**Daha**
11	**Akara**
12	**Barah**
13	**Terah**
14	**Chawda**
15	**Pandhra**
16	**Solah**
17	**Satara**
18	**Atharah**
19	**Ekonees**
20	**Vees**
30	**Tees**
40	**Chalees**
50	**Pannas**
60	**Saath**
70	**Sattar**
80	**Aishi**
90	**Nauwad**
100	**Shambhar**

1,000	**Hazaar**
100,000	**Lakh**
10,000,000	**Koti**

Time

One minute	**Ek minit**
One hour	**Ek taas**
Half an hour	**Ardha taas**
Quarter hour	**Pandhra minit**
Half past one	**Deed**
Half past two	**Adhich**
A day	**Ek divas**
A week	**Ek athavda**
Monday	**Somwar**
Tuesday	**Mangalwar**
Wednesday	**Budhwar**
Thursday	**Guruwar**
Friday	**Shukrawar**
Saturday	**Shaniwar**
Sunday	**Raviwar**
Morning	**Sakali**
Afternoon	**Dupari**
Evening	**Sandhyakali**
Night	**Ratri**

TAMIL

In an Emergency

Help!	**Udhaivi véndum!**
Stop!	**Nillu!**
Call a doctor!	**Doctor koopiddunga!**
Where is the nearest phone?	**Pakkatatillé phone engu irrukku?**

Communication Essentials

Yes	**Aama/Seri**
No	**Illai/Véndaam**
Thank you	**Nanri**
Please	**Daivusaidhu**
Excuse me/Sorry	**Mannikavum**
Hello/Goodbye	**Vannakkam/ Paankalaam**
Stop	**Nillu**
Let's go	**Pohalaam**
Straight ahead	**Néré**
Big/Small	**Perisu/Chinannadu**
This/That	**Idhu/Adhu**
Near/Far	**Pakkatilai/Dooram**
Way	**Vazhi**
Road	**Theruvu**
Yesterday	**Nétru/Néthiku**
Today	**Inru/Innikki**
Tomorrow	**Naallai/Naallaiku**
Here	**Ingé**
There	**Angé**
What?	**Ennai?**
Where?	**Engé?**
When?	**Eppo?**
Why?	**Ain?**
How?	**Eppiddi?**
Up	**Mélai**
Down	**Kizhai**
More	**Unnum konjam**
A little	**Konjam**
Before	**Minaalai**
Opposite/Facing	**Edhirai**
Very	**Romba**
Less	**Kammi**
Louder/Harder	**Perisa/Unnum ongi**
Softly/Gently	**Molla**
Go	**Pongo/Po**
Come	**Vaango/Vaa**

Useful Phrases

How are you?	**Neenga eppudi irukénga?**
What is your name?	**Onge peyar enna?**
My name is ...	**Enodia peyar ...**
Do you speak English?	**English pése theriyuma?**
I understand	**Ennakku puriyum**
I don't understand	**Ennakku puriyadu**
What is the time?	**Ippo ena mani?**
Where is ...?	**... Enga irrukku?**
What is this?	**Idhu ennadhu?**
Hurry up	**Seekrama vaango**
How far is ...?	**... Evallavu dooram?**
I don't know	**Ennaku theriyadu**
All right	**Seri**
Now/Instantly	**Ippovai**
Well done!	**Shabash!**
See you	**Apram parkalaam**
Go away!	**Poividu!**
I don't want it	**Ennaku véndaam**
Not now	**Ippo illai**

Useful Words

Which?	**Edhu?**
Who?	**Yaaru?**
Hot	**Soodu**
Cold	**Kulluru**
Good	**Nalladhu**
Bad	**Kettadhu**
Enough	**Porum**
Open	**Thirandirukku**
Closed	**Moodirukku**
Left	**Edudhu**
Right	**Valadhu**
Straight on	**Nérai**
Near	**Pakkatillai**
Quickly	**Seekrama**
Late	**Nerama**
Later	**Apram**
Entrance	**Varuvu**
Exit	**Velivaasal**
Behind	**Pinalai**
Full	**Rombiruku**
Empty	**Kaali**
Toilet	**Kaizhupu arai**
Free/No charge	**Ilevasaasam**
Direction	**Disai/Pakkam**
Book	**Pustagam**
Magazine	**Patrigai**
Newspaper	**Samachara patrigai**

Shopping

How much does this cost?	**Idhodiya vilai ennai?**
I would like…	**Ennakku idhu venum ...**
Do you have…?	**... onga kitta irrukka?**
I am just looking	**Naan summa paakaren**
Does it come in other colours?	**Idh vera colouril kidaikuma?**
This one	**Idhu**
That one	**Adhu**
Black	**Karuppu**
Blue	**Neelam**
White	**Vellai**
Red	**Seguppu**
Yellow	**Manjhal**
Green	**Pachchai**
Brown	**Kappi niram**
Cheap	**Maluvu**
Expensive	**Vilai jasti**
Tailor	**Theyalkaran**

Bargaining

How much is this?	**Idhu enna vilai?**
How much will you take?	**Neengu evalave edithipél?**
That's a little expensive	**Adhu konjam vilai jasti**
Could you lower the price a bit?	**Vilai konjam kurrakkai mudduyuma?**
How about xx rupees?	**xx rubaai seria?**
I'll settle for xx rupees	**xx rubaai tharuven**

Staying in a Hotel

Do you have any vacant rooms?	**Kaali arai irruka?**
What is the charge per night?	**Oru raatriku evaluvu caasu?**
Can I see the room first?	**Naan mudulai araiya parrakalama?**
Key	**Chaavi**
Soap	**Soapu**
Towel	**Thundu**
Hot/Cold water	**Soodu/Jillu thanni**

Eating Out

Breakfast	**Kaalai chittrundi**
Food	**Saapadu**
Water	**Thanni/Jalam**
Ice	**Ice**
Tea	**Chai**
Coffee	**Coffee**
Sugar	**Shakarai**
Salt	**Uppu**
Milk	**Paal**
Yoghurt	**Thairu**
Egg	**Muttai**
Fruit	**Pazham**
Vegetable	**Kayagiri**
Rice	**Arusi**
Pulses (lentils,etc)	**Paruppu**
Fixed price menu	**Ore vilai menu**
Is it spicy?	**Naraya masala irukka?**
Make it less spicy please	**Masala seriya irukka?**
Knife	**Kaththi**
Fork	**Fork**
Spoon	**Spoon/ Theikarandi**
Finished	**Mudivu**

Numbers

1	**Onru/Onu**
2	**Erundu**
3	**Moonru**
4	**Naangu/Naalu**
5	**Anju/Aindhu**
6	**Aaru**
7	**Yezhu**
8	**Ettu**
9	**Ombodhu**
10	**Pathu**
11	**Pathinonru**
12	**Panandu**
13	**Pathimoonru**
14	**Pathinaalu**
15	**Pathinainthu**
16	**Pathnaaru**
17	**Pathinezhu**
18	**Pathinettu**
19	**Pathombadhu**
20	**Iravadhu**
30	**Mupaddu**
40	**Napadhu**
50	**Aimbadhu**
60	**Aravadhu**
70	**Yezhuvadu**
80	**Yenbadhu**
90	**Thonnuru**
100	**Nooru**
1,000	**Aayiram**
100,000	**Latcham**
10,000,000	**Kodi**

Time

One minute	**Oru nimisham**
One hour	**Oru manéram**
Half an hour	**Ara manéram**
Quarter hour	**Kaal manéram**
Half past one	**Onre mani**
Half past two	**Erendarai mani**
A day	**Oru naal**
A week	**Oru vaaram**
Monday	**Thingakazhami**
Tuesday	**Sevvaikazhami**
Wednesday	**Budhankazhami**
Thursday	**Viyaikazhami**
Friday	**Vellikazhami**
Saturday	**Nyayatrikazhami**
Morning	**Kaalai**
Afternoon	**Madhyanam**
Evening	**Sayankaalam**
Night	**Raatri**

MALAYALAM

In an Emergency

Help!	Sahayikoo!
Stop!	Nilku/Nirthu!
Call a doctor!	Doctore viliku!
Where is the nearest phone?	Evide annu aduth phone?

Communication Essentials

Yes	Athe/Seri
No	Illa/Alla/Véndaa
Thank you	Nanni
Please	Dayavuchaidu
Excuse me/Sorry	Kshamikkanam
Hello/Goodbye	Namaskaram/ Veendum kanaam
Stop	Nilku
Let's go	Namuku pokaam
Straight ahead	Néré povuu
Big/Small	Valudu/Cherudu
This/That	Idhe/Adhe
Near/Far	Aduthu/Akalé
Way	Vazhi
Road	Patha/Road
Yesterday	Innalé
Today	Innu
Tomorrow	Naallé
Here	Evidé
There	Avidé
What?	Entha?
Where?	Evidé?
When?	Eppol?
Why?	Entha/Enthukonda?
How?	Engané?
Up	Mukalil
Down	Kizhé/Thazhé
More	Eniyum kooduthal
A little	Kurachu/Alpam
Before	Munpé/Munnil
Opposite/Facing	Edhirvasam/Edhirai
Very	Valaré
Less	Kurachu/Kuravu
Louder/Harder	Uchchathil/Urakké
Softly/Gently	Pathiyé/Swaram thazhthi
Go	Pokoo/Po
Come	Varoo/Vaa

Useful Phrases

How are you?	Sukhamano?
What is your name?	Ningaludé peru entha?
My name is ...	Ente peru ...
Do you speak English?	Ningal English samsarikumo?
I understand	Enikku manasilayi
I don't understand	Enikku manasilakilla
What is the time?	Samayam enthai?
Where is ...?	Evideyanu ...?
What is this?	Idhu enthanu?
Hurry up	Vegamakatté
How far is ...?	Ethra dooramundu...?
I don't know	Enikku ariyilla
All right	Seri
Now/Instantly	Ippol thanné
Well done!	Kémamai!/Nannai!
See you	Pinne kanaam
Go away!	Dooré po!
I don't want it	Enikku véndaa
Not now	Ippo illa/Véndaa

Useful Words

Which?	Edhu?
Who?	Aaré?
Hot	Choodé
Cold	Thanuppé/Kulluré
Good	Nalladhé
Bad	Cheetha/Mosam
Enough	Madhi
Open	Thurannu
Closed	Adachu
Left	Edadhu
Right	Valadhu
Straight on	Néré
Near	Aduthu
Quickly	Végum
Late	Vaiki
Later	Pinné/Pinneedu
Entrance	Munvasam/ Parvésana vathil
Exit	Purathékkulla vazhi
Behind	Pinnalé/Pinnil
Full	Nirayé
Empty	Kaali
Toilet	Moothrappura
Free/no charge	Saujanyam
Direction	Dikku
Book	Pustakam
Magazine	Masika/Varika
Newspaper	Newspaper

Shopping

How much does this cost?	Idhinu enthu vila?
I would like...	Enikku idhu venum ...
Do you have...?	... Ningaludé pakkal ondo?
I am just looking	Naan veruthé nokukayanu
Does it come in other colours?	Idhu vereyum colouril kittumo?
This one	Idhu
That one	Adhu
Black	Karuppé
Blue	Neela
White	Vella
Red	Chuvappé
Yellow	Manja
Green	Pachcha
Brown	Kappi niram
Cheap	Vilakuravu
Expensive	Vilakuduthal
Tailor	Thayalkaran

Bargaining

How much is this?	Idhinu enthu vila?
How much will you take?	Idhu enthu vilaku tharum?
That's a little expensive	Vila kurachu kooduthalanu
Could you lower the price a bit?	Vila kurachu kuraikumo?
How about xx rupees?	xx rupaku tharumo?
I'll settle for xx rupees	Njyan xx rupaku edukkam

Staying in a Hotel

Do you have any vacant rooms?	Muri (room) ozhivundo?
What is the charge per night?	Oru raatriku entha vaadaka?
Can I see the room first?	Eniku aadyam muri kaanan sadhikumo?
Key	Thakol
Soap	Soap
Towel	Thorthé/Towel
Hot/Cold water	Choodu/Thanutha véllam

Eating Out

Breakfast	Prathal
Food	Aaharam/ Bhakshanam
Water	Véllam
Ice	Ice katta
Tea	Chaya
Coffee	Kaapi
Sugar	Panchasaara
Salt	Uppé
Milk	Paal
Yoghurt	Thairé
Egg	Mutta
Fruit	Pazham
Vegetable	Pachchakari
Rice	Ari/Chorué
Pulses (lentils, split peas etc)	Parippé
Fixed price menu	Otta vila menu/ Krithya vila menu
Is it spicy?	Ithu frivullathano?
Make it less spicy please	Erivu kooduthal vendaa?
Knife	Kaththi
Fork	Mullé/Fork
Spoon	Spoon
Finished	Kazhinju/Theernu

Numbers

1	Onné/Oru
2	Randé
3	Moonné
4	Naalé
5	Anché
6	Aaré
7	Yezhé
8	Etté
9	Onpadhé
10	Paththé
11	Pathinonné
12	Panthrandé
13	Pathimoonné
14	Pathinaalé
15	Pathinanché
16	Pathinaaré
17	Pathinezhé
18	Pathinetté
19	Pathompadhé
20	Irupadhé
30	Muppaddé
40	Nappadhé
50	Ambadhé
60	Arupadhé
70	Yezhupadé
80	Yenpadhé
90	Thonnuré
100	Nooré
1,000	Aayiram
100,000	Laksham
10,000,000	Kodi

Time

One minute	Oru nimisham/ Minute
One hour	Oru manikoor
Half an hour	Ara manikoor
Quarter hour	Kaal manikoor
Half past one	Onnara mani
Half past two	Randara mani
A day	Oru divasam
A week	Oru aazhcha
Monday	Thingal
Tuesday	Chovva
Wednesday	Budhan
Thursday	Vyazham
Friday	Velli
Saturday	Sani
Morning	Raavilé
Afternoon	Uchcha
Evening	Vaikunneram
Night	Raatri

Railway Map of India

The external boundaries of India as shown on this map are neither correct nor authentic.